Arcimboldo

Arcimboldo

1526-1593

Edited by
Sylvia Ferino-Pagden

SKIRA
Sénat
Musée du Luxembourg
kunst historisches museum khm

Cover
Giuseppe Arcimboldo, *Summer*, 1563 (detail). Vienna, Kunsthistorisches Museum
(cat. IV.3)

Design
Marcello Francone

Editing
Michele Abate

Layout
Fayçal Zaouali

Translations
Lorenzo Sanguedolce, Dominic Ronayne, Christopher Evans for Language Consulting Congressi, Milan

The translations have been provided by the services of Skira and sVo

First published in Italy in 2007 by
Skira Editore S.p.A.
Palazzo Casati Stampa
via Torino 61
20123 Milano
Italy
www.skira.net

Printed and bound in Italy. First edition

ISBN (hard cover): 978-88-6130-379-9
ISBN (soft cover): 978-88-6130-381-2

Distributed in North America by Rizzoli International Publications, Inc., 300 Park Avenue South, New York, NY 10010, USA.
Distributed elsewhere in the world by Thames and Hudson Ltd., 181A High Holborn, London WC1V 7QX, United Kingdom.

Arcimboldo (1526-1593)

Musée du Luxembourg, Paris
September 15, 2007
to January 13, 2008

Kunsthistorisches Museum, Vienna
February 12 to June 1, 2008

This exhibition is presented at the Musée du Luxembourg in Paris by the Senate of the French Republic, under the presidency of Mr. Christian Poncelet, President of the Senate, from September 15, 2007 to January 13, 2008, and at the Kunsthistorisches Museum, Vienna, under the direction of Dr. Wilfried Seipel, from February 12 to June 1, 2008.

Exhibition curator
Sylvia Ferino-Pagden
Curator of Italian Renaissance Painting
Kunsthistorisches Museum, Vienna

Exhibition organizing committee
Kunsthistorisches Museum, Vienna
Musée du Luxembourg, Paris,
in collaboration with the Galleria degli Uffizi, Gabinetto Disegni e Stampe, Florence

Exhibition scholarly committee
Andreas Beyer
Görel Cavalli-Björkman
Thomas DaCosta Kaufmann
Franz Kirchweger
Philippe Morel
Karl Schütz
Manfred Staudinger

Exhibition coordination
Patrizia Nitti
assisted by Carolina Vincenti

Exhibition catalogue
Edited by Sylvia Ferino-Pagden

Authors
Carmen C. Bambach
Christian Beaufort
Andreas Beyer
Piero Boccardo
Agnès Bos
Görel Cavalli-Björkman
Thomas DaCosta Kaufmann
Vincent Delieuvin
Sylvia Ferino-Pagden
Franz Kirchweger
Claudia Kryza-Gersch
Silvio Leydi
Mario Marubbi
Philippe Morel
Sabine Pénot
Paulus Rainer
Marion Romberg
Veronika Sandbichler
Katja Schmitz-von Ledebur
Karl Schütz
Sam Segal
Ina Slama
Manfred Staudinger
Monika Strolz
Francesca Della Torre Scheuch
Alexander Wied
Elisabeth Wolfik
Karin Zeleny

Texts Proofreading
Katja Meister, Florence Rougerie, Marie-Pierre Griffon, Laurent Bury (Paris)
Karin Zeleny, Harald Jurkovič (Vienna)

Paris Exhibition

Scholarly Committee for the Renaissance Exhibition Programming of the Musée du Luxembourg
Francesco Buranelli
General Director of the Musei dello Stato Vaticano
Pierluigi De Vecchi
Professeur d'Iconologie et d'Iconographie de la Faculté des Lettres de l'Université de Milan
Antonio Paolucci
Former Soprintendente del Polo Museale Fiorentino
Vincent Pomarède
Chief Curator, Department of Paintings
Giandomenico Romanelli
Director of the Musei Civici, Venice
Nicola Spinosa
Soprintendente of the Polo Museale Napoletano
Claudio Strinati
Soprintendente of the Polo Museale Romano

Production and Organisation
sVo-Musée du Luxembourg
Sylvestre Verger, General Administrator of the Musée du Luxembourg and President-Managing Director, sVo

Design
Frédéric Lebard *assisted by* Bérengère Tabutin

Condition Reporting
Marielle Doyon-Crimail
Chantal Bureau

Construction and Mount-making
Volume International
Yves Lafarie
Aïnu
Stéphane Pennec

Lighting
Jean-Louis Tartarin

Graphics
Atelier Patrix

Press Office
Observatoire-Véronique Janneau

The organisers in Paris would like to acknowledge the following individuals at the Senate:

Jean Cabannes
Director of the Cabinet of the President
Philippe Roux Comoli
Vice-Director of the Cabinet of the President
Pierre Alleaume
Head of the Cabinet of the President
Robert Provansal
General Secretary of the Questure
Yves Marek
Technical Advisor to the President
Xavier Canchon
Director of Architecture, Buildings and Gardens
Damien Déchelette
Architect of the Luxembourg Palace

Vienna Exhibition

General Director
Wilfried Seipel

Exhibition Organization
Christian Hölzl

Coordinator
Peter Aufreiter

Exhibition Architecture
Gerhard Veigel

Exhibition Graphics
Angela Hartenstein

Conservation and Restauration
Elke Oberthaler
Monika Strolz
Ina Slama
Eva Götz
Martina Griesser

Press Officer
Irina Kubadinow and team

This exhibition could not have been brought to fruition without the invaluable trust and unfailing support of numerous private and institutional lenders throughout the world. The curator and organisers would like to express their profound gratitude to the following heads of institutions and staff members:

Austria
Vienna
Kunsthistorisches Museum
Wilfried Seipel
General Director
Sylvia Ferino-Pagden
Curator of Italian Renaissance Painting
Karl Schütz
Director, Gemäldegalerie
Helmut Trnek
Director, Kunstkammer
Christian Beaufort
Director, Hofjagd-und Rüstkammer
Nationalbibliothek
Johanna Rachinger
General Director
Ernst Gamillscheg
Head of the Manuscripts Department
Museum für Angewandte Kunst
Peter Noever
Director
Kathrin Pokorny-Nagel
Director of the Library
Katja Miksovsky
Curator for Ceramics and Glass
Albertina Museum
Klaus Albrecht Schröder
Director
Achim Gnann
Curator
Universitätsbibliothek
Maria Seissl
Director of the Library and Archives

Belgium
Brussels
Musées Royaux des Beaux-Arts de Belgique
Michel Draguet
General Director

Czech Republic
Prague
Národní Muzeum
Michal Lukeš

General Director
Věra Přenosilová
Director, *Historické Muzeum*
Národní Galerie, Graficka sbirka
Milan Knízák
General Director

Denmark
Copenhagen
Kunstindustriemuseet
Bodil Busk Laursen
Director
Charlotte Malte
Registrar

France
Blois
Château et Musées de Blois
Elisabeth Latrémolière
Chief Curator
Paris
Bibliothèque nationale de France
Bruno Racine
President
Nathalie Léman
Head of Exterior Exhibitions
Bibliothèque de l'Ecole nationale des Beaux-Arts
Henry-Claude Cousseau
Director
Musée du Louvre
Henri Loyrette
President-Director
Vincent Pomarède
Chief Curator, Department of Paintings
Marc Bascou
Chief Curator, Department of Works of Art

Germany
Berlin
Kunstbibliothek, Staatliche Museen zu Berlin
Peter-Klaus Schuster
General Director
Moritz Wullen
Museum Director
Bayerische Staatsgemäldesammlung
Reinhold Baumstark
General Director
Cornelia Syre
Chief Curator

Great Britain
London
British Museum
Neil MacGregor
Director
Oxford
Ashmolean Museum
Christopher Brown
Director
Timothy Wilson
Keeper of Decorative Arts

Italy
Como
Cathedral
Mons. Lorenzo Bataloni
Archpriest, Diocese of Como
Don Guido Calvi
Director of the Ufficio Arte Sacra, Curia Vescovile Diocesi di Como
Daniele Pescarmona
Soprintendenza of Milan
Cremona
Museo Civico Ala Ponzone
Ivanna Iotta
Director
Mario Marubbi
Curator
Florence
Galleria degli Uffizi
Cristina Acidini Luchinat
Soprintendente
Marzia Faietti
Director of the Gabinetto Disegni e Stampe degli Uffizi
Museo Nazionale del Bargello
Beatrice Paolozzi Strozzi
Director
Genoa
Palazzo Rosso
Guido Gandino
Director of the Museums
Piero Boccardo
Director of Collections
Milan
Pinacoteca di Brera
Luisa Arrigoni
Director
Carla Enrica Spantigati
Soprintendente
Simonetta Coppa
Curator
Monza
Duomo di Monza
Mons. Leopoldo Gariboldi
Archpriest of the Duomo di Monza
Carlo Capponi
Ufficio Beni Culturali Ecclesiastici e Arte Sacra
Venice
Gallerie dell'Accademia
Giovanna Nepi Scirè
Soprintendente and Director of the Gallerie dell'Accademia
Roberto Fontanari
Curator

Spain
Madrid
Biblioteca Nacional
Rosa Regàs Pagès
Director
Maria Luisa Cuenca
Department Head

Sweden
Stockholm
National Museum
Solfried Söderlind
Director
Torsten Gunnarsson
Director of Collections
Skokloster
Skokloster Castle
Barbro Bursell
General Director
Carin Bergström
Director
Elisabeth Westin Berg
Vice-Director
Bengt Kylsberg
Curator

United States
Boston
Museum of Fine Arts
Malcolm Rogers
Director
Clifford Ackley
Curator
Kim Paschko
Chief Registrar
Denver
Denver Art Museum
Lewis Sharp
Director
Timothy J. Standring
Deputy Director
Houston
The Menil Collection
Josef Helfenstein
Director
New York
French & Company
Henry V. Zimet
President
Pandora Old Masters Inc.
Lester Carissimi
Christian Lapeyre
Metropolitan Museum of Art
Philippe de Montebello
Director
Carmen C. Bambach
Curator, Department of Drawings and Prints

Special acknowledgment must also be afforded to those who have made this endeavour possible thanks to their enthusiastic support and valuable expertise:

Piera Antonelli, Andreas Antoniuk, Alfred Auer, Christina Bacchi, Sophie Bakalowits, Marc Bascou, Mons. Lorenzo Bataloni, Johanna Böhm, Guido Caneto, Tullia Carratù, Hugo Chapman, Dario Cimorelli, Angela Cipriani, Giovanna Damiani, Andrea Daninos, Rita del Tata, Margherita Druml, David Ekserdjian, Roberto Fontanari, Francesco Frangi, Rainald Franz, Mons. Leopoldo Gariboldi, George Goldner, David Graham, Bengt Kylsberg, Eckart Lingenauer, John Mallet, Laura Miani, Catherine Monbeig Goguel, Alessandro Morandotti, Giovanna Nepi Scirè, Open Care, Milan, Patricia Ozan, Carlo Pedretti, Annalisa Perissa Torrini, Daniele Pescarmona, Johanna Rachinger, Lena Rangström, Elisabeth Royer, Francis Russell, Elena Santiago, Alessandra Seregato, Maria Sframeli, Fulvio Simoni, Solfried Söderlind and Timothy Wilson, as well as to all the lenders and contributors to this project who have wished to remain anonymous.

Patrizia Nitti, who has long been the successful director of the exhibition programme of the Italian Renaissance at the Musée du Luxembourg first suggested Giuseppe Arcimboldo as a possible subject for an exhibition. Naturally, we did not want to miss the opportunity to honour this extraordinary Milanese artist, who served as a much valued court painter for two illustrious Emperors of the Habsburg House, Maximilian II and Rudolf II. In fact, in our own collection we not only have four particularly beautiful examples of the famous and fantastic "composite heads", which to this day have thrilled our visitors, as well as a group of real portraits attributed to him, but in addition, we possess an extremely rich collection of rare art objects that illustrate the delightful realm between art and nature, which was extremely inspirational to Arcimboldo.

Until now, the only large exhibition dedicated to the artist, The Arcimboldo Effect *at the Palazzo Grassi in Venice in 1987, was not actually monographic, because in it he was celebrated as the prime precursor of Modernism. Since then, he has enjoyed great appraisal in the fields of advertising and virtual media as a timeless "icon" of surreal fantasy.*

The objective of this exhibition is to carry him back to his time: from his artistic beginnings in Milan, from the cultural environment in the Viennese and Prague courts, where he created his unusual "scherzi", "grilli" and "capricci", to his last years again in Milan (1587-1593), which he spent as a famous and ennobled prince of painting.

Special attention will be paid to his first patron and sponsor, the tolerant, peaceloving and agreeable Emperor Maximilian II – perhaps because of his relatively short reign – has often stood in the shadow of his father, Ferdinand I and above all of his son, Rudolf II, who were unique among Habsburg rulers as patrons of artistic, humanistic and scientific achievements.

Our thanks go to the national and international institutions and private donors for the sometimes difficult and costly loans. Patrizia Nitti and her colleague, Carolina Vincenti were of great help therein. For the enthusiastic and friendly as well as professional collaboration of the sVo-Art Societé, commissioned by the French Senate with the realization of this project, we give special thanks to the director, Sylvestre Verger, his associate Anne Eschapasse, supervising all fields, from the scientific to the organizational, with a broad vision and deep understanding, as well as the equally kind and knowledgeable Ariane de Guernon whose experience makes her a woman for all seasons.

We would like to thank the Arcimboldo experts and internationally recognized scolars in this field, as well as our in-house curators, restorers and collaborators for their efforts in making this catalogue a scientifically valuable instrument in research on Arcimboldo.

We thank the President of the French Senate, Christian Poncelet, for the trust he granted our establishment in the name of the Musée du Luxembourg to be able to play such a decisive role in regards to the contents of this exhibition project. Thanks go to Yves Marek, conseiller technique du Président du Sénat, for the support and subtle coordination of the assignments of the Musée du Luxembourg. With this, we are confident that this exhibition will enjoy great public appeal in Paris and in Vienna.

Wilfried Seipel
General Director
Kunsthistorisches Museum

Sylvia Ferino-Pagden
Curator of Italian
Renaissance Painting
Kunsthistorisches Museum

The Musée du Luxembourg, located inside the grounds of the Palais du Luxembourg and placed under the responsibility of the Senate, was founded in 1750, making it one of the earliest museums of painting in Europe. The public could go there to see works by Leonardo da Vinci, Titian, Veronese, Rembrandt, Van Dyck, Poussin and Raphael, until it was turned, in 1818, into the Museum of Living Artists and, in a way, the first "museum of modern art". At this time the painters whose works were on show included David, Gros, Girodet, Vernet, Ingres, Delacroix...
Between 1884 and 1886, the Senate constructed the building that now houses the museum. It was then left the important Caillebotte bequest, which made necessary the first extension of the museum.
It is because of this dual line of historical descent that I felt it was important for the programming of the museum to celebrate both modern art and the ItalianRenaissance, with a series of events that commenced with the memorable exhibition Raphael: Grace and Beauty *and continued with* Botticelli: from Lorenzo the Magnificent to Savonarola, Profane Veronese *and* Titian, the Face of Power.
Today, the Senate is happy and proud to stage, and to offer to the Parisian and international public, which has now beaten a path to the Musée du Luxembourg, an exhibition devoted to another of the great artists who bears witness to what Italy has given Europe, Arcimboldo.
It is the first major monographic exhibition devoted to this extraordinary painter, whose work has given rise to so many interpretations. So innovative an artist that in the 20th century he became one of the sources of inspiration of the Surrealists, he is nevertheless a man of his time, something which the exhibition makes absolutely clear. He combines all the talents of a Renaissance artist: in turn architect, court painter, organizer of festivals and decorator, he illustrates perfectly the advances that were being made in the natural sciences and botany.
Painter to the Habsburgs and an essential figure in the debate between northern and Italian artists at the court of Vienna, Arcimboldo is also part of the Austrian heritage. I am deeply grateful to Mrs Sylvia Ferino for having agreed to our request to serve as the commissioner of the exhibition, for having brought all her passion and her erudition to the task, and for having associated with the enterprise the Kunsthistorisches Museum in Vienna, which is at once one of the main lenders of works and the host of its second stage.
I would also like to express the Senate's gratitude to all the museums, from a dozen different countries, that have lent works, and to the private lenders who have made a gesture of goodwill to our museum whose value we fully appreciate. I must also thank Mrs Patrizia Nitti, director of the Renaissance projects of the Musée du Luxembourg, who has coordinated the bringing together of all his works with great tenacity and efficiency. In addition, I am grateful to the Italian authorities and to the distinguished members of the committee of experts that the Senate has assembled for their always generous assistance, as well as to the authors of a catalogue filled with new insights.
Finally, I must express my appreciation for Mr Sylvestre Verger and the company sVo, who have organized this exhibition with a proven professionalism that fully meets the standards of quality to which the Senate has wished to adhere ever since it took responsibility for the museum.

Christian Poncelet
President of the Senate

Looking back over the seven years of programming devoted to the art of the Italian Renaissance at the Musée du Luxembourg, a tribute that the museum has wished to pay to the origins of the building in which it is housed, once the Parisian home of Queen Marie de Médicis, even outsiders will find it easy to understand the initial need to focus on the most classic and probably most popular figures of the period (the exhibitions on Raphael, Botticelli, Veronese and Titian clearly reflected this necessity). But they will now be able to discern a tendency – and one that will also find expression in new and upcoming proposals – to look at artists who played an equally important role in those years but have less of a hold on the collective imagination, and thus are in need of both critical and cultural reappraisal. And thus to be presented to the general public in the manner for which our museum is now renowned.
So the exhibition on Arcimboldo, the first ever to focus exclusively on the artist, belongs to a new season in our programming in which not just the French and international public, but also the Italian one, and specifically that of Milan (Arcimboldo's city, where he worked on the stained-glass windows of the cathedral in his youth), who have followed our exhibitions in the past with interest, will be able to regain possession of a great artist. An artist whose role within the complex cultural dialectics that characterized the relations between religious art and secular art during his time is not known to many.
Some have spoken of an "illusory universe" in relation to Arcimboldo's work and the function of choreographer of games and celebrations at the Viennese court may have bolstered the "senseless sense" of his research. But – and here too I refer readers to the critical essays in the catalogue – it seems evident that Arcimboldo's familiarity with Leonardo's drawings, through his connection with Bernardino Luini, allows us to place his cultural references in a broader and infinitely more complex context. One that permits, in fact, a historical interpretation of the perception of his work.
Roland Barthes worked on the concept of "repulsion" in connection with Arcimboldo, and today we are even told that no other artist of the past was better able to express the modern dimension of multiculturalism through his contaminated forms. This is just to say that the critical view of Arcimboldo is continually evolving and that the proposal today of a major monographic exhibition of his work is part of a project that is not limited to sensationalism but sets out to investigate more thoroughly the conceptual and cultural boundaries of a long, complicated and in the end many-sided period that lies under the blanket, splendid in appearance but not lacking in mysteries, of the Renaissance.
The word "mystery" is one that applies to Arcimboldo too. Apparently well-known to the general public, Arcimboldo is in reality still a mysterious artist. The public today finds it difficult to fit him into a specific period, even though his eclectic abilities were widespread among the artists of his time. In this connection it is worth recalling the letter Leonardo da Vinci wrote in 1482 to the duke of Milan, in which he describes his numerous talents, among which he includes his expertise as a hydraulic and military engineer and as an architect. He also boasts of his skills as a sculptor and musician. He concludes the letter by saying that he can paint as well, a field in which his work will stand comparison with anyone else. Arcimboldo was equally at his ease in designing coats of arms, tapestries and stained-glass windows, painting pictures, staging festivities, dreaming up costumes and observing nature. His work entails a curious interweaving of nature, science and art. The composite elements of which his famous "Seasons" are made up have stirred people's curiosity down the centuries. Initially they attracted the attention of the European courts, and then of those "unquiet" spirits of the 20th century, the Surrealists. Today his images are used by advertisers for their astounding modernity.
Why so much interest? In the first place because he was one of the main protagonists of a strictly profane art that reached its peak during the second half of the 16th century, before being swept away by the Council of Trent. The Counter-Reformation spread its pall of rigorous prohibitions and dictates towards the end of the century, smothering that current of free interpretation of nature. Arcimboldo's vision of the world – as far as we can tell from his artistic work – was an anti-dogmatic one: he played with its elements, expressing their disorder, their variety, their mutability, their constant flow. Thus he became the master of the grotesque, of dream, of metamorphosis.
It is not difficult to extend this reflection to the idea that it is precisely his exploration of these themes that brings him so close to modern

sensibilities. A man of the late Renaissance who spoke a language that is still relevant today. An apparently simple and playful painter who reflected the intellectual and innovative fervour of Mannerist Milan and who – as has been pointed out – cleared the way in Italy for the realist painting that was to culminate a few decades later in the work of Caravaggio.

Patrizia Nitti

Contents

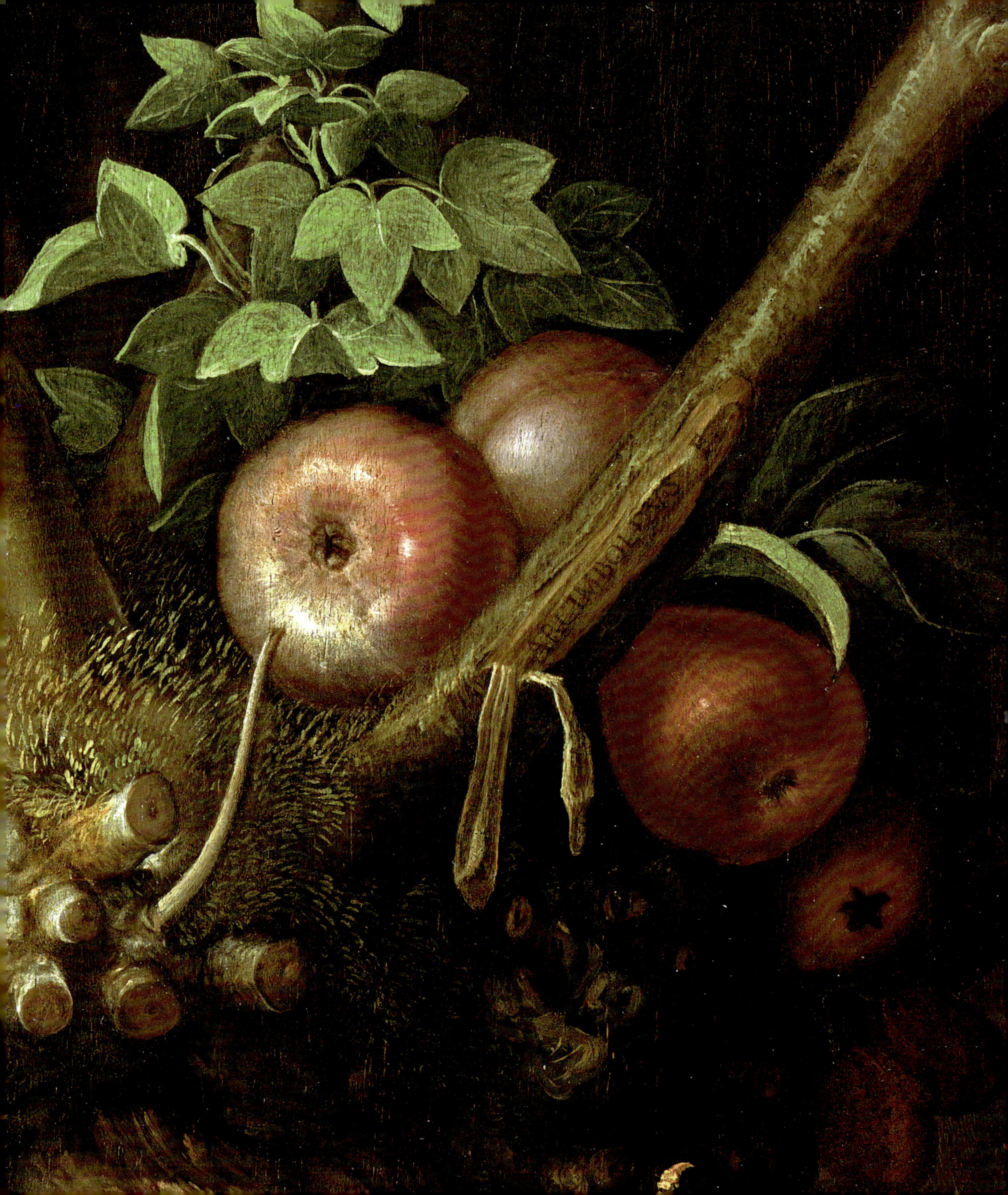

Giuseppe Arcimboldo: Court Artist, Philosopher, "rhétoriqueur", Magician or an Entertainer?

Sylvia Ferino-Pagden

To this day, transforming the human face has remained one of the best visual devices to raise wonder, confusion or joy, or at least to attract attention, because it makes us pass from the ordinary perception of the real world to other perceptive dimensions like illusions, visions, dreams, but also uncertainty, deceitful appearances and even nightmares. All those sensations can be induced by Giuseppe Arcimboldo's composite heads. The first confrontation creates a surprise effect which takes viewers unaware and bewilders them, the disoriented eye goes to and fro between the overall shape and the details, until it finally identifies the trick, which gives rise to amusement, joy or repulsion. Arcimboldo's contemporaries must already have felt that way, as attested by the writings of the historian Paolo Morigia, but also those of the artist and theoretician Gian Paolo Lomazzo, just like Gregorio Comanini's dialogue, which all celebrate his inventions as "scherzi", "grilli" and "capricci"[1].

Nowadays, Arcimboldo is considered the epitome of "Mannerism"[2], the period formerly called the Late Renaissance, which was isolated as a style of its own in the 20th century. From this time it became common practice to draw a parallel between our times and the 16th century, during which all established systems were challenged in the political, religious and philosophical realms, a century which favoured the intellectual "concetti" and "artificiality" of a self-referential art delighting in exaggerations, deformations, anamorphoses, hieroglyphics and secret codes, in the monstrous and the paradoxical, and which brilliantly eluded all attemps at deciphering it[3]. Was that because game-playing, "scherzo", was its central theme? Was not that precisely the reason why, in the 20th century, Arcimboldo was chosen by the Surrealists, the Dadaists and their successors as the founding model for their fantastic creations?

Since he was identified as a source of inspiration for "Fantastic Art, Dada, Surrealism" in the 1937 exhibition of the same title in New York's Museum of Modern Art, Arcimboldo has been promoted the master of illusions, of paradoxes and – to take up the words of Roland Barthes' excellent essay – "rhétoriqueur" and magician[4]. In 1987, on the occasion of the major show in Venice, *The Arcimboldo Effect*, he was finally hailed as a precursor of modernity[5]. Since then, his fantastic compositions have been used in business and advertising; even in the virtual world, he seems to have been raised to the pinnacle as "our eternal contemporary"[6]. What strikes us in Arcimboldo's composite heads is first of all their timeless modernity and the multiplicity of their references: be it the profile portraits he constructed from vegetal elements, as in the *Seasons*, or mainly from animals as in the *Elements*, the professional portraits like *The Cook* or *The Waiter* he composed from emblematic instruments in traditional three-quarter views or the individual portraits of real-life people, like *Librarian* Wolfgang Lazius or *Jurist* Ulrich Zasius[7], in which he ironically chose and arranged objects characterizing their professional interests, so as to hint at their personal weaknesses, in a witty style bordering on caricature.

The real inventor of the autonomous still-life is therefore neither Caravaggio with his famous *Fruit Basket* in the Ambrosiana, nor Figino with his *Peach Basket*[8]: the title should have been granted to Arcimboldo with the invention of his *The Vegetable Gardener* (now in Cremona) or his *The Cook* (now in Stockholm) if he had not deprived himself of the honour by transforming his reversible still-lifes into a game of hide-and-seek, with those startling faces when they are turned upside down[9].

In the more poetic and more paradoxical creations of his late years, the paintings of *Flora* and *Vertumnus* which were sent from Milan to Emperor Rudolf, Arcimboldo took hold of antique myths and poems, with the support of the humanists who observed his works *in statu nascendi* and praised them in their writings. Arcimboldo's curious "capricci" are still seen as the *par excellence* expression of Rudolf II's very idiosyncratic and refined artistic interests; over the last two decades, his composite heads have been present in all the exhibitions devoted to the greatest patron of science and art among the Habsburgs[10]. But in 1562, when Arcimboldo came to the court of Emperor Ferdinand in Vienna, Rudolf was only ten years old and moreover, between 1563 and 1571, he was sent to the court of Spain in order to receive the education of a devout catholic. The fact that Arcimboldo was summoned by Maximilian rather than by Ferdinand I is confirmed by several documents as well as by Morigia's and Lomazzo's writings.

Maximilian was exceptionally keen on the study of nature as a

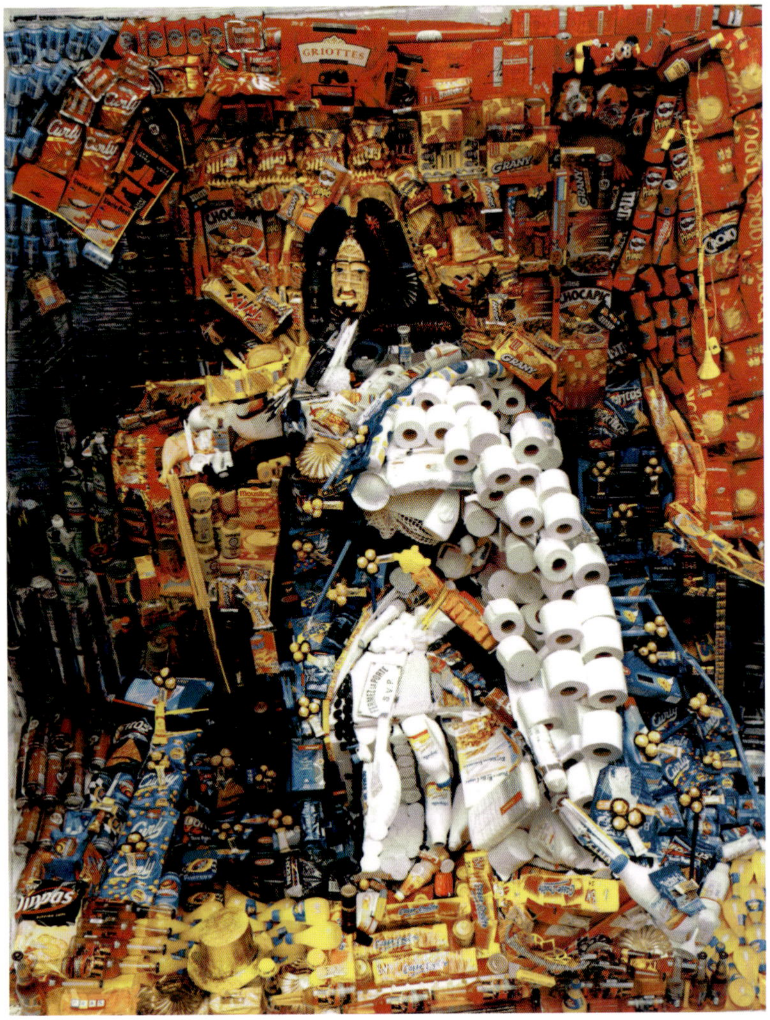

Fig. 1. Bernard Pras, *Louis XIV*, 2003.
Photograph, Cibachrom

whole, even though he had a specific interest in extremely rare or unknown species and their monstrous deformations. Arcimboldo's drawings after live animals are very realistic and matter-of-fact, we are surprised by their sobriety and their "lack of affectation"; they lack the deliberate artificiality of the refined sheets drawn for Rudolf by artists like Joris Hoefnagel who, in order to create more sophisticated works of art, copied and stylized the studies from nature made by others. Those latter pictures thus correspond to the *maniera* defined as an aesthetic ideal, which dictated Rudolf's tastes as far as sculpture and painting were concerned, an ideal which Arcimboldo's heads could not reach, neither as painted works, nor as art, except as curiosities or even monstrosities.

No pictures are known which Arcimboldo may have created while he worked as court artist for Rudolf II. The paintings he sent from Milan to the emperor are different from the heads he painted for Maximilian, if only because of their complex and explicit reference to Antiquity and because of their much greater elegance. Through their thematic choice, they are the only ones which fully embrace the aesthetic of the paradox expressed in their companion poems. On the contrary, despite their equally paradoxical basic structure, the works executed for Maximilian seem much more naive, realistic, natural or even comic, reflecting another aesthetic ideal. But whose ideal was that? Maximilian's or Arcimboldo's?

In today's art, Arcimboldo's principle of composition (in the proper meaning of the word) has been perpetuated under a more refined guise, if we can trust the photographs of more or less famous people, like *King Louis XIV*, *Salvador Dalí*, *Albert Einstein*, *Lolo*, *Dutronc* among others, created by Parisian artist Bernard Pras, which are both disturbing and wonderful, in which one cannot in the least recognize the abundant installations from which they derive, for which the artist selects objects according to their respective themes (*fig. 1-2*)[11]. Pras arranges the various elements of his portraits in specific places which often take an active part in the staging of these composite appearances; it still takes the intervention of the camera's eye to link them together so that a recognizable portrait emerges. This is not the place to consider which dominant criteria influenced the artist in his choice of particular elements for individual portraits, nor which infinite fund of objective correlatives he draws from during the process. Still, Pras creates such effective pictures that one thinks he has a deep understanding of Arcimboldo's method for a composite art which is thus "propelled" into the present.

But just like in Pras' photographs, Arcimboldo's composite heads, on which much of his celebrity relies nowadays, are only part of the various works he had to execute as a court artist. During his youth in Milan, he had to conceive religious scenes, stained-glass windows, tapestries, banners and frescoes, but in Vienna and later in Prague, he was asked to produce portraits of members of the court, paintings for the emperor's museum, short-lived festivities and pageants, illustrations of rare plants and animals, to expertize and buy precious works of art and natural curiosities, to create sketches for interior decoration or pictures of silk culture and other similar processes which transform nature into art.

That is why, when we were asked to put Arcimboldo in the limelight again, twenty years after a major exhibition in Venice, we decided to seize the opportunity: an artist which had inbetween become a timeless icon would at last be replaced in his historical context, following a wish that had already been formulated in 1987 by various critics[12]. Despite the wealth of autograph works on display and the precious contributions to the volume which shed light on Arcimboldo's activity in the Habsburg court, the Venetian catalogue was not really a monograph, since it focused on those aspects of his work which could more easily be related to modernity[13].

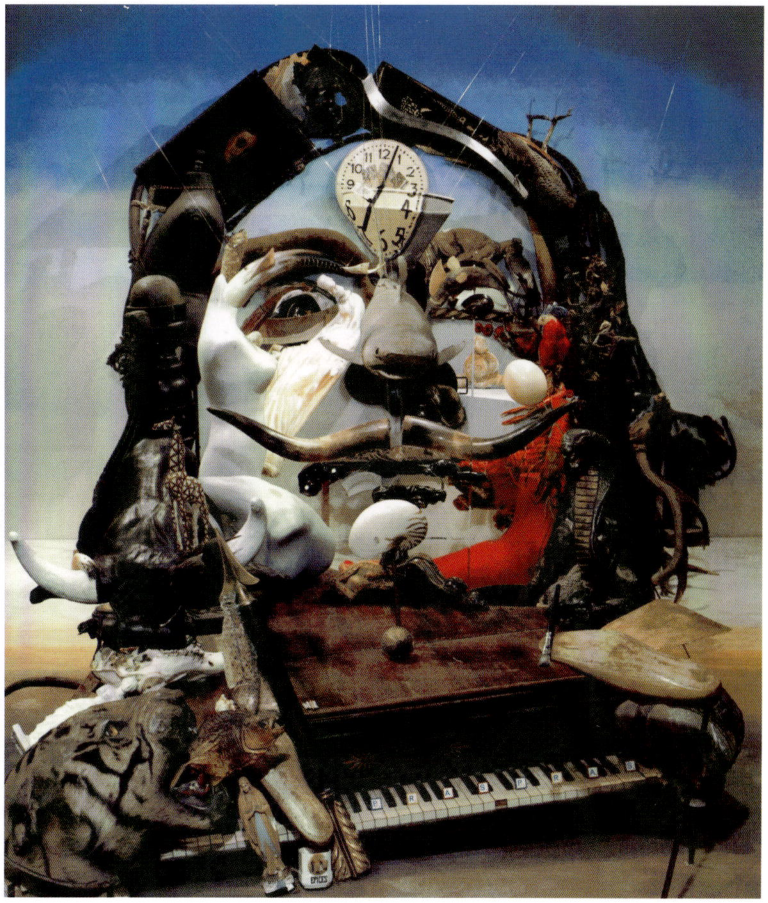

Fig. 2. Bernard Pras, *Salvador Dali*, 2004.
Photograph, Cibachrom

We shall therefore start by scrutinizing those documents already known, to which some new ones have been added[14], in order to reach a better understanding of Arcimboldo's artistic personality, by addressing unanswered questions: Where did he really come from? Through which prowesses, accomplished in his Milanese period, did he deserve the "international fame" which had him hired by the Habsburg court? What kind of spiritual and cultural climate did inspire his "grilli", "scherzi" or "bizarrie", which may have derived from the commissioning of realistic portraits? How should we interpret them? Beyond the considerable generic diversity of his works and sketches, is it possible to identify a personal expression which could unite them, a kind of artistic signature? *In fine*, how should we imagine his "persona"? And why was Arcimboldo completely forgotten after his death, to be rediscovered only in the 20th century? If we read the accounts and praise in the writings of his humanist, chronicler, artist and theoretician friends, in particular those of Morigia, Lomazzo and Comanini who based their works on Arcimboldo's own testimony, we can obtain a fascinating vision of the painter's active participation in his modern fame and, through this, of his artistic personality[15].

It is to be noticed that, in the paragraphs celebrating his role as the Habsburgs' court artist, none of his early works is mentioned. Was that because Arcimboldo saw his time in Milan as forgettable? Though research on Milanese art round 1500 has been especially active in recent years[16], we cannot get an accurate idea of Arcimboldo's personal artistic expression, essentially because his cartoons for stained-glass windows or tapestries were transposed and realized by other artists or because he worked in partnership, as with the Monza frescoes. He seems to be constantly hesitating between two forms: a classical one and a faintly Mannerist one. That is why the "international" repute which he may have acquired in Milan and which led to his appointment in Vienna still remains a mystery.

However, Arcimboldo's formation in this artistic background was extremely important for his future career, since Lombard painting is seen as the cradle of "naturalism", deeply influenced by Leonardo's studies from nature[17]. Leonardo's "comic" heads, his sketches of plants and animals, being circulated among his followers, were specifically used as models for all sorts of creations, including Arcimboldo's[18]. Leonardo's "comic" heads may have influenced Arcimboldo's composite heads, as can be seen through a simple comparison between one of Leonardo's drawings with the *Four Seasons in one Head*, here on show for the first time (*fig. 4-5*).

Recent research has legitimately focused on the cultural climate in Milan which was the background for composite pictures, in relation with carnivalesque popular culture and the ludicrous creations of the artists gathered in the Accademia della Val di Blenio, who tried to escape religious censorship by hiding their true spiritual and aesthetic aspirations in "caricatures"[19], but the present exhibition will prove, thanks to eloquent Italian testimonies, that Arcimboldo did not invent his method from scratch: others before him created heads with objects of all sorts[20].

For the first time, the animal and plant species depicted by Arcimboldo in his *Seasons* and *Elements* are studied with greater attention. He turns out to be an important illustrator of natural sciences, whose sketches of the rare animals kept (alive or dead) in the courts of Vienna and Prague were sent to the famous natural scientist Ulisse Aldrovandi.

We are relatively well informed about the relations between sovereigns interested in natural sciences and the learned men they employed in their courts, about their frequent exchanges of stuffed animals, dried plants and scientific results. In terms of art historical research little interest has been shown towards those artists who were asked to produce scientific illustrations. Beside his botanical drawings, the group of drawings here attributed to Arcimboldo could also help identify the incredible diversity of sea animals he depicted for instance in his representation of *Water*. A sheet dated 1553 belongs to his early years in Milan (see illustration in my contribution on Arcimboldo's studies after nature)[21].

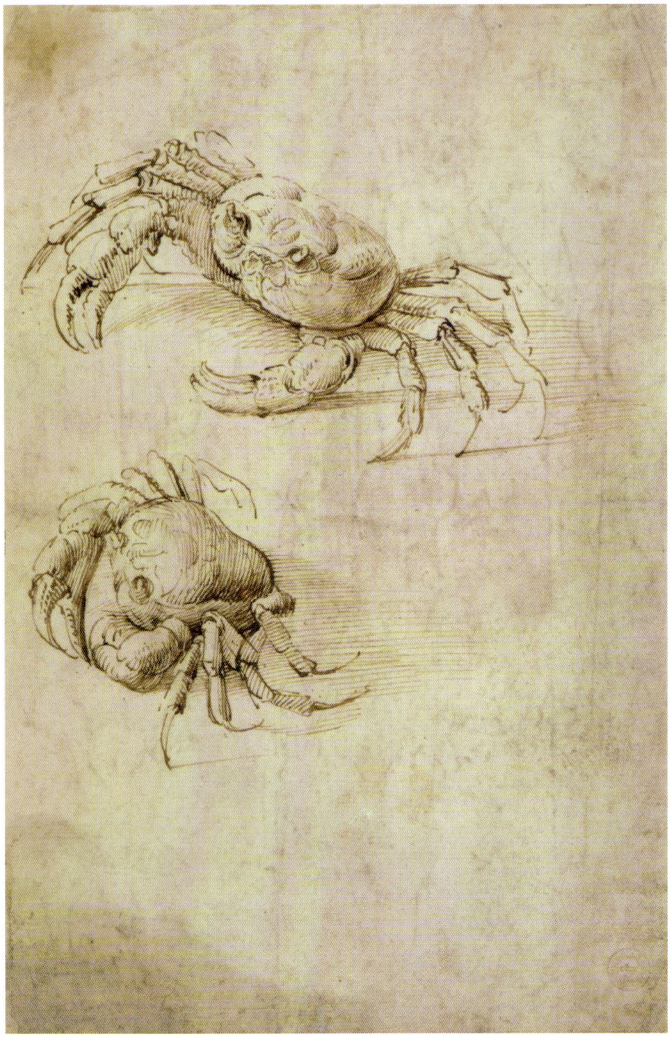

Fig. 3. Leonardo da Vinci (?), *Studies of crabs*. Cologne, Wallraf-Richartz Museum

We still have no proof that Arcimboldo ever painted portraits during his Milanese years. Portrait painting was one of the most important genres the Habsburgs could commission; as Arcimboldo's first attested commission in Vienna was to copy a portrait, it may be thought that he was summoned to the court primarily to fulfill such a dignified task[22], since "portraits of all the members of the Austrian court in the hand of our Arcimboldo" were supposedly displayed among Rudolf's collections[23]. If compared with the famous composite heads, the group of portraits which have been tentatively included in this exhibition may seem disappointing, because of the conventionality imposed by their subject, and perhaps also because of their less impressive quality; nevertheless, they can hold their own if faced with some parts of the Monza frescoes attributed to Arcimboldo[24]. From a strictly technical point of view, the so-called group of the "archduchesses" shows a close relation with the artist's other works[25]. Non the less, the pictures allow us to exclude the idea that Arcimboldo might have been called to the court because of his skills as a traditional portrait painter.

True, we do not know whether his talent for the conception and organization of magnificently staged pageants had already manifested itself in Milan; it most probably led to his summoning to Vienna[26], for contemporary descriptions give proof of his profuse and costly activity in that field when he served Emperor Maximilian and his successor Rudolf II. Arcimboldo himself valued those achievements so much that he had them transcribed in detail by his humanist and artist friends, Morigia and Lomazzo in particular.

Mythological and historical motives from the Antiquity, applied to the present and identified with the sovereign, were repeatedly used in countless variations for the scenario of those pageants, as well as the full allegorical and symbolical repertoire of humanism[27]. All that survives are the virtuoso sketches for costumes, monsters' trappings and graceful projects for carriages[28]. Was Arcimboldo primarily a creator of short-lived marvels? That could explain the confusing fact that only a very small part of his work has been preserved from the twenty-five years during which he worked for the emperors. The interest in Arcimboldo's creations therefore tends to concentrate on his composite heads, their origins and interpretation, inspiring innovating debates in scientific literature, as well as in this catalogue.

According to DaCosta Kaufmann, the political and allegorical references which were particularly present in Arcimboldo's festive works may also have been the main source of inspiration for his composite heads[29], in so far as the *Seasons* and *Elements* series were presented to the emperor on New Year's Day 1569, together with explicative panegyrical poems by Giovanni Battista Fonteo. Mixing various traditions and tracing them back to the Roman empire seen as *caput mundi*, Fonteo described the *Seasons* and the *Elements* and their interaction between microcosm and macrocosm as political allegories of Maximilian's and the Habsburgs' exceptional rule[30]. Arcimboldo's composite creations were supposedly born from the close relation between the humanist artist and the sovereign; only later were they taken up by Fonteo whom the emperor had requested to give a literary expression to the panegyrical concept[31].

This point of view is now almost unanimously accepted and adopted by several of the contributors to this catalogue[32], but in 1978, Roland Barthes already suggested another reading, from a linguistic perspective: comparing the composition method with the various uses of rhetorics (metaphor, allegory, metonymy, allusion), he qualified Arcimboldo as a visual "rhétoriqueur". The analogy also lies in the way Arcimboldo creates a strange novelty through substitution, through displacement, but also through the fragmenting of familiar objects, through the new relations which result from their juxtaposition. Because of their specific combination in the general arrange-

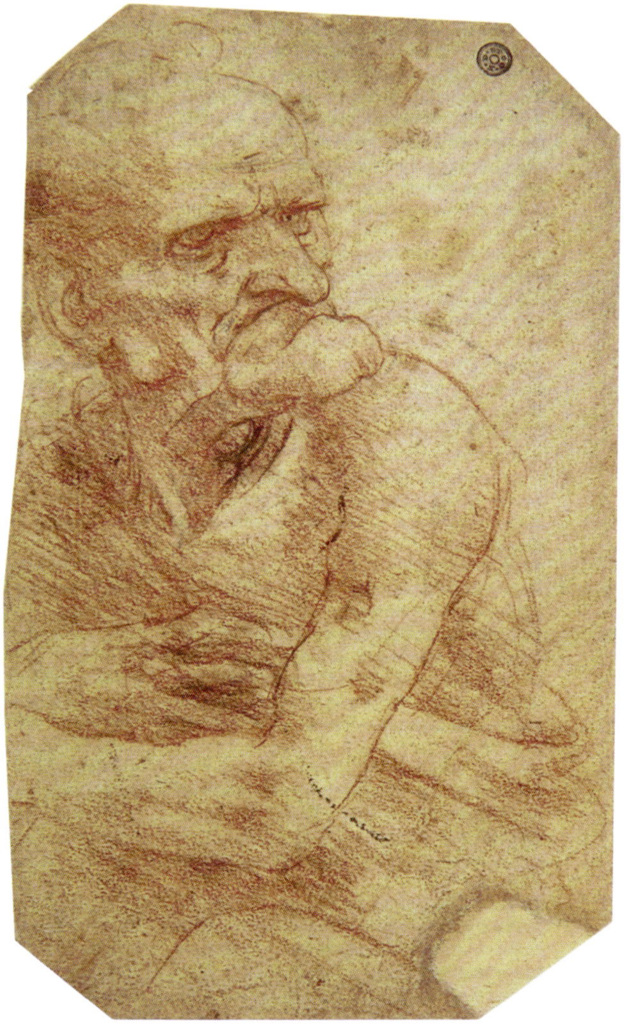

Fig. 4. Leonardo da Vinci, *Study of an old man*. Rome, Istituto nazionale per la grafica

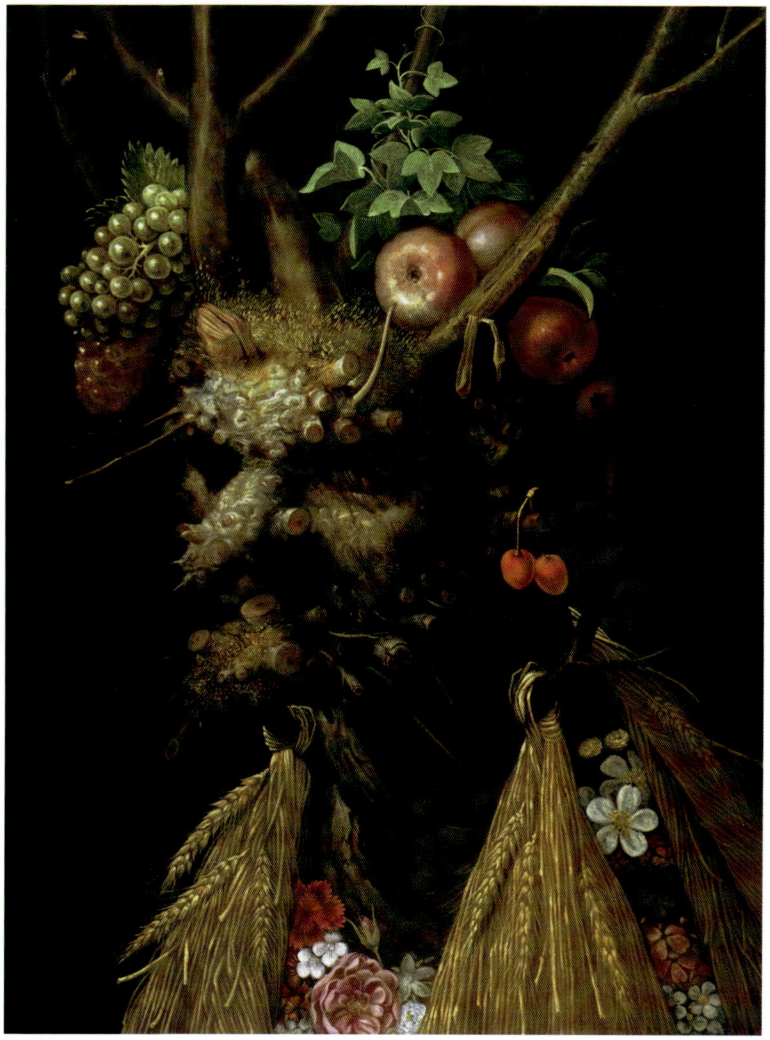

Fig. 5. Arcimboldo, *The four seasons in a head*. Private collection

ment, the viewer is led to adopt new ways of seeing. Beyond the artistic aspect of Arcimboldo's works, Barthes sees a scientific process, an act of acquiring knowledge in the unease roused by those heads, in particular through the process of accumulating many objects, which gives birth to something ugly and monstrous. Using the contemporary poems inspired by *Flora* and *Vertumnus*, Barthes' analysis of rhetorics as applied to Arcimboldo's times allows to show that the painting's subject is indeed the constant movement back and forth between details and overall shape, between two instances of enunciation, between unity and multiplicity, and the resulting metamorphosis. The invention of those heads, inspired by an aesthetic of paradox, could thus be attributed to pure artistic virtuosity, a predilection for playful confusion which is characteristic of Mannerism and its instability of values.

Those different interpretative possibilities (the expectations of a humanist court vs. individual artistic creativity) could harmoniously unite in Arcimboldo's figure. Whatever their artistic ingenuity and unicity, Arcimboldo's paradoxical composite heads cannot be separated from the immediate context of his numerous functions as a court artist. Serving duke Albert V of Bavaria, Samuel Quiccheberg wrote in 1565 that Maximilian especially enjoyed the role of "collector of the things nature [lavished] here below"[33]. If we admit that one of the first tasks entrusted to Arcimboldo as soon as he arrived in Vienna was to depict the plant and animal species so dearly beloved to Maximilian, present in his botanical and zoological gardens (some of those studies date back to the first year of the artist's stay in Vienna), a first important requirement is met, concerning the accumulation of separately studied objects, even though that does not explain their conflation into a human head.

A reason why no passages symbolize the Habsburgs in Arcimboldo's *Seasons* may be that in 1583, their commissioner had not yet been elected emperor. The incarnation of *Fire*, dated 1566, deliberately (rather than accidentally) gives pride of place to the collar of the Golden Fleece, which must be given a political interpretation.

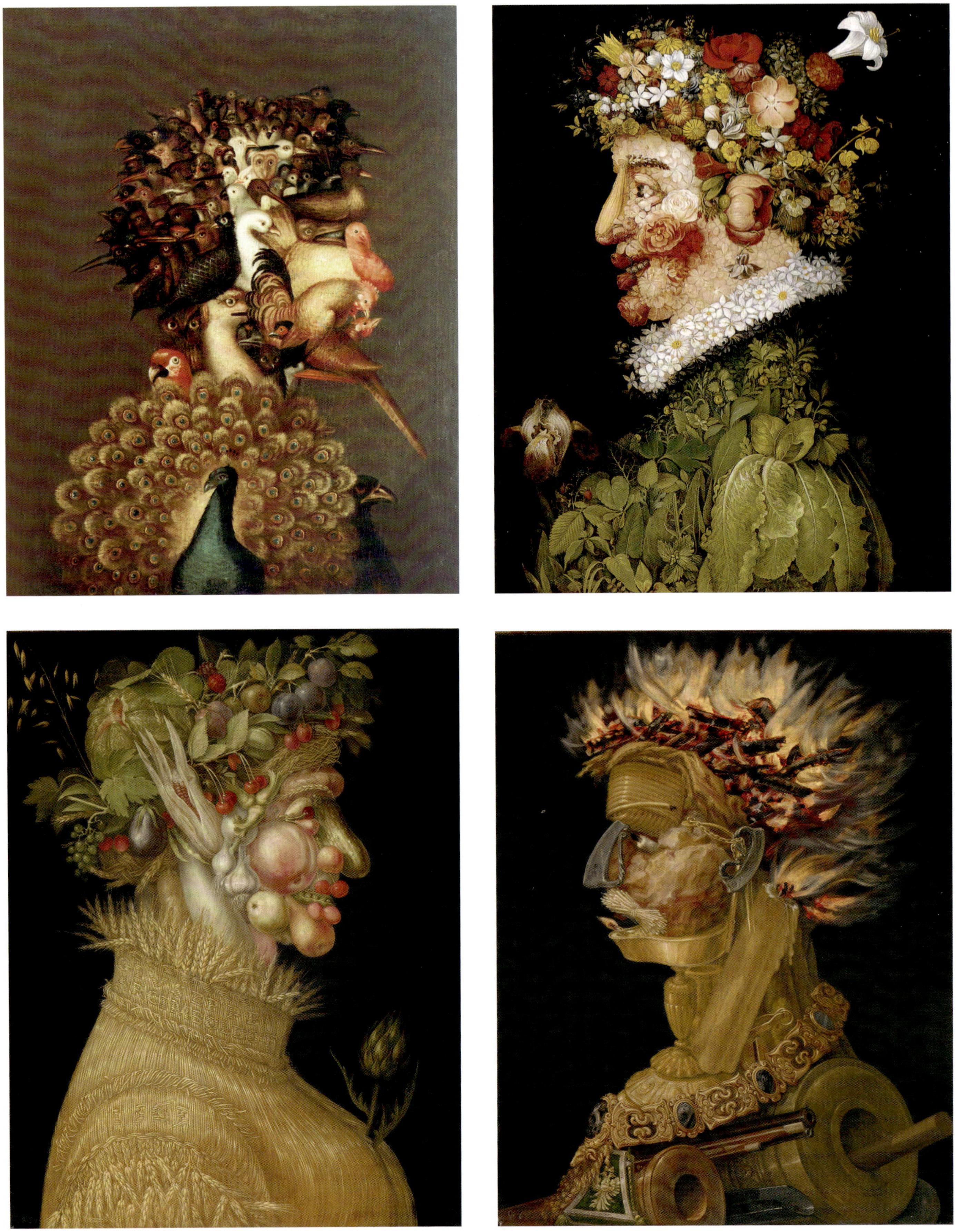

Fig. 6

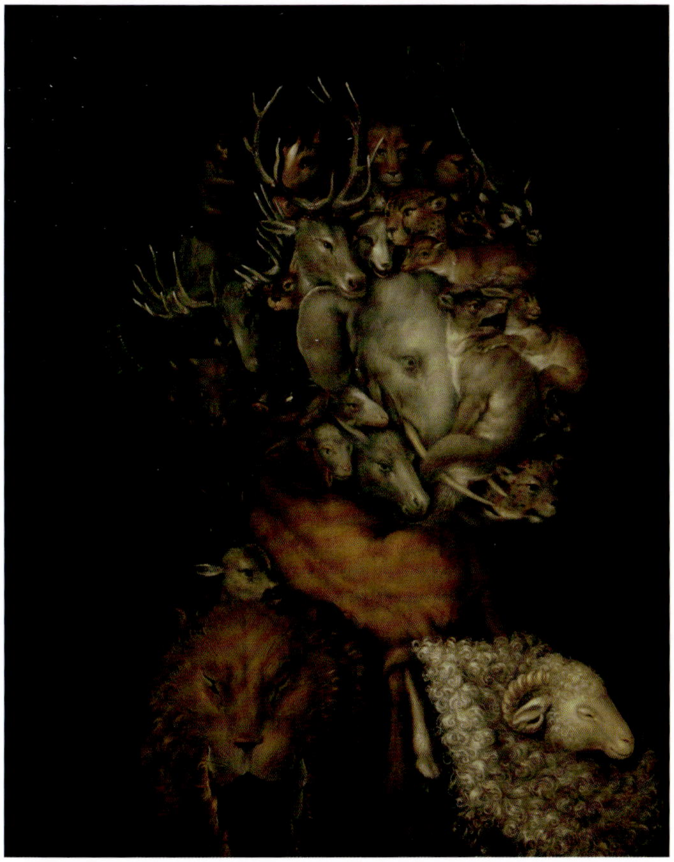

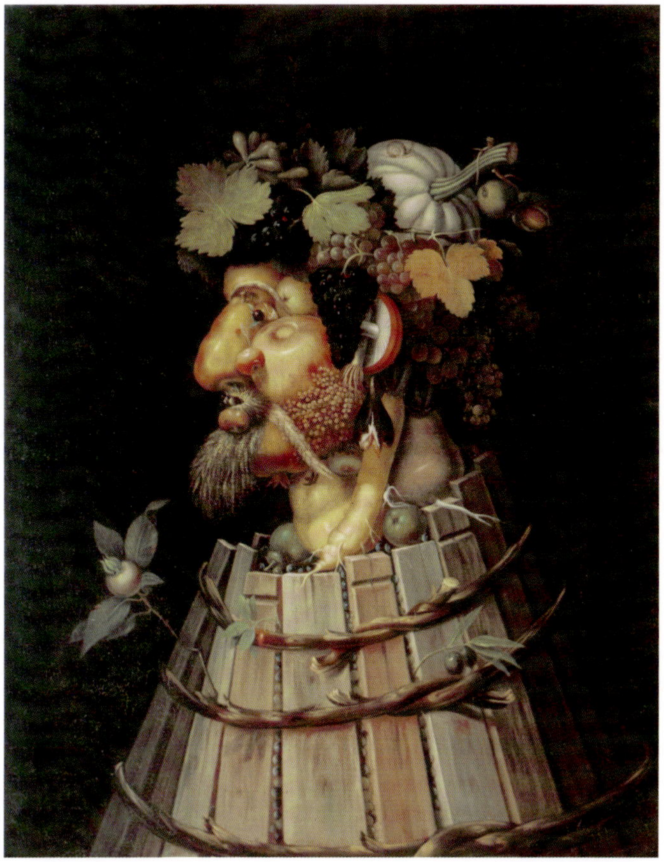

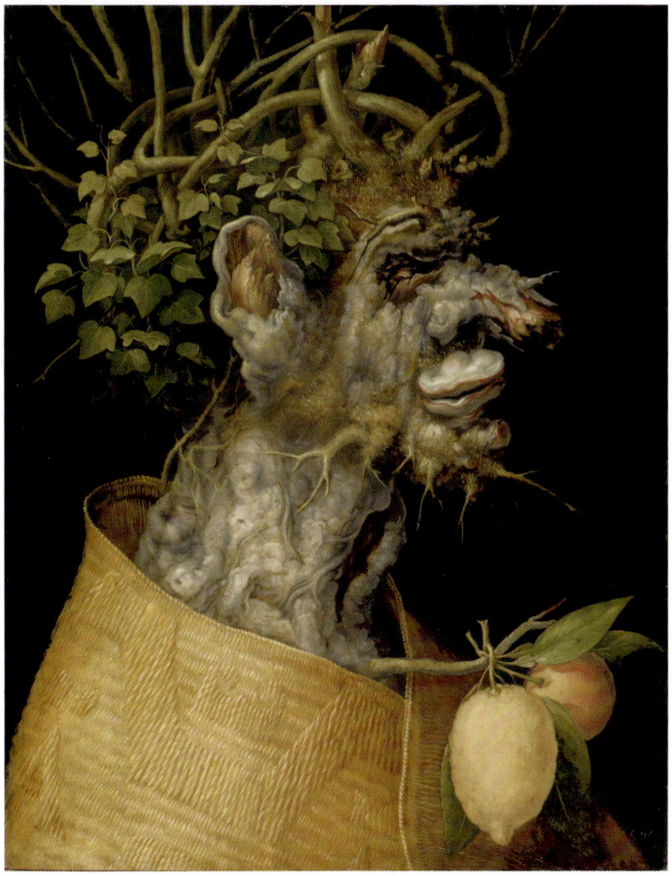

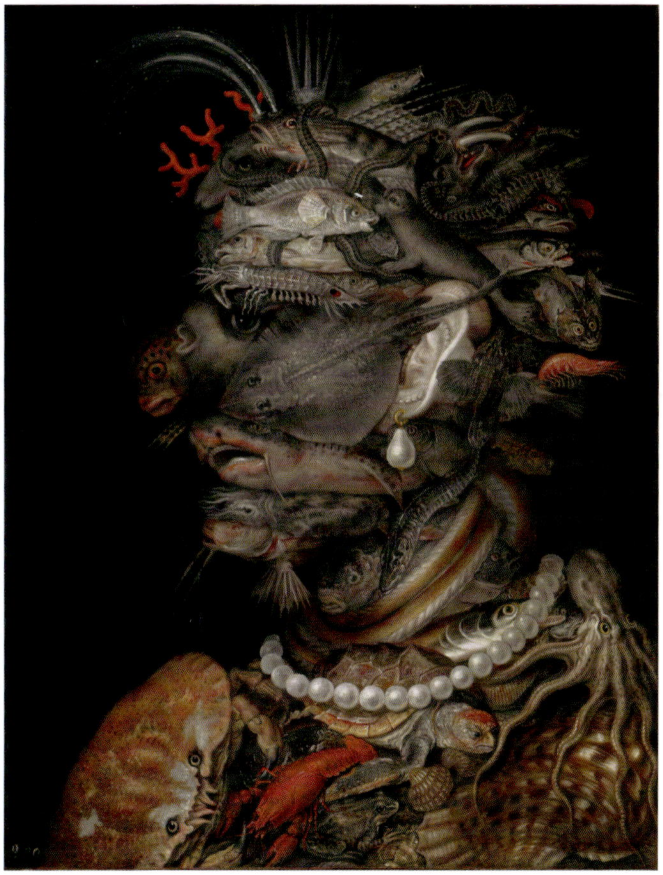

Between 1566 and 1568, Arcimboldo was in Milan and, from 1568 onwards, the Milanese humanist Fonteo also worked in Vienna. According to Lomazzo, who repeated Arcimboldo's own version, the poet was introduced there by the artist[34].

The other paintings of the *Elements* include more explicit political allusions which may reflect a growing desire to honour the emperor. Spontaneously or under the influence of his humanist friends in Milan, Arcimboldo may well have decided to have a literary description written by a humanist in order to give more weight to his works, so that the emperor could identify with them as official products and use them as propaganda for his courtly art, or even boast of them by sending replicas to his relatives and to other sovereigns.

Julius von Schlosser insisted on the fact that even the copies of the *Seasons* sent to other princely courts were always mentioned in the context of cabinets of art and curiosities[35], but we may suppose with Lomazzo that the emperor himself wanted to see them displayed in his museum, "degno di perpetua memoria".

It was even imagined that those paintings were destined to adorn the walls of a huge room (in the order suggested by Fonteo), in the centre of which stood an extraordinary fountain whose decorative programme also exalted the glory of the sovereign and whose bronze statues by Wenzel Jamnitzer, representing the four seasons, have been preserved[36].

In Maximilian's opulent cabinet of art and curiosities, his "archives of wisdom", the rare works of nature or *naturalia* were exhibited together with *artificialia*, elaborate works of art. In this specific context, Arcimboldo's composite heads could be seen as painted "Kunstkammer-objects".

From that perspective, it may have been the artist himself rather than the emperor who employed the humanist to serve his own ends, in the same way as he had poems written by Comanini, Gherardini and others about his *Flora* and *Vertumnus*. This should lead us to question the classical triangular pattern of patron, artist and counselling humanist, which would allow us to reach the more likely vision of an artist who was fully conscious of the value of his artistic inventions. According to Lomazzo's account, Fonteo claimed paternity for one of Arcimboldo's creations: this may hint at the artist's outrage at such a violation of artistic "copyright", which may explain why Fonteo left the court in 1572.

Our conception of Arcimboldo could thus be completed as that of a learned, cunning artist, who could fight for his interests, who was not only ennobled during his career, being elevated to the rank of Palatine count, but who saw himself as a humanist, an adviser, occasionally posing as a poet, under the alias of G.A. da Milano, to sing the praise of his own paintings. Morigia reports that Arcimboldo retraced his genealogy to pre-carolingian origins, through a germanic Arcimboldi family. However, documents have shown that Giuseppe was absolutely not related to the aristocratic family of the same name in Milan, though he thus tried to justify the nobiliary title conferred by the emperor in 1580. This ingenuous trick is proof of the artist's cleverness, just like his awareness that his posthumous fame would owe as much to the writings of humanists as to his own works. Let the visitors of our exhibition and the readers of this catalogue decide by themselves whether, in a time of major talents, Arcimboldo was no more than a "competent journeyman" whose success and reputation are due to only one kind of activity, as Charles Hope observed in his contribution to the Venetian show[37]. Perhaps the title chosen by DaCosta Kaufmann for one of his many essays (*Giuseppe Arcimboldo, The Habsburgs' Leonardo*) should be considered more than a pleasant exaggeration, if we think of the inventions praised by Lomazzo, such as the "perspectival lute" or the "colour harpsichord"[38].

The contributions gathered in the various sections of this catalogue aim at providing a balanced overall vision of Arcimboldo's œuvre which, though quantitatively limited, is Protean by its diversity. Given the number of contributors and the diversity of their methodological approaches, a certain degree of overlapping and disagreement was almost inevitable. That is probably what distinguishes an exhibition catalogue from a traditional monograph by one author. Though this catalogue has a "composite" character similar to Arcimboldo's heads, we hope that it can nevertheless (or precisely, for that reason) be a scientific tool and a valuable instrument for future research into Arcimboldo.

[1] Falchetta in exhibition catalogue Venice 1987; Beyer in this catalogue.
[2] Hulten in exhibition catalogue Venice 1987, 19.
[3] Majorino 1991.
[4] Barr Jr in exhibition catalogue New York 1937; Pieyre de Mandiargues 1978; Porzio 1978; Barthes 1978.
[5] Exhibition catalogue Venice 1987.
[6] Borri 1995, 443-453.
[7] See Görel Cavalli-Björkman's contribution to this catalogue.
[8] Berra 1996a, Berra 2000; Ebert-Schifferer 2002, 1-27.
[9] That is the reason why the French writer André Pieyre de Mandiargues called them "anthropomorphic" still-lifes, in 1978.
[10] Exhibition catalogue Essen-Vienna 1988.
[11] Christian-Louis Eclimont, *Bernard Pras "Inventaires"*, Paris 2007.
[12] Since then, works by Arcimboldo have regularly been included in many exhibitions, with great effect on the public, though their presence was more or less relevant to the themes and objectives announced. In important historical celebrations of Emperor Rudolf II (in Vienna, Prague and recently Dijon) as well as in countless thematic exhibitions (the *Five Senses* in art, *Capriccio* as an art form, *Melancholy*), his composite heads were presented from different points of view and with new interpretations.
[13] What was criticized above all was the general conception of those exhibitions, because they underlined purely visual and superficial relations between Arcimboldo and modernity, without any grounding in the content of the works. See Beyer 1987, 343-344; Hope 1987, 41-44; Gemin 1988, 139-140.

[14] Geiger (1954) 1960, 127-146. The documents gathered by Silvio Leydi and Manfred Staudinger in the Appendix bring valuable new information.
[15] See Andreas Beyer's essay in this catalogue.
[16] Bora 1977; Kaufmann 1988; Fiorio 1988; Miller 1989, 189-190; Bora 1998; Berra 1998; Guazzoni 2005.
[17] Exhibition catalogue Cremona 2000; exhibition catalogue Cremona-New York 2004.
[18] "molto si dilettò di disegnare, i quali si veghono ancora in diversi luoghi, tra quali forsi da cinquanta, disegnati di sua mano, ne tien Aurelio Lovino uno libricciuolo" (Lomazzo, Libro VI, Cap. XXXIII). See Linda Wolk-Simon in exhibition catalogue Cremona-New York 2004, 64-69.
[19] Porzio 1993, 37-42; Berra 1998, 57-76.
[20] Nevertheless, it remains difficult to prove that Carlo Urbino da Crema, mentioned by Lomazzo, was one of his predecessors. Hope 1987, 44; for a contrary opinion, Kaufmann 1988, 14-15, 17, n28-33.
[21] Österreichische Nationalbibliothek, Cod. min. 42. The heterogenous graphic treatment of the various sketches gathered on that page can be interpreted in the following way: Arcimboldo may have added the lizard above, in a blue wash which betrays his style.
[22] The self-portrait, an oil on linen, reproduced in black and white in Geiger's book, is now lost.
[23] Quotation after Fučikova 1986, 15.
[24] See Karl Schütz' contribution to this catalogue.
[25] Kaufmann rejects the hypothetic attribution of those portraits to Arcimboldo.
[26] See Silvio Leydi's contribution to this catalogue.
[27] See Andreas Beyer's contribution.
[28] That is why we decided to include in this exhibition a few coloured prints of pageants devised by other artists, so as to give some idea of their lavishness.
[29] Kaufmann 1976, 275-296; exhibition catalogue Venice 1987, 89-109; 1990, 59-86; 2005, 28-32; see also his contribution to this catalogue.
[30] Kaufmann 1976. The symbols and insignia included in the heads (the collar of the Golden Fleece in *Fire*, the lion and fleece in *Earth*, the peacock and eagle in *Air*) indisputably referred to the panegyrical function.
[31] See Kaufmann's contribution.
[32] Hope 1987, 41-44, formally declared against this hypothesis.
[33] See Franz Kirchweger's contribution to this catalogue.
[34] Lomazzo 1590 (1973), 363.
[35] Von Schlosser 1908.
[36] Alfons in exhibition catalogue Venice 1987, 41-44.
[37] Hope 1987, 44, thus coming round to the opinions of such prestigious art historians as Roberto Longhi, Giulio Briganti and others. See Berra 1996 (Paragone), 136-137, note 1.
[38] Kaufmann 1998.

Fig. 6, pages 20-21. Comparison of the *Seasons* and *Elements*

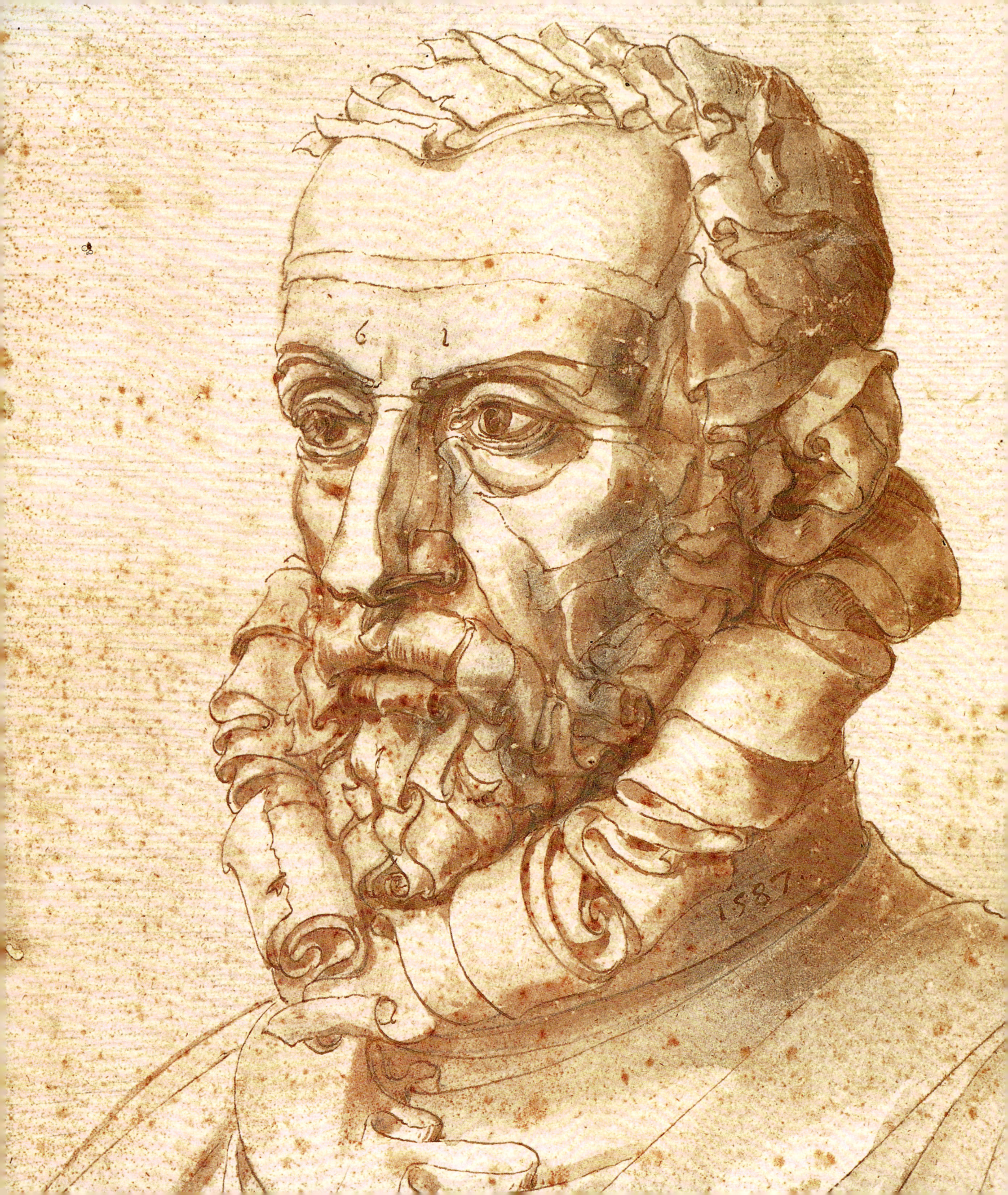
1587

Andreas Beyer

"... il gran pittore Giuseppe Arcimboldi" On the Construction of Arcimboldo's Fame

An artist's fame is never sure to endure forever; it is granted for a limited amount of time, as in a precarial contract – artistic acclaim is a matter of mood. Another proof is the ambiguity of the Italian word *fama* (meaning both fame and rumour); likewise, the phrase *fortuna critica*, in use far beyond the Italian-speaking world, links an artist's reception to the goddess of happiness and destiny[1]. Giovanni Battista Passeri, the biographer of artists, captured it in words in the late 17th century: "In many cases, *fama*'s trajectory also depends on chance, and requires above all the support of propitious and favourable circumstances"[2]. Giuseppe Arcimboldo is no exception; and perhaps this applies to him even more as he spent the most fruitful and significant period of his career in a foreign country and was aware of the limitations of the supposed guardians of his posthumous fame. Enjoying the highest regard during one's lifetime does not preclude sinking into posthumous oblivion nor even *damnatio memoriae*.

The author of one of the earliest, most famous monographs about Arcimboldo, Benno Geiger already lamented: "Arcimboldo's fame, which had remained very much alive in late 16th-century Milan and which had an enthusiastic promoter in the blind seer Lomazzo, vanished from Italy and elsewhere at the beginning of the following century. He was mentioned only once, as a portraitist, by Malvasia in his *Felsina Pittrice* (1678) ... He was totally ignored in the 18th century, if we except Lanzi who made a belated and erroneous reference to him. Austrian archivists dug up his name in the 19th century, but still without any association to his painting"[3]. Since then, research into Arcimboldo has improved considerably. The contours of his life and work have become increasingly clear and his eminent role in Rudolf II's Mannerist artistic milieu has been established more accurately[4]. Besides, since the legendary exhibition curated by Alfred H. Barr Jr. at the New York Museum of Modern Art in 1937 ("Fantastic Art, Dada, Surrealism") up to the "Effetto Arcimboldo" show in 1987 at the Venetian Palazzo Grassi, Arcimboldo's artistic reputation has been abundantly vindicated.

Only through diligent research can we now reconstruct the achievements of an artist who rightly ranks among the central figures of European court painting: this is also due to changing tastes, which more often than not explain the vagaries of *fortuna*. And yet, Arcimboldo's major works had remained visible and his name had by no means disappeared from specialised literature. To some extent, the artist himself seems to have taken care of his own artistic *memoria* in writing, supported by the belief that words could, better than pictures, guarantee the survival of his work. In the 15th century, humanist Guarino da Verona recognized the preeminent value of writing to spread a reputation: "If we compare the various means of ensuring fame, it eventually appears that written accounts surpass any painting or statue. Simply put, pictures reveal the body, while written accounts reveal the mores and the soul. Pictures are mute, while the voice of writing reaches across land and sea. Paintings and statues can only be exhibited in a few locations, but written accounts roam easily across the entire world and are capable of multiplication"[5].

It seems that, by the late 16th century, the written word was considered *the* proven means of spreading *fama*, which was indispensable to the career of a court painter. But from then on, artists themselves had to take this duty in hand[6]. Giorgio Vasari's collection of *Lives of the Most Excellent Painters, Sculptors and Architects*, published between 1550 and 1568, provided a model and a format allowing all artists to rescue their lives and achievements from oblivion, magnify them and insert them within a genealogy of art whose aim was the constitution of a definitive canon. However, Giuseppe Arcimboldo's absence from Vasari's *Lives* should not come as a surprise. He was still too young to appear in the revised and expanded second edition, in 1568. Besides, the book did not grant much space to Milan's artistic production; for political reasons, Vasari's account focused almost exclusively on Tuscany and its artists. True, Arcimboldo finally reached one of the most promising locations for an artistic career when he was invited to the imperial court in 1562 but this was also the reason why he would be forgotten: in his Milanese homeland, his achievements abroad remained virtually unknown until his return in 1587[7].

It is therefore quite understandable that, on his return home after staying in a foreign country for a quarter of a century, Arcimboldo decided to have his life's work recorded for posterity. This was part of a process of "self-fashioning", in the words of Stephen Green-

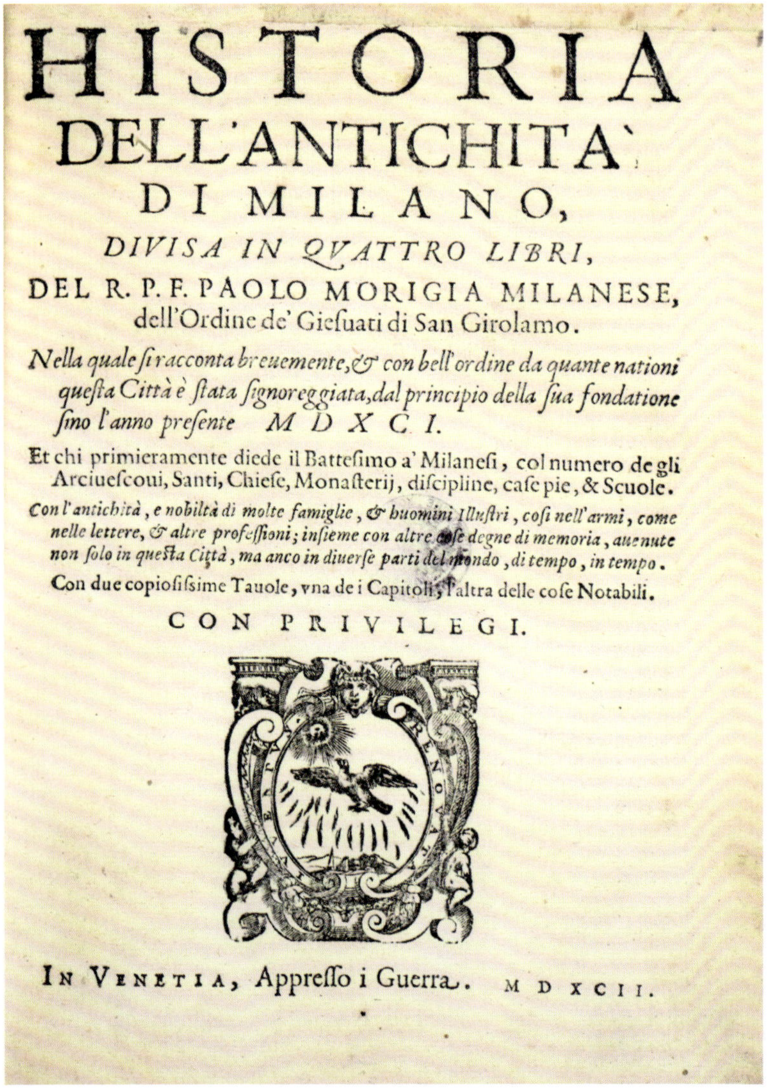

HISTORIA
DELL'ANTICHITA'
DI MILANO,
DIVISA IN QVATTRO LIBRI,
DEL R. P. F. PAOLO MORIGIA MILANESE,
dell'Ordine de' Giesuati di San Girolamo.

Nella quale si racconta breuemente, & con bell'ordine da quante nationi questa Città è stata signoreggiata, dal principio della sua fondatione sino l'anno presente M D X C I.

Et chi primieramente diede il Battesimo a' Milanesi, col numero de gli Arciuescoui, Santi, Chiese, Monasterij, discipline, case pie, & Scuole.

Con l'antichità, e nobiltà di molte famiglie, & huomini Illustri, così nell'armi, come nelle lettere, & altre professioni; insieme con altre cose degne di memoria, auenute non solo in questa Città, ma anco in diuerse parti del mondo, di tempo, in tempo.

Con due copiosissime Tauole, vna de i Capitoli, l'altra delle cose Notabili.

CON PRIVILEGI.

IN VENETIA, Appresso i Guerra. M D X C I I.

Fig. 1. Paolo Morigia, *Historia dell'antichità di Milano*, Venice 1592

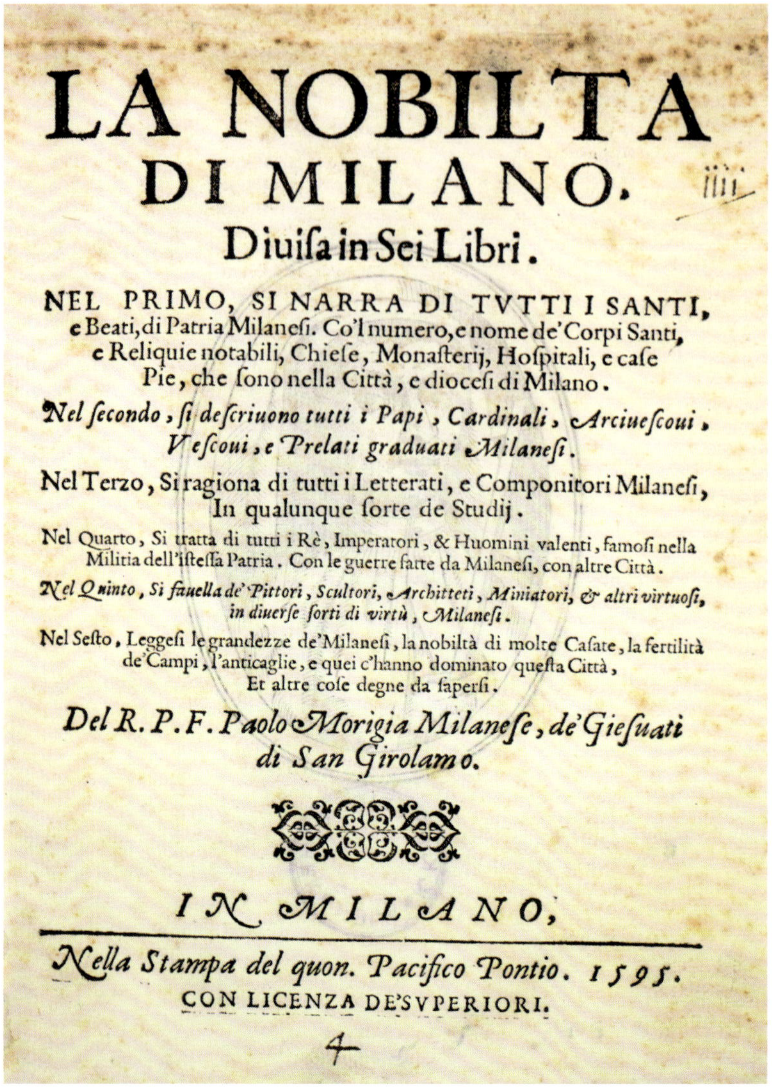

LA NOBILTA
DI MILANO.
Diuisa in Sei Libri.

NEL PRIMO, SI NARRA DI TVTTI I SANTI, e Beati, di Patria Milanesi. Co'l numero, e nome de' Corpi Santi, e Reliquie notabili, Chiese, Monasterij, Hospitali, e case Pie, che sono nella Città, e diocesi di Milano.

Nel secondo, si descriuono tutti i Papi, Cardinali, Arciuescoui, Vescoui, e Prelati graduati Milanesi.

Nel Terzo, Si ragiona di tutti i Letterati, e Componitori Milanesi, In qualunque sorte de Studij.

Nel Quarto, Si tratta di tutti i Rè, Imperatori, & Huomini valenti, famosi nella Militia dell'istessa Patria. Con le guerre fatte da Milanesi, con altre Città.

Nel Quinto, Si fauella de' Pittori, Scultori, Architetti, Miniatori, & altri virtuosi, in diuerse sorti di virtù, Milanesi.

Nel Sesto, Leggesi le grandezze de' Milanesi, la nobiltà di molte Casate, la fertilità de' Campi, l'anticaglie, e quei c'hanno dominato questa Città, Et altre cose degne da sapersi.

Del R. P. F. Paolo Morigia Milanese, de' Giesuati di San Girolamo.

IN MILANO,

Nella Stampa del quon. Pacifico Pontio. 1595.

CON LICENZA DE' SVPERIORI.

Fig. 2. Paolo Morigia, *La nobiltà di Milano. Divisa in sei libri… Del R.P.F. Paolo Morigia Milanese, de' Giesuati di San Girolamo*, Milan 1595

blatt: an attempt at firmly establishing one's status and achievements according to criteria fixed by the artist himself[8]. Arcimboldo evidently did this in the form of self-promotional talks that he conducted in his home with his Milanese friends, talks which became part of the art literature of the late cinquecento. Paolo Morigia, Giovanni Paolo Lomazzo and Gregorio Comanini took notes of what the illustrious repatriate told them about his life at court, his standing, his ingeniousness, his works, his various functions as a court artist and above all his fame. The nature of these interactions recalls Arcimboldo's older contemporary Benvenuto Cellini who also "dictated" his life, much of which he had spent abroad – though it first appeared in print in 1728[9].

It is true that later source study confirmed many of the information thus provided. But it is also true that this lifestory brings together all the *topoi* of a court artist's career, Arcimboldo's being a case in point. Morigia, who traced back a long-winded and complicated genealogy of the Arcimboldi House, as far as its pre-Carolingian origins, affirmed that he had heard it from the artist himself: "All that is said of this illustrious and ancient house I have derived from the accounts and information received from the virtuous, and noble Giuseppe Arcimboldi, a credible nobleman of unimpeachable conduct, who served two Emperors in Germany, as we shall see. He copied the ancestry and origins of the Arcimboldis from an old parchment written in German, which Emperor Maximilian's doctor read to him. Furthermore, he asserts that he travelled in two places where he found the name Arcimboldo in use In the city of Augsburg, in the vicinity of the main church, lies a large cemetery in which stands a big chapel, and when one steps through the gate, one can see an old sepulchre of red marble, on which the crest of the Arcimboldis is carved in archaic letters; similarly, he claims he saw a large, ancient gravestone in the city of Regensburg in the great cemetery of the cathedral, where one can glimpse the carved letters of the crest of the Arcimboldis, and that in many German cities there are many Arcimboldis."[10] By linking his own lineage to that of the *Reich*, Giuseppe Arcimboldo, who was descended from a Milanese family of distinguished artists, could present the nobiliary title he was awarded in the North – the nobility of his blood was confirmed in 1580 and he was later elevated to the rank to palsgrave or *comes palatinus*, a title which could only be granted by the Emperor[11] – not only as a result of his artistic achievements, but as a natural extension of his ancestry. The widespread desire of artists to establish their eligibility to become noblemen through old family lines crops up in the case of Michelangelo as well, who conducted research to establish his ancestors as relations of Matilda of Canossa. Benvenuto Cellini allowed his convoluted family tree to reach Caesar[12].

Elsewhere in the *Historia dell'antichità di Milano* Morigia continues his account which may be read as an autobiography of the artist, since the author dutifully recorded Arcimboldo's claims: "Now that I have dealt with the House of Arcimboldi to some extent, I cannot and do not want to neglect to say something about another Arcimboldi by the name of Giuseppe, who for the sake of justice deserves to be praised. He is a painter of uncommon gifts, learned and distinguished in many fields. Having given proof of his talent for painting and all sorts of *bizarreries* not only in his homeland but also abroad, he won such high praise that his fame hurried to Germany and reached the Imperial Court and the ear of Maximilian of Austria (sic! Ferdinand I), who was elected king of the Romans and, after his father, raised to the dignity of emperor; so much so that this Maximilian insistently requested that Arcimboldi be allowed into his service. Giuseppe finally agreed to serve Maximilian after many requests and, in the year 1562, left his homeland and went to the court of the Emperor, where he was very highly esteemed, and well-treated by Maximilian. The Emperor took him into his service with honourable pay and demonstrated the great affection that he had for him. Our Arcimboldi lived at the imperial court, giving great satisfaction not only to Maximilian, but to the whole court, devoting himself not so much to painting as to many other inventions, such as tournaments, jousts, games, decorations for weddings, and coronations, notably when archduke Charles of Austria took wife. For such festivals, this great mind devised a large number of varied, ingenious, charming and rare inventions, that universally filled with wonder all those great Princes, who had gathered there, and to the great content of Maximilian, his principal master."

To address just one of these many elements composing the traditional image of a Renaissance court artist, it is notable that Arcimboldo boasted of his direct access to the Emperor. For him, as an artist, the natural hierarchy apparently did not apply and he almost belonged to the *familia* of the emperor. The title *familiaris* was not conferred in Northern European courts but the intimacy here mentioned between Arcimboldo and the sovereign was usually allowed to artists whose credentials had been established in the papal court or other Italian courts[13]. "I do not want to neglect to mention that when Maximilian succeeded his father in the imperial line, Arcimboldi was never denied the right to meet the emperor at any time. Indeed, he was one of those who enjoyed the emperor's particular favour and, in short, the entire court of Austria consorted with him in a trusting relation and loved him for his art and his noble, civilized bearing. When Maximilian died, his son Rudolf, who succeeded him as Emperor, showed Arcimboldi no less love and benevolence than his father. Now when the noble and honourable Giuseppe had served both of these great rulers and the House of Austria for 26 years, having requested many times during the course of two years that he might take his leave, so that he could return to his homeland to enjoy his old age, this grace was finally granted by his imperial majesty, who only reluctantly accepted to deprive himself of his beloved artist. So Arcimboldi returned home in the year 1588 (sic! 1587), and though he lived in Milan, he has remained in the service of the emperor in all the things (except painting) which His Catholic Majesty favours and enjoys in Milan. I do not want to neglect to mention that Arcimboldi also receives a yearly pension from the emperor as a reward for his faithful and welcome service. ... One cannot neglect to mention that this Arcimboldi is not only a proficient painter, but also the inventor of many artistic curiosities, for he could create a likeness simply from books and another from birds and yet another from flowers only, which is superb and marvellous to behold. And all such drawings and *bizarreries* now reproduced as engravings, are inventions of this Milanese of ours"[14].

A painter who started writing treatises when he lost his sight, Giovanni Paolo Lomazzo also praised his cosmopolitan countryman – many passages echo Morigia in his *Trattato* as well as in *L'Idea del tempio della pittura*. However, Lomazzo proceeds in no way as a historical biographer, but rather incorporates his homage to Arcimboldo within his somewhat esoteric theory of painting as an ideal, circular temple, with seven columns and a dome divided into in seven segments. Each of these seven parts is ruled by a "regent", who presides over the seven Orders of Painting: proportion, movement, colour, light, perspective, composition and form[15]. Arcimboldo is not included among the artists designated as "regents"; but Lomazzo acknowledges the illusionistic force of his *Four Elements*, a power which, in this theory founded on astrology, is under the influence of fickle Mercury[16]. Unlike Morigia, who appears to have assumed the office of a chronicler, Lomazzo wants to stress the truly artistic aspects of Arcimboldo's work; like his countrymen, he may have seen with his own eyes but few examples of this work, at most

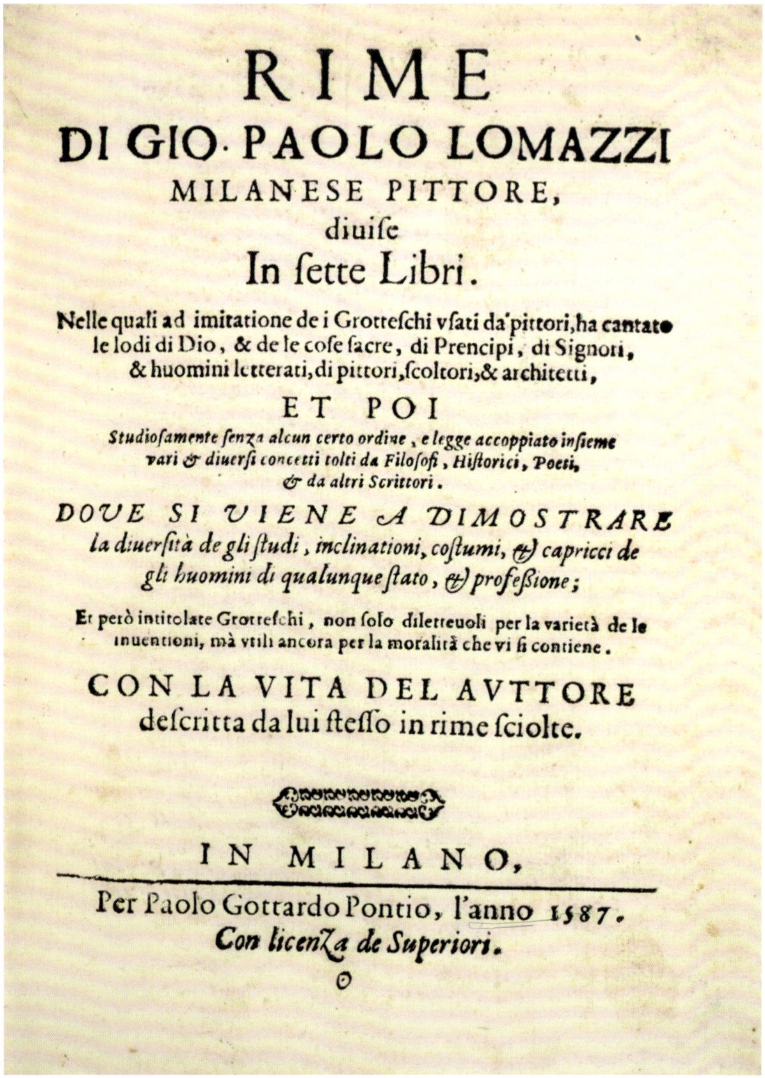

RIME
DI GIO. PAOLO LOMAZZI
MILANESE PITTORE,
diuiſe
In ſette Libri.

Nelle quali ad imitatione de i Grotteſchi vſati da'pittori, ha cantato le lodi di Dio, & de le coſe ſacre, di Prencipi, di Signori, & huomini letterati, di pittori, ſcoltori, & architetti,

ET POI

Studioſamente ſenza alcun certo ordine, e legge accoppiato inſieme vari & diuerſi concetti tolti da Filoſofi, Hiſtorici, Poeti, & da altri Scrittori.

DOVE SI VIENE A DIMOSTRARE la diuerſità de gli ſtudi, inclinationi, coſtumi, & capricci de gli huomini di qualunque ſtato, & profeſſione;

Et però intitolate Grotteſchi, non ſolo diletteuoli per la varietà de le inuentioni, mà vtili ancora per la moralità che vi ſi contiene.

CON LA VITA DEL AVTTORE
deſcritta da lui ſteſſo in rime ſciolte.

IN MILANO,
Per Paolo Gottardo Pontio, l'anno 1587.
Con licenza de Superiori.

Fig. 3. Giovanni Paolo Lomazzo, *Rime di Gio. Paolo Lomazzo milanese pittore divise in sette libri*, Milan 1587

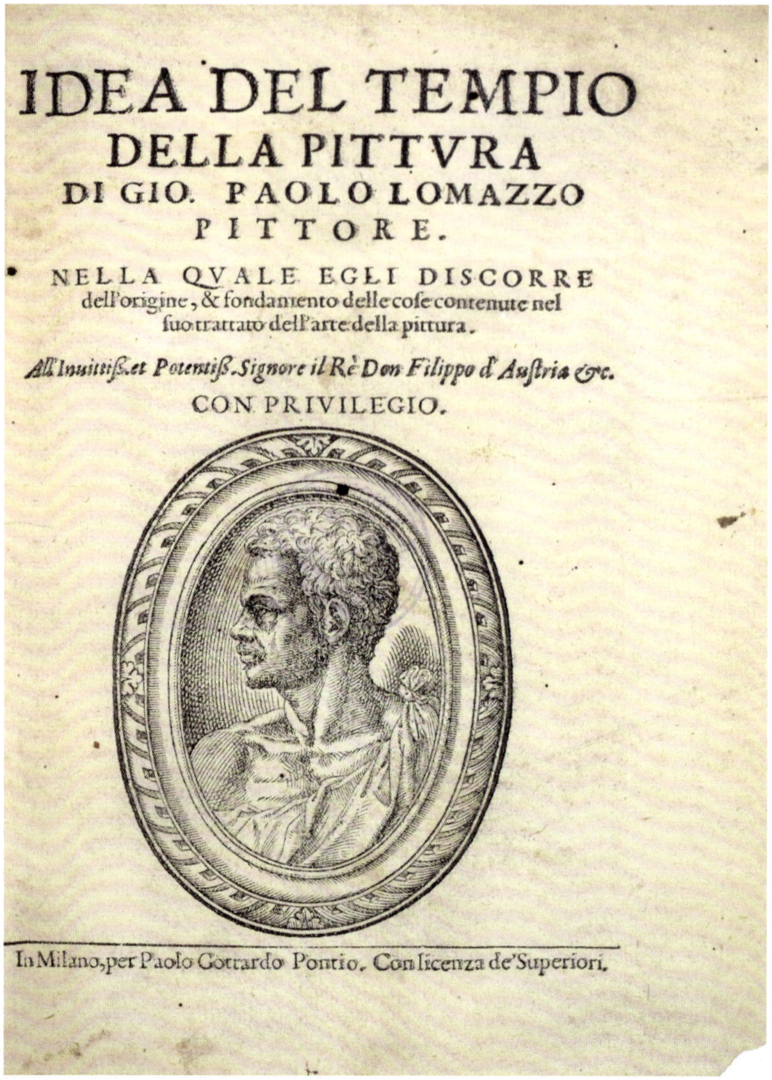

IDEA DEL TEMPIO
DELLA PITTVRA
DI GIO. PAOLO LOMAZZO
PITTORE.

NELLA QVALE EGLI DISCORRE
dell'origine, & fondamento delle coſe contenute nel ſuo trattato dell'arte della pittura.

All'Inuittiſs. et Potentiſs. Signore il Rè Don Filippo d'Auſtria &c.

CON PRIVILEGIO.

In Milano, per Paolo Gottardo Pontio. Con licenza de'Superiori.

Fig. 4. Giovanni Paolo Lomazzo, *L'Idea del tempio della pittura di Gio. Paolo Lomazzo pittore*, Milan 1590

those paintings which Arcimboldo sent to the court from Milan (the *Flora* and the *Portrait of Rudolf II as Vertumnus*). Hence the need, for the artist, to be his own defendant and to provide the key to his own works: "The museum of His Imperial Majesty Maximilian II is especially exceptional and worthy of enduring remembrance. In order to enlarge and improve this museum, Maximilian called on the great painter Giuseppe Arcimboldo, so that with a few paintings he might enrich it with the greatness of his talent, with his masterly command of perspective, his *disegno* and especially with his fanciful ideas, which are absolutely unique in the world. So there he painted the images of the four elements, which I mention in the sixth book of my treatise. Besides, he depicted the four seasons as human heads, assembled from the objects of each season: spring from flowers, summer from cloves of garlic and vegetables, autumn from fruit and winter in the form of a tree; and all of these paintings were executed with great care and infinite care. He also painted Janus, who represents the year itself and whose profile resembles summer on one side and winter on the other, with a snake round his neck, holding its own tail in its mouth, to show that it is an incarnation of the year. This said painting is framed and displayed with the others in the Imperial Museum. Additionally, he represented cooking as a woman, with her instruments and utensils, and a cellar-master in the form of a standing man, likewise assembled from the equipment of a cellar. The emperor is particularly fond of the latter, and of the portrait of his vice-chancellor which, from a distance, many consider an ordinary likeness but, coming somewhat closer, realize that it is assembled entirely from animals: the nose from a bird, the brow from fruit and so on. Everything is so wonderfully composed that it is, to be honest, a marvel to behold everything that he has painted with such great skilfulness."

Lomazzo further attests to Arcimboldo's role of an arbiter of taste, as befitted a respected court artist: "The emperor came to appreciate him so much that he asked for his opinion in all matters and formed his taste according to Arcimboldo's judgment. For this man's ideas were truly exceptional ... he was of an extremely keen intellect in all things and invented devices with allowed to cross rivers easily where neither bridges nor boats were available. He invented codes that no one could decipher without an instrument which he had made. This great man was no less beloved by Maximilian's successor, the emperor Rudolf II, who passed him a great many commissions. When he grew older, Arcimboldo begged the emperor to release him from his service, which Rudolf II very reluctantly granted, under the condition that, from his homeland Milan, he would still send works of art to his lord"[17].

When he reminisced among his Milanese writer friends, Arcimboldo was trying to ensure that his name would go down into history. He apparently could not trust that his work would be adequately remembered in the cities where he had been most active. Indeed, he seems to have been overlooked by the first art biographer of the court of Prague, Karel van Mander. His *Schilder-Boeck*, published in Alkmaar in 1604, can be seen as the Northern European equivalent to Vasari's *Lives of the Artists*, or even as its revision. The artists of the imperial court – Bartholomäus Spranger, Hans von Aachen or Vredeman de Vries – are given pride of place and their biographies are more than just a simple enumeration of basic informations[18]. Formulating his universalist theory as historical dogma, Van Mander celebrates the courtly art in Prague as a felicitous example of the Holy Roman Empire's faculty to sustain artistic production under the blissful rule of Rudolf II. Van Mander also equates the *translatio imperii* that began in the time of Charlemagne with the transfer of art from Southern to Northern Europe, establishing the preeminence of Northern European over Italian art. This implies a certain amount of deliberated falsifications and omissions, the greatest victim being Giuseppe Arcimboldo.

Van Mander did not forget him, but had to ignore him. The virtuous harmony existing among the artists in the court of Rudolf II, which he cites as a prerequisite for the actualization of their full potential, had to remain free of Italian domination or influence: "The exclusive relationship between Spranger and Emperor Rudolf II, as van Mander portrays it, did not allow to refer to Arcimboldo, much less to concede him a prominent status. The point was to show that the elevation of painting to the level of a liberal art in the court of Rudolf II was exclusively due to Northen European art and, as it were, to its victory over Italian art"[19]. In van Mander's work, Arcimboldo fell under a veritable *damnatio memoriae*. As if the artist had guessed that there can be no real certainty when it comes to matters of *memoria*, he himself saw to a preemptive revision and snatched his role from

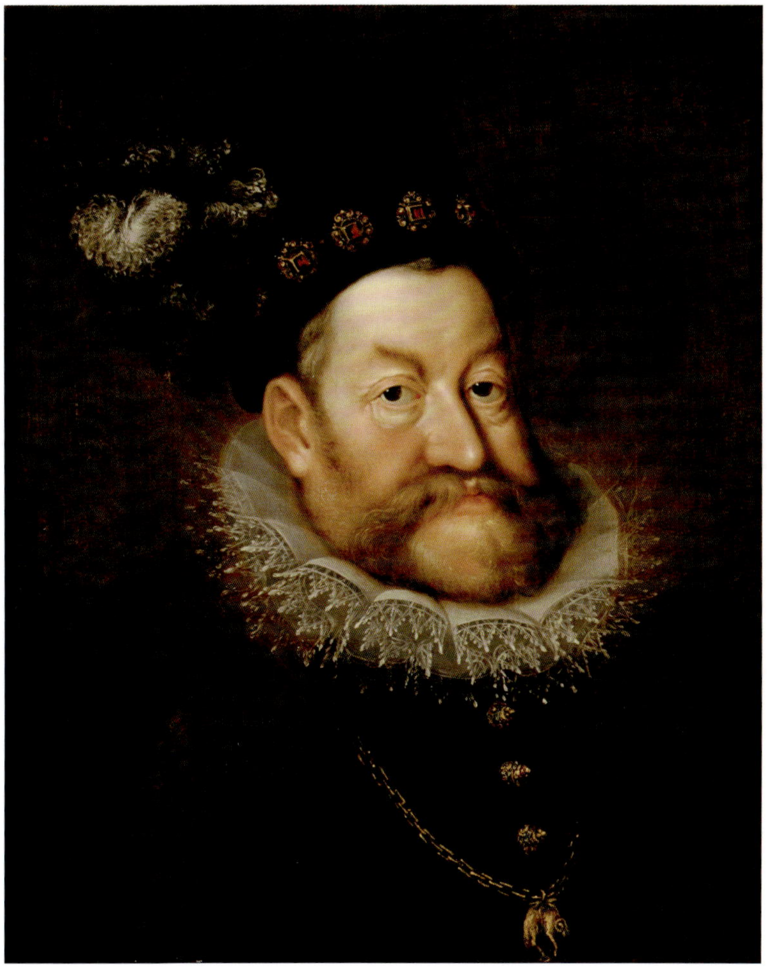

Fig. 5. Hans von Aachen, *Portrait of Emperor Rudolf II*. Vienna, Kunsthistorisches Museum, Gemäldegalerie

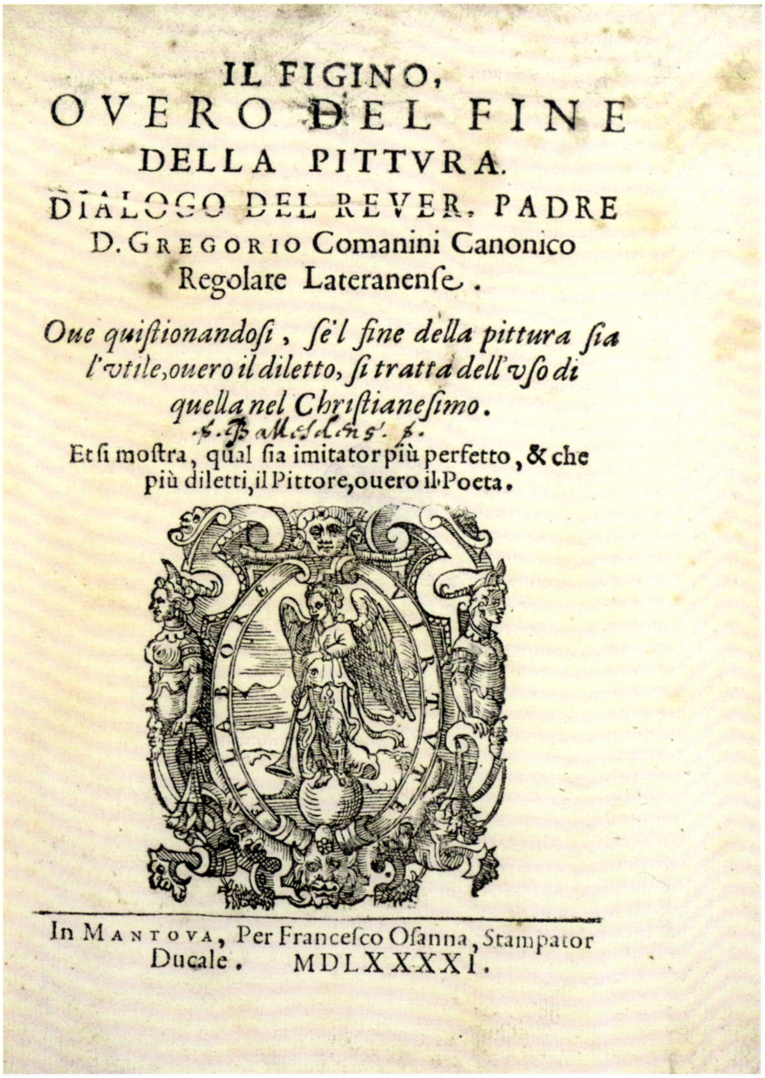

IL FIGINO,
OVERO DEL FINE
DELLA PITTVRA.
DIALOGO DEL REVER. PADRE
D. GREGORIO Comanini Canonico
Regolare Lateranenſe.
Oue quiſtionandoſi, ſe'l fine della pittura ſia l'vtile, ouero il diletto, ſi tratta dell'vſo di quella nel Chriſtianeſimo.
Et ſi moſtra, qual ſia imitator più perfetto, & che più diletti, il Pittore, ouero il Poeta.
In MANTOVA, Per Franceſco Oſanna, Stampator Ducale. MDLXXXXI.

Fig. 6. Gregorio Comanini, *Il Figino overo del fine della pittura. Dialogo...*, Mantua 1591

oblivion by dictating to Morigia and Lomazzo what he himself recognized as his decisive contributions to the blossoming of Rudolfine art. Though Arcimboldo made no reference to Bartholomäus Spranger, he certainly deplored that monopoly position, which illustrates the selective tendency of such glorifying literature.

It is remarkable that van Mander considered Goltzius to be the anointed artist who might vanquish the primacy of Italian art and ensure the continuation of art after Michelangelo (the terminus ad quem of Italian art, according to Vasari). By his engravings, Hendrick Goltzius had contributed to the circulation of Spranger's work and thereby expanded the renown of the courtly art of Prague. Van Mander called Goltzius a "unique Proteus ... in art ... capable of appropriating all styles"[20]. This reference to Proteus, the prophetical "old man of the sea" who could assume a variety of forms, articulates the conviction that an artist is primarily defined by his unlimited transformative ability. Goltzius allegedly adapted to the styles of very different painters and managed to master all sorts of techniques. Van Mander portrayed him as the most universal of all artists, who achieved the perfect synthesis of all techniques and all styles –ancient as well as Italian or Northern European. This protean eclecticism became a characteristic of Mannerism, which deliberately resorted to every artistic tradition, in theory as in practice. Such creative syncretism was the only way to overcome the end of art[21].

An irony of artistic praise is that what van Mander attempted to canonize at the beginning of the 17th century had already been reclaimed for Arcimboldo by his Milanese promoter, Gregorio Comanini. In his book *Il Figino*[22], a poetic-academic dispute over the goals of painting, Arcimboldo was portrayed as a representative of an artistic practice whose "fantastic" and wondrous inventions perfectly embodied the contemporary ideal of free and independent creativity. His work was lauded by Comanini as a successful synthesis of a realistic and a fanstastical world view: "The virtue of fantasy, whose exercise lies in receiving, recording and conjoining the appearances transmitted to our abstract senses by our outermost senses, was infinitely strong in Arcimboldi. For in the images which bring together comprehensible things that he has seen, he makes curious caprices and idols out of them, which no longer derive from the power of fantasy; and those things which it seems impossible to unite, he assembles with great skill and allows to become what he wishes. In order to paint with such exquisite inventiveness, that is, for the creation of such erudite allegories, the artist requires a certain knowledge of universal literature, thanks to which he can transform himself like a new Proteus and can disguise himself in other vestments, as might behove a mimic. These pictures are all the more amazing as nobody had ever created anything similar."

[1] Warnke 1985, 112ff.
[2] Passeri 1937, 72.
[3] Geiger 1960, 98f.
[4] See the authoritative studies by Kaufmann 1978a.
[5] Cited in Garin 1966, 205.
[6] See Warnke 1985, 112ff.
[7] See the contribution by Silvio Leydi in this catalogue.
[8] Greenblatt 1980.
[9] See Nova 2003.
[10] Morigia 1592, 556; see also Geiger 1960, 18.
[11] See Geiger 1960, 139 and Warnke 1989, 205 and 219.
[12] See Warnke, 209.
[13] See Warnke 1989, 142ff.
[14] Morigia 1592, 566f; see also Geiger 1960, 32f.
[15] See Klein 1975.
[16] Lomazzo 1584 (1974), vol. 2, 304. See also Falchetta, 143-198, here 179.
[17] Lomazzo 1590 (1973), vol. 1, 361ff.
[18] See Müller 1993, 77ff.
[19] Müller 1993, 220.
[20] Van Mander 1617 (1991), 339.
[21] See Melion 1989, 113ff. and also Beyer 2000, 287-299.
[22] Comanini 1591. See also Falchetta 1987, 182ff.

"... il gran pittore Giuseppe Arcimboldi"
On the Construction of Arcimboldo's Fame

I.1
Giuseppe Arcimboldo
Self-portrait
Pen, blue wash
231 × 157 mm
Above left: "Ioseffi Arcimboldi imago"
Prague, Národní Galerie, inv. no. K5338

In this folio Arcimboldo studies himself up close: frontally with the severity of the observer's (initially himself in the mirror) searching gaze. Berra presumes that the extreme close-up view is due to a convex mirror.
In it he portrays himself as a handsome man with even features, with a short, Spanish beard, a fine cap, elegant white lace collar and a patterned brocade shirt. It seems he has dedicated a lot of attention to his appearance, to underline his position as a noted court painter or even more to appear as an elegant member of court. That he wished with this elegance to show his claim to noble origins – Emperor Rudolf conveyed on him a noble title in 1580 (see Staudinger document in this catalogue) – is not to be excluded. The much observed similarity with the profile image of his father from the hand of the latter's friend Bernardino Luini (cat. no. II.1) is to be especially seen in the even features, the high forehead and the long nose.
There is disagreement in research regarding his age in the drawing: the accepted dating of the folio ranges from 1565 to 1587, which means some estimate the artist to be forty years old, while others consider him to be over sixty. All the same in the comparison to the "Paper-head", in which he himself puts his age down to be "61", he here appears considerably younger. In my opinion he is between 45 and 50, and the drawing hence originated around 1571-76. DaCosta Kaufmann is of the same opinion.
The drawing technique is similar to that of his studies for festive decorations (cat. no. VII 1-32), many of which were made in the early 1570s. This is also shown by his use of blue-grey to blue wash which he obviously loves and that gives the sheets an especially elegant note.
In the case of the self-portrait this blue tone also underlines the impression of melancholy clouding Arcimboldo's features, and that at the time stood as the temperament that featured above all with "Saturn born" artists. Konečny sees in the hieratical rendering an allusion to Dürer's *Selfportrait as Christ* and in a broader sense to a God-given creative force.
The mixture of broad generous brush washes and small pointed, often bitingly sharp pen strokes, that accentuate the individual wrinkles over the brows around the eyes, give an overall indication of Arcimboldo's art; an art in which contradictions combine and separate continuously.
Hence even after examining this work it is still difficult to grasp Arcimboldo as a portrait painter. Even if he was paid as "Hofconterfetter", the single portraits in the Kunsthistorisches collection, attributed to Arcimboldo by Günther Heinz, reveal a concept of portrait less fine and painstaking than in this trenchant and expressive drawing (compare cat. nos. III.4-11). Rather, one can compare this drawing to the painted self-portrait once in a Viennese private collection, that we only know from the black and white picture on the frontispiece of Benno Geiger's *Monography*; though until the original of this painted self-portrait turns up, it will be difficult to have a clear picture of his painted portraits.

Sylvia Ferino-Pagden

Provenance: Böhm Collection, auctioned in Dorotheum in November 1914 and in April 1918; Jindřich Waldes Collection, Prague

Bibliography: Konečny 1995-96, 132-137; Kaufmann 1997, 425, no. 1.169; 1997, 19; Konečny 1997, 113; Berra 1998, 199, no. 40; Fučikova 2002, 44, no. 9.

I.2
Giuseppe Arcimboldo
Self-portrait on Paper ("The Man of Papers")
Pencil (traces), pen and ink, brush and watercoloured ink, grey wash; mounted white paper
442 × 318 mm
At the centre, on the forehead, "6 1", and under the collar, "1587"
Genoa, Palazzo Rosso, Gabinetto Disegni e Stampe, inv. no. D 1213

The large folio, which arrived in its current location through the 19th-century bequest of Marchese Marcello Durazzo without any specific attribution and remained unrecognized for a long time, constitutes not just the best example of the peculiar and bizarre art of Giuseppe Arcimboldo in the graphic field, but also provides a precise chronological reference that has made it possible to push the date of the artist's birth back from 1527 to 1526.
Like the drawing in the Národní Galerie in Prague (cat. no. I.1), a comparison with which has already provided a first confirmation of the fact that we are dealing with a self-portrait here, this work shows us what Arcimboldo looked like. But while in the former the artist has presented an entirely natural image of himself from the front, in the drawing in Genoa, where the head is turned three quarters, he has deployed his skill in rendering forms in a metamorphic way. In fact, even though fairly well-disguised by an expert draughtsmanship, the true and unusual characteristics of this extraordinary portrait become fully apparent when it is examined from close-up: the features of the lips, the nose, the eyes and the single ear that is visible, as well as the hair, beard and wrinkles, are perfectly evoked by simulating a sort of mask of sheets of paper, carefully arranged in such a way as to flawlessly imitate a human face; other, longer strips reproduce the drapery of a robe or of the cloak, while the ones rolled up at the bottom of the face allude to the ruff.
The artist, who in the exercise of his creative activity had studied figures, costumes and allegorical floats on sheets of paper, just as he had used others for his literary and poetic efforts (Berra 1996, 58), has succeeded here, by representing in illusory fashion that same material so closely linked to his work, in constructing and presenting a sort of allegorical portrait of himself. A portrait that is plausibly comparable to the other one he made of a certain "Doctor Zasio", now unfortunately lost but which, according to the documents, was "made up entirely of deeds, forms, receipts, letters and memorials" (Rudolf 1995, 166).
The four digits "1587" drawn on the collar are certainly a date, and it is that of Giuseppe Arcimboldo's return to Italy for good after twenty-five years of activity at the imperial court, most recently in the service of Emperor Rudolf II, who five years earlier had given him the title of palatine count in recognition of his talents and of his long and loyal service *"in picturis artificiosis et in aliis rebus plurimis"* (Porzio 1979, 107).
But a more important chronological reference should be seen in the digits "6 1" that are fairly clearly visible on the forehead, where they simulate small wrinkles. This is in fact the age of the artist, whose birth, previously dated to 1527 by working backwards from the year of his death, 1593, at the age of around sixty-six, has now been set at 1526 precisely because of this *Self-portrait*, in which Arcimboldo declares himself to be sixty-one years old in 1587.

Piero Boccardo

Provenance: *Legato Marcello Durazzo (1848)*

Bibliography: Boccardo in Genoa 1990, 66; Boccardo in Genoa 1991, 93; Berra 1996a, 54-55; Konečny 1995-96, 137 no. 24; Konečny 1997, 120 no. 40; Berra in Lugano 1998, 199-200; Boccardo 1999, no. 20; Boccardo in Milan 2000, 437.

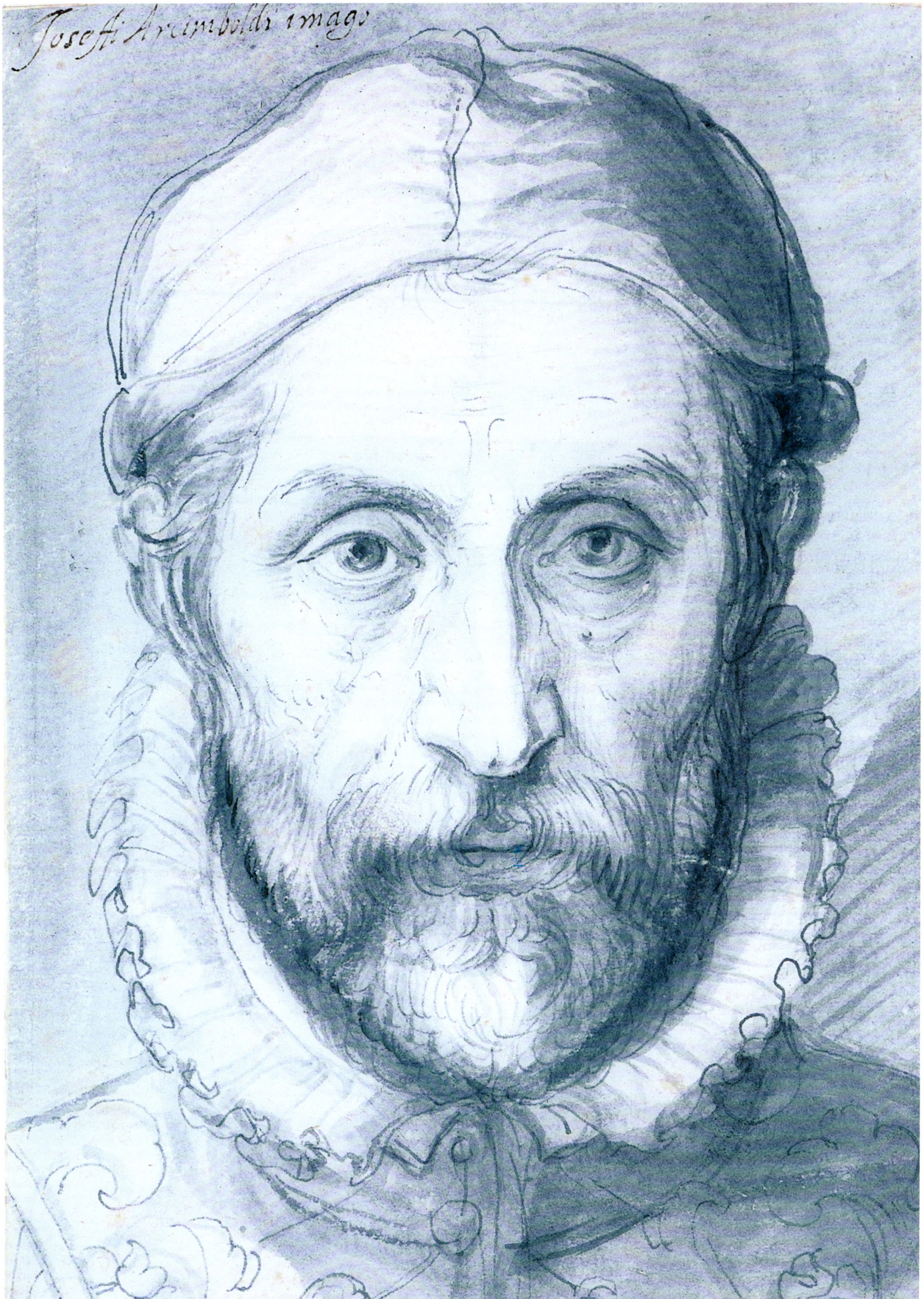

I.1

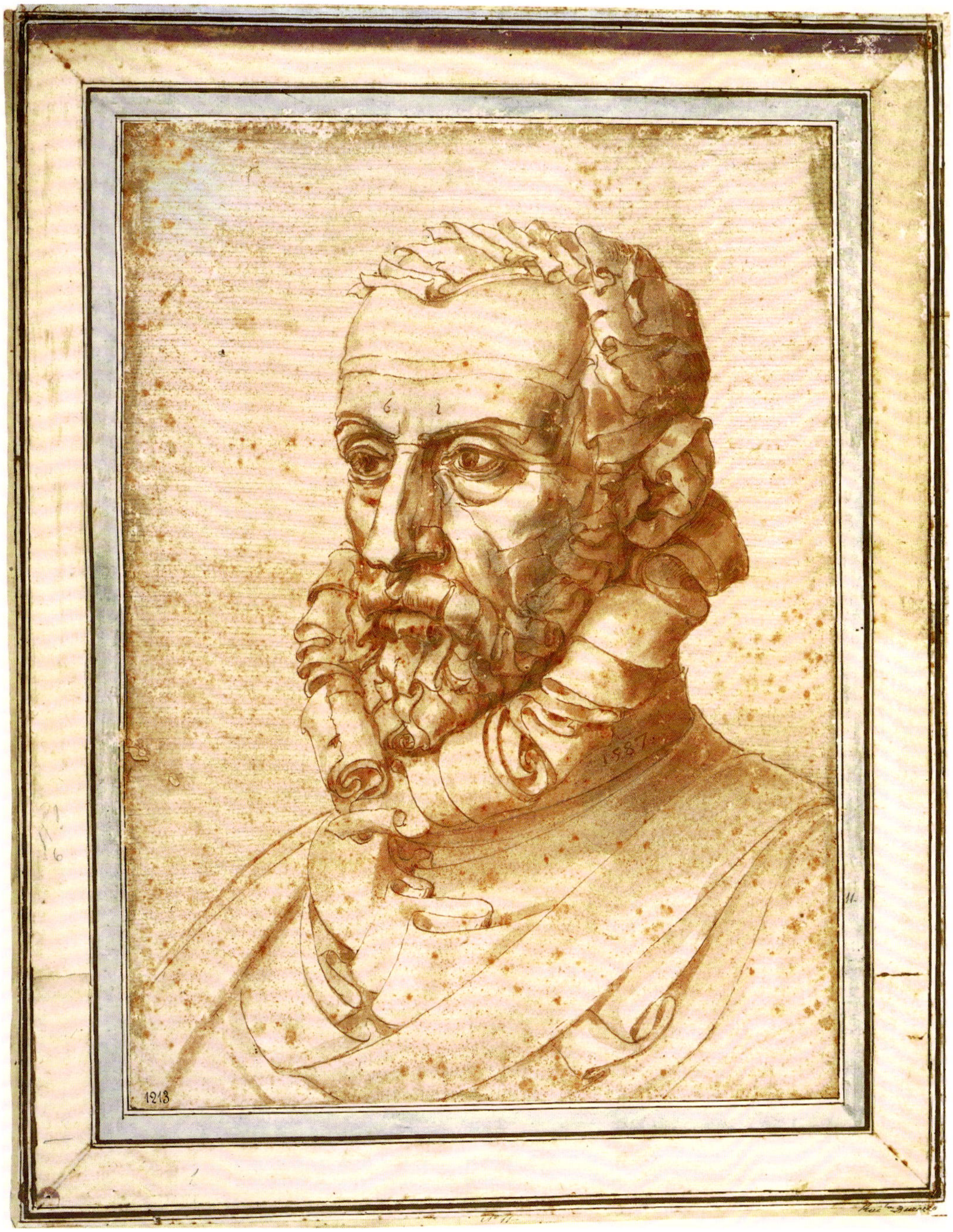

I.2

I.3
Giovanni Paolo Lomazzo
Self-portrait as Abbot of the Accademia della Val di Blenio, 1568
Oil on canvas
56 × 44 cm
Milan, Pinacoteca di Brera

In the rather unusual self-portrait of Giovanni Paolo Lomazzo in the Pinacoteca di Brera, the Milanese painter and theorist of art (1538-92) represents himself in the guise of "abbot" (president) of the Accademia della Val di Blenio (or Bregno). The picture is very likely a commemoration of his having received this title in 1568. The inscription that runs along the bottom of the picture is the decisive element in this identification (Lynch 1964; and above all Isella 1993, 15ff.). It reads something like "Zavargna nabas vallis bregni et P. L. …", while the end of the partially effaced inscription can be interpreted as "pictor 1568". Thus it should be understood as "Zavargna nabas valli bregni et paulus lomatius pictor 1568"; in other words this bust has a dual identity, that of the painter Lomazzo and that of Zavargna, his academic name, accompanied by his title of abbot of the Val di Blenio in the Ticinese dialect.
As Dante Isella has shown (1993), a key to the allegorical interpretation of the costume of abbot of the Accademia di Val di Bregno can be found in the first part of the *Rabisch*, a collection of poems (with an introduction describing the academy's activities) published by Lomazzo in 1589. In a chapter entitled, in the Ticinese dialect, "ceremonies and meaning of the ornaments that the abbot must wear", we learn that he is dressed in the fur of a kid (*cavrett*) as a mark of humility, and the same is true of the straw hat. But we also note that the kid is a symbol and even an attribute of Dionysus, the god who when still a child had been turned into a kid by Jupiter to protect him from Juno. The hat is ringed by a wreath of laurel and vine leaves, Apollinian and Dionysiac symbols alluding to the complementarity of the two sources of poetic inspiration and their indissociable character. The text of the *Rabisch* associates the vine with the poetic frenzy induced by wine, the laurel with its enduring dignity. The thyrsus entwined with ivy – Bacchic except for its metal point – is at once a symbol of power and an allusion to the god's orgiastic force as a characteristic attribute of his thiasus. One of the most enigmatic elements of this costume lies in the medal clearly visible on the brim of the hat. It does not correspond exactly to the medallion or *sigillo* of the academy, described in Lomazzo's *Rabisch* and *Rime*, on which Bacchus is represented seated on a chariot drawn by two lions and holding bagpipes and a container called a *galeon*, with the inscription "Bacco inspiratori abas & consilium vallis bregni", but is an abbreviated version, reduced to just the *galeon* or *galiglion*.

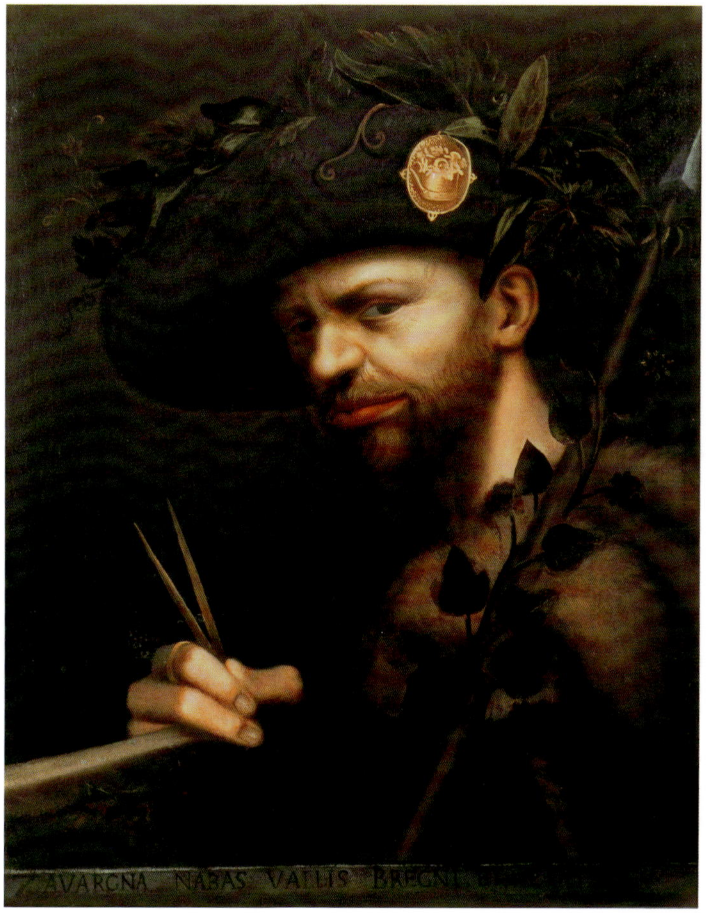

I.3

This vase or container in the form of a watering can but used to drink wine is extolled in several passages of the *Rabisch* and was associated by the members of the academy with Bacchus's ship, covered with vines and ivy and equipped with a fountain of wine, whence the naval name given to the vessel. A number of lines in the *Rabisch* tell us that the *galeon* must always be full of wine, that this should be "*maschio, buono per far figli*" ("male, good for making children") and that it is drunk "*a garganella*" ("poured down the throat"). *Vino maschio* is without doubt pure wine, whose mastery is, in the ancient tradition, one of the characteristics of Bacchus and whose consumption, not generally recommended at a time when it was still the custom to dilute wine with water, is undoubtedly a synonym of drunkenness. This self-portrait should be linked with another, now lost but documented by some of the verses published in Lomazzo's *Rime* (or *Grottesche*), which confirm, if there were any need, the Bacchic allusions of the costume and attributes: "Quando di Bregno fui abbate anch'io, / Mi ritrasse co'l tirso in man di Bacco; / E coronato di quelle ghirlanda / Che Citheron ci manda [...]".

However, the picture in Milan does not limit itself to the somewhat comic traits of the *Nabas:* it also speaks to us of the painter, reproducing his features and identifying him by his initials, and of painting, judging by what Lomazzo is holding in his right hand, a pair of compasses and a canvas of which we see only the back. As Francesco Porzio has explained (Lugano 1998, 179-180; see this reference for a complete bibliography of the picture), the compasses take the place of the brush we might more logically have expected in order to stress the mathematical, and therefore theoretical or speculative character of the art of painting, while the canvas is viewed from the side of the stretcher to indicate its more technical and material aspect. The same hand holds both objects and a finger with a ring is set halfway between them. Not a wedding ring, as Lomazzo was unmarried, but a symbol of union and *accoppiamento*, of "coupling" between compasses and canvas, between theory and practice, in keeping with a formula that recurs in the artist's theoretical writings and that owes a debt to such illustrious predecessors as Leonardo and Dürer. The union of theory and practice is symbolized in a famous engraving by Dürer in which it is personified by Melancholia, as well as in a drawing by Lomazzo in the Albertina representing an *Allegory of Painting* (Lynch 1968) placed under the auspices of several deities, including Bacchus and Saturn. Saturn presides over melancholic inspiration and the highest stage of intellectual life, Bacchus over the *furor* of poetic inspiration and artistic creation. Halfway between the Platonic theory of the four *furores* and a Graeco-Latin theatrical and poetic tradition, this characterization of Bacchus is nothing new in the artistic field, as is clear from the picture of *Saint Luke Painting the Virgin* painted by Marten van Heemskerck in 1532, in which the artist represents himself in the guise of a Bacchic spirit of painting, and from several other self-portraits dating from the end of the 16th century (F. Zuccari, H. von Aachen, Goltzius, etc.). This double connotation can also be found in the self-portrait in Milan, as in addition to the Bacchic attributes of the *Nabas*, some critics have recognized the traits or an expression of melancholia in it. This reinforces a passage in the *Trattato* (II, 7) in which Lomazzo describes the appearance of an individual under the influence of Saturn, which seems in many respects to match his own features. So this self-portrait presents us with an allegory of painting in a derisory and perhaps subversive light, for the Bacchic inspiration put forward in this way is asserted as a principle of play, of irony, indeed of rebellion against the dead weight of post-Tridentine restrictions. Thus the choice by the members of the academy – which included men of letters as well as artists – of a dialect based on that of the Blenio Valley spoken by the *facchini* ("porters") who came down from the valleys of the Alps and Ticino to work in Milan served a dual function: that of a burlesque and macaronic vein and that of a desire to dissemble stemming from the need, in the Lombard city governed with an iron hand by Carlo Borromeo, to conceal their indulgence in literary and convivial pastimes under the sign of Bacchus, something which was not at all in keeping with the climate of the time. Indeed, the archbishop had expended exceptional political energy and religious zeal on promoting and imposing the strictest obedience to the decrees of the Council of Trent and their interpretation in the Church as well as in civil society. Religious ideas and practices, morals and publications were placed under the most rigorous control, while artistic and literary creativity were subjected to rules conflicting with the freedom of invention. It is no surprise that an artist as inventive and atypical as Arcimboldo chose to leave Milan and to remain for a long time at the imperial court, where he found far more favourable working conditions and much greater recognition.

The Dionysiac, creative and transgressive component of Lomazzo's self-portrait takes on a melancholic tinge, divided between an intellectual exaltation and a disenchantment engendered by a situation that was not very favourable to the free expression of genius and imagination. Thus Lomazzo's Bacchic self-portrait may have been intended as an antidote to Borromean austerity.

Philippe Morel

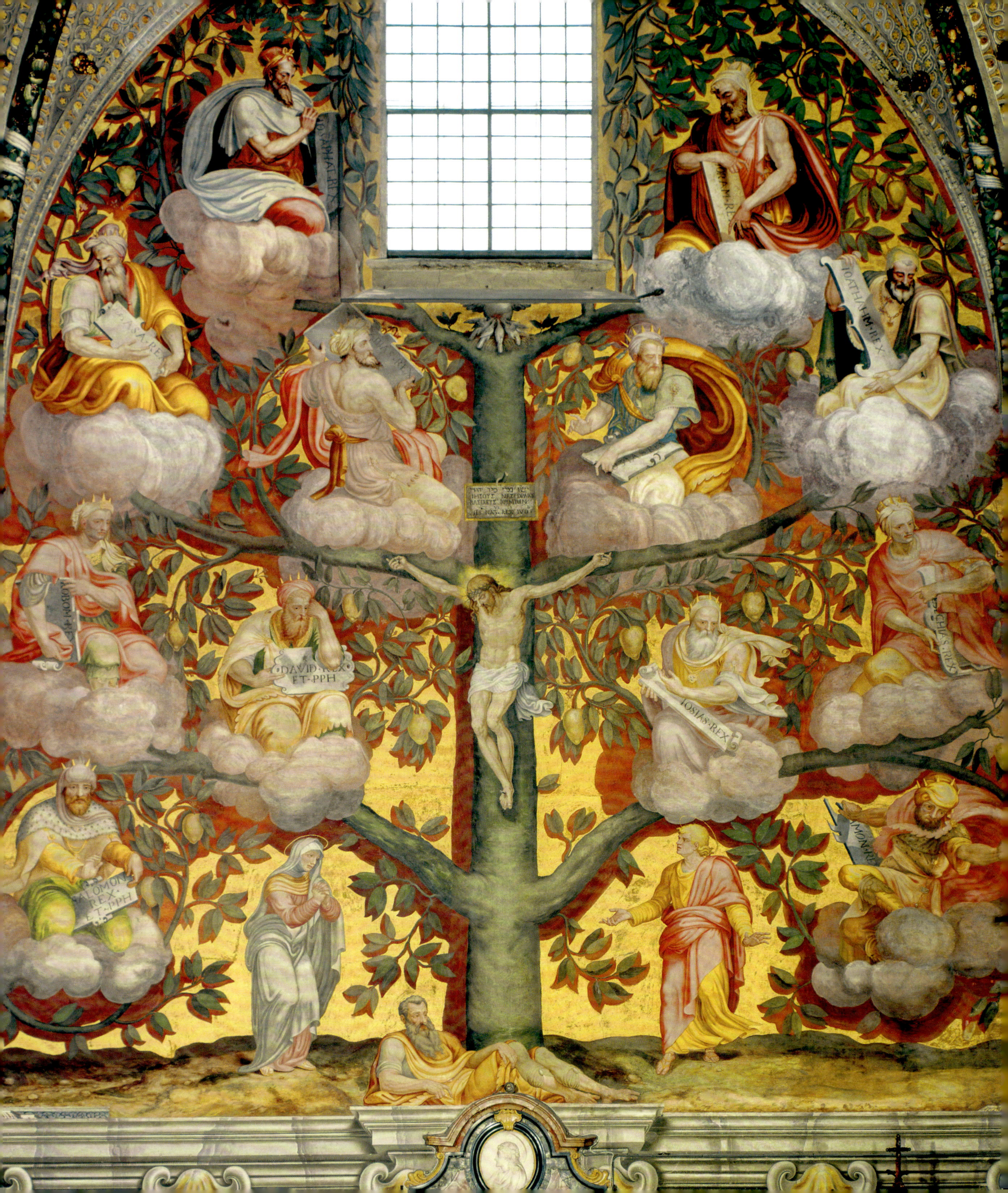
DAVID·REX
ET·PPH
IOSIAS·REX

Silvio Leydi

Giuseppe Arcimboldo in Milan: Documents and Hypotheses

In the pages that follow we shall seek to retrace the history of Giuseppe Arcimboldo's presence in the city of his birth, Milan, through a rereading of the printed sources and an examination of the documents that have already been published, as well as a number of unpublished ones brought to light during the research undertaken for this exhibition. The principal periods taken into consideration, therefore, will be limited to the years between 1526 and 1562 (i.e. from the artist's presumed birth until his move to the court of Maximilian of Habsburg) and between 1587 and 1593 (that is from his definitive return to Milan up until his death). However, attention will also be given to a number of visits to the city paid by Arcimboldo in, judging by the documents, 1566, 1576-77 and 1581.

A thorough reading and interpretation of all the available documents, published and unpublished, has made it possible to establish that Giuseppe Arcimboldo was not descended from the well-known and powerful Arcimboldi family, to which, for example, several of the city's archbishops belonged. This hypothesis, put forward in "modern times" at the beginning of the 19th century by the aristocratic genealogist Pompeo Litta and then uncritically repeated up to the present day, has not in fact found any documentary support. On the contrary, it conflicts with the chronological and historical evidence. Giuseppe seems instead to have belonged to a much humbler family of painters, who included not just his father Biagio, but also at least two uncles, Ambrogio (certainly a painter) and Gian Giacomo, and perhaps another relative, Giovan Stefano Arcimboldo, also a painter.

The Arcimboldi Family in the 15th and 16th Centuries

In order to reconstruct the structure of the Arcimboldi family into which Giuseppe was born in the period spanning the end of the 15th century and the first half of the 16th it is necessary to establish a few fixed points.

To start with, his direct ancestors: the name of Giuseppe's father was Biagio, and that of Biagio's father was Pasio (or Pace)[1]. At present the records do not allow us to go any farther back into the family's past, but already these certainties and the subsequent chronological indications that derive from them can tell us a great deal about the origin of the family, clearing the field of fanciful hypotheses.

Biagio is documented as a painter employed by the *Fabbrica* of Milan Cathedral in 1518[2]. This is the earliest known record of the presence of Giuseppe's father in the city and allows us to place his birth, although with wide margins of uncertainty, at a date that is unspecified but prior to 1498[3]. Thus the birth of Biagio's father, Pasio, of whom we know nothing except that he was a master (but of what guild?) and had already died by 1534[4], must have taken place many years earlier, in the 1470s at the latest[5], and this fact, never emphasized or noted, clashes with the hitherto consolidated tradition that Giuseppe was descended from a noble family.

Up to now, in fact, Pasio (following Pompeo Litta, who published his genealogy in 1823 after decades of research)[6] has been presented as an illegitimate son of Filippo Arcimboldi, himself the son of Guido Antonio, archbishop of Milan from 1489 to 1497, the year of his death. But recent studies have shown that Filippo was born sometime between 1469 and 1473 and died in 1518, and therefore could not have been Pasio's father under any circumstances[7]. It is likely that the source on which Litta drew, in the absence of direct documentation, was the *Anfiteatro Romano* of Giovan Pietro Crescenzi[8], who seems in turn to have relied for the family's origin on a mysterious "old parchment volume by [a] German writer" owned by Giuseppe Arcimboldo[9]. However, no source prior to Litta[10] and not even Giuseppe Arcimboldo himself (through the intermediary of Paolo Morigia) ever makes any mention of this presumed descent from Filippo. A descent that, if true, would on the contrary have lent additional lustre to the already fairly legendary figure of the painter returning to Milan from the glories of Rudolf's court, and would therefore not have failed to be underlined, especially in the light of the fanciful origin of the whole family that the painter himself gave to Morigia after having copied it, as we have seen, "from an old book in vellum written in the German language, which was read to him by the physician of Emperor Maximilian"[11]. The noble title given to Giuseppe Arcimboldo by Rudolf II in 1580 and the heraldic change made to his personal coat of arms, a variant of that of the Milanese Arcimboldi family (for Giuseppe, Or per bend sinister of gules charged with three

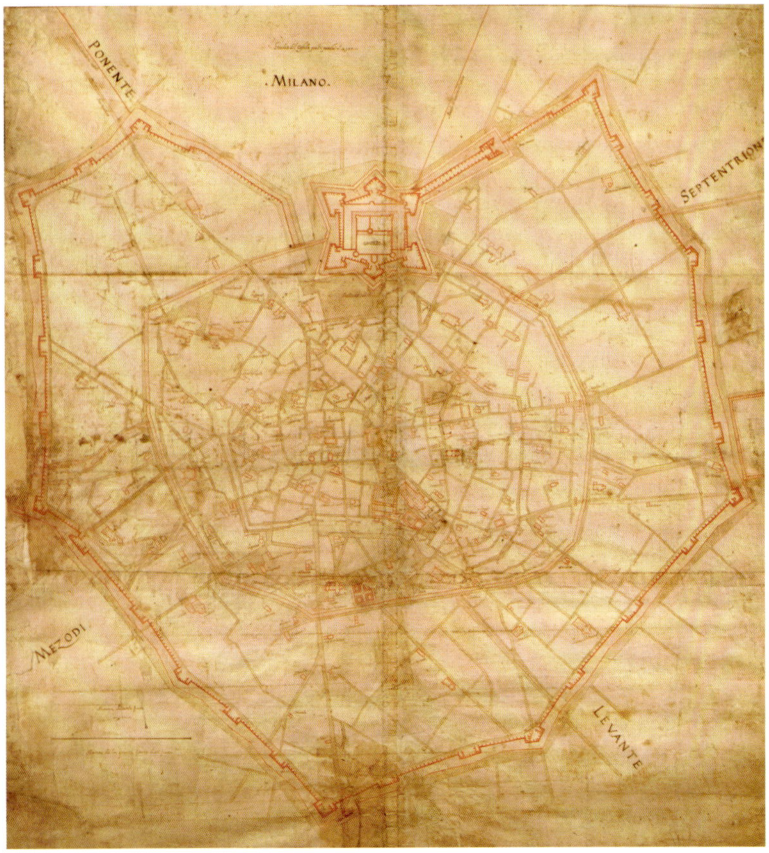

Fig. 1. Giovan Battista Clarici, *Pianta di Milano*, c. 1580. Rome, Accademia di San Luca

mullets; the whole surmounted by a grilled helm, crowned, with crest in the shape of an eagle's head, crowned in turn and surrounded by branches of coral and branches of Or and gules charged with seven mullets of Or on a side)[12] were in any case limited to Giuseppe and his male successors and explicitly granted as a reward for almost twenty years of service to the House of Habsburg. In short, it was a mark of the emperor's personal munificence that, although it echoed in its forms the device of the Arcimboldi of Milan (of which there are several known variants), did not indicate his direct relation to that family but, perhaps, a recognition of mythical and very remote common origins. Moreover, the bestowal of the title of count palatine on Giuseppe in 1592 was dictated by the personal ability of Arcimboldo who, it can be said, bearing an important surname for Renaissance Milan but without belonging to the powerful family that had given the diocese various bishops, succeeded in elevating his rank through his talents and his loyalty to the crown of Austria.

Having cleared the field of the misconception of the descent from the Milanese noble house of the Arcimboldi, it is now possible to look at the family to which Giuseppe belonged from a new point of view. Pasio had at least three sons, of whom at least two took up the career of painter, Biagio and Ambrogio, while all we know of the third, Gian Giacomo, is that he was still alive in 1554[13]. We do not know, however, whether the painter Giovan Stefano Arcimboldi, active in 1555, was a member of the family[14].

Ambrogio Arcimboldi, on the contrary, is fairly well-documented: certainly active between 1534 and 1537, works dated 1549 and 1550 (but not signed) have been attributed to him, concentrated in the area of Lecco and Lake Como (where he lived) and as far as the Valchiavenna[15]. Biagio, resident in Milan, began to work for the cathedral in 1518 and then with more continuity from 1545 onwards as a designer of stained glass and decorator. As well as for lost paintings at the Scuola di San Giuseppe, executed in 1537, he is believed to have been responsible for the cartoon for the tapestry with the *Burial and Profanation of the Body of Saint John the Baptist* in Monza Cathedral, which has been linked with the lower part of the *Assumption of the Virgin* in the Muzeum Narodowe, Warsaw[16].

Taken as a whole, therefore, the activity of the Arcimboldi brothers, sons of Master Pasio, appears to be completely coherent from a chronological as well as stylistic viewpoint. Ambrogio's art shows the strong influence of Bernardino Luini, and there is evidence that Biagio had a close personal relationship with the artist. There is even a well-known portrait of him painted by Luini[17]. One slender lead that might serve to illuminate some aspects of Biagio's life is provided by two payments made by the deputies of the sanctuary of Santa Maria dei Miracoli at Saronno, where a great deal of work was carried out in the first half of the 16th century by, among others, Bernardino Luini and Gaudenzio Ferrari. Here, in the account in Luini's name, appears a payment made on 6 February 1532 to Master Alberto (probably the painter and gilder Alberto Meleguli da Lodi) for the sum of 15 lire to be delivered to a Master Biagio; three years later, in July 1535, a Master Biagio (the same man?) received 2 scudi from the same vestrymen to be paid to Gaudenzio Ferrari[18]. Are not the documented contacts between Biagio Arcimboldo and the Luini family after Bernardino's death and the portrait the latter had painted of Arcimboldo sufficient to identify the Master Biagio paid in 1532 through Luini's account as the father of Giuseppe? And is not the Master Biagio who had to pass on two scudi to Gaudenzio in 1535 the same person? At the moment it is not possible to give a definite answer; what can be said is that if the relations between the three artists were to be further documented and confirmed, the figure of Biagio Arcimboldo would be given greater weight, and with it that of his son.

Giuseppe Arcimboldo: from his Birth to his Departure for the Court: 1526-62

The birth of Giuseppe Arcimboldo, son of the painter Biagio and (according to Litta) Chiara Parisi[19], can now almost certainly be dated to 1526. If any doubt persisted after the discovery of the registration of his death, which took place in Milan on 11 July 1593 at the "age of about sixty-six" (as the record of his decease declared)[20], the convincing attribution of the self-portrait dated 1587 that also bears the number "61" on the forehead, interpreted as his age at the time, dispels almost any remaining uncertainty[21]. Moreover, the first known record of Giuseppe's activity as an artist, the payment by the Cathedral for his designs for stained-glass windows in 1549[22], demonstrates that Arcimboldo was already legally an adult in that year, and therefore over twenty.

Yet nothing is known of his life up until that moment. It can only be imagined that he had learnt the rudiments of the craft in the workshop of his father or his uncles before moving on, in the early 1540s, to an apprenticeship with a master from outside the family, a course taken by many young painters in the Milan of the early 16th century, to complete a training that we can consider to have come to an end around the middle of the forties or shortly afterwards. These are mere suppositions, however: no document and no contemporary source offers any help in this respect, and even Arcimboldo (through his friend Morigia, who was to write a long but already somewhat fanciful biography in 1592)[23] has nothing to say of his childhood. At the age of just over twenty Giuseppe was engaged, after becoming a master and undoubtedly with the support of his father, as one of the artists paid by Milan Cathedral both as a designer of stained-glass windows (which would be executed to his drawings by the German craftsman Corrado de Mochis) and as a painter of various decorations (armorial of the

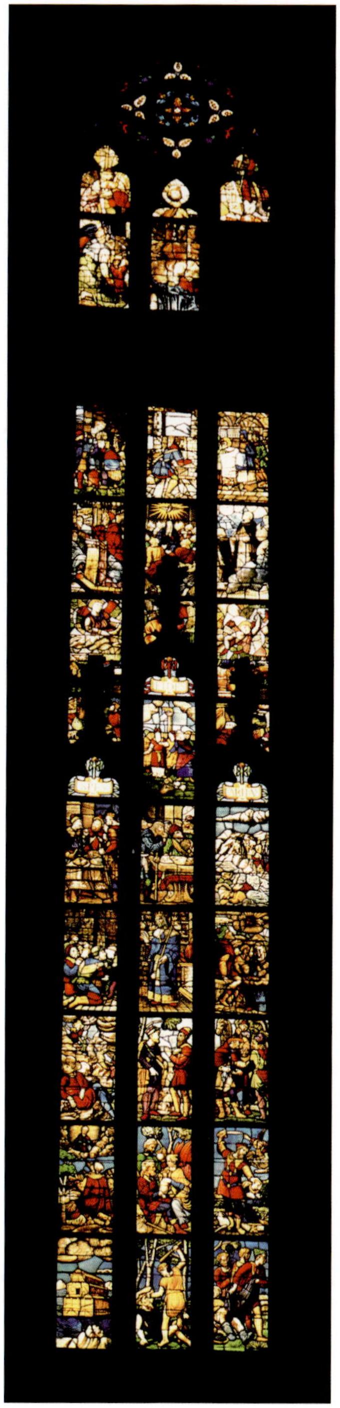

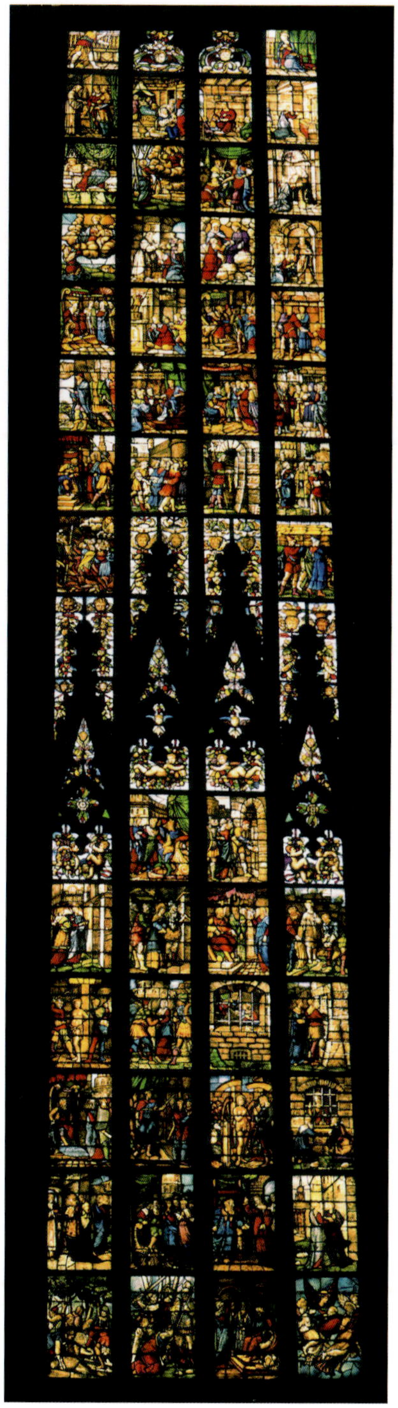

Fig. 2. Stained-glass windows with scenes from the Old Testament, after cartoons by Biagio and Giuseppe Arcimboldo. Milan Cathedral

Fig. 3. Stained-glass windows with scenes from the life of Saint Catherine of Alexandria, after cartoons by Biagio and Giuseppe Arcimboldo. Milan Cathedral

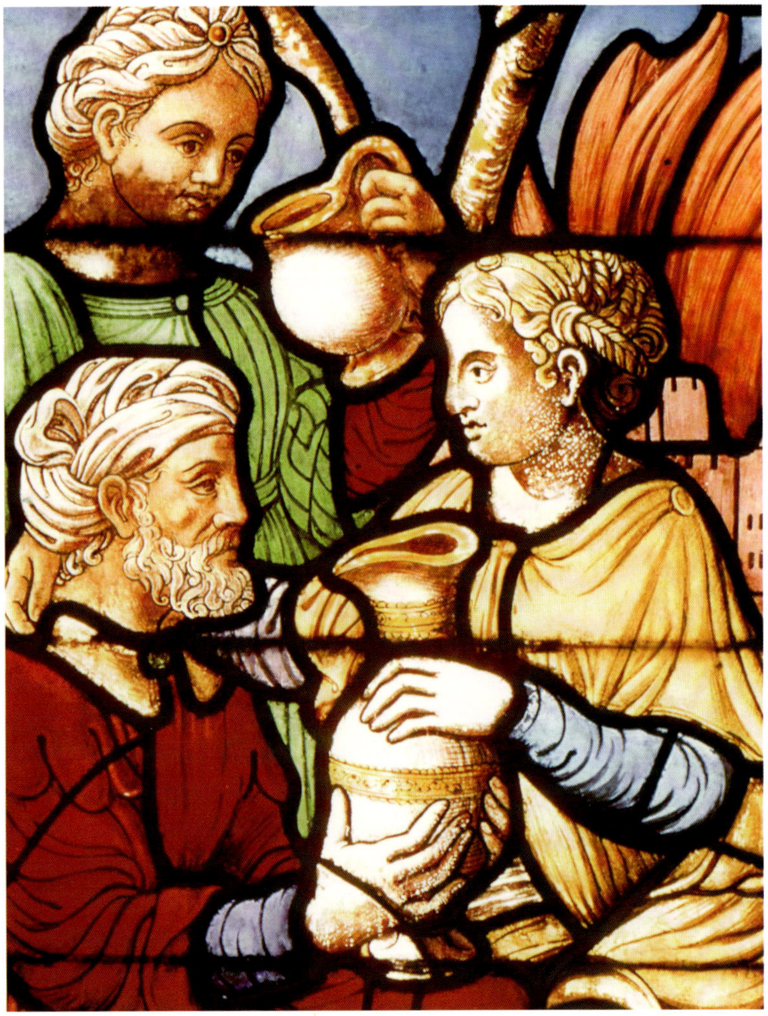

Fig. 4. Detail of fig. 2: *The Daughters of Lot*

Fabbrica, coats of arms on the occasion of lay and religious triumphal entries, part of the doors of the old organ, processional pennants and poles, topographical surveys, tabernacles, canopies). These were works on which his father Biagio was also engaged until at least 1551, the last date on which his name appears among the payments made by the *Fabbrica* of the Cathedral[24]. While the supply of designs for stained-glass windows seems to have been Giuseppe's main activity (payments for as many as 150 are documented between 1549 and 1557), in the same years he was commissioned to carry out a number of less important works: these included reproducing the crest of the *Fabbrica* (a Virgin Mary with an open mantle – an iconography derived from the Madonna of Mercy – enclosing the façade of the Cathedral) on the fronts of buildings and workshops belonging to the vestry board; providing the sacred images displayed on the occasion of oblations offered to the cathedral by the city's guilds; and painting the coats of arms of men succeeding to the posts of bishop or governor in the city. On just two occasions did the Cathedral *Fabbrica* entrust Arcimboldo with a task of greater prestige, although still not in keeping with the ability for which the artist was later to become universally recognized: in 1554, when he painted the doors of the old organ, but only in part and receiving the miserable sum of 10 lire for his work, and in 1558, when for 4 lire he had not only to reproduce the archbishop's coat of arms[25], but also to decorate the outer wall of the southern door. As is clear, these were activities of very low profile, more suited to a decorator than to a painter, which it would be hard to consider artistic if they had not gone hand in hand with other commissions, appropriate to a painter of a certain skill.

Giuseppe's work for the Cathedral was carried out, as we have seen, between the end of 1549 and March 1558[26]. In reality regular payments did not start until 1551, while in 1550 only his father Biagio seems to have been working on the Cathedral, as if the four designs for stained-glass windows supplied by Giuseppe in 1549 had been a sort of trial, even though they were paid for at a higher rate than the thirty executed by Biagio the same year (one and half lire each as opposed to one lira). However, Giuseppe's activity for the Cathedral *Fabbrica*, although regular, could not have been exclusive. Nor was it sufficient to guarantee him a decent income, or even enough to live on: over the course of the ten years he is recorded to have worked for the Cathedral, in fact, Arcimboldo received a total of just 347 lire and 14 soldi, a derisory sum that would not have allowed him to survive even for a year. So it is absolutely certain that both he and his father, from whom he seems to have made himself independent before 1554[27], carried out many other and far more lucrative works, such as the frescoes executed in collaboration with Giuseppe Meda called Lomazzo in Monza Cathedral from 1556 onwards[28] or the cartoon (in reality a canvas) for the tapestry of the *Death of the Virgin* for Como Cathedral, commissioned in December 1558 and not finished until March 1560[29].

Indeed research has brought to light several new documents that allow us to broaden the horizon of Giuseppe Arcimboldo's painting to some extent, even though, it should be pointed out straightaway, they once again relate to modest contributions (to judge by the sums paid to the artist) involving chiefly, it appears, the restoration of works executed by others.

In addition to a number of payments made by the Cathedral of Milan over the years that had escaped the attention of earlier investigations but that do not change the overall situation, in November 1554, for example, Arcimboldo received 49 ? lire from the treasurer of the Luogo Pio di Santa Corona for gilding and painting the structure that framed Titian's *Crowning with Thorns*, i.e. the altarpiece of the chapel of the charitable institution in the church of Santa Maria delle Grazie, now in the Louvre[30]. The payment includes the sum of 36 ? lire for the gilding (with 670 sheets of gold leaf evidently purchased separately) and 13 lire for the painting. From an earlier payment to a Master Andrea Albricci we know that the altarpiece had been removed to permit the addition of carvings (an ornament, a crown and a scroll) and then put back in place[31]. Thus it is reasonable to suppose that Arcimboldo had been entrusted with gilding the new wooden parts made by the otherwise unknown Albricci and retouching the frame, evidently damaged during the carving.

A second previously unknown commission dates from 1556 and concerns Ottaviano Taverna's chapel in the Milanese church of San Francesco Grande. Here Arcimboldo was paid, on 9 September, 60 lire and 19 soldi for unspecified paintings, not by the owner, who had died in 1554[32], but by the confraternity to which Taverna had bequeathed it, the Luogo Pio di Santa Corona once again[33]. The bare record of the payment tells us nothing about what Arcimboldo had been commissioned to do in the sacristy of the church (the Taverna Chapel), but in this case too the small amount paid and previous payments made to the sculptor Giulio da Oggiono for the carving of a marble tabernacle to be set above the chapel's altar suggest that Arcimboldo's intervention may have been limited to covering up the damage caused to the wall by the insertion of the new tabernacle[34]. Unfortunately we have no description of the Taverna Chapel in San Francesco Grande; the sacristy, built by Giacomello Taverna back in 1357, was decorated in its entirety and housed, in addition to Giulio da Oggiono's tabernacle, a large marble portal, various sculptures including two "bowls" (perhaps holy-water stoups) on small columns and the keystone. It also had a painting on the façade[35].

Two more artistic undertakings by Arcimboldo are recorded in the following years: the initial design of the gonfalon of the city of Milan, finished later by Giuseppe Meda (with whom Arcimboldo had already collaborated on the frescoes in Monza Cathedral from 1556 onwards)[36], and perhaps the design of tapestries, which must have been carried out prior to the similar work for Como, this time with *Scenes from the Life of Saint John the Baptist* for Monza Cathedral. This commission, attributed to him on stylistic grounds by DaCosta Kaufmann and Forti Grazzini[37], comprised the last six tapestries in the series (out of nine: the first two or three would date from 1536-37, the third from 1537, but woven to the cartoon that was modified later, around 1550), whose cartoons must have been executed between 1550 and 1560. The last one is thought to be a replica – made to original designs dating from around 1560 – woven by a Flemish factory between 1566 and 1581, perhaps to complete the series with a hanging that was destroyed or never realized. However, some documents that have recently come to light seem to contradict the attribution. These are three payments made to the Milanese tapestry weaver Antonio Maria Bozzolo: in April 1526 he received 408 lire from the vestrymen of Monza Cathedral to settle the accounts for a tapestry depicting *Saint John the Baptist Preaching in the Wilderness* and 250 lire as an advance for the next, *Saint John Baptizing*[38]. In July 1537 Bozzolo was paid an advance of 200 lire for the eighth tapestry ("*pecii octavi tapazarie vite S.ti divi Jo. Baptiste*") of the series of *Scenes from the Life of Saint John* for Monza (*Burial of Saint John the Baptist, Burning of the Body and Scattering of the Ashes*), which the weaver undertook to deliver by Christmas[39]. In addition, we learn from the documents of the *Fabbrica* of Milan Cathedral that since 1533 it had been common practice for Monza Cathedral to lend a series of tapestries to the city's cathedral every year, on the occasion of the feast of the Nativity of the Virgin (8 September)[40]. In the light of these new data it seems difficult to understand why, immediately after Bozzolo's fulfilment of the commission for the tapestries, the Monza Vestry Board should have ordered a second series of tapestries just like the first from the same weaver.

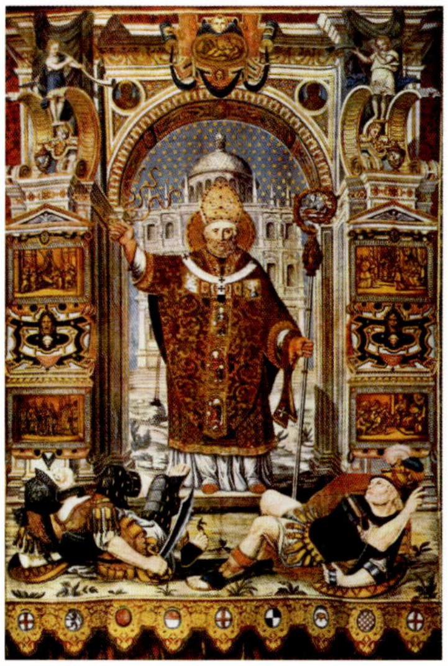

Fig. 5. Giuseppe Meda after a design by Giuseppe Arcimboldo (?), *Gonfalon of Saint Ambrose*. Milan, Castello Sforzesco

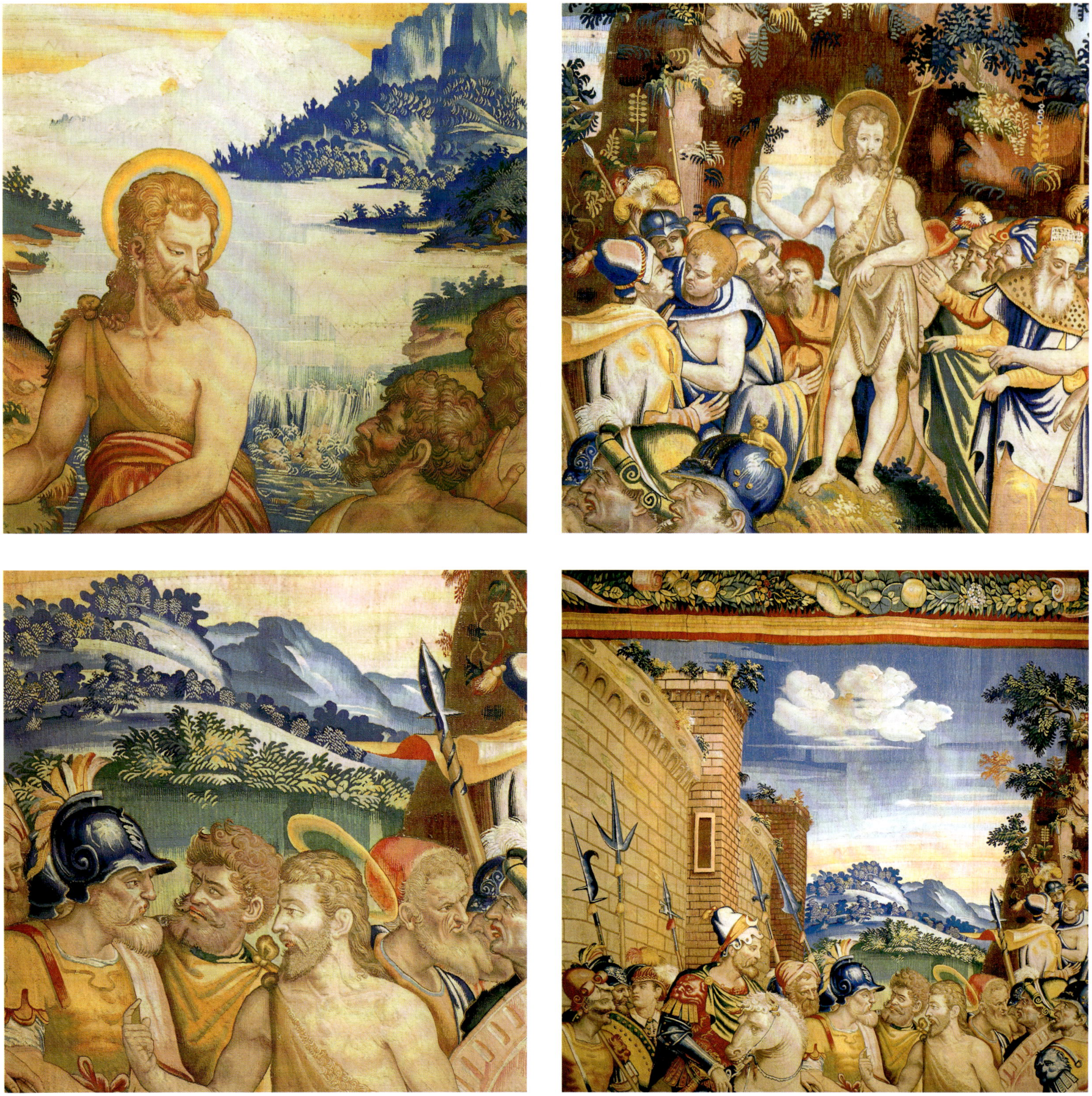

Fig. 6a-d. Tapestry from a series of *Scenes from the Life of Saint John the Baptist*, after cartoons by Giuseppe Arcimboldo (?), details. Monza Cathedral

If the series with *Scenes from the Life of the Baptist* woven by Bozzolo between 1526 and 1537 at least are to be identified with the one now in Monza, it is obvious that Arcimboldo could not have been responsible for the cartoons and almost the whole existing group, which can now be assigned to three phases of weaving (the first between 1536 and 1537, for the first two or three tapestries, the second between 1550 and 1560 for the next five or six and finally the third between 1566 and 1581 for the ninth) would have to be antedated to coincide with the payments made to the weaver. There is, however, one explanation that could reconcile the attribution on the grounds of style with the documents if we imagine that there were two series of tapestries, a first and more old-fashioned one that was concluded with the eighth hanging in 1537 (*Burial of Saint John*) and a second that replaced the first five tapestries, woven in the 1520s and therefore considered too dated, with more modern ones, and the addition of one more[41]. Moreover, Forti Grazzini's proposal of Biagio Arcimboldo as the designer of the *Burial* (documented at the planning stage in 1537) would explain the commission of the new series from Giuseppe, over a decade later: in fact the vestrymen of Monza must have been well aware of the need to update the now aging tapestries devoted to the saint and, at the same time, maintain a degree of visual uniformity so that the differences would not be too glaring when they were put on display. And it would do so without dragging out the execution of the cartoon over too long a period of time (1537-50)[42]. Whence the decision to entrust the continuation of the series (in which the tapestry with the *Burial* must have formed the link between the older hangings and the subsequent ones) to the son of the previous designer, who could obviously have guaranteed continuity as well as innovation, and the weaving to Bozzolo again. The vestry board of San Giovanni must have liked Arcimboldo's work, given that, as we have seen, the frescoing of the right transept was entrusted to him and his partner Meda in 1556: a date that lies about halfway through the process of design of the tapestries (1550-60).

The tapestries in Monza would therefore, like the stained-glass windows in Milan Cathedral, represent the handover of responsibility from Biagio Arcimboldo to his son Giuseppe, now a master in his own right and thus able to take his father's place in the commissions from the two Cathedrals around 1550. It is likely that Biagio, now elderly, was no longer able (or willing) to apply himself to painting and drawing: it cannot be a coincidence that the first payment to Giuseppe (and therefore his first documented work) was made in December 1549 for four designs for stained-glass windows in Milan Cathedral, and that the last documentary evidence of Biagio's activity as a painter (the payment for six designs in February 1551) was made around the same time as that commission.

Although Giuseppe Arcimboldo's activity between the end of the forties and 1562 could not have been confined to the episodes documented and recounted up to now, only one attribution for undocumented works has been put forward and widely accepted: I am referring to the frescoes that adorn the side walls of the chapel dedicated to Saint John the Baptist in the public church of San Maurizio al Monastero Maggiore[43]. The two works (*The Naming of the Baptist* and *Salome Receiving the Baptist's Head*) flank a *Baptism of Christ* by another hand. None of them are attributed with certainty to any artist but they can be confidently assigned, as a date *post quem,* to 1545, the year of the death of Ginevra Bentivoglio, wife of Giovanni II del Carretto[44]. The chapel, commissioned by the couple's sons as a burial place for their mother, has an inscription on the walls with the date 1545 and the names of Alfonso del Carretto and his brothers; it would therefore have been one of Giuseppe Arcimboldo's earliest works, carried out before he had reached the age of twenty and perhaps with the assistance of his father Biagio. But it is also possible that the date 1545 should be understood as a reference to the year of Ginevra's death, allowing us to assign the execution of the frescoes to some time shortly afterwards.

The Move to the Court of Maximilian of Habsburg: Hypothesis for a Choice

Morigia tells us that "Giuseppe agreed to serve Maximilian after many requests, and in the year 1562 left his homeland and went to the court of the Emperor, where he was very highly esteemed, and well-treated by Maximilian"[45]. The well-known passage continues with the assertion that Giuseppe, once at court, devoted himself "not so much to painting as to many other inventions, such as tournaments, jousts, games, decorations for weddings, and coronations", astonishing both Maximilian, "his principal master", and the whole of the court. Morigia's words, of which we know Arcimboldo to have been the direct source ("All that is said of this illustrious, and ancient house [the Arcimboldi] I have derived [...] from the accounts, and information received from the virtuous, and noble Giuseppe Arcimboldo"), are extremely important not just because they confirm, for once and for all, that Arcimboldo's move took place at the desire and request of Maximilian of Habsburg, son of Emperor Ferdinand I[46], and that his destination was the court in Vienna, but also because they make clear, I believe, the reasons and views that led the emperor's son, perhaps not yet named king of Bohemia or of the Romans, to seek his service[47].

No official document relating to Maximilian of Habsburg's request has been uncovered so far: no letter, no payment of travel expenses, no passport. So to try to explain the summoning of Arcimboldo – and not some other painter, such as Bernardino Campi, a famous portraitist who had been active in Milan for years, working for the city's governors among others – it is necessary to draw primarily on sources published at the end of the 16th century by authors who could have known and spoken with the painter and thus offer some clue as to what might have impressed the emperor's son strongly enough to have asked Arcimboldo to come and work for him. And this takes us directly to his career in Milan, about which, despite the new documents and attributions, some of them important and prestigious, we have to admit we still know too little.

Nevertheless, I think it is legitimate to put forward some hypotheses. Let us look at the kind of works he had carried out prior to 1562 (attributed to him with certainty or reasonable probability): they consist almost entirely of drawings (designs for stained-glass windows or tapestries) and frescoes (in San Maurizio and Monza) of large dimensions, or small-scale restorations of other artists' works (such as Titian's altarpiece or the Taverna Chapel), or again decorations of a heraldic character (coats of arms of archbishops, members of the royal family, the governor of Milan, the Cathedral *Fabbrica*) and processional insignia. On the whole none of this appears to foreshadow his subsequent production of paintings, with the exception of the fine representations of nature that can be found in the tapestries in Monza: no portrait, no "cabinet" picture, no private commission[48] except that "portrait of Arcimboldo" cited in 1578 as the first picture in the *post-mortem* inventory of the estate of Count Giovanni Anguissola, which also comprised, confining ourselves to the paintings, four more portraits, a *Passion of Christ* and a total of forty-seven Flemish canvases of large and small size[49]. And in any case, it does not seem that any of this production would have impressed Maximilian, if he had ever come to know about it. But we do know that Arcimboldo, rather than devote himself to painting at the court of Maximilian of Habsburg, was engaged "in many other inventions, such as tournaments, jousts, games, decorations for weddings, and coronations", coming up with a "large number of varied, ingenious, charming, & rare inventions, that universally filled with wonder all those great Princes, who were gathered there, & to the great content of Maximilian, his principal master"[50]. This may be the direction in which we should look to find Giuseppe's specific appeal.

The artist's involvement in public festivals and spectacles in Vienna also led to some controversy with Giovanni Battista Fontana, called Fonteo, who designed the notices for the tourney held to celebrate the wedding of Archduke Charles to Maria of Bavaria in 1571. Fontana, boasting that he was responsible for the entire staging of the event[51], had tried to obscure the reputation and merits of Arcimboldo, to whom credit was nevertheless given by the emperor himself "as this man [Arcimboldo] was truly exceptional in the inventions and above all in the masquerades"[52]. A late record of this specialization of his is provided by the group of 158 draw-

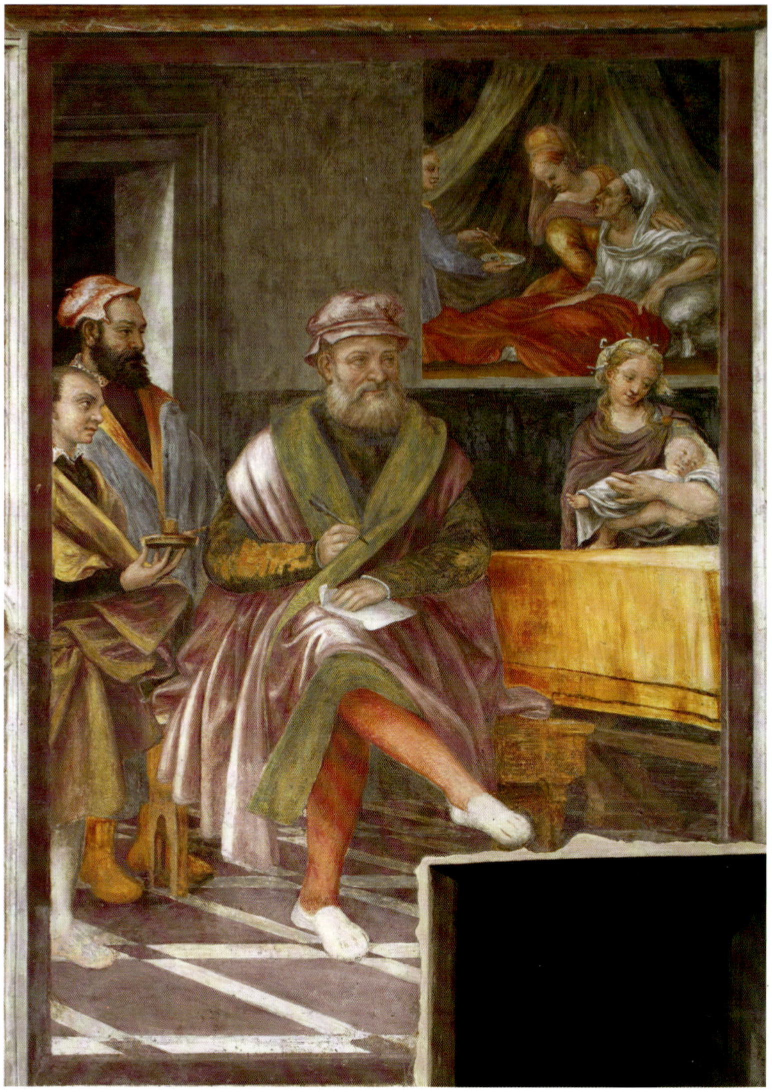

Fig. 8 (and 9, opposite). Attributed to Biagio and Giuseppe Arcimboldo, frescoes with scenes from the life of Saint John the Baptist. Milan, Cappella Carretto

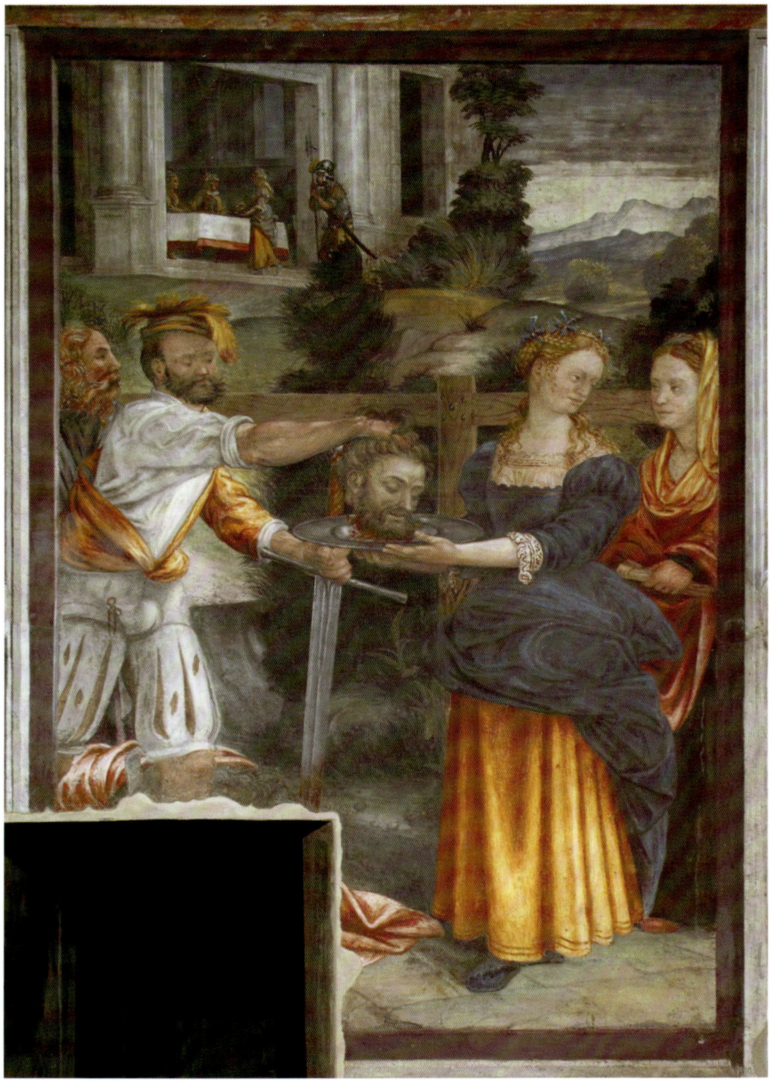

ings in the Gabinetto Disegni e Stampe of the Uffizi, an album that was presented to Rudolf II in 1585. This is a miscellany that cannot be linked to a single festive occasion, perhaps a sort of dummy discarded by the painter – or created or assembled for the occasion – and donated to the emperor. It is this collection that contains a number of drawings which might provide a key to our understanding of Arcimboldi's Milanese period and, at the same time, explain his summoning to Vienna.

I am referring to the representations of several figures intended to accompany the Liberal Arts (Grammar, Dialectics, Rhetoric, Arithmetic, Music, Geometry and Astrology/Astronomy), images that have been linked to the festival organized in 1571 for the marriage of Archduke Carlo and Maria of Bavaria (as part of the procession of Europe)[53]. In reality the same allegories had already appeared in Milan more than a decade earlier, on the occasion of a carnival feast held on 5 February 1559 in the house of Giovan Battista Castaldo to celebrate in a fitting way the governor of Milan Consalvo Fernandez de Cordoba, duke of Sessa, and the captain of light horse Francesco Ferdinando of Avalos, marquis of Pescara. In fact a long description of the festival, written by Ascanio Centorio degli Ortensi, Castaldo's secretary[54], tells us that, at a certain point, "seven Women arrived dressed as Queens in splendid robes of gold and silver, carrying certain signs, which made it absolutely clear to the others who they were, and these were the seven Liberal Arts", each accompanied by an old man. The pairs were: Grammar / Donatus; Rhetoric / Cicero; Astrology / Ptolemy; Arithmetic / Euclid; Geometry / Archimedes; Music / Clinia and finally Dialectics / Porphyry[55].

The scenery for the festival was prepared by Leone Leoni, but we know nothing about who was responsible for the costumes or the figures. It is true that the similarities to Arcimboldo's costume-sketches are very close, but not sufficient in themselves, even in this case, to provide proof of his involvement in the conception of the carnival celebrations of 1559; neither did any member of the court attend the celebrations and we cannot even suppose that the tournament was so magnificent that its echo reached as far as Vienna.

Two years later, however, the same Leone Leoni was entrusted by the marquis of Pescara with the task of preparing another and far more important festival than the one staged by Castaldo, on the occasion of the marriage of Eleanor of Habsburg, daughter of Emperor Ferdinand I, and the duke of Mantua Guglielmo Gonzaga. On 29 April 1561, in Mantua, the barrier tournament organized by the imperial sculptor attracted the principal knights and noblemen of Italy[56] and two days later the same nobles participated in the joust, organized by the supervisor of ducal construction Giovanni Battista Bertani. On this festive occasion the marquis of Pescara acted in a manner of speaking as "host", in so far as he was closely related to both bride and groom, having married the daughter of the first duke of Mantua, Isabella (making him brother-in-law of both Duke Guglielmo and the deceased Duke Francesco and above all of his wife, Catherine of Habsburg, Eleanor's sister). Given his position, Francesco Ferdinando of Avalos undoubtedly did everything he could to put on a display worthy of the situation: calling on Leone Leoni to devise the scenery and Luca Contile to compose the verses in Latin and the vulgar tongue (along with a Cavalier Malaspina whom I have not yet been able to identify), he delegated all the practical side to them, and the two men in turn recruited over two hundred craftsmen "highly skilled in such matters" from Milan so that the work would be completed on time.

If it were possible to imagine that not the least among these two hundred Milanese craftsmen brought to Mantua for the occasion was Giuseppe Arcimboldo, a not unlikely eventuality if he had indeed collaborated with Leoni on the festivities in 1559, then this could explain how news of his ability "not so much in painting but in many other inventions, such as tournaments, jousts, games, decorations for weddings, and coronations" could have reached the court of Vienna and the ears of the father and brother of the Mantuan bride.

Another indication of Arcimboldo's involvement in the organization of spectacles and festivals in mid-16th century Milan might perhaps be found in some drawings that have been attributed to him in *Il libro del sarto*. This is a miscellany of drawn and painted designs for drapes, men's and women's clothing, pavilions, hangings for beds, tailor's patterns, allegorical and festive costumes and banners, interspersed with notes and accounts and also containing skilfully executed drawings glued to originally blank pages, that once belonged to the Milanese tailor Gian Giacomo del Conte (c. 1525-92)[57]. The bearded figure dressed in old-fashioned armour on folio 62r, the dragon set on a capital with the Arcimboldo crest on folio 120r and the design for a cornet's pennant on folio 122r (intended for the troops of the duke of Montemarciano, Ercole Sfondrati)[58] join other drawings that may also have been made by Arcimboldo (107r and 114r, similar in conception to the bearded man on folio 62r)[59] that, along with the numerous figures in costume that fill the pages of the volume, can give us an idea of the complexity of the clients' requirements, of the variety of the sources that were drawn on and of the quality of the designers to whom the organizers of masquerades turned. Thus it is likely that this is the area in which we should look for the specialization of Giuseppe Arcimboldo and for an explanation of the reputation that took him to the imperial court in 1562.

The Brief Returns to Milan

Between the date of Arcimboldo's departure from Milan, 1562, and his definitive return to the city, in 1587, only three brief visits to Italy are documented, although we cannot rule out the possibility that the artist may have crossed the Alps to the south on other occasions.

The first journey must have taken place in the summer of 1566: on 2 June a passport for Arcimboldo was issued at Augsburg and at the end of August "Signor Gioseffo [blank] painter of His Majesty the Emperor Maximilian" was present at Sedriano (a small town situated between Milan and Magenta) to stand as godfather at the modest ceremony of the baptism of Agostina, the daughter of Biagio Mantovani, a servant of Ottone Visconti, and Elisabetta Grancina da Poliano, alongside the godmother, a certain Bianca Bariggia[60]. Above and beyond the confirmation this provides that Arcimboldo was in Italy in the summer of 1566, it would be interesting to discover the reason for the presence of the "painter of His Majesty the Emperor Maximilian" in Sedriano. There may be some connection with the existence of a work by Aurelio Luini in the presbytery of the church of San Bernardino in Sedriano (a *Madonna Enthroned and Child*), a fresco that was certainly painted after 1567[61], given the ties between the Luini and Arcimboldo families that, as we have seen, dated back to Biagio and Bernardino, but the trace appears too faint to be worth pursuing on this occasion.

A decade later Arcimboldo was again in Milan, where he dictated a will to the Milanese notary Giovan Stefano Busti. Unfortunately the notary's records have been almost totally destroyed and the will can no longer be traced[62]. A record of it survives in the later codicils of 1581[63] in which the painter declares his wish to make several additions to the will drawn up in 1576 or 1577. It has to be asked just when it was, during the two years in question, that the painter might have gone to Milan: certainly not between the autumn of 1576 and the following spring on account both of the outbreak of plague in the city and of the death of Maximilian II (on 12 October) and the very long time that elapsed before his burial in the cathedral of Saint Vitus (22 March 1577). The only remaining possibilities, therefore, are that he made the journey in the spring-summer of 1576 or in the same period of 1577; personally I am more inclined to believe that it took place in 1576 rather than the following year, when the new emperor had just been installed and the state of Milan was still suffering from the aftermath of the plague, but only new discoveries in the archives will be able to give the final word on the matter[64].

What is certain is that Arcimboldo was in Milan again in March 1581: on 17 March in fact he drew up, as we have mentioned, several codicils to his earlier will, declaring that, in the eventuality that his son Benedetto, probably born in 1575, died before or after him and before reaching the age of eighteen, the usufruct of the property that was in the hands of Giovanni Filippo Gherardini should be enjoyed by Gherardini himself[65].

The document, in addition to attesting to Arcimboldo's presence in the city, is important from many points of view. In the first place it bears witness to the community of goods between the painter and Giovanni Filippo Gherardini, usufructuary of the property of Arcimboldo deposited with him (and who knows what the painter might have left in Milan and on what occasion?), in that he was probably already the owner of the house the painter lived in. The codicils were in fact drawn up in Gherardini's house, located in Porta Vercellina, in the parish of San Pietro alla Vigna, near the Monastero Maggiore, where Arcimboldo would reside on his definitive return to Italy. Another element of interest lies in the fact that one of the witnesses to the codicils is the merchant and armourer Giovan Antonio Polacini, who had close ties to the Habsburg imperial court and to that of Archduke Ferdinand II of Tyrol[66]. That the two should have known one another comes as no surprise: the members of the Milanese colony, always numerous, maintained cordial relations with one another, if only for an obvious community not only of interests, but of affections and memories; and it is not unlikely that Arcimboldo, given his own position at court, could have assisted artists and craftsmen from Milan, at least in getting the attention of the emperor so as to propose their own creations. As we shall see later, this is precisely the role documented for the painter's last period, after his definitive return to Milan.

The Definitive Return Home: 1587 or 1588-1593

The year 1587 (or 1588?) saw the definitive return of Giuseppe Arcimboldo to Milan, the city of his birth. We do not know the precise date, but it is certain that the journey took place some time after 12 August 1587, when Rudolf II made a one-off payment of 1500 florins to the artist as a mark of gratitude for the work he had done for the House of Habsburg over at least twenty-five years. Morigia asserts that his departure from the Habsburg court – which in 1583 had been transferred from Vienna to Prague – came in 1588 after at least two years of requests to leave from Arcimboldi[67], and that in the meantime he had had his aforementioned natural son, Benedetto, legitimized by Emperor Maximilian II in 1575.

The doubt about the actual date of the painter's return home is not resolved even by an unpublished *status animarum* of the parish of San Pietro alla Vigna, which shows Giuseppe and Benedetto, who must have been about twelve or thirteen at the time, living with Giovanni Filippo Gherardini and his family[68] in the house where Arcimboldo had resided in 1581, at the time of his last known codicil.

In Milan Arcimboldo would find his old friends and colleagues, now getting on in years like him: among them were Giuseppe Lomazzo (i.e. Meda, by that time more of an architect and engineer than a painter), Aurelio Luini, Giovan Paolo Lomazzo, now almost blind, whom Arcimboldo must have known if only because of his kinship with Scipione Delfinone[69], the embroiderer of the gonfalon of Saint Ambrose[70]; and then the Miseroni who had remained in the city (other members of the family had been living in Prague for some time), Giovan Antonio Polacini, who had been his witness in 1581, and above all Giovanni Filippo Gherardini, with whom he would stay until his death. We know that many more of the city's artists came to Arcimboldo's house to admire the painter's latest efforts (at least the *Flora,* the *Vertumnus* and the *Four Seasons in a Single Head* owned by Comanini), to seek recommendations for the court and to submit their own works for his judgement, but perhaps even more to listen to the stories, which we must imagine to have been extraordinary, of someone who had experienced at first hand the splendours and the follies of the courts of Maximilian II and Rudolf II.

Milan had in fact just emerged from the first period of Borromean "rule" (Archbishop Carlo, later to be canonized as Saint Charles, had died at the end of 1584 and Federico did not come to the city until 1595), which had to all intents and purposes exercised a heavy-handed ostracism with regard to many artists who, because of their culture or independent choice, had not been willing to conform to the cardinal's ideas: ideas that extended to every field, not least that of art. Naturally this is not the place to attempt a summary of the influence of Carlo Borromeo's episcopate on artistic developments in late 16th-century Milan[71]. What are striking, however, are the dates of the beginning and end of Arcimboldo's stay at court (1562 and 1587-1588), which coincide almost exactly with those of Carlo's tenure in Milan (1560-1565 and 1584). And we have to wonder whether Biagio's son would have become the Giuseppe Arcimboldo we know if he had not left his own city, escaping the influence of Borromeo and finding the freedom to give expression to his wildest fantasies.

And so, towards the end of the eighties, the now elderly and eminent Arcimboldo, shortly to be honoured with the title of count palatine and still in contact with the imperial court, for which he negotiated or proposed the acquisition of Milanese works of art, or encouraged the city's artists to make their way across the Alps, could not fail to fascinate, as a witness to the eccentricities of Rudolf's rule, the group of artists and men of letters, some of them for many years gathered around the Accademia del Val di Blenio by Lomazzo, who were waiting for nothing more than a breath of new air to dispel the Borromean mists.

It is not hard to imagine the clamour and, at the same time, the silence that must have accompanied his tales of Rudolf II and his dignitaries, as well as of the other people he had encountered in those few years in Bohemia: among them, the English magus and cabbalist Dr John Dee and his earless associate Edward Kelley (who claimed to converse with the angels Uriel and Gabriel), the famous rabbi Jehuda Löw ben Bezalel (in Prague from 1573, founder of the high Talmudic school), the necromancer, alchemist and sorcerer Gerolamo Scotti from Piacenza and the armless calligrapher Thomas Schweicker. Then there was the amazement caused by the endless lists of the wonders assembled in the castle, which Arcimboldo himself was still called on to add to, in the Milanese years, with his own works, acquisitions or indications.

It is certainly no coincidence that the first mentions of Arcimboldo are to be found in writings by Lomazzo that were published after Carlo Borromeo's death but before the painter's final return to the city: in the *Trattato* of 1584, the *Rime* of 1587 and finally the *Idea* of 1590. Other printed verses came out the following year commenting on the *Flora* or the *Vertumnus*, written by Giovanni Filippo Gherardini, Gregorio Comanini, Gherardo Borgogni, Bernardino Baldini, Sigismondo Foliani and the mysterious G.A. from Milan, who may have been Arcimboldo himself[72], but it was not until 1592 that the Jesuit Morigia composed the eulogy, drawing on accounts given to him directly by Arcimboldo, information that he naturally included, in summary form, in his *Historia brieve dell'Augustissima casa d'Austria* of 1593[73].

Arcimboldo's most fertile, and best-documented, contacts in these last years in Milan seem to have been with men of letters, whom he certainly met through Gherardini (even if we still do not know what was his special bond with the latter)[74]. He even seems to have given the Lateran canon Gregorio Comanini one of his works, a head that comprises all four seasons of the year, the only painting by Arcimboldo for the moment documented with certainty in Milan[75]. Obviously artists also frequented his house, some to see his latest works, some to seek introductions at the court, like Ambrogio Figino[76], and some to present their own efforts to the elderly painter, hoping for a positive assessment that might open the way to Prague (as was the case with Fede Galizia, perhaps desiring to follow in the footsteps of Sofonisba Anguissola, who had left for the court of Spain in 1559)[77].

It was in fact the search for works to fill the voracious Habsburg collections that kept Arcimboldo busy in Milan, and it was not just a question of pictures: "however he continued in the service of the emperor, in all those things (as well as painting) that in Milan pleased, and satisfied his Catholic majesty"[78]. We know that shortly before he died Giuseppe had purchased a piece of jasper to be made into a lid for a vase, paying all of 100 ducats for it, a price so high as to suggest that it could only have been an imperial commission[79], while the *scrittoio* in ebony and ivory (among other materials) "of marvellous contrivance, inventions, and secrets" that Giuseppe Guzzi was making to the design "of the exceptional quon[dam] Giuseppe Arcimboldo"[80] was certainly intended for Rudolf II.

Giuseppe Arcimboldo died of kidney failure in the house in Milan on 11 July 1593 at the age of about sixty-six[81]. We do not know with certainty where he was buried, but we can conjecture that his mortal remains were laid to rest in his parish church San Pietro alla Vigna[82]. The epitaph for his funeral was written by Cesare Besozzi, the bookseller and publisher who had married Gherardini's daughter, Clara, in 1578 and therefore knew Arcimboldo well[83]:

Iosepho Arcimboldo viro integerrimo, Pictori
Clarissimo, Comitiq. Palatino;
Qui Ferdinando, Maximiliano II, Rodulpho II.
Imperatoribus gratissimus semper fuit.
Caesar. Besutius tanti viri familiarissimus
L. S.

A second epitaph, penned shortly after his death, was written by Bernardino Baldini[84], physician, philosopher, student of natural sciences and professor at Pavia Università and a member, with Lomazzo, of the Accademia della Val di Blenio. He also wrote verses that accompanied the presentation of Arcimboldo's *Vertumnus* at court in 1591:

Epitaphium Iosephi Arcimboldii.
Integer a vita Ioseph migravit, Olympum
Viseret ut clarum, siderasq[ue] domos.
Caesareus quo pictor, ut hoc effinxit in orbe
Mortaleis, Divum pingat in axe Choros

In the few years that preceded or followed Arcimboldo's death many people who had been close to him in one way or another also died: Scipione Delfinone in August 1590, Lomazzo in January 1592, Aurelio Luini in August 1593, Meda in August 1599, Baldini in January 1601 and the other men of letters who had praised the painter's last works with their verses in the years immediately afterwards. A season had closed. His son Benedetto, who had probably only just come of age at the time of Giuseppe's death, seems to have left no trace of himself in Milan[85], and we do not yet know who inherited the material legacy of the deceased artist. Arcimboldo's last work, the *scrittoio* "of marvellous contrivance, inventions, and secrets" that Giuseppe Guzzi was constructing, was transferred to the house of the Miseroni family and from there, once finished, probably sent to Emperor Rudolf.

Other inventions vanished into thin air, inventions whose names alone speak to us of a multifaceted and astonishing imagination and intelligence: the perspectival lute[86] or the possibility of playing colours as if they were music[87], a means of "crossing rivers rapidly, where there are no bridges or boats available" or "ciphers that cannot be understood without his instrument"[88] and who knows what other marvels designed or even just imagined by Giuseppe Arcimboldo.

[1] The name of Giuseppe's father (Biagio) can be found in many now well-known documents; the name of Pasio (or Pace), can be deduced, for example, from the papers that involve Biagio in the allotment of Bernardino Luini's inheritance from 1534 onwards, when Pasio appears to have already died (ASM, Notarile 7555, 9 November 1534; Miller 1989, 13, doc. 1).

[2] AVFDM, Registri (Libro mastro) 313, fol. 228; see Geiger 1954, 113. Biagio was paid 59 lire for several paintings (probably coats of arms of the vestry board) executed on the vestry board's own houses at Candoglia, location of the quarries which supplied the marble used for the construction of Milan Cathedral.

[3] According to the statutes of the city of Milan, in fact, the age of majority and the consequent ability to receive payments or sign contracts was reached on a person's twentieth birthday (and in any case only following an act of emancipation from parental authority or in the case of the parent's death). So the fact that Biagio was paid directly in 1518 dates his birth to at least twenty years earlier, in 1498.

[4] Pasio's status as a master is recorded in the *pacta* between the community of Acquate and the painter Ambrogio Arcimboldi (Pasio's son and Giuseppe's uncle) drawn up on 1 November 1537 (ASM, Notarile 9816; Shell 1995, 257-258, doc. no. 99). The date *ante quem* for Pasio's death is derived from the *pacta* of 1534 signed by Ambrogio himself (who was in partnership with Sigismondo de Magistris at the time) for the polyptych of the parish church of San Giorgio at Cremeno (ASM, Notarile 10157, 27 August 1534; Coppa 1991, 108 and no. 8).

[5] This is an absolutely minimal estimate arrived at by assigning an age of 20 to Biagio in 1518 and the same age to Pasio at the time of Biagio's birth (although we do not even know whether he was the first-born child). In reality a difference of as long as ten or fifteen years (which would take the date of Pasio's birth to the early 1460s) is entirely possible.

[6] Litta 1823.

[7] For the Arcimboldi family in the 15th and 16th century I now refer the reader to Somaini 2003, although he perpetuates the hypothesis of Filippo's being the father of Pasio. I must point out that Filippo Arcimboldi's will, drawn up on 20 October 1518, makes no mention of any direct descendant apart from his daughter Margherita, already married to Giovanni Bernardino Lampugnani (ASM, Trivulzio, Orfanotrofio femminile [Arcimboldi] 1, fasc. 7). Filippo died the following day, leaving his nephews Francesco and Giovanni, the sons of his deceased brother Nicolò, his universal heirs.

[8] Crescenzi 1640-47, 92: "And Filippo was survived by that Pace, father of Biaggio, of whom Giuseppe Count Palatine of the Empire was son; with Filippo having been succeeded in the fief by his Nephews, I seriously doubt the legitimacy of Pace's birth".

[9] Crescenzi 1640-47, 90. This is undoubtedly taken from Morigia 1592, 556: "All this which I have written up to now on the Arcimboldo family, I have had from Signor Giuseppe Arcimboldi, gentleman of trust, and of uprightness of life, who has served two Emperors in Germany, as will be told, and he has copied this genealogy, and origin of the Arcimboldi from an old book in vellum written in the German language, which was read to him by the physician of Emperor Maximilian".

[10] For example, Margherita is the only descendant of Filippo Arcimboldi di Guido Antonio mentioned in the *Teatro genealogico delle famiglie nobili milanesi* of 1739 (BNBM, MS. AH.XV.3-4). Two handwritten family trees that claim Pasio's descent from Filippo (ASM, Trivulzio, Orfanotrofio femminile [Arcimboldi] 5) are certainly contemporary with or later than Litta and in both appears a second son of Giuseppe, Massimiliano, not mentioned elsewhere. A third family tree, similar to these two but dated 7 April 1823, is conserved in ASCM, Sola Busca (Arconati) 10, fasc. Genealogia (with references to handwritten notes that offer no documentary support).

[11] Morigia 1592, 556.

[12] For the granting of the coat-of-arms, Geiger 1954, 123-124, and Morigia 1592, 567.

[13] ASM, Notarile 12071, no. 155, 1 September 1553 (Gian Giacomo rents from Giovan Battista de Rubeis [or Rossi] a room in a house located in Porta Vercellina, in the parish of Santa Maria alla Porta), and no. 191, 5 March 1554 (Gian Giacomo pays the rent for the aforementioned room).

[14] All we have in connection with Giovan Stefano is a single document, a payment of just 9 lire for unspecified painting work on the altarpiece of the chapel of the deceased Francesco Gallo in the church of Santa Maria alla Porta (ASM, S. Corona, Registri 58, fol. 176, 22 December 1555); this document does not give the name of Giovan Stefano's father.

[15] Rossi 1995, 256-259; Shell 1995, 257, doc. no. 99.

[16] Forti Grazzini 1988, entry 9, 123. The tapestry in Monza dates from 1537.

[17] BML, cat. no. JCR 320, profile turned to the right, signed at bottom right "Bernardino Lovino F." and with the inscription at bottom left "Blasii Arcimboldi pictori Imago". If this really is a portrait of Biagio painted by Luini, the picture provides a further clue to the date of his birth: since it could not have been executed after 1532, the year of Luini's death, and represents a mature but not elderly man, it provides confirmation of the fact that Biagio was born in the 15th century, and probably at an earlier date than that of 1498 which had been postulated as an unequivocal *ante quem.*

[18] ASS, Registri 1, fasc. 3 (Libro dei conti 1526-50), respectively in c. 178 and c. 24; for the latter see Di Lorenzo 1989, 222. At the time Luini was busy frescoing the main chapel of the sanctuary (he died in the spring of 1532); Gaudenzio Ferrari frescoed the lantern of the church's dome between 1535 and 1536.

[19] Litta 1823. It is not known where the nobleman Pompeo could have got the name of Giuseppe's mother's from, but it seems unlikely that it should have been the fruit of pure invention on his part. To my knowledge, however, no document has ever been found that could confirm Giuseppe's maternal descent.

[20] ASM, Popolazione p.a. 104. Casati 1885, 93 (but Casati is wrong in placing the death of Aurelio Luini on the same day: Bernardino's son died just under a month later, on 6 August 1593).

[21] Berra 1996a. The estimation of age at the moment of death, although often fairly accurate, was left to the doctor who drew up the report and therefore cannot always be considered exact. In this case I am more inclined to believe Arcimboldo and to regard the doctor's assessment as approximate (but very close to the truth).

[22] 24 December 1549, payment of 6 lire for four drawings, AVFDM, Registri (Libro mastro) 331, fol. 133; Registri (Giornale di cassa) 407, fol. 171v.

[23] Morigia 1592, 556-557 and 566-567. Some preparatory and manuscript parts of Morigia's biography of Arcimboldo, with interpolations and erasures, including the interesting *Origini della casa Arcimbolda* [continued in another hand] *havuta dal s. Giuseffo Arcinboldi pittore, da lui datta al P. Moriggia*, dated April 1594, can be consulted in ASCM, Sola Busca (Arconati) 10; see Somaini 2000, 5ff.

[24] The last payment to Biagio, dated 24 February 1551, was of 9 lire for 6 designs for stained-glass windows (AVFDM, Registri [Libro mastro] 332, fol. 336; Registri [Giornale di cassa] 408, fol. 109v) under the date 25 February. After this date Biagio seems to have been replaced by his son Giuseppe and his name no longer appears; the last document that mentions Biagio in his lifetime dates from 10 June 1556, when Giuseppe ratified the contract entered into by Giuseppe Meda for the frescoes that the two painters were to execute in the church of San Giovanni Battista in Monza (ASM, Notarile 8882; see Miller 1989, 17, doc. no. 7).

[25] It is likely that these were armorial bearings of the Milanese Filippo Archinto, who was appointed archbishop in 1556 and died in Bergamo on 21 June 1558 without ever succeeding in taking office in the diocese, which he governed solely *in spiritualibus*: Giannini 2000, 248ff. The political disputes within the Milanese Church that prevented Archinto from assuming his post led to the see being left vacant until the appointment of Carlo Borromeo, in 1560.

[26] In fact the last payment was made on 1 March 1558, when he received the modest sum of 4 lire for painting the rebuilt wall outside the door of the cathedral facing onto the Ducal Palace and for the bearings of the archbishop to be placed in the choir of the cathedral (AVFDM, Registri [Libro mastro] 336, fol. 168; Registri [Giornale di cassa] 412, fol. 7).

[27] On 22 October 1554, in fact, Giuseppe, as a resident of the Milanese parish of Santi Cosma e Damiano, located in Porta Nuova, took part in the selection of a representative of the parish to swear loyalty to the new duke, Philip of Habsburg (ASM, ASM, Potenze sovrane post 1535, 3, SS. Cosma e Damiano). On 19 November of the same year Biagio Arcimboldo is recorded as living at San Vittore al Teatro, Porta Vercellina (ASM, Notarile 12915; Miller 1989, 15, doc. 4); but a few months earlier Biagio was resident at Santo Stefano in Nosiggia, Porta Nuova (ASM, Notarile 12915; Miller 1989, 14, doc. 3).

[28] Miller 1989.

[29] Forti Grazzini 1986, 42-47. A document recording the payment to Arcim-

boldo for the design of the tapestry (Ciceri 1811, 99-100) has been known since the beginning of the 19th century, and then was more widely published in Monti 1897, 196; and yet no research had ever been carried out, even if just into checking the source. So the discovery of the administrative record has permitted confirmation of the total amount paid to Arcimboldo (158 lire and 19 soldi) but has shown that it was not made until 1561 (ASDCo, Fabbrica del duomo, Libri contabili 14 [Mastro Biancho 1557-64], fol. 114, Arcimboldo's account). The canvas, painted in Milan, was taken to Como in August 1561 for approval by the tapestry weaver Giovanni Karcher and then immediately sent back to Milan. It was then sent, in November, to Pavia and from there transported to Ferrara by water (*idem*, fol. 192), where Karcher, then in the service of the Este family, wove the cloth, which was finally delivered to Como in June 1562 (*idem*, fol. 237). For his work the tapestry weaver was paid 470 lire and 1 soldo in two instalments (40 scudi, equivalent to 240 lire, in advance on 25 August 1561 and the balance of 230 lire and 1 soldo on 3 June 1562: *idem*, fols. 227 and 237).

[30] ASM, S. Corona, Registri 58, c. 88 and reference to c. 128 (list of the disbursements made by the treasurer Antonio Porro). The payments to Titian for the altarpiece and to Gaudenzio Ferrari for the frescoes of the confraternity's chapel, again recorded in the account books (Registri 55 and 56) of Santa Corona, indicated and in part made known by Canetta 1883, 61-62, have been published in their entirety in Sacchi 1989, 209 and Binaghi Olivari 1994.

[31] ASM, S. Corona, Registri 58, c. 88. Andrea Albricci would receive 36 lire for this work.

[32] ASM, Popolazione p.a. 94, 14 April 1554.

[33] ASM, S. Corona, Registri 58, c. 218 and reference to c. 206 (list of the disbursements made by the treasurer Antonio Porro).

[34] The account in Giulio da Oggiono's name begins with the first payment on 26 August 1555 and ends with the balance paid on 28 May 1556 (ASM, S. Corona, Registri 58, c. 170). The various payments, for a total of 612 ? lire, cover the tabernacle (100 scudi and 24 lire), a marble step (11 lire) and other small, unspecified works (5 lire). For Giulio da Oggiono, a frequent collaborator with Cristoforo Lombardo, see now Sacchi 2005, II, 488ff.

[35] The sources either totally ignore (Morigia 1592 and 1595, Santagostino 1671 [1980] and Biffi 1705 [1990]) or fail to describe the chapel (Torre 1674 [1714], 194, Latuada 1737-38 [1995-2000], IV, 245, and Bianconi 1787, 282), demolished at the beginning of the 19th century along with the rest of the church of San Francesco Grande. Only Bianconi refers to the painted decoration, which he judges to date "from the same time" as the portal on which are carved the date 1357 and the name of the founder, Giacomello Taverna. No mention of 16th-century decorations or paintings. The information on the ornaments comes from a request made in 1807 by the parish priest of Sant'Ambrogio to the War Ministry of the kingdom of Italy to be given custody of the sculptures that were still housed in the sacristy scheduled for demolition; a request that was rejected on the grounds that it was being utilized as a storeroom by the Engineer Corps and was therefore still in use. In 1809 a plan to turn it into a kitchen was submitted (ASM, Ministero della Guerra 670). Not even the inventories drawn up in 1798 at the time of the abolition of the monastery of San Francesco Grande refer to the sacristy (ASM, Amministrazione del Fondo di religione 1862). The ornaments of the chapel-sacristy are recorded by Calderini 1940, 219ff.

[36] The most thorough study of the gonfalon remains the one carried out by Colombo Fantini 1987-88 (with documentary appendix, to which I refer the reader for a complete description of the commission). However, Arcimboldo was to receive in 1567, through a proxy (Gerolamo Cesati), the sum of 50 gold scudi, equivalent to 275 lire, "to recompense him for the work carried out on the first designs of the aforesaid Gonfalon, by virtue of a commission of 23 May of said year [1567]" (ASCM, Località Milanesi 309, final account presented to the civic representatives – the Vicar and the Twelve of Provision – by the treasurer responsible for handling the funds allocated for the work, Erasmo D'Adda, and approved on 15 December 1568).

[37] Kaufmann (1988a and 1988b) assigns only the cartoon of the last tapestry to Arcimboldo; Forti Grazzini (1988) extends the attribution to the last six tapestries, including the one that was certainly woven in Flanders after 1566 (but to an earlier cartoon, datable to around 1560).

[38] Mirabile 2005, 263-268. The two payments in ASM, Notarile 7999, no. 3149, 2 April 1526 (payment of 408 lire in settlement and 50 on account) and no. 3176, 18 April 1526 (payment of 200 lire in advance). The payments also cover the cost of the design of the first tapestry, while the second cartoon would be supplied to Bozzolo by the vestry board.

[39] ASM, Notarile 8010, no. 5700, 11 July 1537. Bozzolo also undertook to meet all the related expenses, including the cost of the design, and promised to produce a tapestry of the same quality as the first in the series, also his work. On 20 September Bozzolo received a second payment of 55 lire, certainly for the same tapestry: ASM, Notarile 10809. The document is only mentioned in Repishti 2002, 51, without archival references or a precise date.

[40] AVFDM, Registri 728 (Liber mandatarum 1533-1536), cc. 9v (20 September 1533), 74v and 75v (3, 5 and 27 September 1534) and 89 (10 September 1535). I would like to thank Francesco Repishti for pointing this out.

[41] In fact it should be remembered that in September 1533 the same Bozzolo had been commissioned by Milan Cathedral to weave the tapestries with *Scenes from the Life of the Virgin*, to cartoons produced initially by Giampietrino and Nicolò Appiani and then by Gaudenzio Ferrari, immediately recognized as setting an example to be followed for their quality and modernity. The contract called for the delivery of three tapestries for the Easter of 1534 and three more for the feast of the Virgin Mary in September; for the subsequent ones Bozzolo was to await the requirements of the clients (AVFDM, Ordinazioni capitolari IX, cc. 57v-58r).

[42] One fact that, in my view, conflicts with the reconstruction proposed by Forti Grazzini, however tentatively, is the subsequent sum that was certainly paid to Bozzolo for the eighth tapestry in 1537 (at least 255 lire in two instalments). This suggests that the weaver was responsible not just for the execution, but also for the design. In this case Giuseppe Arcimboldo obviously could not have had a hand in the cartoon drawn by his father (provided that Biagio was in fact its author).

[43] Forti Grazzini 1988, entry 14, 134; subsequently Guazzoni 2000, 81.

[44] Ginevra died on 21 January 1545 (ASM, Popolazione p.a. 93); Marquis Giovanni II had died in 1535 on the imperial expedition to Tunis: a memorial tablet placed in the chapel on the tenth anniversary of his death records his valour in combat against the unbelievers; Sacchi 2005, I, 319 and *passim*.

[45] Morigia 1592, 566.

[46] In fact the first known document subsequent to his departure from Milan and dating from the spring of 1563 refers to his copying two portraits for Ferdinand I, but explicitly states that Arcimboldo was part of Maximilian's court: Kaufmann 2005, 29.

[47] Maximilian was not elected king of the Romans until 24 November 1562 and then crowned six days later at Frankfurt. Earlier, on 20 September, he had received the crown of king of Bohemia in Prague. None of these titles appears in Morigia's account, and so it appears that the designation to the imperial succession was explicitly recorded as subsequent to the summoning of Arcimboldo (Morigia 1592, 566). Even the assertion that Arcimboldo had moved "to the emperor's court" might suggest, if taken literally, that at that moment Maximilian did not have a court of his own, and thus that the summons had become before the coronations. Yet the thirty years that separate Giuseppe's departure from Milan from the publication of the *Historia* may have given rise to a degree of confusion or inaccuracy in Arcimboldo's account or, more likely, Morigia's text. It must also be said that a journey through the Alps at the height of winter entailed such hardship as to advise against if not exclude it.

[48] Several portraits "from life" are recorded by contemporary sources; they are those of Maximilian II and Philip II (Lomazzo 1584 [1974], 379) or of various members of the imperial court (Morigia 1595 [1619], 461), all works

executed after his departure for Vienna. In Milan the painter's name does not appear in any inventory of works known to me, even after his death: this leads me to think that his output of portraits had been marginal, at least until he moved to the imperial court. In view of the fame attained by Giuseppe during the last years of his life, and after his death, anyone with one of his portraits (or even just a copy or a derivation) in his house would not have failed to point to it with pride. It is true that we do not possess lists of the contents of all the collections of pictures in the Milan of the late 16th and early 17th century and that it was not the custom locally to give the name of the author of the works, but the absence of even the slightest mention suggests a very limited production. Currently a single (self-)portrait has been attributed to Arcimboldo (if we exclude the two drawings in Prague and Genoa and the small profiles of emperors), but the canvas is only known through a photograph: Geiger 1954, frontispiece.

[49] ASCo, Notarile 1021, 13 July 1578; Miller 1989, 22. Although the use of the Italian word *di*, does not allow us to distinguish between "of" and "by", the manner in which the inventory is drawn up leads us to believe that it was almost certainly a portrait painted by Arcimboldo (and not one representing a member of the Arcimboldi family): in fact immediately after it we find "A portrait of Count Giovanni in a white fur; Another of the same in armour; A portrait of a nude woman; A small portrait of a woman with a little bird in her hand". All the personal property of the deceased Count Anguissola was inherited, in the absence of children, by his wife Delia Spinola: see the will of 23 June 1578 (ASCo, Notarile 348).

[50] Morigia 1592, 566.

[51] A brief description of the festival and subsequent controversy can be found in Lomazzo 1590 (1973), 362-363. On Fontana the reader is referred to Savio 1905, Kaufmann 1976a and 1993. It should be remembered that Fontana also wrote the poems that, in December 1568, accompanied the first series of Arcimboldo's *Seasons* and *Elements* presented to Maximilian II.

[52] Lomazzo 1590 (1973), 362.

[53] Kaufmann 1997, 606-607.

[54] Centorio degli Ortensi 1559. On him see at least Longo 1979. On Castaldo, a soldier in the service of the Habsburgs, in addition to the dated but useful D'Ayala 1867, I refer the reader to De Caro 1978 (for the biography) and to Zezza 1999 and Leydi 1999a, 127ff. (for his role as client).

[55] The similarities between the Liberal Arts presented at this festival in Milan and Arcimboldo's drawings in the Uffizi have already been pointed out in Venturelli 1999, 150ff.

[56] For a description of the festivities see Arrivabene 1561 and Malespini 1609, part II, tale XI, cc. 28v ff.

[57] On the *Libro del sarto*, now in the library of the Fondazione Querini Stampalia in Venice (cl. VIII, cod. I, 944) I refer for the sake of brevity to my entry in *Moroni* 2005, with notes and previous bibliography to which should be added a new facsimile edition of the volume (Ediciones Grial, Valencia 2004). On the tailor who owned the volume, Leydi 1999b.

[58] For these attributions see Bora 1998, 55, no. 50.

[59] Venturelli 1999, 169.

[60] Cavalieri 2000, 102. The text of the registration of the baptism drawn up by the parish priest includes a series of crossing-outs, but it appears that it had been corrected once more accurate information had reached its compiler's ears. Thus the first version would have run: "And then on 28 August I baptized Agostina daughter of a servant of Signor Otto Visconte named Biaso Mantovano, according to what was said by the mother of the baby, that is Isabetta Gracina da Poliano, and for godfather Signor Gioseffo [blank] painter of Emperor Maximilian and for godmother Domina Bianca of Gibelino". With the corrections and crossings-out this became: "And then on 28 August I baptized Agostina daughter of Biasio Mantovano and Elisabetta Gracina da Poliano, for godfather Signor Gioseffo [blank] painter of His Majesty the Emperor Maximilian and for godmother Domina Bianca Bariggia of Gibelino".

[61] Cavalieri 2000, 98ff. In the same church there is a fresco with *The Penitent Saint Jerome*, also attributed to Aurelio Luini and dating from some time before 1582, in the third chapel on the right, property of the merchant Benedetto Lamagna or Alemagna (a Lombard but active in France and England).

[62] It is very interesting and significant to note that the contracting parties of the deeds contained in the only two surviving files (ASM, Notarile ultimi versamenti 534 and Notarile 18051) were frequently Milanese booksellers or publishers: Giovan Antonio degli Antoni (printer of works by Bernardino Baldini in 1558 and 1571), Francesco Seroni, Pacifico Ponzio, Giacomo Maria Meda (from Metz), Michele Tini (with whom Gregorio Comanini would print in 1591). It is likely that the presence of such a clientele, perhaps encountered through Gherardini and his circle, to which we will return shortly, had prompted Arcimboldo to entrust this notary with his last will and testament.

[63] ASM, Notarile 15028, 17 March 1581; Miller 1989, 22-23.

[64] In reality it is not even certain that the will was really drawn up in the two years cited, inasmuch as the formula utilized by the notary runs: "*memor sui ultimi testamenti et contentorum in eo rogati per spectabilem dominum Stephanum Bustium anno 1576 seu 1577 seu etc.*" leaving a degree of vagueness with respect to Arcimboldo's memories.

[65] ASM, Notarile 15028, 17 March 1581; Miller 1989, 22-23.

[66] For an initial placing of Polacini, see Leydi 1998.

[67] Morigia 1592, 566.

[68] ASDM, sez. X, Visitationes, Sant'Ambrogio XXXV. The document is not dated, but can be assigned to some time between 1587 and 1589 because of the age it gives for the members of the Gherardini family in comparison with other, later *Stati Animarum* that do bear the date.

[69] It should be remembered that it is to Lomazzo that we owe the first mention of Arcimboldo's works in print: in 1584, and thus prior to the painter's definitive return to Milan, Giovan Paolo referred to both the *Four Elements* and the portraits of Maximilian II and of Philip II (Lomazzo 1584 [1974], 304, 379). It is not unlikely that this information had come to Lomazzo through Giovanni Filippo Gherardini.

[70] Giulio Cesare Lomazzo, the brother of Giovan Paolo, had in fact married Clara Delfinone, Scipione's daughter.

[71] For the entire question the reader is referred to Isella 1993 and Morandotti 2005.

[72] Gherardini 1591; for a preliminary survey of the writers and their relations with Arcimboldo (and with his works of the last years), Berra 1988c. For their biographies see Coccia 1982 (Gregorio Comanini), Ballistreri 1970 (Gherardo Borgogni) and Zambelli 1963 (Bernardino Baldini).

[73] Morigia 1593, c. 63r.

[74] The best review of the Lombard writers and their works can be found in *Sul Tesin* 2002. For an overall picture of the role played by men of letters in the promotion of the arts in 16th-century Milan the reader is referred to Rampi 2002.

[75] Comanini 1591, 49: "Ask to be shown by Comanino the *jeu d'esprit* that the same Painter has made him of the four seasons of the year: you will see a very graceful picture".

[76] Berra 1996b, 124.

[77] Borgogni 1598, cc. 39v-40r and Berra 1996b, 125. For the recommendations of Figino and Fede Galizia see too Berra 2000, 81, no. 1. Morigia records that "as her [Fede Galizia] reputation had reached His Majesty the Emperor Rudolf, he was pleased to have things by hand of this talented Fede" (Morigia 1595 [1619], 467).

[78] Morigia 1592, 566.

[79] ASMn, Gonzaga 1715, fasc. III 1, cc. 293-294 (Maurizio Visconti to Ottaviano Cavriani, from Milan, 26 January 1594): "Arcimboldo the painter of glorious memory of his imperial majesty paid me months ago a hundred ducats for a middle-sized piece with which to make a lid for a vase"; Piccinelli 2003, 223.

[80] Morigia 1595 (1619), 479. The entire passage runs: Giuseppe Guzzi "[...] has made a writing desk, and is still finishing it, of marvellous contrivance, inventions, and secrets, for His Majesty Emperor Rudolf, invention of the exceptional quon. Giuseppe Arcimboldo, who for that [desk], which is expected to be in Ebony, & Ivory, chose this rare and talented Giuseppe Guzzi. As he was doing this worthy work in the house of said Arcimboldo, he is now finishing it in the house of the good Misseroni: & when it is finished, it will be a very precious, and perhaps unique thing, both for its value, and even more for its beauty, inventions, and secrets no longer seen." Unfortunately it has not been possible to uncover any more information about Guzzi than what is provided by Morigia.
[81] ASM, Popolazione p.a. 104. Casati 1885, 93.
[82] No source records the presence in Milan of a tombstone or inscription commemorating Giuseppe Arcimboldo or any other members of his family. The indication of the church of San Pietro alla Vigna as the place of his burial is traditional but not supported by any evidence.
[83] Morigia 1595 (1619), 461.
[84] Baldini 1600, 44. For other poems by Baldini referring to Arcimboldo, see Berra 1996a, 56 and 58.
[85] In 1603 Benedetto Arcimboldo was no longer living in his father's house: see the *Status animarum* of the parish of San Pietro alla Vigna of that year in ASDM, sez. X, Visitationes, Sant'Ambrogio XXXV.
[86] The *liuto prospettico*, as it is called in an inventory of 1621 cited by Geiger 1954, 127.
[87] Comanini 1591, 244-249 and Geiger 1954, 82ff.
[88] Lomazzo 1590 (1973), 363.

II.I
Bernardino Luini (1480-85 – 1532)
Portrait of Biagio Arcimboldo (active 1518-1554)
Black chalk with blue-black wash on grey-brown paper
234 × 146 mm
Inscription below left: Blasii Arcimboldi Pictoris imago
Signed below right: Bernardino Lovino F
London, British Museum, inv. no. JCR 320

The inscription "Blasii Arcimboldi Pictoris imago" on this profile drawing by Bernardino Luini identifies the sitter as his friend, Biagio Arcimboldo, the father of Giuseppe. He is shown as a ripe, bearded man with noble traits, in profile, looking right. While his clothing has only been sketchily represented with rough open strokes, the area of the head is painstakingly worked. The artist uses the full potential of chalk in the mellow light-dark modelling in the area of the face. The head is set in relief against a blue-black washed ground.
Little is known about Biagio Arcimboldo (see the essay by Silvio Leydi in this volume). Between 1518 and 1554 there are records of him in Milan and its surrounds. There is documentation of his work together with his son Giuseppe Arcimboldo on the drawings for the glass windows in the Milan Cathedral in the years 1545 till 1551. His presumed friendship with Bernardino Luini is proven by the documents found in the Milan state archives by Robert S. Miller. Thus, on 9 November 1534 Biagio Arcimboldo was called upon to act as a witness in the matter of the inheritance of the sons of the deceased Bernardino Luini.
Through Bernardino Luini and his sons, Giuseppe may have come into contact with Leonardo's drawings. According to Giovanni Paolo Lomazzo Luini's son Aurelio owned a small book with 50 of Leonardo's caricatures.

Marion Romberg

Provenance: Comte Antoine Francois Andréossi Collection, acquisition of the drawing by Sir John Charles Robinson in Paris, sale for £20 on 1.3.1867 to John Malcolm of Poltalloch, John Wingfield Malcolm Collection

Bibliography: Lomazzo 1590 (1973), 290; Robinson 1876, no. 320; Geiger 1960, 19; Hulten 1987, 52; Miller 1989, 9-10; Kaufmann 1998, 169-176; Berra 1998a, 57-67.

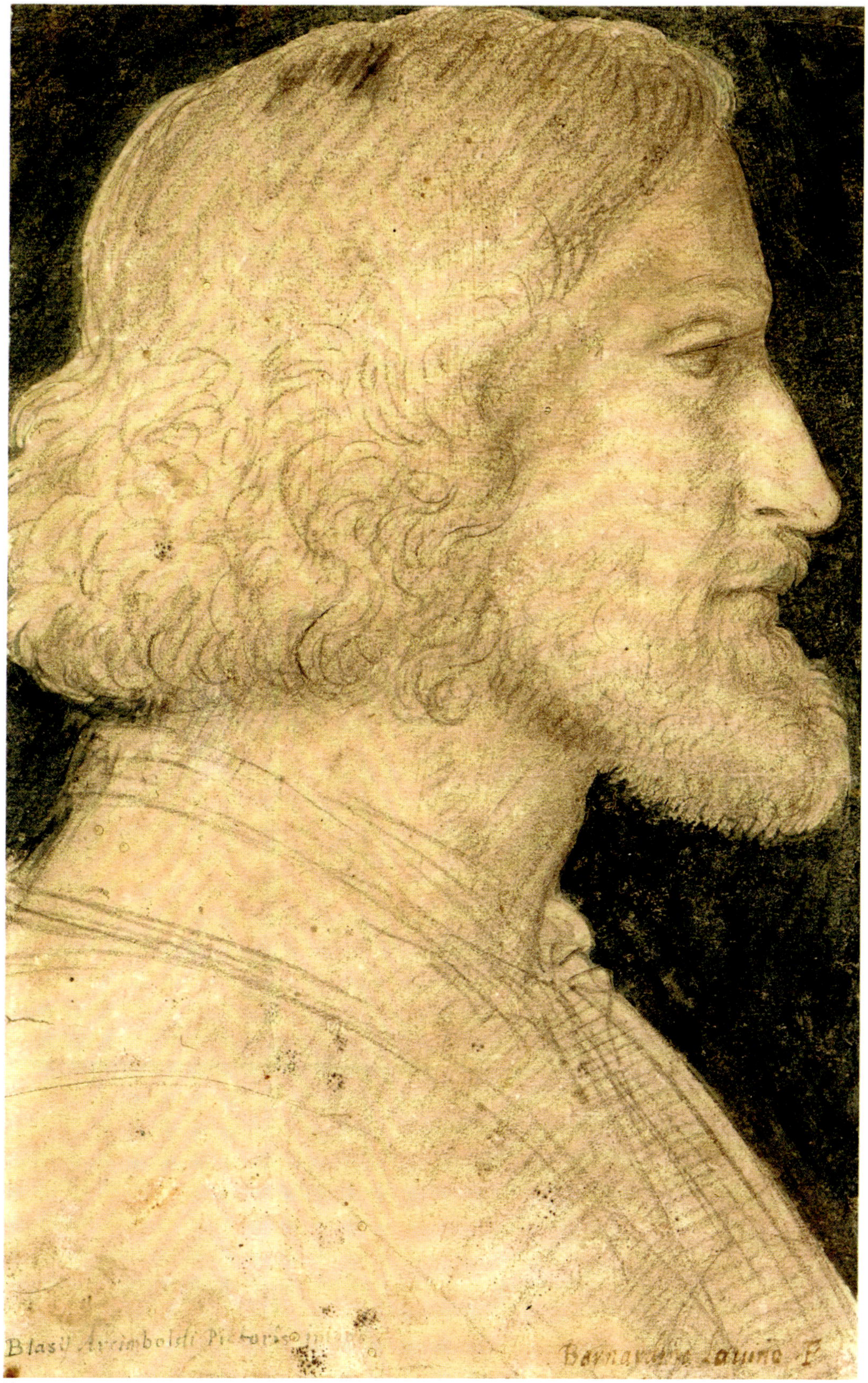
II.1

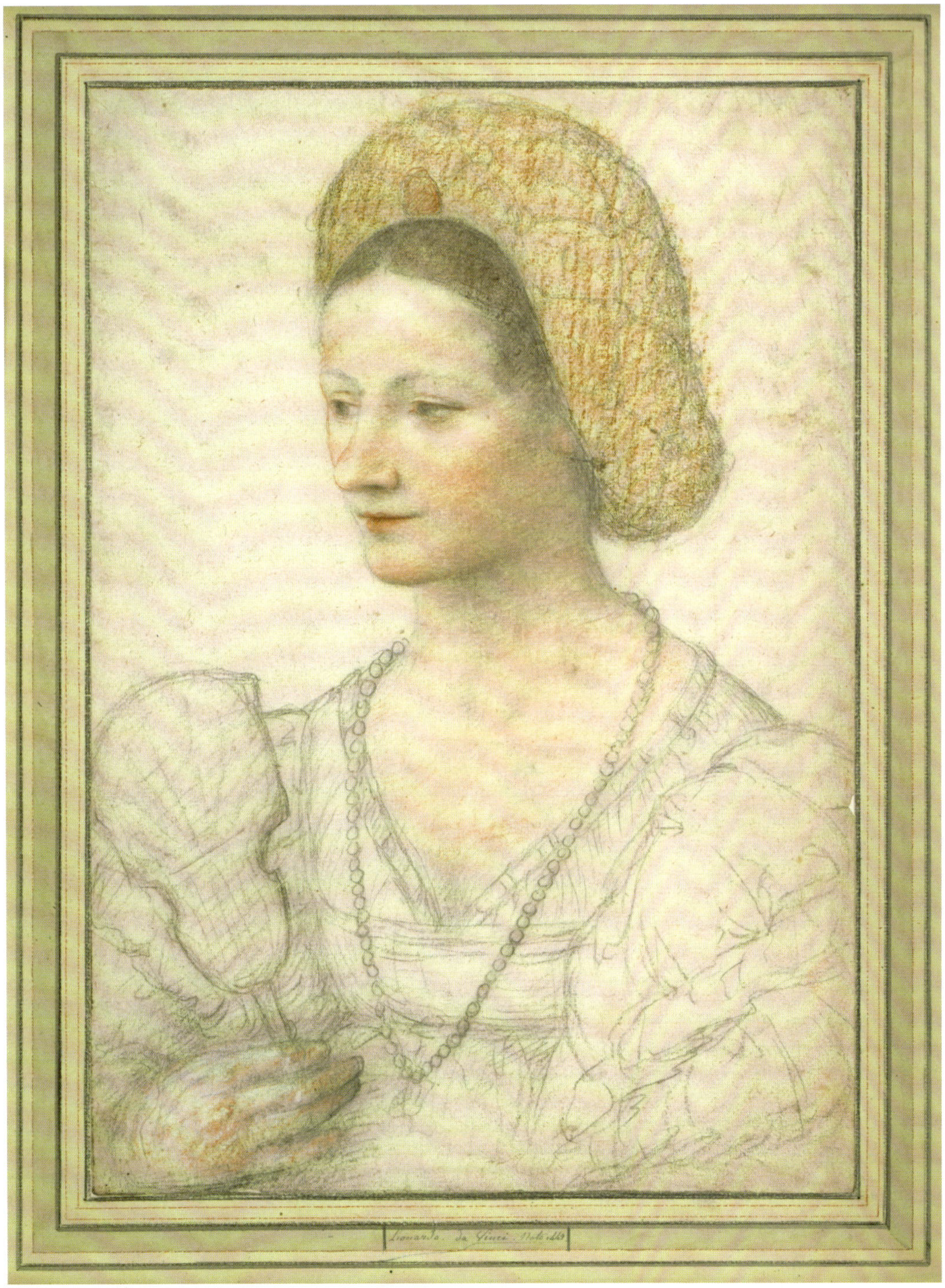

II.2

II.2
Bernadino Luini (1480-85 – 1532)
Portrait of a Young Woman with Fan
c. 1520-1525
Black, red, brown, yellow and white chalk on white paper
414 × 285 mm
Vienna, Albertina, inv. no. 59

This drawing by Bernardino Luini, a friend of the Arcimboldo family, is rightly considered one of the greatest pastel drawings of the 16th century (Bambach 2003, 663). The tenderness and softness of the facial features arise out of a finely executed *sfumato* technique for example to be found in Leonardo da Vinci's cartoon "Isabelle d'Este" in the Louvre. In Lomazzo's treatise on painting Leonardo da Vinci is mentioned as the first who practiced the "nuovo modo" of pastel drawing. Thus it comes as no surprise that up to the 19th century the drawing was attributed to Leonardo.
This was until Gustavo Frizzoni rightly attributed it to Bernardino, a follower of Leonardo – as laid down in a notification in the archives of the Albertina collection.
The subject presents herself to the viewer in a three-quarter view, with a fan or mirror in her left hand. She wears a dress tied under the breast, with puffed out sleeves. Around her neck she wears a pearl necklace, that accentuates the V-shaped cut of her neckaline. Her hair is concealed under a balloon-type yellow headwear. While her garment is drawn with sketchy, open black strokes, in the area of the face and the neck Luini uses the whole colour range of pastel crayons. This easy and natural depiction is achieved of what is depicted is achieved not by modelling the monochrome, but rather in his working soft colour hues. The area where the face joins the neck is masterly worked in grey and brown. The fresh youthfulness of her complexion is accentuated by the use of pink.
There is disagreement as to the identity of the young woman. Part of the research follows Beltrami's and Schäffer's argumentations of 1911, that due to the resemblance of the sitter with the kneeling woman in Luini's lunette fresco in the church of Saint Maurizio, Milan, is to be identified the subject as Ippolita Sforza, the wife of the scholar Alessandro Bentivoglio. Two frescœs in the same church, in the Cappella Carreto, are attributed to Biagio and Giuseppe Arcimboldo. Against this in 1964 Otto Benesch declared he saw a stronger resemblance with Luini's *Portrait of a Lady* in the National Gallery of Art, Washington. The problem of identifying the sitter is accentuated by Bernardino Luini's marked tendency to idealize his characters (Gnann 2004, 138).

Marion Romberg

Provenance: Hofbibliothek, Prince Albert von Sachsen Teschen (L. 174)

Bibliography: Lomazzo 1584 (1974), 170; Beltrami 1911, 360; Schäffer 1911, 144; Benesch 1964, 322; Birke 1992, 32; Bandera-Fiorio 2000, 57; Bambach 2003, 666; Gnann 2004, 138.

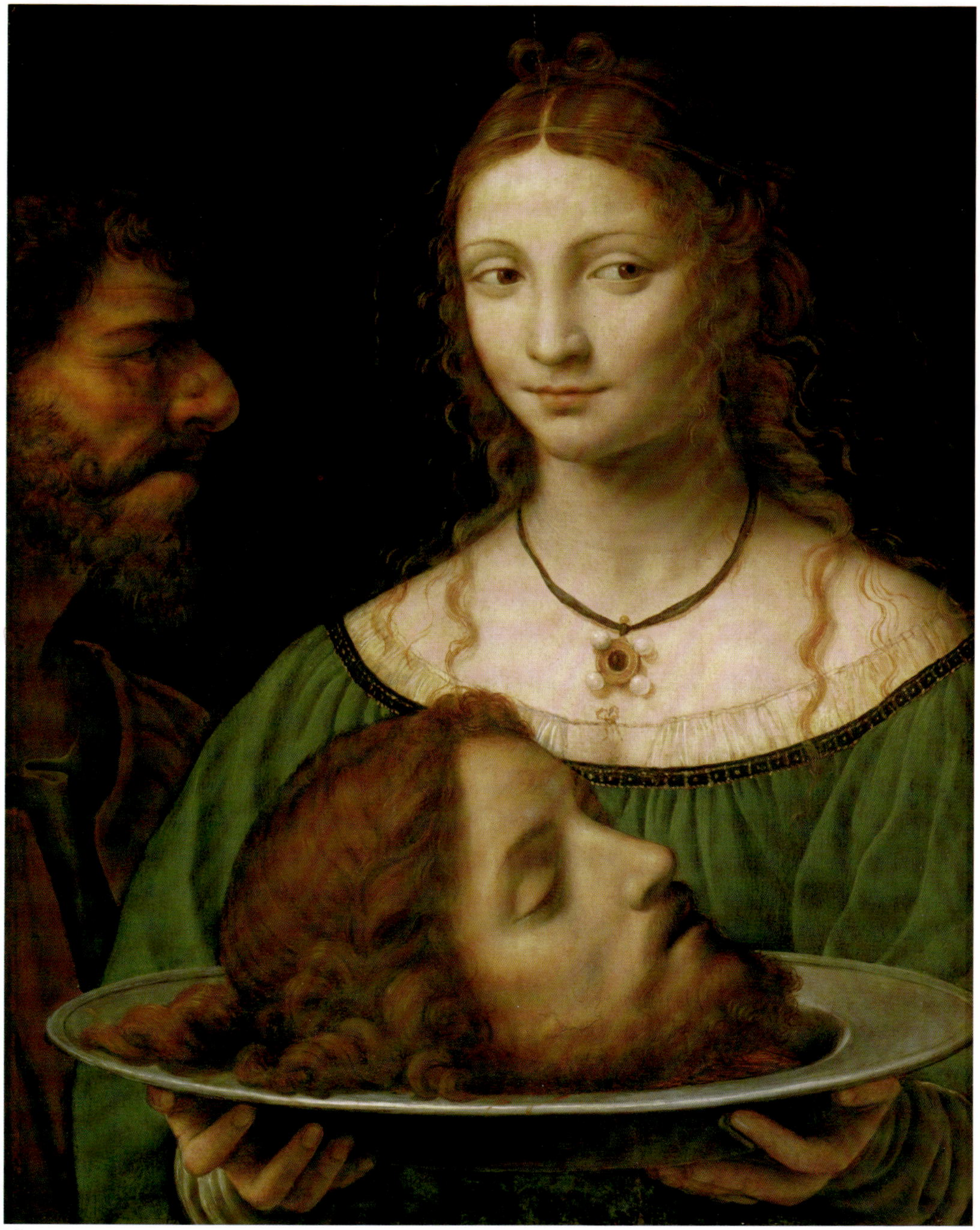

II.3

II.3
Bernadino Luini (1480-85 – 1532)
Salome with the Head of John the Baptist
Oil on wood
55.5 × 42.5 cm
Vienna, Kunsthistorisches Museum, Gemäldegalerie, inv. no. 190

Bernardino Luini's painting of *Salome with the Head of John the Baptist* illustrates the close friendship between Arcimboldo's father Biagio and Bernardino, and the latter's passing on of the stylistic influence of Leonardo to a younger generation.

The story of the beautiful Salome who, through her dance beguiled her stepfather into killing John the Baptist, was turned into the embodiment of the tumultous power of female beauty. The Kunsthistorisches Museum also owns paintings of the same theme by Cesare da Sesto and Andrea Solario. Centre of the representation is always Salome's fickle, ambiguous smile, between accompliceship and innocence, as well as her exquisite beauty set against the brutal ugliness of the Myrmidon, even though the latter appears mostly to bear a human expression of shock.

Due to the quality of the work, the painting was included in the Archduke Leopold Wilhelm's collection as the work of Leonardo himself, like other works of Luini, such as the drawing of a young woman, now in the Albertina collection (cat. no. II.2). Luini's authorship was only recognized in the 19th century.

In no other work of Luini's does the hideous grimace of the executioner seen in profile hark back so much to Leonardo's grotesque heads as here (cat. nos. II.4 and II.6). If one wanted to see Arcimboldo's head compositions on their caricature side as abstract further developments of the grotesque heads devised by Leonardo also including this executioner, in particular his representation of Autumn comes to mind (cat. no. IV.10): the beard and the eyebrows are replaced by corn, the nose with the wart is turned into a pear with pomegranate.

Marion Romberg

Bibliography: Engert 1864, 30; Engert 1896, 16; Williamson 1899, 100; Ottino della Chiesa 1956, 140, fig. 157; Marani 1987, 47; Bairati 1998, 135-142.

II.4
Leonardo da Vinci (1452-1519)?
Caricature of an Old Woman
1485-90
Pen and brown ink
57 × 42 mm
London, British Museum, inv. no. Pp 1.37

Caricature of a Bald Old Man
Pen and brown ink
57 × 40 mm
London, British Museum, inv. no. Pp. 1.38

Kwakkelstein (1994, 107) is convinced of the essentially comic intent of this type of representation, pointing out the satirical character implicit, for example, in details of the hairstyles, headgear or simply the out-of-date attributes and clothing. It seems to have been the artist's clear intention to represent the deformities of faces in which the physical alterations due to aging play an important role. At the root of these drawings certainly lie Leonardo's curiosity about unusual faces and features, his interest in the variety of types of expression and his physiognomic investigations of old age. Critics have suggested that the research into exaggerated and deformed profiles which the artist carried out chiefly in Milan, and which are reflected in his copious production of heads, may have been intended to converge in a lost treatise on physiognomy (Kwakkelstein 1994, 115-116). These profiles, made widely known through the numerous copies executed by his followers, influenced the Milanese milieu, and above all the circle of artists centred on the Accademia del Val di Blenio and Arcimboldo himself (Berra 1998, 57-61). In its uniformity, the series of drawings at Chatsworth is the one that best illustrates this cat-

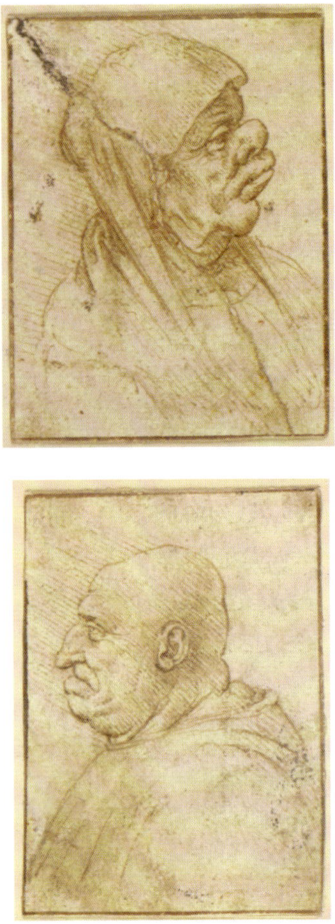

II.4

egory of representations. Copies and engravings made from them – like the famous *Album Mariette* in the Louvre, engraved by the count of Caylus – attest the extraordinary popularity of Leonardo's inventions.
The first folio depicts an old woman viewed in profile and facing to the right, with a veil on her head; the nose is fleshy and the lips jut out and protrude upwards. The deformity of the lineaments of the woman's face, weighed down by the slack tissues, especially in the area of the cheeks and the neck, is investigated with precision. A marked line forms the profile, and then lightens into a fine hatching that defines the chiaroscuro and models the face. The second drawing shows us the profile, facing left, of a bald old man; the drooping nose with its down-turned tip seems almost to meet up with the lower lip, which protrudes upwards in an expression of doubt. The line traces the profile of the back of the skull and outlines the folds of the neck, which terminate in a rounded back or a hood. The hatching, which shapes the profile and grows more dense in the region of the eyes and the ear, progressively thins out until it disappears in the bust and the shoulder.
Copies of these heads, but on a larger scale, can be found on a folio in the Gallerie dell'Accademia in Venice (inv. no. 227; G. Nepi Sciré, A. Perissa Torrini 2003, no. 54) attributed to Francesco Melzi. The profiles also appear in the *Album Mariette* in the Louvre (fols. 10v, 21r), and have been engraved in reverse by Caylus in the *Recueil de Testes de caractère et de charges....*, Paris 1730 (nos. 12, 33) and in Wenzel Hollar's *Characaturas* (Forcione 2003, 695, 698, figs. on 685, 689, 707, 711).
Entering the collections of the British Museum in 1824, the drawings were assigned with some doubt to Leonardo by Popham and Pouncey (1950, 71), who pointed out the difficulty of establishing their originality. Their undoubted quality and the fact that no better versions have turned up since make the opinion of the two scholars still relevant today.

Francesca del Torre Scheuch

Bibliography: Popham, Pouncey 1950, no. 113, II, pl. CVII; Kwakkelstein 1994; Berra 1998, 57-61; Forcione 2003, 695, 698.

II.5
Leonardo da Vinci (1452-1519)
Head of an Old Man and Sketch for a Flying Machine
1487-1490
Pen and light brown ink, watercolour, traces of white paint on pale walnut paper
112 × 75 mm
Venice, Gallerie dell'Accademia, Gabinetto dei disegni e delle stampe, inv. no. 234

Leonardo, attracted by an unusual face, recorded it on a folio on which he had already traced a sketch for a machine. The figure is represented in a three-quarter view, illuminated by light coming from the right. The lineaments are represented by means of a dense hatching that produces a chromatic effect, leaving free the zones of the forehead, the nose, the lips and the chin on which the light falls. The wrinkles and furrows on the face are represented with a thick and continuous line. The puzzled glance is turned to the right: the half-open mouth accentuates the impression that the figure is in a state of bewilderment. This psychological dimension had already been pointed out by Selvatico, who described the folio as a work of "marvellous sincerity" (1854, IV no. 10). The complexity of the subject's psychology conveyed in this drawing is enhanced by the depiction of the face from close-up. On the one hand it reflects Leonardo's fascination with the transformation and the alteration of the physiognomy by means of an accentuation of the features of the face; on the other, Leonardo's interest in the theme of old age in relation to the fundamental problem of the passing of time (Nepi Sciré, Perissa Torrini 2003, 98-99). The representation of the face, executed straight off in ink, as has been demonstrated by infrared reflectography, is striking in the profundity of its psychological investigation (Nepi Sciré, Perissa Torrini 2003, 99). It is neither a portrait, nor a caricature; according to Kwakkelstein (1994, 105-110, fig. 31), it belongs to the category of those folios that can be classified as representations from life, in which the artist recorded the "memorable" faces he came across in the street (Vasari, IV, 26). In a large number of notes and in the *Libro di pittura* (1995, II, 261-262; Viatte 2003, 170) Leonardo speaks in fact of faces that struck him by their distinctive character; as a manifestation of the multiplicity of nature, they are made the subject of representation on the part of painting, which is a science that embraces everything that nature produces (Kwakkelstein 1994, 39).
The folio is unanimously attributed by the recent critics to Leonardo, even though in the past its autography had been cast into doubt by the Commissione Vinciana (Perissa Torrini 2003, 98-99).
As Cogliati Arano (1980, 28; 1992, 319) pointed out, the drawing was executed at two different times: the mechanical sketch was made first, since the head is superimposed on it (Pedretti 1954, 117). Cogliati Arano asserted that the area of artistic research reflected in this drawing corresponded to that of some heads in the Ambrosiana for which she had suggested a date between 1485 and 1490. In these years, moreover, thematic links with groups of studies of mechanics and heads were recurrent in Leonardo's graphic work.

Francesca del Torre Scheuch

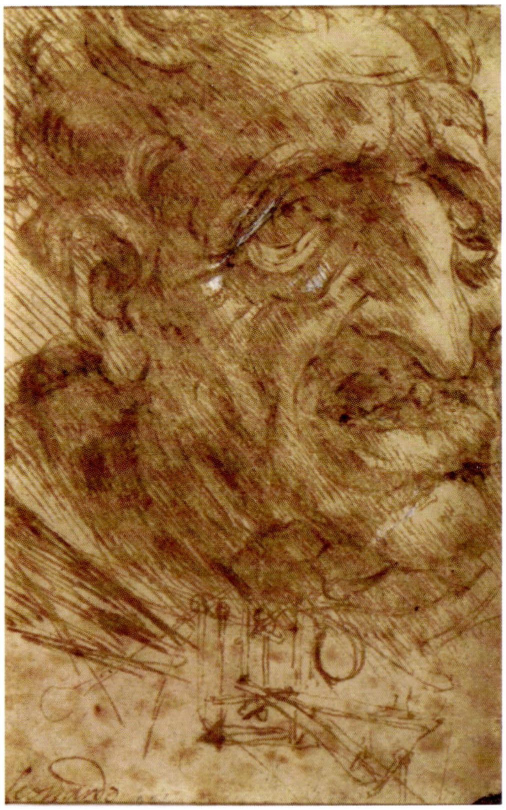

II.5

Bibliography: Vasari (Milanesi) 1878-1885, 26; Nepi Scirè, Perissa Torrini 2003, 98-99, with previous bibliography; Pedretti 1954, 117-128; Cogliati Arano 1980, 28; Cogliati Arano 1992, 319; Viatte 2003, 169-171.

II.6
After Leonardo da Vinci (1452-1519)
(attributed to Francesco Melzi)
Five Grotesque Heads
1515
Pen and sepia ink, white paper
180 × 120 mm
Venice, Gabinetto dei Disegni e delle Stampe, Gallerie dell'Accademia, inv. no. 227

Seven Caricatures
1515
Pen and sepia ink, white paper
180 × 120 mm
Venice, Gabinetto dei disegni e delle stampe, Gallerie dell'Accademia, inv. no. 229

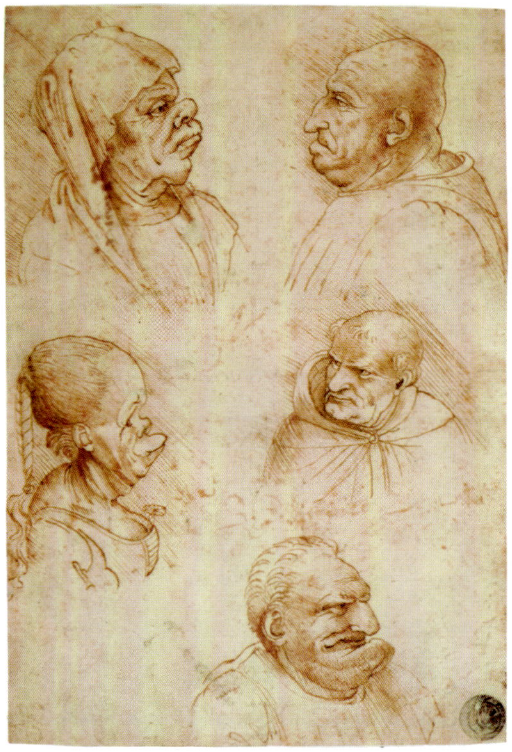

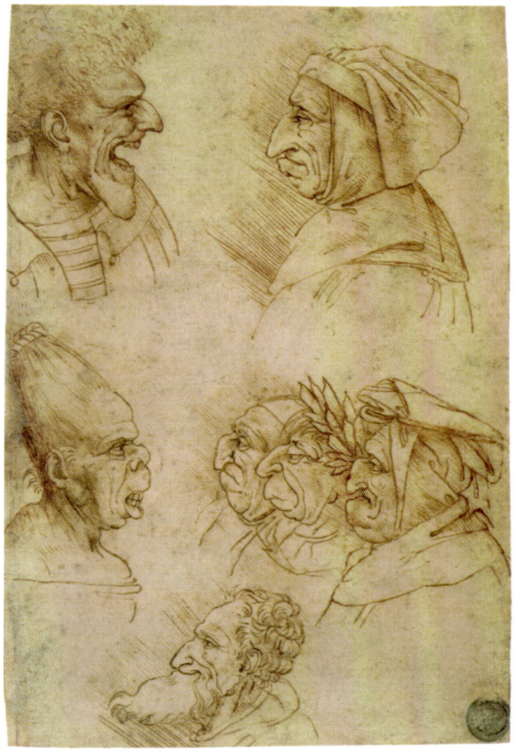

In the gallery of caricatures presented here it is possible to recognize, in the top row and on a larger scale, the two figures depicted in the drawings in the British Museum, which may be Leonardo's originals (cat. no. II.4) (Popham, Pouncey 1950, 71).
The female profile in the second row, whose original is at Chatsworth (Pedretti 2003, 34; Kwakkelstein 1994, fig. 49-a) appears in the *Album Mariette* and was engraved in the *Recueil Caylus* (*Mariette* fol. 21v; Caylus 34; Forcione 2003, 689, 698). The mocking intent is evident in the deformity of the skull, emphasized by the hairstyle, but above all in the detail of the flower sticking out from the neckline of the dress. The original of the monk seen in a three-quarter view, now lost, was at Chatsworth in 1902 (Mariette fol. 5r; Caylus 1; Forcione 2003, 682, 684). The original of the man with the huge chin, at bottom right, is not known but according to Forcione it may have been cut out of the fragment now in the Albertina in Vienna (Mariette fol. 12 v, Caylus 16, in Forcione 2003, 695); it was also engraved in Wenzel Hollar's *Characaturas* of 1786 and reproduced by Gerli in pl. XXIV (Nepi Sciré, Perissa Torrini 2003, 155).
On the second folio seven "monstrous faces" are portrayed in profile: the first two are set opposite one another, while the other five are freely arranged in the lower part of the sheet. The first on the left represents the face of a man, caught in a fit of laughter which emphasized the deformity of his chin. Leonardo's original is now in the J. Paul Getty Museum (Bambach 2005, no. 69). Opposite we see the profile of a man with a protruding lower lip and an aquiline nose that also appears in the *Album Mariette* (fol. 17r) and is reproduced in the *Recueil Caylus* (no. 25; Forcione 2003, 697). The central figures are a woman, whose hairstyle emphasizes the deformity of her skull and profile (Mariette fol. 17v; Caylus 26, Forcione 2003, 697), and three profiles of men, arranged in a row (Mariette fol. 14r; Caylus 27; Gerli XXIV, Forcione 2003, 696), whom Vittore Branca has proposed to identify as the poets Dante, Petrarch and Boccaccio (Perissa Torrini 2003, 154). The last man's head is reproduced in plate XXIV of Gerli's work (1784) and appears paired with the profile of a woman in the folio formerly in the Pembroke collection (Perissa Torrini 2003, 154).
The careful and precise hatching imitates Leonardo's left-handed *ductus*. The artist faithfully reproduces the heads created by the master with particular attention to the modelling of the faces; the hatching around the figures gives them a certain plastic relief, defining the space in an essential manner. The folio shares its provenance and history of attribution with its *pendant*. It is clear that these drawings, which as we have seen bring together various profiles in different associations, are typical academic exercises, and testify to the great success encountered by Leonardo's physiognomic studies throughout the Cinquecento. The folios here exhibited also constitute a demonstration of the didactic intention underlying these products of the master; he made available to his pupils a rich repertoire of *volti mostruosi* – "monstrous faces", an iconographic source of enormous popularity – which they could use for practice and to refine their own skills in the physiognomic research. Even if we do not know exactly what Leonardo's originals looked like, the folio formerly in the Pembroke collection, now dismembered and scattered among various other collections, probably reflected their appearance (Kwakkelstein 1994, fig. 74). So the heads were very likely arranged in pairs, one in front of the other, or in groups of three; it is likely that such juxtapositions were intended to underline their differences and similarities. The drawings were initially attributed to Leonardo by Selvatico (1854, V, no. 8), but are today almost unanimously assigned by Da Vinci scholars to one of his imitators, probably Francesco Melzi (Nepi Sciré, Perissa Torrini 2003, 154-155). Cogliati Arano (1980, 58-59), while acknowledging that the folios are by the same hand as a drawing attributed to Francesco Melzi, preferred to leave the question of its author undecided. The drawing is considered by Clayton (2002, 86, fig. 20) to be by the same hand as a folio in the Royal Library at Windsor, one in the British Museum, to which it had already been referred by Cogliati Arano (1980, 59), and the former Pembroke folio, and thus by Francesco Melzi. The same opinion is shared by Pedretti (2003, 34 no. 51), who notes that this type of drawing has not yet been fully studied and understood. Carefully finished with great attention to detail, they are not mechanical copies, but deliberate reworkings of Leonardo's originals by the copyist. He does not exclude the possibility that they had been executed "under Leonardo's watchful eye", an observation that confirms the view that these folios were the fruit of the master's intense teaching activity.

Francesca del Torre Scheuch

Bibliography: Popham, Pouncey 1950, I, no. 113, II, pl. CVII; Cogliati Arano 1980, 58-59; Kwakkelstein 1994, fig. 49a, 74; Clayton 2002, 86; Forcione 2003, 680-722; Nepi Scirè, Perissa Torrini 2003, 154-155; Pedretti 2003, 13-45.

II.7
Leonardo da Vinci (?)
Flower study
Metalpoint, pen and ink on slightly brownish paper
Subsequently signed upper left: "Leonardo"
upper right: "24"
lower right: Accademia Stempel (Lugt 188)
no apparent watermark
18.3 × 20.1 cm
Venice, Gallerie dell'Accademia, inv. no. 237

Giuseppe Arcimboldo's nature and animal studies arise from a hundred-year-long tradition of various herbariums, such as the *Tractatus de herbis* (London, British Library, Egerton MS 747) and the *Carrara Herbariums* (MS 2020), and above all of nature studies in themselves. One of the highpoints are Leonardo da Vinci's nature studies, which Giuseppe certainly knew from his Lombard origins and his friendship with Bernardino Luini (cat. no. II.1). We know that Leonardo drew "many flowers from nature". The flower study at hand, along with the *Study of a lily* (Windsor, RL 12418) and the *Study with violets* (MS B 2173, fol 14r), are among the few individual pieces that have been passed down to us. It shows various flower studies of grass-like plants. In it are violets as well as flowers from the *Aquilegia* and *Ranunculus* families. With silver point, the artist first defined the contours of the flowers, later concentrating on the interior drawing itself. Through variations in the strength and thickness of the hatching, he masterfully gave the flowers plasticity and natural vibrancy. Despite this high-quality execution, the attribution to Leonardo was first questioned by Carlo Pedretti in 1977. In this drawing, he saw a work of Leonardo's student and successor, Francesco Melzi. Giovanna Nepi Scirè later qualified this attribution, in that she considered it one of Leonardo's uncompleted works, which were later completed by Francesco Melzi.
Along with Leonardo's flower studies, there are countless plant studies from his hand. His scientific interest was so profound that he presumably planned to use these in a natural scientific discourse, as we later find with Jacopo Ligozzi's illustrations in Ulisse Aldrovandi's *Natural history*, or with Giorgio Liberale's drawing for Pietro Andrea Mattioli's *Discorsi* (*Discourses*) on the *Materia Medica* by Dioscorides.

Marion Romberg

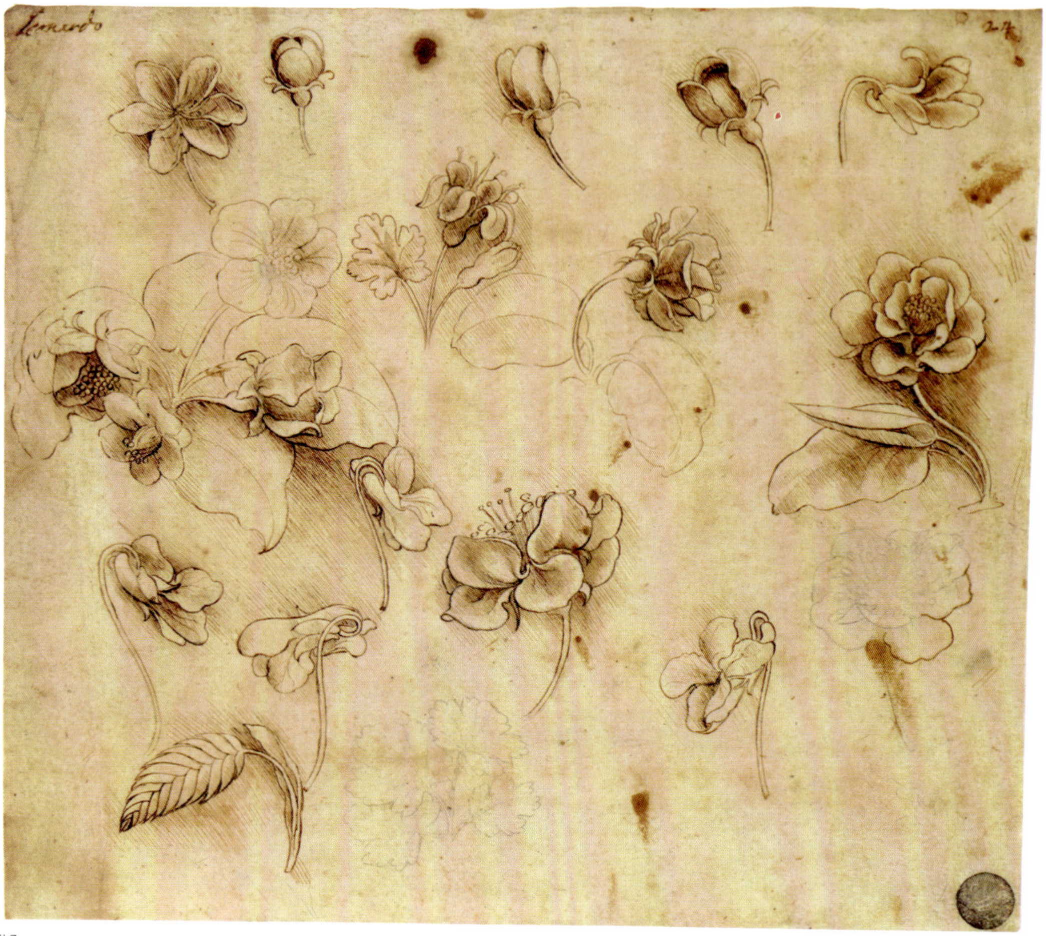

II.7

Provenance: Giuseppe Bossi, 1818; Luigi Celotti 1822

Bibliography: Pedretti 1977, 174; Morley 1979, 553-560; Pedretti 1980; Nepi Scirè 1992, 300, no. 46; Ames-Lewis 1997, 117-124; Tongiorgi Tomasi, Hischauer 2001, 19-22, no. 22; Pedretti, Nepi Scirè 2003, 95 (extensive bibliography); Reeds 2006, 205-237.

II.8
Jacob Hoefnagel c. 1575-1630
A Young Man Caresses an Old Woman, Who Holds a Ring and a Purse in Her Hands
Reverse: The Lover's Hand Withdrawn
Copy of Leonardo da Vinci
Pen, washed, brownish paper; border: pen, washed with blue and brown; Reverse: pencil
Upper right-hand corner contains the mark "Leonardo" in old script in a similar ink; Reverse: above in later handwriting "..an.. (?) Hufnagel / 1602"
310 × 290 mm
Vienna, Graphische Sammlung Albertina, inv. no. 60

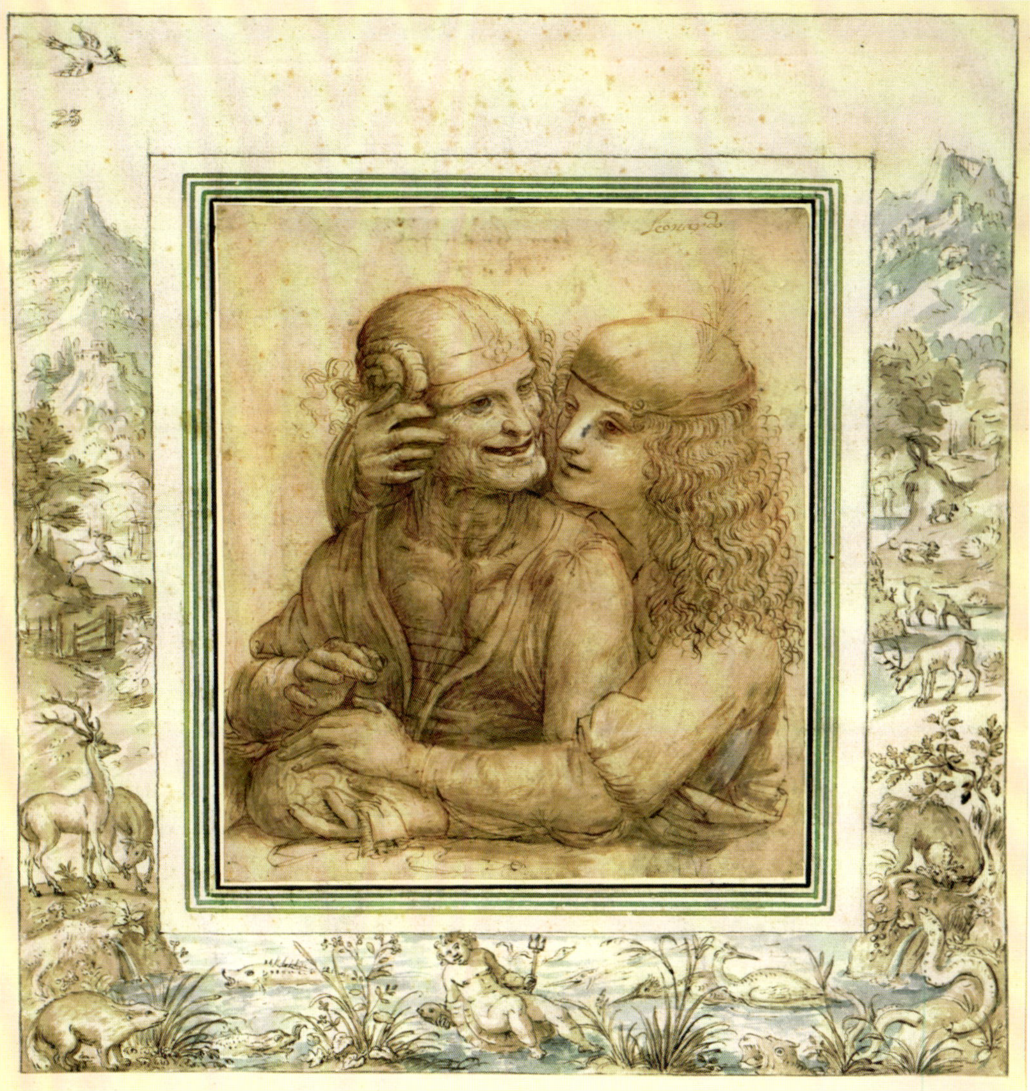
II.8

In a sudden moment of insincere fondness, a young man nuzzles an emaciated, toothless old woman. With his right hand, he brings the woman's head to him, while the left reaches for the actual object of his desire – a tightly filled purse. While she happily allows the young man to embrace her, the gaunt figure demonstratively delays the young man with a ring as remuneration, which accentuates the pecuniary nature of the seduction. The contrast of blossoming youth and the caricatured dissolution of the old woman functions superbly. It characterizes the allegory of the "ill-suited couple", in which old men as well as old women covet young members of the opposite sex. The original source of this Viennese drawing can be determined by the inscription in the upper right hand corner ("Leonardo") as well as by the signature on the etching by Wenzel Hollar found on the reverse. This signature ("Hufnagel"), however, indicates an attribution of the work to the skilled copyist Jacob Hoefnagel (Möller 1928; Vignau-Wilberg 1987, 204). Bert W. Meijer however, disputes the direct connection between the signature on the reverse and the origin of the drawing. He argues that the inscription "Hufnagel" refers rather to the authorship of the border decoration and positions the ill-suited couple in a closer relationship to Leonardo (Lugano 1998, 142).
Originally intended for a treatise on physiognomy and coveted in artistic circles, Leonardo's grotesques were frequently copied. The narrative character as well as the direct manner in which the figures approach each other is atypical of da Vinci's studies of heads. The original source of inspiration was a drypoint etching by the Master of the Amsterdam Cabinet, who employed the motif of the ill-suited couple for the first time around 1475-1480. Leonardo invested the scene with more a satirical, rather than a moral aspect, which he treated as an observation of the grotesque. The figure of the crone with the striking pigtails recalls a drawing attributed to Francesco Melzi, which he copied from Leonardo (Paris, Musée du Louvre, Cabinet des Dessins, inv. no. 28781). Its similarity to the male figure on the left side of the drawing with the five grotesque heads c. 1490 (Windsor, Royal Library, no. 12, 495 recto) is also striking: in the drastic portrayal of decay, the attributes of femininity are all but completely atrophied.
The border decoration, which catches the eye with its ornate composition, was possibly intended as a collector's mark. Four frames of that kind are known, all of whose motifs borrow from the border-work of a Flemish tapestry depicting the story of Noah, for which the painter Francesco Hernandez provided the artwork. Here, bears and deer cavort in an idealized landscape, while a trident-carrying putto rides a sea turtle in the waters of the foreground. The border illustrations are probably the work of a Dutch artist from around 1600 – possibly Jacob Hoefnagel. They display an intense observation of nature, which also shaped Arcimboldo's artistic creations.

Sabine Pénot

Bibliography: Möller 1928, 139-161, plate 214; Vignau-Wilberg 1987, 185-214, plate 9, 201, 203-204; Barryte 1990, 133-139; Lugano 1998, 141-142, cat. no. 6 (Bert W. Meijer).

II.9

Francesco Urbini attributed

Majolica Plate "Testa de cazi (or di cazzi)", 1536

On the underside, dated 1536 in blue, labelled with the mark of Francesco Urbinis, the stylized "cavaletto", flanked by the initials, F.R.

Ø 23.2 cm

Oxford, Ashmolean Museum, WA 2003.136 (acquired 2003)

The profiled head, in ochre tones with white highlights on a blue background is entirely composed of male sexual organs. A band of writing, broken in various places, wraps around it, and the initially illegible text is clarified through a key on the back of the plate (*El breve de[n]tro voi/legerite/ Como giudei se i[n]tender/el vorite*), indicating that it should be read as the Jews read (that is, from right to left):

.OGNI.HOMO.ME.GUARDA.COME.FOSSE.UNA.TESTA.DE.CAZI.

Which means, translated literally: "Everyone looks at me as if I were a dickhead". This sounds like a tautological paradox, which seems to contradict the first-glance apperancet. However, the expression "testa di cazzo" is used in Italy today as an expression of profanity to indicate a rather weak-headed individual with a bad character, whose reasoning originates not in his brain, but rather in his abdomen. Its precise semantic value in the 16th century is difficult to determine. In this representation it is a literal translation of this metaphor in a visual form (friendly indication by Karin Zeleny).

Comparable to this composition is a bronze medal with the portrait of the poet Pietro Aretino, whose back-side portrays a satyr-head, also composed of male genitalia (cat. no. II.10).

Another medal with the presumed portrait of the humanist Paolo Giovio, caricatured as a satyr (cat. no. II.11), displays nearly the same phallus-head on the back side (Waddington 1989, 13-15). Because the bronze medals are not precisely datable (circa 1530-1540) and the majolica plate was executed in 1536, the direction of influence is not completely clear. Because an idiomatic expression is implemented in a picture here, the parallels might have arisen spontaneously.

Even closer to the model of Arcimboldo's methods is the medal of a satyr-head composed of animals with the transcription ATILA, in the British Museum (Waddington 1989, 15f., plate 7, 16f. with interpretation of animal symbolism).

The bronze medal of Aretino (cat. no. II.10) was interpreted as a revenge on the acrimonious derider, for which various clients come into consideration, and also as a play on the homosexuality of the satirist; in any case the relationship of the words "satyr" and "satire" is also significant.

Arcimboldo may have seen the medal in Italy before his departure for Vienna in 1562, but he also may have encountered it later in Vienna, through Strada, Sambucus or Abondio. Whether or not he was acquainted with the majolica plate is unknown. The phallus motif does not appear in Arcimboldo's ascertained works; in this case, only the method is related.

Related to both the plate and the bronze medals, a far more refined drawing of a phallus-head in a private collection, once attributed to Leonardo, now to Francesco Salviati (Monbeig-Goguel 1998, 34, 36, plate 9) may have at least been a model that influenced Arcimboldo. Parronchi (1991) even raises the question of the relationships among the drawing, the bronze medals (cat. nos. II.10-11) and the plate at hand, but comes to no decisive conclusion.

Monbeig-Goguel (1998) was reminded of the antique cults of Dionysus and Priapus, which were strangely assimilated into the Italian Renaissance (Francesco Salviati, Giulio Romano, Perino del Vaga). The majolica plate should also be seen against this background; in its crude salaciousness, wit and satire are more or less auspiciously united.

Alexander Wied

Provenance: auctioned in Paris in 1855; Carpentier Collection, Paris; Roger Peyrefitte Collection, Paris; Carlo di Carlo Collection, Florence

Bibliography: Waddington 1989, 13-15; Parronchi 1991, 52-56; Monbeig-Goguel 1998, 34f., notes 65, 68; Wilson 2005, 10-16 (with additional bibliography, 36f.); London 2007, cat. no. 52 with colour plates and additional bibliography.

II.10

Venetian, second quarter of the 16th century

Portrait medal of Pietro Bacci, alias Aretino (1492-1557)

Bronze

Inscription on back: D. PETRVS. ARETIN. FLAGEL. PRINCIPVM

Inscription on front: TOTVS. IN. TOTO. ET TOTVS. IN QVALIB. PARTE

Ø 47.6 mm

Florence, Museo Nazionale del Bargello, inv. no. 6547

The front of the medal shows the satirist as a profile bust, facing right, with a long beard and full, short hair. His rich attire includes shirt, jerkin, gold chain and *Schaube* (a long, broad overcoat). What is specific here, as opposed to other medals depicting Aretino (for example, of Leone Leoni, Vannel, Toderi 2003, cat. no. 414 with plate), is the reverse side: a satyr-head, composed of a tangle of phalluses and testicles, including one penis that is ejaculating. While the front side recognizes Aretino as "flagellum principum", "scourge of princes", – the epithet derives from Ariosto – the motto on the reverse side is downright blasphemous: the inscription "totus in toto et totus in qualibet parte" ("whole in sum and whole in any part") is taken from scholastic theology and was used by numerous authors in reference to the soul, the world-soul and the trinity or angelic beings. Its use in connection with phalluses (something along the lines of, "in your genitalia you are entirely yourself" or "every single genital reflects your true being") was a disgust to humourless clerics, but must have incited educated freethinkers to booming laughter (friendly indication by Karin Zeleny).

There were various explanations for this phallus-head. Mazzucchelli, the first biographer of Aretino, advances the theory that Paolo Giovio could have had the medal commissioned as revenge for an insulting epigram of Aretino; however, he holds Niccolò Franco as the client; others believe that the offending epigram did not come from Aretino, nor was the medal intended as revenge on him, but rather, they consider it a reference to Aretino's homosexuality (Waddington 1989, 13). In regard to the satyr-head with the (alleged?) portrait traits of Paolo Giovio (see cat. no. II.11).

Waddington (ibid.) saw in the satyr-phallus-head an etymological (and cultural) relation between the words "satyr" and "satire". The epithet "scourge of princes", which accentuates the qualities of the critics, and the reference to Aretino's faun-like, bacchanal love life, eternalized in his pornographic sonnets (*Sonetti lussoriosi*), effectively completes the concept of "satirist".

The idea of the phallus-head was hardly an invention of the unknown medallist. It also appears on the majolica plate from 1536 (cat. no. II.9) and with incomparably more elegance and sophistication in a drawing attributed to Francesco Salviati (Monbeig-Goguel 1998, 26f. with plate).

All three objects – medal, plate and drawing – are only predecessors of Arcimboldo in regard to the compositional method, but not the subject, as the phallus motif does not appear in the painter's work.

Alexander Wied

Bibliography: Waddington 1989, 13f., plate 1; Pedretti 1991, 48f.; Vannel, Toderi 2003, cat. no. 577 with plate and bibliography.

II.11

Anonymous, second quarter of the 16th century

Portrait medal of Paolo Giovio (?)

Bronze

Ø 43 mm, with hole on top

Vienna, Kunsthistorisches Museum, Münzkabinett, inv. no. 15.27bb

The identification of the subject as the humanist, doctor, historian, bishop, biographer and collector from Como, Paolo Giovio (1483-1552) has long been discussed and is based merely on a presumed connection with a medal of Aretino (cat. no. II.10). The profile head with the horns and ears of a faun is composed of animal parts: the forehead is the mouth of a lion, the chin is a scaly fish, the nose is a toad. There is also a vague similarity with the portrait medal of Paolo Giovio by Francesco da Sangallo (for example, in the Bargello in Florence; Vannel, Toderi 2003, cat. no. 714 with plate and Waddington 1989, 14, plate 3), but other arguments speak against an identification of the head as Giovio's.

The back side of the medal shows a satyr-head composed of phalluses, which is identical to that from the back of Aretino medal (cat. no. II.10), along with the inclusion of an additional penis. The motto "TOTVS IN TOTO" etc. is missing.

It is impossible to establish whether the previously mentioned, alleged vendetta voiced in the Aretino medal (cat. no. II.10) found its sequel here – Aretino's counter-revenge on Giovio: there was no hostility between the two men of letters. A blasphemy such as the phallus-head on the back side of the medal, although characteristic of Aretino, could not be expected of the serious Giovio. Similar medals in the British Museum and in Budapest, whose animal motif in the head is further accentuated and more clearly modelled (they may have been models for the more crudely finished "Giovio" medal) bear the inscription ATTILA REX, or ATILA DUX and are intended to represent the Hun king as a terrifying demon (Waddington 1989, 15, notes 15, 20, plate 7, with interpretation of animal symbolism). This "Giovio" medal is probably merely a representation of a satyr, as was in vogue in Italian sculpture and graphics at the time. The front-sides of these ATTILA-heads with their animal symbolism are certainly more interesting than the phallus-compositions on the back-sides of the medals and on the majolica plate from 1536 (cat. no. II.9) as a possible influence on Arcimboldo.

Alexander Wied

Bibliography: Waddington 1989, 13-23; Parronchi 1991, 52-56; Monbeig-Goguel 1998, 15-68; Vannel, Toderi 2003; Wilson 2005, 10-44; London 2007.

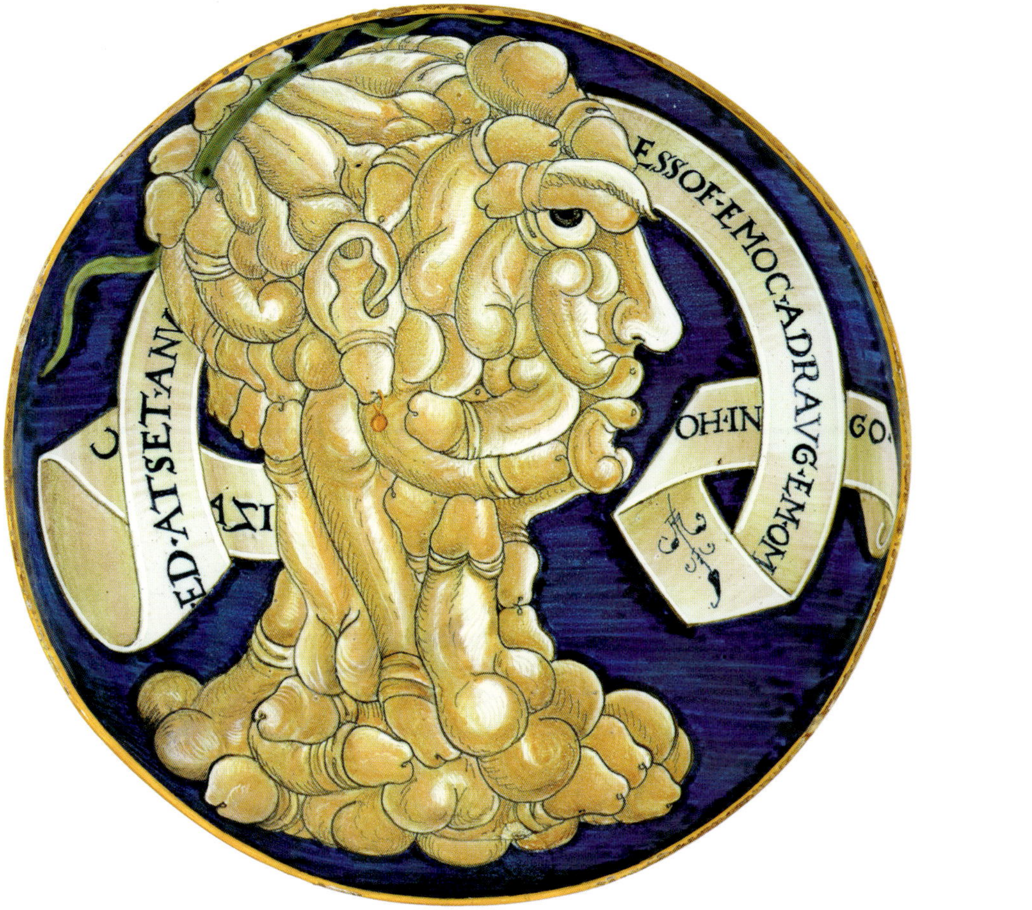

II.9

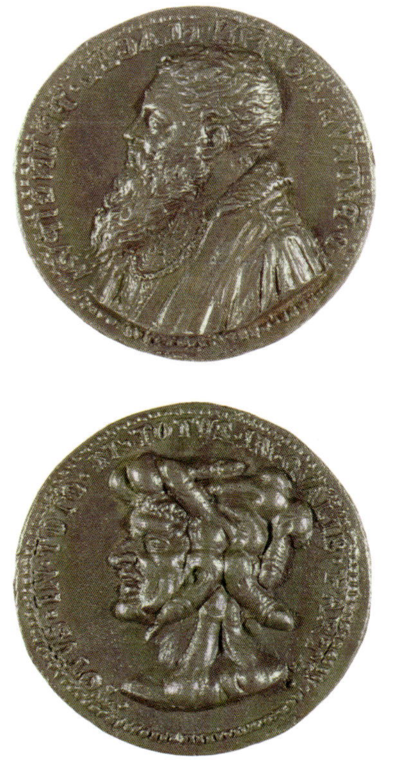

II.10

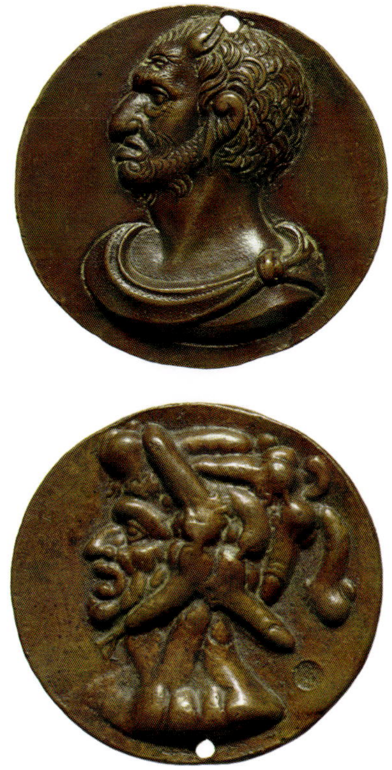

II.11

II.12
Cartoon: Giuseppe Arcimboldo, 1558
The Dormition of the Virgin
Manufactured in Ferrara, woven by Giovanni Karcher, 1561-1562
Tapestry, wool and silk
423 × 470 cm
Como, Cathedral

Already observable in the 15th century, the link between Flemish tapestry manufacturers and Italian painters, that laid the groundwork for the most magnificent tapestries, was perpetuated in the century after that. Hence it comes as no surprise that the most important 16th century masters of tapestry making serving the princely courts of Ferrara, Mantua and Florence were from Brussels. They had the task of setting up tapestry production in Italy. Worthy of note above all are Giovanni Rust as well as the Nicolaus brothers and Giovanni Karcher. The latter, with other tapestry makers who had migrated from Flanders, founded a factory in Ferrara, that went on to produce important series, such as the famous Scipio tapestries after draughts by Giulio Romano (1499-1546).
This tapestry, made out of wool and silk, representing the death of Mary is from this studio. Along with seven other wall hangings, showing scenes from the life of Mary (her marriage, representation in the temple, ascension) and of the Old Testament (Moses with the tables of the laws, the sacrifice of Abraham, the death of Abel, David and the high priests), it is in the possession of the Como Cathedral.
The left lower corner of the tapestry contains a table, localizing and dating the work: FACTUM / FERRARIAE / M D LXII. Concentric to this, above the lower bordure a monogram on a stone can be seen, referring to Giovanni Karcher who worked in Ferrara. Papers and documents from the archives refer to payments proving his authorship: "25 agosto [1561], Giovanni Karcher, arazziere al servizio del duca di Ferrara ma al momento a Como, riceve 40 scudi come acconto per la tessitura dell'arazzo con il *Transito della Vergine* su modello di Giuseppe Arcimboldi, arazzo destinato al Duomo di Como" (see registrations for the years 1561 and 1562, in this exhibition catalogue).
The drawing for this tapestry dedicated to a Christian theme for the decoration of the Como Cathedral was done by no lesser figure than Giuseppe Arcimboldo. As stated in Cathedral archives published by Ciceri in 1811, the artist was already commissioned to do the work in 1558: "Pagate lir. 158.19 al Maestro Giuseppe Arnaboldo [recte Arcimboldo] di Milano pittore per il disegno, e tela di modello per fare il Celone, ossia arazzo, come al Giornale delle spese del suddetto anno" (quoted after Forti Grazzini 1986, 44; see registrations for the years 1561 and 1562, in this exhibition catalogue).
The death of Mary represented in the picture is taken from the traditional source of the *Legenda aurea* of Jacobus de Voragine (circa 1230-1298). Mary's corpse is in the foreground, though not parallel to the picture, as in earlier workings regarding the same theme (i.e. knitted carpet with the death of Mary, The Burrell Collection, Glasgow, 1450-60, inv. no. 46.17), but rather diagonally placed to the picture plane. Hence the sense of depth of the composition is strengthened, though without the the help of foreshortening the lifeless body appears squat. Christ is neither present in the composition nor in the additional side scenes. These are to be found in the framing bordure.
Mary's body is placed on a catafalque with closed eyes and with hands crossed over her breast under a clear sky. Following the representation type of the Dormition, Mary is surrounded by a group of apostles formed in a half-circle. With eloquent gestures they comment the death of the Virgin while they point to her sleeping body. Their gestures and expressions reflect tragic loss and deep sorrow.
The place where this occurs is bordered in the background by imposing architectural elements. The building to the left with the arch, the intarsiated window and the tondo above refer to the decoration of the apse of Como Cathedral. The figures are also reminiscent of works by earlier artists-figures also allow one to reminisce on earlier works of other artists. They call to mind the dense grouping of the actors around a centrally positioned main figure, the expressive positions of the arms or the types of figures, the dialoguing seen in the tapestries and monthly representations following Bramantino's instructions (Civiche Raccolte d'Arte Applicata, Milan).
All told the tapestry contrasts with Arcimboldo's fantastic heads and half figures created at the court of Maximilian II and Rudolf II, offering a more conventional approach. What is highly creative is the bordure. It incorporates five cartouches which complement the central composition of the work. In the upper middle area one finds an oval medallion with the inscription: "CONSORTII LANIFICI NOVOCOME(N)SIS". In the emblem of the upper left bordure neck one has the Annunciation, in the right one the Visitation. The two medallions on the lower horizontal bordure show the birth of Christ, to the right the flight from Egypt. Not unusual is the choice of the elements embellishing the bordure, such as medallions, mascarons, birds, rolls, ribbons, putti or festoons made up of fruit, flowers and leaves, often encountered in the art of tapestry making in the 16th century. A lot more exceptional is the lively, imaginative way in which the traditional divide between bordure and the main scene is overcome. Some motifs in the bordure encroach on the actual picture, creating a plastic effect. This intertwining is the expression of a sensitivity close to a Manneristic style. Whether the bordures as well as the main picture were drawn by Arcimboldo himself cannot be established by today's methods of study.

Katja Schmitz-von Ledebur

Bibliography: Ciceri 1811; Forti Grazzini 1982, 81-84, plate 153-157; Forti Grazzini 1986, 43-47.

II.13
Cartoon: Giuseppe Arcimboldo, c. 1560
Scenes from the Life of John the Baptist:
Sermon to the Soldiers, Baptism in the Jordan River and his Capture
Flanders (Bruges?), between 1566 and 1581
Tapestry, wool and silk
460 × 740 cm
Monza, Cathedral

This wall-hanging belongs to a large series of tapestries, dedicated to the life of John the Baptist. The drawings and cartoons of the series of tapestries created for the decoration of the Monza Cathedral have not survived.
The scene of the baptism in the River Jordan and the capture of John the Baptist balance each other, right and left, in the foreground of to the foreground of the tapestry. Further back in the work one has the representation of the sermon to the soldiers. The simultaneous depicting of events that followed each other in time, as significantly seen in this work, was already common in wall-hangings of the Middle Ages.
John the Baptist is shown preaching facing us in a prominent point in the mid axis of the composition. He stands in front of a grotto and is surrounded by a half-circle of soldiers and civilians, yet one's gaze is drawn by the principal figure. This is followed by the scene to the right edge of the picture, where again John is depicted as the central figure. He is baptising a group of men and women in the River Jordan, including Pharisees and Sadducees (Mathew III. 7). The capture to the left of the picture shows John with the same gesture of pointing to heaven with his right hand (an indication of Christ), the same as in the preaching scene. He is surrounded by soldiers, whose spears threateningly point upwards. One of them holds a rope ready to tie up John, another is about to unsheathe his sword. The front bordure decked with flowers, buds and fruits as well as scrolls is relatively narrow and bears no relation to the picture. As to the attribution, date and origin of this tapestry, various opinions are to be found in the related literature (see essay by Silvio Leydi, in this exhibition catalogue). Five drawings for the series of John the Baptist, created 1550-1555, have been attributed to Giuseppe Arcimboldo. This wall-hanging is to be considered a later work, as corroborated by stylistic changes as well as the differently designed bordure.

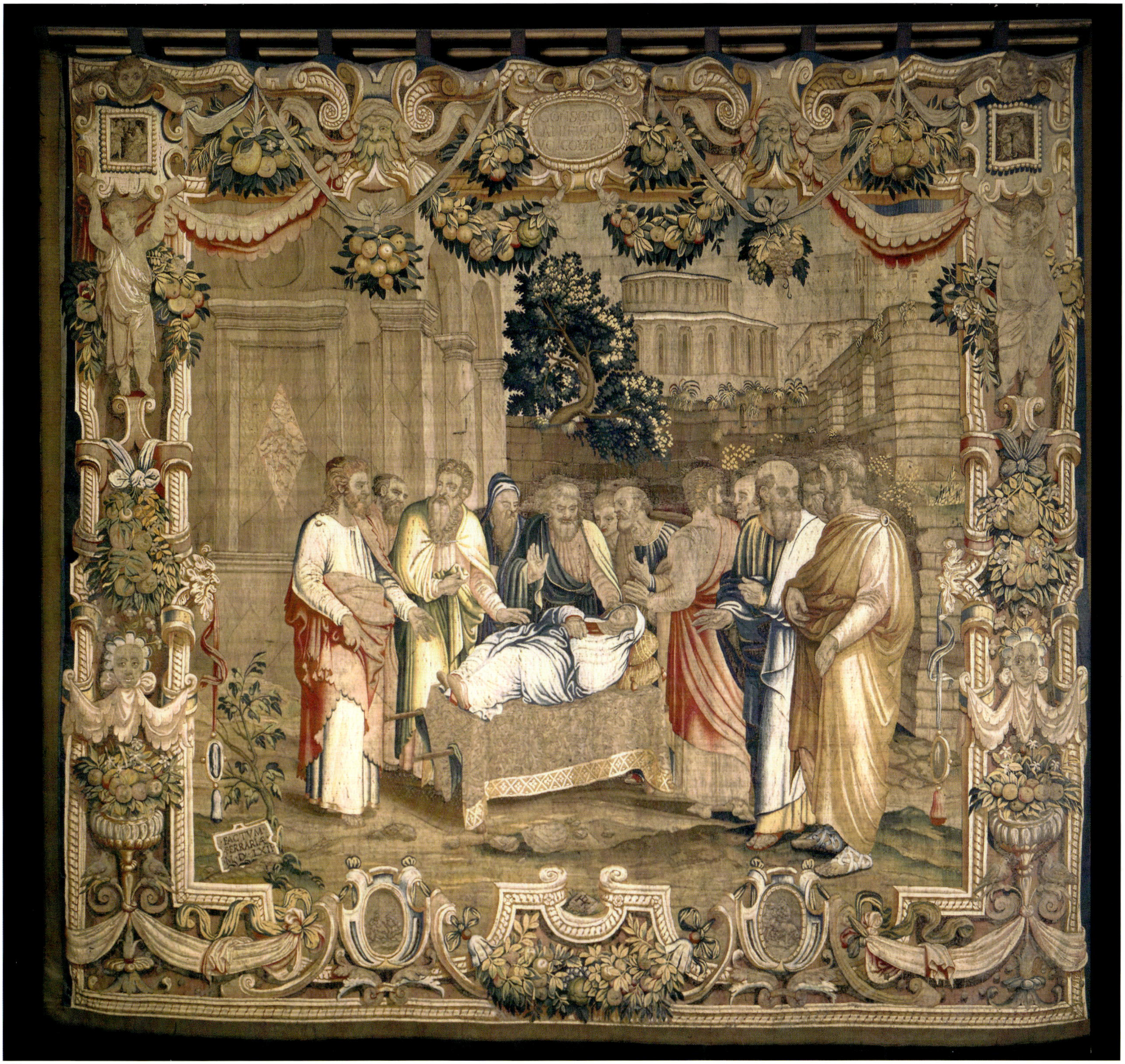

Il.12

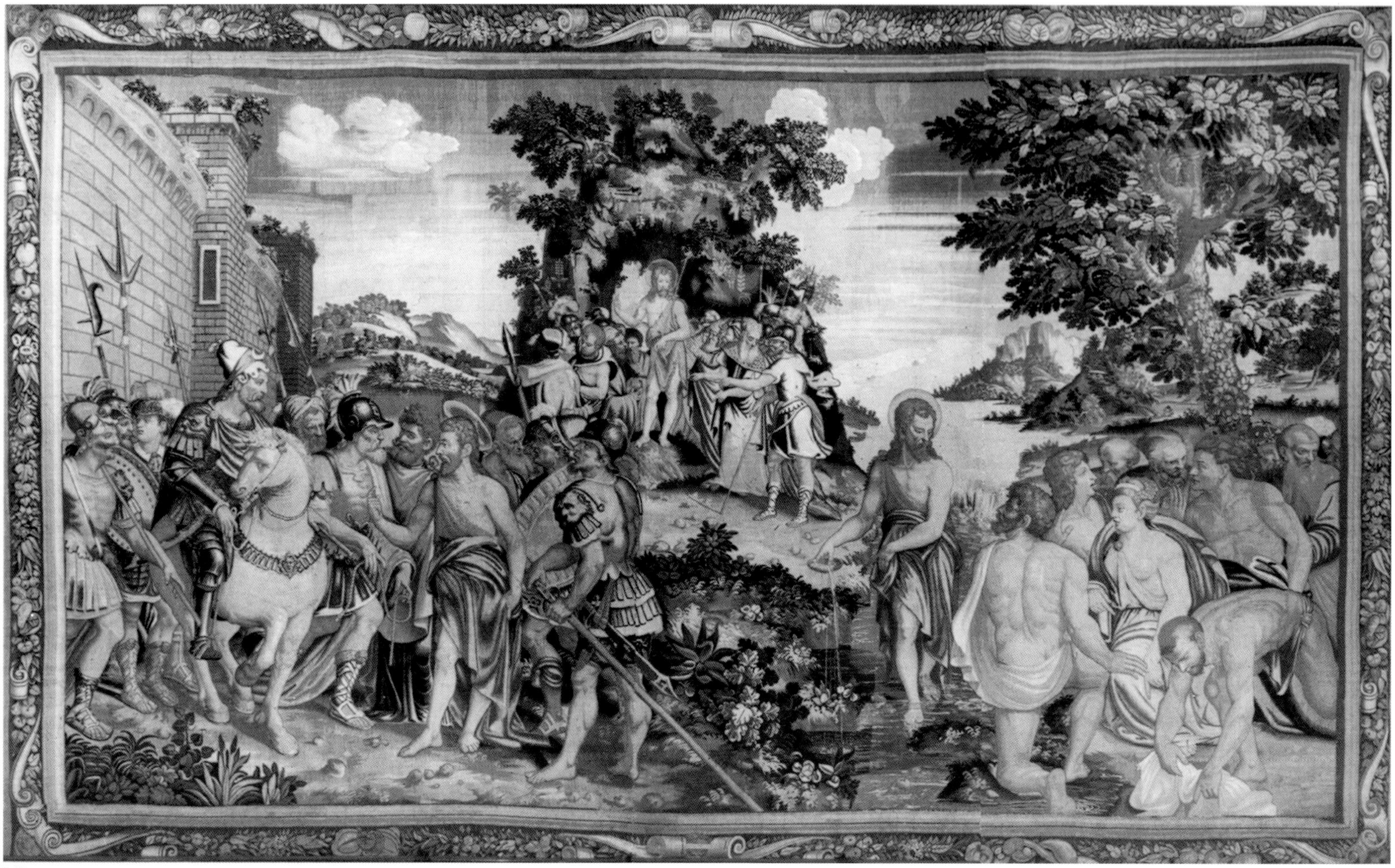

II.13

The attribution of this tapestry to Arcimboldo was already convincingly put forward by DaCosta Kaufmann. He compares figures in the tapestry with the descent of Jesus from the family tree of Jesse in the fresco opposite the southern transept of the Monza Cathedral. The commission to execute this wall painting went in 1556 to the artists Giuseppe Lomazzo (circa 1534-1599) and Giuseppe Arcimboldo. The figure of an old man with beard, long nose, heavy eyelids and jutting cheekbones is to be found both in the frescoes as well as in the tapestry (the figure of John the Baptist). Convincing too is the comparison with the figures drawn by Arcimboldo on the glass windows of the Milan Cathedral. The counter-figure to the womanly figure in the baptism is to be found on the same window in the episode of Lot and his daughters.

Of the entire cycle the tapestry drawn by Arcimboldo shows the most impressive composition. The variation in the order of the numerous groups of figures shows great creativity. While the people set out in a half circle as listeners to the sermon in the upper part of the picture, they surround John as a threatening, compact group in the scene of the capture in the foreground scene close to the picture's edge. The three different scenes of the composition are masterly related while all the same presented separately. On the one hand through the common landscape and the triangular structure with the sermon situated at the top, on the other hand by the architecture foreshortened by perspective on the left and the Jordan to the right. Without doubt the tapestry shows the extreme stylistic maturity of Arcimboldo, which was not achieved in the tapestry representing the death of Mary contained in the Como Cathedral.

Related documentation generates uncertainty as to the dating of the tapestry. One would agree with Forti Grazzini's suggestion that the draft of this tapestry was done slightly later than the other four draughts of Arcimboldo dated around 1550-1555. Forti Grazzini's idea that the work is more recent is based on the inventory of the sacristy of the cathedral for the years 1566 and 1581, where mention is made of the series of tapestries telling the story of John the Baptist. In 1566 the series is said to consist of eight items; against this in 1581 mention is made of nine items. Hence it is probable, that between 1566 and 1581 a new work was in fact added or possibly a lost tapestry was replaced.

In which workshop the tapestry was made is equally unclear. The attribution to an Italian studio would be obvious. Forti Grazzini points all the same to the wall-hanging's striking colouring, atypical of Italian tapestries, which even today shines forth in all the splendour of its colours. The flesh tones for example have been enlivened by gradations of pink, while in the sky the tones of yellow and pinkish-red indicate the first lights of morning. This type of colouring is not characteristic of the technique of the tapestry makers working in Milan or Ferrara, but is rather much more reminiscent of Flemish workshops, especially those of Bruges. This location is also corroborated by the rich variety and the liveliness of the colours as well as their soft, picturesque blending.

Katja Schmitz-von Ledebur

Bibliography: Forti Grazzini 1988, 107-139; Kaufmann 1988a, 428-430; Kaufmann 1988b, 5-17.

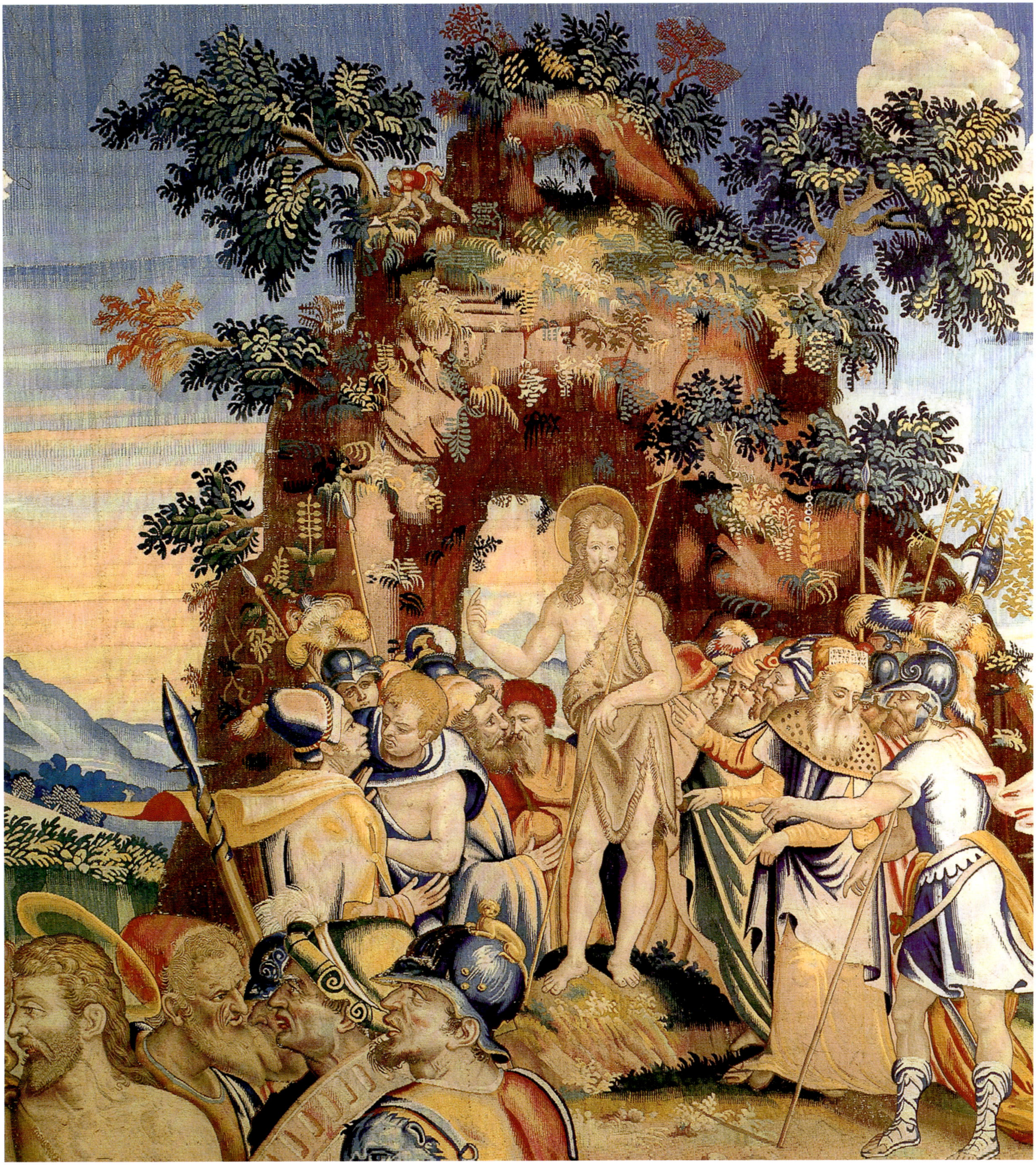

II.13. (detail)

II.14

Giuseppe Arcimboldo (attributed)

Study of a Figure in a Niche (Saint Ambrose; recto); *Architectural Studies: Four Alternative Designs for Fictive Niches and an Unrelated Design with Garlands* (verso)

c. 1560-1567

Pen and brown ink, brush with pale brown and purple wash, over soft black chalk (recto); pen and brown ink, some sketches over black chalk (verso). A patch with unrelated drawings by another hand, glued onto the sheet, contains a cartouche design seen at lower right of recto, and an ornate garland design seen at lower left of verso

351 × 263 mm

Recto is annotated at upper left, in pen and brown ink: "3"; and verso is annotated at upper right by Giuseppe Vallardi with his distinctive classification system, in red chalk: "F 299"

Watermark: a hand surmounted by a six-pointed star (close to Briquet 10796)

New York, The Metropolitan Museum of Art 1995.305 (Casey Fund, 1995)

The attribution to Arcimboldo of the Metropolitan Museum drawing was first suggested by Giulio Bora (cited in Christie's sale catalogue, London, 4 July 1995, lot 37; Bora 1998, 40, 42, 55, note 24, fig. 4, with its whereabouts listed as "già a Londra"), and it was recently reaffirmed by Giuseppe Cirillo (Cirillo 2005, 58, note 97, as "Christie's 1995"), as it is entirely convincing on the basis of style, technical evidence, and context of the documents here discussed. Datable to c. 1560-67 and once owned by the distinguished Milanese collector Giuseppe Vallardi, the Metropolitan Museum drawing relates to the design of a prestigious, though much disputed commission by the Municipio (town-hall) of Milan for a banner representing Saint Ambrose, the heroic patron of the city who is also one of the canonical Doctors of the Church. The ambiguous scenario emerging from the interpretations of the surviving documents indicates that Arcimboldo may have ceded this project to design a banner of Saint Ambrose at the time of his departure from Milan in 1562 for the court of Prague, and that the commission may have been passed onto Carlo Urbino on 18 February 1563, for a document of this date describes the latter artist "as having assumed the job of making a design to be painted on paper and on cloth for the new banner" ("ha preso la carica de fare in pittura in carta et tela il dissegno dil nuovo confalone"; Archivio Storico Civico, Località milanesi, S. Ambrogio, Gonfalone, no. 309/4 [18 febbraio 1563]; here, as transcribed by Robert S. Miller 1989-1990, 226). The documents also tell that the final execution of the banner was to be done by the embroiderer Bartolomeo Rainone, but the entire project was interrupted in 1564, amidst a heated professional controversy, of which modern scholars have given different accounts (compare opinions in Bora 1977a, 54-88; Bora 1977b, 52-54 [notes 58-61], 62-86; Bandera Bistoletti 1986, 92-96; Miller 1989-90, 216-28, note 48; Bora 1998, 52-55; Cirillo 2005, 57-59). From what can be discerned, a casual mention in the legal complaint filed on 6 November 1564 to the Fabbricieri del Duomo of Milan regarding another project, the prestigious commission to paint the organ shutters of the Cathedral entrusted to Giuseppe Meda, partner ("compagno") of Arcimboldo, also seems to shed light on the design of the banner of Saint Ambrose, the project to which the Metropolitan Museum drawing actually relates, as this latter document alludes to a repeatedly competitive situation between Bernardino Campi and Arcimboldo ("in diverse volte a concorentia") regarding the banner of Saint Ambrose ("Sant'Ambrogio"), and to a dispute which was to be settled by the artists' submission of their respective designs to a corporate tribunal (the "Dodici del Tribunale di Provvisione"). This document about the banner of Sant'Ambrogio is in the Archivio della Fabbrica del Duomo di Milano (Ordinazione, XII, fols. 124 recto-125 recto; Miller 1989-1990, 216, 227, note 1). The judges ("stimatori") on behalf of the Fabbricieri del Duomo were Giovanni Francesco Melzi (pupil and heir of Leonardo) and Girolamo Figino, who also ruled that the drawing for the "confalone del nuovo S.to Ambroso" by Giuseppe Arcimboldo, who was in partnership with Giuseppe Meda, was far superior to the design by Bernardino Campi, and that Arcimboldo's was the design chosen for execution. The wording of these documents provides unmistakable proof, "fu per li predicti signori Meltio et Figino indicato il disegno desso Bernardino [Campi] essere molto inferiore al disegno desso magistro Joseph [Giuseppe Arcimboldo] qual fu acetate et messe in opera" (here, as transcribed in Miller 1989-90, 216, 226, but also quoted very diversely in Cattaneo et al. 1973, Vol. 2, 193-197; Bora 1977, 52; Bandera Bistoletti 1986, 92; and Bora 1998, 41). The redesigned banner of Sant'Ambrogio was contracted to be executed (document 14 July 1565) by the more skilled embroiderers Scipione Delfinone and Camillo Pusterla (than Rainone), who were to follow the drawing that was provided. Although completed in early September 1566, Arcimboldo collected two payments on 10 October and 30 December 1567, "for the first drawings made for the said banner" ("per i primi dissegni fatti del sopradetto confalone"). The banner of Sant'Ambrogio is today on display in the Civiche Raccolte d'Arte of Castello Sforzesco, Milan.

The Metropolitan Museum drawing must have been one of the early studies by Arcimboldo for his winning competition drawing of the "nuovo confalone," or new banner. For, confirming the scenario implied in the documents, there exists a large, relatively dry, more or less finished composition drawing much like the final banner in design, now in the Arcivescovado, Milan (inv. no. 36, done in pen and brown ink, brush and brown wash, highlighted with white gouache, on ochre prepared paper; 545 × 375 mm). Although this sheet in the Arcivescovado, Milan, has been repeatedly published with an attribution to Bernardino Campi (as illustrated and discussed in Bora 1977, 84-85, no. 52; followed in Bandera Bistoletti 1986, 92-96, no. 31), it is almost certain that the alternative attribution to Giuseppe Meda, as advanced by Robert Miller, is correct (Miller 1989-90, 216-230 [especially 225, fig. 195]; accepted in Bora 1998, 40, fig. 3; Cirillo 2005, 58). In any case, it can be added here that the papers of the drawings in the Arcivescovado, Milan, by Giuseppe Meda and Metropolitan Museum of Art by Arcimboldo exhibit similar watermarks, a hand surmounted by a star; the first is close to Briquet 10719-10720, while the Metropolitan sheet is close to Briquet 10796. Meda's somewhat lifeless and rather harshly modelled drawing in the Arcivescovado, Milan (which is nevertheless clearly an autograph study for the banner, not a copy) offers an elaboration of details of the key iconographic elements as they are represented in the final banner today at the Castello Sforzesco. These iconographic motifs are also indicated, though in a more inchoate form, in the energetic overall composition of the drawing by Arcimboldo in the Metropolitan Museum of Art. Without doubt, however, the design and the details of the figure and ornament in the drawing by Giuseppe Meda in the Arcivescovado, Milan, seem closer to the composition of the final banner at the Castello Sforzesco, than is the Metropolitan Museum drawing by Arcimboldo.

The driving concept in Arcimboldo's design for the banner is the architectural setting for the figure, which is of great monumentality. His Metropolitan demonstration drawing (a type of early "*modello*") offers two alternative solutions for the illusionistic architectural framework at the sides; this "de choix" feature of the design is often characteristic of drawings for the approval of patrons. On the left half, the small pedimented niche and podium are surmounted by variations of volutes and supported by a monumental, elaborately carved console. Rectilinear elements predominate on the right half of the sheet, but their precise disposition is difficult to judge, since another artist excised a square piece of the drawing and replaced it with the unrelated design of a cartouche. In contrast to the architecture, the figures are broadly painted with light brown wash. The large sketchy nude figure in the centre raises his right hand in blessing, as the fully garbed Saint Ambrose does in the final banner at the Castello Sforzesco. The

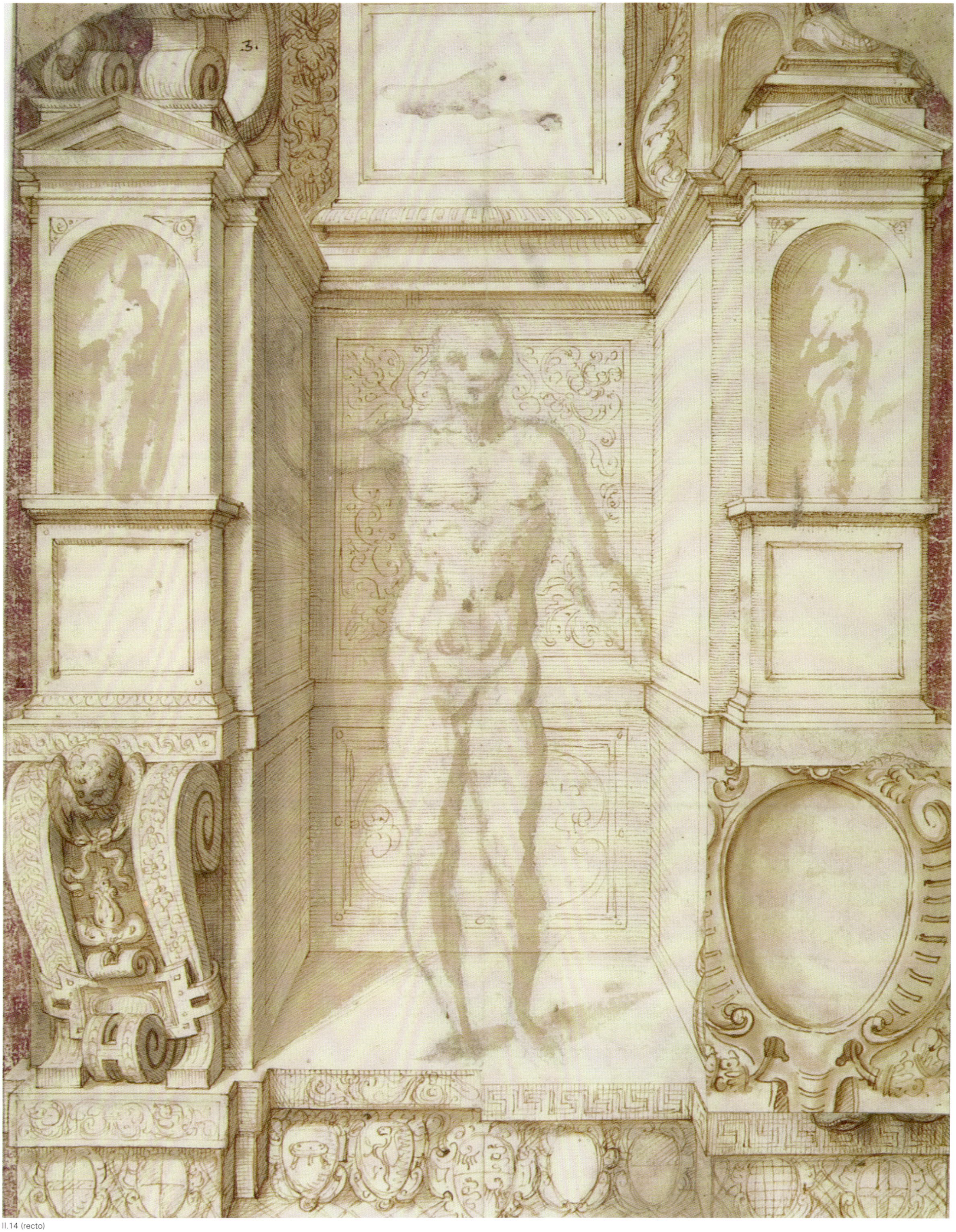

II.14 (recto)

heraldic symbols at the bottom of the Metropolitan drawing, including the coat of arms of the Sforza-Visconti family at centre, below the main niche, all seem to conform to those depicted in the final banner, and apparently also to those in Meda's drawing in the Arcivescovado, Milan.
Although evidencing a particularly close study of Giulio Campi's draftsmanship (in my opinion), the style and technique of the architectural drawings on the main paper support of the verso of the Metropolitan sheet are also clearly attributable to Arcimboldo, as they are exactly comparable to the ornamental passages along the lower border of the recto. These isolated designs of rectangular niches and ornamented pediments on the verso of the Metropolitan sheet were also intended for the fictive architecture flanking Saint Ambrose, and are very similar to the lateral designs portrayed in Meda's drawing in the Arcivescovado, Milan, and in the final banner today in the Castello Sforzesco. But these verso drawings are much disfigured by the distracting patch containing unrelated designs glued onto the sheet (seen at lower left, on the verso) by a different hand, facts which may be overlooked if this drawing is only studied from photographs.

Carmen C. Bambach

Provenance: Edward Pearce (active 17th century); Giuseppe Vallardi (Milan, 1784-1863); Stichting Collectie P. and N. de Boer, Amsterdam; Christie's, London, sale, 4 July 1995, lot 37

Bibliography: Bora 1977a, 54-88; Bora 1977b, 52-54 [notes 58-61], 62-86; Bora 1998, 40-42, 55, note 24, fig. 4 (when in London art market ["already in London"]); Cirillo 2005, 58, note 97 (when at auction at Christie's, London, 4 July 1995, lot 37).

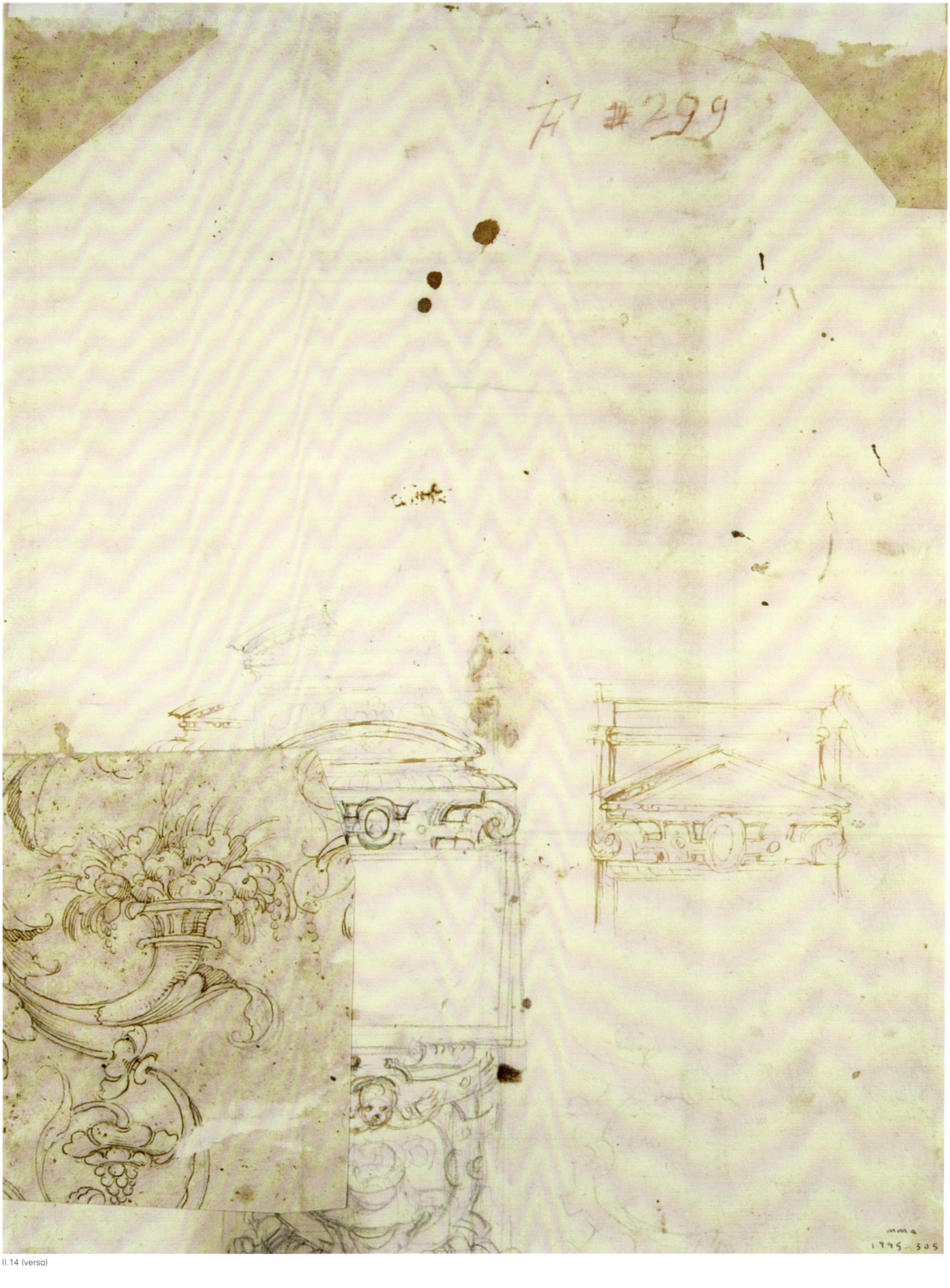

II.14 (verso)

II.15
Giuseppe Arcimboldo
Farm Woman Going to Market
Brown pen, grey-blue wash
Signed bottom left: "Giuseppe / Arcimboldo / Mediolanensis. f."
251 × 181 mm
Madrid, Biblioteca Nacional, inv. no. 7239

This woman, balancing two baskets on a pole placed over her shoulder, was understood by Eugenio Battisti to be a farm woman on the way to the market to sell her products (like the dead hen hanging out of the front basket). Though he did not presume that this was a preparatory work for a painting of a genre scene – like the *Fruttivendole* series by Vincenzo Campi –, but rather saw it in relation to a "*spettacolo teatrale*". This theatre scene was then better defined in relation to Arcimboldo's organization of large festive occasions such as various wedding celebrations in Vienna and Prague, where he not only created masks of the gods, parts of the earth, winds feature, but also farmers, farmers' wives and simple folk (see cat. no. VII.34).
However, the style of this drawing is a far cry from the elegance and graphic expertise of the costume drawings contained in the binder bequeathed to Emperor Rudolf II (cat. nos. VII.1-32), and one would agree with Berra in dating the drawing as fairly early, if only due to the piecemeal graphic technique – small dotting, long drawn out hatchings and wash on top of that. Does this drawing simply illustrate the genre motif of the farm woman that was becoming popular in Lombardy at that time or should one consider it as a mask for a festive occasion?
Indeed in the last series of the Monza wallhangings, the designs of which are attributed to Biagio working together with Giuseppe Arcimboldo, one can find a particularly fine variation of costumes, that bring to mind Arcimboldo's future career in this field. And the representation of a farm woman like this one surely had various uses: for paintings as well as for festive processions. In an essay in this catalogue Silvio Leydi indicates that even in his Milan days Arcimboldo aroused a lot of attention for his organization of festivities. What is more, a motif like this one might have inspired Lomazzo with his famous verses: (1587, 366) "A San Martino portaron a'padroni / I superbi Villan carchi di fame / Co'l palo in collo i promessi caponi" (on Saint Martin's day the proud farmers, laden with hunger, brought to their masters on a pole around their neck, the promised capons).

Sylvia Ferino-Pagden

Provenance: Carderera Collection

Bibliography: Battisti 1956, 56-59, ill. 2; Preiss 1967, 12, ill. 48; Ferrarino, Páez 1974, 14; Pérez Sánchez 1977; Porzio 1979, 48, note. 27; Kaufmann 1983, 199, note. 4; Lugano 1987, 65; Sutton 1987, 231-232; Battisti 1989, Vol. 1, 285; Bora 1989, 82; Kaufmann 1990a, 901; Berra 1996, 58-59, note 12; Berra 1998b, 200, no. 42.

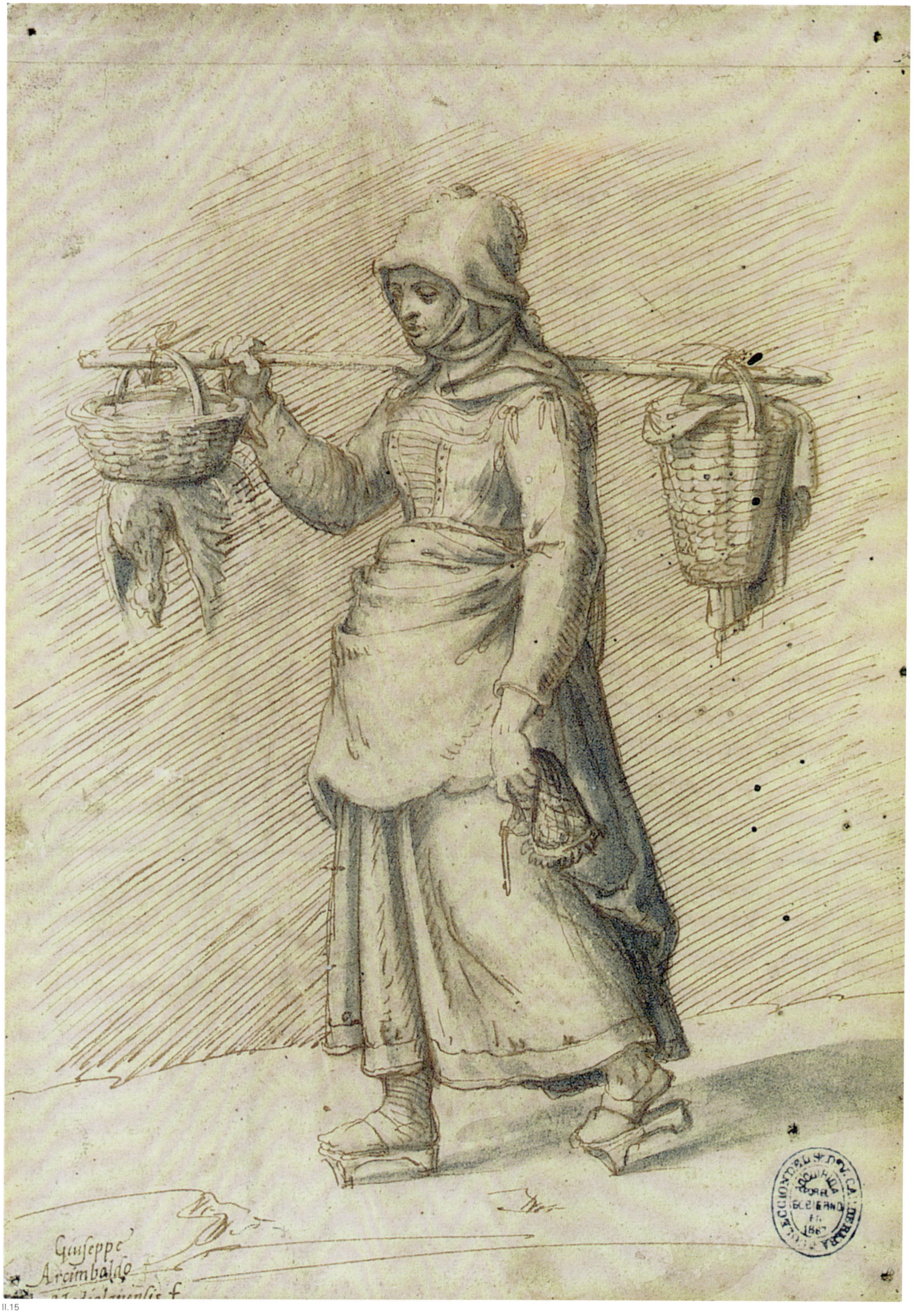

II.15

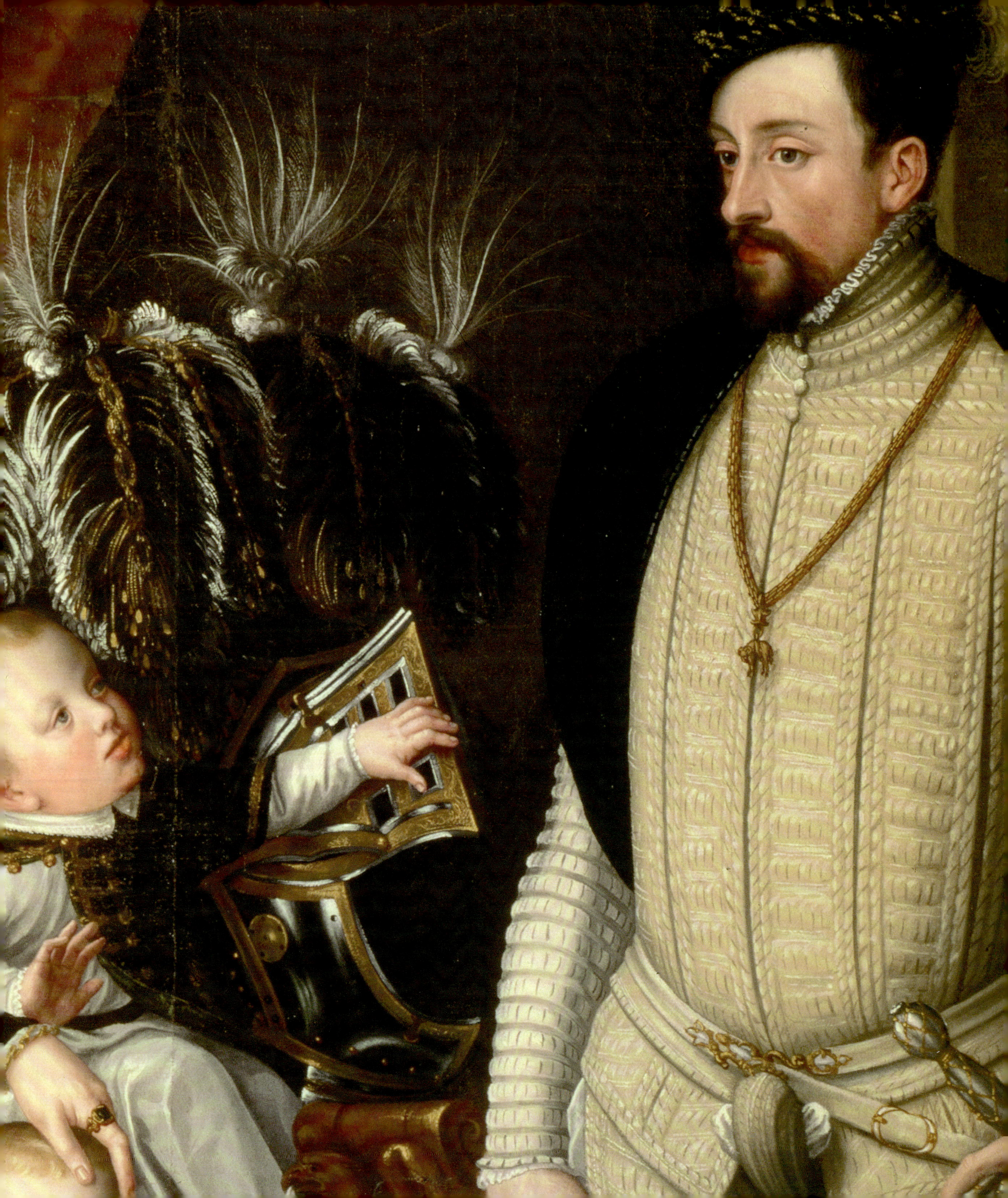

Karl Schütz

Art and Culture at the Court of Emperor Maximilian II

Archduke Maximilian, who would later become Emperor Maximilian II, was born in Vienna in 1527, the first son of Ferdinand I[1] and his wife, Anna of Bohemia and Hungary. As the oldest son of Ferdinand I, Maximilian II[2] became a central figure in the delicate balance between the interests of the Spanish crown and those of the various territories of the "multifaceted Habsburg monarchy"[3], that is between the brothers Charles V and Ferdinand I, respectively. Maximilian was vying with his same-aged cousin Philip (who would later become Philip II, King of Spain) as well as with his younger brother Ferdinand II, who was favoured by their father and whom he jealously observed[4]. Charles V's future plans for the two heirs led to a bitter struggle between the Emperor and his brother, and finally ended with a political compromise in which Philip would become King of Spain (and not the Roman King and Emperor) and Maximilian would succeed his father as King of the Romans (and not as King of Spain). As a result, the separation of the House of Habsburg into two different branches (a Spanish and an Austrian one) was complete. The journey to this point had been a long one for Ferdinand I; he became ruler in Austria in 1521, experienced significant expansion in the kingdoms of Bohemia and Hungary through succession and finally, with his election in 1531 as the King of the Romans, he was appointed as the designated imperial successor. Throughout the years, Ferdinand's policies had been dominated by three major issues: in the Holy Empire the religious schism among the German princes, which the Peace of Augsburg brought to a temporary end in 1555; abroad, was against the Ottomans in Austria and Hungary; and within the family, the difficult relationship with his brother Charles V, and their divergent views on the question of succession as well as the future division of territories between their sons.

In 1558, at the age of 55, Ferdinand I achieved the highest point of his political career. For more than 25 years he had co-authored the policies of the German empire as the representative of his brother, Emperor Charles V, but now he had become the *de iure* head of the Holy Roman Empire in a solemn ceremony in the presence of the prince-electors in Saint Bartholomew's in Frankfurt am Main, the traditional location for the coronation of the King of the Romans[5]. He had already functioned as Charles V's unrestricted deputy since 1556, as the Emperor had abdicated power in Spain and in the Empire and had withdrawn to a villa close to the Hieronymite Monastery of Yuste.

As Archduke of the hereditary lands in Austria and as King of Bohemia and King of Hungary, Ferdinand I held court in several locations[6]. He established Vienna as his Austrian residence, Maximilian I having mainly preferred Innsbruck. Traditionally, the Diets of Bohemia and Hungary insisted that their kings took up residence in the country itself. While Prague had been the capital of Bohemia for centuries, the residence of the Hungarian kings had changed several times; after the loss of a large part of the Hungarian kingdom to the Ottomans, Pressburg became the capital. In the first years of his reign, Ferdinand I found himself, like his brother Charles V, travelling a great deal and mostly visited the Diets at Worms, Nuremberg, Augsburg, Regensburg and Speyer. He travelled to the Netherlands and resided in Linz, Innsbruck, Vienna and in various Hungarian cities as well as Prague, where he had the summer palace Belvedere built for Queen Anna (which was completed decades later, in 1560, by Archduke Ferdinand II). His most important architectural undertaking in Innsbruck was the construction of the palace Chapel which housed the tomb of Maximilian I. With the relocation of the court from Prague to Vienna in 1533, Vienna's importance increased as the centre of Ferdinand I's administration; after around 1550 this became his permanent residence.

The court of this early period had several functions, one of which was to accommodate the needs of the king or sovereign and of his family, while another was the management of the country through its central authorities (such as the financial and judiciary administrations and the military). These functions also included the advancement of the arts and various festive events, as well as the resulting, representative construction in the form of garden enclosures and buildings[7].

Maximilian spent both his childhood and youth from 1529 to 1543 with his brother Ferdinand, who was his junior by two years, and his sisters in Innsbruck. In 1544 both archdukes travelled to Spain in order to stay with their uncle from then on and to take part in the war against the German Protestant rulers in 1546-1547

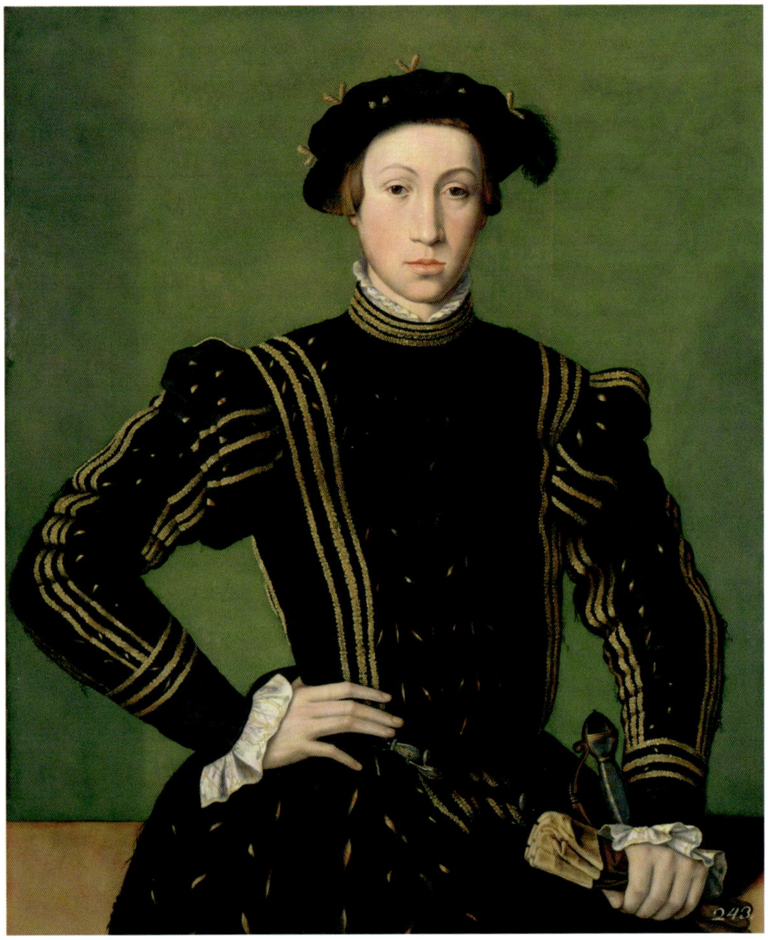

Fig. 1. Attributed to Guillaume Scrots, *Portrait of Maximilian II*, 1544. Vienna, Kunsthistorisches Museum, Gemäldegalerie

(*fig. 1*). While Archduke Ferdinand returned to his father's court and was named Regent in Bohemia, Charles V prepared Maximilian for his succession in Spain. In 1548, he was married to his cousin Maria, the daughter of Charles V and received the title of "King of Bohemia", but had to give up any participation in affairs of state as long as his father lived. After 1548, he functioned as Charles V's regent in Spain, while Charles went to the Netherlands and Germany with his son, Philip.

Although Maximilian wanted nothing more than to be able to return to Germany during his stay in Spain, which he did not care for, Spanish culture nonetheless made a deep impression on him. In 1551 he returned to Austria and brought the Indian elephant Soliman to Vienna to become the first resident of a zoological garden in Ebersdorf, where lions, tigers and bears were later held[8]. His return was celebrated with a great festivity, one of the ephemeral art forms which, as in the case of Ferdinand I and Maximilian II, occupied a central role in the courtly culture of the 16th century[9].

Maximilian II sought a good relationship with the German princes in order to strengthen his position with regard to the question of succession. In his attempts to do so, he aroused the suspicion of his father and even more of Charles V and the Spanish court by pandering to the evangelical Christians and suspected being a kind of Crypto-Lutheran. The conflict surrounding Maximilian's court chaplain, Johann Sebastian Pfauser, who converted to the Lutheran faith, and who had to leave the court in 1560 and was vehemently defended by Maximilian, is just one example among many[10].

Maximilian was elected King of the Romans in 1562 in Frankfurt am Main during the lifetime of his father - *vivente imperatore*. The vote proceeded in a remarkably harmonious atmosphere after the long years of religious conflict[11] because the Protestant princes expected Maximilian to be tolerant regarding their religious beliefs. Maximilian was crowned King of Bohemia in September 1562 in Prague and was crowned King of Hungary in August 1563 in Pressburg[12]. The political authority of Maximilian II was extremely limited during his father's lifetime, which caused Maximilian a great deal of impatience and frustration. Ferdinand I also arranged for the education of Maximilian's sons and had the two eldest (Rudolf and Ernst) sent to the court of Philip II of Spain in 1563 for their education[13]. With Ferdinand's political will and testament and the division of the territories among the three sons after his death in 1564, the Habsburgian lands were split into three domains with their own courts and residences. Maximilian II, as the oldest heir, became emperor and received the kingdoms of Bohemia and Hungary and the archduchy of Austria above and below the Enns River, Ferdinand II received Tyrol and the surrounding territory, while the third, much younger brother Karl II received the so-called inner Austrian lands, Styria, Carinthia, Krain, Gorizia and Gradiska, Trieste and portions of Istria and Friuli. This division of territory in the tradition of the Habsburgian territorial partitions of the late Middle Ages represented a step backwards and contradicted the conventional (explicitly declared for Austria in 1530) principle of primogeniture, where the inseparability of territory was a more valuable commodity than providing for the younger sons[14].

Through this division of territory, the residences in Innsbruck and Graz were revitalized as the seats of their respective sovereigns alongside Vienna and Prague. The inner Austrian lands made up their own state from 1564 to 1619, having as its main goal the defense of the southeast border of the Holy Roman Empire against the Ottomans. Together with the scattered territories in South Germany, Tyrol was independent until 1665, with only one short interruption. Archduke Ferdinand II, who gave up governing Bohemia to improve his control of Tyrol and the surrounding territory, turned his court into an epicentre of Habsburg culture (for which purpose he undertook the construction of Ambras Castle)" of Habsburg culture[15].

All contemporary observers unanimously agreed that Maximilian II was a man of great intellect, known to immediately comprehend everything, and they praised his outstanding mind – "è d'inteletto acutissimo"[16] and "un ingegno uiuo, et d'un giudicio marauigliso; perche subito comprende [...] una felicissima memoria; perche si ricorda di tutto"[17] – his particular gift was with languages, which included a mastery of six or seven languages, namely Latin, German, Spanish, Italian, French as well as Czech and a little Hungarian – "parla sette lingue Alemana, Latina, Italiana, Spagnuola, Bohema, Vngara, et Francese mediocremente"[18] (*fig. 2*). He had many scientific interests; the support of research in the natural sciences, particularly in the area of botany, was especially dear to him. Classically educated humanists were already active as naturalists under Ferdinand I in the Viennese court. These included the emperor's personal physicians Johann Crato von Crafftheim[19] (1519-1585), whom Maximilian II and Rudolf II also kept in their service, and Pierandrea Matthioli of Siena (1500/1-1577), who compiled a commentary of the late antique *Materia Medica* by Dioscorides[20] and in 1540 cultivated rare plants in the newly created garden in Prague, such as the ornamental plant gillyflower *Matthiola incana*[21], which was named after him. The woodcut illustrations for this project were created by Giorgio Liberale da Udine, who was a master of natural science illustration. He followed Matthioli to the court in Prague in 1558, where he was instructed by Archduke Ferdinand II to illustrate the fauna of the Adriatic Sea, which he carried out until 1576. Afterwards, at the court of Ferdinand II in Innsbruck, he worked on the illustrations for an anthology about birds[22]. Wolfgang Lazius, also a physician, acted as court historian for Ferdinand I. It is notable that many of the humanistically educated physicians researched and published in fields other than just natural science. This lively court culture is designated under the collective term "late Humanism"[23] subsuming not only humanism in the strict sense as revival classical studies but comprising all sciences. There were many interconnections between the court and the University of Vienna, though denominational clashes existed in the background. Johann Aichholz (1520-1588), who taught in the medical faculty, allowed the Calvinist Clusius to work in his private botanical garden. The physician Paulus Fabricus (d. 1589), who served at the court as a mathematician, also took part in the poetic competitions and poet coronations of the Viennese Humanists[24]. The late Humanist sphere is characterized by the great mobility of its representatives, who in many cases did not aspire to achieve a secure position in the court, but rather remained for only a short time at the imperial court, where the emperor's religious tolerance towards artists and intellectuals was appealing to them[25].

In 1574, Justus Lipsius (1547-1606) dedicated to Maximilian II his critical volume on Tacitus, inserting an often quoted poem about the Emperor's court: "This unique Viennese court of yours has more learned men than any other kingdom"[26]. After his stay in Rome as the secretary to Cardinal Granvella, the philosopher and

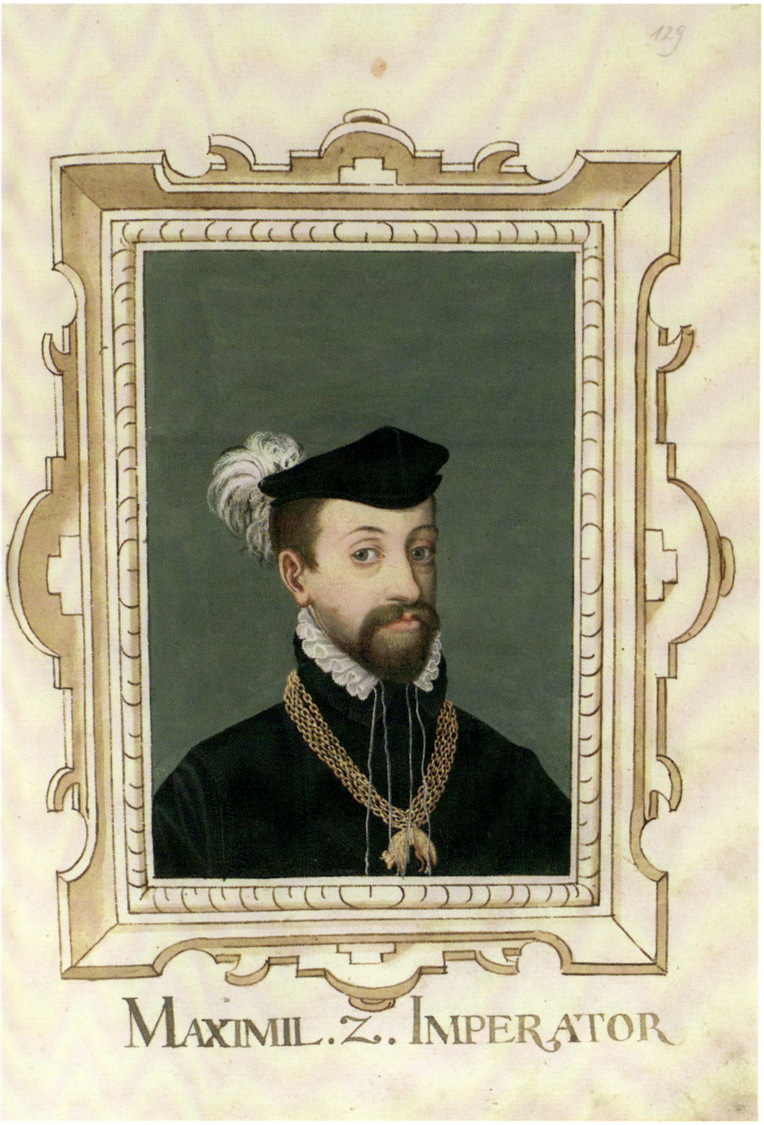

Fig. 2. After an Italian painter, *Portrait of Emperor Maximilian II*, c. 1555-60, from the Portrait codex of Hieronymus Beck von Leopoldsdorf. Vienna, Kunsthistorisches Museum, Gemäldegalerie

philologist Lipsius[27] stopped in Vienna in 1570 and attempted to find a position there, but received a professorship at the University of Jena in 1572.

Nor did the most important composers of their time, Orlando di Lasso and Giovanni Palestrina[28], come to Vienna, although Maximilian II strove greatly for it; because of the chronically limited finances of the Viennese court, the offers made to them were too low.

A similarly prominent figure among the assembled naturalists at the Viennese court was Charles de L'Ecluse (Clusius) (1526-1609), who in 1573 came to Vienna, where Johann Crato provided him with the new role of prefect of the imperial gardens[29]. He described the flora of Lower Austria and was the first to record the unique

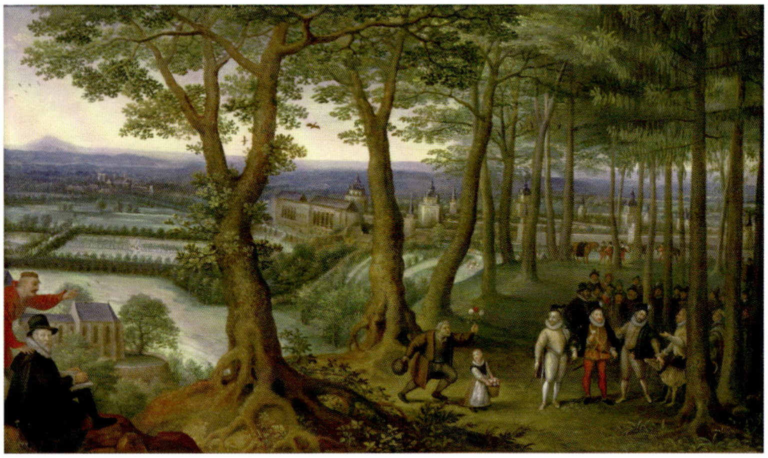

Fig. 3. Lucas van Valckenborch, *Emperor Rudolf II with his Brothers in front of the Neugebäude Palace*, c. 1593. Vienna, Kunsthistorisches Museum, Gemäldegalerie

characteristics of trees such as the European black pine (*Pinus nigra austriaca*). in 1576 he planted the first horse chestnut tree, which was brought by the imperial diplomat David Ungnad from Constantinople to Vienna, and a few years later the potato, which he had received from the New World through the Netherlands. Clusius also noted that wildflowers from the Alps were being sold in the Viennese markets, and were used as table decorations. Clusius stayed for only a few years in Vienna; after the death of Maximilian II, Rudolf II did not employ him further.

Rombertus Dodonaeus was, like Clusius, a botanist and had achieved celebrity in Antwerp thanks to the publication of his *Cruydeboek* in 1554. He came in 1574 as the emperor's personal physician to Vienna, but was apparently uncomfortable in the atmosphere of the court and, as Johann Crato observed, stayed only a few years in Vienna and was released by Emperor Rudolf II in 1580. Another important figure of Late Humanism was Augerius Ghislain de Busbecq, who had already come to the court of Emperor Ferdinand I in 1551 and was sent as an ambassador to Constantinople. In the sixties he accompanied the older sons of Maximilian II, the Archdukes Rudolf and Ernst, to Spain. From 1566 until 1574 he acted as tutor to the younger sons of Maximilian II in Vienna. From Constantinople he brought not only valuable late antique and Byzantine manuscripts as the *Vienna Dioscorides*[30] to Vienna, but also decorative plants new to central Europe, such as tulips and lilacs. Lilac was depicted shortly thereafter for the first time in 1565 in Matthioli's botanical work. The first blooming lilacs in Busbecq's garden in the Seilerstätte caused quite a sensation in 1566; his house was thereafter called "Zur Hollerstaude" and the bastion neighbouring the gatehouse, "Hollerstaudenbastei"[31].

Vice-chancellor Johann Zasius also belonged to the circle of Late Humanists at the court of Vienna. He had been hired by Maximilian II's father and worked until 1570 in the imperial chancellery. He also appointed Hugo Blotius (1534-1608) as head of the court library in 1575. Blotius also worked as a professor of rhetoric at the university of Vienna. He created the oldest inventory of the court library in 1576. At the university, he encountered as co-worker the Hellenist and law historian Georg Tanner (1520-1580). The Humanist Johannes Sambucus (1531-1584)[32] was appointed as court historian since 1566, following the intellectual and politician Wolfgang Lazius. After his death, his rival Blotius acquired his books for the court library under Rudolf II.

The most dazzling figure among the intellectuals in Maximilian II's court was undoubtedly Jacopo Strada (1515-1588)[33], who combined antiquarian skill with a unique artistic activity, whose actual gift lay in his organizational abilities in securing antique artworks for royal collectors. In doing so, he procured works of art primarily for Duke Albrecht of Bavaria, but also Hans Jakob Fugger, Giovanni Giacomo de' Medici, Margrave von Marignano and Cardinal Farnese. In addition, he also acted on behalf of the cities of Nuremberg and Lyon in the fifties. As an artist, he limited himself to initial concepts and left them to be carried out by others, whom he oversaw as *un sopra capo*[34].

In 1554 Strada dedicated his volume on Roman coins to Ferdinand I and received an honorary gift in return; in 1556 he made himself available to Archduke Ferdinand II in Prague to oversee the design of a silver sculpture showing the creation of Adam and Eve (which was not made due to a lack of silver) to be cast by Wenzel Jamnitzer. In 1557 Strada met in Regensburg Maximilian II for the first time, who showed interest in the second volume of his work on coins. In 1558 Strada relocated from Nuremberg to Vienna and entered into the Emperor's service. In 1559-60 he was a member of the commission which oversaw the completion of Maximilian's tomb and came to the decision to create the sarcophagus from stone. Ferdinand I later entrusted him and his expertise with the creation of his own tomb in Prague.

In the first years of his stay in Vienna, Strada was the master architect. Lietzmann[35] suspects that he was the creator of the Stallburg, Maximilian II's residence, which was begun in 1559. After the transfer of power to Maximilian II, he received a second position in the court as an antiquarian and was designated as "His Imperial Majesty's Supervisor of the Art Collection"[36]. His financial situation was so thriving that he acquired a house on Schenkenstraße (today Löwelstraße), which he tore down and replaced with a new *palazzo all'italiana*. On the basis of stylistic similarities with the *Antiquarium* of the Munich residence[37] and of a letter by Hans Jakob Fugger to Strada[38], the *Neugebäude Palace* in Vienna, Maximilian II's greatest artistic project, can be attributed to Jacopo Strada (*fig. 3*). The acquisition of a large collection of antiques on behalf of Archduke Albert V of Bavaria in 1567 in Italy, the design of the *Antiquarium* in Munich for the display of this collection and the simultaneous design of the *Neugebäude Palace* in Vienna represent the high point of Strada's activity; after 1569 the Bavarian court distanced itself from Strada, whose business practices appeared dishonest. The completion of the *Antiquarium* in the Munich residence went on without Strada. In Strada's portrait by Titian[39] – who was said to have had a very low opinion of him: "uno delli solenni ignorati que si possa trouare"[40] – the expensive clothes, a golden necklace, the animated twisting motion with which he presents the viewer an antique statue, and finally the coins on the table, which for the contemporary viewer appear to refer to Strada's numismatic publication as well as his professional success as an art dealer – all represent an unsurpassed depiction of a somewhat dubious character.

The construction history of the *Neugebäude Palace*[41] begins with the acquisition of the estate of Ebersdorf east of Vienna and an enclosed pheasant garden on the Danube. Two years later Maximilian II decided to lay out three gardens further south above and below the steep banks of the Danube, which were later enlarged in an expansion of the original plans with an elongated castle structure parallel to the bank on its upper edge. The upper, roughly square garden with a side length of more than 300 meters was surrounded by an outer wall with turrets and planted with trees; in an interior *giardino segreto* with flower beds was a flat-roofed arcade (through which one could walk with views of the garden) bordered by hexagonal towers in the corners. The lower garden was laid out in terraces; a flower garden connected to a pond (*fig. 4*). All the gardens were provided with an abundant supply of water and equipped with numerous fountains. At the southern end of the enclosure a pump house was erected (today the administrative building of a crematorium). First, in 1568, various fruit trees were planted. From an exact, daily itemization by the court gardener Seiniß in 1581[42], demonstrating the bounty of the harvest, there is an account of "three types of cherries, red, black and French varieties" (8 June), "large apricots [...] a basket full of common apricots, a small basket of blue damascènes and 14 mirabelles" (9 July), "of two types of pears, figs, three types of plums and peaches" (26 August), "four types of peaches, a basket of grapes, two types of plums" (20 September).

After a modification of the plan in 1573, the construction of the *Neue Gepeus* was begun, whose incomplete and empty skeleton is all that remains of the enclosure today, while the garden annexes, after decades of neglect, were abandoned in the 18th century. After Maximilian II's death in 1576, construction proceeded sluggishly; the upper story with its columned balcony and view of the Danube was completed, until Rudolf II, who in the intervening period had relocated his residence to Prague, definitively stopped the works. The *Neugebäude Palace* remained unfinished after almost twenty year of building. The planned interior design was probably not

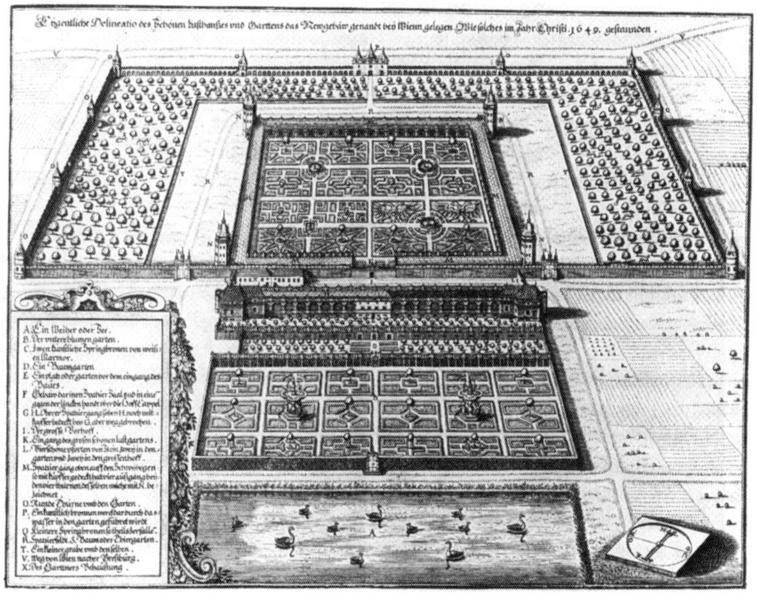

Fig. 4. Matthäus Merian, *View of the Neugebäude*, 1649. Engraving

even begun. Lietzmann[43] has attempted to identify a series of scenes from Roman history, "Giulio Licinio nel giardino di Eberstorf [ha] lavorato nella Turre di Picheto", as a part of the furnishings of the *Neugebäude's* central, jutting body. In 1575 Maximilian II summoned Bartholomäus Spranger and the sculptor Hans Mont from Italy to complete the four unfinished towers of the upper garden. All that remains is a preliminary drawing[44] for a ceiling painting depicting the Olympic gods.

Characteristic of the *Neugebäude,* and unique north of the Alps, is the combination of the architecture and the gardens, which is modelled after the Italian style, such as the Palazzo Te in Mantua, but also the Villa d'Este in Tivoli. The elongated and narrow building is similar to French gallery construction and finds a parallel in the *Antiquarium* in Munich, which can be traced back to a design by Jacopo Strada as well[45].

Since the 17th century a legend has it, that the enclosure of the *Neugebäude*[46] was the location of Sultan Süleyman I's camp during the Turkish occupation of Vienna in 1529 and that the architectural form of the enclosure can be traced back to that Turkish encampment.

The original destination of the *Neugebäude Palace* is uncertain. Obviously it was not planned to be a residential castle outside the city gates as a *villa suburbana*, but rather a *palazzo di natura*, as it was described by Hans Jakob Fugger[47], perhaps to house Maximilian II's art collection[48], who had an interest primarily in antique sculpture as well as in contemporary sculpture and painting. The fountain begun by Wenzel Jamnitzer in 1569, which was completed under Rudolf II after Maximilian II's death (its only remains are

four allegorical features of the *Seasons* cast by Johann Gregor van Schardt)[49], was perhaps intended for the *Neugebäude Palace*.
After the sudden death of Maximilian II in 1576, his eldest son Rudolf II assumed control as his heir in Austria, Bohemia and Hungary and became emperor as well. Rudolf's political and cultural education had been considerably influenced by the many years spent at the court of Philip II in Spain. Upon the insistence of Ferdinand I and Queen Maria, but against the will of Maximilian II, Rudolf, at the age of twelve, was sent with his younger brother Ernst to Spain, where he spent seven years until 1571. As a consequence – in complete contrast to Maximilian II – Rudolf's unwavering Catholicism was never in question. On the other hand, his political opinions remained independent from Spain, as he elevated *dissimulatio* as the highest principle of his political dealings being listened to the opinions of his advisors renowned for his unwillingness to take part in advisory discussions, he listened but remained independent from them making his own decisions and, at least in the first years of his reign, asserting himself decisively[50].
In Spain, the intellectually and artistically gifted but shy and introverted young man was deeply impressed by Philip II's art collection and patronage of the arts, by the painting of Titian and Hieronymus Bosch as well as by the gigantic construction activity at the Escorial, the cloister residence founded by Philip II outside Madrid. Here he developed his understanding of art, and his belief that not just the subject matter is important, but rather the artistic quality of the work. In this way Rudolf II became a true connoisseur and lover of art, who cultivated patronage and art collecting not just as a necessary element of holding court, but out of a true love of art, which aroused in him an enthusiasm bordering on obsession.
Crucial for the further political, but also cultural, development was the relocation of the imperial residence from Vienna to Prague, which was the most important city of the region as well as the capital of the Bohemian crown, ruling over Bohemians, Moravians and Silesians. In terms of political importance, such as economic ability, kingdom of Bohemia far surpassed that of the Austrian Archduchy. From the autumn of 1578 to December of 1581 Rudolf stayed in Prague without interruption. The official announcement of the permanent relocation of the imperial residence to Prague took place during the Bohemian Diet in November of 1583. The decision to relocate had been taken by Rudolf much earlier, however, as demonstrates the construction activity at the Prague Castle since the late 70s. As a result, the work on the construction project taken over from Maximilian II on the *Neugebäude* first slowed down and then suddenly ceased. The artists, who had come to Vienna shortly before to work on its improvement, such as Bartholomäus Spranger and Hans Mont, were summoned in 1580 to Prague. Maximilian II's long-tenured "portraitist" Giuseppe Arcimboldo, Giulio Licinio and Martino Rota also relocated their activities to Prague. Little is known of their work in the 80s, however[51]. Of Arcimboldo's work for Rudolf all that remain are the portrait of the Emperor with the crown of the Holy Roman Empire (cat no. III.11), which was created on the occasion of Rudolf's coronation, and some books with costume designs and carnival processions, dedicated to Emperor Rudolf II in 1585[52]. The famous portrait of Rudolf II as Vertumnus (cat. no. IV.38), often used to demonstrate the almost symbiotic affinity between the Emperor and his court painters, was created after Arcimboldo's return to Milan, as was the painting of Flora, for which the old court painter was named *comes palatinus*.
The activities of the older court painters of Italian origin ended with the end of the 80s; Martino Rota died in 1583, Giuseppe Arcimboldo returned to Milan in 1588, Giulio Licinio returned to Venice in 1589. Bartholomäus Spranger became the leading painter in the court of Rudolf II in that period. His personal style, influenced by international late Mannerism, in which he combined his Dutch origins with years of experience in Italy, forms a point of entry for a specific "Rudolphine" style. Spranger became a leading figure in a courtly art whose visual content was influenced by the personal preferences of the emperor; an art which has long fascinated researchers and audiences[53] and has replaced the interest in the culture of the court of Maximilian II. Hans Ulrich Krafft refers to no other court artists except Spranger during his visit to Prague in 1584 and tells of the emperor's daily visits to the artist's studio, which was located in the Prague Castle[54].
Generous patronage of the work of his court artists, a passion for collecting and a dogged pursuit of his goals, as well as the possession of masterworks of the early 16th century by Dürer and Cranach, Correggio and Parmigianino, depict Rudolf II as a true lover of art. Of equal importance is his interest in the natural sciences, which already played a role in the court of Ferdinand I and were further advanced under Maximilian II, who, with the employment of Tycho Brahe and later Johannes Kepler, shifted the focus from medicine and botany to astronomy and mathematics[55]. Alongside the brilliant and effective empirical thinking, alchemy, astrology and pansophy played an important role[56]; dark, mysterious sciences, whose artistic quality has been found by modern audiences in the enigmatic works of Arcimboldo.

[1] On Ferdinand I in general, lastly: Vienna 2003; Kohler 2003.
[2] Monograph on Maximilian II: Bibl 1929; Edelmayer-Kohler 1992; lastly Sutter Fichtner 2001.
[3] Additionally, Winkelbauer 2003; compare also Duindam 2004, 21.
[4] Sutter Fichtner 2001, 11, 14.
[5] Kohler 2003, 269; Laubach 2003, 131.
[6] Kohler 2003, 118ff.
[7] In general regarding Elias 1981; Müller 2004; especially for Early Modern

Austrian courts Winkelbauer 2003; Pauser, Scheutz, Winkelbauer 2004; Rauscher 2004.
[8] According to the account of Ladislaus Zierotin from 1590 (Lietzmann 1987, 45).
[9] Kaufmann 1978a.
[10] Sutter Fichtner 2001, 36f.
[11] Sutter Fichtner 2001, 47.
[12] Sutter Fichtner 2001, 57.
[13] Sutter Fichtner 2001.
[14] Kohler 2003, 299f.; Winkelbauer 2003, 44.
[15] Lhotsky 1941-45, 179-202; Luchner 1958; Ambras 1977; Scheicher 1979; Ambras 1981; Ambras 2002.
[16] Account of the Venetian ambassador, Giacomo Soranzo, 1563 (Fiedler 1870, 216-217; cited from Lietzmann 1987, 26).
[17] Account of the Venetian ambassador, Giovanni Michiel, 1571 (Fiedler 1870, 277-279; cited from Lietzmann 1987, 26).
[18] Giacomo Soranzo 1563; Bibl 1929, 30; Lietzmann 1987, 26; Sutter Fichtner 2001, 9.
[19] Sutter Fichtner 2001, 101ff.
[20] Lhotsky 1941-45, 176.
[21] Mout 2000, 53.
[22] F. Koreny, in Rosenauer 2003, 567.
[23] Trunz 1931-1965, 147-181; Hammerstein 2000, 9ff.
[24] Mühlberger 1992, 212; Kaufmann 1993, 136ff.; Mout 2000, 54.
[25] Mout 2000, 53; Sutter Fichtner 2001, 101.
[26] Mout 2000, 46, 58.
[27] Oestreich 1989.
[28] Sutter Fichtner 2001, 85, 97.
[29] Bibl 1929, 403; Lhotsky 1941-45, 176; Mout 2000, 54; Sutter Fichtner 2001, 101.
[30] Vienna, ÖNB, Handschriftensammlung (Collection of Manuscripts), *Cod. Med. gr. 1.*
[31] Bibl 1929, 406.
[32] Mout 2000, 55f.
[33] Lhotsky 1941-45, 160ff.; Lietzmann 1987, 110ff.; Lietzmann 1988, 176ff; Jansen 1988, 132ff; Mout 2000, 56.
[34] Lhotsky 1941-45, 161.
[35] Lietzmann 1987, 114.
[36] Jansen 1988, 135.
[37] Wagner Rieger 1951, 142.
[38] Lietzmann 1987, 110.
[39] Vienna, Kunsthistorisches Museum, Gemäldegalerie.
[40] Cited from Lietzmann 1987, 126, note 136.
[41] Lietzmann 1987; Lietzmann 1988, 176ff.; Holzschuh 1989, 366-369; Holzschuh – Hofer, in Rosenauer 2003, 290f.; lastly Hajós 2007, 47.
[42] Vienna, Hofkammerarchiv, NÖHA N.14, fol. 300-304 (Lietzmann 1987, 206ff., Document no. 2).
[43] Lietzmann 1987, 150; compare Stockhammer, in Rosenauer 2003, 495 and note 10.
[44] Vienna, Albertina (Kaufmann 1988c, no. 20.2; Stockhammer, in Rosenauer 2003, 495).
[45] Holzschuh – Hofer, in Rosenauer 2003, 281.
[46] Lietzmann 1987, 9ff.
[47] Lietzmann 1987, 169.
[48] Lhotsky 1941-45, 166.
[49] Vienna, Kunsthistorisches Museum, Kunstkammer.
[50] Evans 1988, 27ff.
[51] Fučikova 1988, 178.
[52] Beyer 1983, 124.
[53] Kaufmann 1988c; Essen-Vienna 1988; Prague 1997; Dijon 2002.
[54] Fučikova 1988, 179.
[55] Horsky 1988, 73.
[56] Trunz 1988, 57.

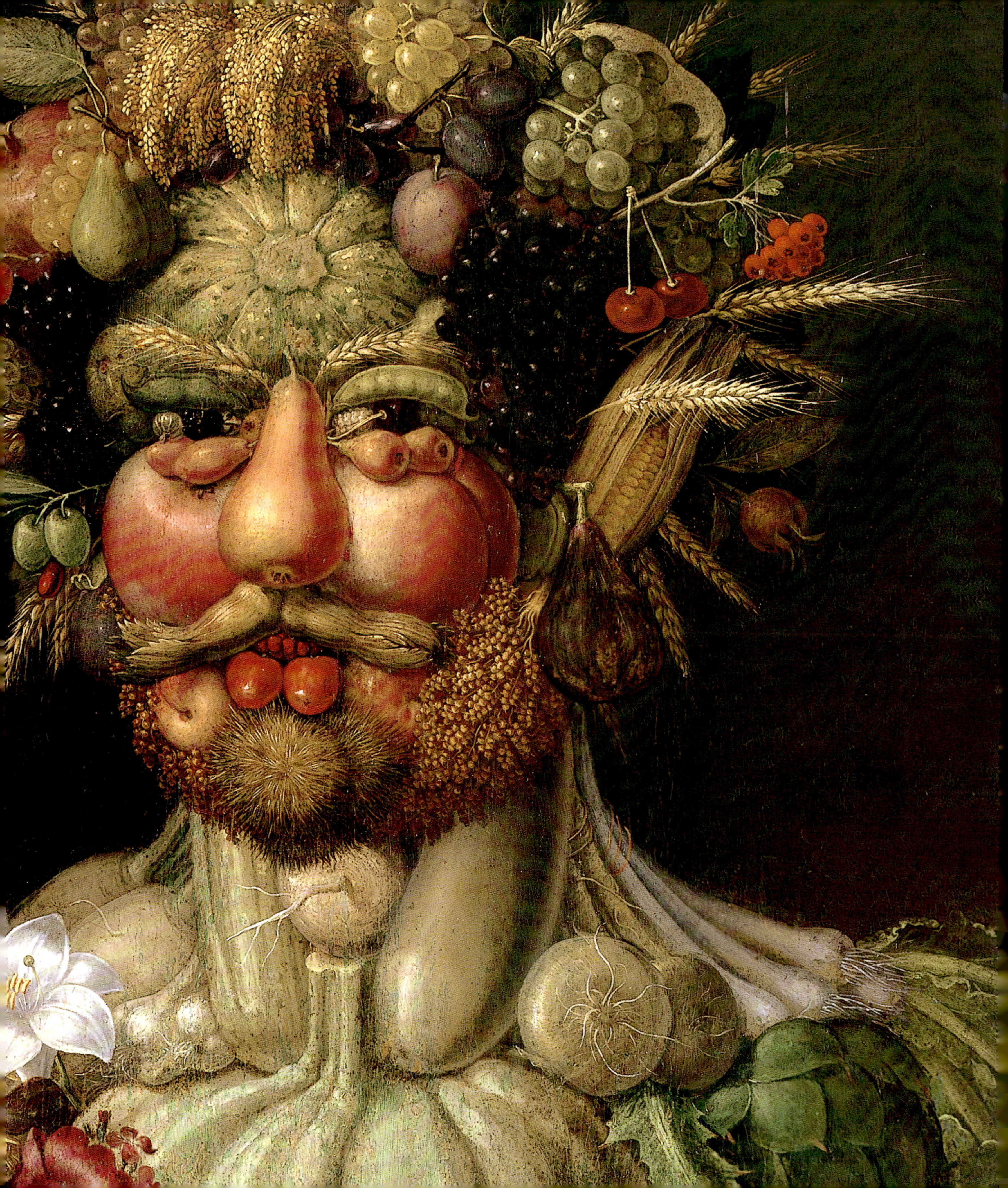

Karl Schütz

Der Rom. Kay. Mt. conterfeter: Giuseppe Arcimboldo as portrait-painter to the Holy Roman Emperor

There is no documented evidence of Giuseppe Arcimboldo's employment in Vienna; neither do we know whey the artist chose a position in Vienna or what led him to be appointed to the emperor's court. There is also no evidence for the supposition that Arcimboldo went to Vienna on the invitation of Maximilian II[1] and that he belonged to this court from the beginning.

The earliest documents supporting his sojourn in Vienna are from 1563: on the one hand, the surviving paintings, whose origins are not recorded in written documents, and on the other, a document about a work that no longer exists. The paintings in question are from the *Seasons* series of 1563, of which *Summer* and *Winter* remain (cat. nos IV.3-4), and the document is a letter from the emperor's treasurer, Swetkowycz, to Ferdinand I, in which he discusses a portrait of the emperor to be copied by Arcimboldo[2]. The emperor had advised his treasurer to send him a portrait taken from the Viennese Kunstkammer and to have another one copied by Arcimboldo – referred to not by his full name, but rather as "maister Joseph irer maj. maller" ("Master Joseph, His Majesty's Painter"). At the time of Swetkowycz's letter to Ferdinand I, Arcimboldo had still not completed it, but continued to work on it for about another week. Swetkowycz pointed out that the painter "gar wol damit beshten wierdt" ("will do just fine"), giving the impression that Arcimboldo's painting ability was being put to the test with this assigned work, as if it were a sort of trial job.

Whether the series of the *Seasons* was intended for Ferdinand I or Maximilian II can not be determined from the existing sources. Nonetheless, the evidence points more strongly towards Maximilian, who, shortly before the paintings' creation, had been crowned as the King of Bohemia in Prague in 1562; a few months later, in December 1562, he was chosen by the princes-electors as the Roman King, and in August 1563 was finally crowned as the King of Hungary.

Regular documentations of Giuseppe Arcimboldo's appointment as the court painter first appear in 1565 in the court registers. Arcimboldo earned a set income of 20 florins per month[3] and additional sums for delivered works[4] – "various portraits and beautiful paintings" as they were referred to around September 1565. These included portraits as well as other unspecified pictures, about which we may only speculate whether they were conventional works or perhaps *teste composte*.

Around 1565 there was reference to many painters at the service of Maximilian II. Along with Seisenegger (who, because of his age and his prolonged activity, did not receive a regular court pay, but rather a *honorarium*)[5], Domenico and Hieronymus Pozzo, Giulio Licinio and Giuseppe Arcimboldo received regular court income. Along with them, other predominately Italian painters were paid on a case-by-case basis[6]. Both Pozzos were busy painting the interior of the Czech Deputies chamber (*Landsrechtstube*) of the Prague Castle in 1564 and were therefore paid by the Bohemian exchequer[7]. Licinio worked on the interior of the chapel of the Pressburg Castle and was therefore paid by the Hungarian exchequer[8]. On the last day of 1565, Giulio Licinio and Giuseppe Arcimboldo received their annual salaries from the court treasury[9]. Other painters are not referred to in this context, indicating that only these two were paid by the court treasury. In addition, a few days later, on 1 January 1566 and on 29 January 1566, Jakob Seisenegger and Arcimboldo[10] received gifts of 34 and 28 florins, respectively. Giulio Licinio had already received a contribution of 100 florins in December. Along with this, Antonio Abondio is mentioned as having received a one-time payment in 1566.

Arcimboldo was active in Vienna since the beginning of his employment at the emperor's court, and not in Prague, as is sometimes presumed. Until the end of 1566, Ferdinand II was still serving as governor in Bohemia[11] and was accordingly mentioned in connection with the activity of Domenico Pozzo.

In June 1566, with accompaniment and with his entire household and personal belongings, Arcimboldo returned to Italy and received a letter of passage (*Paßbrief*) from the emperor[12] as well as 100 florins "for his expenses in Italy"[13]: Because the pass was not issued for the artist alone, but also for his accompaniment and his travel resources, it seems that Arcimboldo had planned a lengthy stay in his homeland. It can be presumed that the series of the *Four Elements* dated 1566 had been created earlier on. In the two following years, the court account books mention Giulio Licinio and Antonio Abondio, not Arcimboldo, as the court painters; he therefore

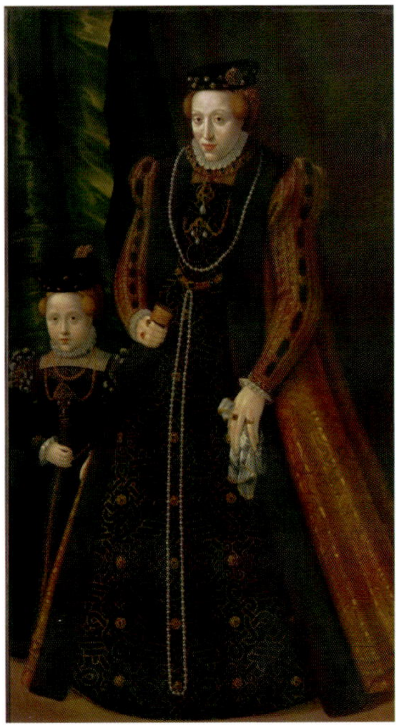

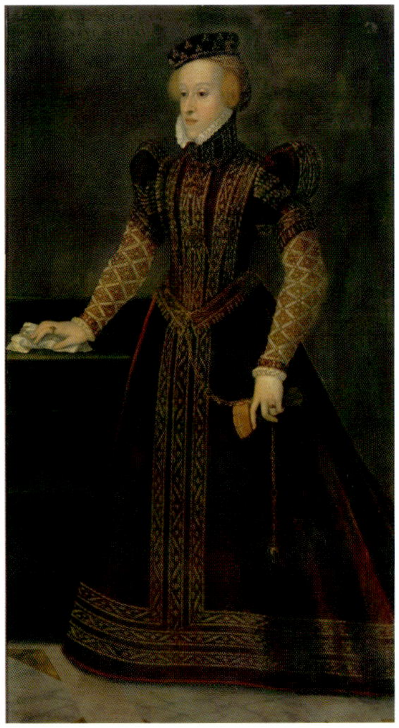

Fig. 1. Jakob Seisenegger, *Archduchess Maria with her elder Daughter Maria Eleonore*, c. 1555. Vienna, Kunsthistorisches Museum, Gemäldegalerie

Fig. 2. Francesco Terzio, *Archduchess Barbara*, 1565. Vienna, Kunsthistorisches Museum, Gemäldegalerie

seems to have remained in Italy. Only in March 1569[14] and in the following year[15] "Joseph Arcimboldo" again appears in the account books as "court painter".

In 1574, the "portraitist and painter of the court of His Majesty the Roman Emperor" Arcimboldo received 65 florins "for painting and work", that he had completed by order of Emperor Maximilian II for the prince-elector, August von Sachsen[16], with no further description of the type or subject of the work. Finally, in 1575, portraits are explicitly mentioned – "numerous portraits" – "based on a list" (which unfortunately no longer exists), that he completed for Maximilian II[17].

In 1576 Arcimboldo was named "portraitist and painter of His Majesty, the late Emperor of Rome" and was paid through the Court Treasurer's Office in the absence of the emperor's valet, Francisco Caprin[18]. In December of the same year Arcimboldo, along with Antonio Abondio, was named "portraitist and painter" in the "order and court" of the new Emperor, Rudolf II; they each earned 20 florins per month[19]. In 1581, Arcimboldo's court stipend was raised from 20 to 30 florins per month. He received the last payment at the end of November 1586, at which time he was given 1500 florins, somewhat more than four regular yearly salaries, as "faithful and well-loved court painter and portraitist to whom, for his steadfast loyalty and ambitious work, we dedicate this contribution and liquidation of the court"[20].

Around the middle of the 16th century, court portraiture throughout Europe had a homogeneous form with few local distinctions and a similarity of tasks, wherein the full-figure portrait dominated as the most representative form. Accordingly, smaller-format portraits, half-figures and busts have more private character, in which case the demand for likeness predominates over the representative function.

As the court painter of Ferdinand I, Jakob Seisenegger (1505-1567) dominated the evolution of the representative portrait in Austria over the course of many decades, from 1530 to 1560. The portraits of Ferdinand I and his numerous children either originated from Seisenegger himself or refer to the portrait types and formats that he coined. Seisenegger followed Italian, and above all Venetian, models[21], as did Francesco Terzio, who worked as the court painter of Archduke Ferdinand II from 1551 to 1571, first in Prague and then in Innsbruck, both simplifying and generalizing his portraits to such an extent that their individual characters seemed interchangeable. This was the situation of court portraiture in Austria that Giuseppe Arcimboldo encountered as he began his court activity at approximately the same time as the Venetian Giulio Licinio. Arcimboldo by no means openly attempted to oppose the portrait ideal of Seisenegger's individual formal solutions, but rather he assimilated the style of the earlier portraits so completely that his portraits carry no personal stylistic characteristics.

Maximilian's personal taste in portraits was formed through the Seisenegger tradition, which he knew from Vienna and moreover through Dutch painters, who in part had been active in Spain. In their youth, after he and his younger brother, Ferdinand II, had joined the court of Charles V in 1544 and travelled through Germany and the Netherlands, the brothers – possibly in 1544 at the Diet in Speyer – were painted by a Netherlandish portraitist[22]. Perhaps this painter was Guillaume Scrots, who at that time was completing a series of portraits of Austrian aristocrats from the entourage of princes, which are in the portrait book of Hieronymus Beck of Leopoldsdorf, a private collection of portraits in gouache compiled between 1570 and 1580[23]. In 1550 and 1551 respectively, during Maximilian II's sojourn in Spain, Anthonis Mor painted the representative portraits of Maximilian and his wife, Anna[24]; he was the leading Netherlandish portraitist, working in Brussels and Spain from 1549 to 1554 as the court painter of Charles V. Maximilian was passionately interested in the creation of family portraits, and he himself chose the colours of the clothing and the jewellery to be worn[25].

In the Viennese Castle in the third quarter of the 16th century there was already a small portrait gallery of half-figure paintings of standardized format, representing both living members of the House of Austria as well as historical figures. The remains of this painting gallery are conserved in the Kunsthistorisches Museum, and some copies of portraits were passed down in the portrait book of Hieronymus Beck[26].

In the account books where Arcimboldo's payments are recorded, no specific work is named; therefore, there is no documentary evidence for his portraits until the copy he made of an existing portrait of Ferdinand I at the very beginning of his activity in Vienna. Based on the assumption that among the works that Arcimboldo created during his decades-long activity as "conterfetter und maller" ("portraitist and painter"), for which he received a regular court stipend, he must have also painted portraits, Günther Heinz[27] attempted to define a group of paintings attributable to Giuseppe Arcimboldo among the enormous quantity of anonymous portraits that were created at the Habsburg court in the period between 1550 and 1580, and which have been preserved till today. Criteria for this attribution were on the one hand the formal structure of these portraits, which combined north Italian elements with a reference to Seisenegger's painting form, and on the other hand characteristic motifs, which Heinz described as a "bustle of small forms"[28], which recall the painter of the *teste composte*, thereby helping to close the gap between these two groups of Arcimboldo's work: those court portraits characterized by a strict thematic coherence on one side, and on the other those paintings distinguished by a great freedom, whose identity is assured by signatures.

The most important painting in the group that Heinz composed is the family portrait of Emperor Maximilian II (cat. no. III.4), which portrays Maximilian with his wife Maria, their eldest daughter Anna, born in 1549, and their two eldest sons, Rudolf, born in 1552, and Ernst, still in the cradle, born in June 1553. According to the number and age of the children, this painting can be dated quite precisely from the end of 1553. If this portrait was actually painted by Arcimboldo, it must therefore be a copy that he created approximately ten years after the creation of the (evidently lost) original. Some characteristics of its execution do in fact indicate the copied nature of the painting.

We have no indication that Arcimboldo was already working for Ferdinand I or Maximilian II before 1563. Evidence of this is the fact that the five coats of arms of the Kings of Bohemia[29] painted for the Cathedral of Milan were not paid for by Maximilian, but rather by the *Fabbrica del Duomo*.

Heinz developed the criteria for an attribution to Arcimboldo based on the details of this painting: "Influenced by Seisenegger, Arcimboldo evidently sought the simplicity of portraiture and only allowed an expression of his artistic individuality in the small details: thus, for example, a decorative border is reinterpreted as an animal in motion, which forms a unique contrast to the naive simplicity of the archduke's representation. With none of the Emperor's other court painters of this period do we see this strange activity of small forms, which is the expression of his creative exploration. The golden cradle of baby Archduke Ernst becomes a grotesque image made of animals and grinning masks that is only paralleled in Arcimboldo's decorative designs for sleighs. This animated microcosm stands in strong contrast to the strictness of the overall form of the portrait's composition, in which Seisenegger's influence can be seen"[30].

Stylistically closely related to the family portrait, on the other hand, is a full-figure individual portrait of Maria[31], which fully corresponds in the details of the clothing and of the stance, specifically in the hand with the handkerchief.

An isolated group, which nonetheless offers very little to be compared with the preceding full-figure portraits, is formed by two series of slightly varied formats, but closely related in view-framing, depicting young girls, possibly the daughters of Ferdinand I (cat. nos. III.5-10). Because of its similarity to other portraits of her, the portrait of the youngest daughter, Archduchess Johanna (later the Grand Duchess of Florence), can be quite safely determined (cat. no. III.9). Born in 1547 and married to Francesco de' Medici in 1565, this portrait shows the Archduchess at about the age of fifteen, and therefore must have been painted right at the beginning of Arcimboldo's activity in Vienna.

It seems evident that if these groups of paintings, similar in style and in characteristics, were actually created by Arcimboldo, it must have been in the first years of his activity in Vienna, and in any case before his protracted return to his Italian homeland in 1566. From his second, much longer sojourn in Vienna and later in Prague, there are no court portraits that can be attributed to his activity: evidently, Arcimboldo was active in other areas, such as the design of pageant decorations, whereas the family portraits were created by other painters, who either held permanent positions as court painters or were appointed for individual works.

As mentioned previously, both Giulio Licinio and Antonio Abondio were employed as painters in the Viennese court simultaneously with Arcimboldo. Licinio received regular payments until 1581 and it is possible that he was also busy with the painted decorations for the *Neugebäude Palace*[32]. In 1589 he received his last payments along with a contribution as "former court painter"[33]. Abondio received his court stipend as "portraitist" from 1566[34] through 1575[35], but was also active as a designer of medals[36]; in 1583 he definitively returned to his Italian homeland. In 1571 Johann (Juan) de Monte[37] received a contribution as court painter of Maximilian II[38] and a regular stipend from 1573[39]. It is questionable whether he is the same man as the portraitist in the Viennese court named Jacopo de Monte from 1587 to 1591, whom we later encounter in 1594 at the Court of Graz as the portraitist of Archduke Karl II, or whether he is a younger relative.

The Netherlandish portraitist Nicolas Neufchatel, who was paid under the name Nicolaus von New Cassel[40] in 1566 for portraits of the Emperor[41] and Archduchess Anna, apparently living in Nuremberg since 1561, was only momentarily employed by Maximilian II. Martino Rota (actually Martin Kolunić, born around 1520 in Sebenico, Dalmatia), working as Maximilian II's "portraitist and painter", was paid regularly. Rudolf II took him on in 1576 and paid him for his service until 1582[42]. However, the most significant painter of this period would be Bartholomäus Spranger, whom Maximilian II had already called to Vienna for the painted decoration of the *Neugebäude Palace*; he later followed Rudolf II to Prague and there, because of his Netherlandish schooling and extensive activity in Italy, founded an internationally oriented Late Mannerism, which remained tied to his name and that of his great patron, Emperor Rudolf II.

[1] Beyer 1983, 92.
[2] Document 2 (28 April 1563, V, 1887, Reg. 4344).
[3] Documents 5 and 7.
[4] Documents 4 and 6.
[5] Document 39.
[6] Document 59.
[7] Documents 32, 33, 38, 40, 42, 44, 45, 46, 47.
[8] Documents 41, 43, 48, 54, 55, 56, 57.
[9] Document 5 (Reg. 5013), document 61 (Reg. 5012).
[10] Document 6 (Reg. 5017).
[11] Bů?ek 2003, 283-295.
[12] Letter of passage from 2 June 1566, document 9 (15, Reg. 11869).
[13] Court treasury account from 2 June 1566, document 8 (7, Reg. 5037).
[14] Treasury account book 1969-70, document 10 (7, Reg. 5163).
[15] Doc. 11 (7, Reg. 5191).
[16] Doc. 12 (7, Reg. 5305).
[17] Doc. 14 (7, Reg. 5312).
[18] Comment on Reg. 5030 (7).
[19] Reg. 4556.
[20] Reg. 5475 and Reg. 11675.
[21] Heinz 1963, 105.
[22] Vienna, Kunsthistorisches Museum, Gemäldegalerie, exhibited in the Portrait Gallery in Ambras Castle (Ambras 1982, no. 51, 57; Vienna 2003, no. VII.19, VII.20).
[23] Vienna, Kunsthistorisches Museum, Gemäldegalerie (Heinz 1975).
[24] Madrid, Museo Nacional del Prado (Vienna 2003, no. VII.4, VII.5).
[25] Sutter Fichtner 2001, 22 and note 45.
[26] Heinz 1975, 174 and eg. plates 210, 227, 233, 234, 299.
[27] Heinz 1963, 108.
[28] Heinz 1963, 108.
[29] Beyer 1983, 92, note 2.
[30] Heinz 1963, 108.
[31] Vienna, Kunsthistorisches Museum, Gemäldegalerie (Heinz 1963, 108, cat. no. 179).
[32] Lietzmann 1987, 148ff.
[33] Reg. 5486.
[34] Reg. 5033.
[35] Reg. 5322.
[36] Vienna 1988.
[37] Lhotsky 1941-45, 175.
[38] Reg. 5267.
[39] Reg. 5307.
[40] Reg. 5032, Lhotsky 1941-45, 175.
[41] Heinz (in Ambras 1982, cat. no. 53) identified it with the portrait of Maximilian II provided in three versions; compare cat. no. III.2.
[42] Reg. 5348, 5392; compare portraits of Rudolf II and his brothers Ernst and Maximilian III (Vienna, Kunsthistorisches Museum, Gemäldegalerie, Vienna 1982, no. 74, 75; here cat. no. III.3).

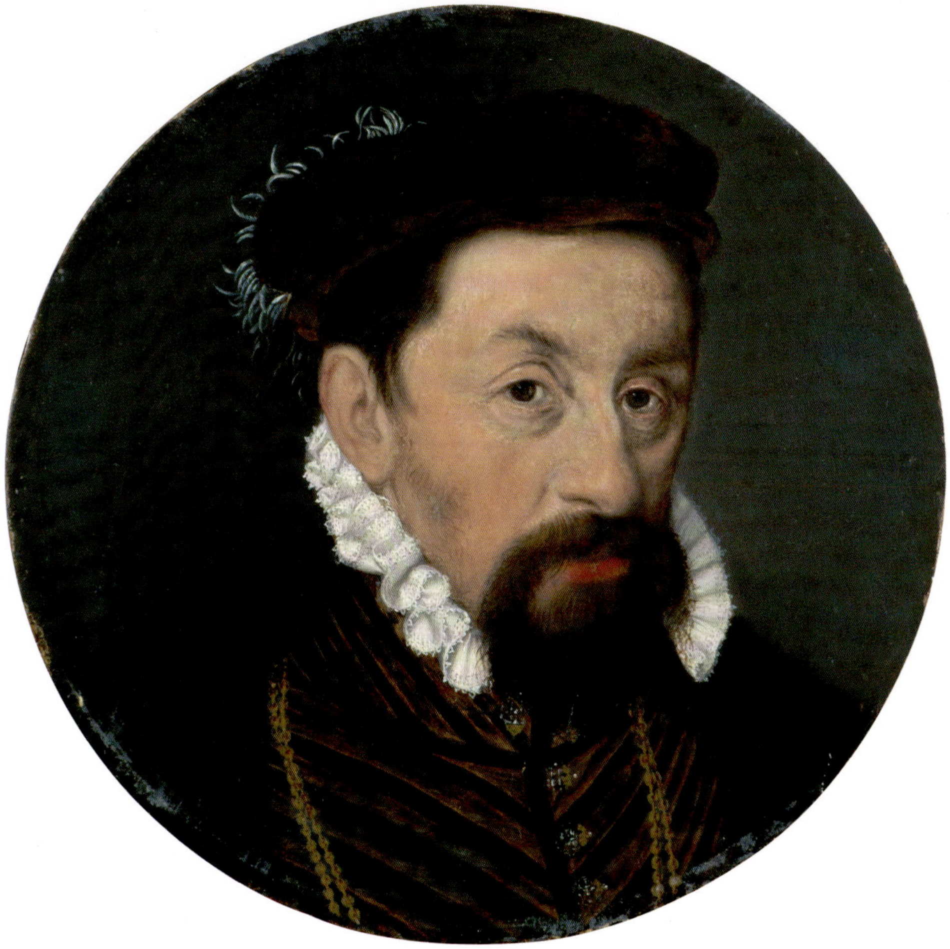

III.2

III.1
Austrian, 1580 circa, after Johann Bocksberger the Elder
(active in Salzburg around the middle of the 16th century)
Emperor Ferdinand I
1580 circa, Original 1550-55 circa
Oil on paper mounted on wood, 13.9 × 10.5 cm
Inscription: FERDINANDVS ROMANORVM IMPE(rator)
Vienna, Kunsthistorisches Museum, Gemäldegalerie, inv. no. 4666

This small-format bust of Emperor Ferdinand I originates from the portrait collection of Archduke Ferdinand II (1529-1595). Because of the division of the Habsburg territories among the sons of Ferdinand I, Ferdinand II resided in Innsbruck since 1567 and had the Ambras Castle built for his art collection. From about 1578 he created a collection of famous personalities from the past and from his own time, ultimately composed of some 1,000 portraits of the same format. On the one hand, it included members of the various ruling families, which he acquired through requests addressed to the European courts; on the other hand a selection of celebrities drawing also from the painting collection of Paolo Giovio.
The original of this bust is a full-figure portrait of Ferdinand I, which Heinz attributes to the Salzburg painter Johann Bocksberger the Elder. Before this it had been considered a work of Jakob Seisenegger, the court painter of Ferdinand I, or perhaps a copy by Francesco Terzio from Bergamo, who had served as the portraitist for Archduke Ferdinand II.

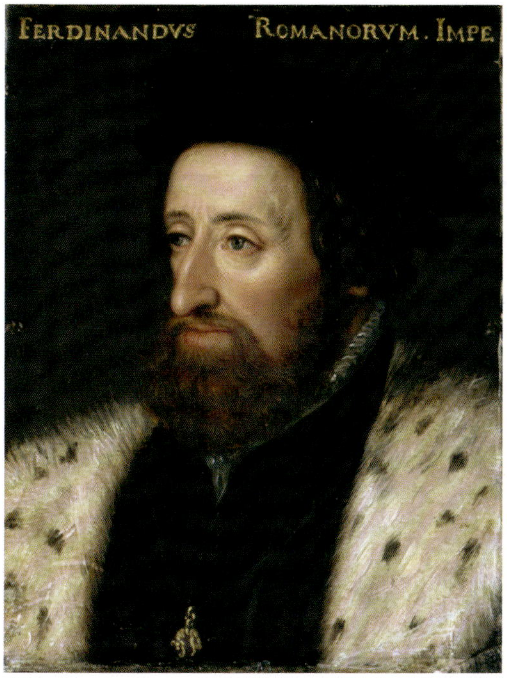

III.1

Because of the age of Ferdinand I in this portrait, in contrast to other portraits, above all that of Titian, which was created after the Battle of Mühlberg in 1548 (original lost, copies among others in the Fugger-Babenhausen collection, Babenhausen Castle and in the Prado, Madrid), Bocksberger's original can be dated between 1550 and 1555.
Over the black, Spanish garb, Ferdinand I wears a half-length, fur-lined cloak, whose broad collar in the form of a "Schaube", resembles the traditional German overcoat.

Karl Schütz

Bibliography: Kenner 1893, 141, no. 151; Ladner 1932, no. H 151; Hilger 1969, 149, no. 15. On Bocksberger's original: Heinz 1963, 107, 185, no. 1; Vienna 1976-82, no. 27; Vienna 2003a, cat. no. XI.16; Berlin 2006, cat. no. III.29.

III.2
After Nicolas Neufchatel (1527-1567)
Emperor Maximilian II
after 1566
Oil on round panel
Ø 19.5 cm
Vienna, Kunsthistorisches Museum, Gemäldegalerie, inv. no. 9080

Nicolas Neufchatel was born in 1527 in Mons (Hainaut) and studied in Antwerp under Pieter Coecke van Aelst; he was forced to leave his homeland because of his Calvinistic religious beliefs and was active in Nuremberg from 1561 to 1567, where he became the most widely known portraitist of the urban patriciates.
In 1566 Nicolas Neufchatel was paid for the portraits of Emperor Maximilian II and Archduchess Anna. There is good reason to believe that the portrait at hand as well as other similar portraits of Maximilian derive from this one. Of the three versions completed by Neufchatel, not one original remains; the various formats of the traditional version are certainly reproductions from his studio.
Along with a half-length version (Vienna, Kunsthistorisches Museum, Gemäldegalerie), whose original

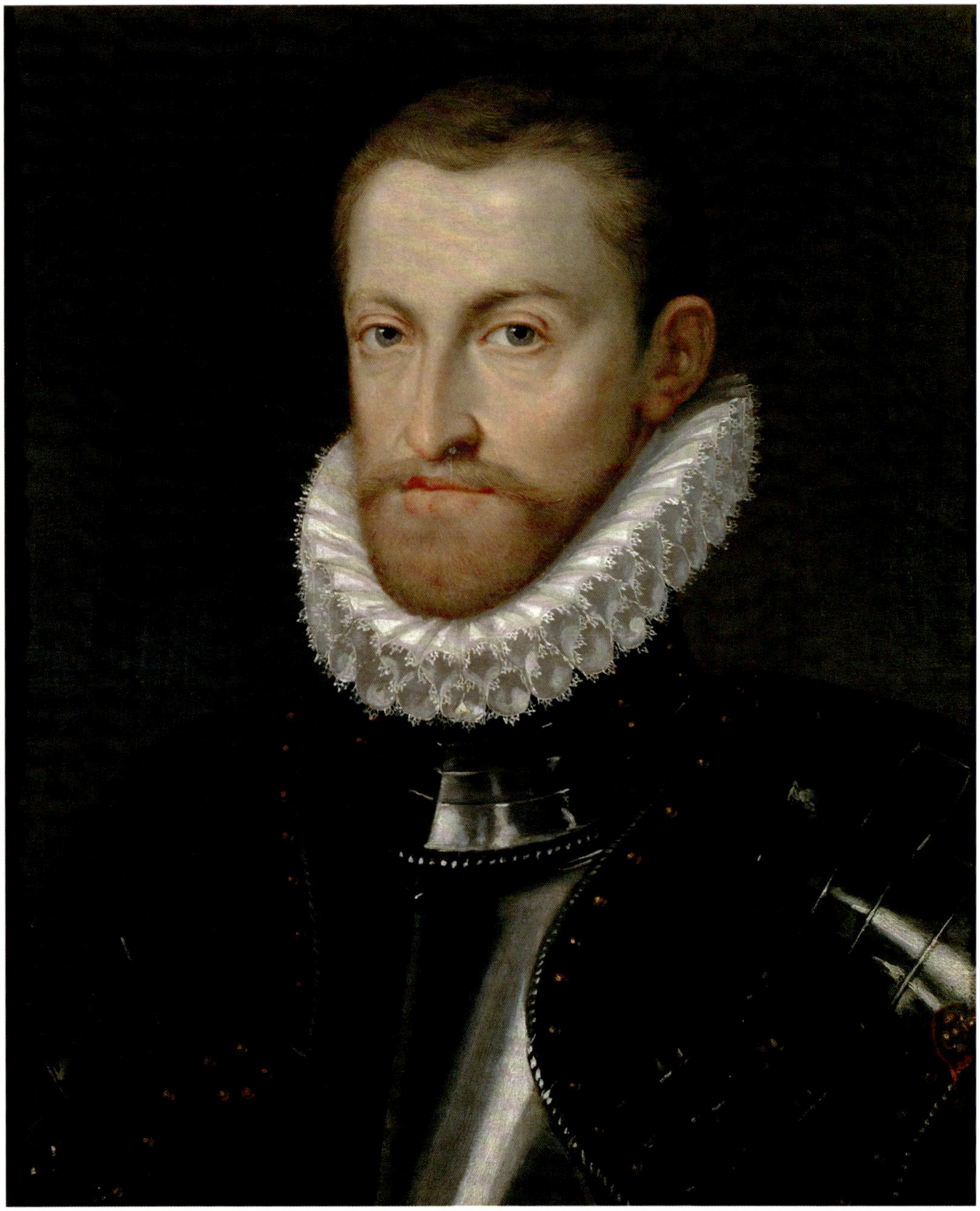

III.3

composition can perhaps be seen in one of the miniatures in the portrait book of Hieronymus Beck from Leopoldsdorf, there exists a version with a similar composition in the Neuhuys Collection, Paris, as well as an additional bust version in the reserve of the painting gallery of the Kunsthistorisches Museum. Another knee-length version was also copied in the portrait book of Hieronymus Beck.
This round version, which focuses on the head of the sitter, was probably created in Neufchatel's workshop.
The picture does not belong to what was once the emperor's old painting gallery, but rather was acquired in 1944 on the Viennese art market.

Karl Schütz

Bibliography: Reg. 5032 (Jahrbuch der Kunsthistorischen Sammlungen des Allerhöchsten Kaiserhauses, 7, 1888); Peltzer 1926, 220; Lhotsky 1941-45, 175; Heinz 1963, 186, no. 4; Heinz 1975, 216, no. 31, 32; Vienna 1976-82, cat. no. 54; Madrid 1998, cat. no. 286.

III.3
Martino Rota (circa 1520-1583)
Emperor Rudolf II in armor, bust
circa 1576-80
Oil on canvas, 51 × 42 cm
Vienna, Kunsthistorisches Museum, Gemäldegalerie, inv. no. 2587

Martino Rota (actually Martin Kolunić) from Sebenico in Dalmatia served as the court painter for Maximilian II since 1568, especially for portraits. Rudolf II acknowledged him in this role in 1576, when he appeared as graphic artist, painter and draftsman for medals.
The portrait of Rudolf II may have been created in 1576 with his crowning following the death of his father, Maximilian II. It belongs to a series of busts of the emperor and his younger brothers, Archdukes Ernst and Maximilian III (all Vienna, Kunsthistorisches Museum, Gemäldegalerie). These busts, smaller versions of larger and therefore more representative portraits, must have been created as first drafts. Two of these larger portraits have been preserved – those of Archduke Ernst (New York, Hispanic Society of America) and Maximilian III (Vienna, Kunsthistorisches Museum, Gemäldegalerie); the portrait of the Emperor seems to have been lost, but a copy remains in the portrait book of Hieronymus Beck of Leopoldsdorf (Vienna, Kunsthistorisches Museum, Gemäldegalerie).
Heinz attributed (1963) the entire group of paintings to Martino Rota due to their similarities with a signed portrait engraving, dated 1577, and the dotted painting technique that recalls his graphics. This attribution was confirmed through three portrait drawings of Rudolf, Ernst and their father, Maximilian II (Budapest, Museum of fina Arts), portraying them in precious armour and perhaps created in 1572 with the coronation of Rudolf II as King of Hungary. The portrait drawing of Rudolf, however, did not necessarily serve as the draft for the painted portrait, which shows him a few years older.

Karl Schütz

Bibliography: Heinz 1963, 115f., 191, no. 37; Heinz 1975, 224, no. 52; Vienna 1976-82, cat. no. 74; Thomas 1983, 25; Kaufmann 1988c, 226, no. 17.1; Essen-Vienna 1988, cat. no. 569; Prague 1997, cat. no. 156; Madrid 1998, cat. no. 287.

Giuseppe Arcimboldo as portrait-painter to the Holy Roman Emperor

III.4

Giuseppe Arcimboldo (?) after unknown artist
Maximilian II, His Wife Anna and Three Children,
1563 c., after a draft from 1553-54
Oil on canvas
240 × 188 cm
Vienna, Kunsthistorisches Museum, Gemäldegalerie, inv. no. 3448

Portrayed next to Archduke Maximilian II is his wife Maria of Spain and three of their children; in front is the oldest daughter, Anna, born in 1549, behind are the sons Rudolf, later Emperor Rudolf II (born 1552) and in the cradle, born in June 1553, Archduke Ernst. According to the number and age of the children, the painting can be quite accurately dated to the end of 1553 or the beginning of 1554.
The originals for this portrait are the full-figure type portraits of Jakob Seisenegger, and in particular the full-figure portraits of Maximilian and Maria, created a few years earlier in Spain by Anthonis Mor (Madrid, Museo Nacional del Prado). The attribution of this portrait to Seisenegger was contested by Löcher, and neither can Francesco Terzio be considered its author. Because of the figuration of small forms that recall Arcimboldo's paintings and decorative drawings, Günther Heinz would attribute the painting to this artist. The family portrait represents the foundation for the constitution of a group of stylistically similar portraits that can be attributed to Arcimboldo, whose traditionally documented ability as a painter of court portraits is otherwise not tied to any other works.
Because we have no record of Arcimboldo's arrival at the Viennese court before 1563, if we wish to correctly attribute this painting we must assume that Arcimboldo had copied the family portrait from the approximately ten-year-old original by an unknown artist. The execution actually shows some signs that the painter was working from a template (see Annexes).
Heinz also attributed to Arcimboldo, on the contrary, an individual, full-figure portrait of Queen Maria (Vienna, Kunsthistorisches Museum, Gemäldegalerie).

Karl Schütz

Bibliography: Löcher 1962, 52; Heinz 1963, 108, 185, no. 3; Vienna 1976-1982, cat. no. 52; Venice 1987, 62; Essen-Vienna 1988, cat. no. 554; Vienna 2003, cat. no. VII.24.

III.5

Giuseppe Arcimboldo (attributed?)
Bust of a Daughter of Ferdinand I: (Archduchess Magdalena?)
c. 1563
Oil on wood
44 × 33.5 cm
Vienna, Kunsthistorisches Museum, Gemäldegalerie, inv. no. 4510

With two other portraits very similar in their conception and technique, as well as in the characteristics of dress (cat. nos. III.6 and III.7), this painting belongs to a series of busts of Ferdinand I's daughters (and of Anna, the daughter of Maximilian II), which includes a total of seven paintings, of varying formats and styles. The closely related portrait of Archduchess Anna (cat. no. III.10) is unquestionably part of the same group. In format as well as in the formal appearance of the other pictures, two portraits differ – one portraying Archduchess Johanna and a second of a younger archduchess (cat. nos. III.8, 9). The seventh painting, portraying another unknown archduchess, deviates even further from the other portraits, and will not be considered here. Günther Heinz (1963, 1976) attributed all seven paintings to Giuseppe Arcimboldo, and in the mid-fifties he dated both smaller portraits of the younger archduchesses from 1560. Since there is no account of Arcimboldo's activity for the Viennese court before 1563, all of these paintings, so long as they are correctly attributed to Arcimboldo, must have been created somewhat later, which would also concord with the apparent age of the subjects. But because of the stylistic differences within the series, the attribution to multiple hands (at least two) should be considered.
The concordance of the individually represented archduchesses is only given tentatively. It seems that the painter may have worked from drawings, possibly from a different hand, which would account for the vague reproduction of the subject's hair and eye colours. The portrait in hand could represent Archduchess Magdalena (born in 1532, the unwed archduchess vowed to live her life under the spiritual guidance of the Jesuits, therefore founding the women's chapter in Hall in Tirol in 1563, as the members of the Community of Jesus were banned from the spiritual guidance of female convents; her younger sisters Margarete and Helena followed Magdalena, who died in 1590). In comparison, a bust by Jakob Seisenegger (Vienna, Kunsthistorisches Museum, Gemäldegalerie) can be included in this group, although we cannot be sure of it (Vienna 1976-1982, no. 62). A series of later portraits, portraying her as abbess, show a long, narrow face with a large, long nose, similar features to those of her father, Ferdinand I.

Karl Schütz

Bibliography: Heinz 1963, cat. no. 24; Vienna 1976-1982, cat. no. 63.

III.6

Giuseppe Arcimboldo (attributed?)
Portrait of a daughter of Ferdinand I (Archduchess Margarete ?)
c. 1563
Oil on wood
44 × 34 cm
Vienna, Kunsthistorisches Museum, Gemäldegalerie, inv. no. 4509

For attribution and portrait identification, see cat. no. III.5.
Archduchess Margarete (1536-1567) remained unwed and followed her older sister Magdalena to the women's monastery in Hall in 1563.

Karl Schütz

Bibliography: Heinz 1963, cat. no. 33; Vienna 1982, 97, mentioned in no. 63.

III.7

Giuseppe Arcimboldo (attributed?)
Bust of a Daughter of Ferdinand I (Archduchess Helena or Barbara?)
c. 1563
Oil on wood
43.5 × 33.5 cm
Vienna, Kunsthistorisches Museum, Gemäldegalerie, inv. no. 4512

For attribution and identification of this portrait, see cat. no. III.5.
A determination of the subject can only be postulated. Heinz considered Archduchess Helena in 1963 and Archduchess Barbara in 1976 (compare cat. no. III.8).

Karl Schütz

Bibliography: Heinz 1963, cat. no. 29; Vienna 1976-1982, mentioned under cat. no. 63.

III.8

Giuseppe Arcimboldo (attributed?)
Bust of an Unknown Archduchess, Daughter of Ferdinand I (Barbara?)
c. 1563-65
Oil on wood
32.5 × 25 cm
Vienna, Kunsthistorisches Museum, Gemäldegalerie, inv. no. 4511

Within the series of archduchess portraits, this one forms the unquestionable counterpart of the cat. no. III.9, which portrays the youngest daughter of Ferdinand I, Archduchess Johanna. It concords with this painting in format, technique and also in

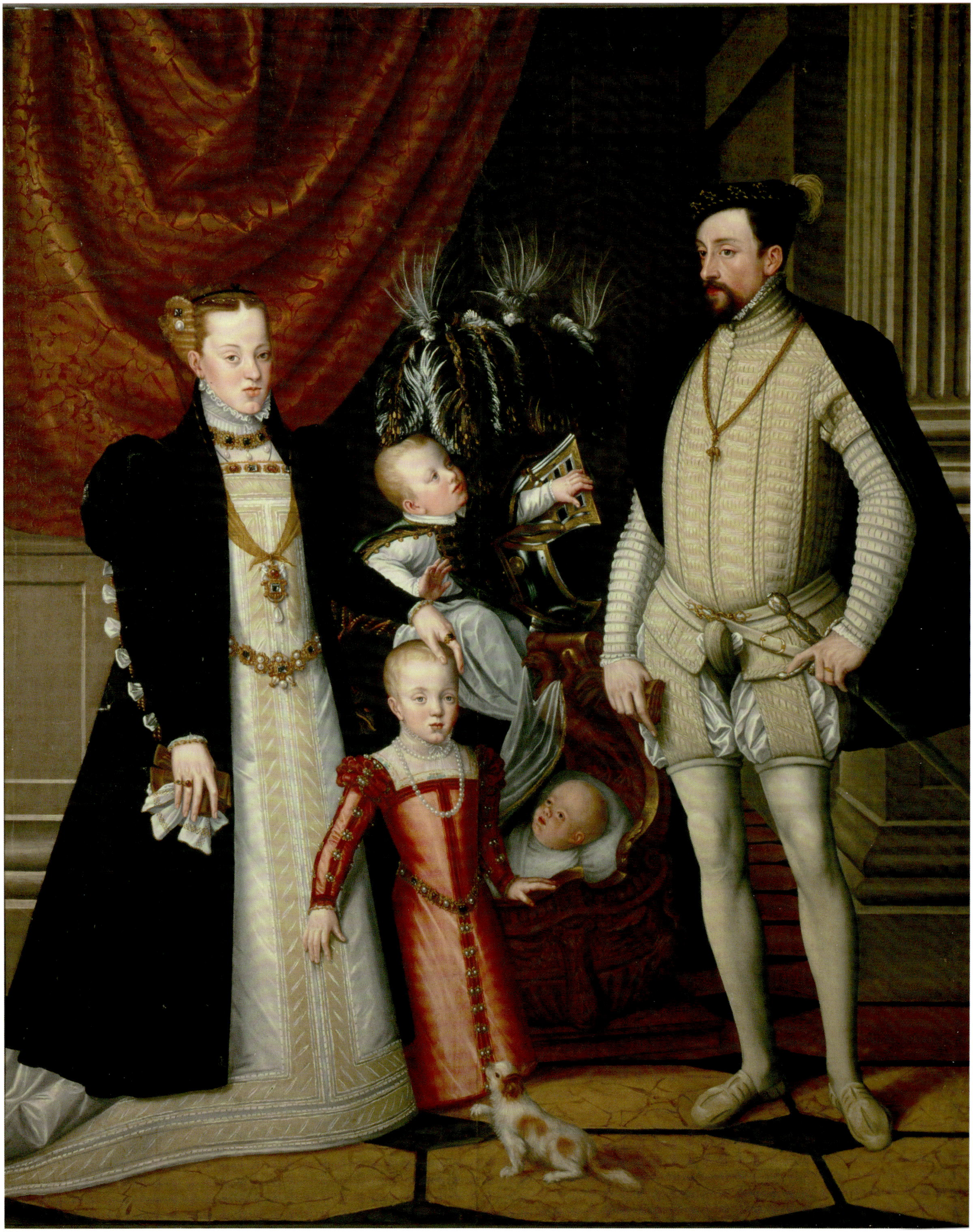

III.4

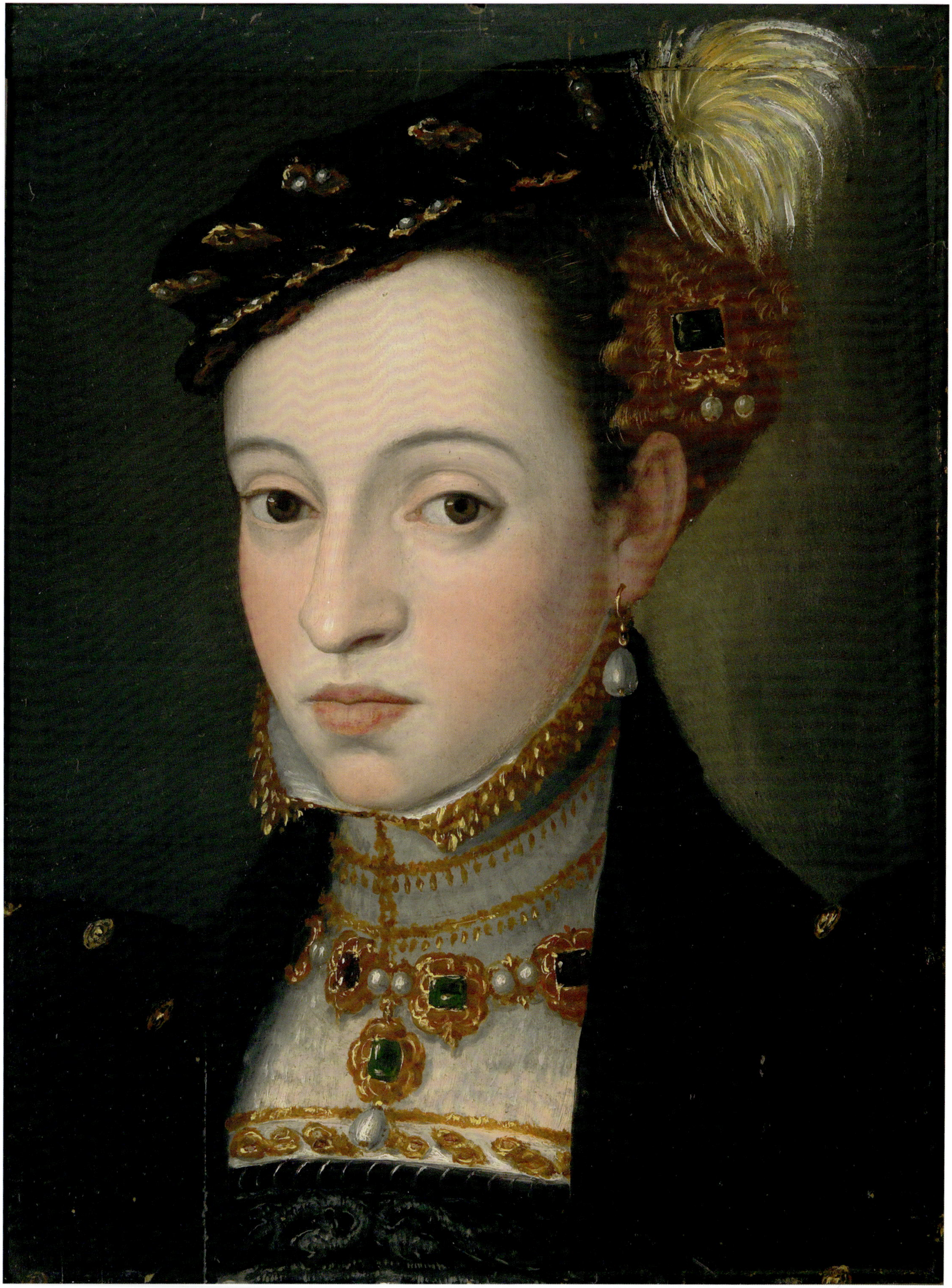

III.5

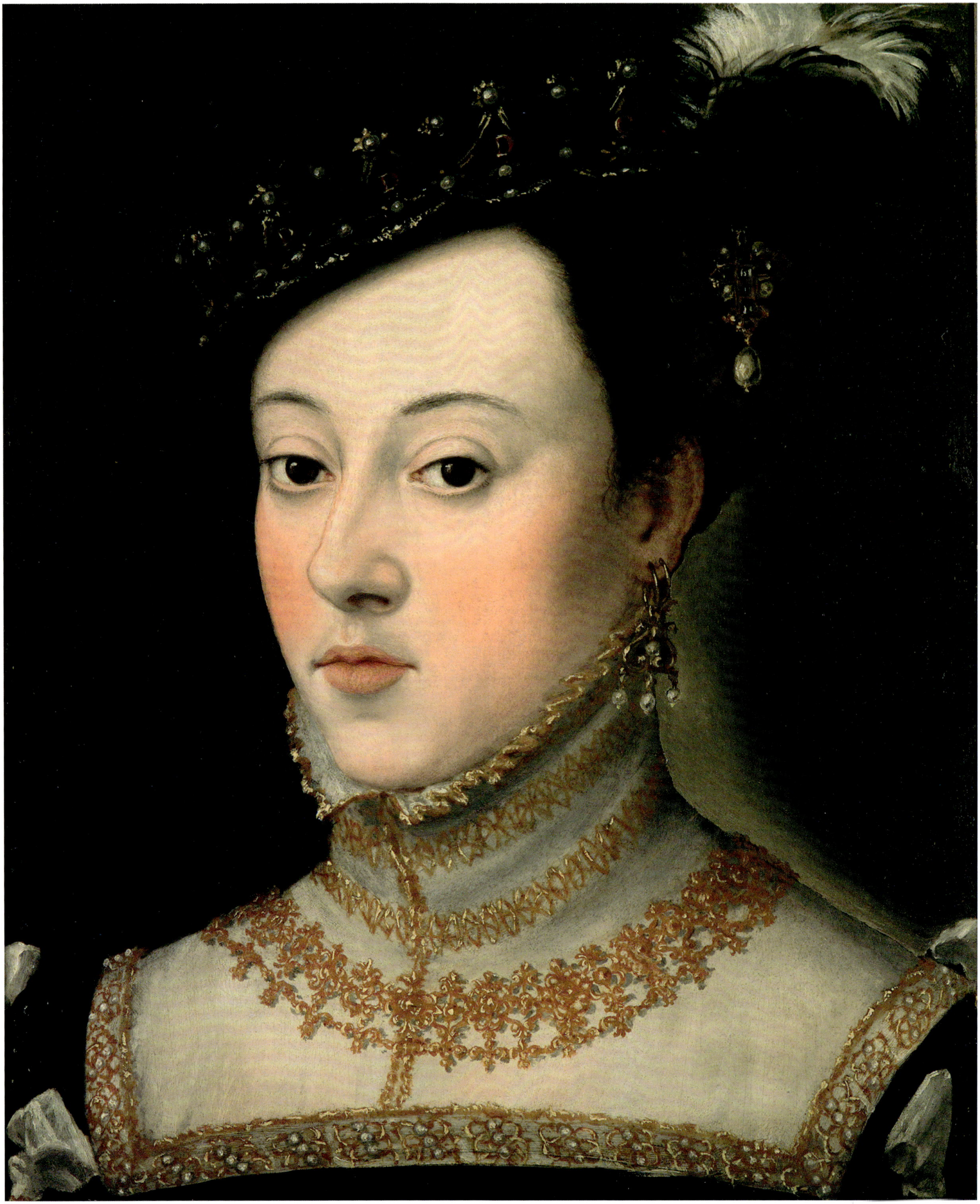
III.6

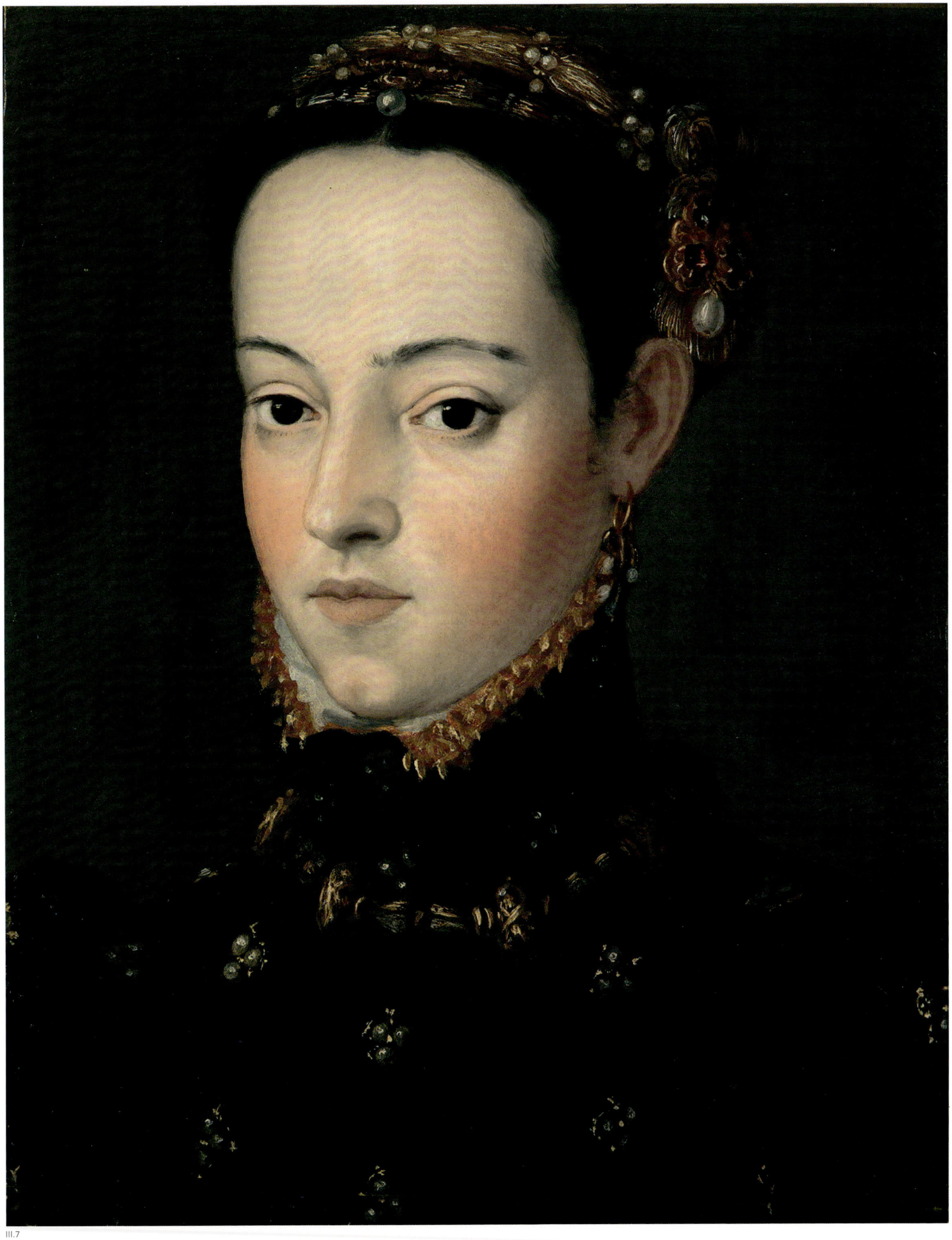

III.7

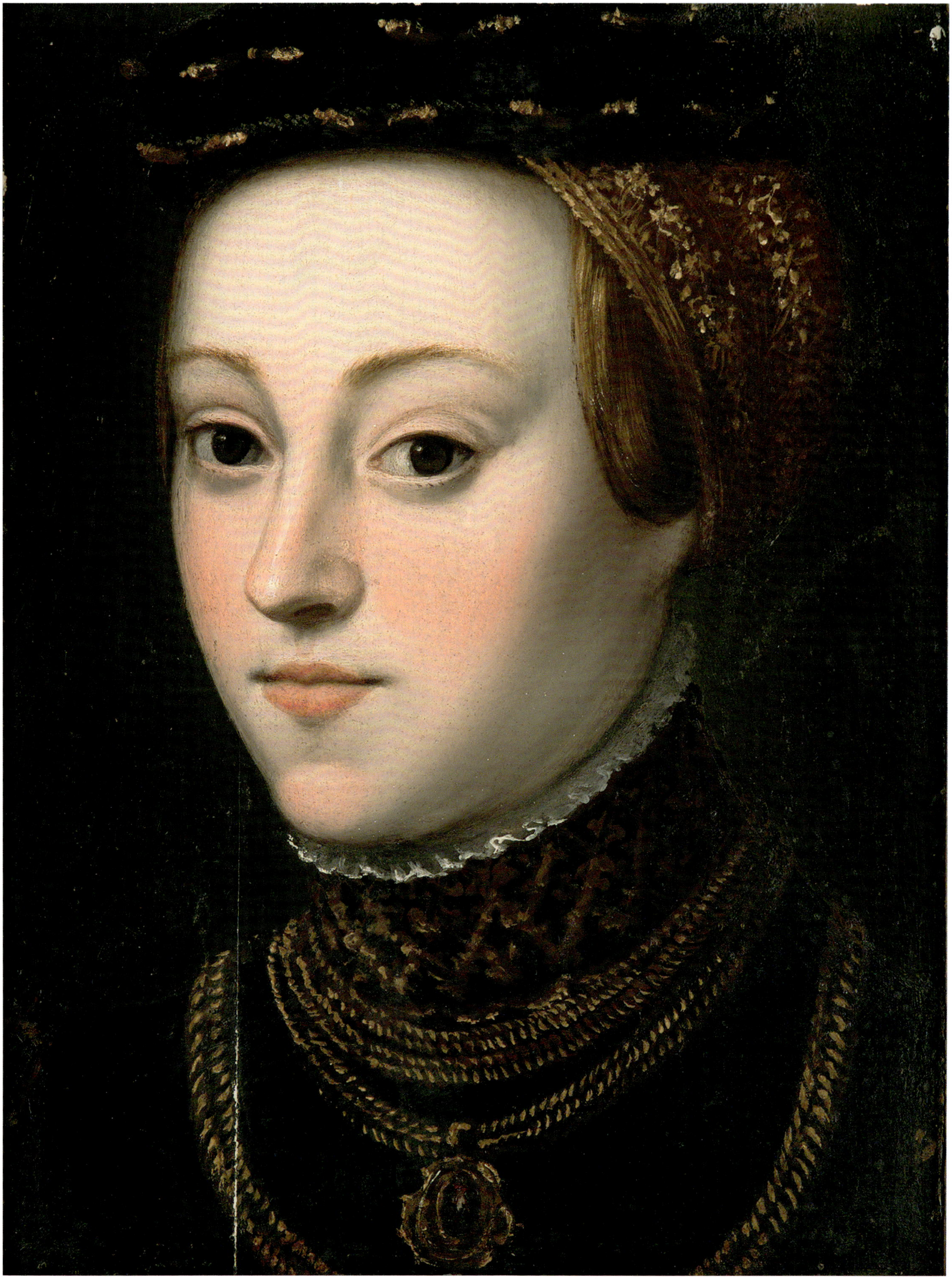

III.8

the mode of portraiture. If we assume that both paintings were created at about the same time, between approximately 1562 and 1565, it could represent one of the two youngest daughters of Ferdinand I, thus either Barbara (born in 1539, married to Alfonso II d'Este Duke of Ferrara in 1565, died in 1572) or Helena (born in 1543, joined the women's chapter [founded by Archduchess Magdalena] with her older, unwed sisters, Magdalena and Margarete in 1564 after the death of her father, died in 1574). Because of its resemblance with a full-figure portrait of Archduchess Barbara by Francesco Terzio (Vienna, Kunsthistorisches Museum, Gemäldegalerie, inv. no. 3994) and a somewhat later bust in the portrait collection of Archduke Ferdinand II, it is most likely a portrait of Archduchess Barbara.
Heinz (Vienna 1976, under no. 63) suggested an identification of the subject as Archduchess Eleonore (1534-1594), who was already married to Duke Guglielmo Gonzaga in 1561.
Again in this picture, as in the closely related portrait of Archduchess Johanna (cat. no. III.9), a series of pentimenti are visible in X-rays, which indicate that this is the first version of the portrait.

Karl Schütz

Bibliography: Heinz 1963, cat. no. 34.

III.9
Giuseppe Arcimboldo (attributed?)
Archduchess Johanna, c. 1562-65
Oil on linden wood
34 × 26 cm
Vienna, Kunsthistorisches Museum, Gemäldegalerie, inv. no. 4513

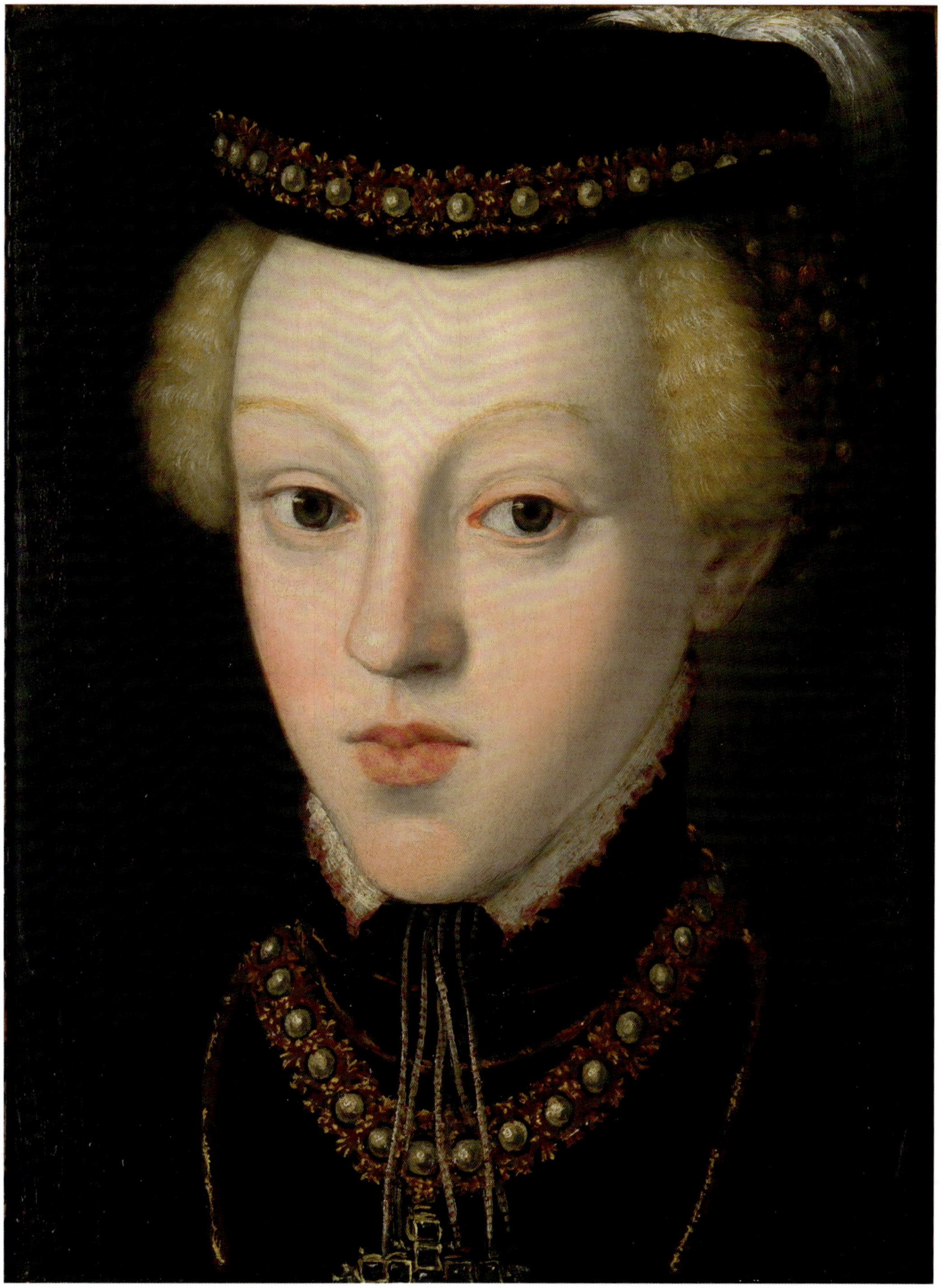
III.9

Archduchess Johanna was born in 1547 in Prague as the youngest and last daughter of Ferdinand I and Anna of Hungary. Anna of Hungary died after giving birth to the last of her fifteen children. In 1565 Johanna was wed to Francesco de' Medici, (ruling since 1564, he succeeded his father, Cosimo I, as Grand Duke of Tuscany in 1574), bearing him many daughters, among them Maria, who would later marry King Henry IV of France, but no son. Johanna died in 1578, and Grand Duke Francesco I married in a second matrimony his longtime mistress, Bianca Cappello.
Within the series of portraits of the daughters of Ferdinand I, through a comparison to other portraits (full-figure portrait by Francesco Terzio, Vienna, Kunsthistorisches Museum, Gemäldegalerie, and the bust in the portrait collection of Archduke Ferdinand II, which was later completed and labeled with name) this one can be safely identified as depicting Archduchess Johanna. The portrait is somewhat smaller in format than most of the other pictures in the series and therefore more tightly framed. It forms an immediate counterpart to cat. no. III.8, in format, technique and fashion. Instead of the low-cut corsage, fashion in 1560 dictated that the dress itself be high-laced and with a banded collar, carrying the shirt's small closing ruffle.
The portrait shows the archduchess at approximately age 16 and must have been painted between 1562 and 1565. Because pentimenti can be seen in X-ray images, the numerous modifications made during the painting process, both in the position of the head as well as in the clothing, indicate that this was doubtless the first version of the portrait.

Karl Schütz

Bibliography: Heinz 1963, cat. no. 31; Vienna 1976-1982, no. 70.

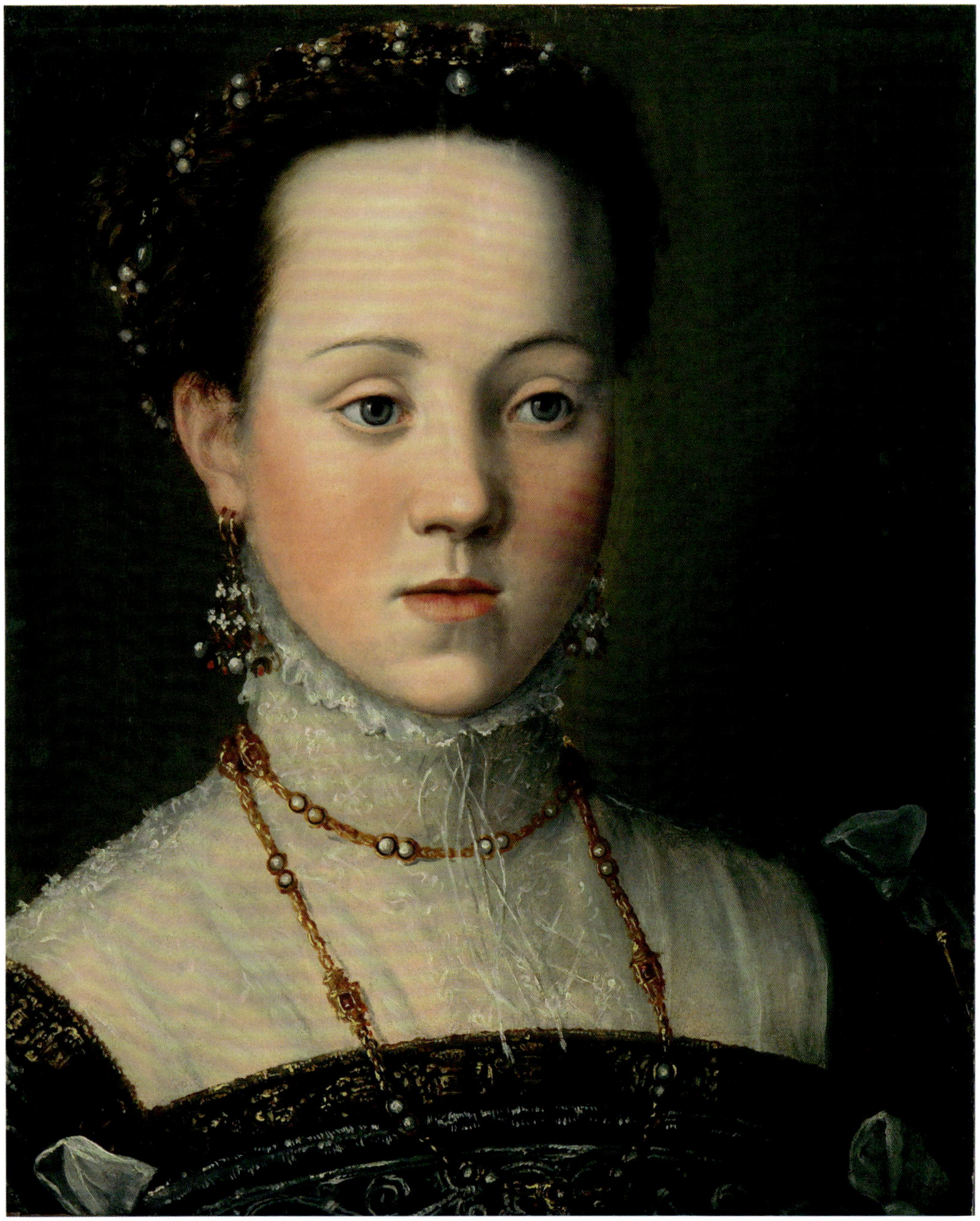

III.10

III.10
Giuseppe Arcimboldo (attributed?)
Archduchess Anna, Daughter of Emperor Maximilian II
c. 1563
Oil on wood
42 × 34 cm
Vienna, Kunsthistorisches Museum, Gemäldegalerie, inv. no. 4514

Among the series of portraits depicting the daughters of Emperor Ferdinand I, because of its size (today believed to have been somewhat reduced), technique and also the fashion of the clothing, this belongs to the group of portraits of Ferdinand's older daughters (cat. nos. III.5-7). Some pentimenti also indicate here that this is the first version of the portrait.
Because of its impressive physiognomic resemblance to the portrait of Anna at approximately age six in the family portrait of Maximilian II (cat. no. III.4) also attributed to Arcimboldo, as well as an individual portrait (Vienna, Kunsthistorisches Museum, Gemäldegalerie, inv. no. 8148), which was completed and labelled with the inscription *E. Anna*, Günther Heinz has determined this painting to be the portrait of the eldest and preferred daughter of Maximilian II.
Anna (1549-1580) was born in Spain, only two years after Archduchess Johanna, who was born in 1547 as the youngest daughter of Ferdinand I. In 1570 Anna became the fourth wife of her uncle, King Philip II of Spain.
Heinz found stylistic arguments for the attribution of this painting to Arcimboldo in details, such as the form of the earrings, which he compared to the hangings in Arcimboldo's decorative drawings, above all with those in the crowning fronds in his designs for sledges, but also in the painting technique of Arcimboldo's characteristic solid colour application.

Karl Schütz

Bibliography: Heinz 1963, no. 35; Vienna 1982, cat. no. 73.

III.11
Giuseppe Arcimboldo
Two portaits of Rudolf II with crown
1575
Black pen and ink on paper
165 × 165 and 155 × 155 mm
Prague, Národní Galerie, Historische Abteilung, inv. no. 40155

In both sketches Arcimboldo defines with sparing pen strokes the profile of Rudolf sunk in the collar of his coronation mantel, though his main attention is on the crowns: to the left the Imperial crown, to the right the Wenceslas crown. Here the artist himself notes down the purpose of these drawings: namely the appearance of the king bearing the respective crown at the various coronation ceremonies. Arcimboldo was present at both. Under the left drawing the following is written: "La Corona dove si corono Re de Romano Rodolpho el primo di Novembre 1575 in Ratisbona corona chera in aquiscrana che fece far Carlo Magno et era di tanta larghezza et gli avanzava doi dita per parte era tutta d'oro e della medema fattura. Io Giuseppe Arcimboldo fui pre[sen]te." ("The crown with which the Roman King Rudolph was crowned on the first of November 1575 in Regensburg. The crown, that is located in Aachen, was commissioned by Charles the Great, and was so big, that on the sides it had a two finger wide gap and was totally made of Gold.") Under the right hand drawing he wrote "La Corona dove si corono Rudolpho Re di Bohemia de medemo garbo come si vede nel pre[sen]te disegno 1575 il giorno de Sto. Matia di Settemb. Io Giuseppe Arcimboldo fui pre[sen]te." ("The crown with which Rudolph was crowned King of Bohemia, has the same fineness, as shown in the said drawing made on the holy day of St. Matthew in September 1575."). The note by Arcimboldo on the colour and material quality of the crowns "raso rosso", or red satin, was taken as an indication, that these sketches were preparatory works for portrait paintings (Larsson 1997, 122). Per-

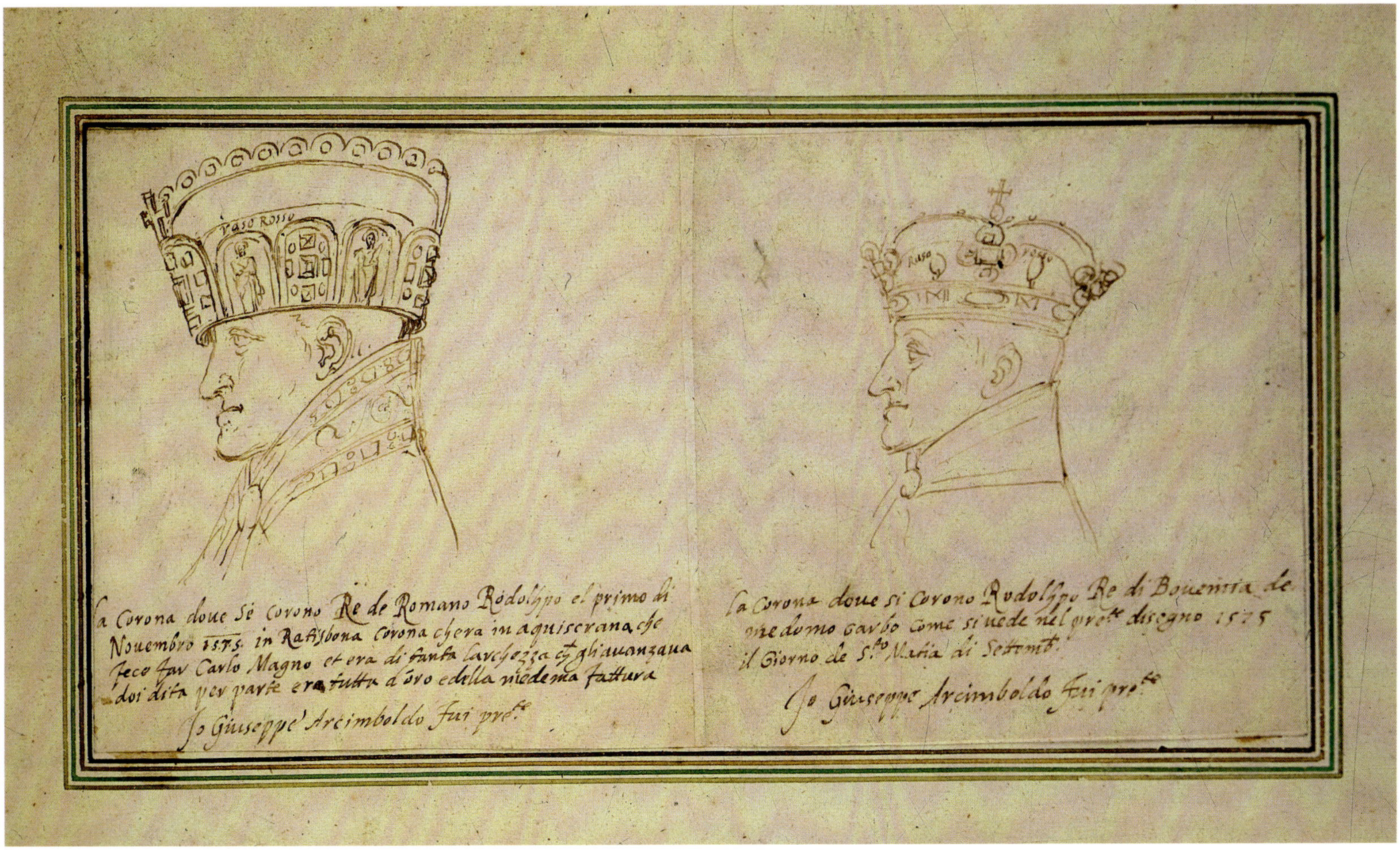

III.11

haps due to the profile view they were for portrait medallions (Fučikova 1986, 15, plate 4-5). Cavalli-Björkman saw the purpose of these drawings as being principally "reports" of historic events, that is of the two coronations.
All these suggestions may be right, though in my opinion a special feature has been overlooked. Already Larsson analyzed the discrepancy well, that Arcimboldo in our opinion particularly in the study to the left captured so masterfully: a discrepancy between the human fragility of the slender head of the bearer and the oversized burden he was compelled to assume with this insignia of power as future emperor. That particularly this inconsistency was worked on by Arcimboldo in his drawings can be related to his professional task as organizer of ceremonies and costume designer, he himself noting down that the Imperial crown was too fingers too large on all sides. This can also be deduced from the "Rudolfskrone" that was commissioned by Rudolf himself in 1602; though it too had an imposing circumference, this was 6 cm less than the imperial crown. This size was also a source of concern for other Habsburg crowned heads, as Goethe ironically commented regarding the coronation of Joseph II in the year 1764: "The crown, that had to be much padded, stood out from the head like an overhanging roof".
These drawings show us something of the appearance of Rudolf at that time: he is as slender and young as in the portrait by Martino Rota also shown in this exhibition (cat. no. III.3) and very different from the later portraits painted by his court painters Hans von Aachen and Joseph Heintz.

Sylvia Ferino-Pagden

Bibliography: Preiss 1967, plate 9-10; Fučikova 1986, 15, plate 4-5; Essen-Vienna 1988, 338, no. 193 (Cavalli-Björkman); Larsson 1997, 122.

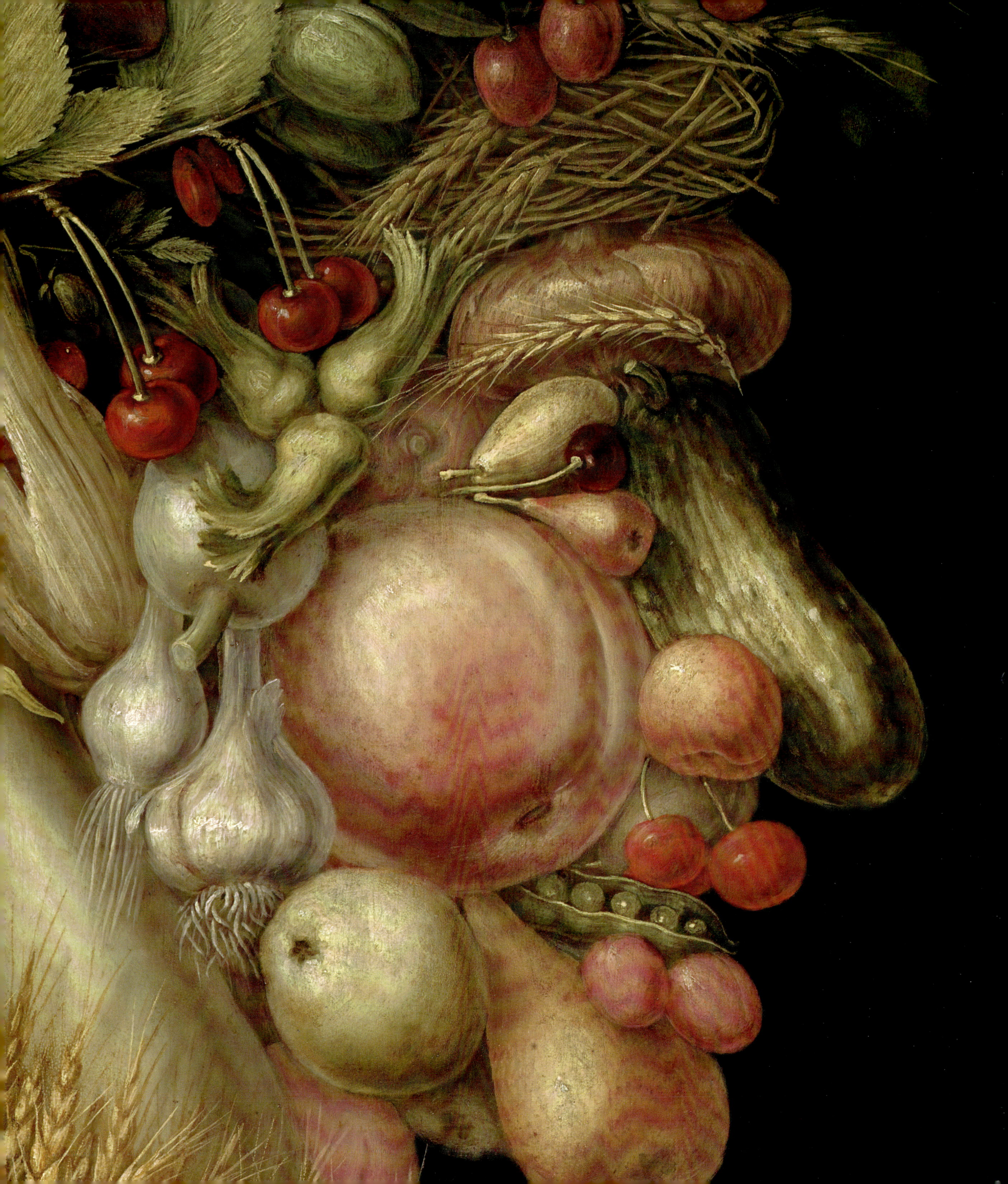

Thomas DaCosta Kaufmann

Arcimboldo's Composite Heads: Origins and Invention

Arcimboldo's most famous creations are no doubt his *teste composte*, his composite heads. These are paintings composed out of disparate but related elements in which clearly identifiable individual elements are conjoined to make up a head and the upper part of a torso. In the various versions of *Summer* (cat. nos. III.3, 5, 9, 13), for example, a cucumber forms the nose, a currant an eye, a peach the cheek, a pear the chin, and cherries the upper lip. A straw fillet crowns the head, and ears of grain comprise the torso, while other vegetables and fruits which grow in summer constitute the rest of the head and hair. In this way the separate features (fruits and vegetables that bloom in the summertime), all rendered in detail, are also associated with the subject depicted (the season of summer). In similar fashion flowers form the head of the season of *Spring*, aquatic creatures that of the element *Water*, birds that of *Air*, animals that of *Earth*, and so forth.

Although Arcimboldo was not the first artist to create composite images, nor to combine their separate elements emblematically, he has long been closely linked with such inventions. His compositions made the form popular in European art. The name Arcimboldesque has been given to a host of imitators active during the later 16th and 17th century, and this is also the designation of a genre for such composites[1]. His works have directly or indirectly inspired imitators up to the present; they may be related to a continuing tendency in the history of art to transform the human face[2]. Their composite quality was what led to the rediscovery of Arcimboldo in the 20th century, his appropriation into the realm of fantastic art and Surrealism, and his association with Mannerism – all matters that are however questioned in this catalogue[3].

In keeping with the historical orientation of the present enterprise, this essay considers the question of the possible sources for Arcimboldo's compositional conception. It attempts to situate Arcimboldo better into historical context. When seen in comparison with their possible antecedents, the characteristics of Arcimboldo's own composite heads and thus his own distinctive conception of the form become more clear.

A plethora of sources has been found for Arcimboldo's images. These range from Mogul miniatures to memory images, from compositions made out of actual food to ancient gems, from Leonardesque drawings to northern European prints[4]. It might even appear that the origins of Arcimboldo's composites are overdetermined. Yet not all of the sources that have been proposed are equally plausible: they need to be reconsidered.

We may begin with one of the earliest suggestions of a source for Arcimboldo: Indian miniatures. In 1933, even before art historians had paid much attention to Arcimboldo, these were proposed by Josef Strzygowski, who was always ready to find eastern sources for western imagery (especially if these could somehow be regarded as "Aryan")[5]. Mogul paintings do represent animals such as horses, elephants, and camels that are made up out of a variety of creatures, and the resemblance with Arcimboldo might seem close. Nevertheless, there is no evidence that any specimens of what became a thriving genre in Mogul India could have been known to this particular European artist before the year 1563. Mogul examples in general post-date rather than antedate Arcimboldo's creations, the earliest of which (the first series of *Winter*) can be definitely set in that year[6]. On the other hand, many European images were exported to the Mogul court[7]. It is also known that European painters – Michael Sweerts the most famous among them – went to India: in fact one artist, Cornelis Claesz. Heda, who had actually served Rudolf II in Prague, worked at an Indian court[8]. It is thus possible that the influence went in the other direction, if the inventions did not just simply occur independently of each other in both places.

A similar problem attends the possibility of Persian influences, which might also be mentioned. Although such images have not hitherto been discussed, in this case direct connections between Rudolfine Prague and Safavid Persia can be established[9]. Heda travelled from Prague in the company of the Persian ambassador to the imperial court. Some Persian miniatures with composite creations may be contemporary with or antedate Arcimboldo[10]. But since the genre of composite miniatures did not flourish in Persia, as it did in India, it is even less likely that these would have been known in Europe, especially before 1563. Again the creation of composites may have occurred independently in different places.

Jurgis Baltrušaitis indeed observed that composites were common both to eastern traditions and to the European tradition stemming

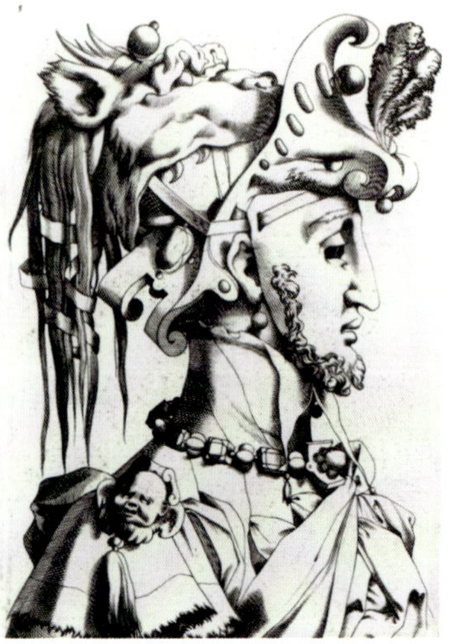

Fig. 1. René Boyvin, *Masked Head*, after Rosso Fiorentino. Vienna, Albertina

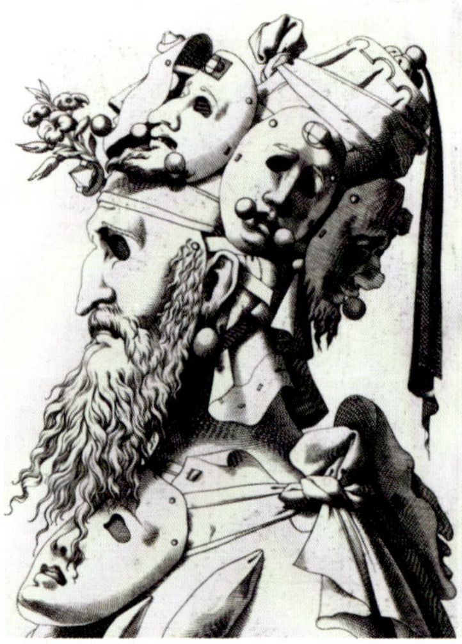

Fig. 2. René Boyvin, *Masked Head*, after Rosso Fiorentino. Vienna, Albertina

from Greco-Roman antiquity. They may be found in Armenian miniatures, Pompeian wall paintings, ancient cameos, and medieval marginal manuscript illuminations[11]. Many of the aforementioned have subsequently been advanced as sources for Arcimboldo[12]. Nevertheless, with the exception of cameos and other ancient gems, on which more presently, there is a similar, recurring problem: how could Arcimboldo have been familiar with any such images?[13]

Connections proposed with northern European art of the 16th century seem more plausible[14]. These include drawings by Hieronymus Bosch (the exact attribution is moot), marquetry by Lorenz Stoer, and prints by René Boyvin and Tobias Stimmer, as well as by anonymous Protestant satirists. While all of the images mentioned represent figures composed of various parts, only those by Boyvin after Rosso Fiorentino, those related to Bosch, and satirical or prophetic images of the Reformation are earlier than Arcimboldo. Bosch's images were also called *grilli*, a term used both to describe composite creations, to which we shall return[15]. However, close comparisons to Arcimboldo are lacking. While Boyvin's images are heads, they are not made out of separate units; only Stimmer's *Gorgoneum Caput* really represents a composite head made out of different pieces, but it was created much after Arcimboldo had begun making composite heads, and may thus derive its idea from his inventions, rather than vice versa.

These images at least bring us close in time and closer in place to Arcimboldo. Several sources have been found in Renaissance Italy, including, perhaps surprisingly, the realm of food. In 16th-century Italy compositions of various sorts, were made out of comestibles, including sugar sculptures[16]. Artists such as Giovan Francesco Rustici, Andrea del Sarto, and Domenico Puligo made elaborate constructions using various kinds of food at banquets of the Compagnia del Paiuolo and of the Compagnia della Cazzuola in Florence, and these may evoke the ideas of Arcimboldo[17].

Other comparisons with comestibles connect Arcimboldo's images to popular sources and the carnivalesque. Eschewing humanist readings of Arcimboldo[18], Francesco Porzio has emphasized his popular sources in Lombardy, including the appearance in a Milanese festival of a wooden horse that disgorged various meats. Porzio relates this to prints by Ambrogio Brambilla of *Lent* and *Carnival*, in which meats are evident, which he compares to Arcimboldo; he relates Arcimboldo's creations accordingly to the carnivalesque, which he compares to Rabelaisian imagery, and to an image of Aretino (cat. no. II.10), to be mentioned further below. Porzio also relates this imagery to the *commedia dell'arte*[19]. Giacomo Berra expands this argument, connecting the Milanese festival, and thus what Porzio and he have seen as Arcimboldo's sources of inspira-

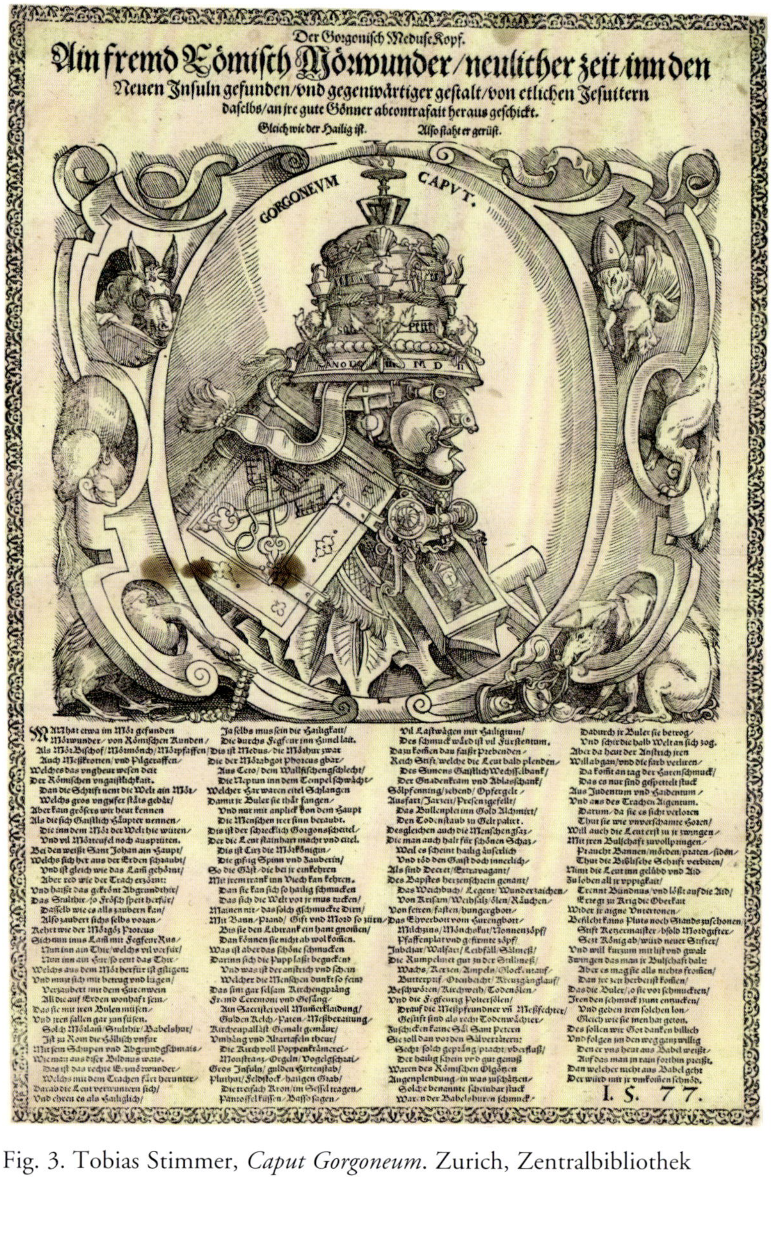

Fig. 3. Tobias Stimmer, *Caput Gorgoneum*. Zurich, Zentralbibliothek

tion, with actual porters, *facchini*, and hence with circles of artists and *literati* in Milan around the painter and theorist Gian Paolo Lomazzo: Lomazzo had formed a pseudo-academy modelled on such porters (the academy of the *Facchini della Val di Blenio*)[20].
While Porzio's critique of the many disparate sources proposed for Arcimboldo is well taken[21], his and Berra's readings in such a vein are however also problematic. First, there is no real visual similarity between constructions out of food, as they are reported (as opposed to the many later ones inspired by Arcimboldo) and especially those contained within objects as seen at the Milanese festival on the one hand and Arcimboldo's pictures on the other. Second, Brambilla's images postdate Arcimboldo's, and given the imperial painter's reputation in Milan, they most likely derived from his; there is also no real grounds for assuming that they replicate the ideation of his images in any case[22]. And although Lomazzo and other writers and artists around him knew Arcimboldo, there is no evidence that Arcimboldo himself belonged to the *Facchini della Val di Blenio*. The connection made with *facchini* misinterprets the meaning of the documents associating Arcimboldo with porters; his relationship with them was no more distinctive than with any of the other groups he served in the context of arranging what were basically fund-raising groups for Milan Cathedral[23]. In any event, it can be demonstrated that his paintings of composite heads originated at the imperial court, not in Lombardy, as has also been argued[24]. Finally, while Arcimboldo was in fact connected with some of the first propagators of the *commedia dell'arte* north of the Alps, these figures appeared in a court, not a popular, context: they did not represent some sort of carnivalesque inversion of the hierarchy, but were in fact involved in a festival that had been designed by Arcimboldo where their antics as acrobats and actors helped to reinforce, not undermine, the foundations of this very hierarchy[25].
Other associations with Lombard traditions seem more persuasive in contrast. The Leonardesque tradition is prime among them. Most pertinent here is a passage appearing in the so-called *Treatise on Painting*, assembled by Francesco Melzi from Leonardo's manuscripts, which describes a way of making an *animal finto* (a fictive creature) such as a serpent seem natural. Leonardo says to take "the head of a mastiff or a hound for a head, the eyes of a cat, the ears of a porcupine, the nose of a greyhound, the brow of a lion, the temples of an old cock and the neck of a turtle"[26]. In his *vita* (life) of Leonardo Giorgio Vasari tells a story, to which Lomazzo also alludes, of how Leonardo painted a head of Medusa on a shield: Leonardo took into a room lizards, newts, maggots, snakes, butterflies, locusts, bats, and other animals of the kind, "out of which he composed a horrible and terrible monster"[27]. The evidence for Arcimboldo's connection with the Leonardesque tradition is clear[28]. So is the idea that his caprices of nature were monsters: Comanini refers to his painting of Vertumnus as a "new monster".

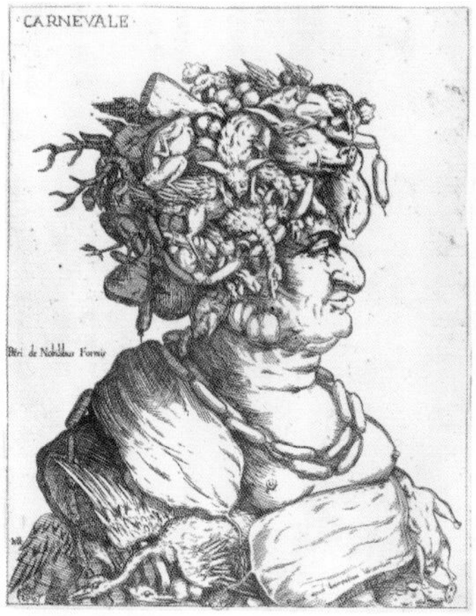

Fig. 4. Ambrogio Brambilla, *Carnival*. Paris, Bibliothèque Nationale de France

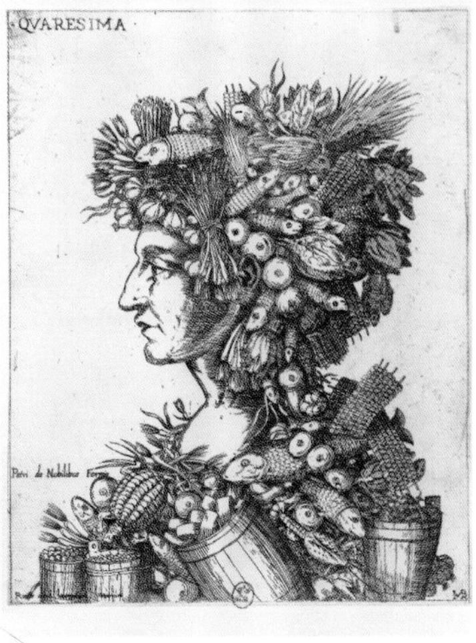

Fig. 5. Ambrogio Brambilla, *Lent*. Paris, Bibliothèque Nationale de France

This discussion of fictive creatures appears in a passage describing how to make fantastic beings[29]. Leonardo's method of composing a fantastic creature out of elements found in nature thus recalls a Renaissance *topos* that is also directly pertinent for considerations of Arcimboldo. This is the *locus classicus* in Horace's *Ars poetica*, which mentions licentious creatures such as one with a human head on a horse's body, whose limbs are covered with feathers, and who looks like a beautiful woman at the top, but has a fish's tail below. Horace's creature became a commonplace reference for the fantastic, for painters and poets to create what they may imagine. It of course also brings to mind the grotesque, a topic with which Arcimboldo was deeply familiar, and about which he had his own distinctive ideas[30].
The literary *topos* of fantastic creatures and grotesques brings us to other forms of monsters, the composites known as *grilli*. This term appears in Pliny's *Natural History*, where it describes humorous pictures, but it is directly applied to Arcimboldo to mean composites[31]. In this sense the term may also be applied to composite images which were known from antiquity. These appear particularly on ancient jewels, especially in cut gems and cameos composed out of various human and animal forms, or monsters, and at times with heads. Some such *grilli* are invertible, so that a composition may be discerned whether the gem be seen in one direction or turned around or upside down[32]. Baltrušaitis traces the appearance of *grilli* from antiquity through the Middle Ages[33].
If *grilli* are to be taken into consideration as sources for Arcimboldo's images, given his humanist and antiquarian interests, it is most likely that ancient gems, not medieval works derived from or comparable to them, would have inspired him. In fact, it can now be determined that several such gems were visible in the imperial col-

lections, where Arcimboldo could have seen them. Several *grilli* in the Vienna collections can now be traced back to an early provenance. A rediscovered inventory of Emperor Maximilian II's *Schatzkammer* indicates that he was a great collector of gems[34].
Some of the closest antecedents to Arcimboldo's heads are however seen in this exhibition: they are images of heads made up of phalloi (male members) which appear on Casteldurazzo plates and on the reverse of a medal of Aretino. In them the phalloi synecdochically depict a satyr's head. These compositions have long been associated with Arcimboldo[35]. More recently Raymond Waddington has called attention to another medal with a composite head of a satyr, which is thought to be a caricature of Aretino's rival Paolo Giovio: here the head of a satyr is composed out of various animals. Waddington explains that this image relies on various physiognomic relationships for the positioning of the animals within the head, and also represents the principle of harmony, *discordia concors*, whereby the various creatures are conjoined. He also argues that the phallic portrait of Aretino evokes another satyr, Silenus, who from the discussion in Plato's *Symposium* was taken as an ugly creature that hid something beautiful within – and thus suggested the idea of a serious joke. This was a key concept of the Renaissance – for Aretino, for Erasmus, and for Rabelais, who refers to it at the beginning of Pantagruel as a key to his work[36].
With such images we are not far from Arcimboldo's composites. Other essays in this catalogue relate how all of the concepts on which the satyr medals (especially that made up of several animals) in particular rely – physiognomy, the serious joke, and harmony – apply to Arcimboldo. The heads made out of *cazzi*, male members, and of animals, are also better understood in relation to Arcimboldo according to what we now know about the natural historical, humanist, and political features of the artist's interests, as explained further in the present catalogue. They are to be situated in an intellectual, witty, and literary context, comparable to that of Aretino with which Waddington associates them, and not with popular culture. As with Aretino, the idea that the intellectual, literary aspect of the *cazzi*, while seeming to be scurilous, are potentially profound, also applies to Arcimboldo.
Whatever his sources may have been, Arcimboldo took the concept of the composite head and developed it further. He took a composition made out of stylized animals, but based his heads on actual studies of nature. The combination of such figures into a harmonious image of discordant creatures he expands into a series of seasons and elements, and develops the idea further in an image of Vertumnus. The emblematic associations[37] suggested by other composites are elaborated in Arcimboldo into series of imperial, and then by transference, princely, allegories. This sort of political allusion also had a lasting life: it is picked up among other places in the presentation of Hobbes's *Leviathan*[38]. Hence while Arcimboldo's images might seem to have scurilous antecedents, they paradoxically present serious matters in seemingly monstrous or humorous form[39]. Not their creation of the type, but Arcimboldo's creative inventions of new forms of composite heads have made his images so compelling.

[1] See Legrand, Sluys 1955; Hope 1987, 44.
[2] Venice 1987.
[3] See the essay by S. Ferino-Pagden in this catalogue.
[4] Legrand, Sluys 1955, 71-76 offers an account of the "origins of the procedure"; Porzio 1978, 14-26 provides a comprehensive survey of the composite idea behind Arcimboldo.
[5] Strzygowski's views are reported in Legrand, Sluys 1955, 73, and Porzio 1978, 14. For the present critique of Strzygowski see Kaufmann 2004, 70-73.
[6] For the dating of the *Seasons*, see Kaufmann 2005. Akbar ascended the throne only about eight years before, as a thirteen-year old, and most painting done in his era is later.
[7] For the general theme of European art and the Mogul court, see Flores 2004.
[8] See Willingen 1870, 152-156 and Supplement B.
[9] See Kurz 1977.
[10] Jaromír Šíp postulated the impact of Persian painting on Savery and art in Prague: see Šíp 1969. I would like to thank Francesca Leoni for discussing with me the issue of composites in Mogul and Persian painting in relation to Arcimboldo.
[11] Baltrušaitis 1981. His point about their ubiquity is made by Porzio 1978, 14, citing Baltrušaitis, "Têtes composées", in *Médicine de France* 19, 1951, 29ff., which was not however available to me.
[12] See Legrand, Sluys 1955, 72f; Porzio 1978, 14.
[13] For instance, Pompeii was not excavated until the mid-18th century.
[14] See Geiger 1954, Legrand, Sluys 1955; Shearman 1967, 204, goes so far as to say that the prints by Boyvin, which had previously been incorrectly attributed to Arcimboldo, inspired Arcimboldo's designs.
[15] Kaufmann 1993.
[16] See Porzio 1978, 46 no. 14 for other examples.
[17] See Porzio, 1978, 19, who elaborates a suggestion made in Kaufmann 1976a, 282: see Kaufmann 1993, 261 no. 39.
[18] In particular Kaufmann 1976a and 1993; see the essay by Kaufmann below.
[19] Porzio 1993. For a further elaboration of this connection with the *commedia dell'arte*, see Paliaga 1995.
[20] Berra 1998a, especially 63-64.
[21] Especially Porzio 1993, 37.
[22] See essay by A. Beyer in this catalogue.
[23] See Kaufmann forthcoming. This hypothesis also seems to seriously misread the nature of Lomazzo's intentions, which, as their best scholar, Dante Isella, has suggested, involved Silenic conceptions not far from Arcimboldo's: see further Kaufmann forthcoming.
[24] See Kaufmann 2005, for the contradiction of assertions by Berra 1998a and Porzio 1993, as well as a similar argument by Hope 1987; on this point see further Kaufmann 1990.
[25] See Kaufmann forthcoming. The distribution of food in a carnivalesque setting may be regarded as much as a measure of social control, as a sign of carnivalesque subversion.
[26] See the translation in *Leonardo on Painting*, 224.
[27] This story is easily accessible in the many editions of Vasari's *Vite*: see for example Vasari 1965, vol. 2, 166. Significantly, this shield was eventually purchased by the duke of Milan, where apparently it was to be seen when Vasari was writing, c. 1550. See Berra 2004, 62.

[28] See the essays by A. Beyer and S. Leydi in this catalogue.
[29] See Kaufmann 2007.
[30] See the essay by P. Morel in this catalogue, as well as the discussion in Kaufmann 1993, 151-173.
[31] See Kaufmann 1993, 106-108. The most thorough account of *grilli* in the Renaissance is offered in Bredekamp 1989.
[32] Examples from the imperial collection are seen in Zwierlein-Diehl 1979 plate 43 no. 804; vol. 3, 1991, 131, no. 2103; no. 2114; A. Bernhard Waecker, "Zur Geschichte der Gemmensammlung", ibid., points to the origins of the gem collections in the Habsburg Kunst- und Schatzkammers of the 16th century.
[33] Baltrušaitis 1981 treats this subject extensively.
[34] For this inventory see Rudolf 1995, 231-253.
[35] Legrand, Sluys 1955, 74 with further reference on 137 no. 14, is credited by Waddington 1989, 21 no. 2 with having been first to notice this association.
[36] See Waddington 1989, for this notion see further the essay by the author below, and further Kaufmann 1990 and Kaufmann forthcoming. The Rabelaisian reference is worth emphasizing, because Porzio 1993, 41, under the influence of Bakthin, invokes him in arguing for carnivalesque elements in Arcimboldo.
[37] The relation to actual emblems and devices is adumbrated by Kaufmann 1976a and elaborated by Porzio 1978, 24-26.
[38] See Bredekamp 2003.
[39] See Kaufmann forthcoming.

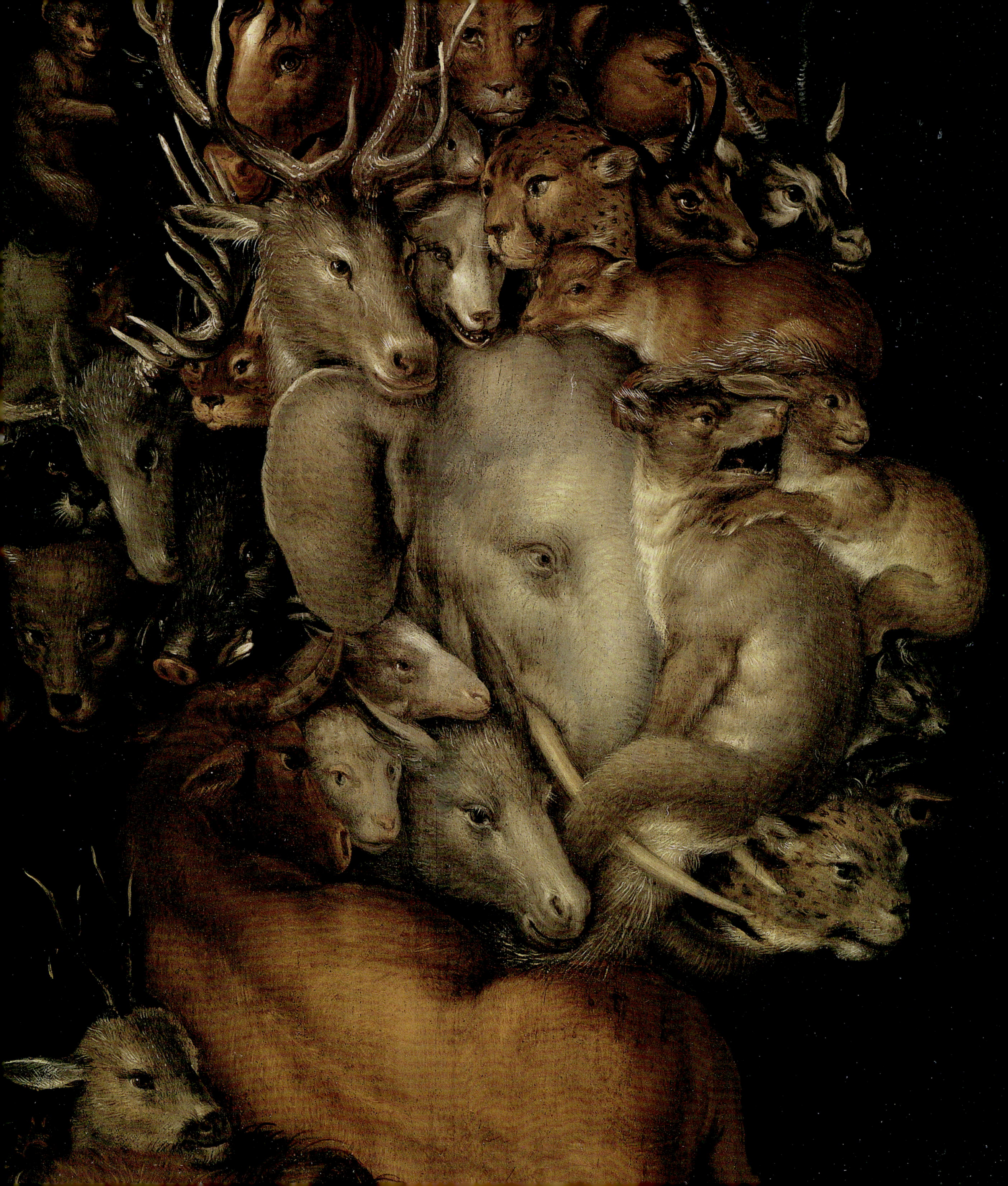

Sylvia Ferino-Pagden

Arcimboldo as "Conterfetter" of Nature

It seems that, in his appreciation of Arcimboldo's activity, Gregorio Comanini already expressed a preference for the composite heads, as pure fruits of the painter's fantasy, rather than for the figurative imitations observed from nature without any artistic intervention[1]. Up to now, modern art research has also concentrated mainly on these fantastic components of the overall forms of Arcimboldo's *Seasons* and *Elements*, with diverging interpretations, from political allegories to the paradoxical "*scherzo*". Attention has very recently started to focus on the various flowers, plants, fruits, but also animals, whose realistic presence, studied with painstaking exactness, constitutes those composite forms. True, the catalogue of the 1987 Venice exhibition included the identification – by Jean Depêche and Pierre Noël – of over 62 sea creatures in the element *Water*, but nobody actually wondered where Arcimboldo might have studied or copied these animals (cat. no. IV.16)[2]. In this catalogue, we have done our best to list the many different species present in the composite heads, as identified by Sam Segal: the faithfully depicted flowers and plants in *Spring*, and fruits in *Summer* (cat. nos. IV.2-3).

Thus we wish to draw attention to the rapid development of scientific research during the 16th century; the exact depiction of plants, animals and stones after nature became a necessary requirement, to enable scientists to systematically order and classify the endless variety of the products of nature. These drawings served as preparations for woodcuts, that then illustrated the first systematic, encyclopedic reference books, like for example Otto Brunfels' *Herbarum Vivae Eicones* which were published between 1530 and 1536 – with illustrations by Hans Weiditz the Younger – or the *Historia Animalium* by physician and scholar Konrad Gessner, whose several volumes were printed between 1551 and 1558.

As they primarily addressed scientific concerns, these illustrations have up to now been given little attention in the traditional history of art and artists. Only the works of artists as prominent as Pisanello, Leonardo, Dürer, Jacopo Ligozzi, Joris Hoefnagel and Hans Hoffmann, while always seen as artistically important, have also been appreciated in their significance for scientific research.

However, it was precisely in the middle of the 16th century that this interest for natural sciences began to establish itself in European courts. Fascinated by the immeasurable wealth of new, hitherto unknown plants and animals from overseas and the New World, Grand Dukes Francesco I and Ferdinando I of Tuscany, Duke Francesco Maria II della Rovere, King Philip I of Spain, Duke Albrecht V of Bavaria and above all Maximilian II and Rudolf II all encouraged scientific research.

Emperor Rudolf II was long considered the most significant promoter of natural sciences among the Habsburgs. This can be supported through of the splendid and artful manuscripts that Joris Hoefnagel executed for him, as well as with the so-called *Museums*. In addition the Emperor particularly encouraged, and furthered, mechanical-technical, physical, astronomical and alchemic innovations. However in the very area of the natural sciences his forerunners had already done much. In 1554-1555, Pier Andrea Mattioli, the famous Sienese naturalist and physician to Ferdinand I, Maximilian II and Archduke Ferdinand of Tyrol, had already brought out a commented and illustrated edition of Dioscorides' *Materia medica* supported by Emperor Charles V. In Vienna and Prague he successfully worked on an improved and extended version in different languages and involved the Udinese painter Giorgo Liberale as scientific illustrator of Adriatic sea creatures as well as other animals[3]. A collection of some hundred painted studies of sea creatures, but also insects etc. mounted on large sheets of parchment is also ascribed to Liberale. Only a few of these were used for woodcuts in Mattioli's luxury edition (1564).

Indeed Liberale's lavish and costly plates reveal the contrasting aspirations of art, set against studies done purely for the sake of scientific knowledge. For instance, the sheet which illustrates the fins of a ray seen from above, partly covered by a decorative frame, displays on its reverse the ventral part of the ray, with the fins protruding over the frame in a *trompe-l'oeil* effect, showing how the aspirations of art enter into competition with purely scientific illustration (cat. no. IV.23). In these parchment illustrations made for Archduke Ferdinand of Tyrol, the contrast between natural scientific illustration and the need to present the objects of nature in an artistic and materially sumptuous manner becomes apparent. This duality between a realistic appraisal of nature and its artistic transposition reflects the aspirations of contemporary monarchs, which probably differed from the prevalently scientific aspirations of naturalists.

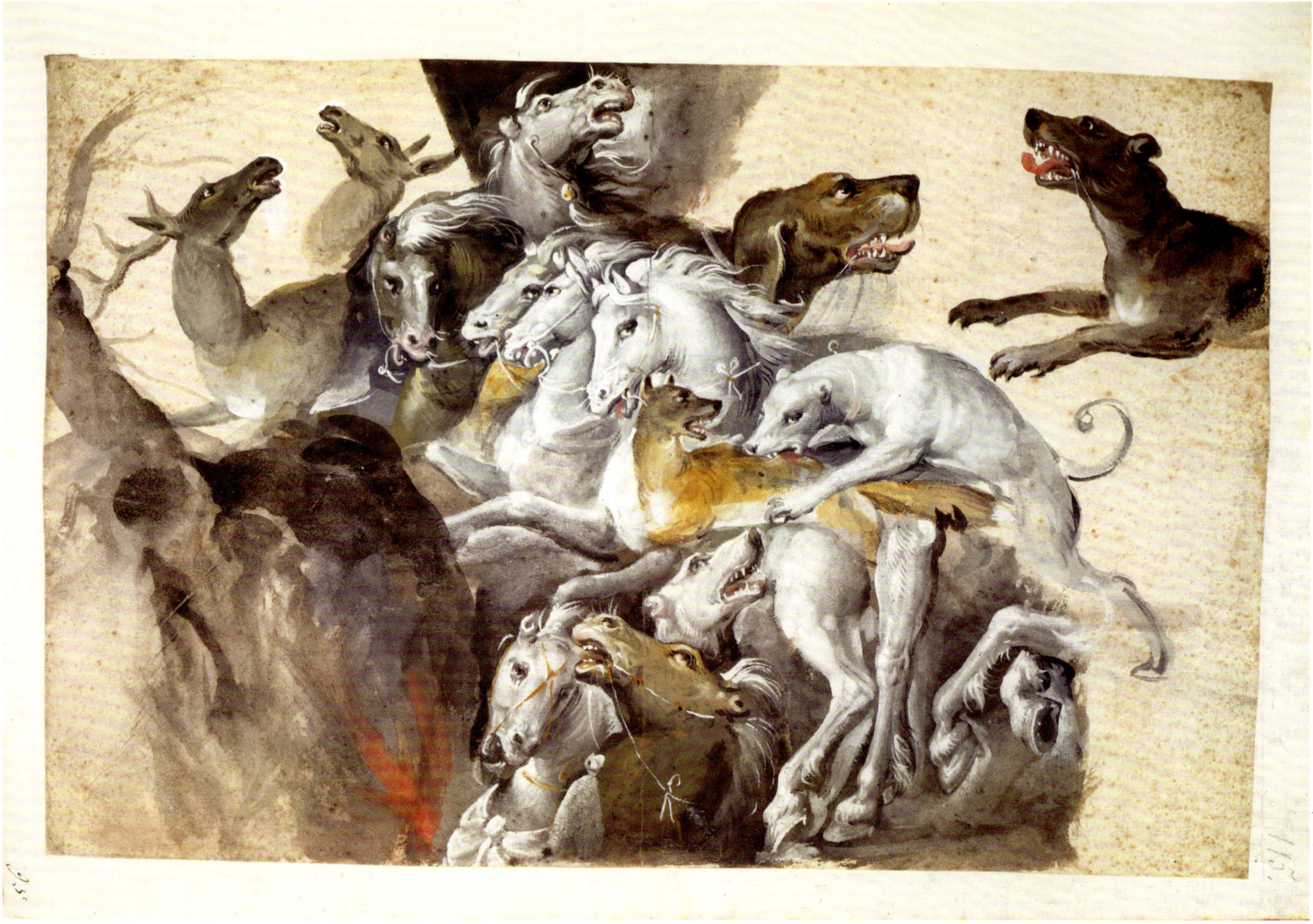

Fig. 1. Giuseppe Arcimboldo, *Composition with Animals*. Watercolour and gouache. Vienna, Österreichische Nationalbibliothek, Cod. min. 42, fol. 115r

The exceptional accomplishments of Emperor Maximilian II, Arcimboldo's principal patron, in the field of natural research, have recently been the object of in-depth study[4]. The Emperor recruited the most famous botanists of his time, such as Carolus Clusius, who was at his court from 1573 to 1577, and also Robertus Dodonaeus, who then moved on to Prague[5]. Maximilian had an equally large interest for animals. In 1552, for his festive entry into Vienna with his new consort Maria, he had a twelve-year-old Indian elephant, a present from his cousin and sister-in-law, Johanna of Spain, steal the show from him[6]. He lavished particular attention on the splendid zoos at Kaiserebersdorf and in the Neugebäuede[7] that were filled with rare species from Africa, Asia and America. The intense exchange of letters with his ambassadors at the court of his cousin Philip II clearly shows how eagerly he awaited plants and animals from the New World[8].

However, it was only when studying the animals in Emperor Rudolf II's so-called *Museum* that one started wondering about the history of those sheets and the possible models for those nature studies[9]. Thea Vignau-Wilberg and Lee Hendrix were the first to identify some of the animals in the *Museum* as elaborate copies or replicas of original studies drawn from nature, glued onto the sheets of a codex now preserved in the manuscript collection of the Nationalbibliothek in Vienna. They related some of these drawings to Arcimboldo's painting *Earth*, guardedly suggesting that they might be his own work[10]. Manfred Staudinger, whose research is presented in this catalogue, discovered that some of these drawings had been sent to the famous natural scientist Ulisse Aldrovandi and that several animal studies in the Codex min. 42 and in Rudolf II *Museum* could be attributed to Arcimboldo[11]. In 1992, Lucilla Conigliello already asserted her conviction that Arcimboldo was the

Fig. 2. Giuseppe Arcimboldo, *Study of a Goat's Deformed Hoof* (?). Vienna, Österreichische Nationalbibliothek, Cod. min. 42, fol. 23r

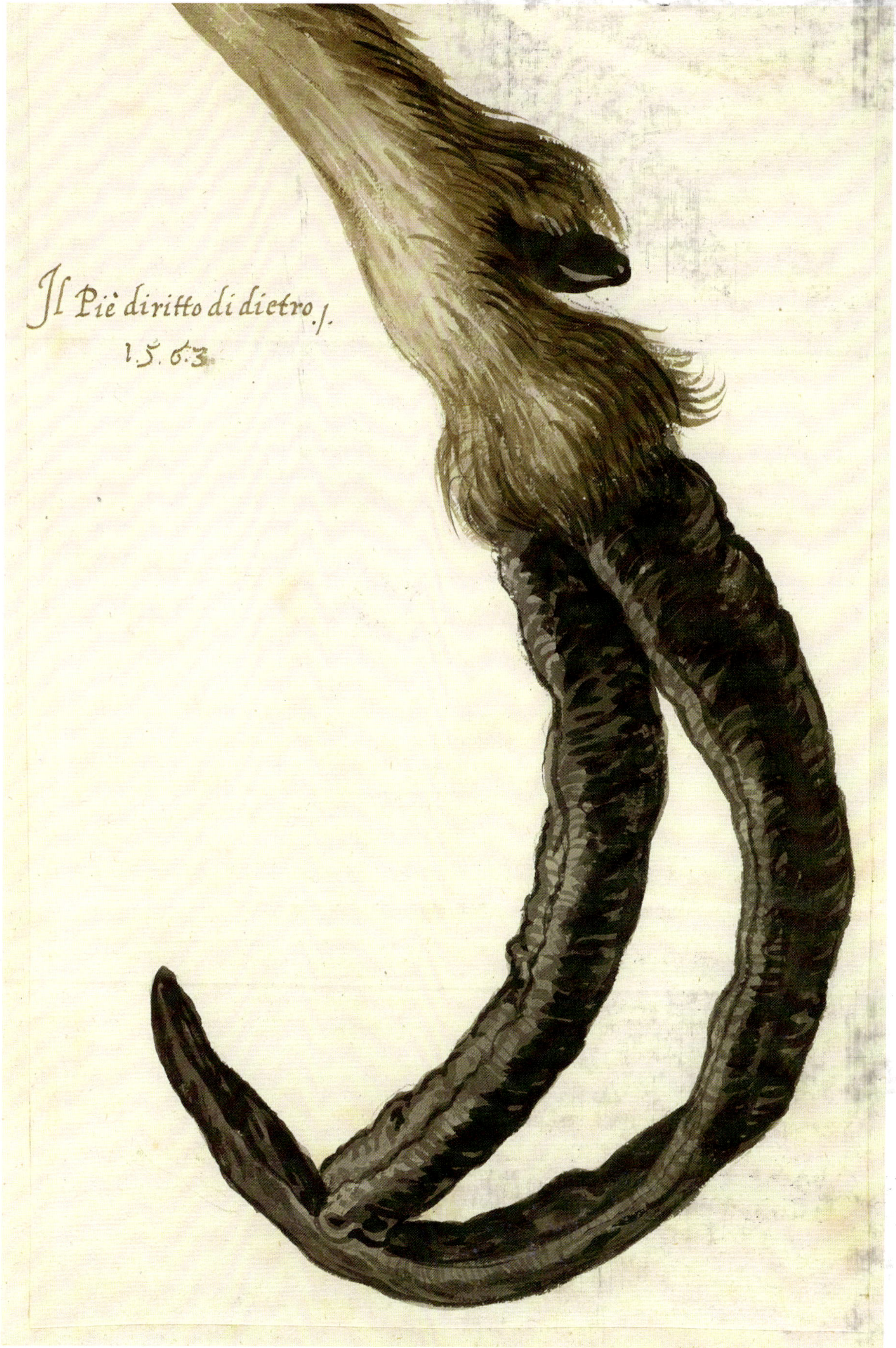

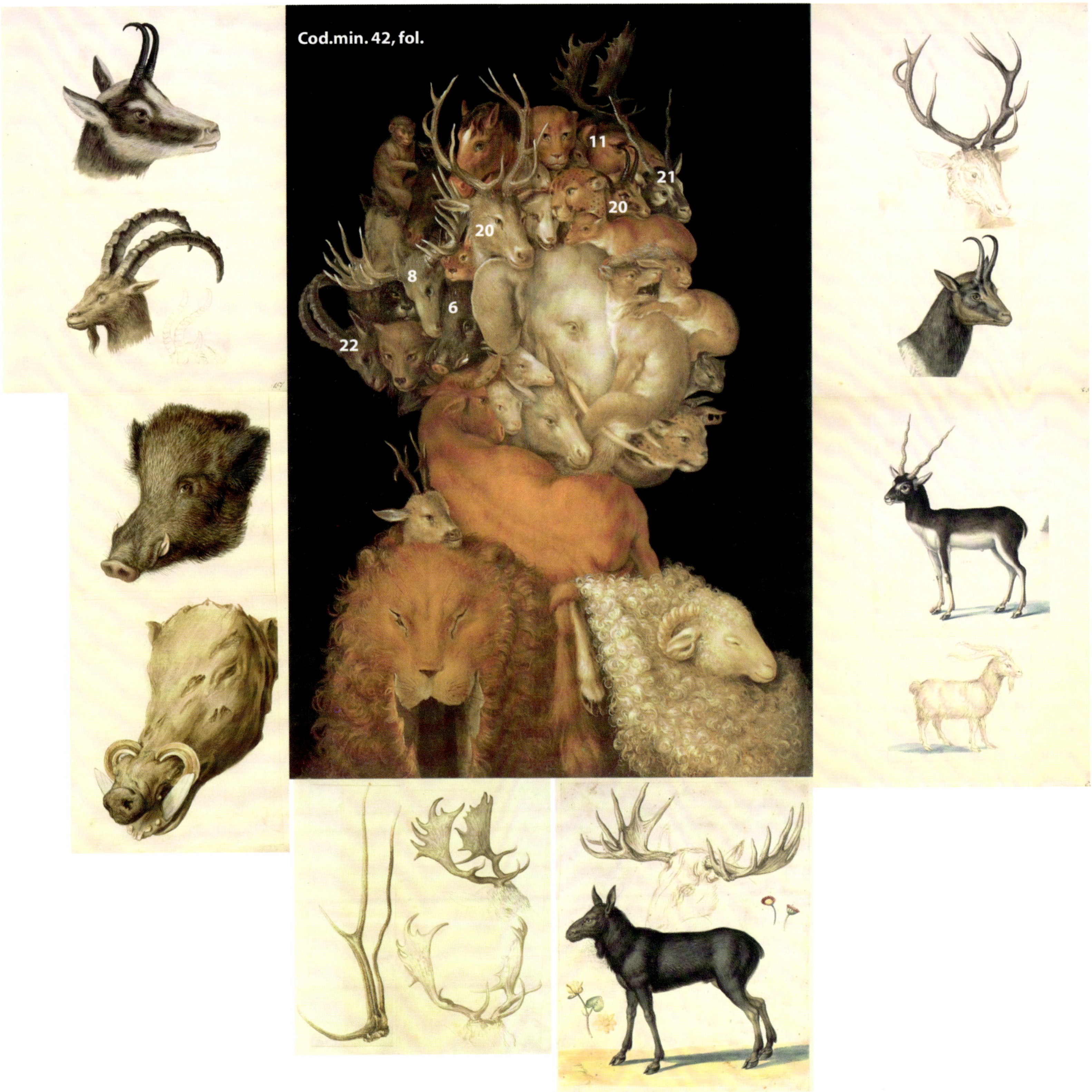

Fig. 3. Giuseppe Arcimboldo, *Earth*. Vienna, private collection. Surrounded with some of the artist's studies from nature in Cod. min. 42, fol. 23r, Vienna, Österreichische Nationalbibliothek

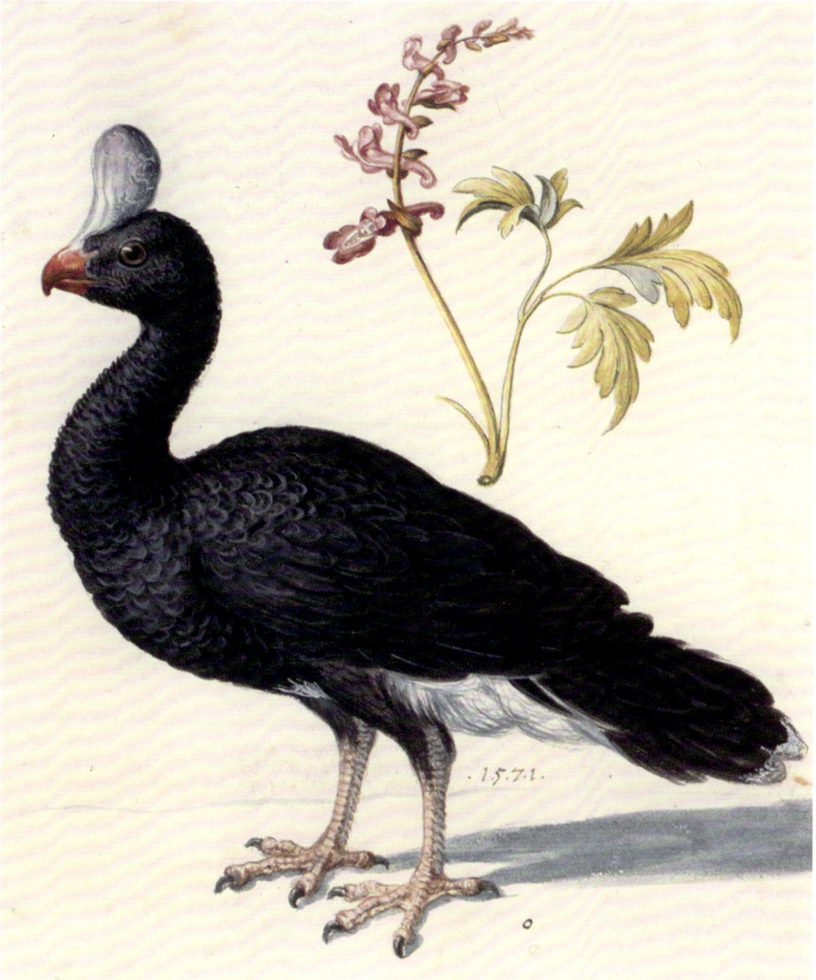

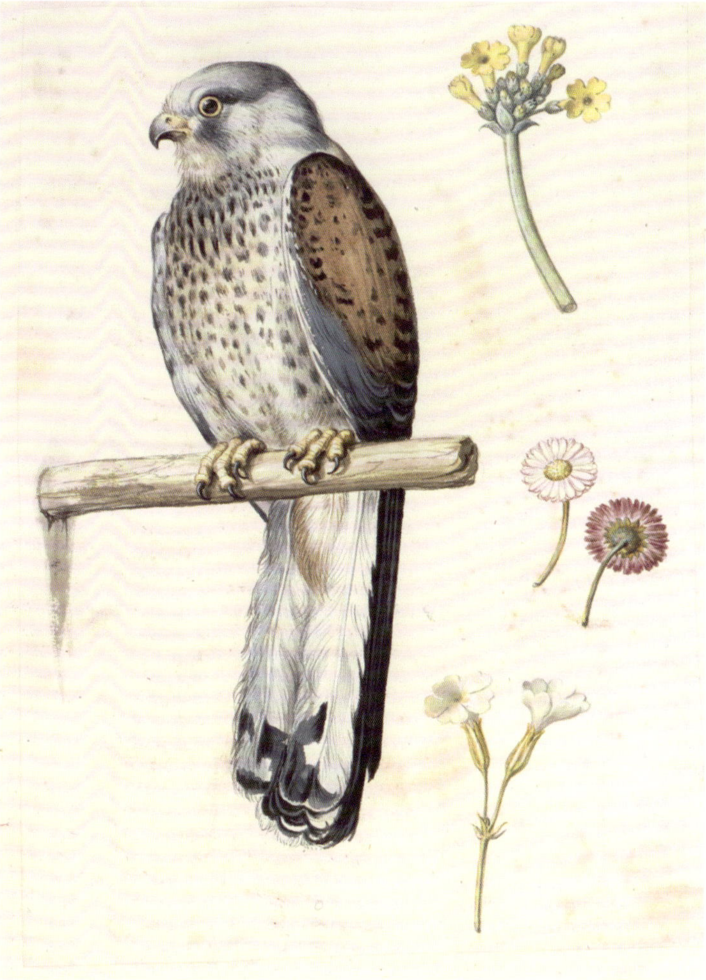

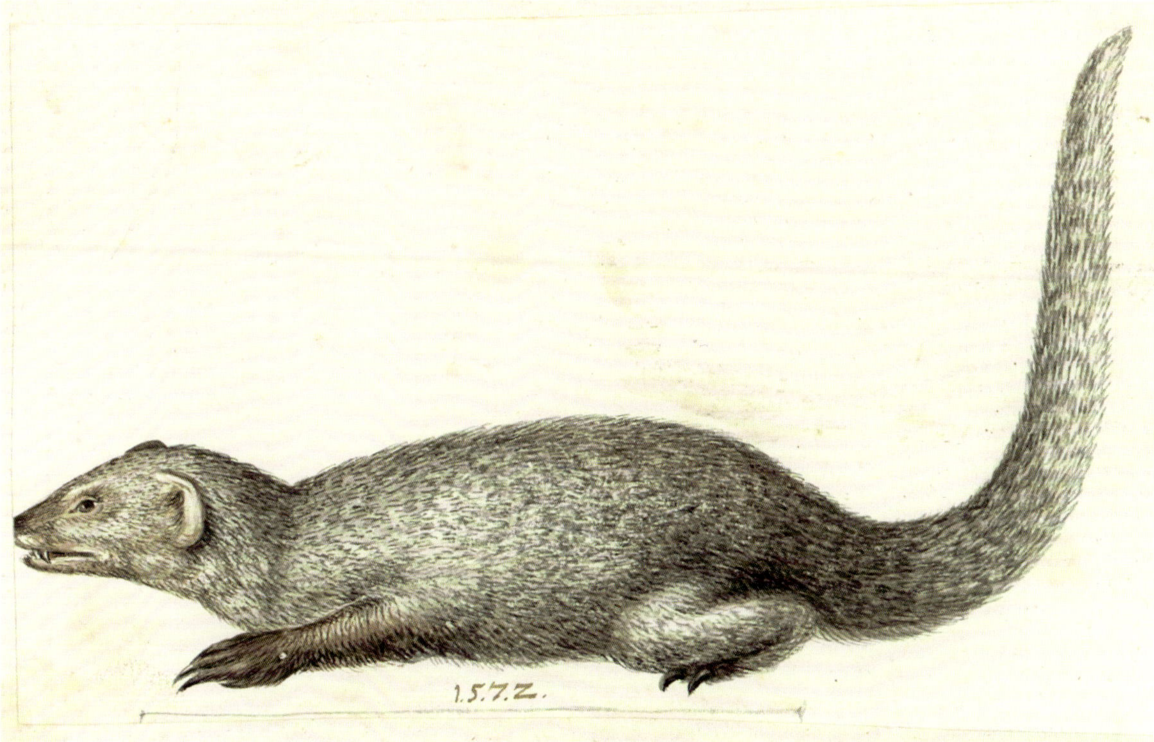

Fig. 4. Giuseppe Arcimboldo, *Study of a Helmeted Curassow*. Vienna, Österreichische Nationalbibliothek, Cod. min. 42, fol. 46r

Fig. 5. Giuseppe Arcimboldo, *Study of a Lesser Kestrel and Flowers*. Vienna, Österreichische Nationalbibliothek, Cod. min. 42, fol. 29r

Fig. 6. Giuseppe Arcimboldo, *Study of an Indian Mongoose*. Vienna, Österreichische Nationalbibliothek, Cod. min. 42, fol. 128r (above right)

author of a group of drawings to be found in this codex[12]. Starting from a very skilful tempera sketch, an unusual scene with agitated dogs, horses and deer (*fig. 1*), she attributed other sheets to Arcimboldo. Studies of the monstrously grown hooves of a goat, with a comment in Italian, surely written in Arcimboldo's hand – one is dated as early as 1563 (*fig. 2*) – are stylistically close to the studies of animals that can be seen in almost identical positions and stances in the composite head of *Earth* (*fig. 3*)[13]. In this catalogue, Manfred Staudinger has identified all the animals in that painting (cat. no. IV.24). This corroborates Comanini's description of a painting of *Earth*, sent to the king of Spain, for which Emperor Maximilian II allegedly allowed Arcimboldo to make direct natural studies of animals[14].

These very studies of animals (now in private hands) which are identically reproduced in the painting of *Earth*, are not dated. Only the *red hartebeest* in the Codex bears the date 1570, increasing the suspicion, due to the different format, that this painting stems from a later series than *Fire* and *Water* in Vienna (cat. nos. IV.16, 18)[15].

This small, above mentioned group of pictures in the same Codex, could be extended to include a considerable number of other studies of mammals and birds (*fig. 4* and cat. no. IV.33): entire animals, in addition to particular studies of heads, antlers and horns, as well as birds, and studies of plants (*fig. 5*).

These works, probably originally drawn on larger sheets and subsequently individually cut according to the theme, show in their sketchiness and in the way they are arbitrarily distributed over the paper, that these are personal studies in the truest sense of the word, made to acquire knowledge through the "portrait" of the different physical correlations and consistency of the subjects, the coat surface, horns, feathers etc.

Arcimboldo's studies stand out from the many other works carried out by other artists in this Codex due to his personal, self-possessed way of drawing, ever sparing in the use of technical materials, that however is capable of extraordinary illusionistic effects. Most of the nature studies drawn by German or Dutch artists in the same volume – Hans Verhagen from Antwerp, Hans Hoffmann, Daniel Fröschel and others – are done in a considerably finer manner with the intricately tiny "tocchi" and finest brushstrokes achieving breathtaking results through lavish use of opaque white. In comparison, Arcimboldo's are "sloppier". He mostly works with watercolour, and at times, particularly for birds, his stroke is loose, sketchy. Even in his particularly painstakingly worked studies he does not resort to opaque white and uses the white paper for the highlights (*fig. 6*). One can also tell his hand from his love of using a transparent, fine wash in elegant grey-blue to blue, if only to hint at a passing shadow. These washes also feature in his studies for masks and costumes (cat. nos. VII.1-32).

Many studies bear a date, generally in the same hand, even if the punctuation differs. Most of them are dated in the seventies and even the early eighties of the 16th century. In a study clearly in Arcimboldo's hand, using the aforementioned blue wash to depict a lizard, a salamander and a chameleon, a "1553" is noted down (*fig. 7*)[16]. Nevertheless, it is not clear whether the date indicates the creation of the drawing or the arrival date or date of finding of the dead chameleon. In the first case, it would be an early example of realistic nature study, an approach that was to fully unfold in Arcimboldo's time as court painter in Vienna[17].

In the painting *Air* (cat. no. IV.20), one can hardly recognize the birds, whose studies are here attributed to Arcimboldo. This is due to the lack of accuracy within the painting, even though the studies are for the most part dated in the 1570s.

Despite the extreme diversity of sea creatures represented in *Water*, no studies in the Codex can be ascribed to Arcimboldo. How much he relied on readily available, illustrated compendiums, or preparatory drawings like the ones Giorgio Liberale must have done on parchment, should receive further research[18].

The attributions of plant studies also pose problems. Isolated buds and flowers of various species appear on sheets with animal representations (*fig. 4-5*) though the step from here to the clean, highly realistic plant studies made by Arcimboldo at the end of the Codex is a long one, and still needs to be intensively looked into[19].

On this point the complaint by Franciscus Paduanus in his letter to Aldrovandi is particularly enlightening: "Today I received from Giuseppe Arcimboldo of Milan, the emperor's principal painter, coloured pictures drawn after nature of several exotic birds and quadrupeds [...]. But as I said before, I am forced to avail myself of the help of a painter, who harrows and tries my patience. For he was careless to the following extent: When a nobleman a few days ago brought to the emperor the plant that Carolus Clusius calls *Tusai* or Persian lily in the first chapter of his *Rariorum aliquot stirpium, per Pannoniam, Austriam, & vicinas quasdam provincias observatarum historia*, luckily I managed to get hold of it when it was still fairly fresh. I immediately brought it to be painted; he promised to do so, but did not keep his promise. He travelled off to a wedding, he stayed away for some days, and meanwhile the flower yellowed, the leaves fell off and the plant withered and died. And though you surely will have seen this plant elsewhere, I was fairly vexed at his callousness"[20].

In his contribution, Manfred Staudinger publishes and comments a list of twenty animals that was sent to the most famous naturalist of the 16th century, Ulisse Aldrovandi, active in Bologna. It gives valuable information on what species were to be found at the court of Emperor Rudolf in Prague.

All the same, the few still identifiable sheets in the Fondo Aldrovandi differ from the "original studies" due to the lavish

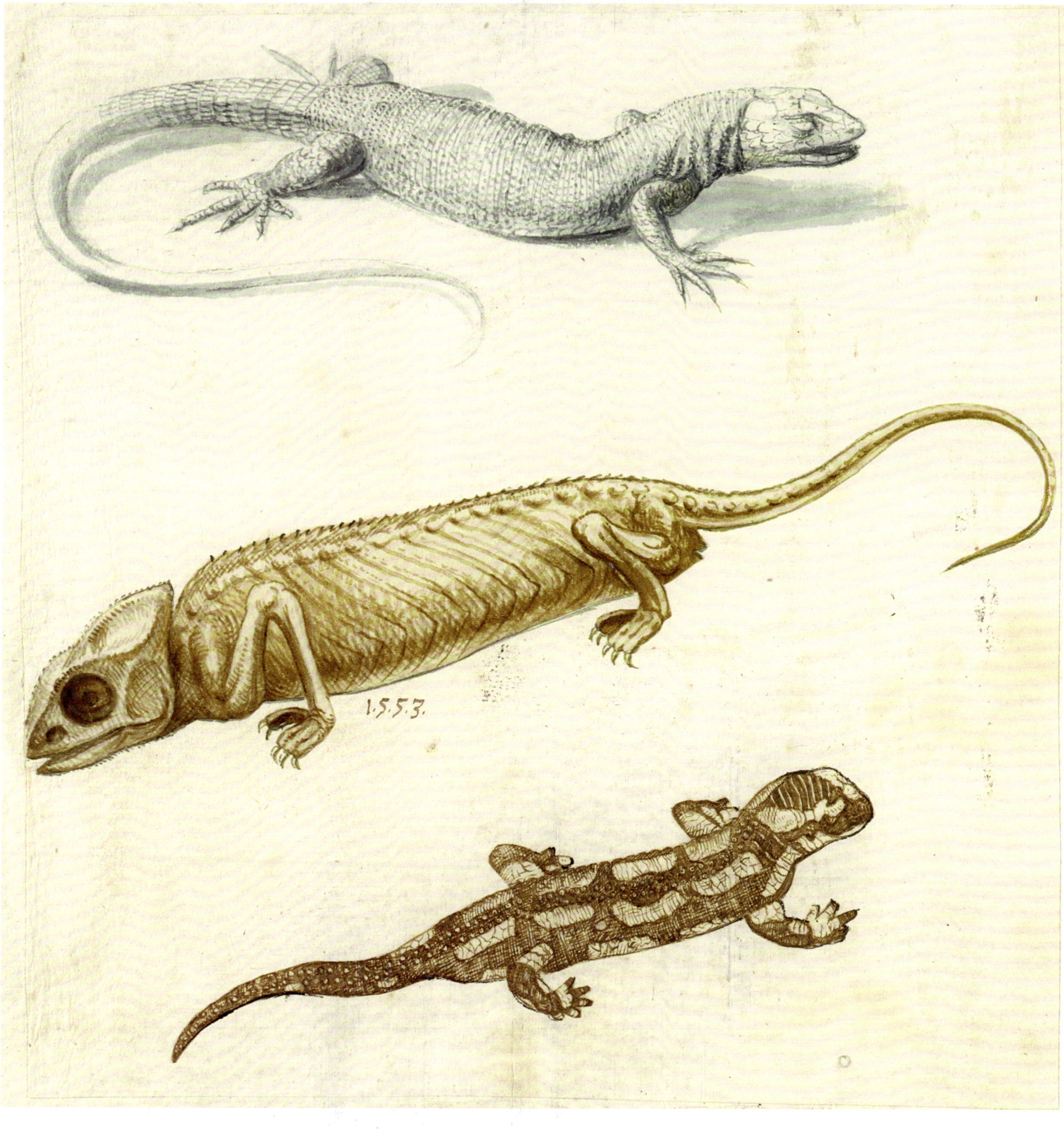

Fig. 7. Giuseppe Arcimboldo, *Study of a Lizard, a Chameleon and a Salamander*. Vienna, Österreichische Nationalbibliothek, Cod. min. 42, fol. 128r (left)

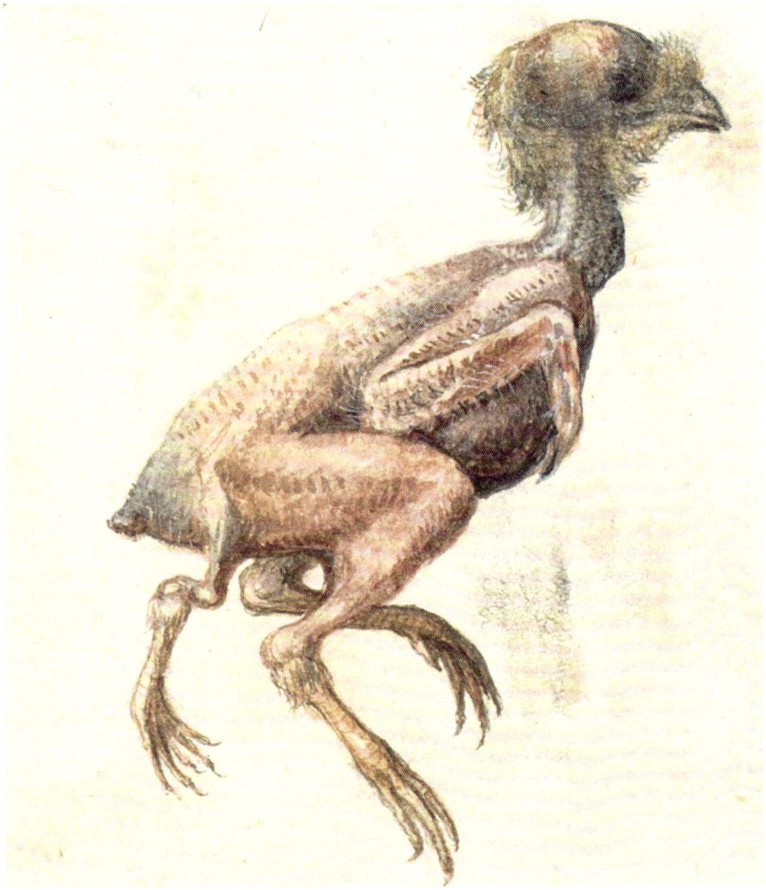

Fig. 8. Giuseppe Arcimboldo, *Study of a featherless three-footed Chick*. Vienna, Österreichische Nationalbibliothek, Cod. min. 42, fol. 46r

bodycolour technique on a coloured ground and the addition of strips of ground covered with grass. These "artistic" scenes are closer to the illustrations in Rudolf II's *Museum*, where we partially find the same animals in the same positions, also in the lavish bodycolour technique, set in scenes with coloured grounds.

Here the question naturally arises whether those watercolour sketches after nature were "edited" by Arcimboldo, reworking them with bodycolour for other purposes. According to Manfred Staudinger, it is quite likely that the artist painted them himself to meet higher artistic requirements, for Rudolf 's *Museum*. As concerns those nature studies, Arcimboldo himself may have copied the mostly rare objects of nature, to allow the scientists to become acquainted with them[21].

Ulisse Aldrovandi left behind him an incredible legacy; not only his collection of *naturalia*, stuffed animals, minerals and dried plants, the result of exchange with other courts interested in science in general and the natural sciences in particular, but also over 148 generally unpublished manuscripts and 15 volumes of illustrations, now in the Bologna University library and available on line[22]. They give an idea of his tireless activity in the building up of a richly ramified information network, comprising not only valuable indications as to the exchange of drawings and descriptions of animals and plants in stuffed, dried or drawn form, with international experts involved in this field – such as Mattioli in Prague – but also discussion forums with other researchers over the relevance of various published or unpublished research reports.

Singularities, abnormalities and monstrosities had a special significance for this scientist who grasped things in a purely empirical manner[23], but this was also part of a general interest for such "wonders" of nature. The studies here attributed to Arcimboldo also include threelegged chickens and birds (*fig. 8*). A particular sensation throughout Europe at this time was the famous "hairy man" Pedro Gonzalez: paintings still exist of him and his equally hairy children in the most important court portrait collections (cat. no. IV.27). However, among the numerous paintings which vary in format and composition (a family portrait was even included in Rudolf 's *Museum*), none has yet been ascribed to Arcimboldo, even though the family was invited by Aldrovandi to Bologna, so that he could study the syndrome with his own eyes.

Even though Aldrovandi managed to win over the most famous artist in the field of nature studies, the Veronese painter Jacopo Ligozzi[24], most of his *tavole* were only created by second-rank illustrators, if only for economic reasons. Aldrovandi himself complained of their lack of talent, and many of them had to be schooled in the specific methods of illustration[25]. Here also appears the problem of a depiction of nature which had to meet scientific requirements and artistic objectives. In the humanistic courts, "nature" was basically seen in relation to "art", which also explains Arcimboldo's task as court painter to firstly depict *naturalia* in their actual presence, and then to work them up "artistically". This projects a new light on Maximilian's and even Rudolf's delight in Arcimboldo's composite heads, which were derived from the direct observation of nature, but transfigured by art. The pleasure which the emperors took in sending copies of the *Seasons* and the *Elements* to their relatives and regents in the courts of Saxony, Bavaria and Madrid, also takes on a new meaning: with these jocular paradoxes they not only wanted to boast about the abilities of their court painter, but also to propagandize their achievements in the controversial field of natural sciences[26].

[1] Comanini 1591, 256.
[2] Venice 1987, 96-97.
[3] Staudinger, Irblich in Vienna 1995, 64-76; Vienna 1996, 209-225; Mazal 1982, 12-38.
[4] Rudolf 1995, 175-187. See also Karl Schütz' contribution in this catalogue.
[5] Mout 2000, 46-64; Hendrix 1997, 158.
[6] Sutter Fichtner 2001, 96; Opll 2004. It died a year later and was reportedly turned into a three-sided stool. See *1200 Jahre Kremsmünster*, Stiftsführer, Linz 1977, 166-167.

[7] Rudolf 1995, 182.
[8] Rudolf 1995, 181-182; Pérez de Tudela, Jordan Gschwend 2001, 8f., 17f.
[9] Staudinger, Irblich, Vignau-Wilberg, Hendrix 1990; Koreny (ed.) 1986-87.
[10] Vignau-Wilberg 1990, 40-41; Hendrix 1997, 158.
[11] Staudinger 1996, 233.
[12] Conigliello 1992, 44-49 and ill. 23-34.
[13] Independently from her publication I came to the same conclusion, this attribution being the basis for even more justified further attributions. A complete view of a goat with similarly grown hooves is also to be found in Aldrovandi's animal studies.
[14] Comanini 1591 (1962), 266. According to Rudolf (1995, 182-187) *Earth* and the other pictures of the series got to the court of Philip II only after 1580.
[15] Hendrix 1997, also dates the *Earth* around 1570.
[16] Österreichische Nationalbibliothek, Handschriften-, Autographen- und Nachlass-Sammlung, Cod. min. 42.
[17] The very different graphic executions of the single studies on this sheet might mean that Arcimboldo added the lizard, clearly in his hand and painted with blue wash, at a later date.
[18] A possible model for the elephant seal can be found in both the *Historia* by Olaus Magnus from 1555 as well as in the *Icones* by Conradus Gesner from 1560, see Venice 1987, 94.
[19] On fol. 161 of the Cod. min. 42 we find a shoot sprouting from a bud with the caption: "1579 in Praga", that could derive from Arcimboldo.
[20] BUB, ms 136, tom. 11, fol. 5r-5v: "Habui et hisce diebus a Josepho Arcimboldo Mediolanum [sic, pro Mediolanensi] Caesaris pictore primario plurium auium et quadrupedum peregrinorum imagines ad uiuum coloribus delineatas ut illas solummodo in tui gratiam effigiare curarem sicuti per literas ad Illustrissimum Bernardinum Blasettum datas de istorum nominibus significaui.
Sed cuiusdam pictoris opere, ut a principio dixi cogor uti, qui me in patientia exercet et probat. nam fuit adeo negligens quod cum Caesari proximis hisce diebus plantam illam quam Tusai siue lilium Persicum Carolus Clusius libro rariorum stirpium per Pannoniam obseruatarum capitulo primo appellat nobilis quidam attulisset nescio quo fabu [sic, pro fato?] adhuc probe uirens ad manus deuenerit meas. hanc statim illi ad effigiandum obtuli, spopondit, sed postea promissis non stetit. nam cum alio nuptiarum caussa secessisset per plures abfuit dies, interim flauescentibus floribus, decidentibusque foliis planta emaciata totaque corrupta est.
Et quamuis alias te hanc uidisse plantam non ambigam, huius tamen inscitiam certe indignabundus tuli" (transcribed by Karin Zeleny). Berra 2000 referred already to this passage in the letter. See also document 29 in Staudinger's Register.
[21] Tomasi Tongiorgi 1996, 143.
[22] http://www.filosofia.unibo.it/aldrovandi/. On Aldrovandi see Olmi – Tomasi Tongiorgi 1993; Crea (ed.) 1993; Frati 1907.
[23] Aldrovandi 1642.
[24] Tomasi Tongiorgi in Washington 2002, 38ff.
[25] Olmi, Tomasi Tongiorgi 1993, 9-31.
[26] This is surely the case with the paintings of the *Seasons* that were sent to Spain. Earlier copies of the series now in Denver and Houston are still in Spanish private collections.

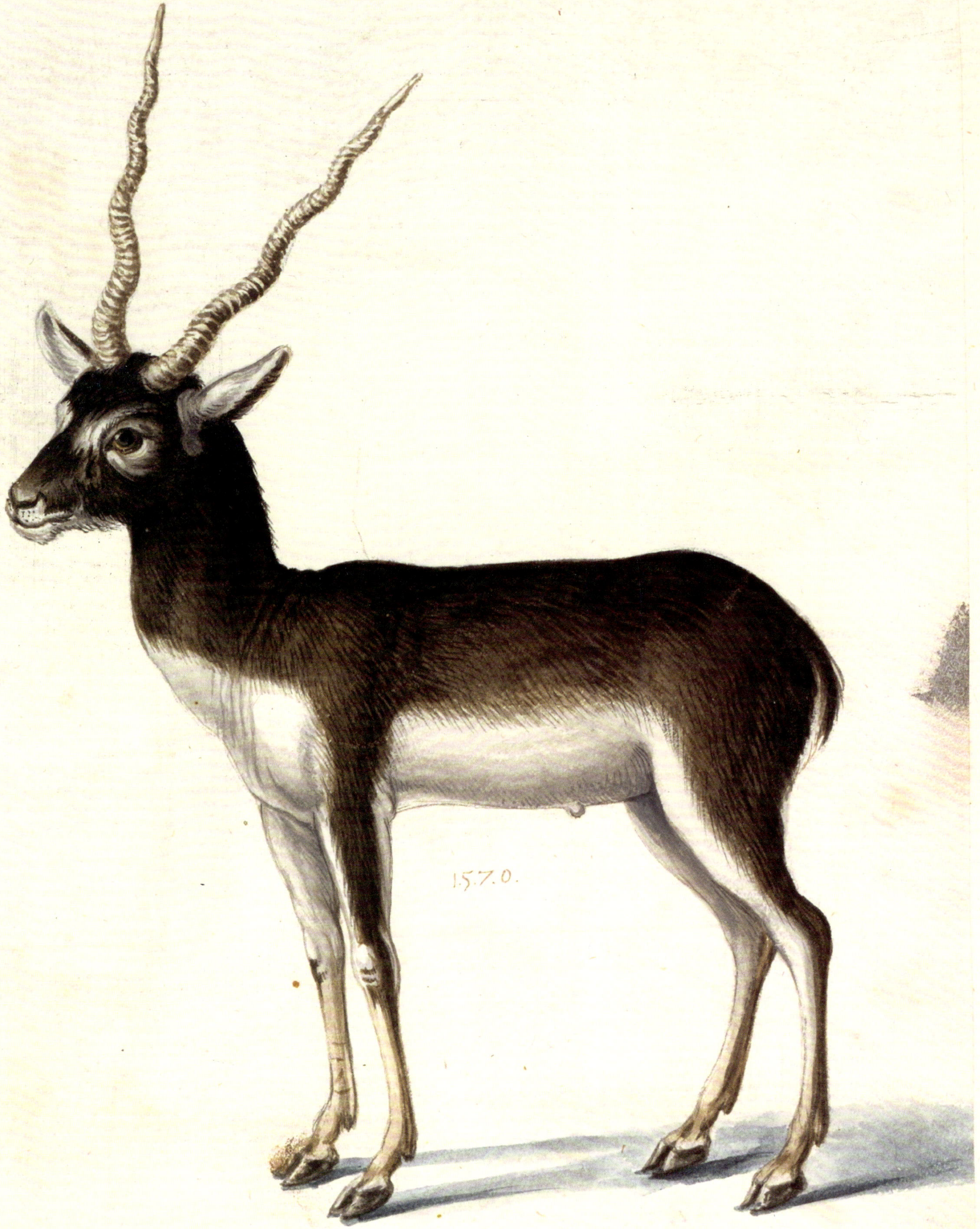
1570.

Manfred Staudinger

Arcimboldo and Ulisse Aldrovandi

Between 1583 and 1585 Franciscus Paduanus sent from Prague pictures of exotic animals in the emperor's court to Ulisses Aldrovandi in Bologna and wrote that he had received them from Jakob Scutellarius. Included was also a list of these animals[1].

Paduanus, occasionally also known as Patavinus, was originally from Friuli and was the physician of Hans Kinsky, burgrave at Karlstein. He had good contacts with the Roman Church and spent some time in Prague between 1583 and 1593. Jakob Scutellarius came from Parma and was the emperor's personal physician from April 1581; he died towards the end of 1589 in Prague. In another letter to Aldrovandi dated September 1585, Paduanus wrote that Giuseppe Arcimboldo had painted pictures, sent by other means, of exotic birds and mammals "*ad vivum delineatus*"[2] (doc. 29). These two pages are today still found in the Biblioteca universitaria di Bologna, Fondo Ulisse Aldrovandi, *Tavole di animali*, vol. 5/1, fol. 20 and vol. 6/2, fol. 87.

The originals of these animal pictures are as a rule found in cod. min. 42, whose studies were glued in and at the time only loosely so that the artists could use individual ones as models. However, they did not serve only as ingredients for separate oil paintings, but they also formed the foundation for a collection of animal pictures on parchment (today cod. min. 129 and cod. min. 130 of the Österreichische Nationalbibliothek). The gouache paintings on parchment are sometimes superior to the 'originals', as far as content and quality[3] are concerned, which allows to conclude to their common paternity and to their temporal proximity.

From the aforementioned list, the following entries could refer both to Aldrovandi's pictures as well as to the animal studies of the imperial court:

Colombo d'India

L'Asino d'Africa

Il Capriolo d'Africa

La Capra del Bezoar

Il Tasso marino

"Il Colombo dell'Indie" or "Colombo d'India" doubtless refers to the picture of the Blue-headed Quail-Dove (*Starnoenas cyanocephala*). Today it is indeed no longer in the collection of the Fondo Ulisse Aldrovandi; however, the relation of the woodcut released in 1600 (Aldrovandi 1600, 482) (*fig. 1*) to the picture in cod. min. 42, fol. 41 below is thoroughly clear (*fig. 2*). This outstanding watercolour study was painted on paper from a live model and is dated "1577". It also served as an original for the meticulous copies on parchment in cod. min. 130, fol. 63r.

Aldrovandi wrote that he had received the picture years earlier from the imperial court in Vienna. The famous doctor, Hieronymus Paduanus (Patavinus) had allegedly sent it to him under the heading, "Indian dove with duck's bill"; however, apart from the feet and its size, it has nothing in common with a dove[4]. This note indicates that a description had been sent along with the picture, as conform to the scientific practice of the time. Alas, it is all too frequent that images and texts go separate ways; it is therefore unknown whether this description still exists today.

The indication "L'Asino d'Africa" seems to be a bit extravagant, and it was not recorded by any of Paduanus' contemporaries. One could think of an African wild ass, but that ultimately leads nowhere. The folio in cod. min. 129, fol. 24r offers not the same, but a similar inscription, "ANIMAL D'AFRICA", and shows a Red Hartebeest (*Alcelaphus buselaphus*). A copy of it, or of a hypothetical watercolour, can be found in the *Tavole di animali* vol. 5/1, fol. 20 above (*fig. 3*). It in turn served as a model for the woodcut that Aldrovandi published in the chapter, "De Bove Strepticerote" (*fig. 4*). Regarding this, he wrote that a few years earlier he had received from the court of Rudolf II wonderfully executed pictures of exotic animals, not unlike the one of a cow shown here[5].

The clue for the identification of the "Capriolo d'Africa" is found on the folio cod. min. 129, fol. 25r, which is inscribed with "CABRILLAS DE INDIAS". Portrayed are three Red-flanked Duikers (*Cephalophus rufilatus*), a small male, a small female and a baby. These animals were mentioned in the reports of the ambassador Hans Khevenhüller dated 17 September and 16 December 1575 from Madrid[6] and may have arrived in Vienna as a gift of the king of Spain.

The watercolour study on paper in cod. min. 42, fol. 19 below (*fig. 8*), which shows only the male red-flanked duiker, served as a model for:

a) the animal decorations of the small oil painting from around

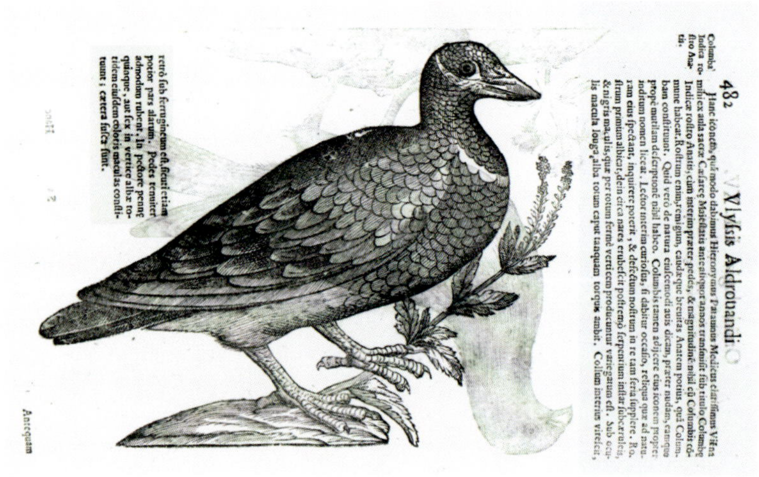

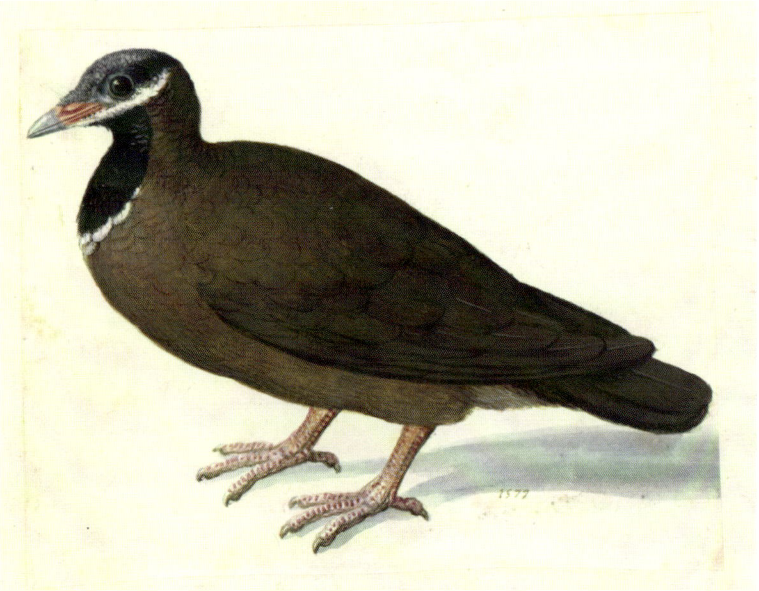

Fig. 1. Blue-headed Quail-Dove, in Ulisse Aldrovandi, *Ornithologiae tomus alter*, Bologna 1600, 482

Fig. 2. Giuseppe Arcimboldo, Blue-headed Quail-Dove, in Cod. min. 42, fol. 41 (bottom)

1560 (?), *The Expulsion from Paradise* (Vienna, Kunsthistorisches Museum, Gemäldegalerie, inv. no. 917),
b) the oil painting of *Venus and Bacchus* from 1590 by Bartholomäus Spranger (Hannover, Niedersächsische Landesgalerie, inv. no. PAM 956/982), where on the left behind a cheetah a red-flanked duiker can be seen, and
c) the picture sent to Aldrovandi in the *Tavole di animali* vol. 6/2, fol. 87 above (*fig. 7*), which served as a model for the woodcut published in the *Paralipomena* and labelled as "Hippelaphus" (Aldrovandi 1642, 127; *fig. 5*).

"La Capra del Bezoar" is identifiable as the Blackbuck (*Antilope cervicapra*). In the chapter entitled "De Capra sive Hirco Bezaartico", Aldrovandi shows a clearly recognizable Blackbuck (Aldrovandi 1621, 755f.; *fig. 6*).

The model for this woodcut can be found in the *Tavole di animali* vol. 5/1, on fol. 20 below, therefore on one of the folios originating in Prague (*fig. 3 in the previous contribution*), and is in turn based on cod. min. 42, fol. 21 above. The watercolour on paper dated as "1.5.7.0." was also copied onto parchment (cod. min. 129, fol. 21r) and served as one of the models for the animal decorations in the previously mentioned *The Expulsion from Paradise* in the Kunsthistorisches Museum in Vienna.

The Blackbuck produces bezoar, as do certain other animals. This identification provides the first documentation that this characteristic was already known in Europe in 1580.

"Il Tasso marino" indicates a badger brought to Europe from overseas, where it originated[7]. In a list from 9 February 1580 of the approximate annual expenses of the Ebersdorf regime for the attention of Vidame Wolf Fuert in Vienna, Hans Berchtoldt, the caretaker there, named a "Merdaxl" among other animals such as lions, tigers, lynxes, bears, apes and parrots (doc. 19). Aldrovandi used the same name, *Taxus marinus* in a legend from his chapter on the badger (*fig. 9*)[8].

The model for the woodcut can be found in the *Tavole di animali* vol. 6/2, fol. 87 below (*fig. 7*). This is one of the folios from Prague that had been sent to him by Hieronymus Paduanus and that originate from Giuseppe Arcimboldo. Unfortunately its model, perhaps a watercolour on paper in cod. min. 42, did not survive; however, to compensate for this is a miniature copy on parchment in cod. min. 129, fol. 53r. With the help of this folio, the species can be identified as a Mountain Coati (*Nasuella olivacea*). The Mountain Coati inhabits numerous, apparently isolated regions in the mountains of Venezuela, Colombia and Ecuador, in elevations from 2000 to 3100 meters[9]. In Aldrovandi's *Paralipomena*, published in 1642, there is a short chapter on the *Taxus montanus*, which could now actually include the description of this picture[10].

Without the possibility of referring to this text, and naturally without any knowledge of the models, in 1766 Linnaeus cited this

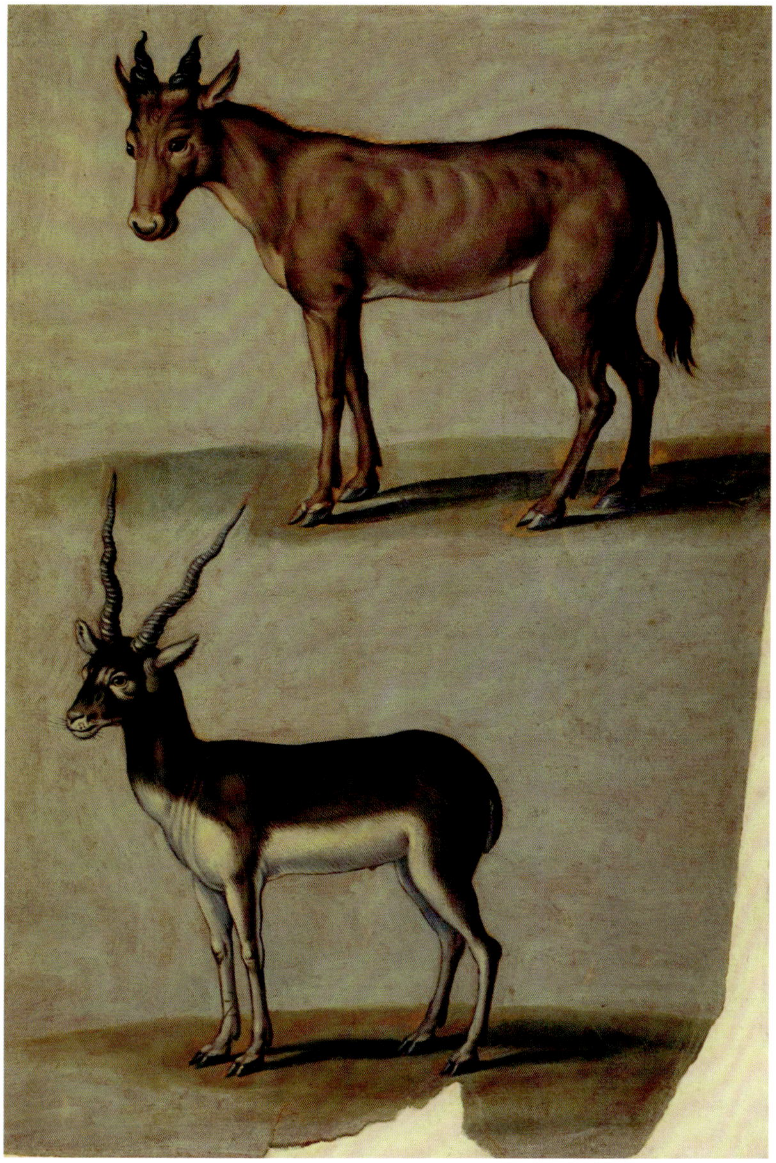

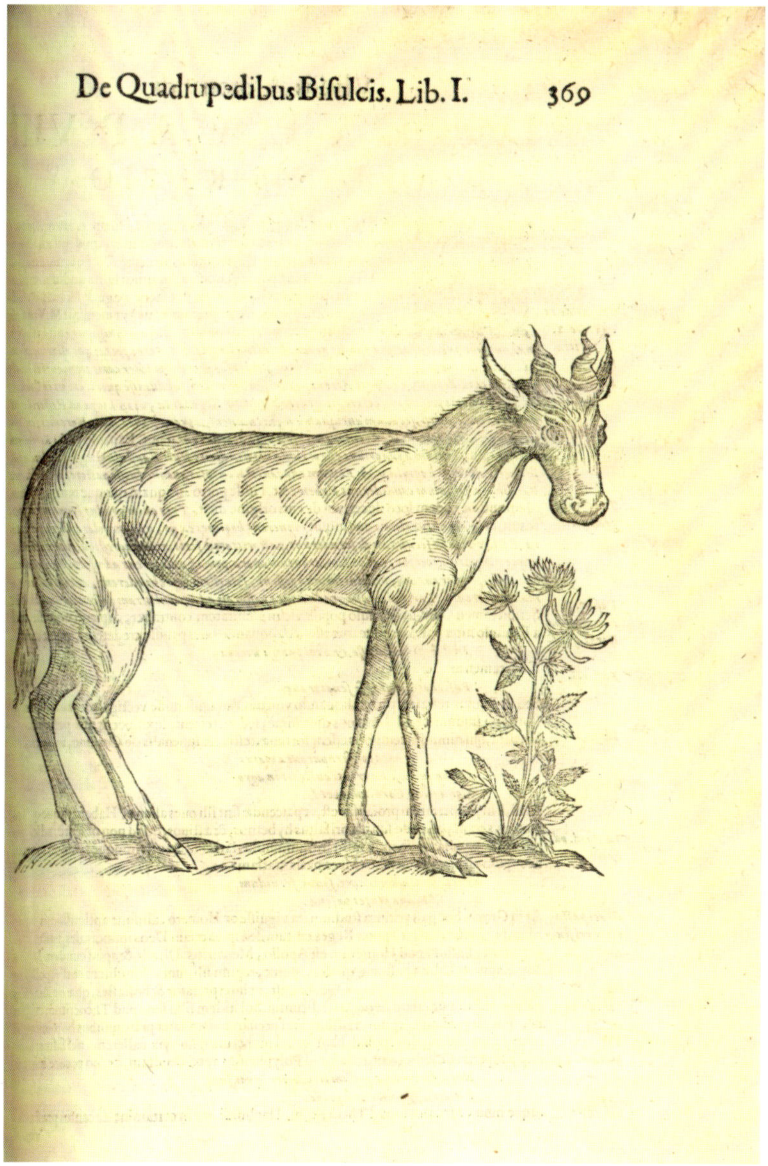

De Quadrupedibus Bifulcis. Lib. I. 369

Fig. 3. Red Hartebeest and Blackbuck, in Fondo Ulisse Aldrovandi, Bologna University Library, *Tavole di animali*, vol. 5/1, fol. 20

Fig. 4. Red Hartebeest, in Ulisse Aldrovandi, *Quadrupedum omnium bisulcorum Historia*, Bologna 1621, 369

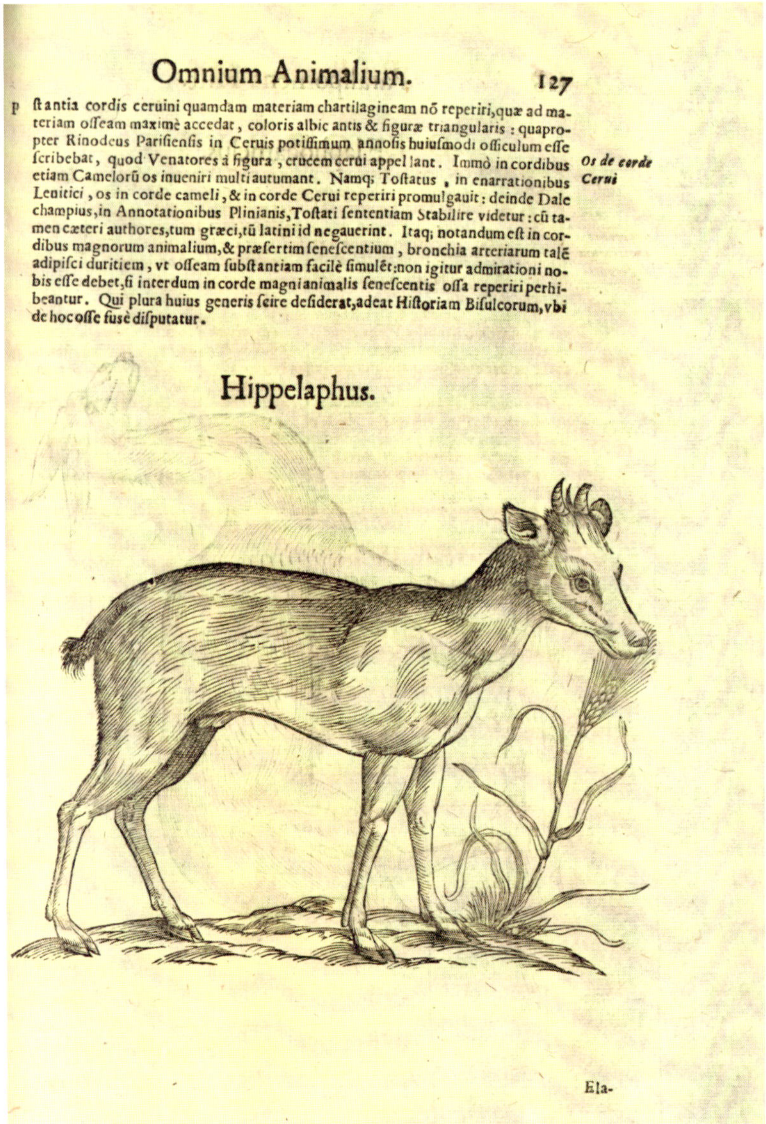

Omnium Animalium. 127

p ſtantia cordis ceruini quamdam materiam chartilagineam nõ reperiri,quæ ad materiam oſſeam maximè accedat, coloris albicantis & figuræ triangularis: quapropter Rinodeus Pariſienſis in Ceruis potiſſimum annoſis huiuſmodi oſſiculum eſſe ſcribebat, quod Venatores à figura, crucem cerui appellant. Immò in cordibus etiam Camelorũ os inueniri multi autumant. Namq; Toſtatus, in enarrationibus Leuitici, os in corde cameli, & in corde Cerui reperiri promulgauit: deinde Dalechampius, in Annotationibus Plinianis, Toſtati ſententiam Stabilire videtur: cũ tamen cæteri authores, tum græci, tũ latini id negauerint. Itaq; notandum eſt in cordibus magnorum animalium, & præſertim ſeneſcentium, bronchia arteriarum talẽ adipiſci duritiem, vt oſſeam ſubſtantiam facilè ſimulẽt: non igitur admirationi nobis eſſe debet, ſi interdum in corde magni animalis ſeneſcentis oſſa reperiri perhibeantur. Qui plura huius generis ſcire deſiderat, adeat Hiſtoriam Biſulcorum, vbi de hoc oſſe fusè diſputatur. *Os de corde Cerui*

Hippelaphus.

Ela-

Fig. 5. Red-flanked Duiker, in Ulisse Aldrovandi, *Monstrorum historia cum paralipomenis historiae omnium animalium*, Bologna 1642, 127

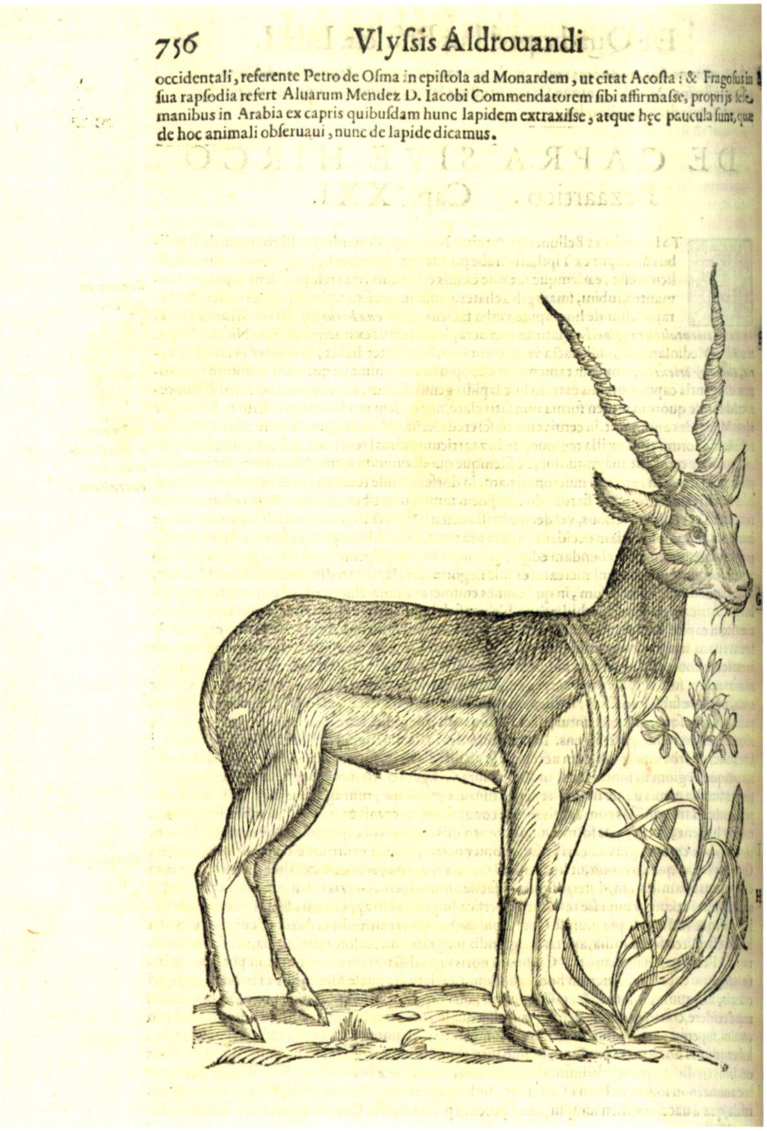

756 Vlyſsis Aldrouandi

occidentali, referente Petro de Oſma in epiſtola ad Monardem, ut citat Acoſta: & Fragoſus in ſua rapſodia refert Aluarum Mendez D. Iacobi Commendatorem ſibi affirmaſse, proprijs ſeſe manibus in Arabia ex capris quibuſdam hunc lapidem extraxiſse, atque hęc paucula ſunt, quæ de hoc animali obſeruaui, nunc de lapide dicamus.

Fig. 6. Blackbuck, in Ulisse Aldrovandi, *Quadrupedum omnium bisulcorum Historia*, Bologna 1621, 756

woodcut in its 12th edition as a member of the South American Coati (*Nasua nasua)*, and since then it has continued to be identified as such[11].

[1] See the Annex in the present catalogue, doc. 26, doc. 27, doc. 28. Aldrovandi had his scribes complete abstracts that were logged under multiple ordering criteria in order to make them easier to locate. This is indicated to some extent in doc. 28 by the number "10.237" on ms 136, tom. 10, fol. 237 (here doc. 27).

[2] In the 16th century, "drawn from life" meant approximately "from nature" or "from an original created by nature" as opposed to an original created by man (artificial). This expression does not indicate whether the animal was living or already dead.

[3] The two criteria can be retained, i.e., for the picture in the cod. min. 129, fol. 25r. It shows a female blackbuck and her cub and, compared with the cod. min. 42, fol. 19 below, the male is better rapresented (back bone, rear paws, etc.).

[4] "Hanc iconem, quam modo dabimus Hieronimus Patauinus medicus clarissimus Viennae mihi ex aula sacrae Caesarae Maiestatis ante aliquot annos transmisit sub titulo Columba Indica rostro Anatis, cum interim praeter pedes, & magnitudinem nihil cum Columbis commune habeat."

[5] Aldrovandi 1621, 368: "Ante aliquot annos ex aula Imperatoris Rodulphi II missae mihi fuere exoticorum aliquot animantium icones diligenter admodum, & pulcherrimè expressae, atque inter eas huius quoque quod hic exprimitur, quod non incongruè bouem dicemus strepticerotem, à cornuum constitutione, sunt enim turbinata, quemadmodum figura ipsa ostendit."

[6] see Hans Khevenhüller in http://documenta.rudolphina.org/

[7] In the 16th century, the attribution "marino" or "sea" had almost the same meaning as "India" or "Indian" and was applied to goods (or in this case animals) that arrived from the East and West Indies by trade ships.

[8] Aldrovandi 1637, 267: "Taxi suilli icon in musaeo publico repetta cum Taxi

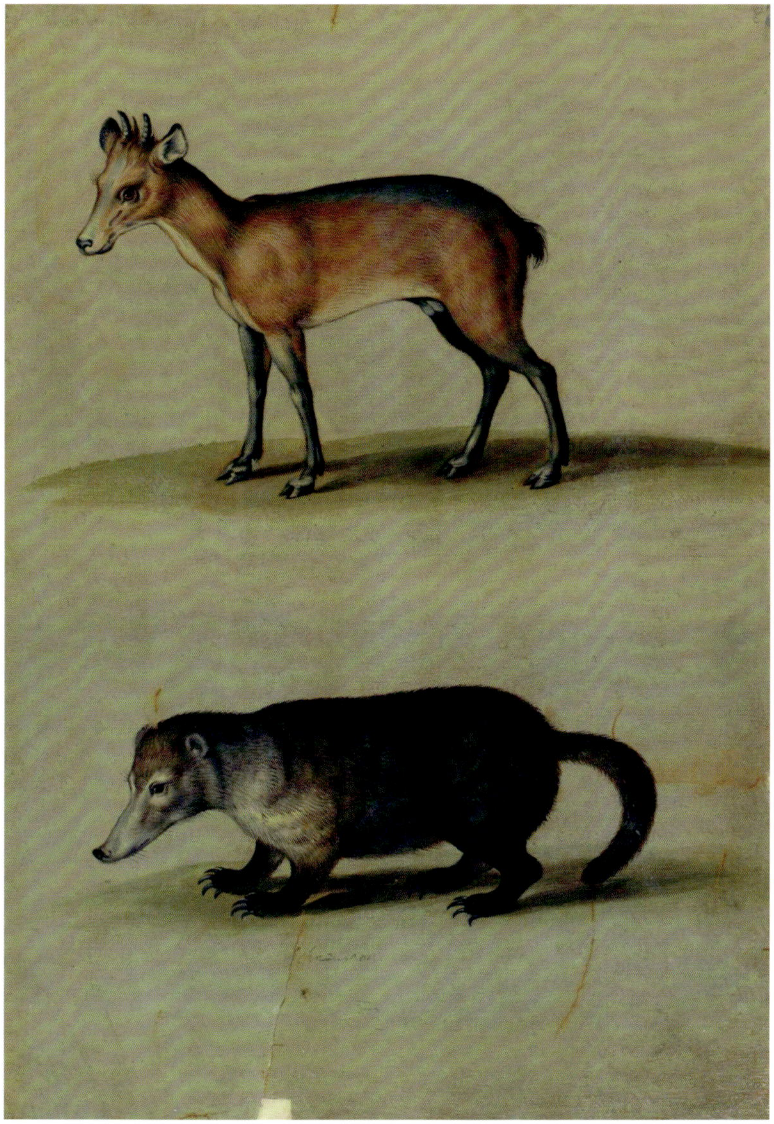

Fig. 7. Red-flanked Duiker and Mountain Coati, in Fondo Ulisse Aldrovandi, Bologna University Library, *Tavole di animali*, vol. 6/2, fol. 87

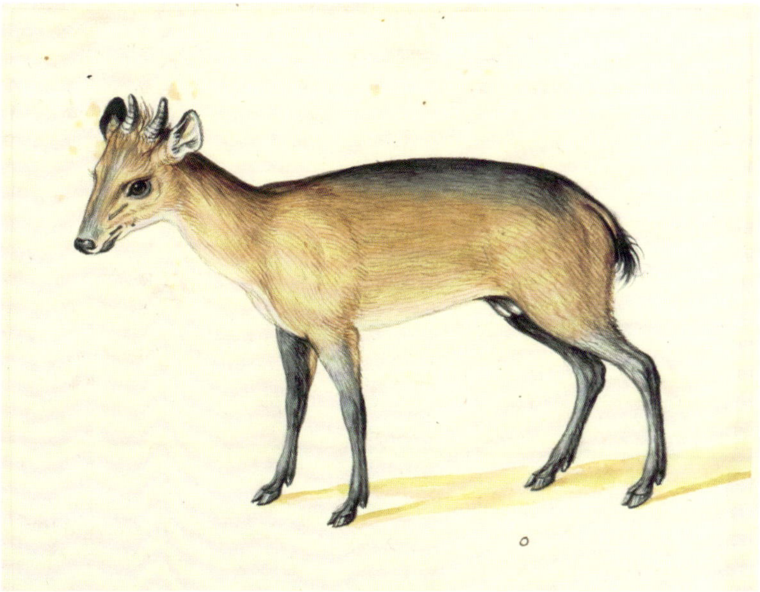

Fig. 8. Giuseppe Arcimboldo, Red-flanked Duiker, in Cod. min. 42, fol. 19

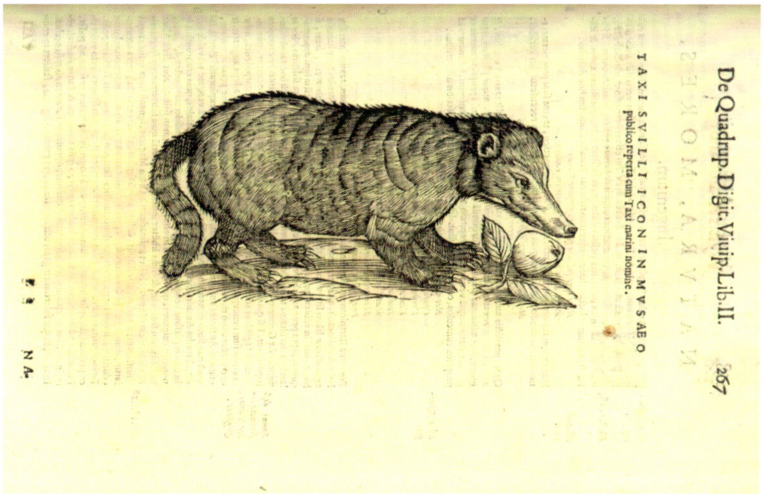

Fig. 9. Mountain Coati, in Ulisse Aldrovandi, *De quadrupedibus digitatis viviparis*, Bologna 1637, 267

marini nomine." He writes very vaguely of this (p. 265): "In regione Americana, quoddam animal nomine Heyrat vagatur, quod nomen bestiam mellis auidissimam significat, huiusmodi animal est colore castaneo, & magnitudine cati, & quotidie opificium apum inquirens in arboribus versatur."

[9] Nowak - Paradiso 1983, 983.

[10] Aldrovandi 1642, 146: "Indi nouae Hispaniae Melem montanum puauhpecotli nominant. Animal est duos plus minus dodrantes longum, rostro prolixo, tenui versus superna contorto, prolixa ite[m] cauda, pilo longo, circa alum albicante, caetera fusco, vel nigro, & candenti, sed circa dorsum nigriore, atris pedibus, & incuruis vnguibus."

[11] Linné 1766, 14.2 "Viverra Nasua, Marcgr.bras.p228 Coati, Dod.act.p181t181 Coati-mondi, Aldr.digit.p267 Taxus suillus".

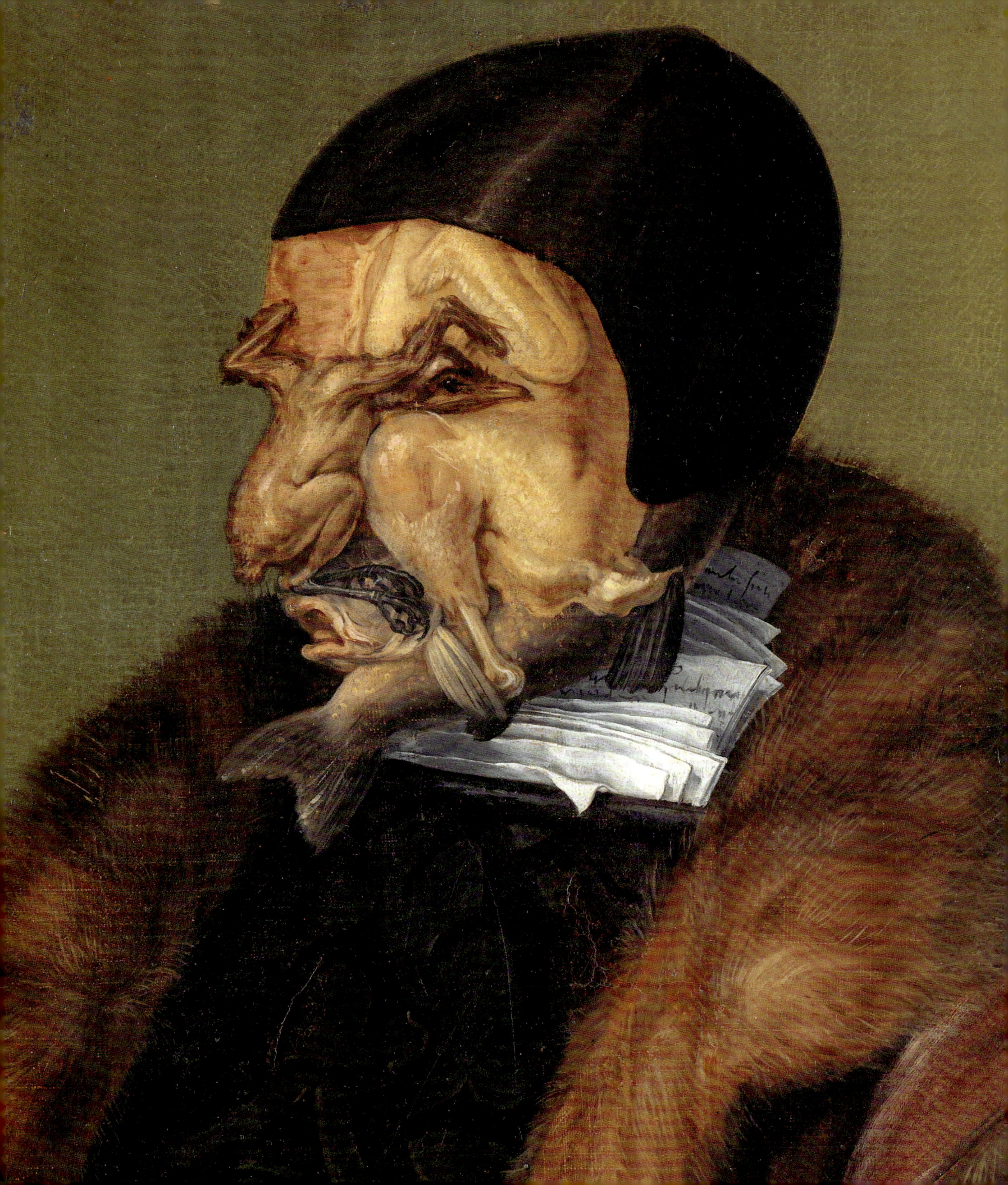

Görel Cavalli-Björkman

Anamorphous Portraits and Reversible Heads

Arcimboldo's pictures composed of food, fruit, flowers and other natural objects became enormously popular at the Habsburg court and as their reputation spread to other European courts he was required to make several versions of them. The demand for his paintings was so great that other contemporary artists also made copies of them, which means that today it is not easy to determine which works come from his hand. Some compositions have only survived as copies.

The immediate reaction of his contemporaries to a painting by Arcimboldo was fascination and attraction. They encountered something surprising and different and the works were often referred to as *capprici, scherzi* or *grilli.* A present day viewer may compare Arcimboldo's compiled heads with a party game (the ridiculous families) where the participants have to find out whom the portrait represents. Arcimboldo always speaks in riddles or metaphors.

To acquire a better understanding of Arcimboldo's complex and puzzling iconography it is worth taking a look at contemporary thinking and the scientific theories that were current around 1560 when he was active. The fashionable sciences were chiromancy, physiognomy and geomancy, which involved believing that it was possible to deduce inner characteristics from the external lines on the hand or the features of a face or landscape. A great deal was also being written about cryptography, secret writing, of which riddles are a playful variant. Arcimboldo seems to have been no stranger to cryptography. Lomazzo tells us that the artist "was the inventor of ciphers which could not be understood without his own key". As Sven Alfons has pointed out, there is no other information about these ciphers or the contexts in which they were devised[1]. But the rest of Giuseppe Arcimboldo's œuvre suggests that he may have had a personal inclination for this mysterious and disguised writing. One could imagine that his cipher was based on ideograms and therefore almost hieroglyphic. Egyptian hieroglyphs were viewed by the humanists as ideograms that contained concealed and coveted wisdom. One development of hieroglyphs can be seen in the emblematic literature that was cultivated at the beginning of the 1560s in Arcimboldo's closest circle. This had been given its characteristic and fully developed form by Andreas Alciatus, whose *Emblemata* was published for the first time in 1531. The popularity of the book can be gauged from the fact that by 1560 it had been reissued in 47 editions. The contemporary belief was that a direct link existed between hieroglyphics and the art of painting and the creation of images. The same covert wisdom could be concealed in the painted images as in the texts. The artist was viewed as offering disclosure, as a medium of "deeper insights". Those who planned the ideational content of a picture were in their turn considered to occupy a higher plane than painters. Arcimboldo, who was responsible for both the ideas behind his images and also their execution, was held in high esteem and his symbolic works were acclaimed by contemporary writers. He was apostrophised by Gregorio Comanini as "the learned Egyptian"[2].

Anamorphous Portraits

Arcimboldo was originally appointed official portraitist to the emperor, which meant that he also received less attractive duties such as copying ancient Habsburg portraits. He later abandoned the conventions of court portraiture and depicted his subjects in accordance with the same principles used in the series of *Elements* and *Seasons.* As the artist also acted as stage designer and created costumes for the court ceremonials, there is no wonder that he also in his portraiture had a tendency to allow the individual to appear behind a mask. Masks can be seen as devices that permit personal distance, deindividualization and ambivalence. This reaches well beyond the confines of the stage and is deeply ingrained in the art of portraiture during the Renaissance and beyond. In court cultures these masks could play such an important role that the subjects lost their identity and became symbolic figures.

The intricate content of the *Seasons* and *Elements,* painted in the 1560s while Arcimboldo worked for Maximilian II, has been explained with the help of poems by Arcimboldo's friend, the Milanese scientist and historian Giovanni Battista Fonteo[3]. Fonteo asserted that the figures depicted were members of the House of Habsburg. There is a particular humour and irony in these allegorical pictures that were almost certainly obvious to contemporary viewers. The pictures also have political implications. The emperor and his court could amuse themselves by looking for symbols and

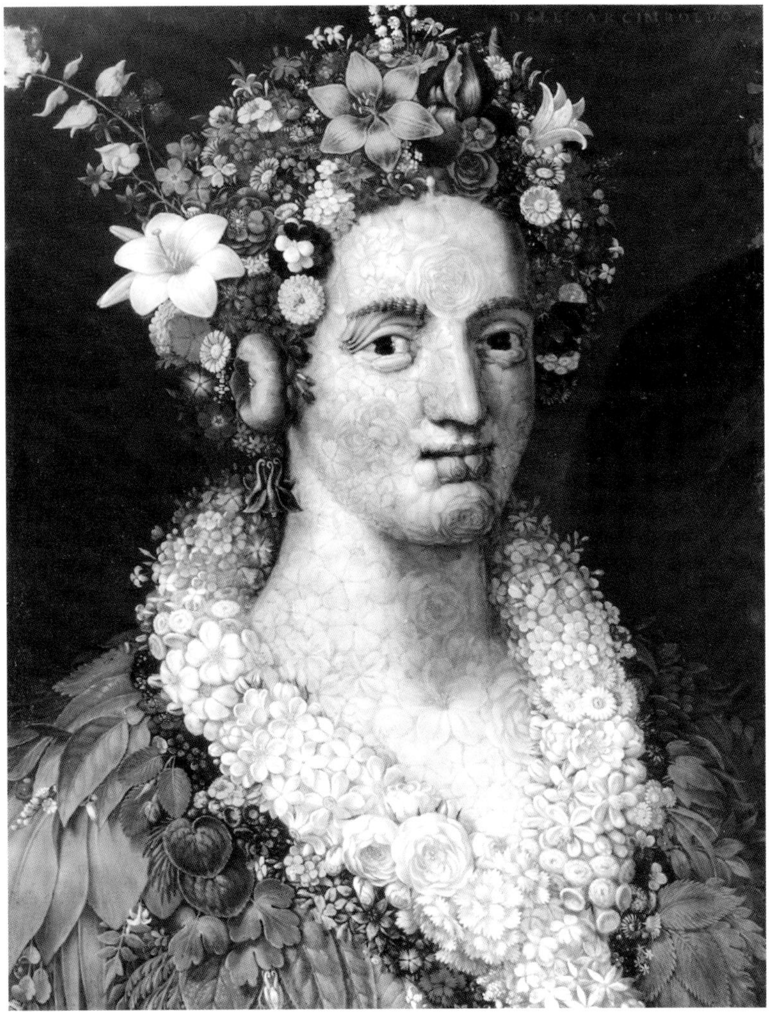

Fig. 1. Giuseppe Arcimboldo, *Flora*, 1589. Stockholm, formerly in the collection of Dr. Axel Wenner-Gren

trying to unveil the symbols of power hidden in the crowd of animals and plants. In these heads Arcimboldo makes use of the traditional half-length profile portrait which was still very frequent in Milan during the three first decades of the 16th century.

After Arcimboldo's return to Milan, the city of his birth, in 1591, he took his figures from classical mythology. He depicted Rudolf II as *Vertumnus,* the ancient Roman god of vegetation and transformation, composed of flowers, fruit and vegetables (cat. no. IV.38). The name Vertumnus can be derived from Latin *vertere* = change, replace. In composing this image Arcimboldo probably found his inspiration in the classical writer Propertius[4], who characterizes Vertumnus as the god that rules over the entire year, *annus vertens.* At the same time he is a symbol of human transience. The painting, which earned the praise of Arcimboldo's friend, the poet Gregorio Comanini, was greatly to the contemporary taste for ambiguity as it is at the same time a portrait of the emperor. Various interpretations have been proposed for this portrait which according to Thomas DaCosta Kaufmann forms the glorious culmination of the suites of elements and seasons[5]. However, nobody has offered a better explanation of the contents of the paintings than Comanini in his poem. Its opening contains a depiction of the creation of the world and he relates the human body to the structure of the globe – microcosmos and macrocosmos[6].

Vertumnus, which was sent to Rudolf II in Prague, can be found in the list made by Königsmarck in 1648 of the paintings brought from Prague to Sweden. However, it is not possible to determine whether the painting was already at Skokloster during its occupancy by Carl Gustaf Wrangel or whether it first arrived there in connection with the Brahe family. During the period in which Per Brahe the younger owned the manor of Bogesund in the mid-17th century, one painting is described in the inventory as "A work composed of fruit" and an inventory dating from 1728 refers to "a flower face in tatters". However, these descriptions could equally well apply to some other Arcimboldo painting that had been brought to Sweden among the spoils from Prague.

Apart from *Vertumnus* Arcimboldo also painted the *Flora* in Milan in 1588 followed by a second version two years later. In their poems to the painting Comanini and Gherardini speculate about the identity of the painted figure. They make playful attempts to probe the double nature of the symbol and in their language they use metaphors, the devices that offer an aesthetic match for Arcimboldo's visual language. Lomazzo published his description of *Flora* in 1590. The painting had therefore probably not long been completed. This fits in with a painting dated 1589 and which until 1965 belonged to a private Swedish collector together with another unsigned and undated version[7]. A later inscription in capital letters on one of the paintings reads: LA FLORA DELL'ARCIMBOLDO. In the top left corner is the date 1589 (fig. 1). The other painting is similar in composition but richer in detail (fig. 2). For instance, among the flowers can be seen a grasshopper, a lizard, a beetle, butterflies, caterpillars and ladybirds. On one of the insects, positioned like a signature in the lower right-hand corner, the artist has arranged the black patches on the wing cases to form a face with eyes, nose and mouth, a playful hint of ambiguity. In this composition Flora's bosom is bare perhaps a reference to the iconography of the courtesan *Flora Meretrix.* Both paintings belonged to the emperor's collection and they came to Sweden among the spoils taken from Prague in 1648.

A third version of *Flora,* discovered by Legrand and Sluys in a private collection in Paris, matches in every essential respect the signed and dated version from 1589 (cat. no. IV.37)[8]. A few insignificant differences can be observed in individual flowers. Legrand and Sluys wanted to attribute this painting to Francesco Zucchi, while Sven Alfons maintains that in all probability the replica was painted by Arcimboldo himself[9].

When it comes to *Vertumnus*, *Flora* and other composite heads Arcimboldo could have had several sources of inspiration. One was, as mentioned above, classical mythology and Ovid's *Metamorphoses*. Another was surely the interest for nature and its classification that was predominant at the courts of Maximilian and Rudolf. The different parts of an Arcimboldo painting come very close to scientific images. Fruits and flowers are drawn from nature and imitated with the greatest possible diligence as is remarked already by the artist's contemporary, Gregorio Comanini[10]. Also Lomazzo praises "the naturalistic quality" of Arcimboldo's figures. We know that Arcimboldo had direct experience of the elements that make up his figures. He could study pictures of them as well as real objects in the imperial collections and gardens. Renaissance and early Baroque flower painting evolved from several pictorial traditions, one being the illustrations linked to the development of botany. The plant identification and classification of Matthioli, Dodoens and Clusius surely underlie the floral portraits by Arcimboldo where every plant can be recognized. The foundation of botanical gardens in northern Italy in the middle of the 16th century led to an increased scientific interest in nature and cultivating plants all over Europe. It is known that Maximilian showed a special interest in botany and that he loved to frequent the gardens of his residences. All this must have had an impact on Arcimboldo's art.

But *naturalia* was not all when it comes to the scope of 16th century collections. Another interest was to collect *artificialia*, the fruits of human creativity and invention. These could be antique coins and gems or practical objects like weapons, armoury and artisan's tools. Arcimboldo illustrates this point with his *Cook* and *Cellarer*, made up of household equipments (cat. nos. IV.31 and IV.34). They were painted for the Elector of Saxony, who owned tens of thousands of such utensils.[11]

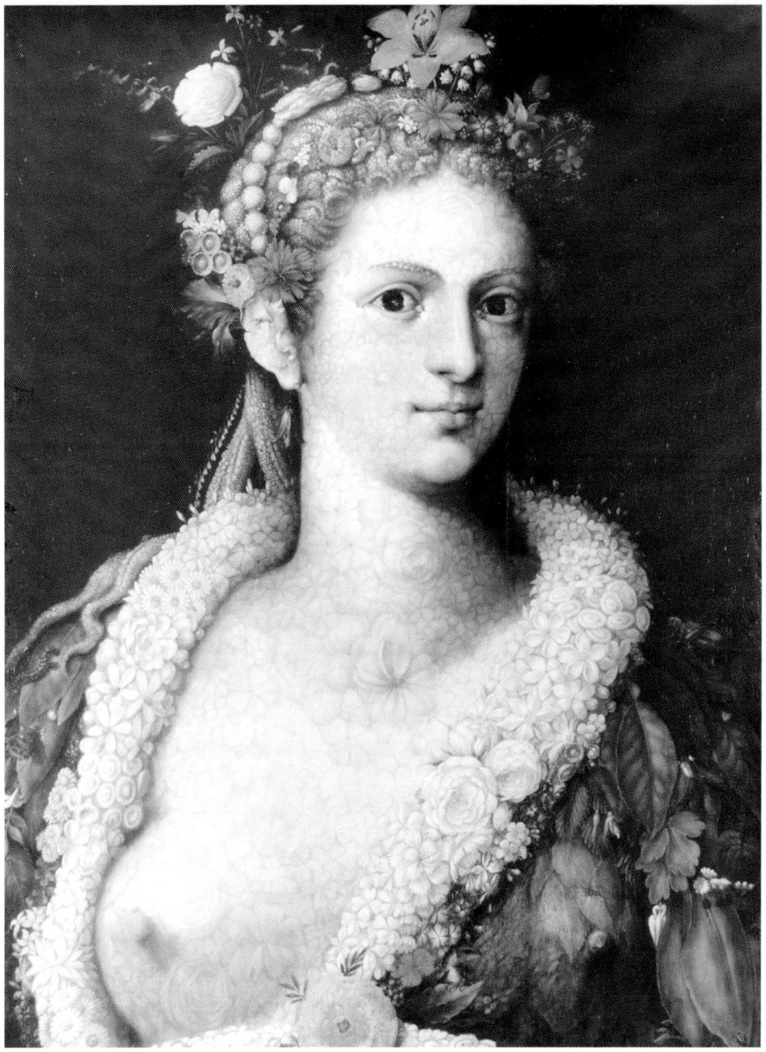

Fig. 2. Giuseppe Arcimboldo, *Flora*. Stockholm, formerly in the collection of Dr. Axel Wenner-Gren

Among the artefacts came also products of human learning such as manuscripts and printed books. A portrait by Arcimboldo dating from 1562, called *The Librarian* (or the *Bookman*), has been interpreted by Sven Alfons as a portrait of Wolfgang Lazius, a learned collector and scientist who was in charge of the Emperor's Kunstkammer and who arranged his numismatic collection and his library (cat. no. IV.29)[12]. The painting is listed in a Prague inventory dating from 1621 as "Ein conterfeet von büchern vom Arsimboldo"[13]. In Sweden there are and have been several corresponding works but it is the version at Skokloster that is probably referred to in the inventory and which arrived in Sweden among the spoils taken from Prague in 1648.

In the spirit of the age, the *Librarian* (or the *Bookman*) can be interpreted symbolically as a satirical depiction of the folly of scholarship. Books were a traditional symbol of learning and wisdom but in this composition the artist makes fun of the subject by depicting him as a fool with an open book on his head and eyes made of key rings. This type of picture originates from a well-known woodcut by Sebastian Brant (1494), which portrays a learned fool in the chamber that throughout the 15th century had formerly provided the background for depictions of Saint Jerome, Augustine and other learned men (fig. 3). The cinquecento preferred to concentrate on libraries and books. This was a time when the printing press was on its way to give increased availability to knowledge. In a rather short time printed materials and books could circulate in a world of their own. Abundance influenced production as well as reception. In Arcimboldo's picture of the *Bookman* this aspect seems to be the dominant factor. In composition this painting is different from the other composite heads as it has more the character of a still-life than a portrait.

The Jurist (1566), which today belongs to the Swedish National Portrait Collections at Gripsholm, is a half-length depiction of a male figure whose face is composed of fishes and plucked fowl and

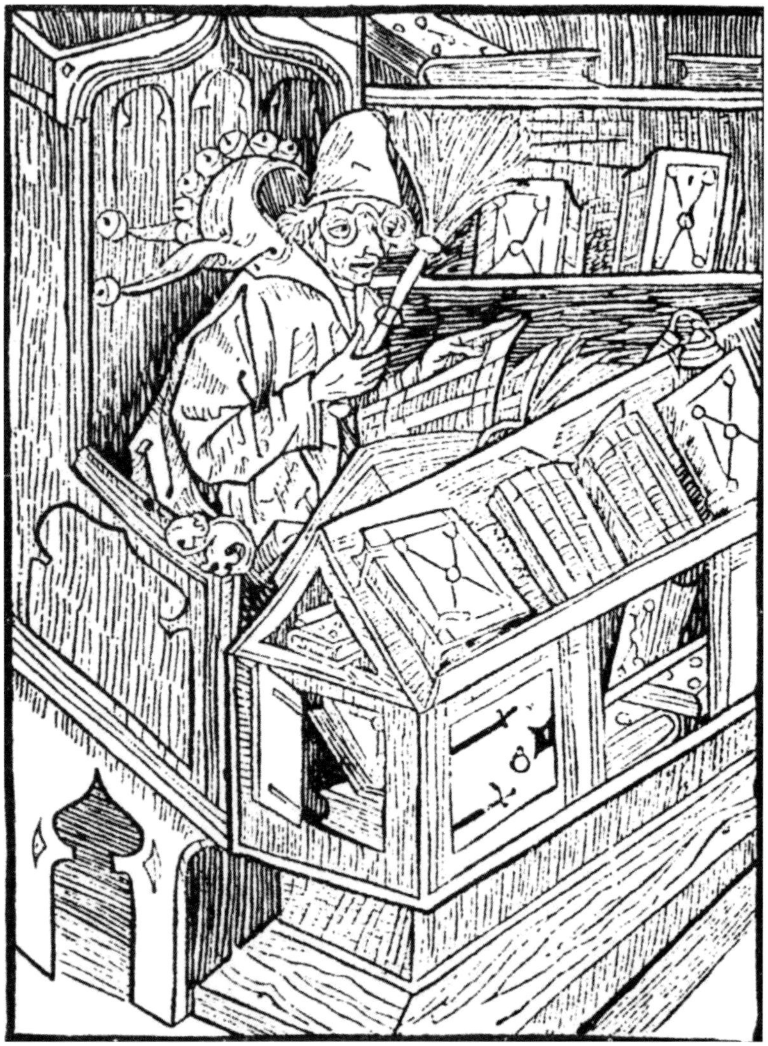

Fig. 3. *The Book Fool*, in Sebastian Brant, *Das Narrenschiff*, Basel 1494

whose body consists of books and manuscripts (cat. no. IV.30). The two volumes that form the base of the figure bear the inscriptions: ISERNIA and BARTHO. The painting was published by Olof Granberg in 1902 as a caricature portrait of John Calvin, and gained international circulation in this form, even among Calvin's biographers[14]. However, in 1957 Sven Alfons offered another interpretation of the portrait[15]. He interpreted the subject as Johann Ulrich Zasius, an administrator with legal training, who was in charge of the imperial family's finances. He also identified the inscriptions referring to two well known medieval jurists.

Composite Heads and Still Lifes

Another type of Arcimboldo image can be found in those that can be turned upside-down to depict two different objects at the same time, both portraits and still-lifes. André Pieyre de Mandiargues has called these pictures "anthropomorphic still lifes"[16]. *The Cook*, which has been dated to 1570, was bought by the Swedish National Museum of Fine Arts in 1994 (cat. no. IV.31). This work can be traced to the spoils taken from Prague in 1648. It is probably also listed in an earlier Prague inventory (1621), where it is referred to as "eine Kopfwechslung" i.e. a reversible head. If you turn the grotesque figure upside down, two hands can be seen lifting the lid of a cauldron with roast animals. It has been speculated whether the figure could be a depiction of a specific individual at the Habsburg court. A similar head from around 1590, which has been called *The Vegetable Gardener*, today in Cremona, also seems to allude to a specific individual (cat. no. IV.32). If the picture is turned upside-down we see a dark green bowl full of root vegetables of various kinds. A few years ago another of these reversible heads appeared on the art market – also shown in this exhibition – ascribed by Thomas DaCosta Kaufmann to Arcimboldo (cat. no. IV.33).

Particularly the last mentioned painting agrees with the *Vertumnus* composition. The vegetables and fruits in these still lifes are arranged with scientific as well as formalistic ingenuity in accordance with 16th century tradition[17]. Characteristic for these pictures is also that they have been painted more freely and more painterly than the early works from the 1560s. The problem is really when they were made. The entry in the Prague inventory dating from 1621 speaking of "eine Kopfwechslung" which I have related to *The Cook,* which later turned up in Sweden as part of the war booty from 1648, could indicate that they were made in Prague already between 1576 and 1587. The recently discovered painting in New York is dated to around 1589 by Thomas DaCosta Kaufmann (see his contribution in this catalogue). Berra, in an interesting essay, relates these paintings to the still life tradition in Milan after Arcimboldo's return to his home city where artists such as Vicenzo Campi and Fede Galizia were active. It was this tradition that became a point of departure also for Caravaggio. Berra argues that Arcimboldo's reversible fruit basket was the immediate source of inspiration for Caravaggio's well known painting of a young boy with a fruit basket[18].

The dominant factor in Arcimboldo's art is compositional invention. Like other Mannerists he fabricated one art out of the materials of another. With time and in the hands of followers and copyists his inventions have hardened into clichés. This is typical of art forms that resemble rhetorical figures. Arcimboldo seems to have taken pleasure in playing with the semantics of language, as remarked by Giancarlo Maiorini[19]. Rhetoric has taken precedence over meaning. But still we are trying to interpret his message. We want to find out what is hidden in his figures. Are they just marvels as other objects in the Emperor Kunst's und Wunderkammer? Does Arcimboldo like Bosch and Bruegel before him create monsters or extraordinary creatures or is his aim to depict what is miraculous in ordinary things?

Numerous texts have been preserved that lend support to the political interpretations that have been made of the works painted by Arcimboldo while in the service of the Habsburg emperors. Another way of describing his art is to draw parallels with the mystical narratives of antiquity. The natural mysticism and the metamorphoses that find expression in his paintings are reminiscent of Ovid's metamorphoses in which Daphne is turned into a tree to escape Apollo or Zeus into a swan when he wants to ravish Leda, the nymph. We must bear in mind that Arcimboldo was a highly educated artist. His familiarity with the ancient Greeks was apparent in the processions which he organized for the Habsburgs. As several authors have pointed out, increasing interest in Platonism was being shown in Arcimboldo's circles.
It is likely that Plato's *Timaeus* with its ideas about the origin of the world has inspired Arcimboldo in his creations of the series of *Seasons* and *Elements*[20]. Plato's basic idea is that of "an eternal god" who created from chaos a world in which everything was composed of the four basic elements: fire, water, air and earth. Reference to classical sources could also be applied to Arcimboldo's series of anthropomorphic still lifes. Considering that these paintings were made to amuse a circle of well read humanists in whose lives the classical authors were a constant presence, Arcimboldo could be looked upon as a parallel to the ancient painter Piraikos. According to Pliny, Piraikos was a specialist in "low motifs" and his paintings were regarded as social satires.

[1] Alfons 1957, 13.
[2] Comanini 1591, 42.
[3] Kaufmann 1976a.
[4] An exhaustive interpretation of this context is offered by Kaufmann 1985b.
[5] Kaufmann 1976a.
[6] Comanini 1591.
[7] The other version is somewhat larger and measures 80.4 × 60.6 cm.
[8] Legrand, Sluys 1955, 93.
[9] Alfons 1957, 133.
[10] Comanini 1591.
[11] Evans 1987, 42.
[12] Alfons 1957, 65.
[13] Jahrbuch, 25 (1905), reg. 19421, no. 1220.
[14] Granberg 1902.
[15] Alfons 1957, 55-59.
[16] Pieyre de Mandiargues 1978.
[17] Concerning forms of nature corresponding to parts of a face see della Porta 1588.
[18] Berra 2000, 60-85.
[19] Maiorini 1991, 50.
[20] Kriegeskorte 2000, 58.

IV.1

Giovanni Battista Fonteo (Fontana)

Carmen cum Distichis et Divinatio, cui titulus Clementia est

1568

303 × 203 mm, 15 folios

Vienna, Österreichische Nationalbibliothek, Handschriften-, Autographen- und Nachlass-sammlung, Codex 10152

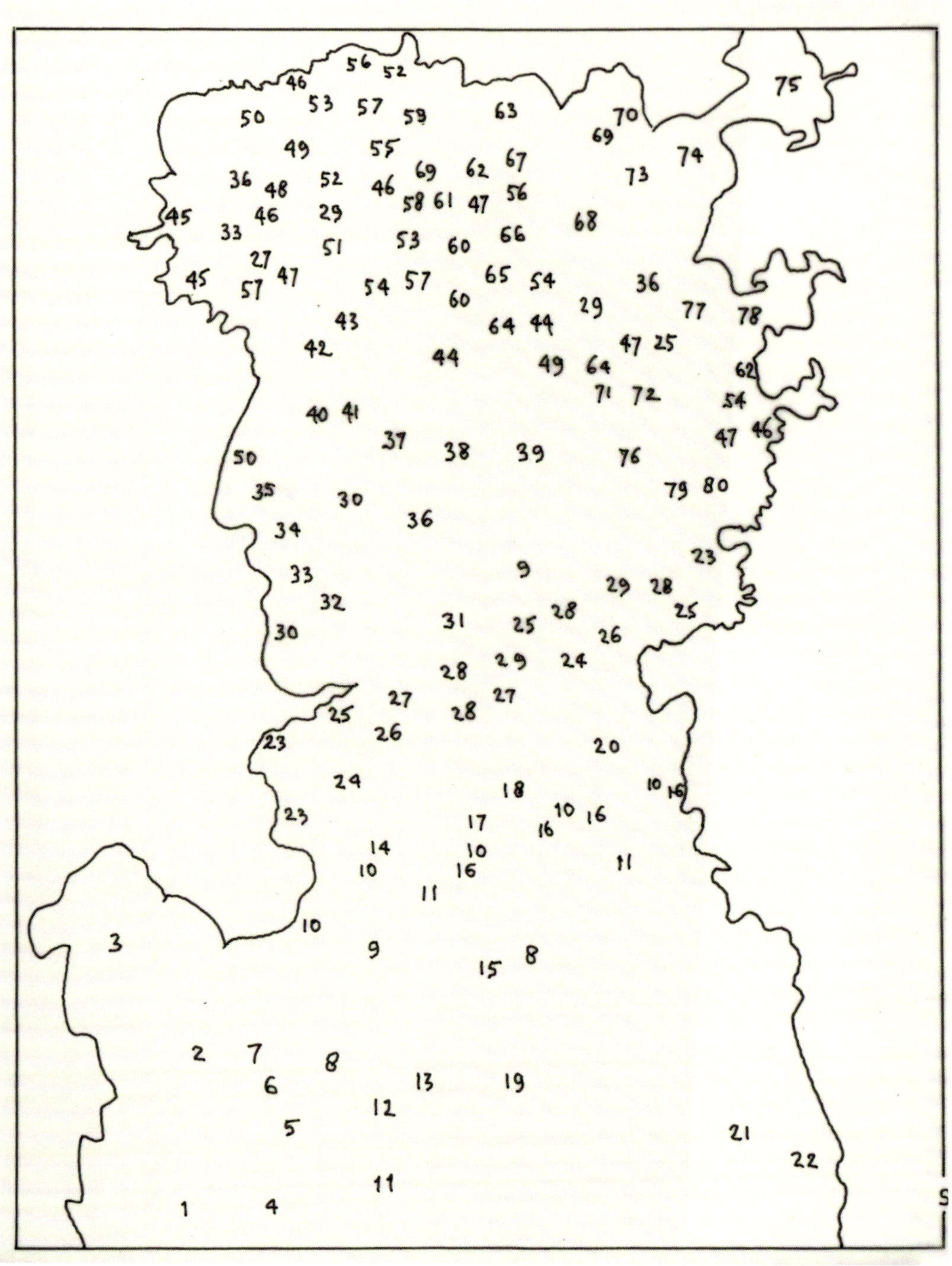

This three-hundred-eight-line poem in elegiac distich was dedicated to Emperor Maximilian II and completed by December 30, 1568, the date on its title page: its subject is the painting of the four elements and seasons in human form by the imperial painter Giuseppe Arcimboldo (part of the title reads *In quatuor temporum, et quatuor elementorum ad humanam effigiem a Josepho Arcimboldo caesareo pictore expressorum*). According to remarks made by the author, Fonteo, in *Europalia* (cat. no. VII.34), where a revised and annotated version appears, it was presented along with the two series of paintings when they were given to the emperor as New Year's Day present at the beginning of 1569. As Fonteo also indicates in *Europalia*, the poem was intended to explicate the paintings. Since the poems, including two by the artist himself among many by his friends and associates, were presented along with *Flora* and *Vertumnus* when they were given to Rudolf II, and this was done with Arcimboldo's conscious approval, and Fonteo supplies another such poem himself for an unfinished picture at the end of *Europalia*, it is most likely that this *Carmen*, written by Arcimboldo's spokesman for festivals around this time, was also so regarded by the artist himself (see Berra 1988; Kaufmann forthcoming). In any case, it provides a key to the interpretation of Arcimboldo's paintings.

The complicated argument and structure of the poem (with the seasons and elements responding to each other) suggests a reading of Arcimboldo's paintings of the seasons and elements as imperial allegories. The poem also points to imperial symbolism visible in various pictures. The general theme is that as the emperor rules over the body politic, so does he rule over the macrocosm of the elements and elements; as the seasons come and go, so will Habsburg rule be eternal. The harmonious conjunction of the seasons with the elements also betokens the harmonious rule of the world under the clement emperor.

Thomas DaCosta Kaufmann

Bibliography: Kaufmann 1978, 76-102; Porzio 1979, 30-32; Venice 1987, 151-159; Kaufmann 1993, 100-128, 197-205.

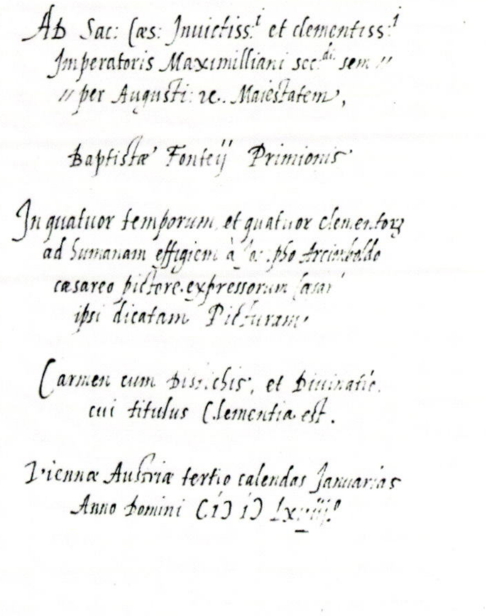

IV.1

IV.2
Giuseppe Arcimboldo
Spring
1563
Oil on oak wood
66 × 50 cm
Signed lower right: GIVSEPPE/ ARCIMBOLDO. F
Madrid, Real Academia de Bellas Artes de San Fernando

Spring, which is currently located in Madrid, could have been originally a part of the Viennese series, *Four Seasons*, as assumed by Mandiargues (1978) and DaCosta Kaufmann (1985a); Arcimboldo painted it in 1563 for Archduke Maximilian, and from 1564 Emperor Maximilian II (cat. nos. IV.3-4). The picture arrived in Spain possibly as a gift to King Philipp II. A fragmentary inscription on the back reads: "LA PRIMAVERA /Va accompagnato con L'Aria ch....una testa di uccelli"; it states, that *Spring* was accompanied by *Wind* (which together formed a pair). Rudolf (1995, 185) on the other hand, presumed that this *Spring* belonged to the series of the seasons (and elements) in the Alcázar and arrived in Madrid by means of the art market.
Of all the season-heads, *Spring*, from a "methodical" perspective, offers less surprises than the other three season allegories. The shift effects and paradoxes of the optical transformation, the manner in which animals and plants become parts of the body and as we see them in *Earth*, *Water* and even in *Lawyer* and in *Cook* in an extreme form are less original here. The form of the head is simply filled out with flowers, the breast with leaves. The surprises are above all in the details, such as in the composition of the lips and teeth, the peony for the ear; particularly, the green leaf arrangement of the breast and the flower-bonnet on the head are of exquisite delicacy. A splendid iris becomes the amulet on the breast, a white lily appears as a feather in the hat. At the same time, however, *Spring* surpasses all of Arcimboldo's other composite heads in its richness of species. Sam Segal counted 80(!) different varieties of flowering plants (see table list below) in his botanical list of species (which he thankfully managed to complete in time). Only *Water* with 62 species comes close to *Spring*.

Alexander Wied

Bibliography: Pérez Sánchez 1964, 314-316; Kaufmann 1985a, 211, cat. no. 2-3; Orso 1986, 162f., 203; Kriegeskorte 1986, 58 with colour plates; Kaufmann 1987, 99f.; Kaufmann 1988c, 165, cat. no. 2-3; Barthes 1990, 151-154; Bremond 1995, 76, fig. 75.

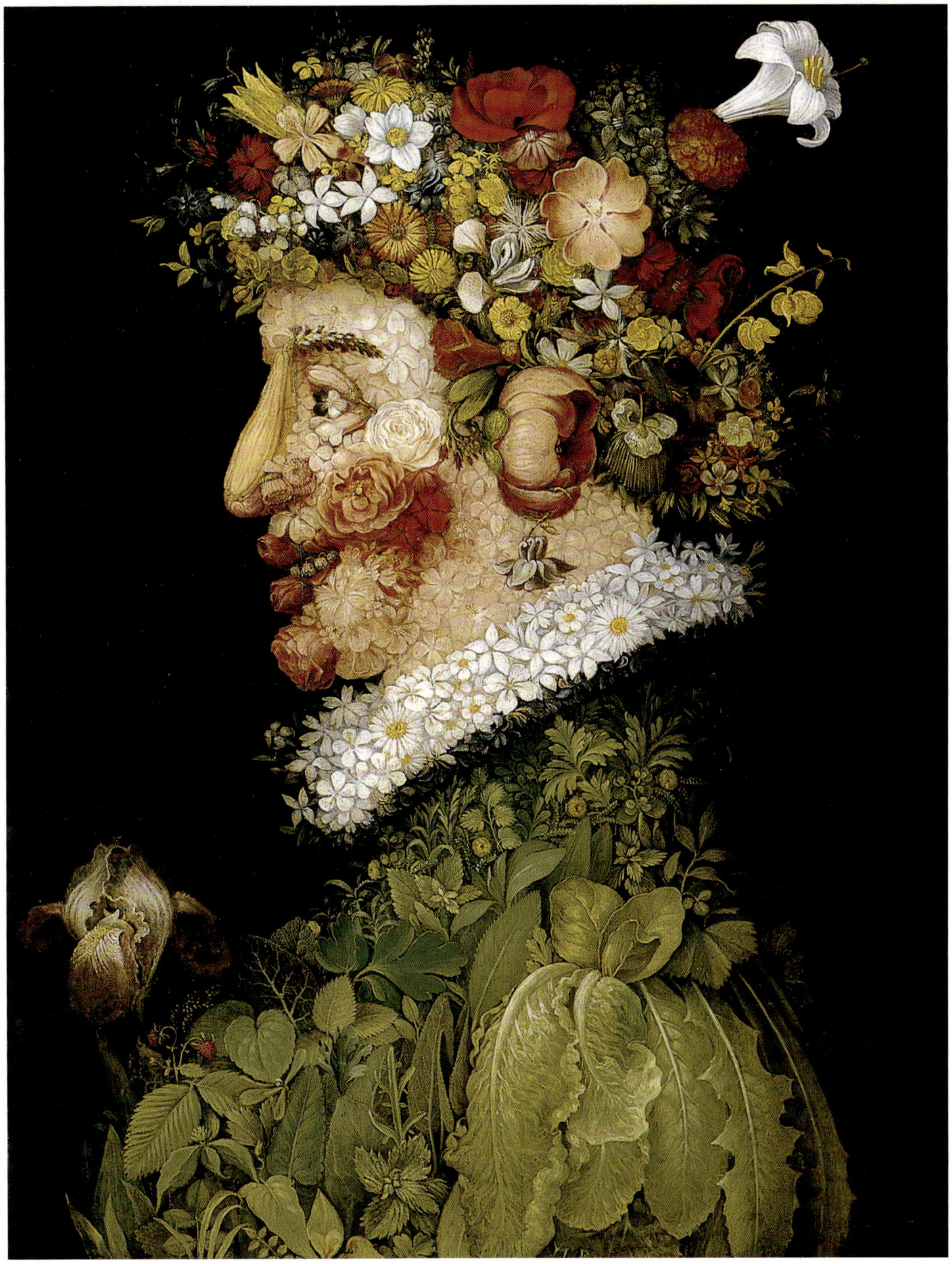
IV.2

Determined through digital images.
Distribution of botanical species: Am = America, As = Southeast Asia,
E = Europe, EA = Eurasia, N = Northern Hemisphere, Co = Cosmopolitan (on all continents),
C = Central Europe, S = Southern Europe and Mediterranean region, W = Western Europe;
Cu = developed in culture.

1 Rose, Rose, Rose, *Rosa spec.*, N As Cu
2 Strawberry, Erdbeere, Fraise, *Fragaria vesca,* EA
3 German Flag, Deutsche, Flambe, *Iris germanica*, C, Schwertlilie
4 Spinach, Spinat, Epinard, *Spinacea oleracea,* As
5 Betony, Betonie. Bétoine, *Stachys officinalis,* EA
6 Pourslane, Gelber Portulak, Pourpier potager, *Portulaca oleracea,* As
7 Violet, Hain-Veilchen, Violette, *Viola riviniana*, E
8 Feverfew, Mutterkraut, Matricaire, *Tanacetum parthenium,* As
9 Columbine, Akelei, Ancolie, *Aquilegia vulgaris*, S C As
10 Wormwood, Wermut, Absinth, *Artemisia absinthium,* EA

11 Purple Dead-Nettle, Acker-Taubnessel, Ortie rouge, *Lamium purpureum,* E
12 Echinophora, Echinophora, Panais épineux, *Echinophora spinosa*, S
13 Sage, Salbei, Sauge, *Salvia officinalis,* S (C)
14 Box, Buchsbaum, Buis, *Buxus sempervirens*, S C As
15 Plum, Pflaume, Prune, *Prunus domestica*, As
16 Lavender Cotton, Cypressenkraut, Petit cyprès, *Santolina chamaecyparissus*, S
17 Salad Burnet, Bibernelle, Pimprenelle, *Sanguisorba minor*, EA
18 Rue, Weinraute, Rue, *Ruta graveolens*, S
19 Salad, Gartensalat, Laitue, *Lactuca sativa*, As
20 Mugwort, Beifuß, Armoise, *Artemisia vulgaris,* N
21 Dandelion, Kuhblume, Pissenlit, *Taraxacum officinale coll.*, EA
22 Swamp Dandelion, Sumpf-Kuhblume, Pissenlit des marais, *Taracaxum palustre coll.*, EA
23 Jasmine, Jasmin, Jasmin, *Jasminum officinale*, As
24 Snowball, Schneeball, Viorne obier, *Viburnum opulus*, EA
25 White Campion, Weiße Tagnelke, Compagnon blanc, *Silene latifolia*, EA
26 Ox-eye Daisy, Wucherblume, Marguerite, *Leucanthemum vulgare*, EA
27 White Stock, weiße Levkoje, Giroflée blanc, *Matthiola incana alba*, Cu
28 Burnet Rose, Gratröschen, Rose de arêtes, *Rosa pimpinellifolia* ?, W C
29 Greater Jasmine, Großblütiger Jasmin, Jasmin à grand fleurs, *Jasminum grandiflorum*, Cu
30 Apothecary's Rose, Apotheker-Rose, Rose à cent feuilles, *Rosa gallica Officinalis*, S Cu
31 Sweet Briar, Wein-Rose, Eglantine, *Rosa rubiginosa*, E
32 White Carnation, weiße Nelke, Oeillet blanc, *Dianthus caryophyllus albus*, Cu
33 Lily-of-the-Valley, Maiglöckchen, Muguet, *Convallaria majalis*, N
34 Pink Stock, rosa Levkoje, Giroflée rose, *Matthiola incana rosea*, Cu
35 Annual Daisy, Garten-, Pâquerette des jardins *Bellis annua*, S, Gänseblümchen
36 Carnation, Nelke, Oeillet, *Dianthus caryophyllus*, C As
37 White Rose, Weiße Rose, Rose blanche, *Rosa x alba,* Cu
38 Heliotrope, Skorpionskraut, Herbe au verrues, *Heliotropium europaeum,* S As
39 Peony, Pfingstrose, Pivoine mâle, *Paeonia mascula,* C As
40 Pansy, Stiefmütterchen, Pensée, *Viola tricolor*, EA
41 Foxglove, Fingerhut, Digitale, *Digitalis purpurea*, W C
42 Lavender, Lavendel, Lavande, *Lavandula angustifolia*, S
43 Dog Rose, Hundsrose, Rose des haies, *Rosa canina*, EA
44 Pomegranate, Granatapfel, Grenade, *Punica granatum plena*, Co
45 Periwinkle, Immergrün, Pervenche, *Vinca minor*, C S As
46 Black Mustard, Schwarzer Senf, Moutarde noire *Brassica nigra* ?, EA
47 Meadow Buttercup, Scharfer Hahnenfuß, Bassinet, *Ranunculus acris*, N
48 Liverwort, Leberblümchen, Hépatique, *Hepatica nobilis*, EA
49 Marsh-Mallow, Wilder Malve, Mauve sauvage, *Malva sylvestris*, E
50 Orange Lily, Feuerlilie, Lis jaune *Lilium bulbiferum*, S C
51 Blue Stock, blaue Levkoje, Giroflée bleue, *Matthiola incana coerulea*, Cu
52 Stock, Levkoje, Giroflée, *Matthiola incana*, S As
53 Orange Pot Marigold, orange Ringelblume, Souci orange, *Calendula officinalis aurantiaca*, S C As
54 Bachelor's Button, Garten-Hahnenfuß, Boutons d'or, *Ranunculus acris plenus*, Cu
55 Christmas Rose, Schneerose, Hellébore noire, *Helleborus niger*, C
56 Cornflower, Kornblume, Bluet, *Centaurea cyanus*, S (E)
57 Yellow Pot Marigold, gelbe Ringelblume, Souci jaune, *Calendula officinalis flava*, S C As
58 dark Columbine, dunkle Akelei, Ancolie noire, *Aquilegia vulgaris atrata*, Cu
59 Sweet Chamomile, Römische Kamille, Camomille romaine, *Chamaemelum nobile*, E
60 Bindweed, Acker-Winde, Campanelle, *Convolvulus arvensis*, Co
61 Wallflower, Goldlack, Giroflée jaune, *Erysimum cheiri*, S As
62 Knot-grass, Quirliges, Illecebrum, *Illecebrum verticillatum* ?, W C, Knorpelkraut
63 Red Poppy, Feuer-Mohn, Coquelicot, *Papaver rhoeas*, N
64 Female Bockrose, Salbeiblättrige, Ciste femelle, *Cistus salvifolius* ?, S As, Zistrose
65 Westcounty Cyclamen, Geschweiftblättrige, Cyclamen, *Cyclamen repandum*, S, Erdscheibe
66 Superb Pink, Pracht-Nelke, Oeillet frangé, *Diantus superbus*, S C
67 Mullein Pink, Kranz-Lichtnelke, Coquelourde, *Lychnis coronaria*, S As
68 Flower of Jove, Jupiter's Lichtnelke, Oeillet de Dieu, *Lychnis flos-jovis*, C
69 Borage, Borretsch, Bourrache, *Borago officinalis*, S
70 Candytuft, Bauernsenf, Corbeille d'argent, *Iberis sempervirens* ?, S
71 Spreading Bellflower, Wiesen-Glockenblume, Campanule étalée, *Campanula patula*, E
72 Nettle-leaved Dead-Nettle Nessel-Glockenblume, Gantelée, *Campanula trachelium*, EA
73 Alkanet, Ochsenzunge, Langue de boeuf *Anchusa officinalis*, C W
74 African Marigold, Sammetblume, Tagète rose d'Inde, *Tagetes erecta*, Am
75 White Lily, Weiße Lilie, Lis blanc, *Lilium candidum*, S As
76 Caper bush, Kappernstrauch, Câprier, *Capparis spinosa*, S
77 Hollyhock, Eibisch, Rose trémière, *Alcea rosea*, As
78 Rush broom, Spanischer Ginster, enêt d'Espagne, *Spartium junceum*, S
79 Damask Rose, Damascener Rose, Rose de Damask, *Rosa x damascena*, As Cu
80 Primrose, Schaftlose, Primevère, *Primula vulgaris*, EA, Schlüsselblume

Plants represented in the Munich version, but not in the Madrid painting:

Soft Cranesbill, Zottiger, Tête rouge, *Geranium molle*, EA, Storchschnabel
Meadow Cranesbil, Wiesen-l, Grâce de Dieu, *Geranium pratense,* EA, Storchschnabe
Bindweed, *Blumen auch in Madrid*, *Convolvulus arvensis-*

Flowers represented in the Louvre and Munich versions, but not in the Madrid painting:

Austrian Briar, Gelbe Rose, Rose jaune, *Rosa foetida,* As
Bittersweet, Bittersüß, Douce-amère, *Solanum dulcamara*, EA

Flowers representend in the Munich version, but not in the Madrid painting:
Fleabane, Ruhrwurz, Herbe de Saint Roch, *Pulicaria dysenterica,* W C As

The flowers depicted in the crown of the Louvre painting cannot be identified.

We could assume that Arcimboldo largely painted the flowers from nature and not from foreign models. Because the plants bloom at different times of the year, he must have sketched out the individual flowers in nature studies (sadly no longer existing) for a later use, as Jan Bruegel the Elder did about fifty years later in his flower bouquets.

Sam Segal

IV.3
Giuseppe Arcimboldo
Summer
Oil on linden wood
67 × 50.8 cm
Signature as pattern in straw meshwork on collar and shoulder: GIVSEPPE / ARCIMBOLDO · F 1563
On the back in antique writing, date and title: 1563. AESTAS
Vienna, Kunsthistorisches Museum, Gemäldegalerie, inv. no. 1589

In the profile bust of *Summer*, the cheek and neck area are composed of a large peach, quince, garlic, white young onions, yellow beets and white eggplant; the mouth and lips are formed of cherries and the open peapod within imitates a row of teeth. The nose is a young wild cucumber and the chin is a pear; the eye shines as a glassy sour cherry between two small pears. The bulge of the forehead seems to be made of brown-skinned onions; even the eyebrows – a curved grain-ear – are not overlooked. On the temple are three hazelnuts in their covers, and in the place of the ear is a dried corncob. The ensemble is completed with a head covering, effectively a cap or a hat made of fruit and vegetables bedded in greenery, from which emerge oat spikes resembling a hat feather. Recognizable are cherries or sour cherries, a violet eggplant, grapes, plums, a melon, raspberries and blackberries, perhaps a medlar; the green, plum-shaped forms could be almonds. The clothing in woven straw has a single artichoke and the woven signature and date sophisticatedly integrated into the composition as jewellery. Perhaps Arcimboldo was familiar with the passage in Plinius Sec. the Elder, *Naturalis Historia* XXXV, 62 about Zeuxis, who became so rich "that in order to flaunt it in Olympia, his name was woven in golden letters into his square-patterned over-garments".

With the striking composition, Arcimboldo's intent was certainly also to create small surprise-effects through the representation of botanical rarities: the corn (*Zea mays L.*), for example, today produced in mass-agriculture around the world, was still rare at the time. It is a grain from the family of sweet grasses (*Poaceae*) and originates in Mexico, where it has been cultivated for thousands of years in approximately 200 species. Corn was brought to Europe from the Caribbean by Columbus. Since 1525, corn was cultivated in Spain, and shortly thereafter in Northern Italy, where Arcimboldo became acquainted with it. In the art chamber of the Trausnitz Castle in Landshut, one can compare the *Summer* (cat. no. IV.13) that hangs there with two small ears of the same type of corn that are also displayed. There is also an ear of corn in *Vertumnus* (cat. no. IV.38). Not as new, but strange enough to the northern aesthetic, was the eggplant (or aubergine) (*Solanum melongena L.*); it belongs to the nightshade family and contains raw nicotine. It originates in tropical Africa, Arabia and Northwest India. The Saracens in Andalusia seem to be the first to have cultivated it in Europe. It had been used in Italy since the 15th century, but was already mentioned by Albertus Magnus in the 13th century (*De vegetabilibus* 3, 97 as *melangena*) and described by Mattioli in 1571 and Dalechamps in 1587 (Appendix 23) (Marzell 1979, vol. IV, 361f.).

Illustrating the (comparatively small) supplies of luxury fruit – and this only in the early crops of May/June – are the lists of the gardener Nicolaus de Seiniß from Maximilian's Garden Castle *Neugebäude* at the courts of Vienna and Prague from 1581, in which he speaks of "artichokes..., three types of cherries of the French variety" and "black cherries", again repeating "varieties" and "two types" up to "five types of cherries", and also "morelles" and "sour cherries" (Lietzmann 1987, 206f.).

The picture originally belonged to a series of the *Four Seasons*; *Summer*, the only dated picture in the series, carries the date 1563. For the first time, Arcimboldo composes heads from all kinds of objects, whose selection gives meaning to the allegory. As attested by, among others, a majolica plate dated 1540 (cat. no. II.9), this compositional method was certainly not invented by Arcimboldo, but the sophistication and imagination with which the painter applies the themes in the picture-puzzles are a very personal achievement, and the many later copies serve to reveal in their weaknesses and simplifications Arcimboldo's true originality.

The figure of *Summer* is composed of grains and various fruits and vegetables, representing the wealth and bounty of summer, whereas *Winter*, also in the Gemäldegalerie of the Kunsthistorisches Museum (cat. no. IV.4), is composed of a tree trunk, a tree-fungus, ivy and lemons. Both of the remaining seasons are known from their repetitions, primarily from a second, completely conserved autograph series in the Louvre in Paris (cat. nos. IV.8-11), which Arcimboldo completed in 1573 for Emperor Maximilian II as a gift for the elector August von Sachsen. The *Spring* in the Real Academia de Bellas Artes de San Fernando in Madrid (cat. no. IV.2), composed of various flowers and leaves, was actually once part of the original series to which the two Viennese pictures belong. The original version of *Autumn* (with the exception of the autograph copy in the Louvre series, cat. no. IV.10), whose body is made of staves and whose head is composed of various fruits, grapes and beetroots, has been lost; one exemplar in a private American collection is considered by DaCosta Kaufmann as a possible original (survey from 4 December 1999; cat. no. IV.6).

The cycle of the seasons is also an allegorical representation of the four ages of life. In correspondence to the *Four Seasons* was the series created three years later in 1566, the *Four Elements* (see cat. nos. IV.26-28). Through a paired arrangement of the qualities in the objects, warm-cold and damp-dry, the elements correspond to the seasons. Thus, the warm-dry summer corresponds to fire, the cold-damp winter to water, the warm-moist spring to air and the cold-dry autumn to earth. Thereby, through the arrangement of the heads, turned to the left or to the right, corresponding pairs face each other and form a unit. It is certainly not by chance that not only in the season-heads from 1563, two face left and two face right, but also in the series of the elements created three years later, in 1566, so that, if desired, they could be arranged into another possible paired-grouping in which each head in one series would face its corresponding head in the other, as follows: *Spring – Air, Summer – Fire, Autumn – Earth, Winter – Water.*

(Additionally, the *Four Elements* are also relatable to the *Four Temperaments*, for example, as according to Jacques de Gheyn II: Sanguinicus – Air, Cholericus – Fire, Melancholicus – Earth, Phlegmaticus – Water [Hollst. Part I, 135-138]. This refers to Empedocles' theory of elements: the correspondence of the elements to the bodily fluids (Jongh 2004, 81), a doctrine that persisted in European medicine from Galenus until the early modern times. Lazius' writings, with which Arcimboldo may have been familiar, will be discussed later.

Arcimboldo's allegories require interpretation on various levels of understanding. The primary one is the level of humour, the visual wittiness, the bizarre, the astonishing. "The Renaissance concept of *ut pictura poesis* finds a brilliant double-strategy here, in the paragon of picture and word, of *mimesis* and *invenzione*... It is very possible that the artist was thus contributing to the debate of modernity against the antique, whose hieroglyphs equally employed intellect along with grotesque and mythological fable-figures of an emblematic fantasy". (E. Mai in Cologne-Zurich-Vienna 1996-1997, 197). Contemporaries such as Comanini, who studied Arcimboldo's works from the very onset (1591, see bibl.), speak of the highly noteworthy *invenzioni e capricci*, using expressions like *bizarrie, scherzi, quadri ghiribizzosi* and *grilli* as well. Lomazzo names the heads *teste composte*. Comanini defines the heads as the results of the imagination, of the individual idea, which corresponds to nothing outside of the subjective experience: *di capriccio, & d'invention sua, & che non habbia l'essere fuori del proprio intelletto* (cited from DaCosta Kaufmann 1987, 90). The authors thereby never lose sight of the symbolism in these inventions, which they take very seriously. This second level of meaning is the allegorical-symbolical. The heads are not only allegories of the elements and seasons, but they also contain allusions to the Habsburg emperor Maximilian II (1527-1576), to whom they were dedicated. The series was begun in 1563 and continued for Maximilian II in 1564, after the death of emperor Ferdinand I. DaCosta Kaufmann has been able to locate a contemporary source from which an allegorical interpretation in the context of court art can be derived, explaining the paintings as a form of tribute to the sovereign. The humanist, Giovanni Battista Fonteo, who was active in the emperor's court at the same time as Arcimboldo, dedicated a series of panegyrical poems to Emperor Maximilian II, which relate directly to Arcimboldo's paintings. With the presentation of the paintings – which was at the time a complete series of eight heads – on New Year's Day in 1569, Fonteo's poems were also delivered. It is presumed that the emperor hung Arcimboldo's cycle in his bedroom in the Viennese Castle (Rudolf 1995, 183). These poems and other comments by Fonteo were meant to prevent any misunderstanding by the emperor regarding the hidden meaning of the pictures. In a complicated system of references and allusions that is no longer comprehensible today, the universal analogy of microcosm and macrocosm forms a bridge across the harmonious cycle of nature and the seasons to the augury of eternal Habsburg rule. In 1976 DaCosta Kaufmann conducted detailed research on this imperial allegory of the seasons and elements. Apart from the general concept, these observations delve into the minutest details; thus, for example, the head of *Water* wears a small crown. The straw collar of *Winter* displays a half-visible M (for Maximilian) on the lower left edge; the firesteel is woven into the pattern of the straw multiple times, which forms a part of the *Imprese* of the Order of the Golden Fleece. The *Winter* as an imperial head refers to the Romans, the founders of the Holy Roman Empire, who made winter the beginning of the year – *caput anni*. The allegory of the ruler culminates later in Arcimboldo's *Vertumnus*, a portrait representing Rudolf II, composed of field crops (cat. no. IV.38). It is quite possible that Rudolf's alchemical-mystical-kabbalistic view of nature was prepared in the spiritual climate of his father, Maximilian II and converged with Arcimboldo's ideas.

A third level of interpretation was proposed by Pontus Hulten (1987, see bibl.): the metaphysical transformation of nature. Arcimboldo was assumed to be a pantheist, spiritually akin to Giordano Bruno. Man is a part of nature just as nature is a part of man. Arcimboldo illustrated the thought that man was comprised of the same elements as the world – thus touching upon the correspondence between microcosm and macrocosm.

Although Arcimboldo's creations were emulated well into the 17th century in painting and graphics, his pictures were only rediscovered in 1920s and 30s have become famous since Benno Geiger's book (1954-1960), in which they were misinterpreted as prefigurations of Surrealism. Roland Barthes' essay from 1961 (1990, see bibl.) certainly comes close to this, but recommends a final analysis of Arcimboldo's "methods" of metaphor. He describes Arcimboldo's heads as "mobile" insofar as they suggest an elevation or a recession.

The way in which Arcimboldo's works weave visual imagination, fantasy, humour and artistic playfulness with an allegorical background certainly gives them their attractiveness.

Alexander Wied

Provenance: Emperor Rudolf II's art chamber, in the Prague inventory from 1621, no. 901: "The four seasons twice, with all types of birds, flowers and fruits as a face by Arcimboldo (Orig.)." It is missing in the revision from 1635 (A 182), but identical to the *eight antique pieces of all types of birds, animals and histories 8 pieces* (AA 67). Treasure chamber specifications from 1748 no. 59: "A head composed of garden fruits from the school of Leonardo da Vinci". 1772 from the treasure chamber. Inventory 1833, Ambras Depot no. 68; Engerth I, 18; gallery no. 349

Bibliography: Pieyre de Mandiargues 1978, 48-62; Kriegeskorte 1986, 62 with colour plate; Kaufmann 1985a, 210, cat. no. 2-1; Venice 1987, 76; Essen-Vienna 1988, vol. 2, cat. no. 555; Barthes 1990, 147, 150, 152; Kaufmann 1993, 100-137, 103ff., 108-110, plates 44-47; Porzio 1993, 37f., plate 1; Tokyo, Hiroshima, etc. 1994-1995, 10, plate 1; Prague 1997, 11f., colour plate 6, 605, cat. no. IV.5 with older bibliography; Lugano 1998, 29, plate 28; Vienna 2003, cat. no. X.23, 528 with plate and bibliography (K. Schütz).

IV.4
Giuseppe Arcimboldo
Winter
Oil on linden wood
66.6 × 50.5 cm
Signed lower right: GIVSEPPE/ARCIMBOLDO. F.
On the back in antique writing: 1563 HJEMS
Vienna, Kunsthistorisches Museum, Gemäldegalerie, inv. no. 1590

The *Winter* originally belonged to a series of the *Four Seasons* of which the *Summer* in the Kunsthistorisches Museum (cat. no. IV.3) carries the date 1563.

The profile bust of *Winter* is composed entirely of a gnarly tree-trunk. The nose is the cracked growth of a branch, moss forming the stubble of a beard and intricate branches forming the scrubby hair, in which an evergreen ivy grows. The mouth is composed of two tree fungi. The vacant, squinting eye is ingeniously created through a crack in the bark. From the breast protrudes a sprig carrying two lemons. Again, the clothing is made of woven straw, in which one can make out a large M (for Maximilian II) and the firesteel referring to the Order of the Golden Fleece. Berra (1998) proposes that the anthropomorphism of the tree-trunk is not only attributable to a model that was perhaps found in the woods, but also to the physiognomic experiments of Leonardo, without which it would be unimaginable.

Alexander Wied

Provenance: Kunstkammer of Emperor Rudolf II, in Prague inventory from 1621 under no. 901 - 65; Engerth I, 19; gallery no. 348

Bibliography: Geiger 1954, 58f., plate 50, 50a; Kaufmann 1976a, 275ff.; Kaufmann 1977, 337f.; Neumann 1979, 196f.; Kaufmann 1985a, 210, cat. no. 2-1; Hulten 1987, 22, 26, 28; Essen-Vienna 1988, cat. no. 112; Barthes 1990, 137, 142, 149, 151, 153; Schneider 1992, 123; Kaufmann 1998a, 169f., plate 1; Berra 1998a, 57; Vienna 2003, cat. no. X.24, 538f. with plate and bibliography (K. Schütz).

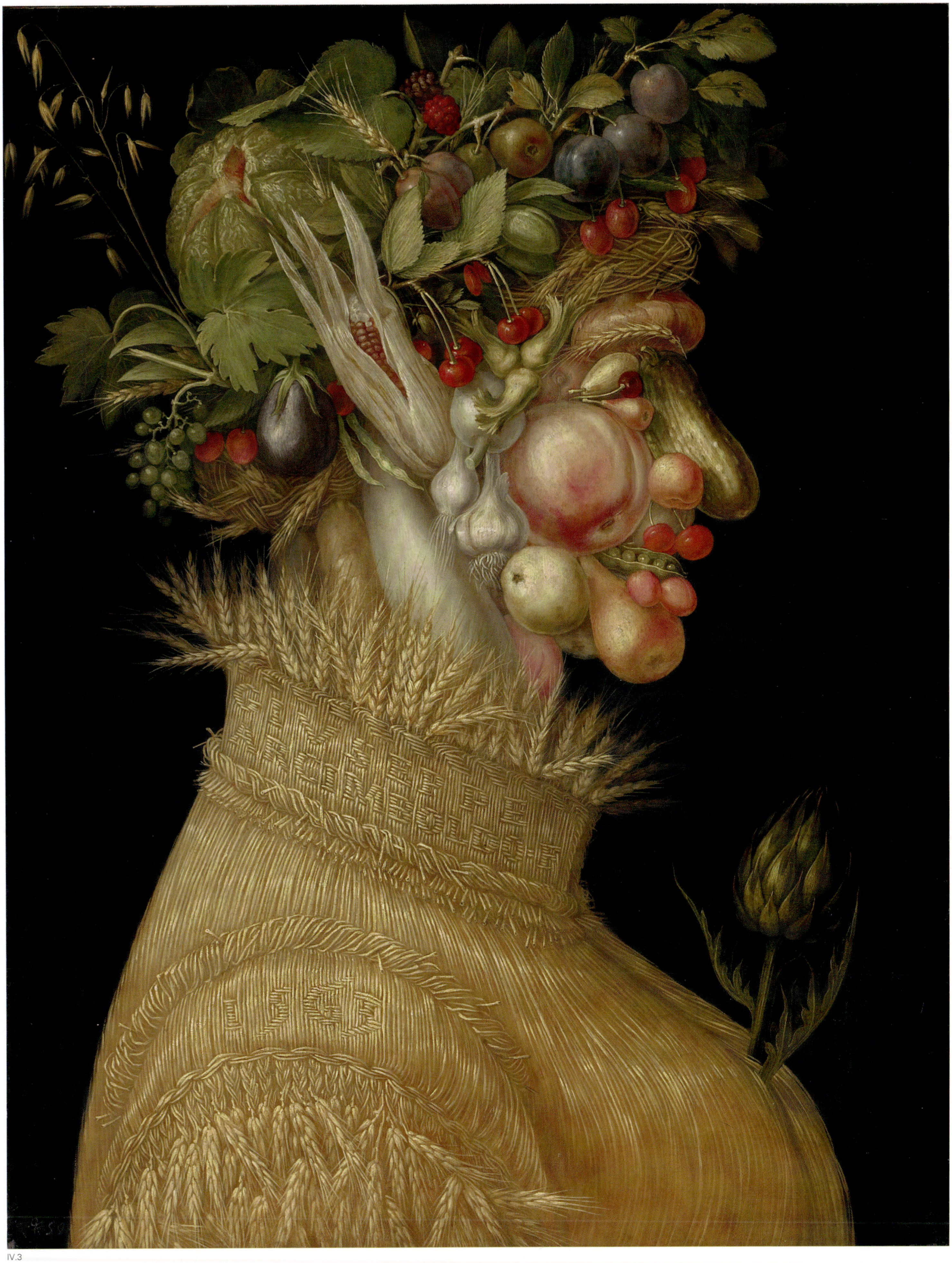

IV.3

IV.5
Giuseppe Arcimboldo
Summer, 1572
Oil on canvas
92.2 × 71.1 cm
Denver, Denver Art Museum. Funds from Helen Dill bequest, inv. no. 1961.56

This signed and dated version of *Summer* is very close in dimensions to a version of *Autumn*, now on display in Denver (private collection, U.S.A.). Both pictures share a provenance from the Bridel-Boiceau Collection, Lausanne, where they arrived after being a French collections from the time of the Napoleonic wars. Because of its similar dimensions and support, a version of *Winter* (Houston, De Menil Collection) shown in this exhibition probably also comes from the same series.
Geiger (1954, 145, and plate 51) and Legrand and Sluys (1955, 52) published this painting as a work by Arcimboldo. However, the present author (Kaufmann 1988c, 165) previously had considered it, along with the related versions of *Autumn* and *Winter*, to be a workshop replica. It was also presented with a question mark in the last major exhibition (Venice 1987, 174) devoted to Arcimboldo.
The negative opinions of this painting may now have to be revised. First, this painting is not a replica, but a variant of the composition of *Summer*. Like the other members of its series, its dimensions are elongated. The blades of grass and weeds projecting out of its head have accordingly been extended, and fill up more of the space of the picture. Other slight differences in detail in comparison with the earlier depiction of *Summer* are visible throughout.
As comparison with other paintings in this exhibition may also indicate, the execution of this work may also be evaluated more positively. Inspection in the 1980s and in 2004 in Denver revealed fine qualities in its handling of paint. These qualities are superior to those found in works which are probably replicas, if not even copies after Arcimboldo, for example the series of *Four Seasons* dated 1573 (formerly Craven Collection, Hampstead Marshall) which are probably copies after the series of similar date by the artist in the Louvre (cat. nos. IV.8-11; for the basis for this attribution see Kaufmann 1977). Close comparison in Paris (in 1999) of *Autumn* with the version of the same subject in the Louvre indeed suggested to this author these pictures to be assigned to the same artist, namely Arcimboldo, although, as in all of Arcimboldo's repetitions, there are slight differences in handling to be found.
The date of 1572 would indicate that this painting and the related versions of *Autumn* and *Winter* represent the first series of *Seasons* to have been executed after the initial versions were done for Maximilian. Their quality as variants, rather than replicas, would suggest that the artist had made this series for another important collector or patron. Because of its possible relation to the version of *Winter* from Houston, which bears an inscription in Spanish and a Habsburg device, it is possible that this painting also shares a provenance from Spain; its arrival in France would have been occasioned by the disruptions of the Peninsular wars, which caused many works of art to be transferred out of Spain. Hence it may have come ultimately from the Spanish royal collections.

Thomas DaCosta Kaufmann

Bibliography: Geiger 1954, 145 and plate 51; Legrand, Sluys 1955, 52; Venice 1987, 174; Kaufmann 1988c, 165.

IV.6
Giuseppe Arcimboldo
Autumn
1572
Oil on canvas
92.71 × 71.76 cm
Private collection, U.S.A. (on loan at the Denver Art Museum)

The dimensions and support (canvas) of this version of *Autumn* are almost identical to those of the painting of *Summer* dated 1572 (Denver, Art Museum, cat. no. IV.5). It also shares with this picture a provenance from the Bridel-Boiceau Collection, Lausanne, and it is framed identically. It thus most likely belonged to the same series as did the Denver *Summer*. Since the version of *Autumn* from Arcimboldo's initial series of *Seasons*, dated 1563 (cat. nos. IV.2-4; Vienna, Kunsthistorisches Museum, and Madrid, Accademi de San Fernando) is lost, this version of *Autumn* is important as representing the earliest surviving Arcimboldesque depiction of that season.
Comparison of this painting of *Autumn* with an authentic version dated 1573 (Paris, Musée du Louvre, cat. no. IV.10) indicates a similar manner of pictorial construction, same materials, and similar touch, with little to distinguish the handling of paint. On the other hand, notable discrepancies do exist between significant details in the two paintings (as they do between the versions of *Summer* in the same sets): they have different tonalities and even hues, as well as treating the individual forms slightly differently. For instance, the colours of the fruits in the 1572 version are represented with greater contrast, the grapes being painted in dark purple, while the planks of wood which constitute the barrel of the torso are depicted in both grey and brown tones, not just in those of one hue, as in the 1573 version. Since the dimensions of the 1572 and 1573 versions are also different, it is unlikely that they are copies of the same source. These qualities speak for both sets being authentic paintings by Arcimboldo himself: the variations suggest that the artist has slightly varied his works over time.
The series executed in 1572 to which this version of *Autumn* belongs moreover seems far superior to those in another series also dated 1572 (Private Collection, Bergamo; see Kriegeskorte 1988, 34). The proportions of the Bergamo series have also been altered. In contrast with the present painting, and its mate in Denver, this series seem to be copies or at best workshop replicas, perhaps even of this painting and that in Denver. The author's previously stated opinion (Kaufmann 1988c, 165) that the paintings from the Bridel-Boiceau collection were replicas therefore needs to be revised.
This version of *Autumn*, along with the Denver *Summer*, are very close in dimension to the painting of *Winter* in the Menil Collection (cat. no. IV.7). They are also painted on a similar support. Although they do not share the same recent provenance, they probably belonged to the same series, and thus, like the Menil *Winter*, may have come from Spain, and perhaps even from the Spanish royal collection. The choice of canvas for a support would also coincide with its having been shipped a long distance.
The Menil painting is however more loosely executed than are the versions in Paris, and than this picture. Comparison of the various versions of *Winter* with other seasons in the different sets, as well as of the various sets with each other made possible by the present exhibition may help resolve questions of the constitution of the various series, and of their attribution to Arcimboldo.

Thomas DaCosta Kaufmann

Bibliography: Geiger 1954, 145 and plate 52; Legrand, Sluys 1955, 52; Kaufmann 1988c, 165.

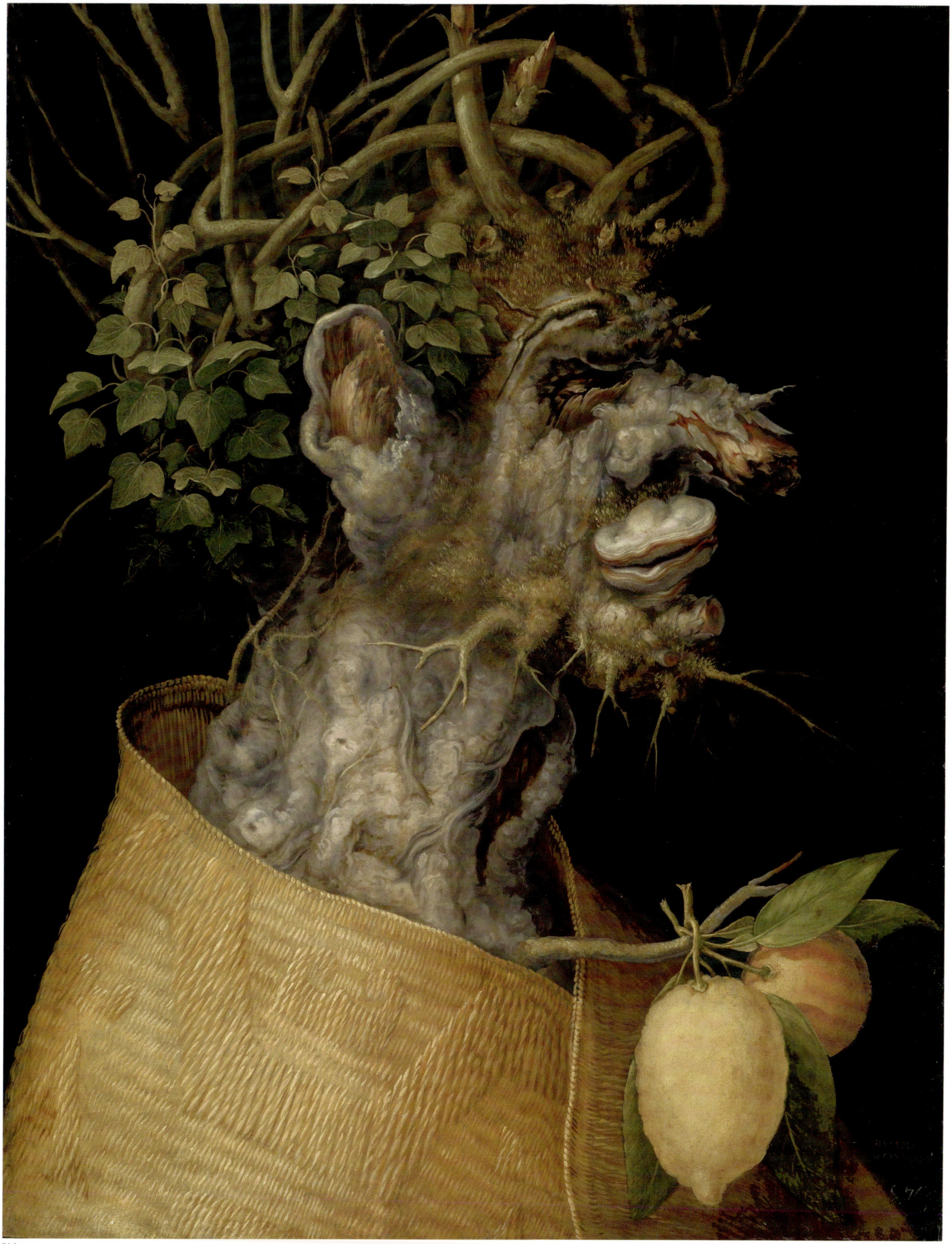

IV.4

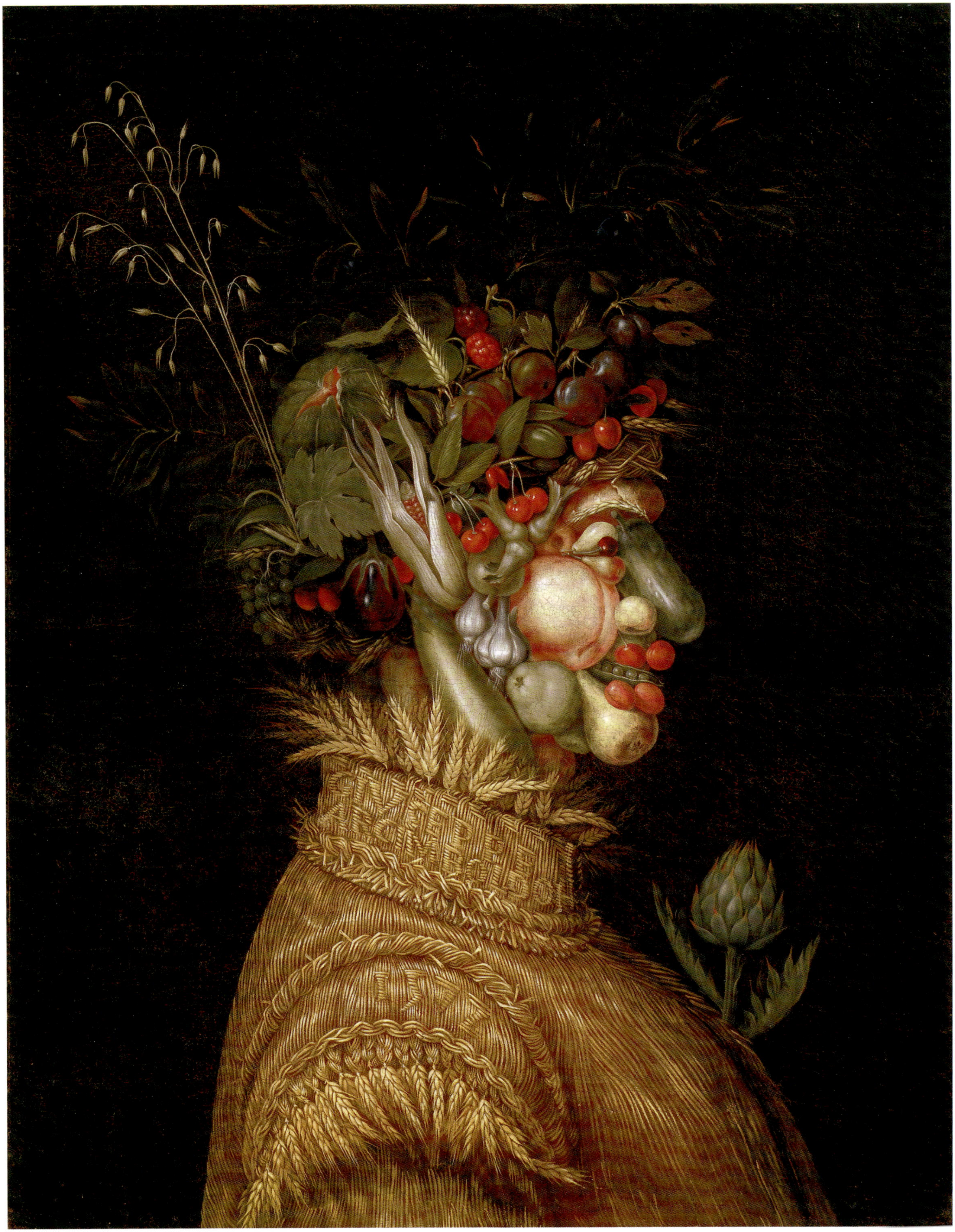

IV.5

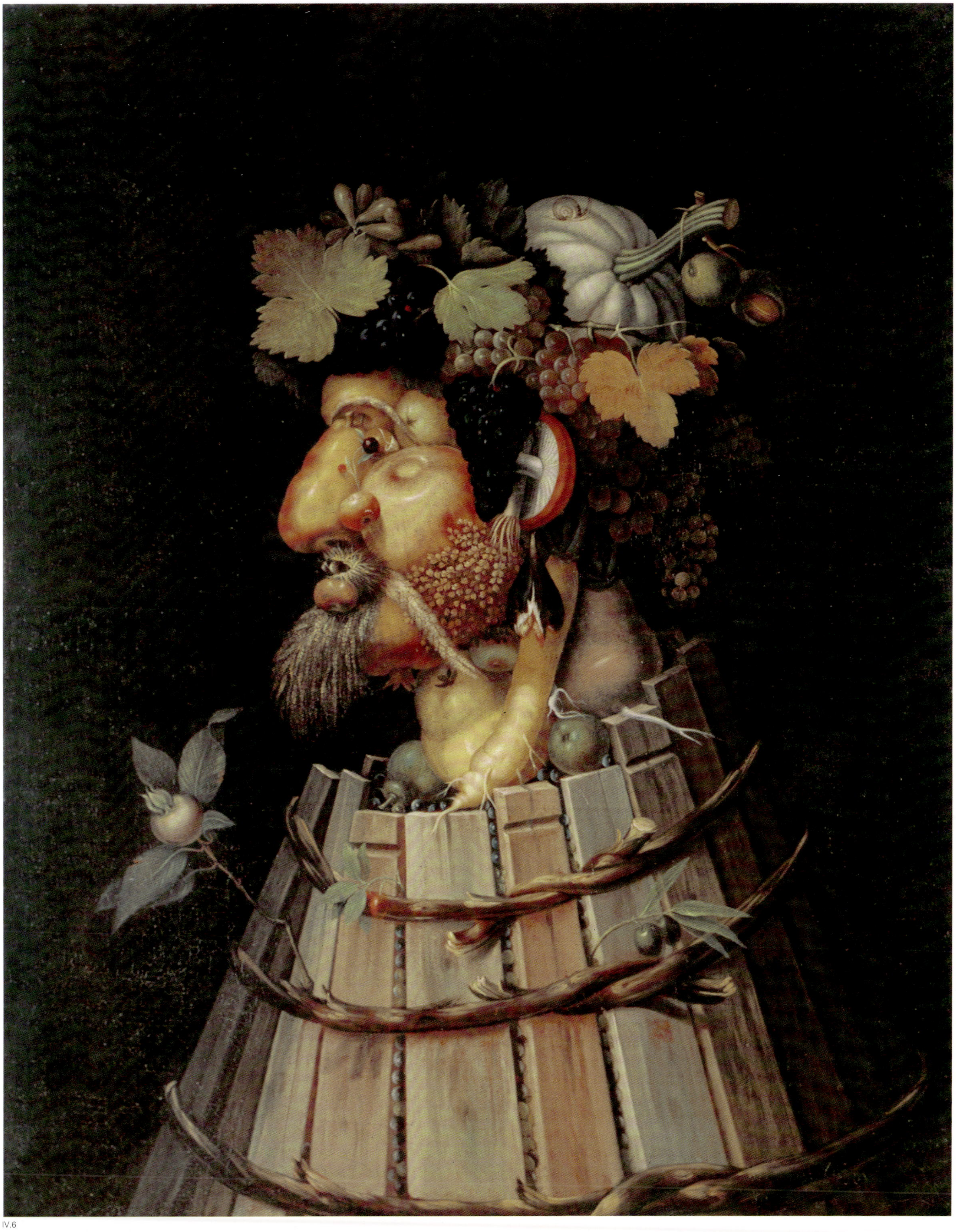

IV.6

IV.7
Giuseppe Arcimboldo
Winter
probably 1572
Oil on canvas
93.2 × 71.5 cm
Houston, The Menil Collection, inv. no. X3060

This painting was attributed to Arcimboldo by Geiger (1954, plate 53), but previously regarded by the present author (Kaufmann 1988c, 165) as a workshop replica. Subsequently, the painting has been exhibited as a work by Arcimboldo without, however, any further comment about the attribution (Kenseth 1991, 252, and plate 2).
The larger dimensions of this depiction of *Winter*, and the consequent extension of details in the branches in the head do suggest that this painting is a variant, rather than a replica, of Arcimboldo's earlier version of the theme (cat. no. IV.4). Other differences in details and qualities of execution support the hypothesis that it may be by the artist himself. It is superior in quality, for instance, to another almost identical version with similar motifs but slightly smaller dimensions (Private collection, Europe) which has been exhibited alongside it (see Venice 1987, 172 and 173), when both examples were however shown as questionable works by Arcimboldo.
The probable date and particular symbolism of this picture also speak for its *Eigenhändigkeit*. The date of execution, 1572, is arrived at by its association with the version of *Summer* from Denver, whose dimensions it approximates. As for its symbolism, the presence of the motif of the fire iron woven into the wicker cloak is significant. The fire iron, which belongs to the chain of the Golden Fleece, the "House Order" of the Habsburgs, is a Habsburg *impresa*. It appears as such in *Fire* (cat. no. IV.27), as well as in Arcimboldo's earlier painting of *Winter* in Vienna (cat. no. IV.4). As in other versions, the motif is probably related to the owner of the paintings – the fire iron and M in the Vienna version stand for Maximilian, the arms of Meissen for the Duke-Elector of Saxony in the Paris version (see Kaufmann 1993 and Kaufmann 2007a). The selection of *Winter* to bear the device is related to the Romans' choice of this season as the start of the year, the *caput anni*, and hence it is especially important: it signifies the beginning of the cycle of time, and, with the rest of the seasons, the eternal rule of the Habusburgs (see Kaufmann 1993, 123-124), but is the ruler's personal season.
As in the Vienna version, the fire iron in the garment identifies this season as the Habsburgs' own, but the absence of the M suggests that this version was however done for Maximilian II. The inscription in Spanish (*Inbierno*, meaning winter) at the top of the painting points instead to a provenance from Spain. The presence of the Habsburg *impresa* might therefore indicate that it came from the Spanish royal collections. It is known that versions of the *Seasons* were present in the Spanish royal collections from an early date (Rudolf 1995, especially 185-187). Like *Summer* exhibited here, this painting may be one of this series.

Thomas DaCosta Kaufmann

Bibliography: Geiger 1954, 146, fig. 55; Venice 1987, 172; Kaufmann 1988c, 165.

IV.8
Giuseppe Arcimboldo
Spring
1573
Oil on canvas
76 × 63.5 cm
Paris, Musée du Louvre, inv. no. R.F. 1964-30

The *Four Seasons* in the Louvre were acquired in 1964 from the Parisian collection of Jean Neger. Two clues have made it possible to retrace the history of these works: the crossed swords of Meissen, the armorial bearings of Saxony that appear on *Winter*'s cloak, and the date of 1573 inscribed on *Summer*'s shoulder, under the artist's signature. Thomas DaCosta Kaufmann (Kaufmann 1977, 337) has linked these elements with a note dated 28 July 1574 in the ledgers of the imperial court, recording a payment of sixty-five gulden to Arcimboldo for paintings commissioned by Emperor Maximilian II (1527-1576) for Augustus the Elector of Saxony (1526-1586). The relative vagueness of this document is fortunately made up for by the 1595 and 1610 inventories of the Kunstkammer in Dresden, in which several of Arcimboldo's works are listed: the *Four Seasons*, *The Cook* and *The Cellarman*. The allegories were mentioned by the traveller Philipp Hainhofer in 1629, and then by Tobias Teubel in 1683. After this date there is no further trace of the pictures, which were probably removed from the collections in Dresden in the 19th century.
Two other versions of the *Seasons* with the coat of arms of Saxony are known. One, signed and dated, was for a long time in the collection of the family of the Earls of Craven in England, who had been left it by Elizabeth (1596-1662), daughter of King James I of Great Britain and wife of the Elector Palatine Frederick V, king of Bohemia from 1619 to 1620. After Frederick V's defeat at the battle of the White Mountain in 1620, Elizabeth left Prague, probably taking these *Seasons* with her to England. DaCosta Kaufmann (Kaufmann 1977, 337-338) considered them to be copies, which would explain, despite their quality, a certain stiffness of composition, especially in the *Summer*, and a slight dryness of tone. The second series, a mediocre copy, is mentioned in a description of the Kunstkammer of the duke of Schleswig-Holstein at Gottorf by Adam Olearius in 1674.

Vincent Delieuvin

Bibliography: Kaufmann 1977, 337-342; Ferrari 1978.

IV.9
Giuseppe Arcimboldo
The Summer
1573
Oil on canvas
76 × 63.5 cm
Paris, Musée du Louvre, inv. no. R.F. 1964-31

Thomas DaCosta Kaufmann has clearly set out the political circumstances in which Arcimboldo's *Seasons* were offered to Augustus of Saxony (Kaufmann 1977, 340-341). In 1570 and again in 1573 this Protestant prince spent time at the Catholic court of the emperor, thereby defending his position as elector against the claims of his cousin Johann Wilhelm of Saxe-Weimar. For his part, Maximilian II, anxious to establish a balance between Catholic and Protestant forces, favoured relations with this ruler, who also supported the election of his son Rudolf as king of the Romans in 1573.
Augustus had been able to admire Arcimboldo's creations at the imperial court, and probably to understand their symbolical and political significance. In 1570 he had taken part in the celebrations organized by the artist in Prague on the occasion of the marriage of the emperor's daughter Elizabeth to Charles IX of France. The *Seasons* may have been presented to him at the time of his stay in 1573 or shortly afterwards. The prince found that the imperial symbols had been replaced by his own in the new version of the pictures. The correspondences between the microcosm, the macrocosm and political power, illustrated in the *Seasons* and the *Elements* and made clear to Maximilian by Giambattista Fonteo, were now organized around the figure of Augustus, also the sovereign of a political and natural order and member of a dynasty whose reign was predicted to last for eternity.
A flattering political allegory, the *Seasons* were also striking images of *discordia concors* and were undoubtedly intended to convey to the Elector of Saxony Maximilian's desire for peace and his ability to fuse the diversity of his empire into a coherent unity.

Thomas DaCosta Kaufmann

Bibliography: Kaufmann 1977, 337-342.

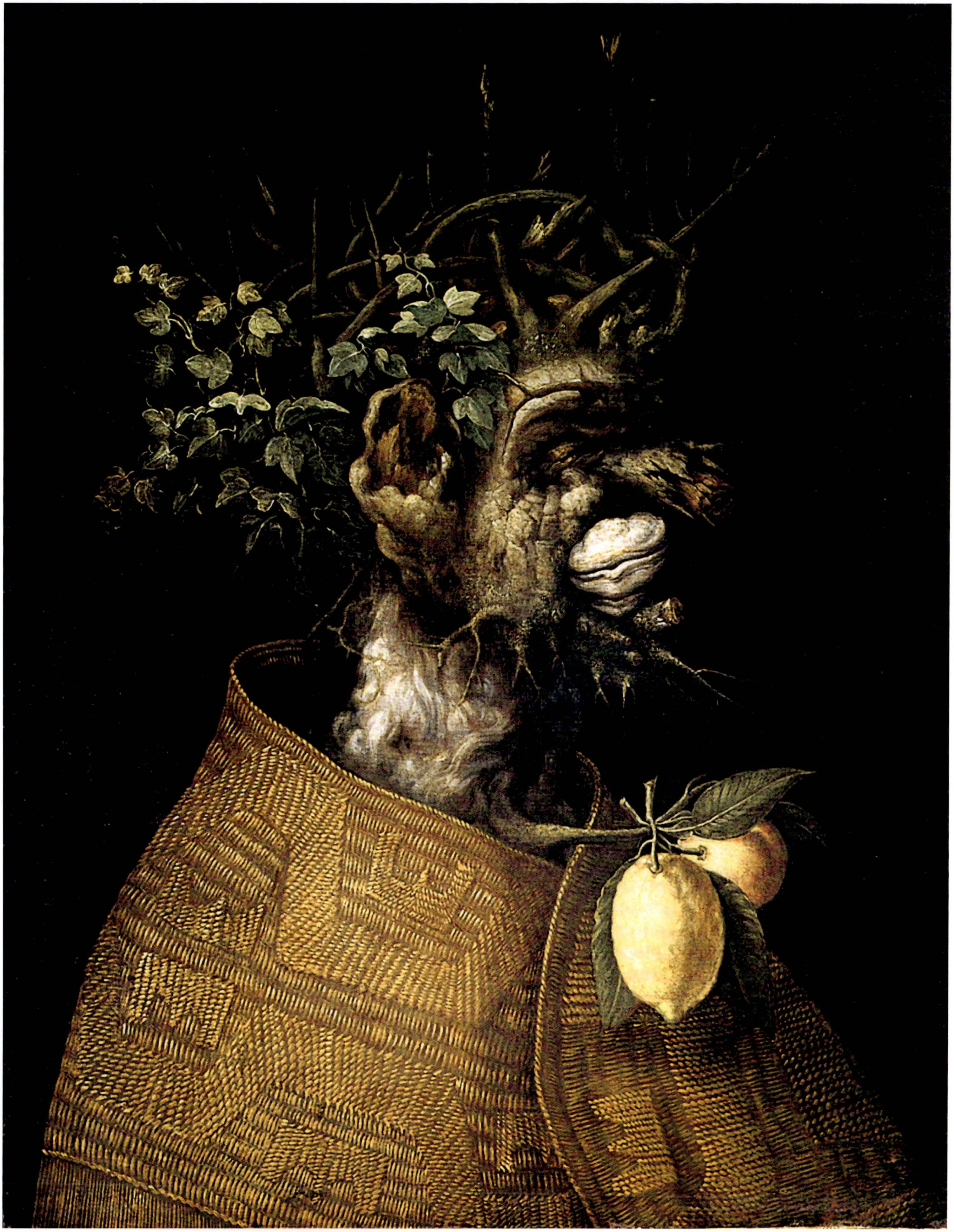

IV.7

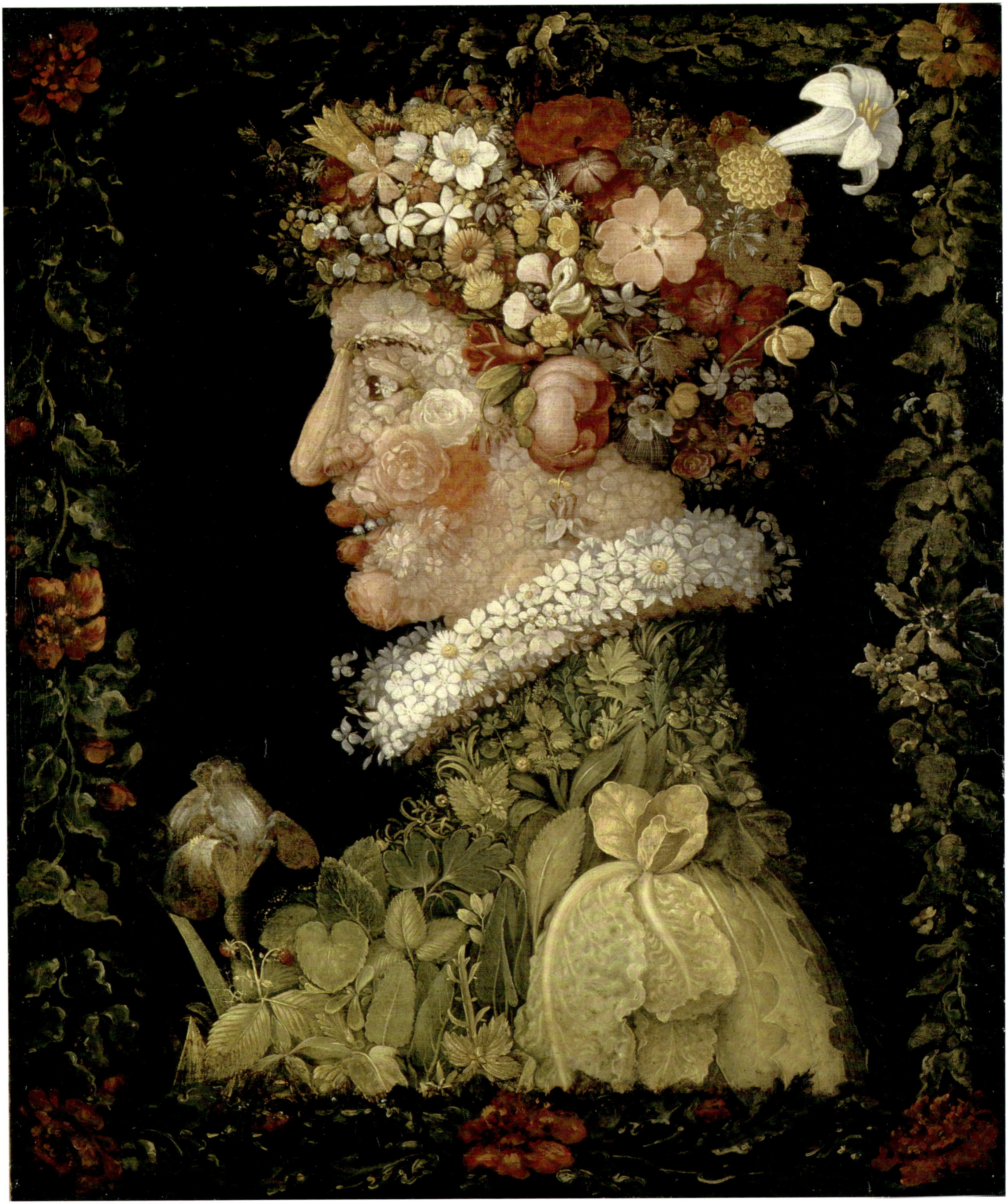

IV.8

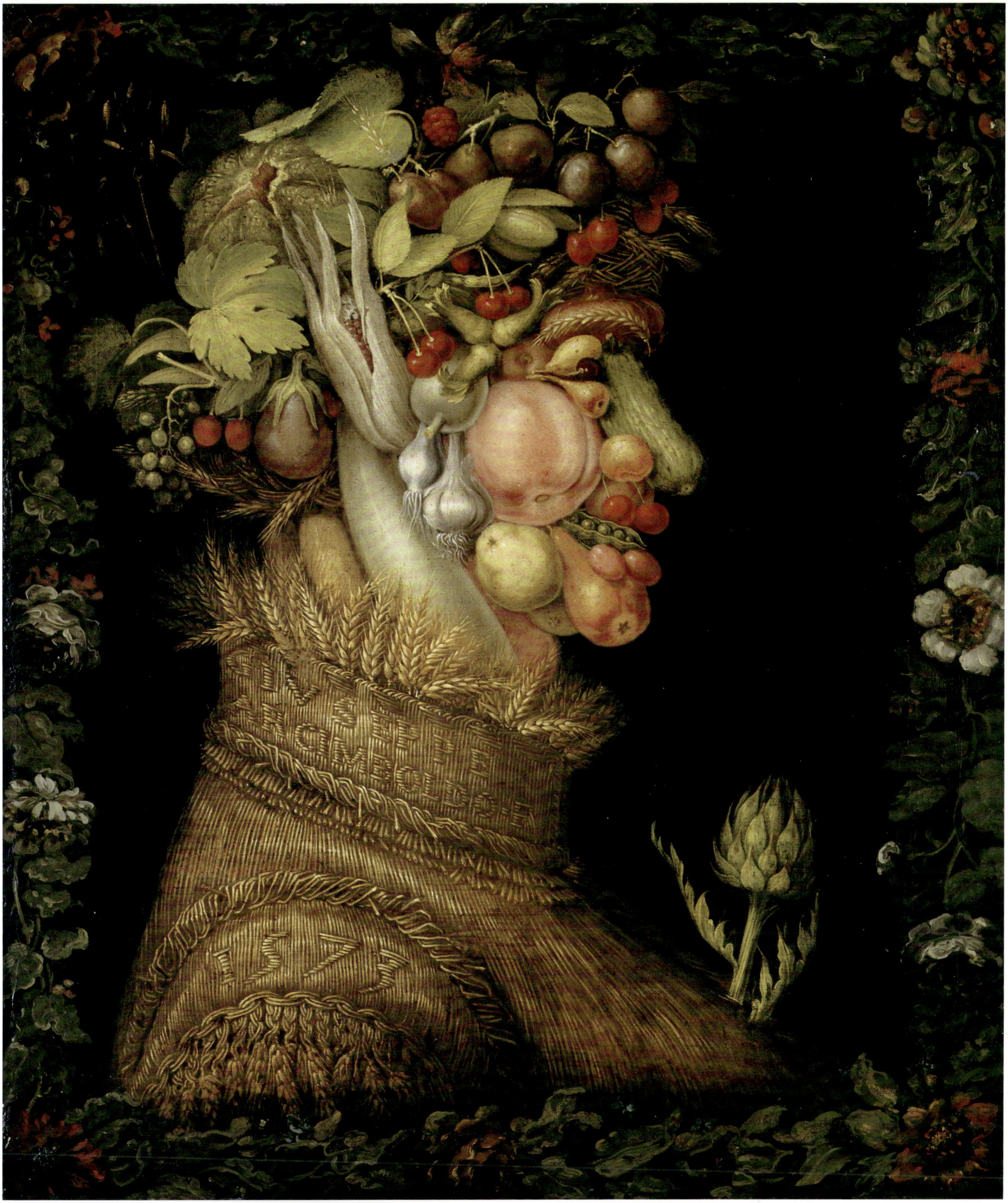

IV.9

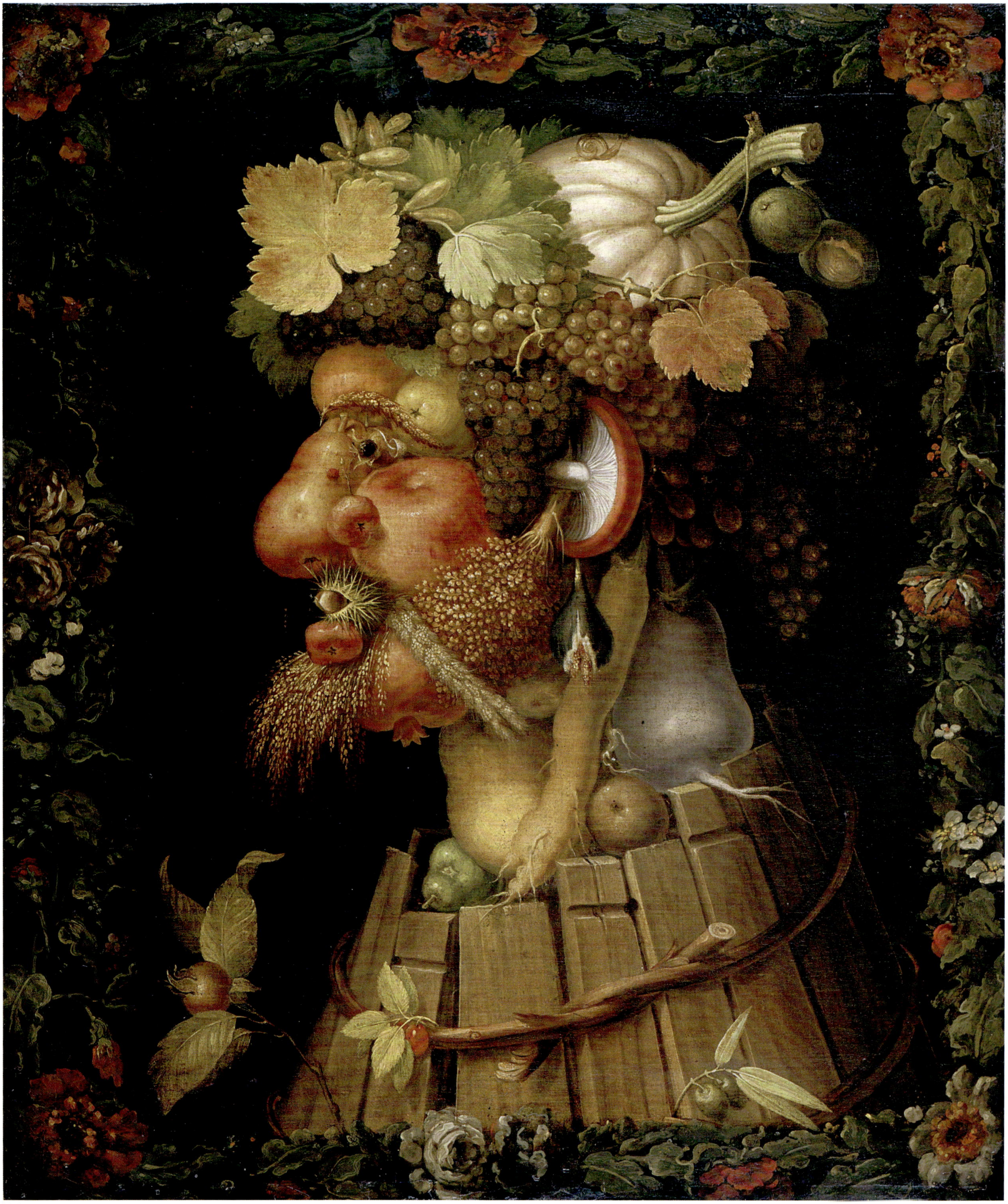

IV.10

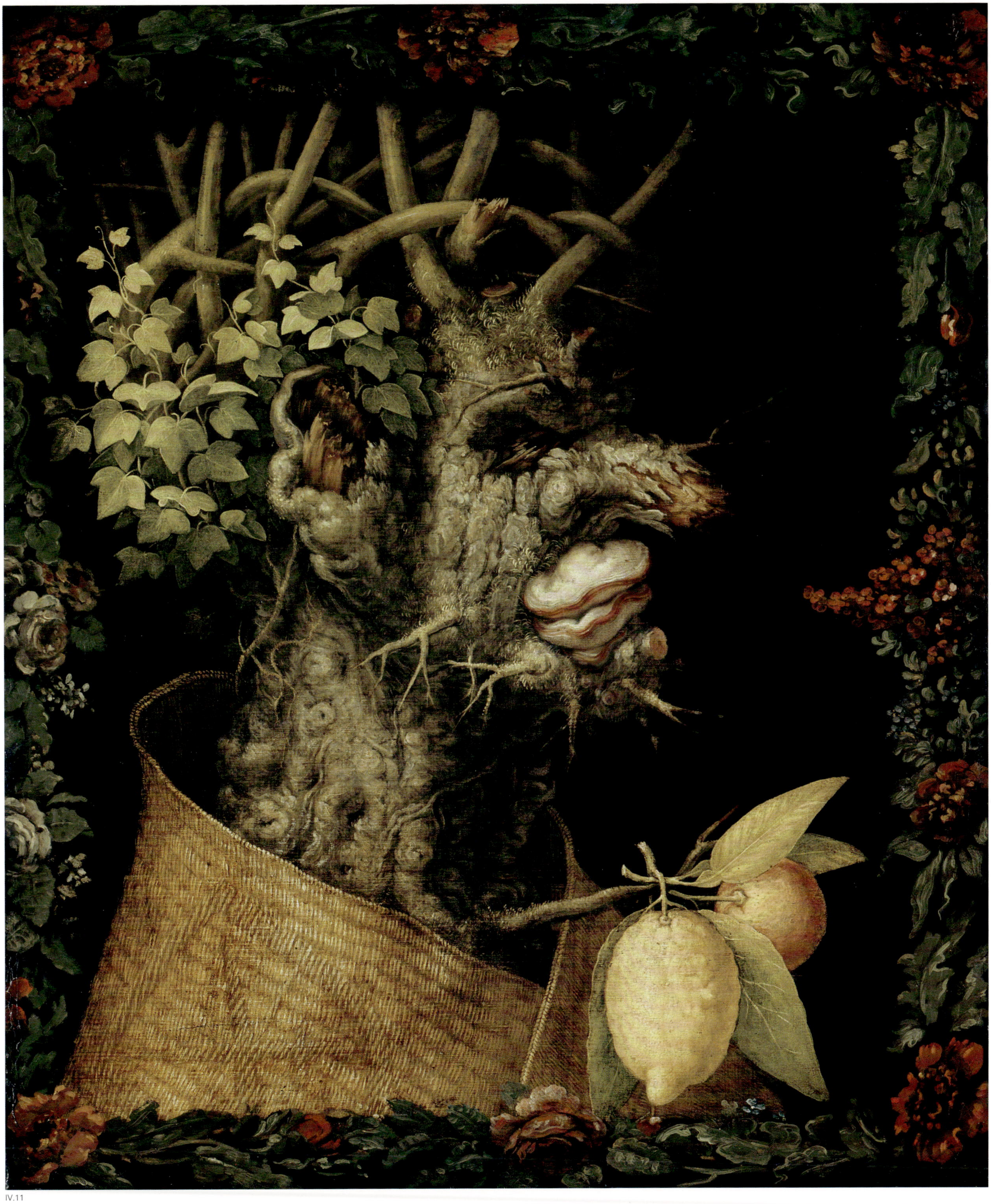

IV.11

IV.10
Giuseppe Arcimboldo
The Autumn
1573
Oil on canvas
76 × 63.5 cm
Paris, Musée du Louvre, inv. no. R.F. 1964-32

For the new year of 1569, Maximilian II received a version of the *Seasons* accompanied by the *Elements* and Fonteo's poem. The perfect coherence of the whole should not make us forget that the *Seasons* were painted independently back in 1563, and that they had been repeated several times, probably making them the series Arcimboldo reproduced most often. It is also the series of which the largest number of autograph versions and old copies are known to us today. The emperor himself possessed at least two of them, and sent one to his cousin Philip II of Spain (Perez Sanchez, 1987, 64), as well as to Augustus. In his *Figino* (1591), Gregorio Comanini tells us that Arcimboldo had offered a picture resembling the *Four Seasons* to him too (Barocchi, I, 1971, 391).
In fact this series has an intrinsic unity, with formal characteristics that distinguish it from the *Elements*. The flower, fruit or vegetable that stands out clearly from the breast, like a precious jewel, has a presence in the composition that the flatter ornaments of the *Elements* lack. And more significantly still, it is from the extremely varied expressions of the vegetable heads that the iconographic originality of the *Seasons* stems. In the first place they represent the four ages of man: childhood, adolescence, maturity and old age. They also reflect the temperament connected with each season (Porzio, 1979, 34): the sanguine character of spring, the choleric one of summer, the melancholic one of autumn and the phlegmatic one of winter. This triple identity of the *Seasons* invites us to seek correspondences with other aspects of nature such as the four elements, the four principles, etc.
This idea that nature functions by correspondences was an increasingly popular one in that period. Fonteo, for example, made use of the *Seasons* and the *Elements*. In Francesco I de' Medici's *studiolo* in the Palazzo Vecchio in Florence (1570), Vincenzo Borghini represented the iconography in even greater detail. The peculiarity of Arcimboldo's *Seasons* lies in the ingenious fusion of these correspondences into a single, coherent and independent image. Thus there is nothing to be surprised about in the fact that Augustus of Saxony had only received these pictures, without the *Elements*.

Thomas DaCosta Kaufmann

Bibliography: Perez Sanchez 1987; Comanini 1971; Porzio 1979.

IV.11
Giuseppe Arcimboldo
The Winter
1573
Oil on canvas
76 × 63.5 cm
Paris, Musée du Louvre, inv. no. R.F. 1964-33

The *Seasons* in the Louvre differ from the original Viennese model in the nature of the support, with canvas taking the place of wood. While the *Spring* in the Real Academia de Bellas Artes de San Fernando in Madrid and the three *Seasons* in the Bayerische Staatsgemäldesammlungen in Munich – these last of questionable attribution – are painted on wood, the majority of the other known versions are painted on canvas. This support may have been chosen for the convenience of the transport for which these works were intended by the man who commissioned them.
The series in Paris is the only one to have a border formed of garlands of leaves and flowers around the heads. This feature is clearly a later addition as the greenery is depicted in a perfunctory fashion with a broader brush and in places clumsily superimposed on Arcimboldo's painting, still visible underneath. The Louvre's scientific laboratory has put forward the hypothesis of an addition in the 17th century, perhaps at the time of the restoration and enlargement of the original canvas.
A comparison with the pictures in Vienna reveals slight differences in the composition. In the *Summer* in the Louvre, the artichoke is shorter and the two small beans under the ear of maize are missing. The interlacing of the branches in the *Winter* is different in the Viennese version, and the opening of the cavity forming the eye is slightly larger. Roland Barthes has compared these pictorial variations to the musical world: "Here we are totally in music: there is indeed a basic theme (the summer, the autumn, Calvin), but each variation has a different effect" (Barthes, 1978, 51). And in fact the *Winter* in Paris, with its half-open eye, looks more alive or awake than the one in Vienna.
The depiction of the vegetables is just as delicate and fine, but with a hazier touch. The tones are brighter, with the lighting more diffuse and even. According to DaCosta Kaufmann (DaCosta Kaufmann, 1977, 338), these changes bear witness to an evolution in Arcimboldo's style, although one that is difficult to grasp owing to the lack of sufficient materials and chronological evidence.

Thomas DaCosta Kaufmann

Bibliography: Barthes 1978, 13-68; Kaufmann 1977, 337-342.

IV.12
Arcimboldo Workshop
Allegory of Spring
Oil on wood
84 × 57 cm
Landshut, Trausnitz Castle, inv. no. L 82/268 (on loan from the Bayerischen Staatsgemäldesammlungen, Munich, inv. no. 2037)

Provenance: 1598 in the Münchener Kunstkammer inventory taken by Joh.Bapt.Fickler, no. 2765: "Spring is crowned with all kinds of flowers and irises, its clothes covered with green foliage, the cress on a shirt of white flowers" – Inventories from 1607, 1635-38 and 1641-1642

Bibliography: Diemer 1980, 130; Kriegeskorte 1986, 60 with colour reproduction; Diemer *et al.* 2004, 197, 132 sq., 139; Sangl 2004, 75.

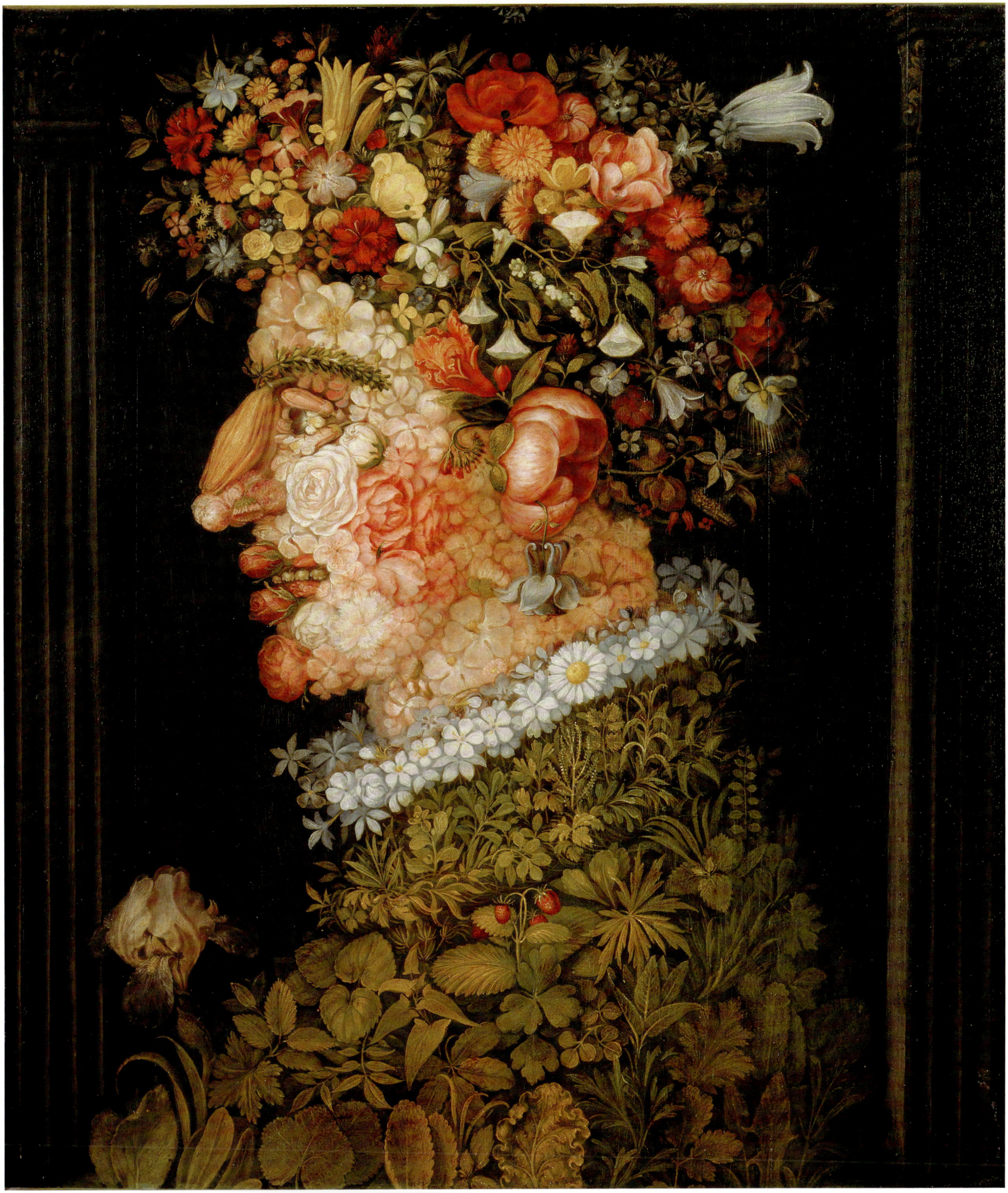

IV.12

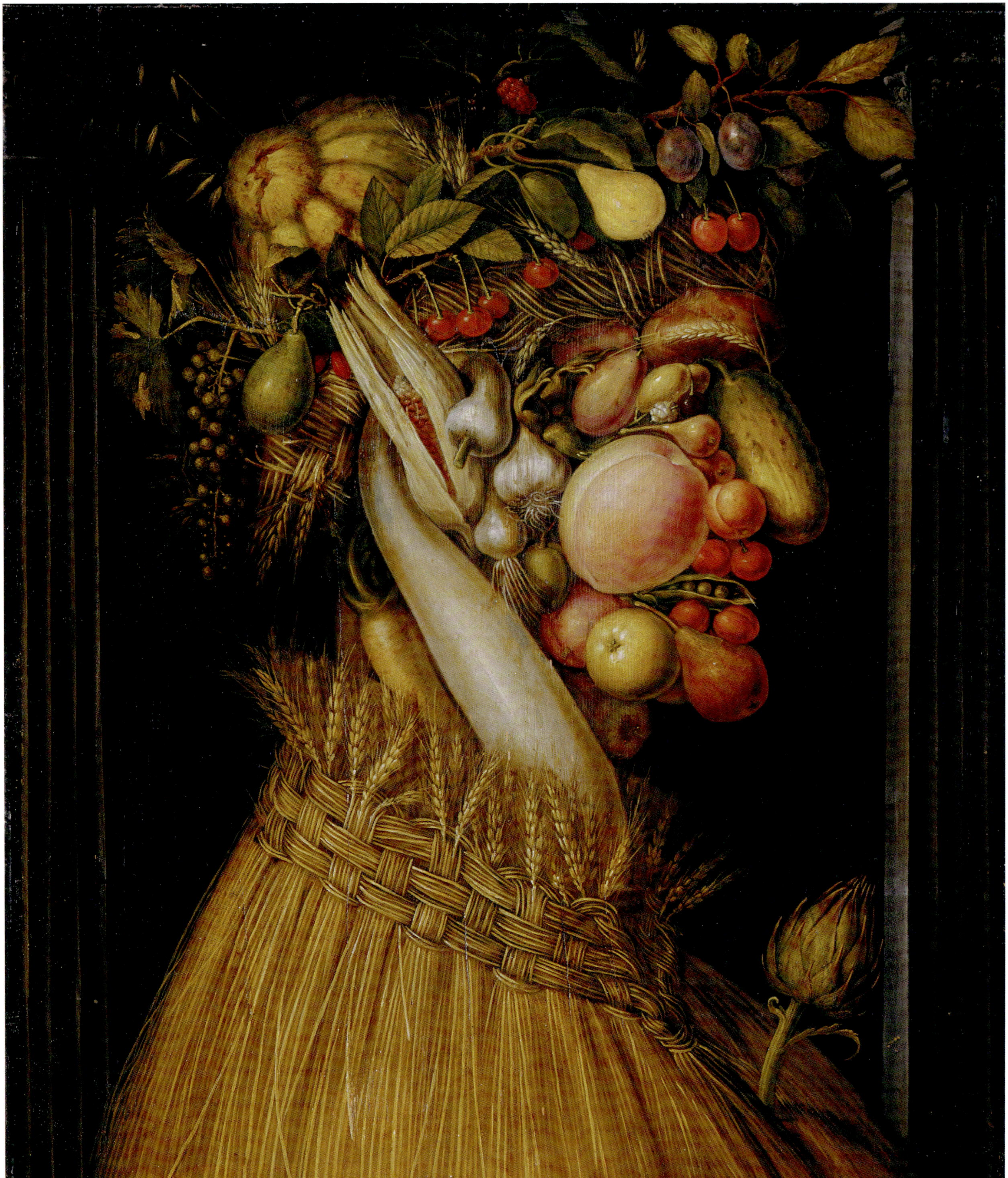

IV.13

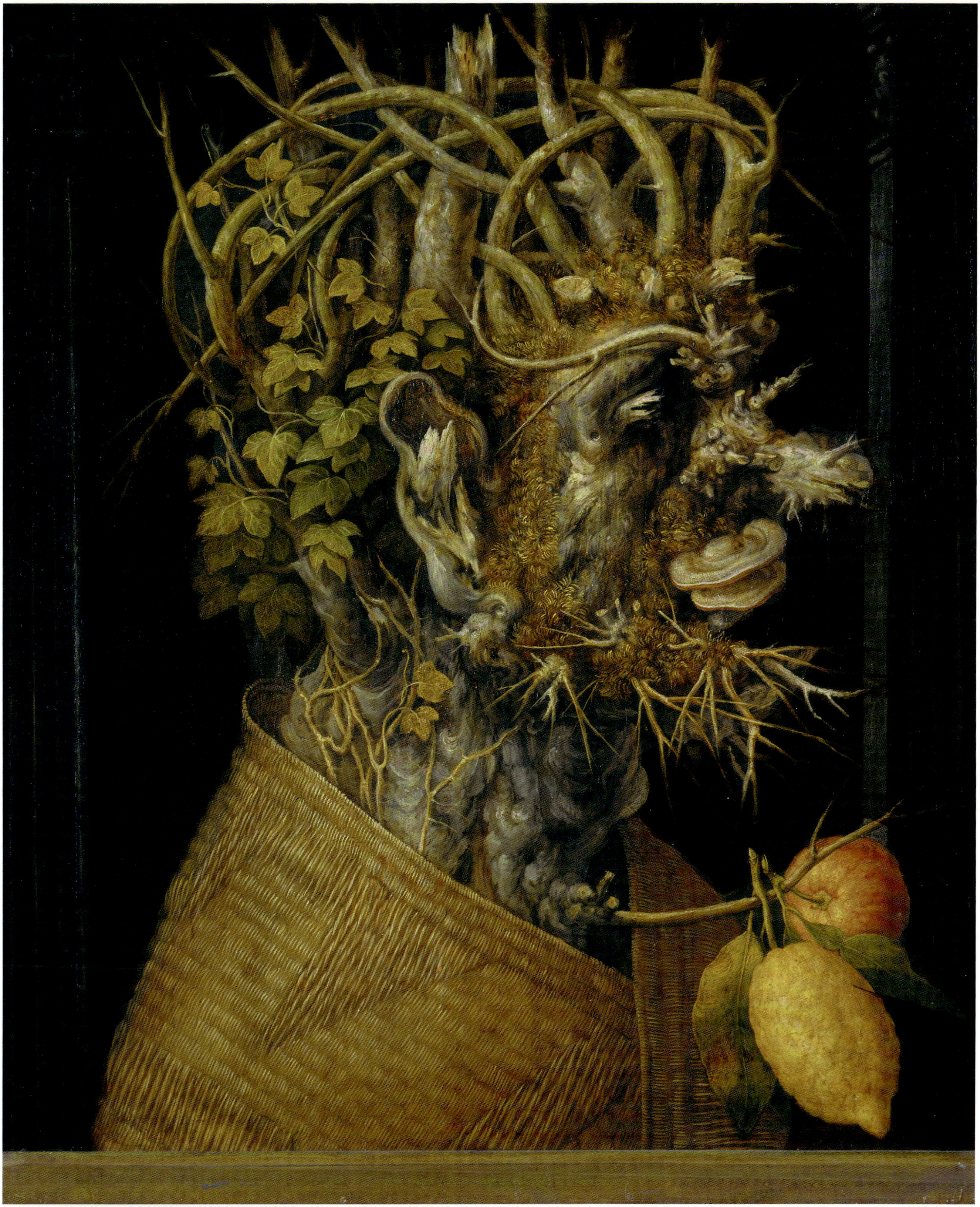

IV.14

IV.13
Arcimboldo Workshop
Allegory of Summer
Oil on wood
84 × 57 cm
Landshut, Trausnitz Castle, inv. no. L 2003/1298 (on loan from the Bayerischen Staatsgemäldesammlungen, Munich, inv. no. 2038)

Provenance: 1598 in the Münchener Kunstkammer inventory taken by Joh.Bapt.Fickler, no. 2766: "Summer, with apples, melons and cherries everywhere, the body covered with grain ears and straw" – Inventories from 1607, 1635-1638 and 1641-1642

Bibliography: Diemer 1980, 130, 132f., 139; Kriegeskorte 1986, 64 with colour reproduction; Diemer *et al.* 2004, 197; Sangl 2004, 74.

IV.14
Arcimboldo Workshop
Allegory of Winter
Oil on wood
84 × 57 cm
Landshut, Trausnitz Castle, inv. no. L 82/269 (on loan from the Bayerischen Staatsgemäldesammlungen, Munich, inv. no. 2040)

Completely anomalous both in its many details and its format, this series of the Four Seasons is distinct from the autograph versions (Vienna cat. nos. IV.2-4; Louvre: cat. nos. IV.8-11). It belongs to the collection of the Bayerischen Staatsgemäldessammlungen; three of them can currently be seen at the newly furnished Kunstkammer in the Trausnitz Castle; the fourth, the *Autumn*, because of its poor condition, is deposited at the Alte Pinakothek in Munich.
The fact that the paintings were already present in 1598 in the Munich Kunstkammer is an indication that these are not arbitrary copies from a later period, but rather pieces that satisfied the quality standards of the Bavarian Dukes. We do not know when and for which duke these paintings were made, whether for Albrecht V (1528-1579) or his son, Wilhelm V (1548-1626), who governed from 1579 to 1597. In any case, they were already present at the beginning of the reign of Duke Maximilian I in 1598.
The interest in Arcimboldo could on the one hand be related to his stay in Bavaria in 1582 and on the other hand to the friendship and blood relation of the House of Wittelsbach with the House of the Habsburg Emperor, where the series of the *Seasons* and *Elements* were found together with other works by Arcimboldo.
Whereas Kriegeskorte (1986) published the Munich series as originals by Arcimboldo, the index of the Trausnitzer Kunstkammer by Sigrid Sangl (2004) is more cautious in regard to the question of the authorship of the Munich series: "After Arcimboldo", in order to avoid the deprecative term "copy". These are by no means copies; they are varied repetitions, which clearly indicate another hand. The colours are altogether more muted, less contrasted. Particularly striking are the modifications in *Winter*: the branches as the hair are even scrubbier, more overgrown, the beard is longer, the nose more gnarled, the moss on the face is clearer and the neck is shortened, so that the entire head recedes somewhat deeper into the picture. In the straw collar the stylized M and the Feuereisen of the Viennese *Winter* (cat. no. IV.4) are replaced by right triangles. In *Summer* the signature woven into the collar is missing. Together with many variations of the details, all of the pictures are framed on the sides by fluted pillars. The flutings of the pilasters provide an optical association with the column in the group portrait *Emperor Maximilian II with his Family* (cat. no. III.4).
It is therefore more likely that the series was created by a very talented member of the studio, upon whose skill Arcimboldo could rely and to whom he could confidently entrust the reproduction for the Duke of Bavaria.
Fortunately, this exhibition offers the possibility for a direct comparison of the series.

Alexander Wied

Provenance: 1598 in the Münchener Kunstkammer inventory taken by Joh.Bapt.Fickler, no. 2768: "Winter has a bare forest on his head, a brittle nest in his beard, a plaited mantle around his body" – Inventories from 1607, 1635-1638 and 1641-1642

Bibliography: Diemer 1980, 130, 132f., 139; Kriegeskorte 1986, 68 with colour reproduction; Diemer *et al.* 2004, 197; Sangl 2004, 74f.

IV.15
Giuseppe Arcimboldo
The Four Seasons in one Head
Oil on poplar wood
60.4 × 44.7 cm
Private collection: procured through New York, Pandora Old Masters

In the famous dialogue of Don Gregorio Comanini, *Il Figino*, published in 1591, Figino allows his dialogue partner to make the following statement: "Please have Comanino show you that piece of art that he made of the four seasons. There you will see a very special painting! A very knotty trunk represents the breast and head, some holes for the mouth and eyes, and a protruding branch for the nose; the beard is made of strands of moss and some twigs on the forehead form horns. This tree-stump, without its own leaves or fruit, represents winter, which produces nothing itself, but depends on the production of the other seasons. A small flower on his breast and over his shoulder symbolizes spring, as well as a bundle of ears bound to some twigs, and a cloak of plaited straw covering his shoulders, and two cherries hanging from a branch forming his ear, and two damsons on the back of his head represent summer. And two grapes hanging from a twig, one white and one red, and some apples, hidden among evergreen ivy sprouting forth from his head, symbolize autumn. Among the branches in the head, one in the middle is loosing a bit of its bark, and pieces of it are bent and falling off; on the white area of this branch is written 'ARCIMBOLDUS P.'. This is how the painting is, in any case, and if you see it, it will please you wonderfully."
Reading this description while viewing this painting, publicly presented here from a private collection for the first time, it becomes immediately clear that Comanini was looking at precisely this composition. In order to be able to rule out the possibility of this being a falsification created according to this description, or a copy of the lost original, only a comparison of style and painting techniques with Arcimboldo's authentic works can help.
As in all versions of the *Winter* – from the Vienna example, dated as early as 1563, to the Paris version from 1573 – the head is composed of a moss-covered, gnarled tree trunk with a peeling bark, similar to our painting in which the elements representing *Winter* are elevated to a supporting structure. Contrary to Comanini's description, the straw cloak is not plaited here, as it appears in the versions of *Winter*, but it is rather composed of loose ears knotted into bundles.
As in the different versions of *Winter*, the bark in the eye openings is breaking off, exposing the wood grain behind it as eyelids. Especially striking in our picture is the quantity of cut-off branch stumps that seem to suggest wart-like formations

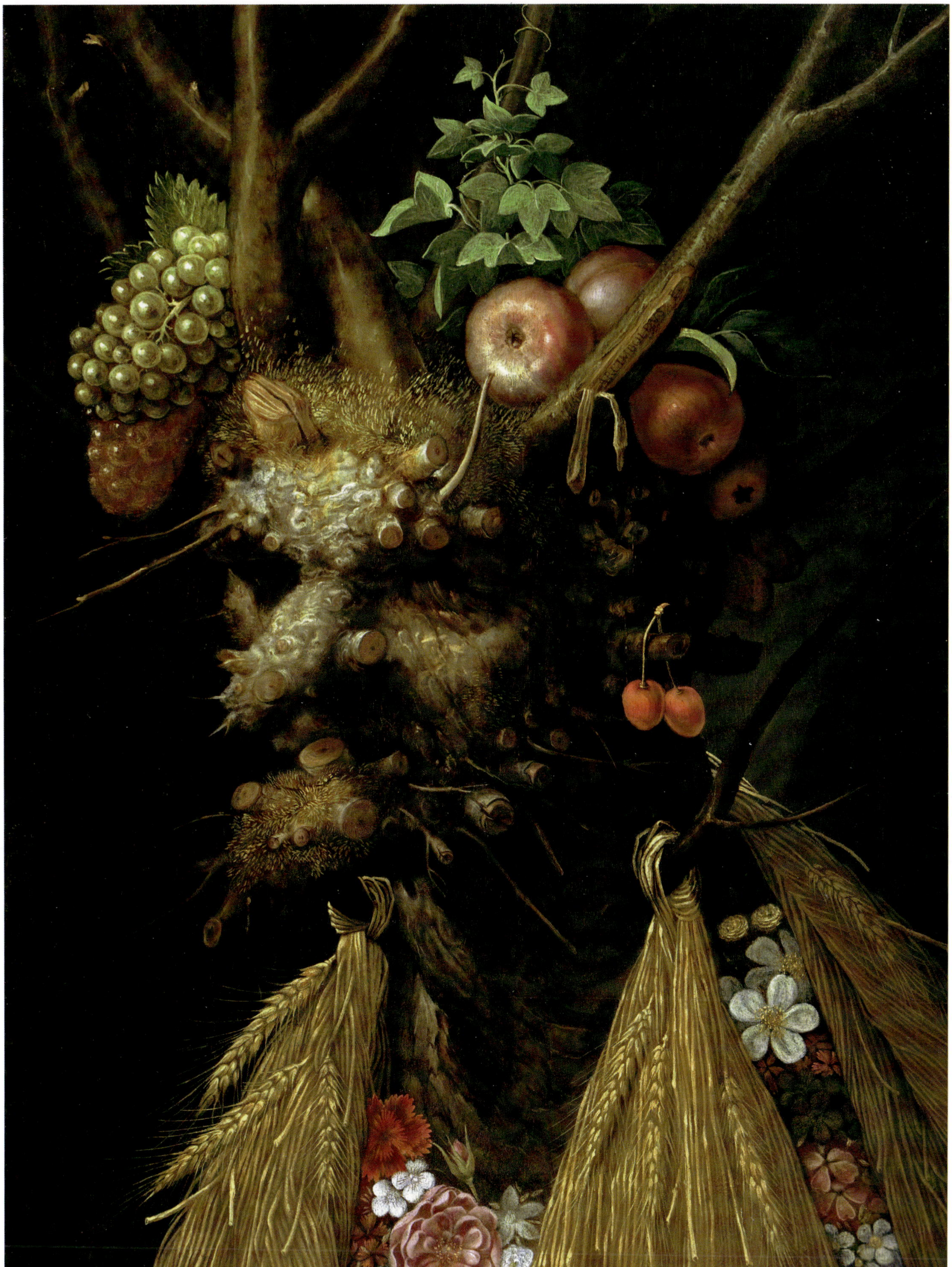

IV.15

on the forehead and nose and even tooth-stubs on the mandible. Morphologically, this bark surface is very similar to that in the *Winter*, just as the fruits, ears, ivy and flowers that are represented here are most closely related to Arcimboldo's signed paintings. The brushstroke in the filling elements, softly modulating with saturated pigments, offers as much of a comparative basis as the loosely vibrating "tocco" of the brush point in the moss-hair and tips of the plants. Furthermore, it is the high quality of execution in the small details that seems to reveal not only Arcimboldo's imaginativeness, but also his own hand.

Despite its generally very good state of conservation, this painting seems to have been slightly damaged in the hanging grapes on the left and in the plums bathed in shadow on the right. Perhaps also the garishly luminous red cherries on the left ear were somewhat spruced up.

The major difference between this painting and the *Seasons* and *Elements*, which are all given in profile, is the almost portrait-like composition of the head in three-quarter rotation to the left. In this, it resembles the so-called occupational portraits, especially the *Lawyer* (cat. no. IV.17). In no other painting of Arcimboldo's is the head so effectively and sculpturally raised up from the background. The mysterious light-dark modelling intensifies the expression of gentle melancholy and thereby also the direct association with Leonardo's works, as they are found in no other creation of the master. In this picture one can almost see one of Leonardo's old men, covered in bark. In particular, it recalls the reverse image of a drawn portrait of an old man in the Istituto Nazionale della grafica in Rome.

In response to the question of placing this work in Arcimboldo's career, the medium of poplar wood would indicate its creation in Italy. In Comanini's dialogue, the work seems to have been created after the equally well-described paintings of the *Flora* and the *Vertumnus*, which he sent to the emperor after his return to Milan in 1589 and 1591 respectively, and after the painting of the *Earth*, which he clearly indicates as having been sent from "Germania" to the king of Spain.

From Comanini's dialogue, it is made apparent that he painted this work for Comanini himself. Unfortunately, we know in general too little about the life of the Mantuan man of letters to be able to draw an accurate conclusion about his property or even about his testament. If the painting referenced in the 1656 inventory of the rich and famous Veronese collection of Giovan Pietro Cortoni, *Le quattro Stagioni che formano una testa* is identical to ours, which is supported by the similar measurements of comparison, we must at least assume that it was created after Arcimboldo's return to Italy and was again listed there in the 17th century.

This seems to rule out the idea that this head could have been a first attempt in the composite genre, inspired by the recent discovery of Leonardo's grotesques which were already widely circulated. Much more, I consider this unification of the seasons in a single picture as a sort of summa of all of Arcimboldo's prior individual naturalistic experiences; the individual elements here, as compared to the *Seasons* and *Elements*, serve a larger, unifying, general expression in which the main focus is directed towards the *naturalia* that characterize them. But wouldn't it serve to postulate another reason for this? In his *Vertumnus,* Arcimboldo created an allegory of Emperor Rudolf. His reign comprised the cycle of the four seasons, and as a God of Antiquity he was capable of unifying the four seasons in himself. This portrait is subsequently depicted frontally, as one would imagine a portrait of a ruler to be. Rudolf as Vertumnus is full of simultaneously blooming and ripening fruits, just like a closed circle of eternal prosperity and avail, entirely in the sense of an imperial panegyric.

As the god Vertumnus was capable of transformation, he could also assume the form of an old woman to seduce his beloved Pomona. Here, the question of the possible gender of our representation arises, as it has elsewhere with most of the other amorphous heads. Judging by the tree-structure, our composite head, as with *Winter*, would most likely be masculine; however, wouldn't the prominently ablaze cherry earrings be rather feminine? For this reason, one is almost tempted to see Vertumnus in the form into which he transformed himself to ensnare Pomona. However, is it plausible that Comanini, the recipient of this painting and to whom we also owe its description, would have omitted such a literary association? Perhaps the artist indeed had another "scherzo" in mind. Don't the branches sprouting from the head of this creature also remind us of the "stanchions" and "ends" of a deer antler? And with this, is not another relationship presented: to the world of animals, the elements and through it also to the temperaments and emotions that characterize man?

Could this painting not be seen as a quintessence of the interests that supported Arcimboldo's microcosm and macrocosm, to which he dedicated his life. Is he not dolefully brooding here, at the end of his life, having arrived at his winter, over his past seasons?

From the branch protruding from the upper-right side of the head hangs the bark, scraped off in two tatters. In the veins of the wood lain bare appears Arcimboldo's carved signature, "ARCIMBOLDUS P.". If neither the association between decortication and skinning is convincing enough, nor that which follows with Michelangelo's headstrong signature in the *Last Judgment,* where he tattooed his face in the skin of Saint Bartholomew, shouldn't then this painting, in which Arcimboldo carved his name not in the skin, but rather in the substance of the tree, be considered a sort of artful and, in the deepest sense of the word, playful self-reference?

Sylvia Ferino-Pagden

Provenance: Inventory of the collection of Giovan Pietro Cortoni, Verona 1656, fol. 1: "Arcimboldo pezzi uno-n.o 1 Le quattro Stagioni che formano una testa, Largo P. 1 o 4 alto P.1 o 9"

Bibliography: Comanini 1591 (1962), vol. 3, 268f.; Campori 1870, 192–202; Montanari 1994, 44; Berra 1996a, 116–117 on Comanini's description.

IV.16
Copy after Giuseppe Arcimboldo
Air
c. 1566
Oil on canvas
74.4 × 56 cm
Private collection, Switzerland

This painting is identifiable with a picture of *Air* by Arcimboldo according to descriptions of Lomazzo (Lomazzo 1584 [1974], 304) and G. B. Fonteo (Kaufmann 1993) who mention a head by Arcimboldo made out of birds. Other prints and drawings (Kaufmann 1988c, 166) confirm that an image similar to this one accompanied other Arcimboldesque images of *Elements*. The provenance of this work from the Wenner-Glen collection in Sweden may also indicate that it came from Prague. Several works (Zimmermann 1905, nos. 1085, 1111, 1245) listed in the 1621 inventory of the Prague collections may correspond to this painting.
Fonteo suggests that like the other pictures in the series of *Elements* this was also an imperial allegory. The eagle in the chest of *Air* is indeed, as he suggests, the imperial bird, and the peacock was also the avian chosen as the heraldic beast of the Habsburgs (Kaufmann 1993). The prominent display of this bird on a triumphal arch erected for Maximilian II's entry into Vienna in 1563 (Wunsch 1914 pl. II) attests to its significance contemporaneous with the original invention of the *Elements* at this time: the earliest versions are dated 1566 (see the entry on *Fire*).
Like *Earth* and probably *Water* in the series, *Air* is also based on studies from nature. Many of the birds whose heads are seen in this composite were drawn by Arcimboldo, along with many other avian species (Kaufmann forthcoming). However, because they are crowded together, the individual species represented here are harder to identify.
Slight differences in dimension, and, more important, in support distinguish *Air* from the other surviving *Elements*. Sven Alfons (Alfons 1957, 48) also noted differences in execution, and pointed to its lesser quality; Francesco Porzio (Porzio 1979, 48) also illustrated it as a copy. Juxtaposition of this with other images by the artist (seen in Venice 1987) also suggested differences in execution. If not a copy, this is perhaps a workshop version, from a later series of elements, or perhaps a repetition made for the emperor.

Thomas DaCosta Kaufmann

Bibliography: Legrand, Sluys 1955; Alfons 1957, 48, 50; Lomazzo 1584 [1974], 304; Porzio 1979, 60, 66; Venice 1987, 98, 99, 103; Kriegeskorte 1988, 16, 17, 24; Kaufmann 1988, 165-167; Kaufmann 1993, 109, 114, 122; Kaufmann, 2007; Kaufmann, forthcoming.

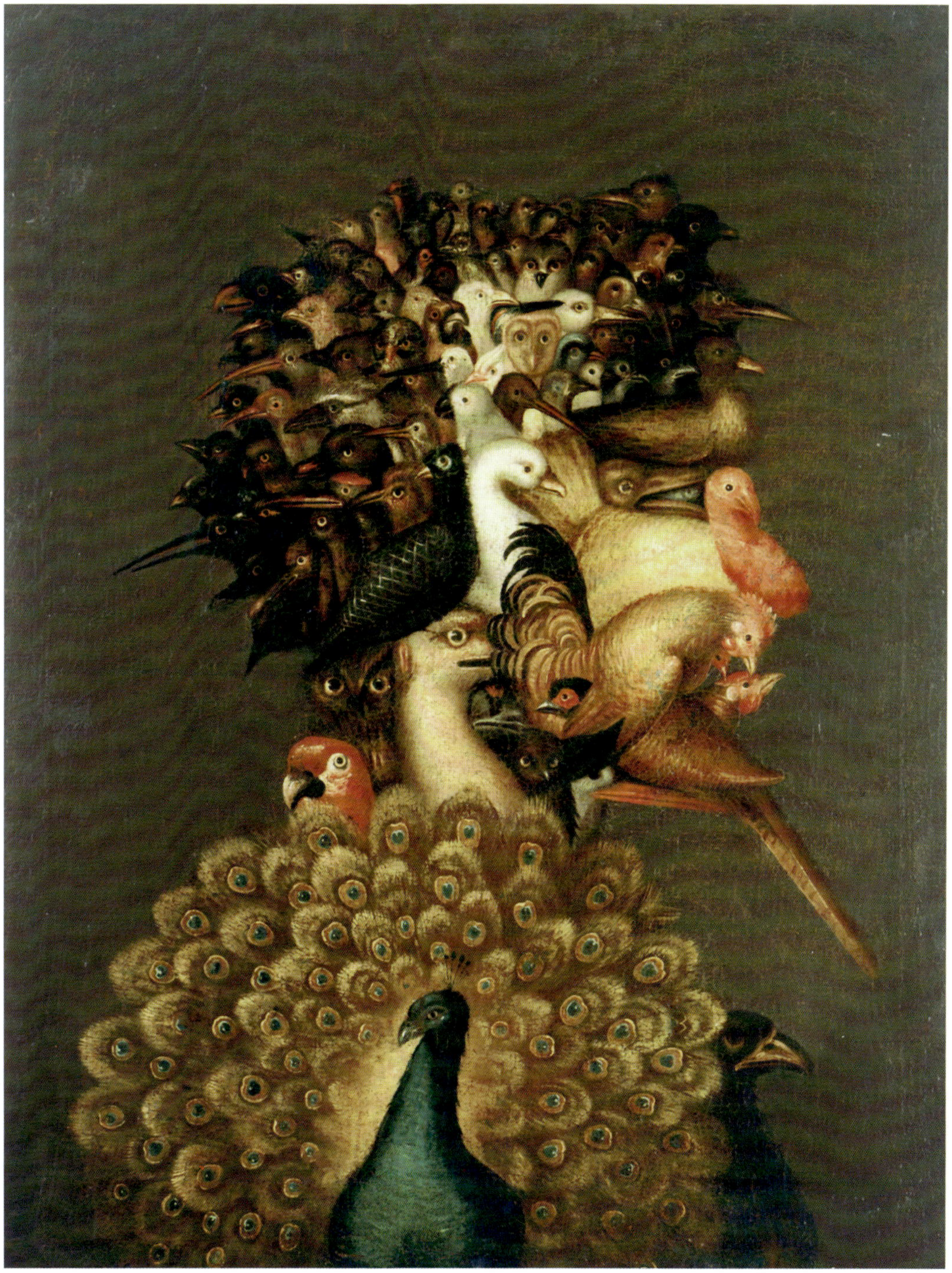

IV.16

IV. 17
The copy planned at this place was retracted in the last moment by the owners.

IV.18
Giuseppe Arcimboldo
Fire
1566
Oil on linden wood
66.5 × 50.8 cm
Signed lower right: Josephus Arcimboldus/ Mlensis.F:
Labelled and dated on the back: IGNIS 1566.
Vienna, Kunsthistorisches Museum, Gemäldegalerie, inv. no. 1585

Like *Water* (also in the Kunsthistorisches Museum, cat. no. IV.21), *Fire* belongs to a series of the *Four Elements. Earth* is now in a private Viennese collection (cat. no. IV.20), *Air* has been lost and only exists in copies (cat. no. IV.16).
The allegory of *Fire* combines objects that are more or less directly related to fire in a bizarre profile head: The cheek is formed by a large firestone, the neck and chin are formed by a burning candle and an oil lamp, the nose and ear are contoured by two firesteels; a blond moustache is formed by a crossed bundle of wood shavings for kindling, the eye is an extinguished candle stub, the forehead area is a wound-up fuse, the hair of the head forms a crown of blazing logs. The breast is composed of fire weapons: mortar and canon barrels together with the respective gunpowder shovel and a pistol barrel. Prominently positioned in the picture is the collar of the Orden of the Golden Fleece, beneath which the imperial double-eagle can be seen: a clear reference to the Habsburg House and the beneficiary of the series, Emperor Maximilian II. The emperor rules fire not only as an element, but also in weapons.

Alexander Wied

Provenance: painted for Emperor Maximilian II, 1566; Emperor Rudolf II's Kunstkammer in Prague; Prague inventory 1621 under no. 901; treasure chamber specification 1748, no. 63: "A head composed of fire and fire-making instruments from the da Vinci school"; inventory 1833, Ambras Depot no. 67; Engerth I, no. 16; gallery no. 351

Bibliography: Kaufmann 1985a, 212, cat. no. 2-5; Kriegeskorte 1986, 18, colour plate, 25; Venice 1987, 91 with colour plate; Essen-Vienna 1988, plate 2, cat. no. 556; Barthes 1990, 144f., 150, 153; Fučikova 1991, 65; Porzio 1993, 37f., plate 2; Schneider 1994, 123 with colour plate; Tokyo, Hiroshima etc. 1994-1995, 10, plate 2; Rudolf 1995, 182f., 186, plate 154; Cologne-Zurich-Vienna 1996-97, 197-199 with colour plate (Ekkehard Mai); Stockhammer 2003, cat. no. 260, table 147; Vienna 2003, cat. no. X.26 with plate and bibl. (K. Schütz).

Copies:
On the copies: The following list makes no claim to completeness; also, the distinctions between copies, workshop reproductions or replicas (with questionable participation by the master) and variations are sometimes blurred. Besides this, double naming is possible, as only an autopsy or a good visual representation would guarantee a faultless differentiation among the individual copies, which was not always possible in this case.

A complete series of the *Four Seasons*, with variations in many details, in possession of the Bayerischen Staatsgemäldesammlungen, of which three are in Landshut, Burg Trausnitz, the *Autumn* in the Depot of the Alte Pinakothek in Munich (cat. nos. IV.12, 13, 14)

Series in Berlin, private collection, oil on canvas, each 76.6 × 57 cm, dated 1572 (Kriegeskorte 1986, 28-34)

Series, signed and dated 1573, on the sleeve of the *Winter* is the Saxon coat of arms, at Sotheby's 7 November 1973 (plate in *The Burlington Magazine*, June 1973, XXIV)

Christie's South Kensington 7 June 1996, lot 381, each 69.2 × 49.5 cm, dated 1572

Copies after the Louvre series:
Former Craven Collection, Hamstead Marshall (later Cornelia Collection), Oil on canvas, 72.5 × 59 cm, dated 1573
(Kaufmann 1977, 337, 340, plates 5,6 and Venice 1987, 109 with colour plate, [there not challenged as original])

Series in the Kunstkammer in Gottorf (Kaufmann 1977, 337f.; 340)

Valencia, private collection, canvas, 75.5 x 56.5 cm, dated on the shoulder, 1572
(cat. no. 20 with colour plate in Valencia 1999)
Sarasota, Ringling Museum (Geiger 1960, plate 57)
Lausanne, former Maurice Bridel-Boiceau Collection (with interwoven signature and date 1572) (Geiger plate 55)
Paris, private collection (colour plate I-3, 35 in Tokyo, Hiroshima etc. 1994-95)

Copies of *Winter*:
Formerly New York, David M.Kötzer Collection (Geiger 1960, plate 59)
London, Christie's 7 June 2006, lot 32 with colour plate (oil on canvas, 76.2 × 62.2 cm)
Paris, private collection (colour plate I-5, p. 37 in Tokyo, Hiroshima etc. 1994-95

Copies of *Water*:
Brussels, Musées Royaux des Beaux-Arts, inv. no. 8930, see cat. no. IV.31

Copies of *Fire*:
Valencia, private collection (plate 76 in Valencia 1999)

Basel, private collection, see cat. no. IV.30

IV.19
Copy after Giuseppe Arcimboldo
Fire
Oil on canvas
75 × 66 cm
Basel, private collection

According to Kriegeskorte this painting is the "second version", in Venice 1987 as "Arcimboldo?" with a dating of circa 1572. In general, repeated versions on canvas can be classified as copies. Compared to the original in Vienna (66.5 × 50.8 cm, cat. no. IV.18), the format is somewhat larger. Overall, the picture is darker and has a more dismal effect. Compared to the original, the execution is simplified. This *Fire* probably belonged to a series, from which the *Air* has survived (in the same Basel collection, see cat. no. IV.16).

Alexander Wied

Bibliography: Kriegeskorte 1986, 70 with plate; Venice 1987, 175 with plate.

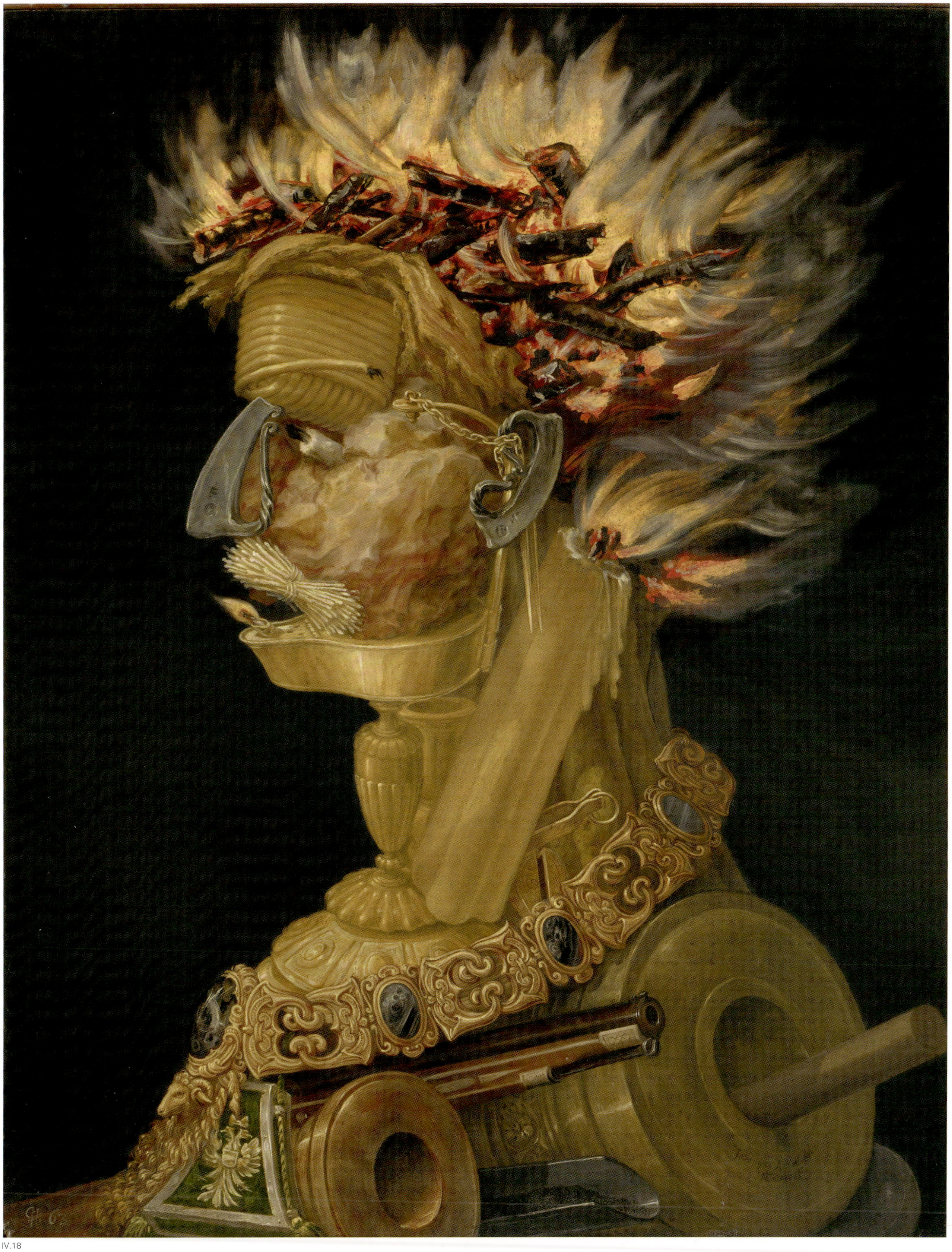

IV.18

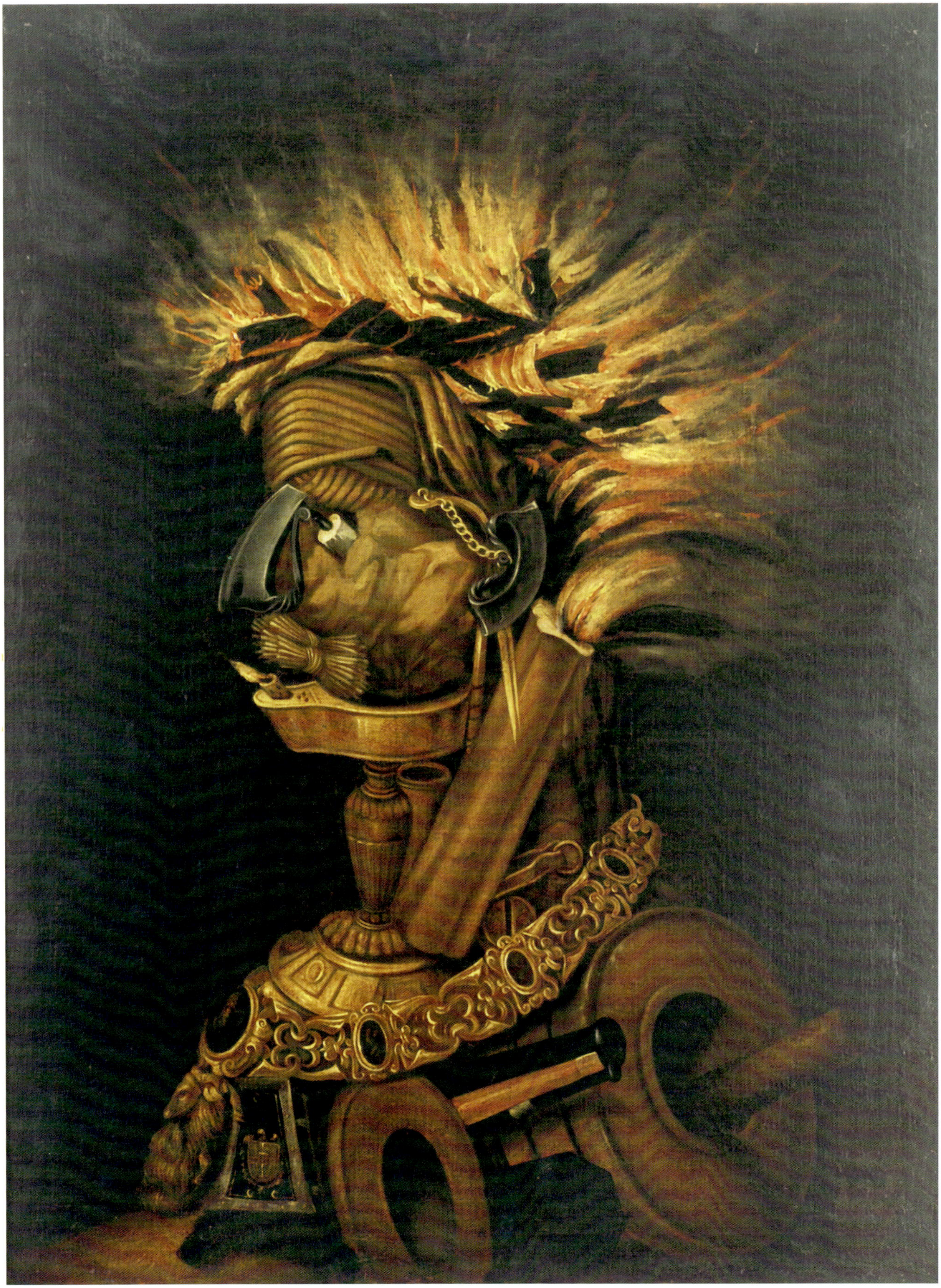

IV.19

IV.20
Giuseppe Arcimboldo
Earth
1566 (?)
Oil on panel
70.2 × 48.7 cm
Private collection, Austria

Arcimboldo's original version of *Earth* is identified as a painting composed out of animals in a poem by G. B. Fonteo which accompanied the *Elements* and *Seasons* when they were presented to Emperor Maximilian II; it is also so identified by Fonteo's descriptive comments in the commentary to a later version of this poem (see the Fonteo documents herewith). The composition of the head out of various creatures, its profile view, approximate dimensions, and support all correspond to the series of *Seasons* and *Elements*. This identification is also supported by other iconographic details from the imperial court circle (Kaufmann 1993). This identification revises previous ascriptions of *Earth* from the series of *Elements*, which had been based on descriptions in Lomazzo (Lomazzo 1584 [1974], 304; Alfons 1957, 51ff.), and on prints with inscriptions to Arcimboldo.
Earth is the most complex of either series. Like the other paintings in both series it is identified by Fonteo as an imperial allegory: this suggests that the emperor rules over the elements and seasons. Several details do make the imperial, Habsburg references, and were already noted by Gregorio Comanini in a painting resembling this one which is described in *Il Figino* (Barocci 1962): these include the antlers which form a kind of coronet, the lion skin, signifying the Herculean skin, and the fleece, standing for the Golden Fleece. Hercules is a traditional association of the Habsburgs, and lion skins appear in similar positions on the shoulders of several busts of emperors; the Golden Fleece is the "house" order of the Habsburgs.
Speaking of a painting sent to the king of Spain, which was probably a later version of *Earth*, Comanini indicates that the placement of creatures in the face derives from considerations of natural history, as presented by the ancient Roman writer Pliny. This indicates that he applied physiognomic notions to the composition of the head. Comanini also says that all the animals in the head were taken from life, because the emperor gave Arcimboldo permission to draw creatures in his menageries. Comanini's accuracy in these regards can be verified. A painting of *Earth* was sent to Spain (Rudolf 1995, 182-187). Many studies of animals by Arcimboldo exist, and many of these studies were used as sources for the creatures seen in *Earth* (see the essay by Staudinger in this catalogue, and also Kaufmann forthcoming). The earliest of these studies antedate the earliest possible version of *Earth*.
Arcimboldo thus proceeded as did many 16th-century natural historians. On the one hand the artist relied on ancient precepts, here the work of Pliny; on the other hand, he directly employed studies of nature. The replication of his nature studies indeed indicates that they were not necessarily made solely in connection with the process of painting the heads, but may have served other functions as well.
The version of *Earth* exhibited here has a provenance from the imperial collections, and it is thus likely that it was made for Maximilian II, or possibly Rudolf II. However, while there is no doubt about its authenticity, discrepancies with *Water* and *Fire* of 1566 do exist as far its dimensions, and more fluid handling are concerned, so it is possible that it might not have belonged to the original series. Inspection of the back of the panel for inscriptions similar to those found on *Fire* and *Water*, may resolve the question.

Thomas DaCosta Kaufmann

Bibliography: Geiger 1954, 63-64, 143; Legrand, Sluys 1955, 53-54; Alfons 1957, 142-150; Lomazzo 1974, 304; Porzio 1979, 31, 62, 67; Venice 1987, 92-93, 103; Kriegeskorte 1988, 20, 21, 26; Kaufmann 1988, 172-173; Vignau-Wilberg 1990, 40-41, 61; Kaufmann 1993, 100, 109-113, 119, 122; Rudolf 1995, 182-187; Prague 1997 164; Kaufmann 2007; Kaufmann forthcoming.

IV.21
Giuseppe Arcimboldo
Water
1566
Oil on alder wood
66.5 × 50.5 cm
Labelled on the back: AQUA
Vienna, Kunsthistorisches Museum, Gemäldegalerie, inv. no. 1586

Water belongs to a series of the *Four Elements*. The Kunsthistorisches Museum also possesses *Fire* (cat. no. IV.18). *Earth* arrived at the Landesmuseum Joanneum in Graz as a gift of Emperor Franz Joseph I in 1872 and was exchanged in 1954, arriving at its present location in a Viennese private collection (cat. no. IV.20), whereas *Air* has been lost and only exists in copies (cat. no. IV.16).
Water is composed of an astounding multitude of aquatic animals. In this picture, Arcimboldo gave no consideration to the relationship of sizes among the individual animals, as can be seen by comparing the large seahorse with the comparatively small seal. A similar disregard for the proportions of animals can also be seen in *Earth* (cat. no. IV.20), whereas the size of the fruits and vegetables in *Summer* (cat. no. IV.3) corresponds more closely to reality.
Kaufmann provided a zoologically detailed, numbered listing of the aquatic animals (1987, 96f.). The listing is repeated here:

VERTEBRATES

I FISHES

1. *"Murena murena" (Muraena helena)*, Mittelmeermuräne, Moray eel *
2. *Mola mola*, Mondfisch, Ocean sunfish *
3. *Hippocampus hippocampus*, Seepferdchen, Seahorse *
4. *Salmo trutta*, Meerforelle, Adriatic trout *
5. *Belone belone*, Hornhecht, Garfish *
6. *Sciena umbra*, Seerabe, Rabenfisch, Brown meagre *
7. *Esox lucius*, Hecht, Pike *
8. *"Lota elongata" (Molva macrophthalma)*, Leng, Mittelmeer-Leng, Blue ling *
9. *Cyclopterus sp.*, Seehase, Lumpsucker, Lumpfish *
10. *Cyclopterus sp.*, Seehase, Lumpsucker, Lumpfish *
11. Representatives of *Bothoidae* (Plattfisch, am ehesten Scholle), Flat fish*
12. Representatives of *Labroidae* (*Labrus turdus, Labrus merula*), Lippfisch (Wrasse)*
13. Representatives of *Trigla sp.*, Knurrhahn, Tubfish *
14. Representatives of *Trigla sp.*, Knurrhahn, Tubfish *
15. *Agonus sp.*, Thwaite shad, Panzerwange
16. *Pegasus sp.*, Seemotte, Seamoth (short dragonfish) *
17. *Raja sp.* (*Raja clavata*?), Rochen (Nagelrochen?), Ray (Thornback ray?) *
18. Kopf eines Knochenfisches, Head of a Teleostean
19. Kopf eines Knochenfisches (Wels?), Head of a Teleostean (Catfish?)
20. Kopf eines Knochenfisches, Head of a Teleostean
21. Kopf eines Knochenfisches, getrocknet, Head of a Teleostean (after desiccation)
22. Kopf eines Knochenfisches, Head of a Teleostean
23. Kopf eines Knochenfisches, Head of a Teleostean
24. Kopf eines Knochenfisches, Head of a Teleostean
25. *Callionymus sp.*, Rückenflosse von Leierfisch, Dorsal fin of Dragonet
26. Schwanzflosse eines Knochenfisches, Tailfin of a Teleostean
27. Schwanzflosse eines Knochenfisches, Tailfin of a Teleostean
28. Kiemen eines Knochenfisches, Gills of a Teleostean
29. Haut von *Scyliorhynus caniculus*, Kleingefleckter Katzenhai, (Skin of small spotted dogfish)
30. Hai mit Barteln (Heterodontidae?, Stierkopfhai?, Hornhai?) (Shark with Barbel - Heterodontidae?, bullhead shark?, hornshark?)

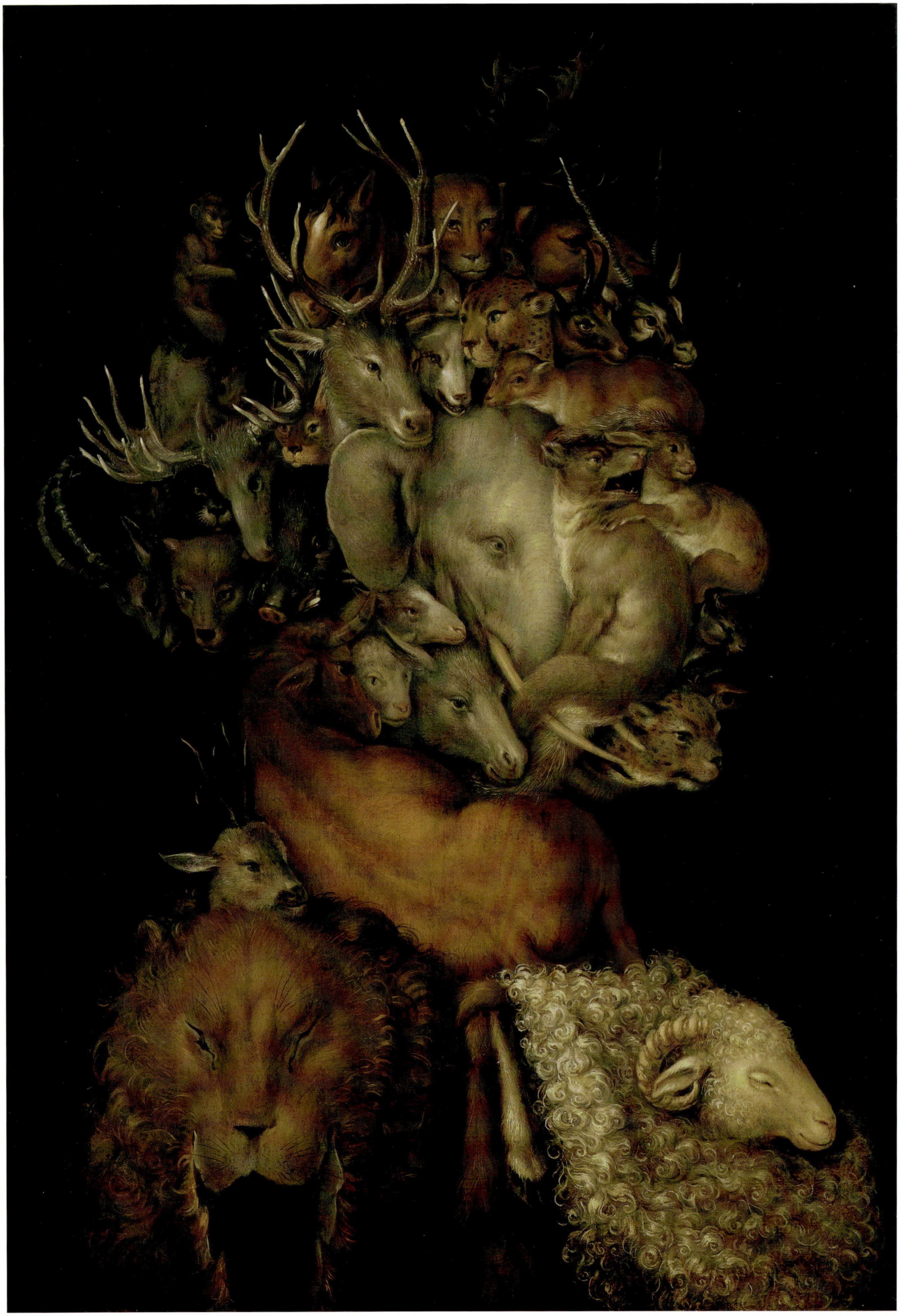

IV.20

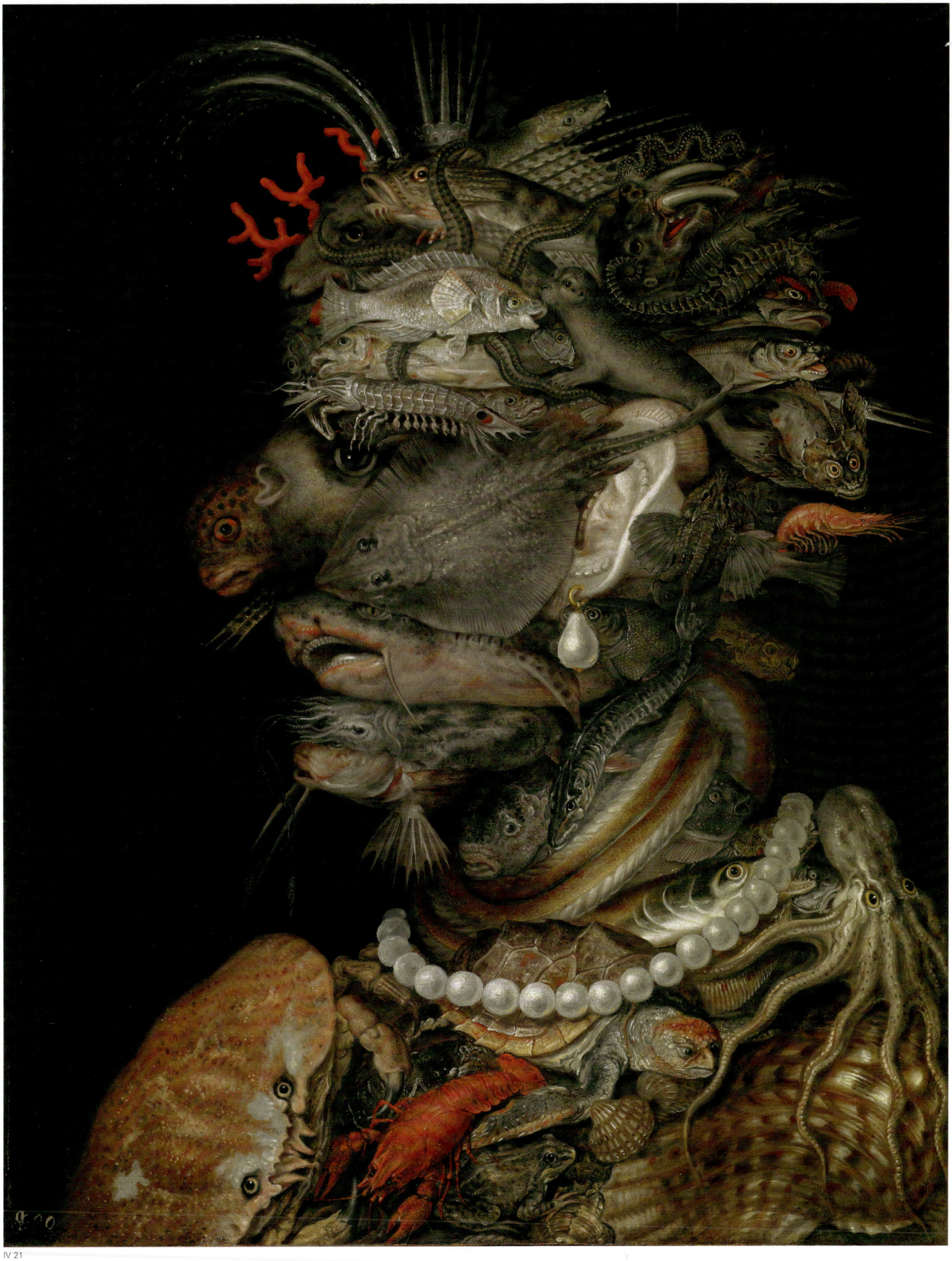

IV 21

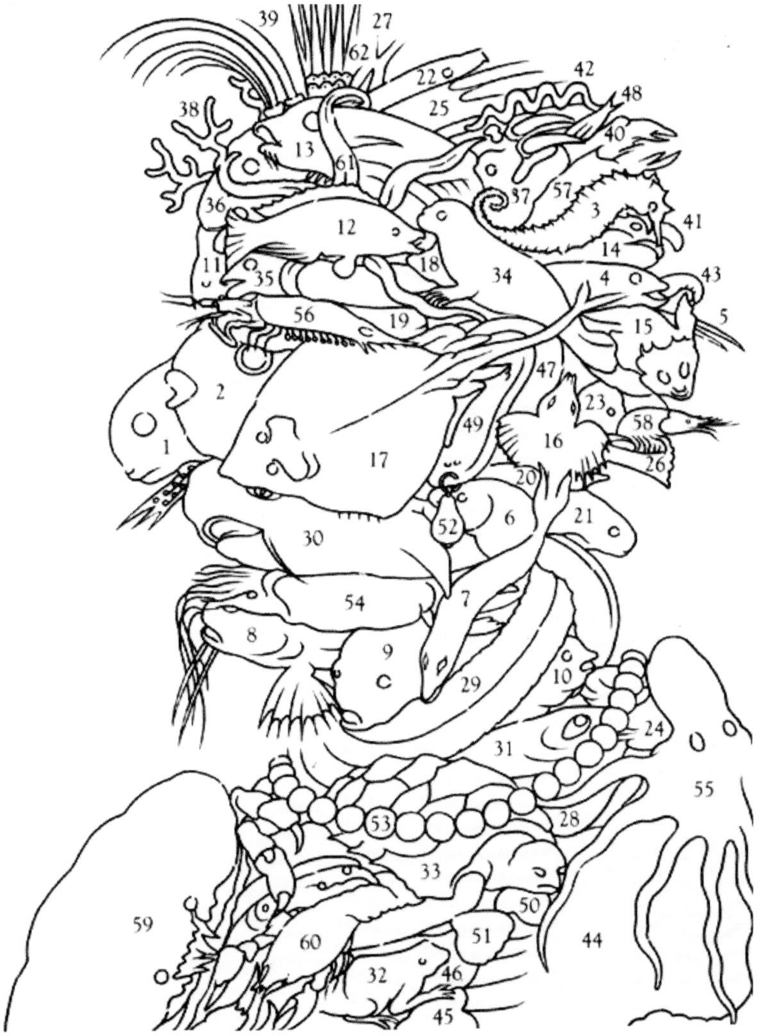

31. Hecht(?) mit überzähligen Kiemen, Pike with supernumerary gills

Those marked with (*) indicate the subclass of Teleostes (Knochenfische), "sp." means species

II AMPHIBIANS
32. *Rana temporaria*, Grasfrosch, European frog, Anura

III REPTILES
33. *Caretta caretta*, Unechte Karettschildkröte, Loggerhead turtle, Chelonians

IV MAMMALS
34. *Pelagius monachus*, Mönchsrobbe (Pinnipedia, Flossenfüßer) Monk seal
35. Seehundkopf, Seal's head (Pinnipeds=Flossenfüßer="fin-feet")
36. Seehundkopf, Seal's head (Pinnipeds=Flossenfüßer="fin-feet")
37. Flossenfüßer, ähnlich einem Amphibium, Sketch of a pinniped similar to an amphibium

INVERTEBRATES
I PHYLUM: CNIDARIA (Nesseltiere, Hohltiere, Coelenterata)
38. *Corallium rubrum*, Rote Edelkoralle, Red coral
39. Seitenansicht einer Seefeder (Pennatularia, Seefedern), Profile of a sea pen

II PHYLUM: PLATHELMINTHES (Flatworms)
40. *Planaria*, (Turbellaria planarians, Strudelwürmer)

III PHYLUM: ANNELIDA (Ringelwürmer, Gliederwürmer, Borstenfüßer) (Annelids/segmented worms)
Class: POLYCHAETA (Vielborster, Borstenwürmer) (Polychaetes)
41. A representative of the family *Phyllodocidae* (Paddelwürmer, Ruderwürmer) (Phyllodocids)
42. Unidentified representative of the Annelida (Ringelwürmer) (Annelids/segmented worms)

Class: CLITELLATA (Gürtelwürmer)
43. A representative of the Hirudinea (Egel), (Sea leech)

IV PHYLUM: MOLLUSCA (Mollusken, Weichtiere) (Mollusks)
Class: GASTROPODA (Schnecken, Bauchfüßer) (Snails, slugs, abalone, limpets, cowries)
44. *Tritonium nodiferum*, Knotiges Tritonshorn (Triton)
45. *Buccinum sp.*, Common whelk, conch (Prosobrancha, front gills)
46. *Buccinum sp.*, Common whelk, conch (Prosobrancha, front gills)
47. Undetermined
48. Wegschnecke (Pulmonata, Lungenschnecken), Slug

Class: LAMELLIBRANCHIATA (Mussels)
49. *Arca sp.,* Archenmuschel (Filibranchia, Fadenkiemer), Blood clarn
50. *Cardium sp.*, Herzmuschel (Eulamellibranchia, Lamellenkiemer), Cockle
51. *Cardium sp.*, Herzmuschel (Eulamellibranchia, Lamellenkiemer), Cockle
52. Austernperle, Oyster pearl
53. Austernperlen, Oyster pearls

Class: CEPHALOPODA (Kopffüßer) (Molusca)
54. *Sepia officinalis*, Gemeiner Tintenfisch (Decapoda, Zehnarmige Tintenschnecken), Cuttlefish
55. *Octopus*, Oktopus (Octopoda, Achtarmige Tintenschnecken, Kraken), Octopus

Class: CRUSTACEAE (Krustentiere, Krebse) Crustaceans, crabs
56. *Squilla mantis*, Heuschreckenkrebs (Hoplocarida, Fangschreckenkrebse, Maulfüßer), Mantis prawn
57. *Astacus fluvialis*, Flußkrebs, Freshwater crayfish
58. *Palaemon sp.*, Garnele (gekocht) (Decapoda, Zehnfußkrebse, Peracarida, Ranzenkrebse), Prawn
59. *Cancer pagurus*, Taschenkrebs (Decapoda, Zehnfußkrebse, Peracarida, Ranzenkrebse), Hermit crab
60. *Astacus astacus* (gekocht), Edelkrebs (Decapoda, Zehnfußkrebse, Peracarida, Ranzenkrebse), Freshwater crayfish

PHYLUM: ECHINODERMATA (Stachelhäuter) Echinoderms
Class: SEESTERNE, STARFISH
61. Seestern, Starfish

Class: ECHINOIDEA
62. Krone, geformt aus den Stacheln eines Lanzenseeigels (Cidaroida), Crown made of rays that look like the aculei of a Cidaroid

(Translation with the aid of: Theodor C.H.Cole, Wörterbuch der Tiernamen. Latin-German-English, German-Latin-English, Heidelberg/Berlin 2000, [friendly advice from Mr. T. Werkner, Vienna] and corrections [only for the fishes] by Dr. Ernst

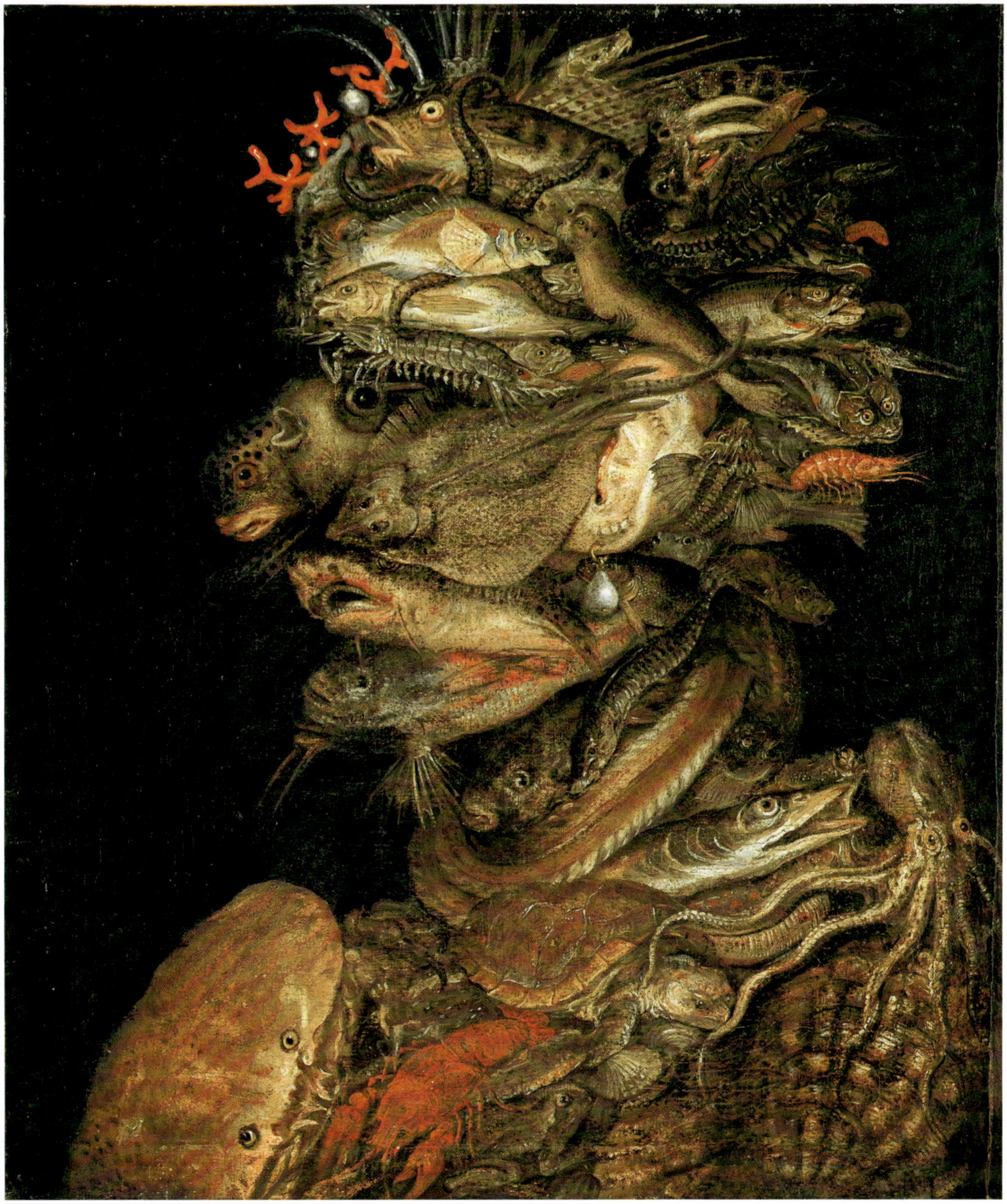

IV 22

Mikschi, Naturhistorisches Museum, Vienna)
Notes: Not all animal representations allow an exact determination. The precision of the representation allows at best only an identification to the genus, not the species; however, among the fishes there are exceptions, such as for example the pike.
The animals are reproduced without regard to the true proportions relative to one another.
There are also some artistic freedoms that allow Arcimboldo to deviate from nature, such as the barbels in 30, the increased number of gills in 31, the "walrus head" in 37 and the humanized eyes of the crab in 59. The majority of the sea animals are of Mediterranean origins, some of them already rare. Only *Pegasus*, the short dragonfish (no. 16), comes from the Indian Ocean.
Regarding no. 15: *Agonus sp.* is correct, but the English name "Thwaite shad" (herring) is incorrect. It is a member of the Scorpaeniformes (Scleroparei or Dactylopteriformes).
Regarding no. 29: visually, it appears not to be the skin of a dogfish – not even the skin of a fish, but rather a fish that has been cut open, perhaps an eel.
Regarding no. 39: the resemblance to sea pens is slight. It can be hardly assumed that Arcimboldo had ever seen such an animal. It is more likely, as already suggested in the first impression, two small water fountains. On one hand this could possibly be associated with spouting whales, and on the other with fountains and trick fountains.
The unusual multitude of species here is astonishing, as well as the inclusion of invertebrates, not only of the snail and the crab, but also of worms. On the other hand, common edible fish are missing, such as codfish, herring, sole, as well as freshwater fish such as trout, carp, grayling which were especially popular on the tables of princes since time immemorial. Finally, the following was indicated regarding deliveries to the court table of

Emperor Maximilian II: "Salmon, grayling, white-fish" (Fichtner 2001, 95 see bibliography). The only fresh water fish is the pike.

Alexander Wied

Provenance: painted for Emperor Maximilian II, 1566; Emperor Rudolf's Art Chamber; in the treasury chamber specifications from 1748, no. 80: "A head composed of fishes, again from the school of Leonardo da Vinci"; 1772 from Prague in the Viennese treasure chamber; inventory from 1883, Ambras Depot, no. 66; Engerth I, 17; Gallery no. 350

Bibliography: Geiger 1954, 65f., plate 78; Legrands, Sluys 1955, 51, no. 3; Alfons 1957, 48f.; Vienna 1965, 5, no. 427; Kaufmann 1976a, 275ff.; Porzio 1979, 30ff.; Kaufmann 1985a, 212, cat. no. 2-4; Kaufmann 1987, 96f.; Venice 1987, 95; Barthes 1990, 145, 150, 152f.; Kaufmann 1993, 103ff., 108-110f.; Essen-Vienna 1988, cat. no. 113; Fučikova 1991, 65, colour plate 168; Rudolf 1995, 183; Vienna 1995, 63, cat. no. 9, colour plate 27; Prague 1997, 605, cat. no. IV. 5 (with bibliography); Vienna 2003, cat. no. X.25, 540, with plate and bibliography (K. Schütz).

IV.22
Arcimboldo Workshop (?)
Water
Oil on canvas
63 × 53 cm
Brussels, Musées Royaux des Beaux-Arts, inv. no. 8930

This version of *Water*, classified in the museum catalogue since 1984 as the work of a successor of Arcimboldo, is of exquisite quality. Porzio (1979) still attributes it to Arcimboldo himself. This version remains quite faithful in most details to the Viennese original (cat. no. IV.21); the most noticeable difference is that the pearl necklace is missing, and the squid is missing from the chin area. Added in the copy, however, were two pearls at the top of the head, one of them particularly large, and the highlights on the red coral branches. This exemplar, although quite early chronologically, could still have been created in Arcimboldo's workshop. The high-quality execution is somewhat sharper, more graphic, than the Viennese original, which appears to have a more silky surface.
The doubled canvas, stretched like a drum, indicates a restoration, which through pressing had evidently caused a loss of pastosity.

Alexander Wied

Provenance: Legat Max Janlet, Brussels 1977

Bibliography: Porzio 1979, 67 with plate; MK Brussels 1984, 6; Venice 1987, 175 with plate.

Arcimboldo and Ulisse Aldrovandi

IV.23
Giorgio Liberale, attributed
Sea Animals
Parchment
Vienna, Österreichische Nationalbibliothek, Handschriften-, Autographen- und Nachlass-Sammlung, cod. ser. n. 2669

The study of marine fauna is the theme for cod. ser. n. 2669 of the Österreichische Nationalbibliothek. They are large-format pictures (approximately 640 × 870 mm) on parchment, which capture the quickly fleeting range of forms of sea animals with unprecedented precision. The motivation behind their creation was probably the project of an illustrated edition of Dioscurides' *Materia medica*, which Pietro Andrea Mattioli (1500-1577) pursued for a period of his life and for which he found in the person of Archduke Ferdinand II (1529-1595) a patron and sponsor.
The pictures themselves are neither dated nor signed and are attributed by Guglielmo Coronini Cronberg to Giorgio Liberale from Udine (Cronberg 1971); however the precise circumstances surrounding their creation are still largely unclear. They were possibly created in 1558 in Görz or, in the case that preliminary studies on paper were used, in Prague. Their connection with *Materia medica* is certain, as at least two pictures have been recognized as models for the woodcuts (cod. ser. n. 2669, fol. 57r for Matthiolus 1565, 314; cod. ser. n. 2669, fol. 78v for Matthiolus 1565, 341. Compare Staudinger 1996, 222-224).
Whereas in *Materia medica* the healing properties of each animal was the reason for their representation, a new concept was at work behind the codex. Henceforth, the idea was to create a comprehensive collection of animal pictures as close to life-size as possible, which were no longer represented in the dualistic "earth – water" relationship, but rather seen in their natural variety of forms – here we need only refer to the numerous representations of sharks. Especially with the fishes, apart from the very limited durability of the preparations, there was hardly any chance of conserving the colours, and so parchment painting became the only truly lasting form of representation.

fol. 32r, 32v: *Bottlenosed skate*
Rostroraja alba (Lacepède, 1803)
The grey-brown, white-spotted skate measures approximately 120 cm from the tip of its mouth to the end of its tail, and although it is drawn diagonally, the point of the left pectoral fin is bent up. Located directly behind the eyes and in slight protrusion are the blowholes. Behind the pectoral fins, at the base of the tail, are two large appendages, which indicate that this skate is a sexually mature male. The tail is armed with three rows of barbs and features the two dorsal fins in the rear. The ventral and dorsal fins, as well as the appendages are bordered in red.
The whitish underside with fine, grey spots is painted on the back side of the folio with exactly the same contours as the front side, so that the tip of the left pectoral fin seems rounded here. On its head are the wide mouth and the five gills to the side, just behind it. Against the whitish colouring, the red anal orifice stands out; it is also evident that the appendages are formed from a part of the ventral fins (Müller 1983; Staudinger 1996).

fol. 91r: *Mediterranean lobster*
Palinurus elephas (Fabricius, 1787)
The Mediterranean lobster's body measures 47 cm and is represented in its actual dimensions. The abdomen and the tail are reddish brown, the pectoral armour is brown and the walking legs are coloured yellowish-red. The second (long) antenna pair is unclearly banded.
The large antennae are unnaturally bent. While unknown to the painter, the end of the basal section has a joint that allows the animal to reach his feelers behind it (Campbell 1983).

fol. 47r:
a: *Garpike*
Belone belone (Linnaeus, 1761)
The garfish is approximately 77 cm long and has a blue-green dorsum; the ventral region is silver-coloured and the gill cover is represented as reddish-yellow. The writing in pencil beneath the head reads "Agone" and today is the common name for a freshwater fish *Alosa agone* (Scopoli, 1786), an entirely different species that belongs to the herring family (*Clupeidae*).
Garpike grow up to 90 cm long, live in the open sea and approach the coast during spawning season. All of its bones are a striking green (Müller, 1983).

b: *Fish*, undetermined

c: *Seahorse*
Hippocampus punctulatus (Guichenot, 1853)
Both of the seahorses, the male on the right with a clearly visible brood pouch, are about eight centimeters long and represented in their natural dimensions. The iris is yellowish, the body is coloured a uniform green and the lappets that look like fringes are clearly visible. The small pectoral fin directly behind the head is missing.
The northern seahorse (and also the iris) is brown with lively, white speckles. In mating, the female sprays her eggs into the male's brood pouch where he carries them to term.

d: *Red bandfish*
Cepola macrophthalma (Linnaeus, 1758)
The band fish is 53 cm long and is represented with

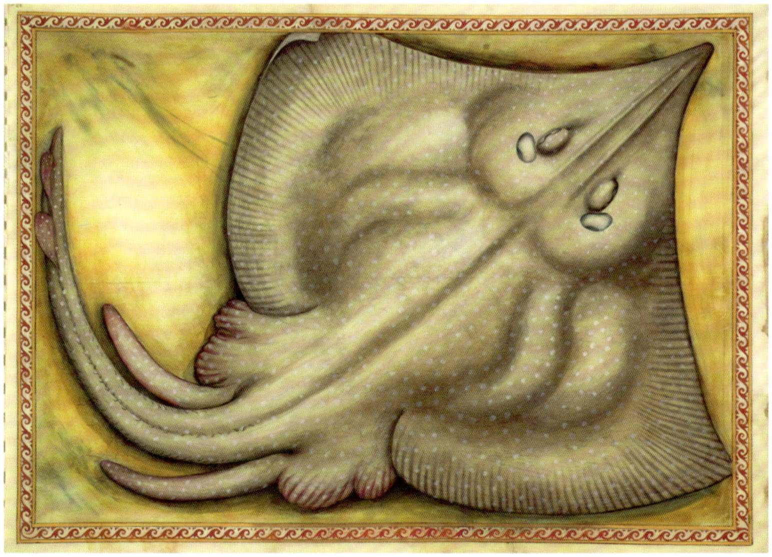
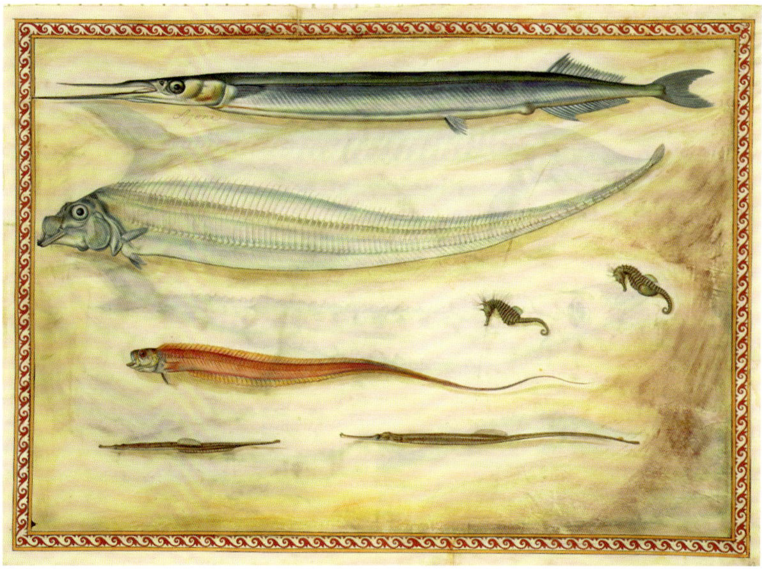
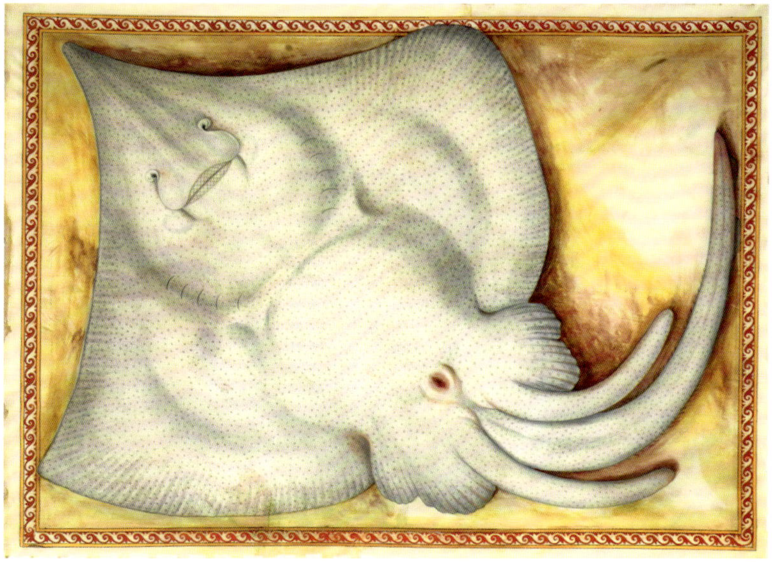
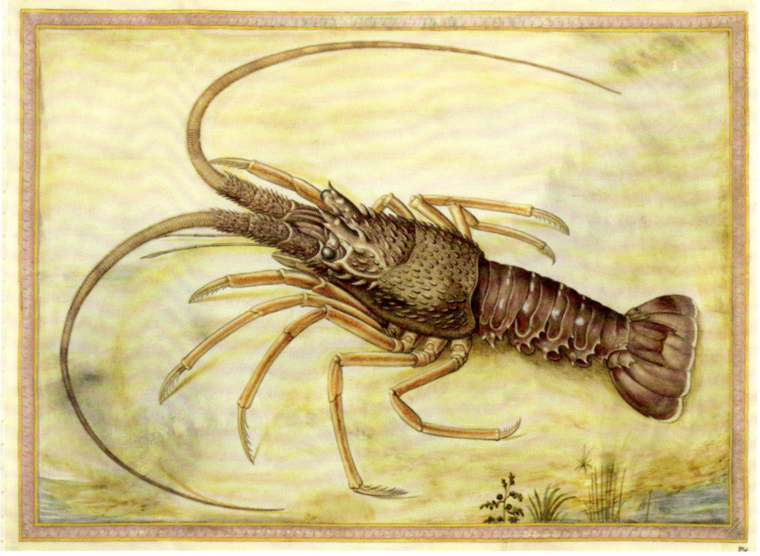

IV.23

a thread-like, tapering tail. The body is red, the dorsal and anal fins are reddish-yellow, the head is grey mixed with yellow and the iris is reddish-brown. Band fish grow up to 50 cm long. Behind the head, the pectoral fin is missing. The tail must have been shorter and terminated with a small tail fin. The fish inhabits seaweed fields near the coast, where it "stands" on its tail, lurking for small prey.

f: *Pipefish*
Syngnathus sp.
Approximately 20.5 cm long with a dorsal and tail fin, as well as a 6.5 cm long anal fin; colour: brown.

g: *Pipefish*
Syngnathus sp.
Approximately 34 cm long with a dorsal and tail fin but no anal fin; colour: brown.

fol. 79v: *Common octopus*
Octopus vulgaris (Lamarck, 1798)
The depiction of this animal with its mantle, siphon-head and tentacles is approximately 80 cm long and could be represented here in its natural dimensions. The skin is whitish with a few blue or yellow toned areas. The eight tentacles of equal length are each lined with two rows of suctions cup and decoratively spread out, so that the span can be clearly seen.
The common octopus is found all over the world and grows up to 130 cm. It is shown in its relatively dark, natural colouring; however, it can change its colour and patterning according to its affection. With its large eyes, it can perceive the orientation of the light's polarization, which is much more important in the sea than the ability to perceive colours (Campbell 1983).
In the present representation, its posture is unnatural and more influenced by tradition; the animal must have lost some of its colouring in transport. The absence of eyes shows that the painter was not familiar with a living or recently deceased exemplar.

fol. 39v: *Ocean sunfish*
Mola mola (Linnaeus, 1758)

fol. 40r, 40v: *Loggerhead sea turtle*
Caretta caretta (Linnaeus, 1758)

fol. 42v: *Spot-fin porcupinefish*
Diodon hystrix (Linnaeus, 1758)

fol. 64r, 64v: *European seabass, Wolf-fish*
Dicentrarchus labrax (Linnaeus, 1758)
Anarhichas lupus (Linnaeus, 1758)

Manfred Staudinger

Bibliography: Müller 1983; Campbell 1983; Staudinger 1996.

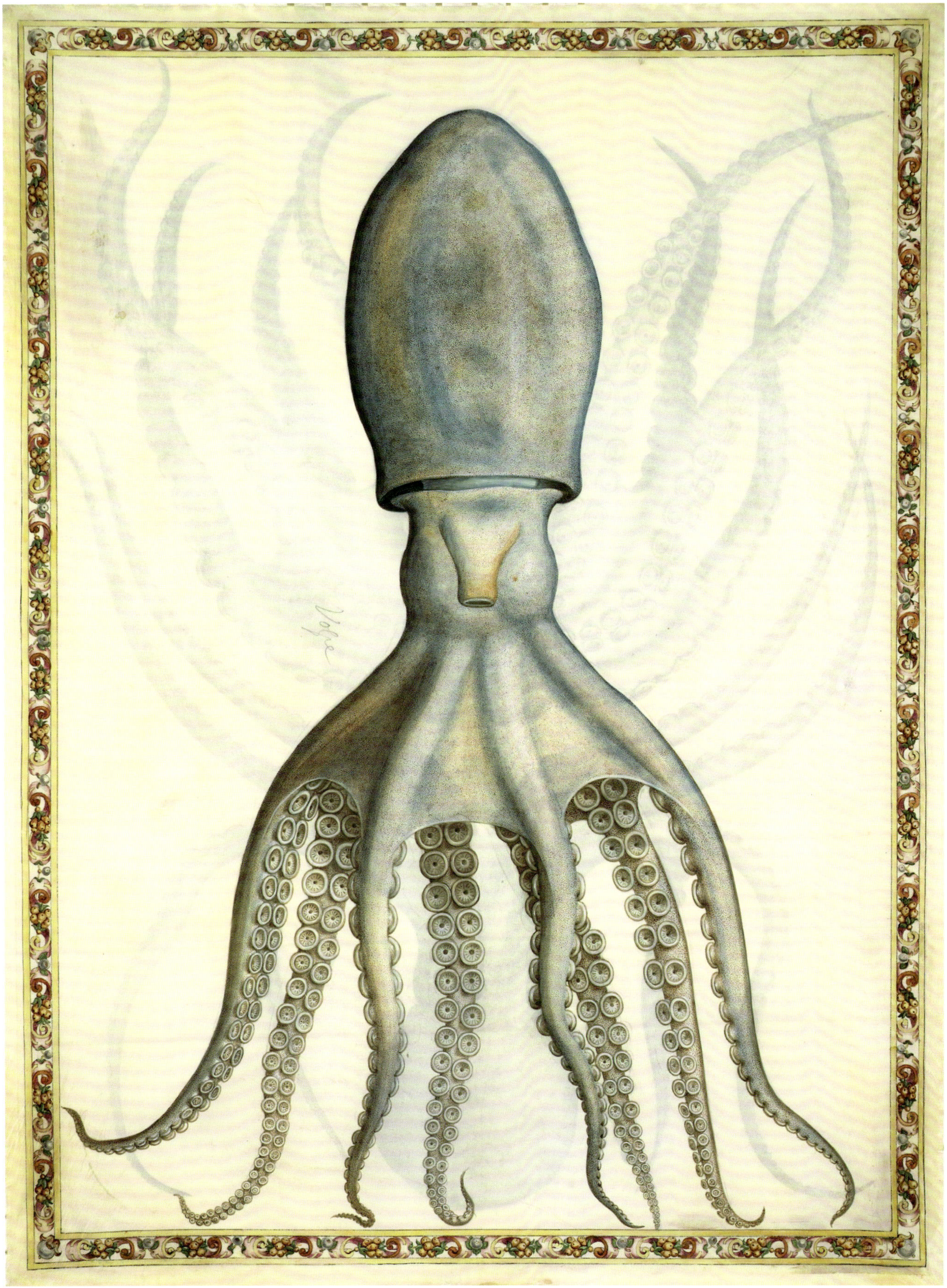

IV.23

IV.24
Giuseppe Arcimboldo
Nature Studies
Watercolour on paper or parchment
Vienna, Österreichische Nationalbibliothek, Handschriften-, Autographen- und Nachlass-Sammlung, Cod. min. 42

The contents of the volume Cod. min. 42 of the Österreichische Nationalbibliothek are representations of animals and plants. The glued-on studies originated from between 1550 and 1612 (?). The pictures from fol. 115 onwards are in glued-in landscape format and are mainly painted with watercolours or opaque colours on paper or on parchment (36 studies). In some cases the backing paper has been cut away, partially to make the rear side of the glued-in study visible, partially to reduce the thickness of the volume. Only a few pictures are signed; however, many are dated. The volume mainly comprises:
1. Mammals, partially with writing and date (5 studies, between 1563 and 1578), fol. 1-24, 116
2. Birds, many dated (14 studies between 1571 and 1585), only a few signed, fol. 26-59. 117-119. 170
3. Plants, on white or blue-grey paper, many fruit bearing executions of trees and shrubs with leaves, writing in Latin (and Greek), many dated with 1552 or 1553, partially with numbers in a circle, fol. 64-102
4. Flowers, no writing or date, partially full plants with (bulbs and) roots, few fruits (figs, cherries, strawberries), fol. 130-160
Also including (not aspiring to be exhaustive):
- pen drawings, miniatures, 21 in number, the first containing an inscribed plaque "Wiriex Inueniter", 64 x 85 mm, fol. 60-62
- sheets signed by "Hans verhagen den stommen van Antwerpen" (fol. 26, 116, 118, 121), by Georg Hoefnagel (fol. 62), by Daniel Fröschel (fol. 32, 53, 54), by Simon Mormion (fol. 55)
- heads of field flowers, fol. 163-167
- contour cut out pictures of birds, fishes and fruits fol. 59, 122-124, 168
- leaves with insects, fol. 125-127
- meat grill, fol. 25
This should suffice to indicate the varied content of the volume.
As proven by the marks on the otherwise bare rear sides of the volume, for a long time the studies were included loose and mostly in other positions. The cutting of the paper and the gluing in were part of the same operation, as the example of the sheets of the little bittern (fol. 39r above) and pheasant (fol. 41r above) show (see below). Whether all sheets were glued in at the same time, as well as the point in time this occurred has not been established.

fol. 6r above: *Boar and head study of a boar*
Sus scrofa (Linnaeus, 1758)
Study of a mummified boar head with upper tusk grown into the snout, copied in Cod. min. 129, fol. 32r (Staudinger 1990, 160-161).
This head was stored in the Kunstkammer of Kaiser Rudolf I, as shown in the inventory drawn up by Daniel Fröschel: "1 Boar snout and skeleton, where the upper tusks with their tip over the snout have penetrated the flesh and crookedly grown into the bone". (Bauer, Haupt 1976, 8, no. 100: "1 wildschweinmaul und gebain, da die obern waffen gantz krumb mit den vordern spitzen ober dem rüssel wider durch flaisch und gebainn hineingewachsen.")

fol. 8r above: *Elk*
Alces alces (Linnaeus, 1758)
Picture of a young elk without antlers, above a head of an elk with antlers, both copied in Cod. min. 129, fol. 18r. On the back of this watercolour study an elk's antlers is drawn, as can be shown by X-ray (Staudinger 1990, 132-133).
In the study of the head, the uncertainty of where to put the ears indicates that it is not the study of a living animal, rather that it was drawn with a skull as a model.
The study of the elk is convincingly influenced by Albrecht Dürer, to be clearly seen in the leg positions as well as in the skin lappet, that rather than being below the throat is below the neck (Koreny 1985, 22). The head is held up high, and the withers are too low, so that the line of the back is almost horizontal rather than sloping off to the back. Whether the slim figure shows a young animal or is simply a matter of representation is unsure.

fol. 9r above: *Red deer*
Cervus elaphus (Linnaeus, 1758)
A representation of a red deer turned to the right, its head turned slightly off to the right. In hunting terms a magnificent ten-pointer, probably from an imperial zoo, Ebersdorf close to Vienna or Stern close to Prague. A study of a set of antlers is to be found on fol. 20r above (see below).

fol. 11r left: *Antlers*
Cervus elaphus (Linnaeus, 1758)
An enormous set of antlers probably of a red deer. This could be the result of a damaged growth mechanism.

fol. 11r right: *Fallow deer*
Dama dama (Linnaeus, 1758)
Study of a normally developed fallow deer antlers, animal also belonging to an imperial zoo, Ebersdorf, Vienna or Stern, Prague. The antlers of the head turned to the right are represented more from the side in the upper part, and more from the front below.

fol. 19r above: *Reindeer*
Rangifer tarandus (Linnaeus, 1758)
The reindeer is turned to the left and "shows" the bottom of the hoof of the right foreleg. The watercolour shows a small circle with ink, to be seen in other pictures in this volume as well as in the inventory of the Kunstkammer of Emperor Rudolf II.
The picture shows what was probably a domesticated reindeer, with antler branches that are just growing again after the shedding, and that is in the middle of its change of fell. The reindeer was very probably a present from a prince to the emperor, though this cannot be corroborated by written material.
A similar picture of a reindeer is also to be found in Cod. min 129, fol. 26r (Staudinger 1990, 148-149).

fol. 19r below: *Red flanked Duiker*
Cephalophus rufilatus (Gray, 1846)
The red flanked duiker is represented turned to the left. The picture also shows a small circle with ink, that is also to be found on other pictures of this volume as well as in the inventory of the Kunstkammer of Kaiser Rudolf II.
Three copies exist of this watercolour of the so-called "Capriolo d'Africa" (see also my contribution "Giuseppe Arcimboldo's Nature Studies" in this catalogue), the very similar representation in Cod. min 129, fol. 25r (Staudinger 1990, 146-147) though is not one of these (see catalogue entry for the said sheet).

fol. 20r above: *Red deer*
Cervus elaphus (Linnaeus, 1758)
Study of the antlers of a red deer; the head is half-turned to the right. The entire animal is to be found in fol. 9r above (see above).

fol. 20r below: *Chamois*
Rupicapra rupicapra (Linnaeus, 1758)
Head study of a chamois. The head is turned right, directed slightly forward.

fol. 21r above: *Blackbuck*
Antilope cervicapra (Linnaeus, 1758)
This male Blackbuck is turned left, shown standing and the watercolour is dated "1.5.7.0.".
The picture is the model for Cod. min. 129, fol. 21r, and the animal is also to be found in a small oil painting *The Banishment from Paradise* (Vienna, Kunsthistorisches Museum, Gemäldegalerie, inv. no. 917; Staudinger 1990, 138-139). A further copy similar to this watercolour "Capra del Bezoar" is to be found in Bologna (see my contribution "Giuseppe Arcimboldo's Nature Studies" in this catalogue).

fol. 21r below: *Goat*
Capra hircus (Linnaeus, 1758)
The goat is shown turned to the right.

fol. 22r above: *Chamois*
Rupicapra rupicapra (Linnaeus, 1758)
Study of a head of a chamois.

fol. 22r below: *Ibex*
Capra ibex (Linnaeus, 1758)
Study of a head of an ibex.

fol. 23r: Lower leg with the abnormally-grown hoof of the right hind leg of a cloven hoofed ungulate, with writing "Il Pie diritto di dietro" and dated "1.5.6.3.".

fol. 24r left: Lower leg with the abnormally-grown hoof of the left hind leg of a cloven hoofed ungulate, with writing "Il Pie mancho di dietro".

fol. 24r right: Lower leg with the abnormally-grown hoof of the right fore leg of a cloven hoofed ungulate, with writing "Il Pie diritto di dinanzi".

fol. 28r: *Aplomado falcon*
Falco femoralis (Temminck, 1822)
The adult Aplomado falcon sits on a gloved hand and is turned left. It is ringed, and the sheet is dated ".1575." and marked with a small pencilled circle. Unfortunately the sheet has been clumsily cut, so that something like a third of the tail is missing. The uncut watercolour study was the model for Cod. min. 130, fol. 10r.
The sources speak of between 1580 and 1602 with at least three transfers of an Aplomado falcon from Madrid to Vienna and Prague. They were organized by the imperial ambassador to Spain, Hans Khevenhüller and for example brought over by Rodrigo de Morales, falconer of the king of Spain (Staudinger 1990, 296-299).
From the dating of this picture one can see that Emperor Maximilian II had already received such falcons, that are indigenous to central and south America, as well as the Caribbean islands.

fol. 29r above: *Lesser kestrel*
Falco naumanni (Fleischer, 1818)
A male roughly one-year-old lesser kestrel sits facing half left, on a log jutting out from the wall. The study is marked with a small pencil drawn circle. The lesser kestrel differs from the very similar common kestrel by the clear blue-grey coloured large coverts. Surprisingly the left primary is missing as if cut off and the extreme left tail side seems to have a black background.

fol. 36r above left: *Black crowned crane*
Balearica pavonina (Linnaeus, 1758)
The Black crowned crane is shown standing turned half left. The adult bird is dark grey; the facial mark is red in the lower half and reaches up to the crown; the iris is light yellow. This study of a dead bird serves as a model for Cod. min. 130, fol. 34r (Staudinger 1990, 356-357).
The head of the royal crane is stored in the Kunstkammer of Emperor Rudofl II, as shown in the inventory drawn up by Daniel Fröschel: "1 bird head with half a beak, in the size of a peakcock's head, with a black plumage in down feathers; at the back of its head, reaching up it has a bunch of fine feathers like brushes and pied like the quills of a porcupine; it is mentioned by Carolus Clusius Pavo Marinus" (Bauer, Haupt 1976, 12, no. 185: "1 vogelkopf mit halbem schnabel, in der größ eines pfawenkopfs, mit einer schwartzen hauben von pflaumfedern, hatt hinden am kopf uber sich stehendt ein strauß subtiler federlein wie börsten, gescheggicht wie die stachel oder meerschwein haben, pavo marinus von C: Clusio genannt.")

fol. 36r above right: *Night heron*
Nycticorax nycticorax (Linnaeus, 1758)
The adult night heron is shown striding left. This painting dated "1585", the picture of a dead night heron in winter plumage, serves as a model for Cod. min. 130, fol. 41r (Staudinger 1990, 370-371).

fol. 36r below: *Partridge*
Perdix perdix (Linnaeus, 1758)
This albino partridge is shown standing, facing left. This study dated "1578" is copied in Cod. min. 130 fol. 75r above (Staudinger 1990, 438-439). The partridge is apparently not subject to a total loss of pigment, and indeed one does not know what triggers off this singular aberration (Rokitansky 1967, 233).

fol. 37r above left: *Little bittern*
Ixobrychus minutus (Linnaeus, 1766)
This male little bittern is shown standing facing left. The watercolour study on paper was painted after a dead bird, and carries the date "1577"; it serves as a model for Cod. min. 130, fol. 42r (Staudinger 1990, 372-373).

fol. 37r above right (above): *Little owl*
Athene noctua (Scopoli, 1769)
The little owl is turned half-right and shown with a bright yellow iris.

fol. 37r above right (below): *Great tit*
Parus major (Linnaeus, 1758)
The great tit is shown sitting turned right.

fol. 37r below: *Jackdaw*
Corvus monedula (Linnaeus, 1758)
The albino crow is shown turned left; the study after a living bird bears the date "1.5.7.4." and is a model for Cod. min. 130, fol. 75r below (Staudinger 1990, 438-439).

fol. 39r above: *Little bittern*
Ixobrychus minutus (Linnaeus, 1766)
The young little bittern is shown standing, turned left and with a small fish in its beak. This very loose study of a living bird is dated "1577" and marked with a small pencil drawn circle. On the back of this sheet one finds the cut off tail top of the pheasant as in sheet Cod. min. 42 fol. 41r top. The rather barbaric cut of this bird study is to preserve the studies on the back of the sheet wherever possible, even after the adhesion of the same (Staudinger 1990, 380).

fol. 39r bottom left: *Blue Tit*
Parus caeruleus (Linnaeus, 1758)
The adult bluemouth is shown sitting, turned left. The study is dated with "1576".

fol. 41r above: *Pheasant*
Phasianus colchicus (Linnaeus, 1758)
The pheasant is shown turned right. Aside its partial albinism its plumage shows a total lack of yellow, so that the usually green colouring on the head and neck as well as the edges of the body feathers are coloured blue rather than green. The missing tip of the pheasant's tail is to be found on the back of the sheet glued on fol. 39r above.
The study, of a living male pheasant, is dated "1577" and also bears a small circular ring, which also appears in other pictures in the volume as well as in the inventory of the Kunstkammer of Kaiser Rudolf II. It is used as a model for Cod. min. 130, fol. 46 r (Staudinger 1990, 380-381).

fol. 41r: *Blue-headed Quail-Dove*
Starnoenas cyanocephala (Linnaeus, 1758)
The partridge dove is shown standing facing left. This masterly watercolour study is dated "1577" and was painted from a living partridge dove.
Under the description of "Colombo dell'Indie" Ulisse Aldrovandi received a copy of this study in Bologna (see on this my contribution in "Giuseppe Arcimboldo's Nature Studies" in this catalogue), that also served as a model for Cod. min. 130, fol. 63r below (Staudinger 1990, 414-415).

fol. 46r above: *Helmeted curassow*
Pauxi pauxi (Linnaeus, 1766)
The helmeted curassow (*P. p. gilliardi*) is shown turned to the left: this watercolour study of a living bird bears the date ".1.5.7.1." and also shows a small round ring, to be found in other pictures in this volume.
The helmeted curassow (*P. p. pauxi*) in Cod. min. 130, fol. 55r, represents another subspecies and thus cannot be a copy of this study (Staudinger 1990, 396).

fol. 46r middle left and fol. 46r below: *Quail*
Coturnix coturnix (Linnaeus, 1758)
A quail with three feet, in the first picture still alive, with its plumage; in the second dead and with its feathers plucked, to better show the anomalies and to be able to judge them. Both pictures

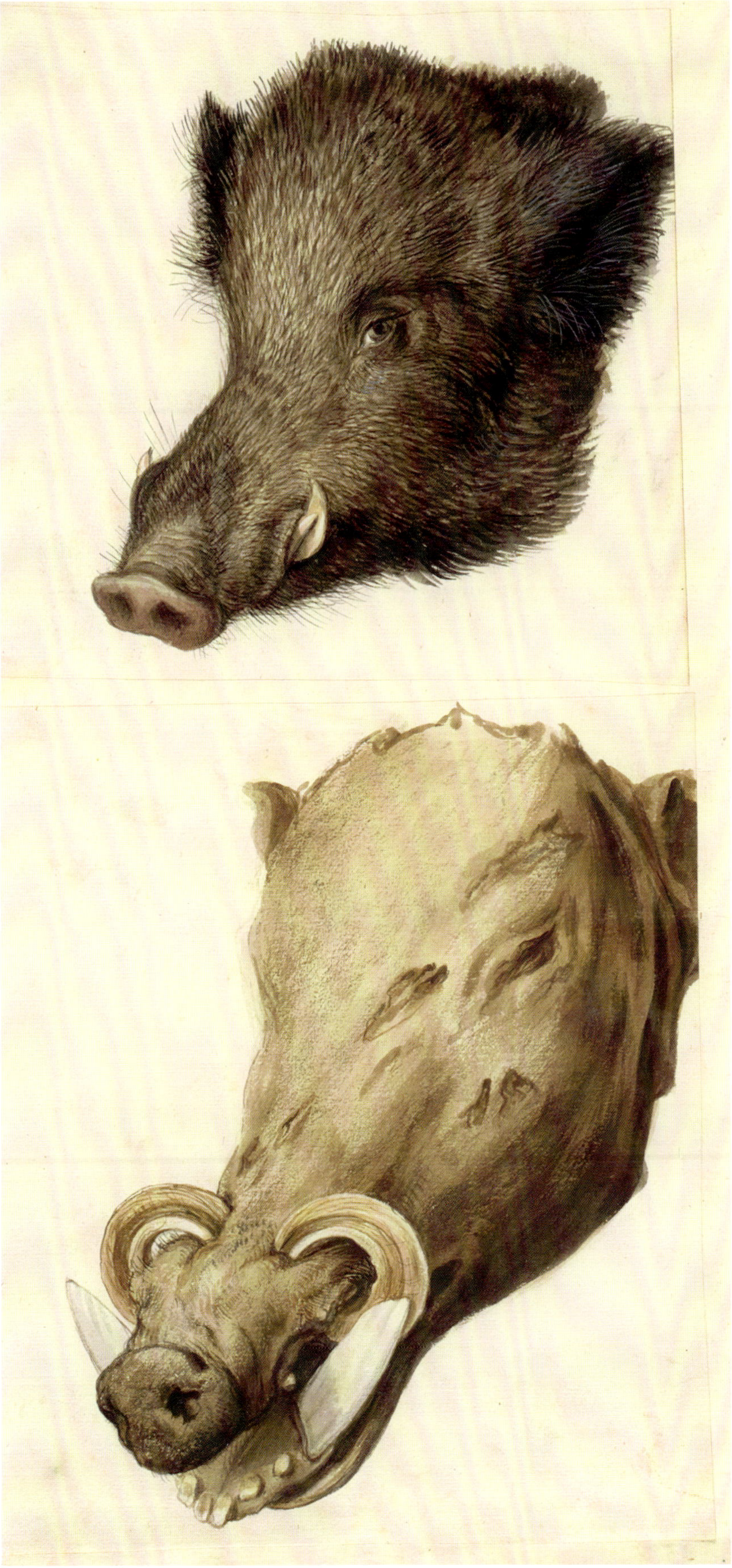

IV.24, fol. 6

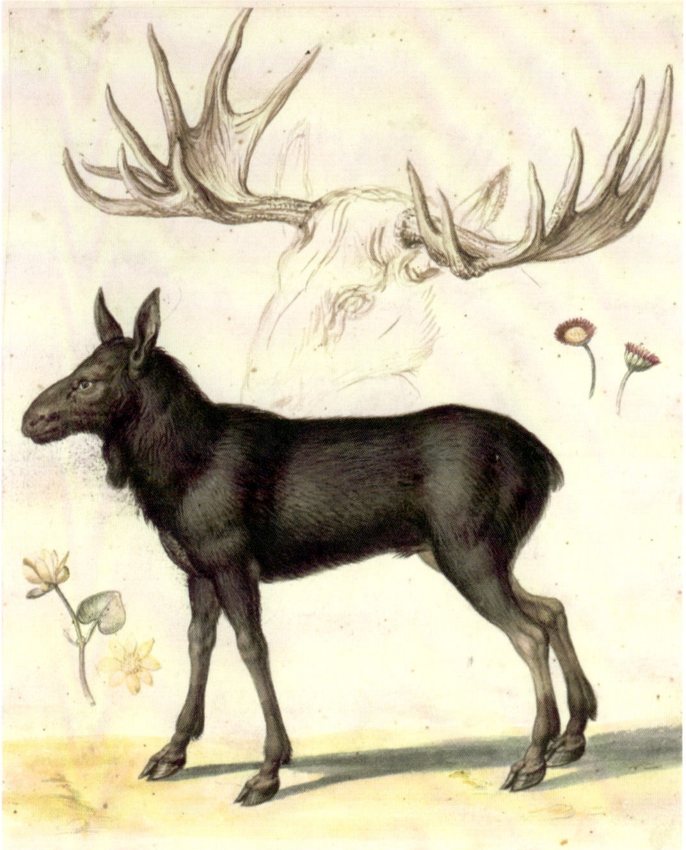

IV.24, fol. 8

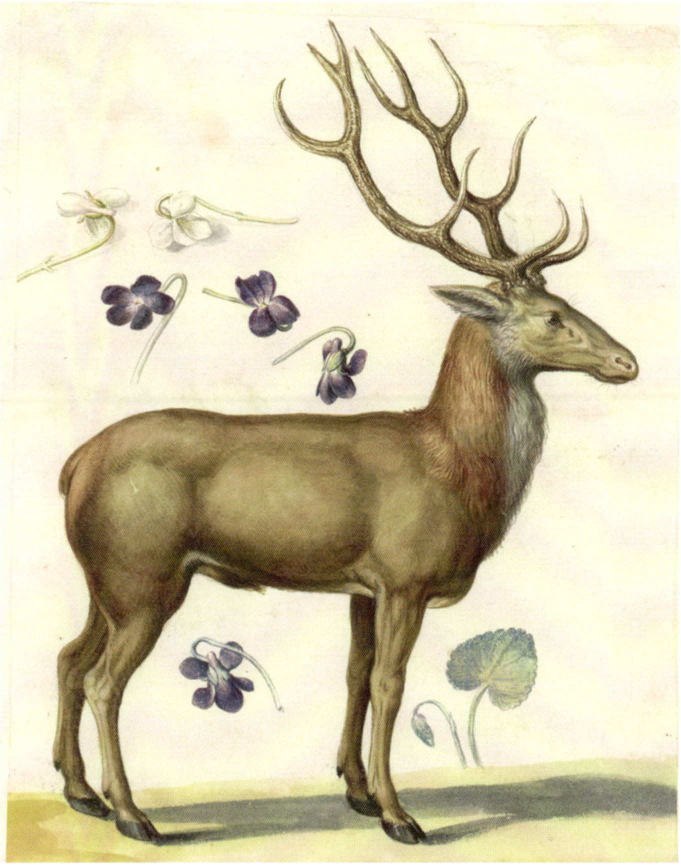

IV.24, fol. 9

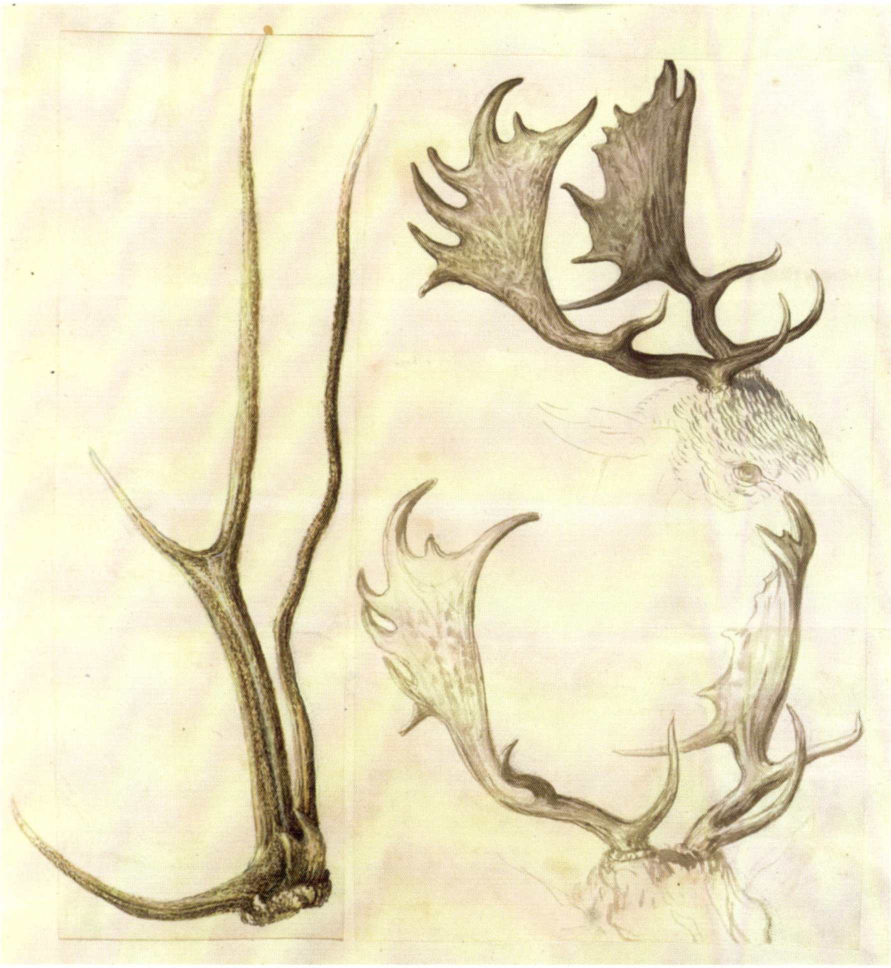

IV.24, fol. 11

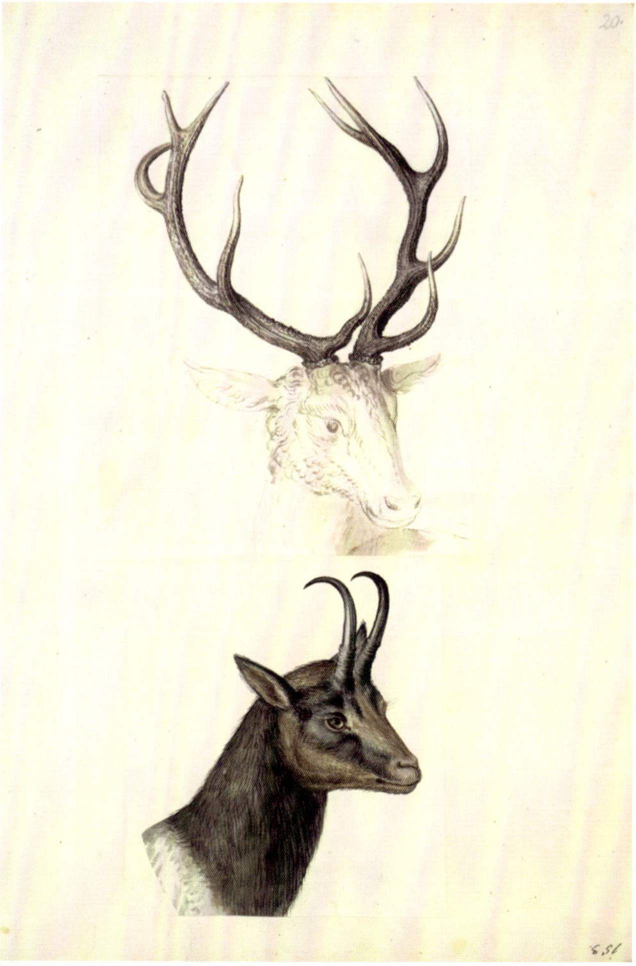

IV. 24, fol. 20

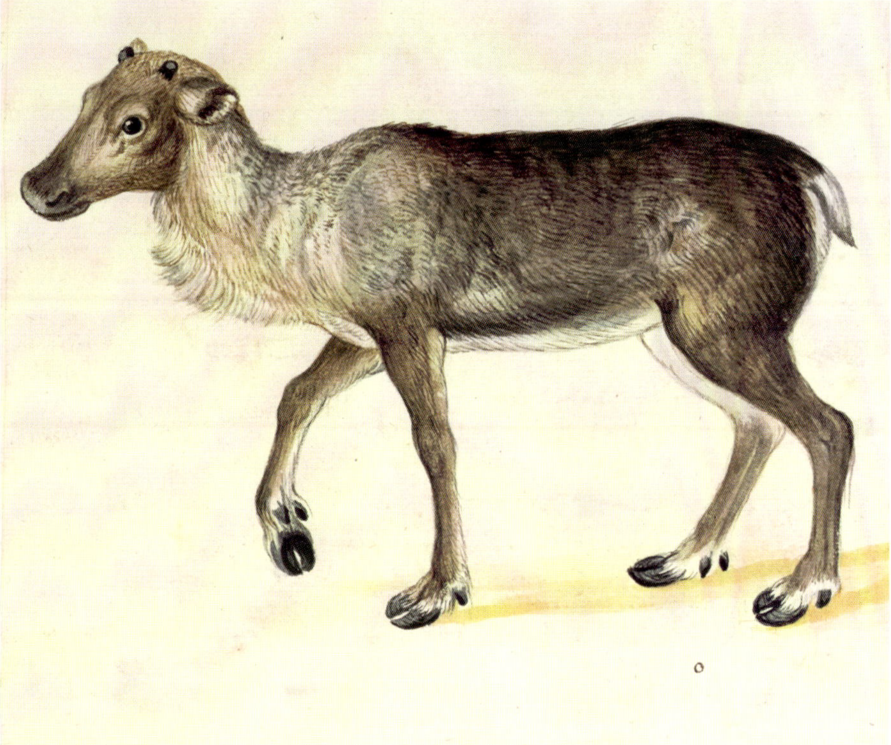

IV.24, fol. 19

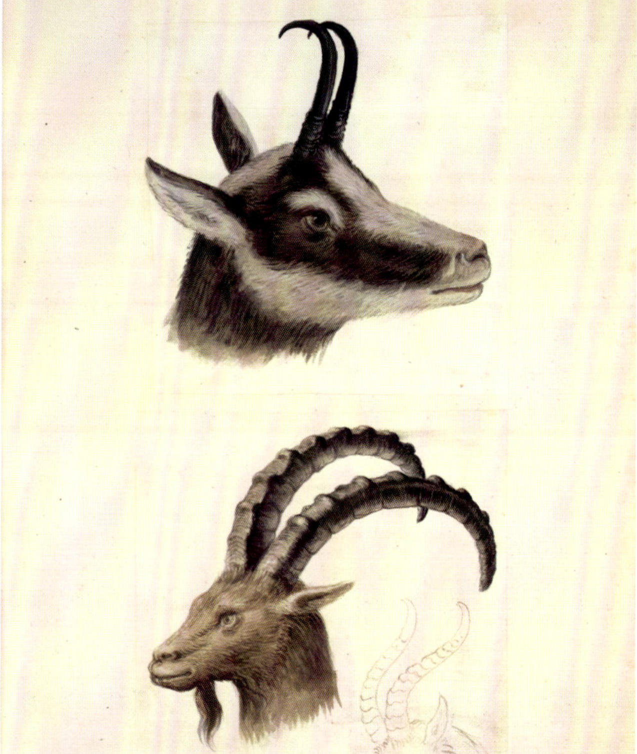

IV.24, fol. 22

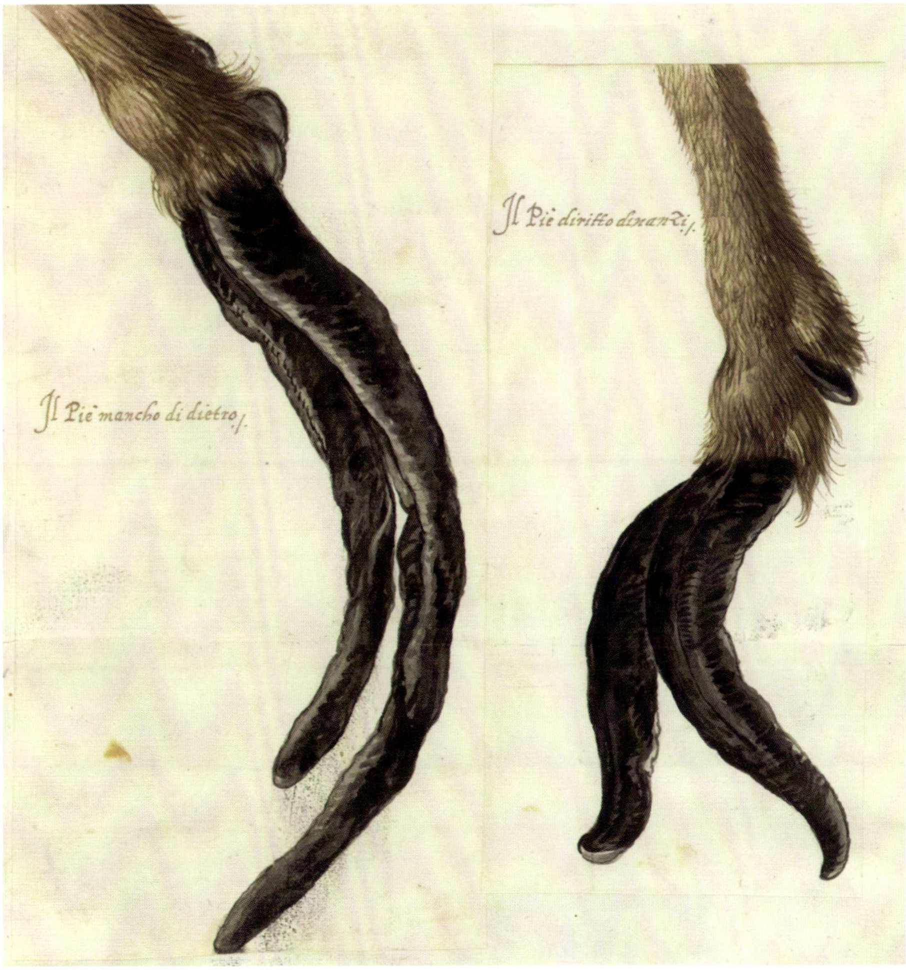

IV.24, fol. 24

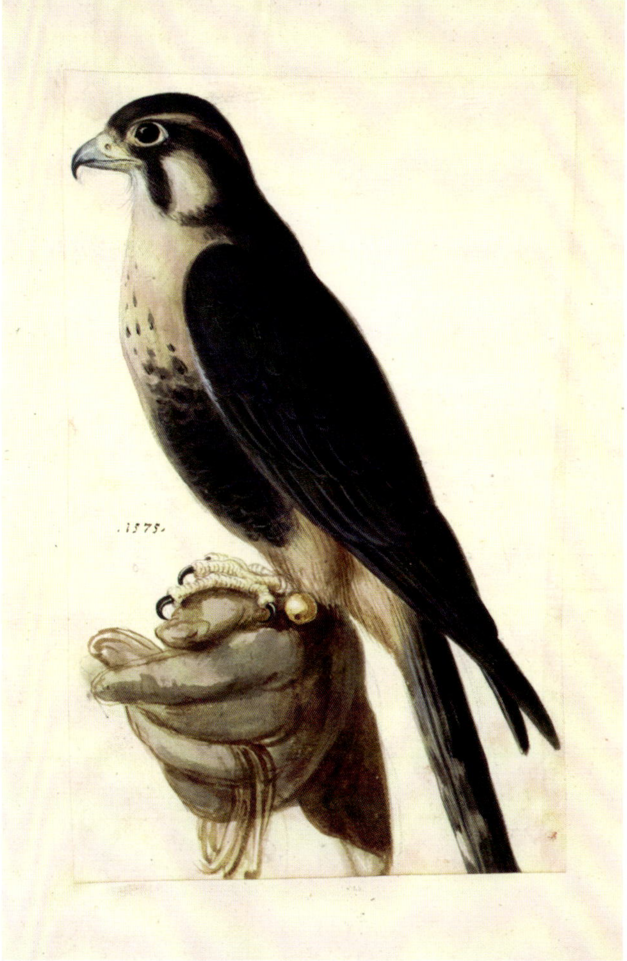

IV.24, fol. 28

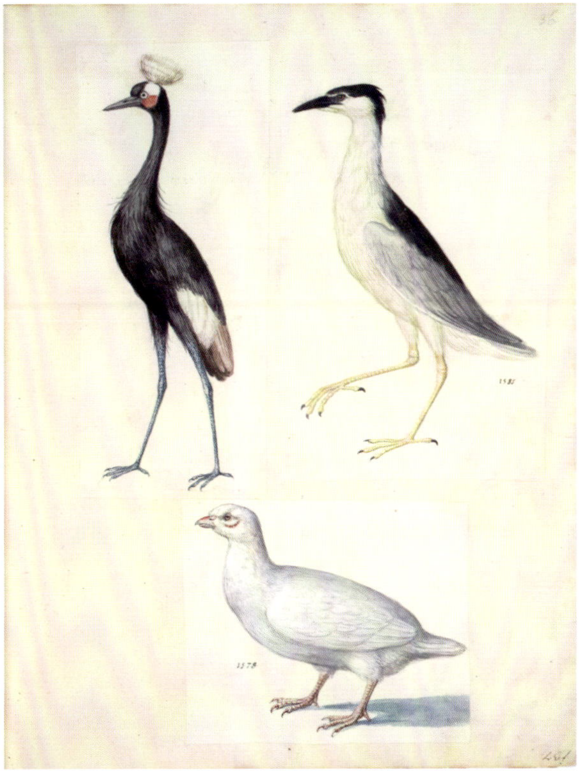

IV.24, fol. 36

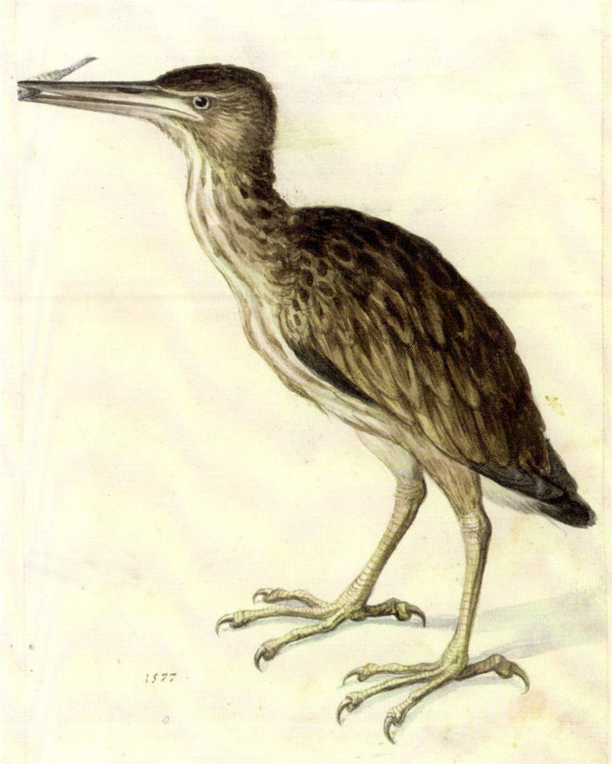

IV.24, fol. 39

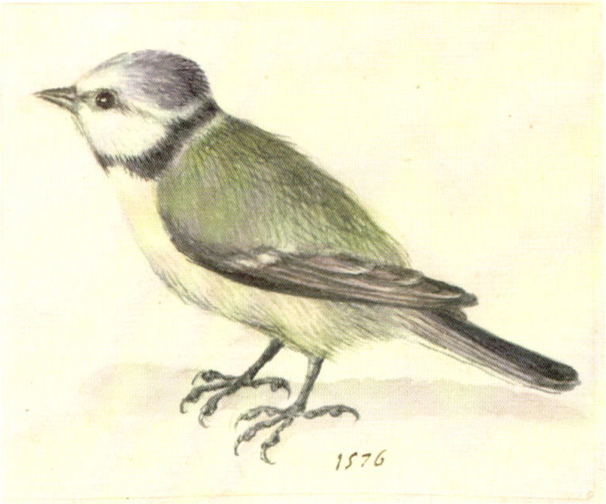

IV.24, fol. 39

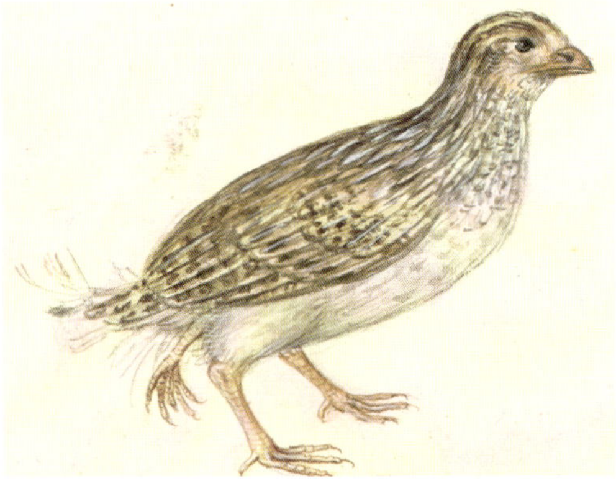

IV.24, fol. 46

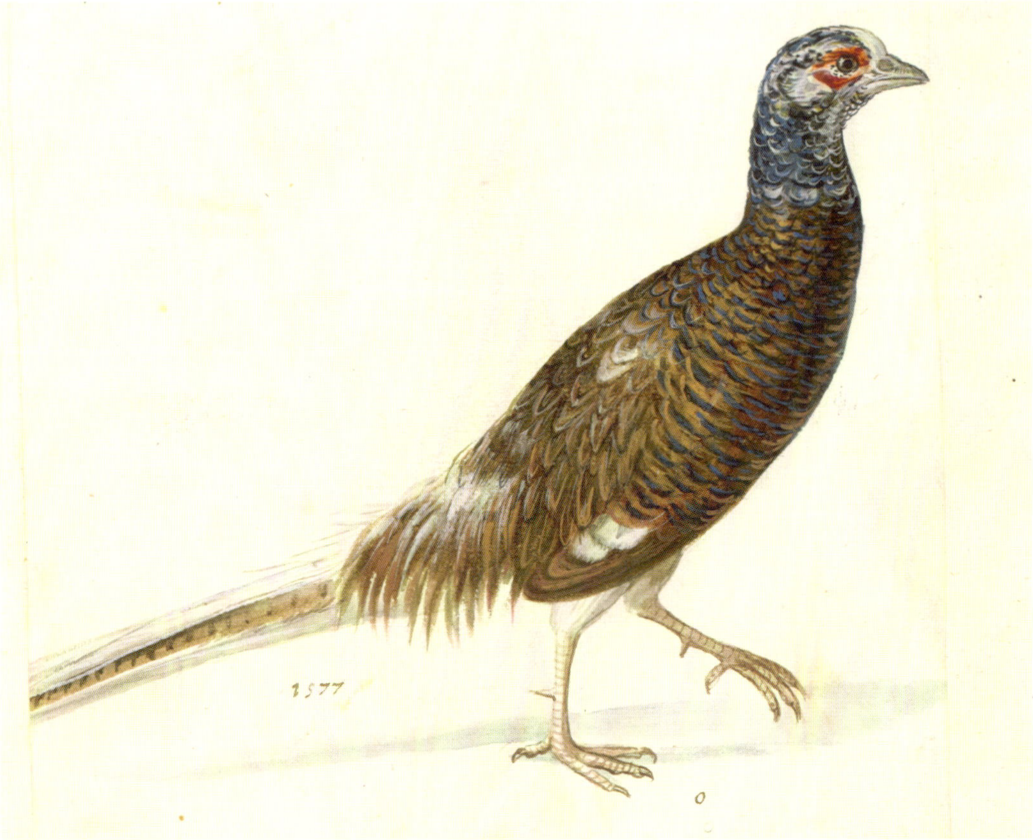

IV.24, fol. 41

are copied from Cod. min. 130, fol. 76r (Staudinger 1990, 440-441).
This quail is also part of the Kunstkammer collection of Kaiser Rudolf II, as listed in Daniel Fröschel's inventory: "A small hen with three feet, embalmed, that came to the Kunstkammer in 1609" (Bauer, Haupt 1976, 9, no. 134: "1 hüenlin mit 3 füßen, gepalsamirt, A°. 1609 zur kunstkammer kommen").

fol. 115r: *Steed and dogs*

fol. 128r left: *Lizard, chameleon and fire salamander*
The lizard is to the right, the chameleon to the left and salamander again to the right (from top down). The sheet is dated "1553" directly beside the chameleon.

fol. 128r right above: *Indian gray mongoose Herpestes edwardsii* (E. Geoffroy Saint-Hilaire 1818)
The Indian mongoose is turned left, lying down or in wait, with upright tail. The study bears the date "1.5.7.2.", and at the bottom edge of the paper sheet the section from the ears to the tail attachment is drawn in pencil, bearing a written "6". On the left, the tip of the nose of the mongoose is somewhat cut off with the paper. The study was also the model for the picture in Cod. min. 129, fol. 64r, where the mongoose is shown in between a mouse or rat and a lizard. It could be an indication of the catch of a tame, live Indian Mongoose, presumably living in the court in Vienna or Prague. The vertically positioned tail could indicate an observed trait (Staudinger 1990, 224-225).
The Indian mongoose is extant from Persia to the Arabian peninsula up to Assam and Ceylon. It was introduced in Malaysia and Mauritius. The English poet Rudyard Kipling built a literary statue to the mongoose in Rikki-Tikki-Tavi as a brave killer of snakes.

Manfred Staudinger

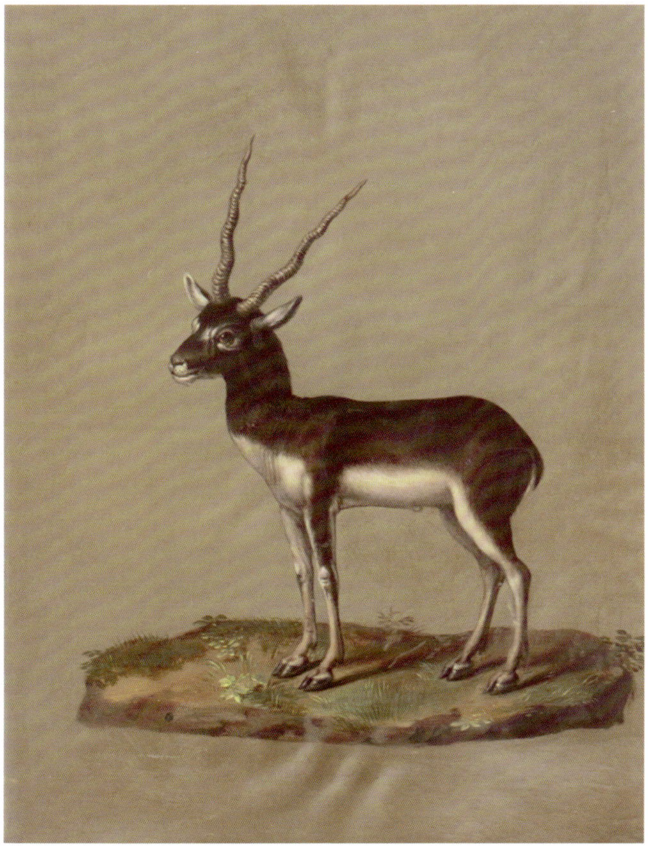

IV.25, fol. 21

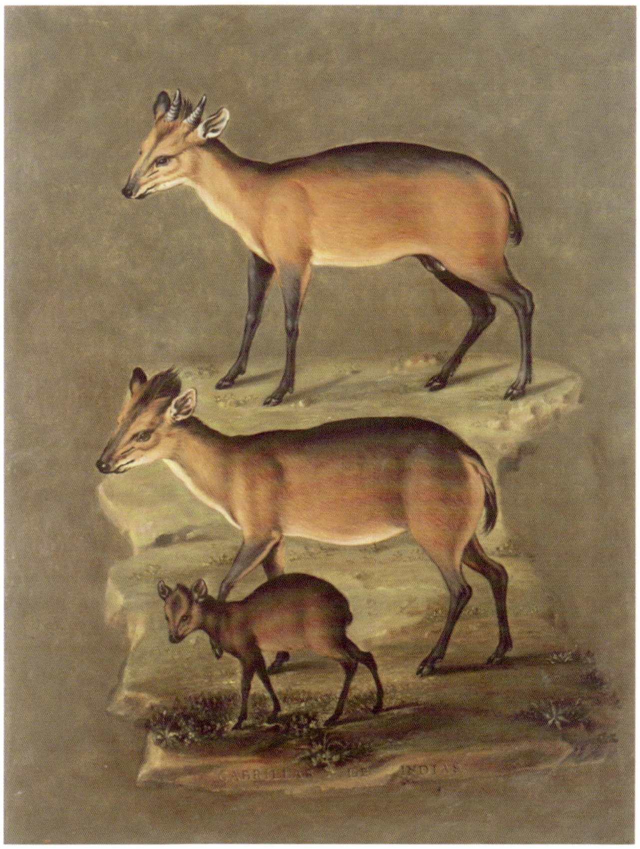

IV. 25, fol. 25

IV.25
Mammals
Gouache on parchment
Vienna, Österreichische Nationalbibliothek, Handschriften-, Autographen- und Nachlass-Sammlung, cod. min. 129

IV.26
Birds
Gouache on parchment
Vienna, Österreichische Nationalbibliothek, Handschriften-, Autographen- und Nachlass-Sammlung, cod. min. 130

An equally ambitious undertaking was what was later known as the "Museum of Emperor Rudolf II", or the codices min. 129 and 130 in the Österreichische Nationalbibliothek. Its beginnings stretch back well into the time of Emperor Maximilian II; however most of the folios were created in the period between 1576 and 1611. None of the folios are signed, and only one is dated with "1610".
The earlier concept that this collection had been created in gouache painting on parchment by a copyist or by a second-rate artist has long been abandoned. Much more, it was created over a longer period of time with cooperation by Giuseppe Arcimboldo, Hans Hoffmann, Dirck de Quade van Ravesteyn and Daniel Fröschel.
The acquisition of exotic animals formed the foundation for the zoological garden, first established in Ebersdorf near Vienna and later in Prague, and was a significant prerequisite for the overwhelming quality of the representations. The imperial ambassadors had been advised to acquire everything that was new, or rather unknown and interesting. According to a report from Madrid by Hans Khevenhüller on 17 September 1575: "The King (Philip II of Spain) has two very beautiful little goats from India that were given to him by Don Juan de Borja, quite unfamiliar and remarkable; the male is a little temperamental, but the female is tame and pregnant. The King loves them very much and frequently has them with him, which is why I would not be able to ask for them. However, I will attempt to indirectly suggest that they be sent to Your Majesty, and if that is not possible, I will try to have a painting of them sent"[1]. And again on 16 December of the same year: "With this I send the picture of the form and dimensions of the small Indian animals that I previously described. The kid is approximately five weeks old; the male is so angry that there is another man, and he now has to contend with his kicking and butting"[2]. With this, it is possible for the first time to date this picture with the three Red-flanked Duikers (cod. min. 129, fol. 25r.).

Cod. min. 129, fol. 21r: *Blackbuck*
Antilope cervicapra (Linnaeus, 1758)
This Blackbuck, a male, faces left and is portrayed standing on a sod (compare Staudinger 1990, 138-139). The picture is an exact copy of cod. min. 42, fol. 21 upper image, dated 1570.
The Blackbuck is native to the Indian subcontinent, where it once flourished in herds of thousands. It is the fastest antelope in India and can only be outrun in a short distance by a sprinting cheetah. Like certain other animals, it produces bezoar.

Cod. min. 129, fol. 25r: *Red-flanked Duiker*
Cephalophus rufilatus (Gray, 1846)
There are three Red-flanked Duikers depicted – a male, a female and a baby – facing left upon a large sod (compare Staudinger 1990, 146-147). On the front edge of the platform-like piece of ground is the inscription in capitalized letters: "CABRILLAS DE INDIAS" ("small goats from India").
The male's body is reddish-brown, with a lighter underside. The back and the front sides of the legs are dark grey, as is a stripe from the nose to the forehead. Between the horns, which are only smooth at the tip and clearly show rings in the lower portion, a darker shock of hair can be seen. The ears are black on the outside with a brown centre at the base, and a longitudinal line inside, in the middle; the lower part has a black spot. The female appears generally somewhat darker and less contrasted and has a broad, dark line that runs over the bridge of the nose to the pronounced shock of hair. The baby is dark grey with a little reddish-brown, primarily on the ventral region and on the head.

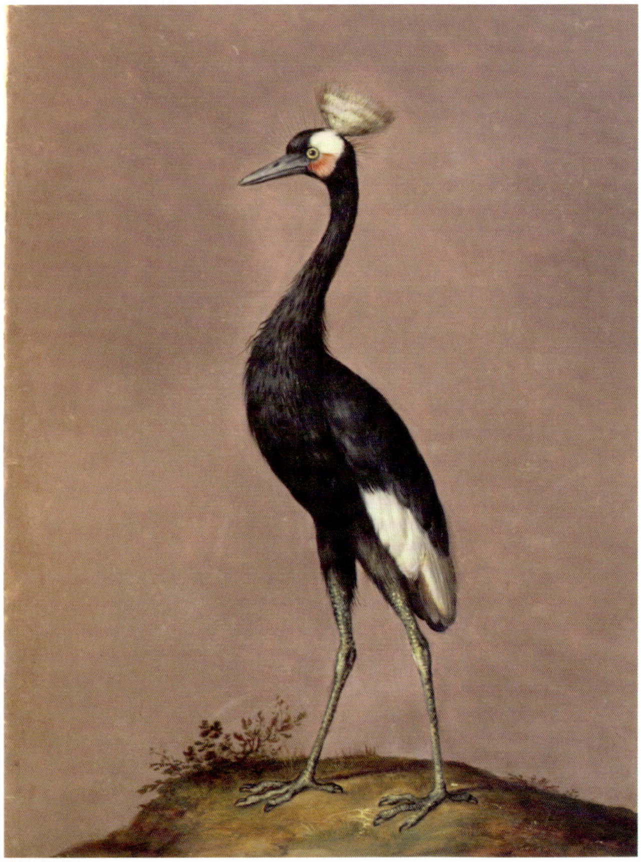
IV.26, fol. 34

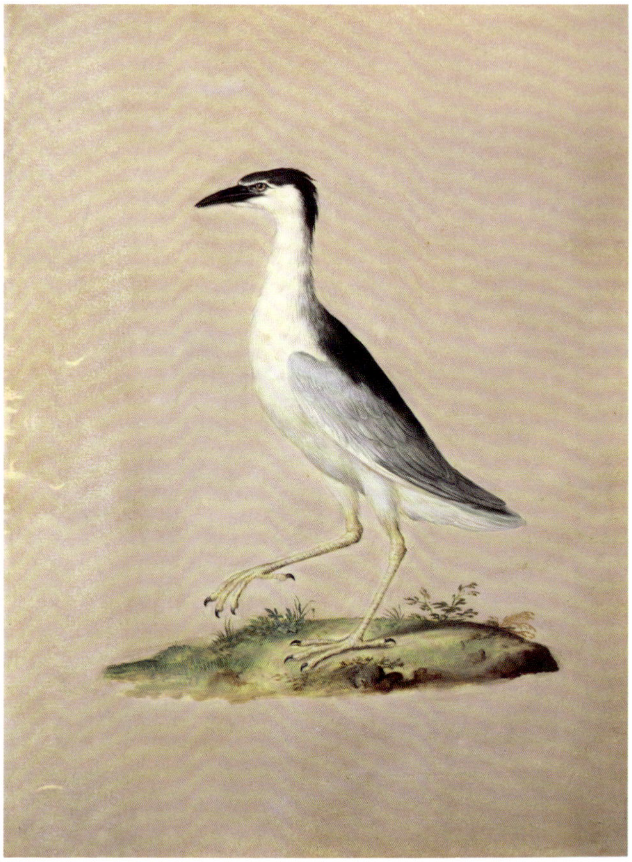
IV.26, fol. 41

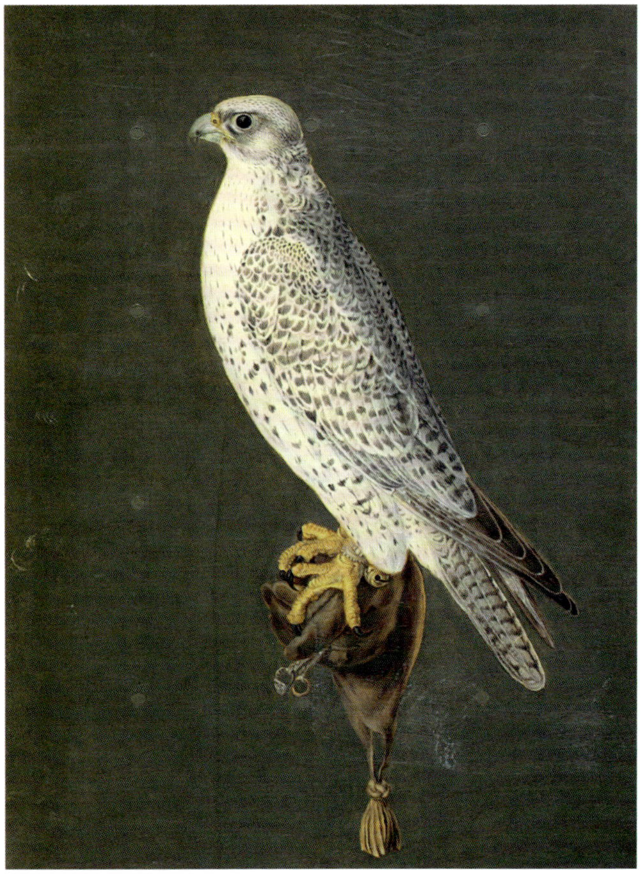
IV.26, fol. 8

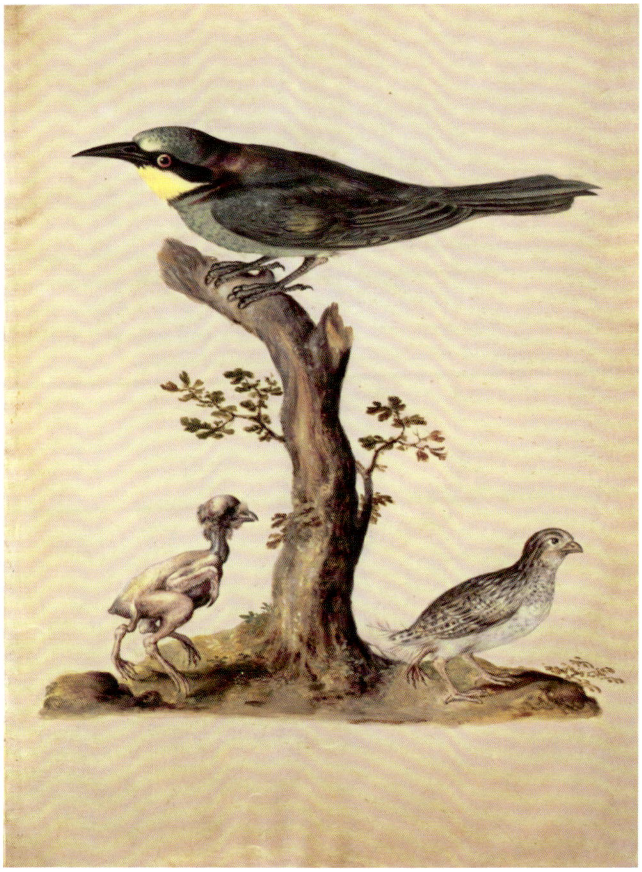
IV.26, fol. 76

There is no known preliminary study for the female and the baby. The male can be seen in a very similar posture in cod. min. 42, fol. 19 below; however, our picture shows significant improvements. The watercolour study differs and is less convincing in the slightly curved rear legs, the slender body and the anomalous form and drawing of the head and ears.
This Red-flanked Duiker, which stands 35 cm at the shoulders, is a very small duiker and lives in forests from Western to Central Africa (Nowak – Paradiso 1983).

Cod. min. 129, fol. 26r: *Reindeer*
Rangifer tarandus (Linnaeus, 1758)
The reindeer faces left and stands with a lowered head upon a sod (compare Staudinger 1990, 148-149). The picture shows a possibly domesticated reindeer, whose antlers have just re-grown after shedding and who is in the process of molting. The reindeer was most likely a gift of a prince to the emperor; however, there is no written documentation of this.
A similar picture of a reindeer is found in cod. min. 42, fol. 19 above; however, the watercolour study cannot be considered a model and the quality of the representation in the present study is not achieved. Wild reindeers inhabit the mountainous regions of Southern Norway and Eastern Finland and eastwards into the tundra and forest tundra. Domesticated reindeers are mostly prevalent in Lapland and Siberia.

Cod. min. 130, fol. 34r: *Black crowned crane*
Balearica pavonina (Linnaeus, 1758)
The black crowned crane faces left and stands on a sod (compare Staudinger 1990, 356-357). It is dark grey; the facial patch is red in the lower half and extends upwards to the crown; the iris is light yellow; the legs are greenish.
The picture is a copy of cod. min. 42, fol. 36 upper left. The watercolour study was probably painted from a dead black crowned crane as a model. In Emperor Rudolf II's art chamber, the remains of two black crowned cranes were found, which were named "*Pavo Marinus*" with reference to Carolus Clusius.
The black crowned crane breeds in sub-Saharan Africa. The dark form depicted here originates in Western Africa.

Cod. min. 130, fol. 41r: *Night heron*
Nycticorax nycticorax (Linnaeus, 1758)
The black-crowned night heron faces left and stands on a sod (compare Staudinger 1990, 370-371). It has a black beak, a bulging forehead and a reddish iris. The picture is a copy of cod. min. 42, fol. 36 upper right, a watercolour study on paper, which is dated "1585".
In comparison to the length of its stride, the black-crowned night heron's toes are too short and the position of its wings and the upward-curved tail exclude the use of a living bird as a model. Nevertheless, in some details of the representation the watercolour study is preferable.
The black-crowned night heron is a widely diffused breeder in Europe.

Cod. min. 130, fol. 8r: *Gyrfalcon*
Falco rusticolus (Linnaeus, 1758)
The gyrfalcon, an adult exemplar with white-grey plumage, faces left and sits on a leather bag (compare Staudinger 1990, 97-98). A silver ring with a double-eagle crest and a small gold ring are attached by a small plate to the bag, which flows into a leather tassel below. The beak is a light, bluish-grey; the iris is dark; the nose skin, the feet and the toes are coloured yellow. A golden manacle can be seen on the left foot.
This high-quality picture was certainly painted from a live bird as a model. The gyrfalcon or hunting falcon was one of the most coveted falcons and in Emperor Maximilian II and Rudolf II's time it was also used in falconry on various birds.

Cod. min. 130, fol. 76r: *Quail*
Coturnix coturnix (Linnaeus, 1758)
The quail faces left and is depicted, practically floating, just above the ground next to a tree (compare Staudinger 1990, 440-441). It is plucked; a third leg (*duplicitas posterior*) has grown on the right side of the pelvis, or just behind it. This is the same quail that can be seen on the right, un-plucked, next to the tree.
The picture is an exact copy of cod. min. 42, fol. 46 bottom, a watercolour study that was painted from the dead, plucked quail as a model around 1609.
The three-legged quail is also listed in the inventory of the art chamber: "1 hüenlin mit 3 füßen, gepalsamirt, A°. 1609 zur kunstkammer kommen" ("one small hen with three feet, embalmed, added to the art chamber in 1609"; Bauer, Haupt 1976, 9, no. 134). From this dating, it can be concluded that the model with the un-plucked bird must have been created previously. The temporal proximity of this present plate of the museum to the watercolour study of the embalmed quail, however, can not be deduced.

Manfred Staudinger

Bibliography: Bauer, Haupt 1976; Staudinger 1990.

[1] Report of the imperial ambassador Hans Khevenhüller, 17 September 1575, Madrid: "Der Khönig hat zway gar schöne Gaissl aus India, so im der Don Juan de Borja presentiert, gar frembd und selzam. Das mandl etwas pöss, das Weybl aber frömb vnnd tragendig, welche den Khönig feindtlich lieb vnnd steets umb ihn hatt, derhalben ichs nit begern dörffen. Wille aber per indirectum die sachen dahin richten, ob müglich soliche Euer Kay. Mt. geschickht würden, wo nit sehe ich dero Conterfäth zu übersenden bekhommen khön." HHStA, State Department, Spain, Diplomatic Correspondence, Carton 9, Khevenhüller 1575-1576, fol. 197v.
[2] Report of the imperial ambassador Hans Khevenhüller 16 Dezember 1575, Madrid: "Hiemit hab Ich derselb[en] der Indianischen Tierl formb vnd grüss conterfeth darvon Ewr Kaj: Mt: Ich zuuor geschriben vbersenden wollen. Das Jung ist bey fünff Wochen alt, dz Mändl so pös dz auch ainen Mann mit seinem anlauffen vnnd stossen zuschaffen gibt." HHStA, State Department, Spain, Diplomatic Correspondence, Carton 9, Khevenhüller 1575-1576, fol. 219v.

IV.27
Anonymous
The "Hairy Man from Munich"
Paper on cardboard
13.2 × 9.5 cm
inv. no. 5417

Anonymous
The Wife of the "Hairy Man from Munich"
Paper on cardboard
12.7 × 10 cm
inv. no. 5419

Anonymous
The Daughter of the "Hairy Man from Munich"
Paper on wood
13.2 × 9.5 cm
inv. no. 5419

Anonymous
The Son of the "Hairy Man from Munich"
Paper on wood
13 × 10 cm
inv. no. 5420

Among the over 1000 images in the portrait collection of Archduke Ferdinand II of Tyrol in Castle Ambras, three portraits stand out because of their peculiar appearance: they portray Pedro Gonzalez and his two oldest children. "The smoke man from Munich" (later also "the hairy baron from Munich"), as the description reads in the Ambras inventory of 1621, is considered the first documented case of "*hypertrichosis universalis congenita*", the so-called "Ambras Syndrome". The congenital illness, which results in the growth of hair on the face as well as the entire body after birth, was researched by doctor Felix Platter of Basel and the Bolognese naturalist, Ulisses Aldrovandi with Pedro Gonzalez as their first example. The fate of the hair-covered members of the Gonzalez family is noted for its reputation as a natural wonder. They were considered animals, who were both marvelled at and presented as gifts.

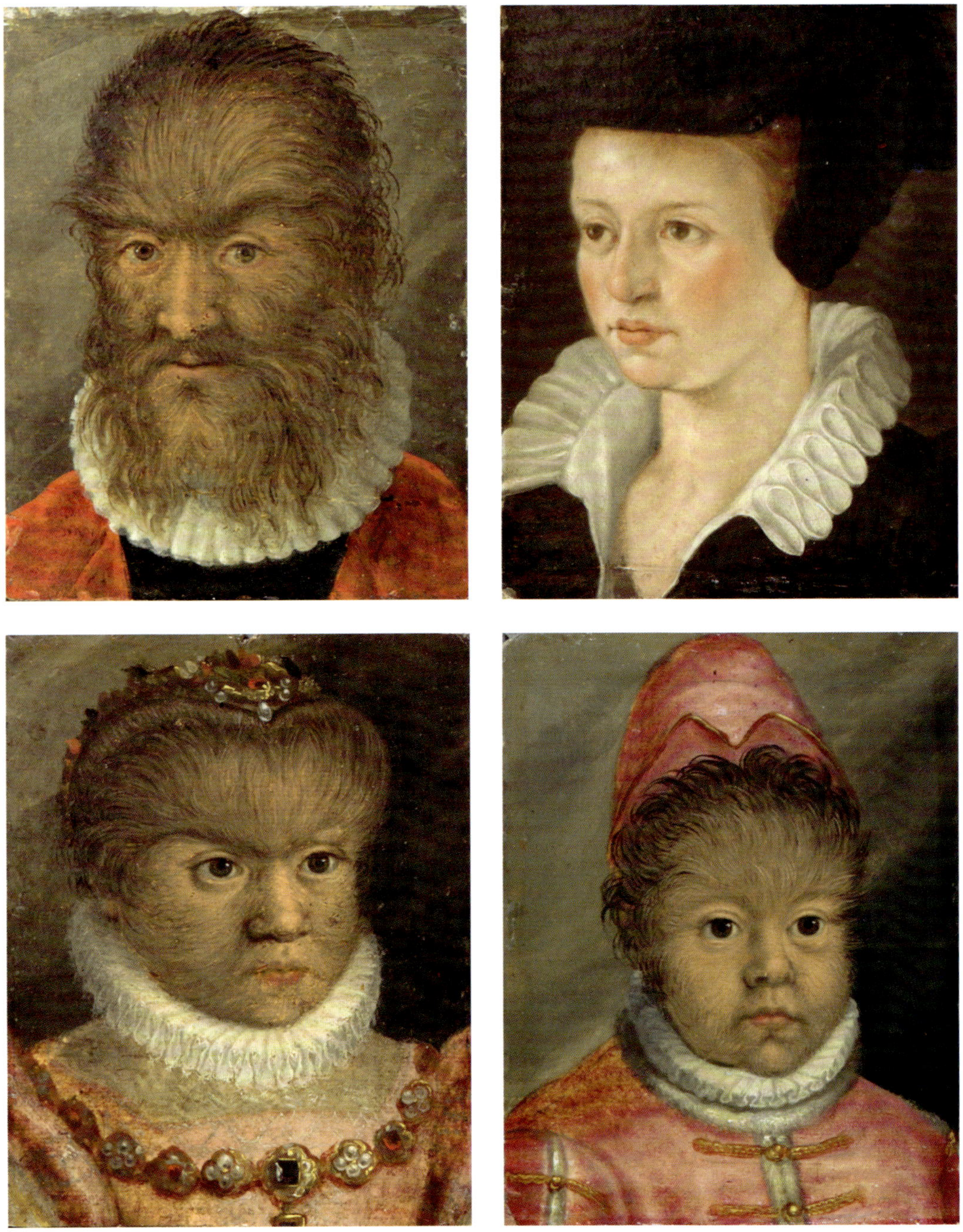

IV.27

Father and son, at least, turned their condition to a certain prestige and material advantage.
Born around 1537 on the Canary Island Tenerife, the hispanicized and baptized Pedro was presented in his infancy as a gift (under yet unexplained circumstances) to the French King, Henry II. The child received a good education and served in the royal court as "sommelier de panneterie bouche" until the end of the 1580s. He apparently possessed the manners of a nobleman and had himself referred to by the well documented title "Don Pedro". Henry II arranged his marriage to Catherine, who supposedly hailed from Paris. As her portrait tablet shows, she did not suffer from "Ambras Syndrome". The caption on a miniature of the couple by Georg Hoefnagel praises her charm in the words of Pedro: "By God's grace I have been blessed with a wife of singular beauty as well as children; the precious fruit of our union". The two oldest children, Maddalena (c. 1575-1642) and Enrico (c. 1580-1656), both of whom inherited their father's condition, are represented in Ferdinand II's collection.
Around 1589, the Gonzalez family was sent by the Duke of Mayenne, after many years of service in the French court, to the Duke of Parma, Alessandro Farnese. Ranuccio Farnese, in turn, bequeathed the son, Enrico, to his brother, Cardinal Odoardo, around 1595. According to a letter by Duke Wilhelm V of Bavaria, Enrico, whom he describes as "most comical and entertaining", lived in the Palazzo Farnese in Rome thereafter. Odoardo had him portrayed by Agostino Carracci (Naples, Museo di Capodimonte) with a dwarf, a Calabrian as well as exotic animals. Upon his request to leave the court, Enrico established himself in the Farneses' earlier holding in Capodimonte on Lake Bolsena. In 1608 the rest of the family followed him there: Pedro obtained the post of personal dresser before he died at the age of nearly 80. Less interested in courtly service than his father, Enrico, who was enjoying a considerable social prominence, pursued financial affairs instead. While we well know that Enrico's older sister Maddalena was marvelled at as a curiosity during her childhood, we know relatively little about her adult life until the date of her marriage (1593).
It was around 1580 that images of the family began to circulate around the courts of Europe (Munich, Graz, Ambras, Prague). Archduke Wilhelm V, who was well-known for his interest in anomalies and monstrosities, possessed a cabinet of curiosities, which was famous as a shrine for remarkable objects of an artistic and miraculous nature. Numerous dwarves, cripples and moors amused the Bavarian court while a series of portraits of curious figures decorated the walls of Wilhelm's picture gallery. Four drawings of the heads of the Gonzalez parents and children arrived from Paris at the court of Wilhelm V. There, they served as the basis for a Munich painter to create four full figure, large format portraits with an imaginary cliff scene (based on the supposedly "wild" subject) as a background. Duke Wilhelm V gave the odd portrait of the "wild men", as it was his custom to call them, to his uncle Ferdinand II of Tyrol, who thereupon had them copied into a smaller format (presumably for his collection) and later had them drawn on cardboard as well as wood.
The fascination that the images of the "hairy people" arouse converges with concepts of mythical savages as well as literary figures (such as Ariost's *Orlando furioso*). The medallion miniatures of the Gonzalez parents and their children, painted by Hoefnagel circa 1580 (Washington, National Gallery of Art), are, for example, associated with fire in the first volume of the *Animalia Rationalia et Insecta*. In a miniature attributed to Dirck de Quade van Ravesteyn (Vienna, Österreichische Nationalbibliothek, c. 1600), whose composition recalls a depiction of the imperial family by Arcimboldo, nearly all of the characteristics of savages are eliminated in favour of a noble depiction of the family. But their presence as illustrations in a bestiary of Rudolf II reconfirms their perception as savages.

Sabine Pénot

Bibliography: Dericks-Tan, Martin 2000, 99; Hellrigl 2002-03, 32-35; Zapperi 2004, 61-73.

IV.28
Lavinia Fontana (1552-1614)
Portrait of Antonietta Gonzalez (or Gonsalvus)
c. 1595
Oil on canvas
Inscription:
"Dall'isole Cannare fu condotto al Serenissimo Enrico re / di Francia Don Pietro huomo selvatico che de presente / si trova presso il Serenissimo duca di Parma del quale / fui io Antonietta, et hora me trovo presso alla Signora / Donna Isabella Pallavicina Signora Marchesa di Soragna."
57 × 46 cm
Blois, Musée du Château de Blois, inv. 997.1.1

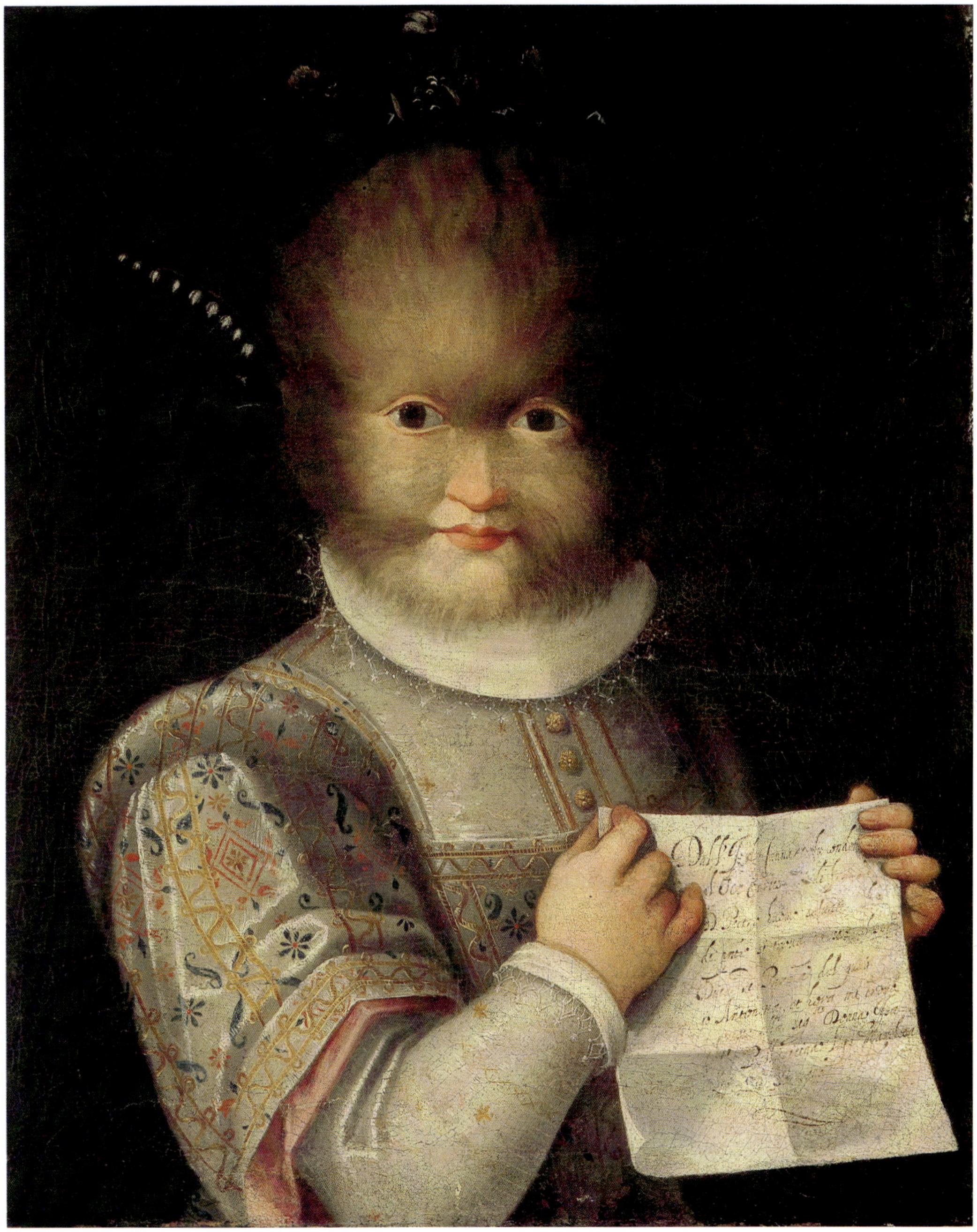
IV.28

The portrait of Antonietta Gonzalez, younger daughter of the famous "hairy man", Pedro Gonzalez (Cantaro, 1993), shows a hybrid being somewhere between a doll-like figure and a hairy creature in court dress. The thick growth of hair that covers the entire face of the eight-to-ten-year-old child, is the result of a genetic malady, *Hypertrichosis universalis congenita.* Born around 1588 in Paris, Antonietta was brought up in the French court, this before she moved to Parma in 1591, year in which the French court made a gift of her and her family to Prince Ranuccio Farnese. A few years later the child drew the attention at court of Isabella di Gerolamo Pallavicino di Cortemaggiore, after which the Prince made the hairy maiden over to the Marchesa of Soragna, resident in Parma since 1593 and who conducted one of the most influential salons in the city. On a sheet of paper, that Antonietta holds in her hand in full view of the observer, one can read the outline of her short though all the same eventful life history: "From the Canary islands Don Pietro, a wild man, was brought to noble Henry, King of France. Today he is with the noble Prince of Parma, to whom I, Anonietta, belong, and now I am with Donna Isabella Pallavicina, the Marchesa of Soragna" (translation after Zapperi 2004).
The work was painted when Antonietta accompanied the Marchesa of Soragna on her visit to Senator Mario Casalli around 1594 in Bologna. Ulisse Aldrovandi closely examined the hairy maiden. The notes of the natural scientist were sustained in the posthumously published *Monstrum Histori* (1642) and illustrated with pictures of the hairy members of the Gonzalez family. Whether the painting, that since 1997 has been in the possession of the Château de Blois in France, is identical to the portrait described as *effigem puellae hirsutae, viri Sylvestris ex Europae filiae* described in the Aldrovandi collection, is still disputed. Probably the latter was inspired by Lavinia Fontana's portrait of the hairy maiden (Murphy 2003, 163). An especially lively, empathetic drawing (Pierpont Morgan Library, New York) made by the Bolognese woman portrait painter served as a study for the painting here displayed. Similarities in the clothing, shown in the pencil portrait, reinforce this supposition, even if the painting does not equal the drawing in liveliness and sensibility.
Together with the four portrait panels from the collection of Ferdinand II. of Tyrol (see cat. IV.27), that show the appearance of the parents as well as Antonietta's older siblings, that also suffered from the socalled "Ambras Syndrome", these pictures feature as singular documentation of the rare and legendary malady, to which the members of the Gonzalez family owed their fate of becoming a court attraction throughout Europe.

Sabine Pénot

Bibliography: Cantaro 1993, 85-102; Fortunati 1998, 27-28; Murphy 2003, 164-165; Zapperi 2004, 100-111; Washington D.C. 2007, cat. no. 26, 152-153.

IV.29
Giuseppe Arcimboldo
The Librarian
Oil on canvas
97 × 71 cm
Skokloster Castle

In order to please Maximilian II and his court, Arcimboldo made a number of portraits of people in the immediate entourage of the Emperor. Those portraits were often composed with the specific tools of their trade or profession. This portrait depicts an old man composed largely of books piled one above and against each other. An open book on the top of his head forms his hat. The figure is held together by a cloak shaped from the drapery in the background. The painting corresponds to the description of *The Librarian* found in the Vienna inventory from 1621: "Ein conterfeet von büchern vom Arsimboldo" (Jahrbuch, 25, 1905). The painting was later taken to Sweden with the spoils from Prague in 1648. Subsequently the painting was owned by Queen Christina. In Sweden there are and have been several corresponding works but it is the version at Skokloster that is probably referred to in the inventory. A version that belonged to the Diocesan Library in Linköping and which was destroyed in connection with the fire there in 1996 was a later copy. Another example in a somewhat larger format (100.2 × 72 cm) was formerly in private ownership in Sweden. Since the Skokloster painting is not of the same artistic standard as other original works by Arcimboldo it may possibly be a copy of a lost original that had already been made in Prague in 1562.

The librarian has been interpreted by Alfons as a portrait of Wolfgang Lazius, a learned collector and scientist who was in charge of the Emperor's Kunstkammer and who arranged his numismatic collection and his library (Alfons 1957, 65). In the spirit of the age, *The Librarian* or the *Bookman* can be interpreted symbolically as a satirical depiction of the folly of scholarship. Books were a traditional symbol of learning and wisdom but in this composition the artist makes fun of the subject by depicting him as a fool with an open book on his head and eyes made of key rings. His beard is a feather duster and his fingers consist of strips of paper stuck into the volumes to mark various places. This type of picture originates from a well-known woodcut by Sebastian Brant from 1494, which portrays a learned fool with a feather duster in the chamber that had formerly provided the background for depictions of the Saint Jerome and other learned men. In composition therefore *The Librarian* is different from the other complex compositions as it has more the character of a still-life than a portrait.

Its subject, Wolfgang Lazius, was born in Vienna in 1514. He studied medicine and served, for instance, as a military physician in Hungary. He returned to Vienna in 1541 as a professor at the university there, where he served two terms as Rector. In time he transferred his interests to historical research. He made extensive journeys to collect manuscripts; he transcribed original documents, collected and made drawings of coins, weapons and prehistoric remains. In 1554 he was appointed court historiographer by the emperor and acted as the overseer of the imperial collections. He acquired his own substantial collection of books, which later became part of the imperial library. His interests were wide-ranging and included Greek and Roman antiquities, medieval history as well as the history of Austria and Hungary, numismatics and the annals of the House of Habsburg. He wrote about the war against the Turks, described folk costumes and also made a major contribution as a cartographer. He published the results of his studies in fifty or so works. He has been described as somewhat uncritical in his publications and it may have been this smug attitude that made him a laughing stock in court circles and the subject of *The Librarian.*

Görel Cavalli-Björkman

Provenance: Prague 1621; Kristina 1652; Ulriksdal 1814; Gripsholm 1822

Bibliography: Granberg 1911, no. 321; Alfons 1957, 65; Geiger 1960, 48, 145; Becker 1980, 462; Alfons 1987, 80, 86-87; Cavalli-Björkman 2005, 178-180.

IV.30
Giuseppe Arcimboldo
The Jurist
Signed: 1566, Giuseppe Arcimboldo F
Oil on canvas
64 × 51 cm
Mariefred, Gripsholm Castle

This painting is a half-length male portrait. The face is made up of fishes and plucked fowls, the head is covered by a black hat and the fur-lined cloak is open at the front to reveal that the torso consists of books and manuscripts. The manuscripts project above the neckband to form a collar. The figure is terminated below by two volumes. On the uppermost of these is the text: ISERNIA. On the one below one can discern less clearly the inscription BARTHO. The composition is very witty and the eyes of the man coincide with the eyes of a little chicken. This painting, which belongs to the Swedish National Museum of Fine Arts, is displayed at Gripsholm Castle.

The painting was published by Olof Granberg in 1902 as a caricature portrait of John Calvin, and gained international circulation in this form, even among Calvin's biographers (Granberg 1902). However, in 1957 Sven Alfons offered another interpretation of the portrait (Alfons 1957, 55-59). He identified the subject as Johann Ulrich Zasius, an administrator with legal training, who was in charge of the imperial family's finances. Alfons arrived at this conclusion by combining two contemporary statements. Lomazzo describes a painting that aroused the emperor's particular appreciation: "This telling portrait of the emperor's vice-chancellor, which from some distance was considered by his majesty and others to be as good a likeness as possible, and which seen from closer quarters turned out to be totally composed of creatures, so that the nose was a fowl, the chin a trout and in like manner the other facial features beasts of other kinds, so excellently assembled that, to tell the truth, it was a miracle to behold" (Lomazzo 1590 [1973], 154). In one paragraph Comanini describes the painting as follows: "The portrait that he painted at the behest of Emperor Maximilian made great mockery of a certain scholar whose entire face had been eaten by the French disease, so much so, in fact, that only a few little hairs remained on his chin… He composed his face entirely of meat and fried fish; and it turned out to be a successful picture that everyone who looked at it immediately recognized the true face of the law scholar. I need not describe to you the pleasure that it aroused in His Majesty and the mockery it incited at the imperial court. You can imagine it for yourselves" (Comanini 1591, 50ff.). The name "Bartho" should probably be construed as Bartholus and is a reference to Bartolus da Sassoferrato, the most influential medieval jurist, who was born in 1314 and died in 1357. Through his commentary on Roman law he was to dominate legal studies during the late Middle Ages and into the 16th century. His works were printed a number of times from 1470 onwards. "Iserna" in the inscription also turns out to refer to a work on jurisprudence. Andreas de Isernia was another medieval legal scholar. He was born in the Italian city of Isernia around 1220 and died in 1316. His works were still current at the time the painting was created. As the puzzling subject supports himself on volumes by both these writers, it is natural to conclude that he was a jurist. How does this fit in with the suggestion in Lomazzo's description that the subject was the emperor's vice-chancellor? It has been shown that this position was occupied at the time the portrait was painted by the Johann Ulrich Zasius referred to above. It could also be determined that Zasius, in spite of his three marriages, was not favoured by any form of physical beauty. He had been disfigured by an accident in which he had been thrown from a carriage drawn by runaway horses and injured the right side of his face. In addition

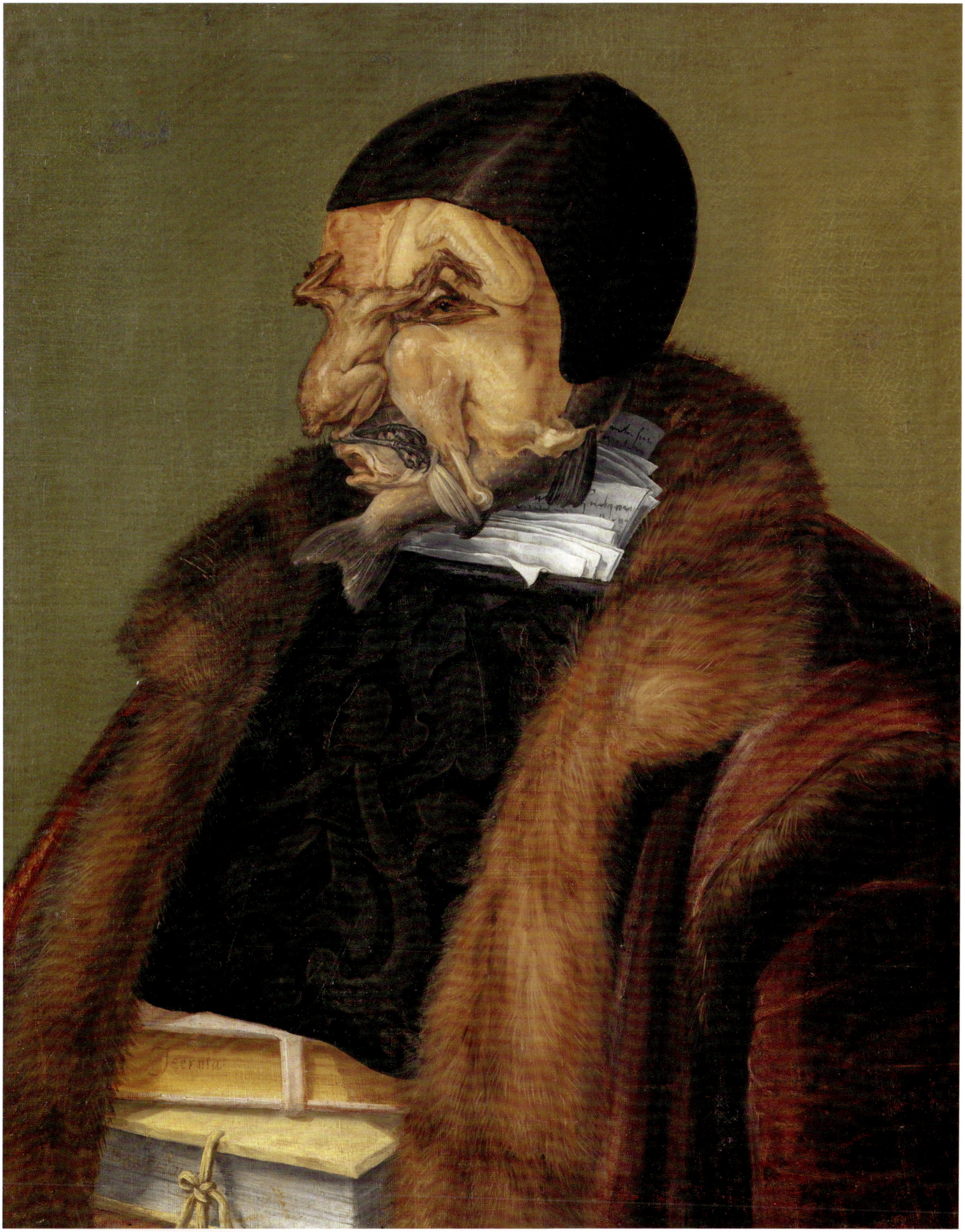

IV.30

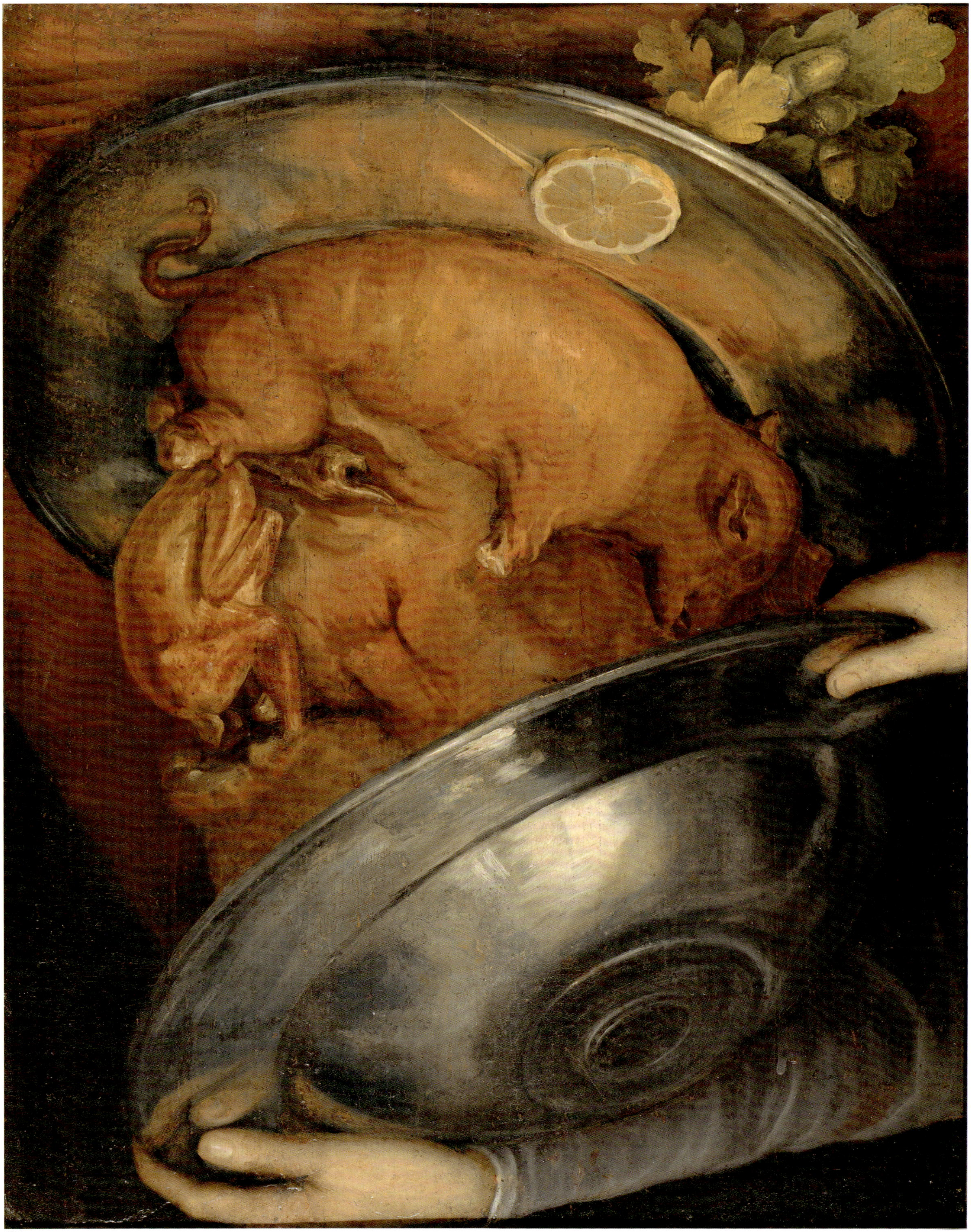

IV.31

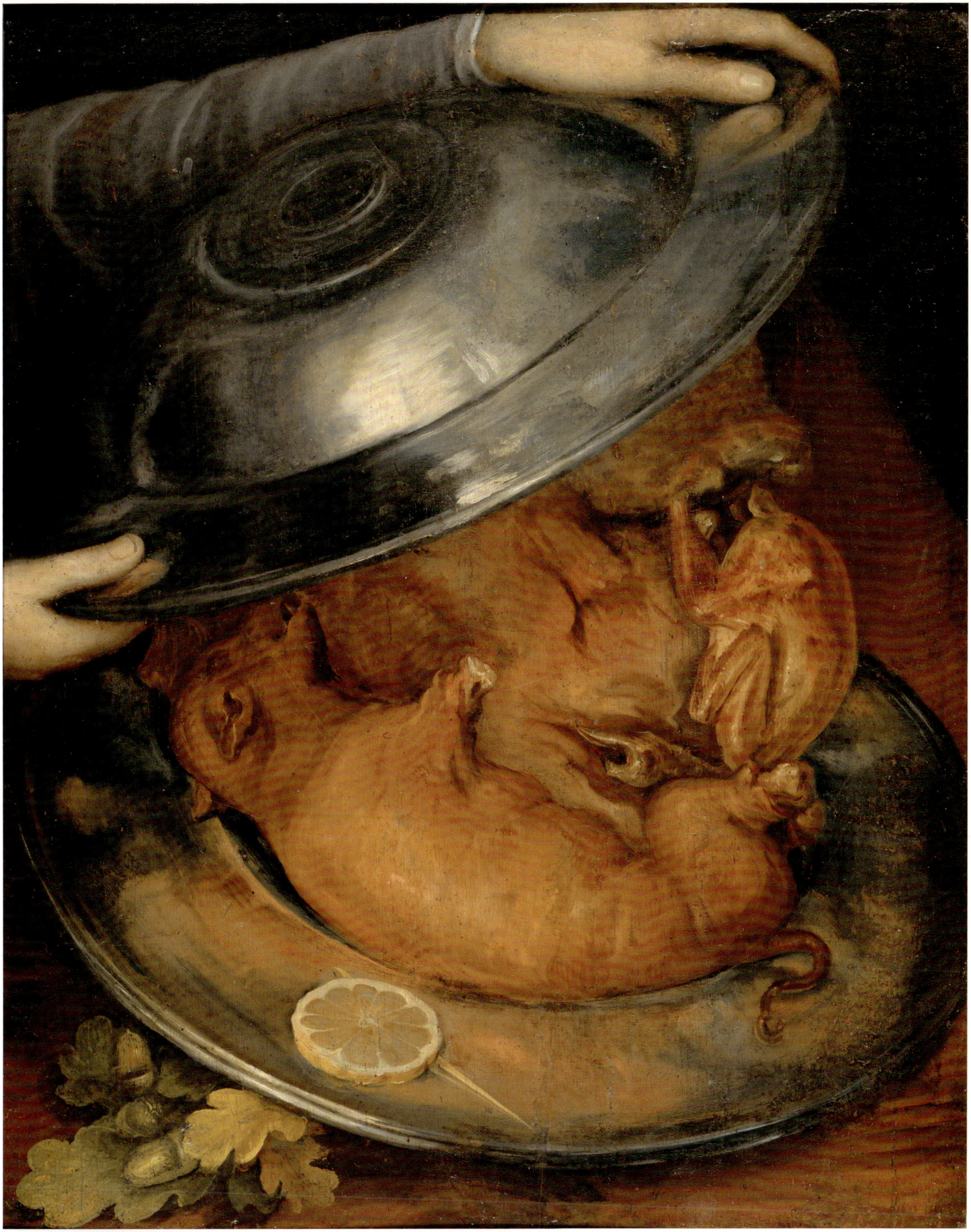

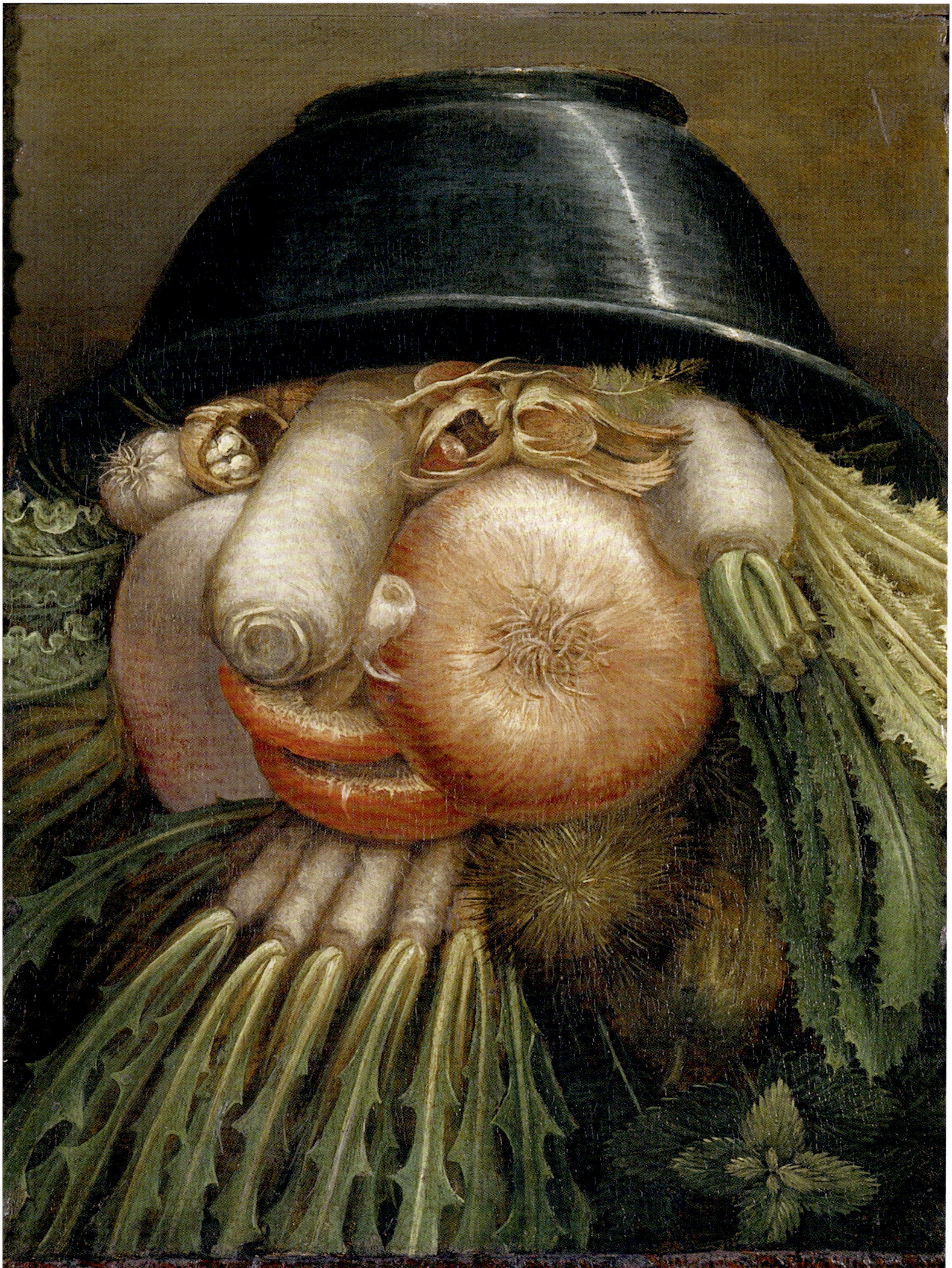

IV.32

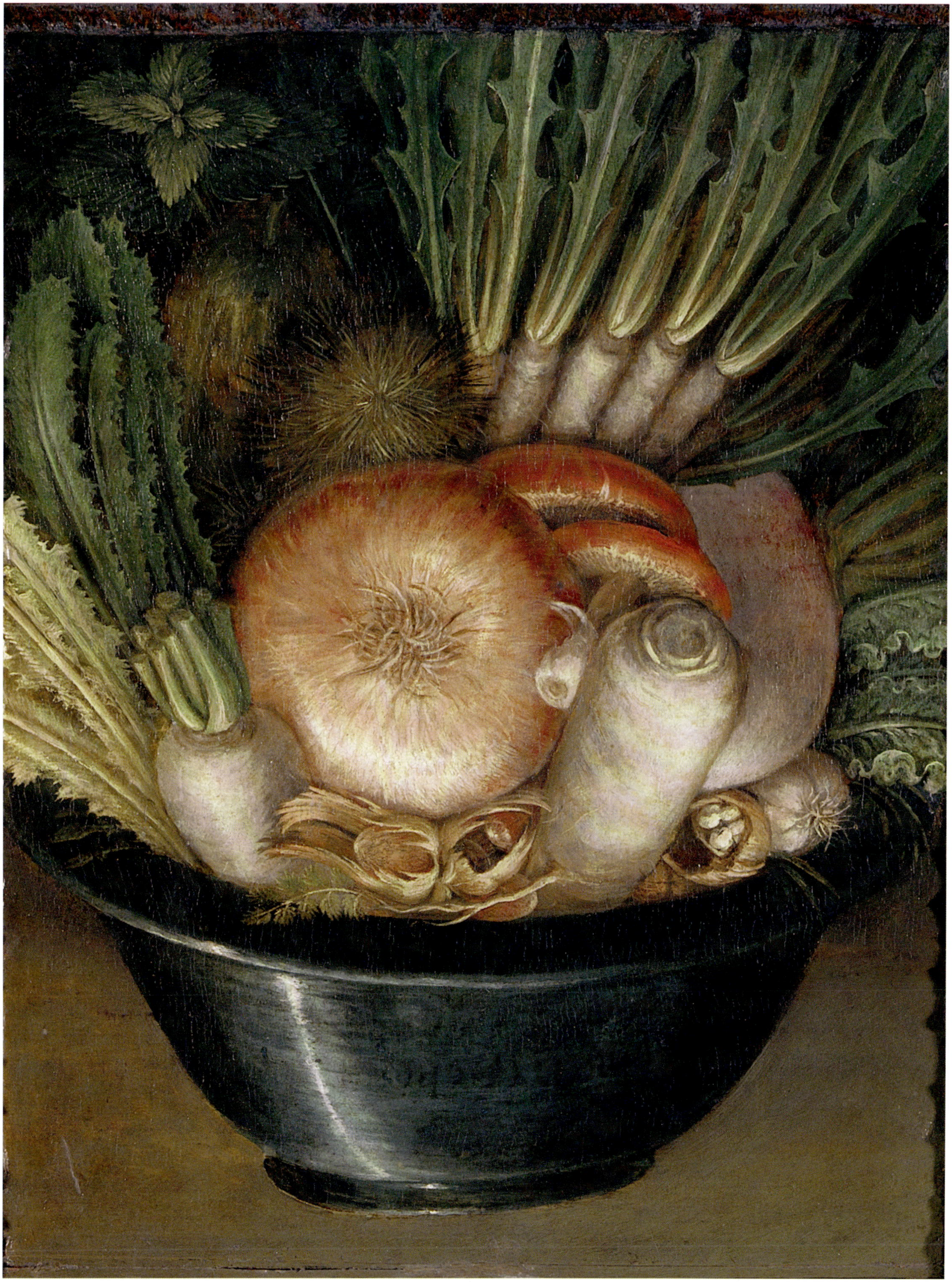

tories of Rudolf's court, as well as from the public, given that the painting has appeared in numerous international exhibitions.
The genre of the type of *capriccio* or grotesque (or *rabisch*, to use the term adopted in contemporary Milanese writing on art) that consists of an invertible head had already been codified by Giovan Paolo Lomazzo, who in his *Trattato* asserted that "figures can again be made in the same way that are perfect to see, [and] that when turned upside down [the picture, *Author's Note*] appear to the eyes as other figures, very different from the ones seen before" (Lomazzo 1584 [1974], 305). Arcimboldo's invention was in line with his more famous allegories of the *Elements* and the *Seasons* which the accompanying poem by the humanist Fonteo defined as "whims" (*picturae grillum*) on the basis of the Plinian source or as "chimeras" (Kaufmann 1976a). A sort of alchemical transmutation that in essence followed the literary model of Ovid's *Metamorphoses*, something he had already experimented with in the *Elements* and the *Seasons.* The basin filled with simple vegetables, turned upside down, is transformed into a merry and ambiguously phallic portrait, at least according to Calvesi's interpretation (1987), that makes use of a fairly blatant arrangement of an onion, a turnip and a turgid radish to suggest in a none too veiled manner the lewd image of the male sexual organ as it had already appeared in concealed fashion in the festoons of fruit in the Loggia of Psyche at the Farnesina. The upturned bowl turns into a sort of helmet, the abundant foliage into thick hair and a flowing beard. Two mushrooms are now the vegetable gardener's fleshy lips, walnuts and hazelnuts his eyes, the onion and turnip the lips and the radish the nose-phallus, in a surprising analogy – as Berra has shown (2000) – to the declaration made in Gian Battista della Porta's *Physiognomonia* that *nasus correspondet praeputio* (della Porta 1586, 71).
Similar *jeux d'esprit* were also present in the imperial collections and in this connection we cannot fail to cite the nobleman Ottavio Landi, who in 1573 described a vase of flowers in Maximilian II's collection that, when turned upside down, became an incredibly ridiculous face, or the portrait of Johann Ulrich Zasius "made up entirely of deeds, forms, receipts, letters and memorials" (Rudolf 1995, 166 no. 3, taken up in Berra 1998a, 59, and Berra 2000). The inventory of the Treasure Chamber in Prague also records originals by Arcimboldo very similar to the picture in Cremona, such as a "head composed of herbs" or a "face composed of turnips" (Zimmermann 1905, XLIII; Venice 1987, 134 no. 1062, 135 no. 1080). The vagueness of these descriptions does not permit us to make any reliable judgement with respect to the possibility that the second picture cited above might correspond to the painting now in Cremona. The hypothesis has recently been put forward (Kaufmann 1988c), but does not appear to have been unanimously accepted (Berra 2000).
In contrast to what has hitherto been claimed, the letters that it seems possible to make out on the basin do not form a signature and the reading of them as "Arcimboldus" is probably a suggestion due to the chance sequence of a number of marks, perhaps not even the result of successive interpolations by a would-be forger. Laboratory tests carried out on the panel by Mario Lazzari on several occasions have in fact demonstrated that these signs do not all pertain to the original layer of paint and are concentrated in a localized area of abrasion. X-ray photography has also uncovered the traces of an earlier version with the bowl and vegetables in a different position, leaving open the possibility that it was only while working on the picture that the painter had the idea of making the head reversible, or at least that it became so only by degrees and through successive adjustments. A first, carefully drawn composition has remained in the state of a sketch, and on top of this the painter outlined the final version, with the help of a number of incisions. Infrared reflectography in particular has revealed the presence of a tuft of leaves that originally partially covered the basin, and of other leaves in a different position than the present one that were subsequently concealed by the superimposition of the onion, the husk on the cheek and the roots that simulate the beard.
As far as the date is concerned, the propensity is to place the execution of the *Vegetable Gardener* close to that of the *Portrait of Rudolf II as Vertumnus* of 1590, and in any case after the painter's return to Milan (1587). Indeed the technical precision and care taken over the execution seem to date the picture in Cremona to some time after the series of *Elements* and *Seasons*, but perhaps earlier than the *Vertumnus* on the grounds of a still naturalistic and experimental approach that takes on a more controlled formal rigour in the phytomorphic portrait of Rudolf.

Mario Marubbi

Bibliography: Camelli 1931, 310; Puerari 1951, 178; Calvesi 1987, 40, 44-46; Kaufmann 1988c, 170; Porzio 1990, 118; Berra 1996, 118-119; Danesi Squarzina 1996, 50; Kaufmann in Prague 1997, 393; Paliaga 1997, 101; Berra 1998a, 201-202; Berra in Cremona 2000, 210-211 (with complete bibliography); Lazzari in Cremona 2000, 141-142; Berra 2003, 84-85; Berra in Marubbi 2003, 144-145; Marubbi in Gregori, Bayer 2004, 214-215.

IV.33
Giuseppe Arcimboldo (?)

Reversible Head with Basket of Fruit, c. 1590
Oil on panel
55.9 × 41.6 cm
New York, French & Company

If seen as a composite head, this painting represents another type of "ridiculous head" familiar in Arcimboldo's œuvre. Turned upside down, it becomes a basket of fruit, comparable to the bowl of vegetables seen in the painting from Cremona also in this exhibition. This invertible quality is also shared with the Cremona painting, as with another painting invertible as a platter of meat (Stockholm, National Museum also in this exhibition cat. n. IV.31).
The possibility of reversibility was associated with Arcimboldo's composites by Lomazzo (Lomazzo 1974, 305). Invertibility seems to have been Arcimboldo's invention, and is recorded as present in a painting documented in a letter of 1573: this describes a painting owned by Maximilian II (first published in Rudolf 1995, 166).
Numerous details support the attribution of this recently discovered work to Arcimboldo. The name "ARCIMBOLD" is scratched into the back of the panel on which this picture is painted. It is executed on linden wood, a material commonly used as a support for paintings in sub-Alpine regions, both north of the Alps, including Lombardy. A stamp on the back (Transka Fideicommiss Wasa) indicates that it was owned by the trust of an old Swedish family, and the painting emerged on the market at an auction in Sweden in 1999. This Swedish provenance points to the collections of Rudolf II in Prague, because many works of art were stolen thence by Swedish troops during the sack of the Hradčany in 1648. This picture may perhaps be identified with a painting of a face of fruits recorded as being by Arcimboldo in the inventories of the Prague collections drawn up in 1621 (no. 1087: "Ein angesicht von allerlei obst vom Arsimboldo. [Orig.]") and 1635 (no. 35: "Ein contrafaict von früchten von Arcimboldo" [(Zimmermann 1905, XLIII, LIX)]. Similar paintings, without however Arcimboldo' name attached to them, are recorded in Swedish inventories from 1648 and following.
The features in the face of this picture when viewed as a composite head closely resemble comparable details in Arcimboldo's painting of Vertumnus. In both works the cheeks are composed of two apples, the nose of a pear, the lower lip of cherries, one eye a berry and the other a nut, while grapes make up the dangling locks of hair. These similarities indicate that this picture was conceived in close proximity to, and probably executed close in time to the *Vertumnus*, c. 1590.
However, the problematic present appearance of the *Vertumnus* makes specific comparison of the

facture of these two paintings difficult. Moreover, other possible comparanda, such as the well known *Seasons* and *Elements*, date several decades earlier, and reveal certain differences in touch, although a similar attention to structure, and handling of highlights, as well as attention to detail, and careful modelling, may be observed in all these pictures. More specific points of comparison must therefore be sought in later pictures by Arcimboldo: the treatment of highlights on the leaves, and the liquescent handling of grapes seem similar in Arcimboldo's *Flora*, which must be close in date to this work, c. 1589.

When seen as a still life this depiction of a fruit basket is therefore an important early representative of this genre. It antedates the famous *Basket of Fruit* (Milan, Ambrosiana) by Caravaggio, who might very well have known it (Berra 1996b; Berra 2000). It also anticipates paintings of fruit still life by Fede Galizia and Ambrogio Figino. It is known that Arcimboldo mediated the acquisition by the imperial court of works by both of them (Berra 2000; Kaufmann 1990, 78-80). It is thus possible that Arcimboldo, to whom this painting should be attributed, had an impact on both of them. It is also possible that this picture and other works may have had an impact on nature painting in Prague (Kaufmann 2007).

The date of execution proposed for this invertible painting, c. 1590, would mean that it would have been painted relatively close in time to works by the Italian masters just mentioned, as by others active in the last decade of the 16th and first decade of the 17th century. This late date, as well as unfamiliarity with other pictures by Arcimboldo of the time (the Vertumnus has problems of appearance; authentic versions of *Flora* [see Kaufmann 1988c, 170-171] have not been possible to see in person since the 1980) may have led some critics (but only in oral opinions) to think that this is a painting by an artist of a later generation, rather than one that in fact more likely had an influence on them. Exhibition here should help establish the quality of this work.

It has been observed that in its inverted form as a basket of fruit this painting might correspond to a depiction of the season of Autumn from a series of four seasons seen as composite heads. This form is also known from a print of a reversible head of a bowl of fruits by the early 17th-century Nuremberg artist, Paul Flindt (Berra 2000). Regardless of the validity of this proposal, the existence of the print again indicates the reception, and hence importance, of Arcimboldo's image. This image may be interpreted in many further ways, as has been recently demonstrated (Kaufmann, 2007).

Thomas DaCosta Kaufmann

Bibliography: Berra 2000; Kaufmann 2007; Kaufmann forthcoming.

IV.34
The Waiter
Oil on canvas
87.5 × 66.6 cm
Signed Giuseppe Arcimbol F and dated 1574
London, Private Collection

The Waiter is an anthropomorphic assembly of objects related to winemaking such as a cash tap, a ceramic ewer, a leather bound glass, a chianti flask, an awl, a tasting cup, a gradual dipstick, a pewter and a wooden wine-funnel and a hotte. The painting which is signed and dated in 1574 has the coat of arms of King Philip II of Spain on the base of the dish on the left. The labels around his neck are inscribed "Gerischer Wein" "Osterreicher.. Rheinische(er).. Nechte(rischer)...

The composition is related to a painting mentioned by Lomazzo (1584 [1974] and 1590 [1973]), which was commissioned by the Emperor Maximilian II for Augustus, Elector of Saxony in 1574 and which had the coat of arms of Saxony. This coat of arms can be noted in the bottom of the bowl that makes the shoulder part of the figure with ten crossbeams alternately black and golden, crowned with the squared wreath. The counterpart to this painting was a representation of a *Cook*. Both paintings were owned by a certain Dr. M. Müller in Prague. After his death his collection was dispersed. These paintings were executed on panel and measured 67 × 52 cm. Arcimboldo possibly made replicas of his paintings for the Kunstkammer in Dresden. Hainhofer who visited the Kunstkammer in Dresden in 1629 wrote that he saw "selzame Snackenköpfe des kochs und dess killers, von Ihnen appropiijrten gebrüchlichen instrumenten."

Görel Cavalli-Björkman

Bibliography: Lomazzo 1584 (1974); Lomazzo 1590 (1973); Doering, Hainhofer Reisen, Vienna 1901; Geiger 1954, 52, fig. 42; Alfons 1957, 93; Porzio 1979, 37-38; Rheims in Venice 1987, 118; Kaufmann 1988c, 168-169, Christie's, *Important Old Master Pictures*, 10 December 1993, London, no. 84.

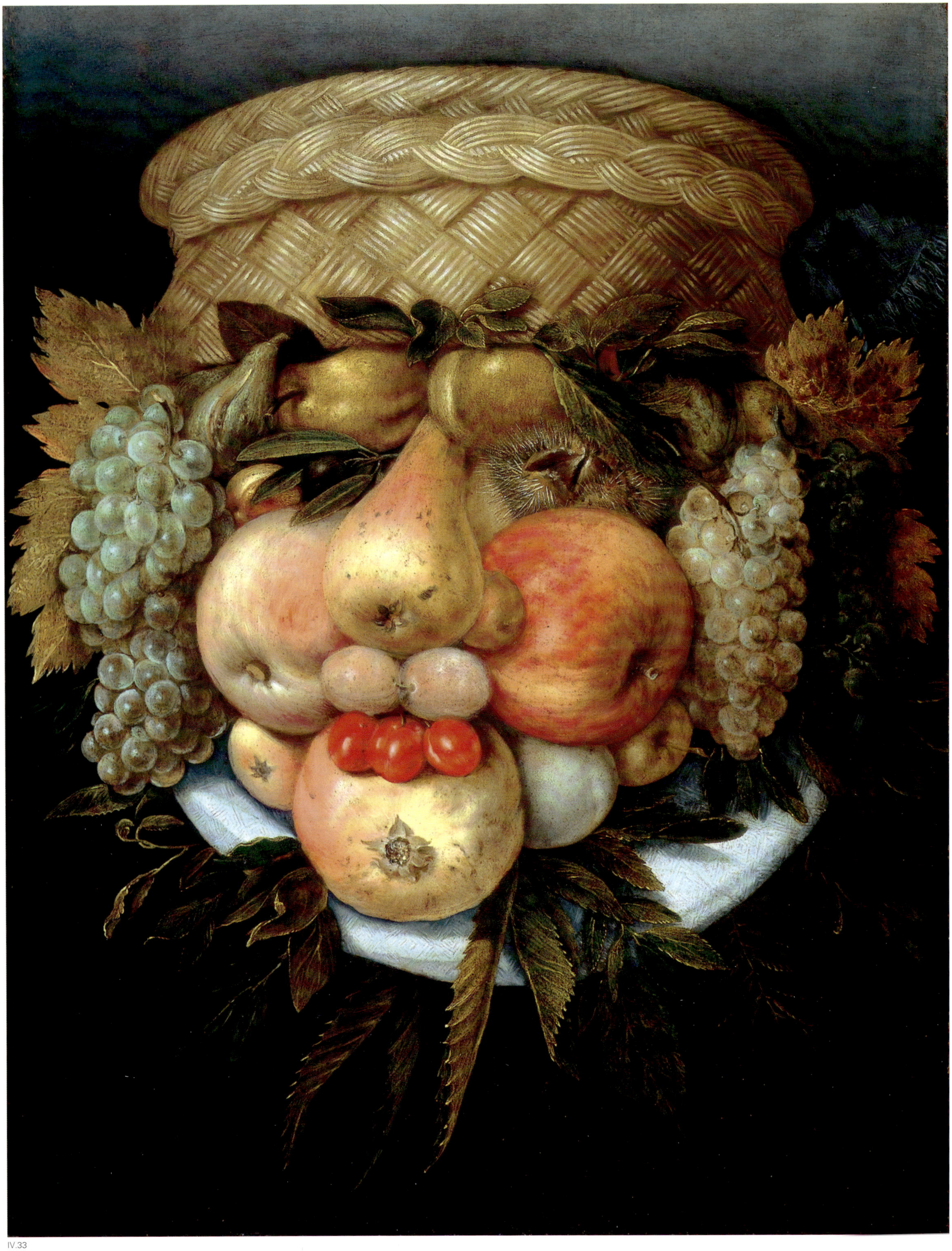

IV.33

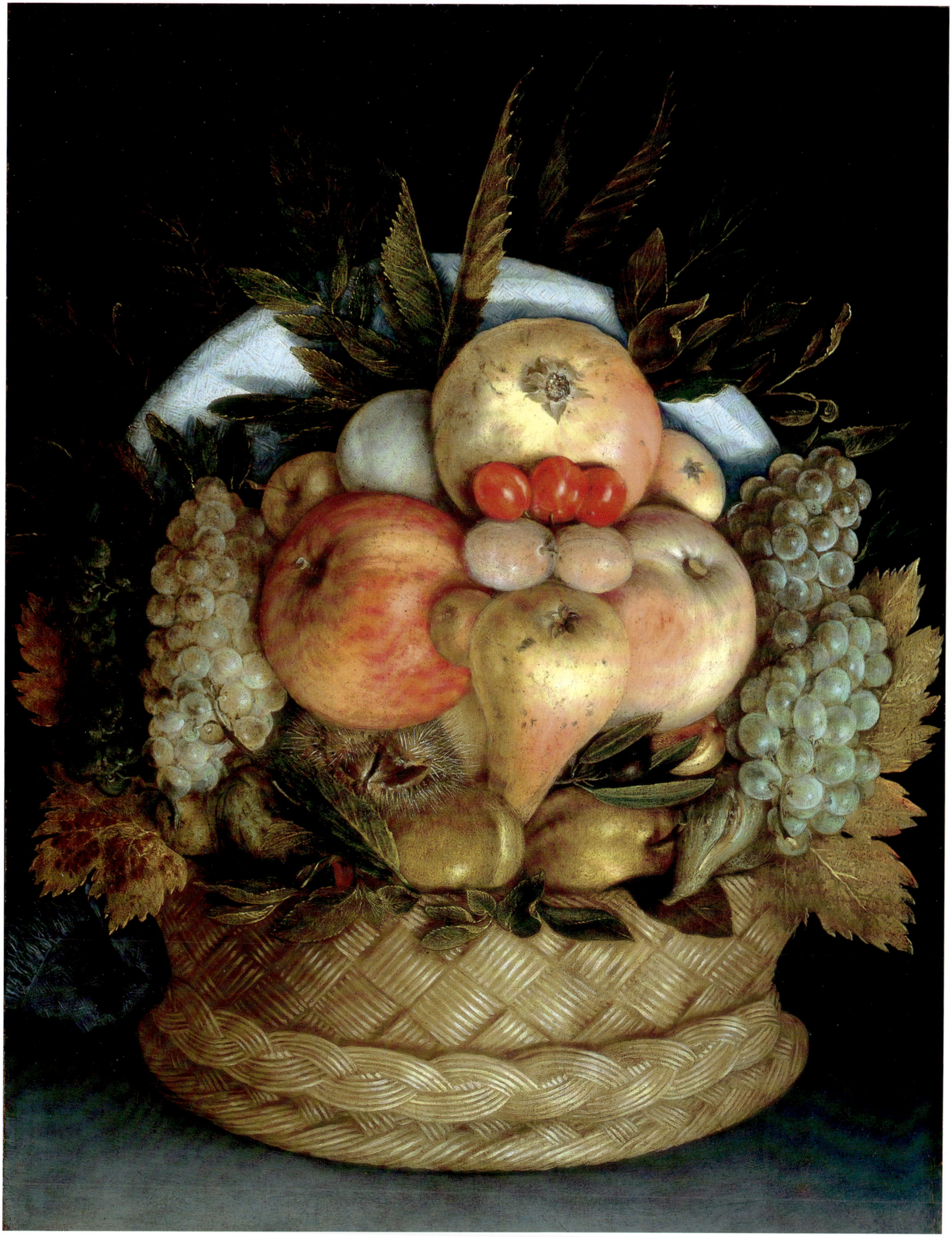

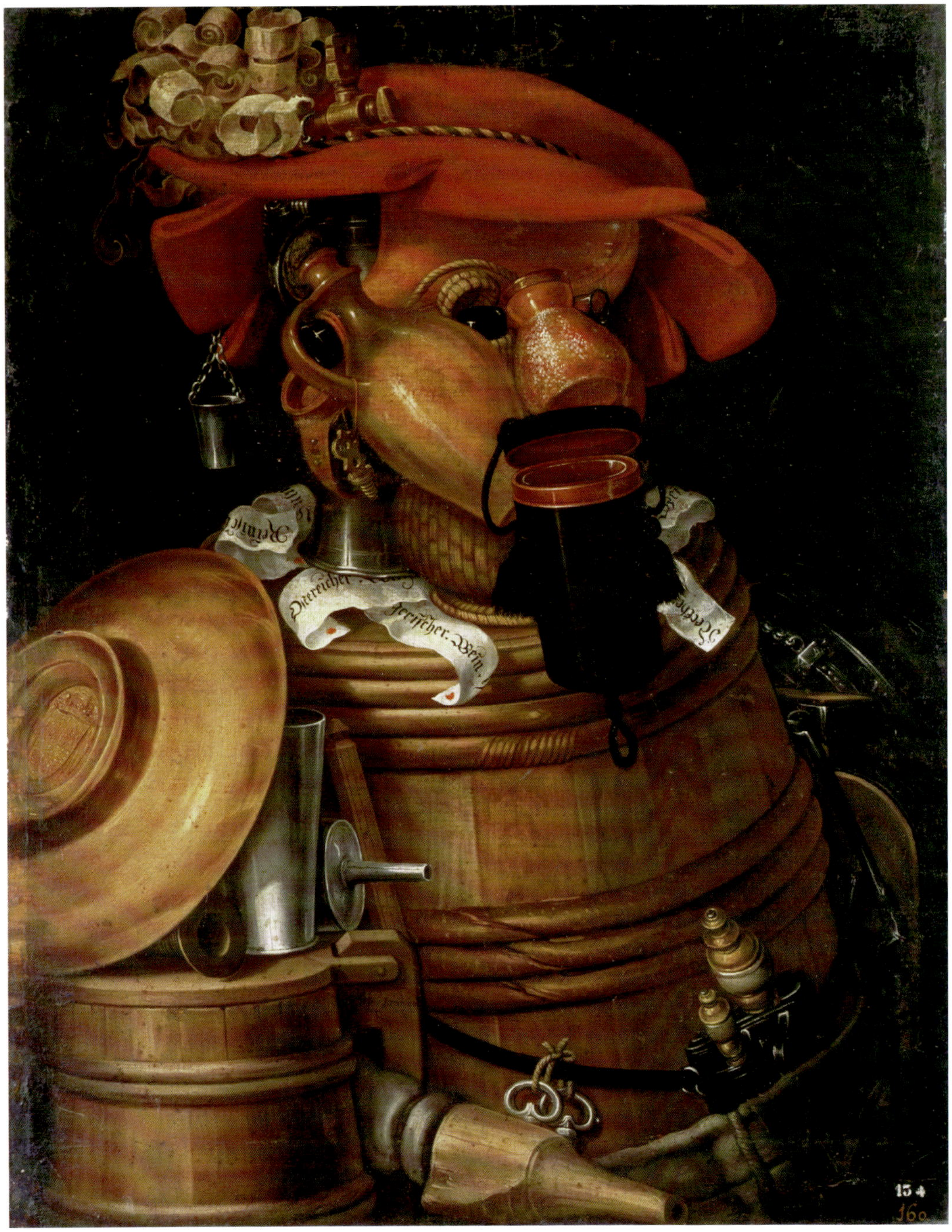

IV.34

IV.35
Carlo Urbino attributed
The Art of Cooking (verso)
Ink drawing in brown India ink over charcoal sketch
199 × 146 mm
Paris, École Nationale Supérieure des Beaux-Arts, inv. no. M.2249

The ink drawing from the École des Beaux Arts in Paris shows on each side a different draft for the composite portrait, *The Art of Cooking*. While the sketch on the front fills the entire page, the draft on the backside is contained within the upper left corner and depicted fragmentarily. Like the copper engraving of *The Art of Cooking* (cat. no. IV.36), the organic, composite construction suggests the hand of Giuseppe Arcimboldo. In Lomazzo's *Idea del Tempio* (1590) we read that Giuseppe painted a female *Kitchen* and a *Waiter* (cat. no. IV.34) as a pair for the imperial collection. If read together, the recto and verso sides could also be considered a pair. The finer, thinner facial traits and the kettle representing the breast on the recto side convey a certain femininity in comparison to the *Art of Cooking* on the verso side. With a bold, free line, the artist draws the individual components of pan, sieve, ladle and cup in order to combine them in the anthropomorphic portrait of a profession.

In the literature, this drawing has been attributed to an unknown Flemish artist, to Giuseppe Arcimboldo himself and to Carlo Urbino. The weakness of the execution makes it impossible to attribute this drawing to Giuseppe. Furthermore, the inconsistencies in the composition of the individual elements would more likely indicate the hand of a successor of Giuseppe. As opposed to Arcimboldo's anthropomorphic portraits, which are always the result of an adroit selection and arrangement of the different objects, the eye of the "female" *Art of Cooking* is classically drawn inside the cup's handle. The nose is not traceable to any cooking utensil; rather, the characteristic sweep of the wing of the nose was added by the artist.

Lomazzo (1584) and later also Luigi Lanzi (1796) already mention a representation of *Art of Cooking* by Carlo Urbino. This was identified by Hope (1987) in the copperplate dated 1569 (cat. no. IV.36). On the other hand, Cirillo 2005 recognized Carlo Urbino's highly personal drawing style in this Parisian drawing. It is entirely unlikely that it was derived from Arcimboldo's composite works.

Marion Romberg

Provenance: 1925 Jean Masson, from 1935 École des Beaux Arts

Bibliography: Lomazzo 1584 (1974), 304; Lomazzo 1590 (1973), 362; Lanzi 1831, 427; Legrand, Sluys 1955, plate 14; Alfons 1957, 92; Geiger 1960, 58, plate 44; Preiss 1967, plate 11; Gatti 1977, 106; Hulten 1987, 113; Hope 1987, 41-44; Hofmann 1987, 345, no. 27; Agosti 1998, 128-129; Coron 2001, 251; Cirillo 2005, 175-176, plate 80.

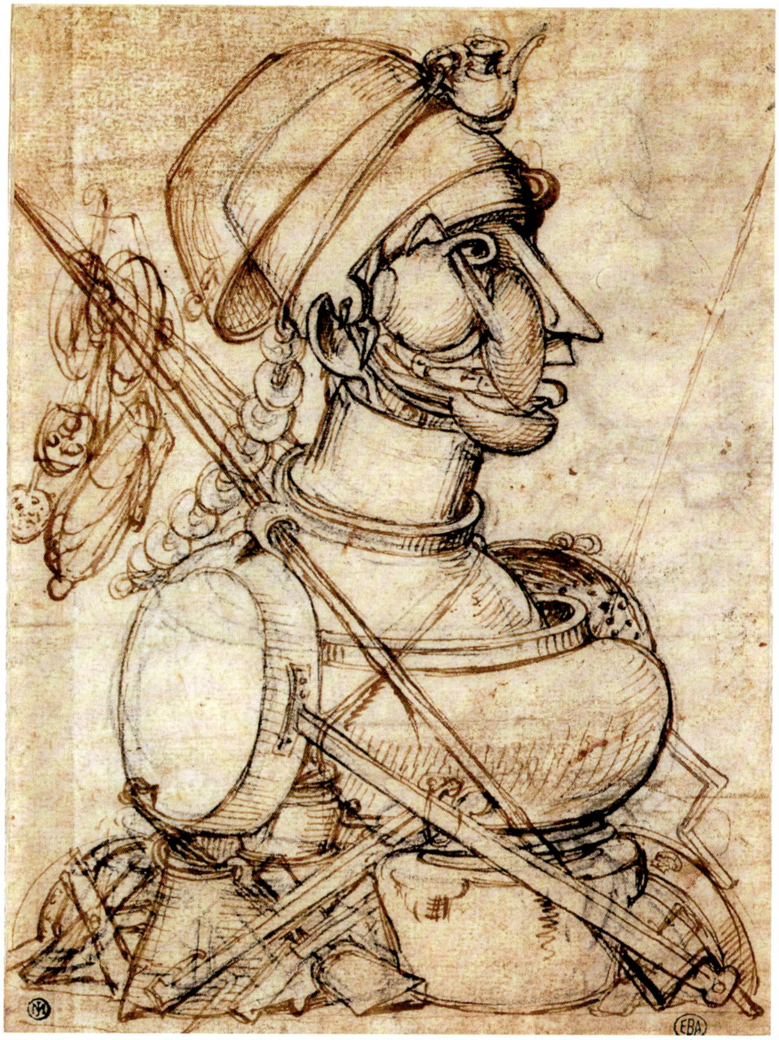

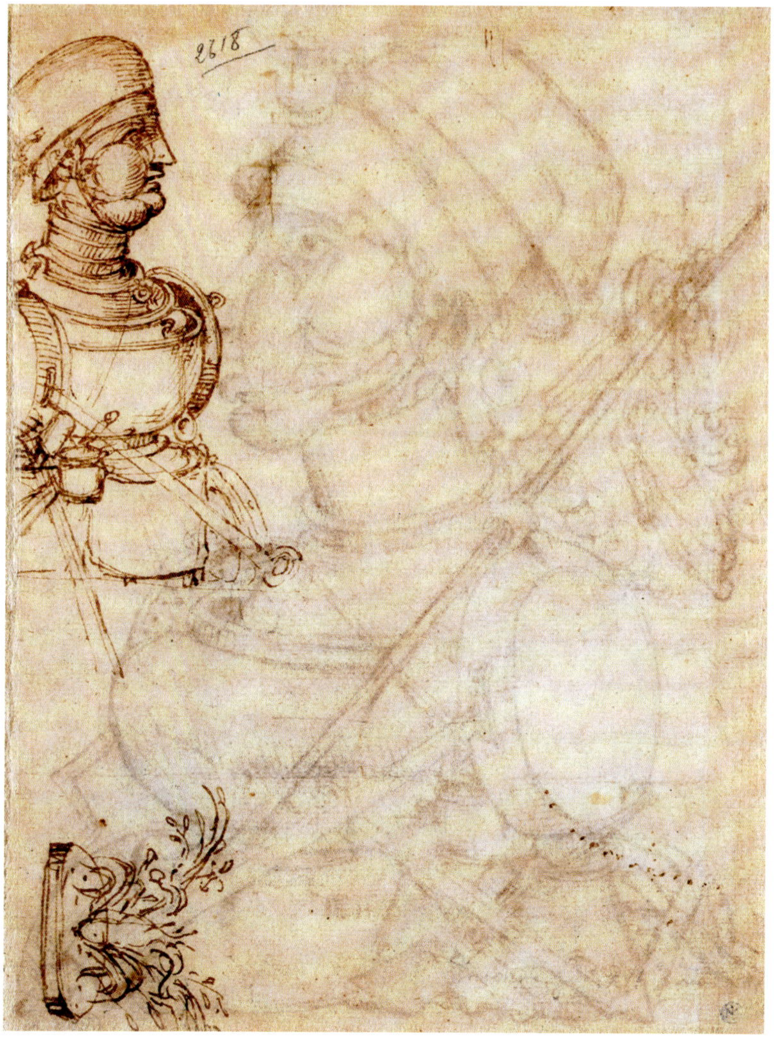

IV.35

IV.36
Anonymous
Humani Victus Instrumenta: Agricultura
1567
Copper engraving
373 × 250 mm
Previously in private collection of Benno Geiger

Anonymous
Humani Victus Instrumenta: Ars Coquinaria
1569
Copper engraving
379 × 277 mm
Previously in private collection of Benno Geiger

The two copper engravings of *Agriculture* and *Art of Cooking*, previously in the private collection of Benno Geiger, recall the organic, abstract construction of the amorphous portraits of Giuseppe Arcimboldo, such as *Fire* (cat. no. IV.18) and *Librarian* (cat. no. IV.29). In his *Trattato* from 1584, Lomazzo mentions Giuseppe in relation to an *Agriculture*, which is composed of "all of the instruments of this trade" (Geiger 1960, 54). A description by Ludwig Lanzi (1796) "of agriculture represented by plows, sieves, sickles and similar instruments" gives us a somewhat clearer picture. The engraving contains these instruments and many more. On top, it bears the inscription, "Realistic representation of an astonishing monster, which was recently seen by farmers in a well tilled field, 1567" (Geiger 1960, 55). This engraving, as well as the pendant of *The Art of Cooking*, were distributed by the Venetian publisher, Giovanni Francesco Camocio. In a letter of passage issued by Maximilian II to Giuseppe Arcimboldo on 2 June 1566 it is stated that the latter was to sojourn for an extended period in Italy, particularly in Milan (see the sources given by Leydi and Staudinger in this volume). From Morigia we know that Arcimboldo's copper engravings were widely distributed. Therefore, it is not impossible for Giuseppe to have commissioned Camocio with the engraving during his stay in Italy.
According to Lomazzo's *Idea del Tempio* (1590 [1973]), Giuseppe had painted a female *Kitchen* – "*la cucina in forma di femina*" – which was intended as a pair along with the *Waiter* (cat. no. IV.34). The gender-neutral impression of the present copper engraving therefore negates a connection with Lomazzo's statement and emphasizes his emblematic intention through the brief *inscriptio* "The tools of the human life" and finally through the sonnet in the *subscriptio* – "It is neither a portrait nor a likeness" (Geiger 1960, 55).
A clue regarding this copper engraving is possibly hidden in an earlier passage from Lomazzo's *Trattato* from 1584. He connects a portrait of a figure of the *Kitchen* or rather the *Art of Cooking*, with all their instruments, to Carlo da Crema, also known as Carlo Urbino. In 1987, on the basis of Lomazzo's testimony, Charles Hope attributed to Carlo Urbino not only *The Art of Cooking*, but also *Agriculture*. An attribution to him must be scrutinized. The methodical consequences in the skeleton of the individual objects as well as in their composition into an organic, abstract portrait imply that this work may have derived from a drawn or painted original by Giuseppe. The difficulty in convincingly emulating or copying Arcimboldo's composite heads is indicated by the two exhibits from the Kunstindustriemuseum in Copenhagen

(inv. no. I1/108 and I1/109). These are later, lower quality paraphrases by the publisher, Angelo Salvadori. Following this line of thought, it can not be excluded that the copper engraving was created on the commission of or after a work by Giuseppe Arimboldo. Lomazzo's statement about Carlo Urbino may lead back to the question of Urbino's activity as a copyist of famous originals for artists such as Bernardino Campi and especially to the drawing of *Art of Cooking* in the École des Beaux-Arts in Paris (cat. no. IV.35).
The popularity of Giuseppe's anthropomorphic portraits is also documented by a woodcut in the Germanisches Nationalmuseum in Nuremberg (inv. no. HB 2026) as well as a sideways adaptation of *The Art of Cooking* on a cabinet in the Danish Rosenborg Castle.

Marion Romberg

Bibliography: Lomazzo 1584 (1974), 304; Lomazzo 1590 (1973), 362; Lanzi 1831, 427; Alfons 1957, 90-92; Geiger 1960, 54; Hulten 1987, 114-115; Hope 1987, 41-44; Maiorino 1991, 54; Bora 1998, 37-56.

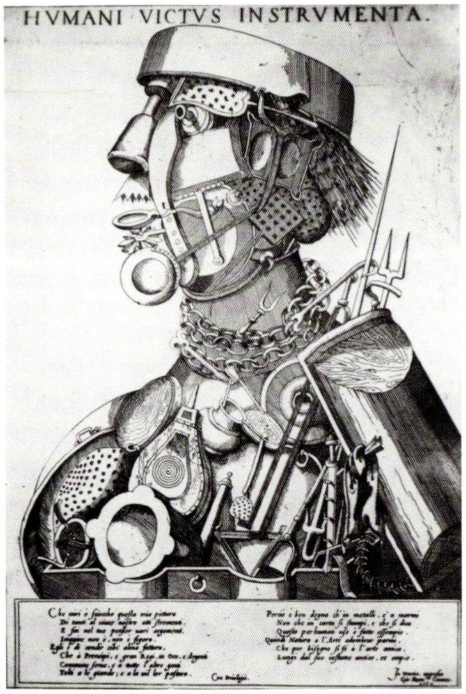

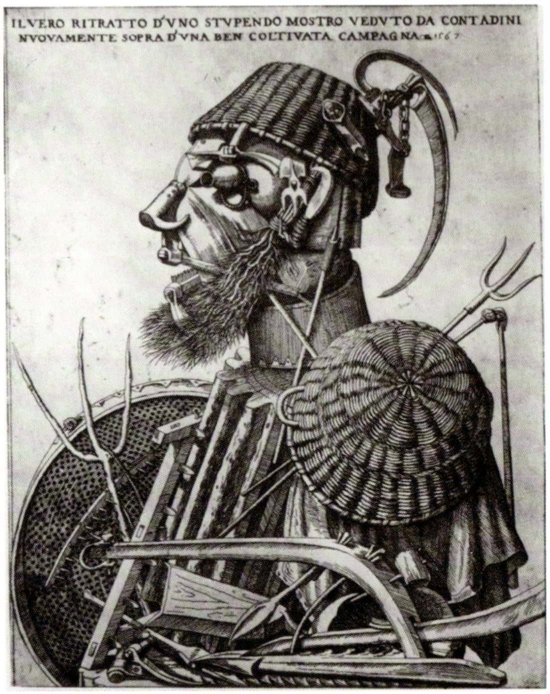

IV.36

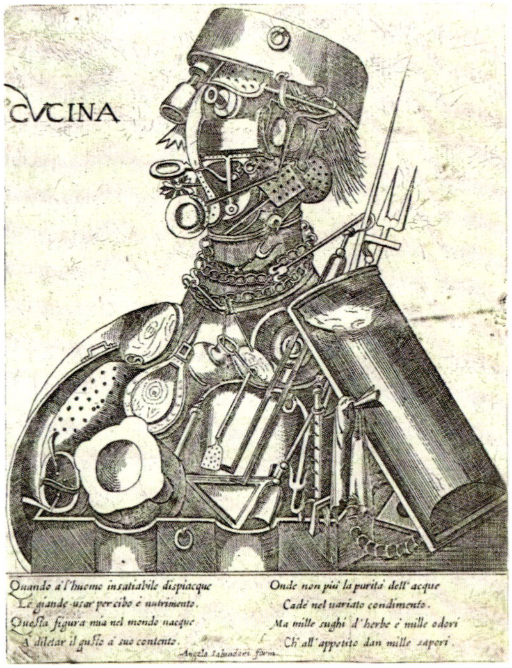

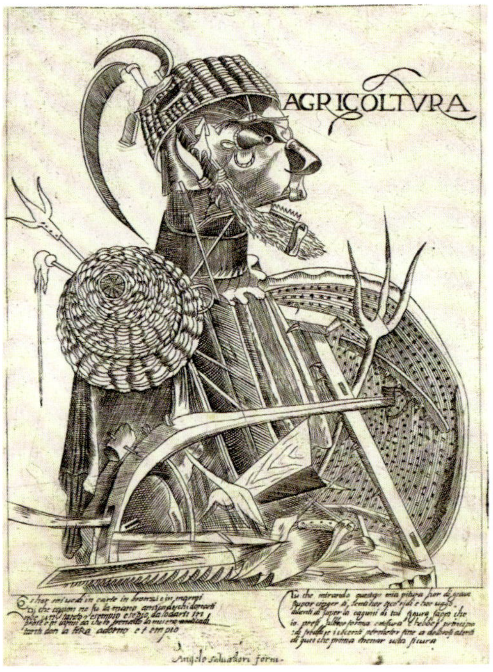

IV.37
Giuseppe Arcimboldo
Flora, c. 1591
Oil on panel
72.8 × 56.3
Paris, Private collection

This depiction of the Flower Goddess can be compared with two other paintings with the same motif that arrived in Sweden among the spoils taken from Prague 1648 and which remained in private Swedish ownership until 1965. The first painting was signed and dated 1589 with a secondary inscription: LA FLORA DELL'ARCIMBOLDO. The second painting also arriving from Prague to Sweden was somewhat larger, with neither signature nor date. In the inventory of Queen Christina's collection drawn up in 1652, both paintings are listed under the heading "*medelmåttiga Schillerir*" i.e. medium-sized paintings as nos. 293, *ditto on panel, which is a female figure with flowers over all*, and 294, *ditto with a female figure*. Prague is given as their provenance. In the inventory in French from the following year signed by Du

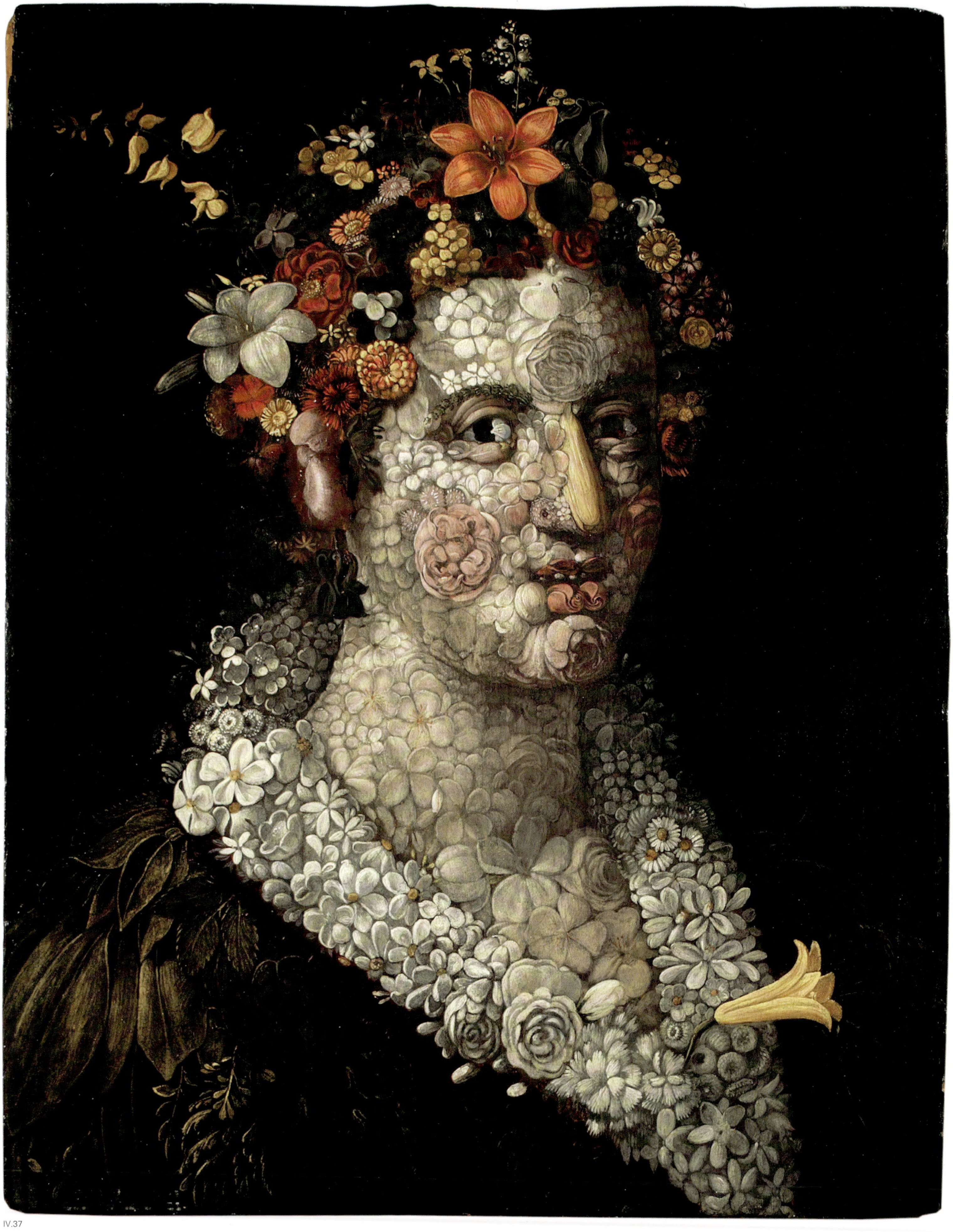

IV.37

Fresnes, the two paintings are numbered 295 and 296: *Un tableau de moyenne grandeur, une femme couvert de fleurs, sur bois* and *Dito, representant une femme.* It is probable that Queen Christina gave them away before she left Sweden and that they were preserved at some country manor until they were bought in the 1860s by the collector Christian Hammer. In 1870 they are listed in his property as: *Arcimbaldi, Giuseppe, two female heads, formed by flowers. On panel: from the collections of Count Fersen and Gyldenstolpe* (Alfons 1956, 132). Hammer sold most of his collection in Cologne in 1894. Both paintings were listed in the catalogue but were not sold at the auction. They were most probably returned to their owner. In 1905 they are listed in Bukowski's auction catalogue and subsequently in 1910 in a catalogue of the collection of a certain Oscar Wollert. They were bought at an auction at the Svensk-Franska konstgalleriet in 1932 by Dr Axel Wennergren. Both paintings were sold at Sotheby's in London on 24 March 1965 (lots 32 and 33).

The Paris painting seems to be the painter's own replica of the signed Prague painting referred to above. Individual flowers display minor deviations. The major difference can be found in the somewhat less uniform flesh tints in the Paris painting and the clearer emphasis on the individual blossoms. The collar of white flowers is terminated at the bottom by a yellow lily, a symbol of fertility.

The original Flora composition was praised by many, and authors dedicated their texts and poems to the painting. It is described by Lomazzo in the following words:

"Remembering his promise to the emperor he now painted a half-length image of a very beautiful woman, composed of flowers, painted from nature and so placed that in the skin of the face and the various parts of body were placed those most naturally inclined to represent these parts, and with a headdress formed of almost all the others, with the exception of those that are white, which are clustered as a kind of trimming for her dress, on which one can see lifelike renderings of the leaves belonging to most of the flowers included in the painting. From a distance this depicts only a very beautiful woman and close up, even though it still appears to be a woman, it also depicts flowers and leaves, combined and composed. And as indeed this is a peerless work, many ingenious men have extolled it in various poems in Latin and Italian, and among the latter Gio. Filippo Gherardino with a strophe in which he introduces Flora herself, who speaks to the emperor to introduce herself to him, as well as Father Gregorio, the canon of the Order, with the following madrigal:

Son io flora o pur fiori?
Se fior, come di Flora
Ho col sembiante il riso? e s'io son Flora,
Come Flora è sol fiori?
Ah non fiori son io, non son'io Flora,
Anzi son Flora, e fiori,
Fior mille, et una Flora,
Vivi fior, viva Flora
Però che i fior fan flora, e Flora i fiori.
Sai come? I fiori in Flora
Cangiò saggio Pittor'; e Flora in fiori.

(Am I Flora or only flowers? If flowers, how then can I have the same smile as Flora? And if I am Flora how can I then be Flora and only flowers? Oh, I am not flowers, I am not Flora. Indeed I am Flora, indeed I am flowers, a thousand flowers and one Flora, living flowers, living Flora, for the flowers shape Flora and Flora the flowers. Do you know how? The sagacious painter transformed the flowers into Flora and he transformed Flora into flowers.)

Lomazzo adds that this and another madrigal by Gherardino "were sent by Arcimboldo to his Imperial Majesty with the painting, who in recompense showed how highly he valued it and liked it" (Lomazzo 1590 [1973], 156f.; Alfons 1957, 129-133). A third madrigal praising the painting has been discovered by Benno Geiger, written by Gherardo Borgogni in his *Nuova Scielta di Rime* from 1592 (Geiger 1960, 72).

Görel Cavalli-Björkman

Provenance: Paris, collection Lebel

Bibliography: Alfons 1957, 128-133; Geiger 1960, 72; Pieyre de Mandiargues 1978, 94-96; Venice 1987, 158-159, 161; Berra, 1988, 11-45; Berra, 2000, 64.

IV.38
Giuseppe Arcimboldo
Vertumnus, c. 1590
Oil on panel
68 × 56 cm
Balsta, Sweden, Skokloster Slott

Arcimboldo's *Vertumnus* has been celebrated since the time it was painted. In *Idea*, published in 1591 (Lomazzo 1590 [1973]), Gian Paolo Lomazzo says that Rudolf II was eagerly waiting to receive the painting, and poems were written about the picture by other Milanese contemporaries. Many of these were collected in a booklet edited in 1591 by the artist's friend and housemate Giovanni Filippo Gherardini, and sent to Rudolf II from Milan along with the painting when it was sent to the emperor. According to Gherardini's preface, Arcimboldo seems to have known and approved of this action; two poems by the artist are included in the booklet (Berra 1988, Kaufmann forthcoming, and the essay by Kaufmann in this catalogue). Some of these poems were published by their authors elsewhere as well.

The best known of these poems was also published in 1591 by Gregorio Comanini in *Il Figino* (Barocchi 1962). Comanini indicates that the painting of Vertumnus is actually a portrait of Rudolf II in the guise of the god of the seasons. *Vertumnus* may consequently be read as the culmination of the expression of imperial iconography in these earlier series, as explicated by the poems by Fonteo that had been written to accompany the first versions of these works when they were given to Maximilian II (Kaufmann 1993, 100-128). The emperor is represented as god of the seasons, comparable to the god of the elements; fruits and flowers from different seasons flourish in his face, suggesting the peace, prosperity and harmony of his reign; their conjunction betokens the Golden Age, which has returned with his reign.

An aetiological elegy by the Roman poet Propertius (IV: 2 – see Kaufmann 1993, 129-135) reinforces these themes, and supplies sources for the choice of many of the particular fruits seen in the face. It is also imitated in the poem Arcimboldo wrote on his own picture that was included in the booklet compiled by Gherardini (Kaufmann forthcoming). Propertius and some of the poems written on Arcimboldo's picture also set up several comparisons, in the spirit of the *paragone*, between art and nature, between ancient and modern, and between poetry and painting.

Comanini also provides a key to understanding how this picture of the emperor as a composite head is also a serious joke, speaking of it as a monster, a hieroglyph, and a Silenus. The image of Rudolf II as Vertumnus thus also epitomizes the ultimately Erasmian approach of Arcimboldo's most familiar images (Kaufmann forthcoming and the essay above).

During the 1980's cleaning, restoration, and inpainting of this picture were carried out, leaving what may be regarded as controversial results, and in any event making judgement of the surface qualities and execution of this painting difficult (Makes 1988).

Thomas DaCosta Kaufmann

Bibliography: Gherardini 1591; Geiger 1954, 72-78, 157; Legrand, Sluys 1955, 54; Alfons 1957, 134-139; Barocchi 1962; Lomazzo 1973, 364; Kaufmann 1978; Porzio 1979, 39, 41, 44, 45, 74, 75; Venice 1987, 94, 96, 103-104, 165, 185-189; Essen-Vienna 1988, 224-5; Makes 1988; Kriegeskorte 1988, 44-47; Kaufmann 1988; Berra 1988; Kaufmann 1990; Kaufmann 1993, 67, 68, 101, 126-135; Kaufmann 1995, 184, 191; Kaufmann 2007; Kaufmann forthcoming.

IV.38

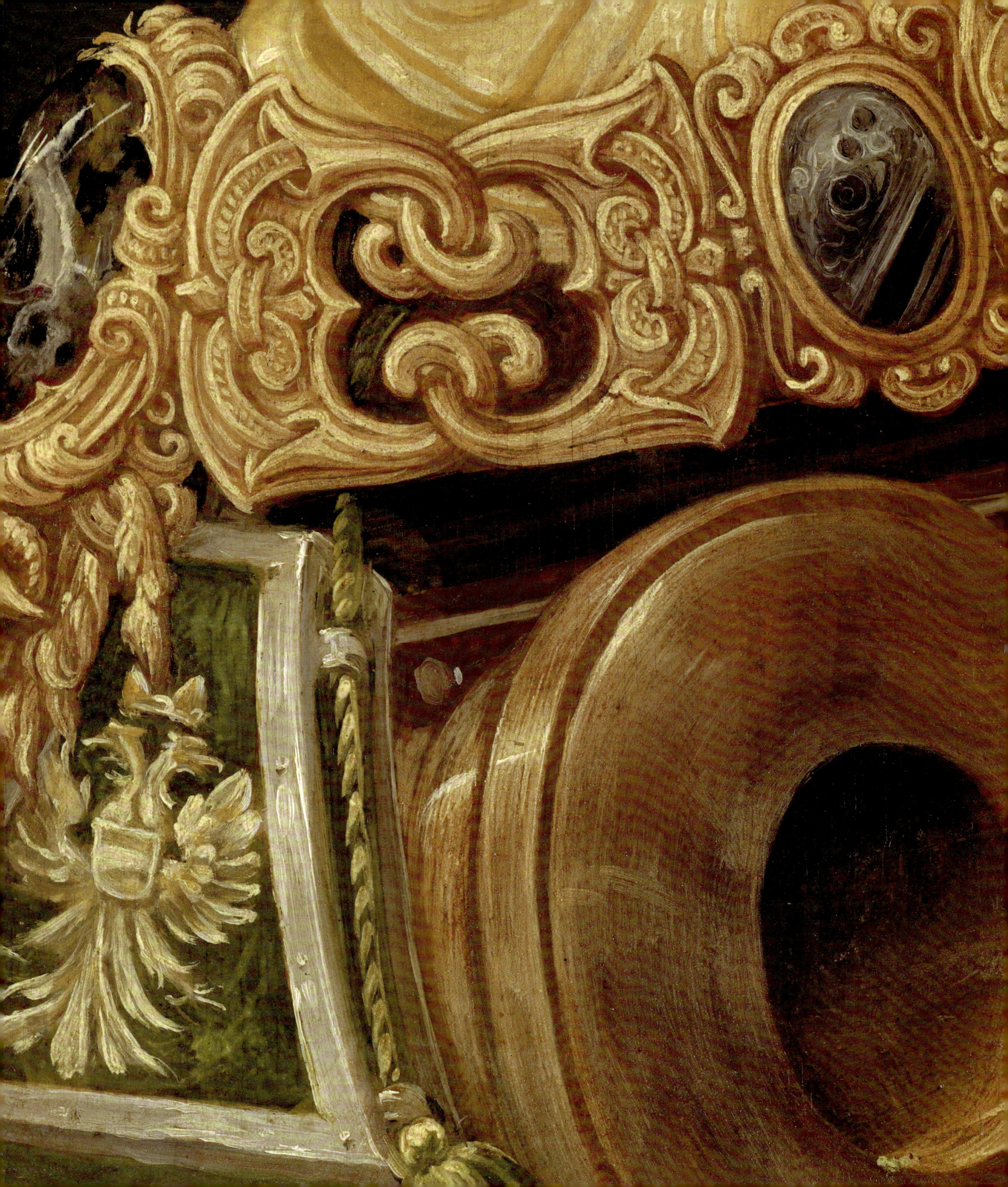

Franz Kirchweger

Between Art and Nature: Arcimboldo and the World of the Kunstkammer

Emperor Maximilian II's "Archive of Wisdom"

In his work, *L'Idea del Tempio della Pittura* (1590), Giampaolo Lomazzo referred to the homage paid to Arcimboldo by Emperor Maximilian II (reg. 1564-1576) (*fig. 1*) who commissioned several works from the ingenious artist in order to enlarge and broaden his outstanding museum worthy of eternal remembrance[1]. The emperor's collection was similarly praised by Samuel Quiccheberg, who worked in Munich for Duke Albrecht V of Bavaria. In 1565, Quiccheberg wrote for him his treatise *Inscriptiones vel Tituli Theatri Amplissimi,* which can be considered the first theoretical design of a museum or collection organization of fundamental significance[2]. Maximilian II comes first in his list of famous collectors: "According to the testimony of many princes, he is also the greatest observer of this adornment that recalls the nature of this world, as well as an excellent provider for the archive, which is overflowing with the most beautiful things, making it seem as if nature itself, which blossoms the most in the new things, had given birth to him in these honourable times"[3]. Artists, agents and scholars worked in his service, in order to enrich the paternal treasure of antique memorials, with "tasteful pictures, created by the most eminent painters" and "so many wonderful things, conserved with such diligence", that the result should cause "the greatest wonder" among all.

Among these authors, no further information is to be found about the appearance and composition of the emperor's highly praised collection, nor on the context in which the pictures mentioned by Lomazzo were presented; however, the mention of Maximilian II's "Archive of Wisdom" in the Quiccheberg treatise as "by far the most demonstrative" example[4] makes it clear that it must have been a collection in the truest sens of Quiccheberg's ideas. Quiccheberg had conceived a universal museum that corresponded to the spirit and understanding of his time, a viewable and accessible encyclopedia of "all earthly existence"[5], in which paintings, sculptures, craftwork, antiques and exotic coins, medals and weights, as well as specially prepared animals, fruits, seeds, metals and minerals, musical instruments, clocks and tools, were organized and assigned their place according to five different classes. Such a "*theatrum amplissimum*" served primarily for the enrichment of knowledge[6], but was also understood as a place of 'memoria', inspiration and moral strengthening for aspiring artists, as indicated by Gabriel Kaltemarckt in his memoirs on the furnishing of a "Kunst-Cammer" (art chamber), published in 1587[7]. In the praxis, other significant aspects were that of entertainment and princely representation[8]. In this sense, Emperor Maximilian II also led noble visitors through his collection, which was apparently located next to his private apartements at the Viennese palace[9]. In 1572, he showed Elector August von Sachsen "piture et altre cose", among which the portrait of Dr. Johann Ulrich Zasius[10], composed of books and documents; in 1574 he also showed Henri de Valois "molte cose belle et singulari, cioè pitture, orologhi, instrumenti d'ogni sorte et cose cussi fatte" in the castle[11]. These little-known descriptions of the structure of the objects could be augmented by some entries in the emperor's chamber inventory dating from 1568 (published in 1995 by Karl Rudolf), in which gems, coins, hand-stones, shells, as well as furs, hides and skins of tigers and of "Indian goats" are listed[12]. They leave no doubt that Maximilian possessed an encyclopedic collection in the spirit of his time[13].

Giuseppe Arcimboldo and the kunstkammer

Among modern scholars, Julius von Schlosser already referred to the documented series of Arcimboldo's composite heads in various early collections (Gottorf, Dresden, Prague)[14] in his ground-breaking study on *Kunst- und Wunderkammern der Spätrenaissance* (1908) – to which can be added another series, present in the Munich kunstkammer in 1598[15]. He thus brought them in the context of these specific collections, whose complex meaning, microcosm-macrocosm analogy and use as "a document supporting the claims of princes to sovereignty over all areas of divine and human creation"[16] have since been greatly reevaluated and also better understood by research[17]. The context of the Habsburg kunstkammer has been repeatedly emphasized as central to an understanding of Arcimboldo's unusual pictorial inventions[18]; it is thus determined that his "manneristic, curious heads" were created as "two-dimensional art chamber pieces"[19]. Documented from the year 1582, the task of acquiring "antiques and art objects" as well as "animals and exotic birds from the new world" for Emperor

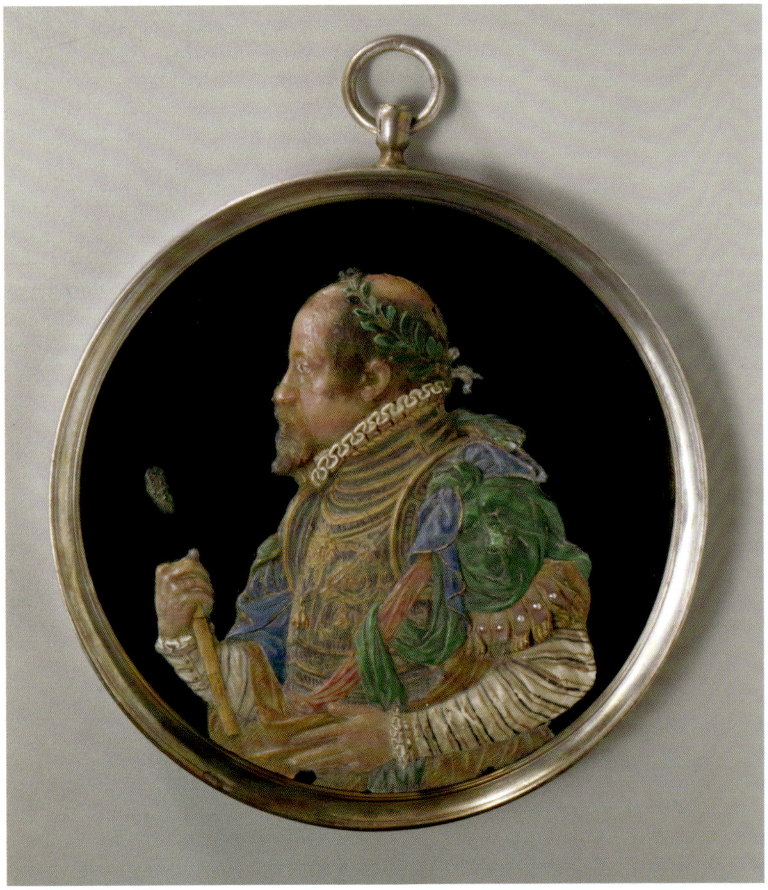

Fig. 1. Antonio Abondio, *Medallion Portrait of Emperor Maximilian II*, wax on obsidian. Innsbruck, c. 1575. Vienna, Kunsthistorisches Museum, Kunstkammer

Rudolf II[20] actually shows Arcimboldo in direct connection with the famous objects of the Habsburgs' collection, which must have absorbed a significant part of the kunstkammer of his father, Emperor Maximilian II[21].

The most important principle characterizing the kunstkammer of the early modern era was the idea to bring together objects of nature, *naturalia*, with those of man, *artificialia*, and to display them comparatively. It was commonly accepted at the time that "many things do not belong entirely to nature or entirely to art, but rather are shared by both", as formulated in Vincenzo Borghini's concept for the decoration of the *Studiolo* painted between 1570 and 1573 at the Palazzo Vecchio in Florence for Francesco I de' Medici[22]. In the cosmos or princely kunstkammers, this relationship between the world of nature and the world of art found its especially manifest expression in the form of those complex structures, which incorporated uncommon natural materials such as ostrich eggs, shells, coral, ores and minerals into the most purposeless objects of display[23]. They gained a very particular significance for demonstrating an artistic-manual proficiency as well as a spiritual-scientific capability, with which man approached the material and through a process of elaboration transformed it into something new and better. This understanding is emphatically supported by the inscription on a silver case dated 1562 by the famous Nuremberger goldsmith, Wenzel Jamnitzer, which appears there on a panel, held by the personification of philosophy on an artificial stone step: "The spirit of man and the science he has created surpass the creations of nature, transforming them into an improved art and eternalizing the otherwise so fleeting human activity"[24].

Only a very general impression of the exact composition of Emperor Maximilian II's collection can be gained, as indicated. In the following examination of the various manifestations of *naturalia* and the interplay between nature and art in the princely kunstkammer, we mainly rely on the thoroughly documented inventory of the Prague kunstkammer of his son Rudolf II[25], whereas two additional significant princely collections from the second half of the 16th century are of comparable value: that of Archduke Ferdinand II of Tyrol in Ambras Castle[26] and that of the Bavarian Dukes in Munich[27].

The Interplay of Art and Nature in the Kunstkammer

In reference to the inventory of natural objects listed, it comes as no surprise that foreign and strange, in other words exotic, species clearly prevail[28]. The fauna of the local environment only had a solid place in the form of horns and antlers of native animal species such as deer, chamois, roebucks and ibexes, which were only considered because of their size or abnormality[29]. Just as in the anomalies and aberrations, such as the animal skull with a tree (*fig. 2*)[30], the double calf-head[31] or the hen with three legs[32], they were considered "*miracula naturae*"[33]. Examples from the native plant world hardly ever appear in the inventories, except again in the form of special cases, such as petrified woods[34] and vines[35], connations of wood[36] or souvenirs of natural phenomena, such as grain that rained from the sky and apples from trees that blossomed in the winter[37]. There is a large proportion of stones and minerals[38]. One occasionally comes across crafted native *naturalia*, such as the horns of chamois, ibexes and aurochs, wild boar tusks[39], native stones made into a rosary[40] or elaborately carved fruit pips[41].

"*Quanta rariora tanta meliora*", the rarer the better, was Emperor Maximilian II's advice to his diplomat in Madrid, Adam von Dietrichstein, who was to acquire objects for his kunstkammer, thus clearly and concisely defining the fascination of his time for the strange and exotic in nature and art[42]. In this sense, the exotic *naturalia* among the inventories of the art chambers stand in the foreground as preparations as well as base material for artifacts. In scope and diversity, the relative inventories of Emperor Rudolf II must have been unique. The list of *naturalia* includes entire skeletons and dried preparations of various exotic mammals, birds and fishes (for example, lions, emus, crocodiles, tortoises, armadillos, sawfish), as well as numerous individual parts, heads, jaws, teeth, beaks, shells, skins and horns of the most varied species[43]. Numerous objects were unknown and "strange", yet the apparent efforts of the archivist, Daniel Fröschl[44], are attested by his consultation of expert naturalists, such as Charles de L'Écluse (Carolus Clusius) and Conrad Gessner[45]. A direct reference to nature studies done on objects in the kunstkammer is found in the starfish, which has been cut open to show "how it is made inside"; there are also two anatomized frogs[46]. From the plant kingdom there are foreign nuts, seeds and beans, as well as cloves[47]. The inventory of the Prague kunstkammer had just as extensive an inventory of exotic natural objects that had been crafted: vessels from rhinoceros horn, coconuts and Seychelles nuts[48], nautilus bowls, ostrich eggs and tortoise shells together with numerous other exotic objects formed one of the most important inventory groups of the entire collection[49]. An interesting position between preparation and art chamber piece was given to a bird of paradise, whose beak was gold plated and enamelled[50], and a fish, whose fins had been gold plated[51].

The inventories in Ambras and in Munich, regarding their scope and diversity of exotic *naturalia,* were clearly more humble, yet the preparations listed show very similar species (crocodiles, snake skins, sets of teeth from seafish, tortoise shells, horns, birds of paradise, sea conchs and snails, corals)[52]. In addition, there were stones and fossilized objects from the sea[53]. A special object displayed in the Munich kunstkammer was the stuffed elephant that Emperor Maximilian II must have sent there[54]. The plant kingdom is represented by coconuts, "Indian" beans[55], cinnamons[56], date trees and by the cedar of Lebanon[57], grains from cotton bushes and fruits and seeds from Palestine[58]. In parallel to the Prague inventories, there are also many types of objects of exotic *naturalia* that have been crafted[59].

The kunstkammer offered a large number of objects that tied the most varied, exotic natural materials together in what was more or less an elaborately conceived and designed context. Rightly, Thomas DaCosta Kaufmann also indicated parallels between Arcimboldo's "fantastic visions of nature and art" and some specific objects that were kept in the kunstkammer as whims and gimmicks of nature, as "*lusus naturae*"[60]. Among them, for example, were the objects found in nature, that had an unmistakable visual association to the forms of other objects: stones that looked like quills[61], nightcaps[62], coral branches[63], snakes[64] or like the member of a boy[65]. Similarly, there are pieces of silver or in the form of dragons and wooden growths resembling animal heads[66] and loaves of bread[67]. On various occasions fantasy was helped by an elaboration of the found objects, in order to strengthen their visual association. A sea stone, which was found with a coral growing from it, had the form of a deer with its antlers[68]; crooked pieces of wood were painted to resemble snakes[69]. Stones carried a special fascination, with their patterns and colourings that could resemble naturally grown landscapes or herbs[70]. These were ground into vessels, incorporated as slabs in furniture and became book covers and picture frames, where they significantly complemented the compositions of painted representations[71].

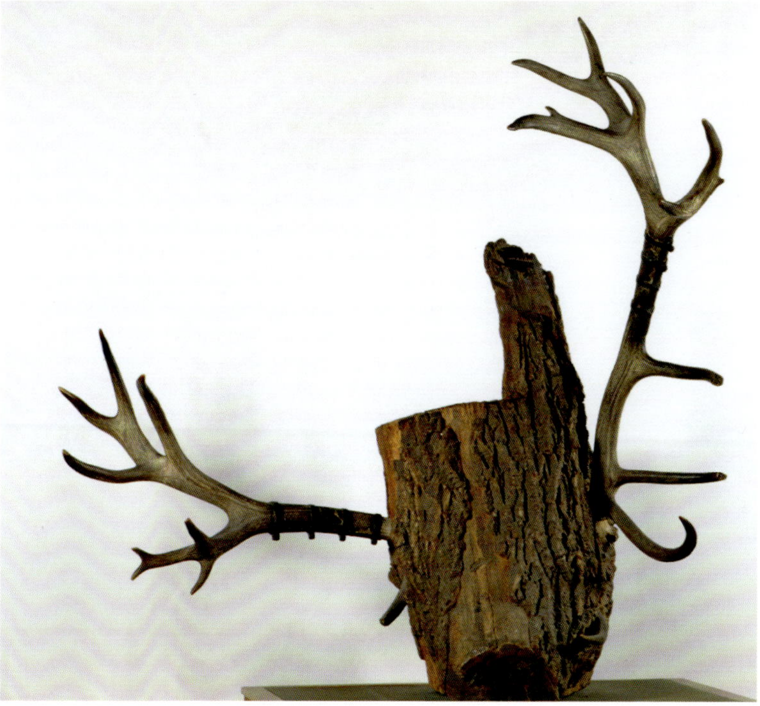

Fig. 2. *Tree Trunk with Antlers*. Vienna, Kunsthistorisches Museum, Schloss Ambras collection

In these cases, the game of nature was once again the starting-point for the game of man with nature; such artistic creations could be found in the kunstkammer in such exceedingly multifaceted forms. In the context of the aforementioned examples, the works that create a great overall pictorial context by combining many individual natural elements seem to be of particular importance. Among them are "Indian" feather pictures, in which the pictorial motifs are composed of many small, colourfully dazzling bird feathers[72], as well as small tables with representations that are composed of the minutest insect parts, grains and feathers[73]. They appear as a European answer to the astonishing pictures composed of exotic feathers. An especially substantial inventory group in the kunstkammer in Prague, Ambras and Munich was comprised of hand stones, familiar in various implementations (cat. no. V.17), in which mostly different stones, ores and minerals were composed into mountain landscapes and finished with figurative decor[74]. A similar meaning inhered, at least in Munich and Ambras, in the gaudy scenarios composed of coral branches, seashells and snail shells, as well as carved coral figures, displayed in their own glass

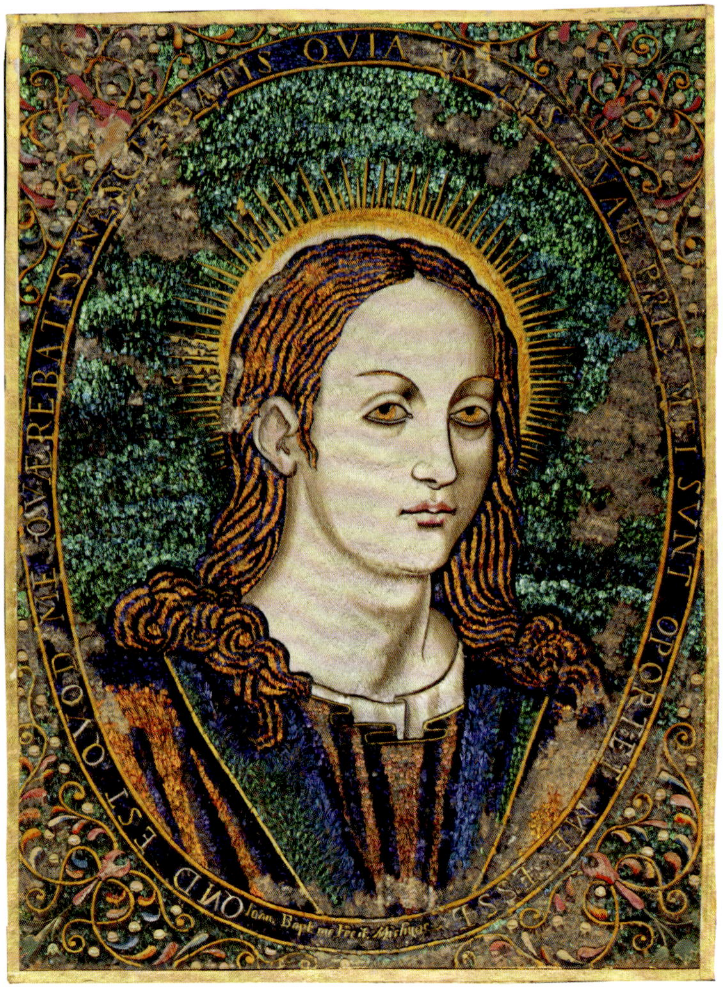

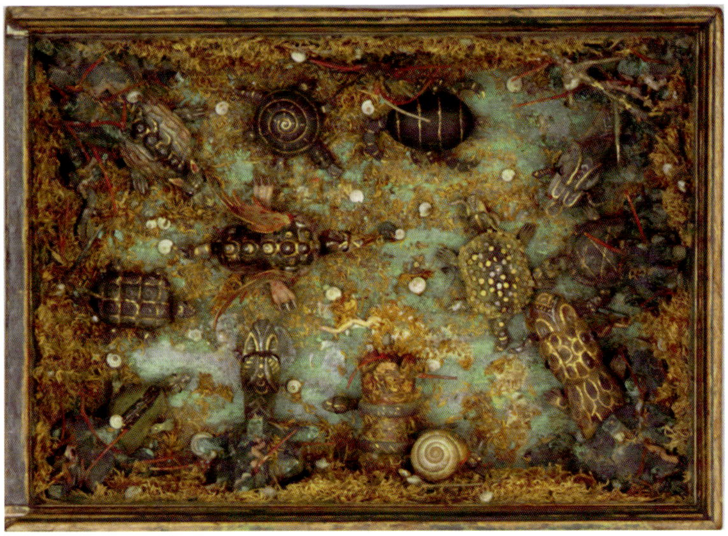

Fig. 3. Juan Baptista Cuiris, *Portrait of Christ made of Humming Bird and Parrot Feathers*. Mexico, Michoacán, 1550-80. Vienna, Kunsthistorisches Museum, Geistliche Schatzkammer

Fig. 4. *Shaker box: Turtles, Snakes and Snails made of Wood, Paper and Plaster, in a Mossy Landscape*, c. 1500. Vienna, Kunsthistorisches Museum, Schloss Ambras collection

cases, which portrayed multifaceted landscapes with Christian scenes (*fig. 3*) or caves with mythological scenes and sea creatures[75]. In the Munich kunstkammer alone there were 27 such compositions.

In these multipartite kunstkammer pieces a subordination of the *naturalia* under a larger, general design concept – as ultimately occurred in the works of Arcimboldo – was consistently present. Also familiar to the kunstkammer was a manifestation that truly seemed to have achieved the complete synthesis of the two poles, art and nature: casts from nature. In the form of natural casts, it was particularly characteristic of the kunstkammer and could especially allow a "host to demonstrate to his guests the dubiety of all sensory perception together with the truth that lies beyond the concrete reality"[76]. The principle of natural casts of plants and animals exists since the beginnings of history and was first taken up again as a technique in northern Italy in the 16th century (cat. no. V.8)[77]; it was carried to a particular zenith by Bernard Palissy with clay in France (cat. no. V.11) and by the previously mentioned Wenzel Jamnitzer with silver in Germany (cat. no. V.10). Numerous entries in the inventories of the kunstkammer in Prague[78], Munich[79] and Ambras[80] refer to small cast animals and herbs in silver, as individual pieces as well as parts of larger works of art, whose naturalistic effect was even partially heightened through painting[81]. The large silver fountain incorporating numerous natural casts created by Wenzel Jamnitzer between 1568 and 1578 for the imperial kunstkammer should be remembered here (cat. no. V.1)[82]. Also frequently mentioned in the kunstkammer inventories are plaster casts from nature: from the arms of the sovereign and other important people[83], to the feet of deer or heads of pigs[84], to hundreds of fishes, crabs, lizards, snakes, frogs and tortoises[85]. It is noteworthy that the result was called "conterfetisch", insisting on its imitative quality[86]. The princes themselves even dabbled in the casting and molding of natural materials. In the inventory of the Munich kunstkammer, we find not only the silver casts made by Duke Ferdinand of Bavaria[87], but also a case with sea plants, fish, crabs, vipers and lizards that Emperor Maximilian II is said to have single-handedly "formed from plaster *conterfetisch*"[88]. These cases could possibly be conceived of as similar to the famous "Schüttelkasten" ("shakers") from the Ambras collection[89]. Another piece listed in the Munich inventory is a majolica plate, which seems to be labelled as a gift of Maximilian II, decorated in the style of Bernard Palissy (cat. no. V.12) with figs, raisins, almonds and gingerbread: "all *conterfetisch*"[90].

This brief overview should provide a notion of the many manifestations of the correlation between the two poles of nature and art – from untouched *naturalia* to molds from nature – in the framework of the "princely kunstkammer", which was also, according to general opinion, the framework for Arcimboldo's works. How definitely involved Arcimboldo was in the sphere of the kunstkammer is documented by the previously mentioned task of acquiring specimens for Emperor Rudolf II. It is even more directly evident in a wax object that he created for the kunstkammer, according to Rudolf's inventory. In addition to a large number of wax embossings – primarily portraits and mythological scenes – there are some works which apparently sought the effect of lifelike imitation, such as the amputated, bloody hand of a woman or "all kinds of fruit from wax with colours" in a silver bowl[91]. Among them is the following entry: "Two wax pomegranates, entirely *conterfettisch*, one made by Giuseppe Arcimboldo and one by Jan Vermeyen, His Majesty's goldsmith" (*fig. 4*)[92]. According to this Arcimboldo created an imitation of a pomegranate in wax for the emperor's kunstkammer before 1587, as was later done by Jan Vermeyen, the chamber goldsmith of Rudolf II[93]. From the context provided by the immediately surrounding objects, it could be concluded that they were both included as artificial imitations of a natural model, intended to cause irritation, surprise and amusement in the viewer.

[1] According to Falchetta 1987, 179.
[2] See in general Roth 2000.
[3] Cited from Roth 2000, 167.
[4] Roth 2000, 165f.
[5] Berliner 1928, 329.
[6] Roth 2000, 37.
[7] Gutfleisch, Menzhausen 1989, 7.
[8] See the bibliography in note 17.
[9] Rudolf 1995, 167. About the problem where the collections were deposited under the emperors Ferdinand I und Maximilian II, see ibid., 225.
[10] Cited from Rudolf 1995, 166.
[11] Cited from Rudolf 1995, 225.
[12] Rudolf 1995, 231.
[13] On the great significance of Maximilian II's personal interests in natural studies, see Rudolf 1995, 175-179.
[14] Schlosser 1908, 88.
[15] Diemer 2004, (no. 2722) "Four fantastic heads, which represent the four seasons: (no. 2765) Spring is crowned with all kinds of flowers and lilies, his clothing covered with green foliage, the shirt collar is made of white flowers. (no. 2766) Summer with pears, apples, melons and cherries on his head, his body covered with grains and straw. (no. 2767) Autumn has grapes on his head, and hanging cucumbers and other similar fruits that grow in autumn; his body is covered with dew and frost. (no. 2768) Winter has a leafless forest on his head, a brittle nest in his beard, a plaited mantle around his body". See also the apparently Arcimboldesque compositions: ibid., nos. 2601, 2885.
[16] Walz 2000, 16.
[17] As an option for extensive literature on this theme see: Scheicher 1979; Lugli 1983; Impey, MacGregor 1984; Bredekamp 1993; Kaufmann 1993, 174-194; Findlen 1994; Grote 1994; Minges 1998; Kaufmann 1999, 389-399; Findlen 2004; Kaufmann 2004; Schramm, Schwarte, Lazardzig 2005.
[18] See, for example Alfons 1987, 67-85; Kaufmann 1998b, 42f.; Kaufmann 1999, 392.
[19] www.liechtensteinmuseum.at/de/pages/artbase_main.asp?module=browse&action=m_work&lang=de&sid=162800972&oid=w-582005152252843
[20] Cited from Geiger 1954, 125.
[21] Rudolf 1995, 170f.
[22] Cited from Walz 2000, 15.
[23] Kemp 1995, 177-196; Scheicher 1995, 115-125.
[24] Cited from Syndram 2005, 22f.
[25] Inventory of the Prague Kunstkammer from 1607-11, see the Bauer, Haupt Edition 1974, 1-140. For an overview of the kunstkammer, see Bukovinská 2005, 199-227.
[26] Estate inventory of Archduke Ferdinand of Tyrol, from 1596, see Boeheim 1888, Reg. 5556, CCXXVI-CCCCXIII. On the Ambras kunstkammer, see Gries 1994, 7-37.
[27] Inventory of the Munich kunstkammer from 1598, see Diemer 2004; on the Munich kunstkammer, see Seelig 1986, 101-138.
[28] Because of space constraints, the inventory entries for the mentioned aspects had to be partially restricted to the most exemplary quotations.
[29] Bauer, Haupt 1976, nos. 73-82; Diemer 2004, nos. 124, 178, 233, 628, 630. In Ambras, the antler trophies of native animal species are only located outside the kunstkammer, as part of the furnishing of the various rooms.
[30] Diemer 2004, no. 129.
[31] Boeheim 1888, fol. 483; Diemer 2004, no. 132; see also ibid., nos. 234, 2113, 2115.
[32] Bauer, Haupt 1976, no. 134.
[33] See note 30.
[34] Boeheim 1888, fol. 406v; Diemer 2004, nos. 539, 609, 2117.
[35] Diemer 2004, 763.
[36] Boeheim 1888, fol. 472.
[37] Diemer 2004, nos. 2094-2107.
[38] Boeheim 1888, fol. 370-371, fol. 377-379; Diemer 2004, nos. 369, 821, 1996, 2007, 2092, 2093, 2150. See here in general Rauch 2006, 157f.
[39] Bauer, Haupt 1976, nos. 53, 55; Boeheim 1888, fol. 404, 405; Diemer 2004, nos. 592, 1008.
[40] Diemer 2004, no. 288.
[41] Diemer 2004, nos. 589, 615, 784, 789, 798, 813.
[42] Distelberger 2000, 19-21.
[43] Bauer, Haupt 1976, nos. 2-12, 29-59, 83-241.
[44] Trnek 2001, 221-231.
[45] Compare Findlen 1997, 214f.
[46] Bauer, Haupt 1976, nos. 212, 218.
[47] Bauer, Haupt 1976, nos. 284-293, 301, 314, 315, 317, 318.
[48] Bauer, Haupt 1976, nos. 293-300, 303, 304 (mounted and un-mounted Seychelles nuts).
[49] Extensively on this: Rudolf 2001, 189-202; Bukovinská 2001, 205-219.
[50] Bauer, Haupt 1976, no. 136.
[51] Bauer, Haupt 1976, no. 227.
[52] Boeheim 1888, fol. 247, 402, 481-483v; Diemer 2004, nos. 810, 816, 887, 1098-1116, 1159, 1182, 1223-1227, 1431, 1488, 1491-1505, 1699-1706, 1729, 2062, 2064, 2065, 3359-3361.
[53] Bauer, Haupt 1976, nos. 242-248, 257, 259-268; Boeheim 1888, fol. 376v-379v (in the 6th case); Diemer 2004, nos. 189-198, 1994, 1999-2005, 2065.
[54] Diemer 2004, no. 3362; see Seelig 2001, 148; Opll 2005, 337-343.
[55] Boeheim 1888, fol. 463v, 464, 469.
[56] Boeheim 1888, fol. 479.
[57] Diemer 2004, nos. 380, 2111.
[58] Diemer 2004, 556, 559.
[59] See Trnek 2000, 30-36; Seelig 2001, 145-161.
[60] Kaufmann 1998b, 43. See also Daston, Park 1998, 255-301.
[61] Diemer 2004, no. 552.
[62] Diemer 2004, no. 599.

[63] Bauer, Haupt 1976, no. 258.
[64] Bauer, Haupt 1976, no. 271; it can not always be clearly determined whether the stones mentioned in the form of crabs, flowers and snakes were found in this form in nature or whether they were successively crafted.
[65] Bauer, Haupt 1976, no. 254.
[66] Diemer 2004, no. 235.
[67] Diemer 2004, no. 291.
[68] Bauer, Haupt 1976, nos. 242, 243.
[69] Diemer 2004, no. 627.
[70] Diemer 2004, no. 2017.
[71] Bauer, Haupt 1976, nos. 1400, 1401.
[72] Diemer 2004, nos. 903, 2017.
[73] Bauer, Haupt 1976, no. 1497.
[74] Compare for example Ambras 2004; Ambras 2006, 169-175, cat. nos. 3.13-3.15.
[75] Bauer, Haupt 1976, nos. 609-617; Boeheim 1888, fol. 401v-403 (9th case); Diemer 2004, nos. 1581-1589; on the feather pictures, in general: Mogne 2004, 38-79.
[76] Four such small tablets are conserved in Ambras (Ambras 2006, 85, nos. 2.30-2.33. They may have originated from the Prague kunstkammer: Bauer, Haupt 1974, no. 2349.
[77] Bauer, Haupt 1976, nos. 1614-1651; Boeheim 1888, fol. 64v, 68, 103, 349v, 363v, 365v-370, Diemer 2004, nos. 122, 123, 1368, 1390, 2009, 2010, 2012, 2023-2091, 2121-2147.
[78] Bauer, Haupt 1976, no. 1625; Boeheim 1888, fol. 413 (12th case); Diemer 2004, nos. 122, 131, 188, 232, 328, 352, 355, 387, 441, 509, 634, 827, 903, 1237, 1381, 1432, 1433, 1489, 1577, 1578, 1601, 1603, 1654.
[79] Scheicher 1979, 16.
[80] Kris 1932; Klier 2004; Lein 2006, 77f.
[81] Bauer, Haupt 1976, nos. 1532, 1548, 1549, 1551, 1552, 1695-1721, 1723, 2335-2337.
[82] Diemer 2004, nos. 570-574, 579, 580, 582, 583. The casts listed in Munich in gold (nos. 575, 578) and in lead (nos. 280, 281, 568) are exceptions for these materials.
[83] Boeheim 1888, fol. 8.
[84] See extensively Klier 2004; as an abstract, also Lein 2006, 77-78.
[85] Schürer 1986, 55-59; for a possible connection with Arcimboldo's allegories, see Alfons 1987, 67-85.
[86] Diemer 2004, nos. 1444, 1459, 1462.
[87] Bauer, Haupt 1976, nos. 1833, 1834, 1840, 1841, 2063, 2064; Diemer 2004, nos. 383, 1445.
[88] Bauer, Haupt 1976, nos. 1842-1845; Diemer 2004, no. 1461.
[89] Some comparison can also be made with the evidence of a snake that was formed from an appropriately coloured piece of marble, which was "gar artlich unnd natural", meaning both artificial and natural at the same time. Bauer, Haupt 1976, no. 1870. See also ibid., nos. 1869, 1871. In general, see also Klier 2004, 113-117.
[90] Diemer 2004, no. 1390.
[91] Diemer 2004, no. 1455.
[92] Ambras 2006, 95-100, cat. no. 2.42.
[93] Diemer 2004, no. 1457. Compare also ibid., nos. 1456, 1458.
[94] Bauer, Haupt 1976, nos. 2063, 2067. – On wax fruits, see also Boeheim 1888, fol. 78; on wooden fruits: Diemer 2004, nos. 555, 563.
[95] Bauer, Haupt 1976, no. 2065.
[96] Staudinger 1995, 263-271.

V.1
Attributed to Johann Gregor van der Schardt
(c. 1530 - c. 1581)
probably from a design by Wenzel Jamnitzer
(c. 1508-1585)
Flora, Ceres, Bacchus and Vulcan
(Allegories of the Four Seasons)
Nuremberg, around 1570
Bronze, fire gilding
H. 71.2 cm, 70.7 cm, 71.8 cm, 71 cm
Vienna, Kunsthistorisches Museum, Kunstkammer, inv. nos. KK1118, KK1122, KK1126, KK 1130

The four statues depict the *Four Seasons* in the form of the deities Flora (Spring), Ceres (Summer), Bacchus (Autumn) and Vulcan (Winter) and are all that remains of a three-metre-high, mechanical silver fountain which the Nurembergoldsmith Wenzel Jamnitzer worked on from around 1568 by appointment of Emperor Maximilian II, and which was delivered in Prague in 1578 to Rudolf II, Maximilian's son. In 1629-1630 the fountain was brought to Vienna by order of Emperor Ferdinand II whereby it escaped the plunder of Prague by Swedish troops, but ultimately not its destruction: between 1747 and 1750 it was melted down in order to finance the new display of the works of art in the treasury. The only remaining pieces of the famous "pleasure fountain" or "beautiful fountain" are the four statues of the gods, which were made of bronze and therefore not suitable to be melted down. The original appearance of the fountain can be pieced together reasonably well from an itemization of the fountain's parts in the inventory of the Rudolfian art collection from 1607-1611 when they were packed in 18 crates as well as from a description of the fountain in a travel diary dating from around 1640. According to the diary, the fountain itself was in the form of a monumental imperial crown, which was carried by four caryatids, representing the four seasons, which explains why these figures were created from bronze, because they had to support the entire structure and required thus a certain stability. The aforementioned travel diary, which probably quotes from a "booklet in parchment" in which the fountain was described, elucidates its various layers of meaning and demonstrates that an encyclopedic concept lay at the heart of the fountain, with the glorification of the House of Habsburg and the Holy Roman Empire as its central meaning. As the basis of this construct of ideas, the four seasons served to demonstrate that only through change things can attain perfection. The seasons are understood to be the basis of human existence in this concept, while the fountain structure with its bowls was dedicated to the four elements. Above everything, Jupiter was enthroned upon an eagle in order to demonstrate in an allegorical fashion that the entire world is subject to the emperor as the highest earthly authority.
Iconographically, the fountain corresponds completely to the ideas of Maximilian's period, which above all dealt with the close relationship between the empire and the House of Habsburg. Like the construction of the *Neugebäude* Castle and the series of images of the seasons and elements by Arcimboldo, also the silver pleasure fountain was about imperial representation and political propaganda in the form of a work of art of the highest quality.
The realization of what was possibly Jacopo Strada ingenious concept was placed in the hands of one of the most famous goldsmiths of the period. Wenzel Jamnitzer, who hailed from Vienna, ran the most important goldsmith's workshop north of the Alps. For the execution of the "beautiful fountain", for which he required a decade, he drew upon numerous colleagues, such as Johann Gregor van der Schardt, a Dutch sculptor working in Nuremberg, to whom the figures of the seasons are unanimously attributed. Their slender proportions and elegant poses correspond to van der Schardt's style, derived from Venetian Mannerism, who was apparently able to follow within certain guidelines his own ideas. Although he had to create load-bearing statues, he still gave each figure a life of its own through different movements and through a subtle shifting of their axes so that they appear in no way stiff or symmetrical, but rather truly alive and highly dynamic. The figures turn gracefully and with a gentle rhythm towards each other, in order to pass on their attributes to the next and show thus their union. As Berger accurately observed, a certain chastity was demanded for the imperial fountain, which is why van der Schardt had to conceal the private parts of the figures with somewhat artificial looking leaves and draperies, which the always antiquity-oriented artist would have otherwise never employed. The exceptional quality of these four figures allows us to assess the tragic waste the destruction of the silver fountain represents, which must have been not only a marvel of the art of goldsmithing, but also a feat of brilliant technical skill, for the several parts, propelled by water, could even move.

Claudia Kryza Gersch

Provenance: 1607-11 in the art collection of Emperor Rudolf II in Prague, brought to Vienna in 1629-30 and traceable since 1640 to the imperial Treasury

Bibliography: Schlosser 1901, 16f.; Planiscig 1924, 194ff., no. 319; Planiscig, Kris 1935, 95, no. 6; Weihrauch 1967, 321f.; Nuremberg 1985, 68f, 231ff. nos. 27-30 (Pechstein); Schürer 1986; Alfons 1987, 70, 81; Vienna 1988, II, 49f., no. 520 (Leithe-Jasper); Honnens de Lichtenberg 1991, 97ff.; Berlin 1995, 320f., no. 94 (Berger).

V.2
Attributed to Johann Gregor van der Schardt
(c. 1530 - c. 1581)
Luna
Nuremberg(?), around 1570(?)
Bronze
H. 51 cm
Vienna, Kunsthistorisches Museum, Kunstkammer, inv. no. KK 5511

The nude, female figure standing erect in elegantly curved *contrapposto* is hard to recognize at first glance. Her face appears to melt into a roughly circular disc. This disc is meant to be the moon and the statuette represents thus the Roman moon goddess, Luna. As the attributes spear and hunting horn reveal, this figure also refers to the goddess of the hunt, Diana, who is usually depicted with a crescent moon above her brow and was equated with Luna. A bronze statuette, comparable not only stylistically, but also in its iconography, can be found in the Rijksmuseum in Amsterdam and features a face whose contours dissolve into a radiating solar disc. This is a portrayal of the sun god, Sol, in the form of Phoebus Apollo, the brother of Diana. Both figures, who each have the same kind of pipe above their heads, which might indicate that they were destined to be used in the context of a fountain, were rightly attributed to van der Schardt by Anthony Radcliffe and Charles Avery in 1977. Although the proportions of the figures and the form of their bases do not fully correspond with each other, it cannot be doubted that these statues belong together. Already in ancient Rome, Sol and Luna were worshipped in the same temple and the integration of such a pair into an astrological table fountain would have fit perfectly into the world of thought of the 16th century. This unusual and remarkable way of presenting Sol and Luna corresponds to the contemporary fashion of personifying abstract concepts and links the statuettes with the allegorical images of Arcimboldo.

Claudia Kryza Gersch

Provenance: 1659 inventory of the art collection of Archduke Leopold Wilhelm in Vienna; 1871 in the imperial Treasury in Vienna; transferred in 1875 to the k.k. Ambras collection in Vienna and in 1891 transferred with that collection to the Kunsthistorisches Museum

Bibliography: Schlosser 1901, 12; Planiscig 1924, 93, no. 163; Halsema-Kubes 1977, 122 (with dedication from Radcliffe and Avery); Vienna 1987, 145, no. I/10 (Boeckel and Stengl); Honnens de Lichtenberg 1991, 104ff.; Scholten 2001, 312; London 2005, 112f., no. 35 (Scholten).

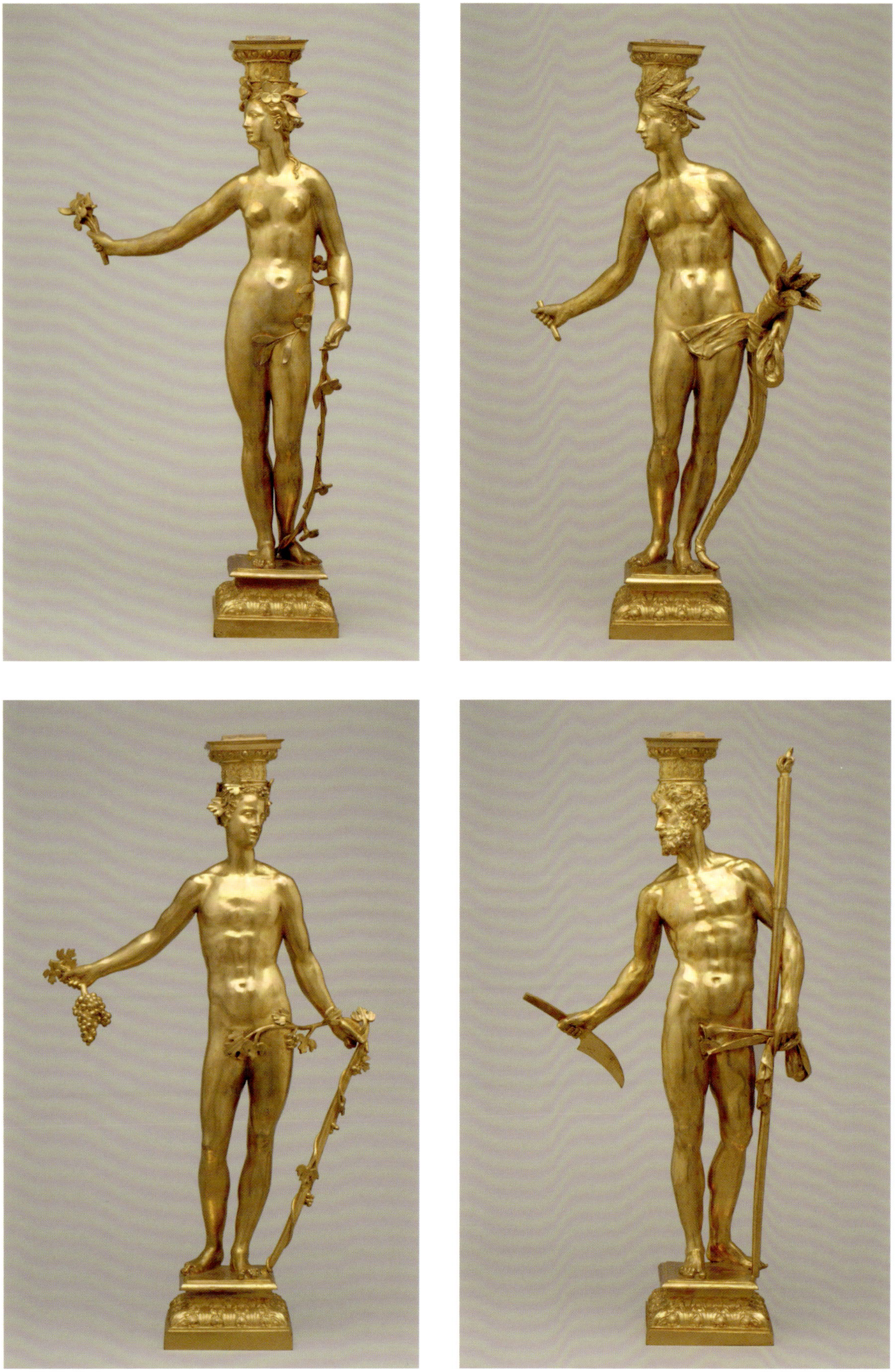

V.1

V.3
Oil Lamp in the Form of a Conch on an Eagle's Claw
Padua, beginning of the 16th century
Bronze
H. 22.3 cm
Vienna, Kunsthistorisches Museum, Kunstkammer, inv. no. KK 5935

The claw of an eagle cast from nature represents a particularly popular element for oil lamps in the Paduan Renaissance, since its grasping form is not only interesting, but provides also good stability for the object, comparable to an antique tripod. Such eagle claws were apparently fabricated in great numbers and provided with a separately manufactured upper part in the form of satyr busts, monkey heads, sirens or something of that sort, which served as oil lamps. The Berliner Kunstgewerbemuseum preserves a single eagle claw whose upper end in the shape of a plug shows how the individual components of such objects could be assembled. In the example at hand, a tree trunk with sawed off branches serves as the link to a conch with a hinged cover. These elements are not examples of natural casting, but were rather modelled freehandly.
Frosien-Leinz suggested that an allegory of the four elements can be seen in this specific oil lamp, where the eagle's claw stands for the air, the tree for the earth, the conch for the water and the fire would be symbolized through the operation of the oil lamp. Frosien-Leinz also refers to the estate inventory of Isabella d'Este from 1542, in which an inkwell in the form of a harpy's foot is listed. Since harpies are described in ancient mythology as half human and half birdlike creatures, it is possible that Isabella's inkwell was in the shape of such an eagle's claw that was, however, interpreted as a harpy's foot. An intended mythical meaning, rather than an allegorical one, which also reached out at the same time to the lost world of Antiquity cannot be dismissed as the possible motivation for the creation of such objects. Interestingly, in the early 18th century many of the everyday objects created in the Paduan workshops in the Renaissance were even considered to be ancient originals.

Claudia Kryza Gersch

Provenance: 1781 collection of the imperial treasurer Josef Angelo de France; purchased for the k.k. coin and antique collection in 1801; transferred in 1880 to the k.k. Ambras collection in Vienna and transferred with that collection to the Kunsthistorisches Museum in 1891

Bibliography: Planiscig 1924, 33, no. 51; Frankfurt 1985, 248, 507, no. 219 (Frosien-Leinz); Vienna 1987, 357, no. VIII/36 (Stengl); Duisburg 1994, 209f., no. 89 (Frosien-Leinz).

V.4
Sea Snail
Padua, beginning of the 16th century
Bronze
L. 7.9 cm
Vienna, Kunsthistorisches Museum, Kunstkammer, inv. no. KK 5940

This enchanting creature is a figment of imagination in which the cast of a snail was combined with a conch in order to create a "Kunstkammer" – curiosity. Unlike unaltered casts from nature, which were created out of zoological and scientific interests, these creations display the romantic, playful side of the era, inspired by the antiquity, as it is also expressed in bronze statuettes of fauns, nymphs and other mythical creatures or in oil lamps in the form of grotesque heads. The element of the bizarre that is inherent in such objects and which was presented with a certain sense of humour, provides a special appeal which the humanistic culture of the Renaissance consciously sought after. In the collections of this period, which during the course of the 16th century developed into the famous "Kunst – und Wunderkammern" (cabinets of art and wonders), objects were combined which above all aroused astonishment – whether they were of natural or artificial origins.

Claudia Kryza Gersch

Provenance: from the k.k. coin and antique collection; transferred in 1880 to the k.k. Ambras collection in Vienna and tranferred with that collection to the Kunsthistorisches Museum in 1891

Bibliography: Planiscig 1924, 39, no. 63; Schallaburg 1976, 104, no. 135 (Leithe-Jasper); Frankfurt 1985, 545, no. 282 (Gramaccini); Vienna 2006, 105, no. 2.49 (Kryza-Gersch).

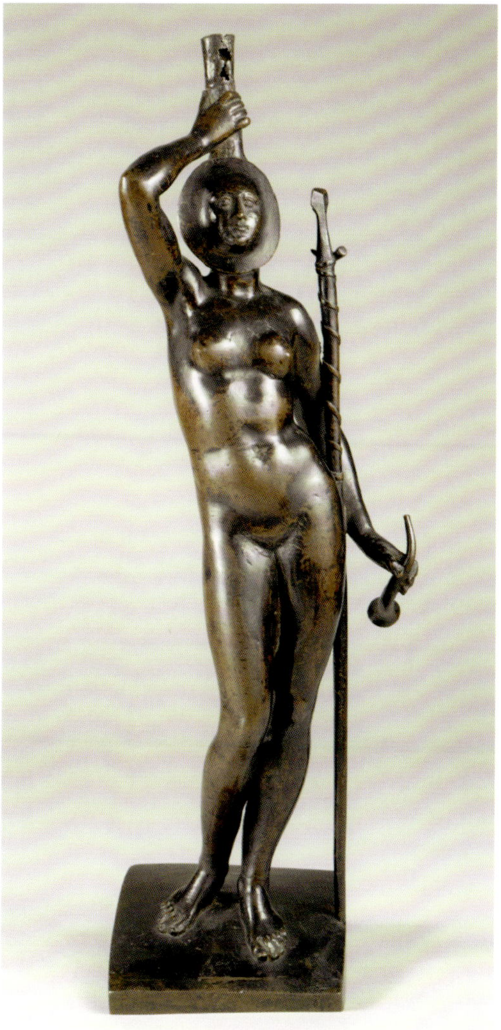

V.2

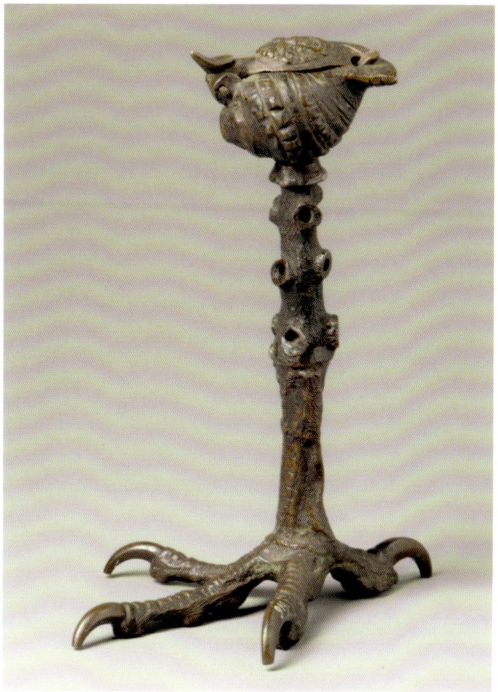

V.3

V.5
Toad
Padua, beginning of the 16th century
Bronze
Ø 8.5 cm
Vienna, Kunsthistorisches Museum, Kunstkammer, inv. no. KK 5938

For this extraordinarily effective cast from nature, which reproduces every detail down to the tiniest wart on its epidermis, a toad with a gaping mouth was used. Because the interior of the creature is hollow, it can be utilized as a container for writing-sand, which was needed for sprinkling over a recently written page so that the ink would dry more quickly. Since one could not close the toad's mouth, it would have hardly served – though it has been suggested – as an inkwell, because the ink would dry out too fast in a container without an adequate cover. The beaked, pointed mouth of the toad is on the contrary excellently suited to evenly sprinkle sand. Along with a crab to hold the ink and a snake for a paperweight, one could arrange thus a veritable zoo on one's writing desk. This corresponded with the enthusiasm for the study of nature, its phenomena and creatures which was so characteristic of the era. It is remarkable, however, that for the Paduan casts from nature, mostly snakes, crabs, toads and lizards were utilized, animals which one would, in general, rather not encounter in a living state. In this context, it is worth mentioning that Aristotle observed in his *Poetics* (IV, 3) that things which the observer perceives with displeasure in reality, become pleasing as soon as they are portrayed consummately in art. This philosophical concept, associated with the Socratic term of "functional beauty", which means that also something ugly can be beautiful if it is useful, may have significantly contributed to the impetus behind the production of cast from nature from such animals.
In order to improve the realistic appearance of casts from nature, some were also painted with colour, as it can be seen in the examples of toads in the Staatliche Kunstsammlung in Kassel. In those cases, the metal used was usually not bronze, but rather lead or iron – the former indicating fabrication north of the Alps, while the latter suggests a later date of the objects, which remained in fashion for a long time.
A second example of such a toad, belonged once to the Kunsthistorisches Museum, but was sold in 1923 and is kept today in the Museum of Cleveland. Further specimens can be found at the Museo Nazionale del Bargello in Florence as well as in the sculpture collection of the Staatliche Museen in Berlin. Casts of frogs were equally popular, though obviously too small to serve as containers and were therefore generally cast in massive metal.

Claudia Kryza Gersch

Provenance: 1659 inventory of the art collection of Archduke Leopold Wilhelm in Vienna; 1750 inventory of the imperial Treasury in Vienna; transferred in 1871 to the k.k. Ambras collection in Vienna and in 1891 transferred with that collection to the Kunsthistorisches Museum

Bibliography: Berger 1883, 473, no. 537; Zimmermann 1889, 573, no. 27; Bode 1907, 27; Bode 1922, 45; Planiscig 1924, 39, no. 66; Kris 1926, 140; Planiscig 1927, 366f.; Schallaburg 1976, 105, no. 138 (Leithe-Jasper); Hunter-Stiebel 1985, 82, no. 65; Washington 1986, 214, no. 57 (Leithe-Jasper); Berlin 1995, 226, no. 42 (Leithe-Jasper); Padua 2001, 202, no. 17 (Leithe-Jasper); Vienna 2006, 105, no. 2.48 (Kryza-Gersch).

V.6
Crab
Padua, beginning of the 16th century
Bronze
Ø 13 cm
Vienna, Kunsthistorisches Museum, Kunstkammer, inv. no. KK 5922

The *Crab* (*Cancer pagurus*) is the largest crab found in the Mediterranean and can reach a shell width of up to 30 cm. Its short tail is folded under its body in such a way that despite its impressive pincers and long legs, it offers a compact but at the same time also interesting form, which is why it was frequently used for casting from nature. The relatively large body could be rendered hollow through a specific process during the moulding of the animal, whereby a cover was formed from the upper part of the shell which could be connected by means of a hinge to the body of the crab. Casts of crabs served primarily as unusual containers which were used for instance for ink. There were also utensils such as candleholders, oil lamps or small table bells, which were indispensable components of the well-equipped, 16th century writing desk. Departing from 1500, these objects were produced through casts from nature particularly in the North of Italy (compare cat. no. V.8). Their appeal arises from their perfect reproduction of nature, which captivated natural scientists and collectors alike, because in the art of the Renaissance consummate imitation of nature was considered one of the highest aspirations. The poet or scholar working at his desk could derive inspiration from glancing at his life-like casts from nature, while also having a useful tool at hand.
The fact that crabs in particular were so often cast was not simply the result of their unusual and somewhat threatening appearance, but is also due to the fact that they could be seen as the symbol for the zodiacal sign Cancer. In older literature it has been attempted to ascribe these crabs to Andrea Riccio. Since there is, however, no clear indication that he occupied himself with the technique of casting from nature there is no basis for such an attribution. It is much more likely one of the many foundries in Padua specialized in the fabrication of these, in no way rare, objects. The Kunsthistorisches Museum has four different examples of these crabs; further examples can be found in the Museo Nazionale del Bargello in Florence, in the sculpture collection of the Staatliche Museen in Berlin, in the Victoria and Albert Museum in London, in the Boijmans Van Beuningen Museum in Rotterdam, in the National Gallery in Washington as well as with art dealers, which attests to the popularity of these unusually formed utensils.

Claudia Kryza Gersch

Provenance: from the k.k. coin and antique collection; transferred to the k.k. Ambras collection in Vienna in 1880 and transferred with this collection to the Kunsthistorisches Museum in 1891

Bibliography: Planiscig 1924, 39, no. 64; Kris 1926, 139f.; Schallaburg 1976, 104, no. 133 (Leithe-Jasper); Frankfurt 1985, 537, no. 261 (Gramaccini); Vienna 1987, 367, no. VIII/64 (Stengl); Duisburg 1994-1995, 243f, no. 112 (Frosien-Leinz); Leeds 2005, 66, no. 13; Vienna 2006, 103ff., no. 2.46 (Kryza-Gersch).

V.7
Crab
Padua, beginning of the 16th century
Bronze
Ø 18.6 cm
Vienna, Kunsthistorisches Museum, Kunstkammer, inv. no. KK 5927

Like the previous catalogue number, this object is an ink container in the form of a crab, which was cast from nature.

Claudia Kryza Gersch

Provenance: probably from the collection of the imperial treasurer Josef Angelo de France; purchased for the k.k. coin and antique collection in 1808; transferred to the k.k. Ambras collection in Vienna in 1880 and transferred with that collection to the Kunsthistorisches Museum in 1891

Bibliography: Bode 1907, 27; Bode 1922, 45; Kris 1926, 137ff.; Planiscig 1927, 366f.; Pope-Hennessy 1965, 138, no. 505; Brüssel 1967, 58, no. 39 (Dhanens); Schlegel 1968, 351ff.; Wilson 1983, 75f; Hunter-Stiebel 1985, 86, no. 69; Washington 1986, 100, no. 16 (Leithe-Jasper); Berlin 1995, 227, no. 43 (Leithe-Jasper); Padua 2001, 213, no. 56 (Leithe-Jasper); Leeds 2005, 66, no. 12; Vienna 2006, 105, no. 2.47 (Kryza-Gersch).

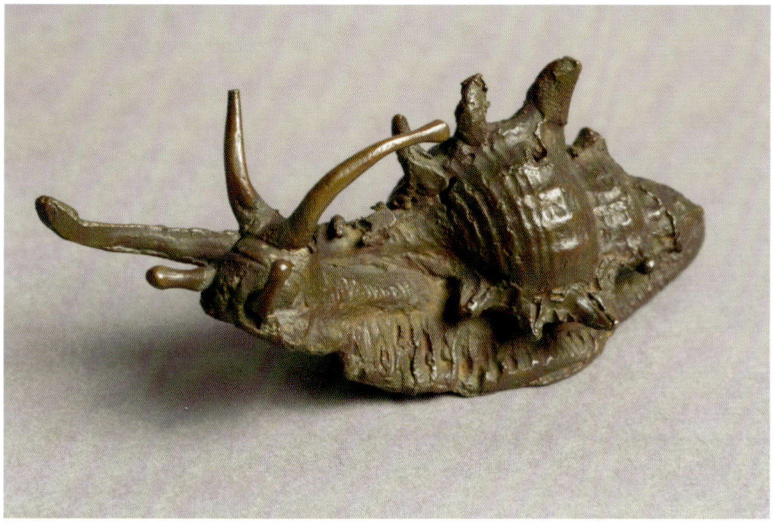

V.4

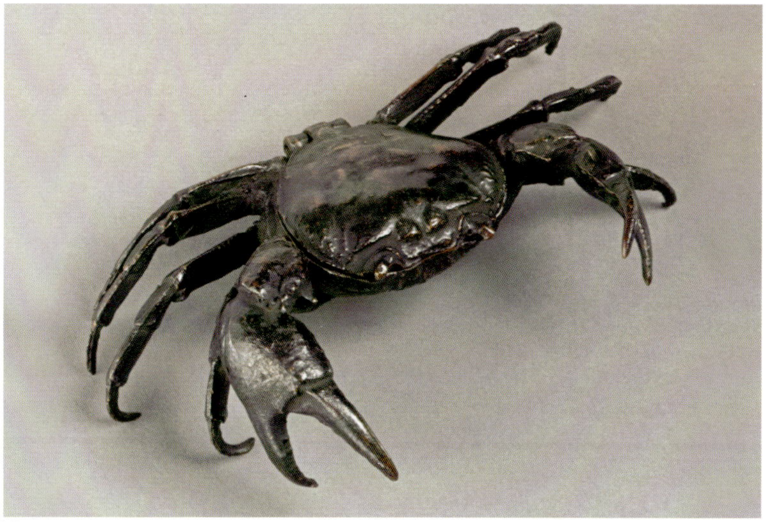

V.6

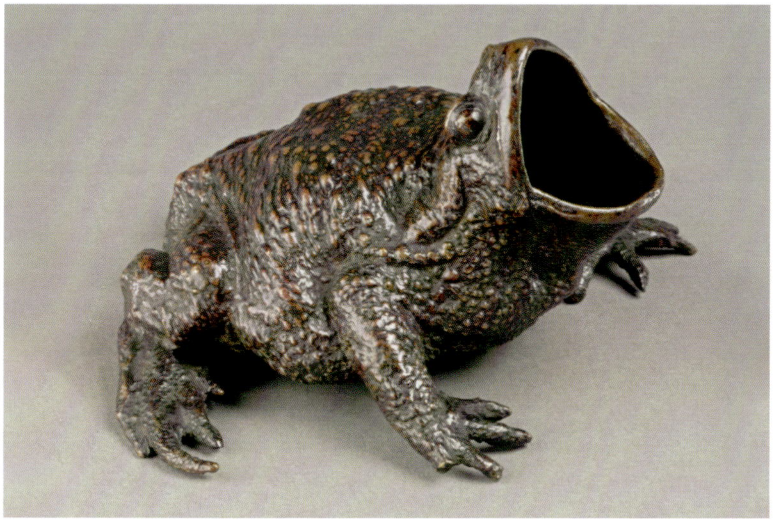

V.5

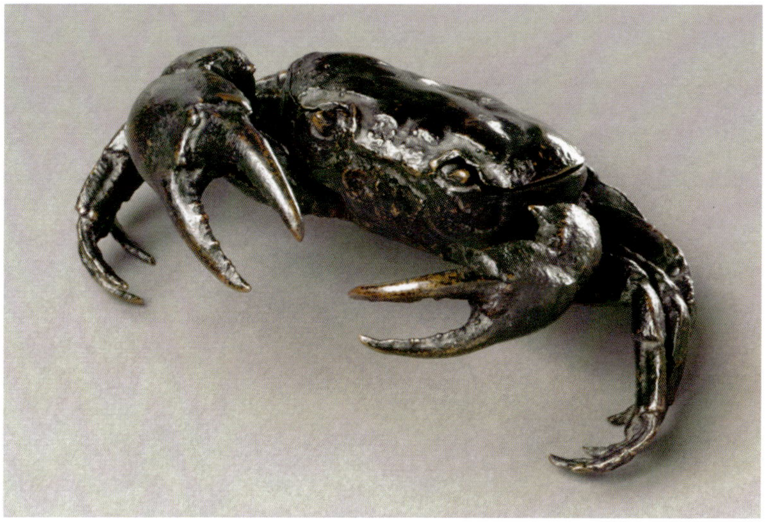

V.7

V.8
Snake
Padua, beginning of the 16th century
Presumedly lead and tin alloy, partially painted
22 × 7 × 2.7 cm
Vienna, Kunsthistorisches Museum, Kunstkammer, inv. no. KK 5907

This extremely realistic representation of a snake was created through casting from nature, a method documented in the *Libro dell'Arte*, Cennino Cennini's famous treatise on artistic techniques from around 1400. The technique had been in use since the 14th century, though already well-known since antiquity. At the beginning of the 16th century, starting from Padua, the casting from nature enjoyed renewed popularity, which was reflected in the creation, primarily from bronze, of numerous works of art and everyday objects. This was no coincidence, as the university city of Padua was a centre of Aristotelianism around 1500 and in that school of thought it is believed that art must imitate nature. As the name of the technique suggests, nature is employed in the creation of the mold, usually in the form of a dead animal, which is plunged into viscous clay after a special preparation so that an exact impression of every physiognomic detail is created. This object would then be gradually encased in increasingly firmer clay so that a feasible mold resulted, which then had only to be baked, whereupon the animal in the centre fell to ashes. After cleansing the mold, it was filled with molten metal and broken apart after cooling. The possibilities of this method of casting are almost unlimited and range from beetles cast in silver to imaginatively assembled articles such as oil lamps and candleholders, for which nature provided a nearly unlimited supply of models.

Snakes, particularly compact, small-scaled vipers with their attractively structured epidermis, were especially popular subjects for the technique of casting from nature, because these animals have not only an attractive surface, but also a relatively uniform body in terms of thickness, which permits filling the mold completely without the risk of fissuring as it cools. Moreover, the flexible body of serpents offered the possibility of being decoratively modified before casting (i.e. undulated or knotted).

This basic type of casting from nature represents the lowest, more or less purely artisanal level of the technique, whose artistic merit can be elevated through the animal's elaborate pose or the creative arrangement of various elements. The cast of a snake, used as the handle of a beautiful Paduan ceremonial basin (compare cat. no. V.9) demonstrates the highest form of applying this technique. Even if some casts of snakes served as paper weights, the delight in the precise reproduction of the reptile as well as its allegorical content were given emphasis over practical purpose. The symbolic power of the snake is multifaceted and complex and encompasses meanings such as cunning, rebirth and medicine, but also devilishness and evil and can therefore possess an apotropaic character. Moreover, the snake belongs to the 48 constella-

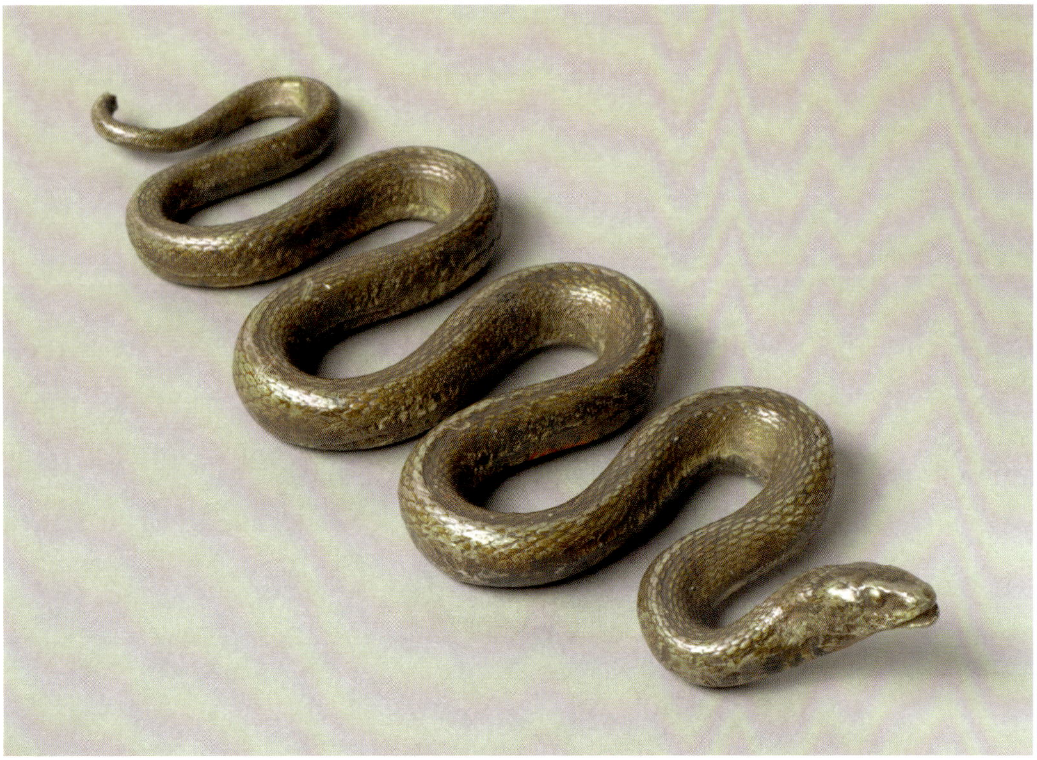

V.8

tions of ancient Greek astronomy, as described by Ptolemy, and can therefore also acquire an astrological significance.

Claudia Kryza Gersch

Provenance: from the k.k. coin and antique collection; transferred to the k.k. Ambras collection in Vienna in 1880 and transferred with this collection to the Kunsthistorisches Museum in 1891

Bibliography: Planiscig 1924, 7, no. 60; Frankfurt 1985, 204, 543, no. 277 (Gramaccini); Vienna 1987, 367, no. VIII/65B (Stengl); Vienna 2006, 107, no. 2.50 (Kryza-Gersch).

V.9
Ornamental Bowl with Snakes
Padua, around 1520-1530
Bronze
H. 33 (26) cm, Ø 62 (42.2) cm
Vienna, Kunsthistorisches Museum, Kunstkammer, inv. no. KK 5501

The classic shape of the monumental cooling vessel can be traced back to ancient examples, such as the so-called *Torlonia-Vase* in Rome, which was known since the early 16th century. The ornamentation, as well as the figural frieze with its nereids, tritons and sea centaurs, was also inspired by antique sources. As is so often the case in this era, the enthusiasm for the ancient world combines itself in this basin with an equally intense enthusiasm for the study of nature. The fancifully formed pair of handles is composed of satyr masks as well as from cast taken from snakes, their shed skin and scallops. This most imaginative application of casts from nature was described by Kris in a famous essay as "style rustique".
A convincing attribution of the bowl to a certain artist or workshop has so far been unsuccessful, although names like Andrea Riccio and Severo da Ravenna have been put forward. On the bottom of the inner surface of the bowl, a stamped crest composed of delicatly raised lines can be made out (although this was later rendered somewhat illegible by the brutal application of an iron bolt), which can be identified as that of the Counts of San Bonifacio, who were living in Padua in the 16th century. To locate the production of the bowl in a Paduan foundry appears therefore appropriate, which would also account for the use of casts from nature.

Claudia Kryza Gersch

Provenance: 1781 collection of the imperial treasurer Josef Angelo de France; purchased for the k.k. coin and antique collection in 1801; transferred to the k.k. Ambras collection in Vienna in 1880 and transferred with that collection to the Kunsthistorisches Museum in 1891

Bibliography: Planiscig 1924, 37, no. 58; Kris 1926, 137; Frankfurt 1985, 204, 534f., no. 258 (Gramaccini); Vienna 1989, 260ff., no. V/32 (Welzig); Padua 2001, 216, no. 59 (Leithe-Jasper).

V.10
Wenzel Jamnitzer
(1508-1585)
Inkstand
Nuremberg, c. 1560-1570
Silver
22.7 × 10.2 × 6 cm
Vienna, Kunsthistorisches Museum, Kunstkammer, inv. nos. KK 1155-1164

In the 16th century, Nuremberg established itself alongside Padua as an important centre for the creation of casts from nature ("style rustique"). First and foremost, Wenzel and Albrecht Jamnitzer excelled as pioneers of this technique (still new to southern Germany) and perfected its application in silver. In 1547, the Nuremberg mathematician Johann Neudörffer praised the quality "of little creatures, small worms, toads and snakes" which the two brothers "cast from silver and adorn[ed] silver containers with them" (comp. Klier, 67). Archduke Ferdinand II of Tyrol, the owner of the small inkstand, appears to have had a special fondness for small, cast animals. The rectangular box, in whose lower half writing implements are stored, is captivating in its contrast between the clean lines of the box's structure and the energetic vitality of the cast from nature appliqués. The profiled areas of the cover are decorated with casts of insects, clams, a crab, a mouse, a toad and two lizards. An ample festoon of various cast flowers and grasses is situated on the lateral surfaces of the box. More small animals frolic among them. This remarkable container can be seen as characteristic work of Wenzel Jamnitzer. In addition to formal and technical criteria, the fact that the owner of the inkstand Archduke Ferdinand II, had often requisitioned natural casts from Jamnitzer supports this attribution. Jamnitzer wrote to the Archduke on 27 January 1557, that he would send "etliche geschmelzte dierlein" ("several little cast animals") to him via

Jacopo Strada (Jb. XI/2 1890, Reg. 7247). In 1565 Ferdinand requisitioned no less than two dozen "allerlei abgegossene thierle, die nider und flach sein, und noch darzue allerlei klaine kreuter, die auch nieder und flach, alles von silber" ("sundry cast animals, all of which are flat and small as well as sundry small toads, which are also to be flat and small, all from silver") (Jb. XIV/2, 1893, Reg. 9720).

Paulus Rainer

Bibliography: Kris 1926, 155; Kris 1932, 30f., no. 44; Hayward 1976, 208; Hernmarck 1978, 218, 273, 345; Nuremberg 1985, 226, no. 21; Rudolf 1995, Klier 2004, 88f.

V.11
Bernard Palissy (or workshop of Bernard Palissy)
(c. 1510-1589/90)
"Rustic" ewer
between 1556 and 1590
Glazed terra-cotta
H 19.2 cm, Ø 20 cm
Paris, Musée du Louvre, Département des Objets d'Art, inv. no. MR 2337

The piece is a reinterpretation of a simple form of ewer, of the kind often found in the sphere of goldsmithry, in a manner that the potter Bernard Palissy developed in the middle of the 16th century and that he called *rustiques figulines* ("rustic vessels"). White shells of different kinds are set on a mottled brown and blue ground, evoking eddies in the sea, while the spout takes the form of a frog whose open mouth serves to pour the liquid and the lid holds a crayfish whose claws frame the amphibian's head and whose tail rests on the handle. These different elements have been moulded directly from nature or from a cast. The quality of the overall composition and the mastery of the technique of moulding allow us to attribute this piece to Bernard Palissy or his workshop. The vogue for this kind of decoration over the course of the second half of the 16th century and into the 17th meant that Palissy was widely imitated and that there are numerous such "rustic" pieces: bowls, plates, dishes... Potters did not use just animals to adorn them, but also plants, moulded in the same way. The purpose of this piece remains uncertain. Its fixed lid, which means that it can only be filled through the slits on each side of the crustacean's claws, suggests that it was not a ewer made for everyday use; it may have been an element in the decoration of a grotto.

Agnès Bos

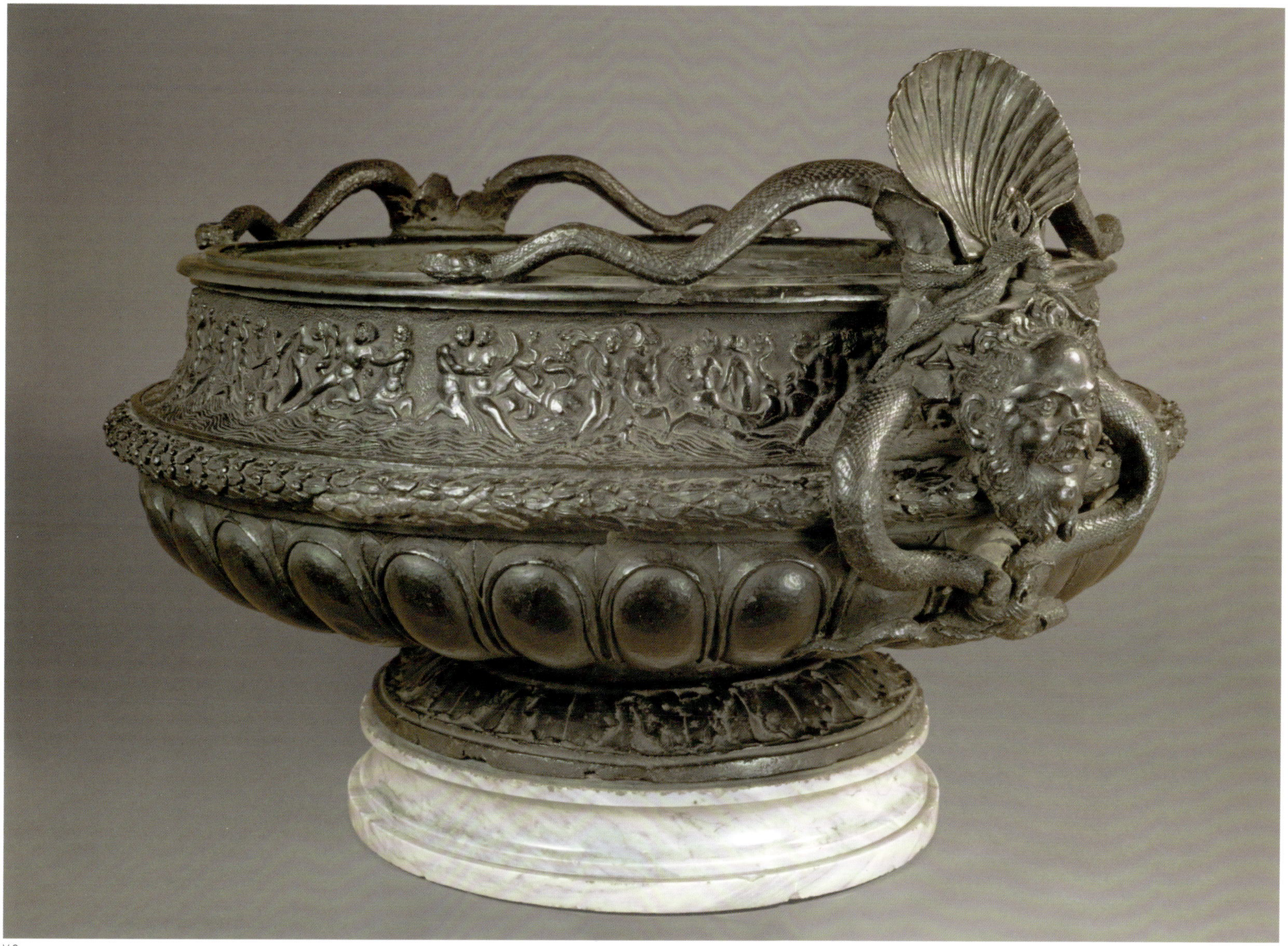

V.9

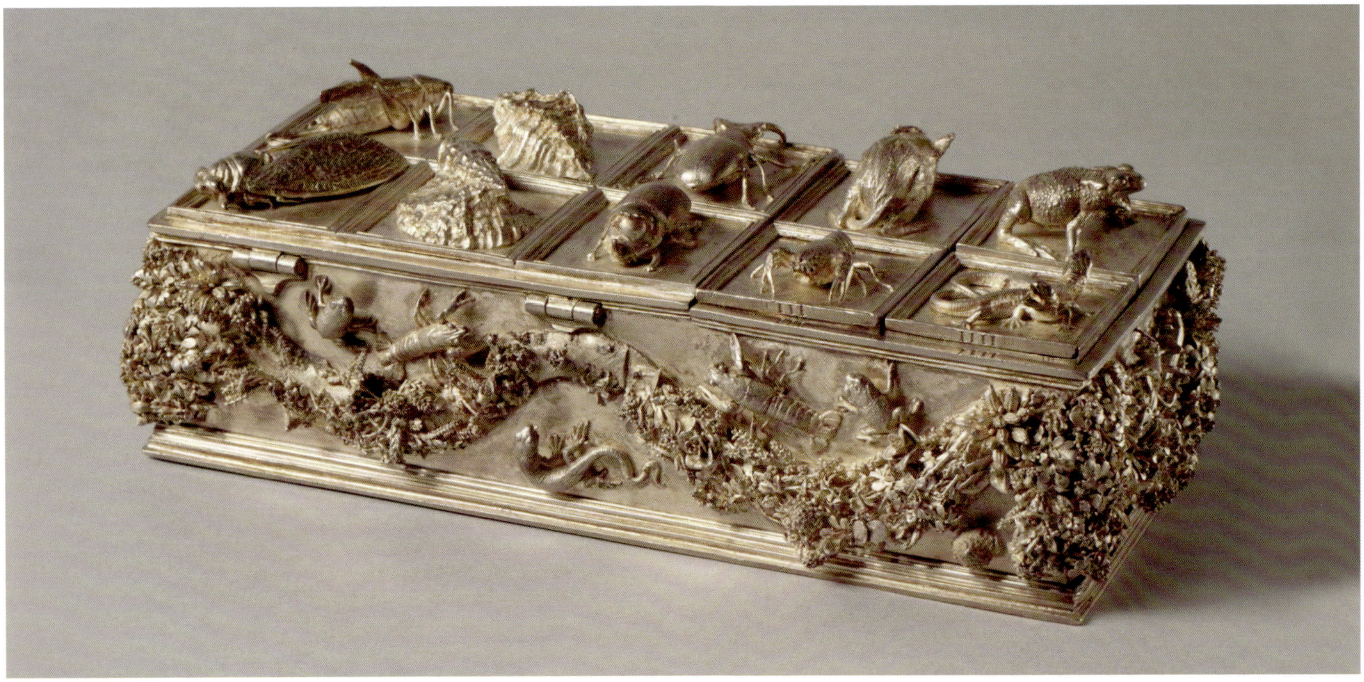

V.10

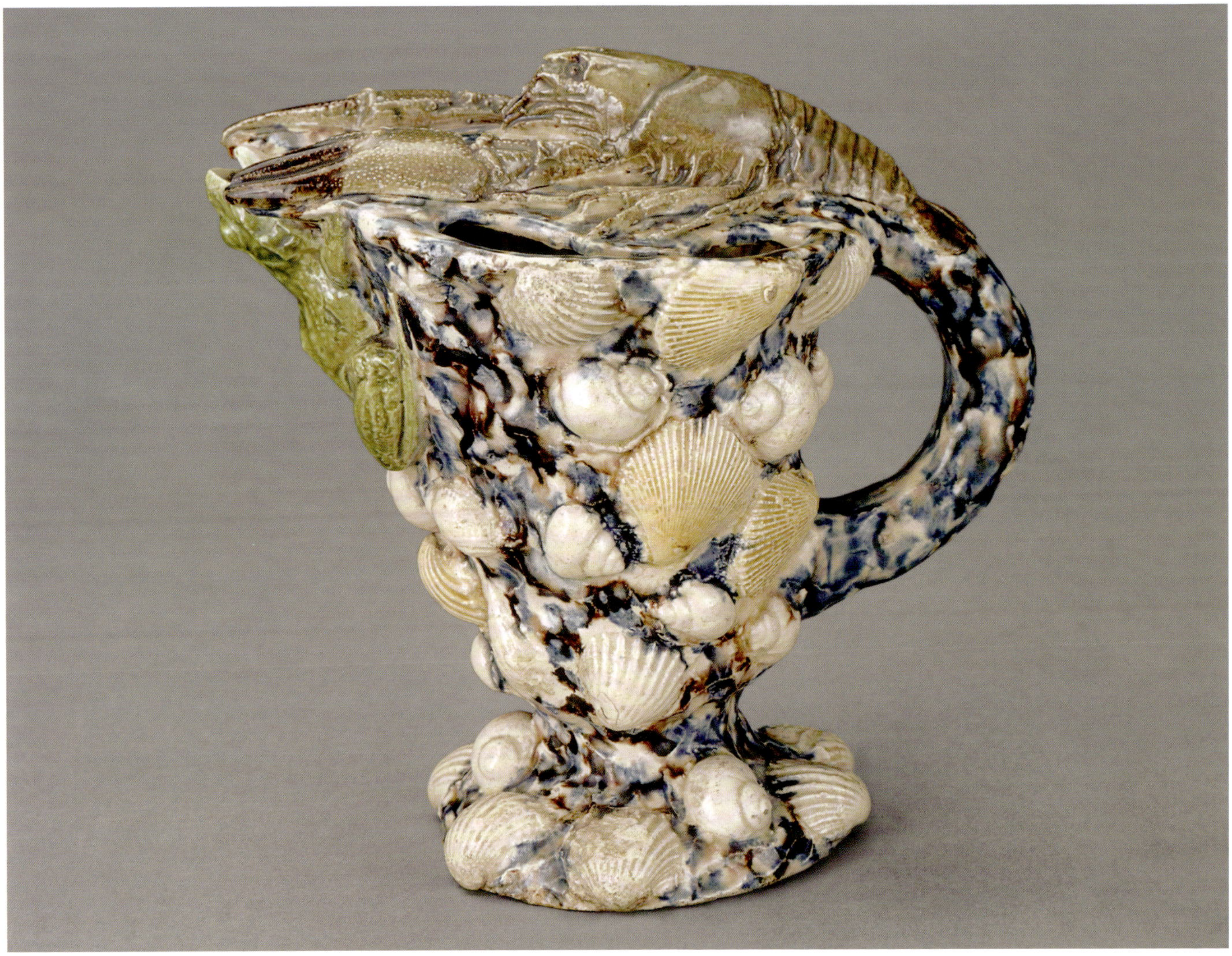

V.11

Provenance: collection of Chevalier Durand, acquired 1825

Bibliography: Delange, Sauzay 1862, pl. 11; Tainturier 1863, 78; Migeon 1901, no. 120; Clément de Ris 1875, 44; Ballot 1924, pl. 39; Amico 1987, 64-65; Amico 1996a, 31-32; Amico 1996b; 90-91; Ecouen 1997, no. 66; Perrin 2001, 259, 76-77; Tours-Limoges 2002-03, no. 14.

V.12
Bernard Palissy (attributed)
Foot-bowl in rustic style
Second half of the 16th century (?)
Ceramic, glazed
53 × 40 cm
Vienna, Österreichisches Museum für Angewandte Kunst, inv. no. Ke 3694

The oval bowl is traditionally ascribed to Bernard Palissy (1510-1589 circa). It bears a decoration in rustic style, developed by this glass painter active in France and much copied. Typical to Palissy's oval bowls, the item in question is also divided up into an island, water and shore area, featuring scenes of naturally shaped animals. A writhing snake occupies the centre of glimmering blue based composition. The area in which it writhes is bordered by water inhabited by fishes and frogs marked by wavy lines. The edge of the bowl, that pictures shore life, is inhabited by lizards, frogs, crabs, mussels, leaves etc. The striking, deceptively realistic effect of the animals was one of Pallissy's particular skills. This is partially due on the one hand to the natural forms common also to the art of goldsmithery and on the other to the lively effects achieved by the reliefs and the fine glazing. The latter gives the amphibious creatures and insects a glimmering wet shine, as if they had just come into contact with water. A decisive point in Palissy's work was also the theme of movement, principally offset by the stiff, lifeless animals. Their careful positioning on the bowl, the open movement and countermovement as well as the restlessness in the order of the single figures masterly work against a static appearance.
A bowl with the same composition, though with different colouring, is to be found in the Louvre (Paris, Musée du Louvre, inv. no. OA 1361). It is attributed to the so-called *Maître du Griffon* (Amico 1996, 128).

Katja Schmitz-von Ledebur

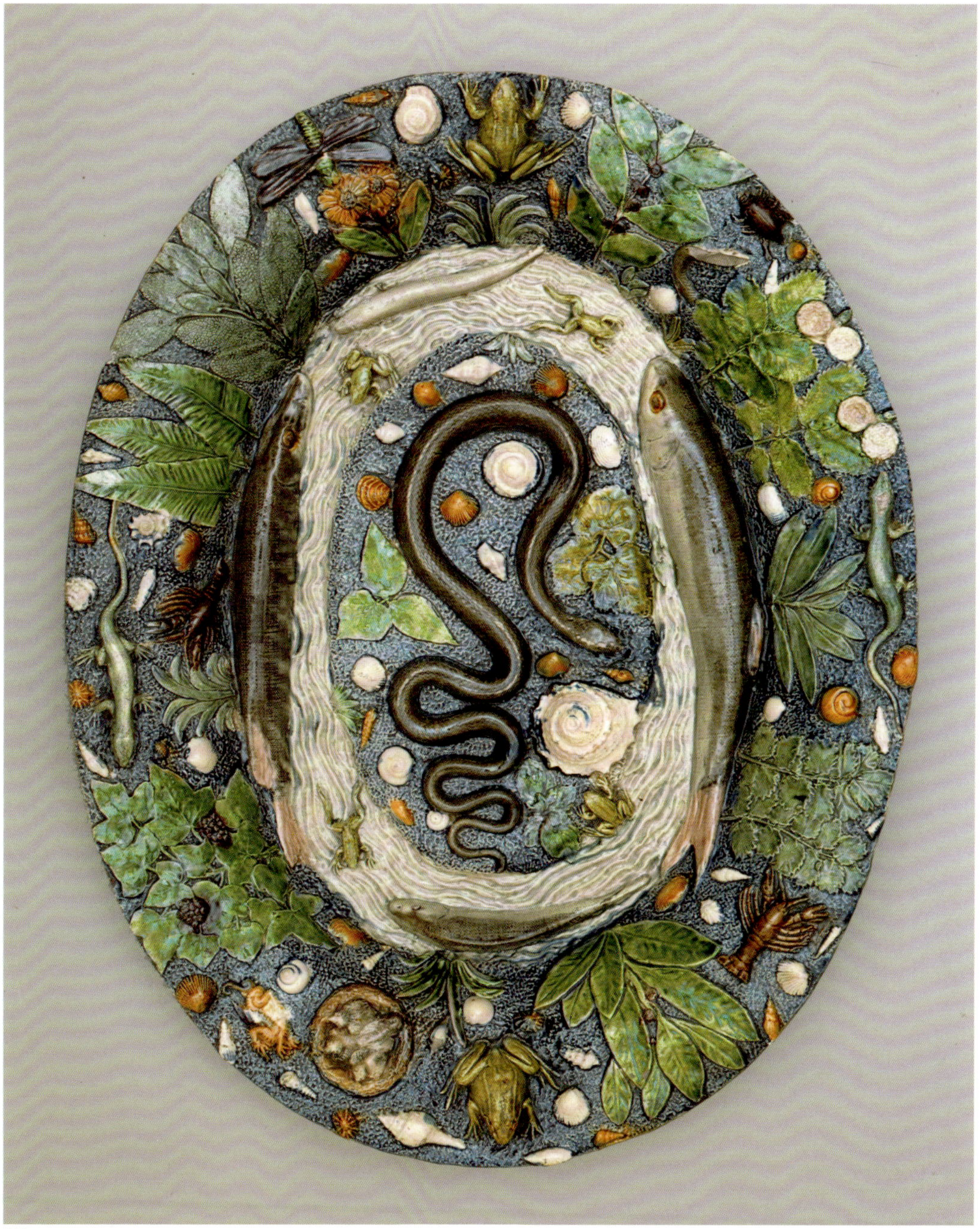

V.12

V.13
Gasparo Miseroni
(c. 1518-1573)
Ten-passed basin with "Head of Medusa"
Milan, c. 1560-1570
Chalcedony, set in enamelled gold
H. 12.3 cm, Ø 32.2 cm
Vienna, Kunsthistorisches Museum, Kunstkammer, inv. no. KK 1668

Gasparo Miseroni, to whom the large, round basin already in Cosimo I's inventory in 1570 can be attributed, created here a perfectly formed masterpiece, which attests to the great esteem he received in the European courts of his time. The thinly ground wall, which in translucence ideally accentuates the beauty of the brown-violet-white colouring of the chalcedony, fans out in ten spiralled passes. In each narrow retraction between the passes there is an external canted rod, decorated with a small leaf motif at its juncture with the border of the upper lip. In the centre of the swirl within the basin, from which the here flattened spiral bars protrude, sits a round medallion with a grotesque mask. With a wide-open mouth, the creature glares at the viewer with winged ears and a leaf-beard. Two snakes grow from the hair, in a common representation of the head of Medusa. However, it is probably a fantastic representation of an extended faun head, as can be seen in a drawing of a pitcher – seen in profile – in Berlin (Venturelli 1998, plate 2).
The monolith basin, in which a low-gorged foot was also carved into the stone, was given a decorative yet conservative support – with two lateral handles and a golden stand-ring to broaden the standing surface – by the Milanese goldsmith, whose name is still unknown, and who also collaborated with Gasparo Miseroni on additional works. The handles are each composed of two snakes, held together in the middle by a ring. Because the handles are each fastened to the border at only one point, the richly enamelled snakes appear to float on or above the basin wall.

Franz Kirchweger

Provenance: 1570 in inventory of Grand Duke Cosimo I de' Medici's Guardaroba in the Palazzo Vecchio in Florence; 1628 as gift of Grand Duke Ferdinando II to Emperor Ferdinand II

Bibliography: Distelberger 2002, 148, cat. no. 63 (with bibliography); Vienna 2003, 399, cat. no. III.3.13 (R. Distelberger).

V.14
Gasparo Miseroni
Bowl in the Shape of a Shell
Milan, c. 1565-1570
Rock crystal, set in enamelled gold
23.5 × 30.2 × 19.4 cm

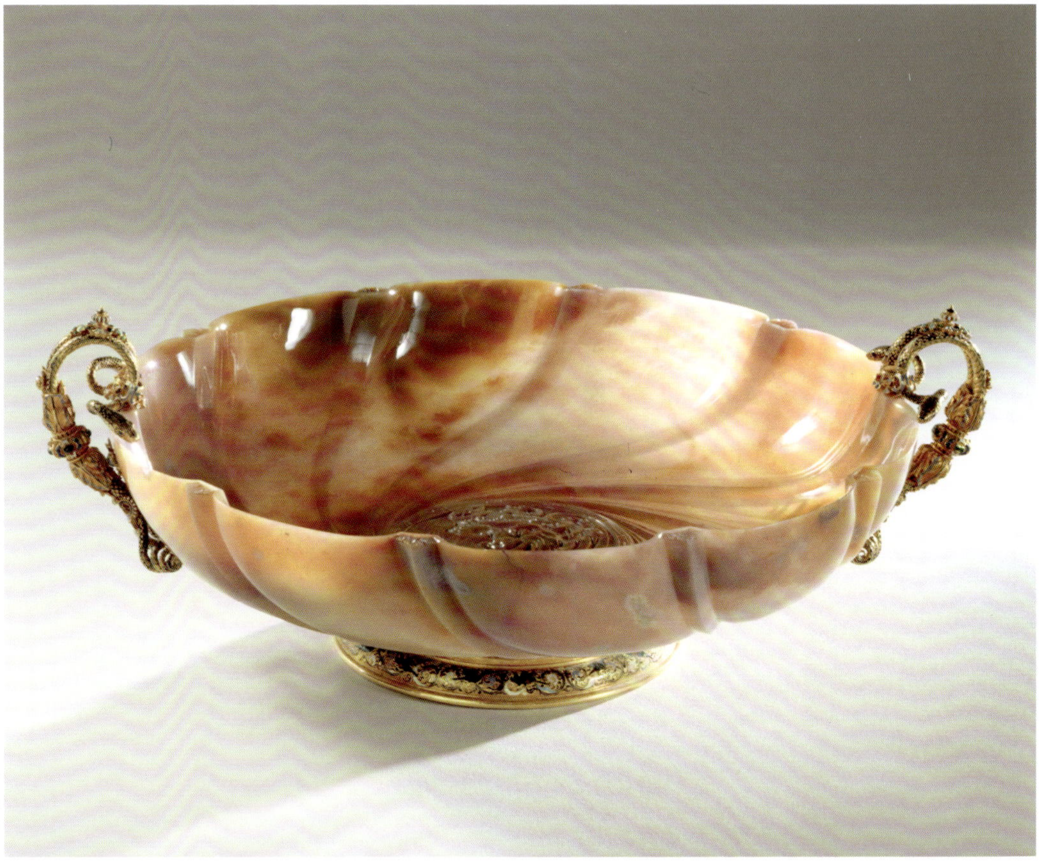
V.13

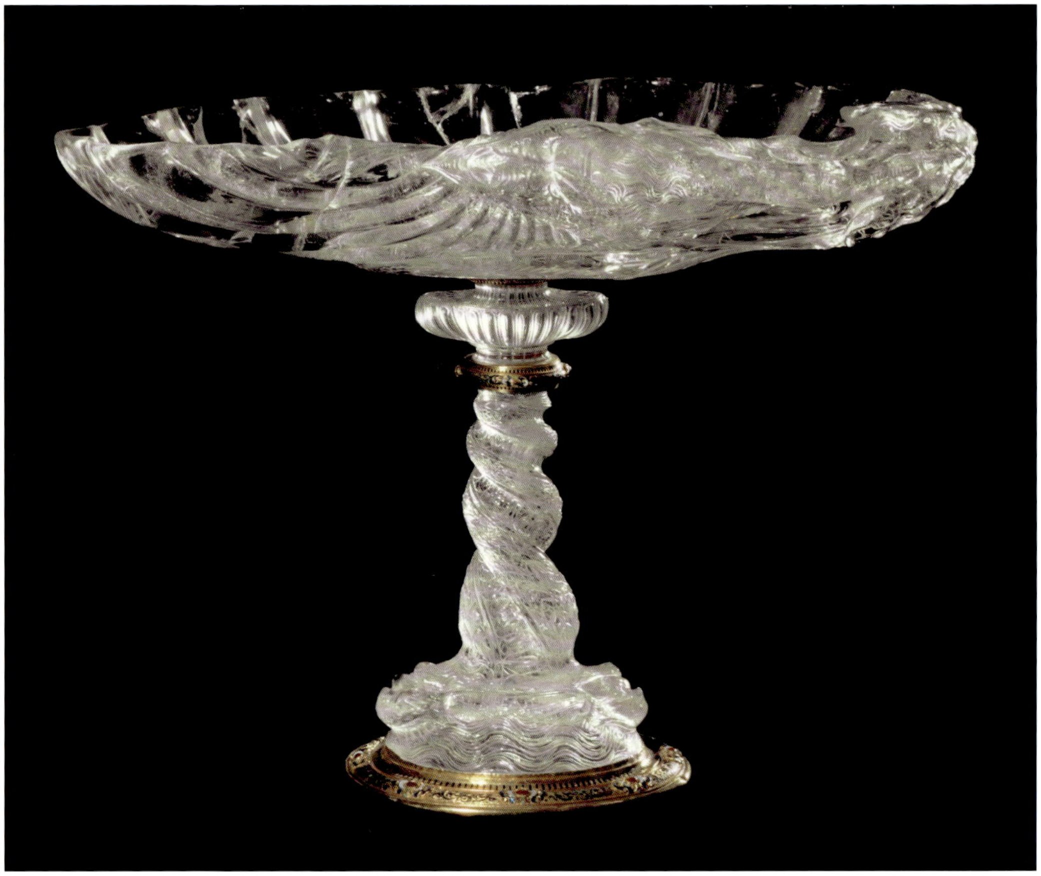
V.14

Vienna, Kunsthistorisches Museum, Kunstkammer, inv. no. KK 2268

Two serpent-like dragons with scaly bodies intertwined in a spiral serve as a stem supporting the flat, oval shell, which forms the cantilevered bowl of this richly designed ornamental container. Another dragon winds its snake-body around the bowl's foot appendix and clamps itself onto the lock of the sixteen-lobed shell. The front of its body, formed in high relief, with its gristly spine and deeply undercut webbed legs also forms the upper-rear edge of the bowl. The form of the dragon inscribed on the bowl remains clearly visible, although it requires a closer examination to comprehend the design's compositional complexity and its richness of detail. This is also true of the decoration of the shell's floor. It contains miniature inlays with the representation of an aquatic environment, upon and above which winged dragons and other fabled creatures fight.
This vessel bowl is considered a masterpiece of the Milanese Gasparo Miseroni (circa 1518-1573). As one of the most important stonecutters of his time, he established the fame of the Miseroni workshop around the middle of the 16th century. The workshop remained active through many generations, providing numerous royal houses with its objects. Between 1565 and 1571, he also frequently supplied rock crystal containers to the court of Emperor Maximilian II (who reigned from 1564-1576) in Vienna. Gasparo was credited for the invention of this type of bowl in the shape of a shell with dragon, of which numerous variations have survived. In 1568, Giorgio Vasari admired this invention of Gasparo Miseroni in a similar bowl in Florence. According to R. Distelberger (2002, 80, 134), the design refers to Leonardo da Vinci's idea of combining various body parts of animals in the formation of the most grotesque and bizarre fantasy creatures possible.
The game of alienation makes an exemplary appearance in the shell bowl: the natural material of the extremely hard, transparent rock crystal is transformed through the stonecutter's artistry into a completely new, albeit zoomorphic natural form.

Franz Kirchweger

Provenance: 1596 in Estate Inventory of Archduke Ferdinand II of Tyrol, fol. 351 (Jb. VII,2, CCLXXX)

Bibliography: Ambras 2001, 45f., cat. no. 21 (R. Distelberger); Distelberger 2002, 135f., cat. no. 53 (with bibliography); Vienna 2003 (R. Distelberger).

V.15
Gasparo Miseroni
Lidded Bowl in Prase
Milan, c. 1565-1570
Prase, set in enamelled gold, rubies, emeralds, pearls, onyx cameos
19.3 × 23.9 × 16.3 cm
Vienna, Kunsthistorisches Museum, Kunstkammer, inv. no. KK 2014

Prase is a gemstone from the quartz family, which has been greatly coveted since ancient times. The Greeks named it for its characteristic leek-green colour. An unusually large piece of this rare stone was used for this lidded bowl.
A small gradation offsets the paunched floor of the bowl from the slightly concave wall, which ends with a thrice-stepped lip. The wall, only slightly more than one millimeter thick, and the soft, convex-concave swell of the lid demonstrate a technical perfection, which, in the examined period, can only be associated with Gasparo Miseroni. The virtuosity of the extremely thin cut, which, in this bowl, is considered "a merit in itself" (Distelberger 2002, 152), as well as details such as the minute lion masks with crowns of leaves on the walls, indicate the hand of this Milanese stonecutter, who was one of the most expert specialist in this field in his time. The three small cameos with black-skinned girls on the knob of the lid could be considered precursors of the Miseroni workshop's later works (Compare Distelberger 2002, cat. nos. 71, 72).
For the stone bowl, there is no question that the goldwork setting was intended from the onset as a striking enhancement and suspenseful contrast. The dark green of the elegantly proportioned, yet frugal stone container thus contrasts with the intensive colour effect of the goldwork elements. The stand-ring and the wide border of the lid feature the enamelled tendril reliefs with stone and pearl inlay that are characteristic of Milanese goldwork. Particularly striking are the two handles in the form of two grotesque harpies, which, among others, refer to designs by Giulio Romano as possible models. The bolt necessary for attaching the harpies to the lion masks was utilized here in a manner that was characteristic of this period, in order to transform the technical solution into a curious effect: the flat screw-nut used for the attachment became the tongue of the lion mask.

Franz Kirchweger

Provenance: 1607-1611 in the Kunstkammer of Emperor Rudolf II in Prague, fol. 228, no. 1439 (Jb. 72, 77)

Bibliography: Essen-Vienna 1988, vol. II, 216, cat. no. 689 (R. Distelberger); Distelberger 2002, 150-153, cat. no. 65 (with bibliography).

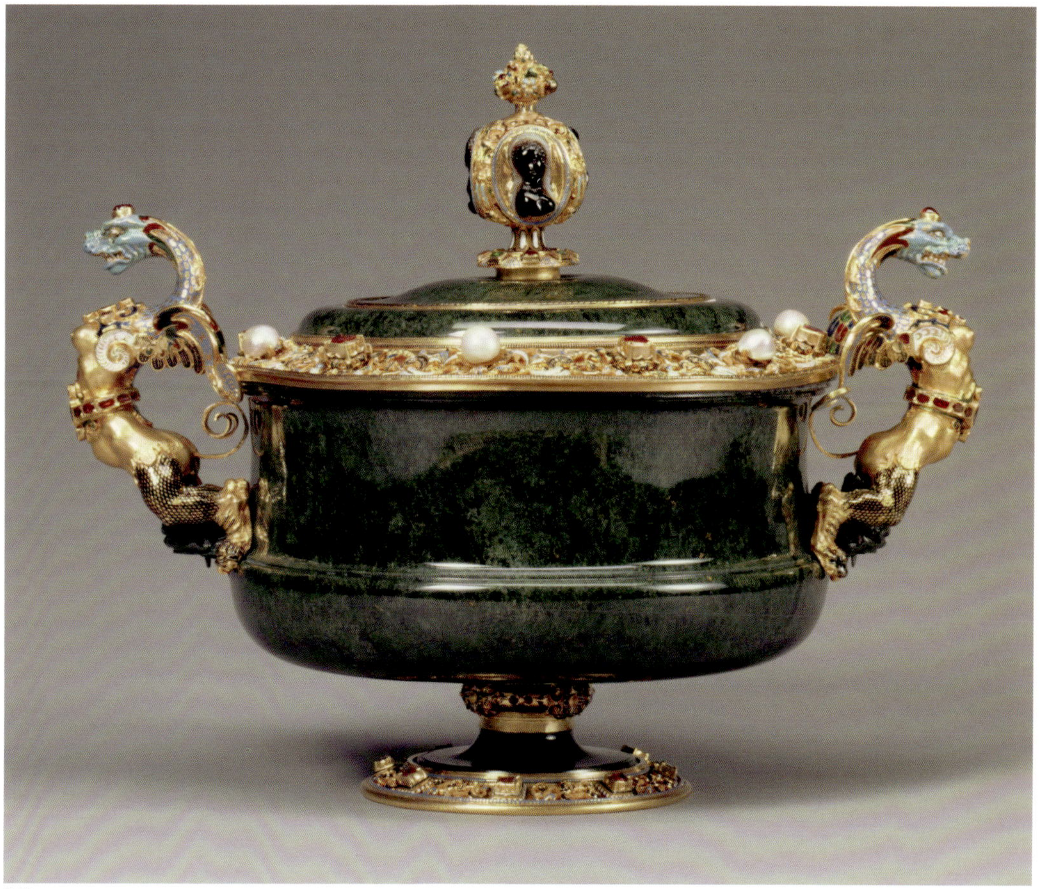

V.15

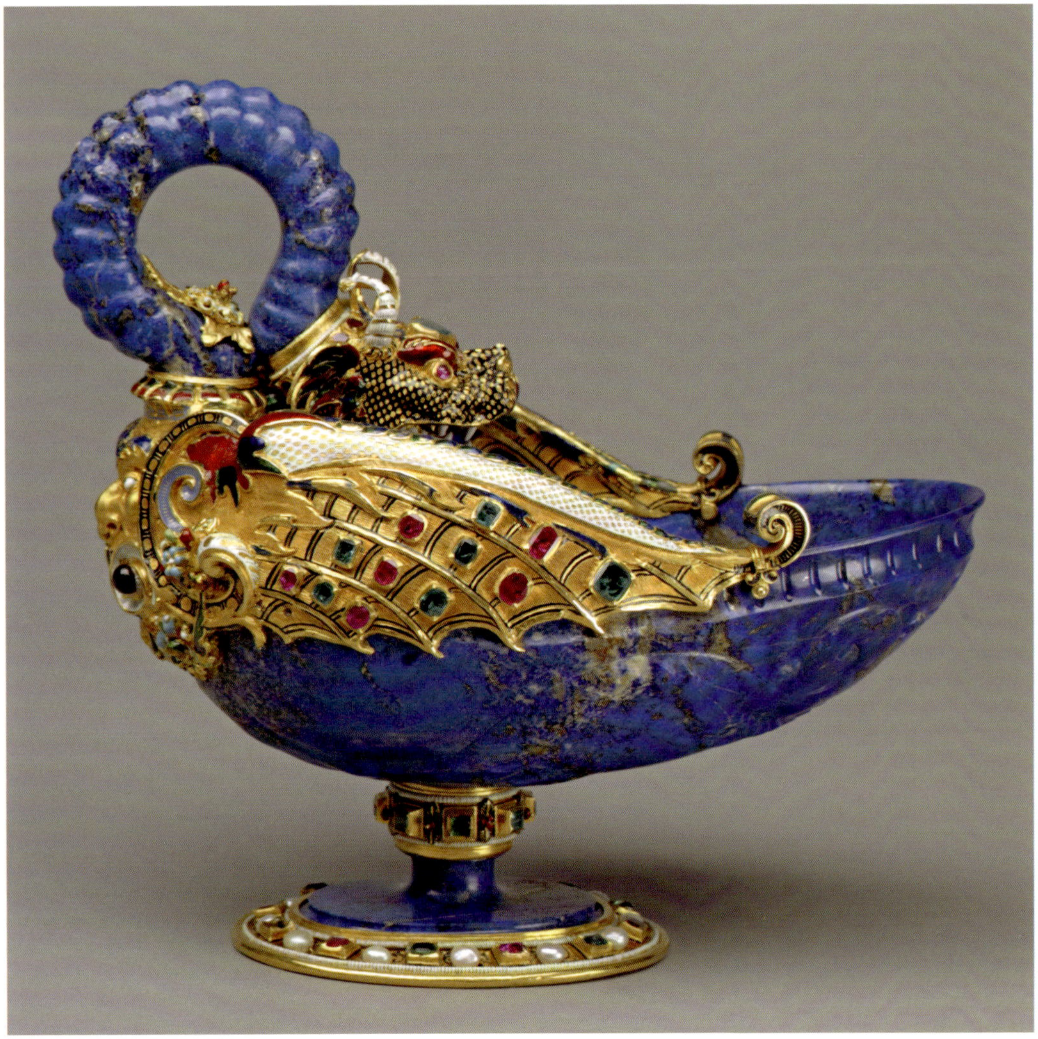

V.16

V.16
Gasparo Miseroni
Drachenschale (Dragon Bowl)
Milan, c. 1565-1570
Lapis lazuli, set in enamelled gold, rubies, emeralds, pearls, garnets
17.2 × 18.9 × 10.9 cm
Vienna, Kunsthistorisches Museum, Kunstkammer, inv. no. KK 1851

Even more so than in the lidded bowl in prase (cat. no. V.15), it is clear that the design of this decorative bowl in lapis lazuli was jointly conceived by the stonecutter and the goldsmith at the outset. Here it was not the goldsmith's job, as was normally the case, to simply assemble the individual pieces finished by the stonecutter, but rather he played a decisive role in giving this bowl the form of a sea dragon of both menacing fantasy as well as unusual decorative richness.

The shell-shaped bowl in lapis lazuli, whose walls show the fish-like webbed legs of the dragon, has an enamelled gold support mounted to the back portion, enveloping the bowl towards the front with two large, outspread wings. Arching above it is the gristly stone neck of the horned dragon with sparkling ruby-eyes and wide-open mouth, seemingly ready to regurgitate upon an imaginary drinker. On its back is a large mask in enamelled gold with a ferocious expression and a sort of snaffle between its teeth. Clamped between coving clasps and multicoloured flower-festoons, the mask's demonic edge is melted into grotesque ornamentation.

The bowl is a variation on Gasparo Miseroni's model of various shell-bowls with zoomorphic decor in which a *mostro marino* with webbed legs lies upon a shell-castle and symmetrically surrounds the container (Distelberger 2002, 82). Numerous details of the gold-work are repeated in other works by Gasparo Miseroni and help to safely attribute this decorative bowl to the production of his Milanese workshop. The Miseronis held close familial relations with various Milanese goldsmiths (Distelberger, 2002, 80). However, it has not yet been possible to tie a specific name to these works.

Franz Kirchweger

Provenence: 1607-1611 in the Kunstkammer of Emperor Rudolf II in Prague, fol. 238, no. 1473 (Ib. 72, 1976, 79)

Bibliography: Essen-Vienna 1988, vol. II, 216, cat. no. 690 (R. Distelberger); Distelberger 2002, 153f., cat. no. 66 (with bibliography).

V.17
Caspar Ulrich (attributed)
Handstone with Crucifixion and Resurrection Scenes
Saint Joachimsthal, third quarter of the 16th century
Silver gilt, partially enamelled, minerals, piece of silver ore
H. 27.4 cm
Vienna, Kunsthistorisches Museum, Kunstkammer, inv. no. KK 4149

The original meaning of the term handstone was used for a piece of ore that was extraordinary in its size or shape and which was intended to be appreciated whilst held in the hand and usually served as a gift from a miner to the owner of a mine. Later, these rock samples were prized for their natural, often bizarre and, in the sense of a miniature world, perfect shape and were collected as unprocessed minerals. During the course of the 16th century, outstanding pieces of ore were artistically modified with increasing frequency and adorned with other materials and goldwork. Not unlike casts from nature, they were also combined with organic items and converted to kunstkammer objects. The first handstones manufactured in this way appear, in all likelihood, to have originated in S. Joachimsthal (Jáchymov) in the Bohemian Ore Mountains, from which most of the handstones in the Kunsthistorisches Museum come. The handstone pictured here stands on a gilt base. An assemblage of various minerals on the lower half forms the background for a mining scene. On the upper end of the artificial handstone kneels a miner, who is praying in the direction of a crucifixion scene. This is cut from a pure piece of silver ore under which a panel is located, engraved with the inscription "DAS BLVT IHESV / CHRISTI REINIGET / VNS VON ALLEN / SVNDEN" (the blood of Jesus Christ cleanses us from all sin). On the reverse side of the silver ore, Christ's resurrection, drawn from Dürer's woodcut of the Great Passion, is portrayed (B. 15). The handstone, which unifies the artificially assembled lower section (populated with enamelled figures) and the upper section of natural, but aesthetically modified ore, can be attributed to Caspar Ulrich, a goldsmith from Saint Joachimsthal.

Paulus Rainer

Bibliography: Storczer 1993, 101-103; Distelberger 1985, 273f.

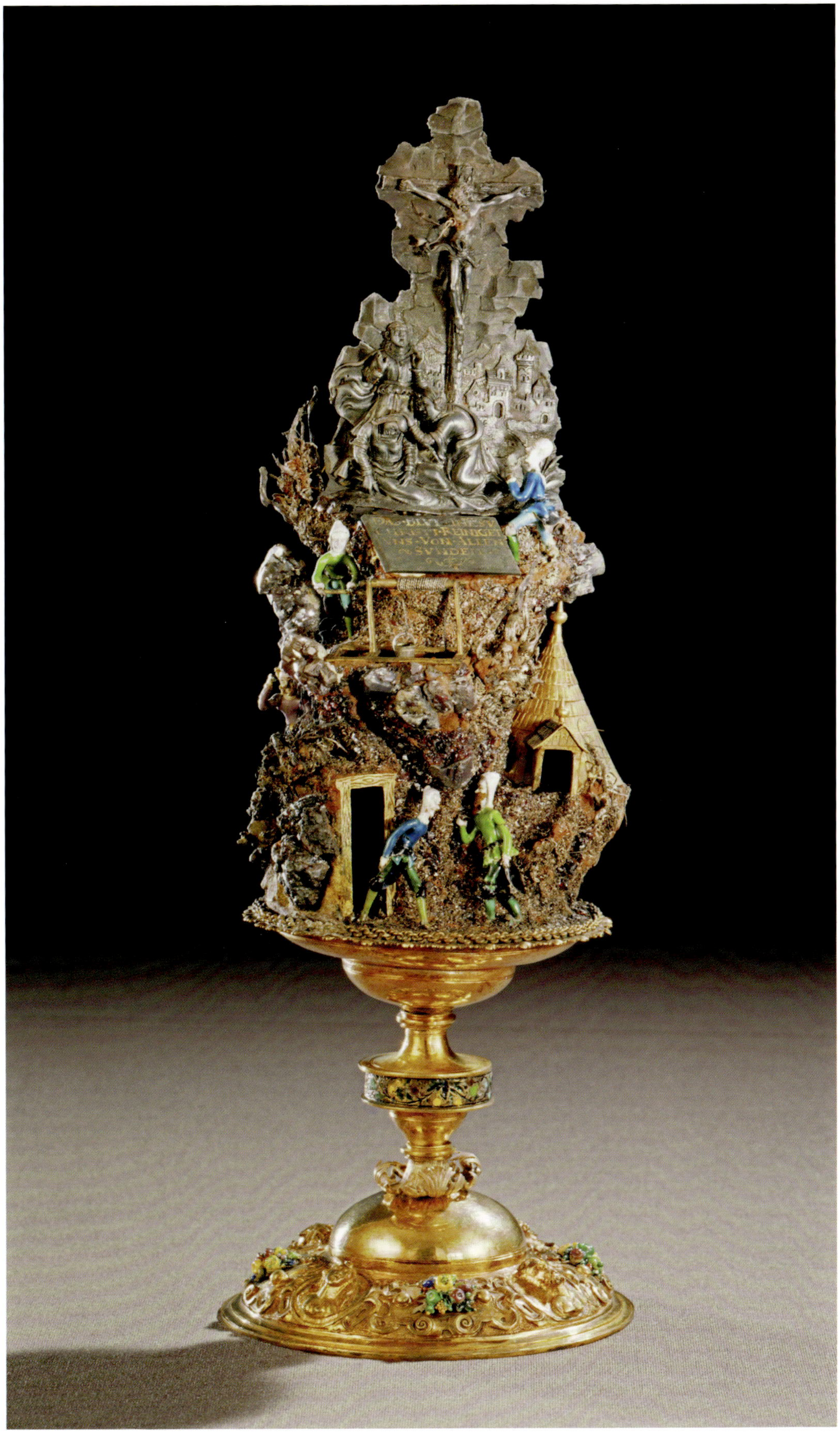

V.17

V.18
Leonhard I Bräm (Brem)
(Master 1531, died 1565)
Cup in the shape of a fool's head
Zurich, dated 1556
inspection and master signs
Coconut, setting: silver, partially gold-plated
H. 18 cm
Vienna, Kunsthistorisches Museum, Kunstkammer, inv. no. KK 911

Coconuts were often used as containers in the 16th century (cat. no. V.19) and thereby frequently completed in animal forms such as owls, ostrichs or peacocks. With this drinking vessel, the alienation effect is even further heightened.
The coconut, positioned diagonally across a low base, through its mounting takes on the appearance of a fool's cap with donkey ears, with a comb formed of nine bells and a collar also laden with bells. In order to fill it and use it as a drinking vessel, the coconut must first be turned over. The two long donkey ears thereby simultaneously served as handles and legs for placing the vessel on the table. A lid once presumably completed the Viennese fool's head cup, as in the closely related example conserved in Basel (Fritz 1983, 101, cat. no. 79, plate 42a). There, the lid was made from the section of the coconut with the germinal holes, using the physiognomic similarity, to give the fool's cap a sort of "face". More representative human facial features are shown on the lid of a silver fool's head cup from circa 1570, now conserved in Bern (Richter 2006, 13, cat. no. 2). If such a lid was applied to the Viennese fool's head cup, as in the Bern example, its removal could also be interpreted along the lines of an unmasking, which transforms the figure into a drinking vessel before the eyes of those present. Even without the lid, however, the cup has elements of ambiguity and mutability, as are generally associated with the figure of the fool. The ambivalence between design and use, which apparently contradicts the conventional experience patterns in association with drinking vessels, is characteristic of the so-called "*Scherzgefäße*" (novelty vessels) and "*Trinkspiele*" (drink games) from the 16th century north of the Alps.

Franz Kirchweger

Provenance: 1596 in Estate Inventory of Archduke Ferdinand II from Tyrol, fol. 358r (Jb. VII,2, Reg. 5556, CCLXXXII)

Bibliography: Lösel 1983, 164, no. 68b (with bibliography); Fritz 1983, 102, cat. no. 80; Ambras 2006, 275, cat. no. 5.34 (K. Seidl; with bibliography).

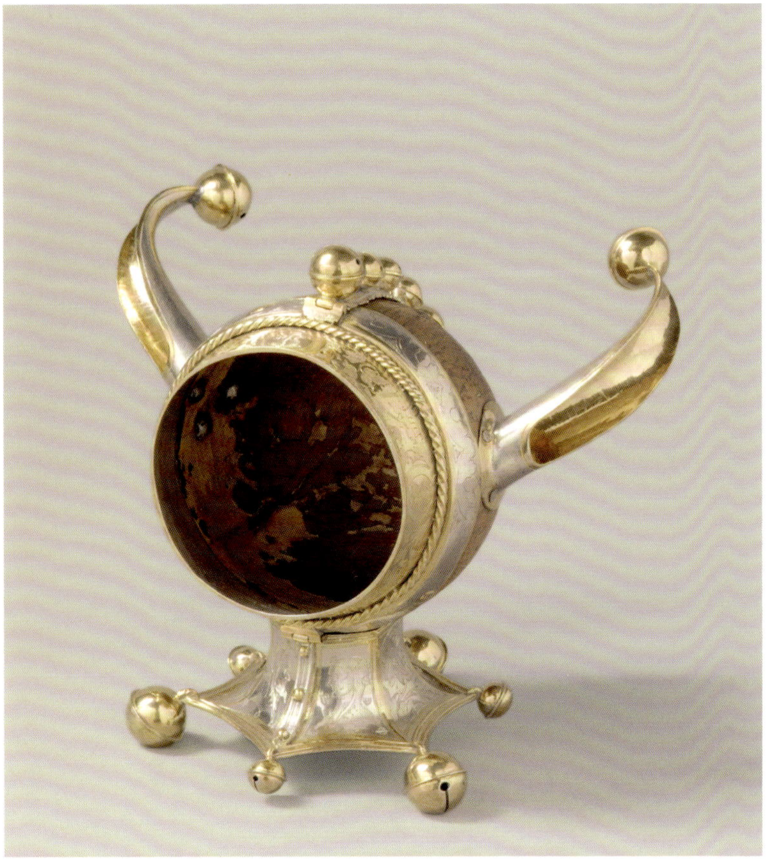

V.18

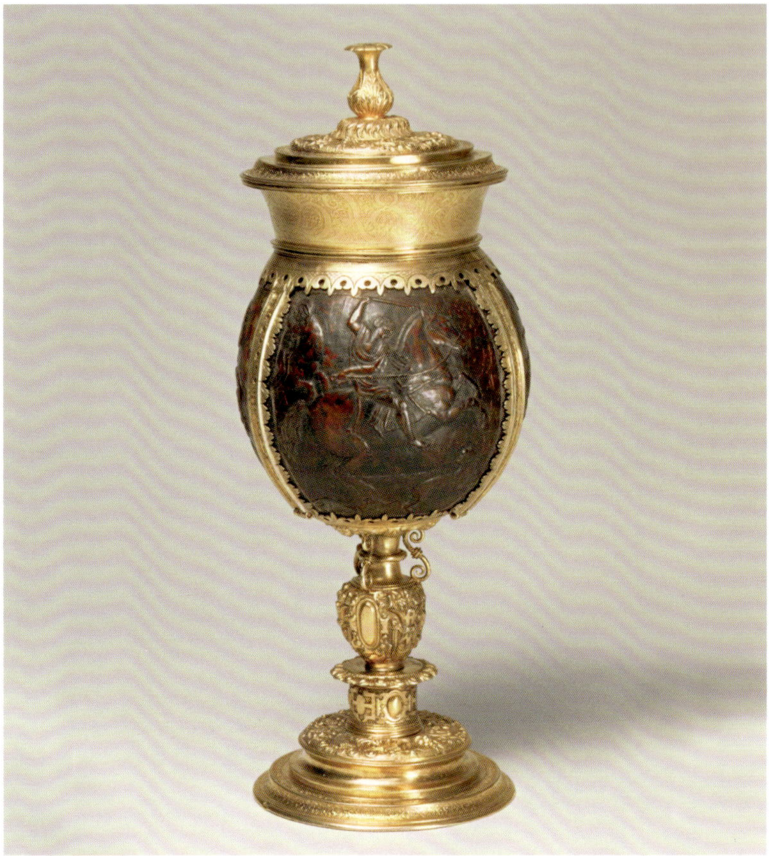

V.19

V.19
Michael Keberlin
Coconut Cup
Augsburg
c. 1568-1570
Assay mark for Augsburg (probably SEL 6) and maker's mark (SEL 797a), Viennese secondary tax mark 1806-07
Coconut, gilt silver
H. 28.5 cm, Ø 13 cm
Vienna, Kunsthistorisches Museum, Kunstkammer, inv. no. KK 919

Like the ostrich egg (compare cat. nos. V.24 and V.25), the coconut was prized not only because of its exoticism but also for its purported medical properties. Marco Polo had already praised the effects of coconut milk, which alleviated, among other things, tapeworm, fever, kidney and bladder afflictions and served as an aphrodisiac as well. The nut's shell was rumoured to possess the ability to reveal poisons, a belief which persisted well into the 18th century. This particular attribute of the ocean nut or Indian nut, as the fruit of the coconut palm was also called, predetermined its use as the cup element in drinking vessels. The vessel could protect the drinker from poisoning and was at the same time an object of prestigious exoticism. The design of the standing cup is typical of southern Germany in the second half of the 16th century. The vessel rises above a repeatedly molded and stepped foot, which is decorated with etched Moresque banding on its lower edge. The second level of the foot is adorned with elaborate interlaced bands and mascarons. From this a short shaft arises, which leads into a vase-shaped nodus. The surface of the shaft and nodus are covered in strapwork cartouches. Three S-shaped volutes lead to the main vessel. This is fashioned from a large coconut shell whose surface is decorated in faux-antique flat relief. Three brackets secure the carved fruit and hold it between two cuffs. A tall, conical, cantilevered brim is affixed on top. This is covered with a dense lattice of etched Moresques. The flat lid of the goblet matches the extensively stepped foot (whose decoration it reflects) and is topped with a vase-shaped knob trimmed with acanthi.

Paulus Rainer

Bibliography: Fritz 1983, 106, no. 111; Innsbruck 2006, 71f., no. 2.16.

V.20
Powder Flask in the Form of a Tortoise
Southern Germany (?), second half of 16th century
Shell of a Greek tortoise (*Testudo hermanni boettgeri*), setting: silver
5.6 × 15 × 8.2 cm
Vienna, Kunsthistorisches Museum, Kunstkammer, inv. no. KK 890

The marksman had to carry on his person the powder necessary for the early hand firearms in a so-called powder flask or powder horn. Normally, small containers were used for the finely ground priming powder that was sprinkled on the powder pan ("Zündkraut") and served to light the propellant, which was normally dispensed by a mechanism that regulates the amount of powder disbursed through the nozzle-spout ("Pulversperre"), in contrast to the containers that were later used for carrying the coarser black powder. This is also the case with this example of the powder flask in the form of a tortoise. For this container, the entire shell of a Greek tortoise was used. The soft parts of the animal were exceptionally reconstructed in silver and applied to the armour in the appropriate positions. The neck and the head of the tortoise were employed together as the nozzle-spout for the powder flask. On the bottom of the shell a long, silver closure lever is attached, which, with the help of a spring mechanism – no longer existing – opened and closed the animal's mouth opening with equal pours of powder from the powder flask. Three rings on the underside were originally used to attach a carrying strap.
Powder flasks were created in the most diverse

forms and materials (metal, leather, horn, bone, wood, ivory, etc.). Exotic materials such as seashells, lobster claws, coconuts and tortoise shells were also very popular. The combination of natural materials and a precious silver setting, as in the present example, made the hunting tool also a curious showpiece for the princely kunstkammer.

Franz Kirchweger

Bibliography: Ambras 2006, 275, cat. no. 5.34 (F. Kirchweger).

V.21
Bottle in the Shape of a Heart
Central America, Mexico (?) or India, Gujarat (?), 16th century; the assembly: Iberian Peninsula, circa 1580
Tortoiseshell, silver
H 26.3 cm
Vienna, Kunsthistorisches Museum, Kunstkammer, inv. no. KK 4100

The tortoiseshell obtained from the carapace of a certain turtle fascinated the people of this period because of its transparency, coloration and patterning. The material, when softened in boiling water, could be pressed into large plates and could even be shaped into three-dimensional forms to produce caskets, bowls, horns, combs and even bottles. Contemporary accounts from the 16th and 17th centuries document this type of production on the west coast and in the north west (Gujarat) of India (Vienna 2000, cat. 83, 84).
Heart-shaped bottles that presented this exotic material in such an unusual form must have been especially strange in Europe. Two such examples are actually conserved in the kunstkammer of the Kunsthistorisches Museum (Vienna 2000, cat. 85, 86). Both bottles must have originally been carried hanging on chains. The silver foot-stand was added later, when the objects were adapted for display in the princely collection. Where the bottles themselves were originally created has still not been ascertained. The engravings with geometric ornaments on the surfaces would more likely indicate their origin in Central America (Vienna 2000, cat. 89).
This heart-shaped bottle, together with its counterpart, can be traced back to the kunstkammer of Archduke Ferdinand II of Tyrol. Similar bottles are also documented in the kunstkammer in Graz as well as in the imperial collection of Rudolf II in Prague (Bauer, Haupt 1976, 25f., no. 424: “Two bottles, also of tortoiseshell, studded with silver, formed into a translucent, yellow heart...”). In Ambras, however, it was associated with glass or earth, although eight tortoiseshells hung on the wall in the library of Ambras Castle, one of them elaborately painted (Vienna 2000, cat. 222, 223). In Prague, on the other hand, this material was

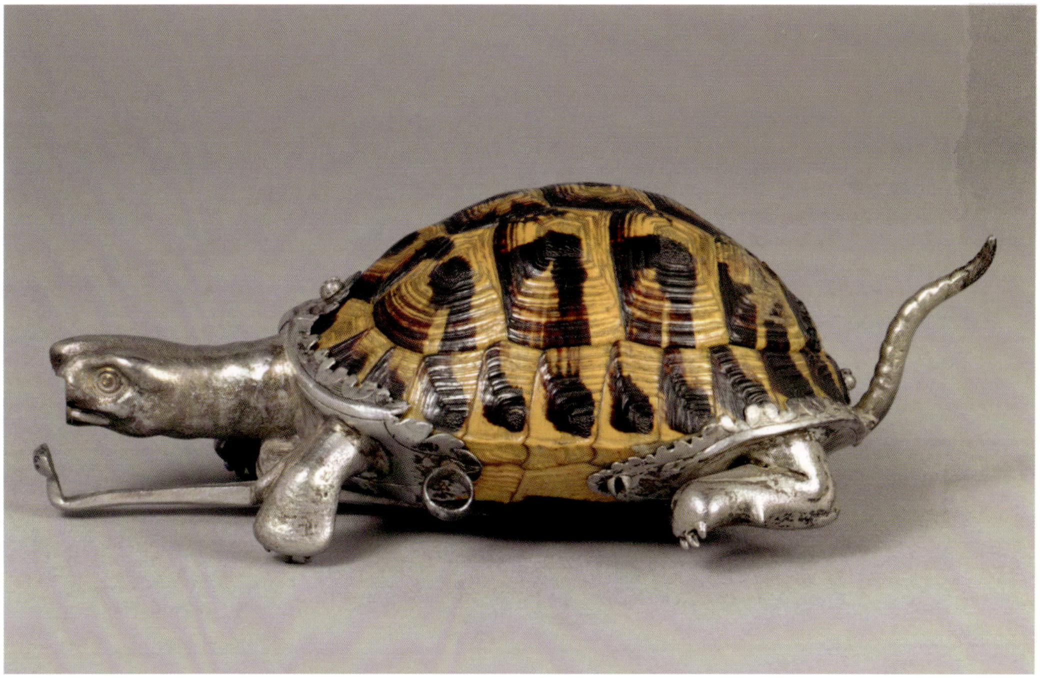

V.20

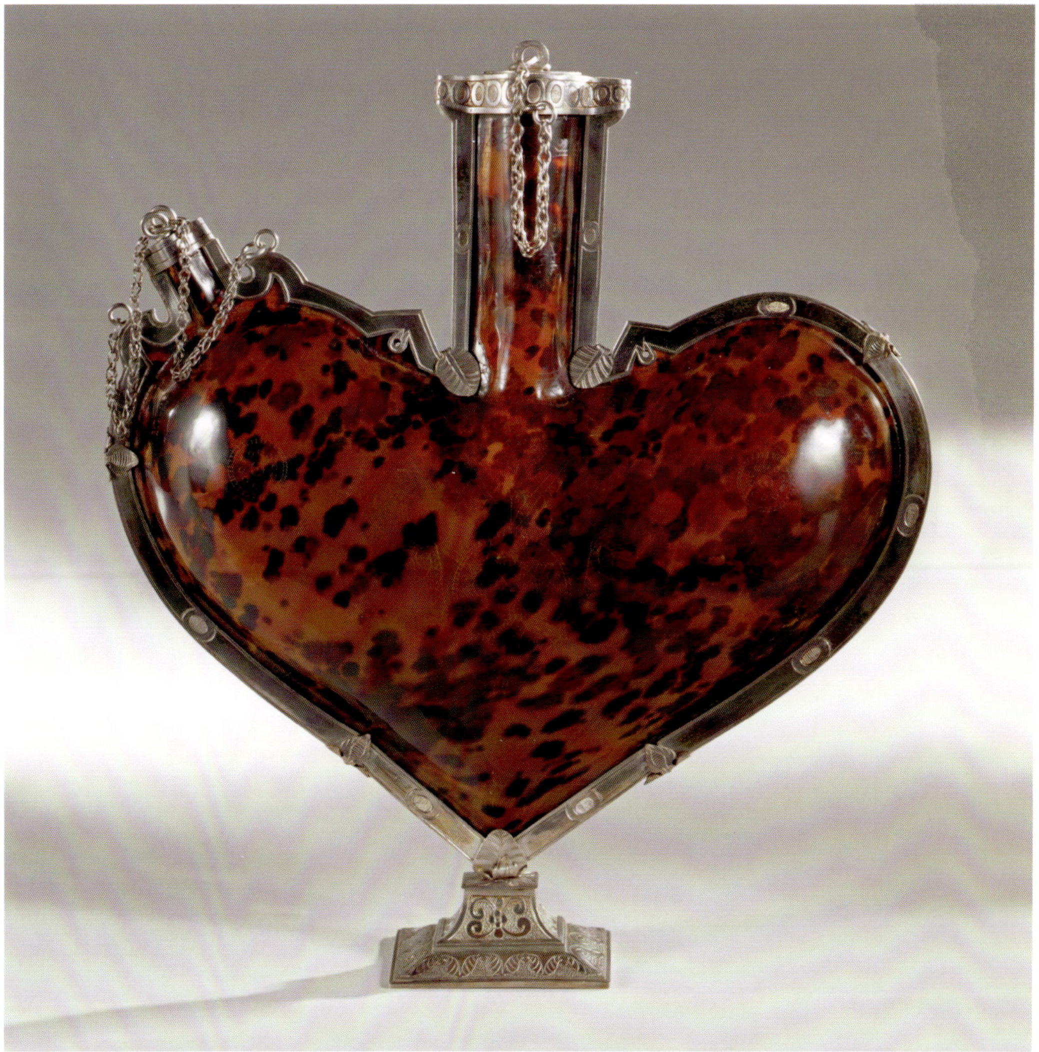

V.21

appropriately called "tartaruga", or tortoiseshell. In his *Allegory of Water* (cat. no. V.26) from 1566, Arcimboldo had already included an extremely precise representation of the Loggerhead Sea Turtle (*Caretta caretta*), also native to the Mediterranean.

Franz Kirchweger

Provenance: 1596 in Estate Inventory of Archduke Ferdinand II of Tyrol, fol. 457r (Jb. VII / 2, 1888, Reg. 5556, CCCVI: "Also, one Indian bottle, shaped like a heart, from cast glass or earth, black and yellow, round with pure silver rings, chains and studded with silver")

Bibliography: Vienna 2000, 174, cat. no. 86 (H. Trnek; with additional bibliography).

V.22
Wenzel Jamnitzer (workshop)
Nautilus Cup in the Form of a Chicken
Nuremberg, third quarter of the 16th century
Nautilus, silver, parcel gilt, painted, cast from nature
H. 18.4 cm
Vienna, Kunsthistorisches Museum, Kunstkammer, inv. no. KK 1060

The shell of the Nautilus pompilius was among the exotic natural objects being imported as jewellery to Europe via Portugal in the 16th century. Since the Renaissance, the shell of this cephalopod was frequently decorated with goldwork in order to emphasize its uncommon value and to augment its visual impact. With its large chamber opening and evenly shaped edge, the nautilus lends itself very well to the creation of drinking vessels and goblets. The outermost layers of the shell would often be removed – as is the case with the drinking vessel at hand – so that its dazzling mother of pearl was revealed; a formative moment in the art of goldsmithing. Here, this unusual natural object forms the body of a rooster and represents a purely aesthetic effort, rather than being motivated by allegorical content. The head of the rooster sits at the tip of the shell's spiral, while the chamber opening is surrounded by an engraved band and serves as the brim of the drinking vessel. The head and neck of the bird, as well as its abdomen and its legs, are cast and somewhat crudely engraved. This stands in stark contrast to the finely wrought lower portion, which serves as the base of the drinking vessel. Here, four lizards crawl through delicately rendered grasses and bushes and glance upwards at the rooster in attack posture. The lifelike appearance of these lizards and grasses arises from the fact that they were created as natural casts. In order to further enhance their natural appearance, they were coloured and the remaining paint is still visible. Due to the quality of its technical execution, the base is rightly attributed to Jamnitzer's Nuremberg workshop (Kris 1932, 31), although it is difficult to establish a connection between the Nuremberg master and the rooster itself.

Paulus Rainer

Bibliography: Kris 1932, 31, no. 45; Hayward 1967, 148; Mette 1990, 20; Mette 1995, 108, 187, cat. no. 12 (with wrong inventory number).

V.23
Endris (Andreas) II Degen
Seashell Cup
Augsburg, c. 1580
Assay mark for Augsburg (SEL 15) and maker's mark (SEL 675)
Shell of a knobbed triton (*Charonia lampas*), gilt silver
H. 40.5 cm
Vienna, Kunsthistorisches Museum, Kunstkammer, inv. no. KK 6863

This exotic art object is described as "a sea snail upon a gilded silver foot with satyr and gilded mouthpiece" in the estate inventory of Archduke Ferdinand II of Tyrol from 30 May 1596 (Jb. VII/2, 1888, Reg. 5556, CCLXXXII). A knobbed triton (*Charonia lampas*) is meant by "sea snail", a kind of mollusk, which by virtue of its rarity and imposing shell was sought after by collectors. This mollusk was named after Triton, the son of Aphrodite and Amphitrite (Hesiod, Theogonie 930-933), who in the visual arts is usually depicted with such a shell which he uses as a trumpet. It is therefore probable that the supporting figure, which carries the precious natural object on its shoulders, is not – as the historical inventory describes – a satyr, but rather Triton himself. Contorted under the enormous weight of the oversized shell, his upper body is bent over a rolling, S-shaped strapwork. This structure supports him on the one hand, but he is also built into it and must therefore submit to his fate. With the bound Triton and the aesthetically modified natural object, the artist succeeds in bending nature, and even the world of the gods, to his purposes and placing them in service of mankind. It has already been suggested that ornament prints by Cornelis Floris and/or Cornelis Bos might have been inspiration to the goldsmith. (Kris 1932, 40; Munich 1994, 242f.). That Archduke Ferdinand II, the owner of this object, had a special fondness for these engravings and the motif of the bound figure is evidenced by a series of similar pages from his collection of etchings in the so-called Ambraser Klebebänden (Ambras Castle Volumes) (for example in the volume *Vasa diversa antique et moderna*, inv. no. KK 6633).

Paulus Rainer

Bibliography: Kris 1932, 39f., no. 60; Munich 1994, 242f.; Vienna 2000, 295, cat. no. 230; Innsbruck 2006, 262f., cat. no. 5.18.

V.24
Ostrich Egg Standing Cup
Leipzig, c. 1560-1580
Assay mark for Leipzig and unclear meker's mark (R3 3037)
Ostrich egg, gilt silver
H. 34 cm
Vienna, Kunsthistorisches Museum, Kunstkammer, inv. no. KK 982

Along with the feathers of the ostrich, the great eggs of the flightless bird played an important role in the long-distance trade of the Middle Ages. Imported at first primarily from Asia Minor and North Africa to Europe via Venice; by the early 17th century, trade had expanded and shifted to South Africa. In the 40th volume of the Great and Complete Universal Lexicon of all Sciences and Arts by Johann Heinrich Zedler (created 1732-1754) it is stated: "This egg is found in great abundance in Africa, particularly on the Cape of Good Hope [...] the whole egg is kept in art and natural cabinets as a rarity [...] The egg can be used as a drinking vessel and for other purposes". Indeed, ostrich eggs found use in the secular world in the art and marvel cabinets of princes as well as in sacristies and reliquaries. Both of these domains are combined in the iconography of the present example: here the christian pairs itself with the profane. A battle between tritons adorns the stepped foot and profane ornamentation also dominates the rest of the silver mounting. The three brackets, however, with which the ostrich egg is bound to the foot, are decorated with miniature, winged angels' heads. The conflict between profane symbolism and Christian allegory is particularly evident on the decoration which crowns the lid. Here, a nest with three small ostrichs is portrayed; among them, the mother rises up alongside the father bird, who winds a snake around his legs. On one hand, this image recalls the battle between the stork and the snake (Pliny, Naturalis historia, X 62), but on the other hand also bears a certain resemblance to the topos of the pelican feeding his chicks. The inside of the lid attests to a Christian meaning and with it confers the pelican motif to the ostrichs. Here, a medallion is mounted with a portrait of Christ and the inscription "christ/ vs".

Paulus Rainer

Bibliography: Kris 1932, 41, no. 62; Bock 2005, 234f., no. 29; Innsbruck 2006, 113, no. 2.55.

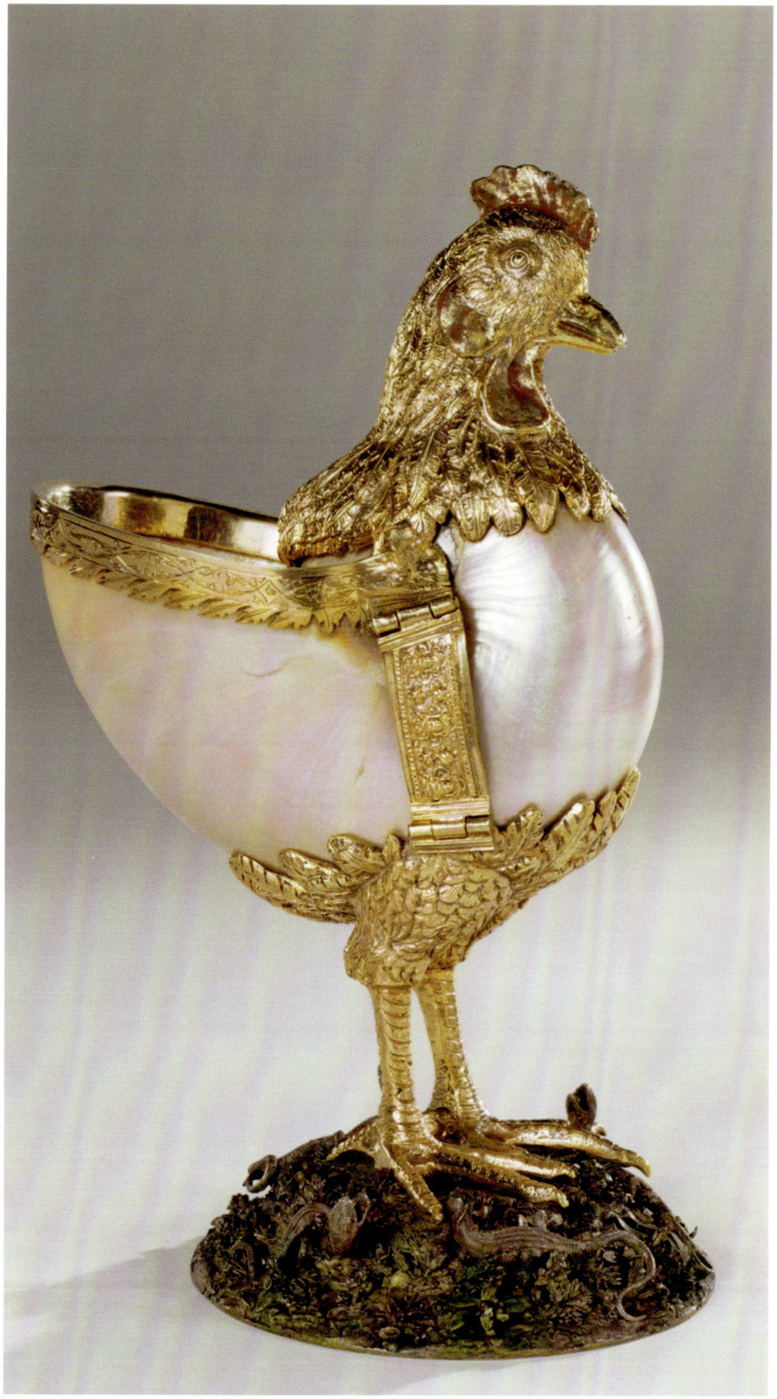
V.22

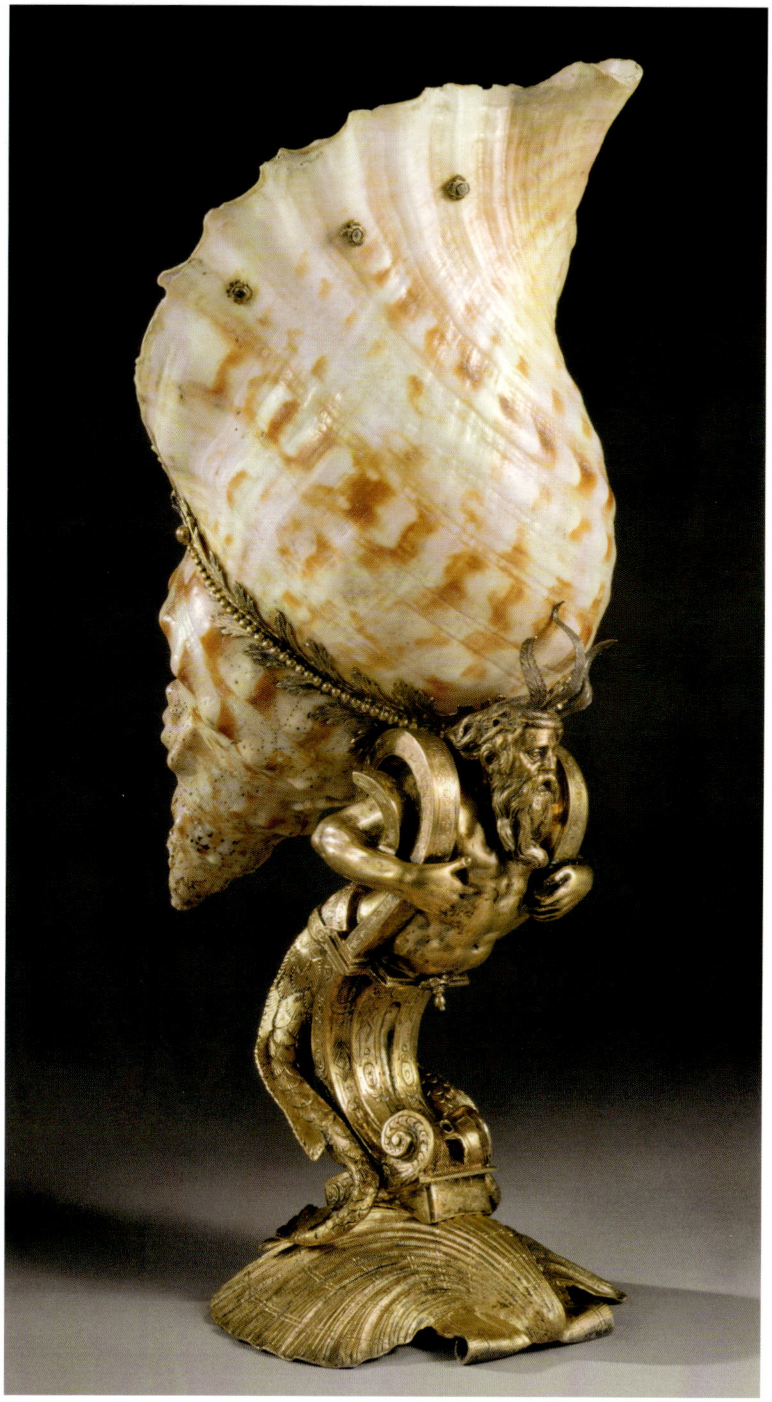
V.23

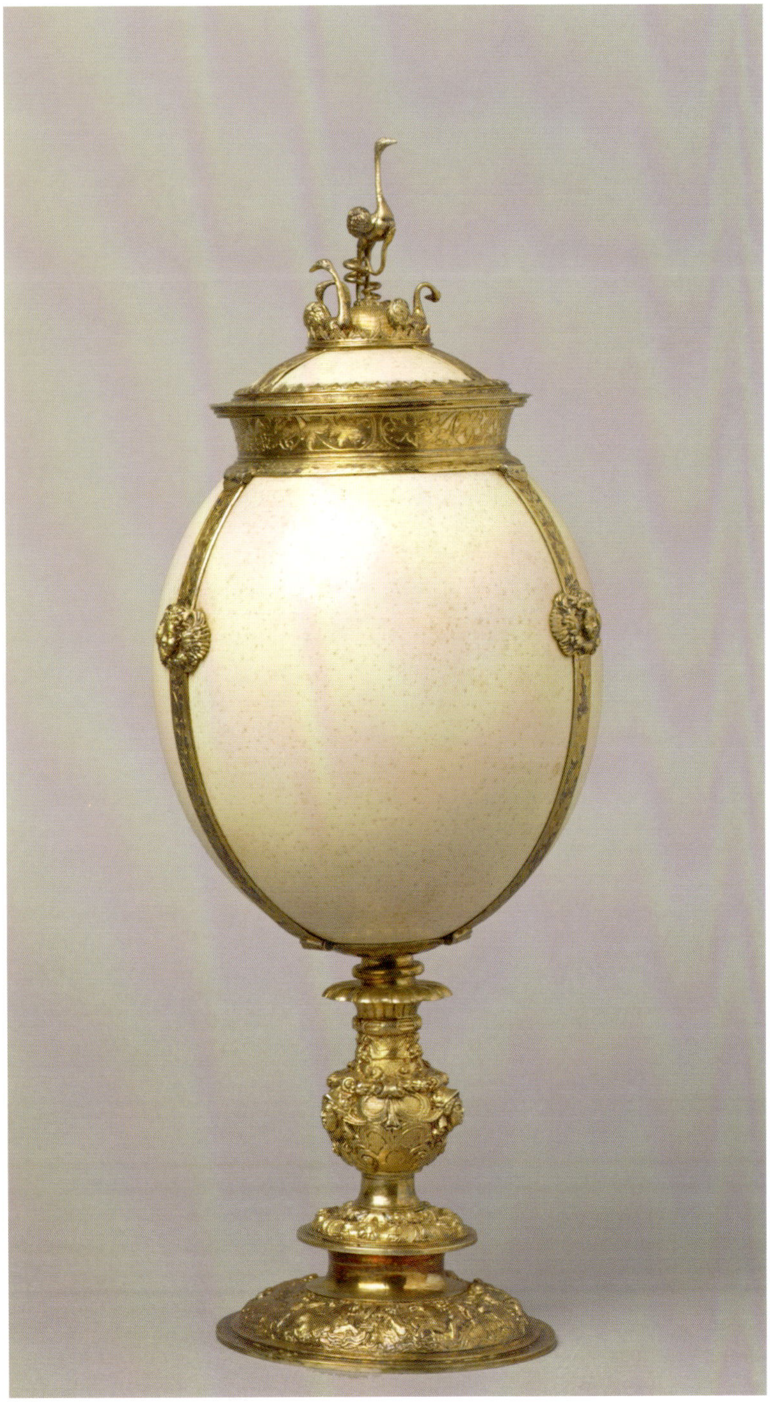

V.24

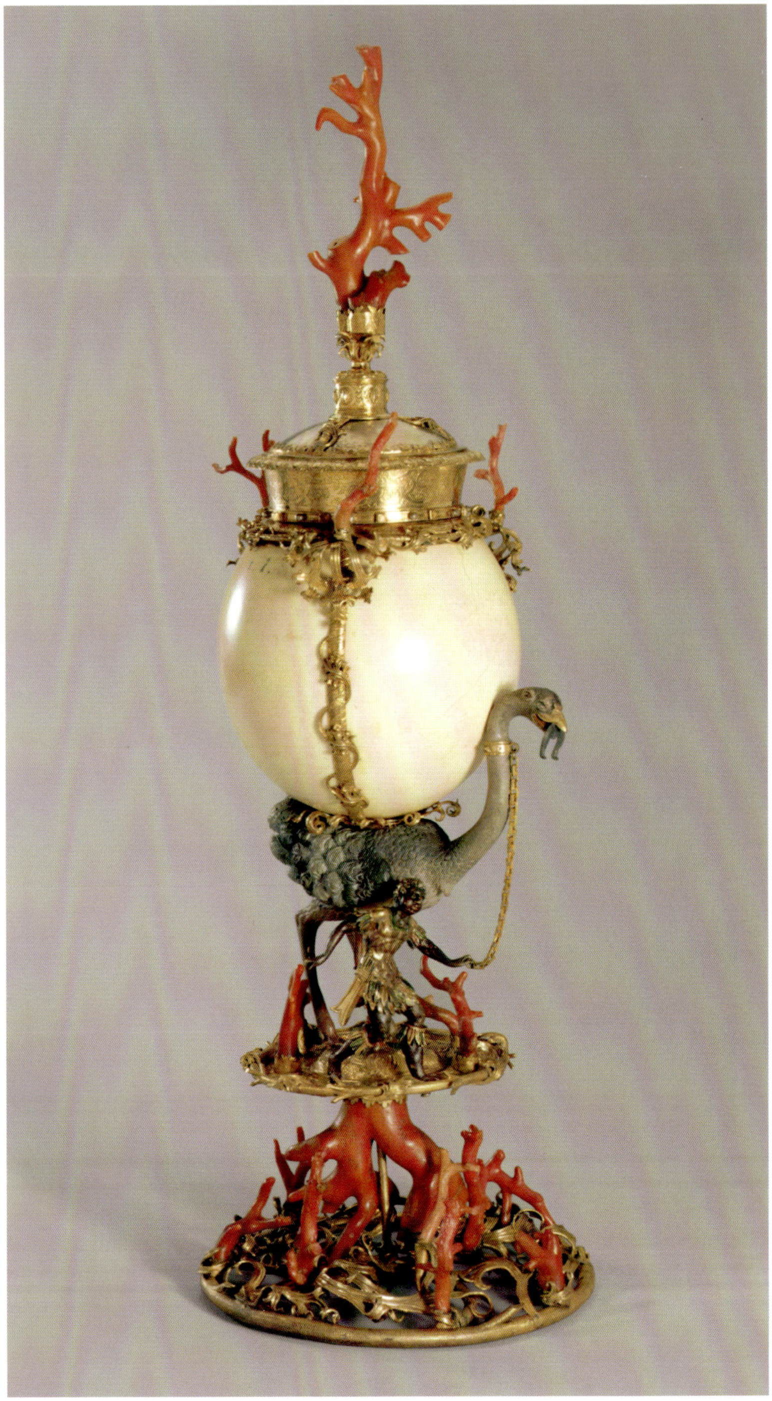

V.25

V.25
Clement Kicklinger
Ostrich Egg Standing Cup
Augsburg, c. 1570-1575
Assay mark for Augsburg (SEL 12) and maker's mark (SEL 735a)
Ostrich egg, coral, silver, parcel gilt, partially painted
H. 56.8 cm
Vienna, Kunsthistorisches Museum, Kunstkammer, inv. no. KK 897

This ornate object presents itself as an extremely exaggerated showpiece in which the extravagance of the materials used is balanced by the creativity of its concept and the craftsmanship of the goldsmith. A bent branch made of gilt silver forms the fragile and bizarre looking circular base. Large pieces of coral visually comprise the shaft of the goblet and appear to support the rest of the structure. Here, on the second level, a moor wearing a breastplate adorned with feathers leads an enormous ostrich by a chain. The latter carries a horseshoe in its beak – a reference to the bird's supposed ability to digest iron (Pliny, Naturalis historia, X 1). The flightless bird carries its own egg, secured with three brackets, on its back. The egg, with its banded brim, serves as the goblet's cup. A similarly secured spherical cap crowned with a thick branch of coral closes on the goblet as a lid. This elaborate object exhibits all the characteristics of a standing cup, but dispenses with any sort of functionality. The bizarre object cannot even be safely grasped in order to lift it. To bring the vessel to one's mouth when full would be almost impossible. In abandoning functionality in favour of increased refinement, the object eludes any use at all and is designed purely as an art piece. In that capacity, it is captivating in its vibrant colour and striking interplay of natural and vegetable in its goldwork. In its effective combination of exotic material with exceptional goldwork, the vessel can also be perceived as a allegory for Africa, referring to the materials of the goblet as well as to the motif, with ostrich and moor, from this continent.

Paulus Rainer

Bibliography: Kris 1932, 40, no. 61; Wagner 1985, 37; Scheicher 1995, 115-125; Seelig 1996, 486-492; Vienna 2000, 295-298, cat. no. 231; Bock 2005, 237f.

V.26
Pen and Ink Casket
Southern Germany, Genoa(?), second half of 16th century
Silver, coral
27 × 34.5 × 23 cm
Vienna, Kunsthistorisches Museum, Kunstkammer, inv. no. KK 1048

The flat silver casket on paw-shaped feet is partitioned into four equal sections for the storage of writing utensils, an inkwell and a duster. The external surfaces feature a rich decor of embossed ornaments. The cartouche work is divided into mascarons, festoons, female busts and personifications of virtues. The top of the lid is primarily decorated with sea creatures, such as tritons, nereids and fishes. These form an imaginary entourage for Neptune, the god of the sea, positioned on a plinth-like appendix in the middle of the case. The small, crowned sculpture is carved out of a branch of deep red coral (*Corallium rubrum*). In the formation of the two-tailed sea-monster and the extended movement of Neptune, the carver followed the natural shape of the coral. This leads us to believe that the small figure was not created in a workshop in Sicily or in southern Italy, but rather farther to the north, possibly in Genoa (Daneu 1964, 96). This type of coral carving apparently arrived from there as unfinished goods, sent farther north where it would be integrated into a larger context. In this case, the Neptune was presumably sent to Nuremberg, where it was fixed a top of the silver casket, which was created there. Archduke Ferdinand II of Tyrol possessed one of the largest coral collections of his time. The twelfth cabinet in the Kunstkammer in Ambras Castle was exclusively dedicated to the theme of coral. Along with crude and polished stems in red, black and white, there were numerous works containing or made entirely from coral. The undisputed highlight of the collection were the seven large cabinets that displayed multipartite, bizarre landscapes composed of shells, limestone, glass

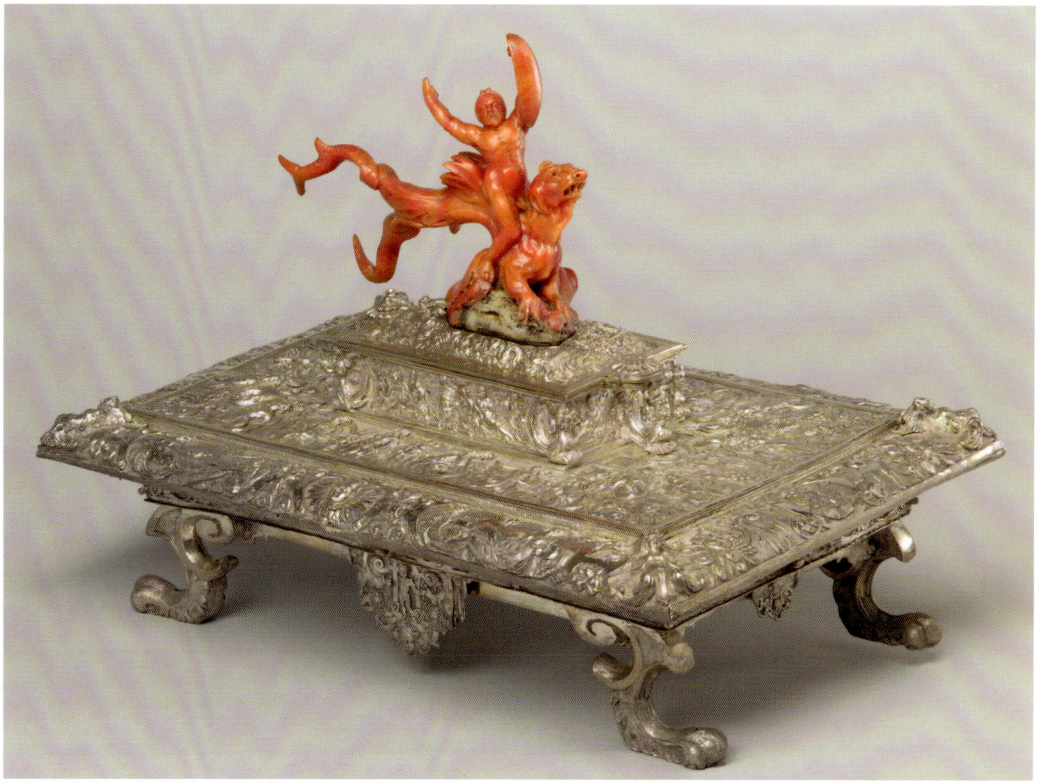

V.26

and coral, modelled after the Manneristic *grotti* of Florentine palaces (Ambras 2006, 267).

Franz Kirchweger

Provenance: 1596 in Estate Inventory of Archduke Ferdinand II of Tyrol, fol. 417 (Jb. VII,2, Reg. 5556, CCXCVII)

Bibliography: Ambras 2001, 94-99, cat. no. 53 (M. Rauch; with bibliography).

V.27
Friedrich Hillebrandt
Standing Cup and Cover
Nuremberg, c. 1593-1602
Assay mark for Nuremberg and maker's mark (R3 4017)
Silver, parcel gilt, partially enamelled, mother of pearl, emeralds, rubies, pearls
H. 44.1 cm
Vienna, Kunsthistorisches Museum, Kunstkammer, inv. no. KK 1136

From the catalogue of gifts, which the Princess Maria Anna of Bavaria received on the occasion of her marriage to Archduke and later Emperor Ferdinand II on 23 April 1600, we learn that her father, Wilhelm V of Bavaria had "ten drinking vessels, with exquisite mother of pearl outside, artificial but with the appearance of grapes within, made of silver and gilded" brought to her (Jb. XVI/2, 1894, Reg. 12524, CLXX). This group of vessels consists of eight double-cups and two standing cups crowned with bouquets. All the vessels are distinguished – as described in the account above – by an embossed interior in the form of grapes, while their exteriors are decorated with small tiles of mother of pearl. These are actually examples of bunch of grapes-cups which have been encrusted in mother of pearl. The iridescent tiles, with their enamelled and precious stone-encrusted appliqués, appear pinned to the inner surface of the goblet. The spaces between the multi-layered body of the vessel are filled with putty. The cup is created using a technique which was known in Europe primarily through the importation of goods from the Indian state of Gujarat. Because these imports passed through the great trading houses of Augsburg and Nuremberg, many goldsmiths in these centres adopted the technique. The pictured goblet, whose cup is modelled after an ostrich egg goblet or coconut goblet, is comprised of raised and grooved walls. The crown of the cover is decorated with a gadrooned vase with a naturalistic bouquet. With this composition and the bumpy molding of the cup's interior, the goblet associates itself closely with two mother-of-pearl goblets from the royal collection of the Hessian Landgraves (today in the Hessisches Landes museum Kassel, inv. nos. B 11.68 and 11.69), which were created by Lucas Hillebrandt, the brother of Friedrich Hillebrandt.

Paulus Rainer

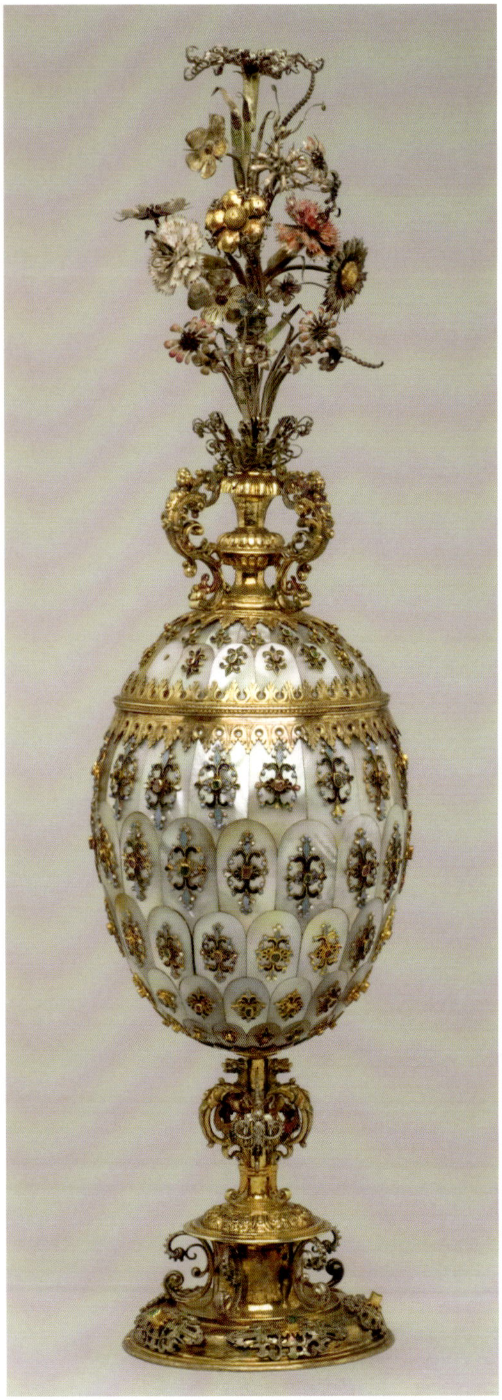

V.27

Bibliography: Kris 1932, 53, no. 84; Pazaurek 1937, 38.

V.28
Francisco Lopez (parts of the mounts)
Elephant with Salt Receptacle
Lisbon, 1550
Elephant: Indian Europe, 14th-15th century
Rock crystal, gold, enamel
7.3 × 9.4 × 4.9 cm
Vienna, Kunsthistorisches Museum, Kunstkammer, inv. no. KK 2320

The reclining, elongated elephant in rock crystal was acquired in 1550 in Lisbon by the Queen of Portugal, Dona Catarina (1507-1578). In that same year she paid the goldsmith, Francisco Lopez, for the rock crystal object, as well as for his work on the assembly. In its original form, the elephant, which must have arrived in Lisbon from southern India via Goa, certainly already had the enamelled tusks and the golden ears, pads and tail. Lopez apparently added only the neck band and modified the object for use as a salt cellar by the addition of a rock crystal bowl attached to its back with a bevelled abdominal strap. This bowl now hides a hole in the back of the elephant, which may previously have held a container for perfume. In 1553 Dona Catarina gave this small object – unique for its type today – to her niece and daughter-in-law, the Infanta Juana (1535-1573).
The elephant had long been well known to the West; however, living specimens rarely arrived in Europe. In the 16th century, they still caused quite a stir. Exemplars such as the Indian elephant sent by King Manuel I of Portugal (1469-1521) to Pope Leo X in Rome in 1514 were immediately recorded in drawings and leaflets and thus made famous (Bedini 1997). A living elephant also came into the possession of Archduke Maximilian, who later became Emperor Maximilian II (reigned from 1564 to 1576). He received the animal as a gift from his cousin, the already mentioned Infanta Juana, during his stay in Madrid. In the winter of 1551-52 it was brought from Spain to Vienna. Here the elephant, given the name Soliman, was brought to the new menagerie in Ebersdorf, where it perished, however, already in 1553 (Opll 2005). From its bones a chair was made (today in the monastery of Kremsmünster), the skin was stuffed and came into possession of Archduke Albrecht V of Bavaria (1528-1579).

Franz Kirchweger

Provenance: purchased in 1550 by Dona Catarina in Lisbon; given as a gift to Dona Juana in 1553; Inventory of Viennese Schatzkammer in 1750, 519, no. 82 (Jb. X,2, Reg. 6253)

Bibliography: Jordan Gschwend 1991, 121-126; Vienna 2000, 178, cat. no. 92 (N. Vasallo and Silva; with bibliography).

V.29
Annibale Fontana
(1540-1587)
and the Saracchi workshop
Lidded Goblet with Representation of the Myth of the Origin of Seasons
Milan, before 1569
Rock crystal, setting: enamelled gold
H. 24.6 cm, Ø 12.3 cm
Vienna, Kunsthistorisches Museum, Kunstkammer, inv. no. KK 1415

The decoration of this simple yet elegant rock crystal goblet is focused entirely on the engravings, which are cut into the polished surface.
The many-figured scenes of the cupola illustrate the story of Proserpina and the myth of the origin of seasons, which is connected to her according to Ovid's Metamorphoses (V, 341-570). In the principal axes on the lid above it sit the personifications of the four seasons in their characteristic landscape surroundings.
R. Distelberger (1975, 107f.) convincingly linked this unusually masterful carving of scenes to the person of Annibale Fontana, who initially worked as a medallist and stonecutter and later as an accredited sculptor in Milan (Lugano 1998, 339f.). In contrast to the Saracchi brothers, to whom he was related and with whom he must have worked very closely, his compositions are not limited to added rows of a single scene along a bottom area but rather show a highly differentiated – in this goblet helical – offset and spatial development. The exceedingly sophisticated modelling and moved bodies of Fontana imply a broad anatomical knowledge. In the field of stonecutting, Fontana concentrated on the especially highly prized arte minuta, or work involving small-figured scenes. Among the various works in rock crystal that may be attributed to him, this goblet holds a special place in that it is the first example of his work in this field.
Fontana's artistry as a "crystal carver" was especially praised by Giovan Paolo Lomazzo in his *Trattato dell'Arte della Pittura* (1584) (Distelberger 2002, 80). Annibale Fontana, belonged to the Accademia della Val di Blenio, directed by Lomazzo since 1568, as did another important Milanese stonecutter of his time, Francesco Tortorino (Lugano 1998).

Franz Kirchweger

Provenance: from the imperial Schatzkammer

Bibliography: Distelberger, 1975, 107-112; Distelberger 2002, 125-127, cat. no. 45 (with bibliography).

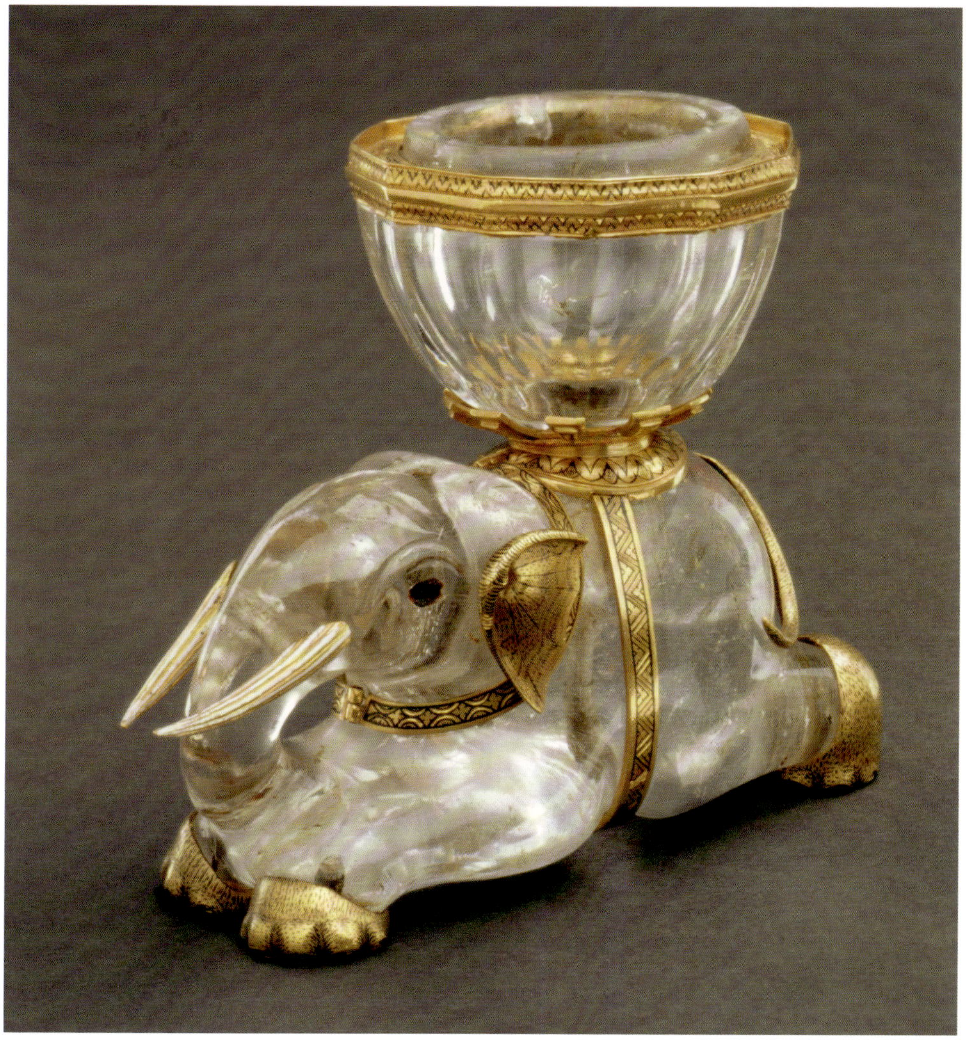

V.28

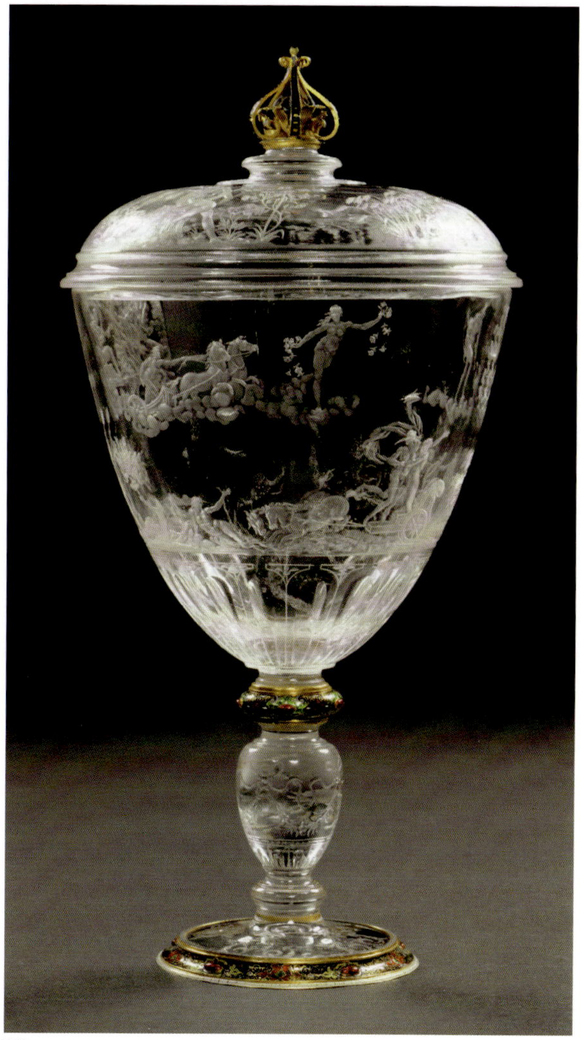

V.29

V.30
Giovanni Ambrogio and Saracchi
(c. 1540 - after 1612; c. 1547-?)
Bowl with Scenes from the Trojan Saga
Milan, circa 1570
Rock crystal
6 × 29.6 × 23.8 cm
Vienna, Kunsthistorisches Museum, Kunstkammer, inv. no. KK 2242

The circular bowl was cut from a single piece of rock crystal. The low-gorged foot has an unpolished edge, implying that a support was originally intended for it. The handle in the form of shells, however, was fabricated out of rock crystal by the stonecutter together with the overall shape.
R. Distelberger (1975, 106f.) could link this bowl to a reference contained in a letter from 1573, in which the brothers Giovanni Ambrogio and Simone Saracchi from Milan offered their services to Duke Albrecht V of Bavaria. There, the bowl representing scenes from the Rape of Helen and the Trojan horse, which had already been sold to the duke, was referenced along with a drawing of the work. Additionally, the brothers explained that Giovanni Ambrogio had created the container and Simone had cut the minute engravings.
Because of this unusually thorough documentation, the bowl of the Viennese collection gains great significance. This becomes the key work for the beginnings of the Saracchi workshop, who, next to the Miseroni, run the most important and productive studio in Milan in the last third of the 16th century and at the beginning of the 17th century. Paolo Morigia dedicated an extensive chapter to the family activity in his work, *Nobilità di Milano* (1595). "Delli Sarachi eccellenti nella virtù dell'intagliare di Cristallo, & altre gioie". The family had a close artistic exchange with Annibale Fontana (cat. no. V.9), whose compositions and figure types frequently served as models for the Saracchi workshop. In the present case, Simone Saracchi copied the four figures in the centre of the bowl, which represent the four seasons, directly from the respective figures of Fontana in his *Persephone goblet* (cat. no. V.9). In a direct comparison, however, it is clear how far behind Simone's engravings were from the exceptional level of Annibale Fontana.

Franz Kirchweger

Provenance: from the imperial Schatzkammer

Bibliography: Distelberger 1975, 104-107; Distelberger 2002, 198f., cat. no. 112 (with bibliography); Milan 2005, 300 (P. Venturelli).

V.31
Ottavio Miseroni
(c. 1568-1624)
Bowl in the Form of a Lion Skin
Prague, c. 1590-1600
Cairngorm
8.9 × 24.6 × 9.6 cm
Vienna, Kunsthistorisches Museum, Kunstkammer, inv. no. KK 2349

In 1588 Emperor Rudolf II (who reigned from 1576 to 1611) summoned the twenty-some year-

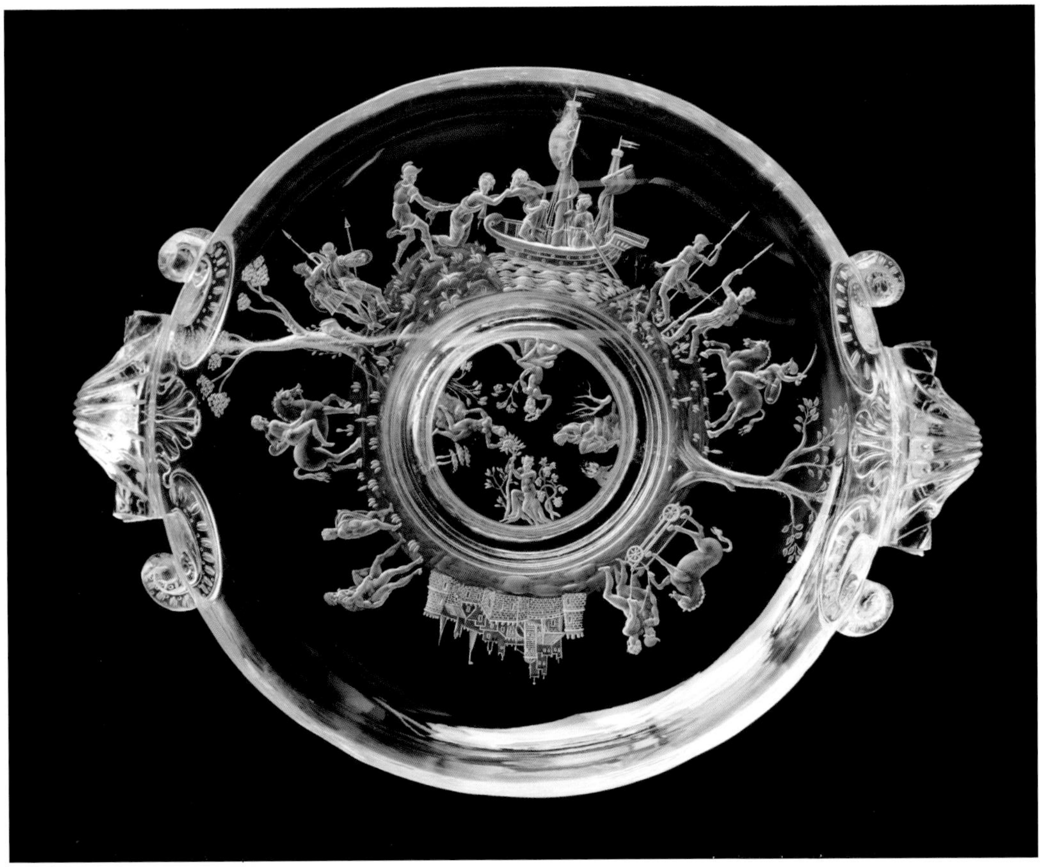

V.30

old Ottavio Miseroni from Milan to Prague and thereby established the position of his city of residence as the most significant centre outside of Italy for the art of stonecutting in this period. Ottavio came from the famous Miseroni family, which ran one of the most important workshops in Milan (cat. nos. V.13-16), which also continued to deliver works, especially in rock crystal, to the imperial court. Building upon the Milanese tradition, Ottavio developed an extremely personal formal language in Prague, as well as a concept that may be spoken of as "a virtuosic denaturalization or alienation" of the stone, "a form of abstraction which speculates on one hand with a heightened effect through this composition and on the other with a pleasurable amazement at the artist's technical virtuosity," (Distelberger 1978, 134).
This intent is also particularly noticeable in this bowl, in which a lion skin, lying on its back, appears to be draped over a laterally oblong bowl. The head lies opposite the drinking lip, and the tail, thrown over the back in an oval shape, forms a low stand-ring. The paws of the lion skin are tied over the container's opening. With this form, which made carving out the stone considerably more difficult, Ottavio certainly intended to demonstrate his exceptional technical mastery. According to R. Distelberger, not only the fact that a relatively impure crystal was used, but also the decision to conceive the vessel this way from the onset, thus eliminating the need for goldwork support, indicate that this must be a relatively early work from his career at the imperial court.
Regarding the manner of representing the lion head on the detached skin, there is a pictorial parallel to this motif in Arcimboldo's *Earth* (cat. no. IV.28), in which it forms the shoulder area.

Franz Kirchweger

Provenance: 1607-11 in the kunstkammer of Emperor Rudolf II in Prague, fol. 209v, no. 1326 (Jb. 72, 72)

Bibliography: Distelberger, 1978, 131; Distelberger 2002, 261, cat. no. 144 (with bibliography).

V.32
Ottavio Miseroni
Bowl in the Form of a Ship
Prague, beginning of 17th century
Rock crystal
13.5 × 22 × 7.2 cm
Vienna, Kunsthistorisches Museum, Kunstkammer, inv. no. KK 2335

The small, elegant bowl in rock crystal has the extended form of a little ship being carried by an "S"-shaped dolphin. In the back third portion, the rolling lip is extended upwards and continues into an openwork bar, which is formed on one side by a leaf mask and on the other side by a central motif flanked by two arched elements – today unfortunately broken off.
Especially worth noting in this bowl is the technical mastery with which the thin-walled container was cut and conceived without a goldwork support. The individually finished sections – the bowl, the dolphin and the almond-shaped, flat stand-plate – are attached to each other with pegs, which gives the delicate bowl its particular lightness and elegance. These technical and artistic means, the motif of the bar over the container's opening and the offset, slanting lip, which show similarities to the design of the bowl in the form of a lion skin (cat. no. V.31) give R. Distelberger (1978, 145) a reason to consider Ottavio Miseroni as the creator of this bowl. The aforementioned arguments also support the validity of P. Venturelli's differing opinion, which considers the work a creation of an anonymous Milanese workshop from the period around 1600 (Mantua 2002, 298, cat. no. 101). The tendrilled decoration, which is concentrated on the stand-plate and on the rear of the bowl's floor, is doubtless in the tradition of the Milanese workshop of Ottavio and his brother, who travelled with him to Prague; they continued to work in this tradition abroad as well. Rock crystal work played a secondary role in Ottavio's creations; its quality never attained the level of virtuosity of the tendrilled *intagli* of the Milanese works. However, he was well capable of the technical virtuosity of an extremely thin cut of the container's wall, as this bowl demonstrates.

Franz Kirchweger

Provenance: from the imperial Schatzkammer

Bibliography: Distelberger, 1978, 145; Mantua 2002, 298, cat. no. 101 (P. Venturelli).

V.33
Cosimo Castrucci
(appears in Prague from 1592 to 1602[?])
Landscape with a Chapel and a Bridge
Prague or Florence, 1596
Commesso (agate and jasper), copper
Signed and dated: "Cosimo Castruccj Flor[en]tino FEcit Anno 1596"
H 18.3 cm, Ø 24.5 cm
Vienna, Kunsthistorisches Museum, Kunstkammer, inv. no. KK 3037

The age-old technique of composing mosaics from flat tiles of hard, coloured stones experienced a new and major resurgence in Florence after 1570. Milanese stonecutters, who came to Florence following the renown of Francesco de' Medici with the intention of working for him there, played an important role in this trend (Distelberger 2002, 174-176). In 1589 Emperor Rudolf II received an inlaid tabletop made out of stone from Ferdinando I de' Medici as a gift, which excited him so much that he not only commissioned the manufacturing of a similar table in Florence, but also intensified his search for a specialist who could create "Commessi di pietre dure" for him in Prague. He ultimately found what he sought in the Florentine Cosimo Castrucci, who was in his service since at least 1592. In clear contrast to the Florentine mosaics, which favoured abstract and figurative ornamental motifs, Cosimo created for the emperor above all works such as the signed and dated representation of the *Landscape with a chapel and a bridge.* It shows the characteristic traits of a high perspective over a broad, idyllic landscape with large, imposing stone massifs in the foreground and – in accordance with an aerial perspective – light, particulate stones in the background. Cosimo used preferentially Bohemian jasper and agate, whose rich coloration and natural markings he tied together in a subtly sophisticated representation.
The interplay between nature and art presented in the *commesso di pietre dure* unquestionably reflected in a special manner the pansophic world view of Rudolf II, who, according to Anselmus Boethius de Boodt (1609) saw a "reflection and spark of godliness" in stones. In the representation of landscapes like this one, according to R. Distelberger, this spirit could manifest itself more palpably than anywhere else: "It can be experienced in the markings and in the beauty of the stones, which have been extracted from the macrocosmic nature and introduced into the work of the artist, who forms them into new images of nature."

Franz Kirchweger

Provenance: from the imperial Schatzkammer

Bibliography: Distelberger 2002, 250-252, 287f., cat. no. 172 (with bibliography); Giusti 2005, 119.

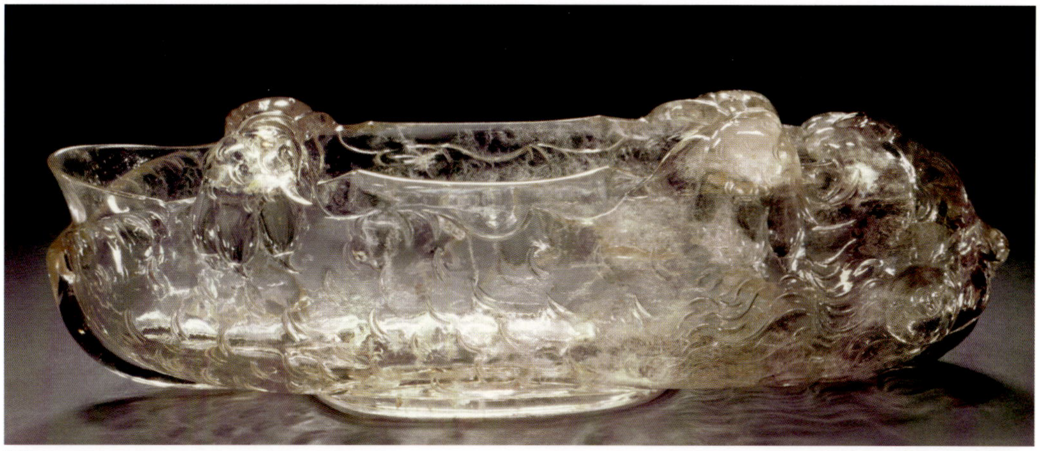

V.31

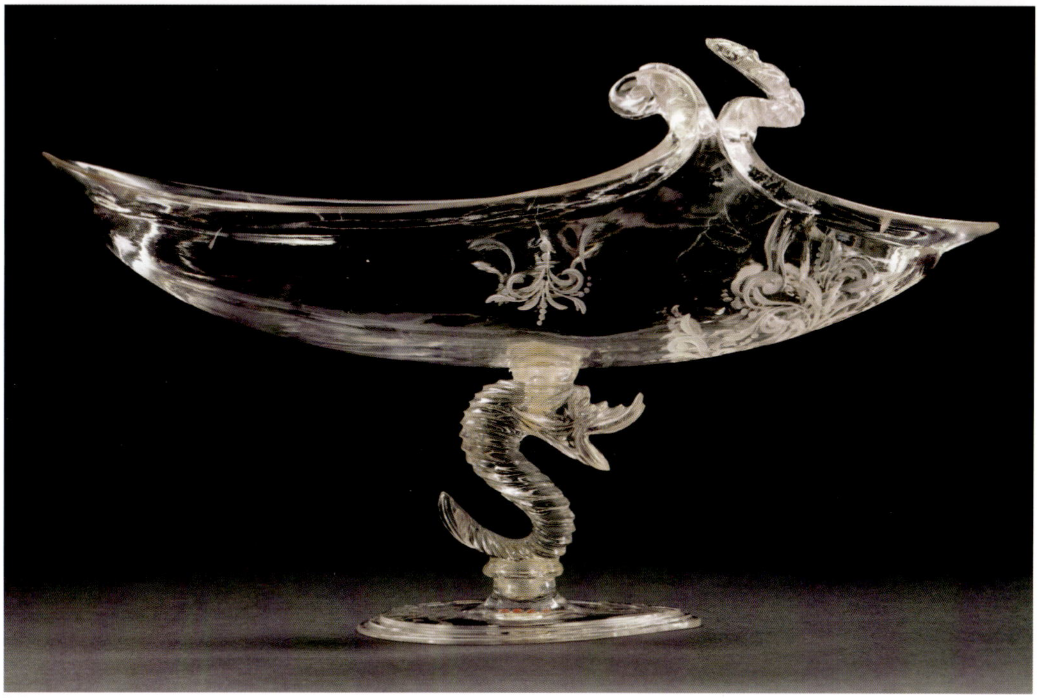

V.32

V.34
Ottavio Miseroni
Saint Mary Magdalen
Prague, c. 1610
Signed "Ott. M."
Reliefcommesso from various agates and jaspers, as well as from carnelian on chalcedony; setting: gold-plated silver
10.5 × 7 cm
Vienna, Kunsthistorisches Museum, Kunstkammer, inv. no. ANSA XII 820

Ottavio Miseroni discovered the principle of the cameo conceived as a *commesso*, in which various types and colours of stones were composed in a relief. His inspiration possibly came from the works of the Castrucci Workshop in Prague (compare cat. no. V.33), or from *commessi*, as they were created in the Florentine court of Great Archduke Ferdinando I de' Medici (1549-1609) (compare Distelberger 2002, 174-176, cat. no. 91).
For the necessarily oval-shaped representation of Saint Mary Magdalen with the salve container, Ottavio Miseroni meticulously combined fifty individual pieces from about a dozen different stones on a plate of chalcedony. Colour and structure of the various stones are effectively combined into a composition, whose impact is clearly more naturalistic, pictorial and material than the other cameos, which – as was normally the case – were cut from a single piece of stone. The chalcedony plate was once blackened on the back, which must have created an even stronger effect of colour contrasts of once.
A rich differentiation also shows the relief flowing through all grades, from the almost fully plastic hands in the foreground to the paper-thin head veils. A rare case for this type of work, this cameo

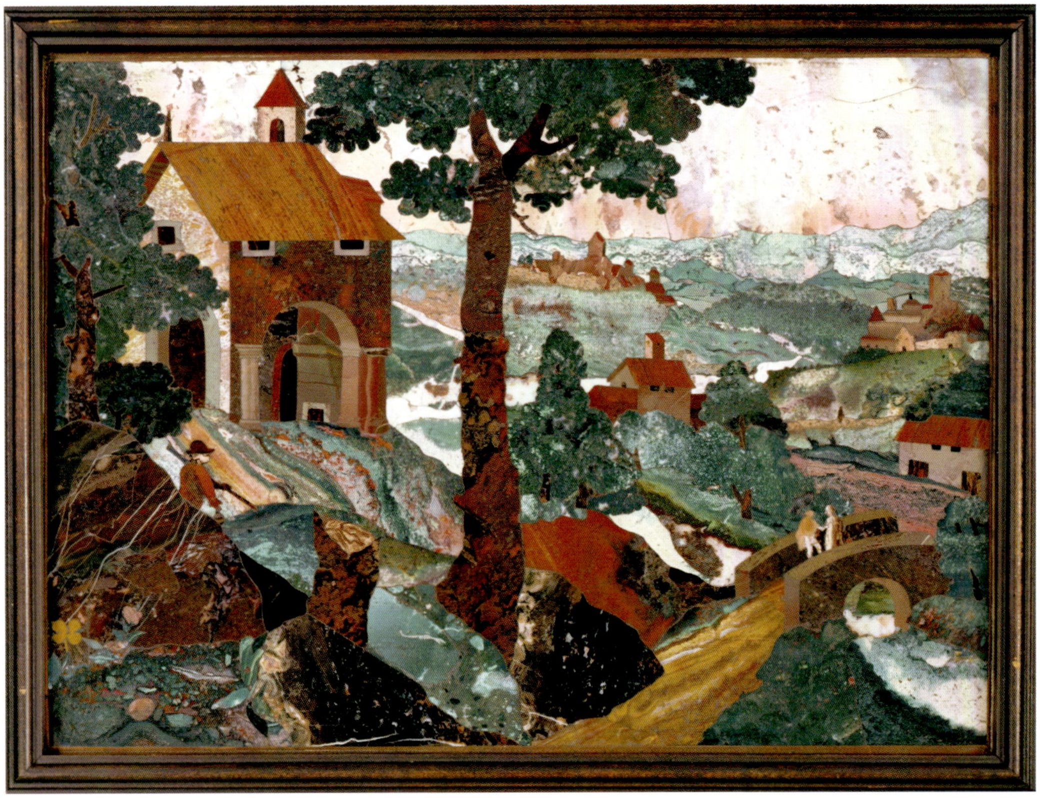

V.33

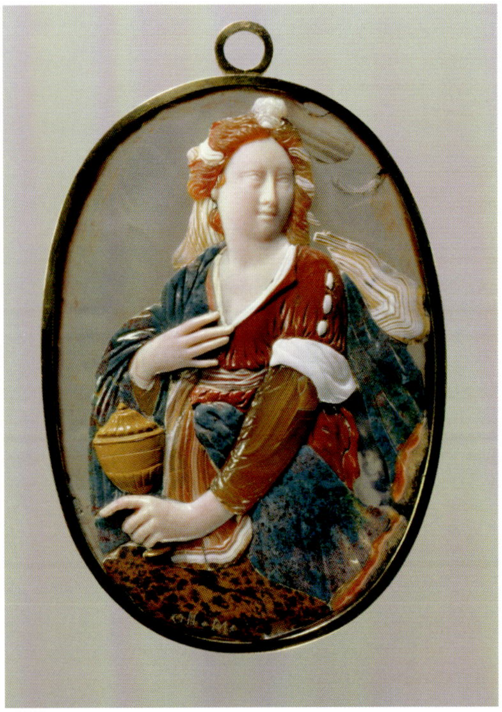

V.34

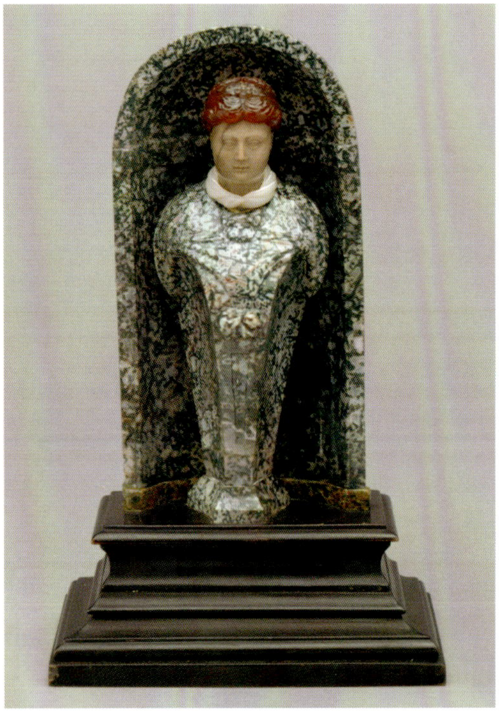

V.35

bears the signature of the master on its lower edge. A painting by Rudolf II's chamber painter, Joseph Heintz the Elder (1564-1609), may have served as a possible model for this representation of Saint Mary Magdalen (Zimmer 1971, 146, no. C1 and plate 117), which Ottavio may have seen either as an engraving or even as the original painting or a draft of it (Distelberger 2002, 278).

Franz Kirchweger

Provenance: from the imperial Schatzkammer

Bibliography: Distelberger 2002, 278, cat. no. 161 (with bibliography).

V.35
Prague workshop of the Miseroni
Herm in a Niche
Prague, c. 1600-1610
Moss agate, carnelian, jasper, mother of pearl; base: painted wood (later addition)
16.2 × 8.3 cm
Vienna, Kunsthistorisches Museum, Kunstkammer, inv. no. KK 1790

This feminine (caryatid) herm in a niche combines two possible forms in the art of stonecutting, which played an important role in the work of Ottavio Miseroni (Milan c. 1568 – Prague 1624) in Prague. On the one hand, it represents the idea of cutting round, plastic figures out of hard stones, such as chalcedony, as we often find in his work and which must have motivated him in works from Milan – not least of all, those from his home workshop – and on the other hand, the principle of the commesso, which can actually be considered his own invention. The reliefcommesso is characterized by the combination of various types and colours of stones in a relief, as in the representation of Saint Mary Magdalen (cat. no. V.34). The crop of the face and the richly differentiated treatment of the hair, are clear indications in the case of this herm of the differences with respect to the other works that are certainly to be attributed to Ottavio Miseroni; it is for this reason that R. Distelberger thought of the activity of another stonecutter active in Ottavio's workshop in Prague, his brother, Giovanni Ambrogio (Zittau 2002, 374f., cat. no. C 13).
Together with this herm, two other equally designed examples exist, each constructed as busts and with decorated moss agate bases and jasper heads with separately produced, fashionably styled carnelian calotte. The transition from bust to neck also hides mother of pearl collars.
In these herms, which today stand in niches of various stone qualities and colours, we are certainly confronted with originally mismatched pieces from a larger context. Perhaps they were once included in a large cabinet in Emperor Rudolf II's kunstkammer, as is suggested in the only oil sketch in the collection of the Kunsthistorisches Museum's Painting Gallery (inv. no. GG 2827).

Franz Kirchweger

Provenance: from the imperial Schatzkammer

Bibliography: Essen-Vienna 1988, vol. 1, 509f., cat. no. 380 (R. Distelberger; with bibliography); Zittau 2002, 374f., cat. no. C13 (R. Distelberger).

V.36
Marble Fruits
Italy (?), late 16th century
Marble, stone
Apples: H. 7 cm; pear: H. 11 cm
Vienna, Kunsthistorisches Museum, Ambras Castle Collections, inv. nos. PA 911-913

The dimension, form and colouring of both the apples and the pear, together with rotting brown sections, leave no doubt that these fruits were intended to create a complete illusion for the viewer. Only upon holding them does it become clear that the fruit is made of painted marble with the addition of stone stems.
These marble fruits were kept by Archduke Ferdinand II of Tyrol along with other illusory stone objects (candies, eggs) in a separate cabinet in the Kunstkammer, where they were described in 1621. Similar stone fruits have been conserved in the Kunstkammer of the Kremsmünster Monastery in Upper Austria.
Realistic artificial fruits were also made of wax and ceramics around the middle of the 16th century (Braunschweig 2000, 38, cat. no. 18). Mentioned later in a description of the contents of a cabinet by the famous Augsburg art agent, Philipp Hainhofer (Gobiet 1984, no. 1513, 832) we have the impression that fruits were also made out of glass and displayed in precious baskets, although in this case, because of the material, the illusory effect would not have been as perfect as with the marble fruits. This is quite different from the so-called nature-casts (compare cat. nos. V.3-9), where the model of nature in its new materiality (silver, bronze) usually remains recognizable as such, as does the concrete function (decoration on objects), and thereby the artistic-creative work clearly stands out; with the marble fruit, on the other hand, the imitation of the natural model is undoubtedly more concerned with playfully deceiving the viewer. Such fruits were probably mixed with real fruit on the table and served to exhilarate the guests when someone picked up an artificial one.

Franz Kirchweger

Provenance: 1621 in inventary from Ambras Castle, fol. 350r (unpublished)

Bibliography: Innsbruck 1977, 35, nos. 33-35; Ambras 2006, 72f., cat. no. 2.17 (T. Kuster; with bibl.).

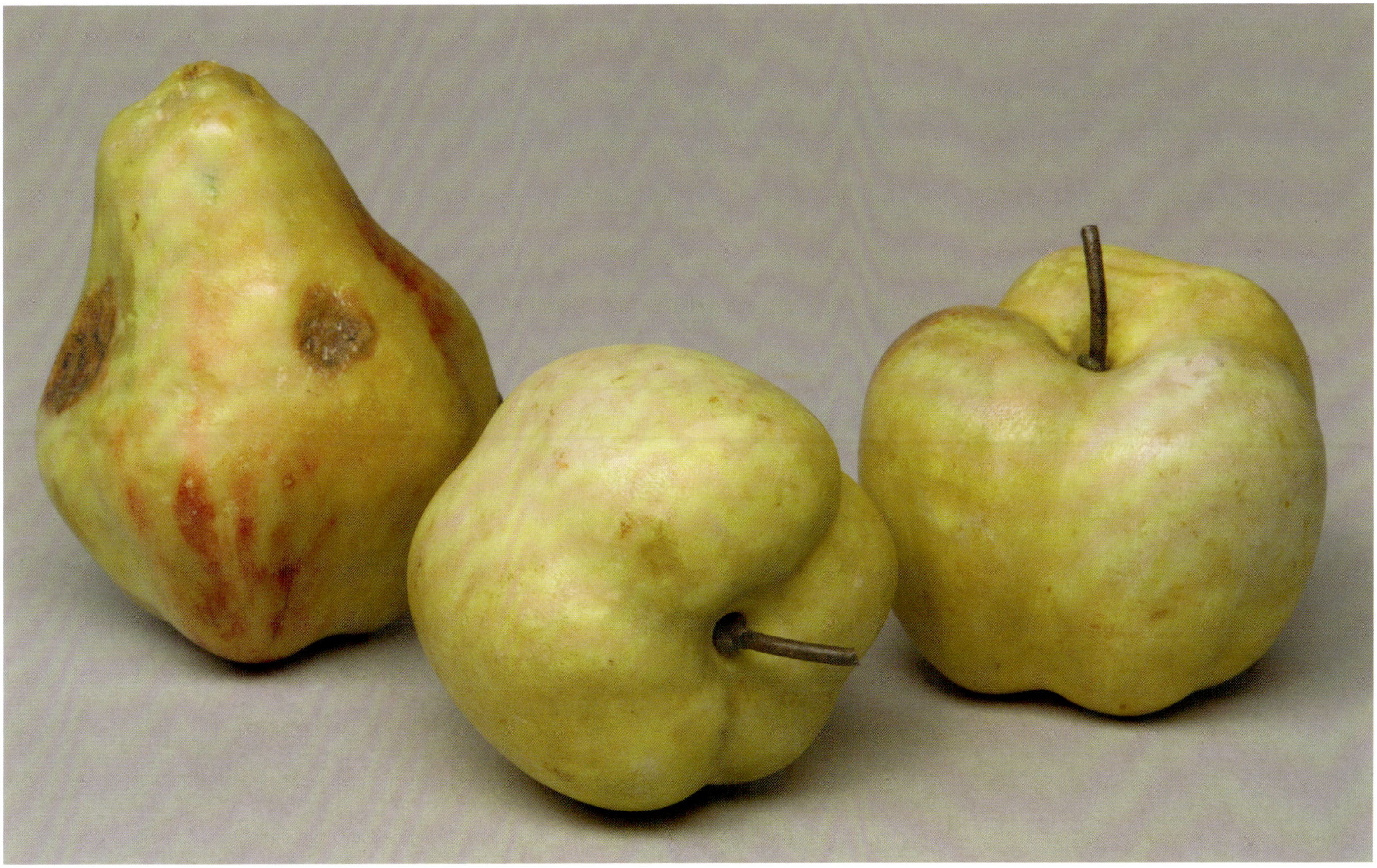

V.36

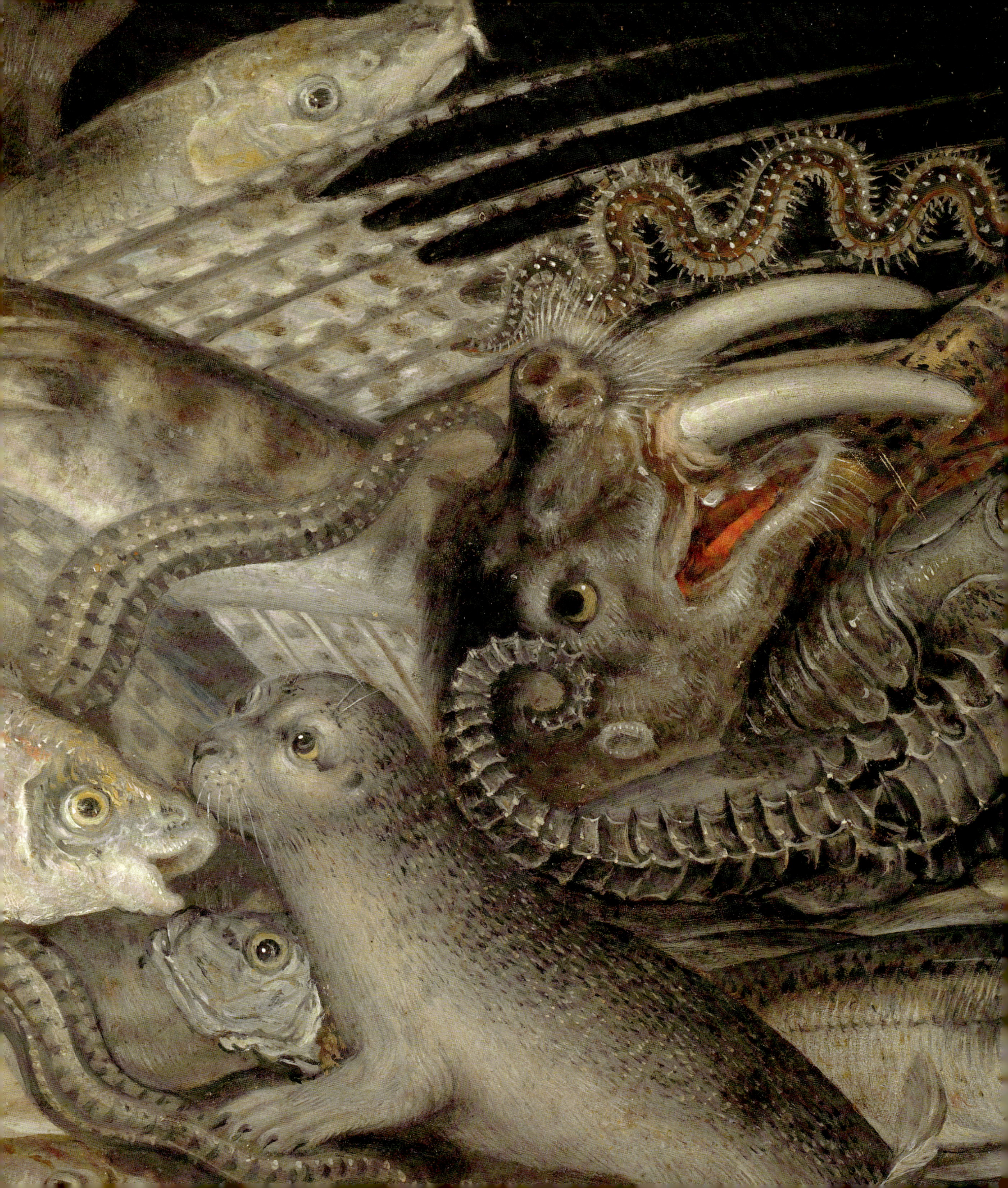

Philippe Morel

Arcimboldo's Composite Heads, Grotesques and the Aesthetics of Paradox

Introduction

It has become common to associate Arcimboldo's work with grotesques, either as a quick way of placing it in its context, or in an attempt to understand better the characteristics and peculiarities of his composite heads, seeking at times to justify such-and-such an interpretation through this parallel[1]. But it seems that this comparison is generally proposed on the basis of flimsy or superficial data, without any real foundation, while it ought to be tackled at a more structural level, that of the respective modes of operation of the two phenomena linked in this way. I will look first at the pitfalls or false trails that lead to the use of the term, the relationship with caricature, the question of decorative taste and certain syllogistic approximations.

Let us dismiss straightaway the most superficial and anachronistic idea that the composite heads can be defined as "grotesque", that is to say ridiculous, extravagant or bizarre, in the sense that the adjective took on from the 17th century onwards, or that they border on "the grotesque", the substantivized adjective coined by historians of literature and liable to be applied to a variety of creations dating from very different periods. These are two usages of the word to which the historical specificity, richness and complexity of the decorations made up of grotesques that are so common in Renaissance art, and that we wish to compare with Arcimboldo's inventions, cannot be reduced[2]. It should be pointed out here that the connection sometimes made between the caricatural heads – themselves regularly described as grotesque beings – of Leonardo or the Leonardesque tradition and Arcimboldo's heads stems from a false resemblance and a genuine misunderstanding (*fig. 1*)[3]. On the one hand, the composite heads have, with a few exceptions, no caricatural function[4]; on the other, Leonardo and his imitators distorted natural and lifelike traits, accentuating ("exaggerating") the defects or characteristic elements of the face, whereas Arcimboldo constructed a face that was not generally lifelike out of thematically homogenous components.

In his *Trattato*, Lomazzo says that both Arcimboldo's composite and invertible heads and scenes of hell, trophies, grotesques "e simili *bizarrie* che tengono della natura del tutto" are destined for *luoghi mercuriali* (probably inns and taverns)[5]. Based on such a generic and ambiguous definition, this association is not very instructive and is discredited by the initial destination of the pictures painted for the emperor and by the more detailed comments that the same author presented, a few years later, in the *Idea del tempio della pittura*.

Contrary to these oversimplified associations, the link that is often established between one and the other phenomenon and a range of notions that were very widespread at the time – *grylli*, chimeras, dreams or caprices – has to be examined with care, even if it turns out that the use of these metaphors is very generic or vague and conducts to a very low quality of information. Finally, an apparently more decisive piece of evidence that has encouraged the lumping together of Arcimboldo's inventions and grotesques is provided by a letter written by the painter around 1587 in which he speaks of grotesques and in particular of their origin: it needs to be made clear straightaway that the letter is not about the composite heads, but accompanies a series of drawings that are not, strictly speaking, grotesques, and that its contents and expressions may not be as rich in meaning as we have sometimes been led to believe.

To close this introduction, I would say that the relationship between the composite heads and grotesques does not depend on these superficial or vague resemblances, but is on an analogical level, of an essentially rhetorical nature, and is to a large extent rooted in an aesthetics of the paradox.

Grylli *and Other Chimeras*

As Kaufmann has pointed out, Fonteo utilizes on several occasions, in his poems and unpublished annotations, the term *grylli* (or *grilli*) to describe Arcimboldo's inventions: "Josippus arcimboldus insignis inventione gryllorum sive chymerarum"[6]. The word *gryllus* is applied by Pliny to the work of the painter of Greco-Egyptian origin Antiphilos: "It was he who painted in some pleasant works a man called Gryllus, wearing a ridiculous costume, from which pictures of that sort came to be called *grylli*"[7]. If in antiquity it was the reference to swine (*gryllos* in Greek) and to the comical dressing-up of man as pig that was claimed in an artistic and literary context[8], this sense dominated by the ridiculous, the parodic and deformity seems to have taken on a distinctly more monstrous and hybrid

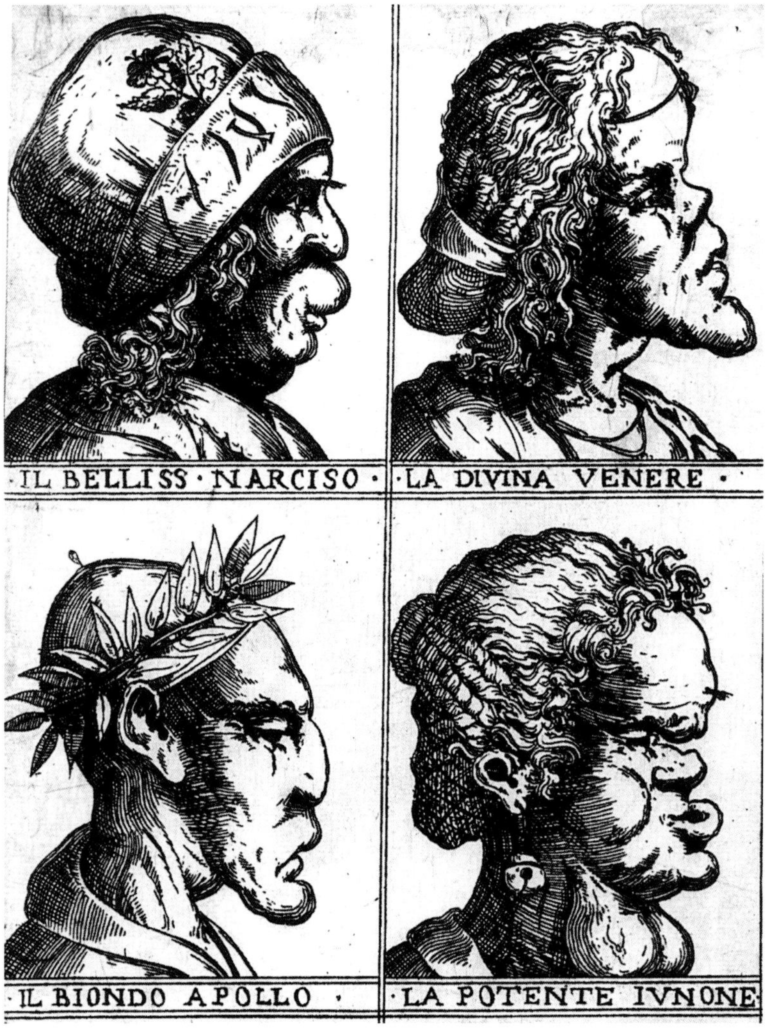

Fig. 1. G.A. Brambilla, detail from *Caricatures of the Gods of Olympus*. Florence, Uffizi, Gabinetto dei Disegni e delle Stampe

character in the Middle Ages, when, following in the footsteps of ancient glyptics, more and more of the figures called *grylli* appeared. The product of truncated, sometimes multiple and often heterogeneous juxtapositions, they proved extremely popular in *marginalia* from the 13th century onwards and can still be found in the paintings of Bosch and his emulators (*fig. 2*)[9]. As the meaning of the Latin word *grillus* was cricket, the Greek and Latin traditions seem to converge in the artistic and literary sense given to the word *gryllus* in the Renaissance, so that we find it identified, like the grotesques, with monsters and chimeras as well as with *cicalate*, *ghiribizzi*, *castelli in aria* and other vain and futile things produced by the imagination and dream.

Even the chimeras that Fonteo associates with *grylli* to designate the composite heads had a variable significance in the 16th century: for Egnazio Danti, "if they are not, on the whole, imitations of nature, they are nevertheless composed of parts borrowed from nature" (the author is thinking of hybrids like the Chimera of Arezzo); for Doni and Armenini on the other hand, chimeras are figures born out of the imagination through the observation of blots and clouds[10].

In both cases we find a collusion between the teratological and the fantastic, for which dream or whimsy are regularly brought in as a basic principle of explanation[11]. Noting, however, that the composite heads are sometimes described as "monsters" (*Vertumnus* is presented as a "new monster" in Comanini's poem), it appears difficult to regard the composite heads as medieval *grylli*, or as hybrids of the kind frequently utilized and created by painters of grotesques, "the principles of elaboration, the procedures of selection and assemblage being profoundly different", especially with regard to the principle of analogical substitution or addition characteristic of many grotesques but without any relation to the arbitrary similarities (which depend rather on the feigned *aemulatio*) that inspire the distribution of fish, fruits, vegetables, etc., in the place of the different parts of the face (*figg. 3-4*)[12]. So the use of these notions is too vague to serve as a real basis of comparison.

In grossa maggia

The same is true of the recourse to the *topos* of the observation of blots and stains (invoked by Doni and Armenini in connection with grotesques) which, contrary to all expectations, has also been made for Arcimboldo, on the grounds of the use that he makes of the word *maggia*, opening the door to a theme of ancient origin that was dear to Leonardo da Vinci. Starting out from the undeniable fact that the word *maggia*, taken from the Milanese dialect, means *macchia*, i.e. blot or stain, Kaufmann and Dolev have chosen to see in it, each in their own way[13], a highly significant allusion to blots as a source for the invention, a point of departure stimulating the artistic imagination and giving rise to the figurative elaboration of the inchoative forms outlined by nature. Thus the artist is able to extract from or project onto clouds – as well as stones, tree trunks and the most diverse stains – a variety of figures[14]. Before turning to the relationship of the composite heads with grotesques[15], also associated with what we might call the poetics or naturalistic maieutics of blots, Kaufmann looks into this last question in the limited context of Arcimboldo's phrase, which concerns the preparatory drawings representing the production and manufacture of silk for a project of decoration submitted to Baron Hoffmann (cat. no. VI.1).

This hypothesis poses two problems: first of all, Arcimboldo does not write that his drawings resemble *maggie*, blots, but that they had been made *in grossa maggia* ("mi e parso de dar' alcuna inventione fatta cosi in grossa maggia per non haver tempo di poter' con quella diligentia far detti schezzi come si convene"[16]. Moreover, as he is clearly drawing on Armenini's exactly contemporary treatise, in such a context the word *macchia* can become a synonym of sketch, improvisation and rapidity of execution ("[...] *a guisa di macchia, che da noi schizzo o bozza si dice*, conciosia che si accenna diverse attitudini di figure e di altre materie in un tempo brevissimo [...]")[17]. This is definitely the sense of the words used by Arcimboldo, who declares that the drawings he has proposed are only *abbozzati* ("sketched") and thus not as finalized as they would have been if he had had the time. Here it is not at all the blot that is the source of the invention, but the sketch that is the first manifestation of the latter; and a sketch that, in this specific case, has nothing to do, as far as its content is concerned, with the frenzy of the imagination in the sense that it was understood by Vasari or Armenini, nor, in its form, with those initially indeterminate drawings of Leonardo (of which Armenini may have been thinking) which really show the effects of their amorphous genesis: it is quite simply a documentary drawing, one that is purely imitative but not yet completed. What could be more different, in all respects, from these drawings accompanied by explanatory captions and illustrating the various technical stages in an agricultural activity, than Leonardo da Vinci's *componimento inculto* and its morphogenesis, so subtly analyzed by Daniel Arasse, which seems to me elaborated in imitation of nature, of its blots and of their figurative gestation[18]!

As for the application of the maieutics of blots to the composite heads, as is suggested by Dolev (who holds that Leonardo and Arcimboldo "were engrossed by the notion of *macchia*"), it is largely a question of misunderstanding. Leonardo suggests imagining landscapes, battles, heads and a whole range of other things on the basis of the *confuse forme* found in nature, while Arcimboldo constructs his composite heads by accumulating and interweaving perfectly elaborated and identifiable forms, handled with a great concern for mimicry. One starts out from *phantasia*, the other from mimesis; one proceeds initially in a fantastic manner, interpreting and fashioning, the other in an imitative manner, describing before composing. And the goal of the undertaking is radically different,

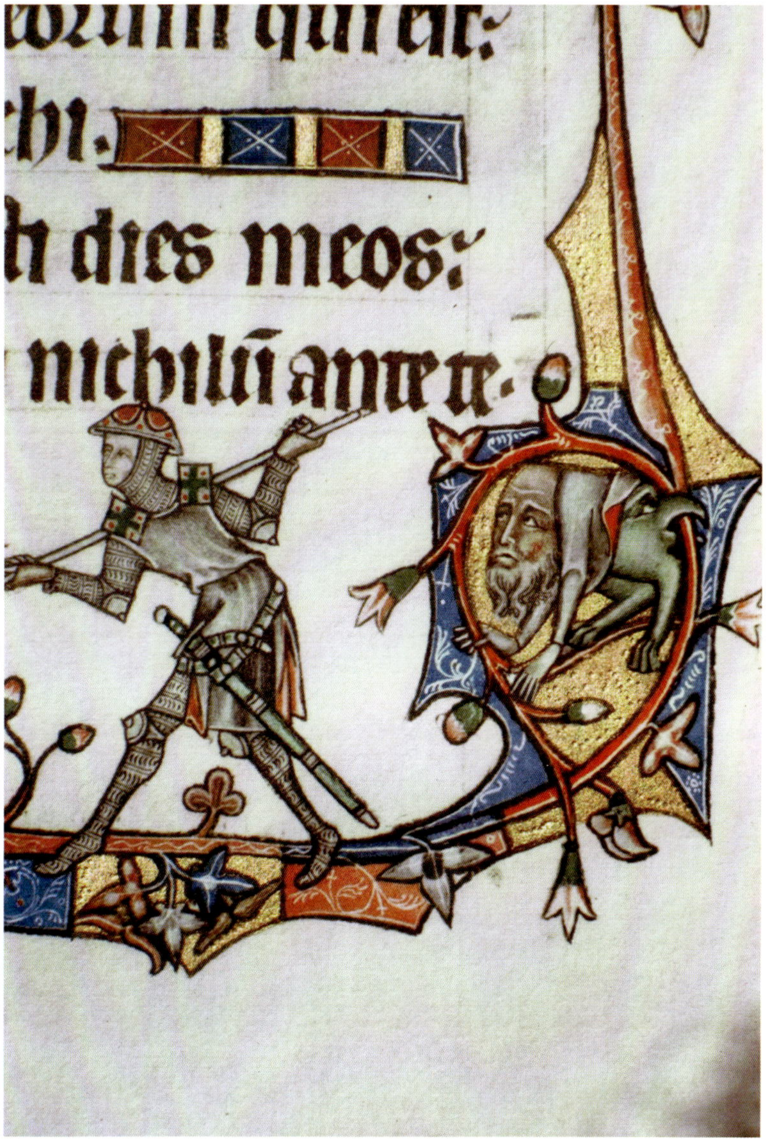

Fig. 2. Unknown artist, *Monster*, Ormesby Psalter. Oxford, Bodleian Library

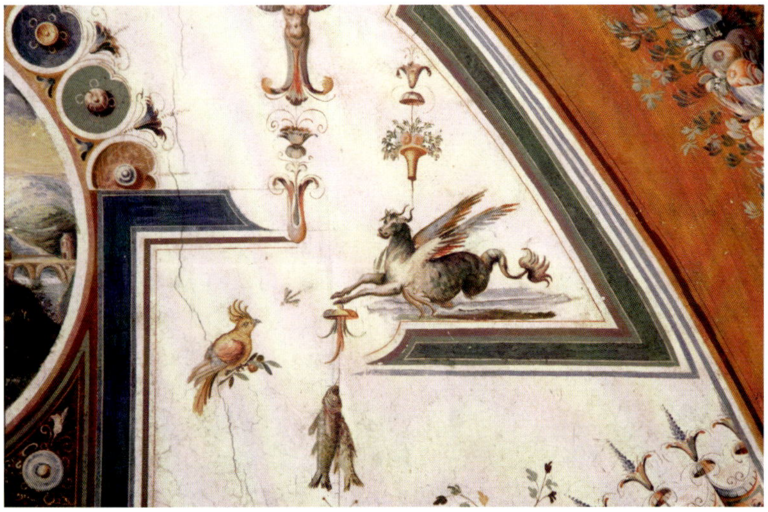

Fig. 3. Unknown artist, *Hybrid Figure*. Caprarola, Palazzo Farnese, Stanza del Liocorno

with Leonardo ending up creating natural and well-defined figures out of the amorphous matter of nature, and Arcimboldo producing faces that are certainly anthropomorphic but nevertheless totally strange and improbable (monstrous according to Comanini) out of this accumulation of plants, things or instruments. Only two peripheral examples could pertain to a sort of naturalistic morphogenesis: the head of *Winter*[19] and the anthropomorphic landscapes of possible Arcimboldesque inspiration (*fig. 5*)[20], which translate onto a large scale and in an almost caricatural manner a solution that Mantegna and Dürer had already exploited in the form of simple rocky profiles.

Mimesis and Hermeneutics

Thus the relationship of Arcimboldo's heads to grotesques does not really lie in either caricature or hybridization, nor even in the poetics of blots. However, they are two types of production characteristic of Mannerist culture which have in common their connection with scientific illustration and, to a lesser degree, the hieroglyphic tradition of the period. Above all, they are both structured to a large extent by certain rhetorical paradigms. Before we focus more precisely on the rules of composition and function of the composite heads, let us take a look at the two other shared characteristics.

Some authors – especially Alfons – have followed Schlosser in insisting on the relationship of the *Seasons* and the *Elements* to Maximilian II's interest in the natural sciences and to his Kunstkammer, for which the pictures were to serve as an encyclopaedic introduction and ideological symbol: the potentially encyclopaedic character of the naturalistic composite heads would have reflected that of the collection and the analogical parallel between seasons and elements would be related to an ancient cosmological system, used for the classification of the collections and the decoration of certain cabinets[21]. A link can also be made between their enumerative dimension and their naturalistic execution ("cavati dal naturale et imitati con quella maggior diligenza che possibili sia"[22]) and the scientific miniatures of Georg Hoefnagel, who produced four volumes of illustrations of animals classified according to the four elements, as similar volumes or catalogues present in the imperial Kunstkammer[23]. As Kaufmann has pointed out, Hoefnagel presented himself as an *inventor hieroglyphicus et allegoricus*, his collections of scientific illustrations were conceived as books of emblems, and some of his drawings have a manifestly allegorical function of an essentially ethical or existential nature[24]. Hieroglyphs and allegories are notions that crop up regularly in the commentaries of Fonteo and Comanini, in which Arcimboldo is described as a *dotto egiziano* ("learned Egyptian") whose *dotte allegorie* ("learned allegories") have to be deciphered.

To some extent this is true of grotesques, whose recurrent link with collecting and scientific illustration is easy to demonstrate, particularly in a Florentine decoration contemporary with Arcimboldo; grotesques of which Ligorio and Lomazzo were able to declare that they were made *ad uso di lettere hierogliphiche*, that they "were filled with symbols and learned things" and that they functioned as emblems or *imprese* (*fig. 6*)[25]. But once again, we have to be cautious. Unlike in the majority of the composite heads, naturalistic and encyclopaedic characterization is not a general rule among grotesques, which constitute a much more polymorphic and heterogeneous phenomenon than Arcimboldo's inventions. The same applies to the presence of a hieroglyphic or emblematic language in grotesques: it is occasional and reveals an analogical relationship to signs and things. In the case of the composite heads, the word hieroglyph and the reference to the secret are somewhat excessive, or seem first and foremost to result from a rhetorical device that is intended to bring out their symbolical and allegorical potential.

The question of allegory obliges me to return to the central, difficult and keenly debated question of the political allegory in some of Arcimboldo's composite heads; a question which it seems to me is in need of a less systematic and clearcut reading than it has received up to now. On the basis of a long poem by Fonteo, his annotations and other contemporary writings by the same author collected in two manuscripts preserved in Vienna, Kaufmann has set out to show that the series of the *Seasons* and the *Elements*, dating from 1563 and 1566 respectively and presented to Emperor Maximilian II in 1569, constituted a political message and a visual panegyric, an allegory of the universal power of the emperor and the harmony that he imposed, indeed a prophecy of the enduring reign of the Habsburgs[26]. Fonteo's encomiastic text leaves no doubt over the message that he wanted to impart to the pictures, by referring them to the person of the emperor that was hidden behind these portraits, but the question that must be asked is whether Arcimboldo's composi-

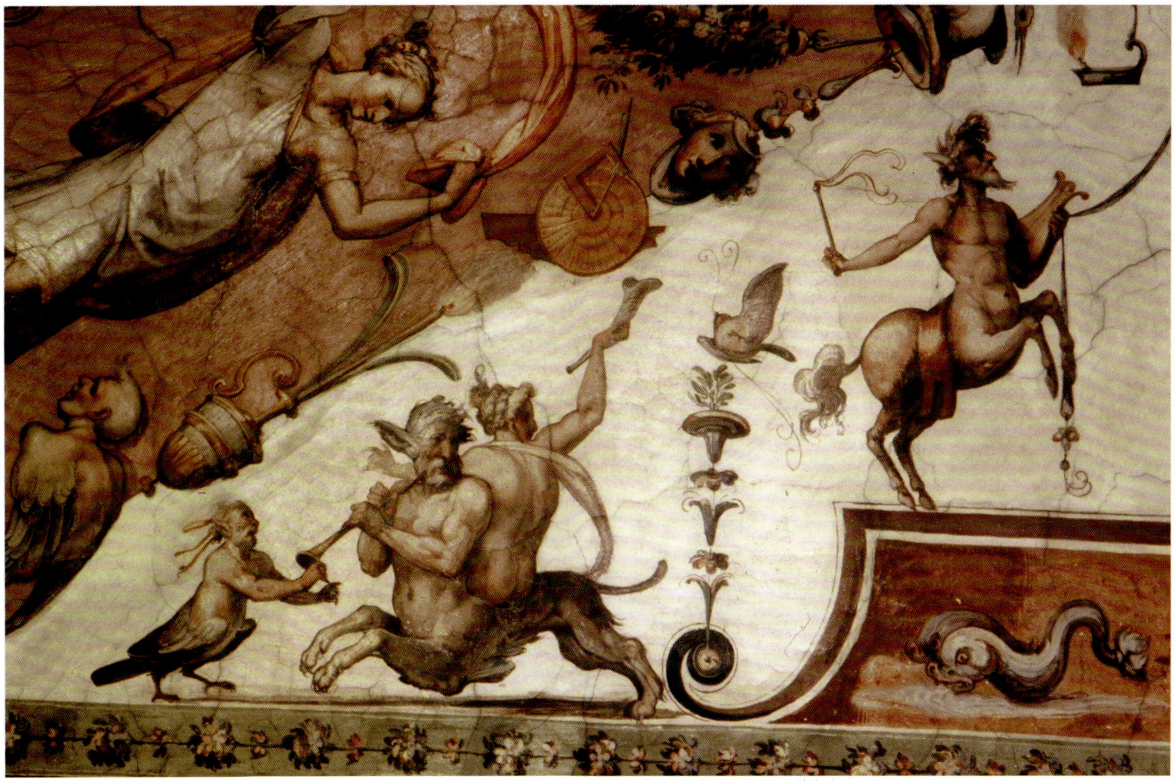

Fig. 4. Alessandro Allori and workshop, *Mixed Beings*. Florence, Uffizi, Corridoio Vasariano

tions "are" an imperial panegyric or "become" one through the interpretative filter of the poem offered to the emperor as an accompaniment to the pictures. Qualifying his initial formulation ten years later, Kaufmann concludes it is in part an *ex post facto* interpretation, while stressing that it must have represented the artist's own thinking, that it must have been formulated with his agreement and above all that it is corroborated by a whole set of politically significant details in the paintings[27]. In response to this analysis, Fonteo's poem has been reduced to the state of literary embroidery and fanciful exegesis by Hope, who sees nothing in these pictures but simple jokes without depth, establishing – against all the historical evidence – a hard-and-fast boundary between painting and poetry[28]. Later on we will see to what point it is difficult to subscribe to this type of judgement (or prejudice), but first it is necessary to go into the allegorical-political hypothesis in a little more detail.

The vast majority of the politically significant iconographic details are in a peripheral location[29] and they are not present in all the pictures[30]. They are not necessary but contingent. Moreover, only *Winter* exhibits this kind of detail in the initial series with a specific allusion to Maximilian, who was not yet emperor[31]. They become more frequent in the series of *Elements*, but are less personalized. Finally, the various copies of the series of *Seasons* given to princes and relatives of the emperor suggest that these creations had their own *raison d'être*, and one that was certainly free of any political significance, outside the specific context of the imperial collection and the association with the elements[32].

So I do not believe that there was a political programme at the root of these composite heads, nor that any political orientation had really determined their conception. After a first discreet and targeted encomiastic allusion, Arcimboldo had to try to work this seam by adding symbols on the periphery of some of the *Elements*, that would be clearly recognizable to the new emperor and his entourage. On the basis of these discreet signs of a fairly banal courtly homage that took shape in the second series, Fonteo built a grand rhetorical construction that made use of *encomio* and hyperbole, commenting on the seasons and elements, insisting on the idea of universal domination and peace and proposing bold or hazardous meanings, such as the matrimonial and dynastic interpretation of the pairings and confrontations of the seasons and elements[33]. Thus Fonteo's poem is not trasparent or faithful to the pictures. It does not describe them, nor does it reflect the initial aim of the painter. It glosses these pictures on the basis of the few elements introduced by the latter and of the semantic potentialities "opened up" and offered by these images as a result. Fonteo's intervention is an example of an exercise that was very common at a time when no opportunity was missed to pay tribute (often out of self-interest) to princes, using the most varied circumstances or objects as medium and pretext. Nonetheless it bears witness to the dynamic relationship that could be established, during the Renaissance, between the work and its commentator, and to the forms of reception that were current in such a milieu. Finally it illustrates the difference that could exist between a "programme" in which everything was prede-

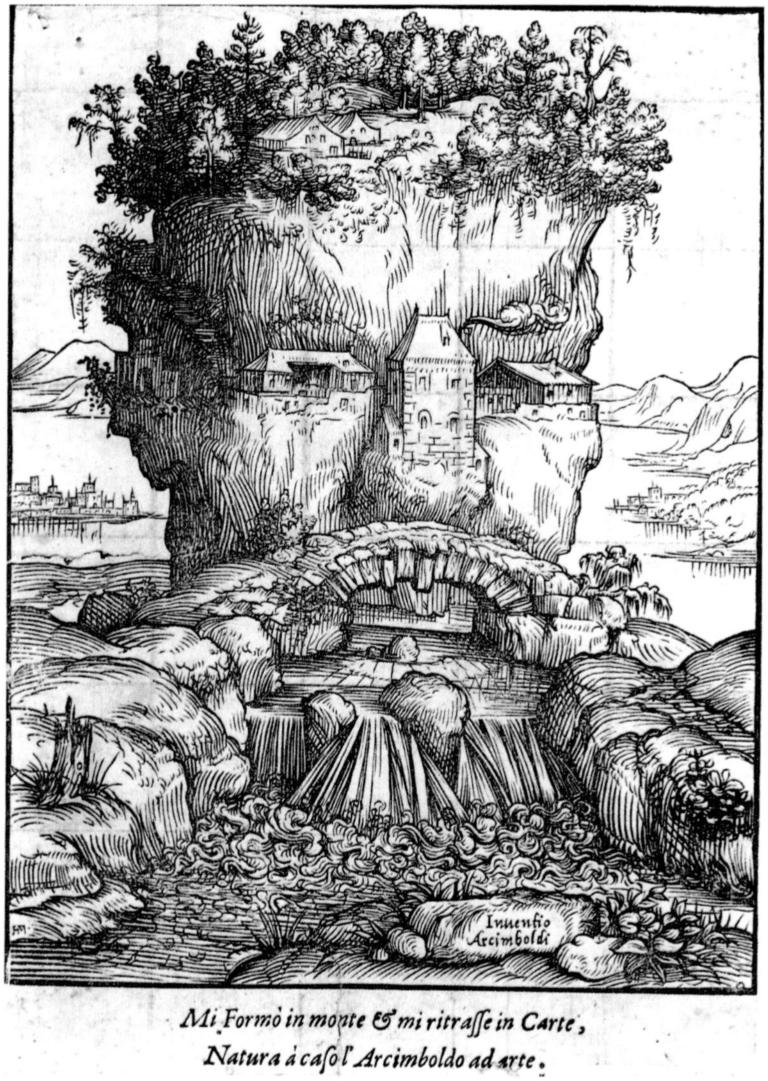

Fig. 5. Anonymous, attributed to Giuseppe Arcimboldo, *Anthropomorphic Hill*

termined, and an "invention" whose semantic potentialities were left to the ingenuity of the commentator or the well-informed observer[34].

Associated with Comanini's poem, which is its exact contemporary, the *Vertumnus* is a different case[35]. A first, separate elaboration (that of the partnership between Arcimboldo and Fonteo on the *Seasons* and *Elements*) was followed by a collaboration between Arcimboldo and Comanini, or a real adherence by the latter to the invention of the artist, of whom he was a great friend[36]. The poet carefully describes a long series of details that he links to the different seasons over which Vertumnus presides. This testifies to the attention paid to a more studied process of selection than in the earlier composite heads; an attention that is accompanied by an obvious desire to praise the painter as well[37], while the parallel with the emperor is separate from this descriptive presentation and is only made in the final section of the poem, through the Silenic device of the passage of the outside (fruits and flowers, monstrous face) to the inside (Rudolf II, of whom Vertumnus becomes the allegorical image here, showing his capacity to embody all and bring together all, his ascendancy over all the seasons and their riches, and personifying a sort of golden age)[38]. It can be said without hesitation that Vertumnus was chosen and depicted with this assimilation in mind, its conceiver(s) being able to make use of Fonteo's earlier eulogy (the emperor reigns over all the seasons) while improving on it (Vertumnus really can personify universal imperial power and its benefits), and Arcimboldo having given the god features clearly comparable to Rudolf's. This has been stressed by Kaufmann as well as by Comanini himself who indicates that it is a question of resemblance, metaphor and symbol in a succinct phrase: "Te rassembr'io, te figur'io, te segno".

But whether it is a question of a secondary effect and the conditions of reception or something that determined the very conception of the work, the political interpretation of the heads does not allow us to understand the overall modes of the invention or fabrication of these composite heads. Passing from political to a sort of moral allegory, Comanini's commentary on *Earth* takes an approach that combines physiognomy, hieroglyphic model and theory of signatures. In doing this, it pertains to the same level of validity, that of the interpretative potentiality that starts out from some plausible indications and does not fear to extrapolate them[39]. The fact remains that if the hermeneutic approach typical of these allegorical readings can arise from these inventions, it is not able to embrace them as a whole or above all to go back to their principles.

Rhetorical Constructions

However, some authors, and Kaufmann in particular, have pointed the finger at what seems to be a more decisive motivation or a more satisfactory definition of the composite heads, declaring that they are visual *concetti* or, to use the terminology of the 16th-century authors, ingenious inventions filled with clever devices[40]. It is in a later article that Kaufmann, rightly insisting on the notion of *serio ludere* and extending an idea outlined by Rosalie Colie, ends up emphasizing the role of paradox in Arcimboldo's work[41], which brings us right back to their relationship with grotesques. The 20th-century author who has undoubtedly laid most emphasis on the rhetorical dimension of Arcimboldo's work but who has been, it seems to me, the least followed as a result of his distinctly unhistorical approach to the phenomenon, is none other than Roland Barthes. And yet, long before him, some of Arcimboldo's contemporaries paid attention to a dimension of his paintings that was much more structural or semiological than hermeneutic[42].

Criticizing the supporters of Aristotle by comparing them to Arcimboldo and his imitators in his third letter on sunspots, Galileo writes: "Questi, che si sottopongono a così *strette leggi*, mi fanno sovvenire di *certi obblighi* a i quali tal volta *per ischerzo si astringono* capricciosi pittori, di voler rappresentare un volto umano o altra figura con l'*accozzamento* ora de' soli strumenti dell'agricoltura, ora de' frutti solamente o de i fiori di questa o di quella stagione: le quali bizzarrie, sin che vengono proposte per ischerzo, son belle e piacevoli, e mostrano maggiore perspicacità in questo artefice che in quello, secondo egli avrà saputo più acconciamente elegger ed applicar questa cosa o altra alla parte imitata"[43]. He does not speak of esotericism, *impresa* or allegory, but places the accent on laws or principles of composition that are all the more arbitrary because they are playful in the way that they determine the selection, arrangement and interweaving of the components. In the eyes of a man with such a sharp and critical mind, and free of any courtly bias with regard to the subject, Arcimboldo's talent and the (relative) interest that he finds in his works do not lie in their symbolic profundity, but in the art of *accozzamento* ("jumbling").

In a text published in 1978, Roland Barthes presented Arcimboldo as a rhetorician and poet, as a workman of language, whose compositions were "a true laboratory of tropes", revealing a linguistic background where the signs were combined, exchanged and led astray[44]. Which could explain, incidentally, the fascination and the desire for emulation that *Flora* and *Vertumnus* have stirred in poets, as well as Arcimboldo's remarkable self-portrait made up of fine strips of paper[45]. We are first going to take up and briefly develop this type of analysis. As has often been pointed out, the composite heads originate in the utterly commonplace rhetorical figure of metonymy, in which one thing is replaced by another thing that is associated with it by a relationship of spatial, temporal, causal or semantic contiguity[46]. But the metonymy (like the personification) would be satisfied with a single bird, a single flower or a single fish, while their accumulation verges on what is known in rhetoric as a process of amplification, or even a pleonasm or better still an asyn-

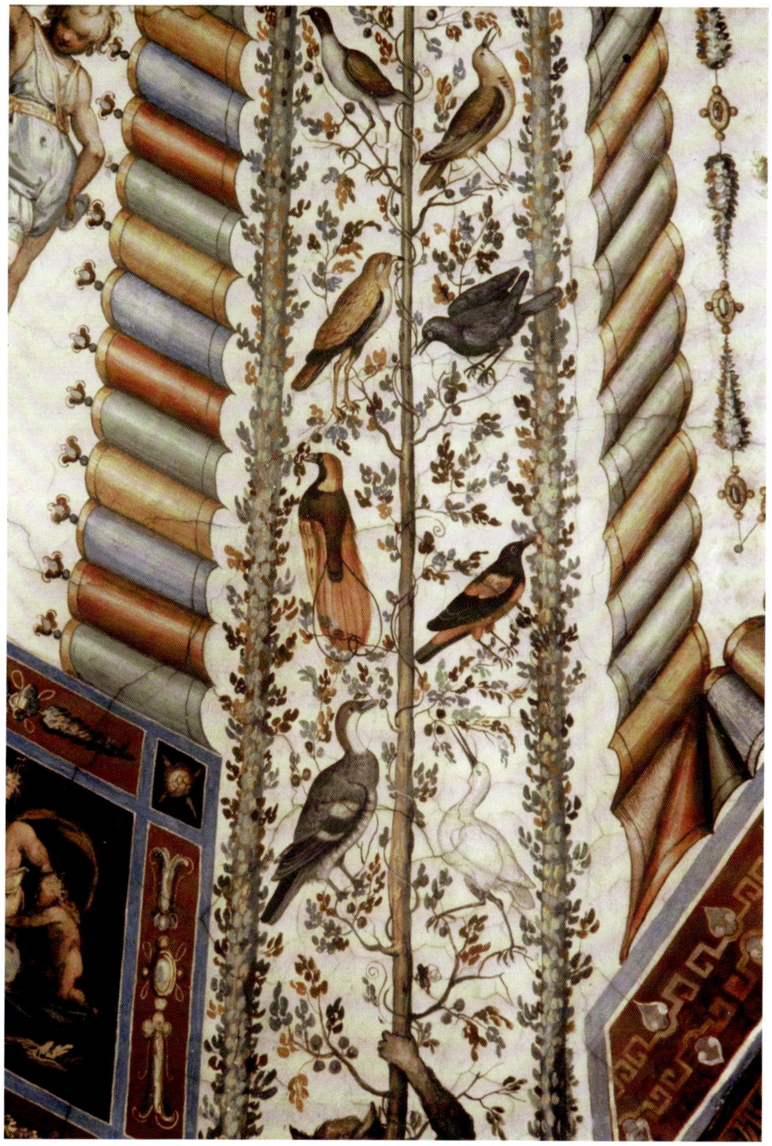

Fig. 6. Alessandro Allori and workshop, detail from the decorative grotesques. Florence, Uffizi, Corridoio Vasariano

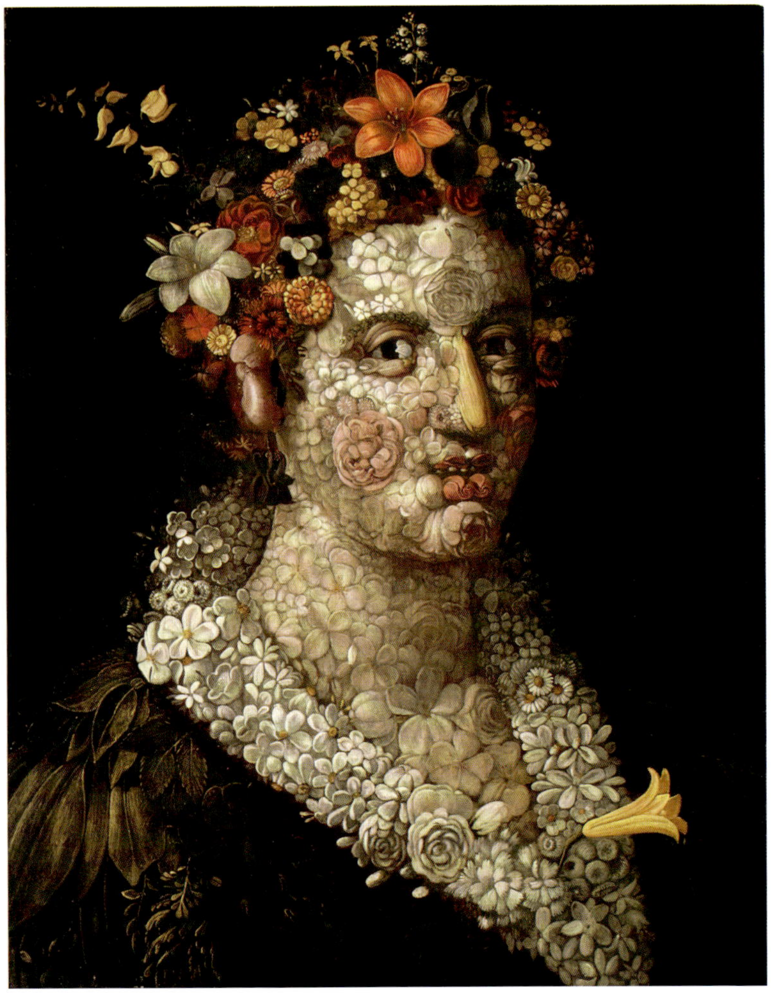

Fig. 7. Giuseppe Arcimboldo, *Flora*. Private collection

deton (unconnected juxtaposition). Thus the metonymy operates here according to a process of asyndetic accumulation that responds equally to a principle of distribution since, in order to compose a face, it is necessary to play on similarities of form, and therefore the metonymic and asyndetic lexical device is traversed by a metaphorical grammatical instance. It is through the play of often random comparisons and highly arbitrary resemblances that the face takes shape, with the mouth formed from a fungus, the nose from a pear, the forehead from a melon[47]. In this way the customary device of allegorical personification is parodied totally.

The interest in and success of these composite heads derive from the interaction of these two extremely common rhetorical figures with another figure that was much in vogue in the 16th century, the paradox, which is produced here by the confusion between detail and whole, natural image and fantastic image. The paradoxical way in which these heads function is revealed precisely by Comanini's poem on *Flora*, which is a literary transcription of the process used to engender the composite head as well as an interpretation of its effects: "imita ben la pittura dell'Arcimboldo", as he himself wrote[48] (*fig. 7*).

The poem tackles the question of identity as the picture is supposed to be a portrait (lines 1-4). Who is depicted? What is the subject? Flowers cannot smile and a human being cannot be made just of flowers. This question of identity is exhausted in the play of an alternation and an ambiguity between two terms; it leads to the antithetical affirmation of being nothing and being everything, to the contradictory, oxymoronic juxtaposition of the one and the multiple (lines 5-8) and to the chiasmic inversion of causalities. From an impossible identity sought at the outset, it comes to the acknowledgement and the affirmation of change, of metamorphosis, as the aim of painting and the result of the skill of the painter (lines 8-10), who becomes the demiurge and the arranger of appearances[49].

So it is a genuine paradox of the portrait that these composite heads propose, in which the question of the identity and the unity of the subject slips into an elusive conceptual metamorphosis, a permanent metonymic circularity between the whole and the part, two terms at once similar and dissimilar that constantly refer to one another. A paradoxical slide between nothing and everything, one and multiple, cause and component, but also between the naturalistic detail and the imaginary and monstrous whole, eicastic imitation and fantastic imitation (Comanini), or again between the view from close-up and the view from a distance (Lomazzo). If we had to come up with a rhetorical definition of the composite heads, they could be described as a metonymic and asyndetic paradox.

This role played by paradox in Arcimboldo's composite heads is confirmed in a passage of the poem Comanini devoted to Vertumnus, the god of harvests, of the cycle of the seasons and of the change of appearance. "Vario son da me stesso / E pur, sì vario un solo / Sono, e di varie cose / Co'l mio vario sembiante / le sembianze ritraggo"[50]. The conceptual contrast between variety and unity or identity has a tendency to turn into a relation of kinship between variety and change and above all into a passage from being to appearing that puts in check the stable and unitary allegorical presupposition of the personification, and the choice of Vertumnus reflects this intention. Another revealing element of Comanini's two poems resides in his use of dialogue (Flora and Vertumnus address the reader, so the poet makes the two "portraits" speak), which has been linked to the model of the elegy Propertius devoted to Vertumnus[51], but which is already present in Comanini's earlier poem on Flora. The influence of the ancient author is indisputable, but above and beyond a simple prosopopoeia, the dialogue established in this way precisely matches the composition of the two pictures, in which, unlike in Arcimboldo's other composite heads, the figures are looking at us; and the dialogue is itself of a "paradoxical" nature, with the paradox implying the active presence of a potential interlocutor or spectator who has to be amused, astonished and induced to question himself[52].

Thus the painter's work is characterized by an aesthetics of paradox and metamorphosis which was constructed over time and attained its most perfect form with *Flora* and even more so with *Vertumnus*: in addition to being an allegorical and political portrait of the emperor, the painting has to be recognized as an allegorical self-portrait of the artist and his art.

So I do not believe that the circular approach (or the *mise-en-abîme*) of paradox, as it is expressed by Comanini, should be limited to the Silenic model that he invokes in other respects, i.e. to the *topos* of the serious, precious or divine content concealed behind ridiculous appearances[53]. Treated in this way, the imperial allegory of *Vertumnus* is in itself a paradox and it remains in the paradoxical grip of being and non-being. Beyond a general opposition to the *doxa*, to commonly held opinion, the notion of paradox can indeed refer to varied and even contrasting discursive practices, such as the Platonic or Erasmian paradox that is intended to reveal a higher truth, while sophistic, logical or purely rhetorical paradoxes that play endlessly on appearances are aporetic or turn into exercises of intellectual and verbal virtuosity[54]. From this point of view, the hidden meaning is part of the game. It is one of those possible, but it is not necessarily the last word. Where ambiguity reigns, you end up losing your footing. In the *serio ludere* understood in this way, the serious does not impose itself on the terms of the game, it is the game itself that turns serious with regard to the questions that it raises and to the *ingenium* and the mastery of the rules that it supposes.

However, one arrives at a form if not alternative, then at least of ambiguity: the paradox asserts itself as a gratuitous exercise of virtuosity, and/or reveals a culture in crisis, in search of new points of reference. "Just as Montaigne portrays not his being, but his passing," writes Daniel Arasse, "the paradoxes of the Mannerist Arcimboldo playfully bring into question the certainties of a clear representation of the unity of the Self"[55]; to which we could add those of a clear and stable representation of the identity of things, exalted by scientific precision and naturalistic accumulation before being disturbed by this delirious asyndetic concentration, tending towards anthropomorphic otherness and the *mise-en-abîme* of vision and thought. The epistemic foundations of the culture of the Renaissance are themselves undermined by this, for if the traditional cosmological scheme of the microcosm and the macrocosm fits well into the background of these composite heads, if man lays claim once again to be the point saturated with resemblances, the privileged reference from which radiate a multitude of similarities, then this central position takes on an allure as strange as it is derisory and the logic of similarities that underlies it gets out of control and turns into masquerade[56].

The more strictly rhetorical side of this philosophical perspective is fully displayed with the grotesques. In their paradoxical constructions, "the initially perceived verisimilitude is revealed, on examination, to elude the realm of the possible and the rules of common sense"[57], and it is indeed on the checking of ordinary reason and on a constant playing with appearances that these decorations and their plastic and rhetorical *tours de force* work: scenes in which it is at once the location, the identity and the iconic status of the figures that are turned upside down in their equivocal and aberrant relationship with background, space, nature or gravity. Arcimboldo's inventions are neither grotesque, nor grotesques, but they share with the latter a constituent relationship to paradox while interpreting it, in their most successful expressions, in a way that is undoubtedly more profound, according to parameters that are as logical as they are epistemic.

[1] See in particular Wescher 1950, 3; Hope 1987, 42-43; Kaufmann 1990b, 67-68.

[2] Morel 1988, 89. Cf. Lugano 1998.

[3] Cf. above all Berra (1998, 57-67), who insistently develops this idea, confusing the themes of inspiration and seeking desperately to find resemblances between the Leonardesque caricatures and Arcimboldo's composite heads, especially the *Winter*, before trying to place the artist's production in the Milanese culture of the period, and in particular that of the Accademia dei Facchini della Val di Blenio.

[4] Which serves to confirm the virtual or tangible imperial interpretation made of them by Fonteo and Comanini (see *infra*). Only the "natural", but composite, portrait of the imperial vice-chancellor of which Lomazzo speaks (1973, I, 362) – which should perhaps be identified with that of the jurist (Johann Zasius?) now in Stockholm and mentioned by Comanini (1962, 269) – is manifestly intended as a caricature. Among the composite heads that

serve as personifications, that of *Winter*, which Berra brings up in this connection, could lend itself to such a valuation, but the comparison remains very problematical and subjective, which is less true of the two inverted heads, the cook and the vegetable gardener.

[5] Lomazzo 1590 [1973], II, 304-305.

[6] Kaufmann 1993, 313, see also Kaufmann 1976a, 280-282: "Volebat pictor Picturae imaginem, per grillum ut solet exprimere, hoc est, ex instrumentis et rebus ad ipsam pertinentibus conficere [...]", "apellantur Grilli huiusmodi picturae Arcimboldianae".

[7] Cited from Pliny the Elder, *Naturalis Historia*, XXXV, 114, trans. by J.M. Croisille: "Idem iocosis nomine Gryllum *deridiculi habitus* pinxit, unde id genus picturae grylli vocantur".

[8] See the note by S. Reinach on the passage from Pliny (*Recueil Millet*, 386-387) to which we could add a passage from Plutarch concerning the companions of Ulysses (mentioned in the 16th century by C. Rhodiginus, as has been pointed out to me by Colette Nativel).

[9] The most common type consisted of a head set on legs, without a trunk, frequently with the addition of a supplementary head on the chest or the behind. See Baltrušaitis 1981, ch. 1.

[10] E. Danti, *Trattato delle perfette proporzioni* (1567), cit. in Morel 1998, 86. Doni 1549, 22v.

[11] For the notions of dreams and fancies applied to Arcimboldo's work, see Comanini 1962, 257, 269-270. Lomazzo 1590 [1973], I, 361.

[12] Morel 1998, 13 and ch. 6 for the question of hybrids.

[13] Kaufmann 1993 (1984); Dolev 1994.

[14] See Janson's fundamental study (1961) for this frequently tackled question.

[15] By means of the notions examined above: dreams, *grylli* and chimeras. Kaufmann 1993, 162-163.

[16] Cit. in *ibidem*, 152, and cf. *ibidem*, 158-160.

[17] Armenini 1973, 2532-2533.

[18] For his part, Daniel Arasse (2006) distinguishes the *componimento inculto* from the poetics of blots.

[19] The head of *Winter* is not the product of a conglomeration, but consists of a single gnarled tree trunk from which spring small roots, broken or severed boughs, an interlacing of branches, a tree fungus and ivy leaves. The fungus by way of mouth, the severed boughs of the nose or ear: all this can fit in with the theme of the "image made by chance" and of nature the painter aided by the painter imitating nature. See Berra 1998, 57.

[20] By Momper, Merian, etc. Lomazzo described *Earth* as follows: "il quarto elemento della terra, di diruppi di sassi, di caverne, di tronchi, e di animali terrestri". Lomazzo 1590 [1973], II, 304. See also certain later drawings by Gheyn.

[21] The quaternary system summed up by Isidore of Seville in a celebrated analogical diagram and developed in several imperial artistic programmes dating from shortly after the pictures, the masquerade of 1571, Jamnitzer's fountain and a decoration in Prague Castle. See Alfons 1987, 67-85 and Kaufmann 1978a, 25-26.

[22] Comanini 1962, 265-266.

[23] Kaufmann 1993, 172; *idem* 1984, 116.

[24] *Ibidem*, 117, 244ff.

[25] See Morel 1998, chs. 5 and 3. Berra (1988, 35) makes a precise link between the *Vertumnus* and an *impresa* or "device".

[26] This is not the place to go into the details of an argument presented in the very important and well-known article of 1976, and then taken up again on several occasions by the same author, culminating in an article published in 1990 in which he discusses the disagreements with his thesis and replies to the critics who had put them forward. On the sometimes disputed dating of the *Elements*, see in particular Hope 1987, 44 (but there is nothing to indicate that Lomazzo's sonnet refers precisely to the pictures painted for Maximilian).

[27] Kaufmann 1987, 103.

[28] Hope 1987, 42-43. According to this author, painters work with things and not with ideas... We should point out, however, that he amends or clarifies his view by writing that Fonteo and Comanini's interpretations of the *Seasons* and the *Elements* "tell us something about the way in which some of Arcimboldo's paintings could have been discussed under certain circumstances during the sixteenth century".

[29] On the breast or the shoulders: the "flint and steel" and the letter M of *Winter*, the peacock of *Air*, the lion and ram of *Earth*, the necklace of the Order of the Golden Fleece and the two-headed eagle of *Fire* (the only personification to display a political symbol at the level of the face, where the pieces of steel form the ear and the nose). As for the identification of crowns on the heads, I consider this unconfirmed and not very critical.

[30] And some of them disappear in the autograph copies offered to other princes (this is true, at the very least, of the *Winters* donated to the elector of Saxony and the duke of Bavaria).

[31] An allusion reiterated and explained at the masquerade of 1571. Maximilian succeeded his father in 1564.

[32] For a different view, cf. Kaufmann 1987, 103-104.

[33] Sought and defined by Arcimboldo to fit the traditional cosmological scheme, to establish an internal order and to determine their arrangement, and certainly not to deliver a political message.

[34] On this question, see in particular *Programme et invention dans l'art de la Renaissance*, proceedings of the conference in Rome (April 2005), ed. by M. Hochmann, J. Kliemann, J. Koering and P. Morel, to be published in 2008.

[35] In the *Idea del tempio*, whose dedication dates from December 1590, Lomazzo declares that the picture representing *Vertumnus* is *poco meno che perfetto*, while the poem, published in the *Figino*, whose dedication is dated September 1591, had earlier been included in the collection of poems on *Flora* and *Vertumnus* published by Gherardini, with an introduction dated January 1591 in which it is made clear that Comanini had already seen the picture in the painter's studio and that the idea of sending his poem to the emperor came from Arcimboldo. Berra 1988, 17-18, 21-22, 28 (the author defined the poem as "Un componimento che aveva il compito di presentare il dipinto del *Vertunno* all'Imperatore").

[36] This may have already been the case with a female personification of which Fonteo speaks, which was planned for the marriage in 1571 and was undoubtedly never finished. Neither Kaufmann (1976, 295) nor Berra (1988, 22) make this distinction between Fonteo's poem and Comanini's. On the closeness of the artistic and intellectual relationship between Arcimboldo and Comanini see, herein, the picture painted *for* the latter and precisely described by him (Comanini 1962, 268-9), which combines the four seasons in a single head: a picture only very recently identified and shown for the first time in this exhibition (oral comm. from S. Ferino-Pagden).

[37] After an introduction based on the oxymoron (beauty/ugliness, variety/unity) which prepares for the Silenic oxymoron instigating the conclusion ("fuor sembro un monstro, e dentro alme sembianze e regia imago ascondo"), he develops a cosmogonic panorama (with, in particular, the separation of the primordial elements) and implicitly presents the artist as a sort of demiurge (by comparing Arcimboldo to Jupiter), before embarking on a highly detailed description of the picture which depicts the union of the seasons in the figure of Vertumnus. Cf. Berra, 1988, 30-31.

[38] See Kaufmann 1976a, 295-296. In an article of 1985 (reproduced in 1993, 129ff.), Kaufmann insists on the painter's borrowings from Propertius's elegy of Vertumnus and seeks in his makeshift interpretation a (not very convincing) argument to make him a god of the elements as well. In Cartari's free translation of the Latin poem, Vertumnus is also declared to be god of the year. See Berra 1988, 24-26, who identifies, with good reason, this translation as the most direct literary source of Arcimboldo's invention.

[39] Comanini 1962, 266-268. The choice of the elephant and the hare for the cheek (timidity) and the nose (flair, daring). Certain passages are delightful, like the one concerning the ox (which I suggest should be linked to the zodiacal melothesia instead by assimilation to Taurus, which rules over the neck).

[40] They have also been described as "products of learned wit", "visual puns", "calembours plastiques", etc.
[41] Kaufmann 1990b, 65-72. Colie 1966, 286-288.
[42] See in particular: "[...] componendo insieme l'imagini delle sensibili cose da lui vedute, ne forma strani capricci et idoli non più da forza di fantasia inventati, quello che pare impossibile a congiungersi accozzando con molta destrezza e facendone risultar ciò che vuole", Comanini 1962, 270.
[43] The italics are mine. A still unpublished text by Massimiliano Rossi (provisional title *La Crusca nell'occhio* [...]) has drawn my attention to this comparison, which can also be found in the Galilean literature (Reeves 1997, 7). M. Rossi also points out that, in the *Considerazioni al Tasso*, Galileo seems to want to compare certain aspects of the *Jerusalem Delivered* with the pictures of Arcimboldo or Jan "Velvet" Bruegel (in a passage cited earlier by Panofsky 1954, ch. 5, no. 6).
[44] Barthes 1978, *passim*.
[45] See Berra 1988, 18-19. And this might also inspire a comparison with that other great rhetorician Giambologna, whose *Rape of a Sabine* triggered a similar outburst of poetry. For the drawing with his self-portrait, see herein. The two poems attributed to G. A. da Milano in the collection of 1591 may have been written by Arcimboldo himself (*ibidem*, 38-39).
[46] This can be a complex and multiple metonymy, as in the *Jurist*, who is represented by the books he reads, the letters he writes and the victuals that he must have received as salary: one of these aspects alone would not have been sufficient to define him as a lawyer.
[47] Metaphors that are all the more arbitrary in that the same fruit serves as a nose in one case, and as a chin in another, something which is called antanaclasis (repetition of the same symbol with a change in meaning). See Barthes 1978, 32.
[48] *Son io Flora, o pur fiori?*
Se fior, come di Flora
Ho col sembiante il riso? E s'io son Flora,
Come flora è sol fiori?
Ah non fiori son io, non son'io Flora.
Anzi son Flora e fiori.
Fior mille, et una Flora,
Però che i fior fan Flora, e Flora i fiori.
Sai come? I fiori in Flora
Cangiò saggio Pittor'; e Flora in fiori.
(Comanini 1962, 258; cf. Berra 1988, 18, for the very slightly different version published by Gherardini).
"Am I Flora, or just flowers?
If flowers, how come
My face bears Flora's smile? And if I am Flora,
How come Flora is nothing but flowers?
Ah I am not flowers, nor am I Flora,
Rather I am Flora and flowers.
A thousand flowers, a single Flora,
But the flowers make Flora, and Flora the flowers.
You know how? The clever painter has changed
The flowers into Flora, and Flora into flowers."
[49] On the painter as demiurge, see the note *supra* on the poem on *Vertumnus*.
[50] "I am myself various / And yet only one varies / I am, and of various things / With my varying appearance / I portray appearances." Comanini 1962, 259.
[51] Kaufmann 1993 (1985), 134; Berra 1988, 26.
[52] See Margolin, in *Paradoxe* 1982, 74.
[53] For a contrary opinion, Kaufmann 1990b. For the reference to Plato at the end of the poem on Vertumnus: "È ch'io quasi un Sileno [...] Son, che fuor sembro un monstro, / E dentro alme sembianze / E regia imago ascondo. / Dimmi or tu, se t'aggrada / Di veder quant'io celo / Ch'or or ne tolgo il velo." Comanini, 264.
[54] See Colie 1966, as well as the articles by Alain Michel and Jean-Claude Margolin in *Paradoxe* 1982.
[55] Arasse 1997.
[56] Cf. Wesher 1950, 7. This privileged position of man-microcosm in the world is very clearly evoked, in connection with Arcimboldo's composite heads, in one of the poems by Gherardini published in the collection of 1591. Cit. in Berra 1988, 31.
[57] Morel 1998, 105.

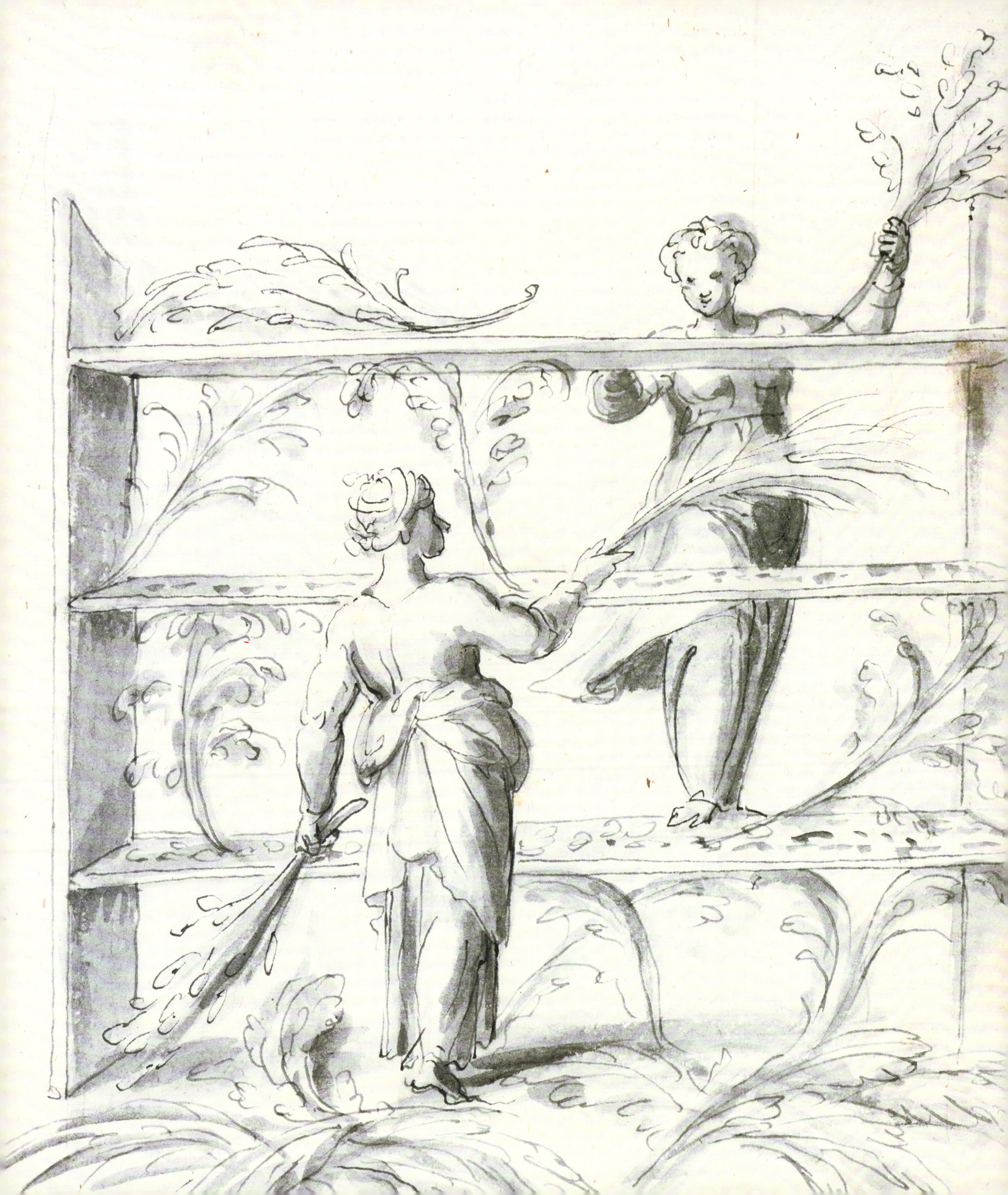

Philippe Morel

Giuseppe Arcimboldo: Silk Cultivation and Manufacture

The group of thirteen drawings by Arcimboldo representing the manufacture of silk and now in the Museum of Fine Arts in Boston is accompanied by a letter from the artist which allows us to understand that it is related to a plan of decoration proposed around 1587 to Baron Ferdinand Hoffmann, the new president of the imperial *Hofkammer*, for some rooms in his palace in Prague. The scenes of farming and handicraft would have been set in the middle of grotesques, a type of decoration whose œancient origin, discovery underground and in no way gratuitous or haphazard character are referred to briefly by Arcimboldo, following in the footsteps of many other contemporary authors, before proposing an updated adaptation of it (Kaufmann 1993 [1984], 151ff.; Fučikova 1987, 121-131; Barthes 1978, for the illus.). The presence of documentary images of this kind within a framework of grotesques, in the place of motifs in a more traditional antique style, at the end of the 16th century should not surprise us. Modestly foreshadowed in some details of the ceiling of the Sala dei Lanifici in the Farnese Palace in Caprarola (which reflect a fundamentally iconographic and symbolical inflection), they can be found in particular in the decoration of the Uffizi, on the ceilings of the rooms of the Armoury, painted in 1588 in a military and technological vein, and on that of the Stanzino delle Matematiche (1600), where scientific instruments, machines and historical episodes related to the subject are represented (Morel 1998, chap. 8). Since Arcimboldo writes "[...] li moderni medensamente potran' mettere nella tessidura *dentro a gli spacii* in vezzo come gli antiqui mettevano altari sacrificii animali ho altra [...]" (in Kaufmann 1993, 152), we can deduce that the scenes would have been set inside frames, rather than standing out – the other possibility – from a white ground surrounded by the figures of the grotesques.

The thirteen drawings accompanied by their captions accurately illustrate the different stages in the production of silk, from the rearing of the silkworms (gathering of the eggs deposited the previous summer and emergence of the larvae towards the end of April [drawing no. 1], growth of the worms during a good month) including the picking [2], selection and cleaning of the mulberry leaves [3] that are their only food (supplied up to ten times a day), their placing on racks that are frequently cleaned [4]. Once they have attained their maximum size, the worms are transferred onto branches (here of broom [5]) on which they can spin their cocoons out of a single filament of silk; inside the pupa commences its metamorphosis, which takes about ten days. When it comes to an end, before the moth perforates the cocoon and breaks the filament, the cocoons are gathered and exposed to a source of heat (here the sun [6]) and then placed in a cauldron of hot water (the most common way of scalding the pupae), to wash and loosen the filaments before the process of unwinding (*trattura*) the silk starts [7]; this is followed by the operations of drying [8] and of "throwing" (*torcitura*) [9], which produces the skeins of raw silk. It will then be wound again, stretched [11-12], dyed [13] and finally woven (cf. a similar series of Chinese drawings from the late 17th century: http://depts.washington.edu/chinaciv/clothing/11sericu.htm).

There are several reasons for the interest in the production and manufacture of silk to which this project bears witness: in the first place the spectacular expansion of *gelsibachicoltura* in Italy during the Renaissance, which made the peninsula the main centre of silk production and manufacture in Europe, and this agricultural activity and cottage industry a fundamental resource for certain regions and towns (Battistini 2003, *passim*). The cultivation of mulberry and silkworms, which is dependent on climatic conditions and a type of soil that are difficult to find north of the Alps, developed first in Southern Italy but then gradually shifted to the central and northern parts of the peninsula, where the fabric was also worked and manufactured, in particular at Lucca, Florence and Venice. Thus the hills of the Tuscan and Emilian Apennines, the northern plain of the Po Valley and the regions of Vicenza and Verona became major centres of production of the raw material, and it was not until the end of the 16th century that they were followed by Milan and its environs. The expansion of the European silk trade, the growing difficulty in importing it from the Levant and the reduction in the export of Calabrian raw silk were among the most decisive factors in this development, which did not involve the manufacturing and merchant classes alone. A number of Italian princes had taken an interest in this agricultural activity since the 15th century and certain states, like the Grand Duchy of Tuscany,

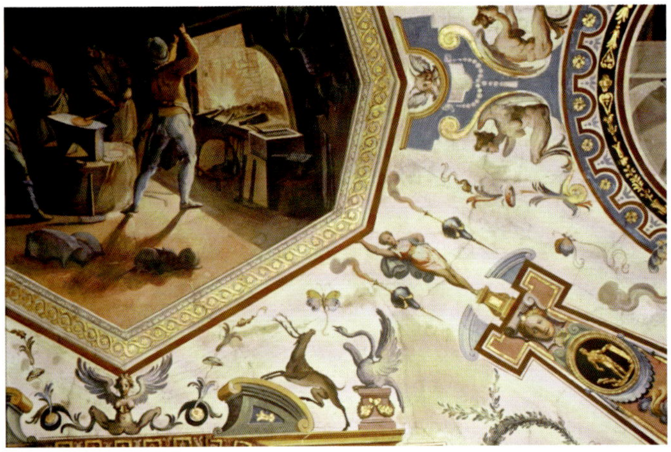

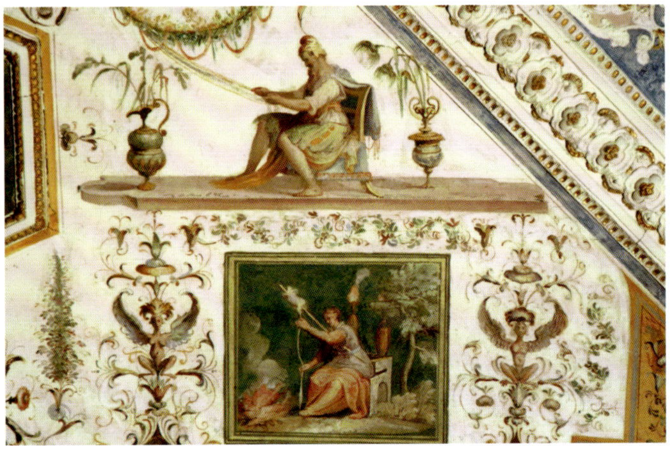

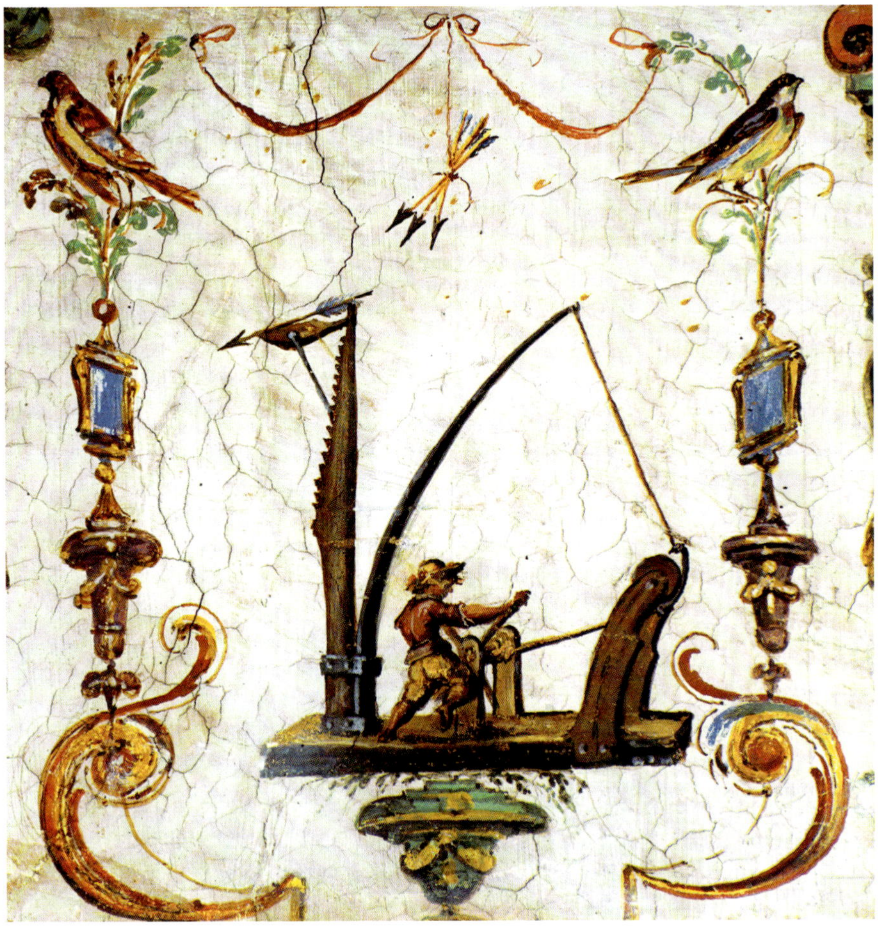

Fig. 1. L. Buti, a forge with grotesques, detail from a painted ceiling. Florence, Uffizi, Sala dell'Armeria

Fig. 2. Unknown artist, detail from decorative grotesques. Caprarola, Palazzo Farnese, Stanza dei Lanifici

Fig. 3. G. Parigi, detail from a painted ceiling. Florence, Uffizi, Stanzino delle Matematiche

had made considerable efforts to encourage it, notably by making the planting of mulberry trees compulsory.

The *gelsomania cinquecentesca* or "mulberry mania of the 16th century" and the rearing of Bombyx connected with it gave rise to several types of publication during the period (Molà 2000, 227-8), ranging from poems in praise of the *Bombyx mori* (by Marco Gerolamo Vida and Alessandro Tesauro) to short treatises on agriculture and craft technology: Agostino Gallo's *Le venti giornate della vera agricoltura e piaceri della villa* (1569, third edition of the original *Dieci giornate*, in which sericulture is dealt with on the sixteenth day), Levantio Guidiciolo's *Avvertimenti* (1564), *Il vermicello di seta* by Giovanni Corsuccio (1581) and the *Dialoghi sopra l'utili sue inventioni circa la seta* by Maggino Gabrielli (1588). This latter work, which describes a process that permitted two harvests of cocoons to be made in a single year, is accompanied by illustrations, but it is Giovanni Stradano's engravings that stand out as the most interesting contemporary visual documents of the subject. With good reason Kaufmann has focused on one of the engravings of the *Nova reperta* where the raising of the silkworm (and its importation into the West under the reign of the emperor Justinian, according to Procopius) figures among the most important technical discoveries and inventions, but it is the series of six engravings entitled *Vermis sericus* that we consider best suited to a comparison with Arcimboldo's drawings (Baroni Vannucci 1997, 289-291, 397, 401-402; McGinty 1998, 116-122). In them the different phases of production are represented, with a similar concern for documentary accuracy (including brief captions) and very few variations, beginning with the gathering of the larvae and ending with the reeling and spinning of the silk. The engravings made by Philippe Galle after Stradano's drawings (which have survived) were commissioned, undoubtedly towards the end of the 1580s (and thus contemporary with the decoration planned for Baron Hoffmann), by Costanza Alamanni, who in this way was following a family tradition exemplified by *La coltivazione,* a poem of Virgilian inspiration by Luigi Alamanni, as well as by the commission of the *Nova reperta* from the same artist.

Fig. 4. Giovanni Stradano, *Silkworm Farm*. The Royal Collection © HM Queen Elizabeth II

Fig. 5. Giovanni Stradano, *Silkworm Farm*. The Royal Collection © HM Queen Elizabeth II

Fig. 6. Giovanni Stradano, *Reeling of the Silk*. The Royal Collection © HM Queen Elizabeth II

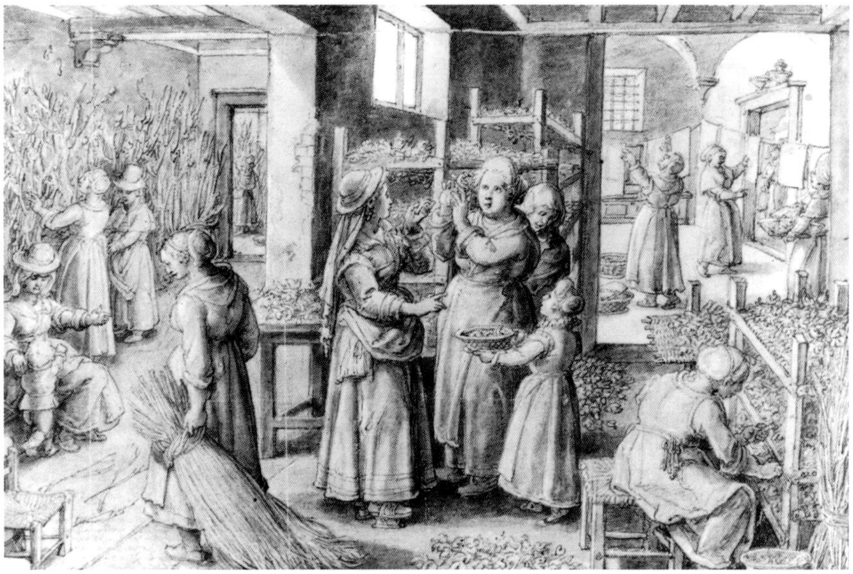

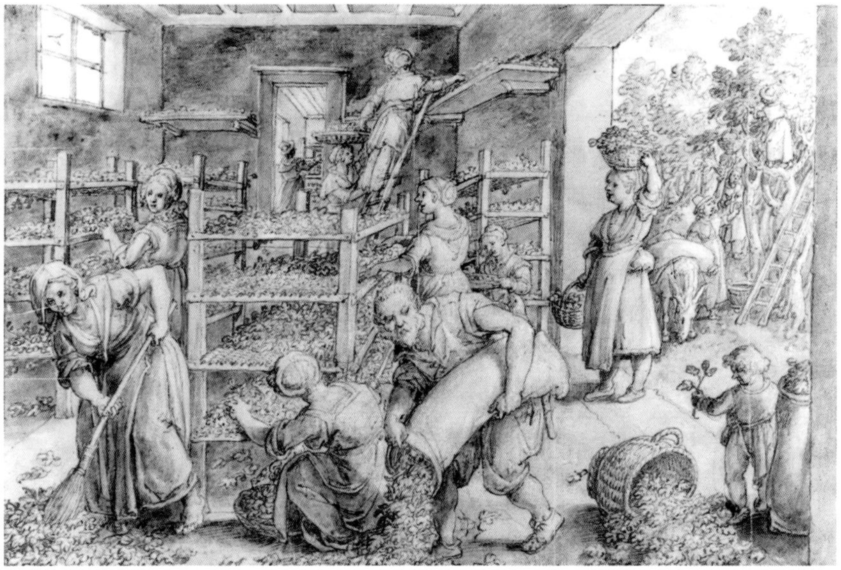

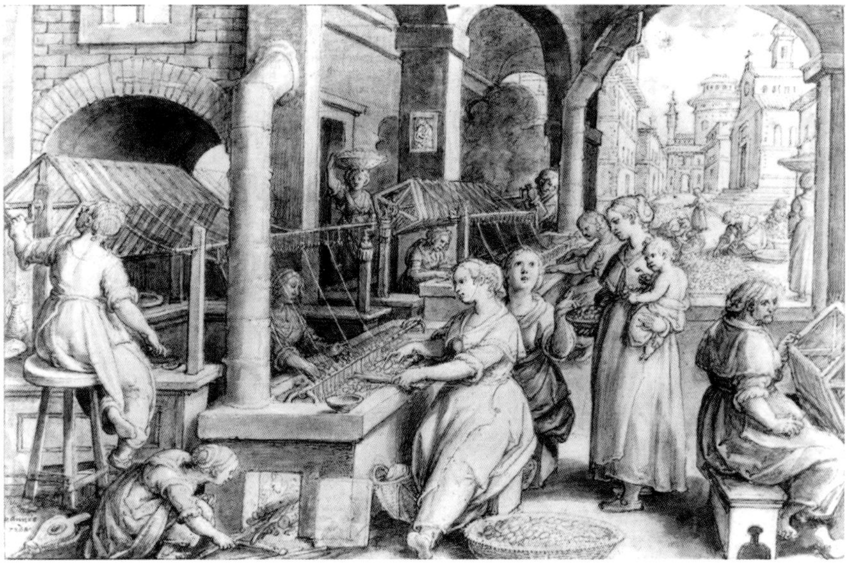

Arcimboldo himself supplied one explanation for the choice of a decoration devoted to the production of silk, which was to have been accompanied by other, similar decorations devoted to wool and to linen: "[...] io dimostro nelli presenti schizzi che e il lavorerio / da sede e per esser' questo piu incognito dentro / Germania ho pensato di haver' posto questo primo / come si potra fare in una altra Camera il lavorerio dalle Lana e in altra Camera si potra / far il lavorevi della tela o vogliamo dire il / principio del Lino come prima si coglie et / lino e poi de man in mane siva facendo la / tela" (Kaufmann 1993, 152-153). The wearing of silk was no longer reserved for the powerful, as it had been in the Middle Ages, and had become fashionable throughout Europe, but its culture and manufacture must have appeared relatively exotic in the eyes of a German-speaking public. It is also possible that Baron Hoffmann had shown a particular taste for the precious fabrics or an interest in commercial or industrial projects in the field. Finally, the two Florentine examples mentioned above and the idea of décor that gave rise to them allow us to imagine, by way of a mere hypothesis, that this iconography linked to silk, wool and linen may have been intended for a set of rooms supposed to house a wardrobe, or better still a collection of garments and other textiles. One thing is certain, as Kaufmann has already pointed out: like the same artist's composite heads, these drawings are a product of the marked taste in Vienna and Prague for naturalistic and scientific illustration of which Hoefnagel's miniatures constitute the most obvious expression, and they can be regarded as a forerunner of the more mathematical and astronomical interests that Hoffmann would later display (Kaufmann 1993, 172-173).

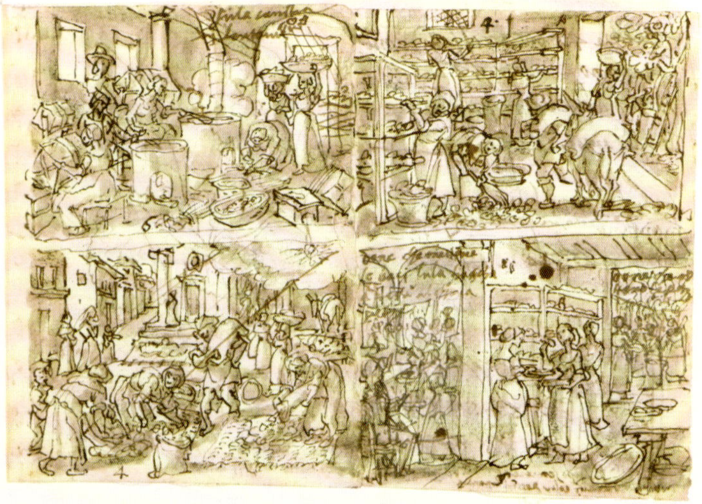

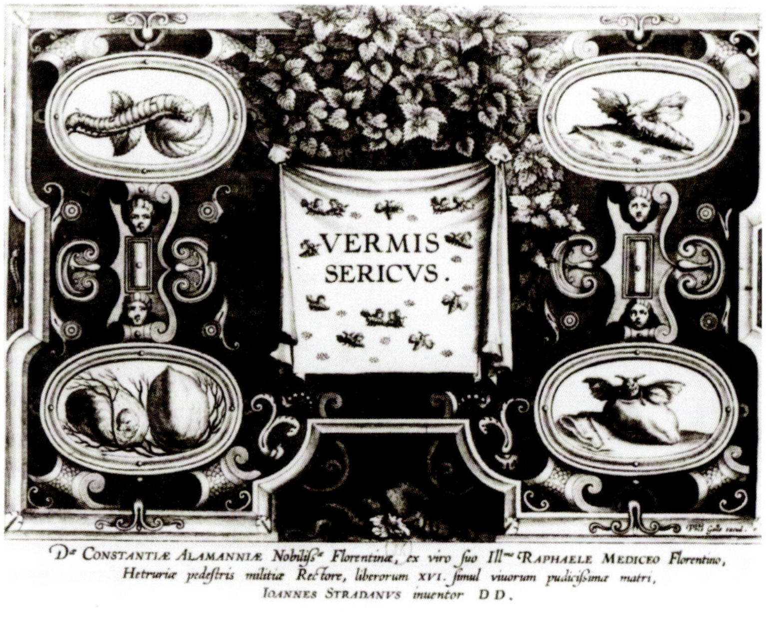

Fig. 7. Giuseppe Barberi, Drawing after a funerary monument for Bonafede di Monte, 1805. Washington, Smithsonian Institution Museum, Cooper Hewitt National Design Museum

Fig. 8. Philip Galle, after Giovanni Stradano, *Vermis Sericus*. Paris, Bibliothèque Nationale de France

Giuseppe Arcimboldo: Silk Cultivation and Manufacture

VI.1
Giuseppe Arcimboldo
Illustrated Volume with a Series of Thirteen Drawings on Sericulture, and Including an Autograph Letter
c. 1586
Pen, blue ink and blue wash on paper
Volume: 32 × 21.5 × 5.3 cm
folio: 30.8 × 19 × cm
Boston, Museum of Fine Arts, William A. Sargent Fund, inv. no. 50.6.15

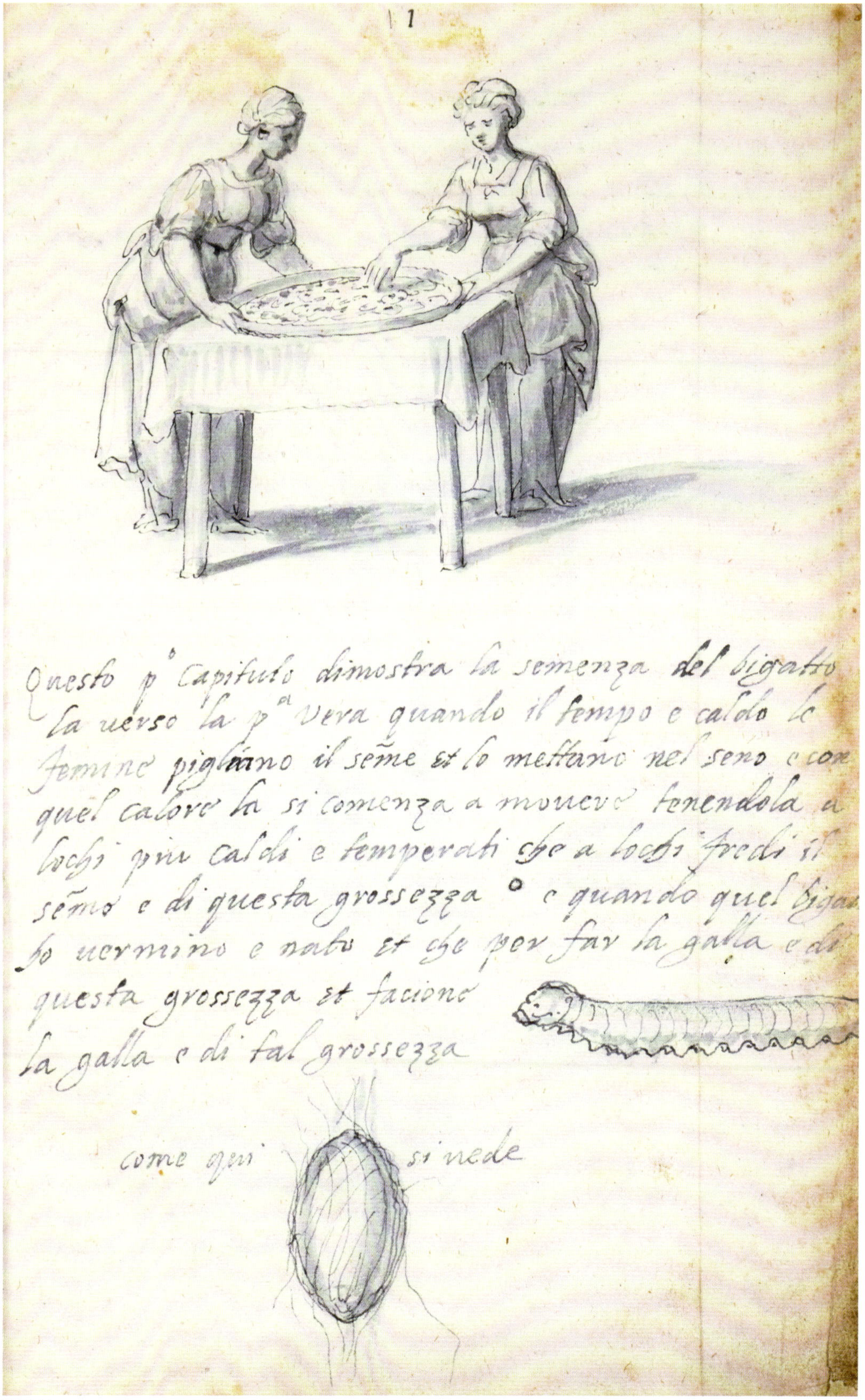

VI.1. fol. 1

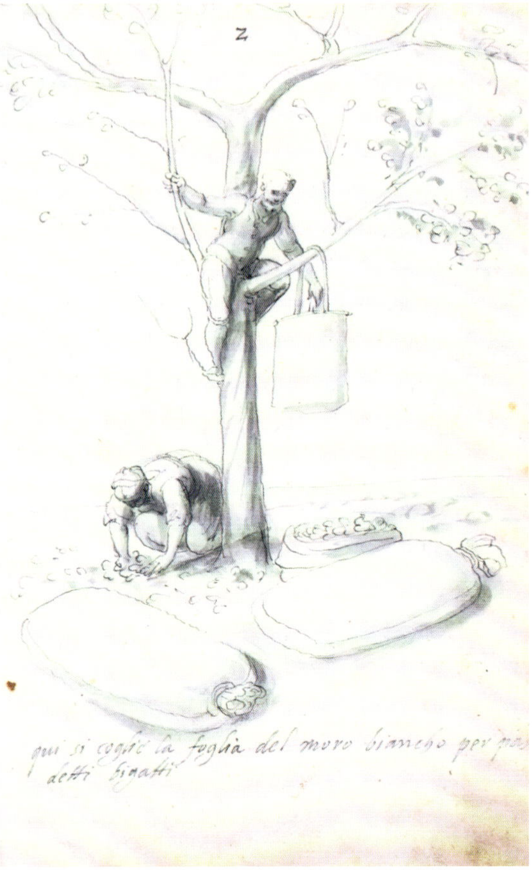

VI.1. fol. 2

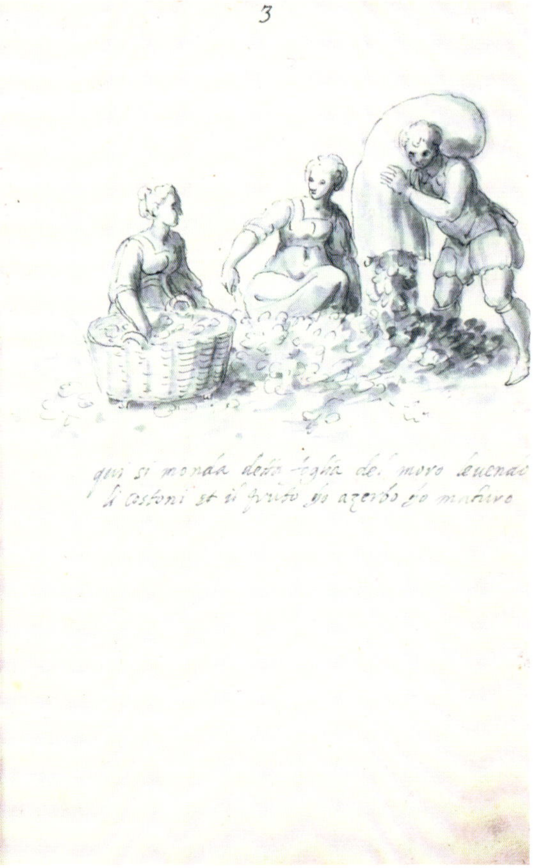

VI.1. fol. 3

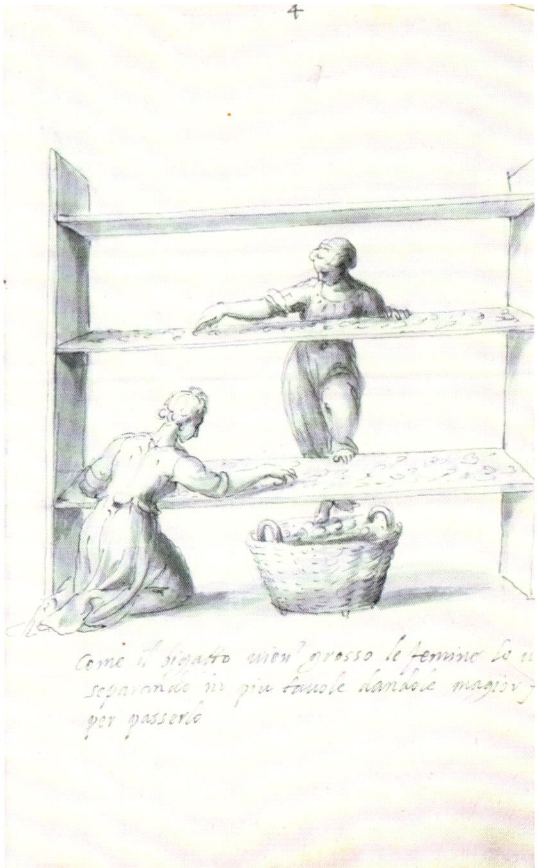

VI.1. fol. 4

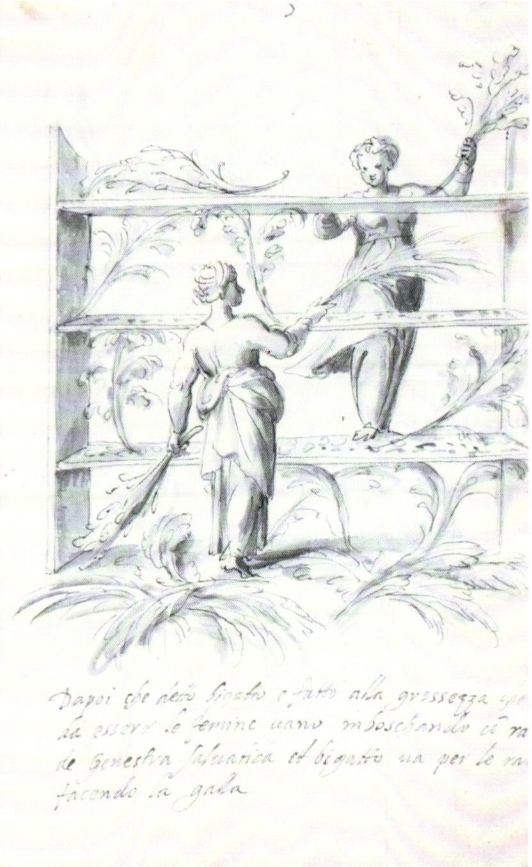

VI.1. fol. 5

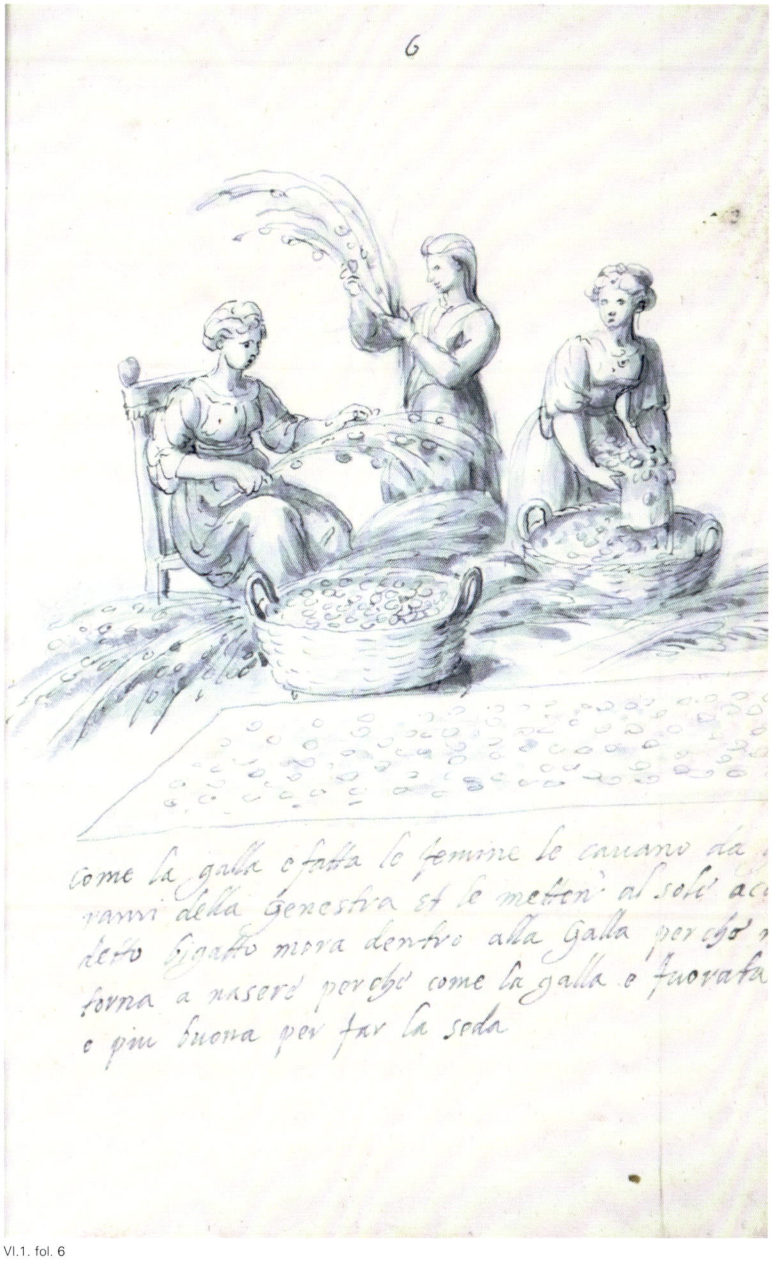

VI.1. fol. 6

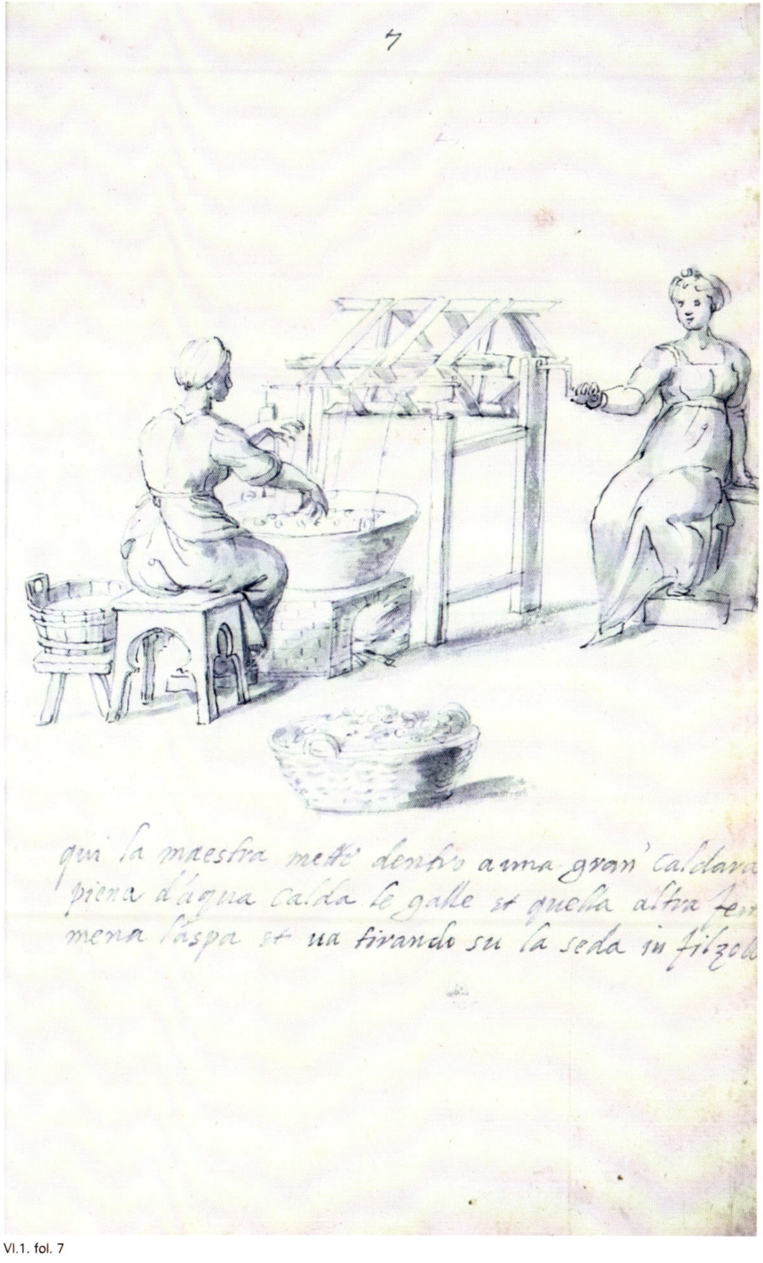

VI.1. fol. 7

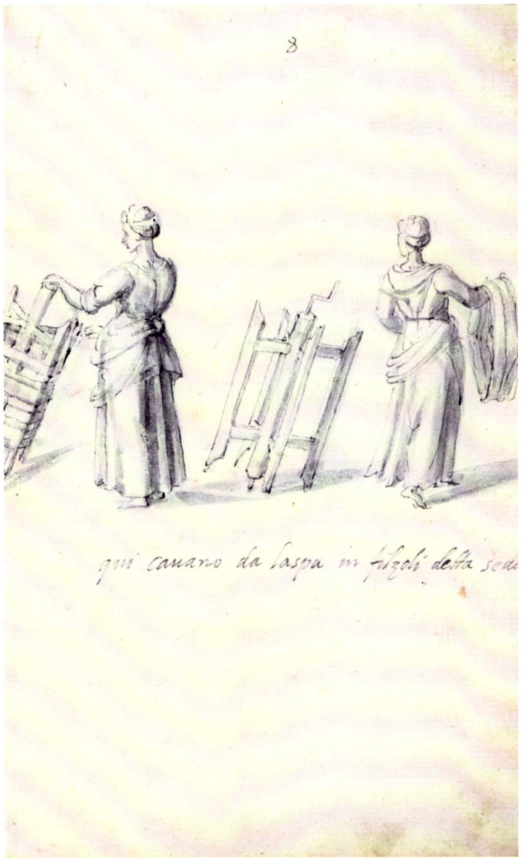

Vl.1. fol. 8

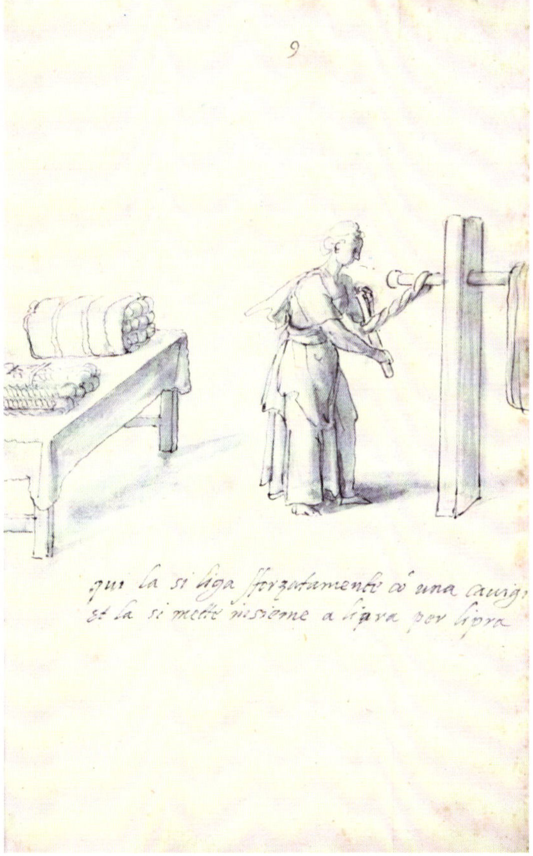

Vl.1. fol. 9

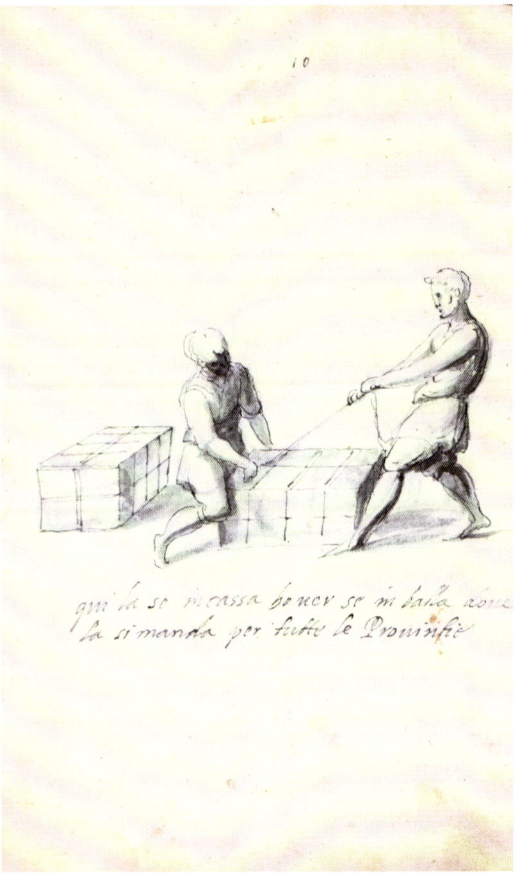

Vl.1. fol. 10

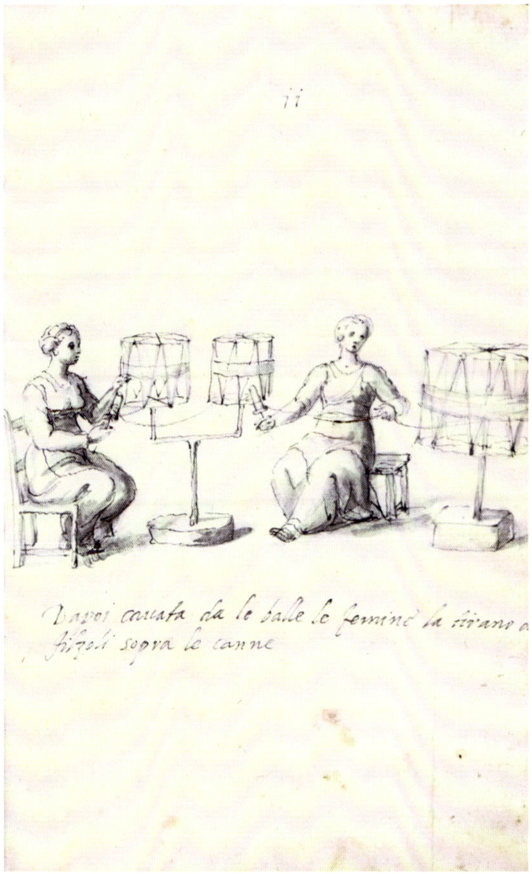

Vl.1. fol. 11

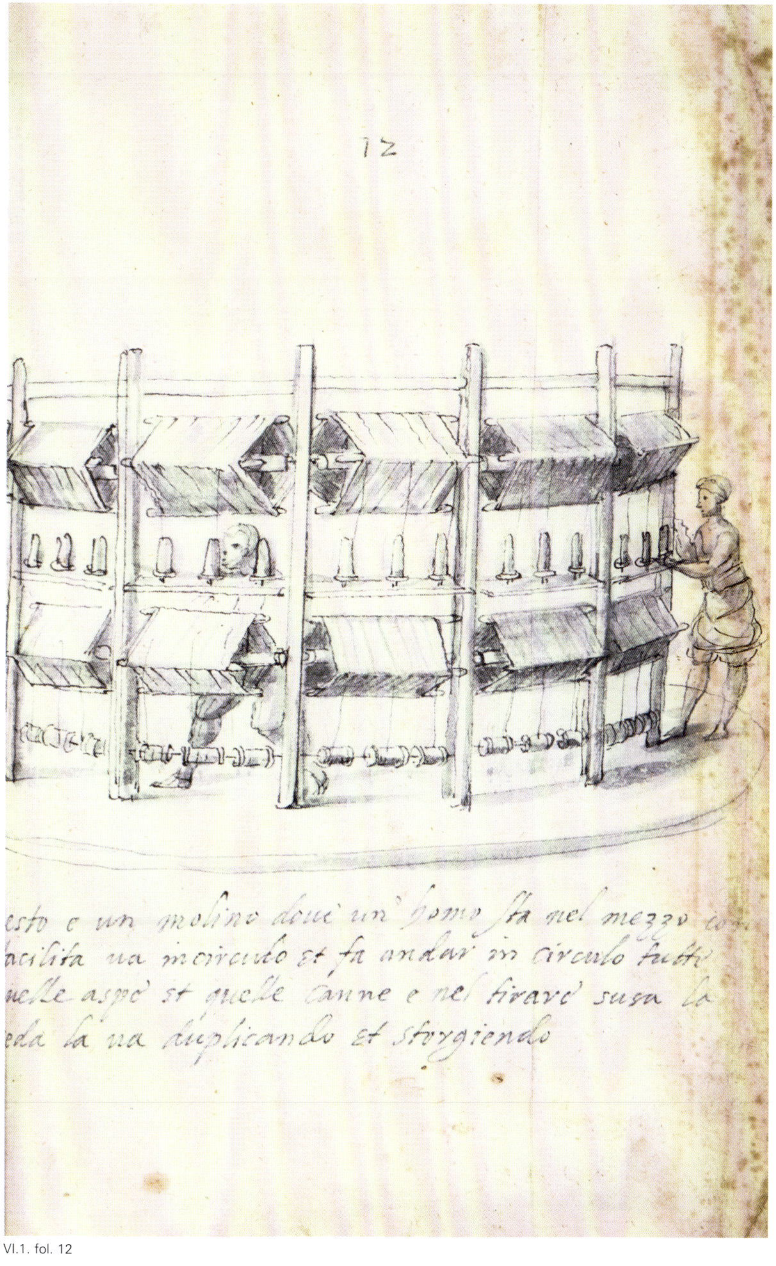

VI.1. fol. 12

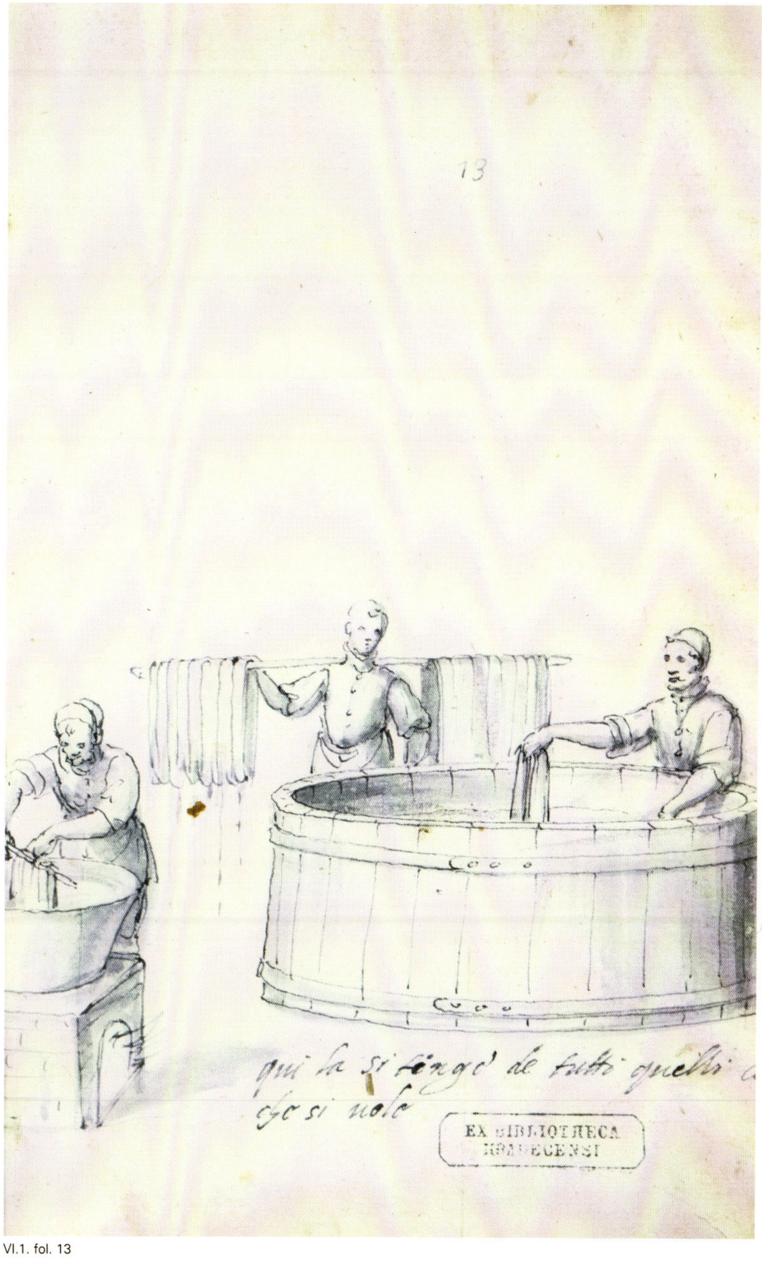

VI.1. fol. 13

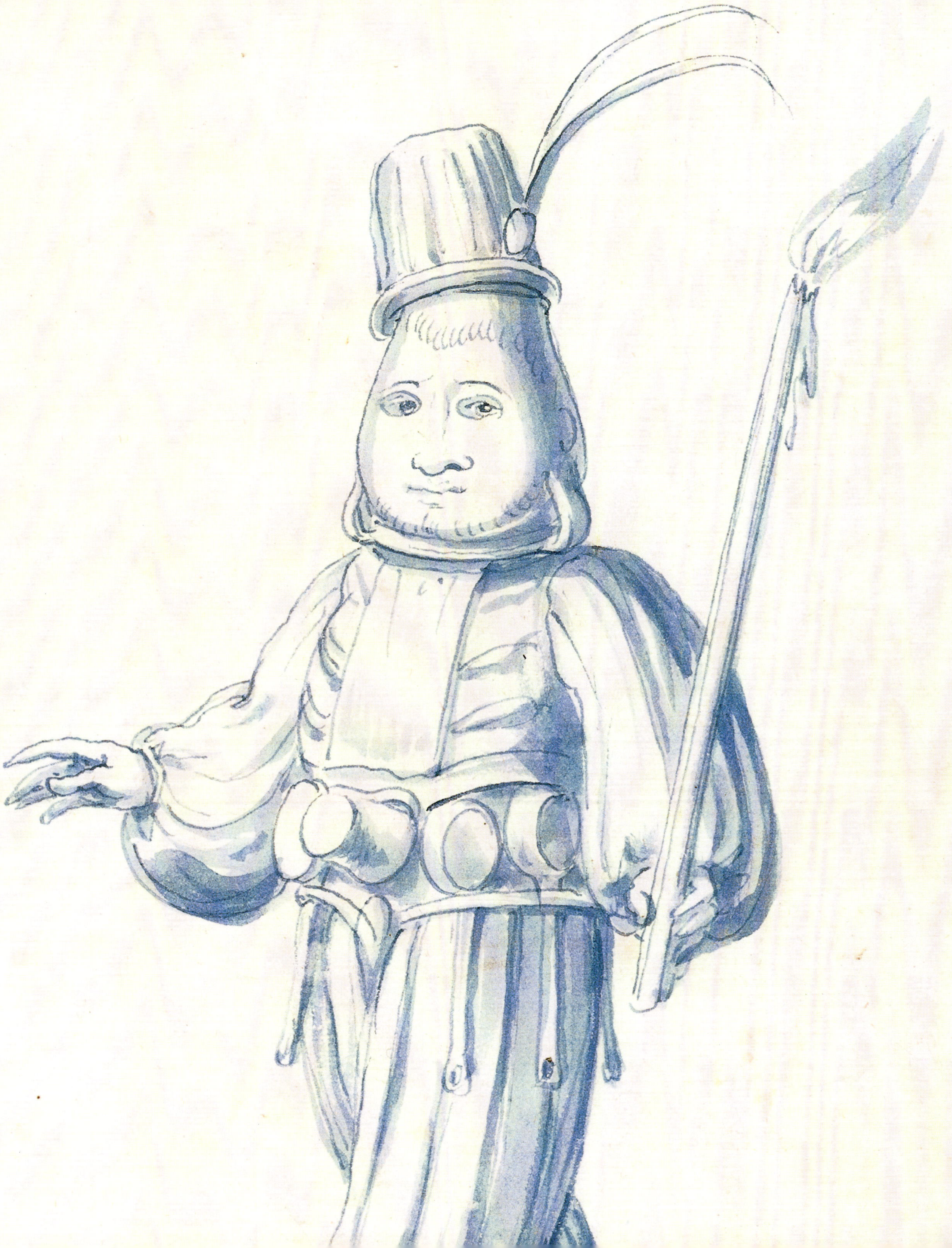

Andreas Beyer

The Princely Stage
Arcimboldo's Costumes and Drawings for Court Festivities and Tournaments

Among the many tasks of a court artist featured the design and organization of festivals and tournaments, which Renaissance princes saw as their favourite means of political propaganda. Pageants were an important occasion to celebrate wealth and generosity, that is the virtue of *magnificentia*, underlining the excellence of their protagonists while allowing others to take part in the general display of splendour. Through illusion and exaltation they created an allegory of power; their mostly ephemeral decorations emphasized the exceptional nature of the present moment and the irreversibility of time, thus intensifying the enjoyment of the instant. Garments, equipment and scenic effects were used to glorify the ruling house and legitimate and fortify the power structures. In tournaments, the image of the magnanimous ruler was completed with that of the victorious commander – each show was part of a "liturgy of secular apotheosis", based on mythological and historical themes from Antiquity associated with the ruler, as well as on the allegorical and symbolic repertoire of humanism. As a theatrical mirror of princely life, festivals and tournaments served a power strategy which aimed at conveying abstract ideals of power by way of sensory persuasion. Renaissance festivals have been aptly described as an art form which was both an event and its own explanation, where art and history meet in a both abstract and concrete sphere[1].

The festive culture[2] which developed in the Italian courts in the early modern period found its transalpine equivalent in the sumptuous tradition of pageants and tournaments of the Burgundian court. The Habsburgs, who claimed to be the heirs of the House of Burgundy, took over the legacy and introduced the tradition into their own court representations. The many tournaments held by Ferdinand II of Tyrol during his time as governor of Bohemia led to the founding of a specific tradition in Prague, even before Rudolf II transferred his court there[3]. By gathering the princes and the aristocracy on the occasion of festivals and tournaments, the Habsburgs achieved the desired effect of thus symbolically unifying their empire made up of many peoples, and concealing the numerous contradictions present behind the feeling of unity and harmony[4].

Three types of tournament were held at the imperial court of the Habsburgs: jousting, tourney and foot tournament. Lavish processions headed for the tournament fields, harking back to the triumphs of antiquity, giving an impression of festive might and splendour. Tournaments marked a rebirth of chivalry, as chivalrous combat had gradually disappeared from actual battle and had been turned from a military into an aesthetic practice. Their new form had to be devised by artists. Gian Paolo Lomazzo, one of Arcimboldo's first biographers, praised the Milanese artist's outstanding work as a painter, but also his special gifts for staging this type of festival: "In fact this man was truly unique in his inventions and more than anything for the conception of masked pageants, so that he was assigned the task of designing the whole festivities on the occasion of the celebrations of the wedding of His Highness Archduke Charles, Maximilian's brother. For the first tournament, in which the Emperor himself took part, he had the happy and unusual idea of having three kings appear, who stood for the three parts of the world, Asia, Africa and America, to honour the princes of the Austrian dynasty. Asia was represented by Archduke Charles, the bridegroom, Africa by Archduke Ferdinand and America by the commander of the Archduke's cavalry. These happening to find themselves in the appointed place when they heard of the coming wedding festivities, they joined together and offered their services as tournament stewards. Arcimboldo then had Europe meet them, under the guise of four figures representing her four most important provinces, namely Italy, France, Spain and Germany. Archduke Ernst stood for Italy, Archduke Rudolf for Spain, the Emperor's cavalry major for France, and the Emperor himself for Germany. The clothes, insignia, symbols and accompaniers of these persons indicated and signified their respective provinces, and I shall not here count up all the devices, constructions, wonders and glories of this tournament, since that would fill an entire volume"[5].

That Arcimboldo instructed Lomazzo to render such detailed accounts of his festive projects shows how important this function was considered at court. Another proof is the fact that not only Arcimboldo's paintings but also his drawings for courtly pageants were included in the imperial art collection. The inventory of Rudolf II's Kunstkammer from the years 1607-1611 lists four

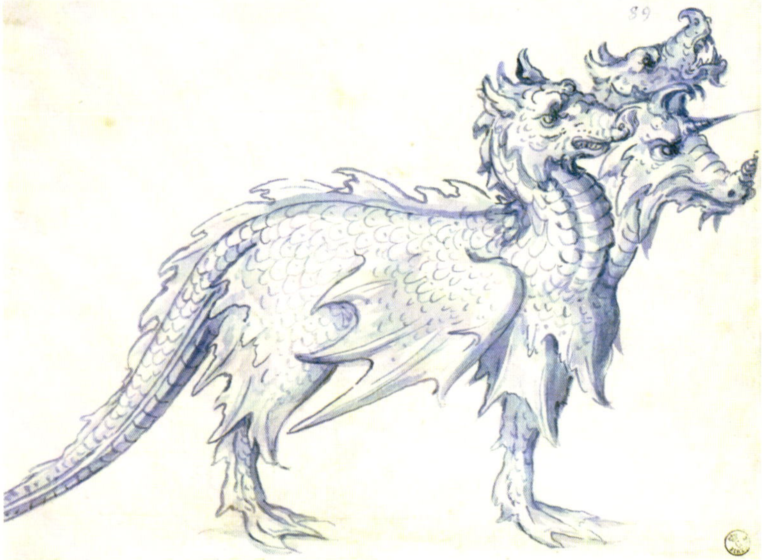

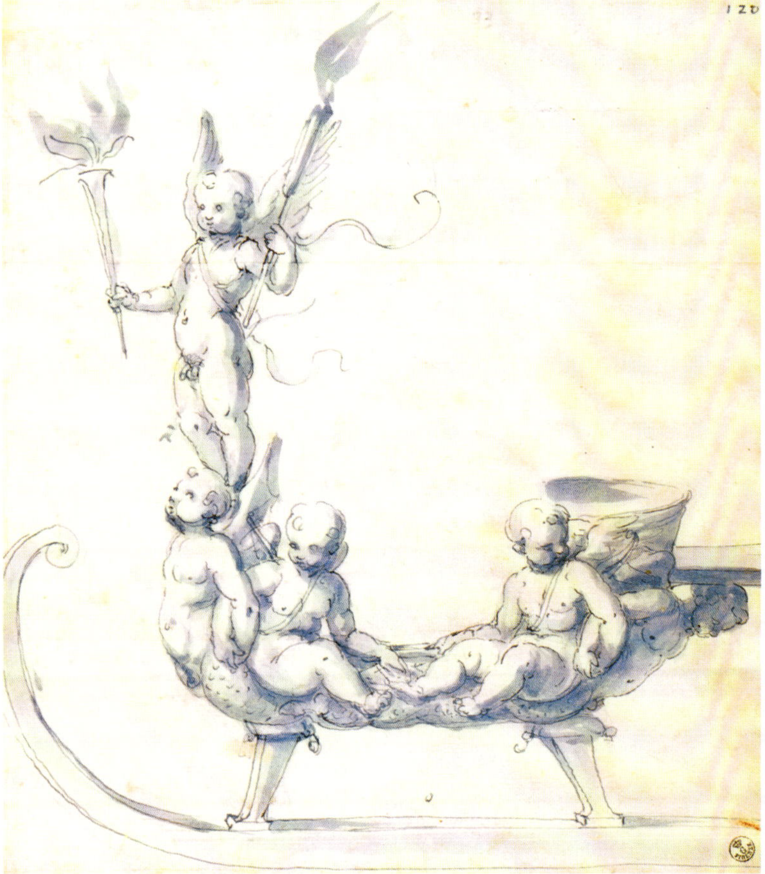

Fig. 1. Giuseppe Arcimboldo, *Sketch for a Cerberus*. Florence, Uffizi, Gabinetto dei Disegni e delle Stampe

Fig. 2. Giuseppe Arcimboldo, *Sketch for a Sleigh with Putti*. Florence, Uffizi, Gabinetto dei Disegni e delle Stampe

folders in which the vestiges of this ephemeral work were stored[6]. These also included "a sketchbook of Arcimboldo with all kinds of farces, adorned with floral patterns" (inv. no. 2767). A selection of sketches of various pageants and tournaments, originally gathered in a red Morocco portfolio, are now preserved in the Gabinetto dei Disegni e delle Stampe of the Uffizi, Florence; one can presume they were brought to Florence via the Tuscan branch of the Habsburg family. The dedication on the frontispiece (cat. no. VII.1) leaves no doubt as to their authorship.

INVICTISSIMO ROMANORUM IMPERATORI
SEMPER AUGUSTO RODOLPHO SECUNDO
DOMINO CLEMENTISSIMO
Iosephus Arcimboldus Mediolanensis Has Pro
Hastiludiis Multas Variasq. Ornamentarum
Inventiones Manu Propria Delineatas Dicavit
ANNO DNI MDLXXXV

TO THE INVICIBLE EMPEROR OF THE ROMANS
HIS SEMPITERNAL MAJESTY RUDOLF II
THE ENORMOUSLY BENIGN RULER
Giuseppe Arcimboldo of Milan
has dedicated many different inventions
drawn for the organization of tournaments
IN THE YEAR OF THE LORD 1585

Most of these sketches are in brown pen and blue wash. Arcimboldo's drawing style can be related to the Lombard tradition, namely to that of the Campi family of painters; the attempt to compare the drawings with the festive projects of the Fontainebleau school is less convincing[7]. However, one should above all remember that the specific character and function of these drawings is necessarily detrimental to their inventive potential. They are models, patterns for tailors, seamsters and craftsmen, from which costumes, masks and other objects were to be prepared. The painstaking mode of drawing inevitably betrays little artistic originality, as opposed to freehand drawings or *bozzetti*. These projects, most of which are drawn with pen and more or less extensively filled in with blue wash, are all in the same tone; Arcimboldo indicates in his own hand, as in the case of the "artes liberales", the colours the costumes are to be made in. Even though in this or that sketch the artist appears to have given free rein to his imagination (inv. no. 3197), the explicitly antiquarian style or *gestus* of these drawings (see the costumes of "artes liberales" inv. 3150, 3151, 3152, 3153, 3154, 3155, 3156) clearly illustrates the importance of historical references in pageants and tournaments. While Arcimboldo's paintings appear to follow the taste of the Rudolfine court for "free art" – and thus actively correspond to the artistic and political ambitions of the ruler – these sketches are of a more affirmative nature; this is why they were attributed a quasi historiographic role, as precious documents of an ephemeral festive culture.

Arcimboldo was also in charge of the festivities for the marriage of Maximilian II's elder daughter Anna with Philip II of Spain, for which he organized the procession of participants in the tournament. A chronicler tells us that the sumptuous pageant was headed by the artist himself: "... a tall man in a difficult role was the Emperor's painter, Joseph, who headed the triumph"[8]. As their train included horses dressed as dragons and an elephant which aroused general amazement, it is very likely that some sketches for those disguises are conserved among the drawings in the Uffizi[9].

Arcimboldo's contribution to the marriage celebrations of Archduke Charles von Steiermark with Maria of Bavaria in 1571 was much greater. Lomazzo's extensive and glowing accounts of the festivities underline that the artist himself set great store by these specific achievements. There exist many descriptions of the event, but a deeper analysis only became possible after Giovanni Battista Fonteo's account was discovered and interpreted by Thomas DaCosta Kaufmann[10]. The festival started with a "ring race" in the open fields beyond the town walls. For this purpose an artificial hill and a field of contest marked by two pyramids were constructed. As protectress of matrimony, Juno was the first to appear, standing on a carriage drawn by peacocks (inv. no. 3268). She was accompanied by three personifications of Africa, Asia and America, as also mentioned by Lomazzo. She was followed by Iris who, as Juno's messenger, descended from a cloud and uttered the cry that opened the contest. Then came Europe, on a horse dressed as a bull, followed by sirens and the seven Liberal Arts. In Fonteo's commemorative poem, they are described as children of Mercury and their parts were played by the emperor's chamberlains. Each of the "artes liberales" appeared associated with two of its typical representatives, so for example Rhetoric was accompanied by Demosthenes and Cicero. The Florentine folder contains projects for those seven costumes (inv. no. 3150, 3151, 3152, 3153, 3154, 3155, 3156).

Diana was preceded by her retinue, the goddess appearing in the company of a unicorn and a group of servants dressed as wild animals. Behind her marched woodmen with horns and Amazons armed with spears, bows and arrows (inv. no. 3512, 3157, 3168). The group around Neptune was composed of men dressed as fishes, showing the sea creatures from the waters surrounding Europe. This was followed by the train of Pallas Athena. It consisted of a carriage decorated with an owl, to which the four vices were bound. The cardinal virtues entered with the personification of victory. Various noblemen and members of the emperor's family embodied Justice, Fortitude and Temperance. The allegory of Gluttony entered along with Venus, surrounded by *amoretti*.

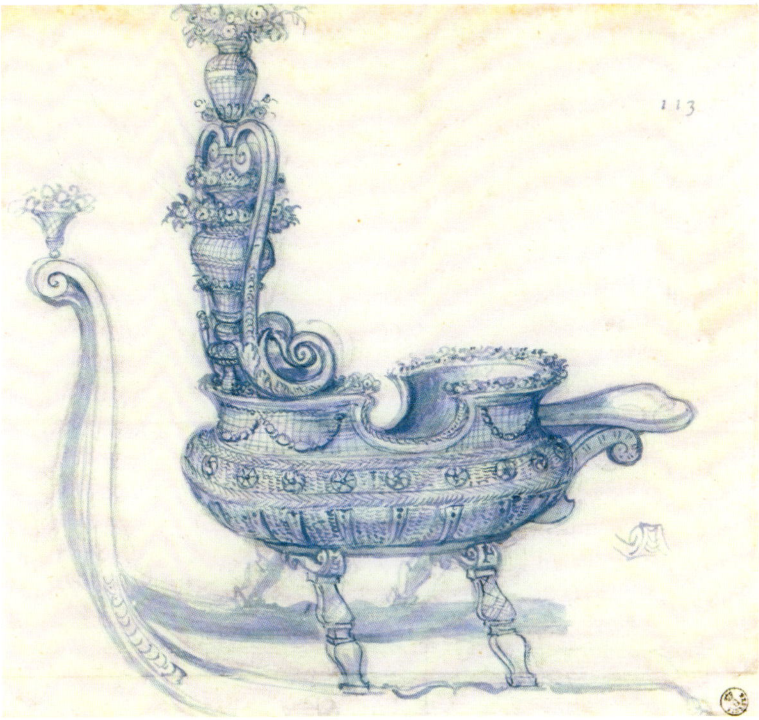

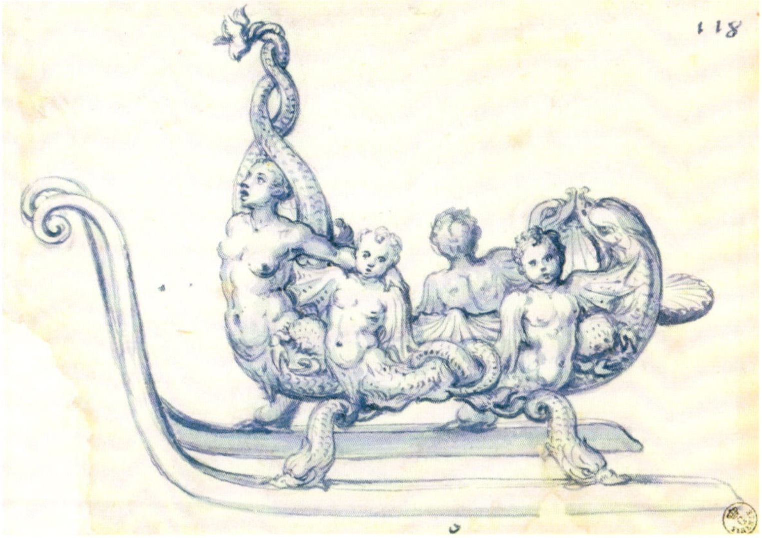

Fig. 3. Giuseppe Arcimboldo, *Sketch for a Sleigh Shaped like a Basket of Flowers*. Florence, Uffizi, Gabinetto dei Disegni e delle Stampe

Fig. 4. Giuseppe Arcimboldo, *Sketch for a Sleigh with a Siren*. Florence, Uffizi, Gabinetto dei Disegni e delle Stampe

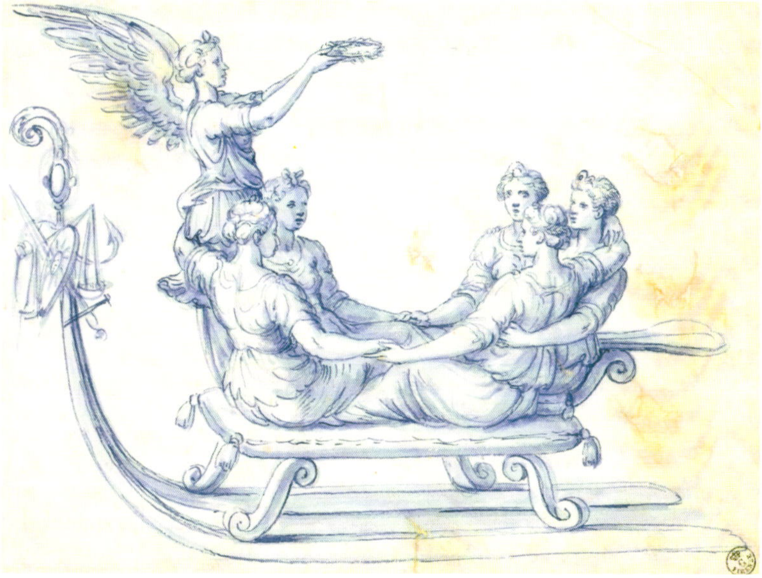

Fig. 5. Giuseppe Arcimboldo, *Sketch for a Sleigh with an Allegory of Victory*. Florence, Uffizi, Gabinetto dei Disegni e delle Stampe

Bacchus, for whose train no drawing seems to have been preserved, was embodied by a man in a barrel and surrounded by personifications of the four winds, the four elements, the four seasons, the four rivers and other foursomes such as the four European peoples dressed as the four ages of life. After the allegory of spring came a float on which the river Po troned, characterized by an Italian entourage. This was followed by the Spanish group, led by Zephyrus and two other west winds. A representation of fire was followed by the sun, bearing the Spanish element, gold. The heir to the throne, Rudolf II, who had been brought up at the Spanish court, appeared as the personification of summer in this group, closed off by the Ebro river. Along with the southwest and southeast winds, the south wind led the Gallic troops, represented by hornblowers. An allegory of the earth was followed by Jupiter, bearing the Gallic present, namely tin. Before the Rhone closed off this formation, more costumed peers followed, including a personification of autumn. The last part of the procession was made up of the German train, led by the north wind. The goddess Luna, who carried the German metal, silver, was preceded by a personification of water. Maximilian II, dressed as winter, led this procession, the Danube bringing up the rear.

In the evening, a banquet and a ball took place, which the invited princes attended in their own costumes, bearing torches (inv. no. 3214, 3176). Those sheets may be sketches for this part of the festivity, which would show that this act too was part of the artistic programme of the allegorical pageant. The celebrations of the first day were followed by a further tournament day. Sketches for the procession to the tournament field have not reached us; yet one can assume that Arcimboldo was fully responsible for it too. Men appeared on stilts, others with excessively long necks, still others with snail shells on their backs, followed by a float supporting a representation of the Etna volcano, with musicians dressed as animals. According to Fonteo's account, two Bavarian princes sat in the middle of the carriage dressed as Pluto and Proserpine, surrounded by the Titans Tantalus, Ixion and Sisyphus.

On the basis on Fonteo's account, Thomas DaCosta Kaufmann gave a very convincing interpretation of the entire festive programme as a Habsburg vision of the Renaissance universe, where the emperor and the Austrian dynasty were assigned a key role. The procession to the "ring race" celebrated the Habsburgs as ruling over Europe and the other parts of the earth, and over the elements and the seasons. The evening "Astral Festival", in which the participants took part dressed as planets, extended the power of the princes and sovereigns to cosmic dimensions. In the spectators' minds, this representation of a united western world led by the Austrian dynasty unequivocally referred to the energy with which the impending "Turkish peril" was to be confronted. In the same folder, another poem by Fonteo draws a parallel with the battle of Lepanto, making the political allusion more explicit. The entire procession of the first day can be interpreted as a reference to the Holy Alliance. The sirens embodied the call for a united western world. The winds bore the Christian ships, the elements led the Turks to their downfall, the metals formed the basis for financing the battle, the seasons finally saw the fleet assemble, emerge, achieve victory and triumphantly return. Fonteo's poem was probably not the actual *titulus* of the festive programme, and may have been written *post festum*[11]. This in no way implies that the whole allegorical pattern did not serve exactly such an ambitious programme.

Acknowledging Arcimboldo's achievements in these activities is fundamental to appraising him as an exemplary court artist of central importance. His part in the Austrian court was not limited to creating puzzling allegories; it was far more political. Artistic freedom and service to the court were part of a two-way trade. When Rudolf II was crowned King of Hungary in 1572, Arcimboldo was once again called in for the celebrations; the figure of a "necromancer" in the Florentine folder may be one of the sketches made for this occasion (inv. no. 3217)[12]. A similar character is mentioned in the description of the festivities as being the inhabitant of one of the grottoes set up near the tournament field, a caution against dwindling fighting strength. Indeed Rudolf II contributed to reviving festivals and tournaments and Arcimboldo probably continued in this major task, organizing another pageant in 1579, and on the occasion of a ceremony of investiture into the order of the Golden Fleece in Prague in 1585[13].

Lomazzo's account of Arcimboldo ends with the following passage: "And all this was the idea and the invention of this inimitable

Fig. 6. Giuseppe Arcimboldo, *Sketch for a Visored Helmet*. Florence, Uffizi, Gabinetto dei Disegni e delle Stampe

Fig. 7. Giuseppe Arcimboldo, *Sketch for a Mask*. Florence, Uffizi, Gabinetto dei Disegni e delle Stampe

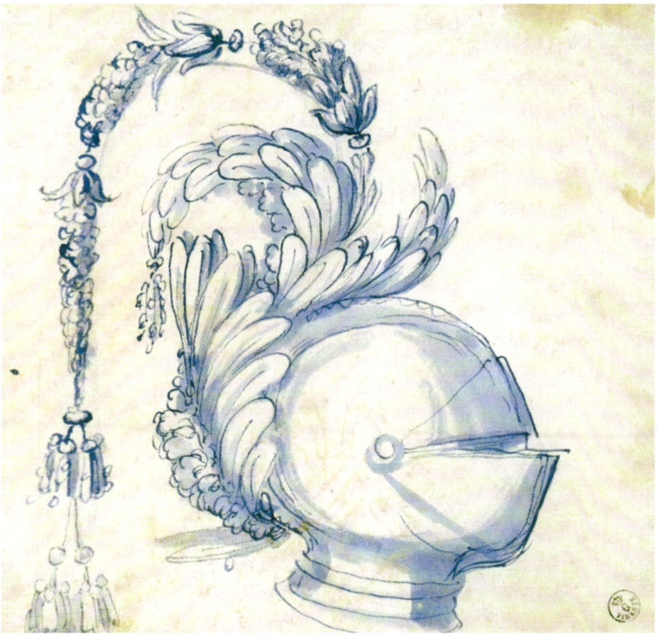

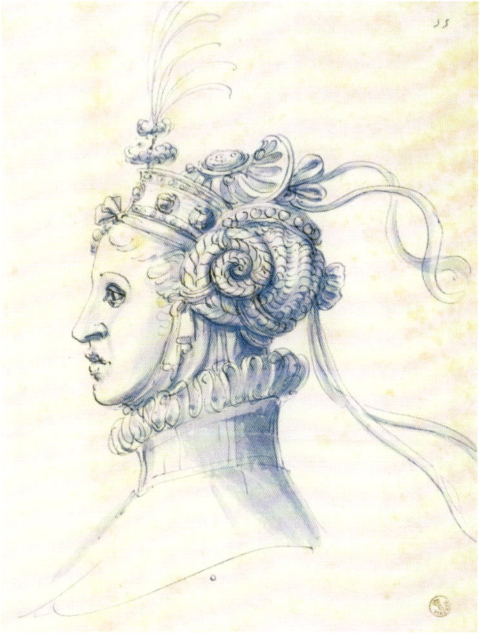

painter, even though a certain Fonteo, introduced into the court by Arcimboldo and assigned by the latter to work on the programme of festivities, was so shameless as to claim he was the author of one of these compositions. The Emperor was much amazed when he heard this, as he knew well that the idea came from Arcimboldo, with whom he had often discussed it"[14]. The authorship here in dispute is yet to be confirmed, but it reminds us of the importance of an activity which Arcimboldo himself never considered as second to his work as a painter.

[1] See basically on this point Alewyn 1985; Berns, Rahn 1995; Buck *et al.* 1981; Ragotzky, Wenzel 1990; Strong 1991; Trevor-Roper 1976.
[2] See on this issue Burckhardt 1989, 397ff. and Helas 1999.
[3] See on this issue Kaufmann 1978a, 19.
[4] See Jacquot 1956, Vol. 1, 9ff.
[5] Lomazzo in Ciardi 1973, Vol. 1, 362.
[6] Year 1607, 1ff. See Neumann 1966, 262-265.
[7] For the stylistic classification see Kaufmann 1978a, 53; Kaufmann 1982b; Fučíková II, in Stuttgart 1979, Vol. 2, 187-192; Legrand 1955; Saxl 1936.
[8] Zirfeo 1570, fol. 16r. After Kaufmann 1978a, 30.
[9] See Beyer 1983, 110 and Kaufmann 1978a, 31.
[10] "Europalia, hoc est: Species, Dignitas, significatio solemnis ejus popae, quam Maximilianus II Imperator invictissimus cum illustri Europae ostentatione ijs produxit ludis, quos egit summo incredibili*que* splendore, atque apparatu, dum Serenissimi Archiducis Caroli fratris nuptialem celebritatem ornandam amplificandam*que* suscepit, diuino*que* simul praesagio foederate aduersus Gloriosos exitus, et Triumphum portendisse uisus est, die ipso quadragesimo ante magnam uictoriam naualem". Codex 10206 of the Austrian National Library. All following material after Kaufmann 1978a, 34ff. See also Beyer 1983, 111ff.
[11] Kaufmann 1978a, 39f.
[12] Kaufmann 1978a, 40ff.
[13] Kaufmann 1978a, 43ff.
[14] Lomazzo in Ciardi 1973, 363. On Fonteo see Falchetta 1987, 147-164.

The Princely Stage
Arcimboldo's Costumes and Drawings for Court Festivities and Tournaments

---

VII.1-32
Giuseppe Arcimboldo
Drawings of tournaments dedicated to Rudolf II.
1585
Florence, Gabinetto dei Disegni e delle Stampe degli Uffizi

VII.1
Frontispiece of the binder preserved in the Uffizi, Florence, with Arcimboldo's preparatory drawings

VII.2
Costume of the allegorical figure "Grammar"
In the upper part of the page the remark: "Grammar, led by the Roman Priscianus and the Greek Aristarchos. Blue garment."
301 × 202 mm
Pen, blue wash, white paper
inv. no. 3150 F

VII.3
Costume of the allegorical figure "Dialectic"
In the upper part of the page the remark: "Dialectic, led by Leon and Chrysippus or Aristotle. White, gold striped garment".
304 × 207 mm
Pen, blue wash, white paper
inv. no. 3151 F

VII.4
Costume of the allegorical figure "Geometry"
In the upper part of the page the remark: "Geometry, led by the Sicilian Archimedes and the Calabrian Archita. Black garment".
304 × 206 mm
Pen, blue wash, white paper
inv. no. 3155 F

VII.5
Costume of the allegorical figure of "Rhetoric"
In the upper part of the page the remark: "Rhetoric, led by the Roman Cicero and the Athenian Demosthenes. Red garment".
304 × 205 mm
Pen, blue wash, white paper
inv. no. 3152 F

VII.6
Costume of the allegorical figure "Arithmetic"
In the upper part of the page the remark: "Arithmetic, led by the Italian Pythagoras and the Greek Euclid. Green garment".
309 × 205 mm
Pen, blue wash, white paper
inv. no. 3153 F

VII.7
Costume for the allegorical figure "Music"
In the upper part of the page the remark: "Music, led by the Roman Boethius and the Greek Arion. Yellow garment".
303 × 204 mm
Pen, blue wash, white paper
inv. no. 3154 F

VII.8
Costume for the allegorical figure "Astrology"
In the upper part of the page the remark: "Astrology, led by the Alexandrian Ptolemy and the Roman Julius Hyginus. White garment, bordered in red with golden stars".
301 × 203 mm
Pen, blue wash, white paper
inv. no. 3156 F

VII.9
Costume drawing of a woman with lance
301 × 206 mm
Pen, blue wash, white paper
inv. no. 3157 F

VII.10
Costume drawing for a woman bearing a lance
294 × 208 mm
Pen, blue wash, white paper
inv. no. 3168 F

VII.11
Costume drawing for a woman bearing a torch
308 × 211 mm
Pen, blue wash, white paper
inv. no. 3176 F

VII.12
Costume drawing of a female figure with torch
305 × 204 mm
Pen, blue wash, white paper
inv. no. 3179 F

VII.13
Costume drawing of a woman with torch
306 × 205 mm
Pen, blue wash, white paper
inv. no. 3174 F

VII.14
Costume drawing for a female figure with torch
303 × 205 mm
Pen, blue wash, white paper
inv. no. 3212 F

VII.15
Costume drawing for a male figure with torch
314 × 203 mm
Pen, blue wash, white paper
inv. no. 3214 F

VII.16
Costume drawing for a male figure with stave
314 × 211 mm
Pen, blue wash, white paper
inv. no. 3207 F

VII.17
Costume drawing for a "necromancer"
210 × 169 mm
Pen, blue wash, white paper. *Controfondato*
inv. no. 3217 F

VII.18
Costume drawing of a cook
305 × 202 mm
Pen, blue wash, white paper
inv. no. 3197 F

VII.19
Costume drawing for man-at-arms
312 × 210 mm
Pen, blue wash, white paper
inv. no. 3201 F

VII.20
Costume drawing for a knight
316 × 209 mm
Pen, blue wash, white paper
inv. no. 3203 F

VII.21
Costume drawing for a knight
313 × 198 mm
Pen, blue wash, white paper
inv. no. 3199 F

VII.22
Costume drawing for a knight
301 × 198 mm
Pen, blue wash, white paper
inv. no. 3202 F

VII.23
Sketch for a sleigh
138 × 174 mm
Pen, blue wash, white paper
inv. no. 3250 F

VII.24
Sketch for a sleigh
137 × 175 mm
Pen, blue wash, white paper
inv. no. 3251 F

VII.25
Costume drawing for a knight on horseback
304 × 210 mm
Pen, blue wash, white paper
inv. no. 3210 F

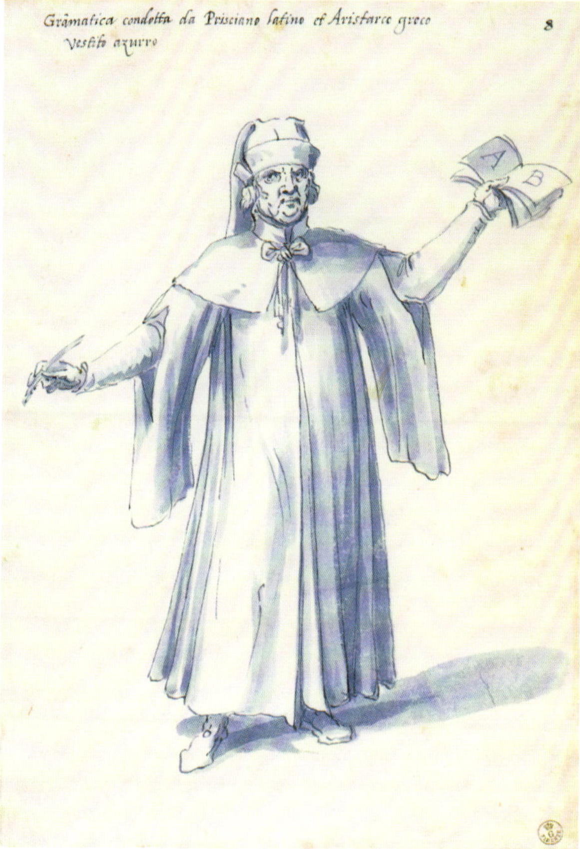

VII.2

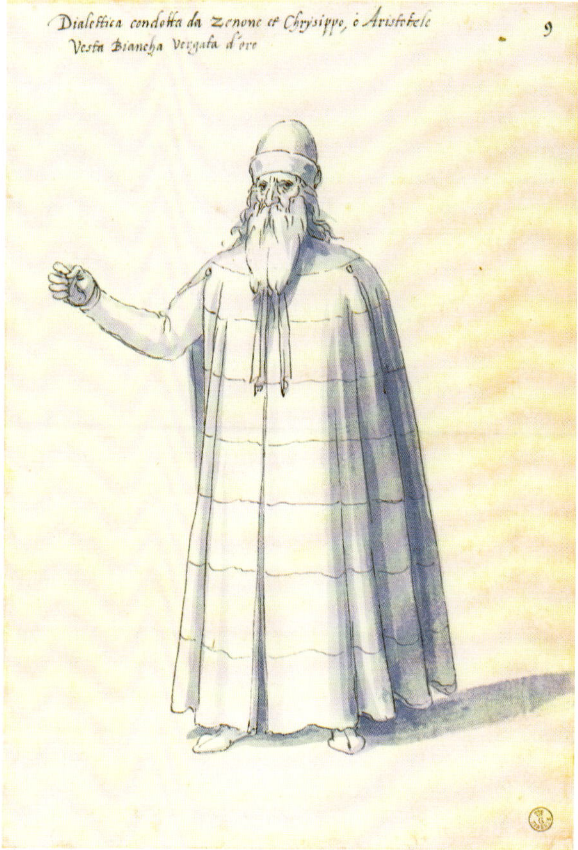

VII.3

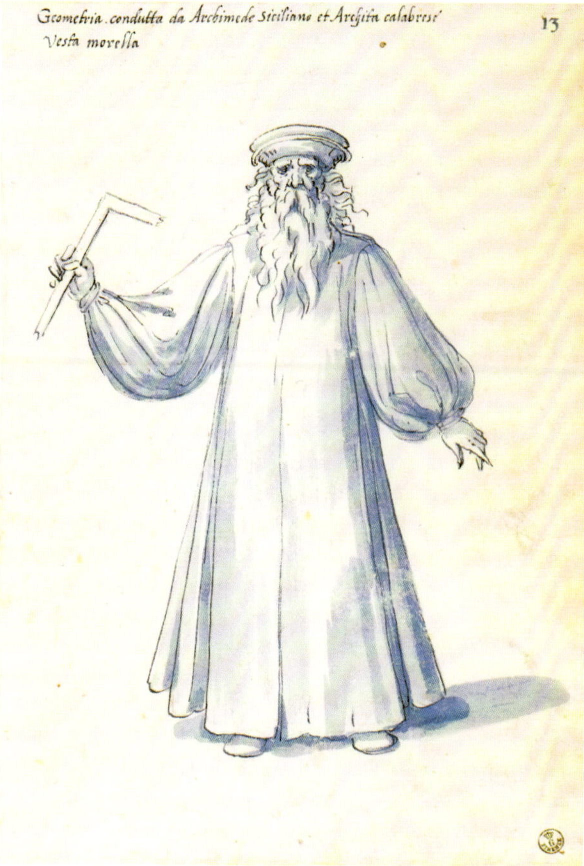

VII.4

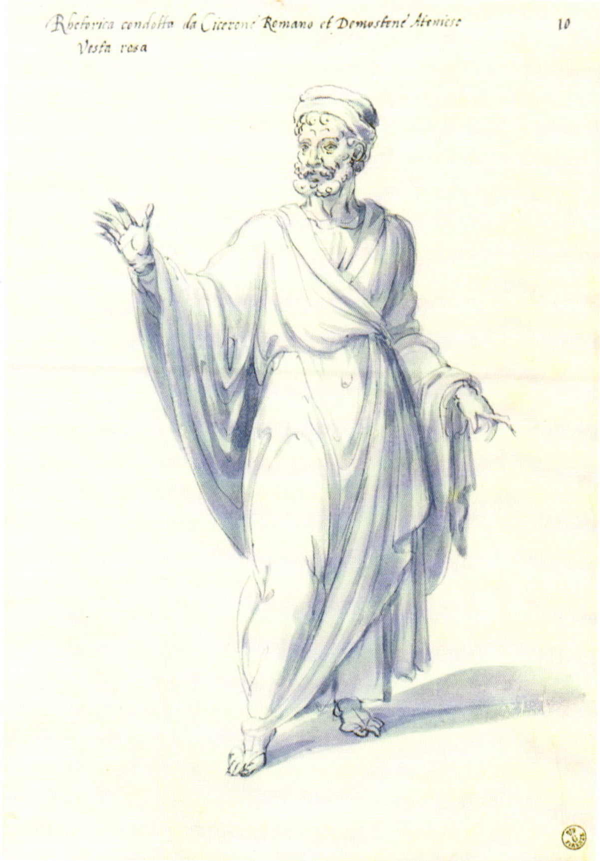

VII.5

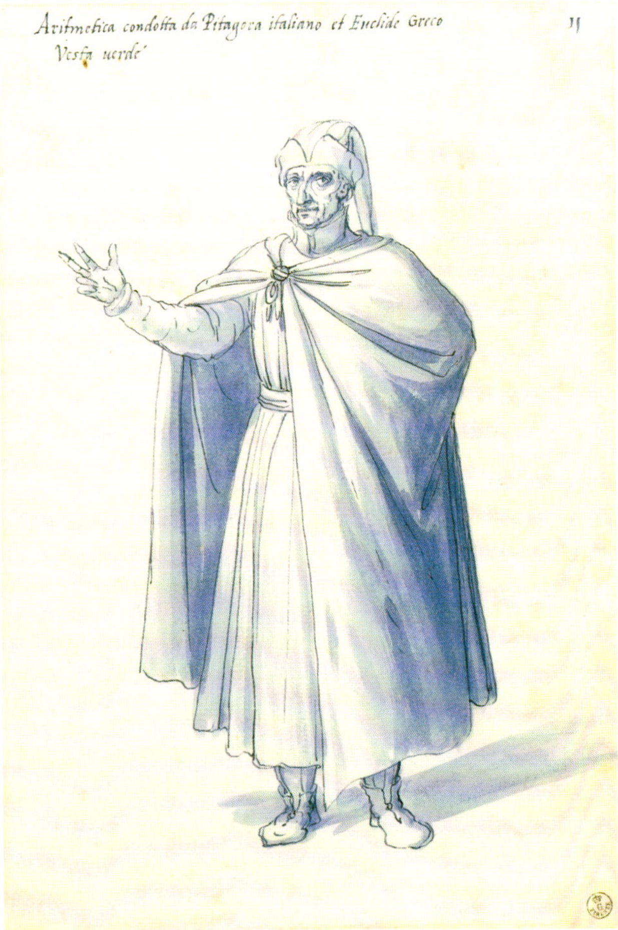

VII.6

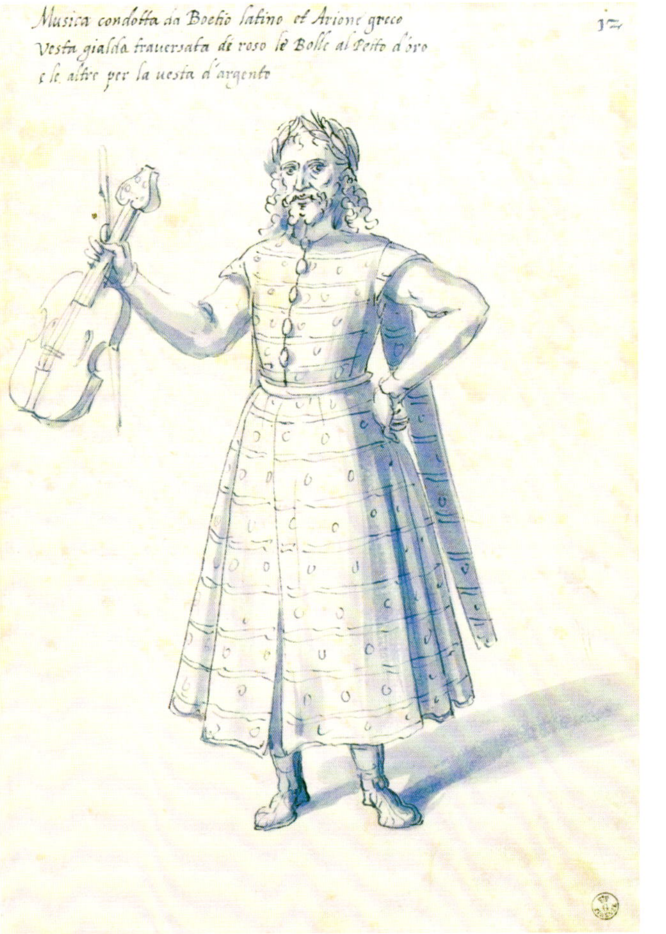

VII.7

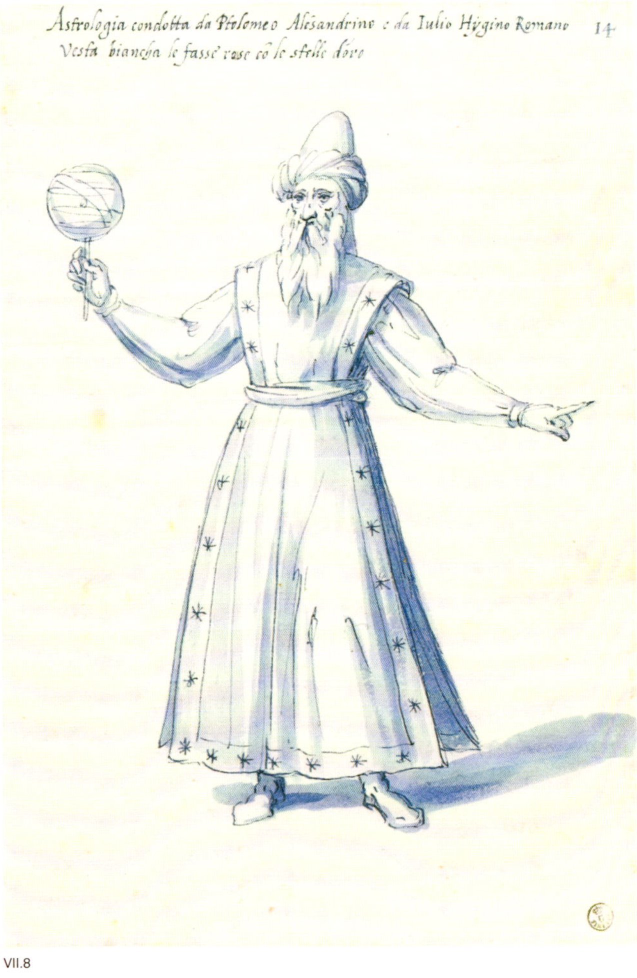

VII.8

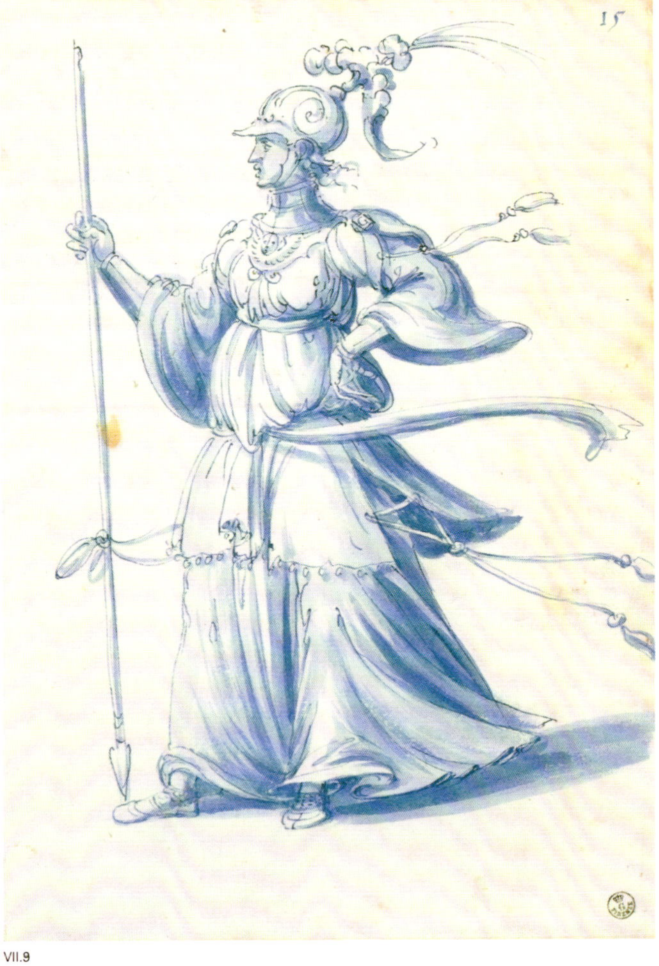

VII.9

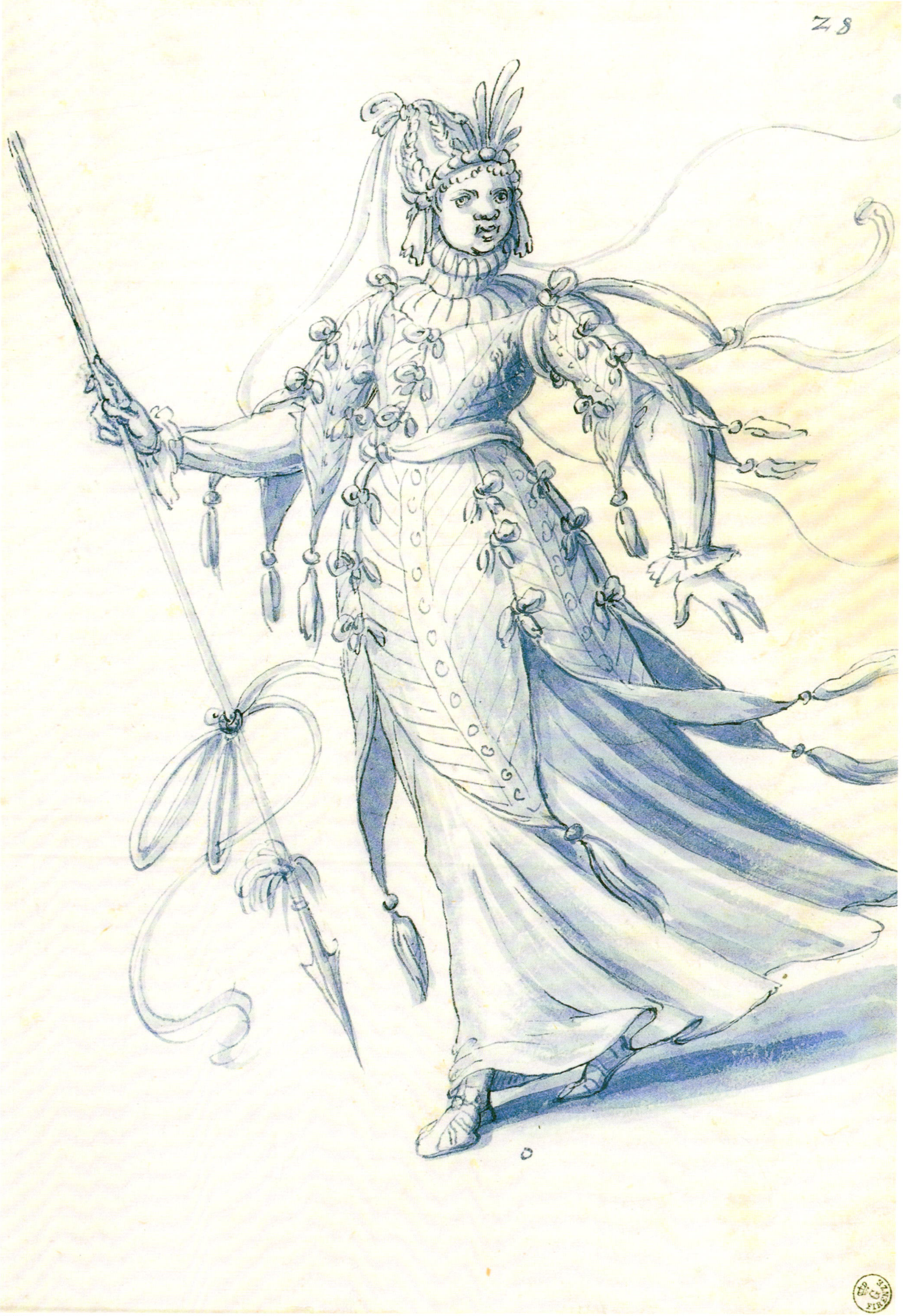

VII.10

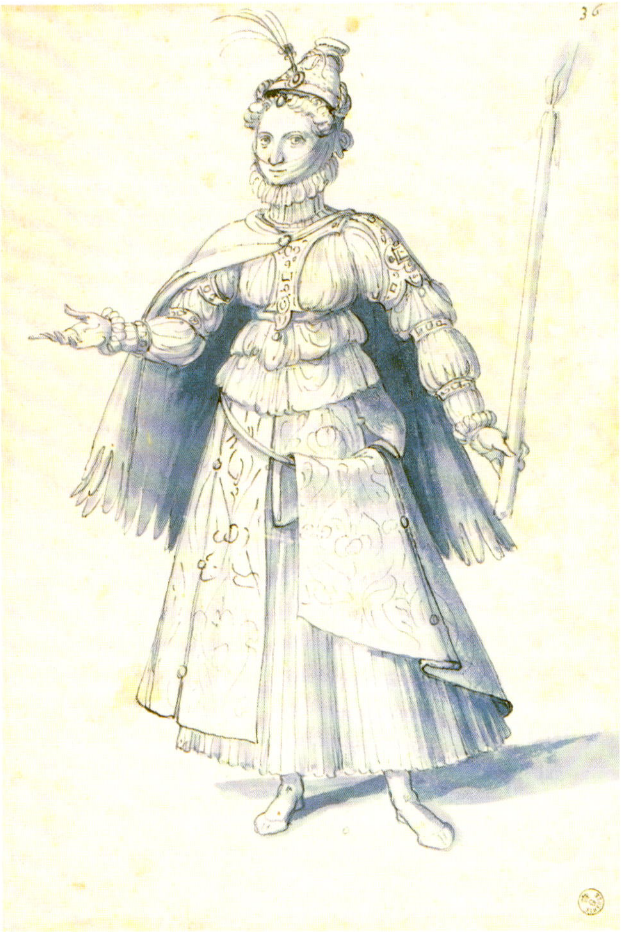

VII.11

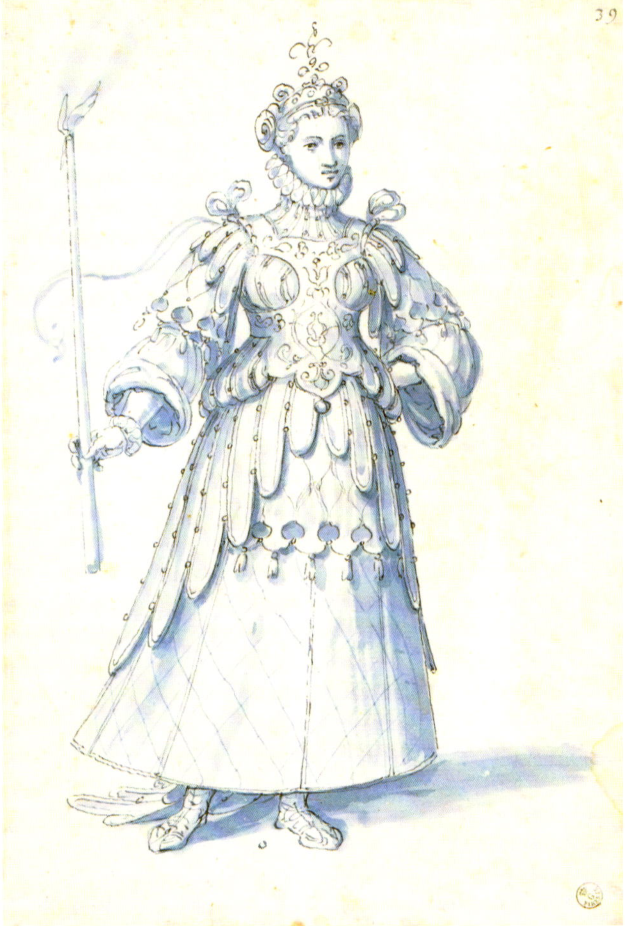

VII.12

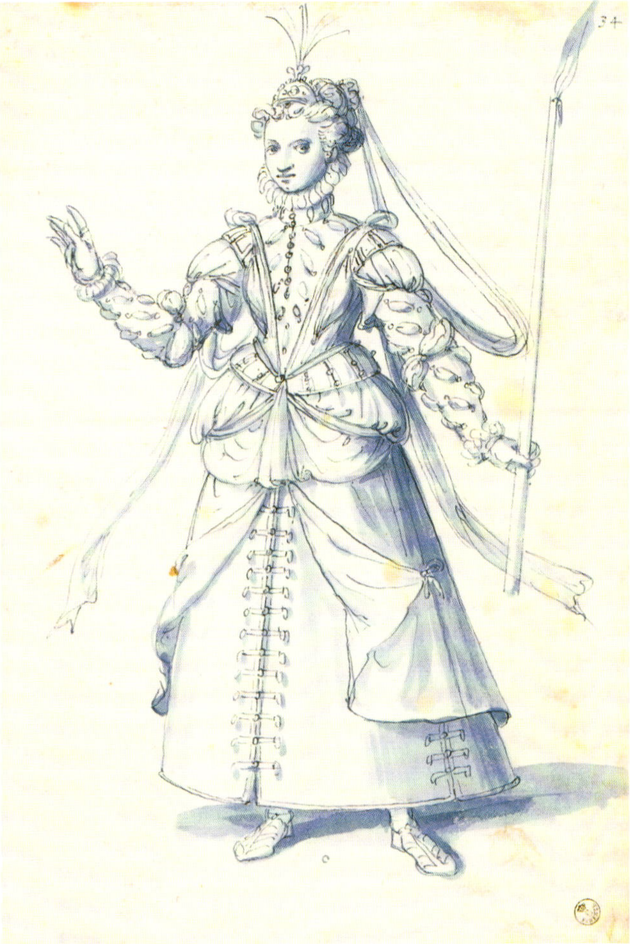

VII.13

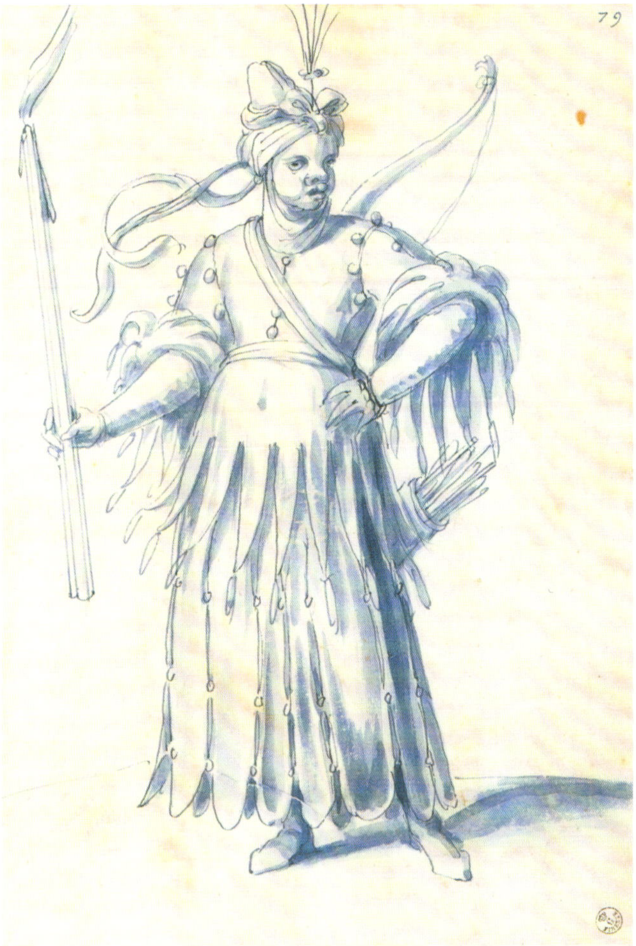

VII.14

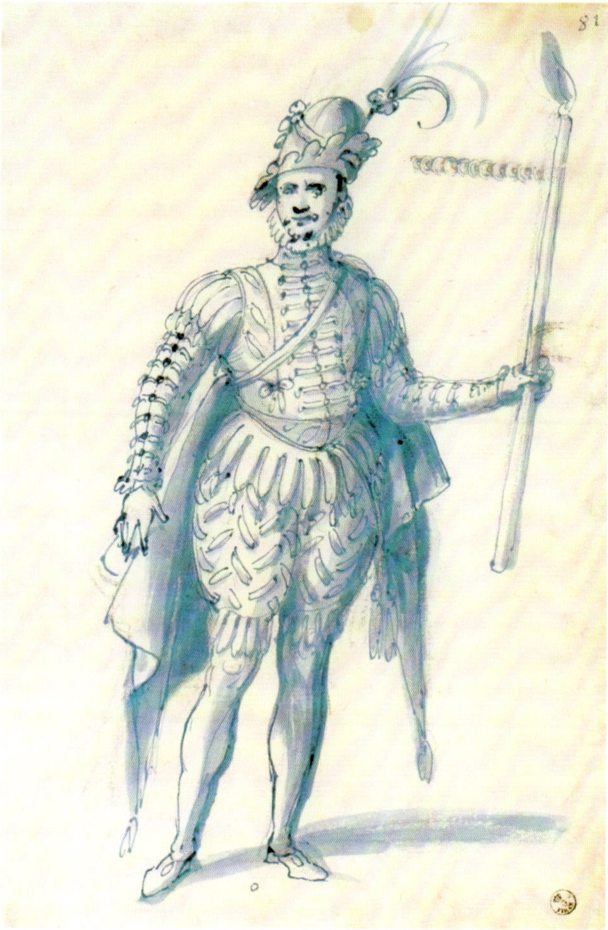

VII.15

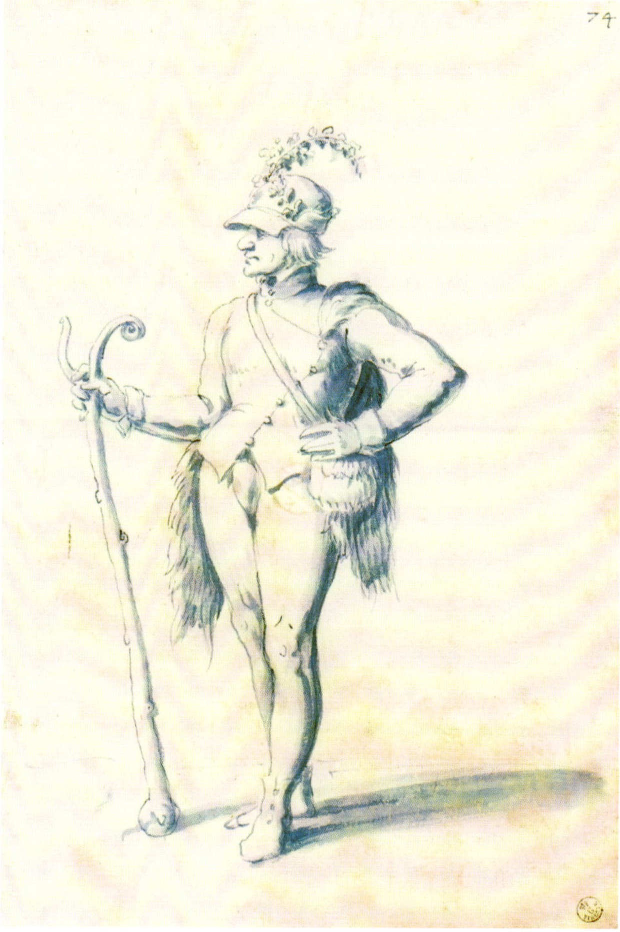

VII.16

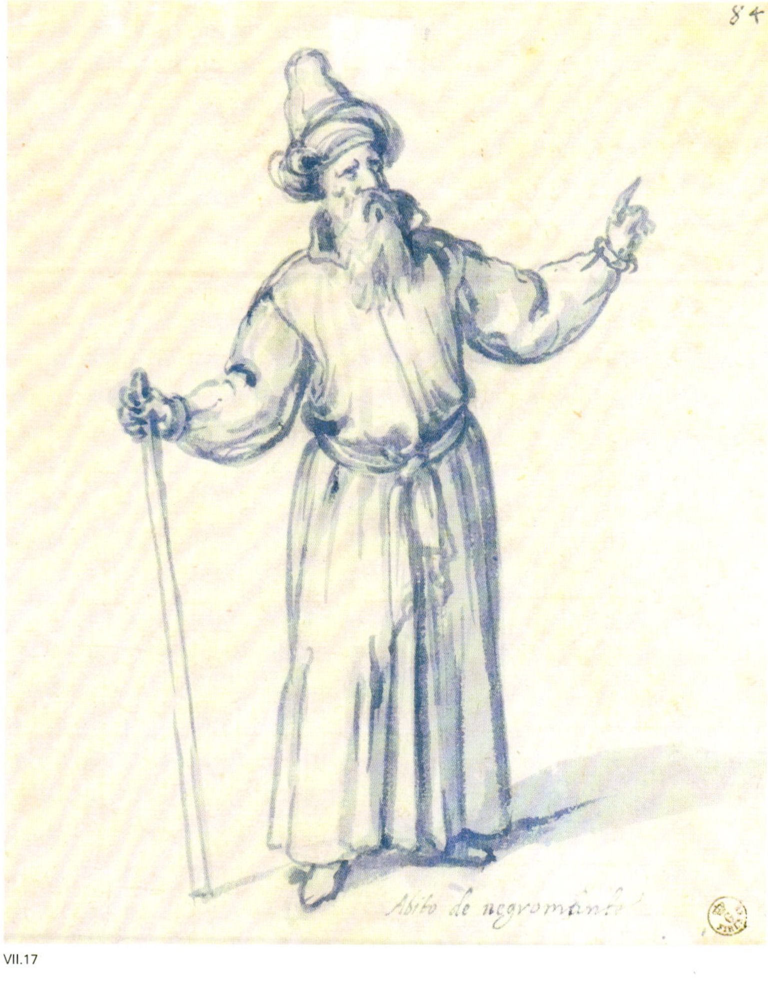

VII.17

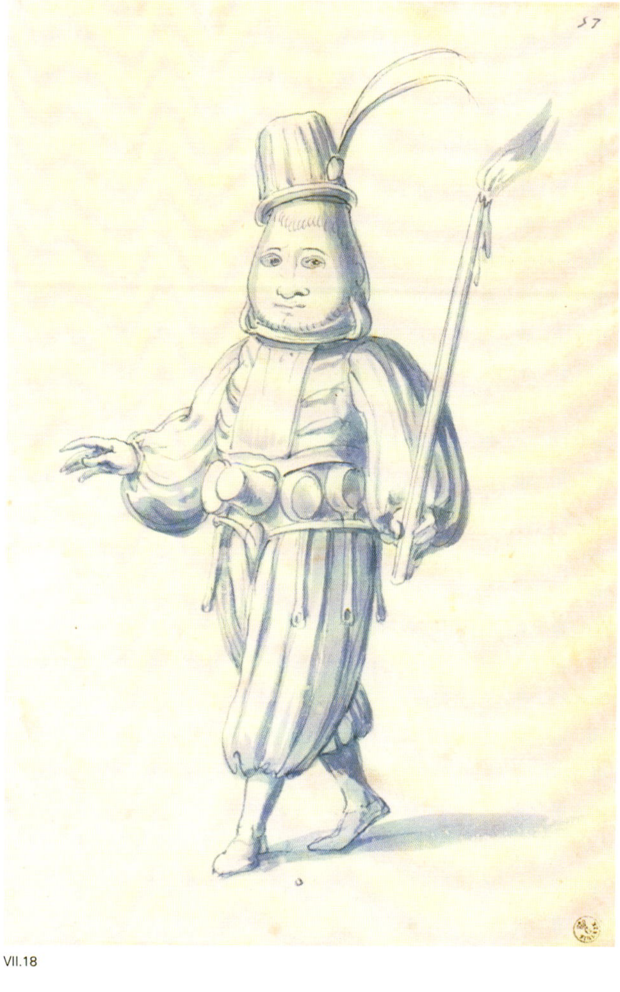

VII.18

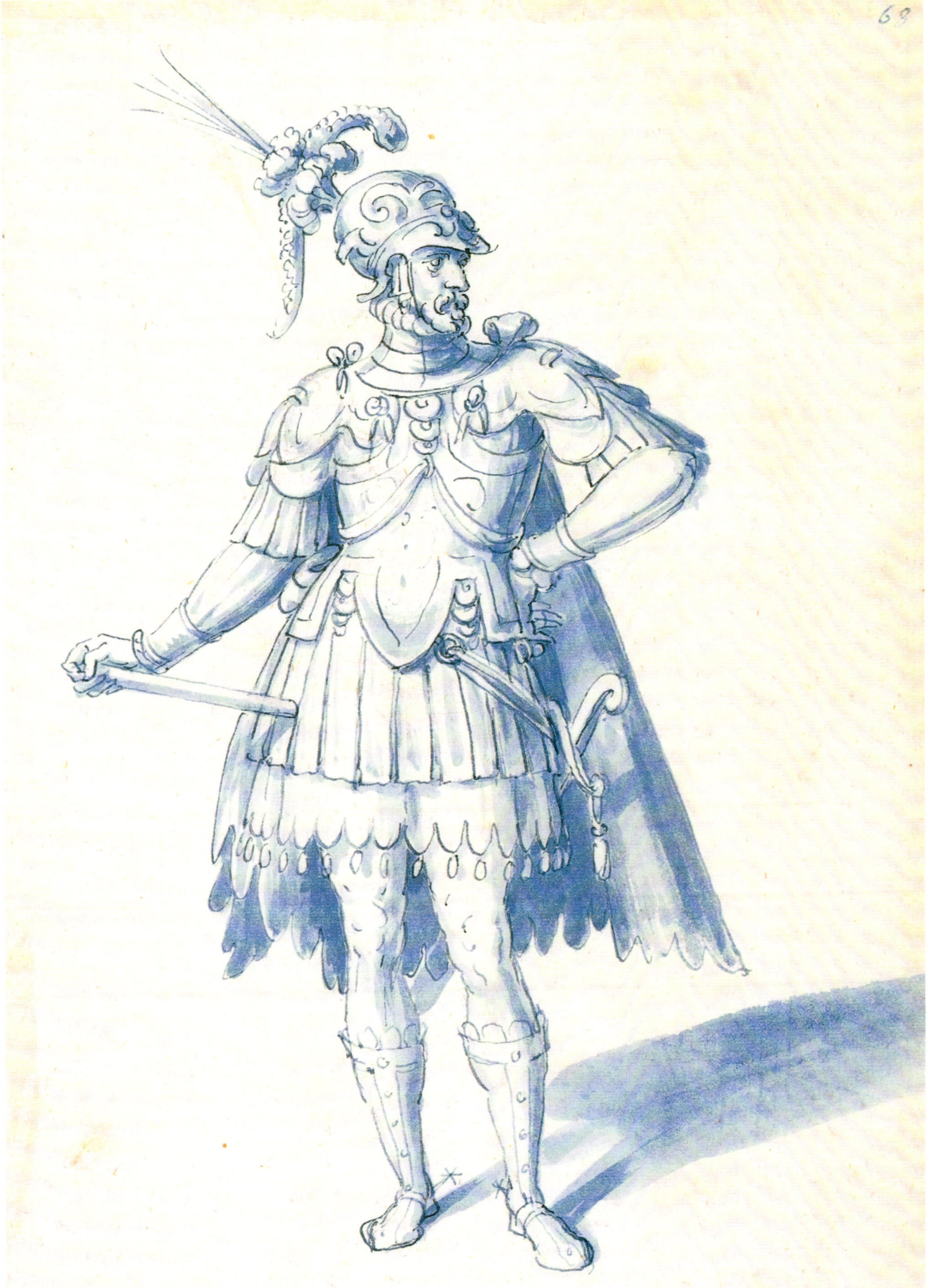

VII.19

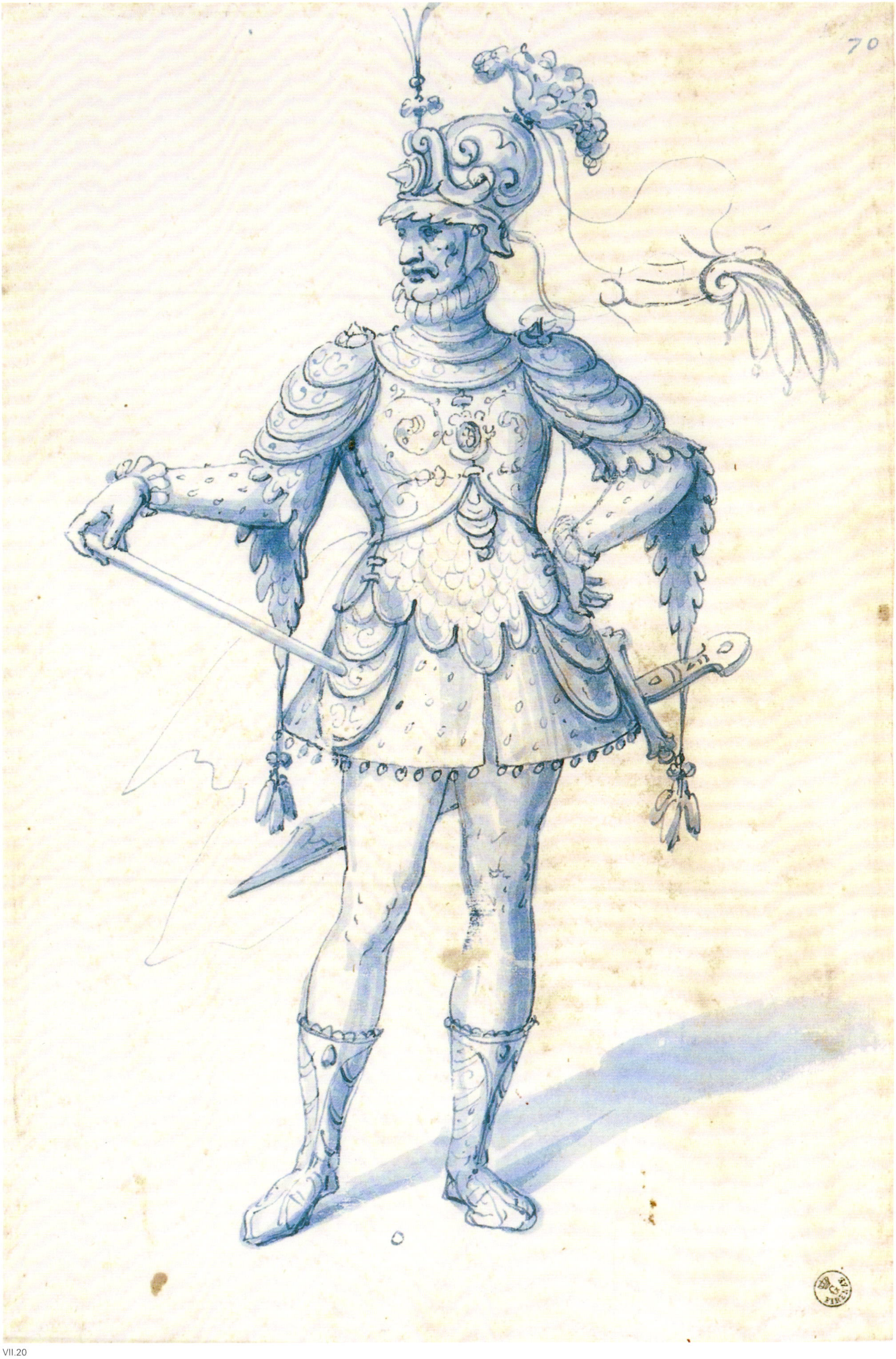

VII.20

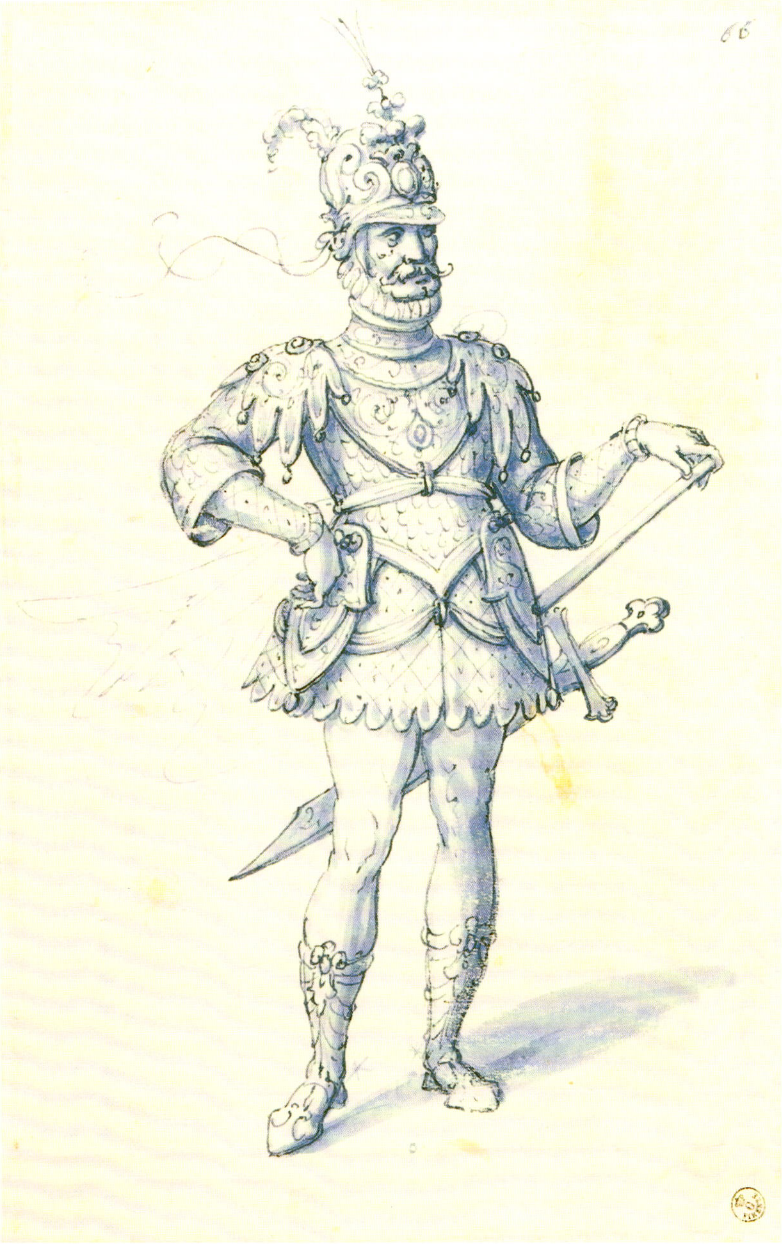

VII.21

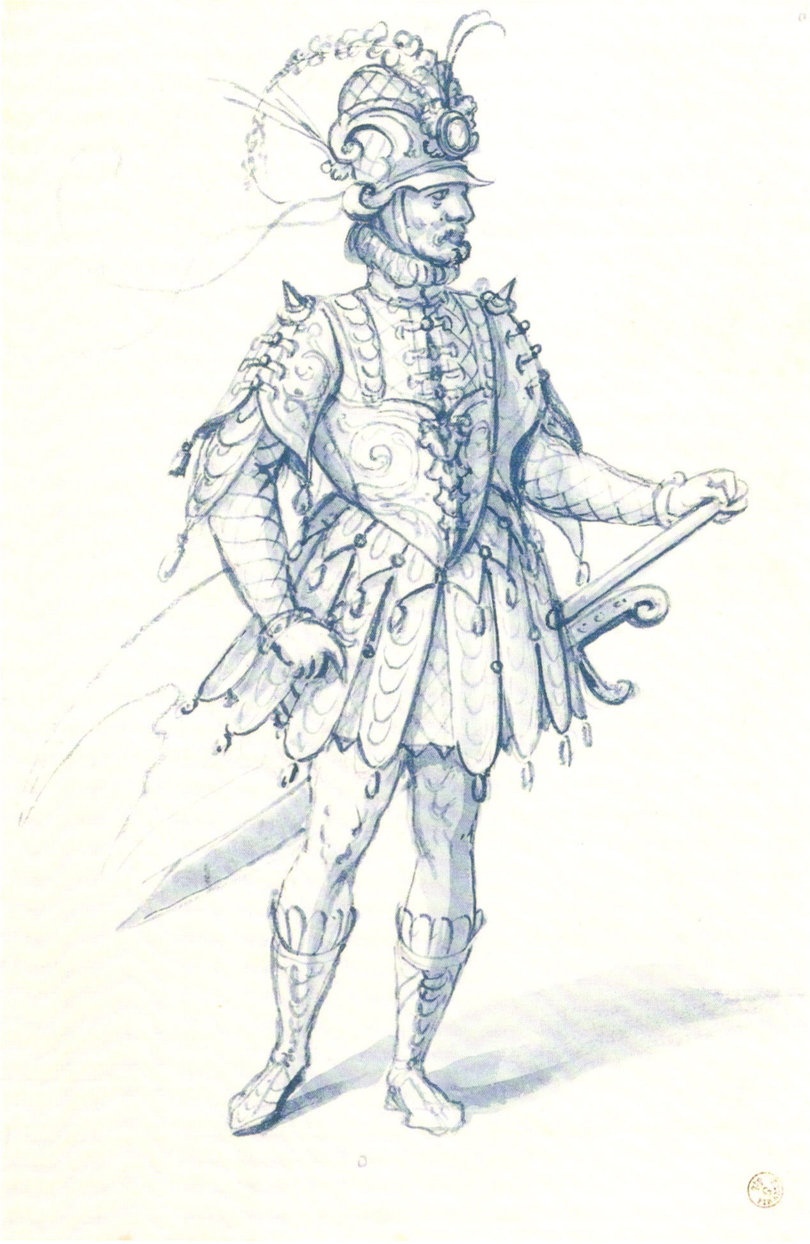

VII.22

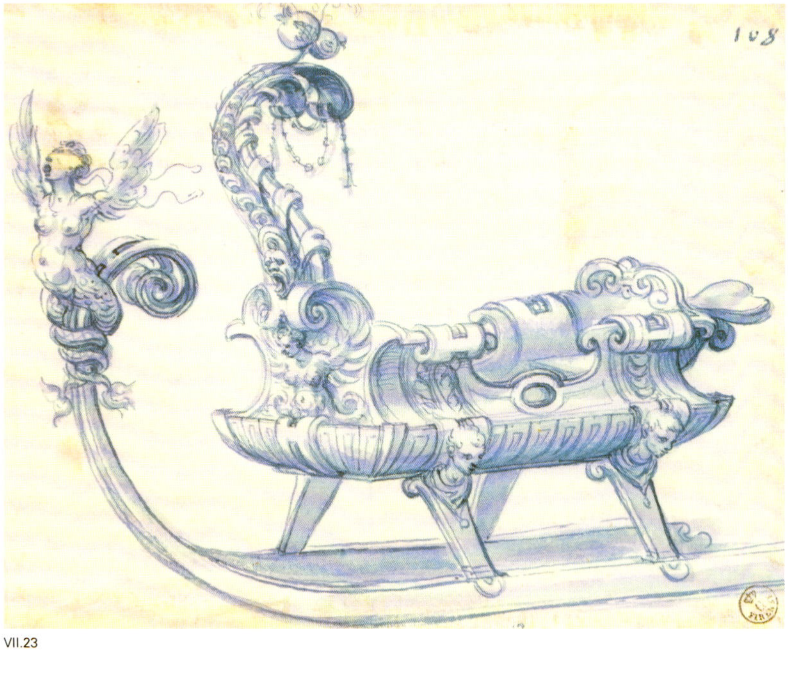

VII.23

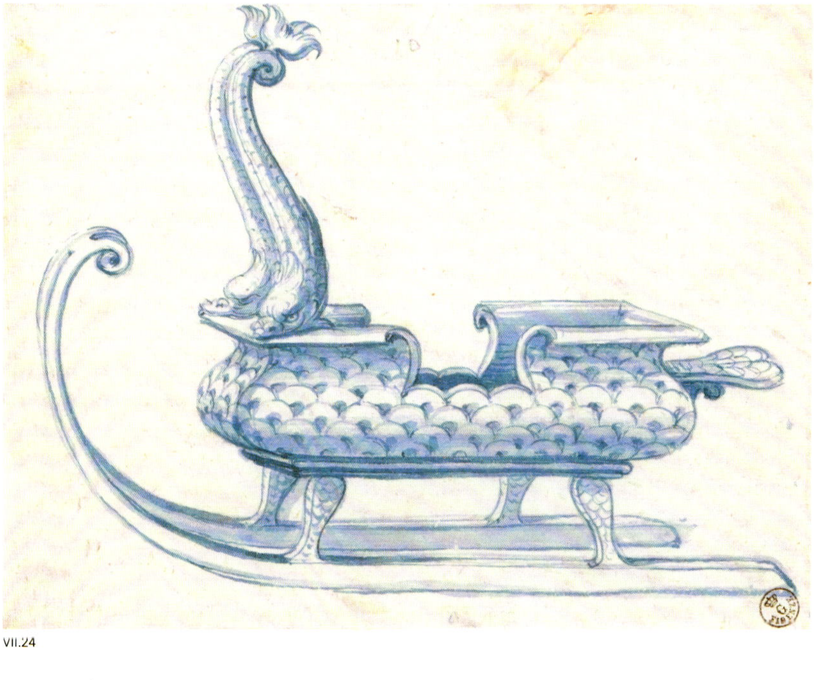

VII.24

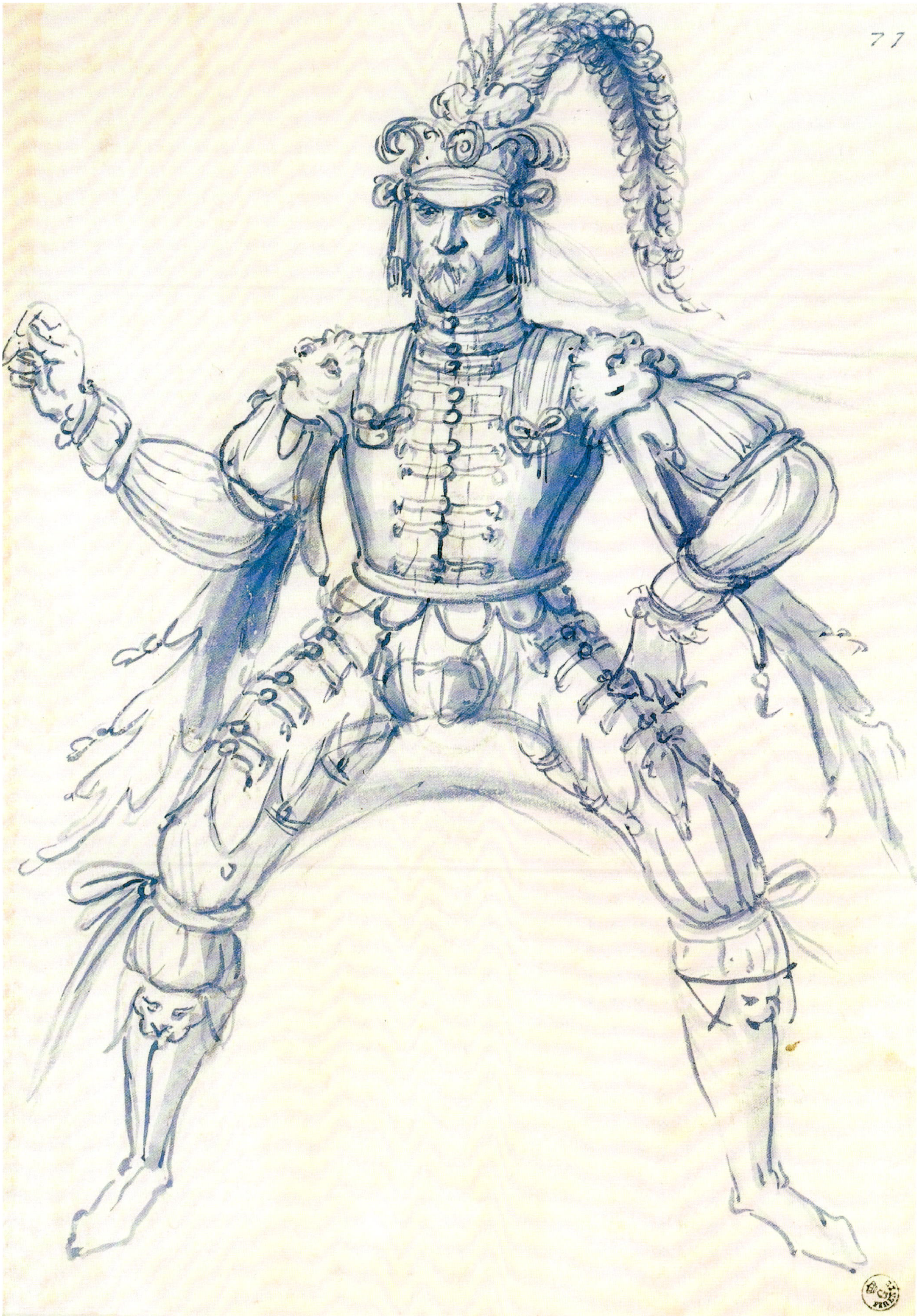

VII.25

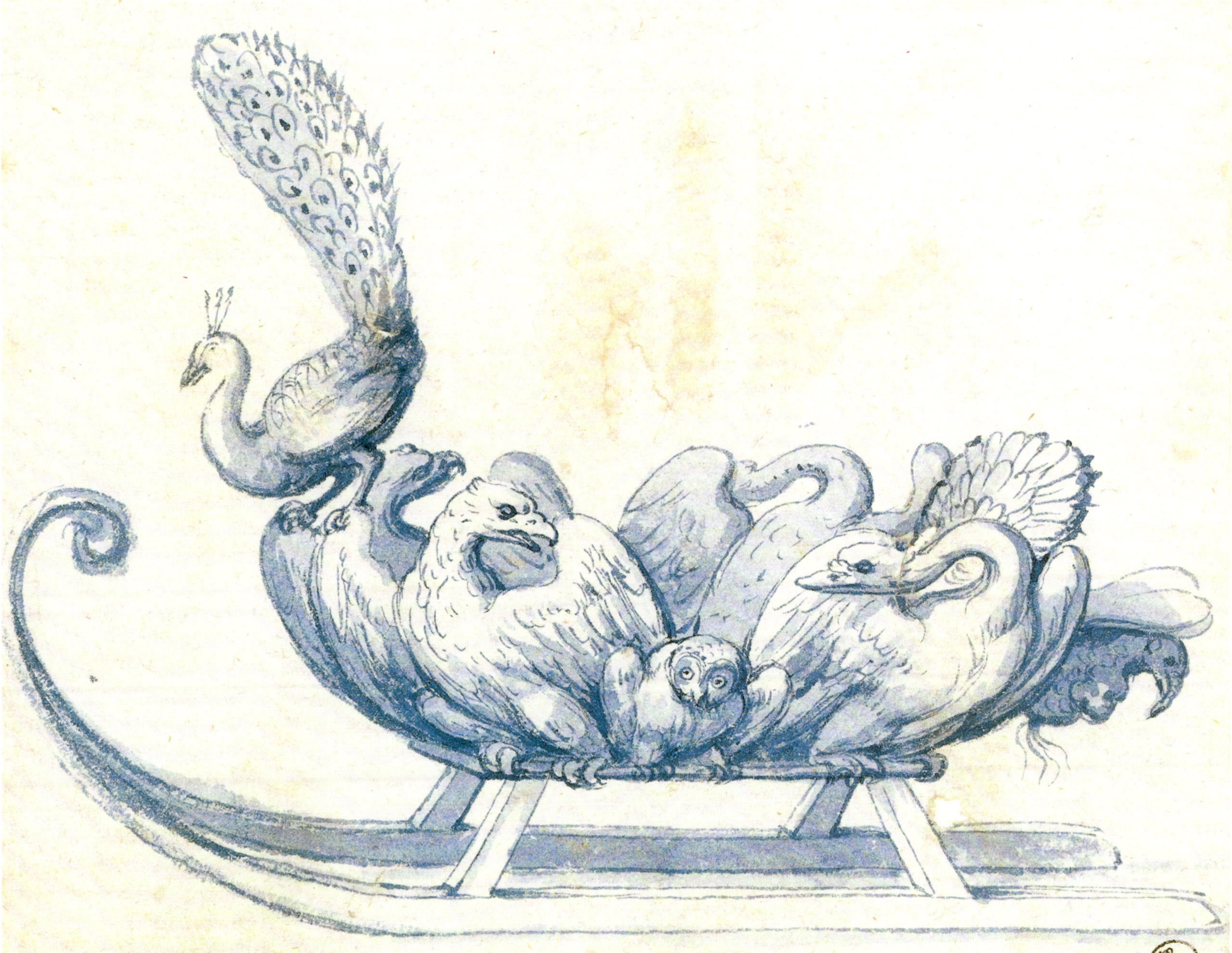

VII.26

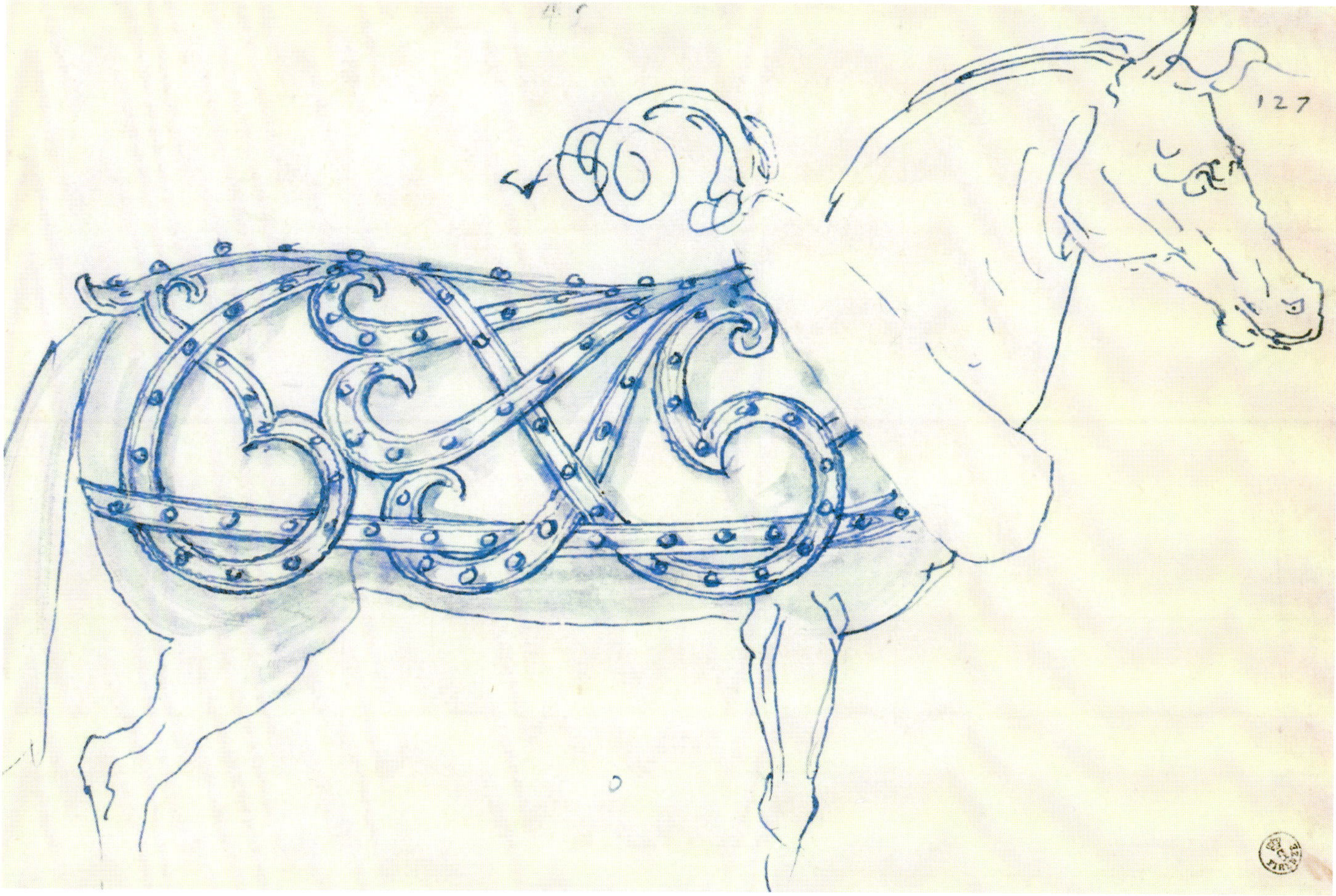

VII.27

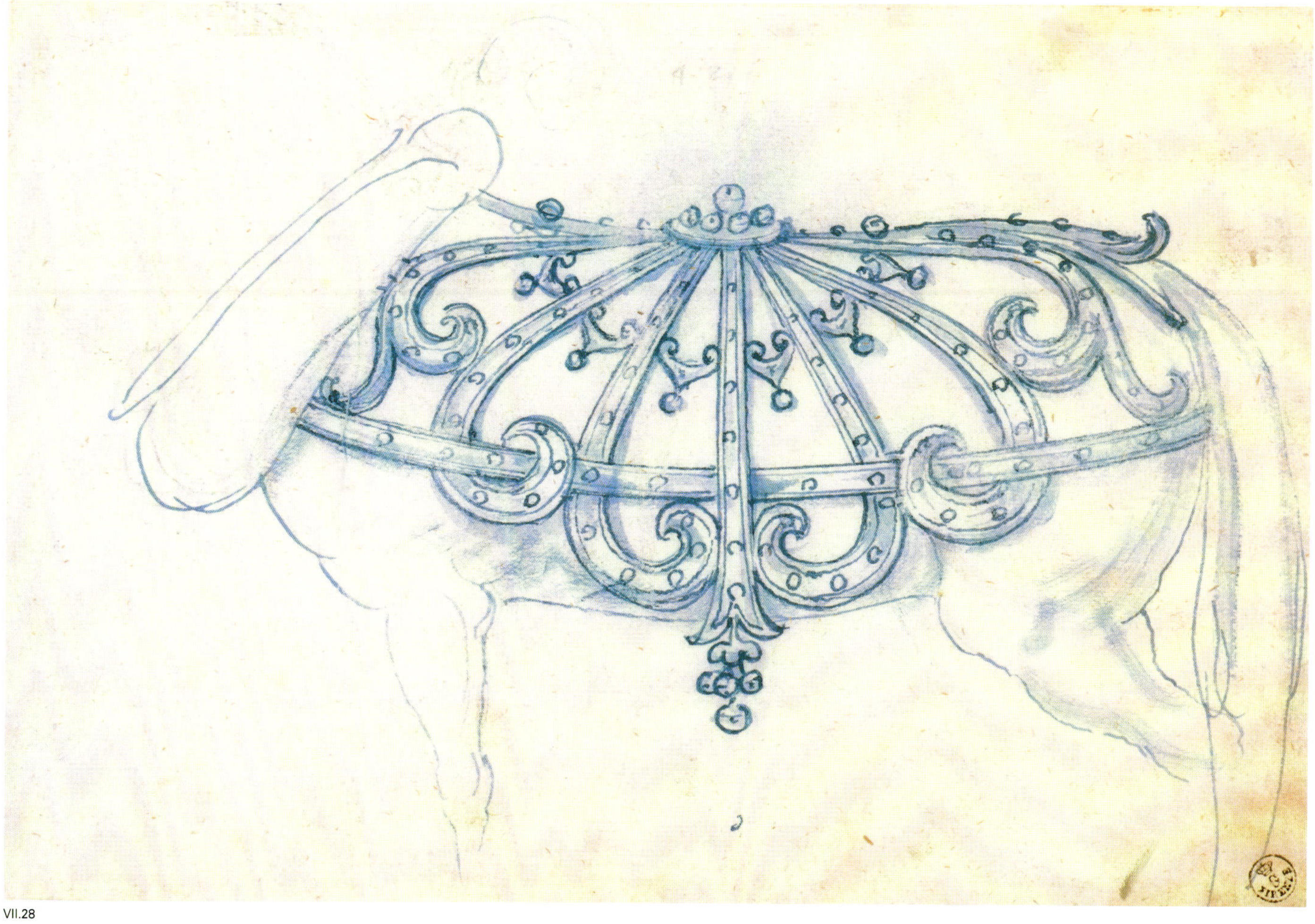

VII.28

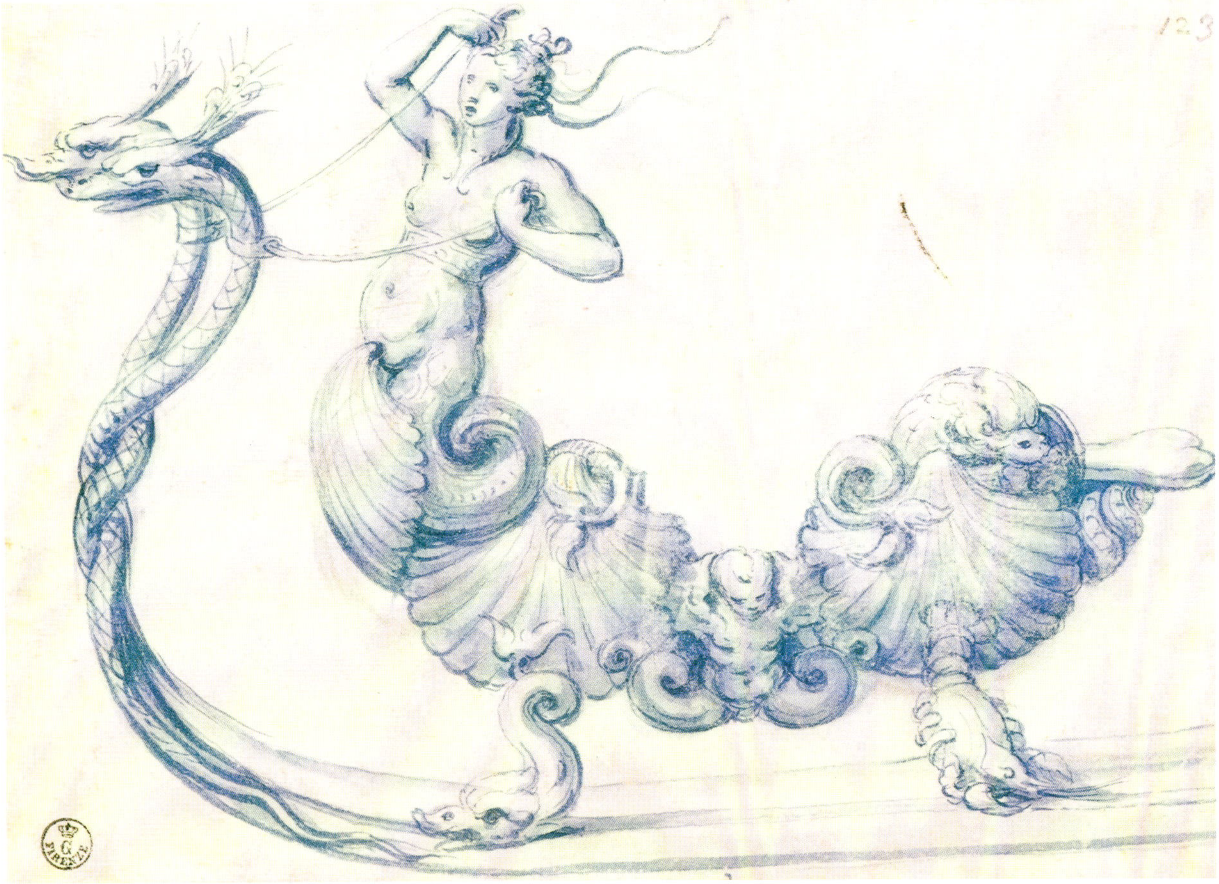

VII.29

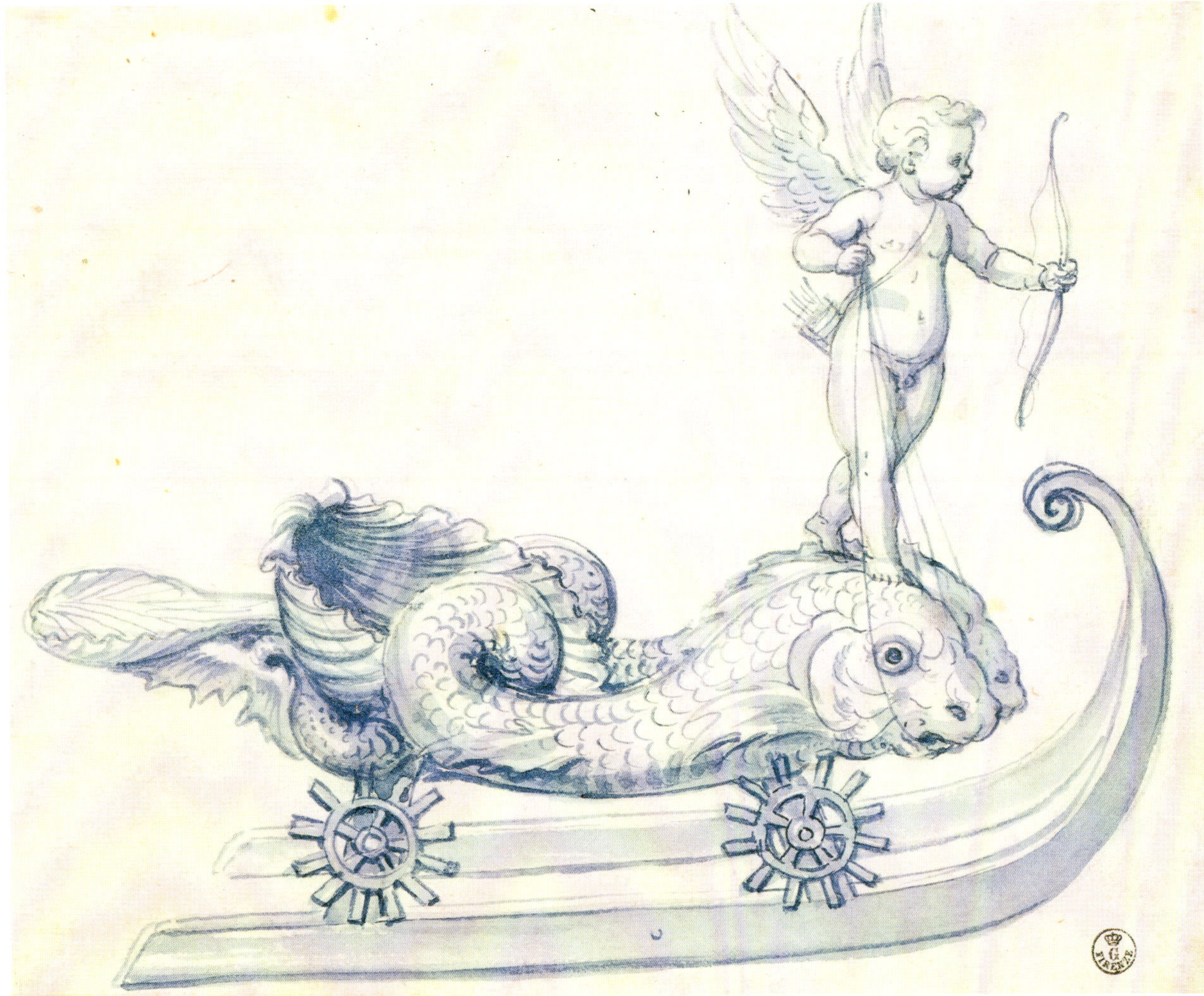

VII.30

VII.26
Sketch for a sleigh
156 × 189 mm
Pen, blue wash, white paper
inv. no. 3268 F

VII.27
Horse Harness
181 × 270 mm
Pen, blue wash, white paper
inv. no. 3285 F

VII.28
Horse Harness
165 × 238 mm
Pen, blue wash, white paper
inv. no. 3286 F

VII.29
Sketch for a sleigh with figures of sirens
150 × 205 mm
Pen, blue wash, white paper
inv. no. 3278 F/A

VII.30
Sleigh with figures
188 × 230 mm
Pen, blue wash, white paper
inv. no. 3278 F/B

VII.31
Saddle for sleigh horse
167 × 227 mm
Pen, blue wash, white paper
inv. no. 3290 F

VII.32
Saddle cover
183 × 235 mm
Blue chalk, lilac wash, gold, white paper
inv. no. 3290 F bis

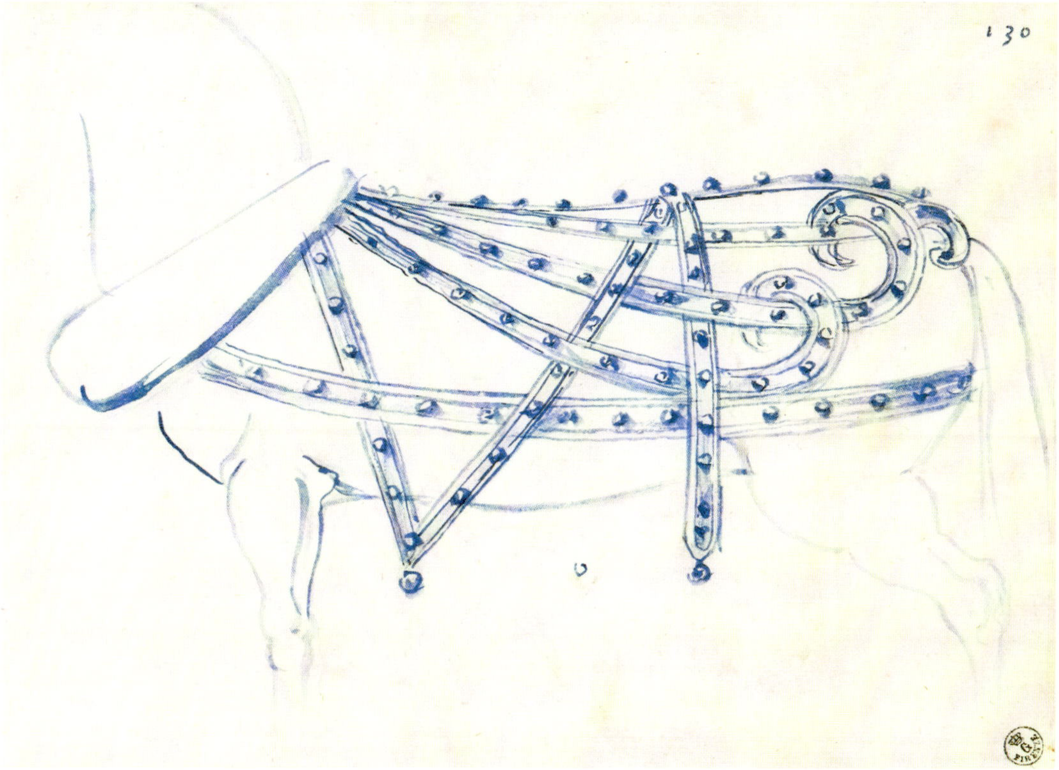

VII.31

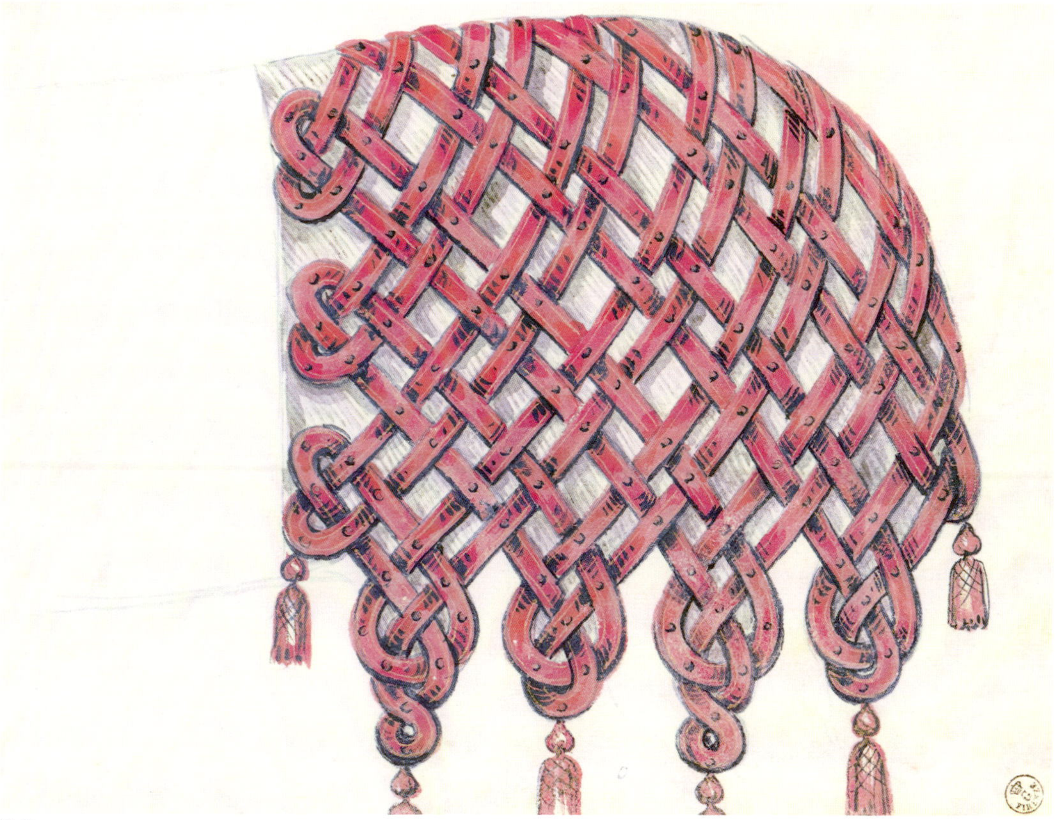
VII.32

VII.33
Heinrich Wirrich
Ordentliche Beschreibung, des Christlichen / Hochlöblichen vnd Fürstlichen Beylags oder Hochzeit / so da gehalten worden durch den Durchleuchtigsten / Hochgeborenen Fürsten vnnd Herrn / Herrn CAROLEN / Ertzhertzog zu Osterreich / Burgund / Steyr / Kärnten / Crayn / Graff zu Tirol / Zilli vnd Göertz / etc. mit dem Hochgebornen Fräwlein Maria / geborne Hertzogin zu Bayrn / den XXVI. Augusti in der Kayserlichen Statt Wienn / dem Hochermelten Fürsten vnnd Fräwlein / auch jrer beyder Hochlöblichen Freundtschafft zu den höhisten Ehren in Teutsche Carmina gestelt: Vnd einem Edlen / Ehr und Vesten / Wolweisen Rath / der Fürstlichen Hauptstatt Grätz in der Steyrmarck dediciert / Durch Heinrich Wirrich ....

[Proper description of the Christian / highly respected and noble *Beylag* or wedding / which was held for the most serene and highborn of princes and sovereigns / Archduke Carl of Austria / Burgundy / Steiermark / Kärnten / Krain / Duke of Tyrol / Zilli and Göertz / etc. with the highborn Lady Maria / rightful Duchess of Bavaria / took place on the 26th of August in the imperial city of Vienna / with the noble, abovenamed Lord and Lady / as well as the most serene friends of both to the highest honour of the German Carmina: and dedicated to the noble / courageous, firm / and honourable council / to the sovereign capital Grätz in Steiermark / by Heinrich Wirrich ....]

dated 1571
Coloured woodcut (leaflet) on paper
292 × 1430 mm
Vienna, MAK Österreichisches Museum für angewandte Kunst,
A II 27, inv. no. 1453

In August 1571 Archduke Karl of Inner Austria, brother of Emperor Maximilian II, married Maria von Wittelsbach of Bavaria. The director of festival events in Vienna was Giuseppe Arcimboldo, who had been employed at the imperial court since 1562. The festivities, which lasted for several days, were recorded by Heinrich Wirrich, *Pritschenmeister* [similar to a director of ceremonies and canter poet] from Solothurn in Switzerland, who served the Emperor until 1572, in his extensive wedding description, which featured coloured woodcut prints. Wirrich, who was bound to the tradition of medieval heraldic poetry, begins his description with his journey from Prague to Vienna, during which he becomes lost and is taken in by dwarves, who interpret one of his dreams as a vision of the allegorical tournament. He travels on to Vienna with one of the dwarves, takes part in the wedding and describes what he sees with the help of the cultured dwarf. Wirrich's importance as a chronicler of festivals lies less in the rich content of his documentation of the complicated events of the wedding than in his more popular depiction of the medial nature of the festivities.
The sequence:
The first illustrated page (*fig. 1*) shows the bride's reception in Vienna on August 24th. The bride's delegation, who sailed by ship from Klosterneuburg to Vienna, lands outside the city walls on the right bank of the Danube (today the 9th district) and is met by Vienna's dignitaries; the mayor Johan von Thaw, ten captains and their men in battle formation, ensigns with ten coats of arms, musicians and lifeguards. The mayor's tent can be seen in the upper right-hand corner of the square. The train of coaches for the continuation of the journey waits in the background. According to Wirrich, Italian envoys in galleys had been greeting the bride on the Danube, as had the Archbishop of Salzburg. The groom approaches and greets the bride on horseback as soon as she disembarked (background right). Thereafter, according to Wirrich, the procession enters the city, where the gathered citizens welcome the bride by enacting a skirmish "wenn ein rechter Ernst da wär" [as if it were for real]. They then spend the night at the Imperial Court. On August 26th the marriage ceremonies are held in the Augustinerkirche by the Archbishop of Salzburg. Afterwards the couple holds a great wedding feast; Wirrich mentions every guest by name. That day's festivities end with a dance in a structure especially erected for that occasion. On August 28th comes the central and, allegorically speaking, most complicated part of the mannerist festival events: the ring jousting "vor dem Roten Thor" [before the red gate]. This was held outside the city in what is today the second district. There the contestants must skewer a trophy ring, suspended between two pylons, with a lance while on horseback. Giuseppe Arcimboldo was once again responsible for concept, artdesign and costumes.
The content of the contest proves to be complex: Juno as the goddess of marriage and wife of Jupiter (depicted here as coming from the upper right on a cloud with two peacocks under her arms), claims the area as her own. Europa, Jupiter's mistress, does not want to leave, though. Juno is followed by three kings, allegoric figures for Asia, America and Africa, who watch the battle from an artificial hill to the right (Archduke Ferdinand, Archduke Karl, the groom, and Wolf von Stubenberg). Europa, who was brought to Crete by Jupiter in the shape of a bull, is accompanied by "her children" Germany, Spain, France and Italy, over whom she now rules. The geographical winds, the four elements, four metals, four seasons (among which Emperor Maximilian II himself is Winter) and four European rivers are assigned to them in a fortress and follow them as an entourage. Juno wants to make room for her "foreign" host and Europa calls for help from her friends "aus Wasser und Wälden, aus Stetten und weiten Felden" [from the water and woods, from cities and broad fields]. Following afterwards are groups representing the seven liberal arts (Grammatica, Dialectica, Rhetorica, Arithmetica, Geometry, Music and Astronomy – one of them embodied by Don Juan de Austria, the future hero of Lepanto), Diana with her animals of the forest and the Sirens as the messengers of Europa. Then Europa herself arrives, followed by Victory with her attributes such as armour and weapons on a column (embodied by the young sons of the Emperor; Rudolf – the future emperor – and Ernst), the four virtues (Justitia, Prudentia, Fortitudo and Temperantia), a group representing Neptunes entourage and finally four knights of the round table. On Wirrich's illustration the jousting and procession are depicted side by side and simultaneously and not in their actual order. In the foreground the sirens with fish tails, reciting songs composed for this festival by Filippo di Monte, are accompanied by trumpeters in the guise of fish. In the following line Diana's allies, men in bear, lion, panther and wolf costumes, fight over various trophies. On the upper end of the racetrack the rest of the Imperial family, who are not an active part of the spectacle, can be seen, as they observe the events from a grandstand. Wirrich revels in the rich and elaborate costumes with hymns of praise:
"von Silber / Perlen / rotem Golt, ein jeder es gern sehen solt, Allding geziert nach solcher weiß, ich meint ich wär im Paradeiß" [of silver, pearls, reddish gold, each one is beautiful to behold, everything decorated in such a way, I thought I was in Paradise].
August 29th was designated as a day of rest. The festivities continued on August 30th with a tournament called "Turnier über die Balia" (*fig. 2*) or "Volia oder auch über den Schranken" on the square before the castle. The *Mantenators* (the challengers in the tournament) were ostentatiously dressed in "ash, yellow and white" (armour, harness and horse). Drummers and 12 trumpeters as well as other men dressed in the same colours moved ahead of them. Wirrich's images of the castle square are useful in terms of architectural history; they depict the contemporary appearance of the castle with the "Schweizer Tor" [swiss gate] to the left as well as the extension of the Northwest Tower in the middle of the background, which was newly built for the children of Emperor Ferdinand I. The conclusion of the festivities on the afternoon of September 2nd comprised a foot tournament before the Imperial Court: after the entrance of the participants, a large artificial mountain pulled by four horses appears, which represents Mount Etna, the volcano. Wonderous imaginary figures with swan necks and snail bodies accompany the horses. Orpheus sits at the center of the mountain, surrounded by musicians in the form of animals, who play imaginary instruments. The mountain is flanked by Ixion, who must eternally push a millstone as a punishment from Jupiter (actually, he is bound to an eternally rolling burning wheel), Tityus, upon whose body vultures eternally feed, Tantalus who, because he revealed the secrets

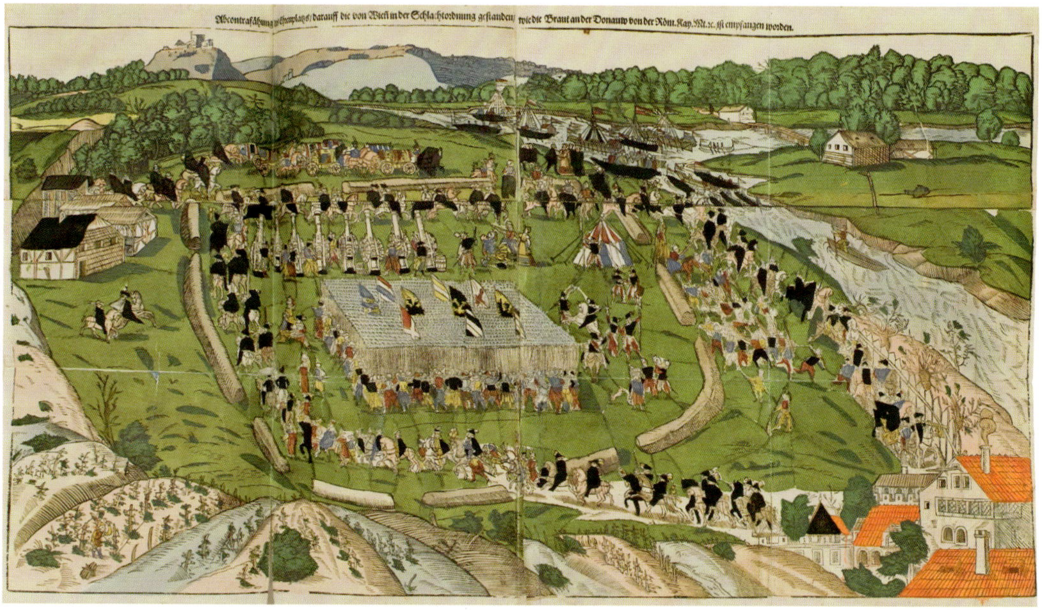

of the gods, now stands (here sitting) in water surrounded by trees heavy with fruit but nonetheless eternally suffers from hunger and thirst. And finally, there are several maidens who represent the Danaides: those virgins who murdered their husbands on their wedding night and as punishment must fetch water to fill a barrel that never becomes full. In conclusion, Archduke Ferdinand II on horseback is said to have leapt out of the volcano's crater as a challenger in the foot tournament. Wirrich writes nothing about the men on stilts at the end of the events, who were a traditional part of such festivals. In this case, it is rumoured that Arcimboldo himself took part in the festivities in this guise.

Elisabeth Wolfik

Bibliography: Vocelka 1976, 47-98; Lindell 1990; Vienna 1999, cat. no. 35; Vienna 2005, cat. no. 2.1.

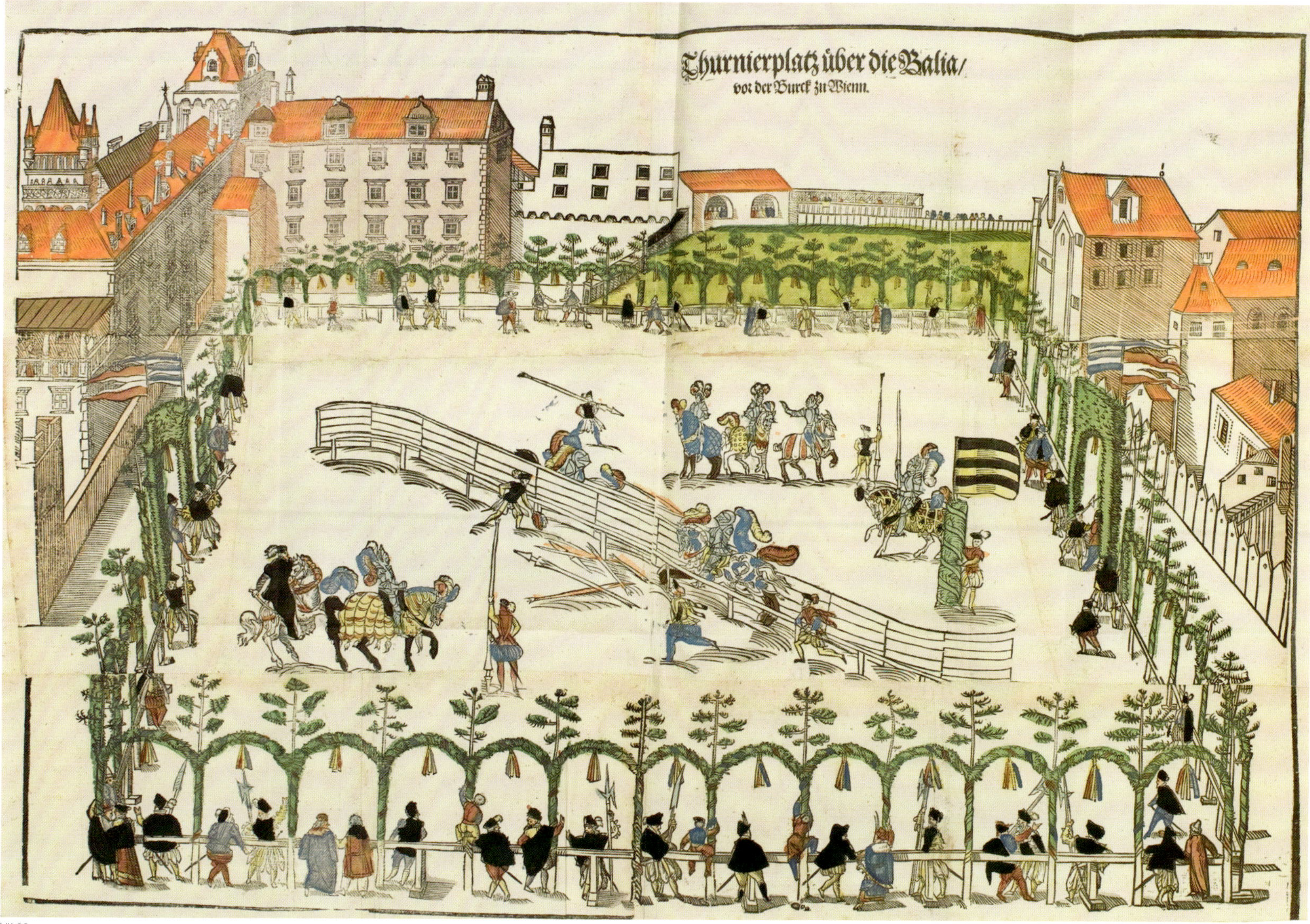

VII.33

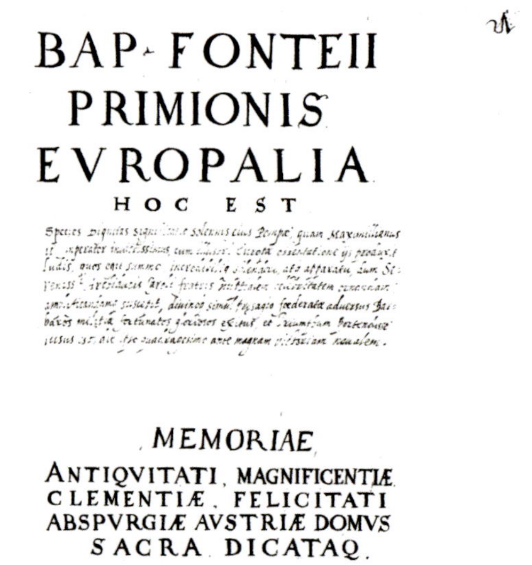
BAP. FONTEII
PRIMIONIS
EVROPALIA
HOC EST

MEMORIAE
ANTIQVITATI, MAGNIFICENTIÆ
CLEMENTIÆ. FELICITATI
ABSPVRGIÆ AVSTRIÆ DOMVS
SACRA DICATAQ.

VII.34

VII.34
Giovanni Battista Fonteo (Fontana)
Europalia, 1571
Vienna, Österreichische Nationalbibliothek, Handschriften-, Autographen- und Nachlass-Sammlung, Codex 10206.

This manuscript compendium contains primarily materials relating to the festival held in Vienna at the end of August and the beginning of September 1571 to celebrate the marriage of Archduke Karl to Maria of Bavaria. It includes a variety of texts by Fonteo: a poem on the events; another poem relating the festival to the battle of Lepanto, which it is said to prophesy; a poem on Rudolf II; a description of the characters, costumes, and programmes of the *Ringlrennen*, which Arcimboldo designed; and several other poems which have been identified as lyrics that were set to music during the festival. In addition the codex includes the programme and a description of the festival, together with its costumes, held in Prague at the end of February and the beginning of March 1570: this tournament was also designed by Arcimboldo. The manuscript also contains a revised and annotated version of Fonteo's poem on Arcimboldo's paintings of the *Seasons* and *Elements* (see cat. nos.), together with important marginal comments which also make reference to some other pictures by the artist; significantly the content of the paintings is related to the festivals. Finally it ends with a short poem on another painting, not yet identified, by Arcimboldo.
Since at the time he was writing these texts Fonteo was a close associate of the artist, this compendium is important both for the knowledge about and for the interpretation of Arcimboldo's art and other activities. It allows for insights into the social and intellectual conditions at the court of Maximilian II in which Arcimboldo's paintings and festivals were designed. It provides many details pertaining to the pictures and festivals, and allows for interpretation of both paintings and events as allegories of imperial rule.

Thomas DaCosta Kaufmann

Bibliography: Vocelka 1976, 78-79; Kaufmann 1978, 33-40, 76-102; Porzio 1979, 30-39; Venice 1987, 88, 156-164; Lindell 1987; Lindell 1990; Kaufmann 1993, 103, 312-316.

VII.35
Giovanni Battista Fonteo (Fontana)
Design for a Festival Entry, c. 1572 (?)
Pen and brown ink, brown and grey wash, over traces of red chalk
c. 290 × 2665 mm
Berlin, Kunstbibliothek, inv. no. Lipp-Hdz 3324

In *Idea* (1590) Gian Paolo Lomazzo (Lomazzo 1590 [1973], 362) says that Arcimboldo was "singular" (*singolare*) in inventions, above all of masquerades, and elaborates particularly on the festivities he designed for the marriage of Archduke Karl in Vienna in 1571 (Vocelka 1976, 47-98). Many festival drawings by Arcimboldo survive (see cat. no. VII.1-32). Among them are some for the 1571 event, as well as others probably for festivals held during the same period (Kaufmann 1978, 28-42). The present drawing may be related to such festival designs. The format itself may be associated with that frequently used for descriptions of tournaments. The extreme length of this drawing suggests that it was originally presented as a roll, used for books from antiquity onwards in Europe, but also traditionally employed in East Asia for paintings, where images emerge as the scroll is unrolled. Tournament descriptions were often presented in the form of rolls: this is frequently the case at the Habsburg courts of the later 16th century (Kaufmann 1976b; Auer 2005, 20-21, 119-132, 164).
The fantastic costumes and creatures (notice the bat-like wings attached to some figures, the monsters, and the like) as well as the procession of the figures and the floats are also evocative of a festival. The turbans on the heads of some of the men, and the dresses with tight bodices and puffed shoulders

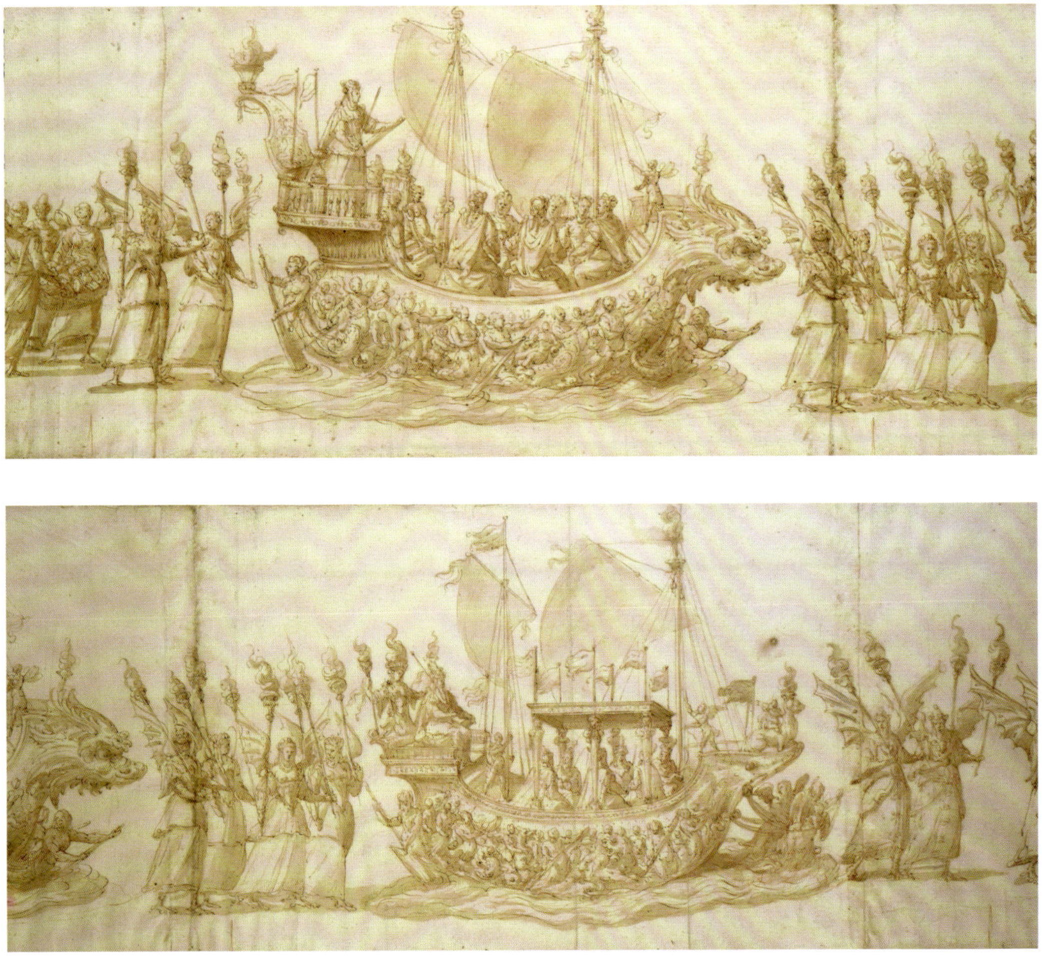

VII.35

worn by some of the ladies, moreover recall features found in Arcimboldo's drawings for festivals. The three-headed Cerberus-like creature seen in this drawing resembles a similar monster drawn by Arcimboldo (see *fig. 1* in the essay by A. Beyer in this catalogue). While the present drawing was first given to Ludovico Pozzoserrato and was also associated with a Venetian festival of the 1550s (by Heinrich Bodmer, on a photograph, now in Warburg Institute, London; see also Hookey 1969, 49, fig. 28), when it was offered for sale in the 1960s it was (Nerman 1967, 20, no. 10) attributed to Giuseppe Arcimboldo, and the Arcimboldo attribution prevailed for a decade (see Barthes 1978, 172).
However, this drawing does not share the stylistic characteristics of drawings by Arcimboldo, nor can it be associated with any of the festivals known to have been designed by him. In fact, it bears an elaborate monogram in the bottom left hand corner which indicates that it was executed by another hand. This monogram is quite visible and may readily be deciphered to read "Fonteo" (Kaufmann 1978, 59 and fig. 35).
Lomazzo (Lomazzo 1590 [1973], 363) says that Arcimboldo gave the task of designing the programes for the first tournament for the 1571 festival to a "certain Fonteo". This person can be identified with Giovanni Battista Fonteo (Giovan Battista Fontana). Although no other evidence exists to support Lomazzo's further charge that Fonteo claimed, to Emperor Maximilian II's astonishment, to have made the designs for the 1571 festival, a copy of this programme, written by Fonteo, is inscribed on succeeding pages to indicate Arcimboldo as its *fabricator* and Fonteo as its *coordinator*.
Fonteo also penned a description of a tournament held in Prague in 1570, which was also designed by Arcimboldo; he may have been involved in that event as well, and he may also have worked with Arcimboldo on a tournament held in Bratislava in 1572. Fonteo had also collaborated with Arcimboldo for at least several years before 1571, since he had presented poems on the artist's pictures of the *Seasons* and the *Elements* to accompany them when they were given as gifts to Maximilian II on New Year's Day 1569 (see cat. no. IV.1). Another of Fonteo's treatises, on laughter, allows further insights into Arcimboldo's paintings, as do his associations with Erasmian circles in Italy (see the essay by Kaufmann on Arcimboldo and humanists in this catalogue; also Kaufmann 1990, Kaufmann 1993).
Although Fonteo may not have done what Lomazzo says he claims he did, namely design the 1571 tournament, the evidence of this drawing indicates that he nevertheless drew designs related to festivals. It is in any event not on the basis of the claim Lomazzo reports, but on the clear evidence of the monogram visible on it that this drawing is to be attributed to Fonteo (misunderstood by Berra 1996, 59n). Although other sources indicate that Fonteo was a learned *letterato*, it is mistaken to assume that he would consequently have lacked any interest in the practical aspects of art: several other instances at the imperial court indicate that it is not strange at all to have been both a man of learning and a draftsman, with an interest in artistic practicalities, too (see the essay "Giuseppe Arcimboldo: Learning, Letters, and Art", in this catalogue; Berra 1996, 59n).
This drawing thus provides important evidence from Arcimboldo's entourage at the imperial court for a humanist's direct involvement in art, hence for collaboration between artists and humanists in practical matters of art, while moreover illustrating a procession from a still unidentified festival.

Thomas DaCosta Kaufmann

Bibliography: Nerman 1967, 20, no. 10; Barthes 1978, 172; Kaufmann 1978, 59-61; Venice 1987, 147; Berra 1996, 59n.

VII.36
Unknown artist
The eight-year-old Archduke Rudolf with the court giant Giovanni Bona at the Vienna tournament of 1560, Austria, after 1560
Watercolour and bodycolour painting on paper
265 × 655 mm
Vienna, Kunsthistorisches Museum, Kunstkammer, inv. no. 6564, fol. 16

This miniature and the following work (cat. no. VII.37) are what remains of a lost painting cycle of the Vienna tournament of 1560, arranged by the later Emperor Maximilian II in honour of his father Ferdinand I from 24th of May to 24th of June. These three originally separate folios were probably first associated together in the 19th century in the imperial collection. In the early 19th century they were arbitrarily included in a tournament book (cod. KK 6564) of Archduke Ferdinand of Tyrol, a gouache paper manuscript from the 16th century.
The entry of the eight-year-old Rudolf with the 2.40 metre tall giant was surely a great success, in that giant and dwarf belonged to court life where they were featured as living Kunstkammer figures. Under the note, "Most serene princely highness Archduke Rudolf", the boy in armour strides onto the tournament field alongside the court giant Bon von Riva (Giovanni Bona) costumed as a "wild man".
According to the accomplished description of the famous Vienna tournament given by Francolin Burgunder, this is the entry of sixth part of the foot tournament. The court giant of Archduke Ferdinand of Tyrol, Giovanni Bona, accompanies the young Archduke to the tournament field. In his right hand the giant holds part of a tree torn up with its roots that he shakes while roaring "make way I am a giant". This announcement was to make way for Archduke Rudolf and his seven-year-old brother, who would measure themselves up to their uncle Archduke Karl in the foot tournament.

Christian Beaufort

Bibliography: Vienna 1978, 22f.; Vienna 1988, cat. no. 804; Stockholm 1992, 108.

VII.37
Unknown artist
Walker on Stilts, Austria, after 1560
Watercolour and bodycolour on paper
402 × 205 mm
Vienna, Kunsthistorisches Museum, Kunstkammer, inv. no. KK 6564, fol. 17

The following scene, on closer examination, reveals itself to be cut out and glued onto another paper. After the description of the tournament published in 1561 we here see an event that took place later on in the games, namely the entry of the tenth part of the foot tournament, headed by Isabella of Carthage, the Phrygian goddess who is followed by the representation of a magic mountain concealing a noble knight who, following the chivalric novels of the Middle Ages, was to defend and restore the honour of womanhood.
The courtly Renaissance festivities often had a programme postulating a humanistic formulation. Yet the message was also intelligible for ordinary people and these carnivals included jesters, stilt-walkers, acrobats, fire eaters, etc.
Here we see a figure on stilts, who moves with agility on thin wooden sticks, nearly twice his own body height. His costume is not easily explicable and also in the description of 1561 figures on stilts were not mentioned. He wears a black felt hat, with downturned rim, decorated in the nape with six cock's feathers. The mask conceals the face of a thin man with a twirled walrus moustache. A small white lace collar lies over a longarmed coat-of-mail, that ends in spiky edges at cratch height over a pair of broadly cut white breeches. His left hand is on his hip and he keeps his balance with the pike that he holds over his shoulder. To be able to move around with stilts below the knee already requires great acrobatics. We also hope for the figure on stilts that his chainmail coat is only an imitation, since a real one would weigh at least 30 kg.

Christian Beaufort

Bibliography: Vienna 1978, 22f.; Essen-Vienna 1988, cat. no. 804; Stockholm 1992, 108; Schloss Ambras 2005.

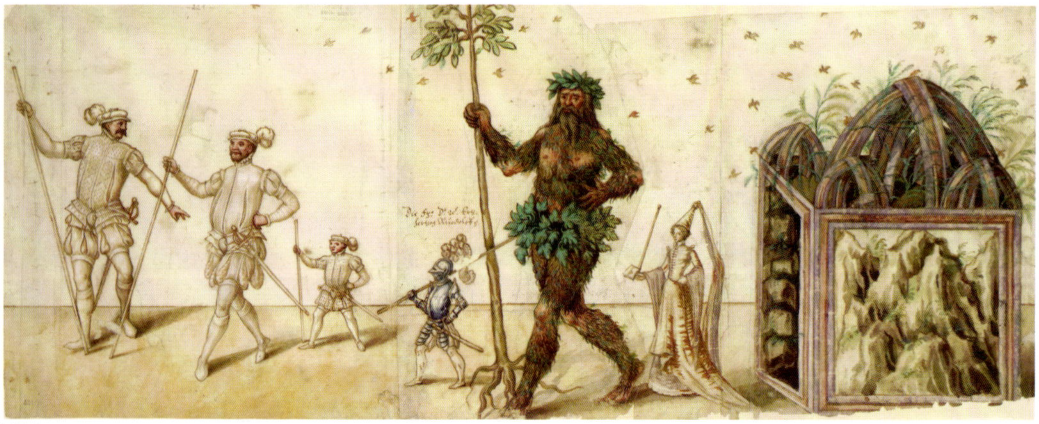

VII.36

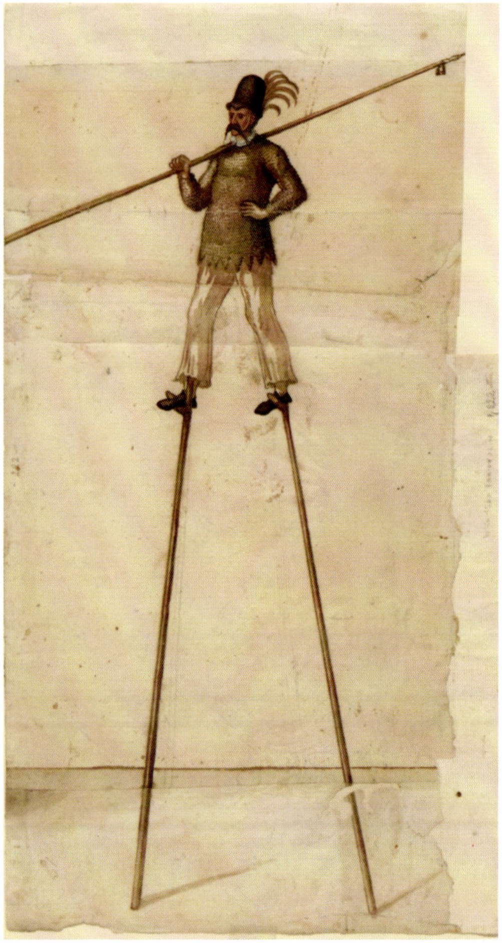

VII.37

VII.38
Sigmund Elsässer
Kolowrat Wedding
Innsbruck: Hans Baur (Johannes Agricola) 1580
Copperplate etching on paper painted with watercolour
Paper I, 74, II* Bl. 335 × 450 mm; sheet in varying formats
Vienna, Kunsthistorisches Museum, Kunstkammer, inv. no. KK 5269

Fol. 26: *Aeneas' Ship and Strophadian Islands*
340/610/370 × 3270 mm

Fol. 27: *Venus and Cupid*
340 × 2700 mm

The so-called *Kolowrat Wedding* was carried out in copperplate etching, painted with watercolour, with explanatory text and captions printed in Gothic script. It depicts the tournament events arranged on the occasion of the marriage of Johann Lipsteinsky of Kolowrat with Katharina of Payrsberg, which took place from 14 to 16 February 1580 in Innsbruck. Although it deals with the marriage of a courtier, – Kolowrat was the chamberlain of the Tyrolean sovereign, Archduke Ferdinand II (1529-1595) – the Archduke used the occasion to stage these events (with allegorical, cosmological and mythological motifs) as a triumph in the style of the courtly festivals of the era. He made them into a demonstration of his sovereign and dynastic authority and documented them through a series of prints. Identical copies of this codex can be found in Brznice and Munich. From the preface, it can be learned that Archduke Ferdinand was "a lover of these and similarly princely amusements", as well as the fact that Ferdinand himself masterminded the entire endeavour and employed painters, sculptors and other artists in his Innsbruck court to realize his ideas. The court painter Sigmund Elsässer was engaged as executive artist from 1579 to 1587. The printing was executed in accordance with the imperial printing privilege by Hans Baur (Johannes Agricola) in Innsbruck.
Fol. 26 and 27 belong to the fifth event of the tournament. On the first page, one can see Count Wilhelm of Zimmern, Lord Steward of Archduke Ferdinand, in the role of Aeneas. Accompanied by "many knightly heroes", he is travelling on a kind of caravel; Lady Fortune, in the form of a figurehead, provides a safe crossing, while a fire-spitting lion's mouth on the prow enhances the martial atmosphere. The stylized scenery depicts the Strofades (today Strivali), two small islands in the Ionian Sea, which were held to be the home of the harpies. These "terrible monsters and birds of prey" are portrayed on a mountain topped with a fortress. On the following overleaf, Aeneas heroically attacks the bird-bodied monsters despite negative auguries. Ships, barques, castles and mountains number among the favoured props of a courtly celebration's equipment, whose visual effect were enhanced here through the use of fireworks.
On fol. 27, the goddess Venus arrives "on a seashell, together with her son Cupid and with her faithful animals, the dolphins". The caption indicates that two men are concealed in the fishes, which pull the silver-plated shell. The procession vehicle in the form of a shell is, like the previous two costumes, constructed from decoration material typical of the theatre: wood for the frame and papier mâché for the exterior molding.
Books, as well as the paper in the form of a roll, served as a print-based medium for the documentation of such festival events: the printed pages were bound or attached to each other in a long strip. Rolls of this kind were especially well suited to the proper representation of the course of a triumphal procession or the events of a tournament.

Veronika Sandblicher

Bibliography: Boeheim 1888, CCLXXXIX; Scheicher 1981, 136-138; Vienna 2005, 164-165, cat. no. 5.14.

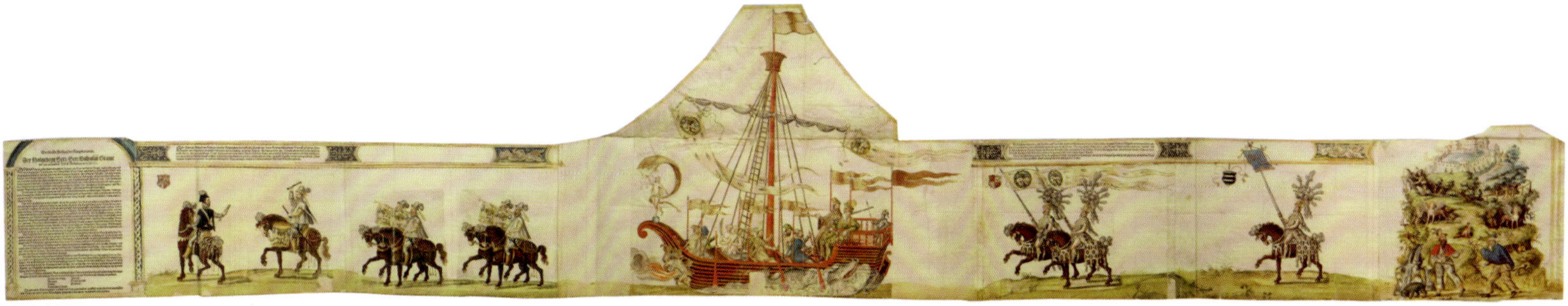

VII.38, fol. 26

VII.39
Sigmund Elsässer
Wedding Festival Book of Archduke Ferdinand II
Innsbruck: Hans Baur (Johann Agricola) 1582 (1580)
Copperplate etching with watercolour on paper
Pap. II, 60, I* Bl.
430 × 269 mm
Vienna, Kunsthistorisches Museum, Kunstkammer, inv. no. 5270

Fol. 51r: *Neptune*
430 × 535 mm (sheet)

Fol. 60r: *Mercury and Carriage*
430 × 545 mm (sheet, cropped)

The so-called *Wedding Festival Book of Archduke Ferdinand II* owes its origins to the second marriage ceremony of the Tyrolean nobleman in May 1582 at Innsbruck; the bride was the Mantuan Princess Anna Caterina Gonzaga. The codex contains 106 colour prints of the events of a tournament, which was arranged for the festivities: ring jousting, foot tournament, "quintaine" tournament, jousting, tilting and Hussar tournament. In contrast to the so called *Kolowrat Wedding* (compare cat. no. VII.38), there are no text passages or captions. The appearance of each person can be identified on the one hand by an affixed crest, and on the other hand by captions printed in Gothic script, which can be found in both the identical copies of the codex (New York, Munich). For the creation of the codex, copper plates were used, which had already been created for the *Kolowrat Wedding*. The knight figures in particular, coloured differently and with different descriptions, were placed in different contexts (along with the new material): a cost-saving device, which demonstrates that such codices of court festivals were not necessarily authentic, but rather mass produced.
At this court festival, Archduke Ferdinand II also cast each person in a role that corresponded to their rank and pedigree, including, among others, the Trojan hero Aeneas as a fearless Hussar and defender of the Catholic faith.
Fol. 51r shows Neptune, the bearded, trident-carrying sea god, clad in plate armour over clothing

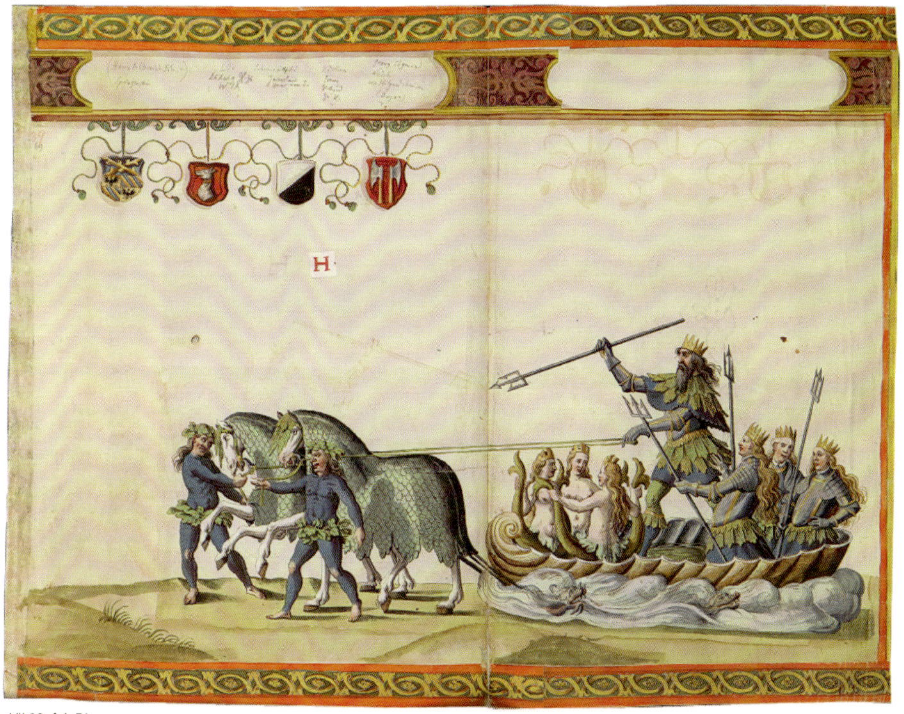

VII.39, fol. 51

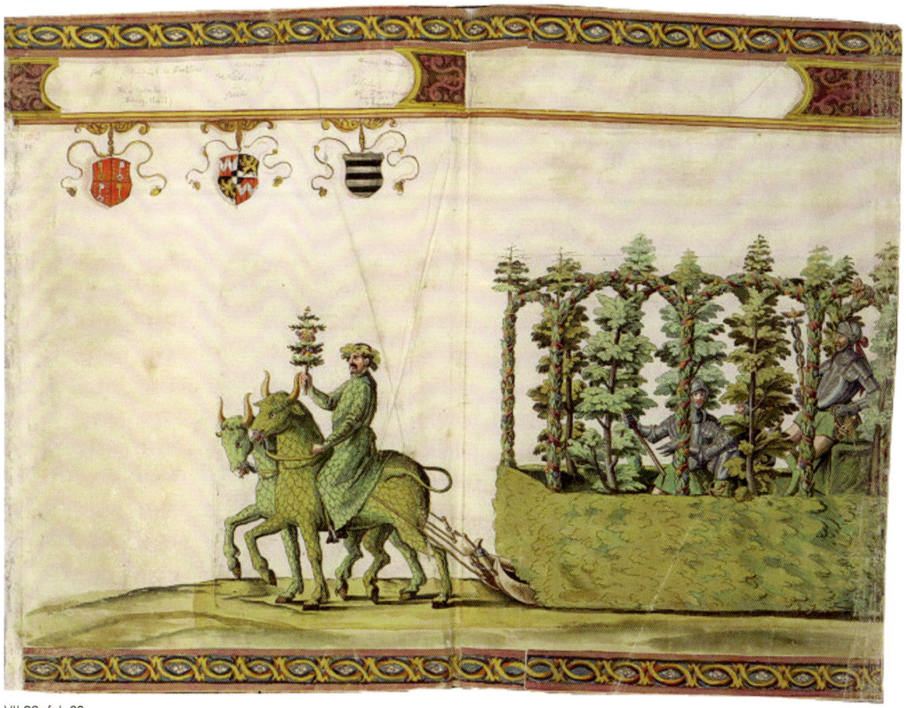

VII.39, fol. 60

made from scales and foliage, gliding over the wave-tops in his clamshell wagon. Accompanying him are three nereids and tritons. The brother of Jupiter, the father of the gods, functioned as ruler and tamer of the seas. In the context of Aeneas' myth, which played a special role in this costumed tournament, Neptune is the saviour of the ships carrying the Trojan heroes and provided the calm crossing from Sicily to Carthage.
The crests reveal the pictured figures to be members of Tyrolean as well as Bohemian nobility: Wia, Köstlan, Schmirsitzky and Lösch (from left to right).
Fol. 60r shows a knight on a sledge elaborately decorated with branches and garlands, in which two men in plate armour are concealed. Like the shell wagon or landscape scenes, the sledge was also an oft-used prop for such festivals. In this case, the sledge is pulled by two horses dressed as oxen, upon which rides a wildman with a sapling in clothing made of foliage. "Barbarians" are typical of the image repertoire of the era (compare cat. no. VII.36; Elisabeth Wolfik, KK 6465, fol. 16). On the one hand, court festivals and tournaments embody the demonic and indomitable power of untamed nature as the polar opposite of cultivated, courtly life. On the other hand they are seen in a general sense as a symbol of barbaric, inimical powers. In the 16th century, the allegory of the Turks as the arch-enemy of Christendom was at the forefront of this concept. In general, the barbarism, which resided outside of civilized culture, customs and society, was represented as challenge to knightly, Christian fighters.

Veronika Sandblicher

Bibliography: Boeheim 1888, CCXIII; Innsbruck 2003, 108-110, cat. no. 50; Innsbruck 2005, 128-129, cat. no. 4.2.6; Sandbichler 2006, 47-89.

VII.40
Anonymous
Morion from an all'Antica Set with Roundshield which once Belonged to Archduke Ferdinand II (1529-1595)
Milan, circa 1560
Blued, worked, gilded and silvered iron, rich gold damascening, formerly gilded brass rivets. The helmet lining (red satin) is missing.
32 × 21.5 × 32.5 cm
Vienna, Kunsthistorisches Museum, Hofjagd- und, Rüstkammer, inv. no. A 802

According to most recent research (Godoy in Genf 2003) the morions and the splendid round shield (cat. no. VII.41, inv. no. A 802a) are stylistically and thematically unrelated and are the work of two different masters. Their former attribution to Giovanni Battista Panzieri, also known as Zarabaglia (Serabaglio) has been invalidated, and it would seem that the morion and round shield were created by two anonymous, Northern Italian masters.
Nonetheless, the use of both pieces as an *all'antica* ensemble is imaginable, even though the decoration of the morion and the round shield are thematically quite significantly different, the former with maritime representations and the latter adorned on both sides primarily with the feats of Hercules.
In the festival processions of the Renaissance ancient scenarios predominated. As a result many *all'antica* armour sets have also come down to us, that are only made up of a helmet (morion) and a roundshield and that were worn with a coat-of-mail, *all'antica* muscle armour or special weave. The iron parts were decorated with embossed, gold damascened and sumptuously executed mythological scenes.
Among all things the helmet offered many artistic possibilities to apply fantastic decor, as attested by the many helmets in the accomplished costume drawings of Salviatis and Arcimboldo.
The crest of the helmet has the form of a winged dragon, reminiscent of the orca in Ariosto's *Orlando Furioso*. At the front the hideous face of a wolflike monster, with a piercing gaze pointing upwards. On the left side of the helmet dome, Amphitrite is seated in a triumphal chariot drawn by two dolphins and driven by a putto. On the opposite side, sea horses draw Poseidon. Fishes and sea monsters populate rough waters, while on the cheek guards and neck guard Tritons fight and blow their instruments.
Evidence of the tradition of fantastic, bizarre helmet forms is already known in painting, drawing and other media as of the second half of the 15th century. To cite but a few examples, one only needs recall the frescœs painted by Piero della Francesca in the choir of the church of Saint Francis in Arezzo between 1452-59, the terracottas with all probability modelled by Verrocchio and glazed by Andrea della Robbia bearing the relief of Alexander the Great (Vienna, Kunsthistorisches Museum, Kunstkammer, inv. no. 7491), up to the drawing by Leonardo in the British Museum (Popham 1947, no. 129).
This is sufficient proof that this kind of fantastically shaped helmets was already present in other media from the 15th century onwards, i.e. a lot earlier than what is known to us as regards real helmets and armour. The "lion's head" morion dated 1480-1490 in New York (inv. no. 23.141) is the earliest evidence of such *all'antica* helmets.

Christian Beaufort

Provenance: from Ambras Castle. Mentioned in the 1596 inventory

Bibliography: Gamber, Beaufort 1990, 188f.; Monbeig-Goguel 1998, 270f., no. 106; Godoy, Leydi 2003, cat. no. 18, 424f.; Beaufort, Pfaffenbichler 2005, 30, 162f., cat. no. 56.

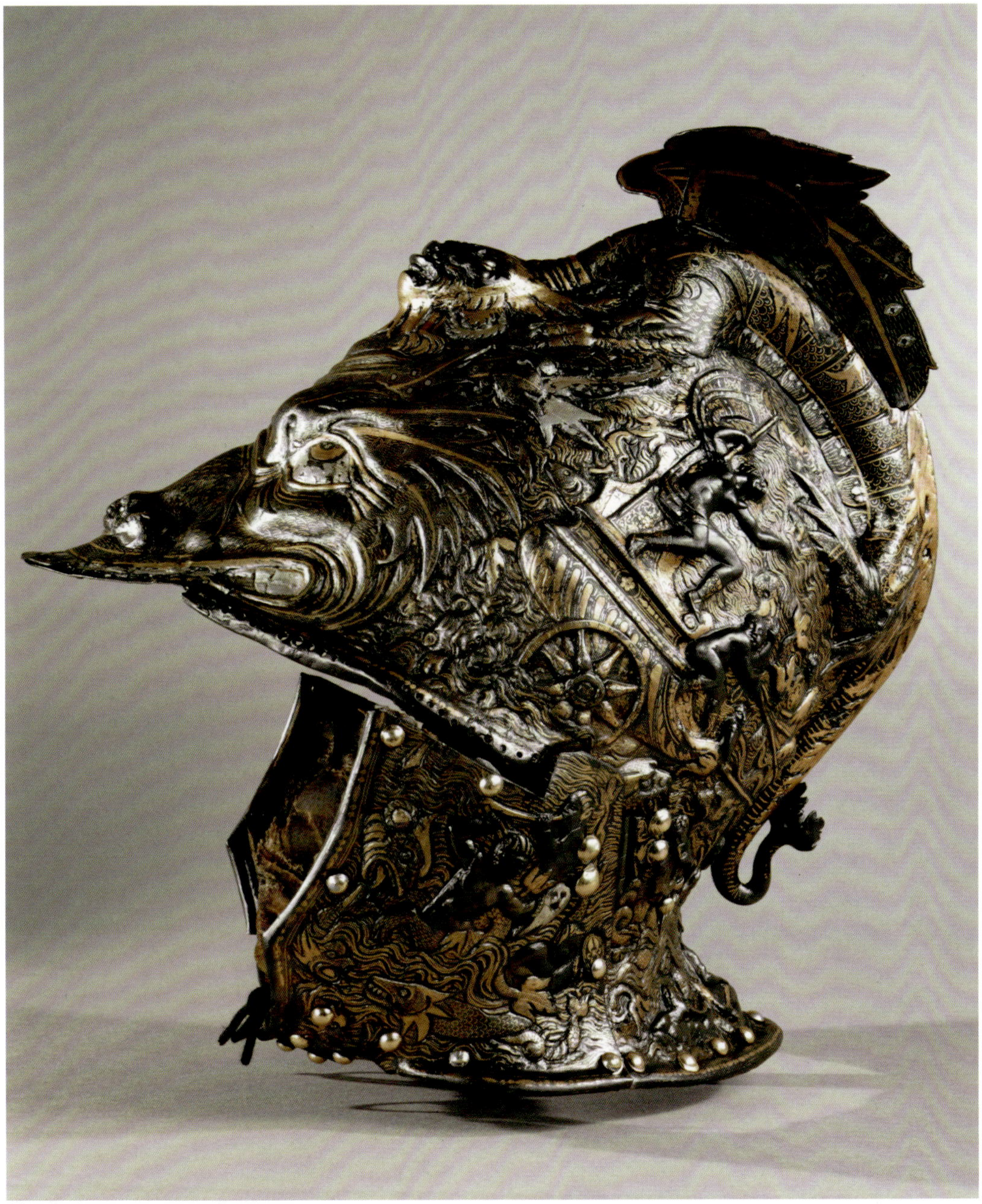

VII.40

VII.41

Attributed to Caterina Leuca, born Cantona (embroideress), (est. circa 1560)

Round Shield from an all'Antica Set with Morion,
Milan, circa 1560
Archduke Ferdinand II (1529-1595)
Blackened, embossed iron, gold damascened, silvered, engraved; red satin with gold-and silk embroidery
Ø 60 cm
Vienna, Kunsthistorisches, Museum, Hofjagd-und, Rüstkammer, inv. no. A 802 a

The splendid round shield (*parma*) and the morion (cat. no. VII.40) are no longer considered a pair but rather the work of two different masters (Godoy in Genf 2003), who remain anonymous despite their extremely elegant work, due to the fact that these pieces can not be attributed to any of the well known artists.
The round shield is very richly decorated on both sides: on the embossed front of the shield Hercules crushes the Antaus, while the border medallion features scenes from the old testament, such as David and Goliath and Samson with the Lions, with mythological allusions, such as Cacus who steals a head of cattle from Hercules, or how Hercules slays the already felled Busir.
Singular is the masterly decorated inner side of the shield. The whole surface in red satin is in golden thread with moresques and an embroidered framework in which also the deeds of Hercules in coloured silk painting are represented: Hercules slays the centaur Nessus, then his struggle with Hydra of Lerna, followed by the abduction of Dejanira by the centaur Nessus and lastly how Hercules tames the three headed dog of Hades Cerberus.
As master of the textile work, Boeheim (1898) suggests Catarina Leuca, born Cantona in Milan, who demonstrably also worked for Catarina Micaela, Duchess of Savoy and a daughter of King Philipp II of Spain. There is no evidence of this assumption, yet there is also nothing to contradict it.

Christian Beaufort

Provenance: from Ambras Castle. Recorded in the inventory of 1596 of Archduke Ferdinand II of Tyrol

Bibliography: Gamber, Beaufort 1990, 188f.; Godoy, Leydi 2003, no. 18, 424f; Beaufort, Pfaffenbichler 2005, 30, 162f., cat. no. 56.

VII.42

Coral Sabre
Italian, circa 1560
Archduke Ferdinand II of Tyrol (1529-1595)
Coral, gilded silver, steel, wood, silk
83.5 × 23.5 cm
Vienna, Kunsthistorisches Museum, Hofjagd- und Rüstkammer, inv. no. A 791

Right from antiquity coral was believed to have magical powers, and it befitted the world of Mannerist ideas to also use it as a weapon, in which – as here – nature and art combine so perfectly.
The magic coral is the hilt of what was considered an ancient "coltellaggio", a slightly bowed long knife, which from the Quattrocento was falsely considered ancient-Roman and as such included as part of the *all'antica* iconography in Renaissance festivities.
The hilt is a powerful, richly ramified branch of blood coral, and the slightly curved blade is gilded and decorated in its upper third, with a wording on it that still has not been interpreted, said to constitute a magic spell. And carrying on with Mannerist associations, the mighty branch of blood coral constituting the sabre hilt resembles man's aorta arching over the heart, here to be found directly at the blade guard. Due to its fragility, the magnificent coral sabre was naturally only a Kunstkammer exhibit, in that even a slight jolt could cause great damage. Hence its listing in the 1596 inventory, where it was described as specifically stored in a cabinet with other coral objects and possessions.
To date only four coral sabres of this kind are known, all part of the legacy of Archbishop Ferdinand of Tyrol and now to be found in the collec-

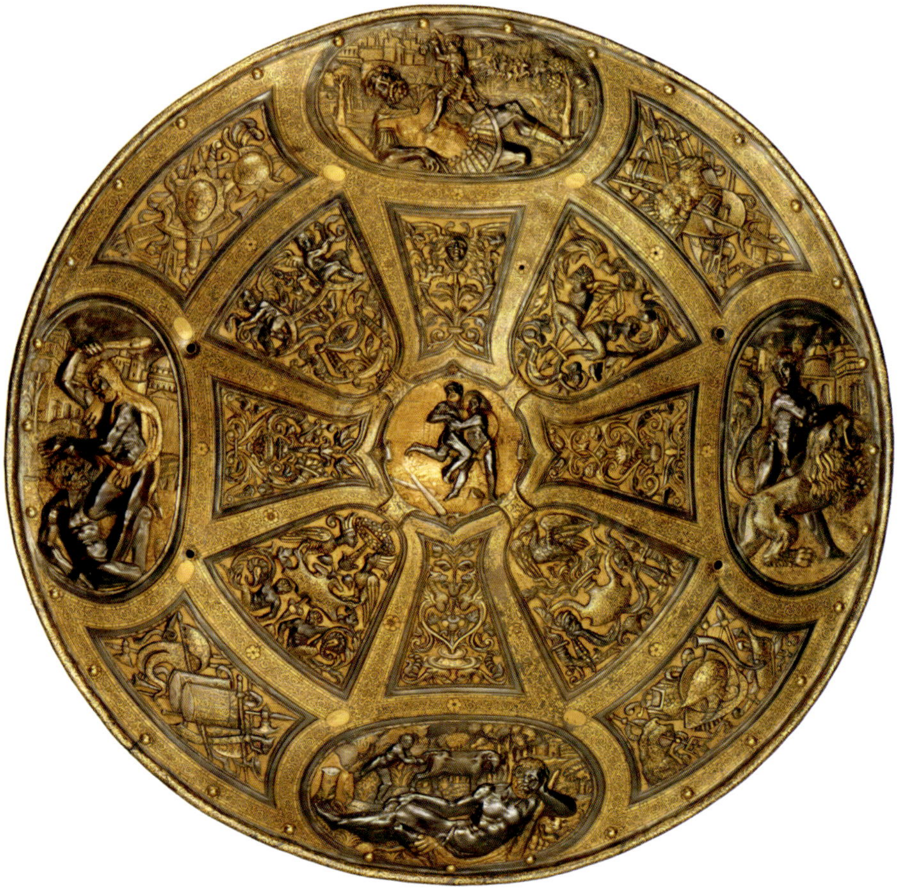

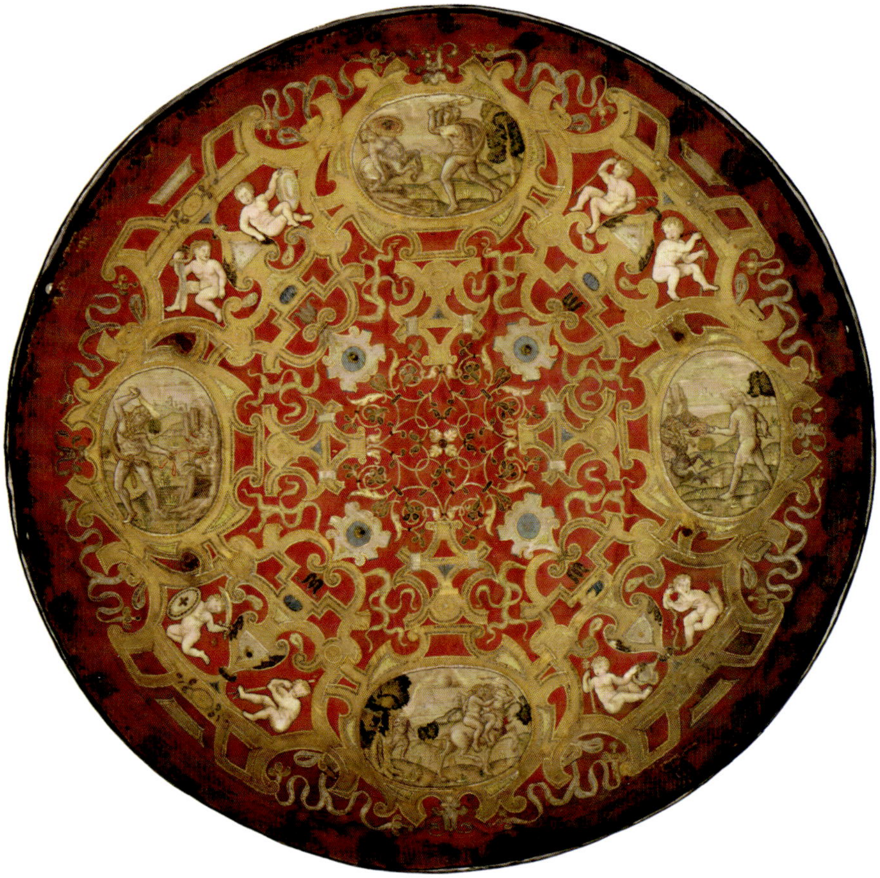

VII.41

tions of the Vienna Kunsthistorischen Museum and Ambras Castle.

Christian Beaufort

Provenance: from Ambras Castle, inventoried in 1596

Bibliography: Hofmann 1987, 370f., no. 74; Checa Cremades 1998, 653, no. 268; Beaufort, Pfaffenbichler 2005, cat. no. 38, 124f.; Moscow 2005, 32f., cat. no. 4.

VII.43
Anton Peffenhauser
(1552-1603)
Plankengestech tournament armour for Archduke Charles of Austria (1540-1590)
Augsburg 1571
Plain steel, leather
163 × 70 × 50 cm
Vienna, Kunsthistorisches Museum, Hofjagd- und Rüstkammer, inv. no. A 885

No Habsburg festivity has provided us with so many tournament suits of armour as the Vienna wedding feast of 1571, where Arcimboldo was praised as the organizer of the artistic staging. No expense was spared for the occasion, that with the marriage of Archduke Charles, the youngest brother of Emperor Maximilian II, and Princess Anna of Bavaria, sealed the political bond between the two large Catholic Houses, Habsburg and Bavaria.

Barely recognizable allusions to the occasion are also to be found on the helmet. Both sides of the helmet comb are decorated with a gold etched love symbol: a female genius offers her burning heart in a bowl. Next to the date 1571 on the helmet one finds the signature of the armourer in the form of his embossed three-legged mark, like the Augsburg city mark.

The bridegroom's tournament armour, in nearly perfect condition, is all that remains of a huge set that the bridegroom could use for competing in all the tournament variants, as well as in the *Plankengestech* tournament, a form of knightly dual combat, where the contestants rode along a board or *Palia* that separated them while trying to unhorse the opponent with their lance or to at least break the opponent's lance.

Christian Beaufort

Provenance: From the Imperial Armoury in Vienna

Bibliography: Graz 1964, 128, Nr. 323; Augsburg 1980, 525 f., Nr. 934; Madrid 2002, 86f.

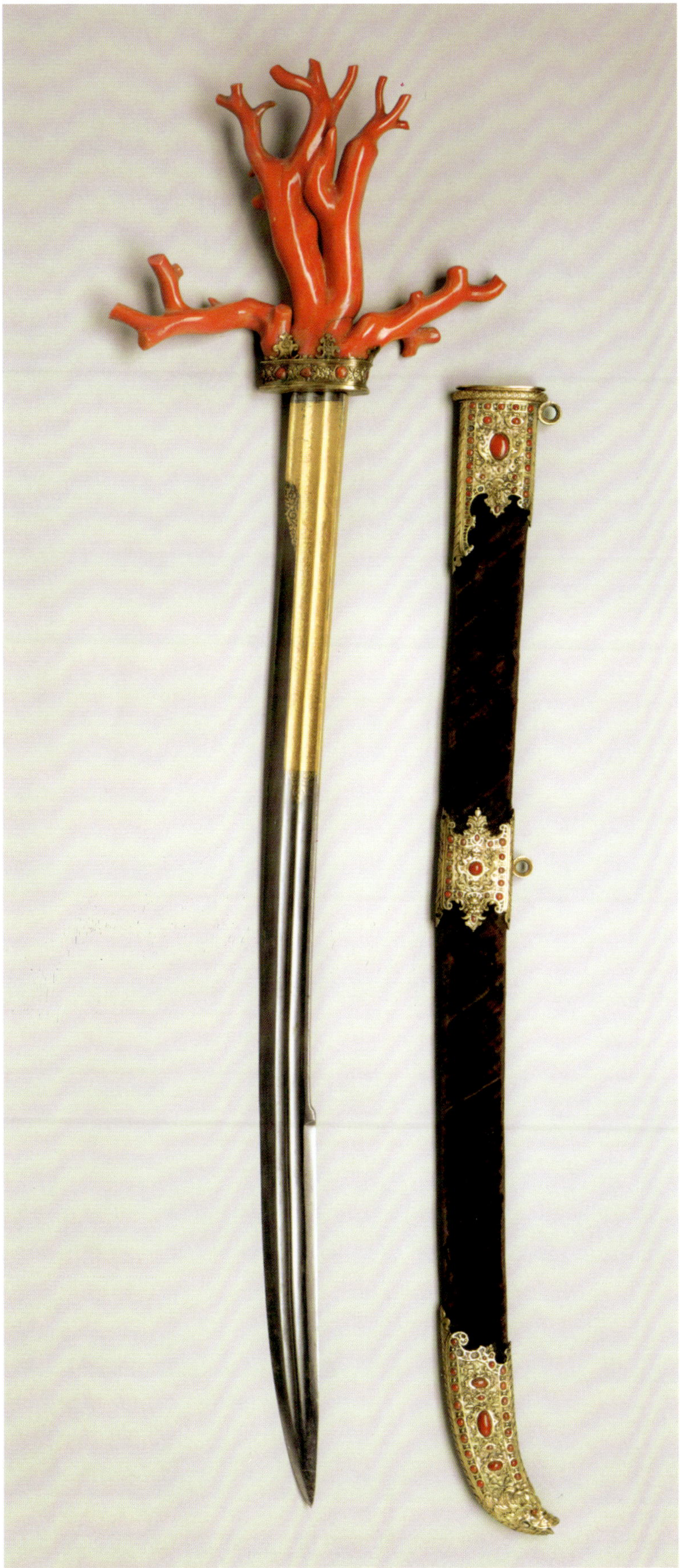

VII.42

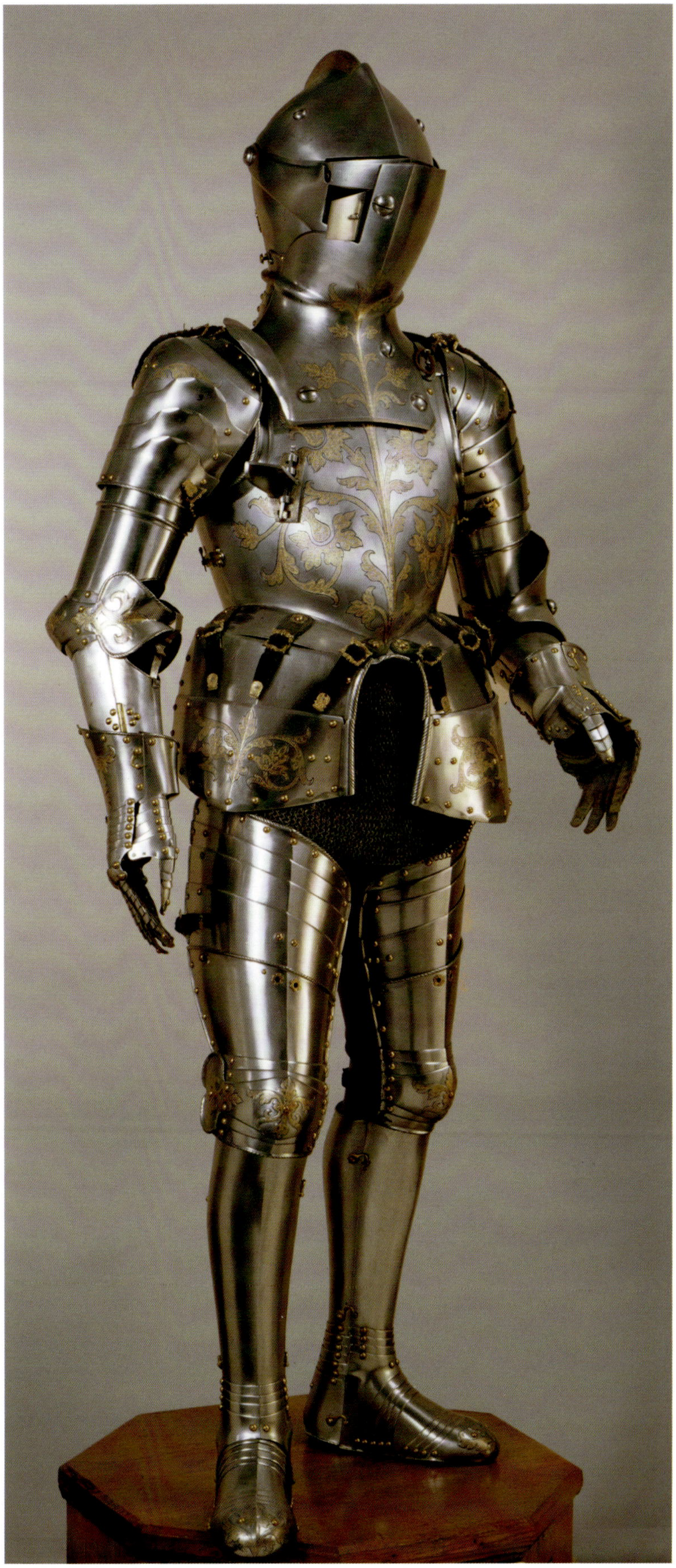

VII.43

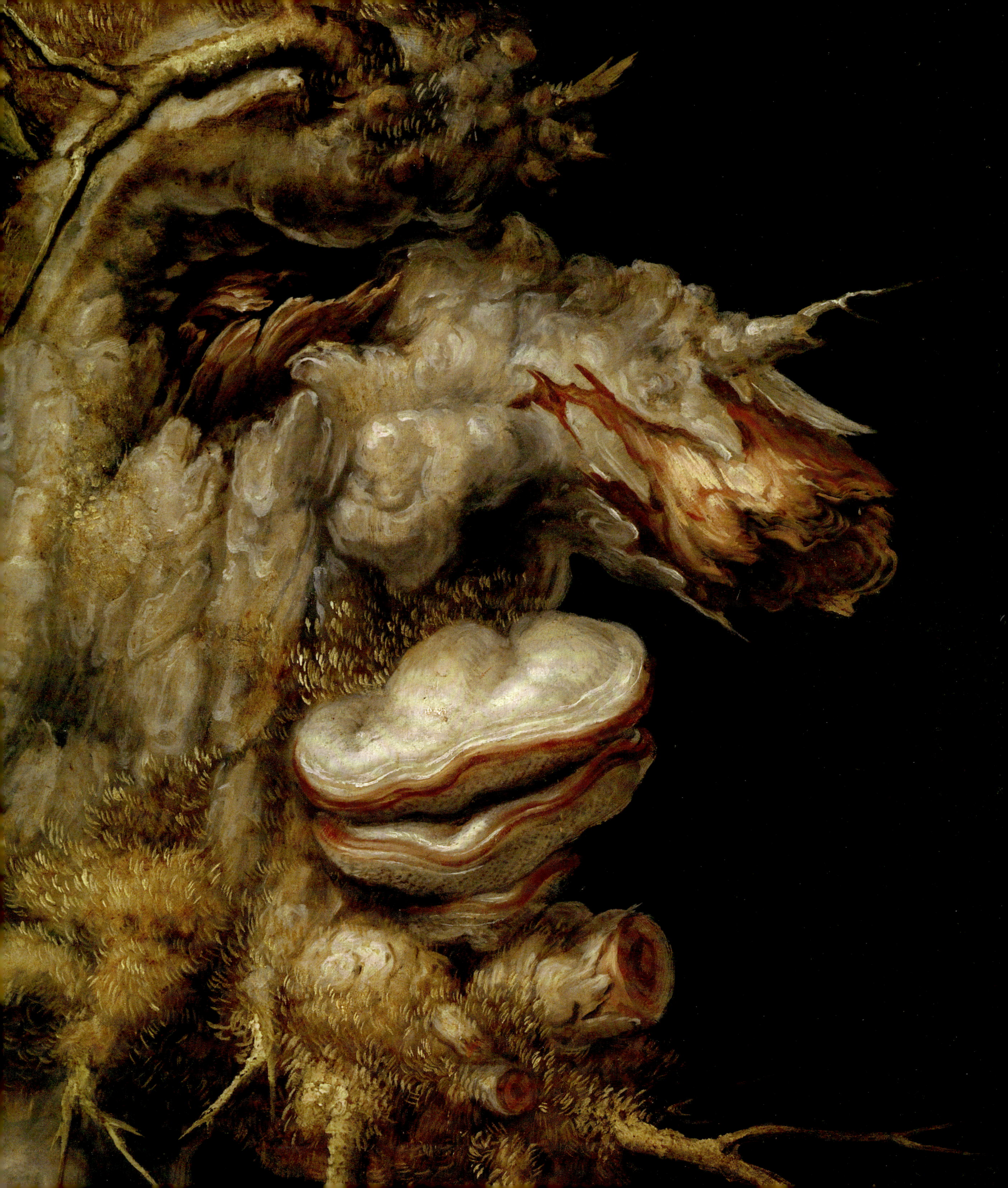

Thomas DaCosta Kaufmann

Giuseppe Arcimboldo: Learning, Letters, and Art

One of Giuseppe Arcimboldo's most remarkable images is his self-portrait as a composite head. In this drawing Arcimboldo does not depict himself as a painter or draftsman, as he might have done had he composed the head out of paint brushes or pens, or canvases or panels. Instead he fashions himself as a man of paper. Arcimboldo becomes literally a man of letters (cat. no. I.2).

Dated 1587, the year that Arcimboldo left Prague to return to Milan, where he was to spend his last years, while still remaining in imperial service, this self-portrait may be taken to stand for an important part of his life and work in both places. Regardless of whether it be viewed as a summary reflection on his previous career at court or an announcement to a milieu of literati that he aspired to join[1], this drawing attests not only to the artist's self-consciousness but also to the reality of his involvement with the world of letters and learning. Other essays in this volume deal with Arcimboldo's tournament and festival designs, natural history studies, and grotesques. But humanist ideals, and more directly, actual humanists were occupied in planning the programmes and paraphernalia for entries and tournaments at the imperial court; they studied natural history as well as ancient letters and history; and their study of antiquity guided attitudes toward grotesques. A mentality informed by humanism and literati culture underlies Arcimboldo's interests in all these matters, and, most important, it creates a context for understanding the creation and reception of his paintings as well. Arcimboldo, his patrons, friends, and associates all participated in a culture coloured by Renaissance humanism and literature, which provides not only the background and sources for his imagery, but also keys to the interpretation of his inventions, most notably his paintings of composite heads.

All of Arcimboldo's imperial patrons were interested in and supported scholarship of various kinds. Arcimboldo arrived at the Habsburg court in Central Europe during the reign of Ferdinand I. Ferdinand had had a close personal relation with the famed humanist Desiderius Erasmus, who had met the thirteen-year old archduke in 1516, when he was residing at the court of his aunt Margaret of Austria in Mechelen (Malines). Erasmus influenced the education of Ferdinand both personally and through his writings, and dedicated to him the *Institutio Principis Christiani*, a book on the education of the Christian prince, as well his paraphrase of the gospel of John, while advising moderation in dealings with Protestant Reformers[2]. In turn Ferdinand granted Erasmus a privilege to print all his works, because he thought they might be useful[3]. The emperor later helped reform the university of Vienna, where several important scholars worked, including figures who also had court connections. Among them was the emperor's personal physician, Wolfgang Lazius, who was at the same time professor of medicine at the university of Vienna, cartographer, and scholar of numismatics and genealogy. Another of Ferdinand's personal physicians was the noted botanist Pietro Andrea Matthioli [see the chapter on Nature studies].

Ferdinand's son and successor Maximilian II (emperor 1564-1576) "gathered around him a whole collection of learned men" – or, as was said in Latin, his was an "*aula compluribus doctissimis viris ornata*"[4]. These were diverse figures from many different countries, religious confessions, and intellectual backgrounds. Lazius continued in imperial service, as did such scholars as Paulus Fabritius, imperial astronomer (*mathematicus*), personal physician to the emperor, botanist, and poet. Among the other scholars at court were Johannes Sambucus, court historiographer, compiler of an important emblem book, and an important book collector; Hugo Blotius, imperial librarian, and avid correspondent; Lazarus Schwendi, military commander but promoter of irenicism; Jacopo Strada, antiquarian, architect, and fountain designer; and Johannes Crato, imperial physician and philosopher. Also found at Maximilian's court were the botanists Carolus Clusius (Charles de l'Ecluse), Rembert Dodoens, as well as Matthioli, who are mentioned in an earlier chapter. Other important thinkers and writers, including Philip Sidney, poet, Guillaume Postel, cabalist, and Peter Canisius, Jesuit educator, all worked in or passed through Vienna, where they had contact with the court.

Rudolf II inherited the group of scholars who had gathered at Maximilian's court, much as he did the original nucleus of artists, including Arcimboldo, who also were to serve him during the first part of his reign. Several of the most important figures who later worked in Prague, among them the renowned astronomers Theodore Hagecius von Hayek, Tycho Brahe, and Johannes Kepler

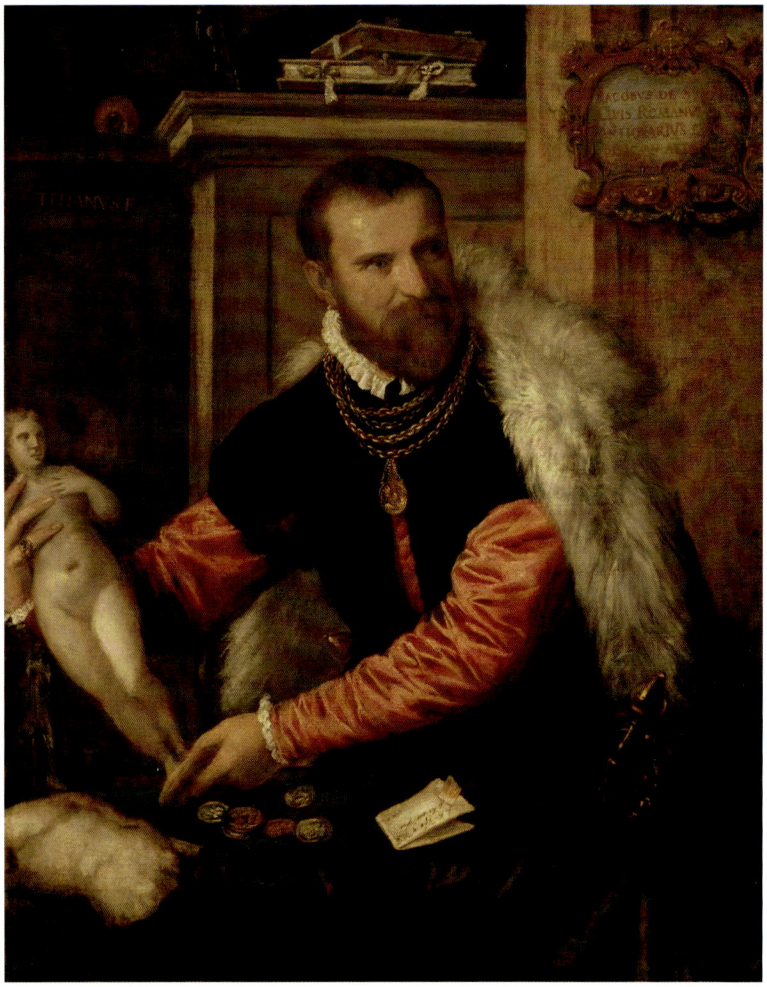

Fig. 1. Titian, *Jacopo Strada*. Vienna, Kunsthistorisches Museum, Gemäldegalerie

also wrote poetry and engaged in other humanist pursuits. Although these men were active at the imperial court after Arcimboldo had already left it, a connection may nevertheless be traced between the artist and this group, too. His drawings for the silk industry were presented to Ferdinand Hoffmann von Grünpichl und Strechau, and are found in a book from his large library; Hoffmann was a man of learning who was well known to literary circles, and he was to mediate between Brahe and Kepler (Kepler dedicated one of his treatises to Hoffmann)[5].

Although some scholars have sought to distinguish between the manners of expression, activities, and interests of humanists or poets and those of artists, and to minimize or downplay the significance of their collaboration and mutual impact, an ever increasing amount of information also indicates that this argument does not hold in many cases, particularly not in regard to the imperial court, and especially not in regard to Arcimboldo[6]. Many of the scholars mentioned hitherto were simultaneously humanists, scientists, and artists (at least of the amateur variety). Johannes Kepler was among other things a draftsman[7]. Lazius made the maps himself that he published in his cartographic works; he also did both the drawings that he employed as models for the illustrations in his books, and the etchings or engravings after them[8]. Another of Rudolf II's physicians, Anselmus Boethius De Boodt, the author of the first scholarly treatise on gems, assembled a large group of nature studies, which he annotated, and he drew many of these studies himself[9]. Drawing was central to Strada's antiquarian endeavours: they were used as the basis for illustrations in his publications on numismatics, and his corpus of drawings was replicated and presented in numerous manuscripts for potential patrons, his so-called *libri di disegni*. These were books on a wide variety of subjects, including devices (*imprese*), numismatics, and fountains[10].

Several scholars collaborated with artists in organizing entries and tournaments. For example, Lazius was called upon to design the imagery of the arches erected for the first royal entry of Maximilian II into Vienna, held on 16 March 1563. Lazius both wrote the inscriptions that appeared on the arches, and invented their visual imagery[11]. A tournament was held on the occasion of the entry[12]. Artists collaborating on the actual execution of the arches for the 1563 entry moreover had intellectual aspirations themselves[13]. One of them, Melchior Lorch, had travelled to Constantinople; like Lazius, Lorch was interested in chorography and the history of the ancient Germans, and later entered the circle of the antiquarian and cartographer Abraham Ortelius[14]. Heinrich Vogtherr the Younger is also documented as having painted the arches for the Vienna entry: Vogtherr was a many-sided artist who had participated in the publication of his father's *Kunstbüchlein*, one of the handbooks published in the wake of Albrecht Dürer's theoretical tracts[15].

Other humanists collaborated with artists on similar events during the reign of Rudolf II. For Rudolf's 1577 entry into Vienna, the first held there after he had gained the imperial title, Paulus Fabritius, court astronomer, and like Lazius simultaneously professor of medicine at the university, designed several triumphal arches. Fabritius supplied the inscriptions and invented the programmes for the arches, which were erected and decorated by a company of artists, including the painter Bartholomäus Spranger, later to become a major figure at Rudolf's court, and the sculptors Hans Mont and Matthias Monmacher[16]. Fabritius not only supplied a demonstation of the Copernican and Ptolemaic systems for the arch, but he also specifically says that he served as humanist advisor on this project. An exchange thus occurred about their "inventions and personifications": the artists convinced the humanist to substitute a figure of Pegasus for a pyramid on top of one of the arches for the sake of variety, ornament, and novelty. The application of rhetorical criteria such as these moreover suggests that the artists were applying poetic (or rhetorical) principles to the visual arts, as in other demonstrable cases in Rudolfine Prague[17].

Arcimboldo may be shown to have associated with some of these men, and he also worked directly with another humanist on other projects. Paolo Morigia provides evidence for what was possibly his earliest contact with a court humanist. Morigia says that Arcimboldo had supplied him material on the origins and history of his family that came from an old book in parchment, written in German, which Maximilian's physician had read to the artist. The physician had ascertained that there were two places named Arcimboldo, that cemeteries in Augsburg and Regensburg had tombs with the arms of Arcimboldo, and that there were many Arcimboldi in many German cities[18]. Arcimboldo's source also supplied mythic origins for the family in pre-Carolingian Germany, and a fantastic etymology for the family name. This German physician was most likely Lazius: the fantastic genealogy, the made up etymology, and the antiquarian interests all characterize his approach to scholarship. Arcimboldo's interest in genealogy also represents a concern shared more generally by humanits[19]. It mirrors Lazius's efforts to create a genealogy of the Habsburgs, which appeared in print most fully in a book published in 1564, and was hence probably in press at the very time that Arcimboldo was arriving in Vienna[20].

While Jacopo Strada was one of Lazius's antagonists, he also collaborated with Arcimboldo. Strada (*fig. 1*) was an art dealer, architect, advisor of collectors, and himself a collector of coins and manuscripts, as well as being a renowned scholar of antiquity. From 1558 Strada appeared on the payrolls of the imperial court. Soon thereafter he became embroiled in a controversy with Lazius, when he severely criticized the commentary on the imperial coin collection which Lazius had prepared[21]. Strada's evident ambitions to be advisor in such matters, which epitomize among other things his striving to be taken seriously as a humanist, came to fruition in 1563, the year of Arcimboldo's arrival at court: in that year he was appointed imperial *antiquarius*. In the role of imperial *antiquarius* Strada advised the emperor on acquisitions and in general seems to have overseen the imperial collections. In 1565 in Vienna he designed an important arcaded structure for Maximilian II, the Stallburg, in which both the imperial horses and art collections were housed. From c. 1568 he was probably involved in designing the Neugebäude, a noteworthy imperial villa located to the east of Vienna, near the imperial palace at Kaiserseberdorf, for which he supplied fountains and other water works[22]. At the Neugebäude Strada also collaborated with numerous artists, probably including Spranger, who was soon thereafter to become a leading painter at Rudolf II's court[23].

One compendium of Strada drawings includes designs for costumes and horse trappings appropriate for festivals, including a drawing for an elephant (*fig. 2*). An inscription indicates that this drawing was made for the tournament of 1571, where Arcimboldo invented and designed costumes for the programme, and a payment to Strada made in 1571 also establishes that he was in Vienna at the time[24]. The inscription on the drawing of the elephant points to the probable function of other sheets in the volume, as well as to his participation, hence collaboration with Arcimboldo.

As noted above (see the essay by A. Beyer in this catalogue), another Italian born humanist, who was also a draftsman, also worked closely with Arcimboldo on the 1571 tournament and on other projects. This was Giovanni Battista Fonteo (or Fontana; Fonteius in Latin) who can be demonstrated to have worked with Arcimboldo at least during the years 1568 to 1572. Fonteo presented poems on the artist's pictures to accompany them as a gift to Maximilian II on New Year's Day 1569, and wrote the cartel, or programme, for the 1571 Vienna tournament. One copy of this programme, probably written in Fonteo's hand, survives, and is inscribed with the names of Arcimboldo as its *fabricator*, and Fonteo as its *coordinator*. Fonteo also wrote a lengthy description of the 1571 celebrations, including a ball and masquerade, and composed poems which were set to music at the festival. His description of the 1570 Prague tournament suggests that he was most likely involved in that event as well, and he may also have worked with Arcimboldo on a tournament held in Bratislava in 1572[25]. Like Strada, Fonteo was not only a humanist, but a draftsman. This is demonstrated by a drawing of a tournament procession which bears a complex monogram containing all the letters of his name[26].

Present at the imperial court at the latest by the end of 1568, Fonteo must have remained part of its entourage for several years. In 1570 he dedicated a treatise on laughter, *De Risu* – about which more presently – to the Venetian ambassador to the emperor, Michele Frangipani. According to references in *De Risu*, Fonteo travelled with the court during its peregrinations through Germany, Austria, and Hungary.[27] In 1571 Fonteo also delivered a funeral oration in Saint Veit's Cathedral in Prague for Melchiore Biglia, a Milanese patrician born c. 1510 who had been papal nuntio to the imperial court from 1565 until his death in Prague 22 April 1571. In this long (ninety folios) oration, which survives in an unpublished manuscript, which has not previously been discussed, Fonteo notes that he had met Biglia three years before, and provides much other information about court personalities and activities.[28]

The manuscripts Fonteo presented to the emperor and to Frangipani (*De Risu*) no doubt were given in anticipation of some sort of payment in gratitude, and suggest that he was not paid a direct salary by the court. Perhaps it was out of a desire for recognition, or a search for further employment that Fonteo may have claimed to have designed the 1571 tournament, which Gian Paolo Lomazzo says was the cause of a break with Arcimboldo[29].

Fonteo had been born in Milan c. 1547[30], a nephew of Primo Conti (or del Conte), erudite master of sacred scripture at the Collegio

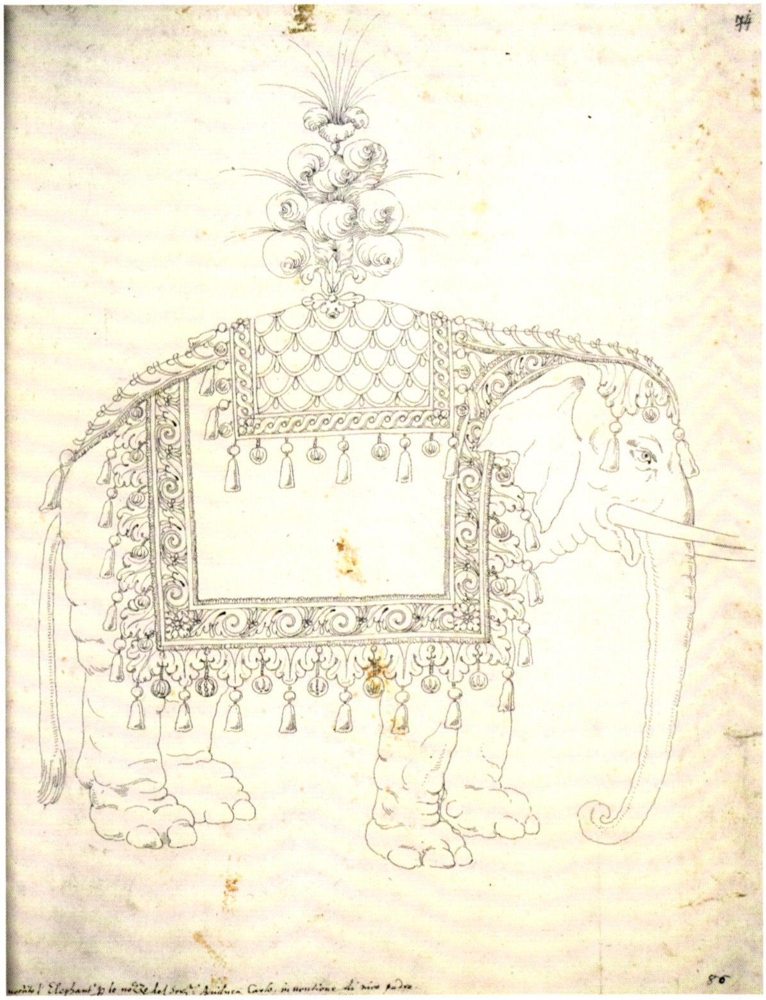

Fig. 2. Jacopo Strada, *Sketch for the Trappings of an Elephant, on the Occasion of a Tournament in Vienna*, 1571. Vienna, Österreichische Nationalbibliothek, Handschriftensammlung, Cod. min. 21

Ambrosiano in Milan, and a participant at the Council of Trent[31]. Fonteo's devotion to his uncle's interests is evinced not only by the fact that he took his name (he signs himself *Primionis*), but by his edition of the spiritual letters and biography of the Angelic sister Paola Antonia Negri, centre of the female branch of the Barnabites and an important spiritual reformer[32]. Negri's letters had earlier inspired Primo Conti, who had promoted them to the Council of Trent[33]. Primo Conti formed the nucleus of a group of Lombard admirers of Erasmus, whose teachings he imparted to his pupils, as is evident in a treatise by the most distinguished of them, Marco Antonio Maioragio, son of Giuliano Conti, otherwise known as Julianus Comes, and thus also another relative of Fonteo. Maioragio also provides a link between the Conti circle and antiquarianism, seen in the person of Andrea Alciati, a prominent Milanese jurist who is however best known as the inventor of emblem books[34].

Fonteo's background thus leads us to literati circles in Lombardy, with which Arcimboldo had already associated before he came north, and with whom he was certainly closely connected after he returned home in 1587. Francesco Melzi, the inheritor of Leonardo's manuscripts, and the compiler of the so-called *Treatise on Painting* attributed to Leonardo, had in 1559 judged a competition for the design of the organ shutters of Milan Cathedral in which Arcimboldo had participated. Bartolomeo Taegio, another important Milanese intellectual, was in 1564 one of the judges for a similar competition for the design of a standard of Saint Ambrose in which Arcimboldo had also engaged. Taegio also provides another link to the Milan of Andrea Alciati, the above mentioned humanist and legal scholar who invented emblem books, and hence to circles around Primo Conti[35].

While Taegio's and Melzi's connections with Arcimboldo are perhaps indirect, other Milanese intellectuals wrote about him, and several were demonstrably close associates of the artist. Morigia, Lomazzo, and the canon Gregorio Comanini, poet and art theorist, all wrote about Arcimboldo. Giovanni Filippo Gherardini, mathematician, musician, and poet, and member of the Accademia degli Affidati of Pavia[36], was named by Arcimboldo to be his beneficiary in a codicil to a will notarized in Milan on 17 March 1581[37]. A document of 17 May 1588 indicates that Gherardini had sold a house to Arcimboldo[38]. It is possible that this is the house in which both Gherardini and Arcimboldo were living c. 1590, when Comanini says he was also there[39].

In 1591 Gherardini published a booklet with poems in Latin and Italian on Arcimboldo's *Flora* and *Vertumnus*. This book contains three poems by Gherardini himself, one of which also appears in Lomazzo's *Idea* of 1590[40]. Another of his poems also alludes to Arcimboldo and Figino and "my Arcimboldo"[41]. The poems Gherardini assembled probably correspond as well to those Lomazzo mentions in *Idea*[42]. They bear on another statement by Morigia that many learned people wrote poems in Arcimboldo's honour, specifically naming as authors those figures whose works are included in the booklet[43]. Several of these poems (by Bernardino Baldini, Borgogni, and others) on Arcimboldo were also printed elsewhere[44].

The practice of writing poems on paintings was widespread in the Renaissance, and it seems to have been prevalent in Milan c. 1590 where attention was paid and poems written on paintings by Fede Galizia, Giovanni Ambrogio Figino[45]. Comanini's art treatise is named after the painter Figino, and it stages a dialogue in which that painter and the learned ecclesiastic and writer Stefano Guazzo participate. This suggests a close connection between humanism and painting in Milan c. 1590.

A large compendium of poems in manuscript (British Library, London), in many different hands, mainly on Figino, also demonstrates this connection. This includes a poem of self-praise by Figino himself, who like Bronzino and Michelangelo was a poet as well as a painter. It now appears that Arcimboldo was, too.

Among the poems in Gherardini's compilation are two by a G. A. da Milano, one a madrigal praising the painting of *Vertumnus*, the other a sonnet praising Arcimboldo's paintings in general. No other contemporaneous Milanese writer seems to have had these initials, and Arcimboldo uses this form of signature, as in Giuseppe Arcimboldo da Milano (cat. no. II.15). Like Figino, he therefore wrote praising himself. Arcimboldo's poetry may be read variously: like his paintings, it reveals his knowledge of antique sources and myths, and leads us to a larger conception of his learning and interests. Its recondite references are signs of Arcimboldo's learning.

Other evidence for Arcimboldo's learning exists. The complicated programmes for the 1570 and 1571 ceremonies held in Prague and Vienna employ many references to antique sources. Arcimboldo's costumes were based on descriptions in a variety of ancient authors, and these stem not merely from his humanist advisors[46]. His antiquarian interests are revealed in a letter which accompanied drawings for silk making proposed to Hoffmann[47]. According to a letter of 8 September 1582 from Rudolf II to Raimund Dorn in Kempten, Arcimboldo was sent to Kempten to inspect all kinds of antiquities and works of art which the emperor wished to purchase[48]. He was to make a selection, and to bring the antiquities back himself, if the objects were not going to be sent. Hence he was obviously highly regarded as an expert judge of antiquities as well as works of art – which speaks for his antiquarian, hence humanistic expertise.

These humanist connections and poems are important for gaining insights into Arcimboldo's paintings. The pictures employ devices like metaphor, metonymy, and allegory much as do the poems written by the artist as well as the witty, complex, highly intellectual poems by several other authors who wrote on Arcimboldo; both poems and paintings are full of conceits (*concetti*). Although obviously distinctive in their qualities, the two media were evidently thought about in similar manner by Arcimboldo. One of the poems relies on an elegy by Propertius – the genre of Arcimboldo's own poem; Propertius's poem also served as the ultimate source for the details in his painting of Vertumnus, to whose meaning it also provides clues.

Arcimboldo's painting of Vertumnus may be regarded as the culmination of messages suggested by the pictures of the *Seasons* and *Elements*. A poem by Fonteo accompanying these paintings when they were given to the emperor indicates that the original versions of these pictures were meant to be understood as imperial allegories. Fonteo describes at length how harmony exists between the paintings of the *Elements* and the *Seasons*, how they are to be seen in harmonious conjunction, how this betokens the emperor's reign, and how the eternal cycle of the seasons suggests the eternity of Habsburg rule. He also adds that the choice of heads is related to the prophetic discovery of a head under the foundations of the Capitoline, indicating that Rome would be *caput mundi*. While many claims by Fonteo may be literary embellishments, it is not impossible that Arcimboldo may have been cognizant of them and agreed to them – even, considering his familiarity with a prophetic poem by Propertius, this last allusion too.

Although the pictures of the *Seasons* and *Elements* were given several years after they had been completed, there is also no reason to doubt that, however much Fonteo may have embellished their content, he conveyed Arcimboldo's intentions. Arcimboldo was soon to employ Fonteo as his spokesman for festivals, and he certainly later approved the practice of supplying explanatory poems for his pictures: he clearly was familiar with the poems that Comanini and others had presented along with *Vertumnus* when that picture was given to the emperor, since, as noted, he added his own poems to the group, which also contains poems on Arcimboldo's painting of *Flora*[49]. Other poems on *Flora* had accompanied it as well to the imperial court.

Comanini's poems on *Flora* and *Vertumnus*, which also appear in his own treatise of 1591, *Il Figino*, functioned like the other poems in Gherardini's booklet and much as Fonteo's poem had done when it was presented along with the *Seasons* and *Elements*. Much like Fonteo's poems were to serve to explain paintings of the seasons and elements to Maximilian II, Comanini's and his contemporaries' poems explicate the paintings of *Flora* and *Vertumnus* made for Rudolf II. *Inter alia*, Comanini identifies the *Vertumnus* as a portrait of Rudolf II.

Rudolf is shown as god of the seasons, and comparable also to god of the elements. All the seasons are however shown existing together in one image alone in this head, and their conjunction signifies that a new golden age of one undifferentiated season has come with the reign of Rudolf II. Rudolf II's rule as Holy Roman Emperor is thus as a ruler of a new Rome, which will enjoy the kind of eternal domination of the world which was foretold for ancient Rome in the elegy by Propertius on which Arcimboldo's picture is based.

Beside their serious message, Arcimboldo's paintings, like his tournaments, for several of which Fonteo also wrote the cartel (see Kaufmann 1978) and grotesques, also obviously have an entertaining side. While Comanini's treatise deals with questions of imitation, his discussion of humour, and of Arcimboldo's pictures, must have been regarded as appropriate topics of conversation at court. The role of humour and especially joking at court is indicated by Baldassare Castiglione's *Cortegiano*, and envisaged by Guazzo, the interlocutor in his dialogue, and the author of treatises on conversation. The role of jokes in providing a pastime or point of conversation is also suggested by Bartolomeo Taegio, who, as noted, was also linked, albeit not immediately, to Arcimboldo. Taegio's treatise on the *Villa* establishes conversation as an aspect of affability and urbanity. Conversation was a form of recreation in which games, sayings (*motti*), and jokes (*burle*), if not too biting, could be employed. This situation may well correspond to the actual context in which Arcimboldo's paintings were viewed. These topics are further discussed in Fonteo's treatise on laughter, which also suggests the dialogue structure, and imagines a context for such activities.

Laughter and jokes are close to Arcimboldo's imagery, but Arcimboldo's composite images may thus hint at much more than mere entertainment. In them the serious is not separated from the ridiculous, but may be contained within it, or represent it when inverted. The serious is also not separated from the playful, or even the ridiculous, in his art.

Writers on Arcimboldo make such arguments. Comanini directly evokes the notion of serious jokes in his poem on Arcimboldo's *Vertumnus*. He also adumbrates what this idea may further signify when he explains why the viewer must halt the reaction of laughter to realize that the picture hides serious content. After mentioning its risible quality, Comanini immediately alerts the viewer of the painting that there is something more to its monstrosity. In revealing that the "kingly image" is a portrait of Rudolf II, Comanini thus makes known that the source for the conceit is the idea implicit ancient Sileni – that an ugly, monstrous, or risible exterior may hide something beautiful, or heavenly.

This is an ultimately Erasmian message – one thinks of the *Adages* and the *Praise of Folly*. In particular, it is suggested by the adage of the Sileni of Alcibiades, whose roots go back to a theme presented first in Plato's *Symposium*, where the image had originally been applied to Socrates. Erasmus developed this adage to apply to a variety of circumstances in which something seemingly ugly contained something beautiful, or, as in his *Praise of Folly*, something risible actually expressed something serious. This concept was well known during the Renaissance (Rabelais among others cites it as a key to interpreting his own work). And we now know that through Fonteo, and through the imperial connections with Erasmus and Erasmian moderation (evinced at the court of Maximilian II)[50], these notions may be applied directly to Arcimboldo.

Arcimboldo's paintings may be regarded as a kind of *scherzo*, or joke, but they are serious jokes. Arcimboldo's own inclinations, the milieu in which they were created, and in which they were also received, would all have led to an understanding of how his images may have operated as such. As Comanini's *Il Figino* demonstrates with reference to Arcimboldo's pictures, the art of painting may both instruct and delight. In this way painting may strive for effects like those of poetry, as was stated in a staple of poetic theory since antiquity: instruction should be mixed with delight, the useful should be mixed with the sweet.

As seen in previous essays, Arcimboldo's paintings engage many concepts of art and nature. Arcimboldo was not just an artificer of fantasy, but a learned painter with literary aspirations who was also a scrupulous imitator of nature. His pictures may be related to the Kunstkammer, or cabinet of curiosities, but in the way that that entity too was enmeshed in a world in which it incorporated and could facilitate not only wonder and curiosity, but naturalistic investigations and at the same time also represent political or social claims[51].

Arcimboldo's intriguing images, made out of his imagination, also may present imperial allegories. At the same time his composite heads and invertible images may paradoxically claim a significant place in the development of the naturalistic genres of animal painting and still life. But the keys to the many ways in which they work – which may be further elaborated – are to be found in the humanist and literary appropriation of the classical tradition[52].

[1] See Berra 1996, for the latter argument about this drawing.

[2] See for these points the brief and useful summary in Seipel 2003, 326, and for the general context Mraz 2003.

[3] This approach is related to what has been described as the climate of moderation in religious matters that existed at the imperial court, where some of the imperial advisers "openly displayed Erasmian sympathies and approved of colloquy". Evans 1979, 19.

[4] Evans 1973, 118. Evans 1973, 118-129, and Evans 1979, 20-24 provides an introduction to this group. See further for more detail on several figures discussed here Louthan 1997 and Mühlberger 1992.

[5] See Evans 1973, 153-154; Kaufmann 1993.

[6] Cf. Charles Hope, 42, following McGrath1985, 130-132. See also Porzio 1993, especially 37-38.

[7] For two prominent examples from the period of Rudolf II, see Grafton, 1991, 178-203; and for Kepler's drawing, see Alpers 1983, especially 49-50. For Tycho Brahe, see most recently Christianson 2006.

[8] It has been argued that Lazius turned to making his own illustrations because of a want of professional artists and engravers in Austria. See Goffart 2003, 61-62. This may be possible, because many artists had to be called to the imperial court; even figures active in Vienna, such as Melchior Lorch, with whom Lazius collaborated on the arches, were only there for a short while – Lorch was formally in the service of the king of Denmark.

[9] See Maselis, Balis and Marijnissen 1999.

[10] There is an extensive bibliography now on Strada. For this aspect of his work and his activity at the court of Maximilian II see Jansen 1992.

[11] Sources for this entry are Lazius 1563; Stainhofer 1566, reprinted, with its illustrations of the arches, in Wunsch 1914, 25-31.

[12] For interpretations of the entry see Louthan 1997, 34-42, and also Chabrowe 1970, 114-122, and 180ff.; see also Kaufmann 1978, 27.

[13] See Uhlirz 1897, no. 15749, 15764, 15778.

[14] For an introduction in English to this dimension of the work of Lorch, see Kaufmann 1982b, cat. no. 13-15. For the Ortelius circle see Meganck 2003.

[15] For this category, see Schlosser 1964, 276-280.

[16] See Kaufmann 1993, 136-150.

[17] Kaufmann 1993, 148-150. The theme of the application of rhetorical and poetical ideals to painting in Rudolfine Prague was elaborated in Kaufmann 1982a, and then in many subsequent publications.

[18] Morigia 1592, 556.

[19] Lazius was also deeply concerned with genealogy: see e.g. Lazius 1564. This had been a preoccupation of the Habsburgs since the time of Maximilian I (reigned 1493-1519). Lacking connections with older royal houses, as well as

ancient noble origins, the Habsburgs, like many other arriviste monarchs, created their own roots, setting them in a legendary past. See Lhotsky 1971, Lazius's research also often resulted in the production of what have been called "incredible genealogies": see the comment on Lazius in Bizocchi 1995, 47. Lazius's antiquarian researches aided his genealogical investigations. In addition to being an avid coin collector and numismatist, Lazius collected books and other antiquities. He evidently travelled to do research as well. Like other humanist antiquarians, Lazius used the visible relics of the past to comment on or construct an account of the past. See Lazius 1558. See further for this subject Cunnally 1999.
[20] See Lazius 1564.
[21] Louthan 1997, 28. See further 1995, 172f.
[22] See in particular Kaufmann 2002.
[23] See Lietzmann 1987, 152ff. and *passim*.
[24] For Strada's involvement in the 1571 tournament, and the evidence for it, see Kaufmann 1978, 61-64, fig. 45, illustrating Österreichische Nationalbibliothek Cod. Min. 21/3, fol. 74r, which is inscribed by Ottavio Strada "E fu vestito l'Elephant per le nozze del Serenissimo Arciduca Carlo, inuentione di mio padre".
[25] For information on and sources for the collaboration of Fonteo and Arcimboldo on tournaments, see Kaufmann 1978, 28-43.
[26] As indicated clearly in Kaufmann 1978, fig. 35: the basis for the attribution is misstated by Berra 1996, 59n. This drawing will be exhibited in the Arcimboldo exhibition, now in preparation, where the monogram will be evident.
[27] Vienna, Österreichische Nationalbibliothek, cod. 10466, *De Risu, sive quo risus sit virtus, Dialogus Ioanni Michaelio Frangipani Veneto penes Caesarem oratori dicatus*, dedicated at Speyer, 1570; see fol. 2v-3r for Fonteo's peregrinations with the court.
[28] "Oratio habita Pragae in summo arcis templo pro funere Melchioris Biliae internuntii pontificii coram regum oratoribus et caesarea curia", Vienna, Österreichische Nationalbibliothek, Cod. 7802.
[29] Lomazzo on Fonteo.
[30] For Fonteo's biography, see Savio 1905.
[31] For Primo Conti see Paltrinieri 1805.
[32] See De Klerck 1999, 144-145.
[33] Fonteo 1576, 70; see further Savio 1905, 342-350.
[34] Maioragio wrote a treatise on eloquence which he named in honour of Conti, *Primus Comes seu de eloquentia*. For Maioragio, see Seidel Menchi 1987, 276; the description of Maioragio is from Albonico 1995, 208; for the link with Alciati, see Seidel Menchi, 234, 276. Maioragio's text is printed in Paltrinieri 1805.
[35] Seidel Menchi 1987, 276.
[36] For the biography and bibliography of Gherardini, see Argelati 1745, col. 679.
[37] This document was first found and published by Miller 1989, 22-23, no. 14. The original will has however not yet been found, and does not seem recoverable.
[38] Berra 2000, 81, no. 1, publishes a document to this effect.
[39] Comanini in Barocchi 1962, 257.
[40] Gherardini 1591. See for this collection, and for Gherardini's biography, Berra 1988, 11-39.
[41] *Canzone*, in Gherardini 1588, 6:
Zeusi non ci è, serbi di lei il mortale
nè suoi colori, l'Arcimboldo mio,
o il Figino gentile
[42] Lomazzo 1590 [1973], 364.
[43] Morigia 1595, 279.
[44] Borgogni 1592, 140 (on Arcimboldo); 1, 2, 15, 16, 17 (on Figino); Borgogni 1594, pt. 2, 19 (on Arcimboldo), 31 (Comanini on Figino); Baldini 1600, 43 and 44 (on Arcimboldo; with an epitaph of Arcimbldo on 44).
[45] In addition to the poems on Figino and Arcimboldo discussed here, see the comments and poems on Fede Galizia in Borgogni 1598, 39f.
[46] See Kaufmann 1978.
[47] Kaufmann 1993, 151-173. This matter will be dealt with anew by Philippe Morel in the forthcoming Arcimboldo exhibition catalogue.
[48] Geiger 1954, 124-125, citing *Jahrbuch der kunsthistorischen Sammlungen des Allerhöchsten Kaiserhauses*, vol. 5, 1887, reg. no. 4565.
[49] See initially for this subject Kaufmann 1978.
[51] See Louthan 1997.
[51] See Kaufmann 1993.
[52] The present essay is a condensed version of arguments presented in my Kaufmann forthcoming; the other themes alluded to in this and the preceding paragraphs are also presented in this book.

Appendix

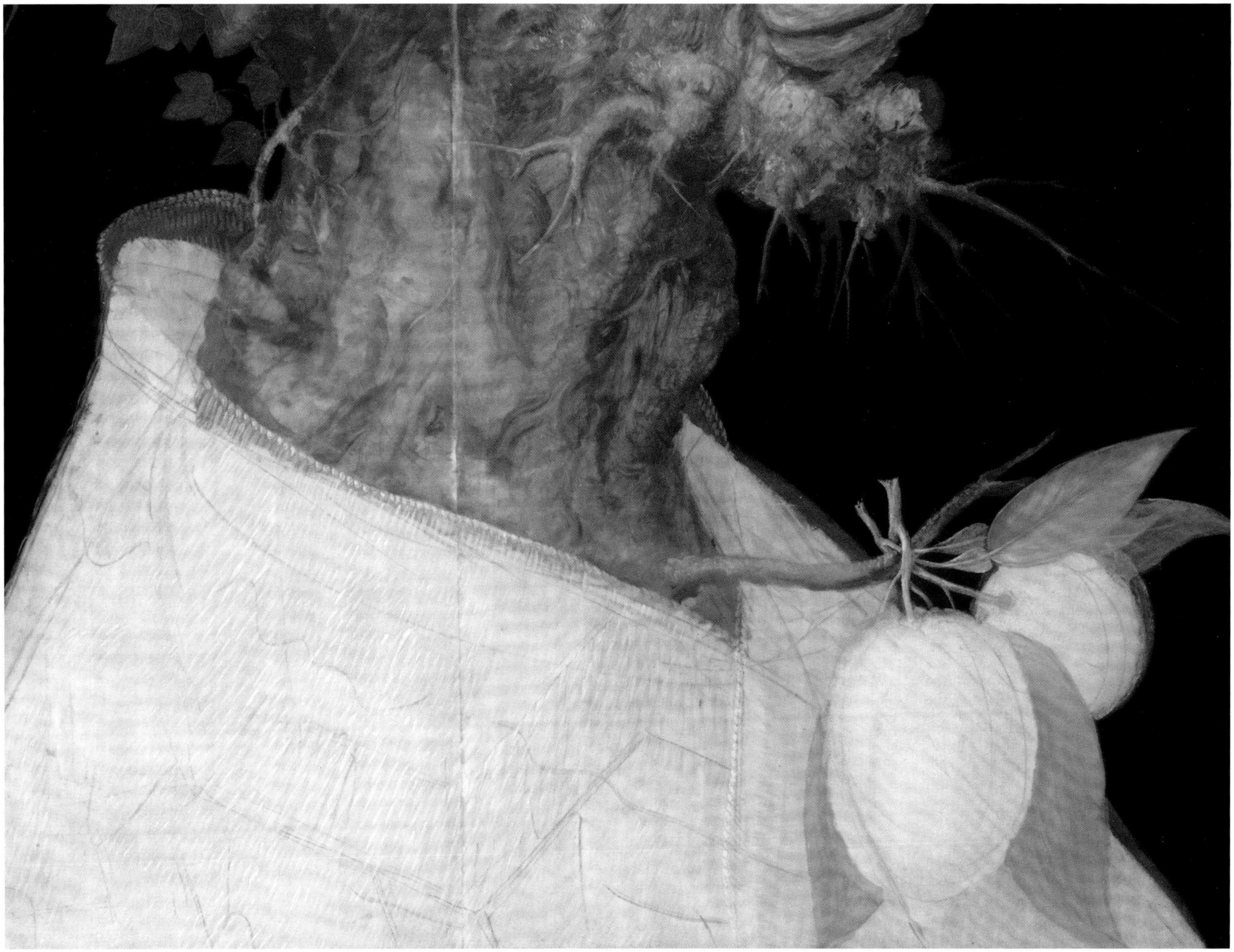

Ina Slama and Monika Strolz

Observations on the Painting Technique of Arcimboldo and his Circle

Up to now little has been known or published on Arcimboldo's painting technique. This present study provides the opportunity of becoming better-acquainted with his paintings from a technical point of view.

Arcimboldo's four *Teste Composte* – *Summer, Winter, Fire, Water* – to be found in the Gemäldegalerie of the Kunsthistorisches Museum – were first examined in terms of the material structure and their state of preservation[1] during their restoration in 1996-97. The more recent studies now also include digital infrared reflectography[2], X-radiography[3] as well as scientific analyses of the paint layers and the supports.

Alongside his famous "heads" Arcimboldo, in his function as court painter, also painted portraits, however, little is known concerning this aspect of his production. Other than a painted self-portrait and several portrait drawings no other likenesses are firmly attributed to him. Consequently, the family portrait of Maximilian II (circa 1565) (cat. no. III.4), as well as six portraits from a series of Archduchesses from the second half of the 16th century (cat. nos. III.5 to III.10), all attributed to Arcimboldo became part of this survey.

Giuseppe Arcimboldo, *Winter* (cat. no. IV.4)
Painting technique and underdrawing

This painting has a light grey, slightly pinkish ground in one layer, consisting of lead white, red lead and carbon black.[4] This is unlike the *Summer*, which is also dated 1563, and shows evidence of a multi layer ground. Examination under the microscope of the paint surface shows that Arcimboldo used various different colours of underpaint for selected paint passages. The rows of ivy and branches composing part of the head are underpainted in brown (*fig. 1*). The colour of the underpaint was utilized as a middle tone for the image, as it remained visible between the applications of the overlying layers. The face and neck, however appear to be underpainted in light beige and grey hues (*fig. 2*). In painting the background Arcimboldo left a reserve for the area of the figure. As it is visible in the infrared reflectogram (*fig. 3*), the reserve is somewhat smaller than the final painted figure and only loosely defines its contours. Those elements which subsequently extended over the reverse into the background colour appear darker, for instance the upper part of the collar or the tip of the nose.

In observing the X-radiograph one notices vertical bands of varying width (*fig. 4*). They are the result of the grain of the wooden support, for which tangentially cut boards were used.[5] *Pentimenti* are visible in the citrus fruits. Both fruits were enlarged in the underdrawing stage, as indicated by the multiple drawn outlines. Additionally one can see that the painted edges of the fruits extend over the contour of the reserve.

In this picture the underdrawing has a special characteristic. It is not – as is normally the case – on top of the ground, but rather was applied over the underpaint layers, at a more developed stage in the painting process. This can be related to the purpose of the underdrawing, which can be best illustrated through the numerous drawn lines in the straw braid of the cloak, which help to define the contours of the braided pattern. Following these indications, Arcimboldo painted the straw with exactly aligned *impasto* brushstrokes (*fig. 5*). Alongside we find loosely directed, wavy lines which were not followed in the paint stage. The run of the collar and the contours of both shoulders were laid down with several slightly varying lines. The head and the neck reveal another way of working. The underdrawing here is more freely set out, offering vague suggestions of roots, ivy leaves or similar elements, which only occasionally fit in with the finished painting.

Giuseppe Arcimboldo, *Water* (cat. no. IV.26)
Painting technique and underdrawing

The light ground in this painting is built up in one layer and contains lead white, carbon black and some chalk. Compared to the other three paintings, *Water* presents exceptions on various points. The proportion of lead white in the ground layer appears to be comparatively less and it contains some vermilion instead of red lead. Looking at the X-radiograph (*fig. 6*) one has the impression that the ground layer was applied by brush rather than with a palette knife. These differences in the composition of the ground layer as well as the different mode of its application clearly show up in the X-radiograph, as does the different wooden support, which consists of alder instead of lime wood, as stated below. Another important difference is the presence of an unpainted margin and a barbe along the top edge of *Water*. The lack of unpainted margins on the other paintings might be the result of a later change in format.

In all probability here too a reserve was left for the area of the figure. When examining the work using infrared reflectography this is less discernable than in the other paintings, which may be attributed to the overall darker colouring.

Very surprising was the fact that no evidence of underdrawing was found. This might be due to the drawing material used and/or to the colouring of the animals, since many of them contain black or have dark outlines, making any identification of an underlying drawing somewhat more difficult. It is hardly imaginable, that this very picture with its sophisticated positioning of elements could not have some type of underdrawing.

Concerning the painting technique, many similarities with the other pictures exist. Here too we find a brown underpaint (*figg. 7, 8*) that is often used as a middle tone. The mode of applying the paint ranges from thinly painted parts to those built up in several layers; white highlights applied *impasto* are to be found along with areas that were painted wet-in-wet (*figg. 9, 10*). Arcimboldo used shell gold for two fishes (*fig. 11*). The overall reduced scale of execution and the level of detail within the image and its method and style of application differentiate the *Water* from the other paintings.

Giuseppe Arcimboldo, *Summer* (cat. no. IV.3)
Painting technique and underdrawing

The ground in this painting consists of several layers, as was confirmed by cross-section analysis of a paint sample. A lower, grey layer is followed by two further brick red ground layers.[6] White and red lead pigments are to be found among the components of all three layers. In this picture too we find – consistent with the observations made on the other three – a reserve for the figure and an underpaint in a warm brown tone for the area of the head (*fig. 12*). Apart from the rather thinly painted background the paint in general was built up in several layers. Highlights have been applied using *impasto*, particularly visible in the area of the straw garment, where Arcimboldo has "woven in" his signature and the date (*fig. 13*). Final accents, such as the delicate strokes used to paint the ears of corn or the corrections of outlines applied on top of the background, appear to have been painted in a tempera-bound colour, since the paint has beaded up in tiny pools over the underlying layer (*figg. 14 to 16*).

Consistent with the findings in *Winter* the X-radiograph of *Summer* shows the same prominent structure of the wooden support which consists of tangentially cut boards (*fig. 17*). Clearer than in the other paintings, here the wood grain is visible on the surface of the painting, particularly in the thinly painted parts (*fig. 18*). The thin scratches or grooves in the preparation that are to be seen both in the X-radiograph and on the picture surface, probably arise from the application of the ground with a knife or spatula. Due to the high proportion of lead in the ground the X-radiograph appears rather dense, this is why from the *pentimenti* present only the enlargement of the aubergine can be recognised. The other *pentimenti* are visible within the picture itself: for the most part they are a question of minor corrections in terms of size or outline of single pieces of fruit or vegetables; for example with the gherkin that forms the nose or the pear on the chin. In the group of plums top right the stalk of the left plum has been moved to the right. In the centre of the head the relief of some leaves are to be seen, later replaced by cherries and smaller leaves.

Infrared reflectography (*fig. 19*) revealed underdrawing in various parts of the painting. The type of underdrawing is very different from that in *Winter*. In the area of the straw garment only sporadic and very fine lines could be detected, while similarly Arcimboldo weaved in his signature and patterns. On the side in the cheek the light toned vegetable with the stalk facing downwards is underdrawn with several lines. In comparison to the painted stage the stalk in the underdrawing is considerably longer. The character of these lines is clearly different from that of the lines found in the rest of the picture which are finer and more precise. These are mostly contours or indications for the placement of twigs etc. They, for example, can be seen in the garlic, in the gherkin, in the plums top right or in the peach, where in addition several diagonally running lines are visible. The light, vertical running marks in the face are due to the wooden structure (*fig. 19*). One notes traces of a strongly diluted paint applied by brush – almost like a wash, partially following the forms, partially flowing downwards. This is visible for example in the area of the corncob and the garlic or on the collar right. It probably served as an initial indication of forms or areas of shadow.

Giuseppe Arcimboldo, *Fire* (cat. no. IV.27)
Painting technique and underdrawing

Fire shows the same layer structure as *Summer*, which is dated three years earlier. The cross-section of a paint sample shows a ground which was built up in three layers in the same colour succession.[7]

The X-radiograph of the picture shows great similarity with that of *Summer* and *Winter* (*fig. 20*). Here too the structure of the tangentially cut boards of the support is prominently visible as well as the spreading of the ground layer due to its lead content. One can presume that the ground was applied with a palette knife or a spatula since there are numerous fine scratches to be seen.

The use of reserves and local underpaint described above are also to be found here. The background is underpainted in a dark grey, the lower part of the painting in brown (*fig. 21*) and the "hair" in a dark red. Arcimboldo used gold leaf to depict the blazing flames of the "fire". The rectangular shaped gold leaves shine through in some parts (*fig. 22*). Some of the gold overlays look more like shell gold (*fig. 23*). The gilded areas are further worked over with detailed brushwork, applying red and white accents with *impasto* and red lake glazes, which are well preserved. In other parts the paint was applied wet-in-wet, as with the medallion of the chain (*fig. 24*) or the dark billows of smoke in the background to the right. In the face Arcimboldo used his finger to modify the application of paint, as the fingerprints in the brown and green glazes document (*fig. 25*).

Several corrections of the figure's contour, extending into the dark background, can be easily read in the infrared reflectogram (*fig. 26*). The left side of the neck has been somewhat broadened, while on the right, neck and nape have been markedly narrowed, being initially broader and rounder. The chain of the Order of the Golden Fleece in the nape has been left uncorrected in its original position and was not aligned with the changed run of the nape. Above the chain the neck has been widened again, as the subsequently applied paint layer shows a poor adherence to the background paint, what might be due to a tempera based medium (*fig. 27*).

Several changes in the composition, which are difficult to interpret, can be found in the lower part of the painting. The deviations from the final image can be seen in the underdrawing (*fig. 26*) and through the relief of the painted surface with raking light. The underdrawing shows a smaller, higher placed muzzle. The curved line to the left of the same is not clearly interpretable, however it could be an indication of a further; larger muzzle. By joining the lines visible close to the gun barrel and the order chain, a form emerges that one could read as the shape of a fire iron. Furthermore, mostly very fine lines are to be found in various points forming outlines, i.e. in the order chain or in the eye. On the forehead many fine, parallel running lines are visible.

Supports and back sides

Since the four paintings form part of a group and share basic similarities concerning their supports in terms of material, workmanship und state of preservation[8], the following will sum up the observations made on all four (*fig. 28 to 31*).

The panels of *Fire, Summer* and *Winter* are made out of lime wood boards. Only *Water* forms an exception with the use of alder.[9] The choice of supports shows that Arcimboldo – as an Italian painter in Vienna and Prague – had clearly been influenced by local painting technique traditions. While the use of lime wood for panels was widespread in the north, it was also used in Italy, although the majority of panels were painted on supports consisting of poplar wood.

The formats of the four panels are largely consistent and differ only slightly in height.[10] The fact that an unpainted margin is only present along the top edge in *Water* could be a clue to a change in format of all four paintings.[11] The paintings share a panel thickness of 8 to 10 mm. A further point in common is that all panels, again with the exception of *Water*, have two inserted cross battens. Within the respective series one finds consistencies in the construction of the supports. The panels from the series of the '*Seasons*', *Winter* and *Summer*, painted in 1563, consist of two vertically glued boards with each join secured with three butterfly keys. The panels of *Fire* and *Water* (dated 1566) consist both of three vertically glued boards. The joins were each reinforced with butterfly keys, using four in *Fire* and seven in *Water*. The back sides of all four pictures are covered with a dark-grey/black coating[12], including an inscription in Latin noting the theme (title) and date. The exception is *Water*, which only notes the theme (*figg. 28 to 31a*).

In summary the construction of the panels appears similar except for *Water*, which is constructed from a different species of wood, exhibits an unusually high number of butterfly keys and, in addition, has neither cross battens nor an inscription regarding the date. This does not necessarily cast any doubt concerning the originality of the cross battens in the other pictures.[13] In comparing the back sides of all four pictures it can be recognised that all the inscriptions were probably executed at the same time. All of them are applied at the same height, regardless whether they are inscribed directly on the panels or – as with *Fire* – on a cross batten.[14] Also in this respect *Water* shows an interesting difference. In the X-radiograph one can see that the writing "Aqva" was initially positioned upside down and was subsequently corrected (*figg. 32a and b*). The cross battens were already extant when the back sides were coated. Presuming that the inscriptions are from the 16th century, which is stylistically possible, the cross battens and coatings would then be original.[15]

Monika Strolz

Giuseppe Arcimboldo (?) after unknown artist,
Maximilian II, his spouse Maria and their three children (Cat. Nr.III.4)

For the fabric support of the life-size family portrait, a herringbone twill canvas was chosen, consisting of two vertically running canvases of near equal width.[16] The measurements of both parts constitute the width of a standard loom. Along all four edges the painting has been somewhat trimmed and reinforced with a strip lining.[17] Till this day it is unlined, which is somewhat remarkable considering its age and size. The painting has a quite thin ground layer which is ochre in colour and this thinness of the ground could very well have been an advantage when rolling, transporting and restretching the painting. The potential damage due to the mechanical stresses, such as build-up of tension or flaking, was thus reduced. The thinness of the ground also influences the paint surface of the picture as it allows the herringbone structure to be integrated (*fig. 33*). A clearly visible underdrawing, executed in two different mediums can be seen in the infrared reflectogram. In the areas of the architecture (floor and pillar) a series of straight lines have been traced with a dry medium (charcoal, mineral or artificial chalk) using a ruler or straight edge.[18] *Figura 34* shows horizontal and perspective tapered vertical construction lines that run together to a vanishing point, located above Archduke Rudolf's chin. However most of these are uncorrected, freely drawn lines, with a slightly varying thickness and intensity of colour. This effect is obtained through the use of a fluid charcoal medium applied by brush.[19] On the basis of *fig. 35*, that shows Maria's head, at least three different brush sizes were used to carry out the underdrawing. The finest was used for the facial features, the next biggest for the outer contours of the heads well as the clothing, and the broadest for the structuring of the drapery. Due to the assuredness of the stroke one can assume that some type of preparatory design existed to aid the artist in setting out the composition. This could have been a reduced preparatory sketch (or an already existing painting?) and a cartoon.[20] One presumes the transfer was carried out by pressing (re-drawing) over the drawn contours of the cartoon, which was prepared on the reverse with charcoal to transfer the line to the paintings surface (ground). The transferred lines were subsequently reinforced with black paint with a brush. The remaining charcoal would then be brushed away to avoid them being mixed with the paint.[21] In the area of the eyes and mouth of Archduke Ernst (seen in the infrared reflectogram) small dark dots set out in regular intervals are recognizable that run closely along the fluidly applied underdrawing (*fig. 36*). It is to be presumed that these are the remains of the transferred lines, that have partially remained in the deeper parts of the canvas and are not dots as the result of a *spolvero* tracing procedure. The pronounced and diagonally running structure that is shown up in the infrared reflectogram is not attributable to the underdrawing, but to the marked type or weave of the canvas support – only single hatching is used for modelling the flesh tones.[22] Due to certain similarities between the family portrait of Maximilian II and the portrait of Maria of Spain (inv. no. GG 8140, *fig. 37*), it was decided to compare the execution of both works. In fact, it was able to be detected that the contours of the portrait of Maria[23] from the family portrait and those of the smaller singular portrait convincingly correspond (albeit reversed, *fig. 38*).[24] Although no underdrawing was detected with the smaller portrait[25], one can argue that a single preparatory study (cartoon) existed and could have been shared by both. Comparisons through normal illumination, X-radiography and infrared reflectography show that the underpaint (*figg. 39a to 39c*) of the family portrait exactly follows its underdrawing. Only a few details differ slightly from those being: Anna's right hand and Maria's left hand which have been enlarged, the "carved" bird on the cradle as well as the dark green marble plates have been readjusted slightly. The underdrawing of the figures was mostly followed in terms of spatial layout, in that these areas have been left blank in the underpaint or they specifically follow the form (*fig. 39b*). Details such as the jewels, the applications on the costumes, the dagger as well as the small dog (*fig. 34*), that were included in the composition at a later stage, have been directly painted onto the background, as is usual for details of this type. Similarly the painting of the floor between the right leg of Archduke Maximilian II and the cradle (*figg. 38, 39a, 39 b*) as well as the pillar to his right were fully completed and the black of the Spanish cape only filled in as a last measure. The reason for this reworking (done by the painter himself) presumably lies in the slight colour and contrast difference between the similar browns of the floor and the cradle and, respectively, the light doublet and the pillar, which as well exhibit nearly the same colour. It appears that an oil based medium, or more specifically an oleo resinous binder was used to develop the paint passages or design areas which are generally laid in with rather summary applications of denser paint. Even transparent colours like the red lake (Anna's dress) or dark green glazes (presumably a copper oleate or resinate) of the marble tiles were applied rather thick. The paint is often modelled on the canvas and overpainted wet-in-wet, in which the colours are also directly mixed on the painting (*fig. 40*). As an effective solution providing a three dimensional representation of the varied materials, such as the embroidered and carved surfaces without resorting to the use of fine glazes, the artist above all used yellow highlights "in relief", to give the various materials their plasticity. The general expression of this paint surface is rather rough in texture, with slightly broken brushwork due to leaner consistency. One can assume that a tempera bound medium was used (*fig. 41*).

Attributed to Giuseppe Arcimboldo (?), *Archduchesses: presumably Margarethe, Magdalena (?), Eleoneore, Barbara (?), Johanna and Anna* (cat. no. III.5 to cat. no. III.10).

Concerning the six portraits shown in this exhibition, that presumably depict the daughters of Emperor Ferdinand I (*figg. 42a to 47a, 45c, 46c*), no documents have been found that confirm where the paintings were made, nor are there indications as to the site in which they were displayed. One can assume that all pictures initially had their own frame. Whether the portraits after the completion of the series were jointly mounted in a wall panel or kept separate is still unknown. After the series was divided up, three of the Archduchesses were placed on show at Ambras castle (Innsbruck), the others since then have been kept in Vienna. The small, well-preserved wood panels show many similarities. Firstly, they are all of similar size and despite slight trimmings they are still close to their original format.[26] The fabrication of all panel supports is similar (five are made presumably of lime wood), except for one panel which is made of oak (cat. no. III.6). The panels consist of one to three (mostly two) on average 4 mm thick, vertically running and tangentially cut boards, that have been glued together using butt-joints. On the reverse of three panels (cat. nos. III.5, III.7 [partial], III.9) there are tooling marks from the plane used to work this surface (*figg. 42c, 44c, 46c*), two others (cat. nos. III.6, III.8) show a fairly clean surface. In addition, one panel has been cradled (cat. no. III.10). With one painting (cat. no. III.5) one can see that the upper and lower edge of the front surface is free of paint and that with four of the paintings the reverse of the panels show noticeably lighter edges. This could possibly be evidence that the paintings were once set into frames (*fig. 42c to 46c*).[27]
The ground layer of four panels (cat. nos. III.5, III.6, III.9, III.10) is white[28] (*fig.* 48) with varied partial coloured underpaint (grey-brown or grey-green, *fig. 49*). Two panels (cat. nos. III.7, III.8) show light grey-brown ground layers (*fig. 50*). Examining the pictures an overall colour scheme can be recognized. During the examination under the microscope the following range of colours could be established: Black[29], various earths, an intense green pigment (malachite?) and lead white (in pure form and in various mixtures) as well as a yellow pigment (lead tin yellow?) and a red lake. The method of paint application is generally similar, even if this changes slightly from painting to painting. All panels show a layered, though relatively homogeneous and fluid application of paint (*fig. 51*). Details and highlights can be seen to have been both integrated into the overall paint scheme and later embellished with final glazings and applied in a purer form to the more finished surface (*figg. 52, 53*). To the background of three of the paintings (cat. nos. III.5, III.7, III.8) a more coarsely ground pigment (grey-green in colour) had been prepared and applied in multiple layers (*fig. 54*).
That the paint surface shows a fine relief in raking light is due, on one hand, to the application of paint in multiple layers, (above all in the area around the nose and eyes, *fig. 55*) it is, as well, attributable to the inherent graininess of the pigments selected. All pictures show details painted wet-in-wet (*figg. 56, 57*). The colours are generally dense and opaque, despite being thinned or diluted with the paint medium. Glazes are only used sparingly, and are for the most part, recognisable in the modelling of the mouth (*fig. 58*) and ears. In five paintings a later correction of the outline of the head can be noticed, wherein the background colour can be seen to extend inwards (*fig. 59*). Despite the similarities between the works, in terms of image and chromatics, it can be seen, when looking closer, that the stylistic variations present can be more aptly attributable to a slightly different way of manipulating the same materials. The X-radiographs (*figg. 45b to 47b*) help clarify the different approaches in painting, often revealing *pentimenti* or reworkings, made by the same painter/painters (?). On the basis of the evidence gleaned from this examination it appears that three of the portraits (cat. nos. III.5, III.7, III.8) are closer to each other and form a special group among the (presumably successively) commissioned series of portraits.[30]

Ina Slama

We would like to thank our colleagues at the Kunsthistorisches Museum for their support: Elke Oberthaler, Eva Götz, Robert Wald, Sonja Kocian (*Painting Conservation Department*); Ruperta Pichler, Elisabeth Wolfik (*Gallery Registrars*); Martina Grießer, Sabine Stanek, Vaclav Pitthard (*Conservation Science Department*); Stefan Zeisler, Michael Eder, Tom Ritter, Andreas Uldrich (*Photo Studio*).

[1] See Fend, Strolz 1999, 282-290.

[2] Infrared reflectography was carried out by Ina Slama and Monika Strolz. The digital assembling and image processing was done by Michael Eder.

[3] X-radiography of the individual paintings was carried out by Elke Oberthaler, Ina Slama und Monika Strolz with digital composites by Tom Ritter.

[4] Scientific analyses of the paint samples of all four paintings were conducted by polarising light microscopy and scanning electron microscopy. Micro chemical staining tests of the cross-sections for organic binding media were performed, but did not prove to be conclusive due to the minute size of the samples and the sampling point directly on the paintings edges.

[5] It was not unusual to cut lime wood boards tangentially (see Klein 1999, 29-36). The difference in cell density of sapwood and latewood does register differently in the X-radiograph (see Mohan, Menu, Mottin 2006, 40). In addition, the minimal unevenness in the panel surfaces is emphasized by the lead white ground.

[6] A comparable paint structure with multiple ground layers was observed in Arcimboldo's painting *Vertumnus*, 1590, Skokloster Palace, see: Makes 1988, 49.

[7] The presence of a light grey ground layer underneath the two red ones was observed during the examination with the stereo microscope. This lowest layer is missing in the cross-section, probably due to the separation of the layers during sampling.

[8] Signs of later conservation treatments can only be notices in two paintings. In *Summer* the join was opened and reglued. In the course of this treatment the reverse of the support was somewhat planed down. In addition, the join was further stabilised with a mahogany strip. With the painting *Winter* the join was also reglued and secured with hemp fibres.
[9] To identify the species of wood used samples were taken from the panels and partially from the butterfly keys and cross battens. The identification was carried out by Prof. Dr. Peter Klein, Hamburg University, Wood Biology Department. I thank him for his readiness to carry out the analyses in an extremely short period of time.
[10] *Summer* has been slightly trimmed on the bottom edge, *Fire* both on top and bottom edges.
[11] Comparing the four paintings, it stands out that the eye level in *Water* is somewhat lower than in the other three paintings. The painting was slightly trimmed along the bottom edge, lowering minimally the overall composition. It is hard to tell whether originally all panels have had unpainted margins and were cut later on. If this indeed had been the case, one could conclude that *Water* was slightly smaller right from the beginning, since the current formats of all four paintings are all fairly consistent.
[12] Since all panels retained, on their back side, unpainted margins of circa 5 mm and barbs, the panels must have had an engaged frame at the time of the application of this coating. Only with those panels, that have had the top and/or bottom edges trimmed, the unpainted margins are somewhat narrower or are missing. A sample was taken from the coating and analysed regarding the pigment and the binding medium used. The pigment proved to be carbon black. The gas chromatography mass spectrometry analysis showed that the binding medium was rabbit skin glue.
[13] To further pursue these questions, prospective examinations and comparisons with other panels by Arcimboldo, his assistants and contemporaries are deemed necessary.
[14] In order to establish whether the four inscriptions are all by the same hand a graphologic examination would be interesting.
[15] My thanks are due to George Bisacca, Restorer in the Painting Restoration Department of the Metropolitan Museum of Art, New York, and specialist in panel paintings. His thoughts and opinions as to the many open questions regarding Arcimboldo's panels have been highly appreciated.
[16] The left part of the canvas has a width of 95 cm, the right side 98.5 cm.
[17] The original paint layers extend over the edges of the stretcher, therefore one can assume that approximately 3 cm have been trimmed away.
[18] Siejek, Kirsch 2004, 56-67.
[19] A careful interpretation of the infrared reflectogram should be made, where some light grey areas of the paint layer show up very dark.
[20] There is no evidence of a direct transfer using a grid.
[21] Ibid, 56
[22] Anna: left bridge of the nose and right ear. Maria: over the right eye, chin.
[23] Inv. no. GG 8140 was reversed and superimposed over the family portrait to determine the contours.
[24] Small differences can also occur due to the slight shifting of the cartoon during the tracing procedure.
[25] The reason for this could also be put down to the type of materials used in the underdrawing.
[26] All panels have been cut to a certain degree along the sides. Cat. no. III.6 has been cut along the top, cat. no. III.9 reduced above and below. Four of the six panels (cat. nos. III.5, III.7, III.8, III.10) are around 42 and 44 cm high and between 33 and 34 cm wide. With the other two panels (cat. nos. III.6, III.9) the height is the same as the width of the larger panels – around 33 and 34 cm. The width is between 24 and 25 cm. Due to the later changes in the sight size (clearly broader rebate cover in cat. no. III.8; recognisable by the yellowed varnish) one can deduce, that these portraits had no longer been presented together for a considerable time period.
[27] Small wedge shaped channels including traces of rust from metal hardware (such as nails) along the left and right edges. It is to be presumed, that this is due to the mounting of the wood panels in frames using slender battens.
[28] The ground layer of panel cat. no. III.10 does not continue to the upper edge of the painting and the painter subsequently integrated these areas with the background colour.
[29] Often carbon black was used, recognizable in the long needle-shaped particles.
[30] Size and type of wood are the same in all cases. The ground though is different. Two of the three panels show a grey-brown priming, the third has a white, non lead containing ground which helps in the interpretation of the X-radiographs. The strong difference in contrasts and the spottiness of the background in the X-radiographs is not due to an irregular application of the underpaint, but rather to the high lead white component of the dense and irregularly applied paint surface. There are also similarities in the colouring and placing of the "Rouge" to the cheeks and chin, the veiled application of the hair and in certain fashion details, such as the blond curled upstanding hair – "Papos" [Orsini, Niccoli 2005, 32f.], adorned with precious jewellery. Numerous pentimenti are noticeable in all three paintings.

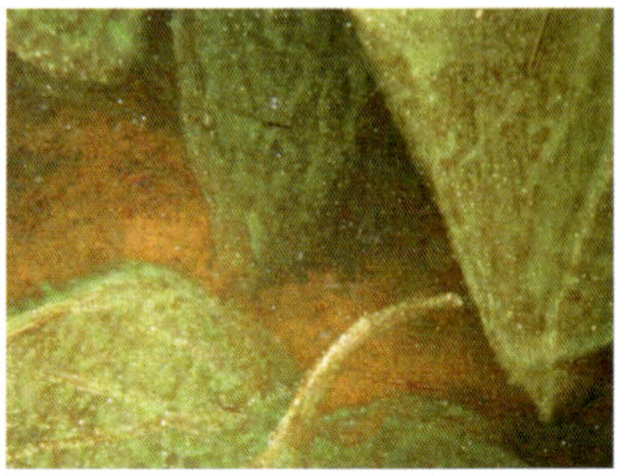
Fig. 1

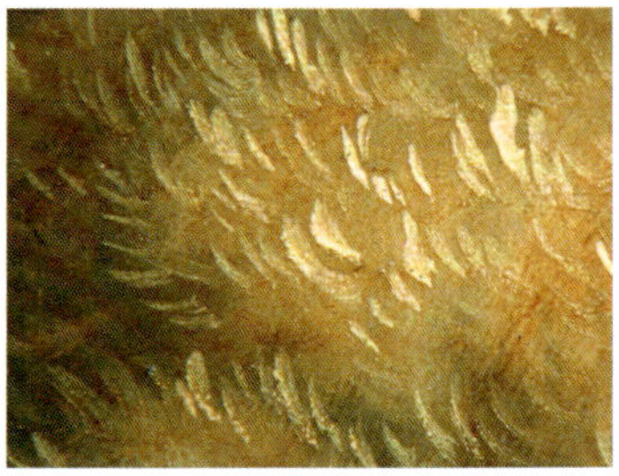
Fig. 2

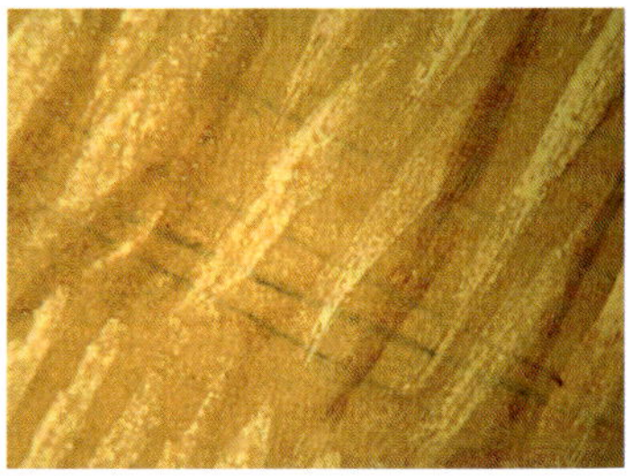
Fig. 5

Fig. 1:
Cat. no. IV.4 Photomicrograph of the ivy showing brown underpaint

Fig. 2:
Cat. no. IV.4, Photomicrograph of the neck showing light underpaint

Fig. 3:
Cat. no. IV.4, Detail of infrared reflectogram

Fig. 4:
Cat. no. IV.4, X-radiograph

Fig. 5:
Cat. no. IV.4, Photomicrograph of the straw garment showing underdrawing

Fig. 6:
Cat. no. IV.21, X-radiograph

Figg. 7, 8:
Cat. no. IV.21, Photomicrographs of two fish: light brown underpaint in the interstices, detailed brushwork

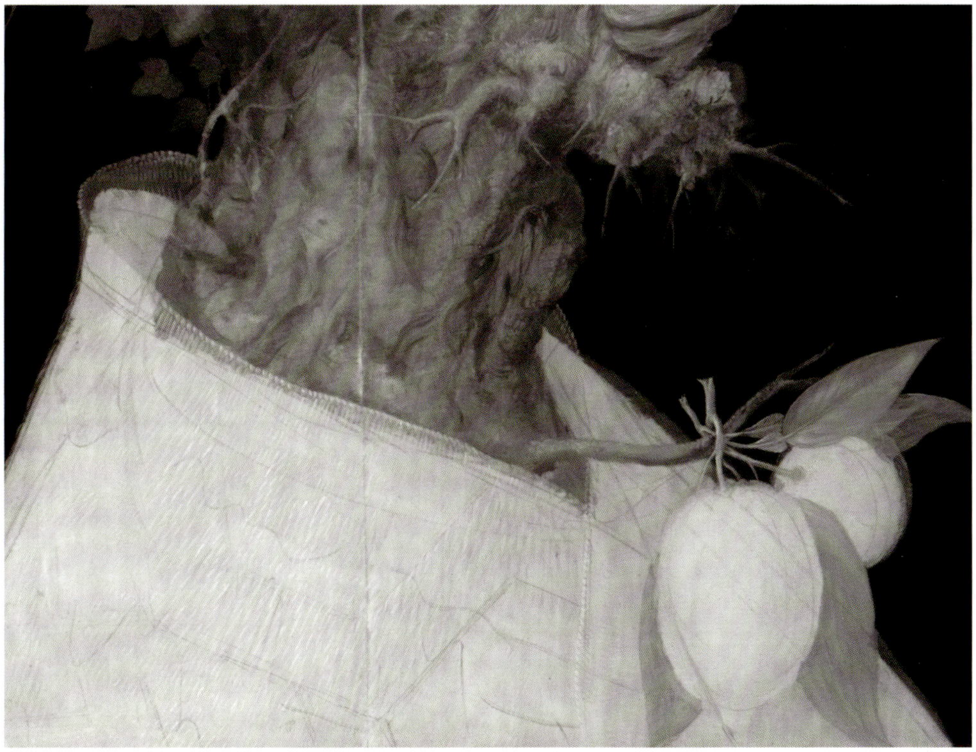

Fig. 3

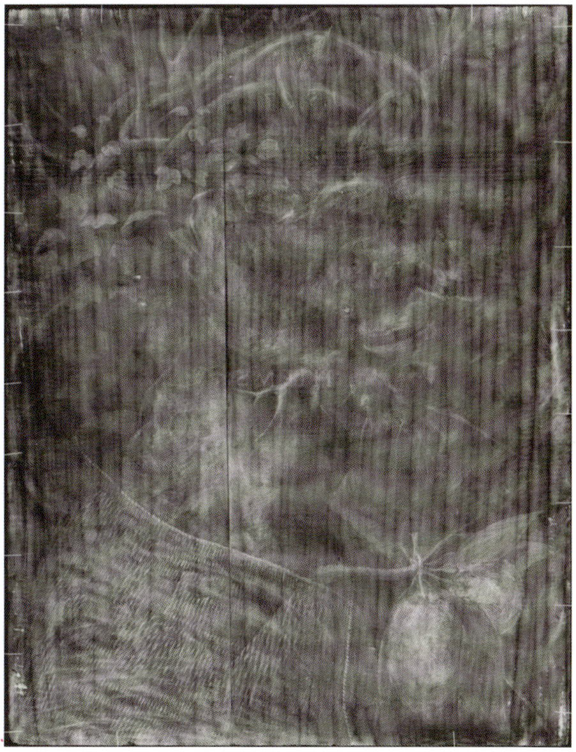

Fig. 4

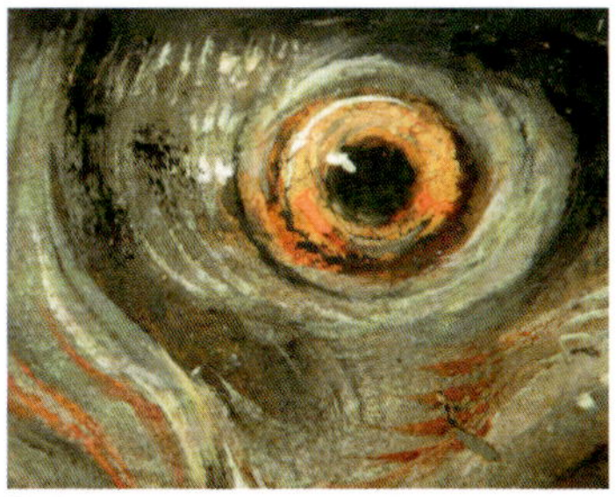

Fig. 7

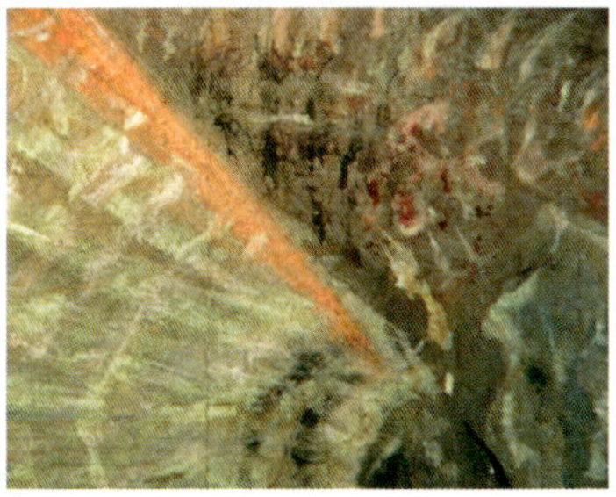

Fig. 8

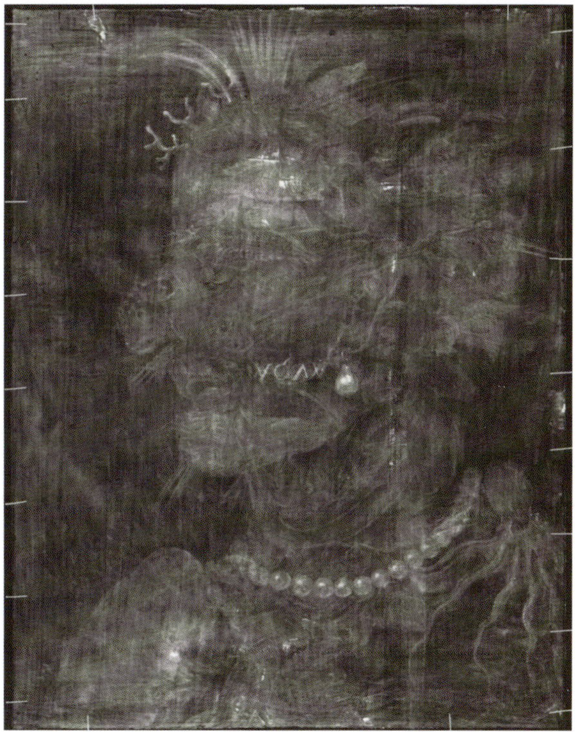

Fig. 6

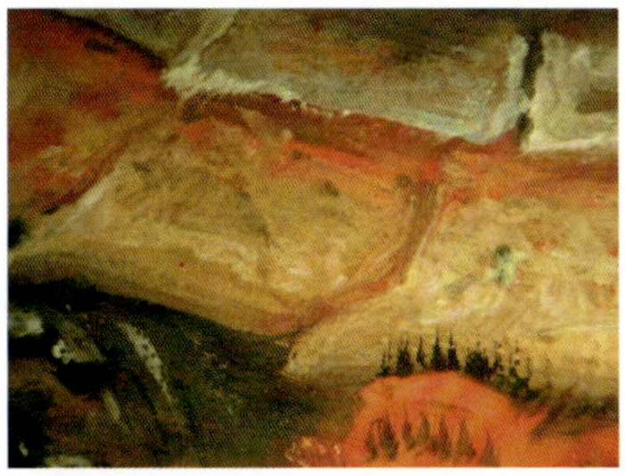

Fig. 9

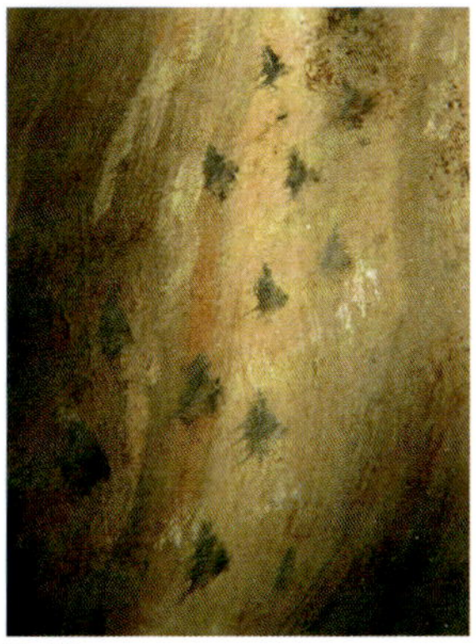

Fig. 10

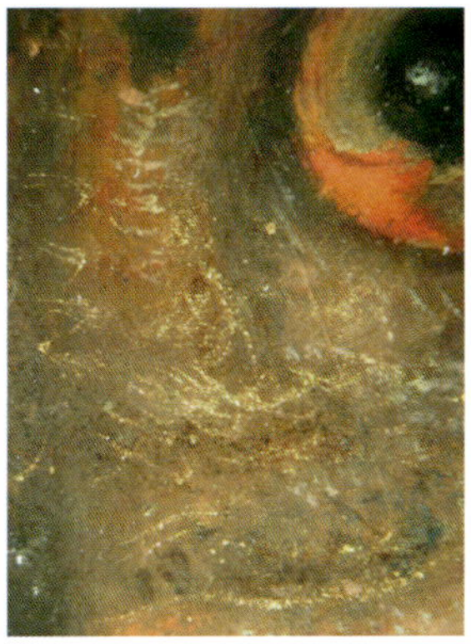

Fig. 11

Fig. 9:
Cat. no. IV.21, Photomicrograph of the turtle: black brushstrokes applied wet-in-wet

Fig. 10:
Cat. no. IV.21, Photomicrograph of the octopus with patterning applied wet-in-wet

Fig. 11:
Cat. no. IV.21, Photomicrograph of the fish that represents the "nose" embellished with shell gold

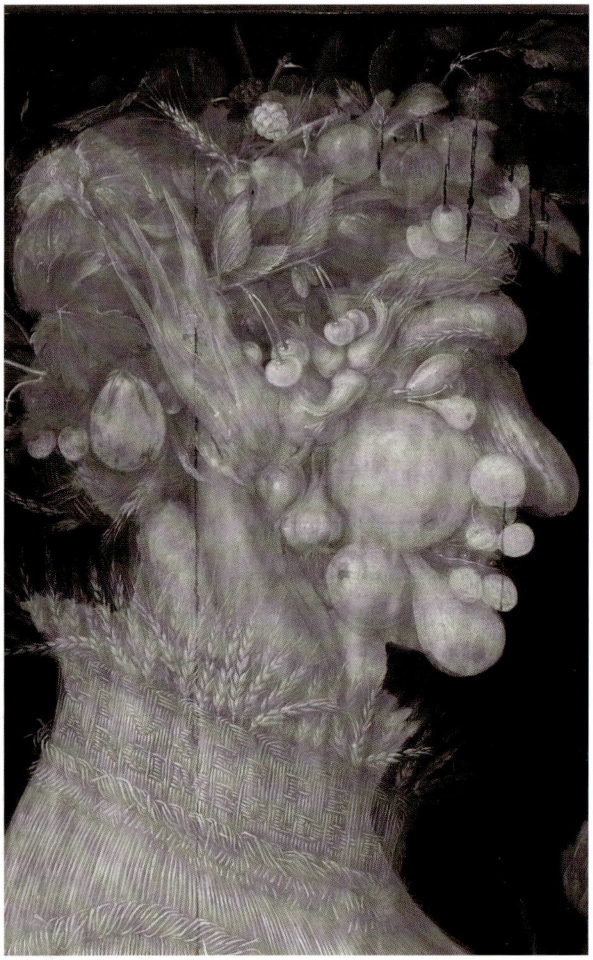
Fig. 19

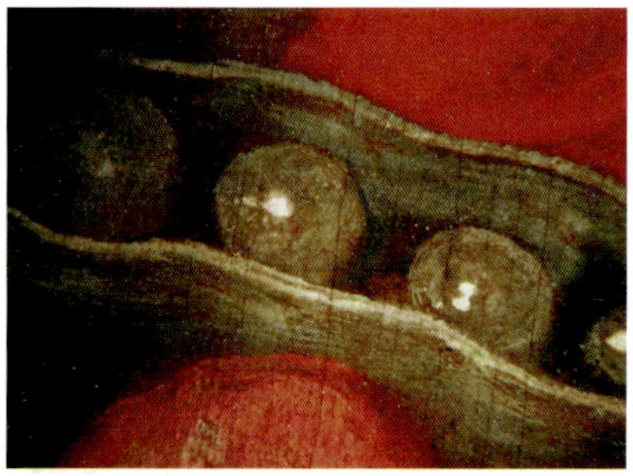
Fig. 12

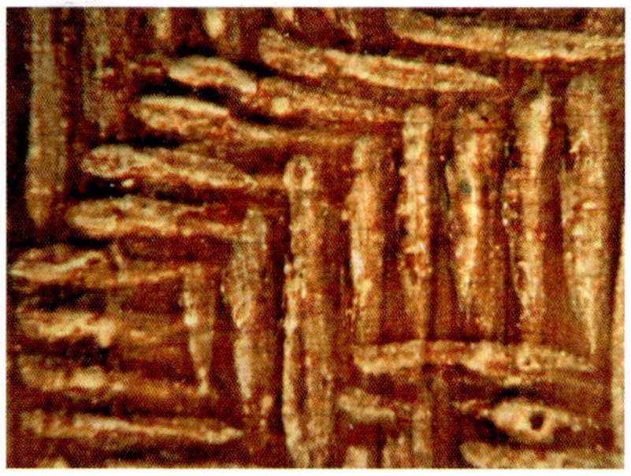
Fig. 13

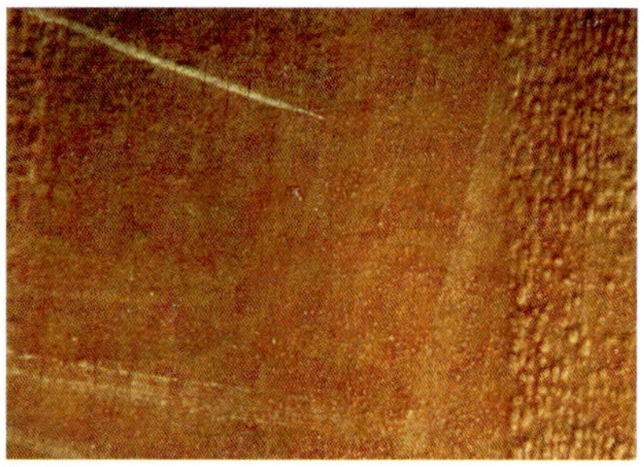
Fig. 18

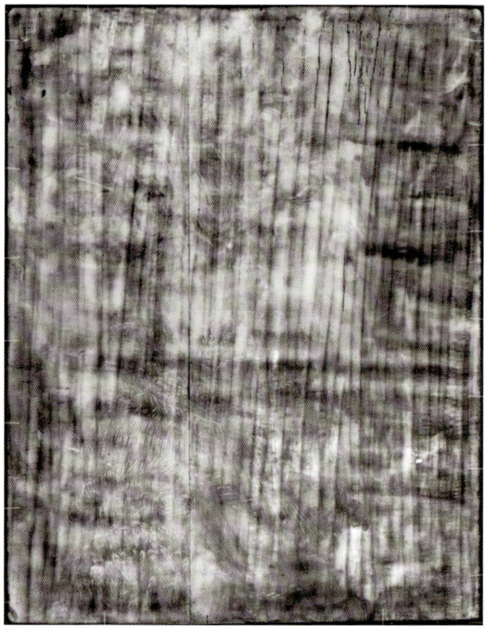
Fig. 17

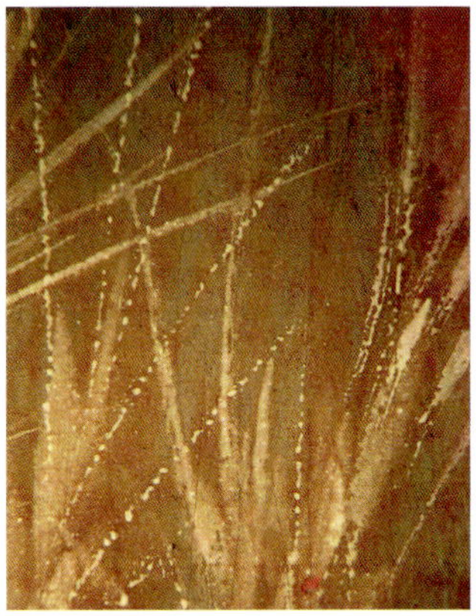
Fig. 14

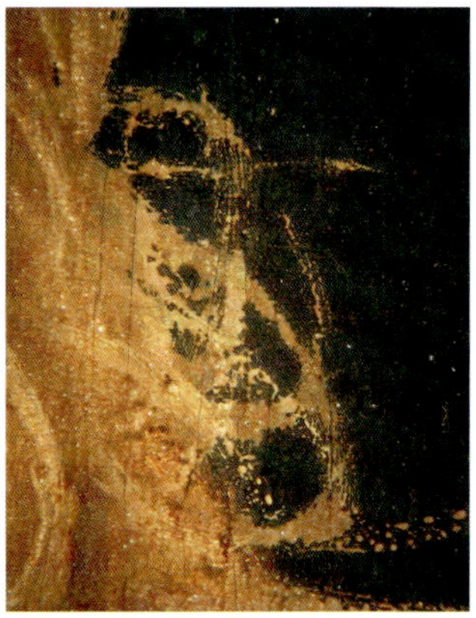
Fig. 16

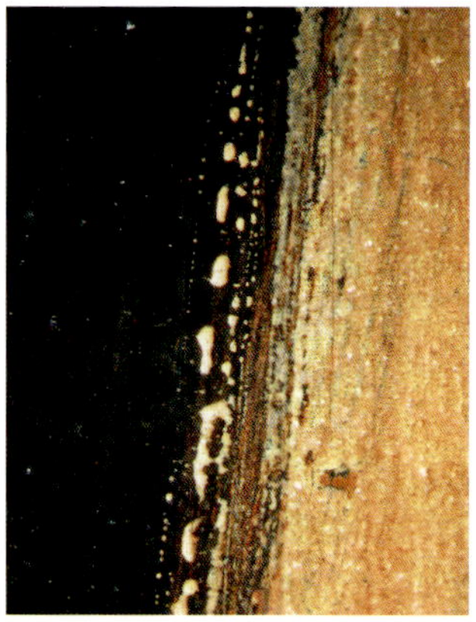
Fig. 15

Fig. 12:
Cat. no. IV.3, Photomicrograph of the "mouth" showing brown underpaint in the interstices

Fig. 13:
Cat. no. IV.3, Photomicrograph of the straw garment, figure '6' of the date with impasto applied paint layer

Fig. 14:
Cat. no. IV.3, Photomicrograph of the ears of corn on the collar showing fine brushstrokes with beaded paint consistency

Fig. 15:
Cat. no. IV.3, Photomicrograph of the shoulder bottom left: the corrected contour painted over the background with beaded paint consistency

Fig. 16:
Cat. no. IV.3, Photomicrograph of the collar: loose brushwork of the straw painted over the background with beaded paint consistency
Fig. 17:
Cat. no. IV.3, X-radiograph

Fig. 18:
Cat. no. IV.3, Photomicrograph of the bottom right showing the differences in the surface structure due to the wood grain

Fig. 19:
Cat. no. IV.3, Detail of infrared reflectogram

Fig. 20:
Cat. no. IV.18, X-radiograph

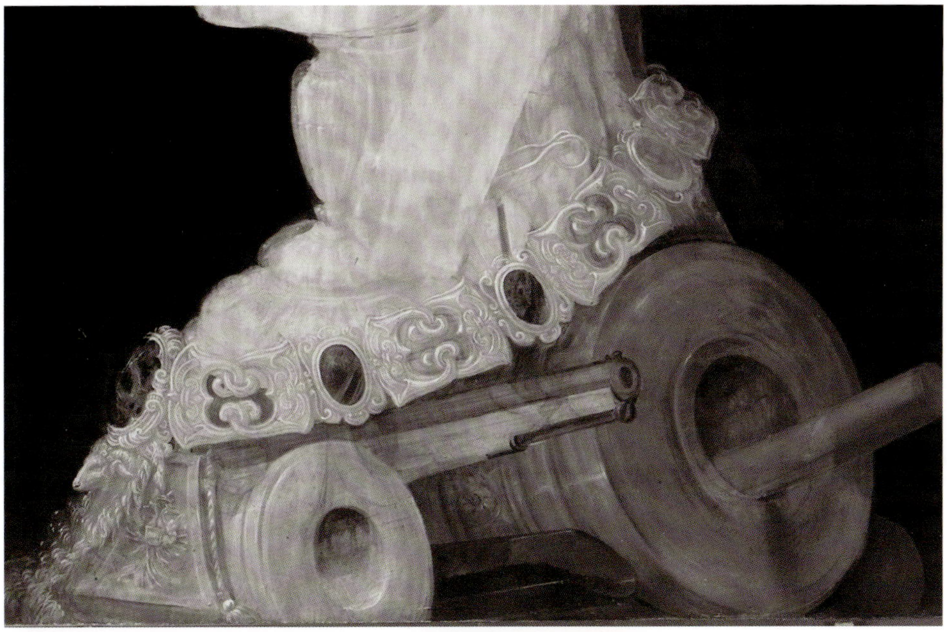

Fig. 26

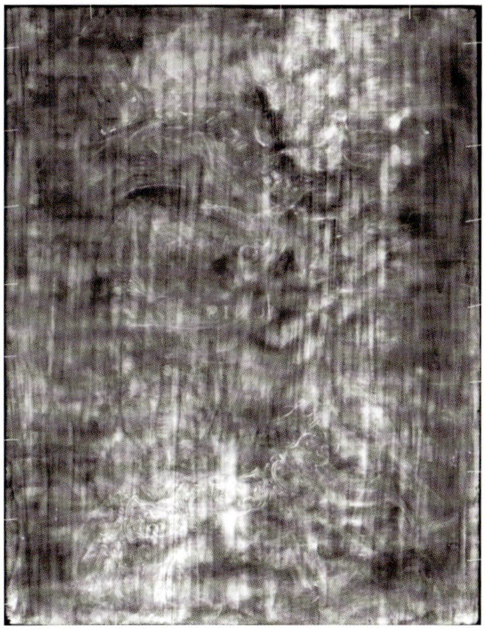

Fig. 20

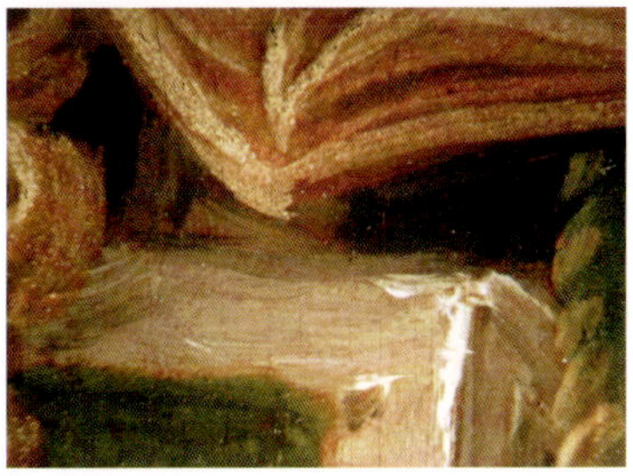

Fig. 21

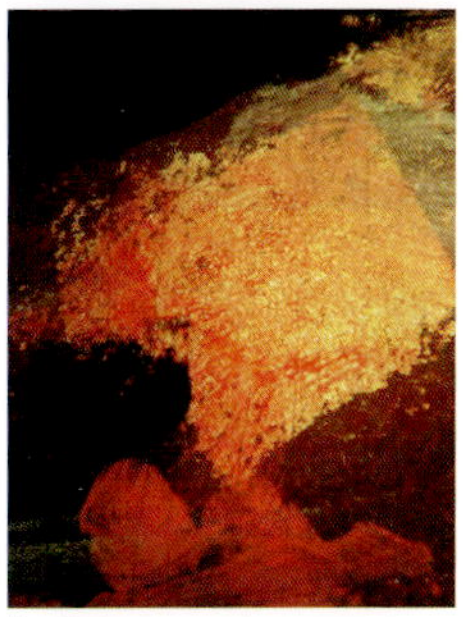

Fig. 22

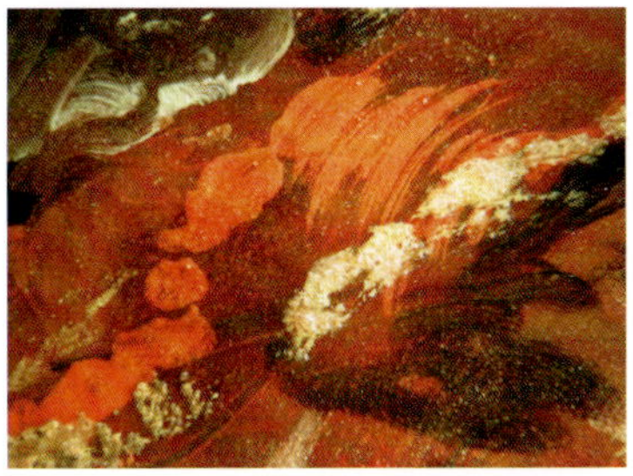

Fig. 23

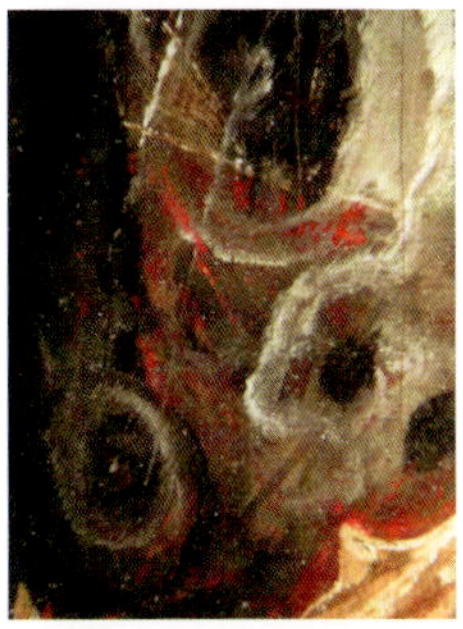

Fig. 24

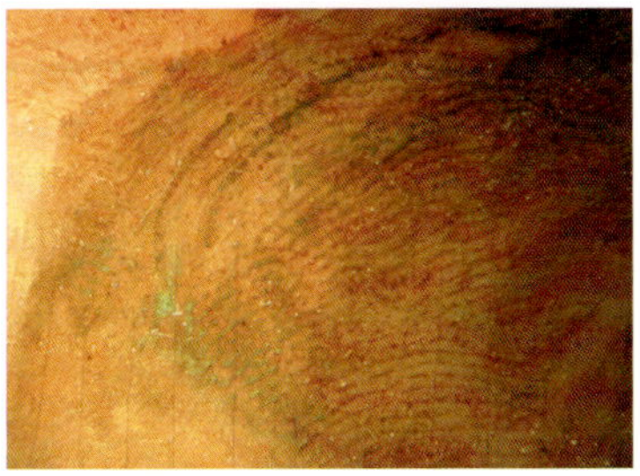

Fig. 25

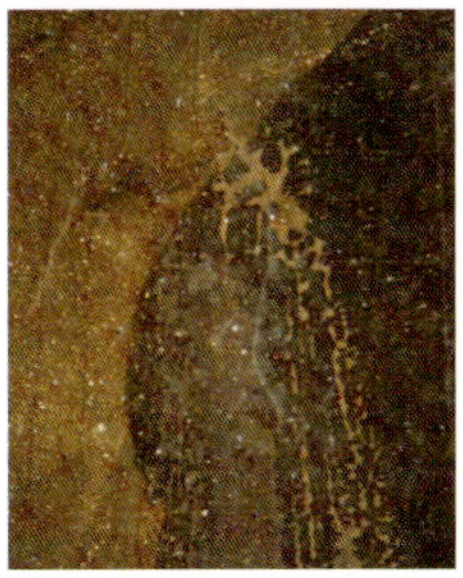

Fig. 27

Fig. 21:
Cat. no. IV.18, Photomicrograph showing brown underpaint in the interstices

Figg. 22, 23:
Cat. no. IV.18, Photomicrographs showing gold leaf and shell gold

Fig. 24:
Cat. no. IV.18, Photomicrograph of the chain showing red underpaint, paint partially applied wet-in-wet

Fig. 25:
Cat. no. IV.18, Photomicrograph of the face: fingerprint in the green glaze

Fig. 26:
Cat. no. IV.18, Detail of infrared reflectogram

Fig. 27:
Cat. no. IV.18, Photomicrograph of the *pentimento* at the neck, with paint layer beading up in tiny drops

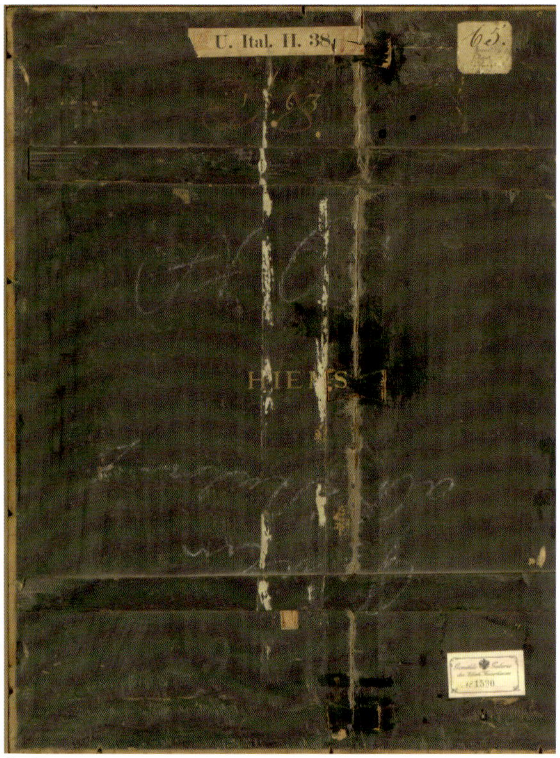

Fig. 28

Fig. 29

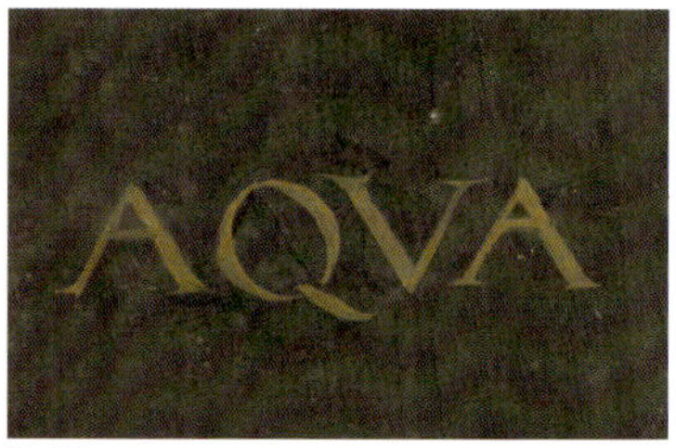

Fig. 32a

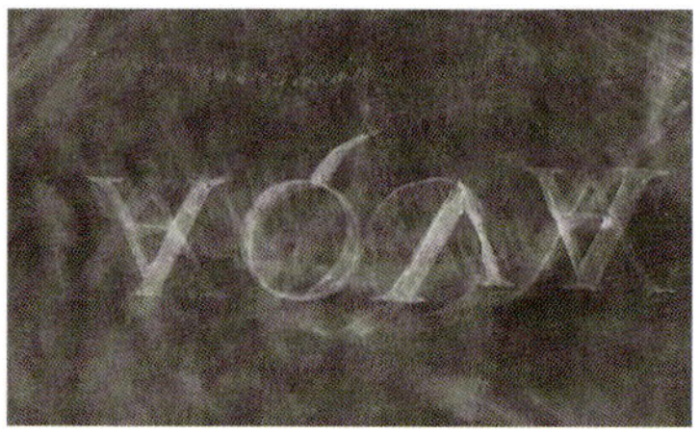

Fig. 32b

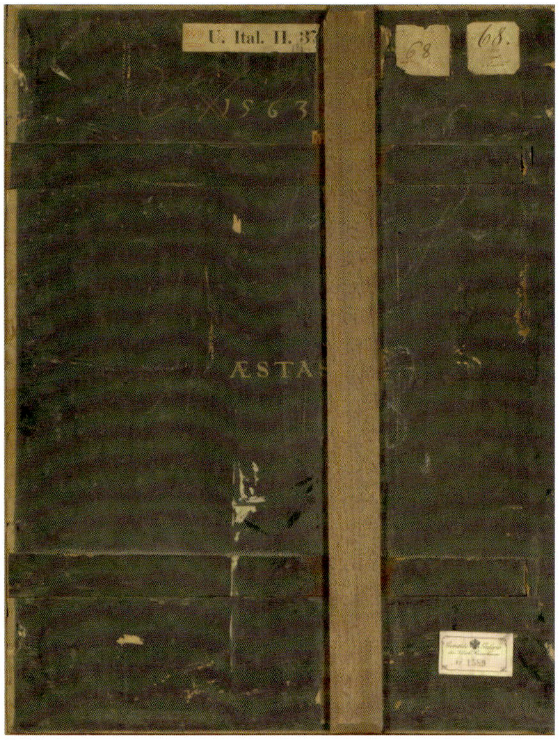

Fig. 30

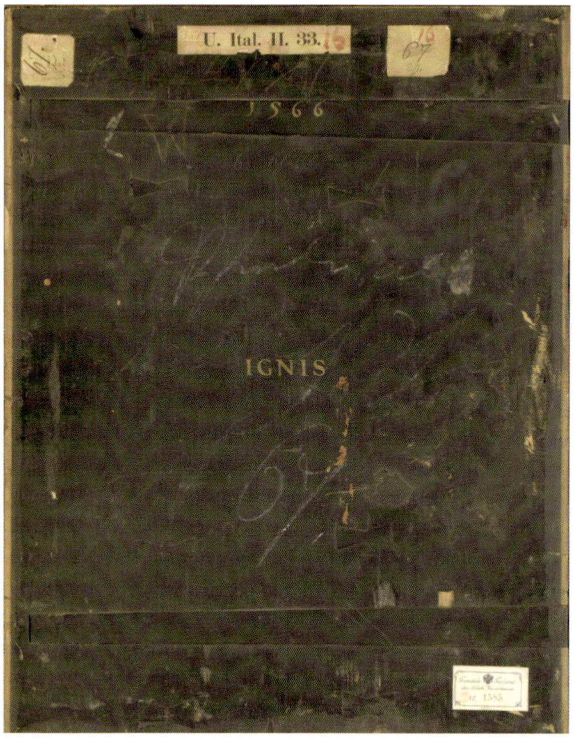

Fig. 31

Fig. 28:
Cat. no. IV.4, reverse of panel

Fig. 29:
Cat. no. IV.21, reverse of panel

Fig. 30:
Cat. no. IV.3, reverse of panel

Fig. 31:
Cat. no. IV.18, reverse of panel

Fig. 32 a and b:
Cat. no. IV.21 Photomacrograph with detail of inscription in normal illumination (a) and detail of the X-radiograph (b)

Fig. 33:
Cat. no. III.4 Raking light photo, herringbone structure of the canvas recognizable

Fig. 34:
Infrared reflectogram, floor with construction lines

Fig. 35:
Infrared reflectogram, fluid underdrawing with brush

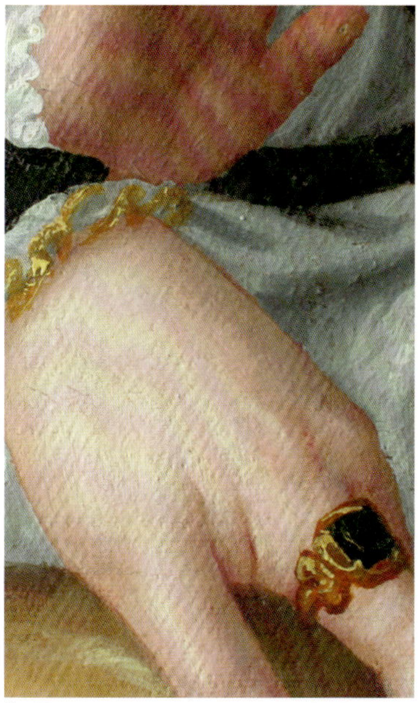

Fig. 33

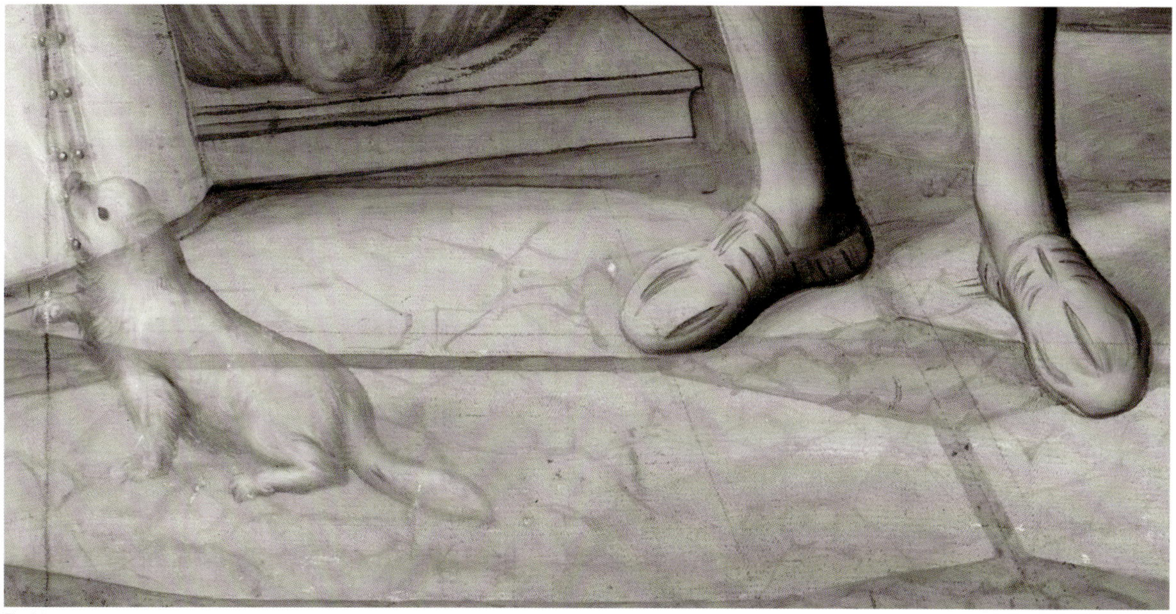

Fig. 34

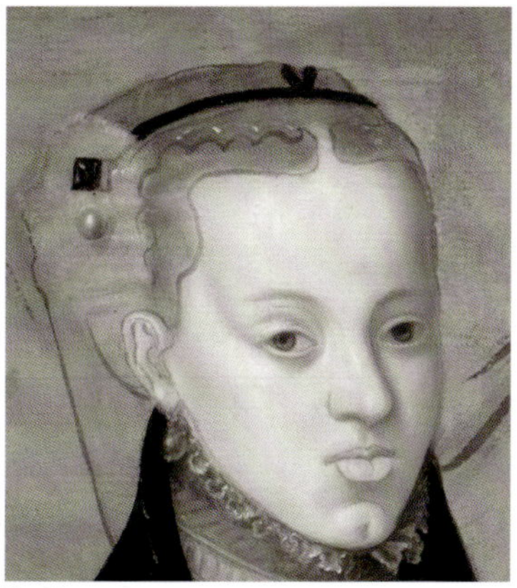

Fig. 35

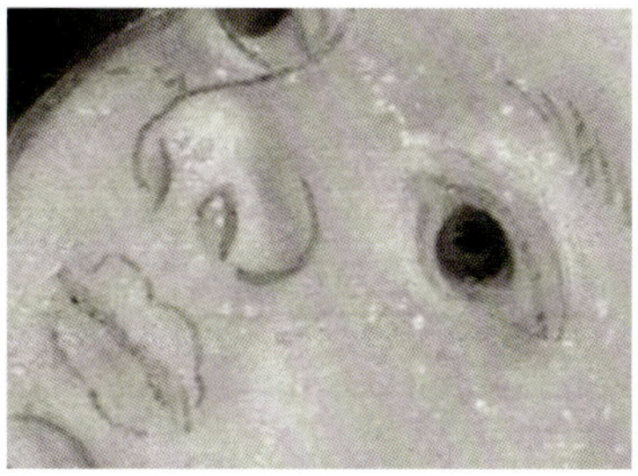

Fig. 36

Fig. 36:
Infrared reflectogram, detail of Archduke Ernst

Fig. 37:
Queen Maria of Spain inv. no. GG 8140

Fig. 38:
Digital overlay of inv. no. GG 8140 and cat. no. III.4

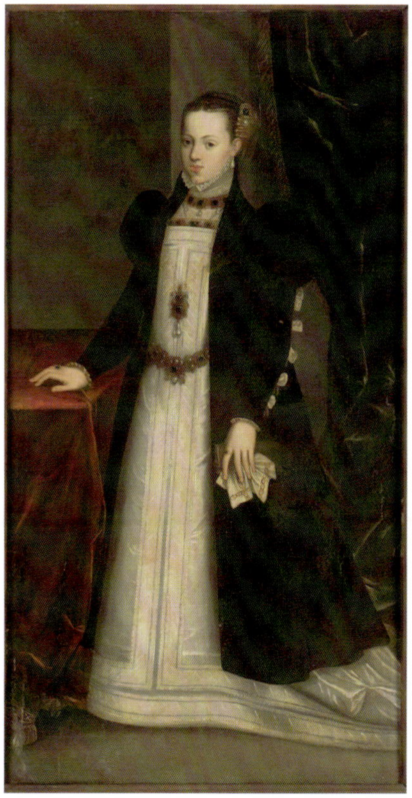

Fig. 37

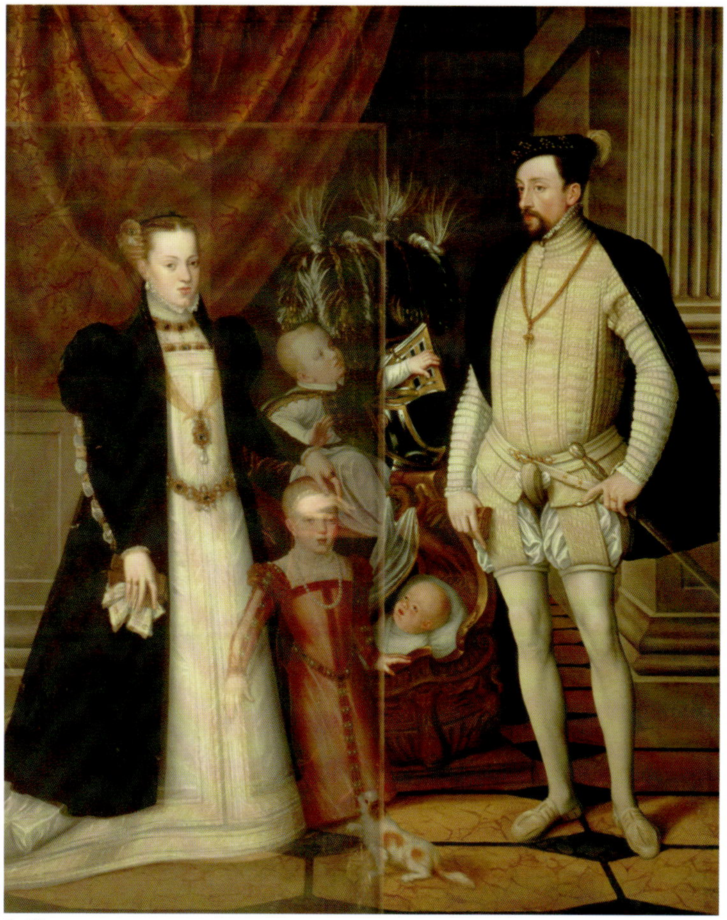

Fig. 38

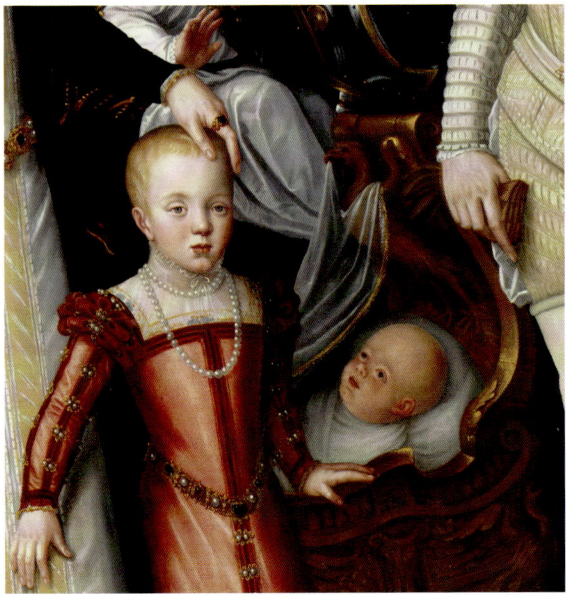

Fig. 39a

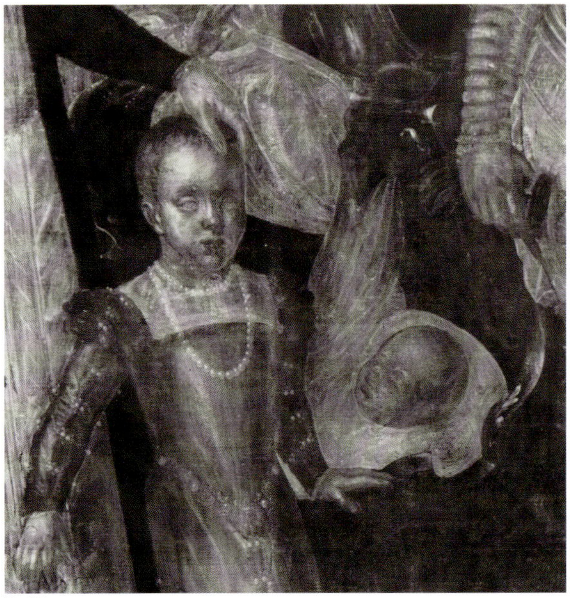

Fig. 39b

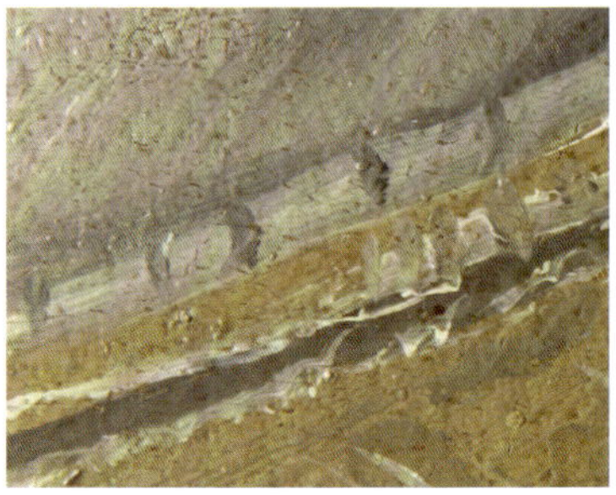

Fig. 40

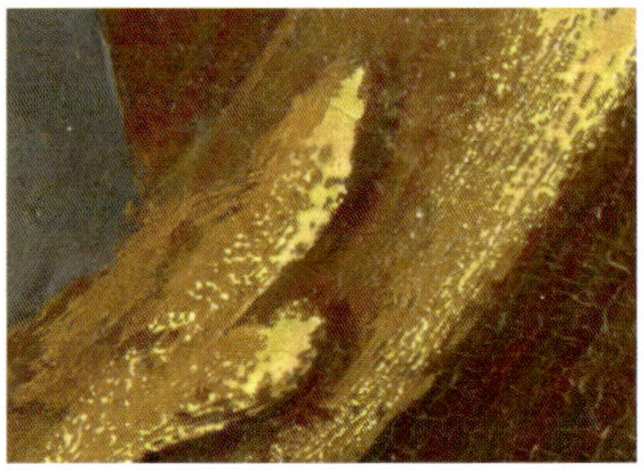

Fig. 41

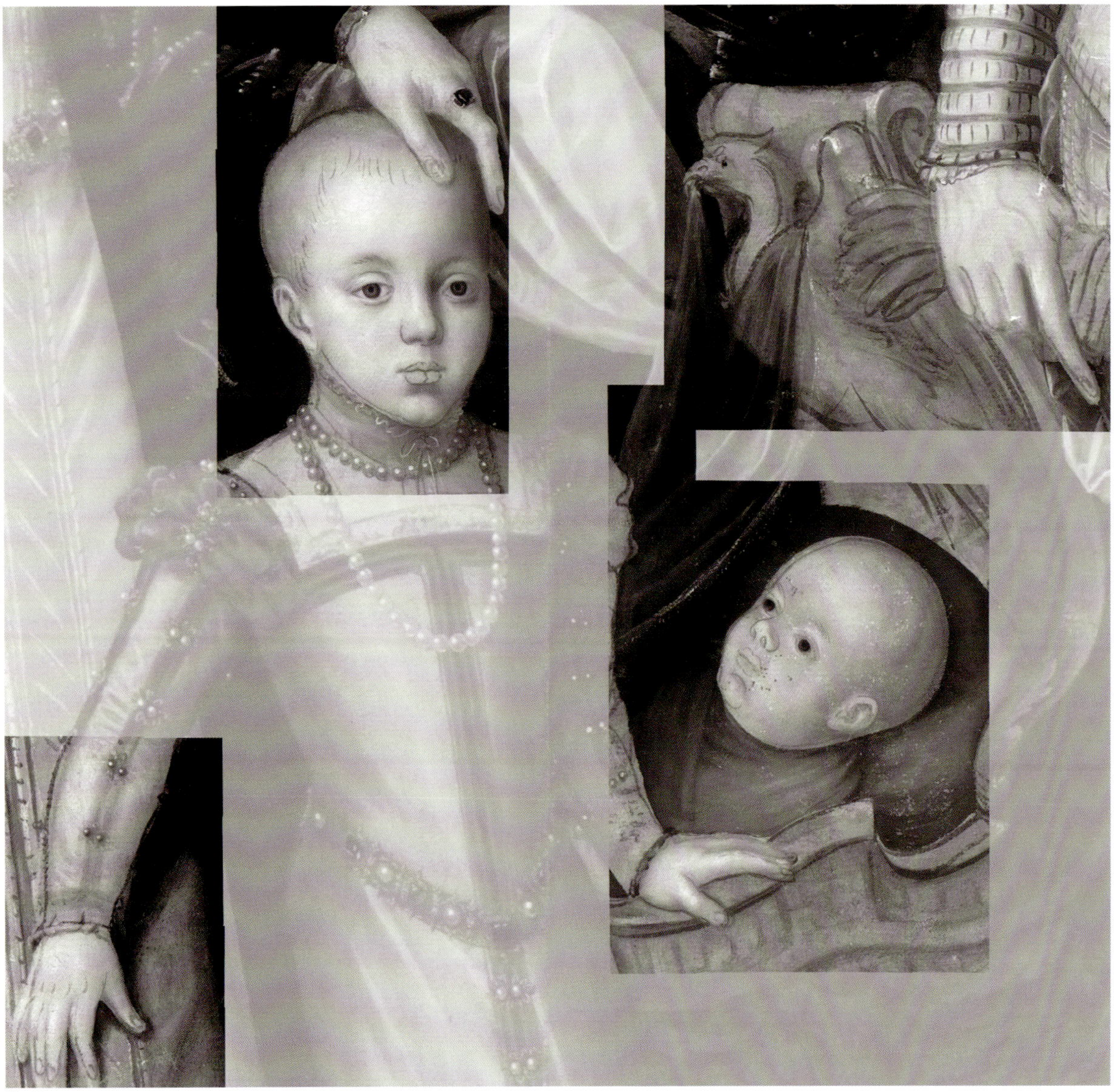

Fig. 39c

Fig. 39a:
Detail, normal illumination photo

Fig. 39b:
Detail, X-radiograph

Fig. 39c:
Detail, infrared reflectogram

Fig. 40:
Photomacrograph, modelling wet-in-wet application of paint, detail of Maria's cloak

Fig. 41:
Photomacrograph, highlights in "relief", detail of the cradle

Fig. 42a:
Cat. no. III.5 *Archduchess Margarethe*

Fig. 42b:
Cat. no. III.5 X-radiograph, *Pentimenti*: feathers with general light underpaint; collar – originally not ruffeled, but flat and larger horizontally. Area of the neck lighter, probably higher cleavage; white blouse plucked out of the slits of her black dress without dark underpaint

Fig. 42c:
Cat. no. III.5 Back of panel with tooling marks in raking light

Fig. 43a:
Cat. no. III.8 *Archduchess Magdalena* (?)

Fig. 43b:
Cat. no. III.8 X-radiograph, *Pentimenti*: the upper edge of the forehead was initially straight. Small changes in the area of the left and right collar of the cloak as well as the left and right puffed sleeves

Fig. 43c:
Cat. no. III.8 Back of panel in raking light

Fig. 44a:
Cat. no. III.7 *Archduchess Eleonore*

Fig. 44b:
Cat. no. III.7 X-radiograph, *Pentimenti*: small white, gold embroidered collar extending further into the face; forehead was higher – cornered hairframe, hair regarding headdress left was laid flatter. Right collar of the dark cloak initially inexistent; neck broader to the right. Left and right shoulder fairly straight in the first version – puffed sleeves added later

Fig. 44c:
Cat. no. III.7 Back of panel in raking light

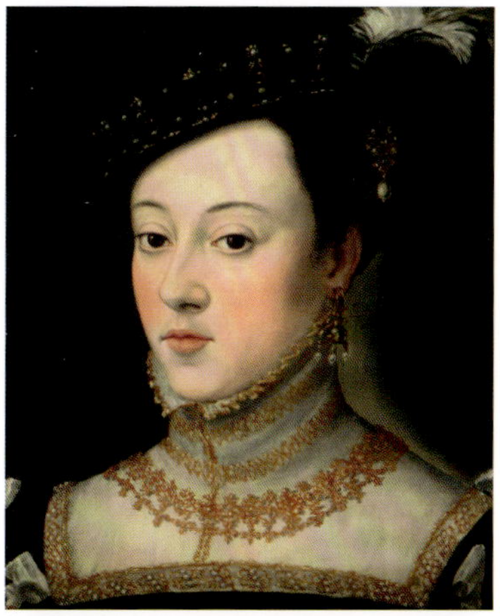
Fig. 42a

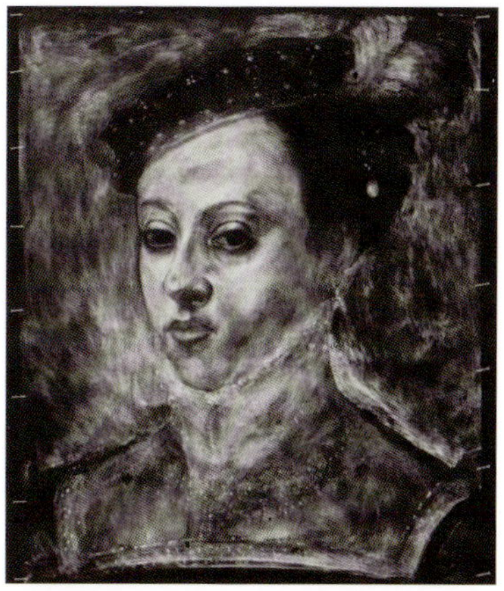
Fig. 42b

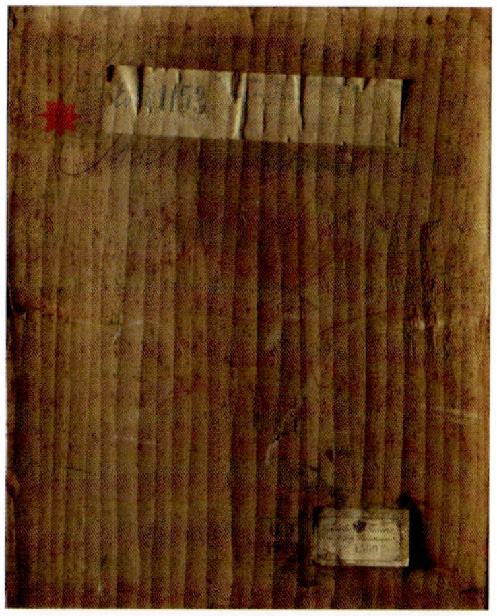
Fig. 42c

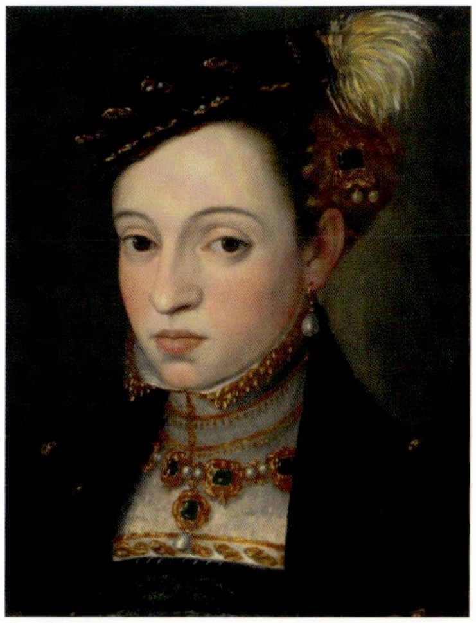
Fig. 43a

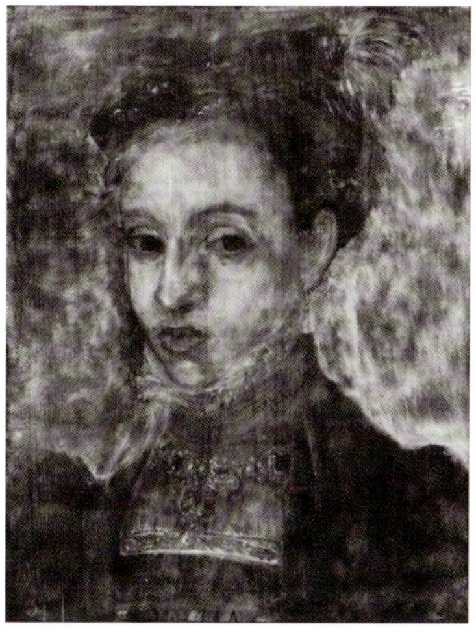
Fig. 43b

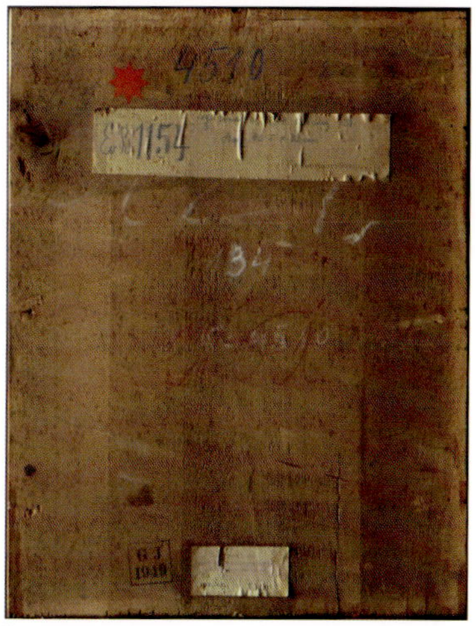
Fig. 43c

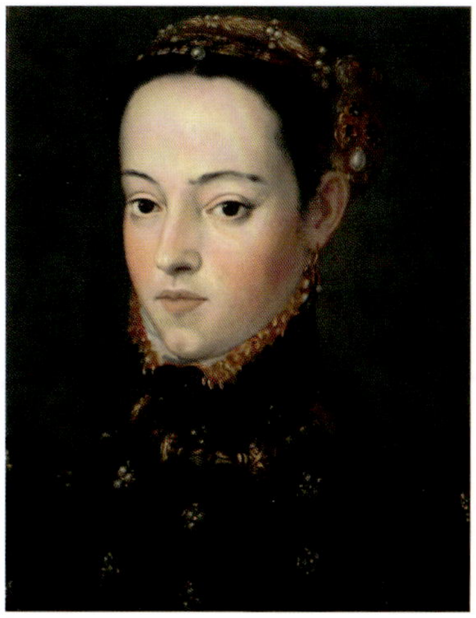
Fig. 44a

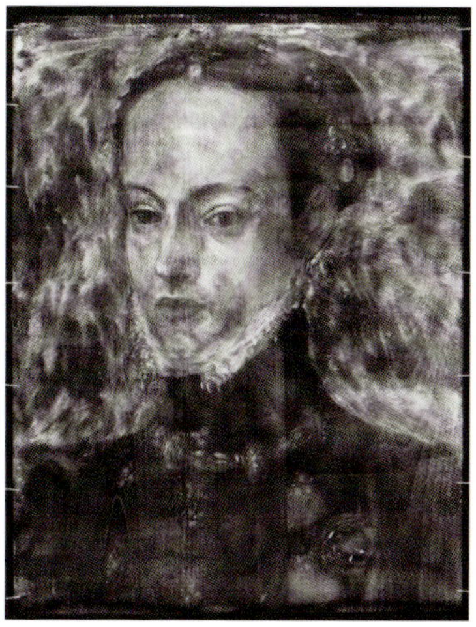
Fig. 44b

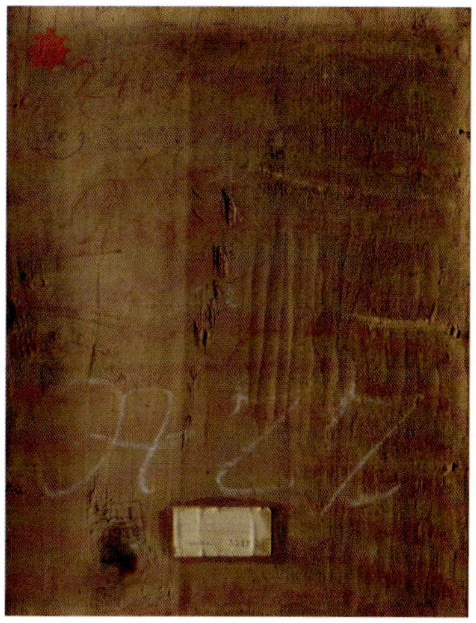
Fig. 44c

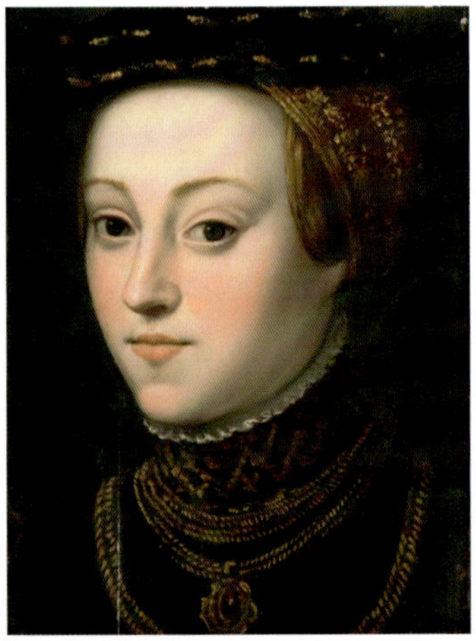

Fig. 45a

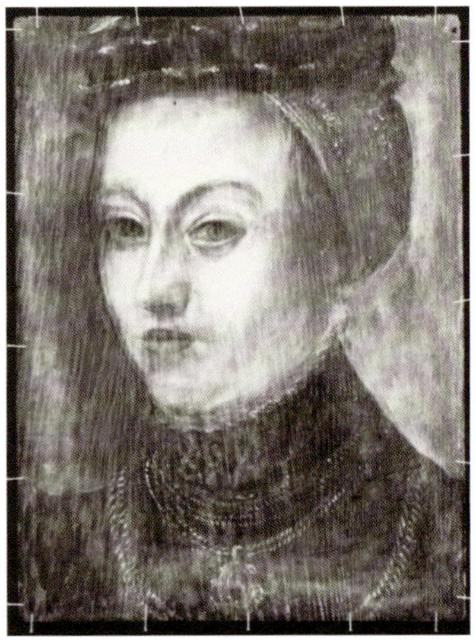

Fig. 45b

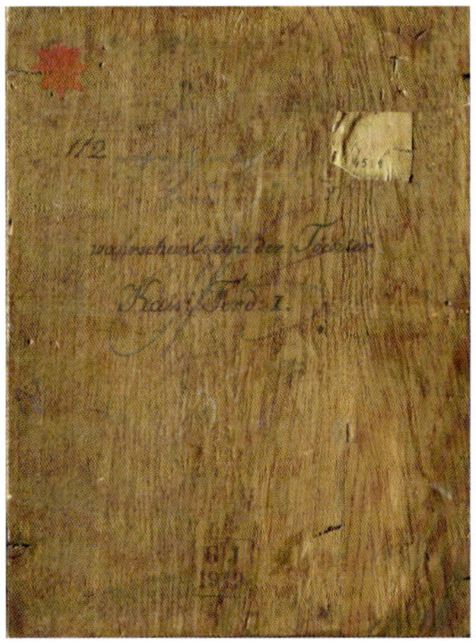

Fig. 45c

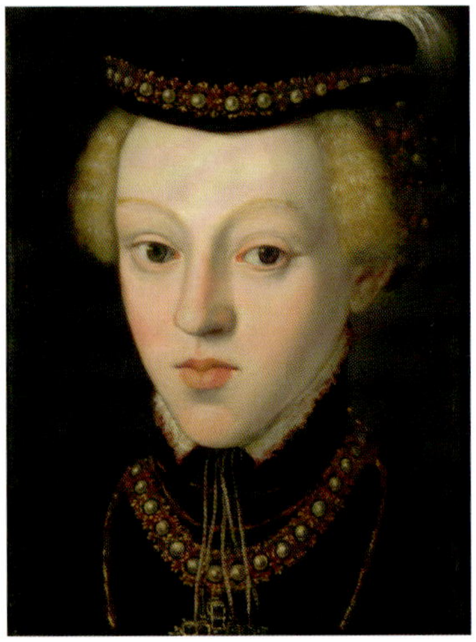

Fig. 46a

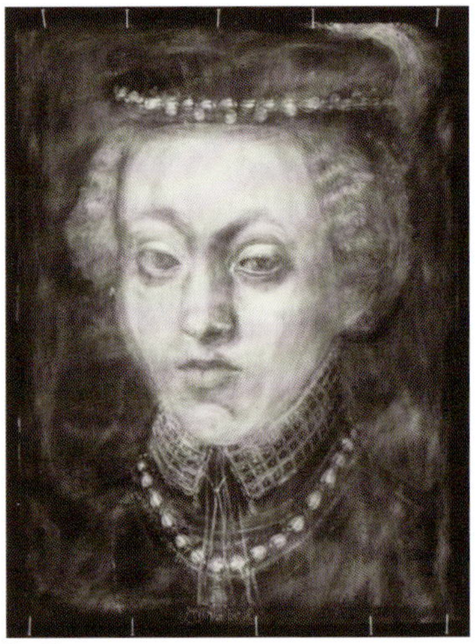

Fig. 46b

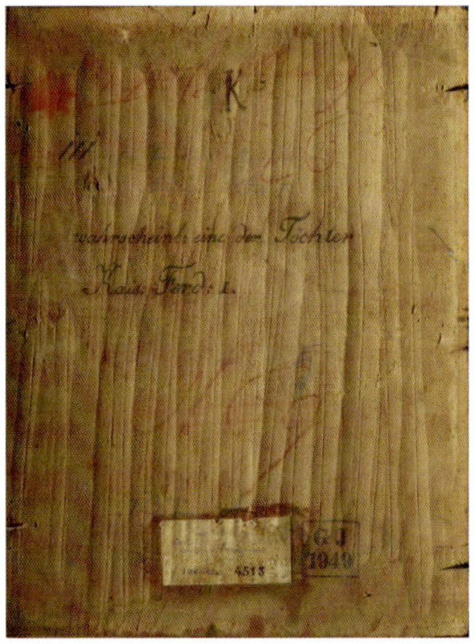

Fig. 46c

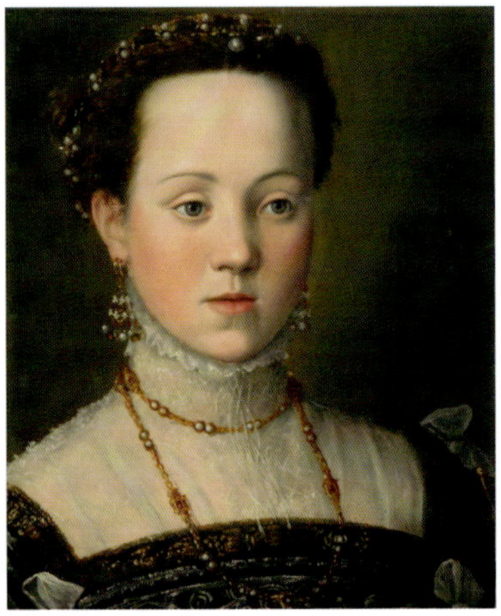

Fig. 47a

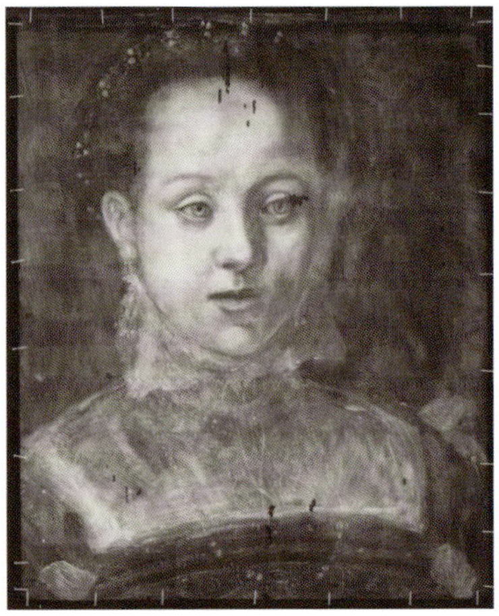

Fig. 47b

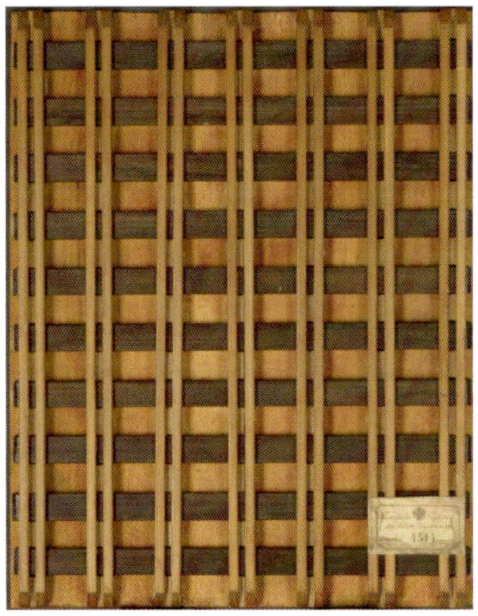

Fig. 47c

Fig. 45a:
Cat. no. III.6 *Archduchess Barbara* (?)

Fig. 45b:
Cat. no. III.6 X-radiograph, *Pentimenti*: in the first version in the area of the stiff collar, another chain can be seen, the left cheek was broader, hair in the underpainting not defined exactly and clearly bordered along the cheek

Fig. 45c:
Cat. no. III.6 Back of panel with inscription in raking light

Fig. 46a:
Cat. no. III.9 *Archduchess Johanna*

Fig. 46b:
Cat. no. III.9 X-radiograph, *Pentimenti*: several over workings: The face was more frontal, the nose wider, right cheek wider, left eyelid deeper, forehead higher, the eyebrow shadows in a dark tone, hair over the left ear. Different shape of collar (small tassels on the ends) with striking appearance – chequered with cross-stitched details – both ends of the collar are held together by a ribbon. The bonnet appears straight in relation to the forehead. Initial decoration with simple bud shaped jewellery, forerunner of the current chain

Fig. 46c:
Cat. no. III.9 Back of panel with tooling marks in raking light

Fig. 47a:
Cat. no. III.10 *Archduchess Anna*

Fig. 47b:
Cat. no. III.10 X-radiograph, *Pentimenti*: change in collar – originally not ruffled, but flat and larger horizontally (*see fig. 42b*). Shoulders moved upwards, jewellery modified from short and broad to long and narrow, change in décolleté.

Fig. 47c:
Cat. no. III.10 Back of panel, cradled

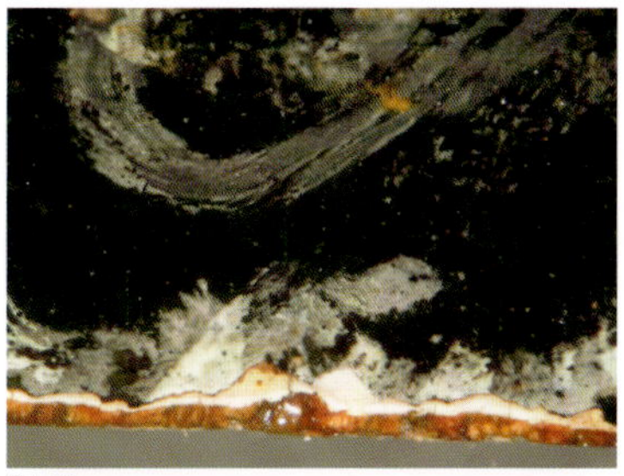
Fig. 48

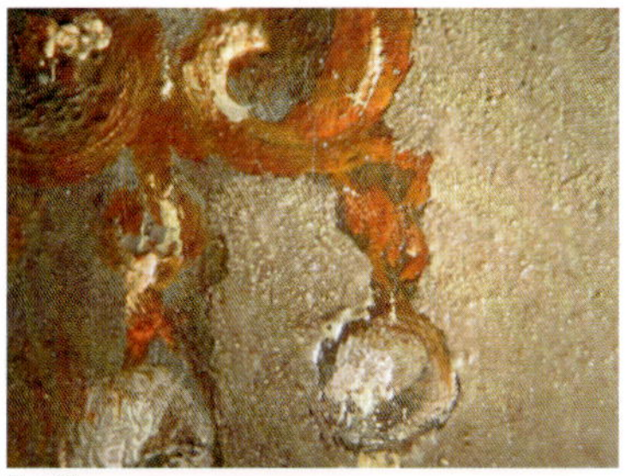
Fig. 49

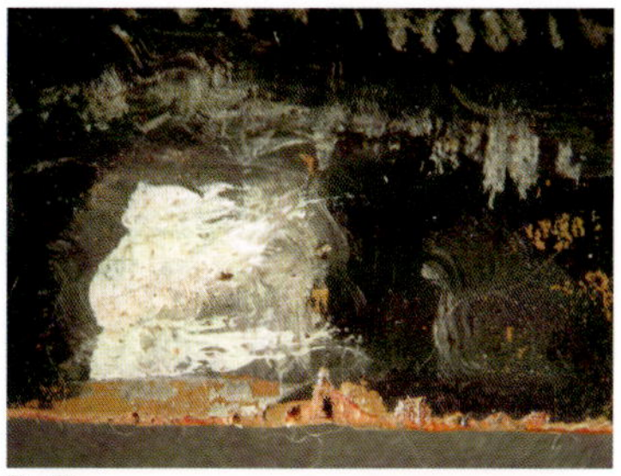
Fig. 50

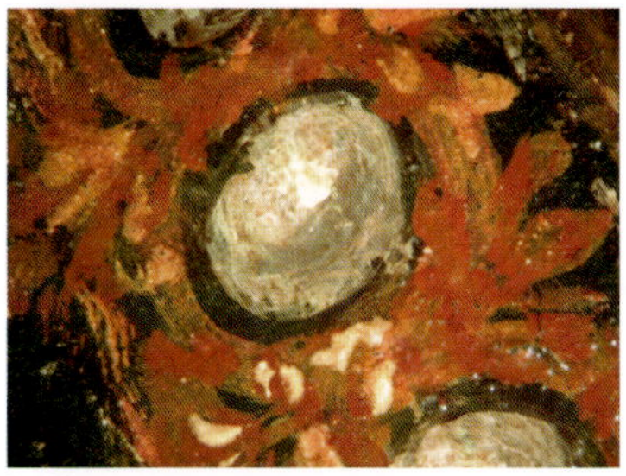
Fig. 51

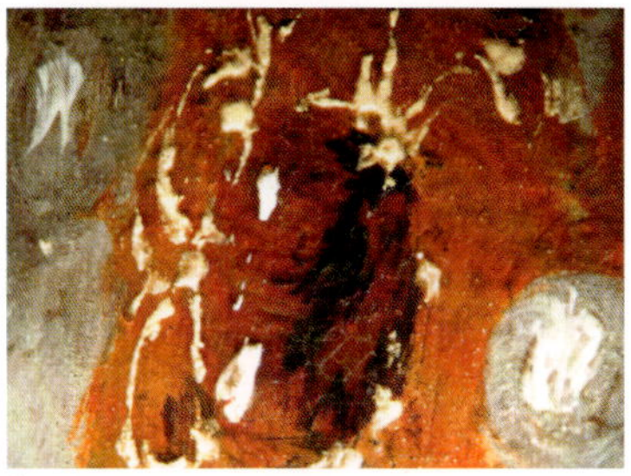
Fig. 52

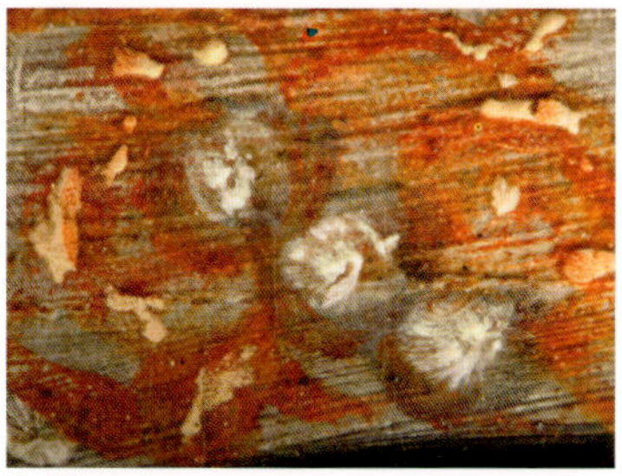
Fig. 53

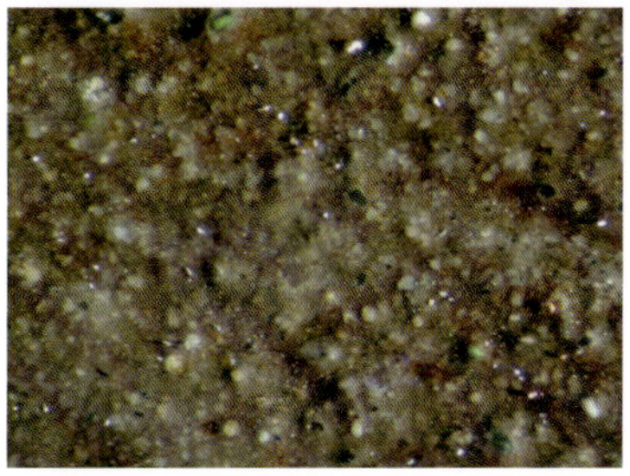
Fig. 54

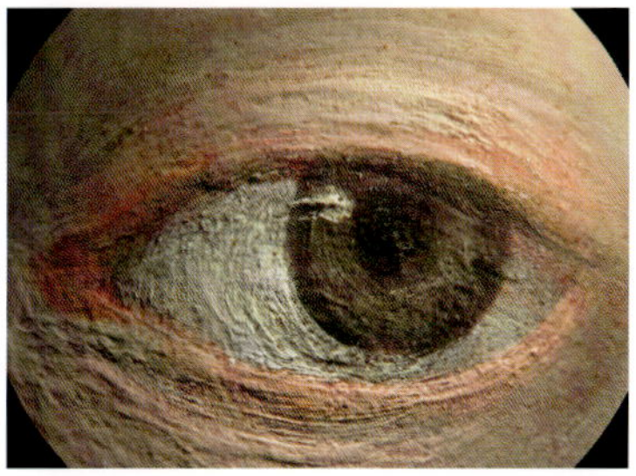
Fig. 55

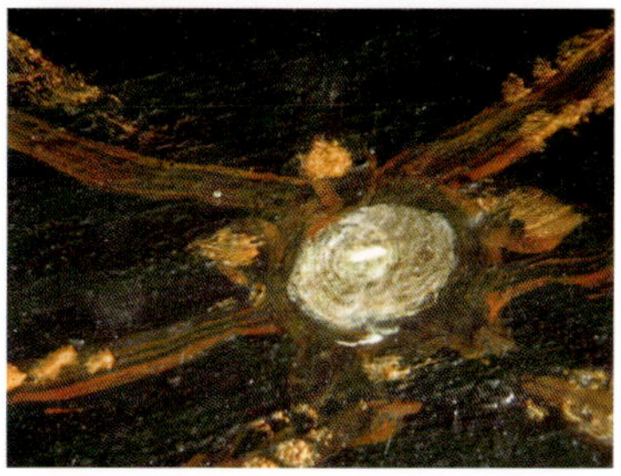
Fig. 56

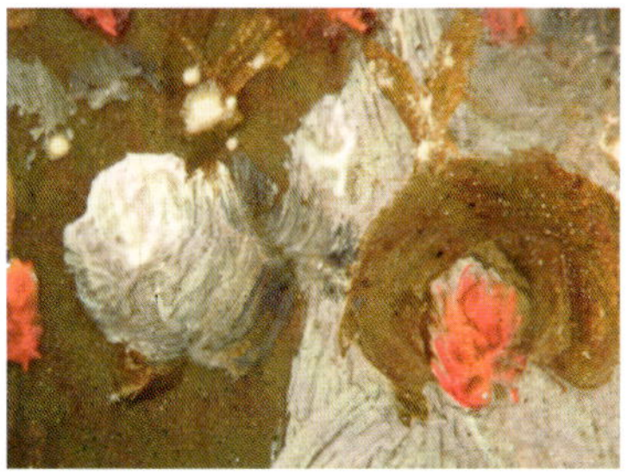
Fig. 57

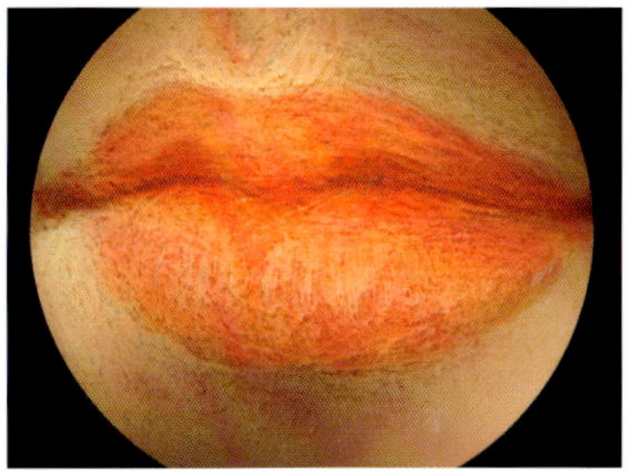
Fig. 58

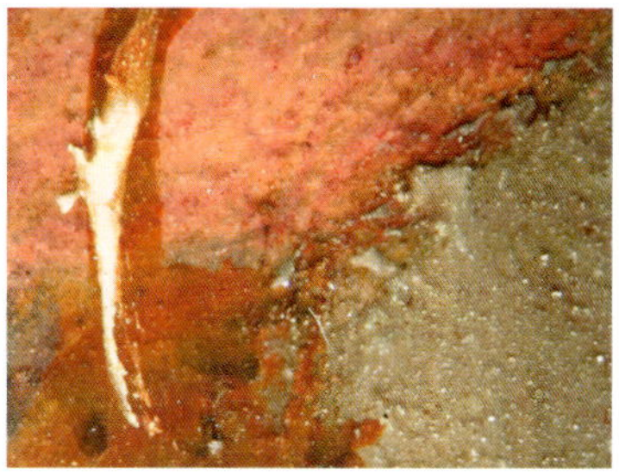
Fig. 59

Fig. 48:
Cat. no. III.10 Photomicrograph, white ground layer

Fig. 49:
Cat. no. III.5 Photomicrograph, grey-brown underpaint and grainy background

Fig. 50:
Cat. no. III.8 Photomicrograph, grey-brown ground layer

Fig. 51:
Cat. no. III.9 Photomicrograph, more fluid application of paint

Fig. 52:
Cat. no. III.8 Photomicrograph, mounting of a ruby – impasto work

Fig. 53:
Cat. no. III.5 Photomicrograph, stitched cuff. Brushwork from a rather dry consistency of paint that is followed by paint layers of varying thickness.

Fig. 54:
Cat. no. III.7 Photomicrograph, coarse grained paint, background

Fig. 55:
Cat. no. III.9 Photomicrograph, eye

Fig. 56:
Cat. no. III.5 Photomicrograph, wet-in-wet paint application, bonnet decoration

Fig. 57:
Cat. no. III.10 Photomicrograph, wet-in-wet paint application, earrings

Fig. 58:
Cat. no. III.5 Photomicrograph, glazes

Fig. 59:
Cat. no. III.8 Photomicrograph, colour of background extending inwards (correction of the outline of the head)

Mario A. Lazzari and Mario Marubbi

Technical Analysis of *The Vegetable Gardener*

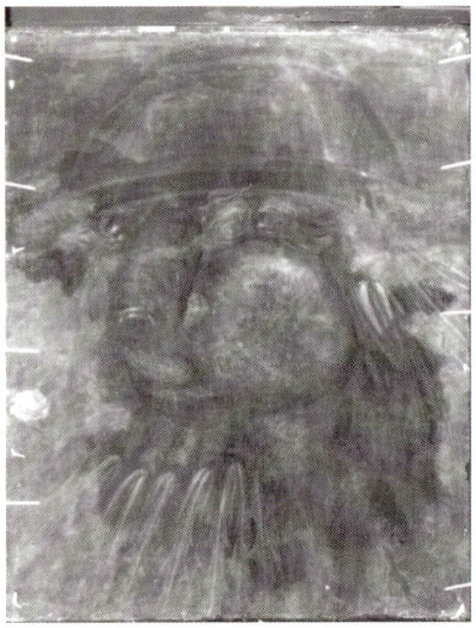

Fig. 1

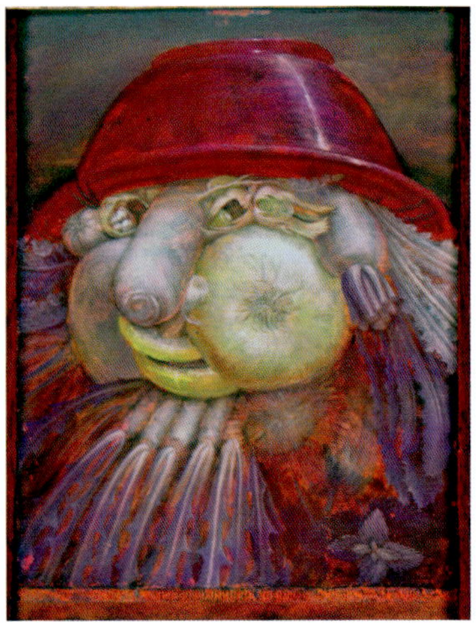

Fig. 2

The *reflectogram taken at 2000 nm* reveals a complicated preparatory drawing in pencil or pen, realized directly on the support. Much of this drawing does not correspond to the finished painting: the graphic lines do not follow the figurative elements of the definitive composition; in addition, near the bowl there are leaves that have not been painted.
However, the *false-colour image taken in infrared* does not show a real layer of paint under the one now visible that corresponds to the drawing revealed by the reflectography: in fact the ground appears fairly even, with a reddish tone interrupted here and there by slightly darker zones, suggesting that the previous layer of paint is merely that of an incomplete sketch.
The *X-ray photograph* confirms what has been deduced from the investigations referred to above, i.e. that underneath *The Vegetable Gardener* lies the sketch of a different composition, but one that is the work of the same artist. The background has an outline that does not match that of the painting now visible, and that, in the bowl for example, recalls the leaves revealed in the reflectograms. At various points, moreover, fine incisions made in the fresh paint can be clearly distinguished. These correspond to the outlines of the present composition, which was evidently painted directly over an incomplete sketch. The presence of these incisions is also confirmed by the *reflectogram taken at 1000 nm*.
In conclusion, the data obtained from the investigations conducted so far allow us to hypothesize the following: that the painter had outlined a composition different from the one we see now; that he had begun to paint the aforesaid composition (probably using a palette with a reduced range of colours), abandoning it shortly afterwards (at many points in fact the drawing is not covered by the first layer of paint); and that in order to block in the present painting he had made fine incisions with a sharp instrument while the pigment was still fresh, in order to position correctly the individual elements that make up the face.
Finally, it should be stressed that the neutral ground appears to have been painted last, blocking in the edges of the bowl; in the reflectograms taken at 1000 and 2000 nm, as well as in the false-colour IR image, we can discern a surface on which the composition of vegetables was set. Whether this was an autograph modification or not is currently under evaluation.

Fig. 1:
Reflectogram at 1000 nm

Fig. 2:
False colour infrared photo

Fig. 3:
Reflectogram at 2000 nm

Fig. 4:
X-ray photograph

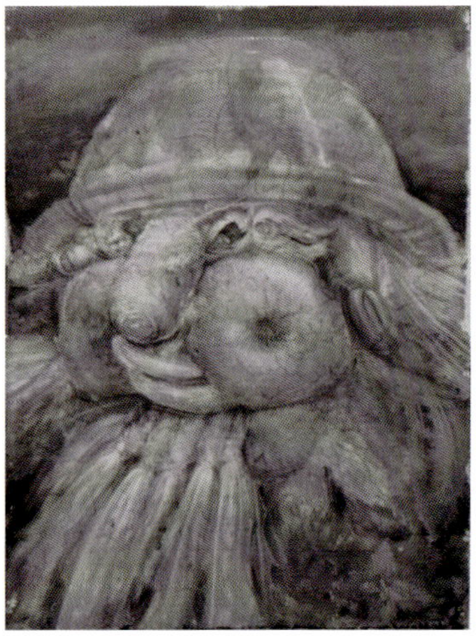

Fig. 3

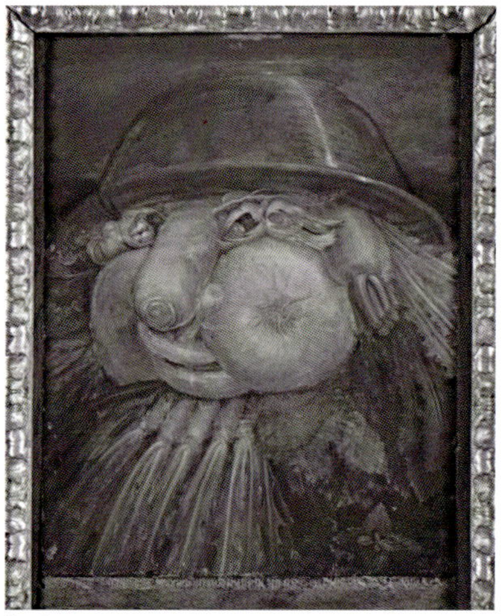

Fig. 4

Silvio Leydi

Giuseppe Arcimboldo in Milan: Documents and Hypotheses
Summary of the Documents Relating to the Milanese Period

In bold type: unpublished documents or new indications

Ordinary text: published documents (where not otherwise indicated, the documents have been published in Geiger 1954)

> [indented and in square brackets: documents or data not directly connected with Giuseppe Arcimboldo but of some interest in relation to his activity, his family or the Milanese historical and artistic context]

List of abbreviations (the names of collections of documents in the archives are always given in full):

APS: Archivio Parrocchiale, Sedriano
ASCM: Archivio Storico Civico, Milan
ASCo: Archivio di Stato, Como
ASDCo: Archivio Storico Diocesano, Como
ASDM: Archivio Storico Diocesano, Milan
ASM: Archivio di Stato, Milan
ASMn: Archivio di Stato, Mantua
ASS: Archivio del Santuario di Santa Maria dei Miracoli, Saronno
AVFDM: Archivio della Veneranda Fabbrica del Duomo, Milan
BLL: British Library, London
BML: British Museum, London

q. = quondam (English: late, son of the late)
S. = scudo/scudi
L. = lira/lire
ss. = soldo/soldi
d. = denaro/denari
fasc. = file
fol. = folio
c. = paper
cc. = papers
n. = note
no. = number
p.a. = old part
sez. = section

Key to collections of documents:
Giornale di cassa = Cash Book
Libri contabili = Account Books
Libro dei conti = Account Book
Libro giornale = Daybook
Libro mastro = Ledger
Notarile = Notarial
Ordinazioni capitolari = Capitulary Ordinations
Popolazione = Population
Registri = Registers
Registro dei battesimi = Register of Baptisms
Rubriche notarili = Notary Account Lists

Milanese measures
coins
1 lira = 20 soldi = 240 denari (1 soldo = 12 denari) (thus L. 5.8.4 = 5 lire, 8 soldi, 4 denari)
1 scudo = about 5 ? lire (or 110 soldi)

linear measures
1 braccio (ell) = about 60 centimetres

Administrative division of the city
The city of Milan was divided for administrative purposes into six *porte* or "gates" (Vercellina, Ticinese, Romana, Orientale, Nuova and Comasina) and into parishes. Thus the location of a house was indicated by the gate and the parish. It should be borne in mind, however, that the boundaries of the parishes (of ecclesiastic competence) did not always follow those of the gates (of civic and therefore lay competence): in some cases a single parish could belong to two adjoining and different gates.

1518
> [10 December, L. 59 to Biagio Arcimboldo, painter, for paintings executed on the houses of the Cathedral Vestry Board at Candoglia (AVFDM, Registri {Libro mastro} 313, fol. 228; *Annali* III, 206)]

1519
> [Milan Cathedral: no reference to Biagio Arcimboldo and no payment for designs of stained-glass windows or other works]

1520
> [29 December (1521 at Christmas). In the account code list of the notary Bernardo Belloni q. Giacomo is recorded a sale by Ermes Visconti to Bernardino Luini: it is probably the bill of sale of the emphyteutic lease later resold to the Visconti heir by the sons of Bernardino Luini on 9 November 1534 (v.). (ASM, Rubriche notarili 446; there is a gap in the notary's deeds)]

1526
birth of Giuseppe Arcimboldo

> [Milan Cathedral: no reference to Biagio Arcimboldo and no payment for designs of stained-glass windows or other works]

> [2 April, Antonio Maria Bozzolo q. Bartolomeo, Porta Vercellina, San Martino al Corpo Foris, receives from the Venerable Presbyter Giovanni Lurasco and Giovanni Antonio de Nigris, canons resident at San Giovanni Battista in Monza, and from Giovan Cristoforo Taegio and Andrea de Sirtori, both living in Monza and all vestrymen of the church of San Giovanni Battista in Monza, L. 408 in full payment for a tapestry depicting *Saint John the Baptist Preaching in the Wilderness* delivered to said vestrymen and for the design of a tapestry that will represent *Saint John the Baptist Baptizing*; he also receives L. 50 in advance for the next tapestry (*Saint John the Baptist Baptizing*) (ASM, Notarile 7999, no. 3149; Mirabile 2005, 263)]

> [18 April, Antonio Maria Bozzolo q. Bartolomeo, Porta Vercellina, San Martino al Corpo Foris, receives from Giovan Antonio Sonzino q. Giorgio, resident in Monza, who pays in the name of the vestry board of the church of San Giovanni Battista in Monza L. 200 on account for the tapestry with *Saint John the Baptist Baptizing* that said Bozzolo is weaving (ASM, Notarile 7999, no. 3176, Mirabile 2005, 267)]

1527
> [Milan Cathedral: no reference to Biagio Arcimboldo and no payment for designs of stained-glass windows or other works]

1532
> [Milan Cathedral: no reference to Biagio Arcimboldo and no payment for designs of stained-glass windows or other works]

> **[6 February, the vestrymen of the sanctuary of Santa Maria dei Miracoli of Saronno hand over to Master Alberto (probably the painter and gilder Alberto Meleguli da Lodi) the sum of L. 15 to pay to Master Biagio (Arcimboldo?). The payment is part of the entry in the name of Bernardino Luini (ASS, Registri 1, fasc. 3 {Libro dei conti 1526-50}, c. 178)]**

> [pre-1 July, Bernardino Luini dies. Date *ante quem* for the portrait of Biagio Arcimboldo painted by Luini and preserved in BML]

1533
> [Milan Cathedral: no reference to Biagio Arcimboldo and no payment for designs of stained-glass windows or other works]

1534
> [Milan Cathedral: no reference to Biagio Arcimboldo and no payment for designs of stained-glass windows or other works]

> [9 November, the heirs of the deceased painter Bernardino Luini (i.e. his sons Tobia, Evangelista, Giovanni Pietro and the child Aurelio, all minors and resident in Porta Comasina, in the parish of San Marcellino) resell to Giovanni Battista Visconti, son and heir of the deceased Ermes Visconti an emphyteutic lease that Ermes had ceded to Bernardino with a deed of the same notary (Bernardo Belloni q. Giacomo, v. 1520, 29 December) for the

sum of L. 625. Present at the drawing up of the deed, on behalf of the under-age brothers, are Giovanni Lomazzo q. Bartolomeo, Porta Ticinese, San Pietro in Camminadella (painter, maternal uncle of the minors), Margherita Lomazzo q. Master Ambrogio (wife of Bernardino Luini, mother of the minors and cousin of Giovanni) and Giovanni Antonio Luini q. Pietro, Porta Nuova, San Protaso ad Monachos (paternal uncle of the minors). Witnesses to the deed are: Bernardino de Bozolis q. Agostino, Porta Vercellina, San Pietro al Dosso; Annibale della Porta q. Giovanni, Porta Nuova, San Bartolomeo Intus; Master Biagio Arcimboldo q. Pasino, Porta Nuova, Santa Margherita (ASM, Notarile 7555; Miller 1989, 13)]

1535

[Milan Cathedral: no reference to Biagio Arcimboldo and no payment for designs of stained-glass windows or other works]

[July, Master Biagio (Arcimboldo?) receives from the vestrymen of the sanctuary of Santa Maria dei Miracoli in Saronno 2 scudi to be paid to Gaudenzio Ferrari (ASS, Registri 1, fasc. 3 {Libro dei conti 1526-50}, c. 24; De Lorenzo 1989, 222)]

1537

[11 July, the tapestry weaver Antonio Maria Bozzolo receives L. 200 on account for part of the payment due to him for the tapestry with the *Burial and Profanation of the Body of Saint John the Baptist* in Monza Cathedral, the eighth in the serie (ASM, Notarile 8010)]

[20 September, the tapestry weaver Antonio Maria Bozzolo receives L. 55 on account for part of the payment due to him for the tapestry with the *Burial and Profanation of the Body of Saint John the Baptist* in Monza Cathedral, eighth in the series (**ASM, Notarile 10809**; cited without references in Repishti 2002, 51)]

1538

[17 October: confessio: Master Biagio Arcimboldo q. Pasino, Porta Nuova, San Protaso ad Monachos, receives from Costantino Bossi q. Luigi, Porta Nuova, San Protaso ad Monachos, prior of the Scuola di San Giuseppe, L. 20 in full payment of the paintings and other works carried out by said Biagio in the guild, situated in Porta Nuova, parish of San Silvestro, in the Andegari district, works valued in all at L. 48. The L. 20 come from a deposit of the same sum registered by the notary Gerolamo Ciseri (non-existent, probably the notary Gerolamo Ciceri, whose records have been destroyed) (ASM, Notarile 7621; Miller 1989, 13-14)]

1540

[Milan Cathedral: no reference to Biagio Arcimboldo and no payment for designs of stained-glass windows or other works]

1541

[Milan Cathedral: no reference to Biagio Arcimboldo and no payment for designs of stained-glass windows or other works]

1542

[Milan Cathedral: no reference to Biagio Arcimboldo and no payment for designs of stained-glass windows or other works]

1543

[Milan Cathedral: no reference to Biagio Arcimboldo and no payment for designs of stained-glass windows or other works]

1544

[Milan Cathedral: no reference to Biagio Arcimboldo and no payment for designs of stained-glass windows or other works]

1545

[3 June, L. 8.15 to Master Painter Biagio Arcimboldo for painting various *Maestà* for 35 candlesticks at ss. 5 each on the occasion of this year's general oblation of Porta Orientale (AVFDM, Registri {Libro mastro} 329, fol. 222; Registri {Giornale di cassa} 405, fol. 189v)]

[10 June, L. 23.10 to Master Painter Biagio Arcimboldo for painting several *Maestà* on the occasion of this year's general oblation of Porta Romana (AVFDM, Registri {Libro mastro} 329, fol. 222; Registri {Giornale di cassa} 405, fol. 192)]

[14 September, L. 6 to Master Painter Biagio Arcimboldo, as per a note with the treasurer Reina (AVFDM, Registri {Libro mastro} 329, fol. 437; Registri {Giornale di cassa} 405, fol. 220)]

1546

[31 August, L. 5 to Master Painter Biagio Arcimboldo for 5 cartoons supplied for the oblations of the carriers and porters made on 16th last (AVFDM, Registri {Libro mastro} 330, fol. 332) (ref. c. 260)]

[13 September, L. 5.6 to Master Painter Biagio Arcimboldo for cartoons supplied for the feast of Saint Mary and for the oblations of the cobblers and measurers of feed (AVFDM, Registri {Libro mastro} 330, fol. 332) (ref. c. 261)]

1547

[Milan Cathedral: no reference to Biagio Arcimboldo and no payment for designs of stained-glass windows or other works]

1548

[the painter Giovanni Luini is paid for designs of stained-glass windows on 5 March (L. 12 for 6 drawings) and 6 August (L. 6 for 3 drawings) (AVFDM, Registri {Libro mastro} 331, fols. 168 and 172); Registri {Giornale di cassa} 407, fols. 13v and 54]

[July-August, Maximilian of Habsburg passes through Lombardy and Milan on his way from Vienna to Spain, where he will take the place of his cousin Philip and marry Maria of Habsburg, daughter of Charles V. He is accompanied by the cardinal of Trent Cristoforo Madruzzo]

[15 October, L. 13.5 to Master Biagio Arcimboldo for having painted two canvas banners for two altars in the cathedral (at L. 5.10 each) and two *Maestà* for the paschal candlesticks of the cobblers (AVFDM, Registri {Libro mastro} 331, fol. 174; Registri {Giornale di cassa} 407, fol. 66v)]

[December, Prince Philip of Habsburg passes through Lombardy and Milan on his way from Valladolid to Flanders, accompanied by the cardinal of Trent Cristoforo Madruzzo]

[24 December, L. 45 to Master Biagio Arcimboldo for having painted 8 banners for the altars of the cathedral, the arms of Prince Philip of Habsburg and other things (AVFDM, Registri {Libro mastro} 331, fol. 176; Registri {Giornale di cassa} 407, fol. 84v)]

1549

[October - November, Archduke Ferdinand of Austria, coming from Mantua (where he had accompanied his sister Catherine, bride of Francesco Gonzaga), is in Lombardy and Milan before continuing his return journey via Venice]

[22 November, L. 30 to Master Biagio Arcimboldo for 30 designs of stained-glass windows (AVFDM, Registri {Libro mastro} 331, fol. 133; **Registri {Giornale di cassa} 407, fol. 165v**; Geiger 1954, 113)]

24 December, L. 6 to Master Giuseppe Arcimboldo for 4 designs of stained-glass windows (AVFDM, Registri {Libro mastro} 331, fol. 133; **Registri {Giornale di cassa} 407, fol. 171v**; Geiger 1954, 113)

1550

[24 March, L. 5 to Biagio Arcimboldo for painting several images in the sacristy of the Ordinaries (AVFDM, Registri {Libro mastro} 332, fol. 111); (**Registri {Giornale di cassa} 408, fol. 21**; *Annali* III, 319)]

[18 April, L. 9 to Master Biagio Arcimboldo for 6 designs of stained-glass windows (AVFDM, Registri {Libro mastro} 332, fol. 127; **Registri {Giornale di cassa} 408, fol. 30;** Geiger 1954, 113)]

[13 May, L. 6 to Master Biagio Arcimboldo for 4 designs of stained-glass windows (AVFDM, Registri {Libro mastro} 332, fol. 127; **Registri {Giornale di cassa} 408, fol. 38;** Geiger 1954, 113)]

[21 June, L. 9 to Master Biagio Arcimboldo for 6 designs of stained-glass windows (AVFDM, Registri {Libro mastro} 332, fol. 127; **Registri {Giornale di cassa} 408, fol. 48, under the date 23 June;** Geiger 1954, 113)]

[27 June, L. 41.11 to Biagio Arcimboldo for paintings made on the occasion of the triumphal entry of Archbishop Giovanni Angelo Arcimboldo (AVFDM, Registri {Libro mastro} 332, fol. 114; Registri {Giornale di cassa} 408, fol. 48, under the date 23 June)]

[23 August, L. 9 to Master Biagio Arcimboldo for 6 designs of stained-glass windows (AVFDM, Registri {Libro mastro} 332, fol. 127; **Registri {Giornale di cassa} 408, fol. 60v;** Geiger 1954, 113)

[31 October, L. 9 to Master Biagio Arcimboldo for 6 designs of stained-glass windows (AVFDM, Registri {Libro mastro} 332, fol. 128; **Registri {Giornale di cassa} 408, fol. 74v;** Geiger 1954, 113)]

[24 December, L. 9 to Master Biagio Arcimboldo for 6 designs of stained-glass windows (AVFDM, Registri {Libro mastro} 332, fol. 128; **Registri {Giornale di cassa} 408, fol. 88;** Geiger 1954, 113)]

1551

[24 February, L. 9 to Master Biagio Arcimboldo for 6 designs of stained-glass windows (AVFDM, Registri {Libro mastro} 332, fol. 336; **Registri {Giornale di cassa} 408, fol. 109v {under the date 25 February}**; Geiger 1954, 114)]

20 May, L. 9 to Master Giuseppe Arcimboldo for 6 designs of stained-glass windows (AVFDM, Registri {Libro mastro} 332, fol. 336; **Registri {Giornale di cassa} 408, fol. 130**; Geiger 1954, 114)

17 June, L. 8.5 to Master Giuseppe Arcimboldo for having painted the image of Mary with the façade of the cathedral on the workshops just built near the ducal palace (AVFDM, Registri {Libro mastro} 332, fol. 330; **Registri {Giornale di cassa} 408, fol. 139**; *Annali* IV, 6)

1 August, L. 9 to Master Giuseppe Arcimboldo for 6 designs of stained-glass windows (AVFDM, Registri {Libro mastro} 332, fol. 336; **Registri {Giornale di cassa} 408, fol. 149**; Geiger 1954, 114)

15 September, L. 9 to Master Giuseppe Arcimboldo for 6 designs of stained-glass windows made in August (AVFDM, Registri {Libro mastro} 332, fol. 336; **Registri {Giornale di cassa} 408, fol. 158v**; Geiger 1954, 114)

[November, Archduke Maximilian of Habsburg is in Lombardy (25 November) and Milan (28 November - 2 December) on his way back from Spain to Vienna; travelling with him are his wife, Maria of Habsburg, daughter of Emperor Charles V, his daughter Anna (born on 1 November 1549) and an elephant]

28 November, L. 10.5 to Master Giuseppe Arcimboldo for having painted 5 insignia of the king of Bohemia and L. 2.5 for 2.5 hundred pounds of ivy to adorn the door of the cathedral (AVFDM, Registri {Libro mastro} 332, fol. 333; **Registri {Giornale di cassa} 408, fol. 178v;** *Annali* IV, 7)

29 December, L. 9 to Master Giuseppe Arcimboldo for 6 designs of stained-glass windows (AVFDM, Registri [Libro mastro] 332, fol. 336; **Registri [Giornale di cassa] 408, fol. 186v [under the date 31 December]**; Geiger 1954, 114)

1552

24 February, L. 9 to Master Giuseppe Arcimboldo for 6 designs of stained-glass windows made in January and February (AVFDM, Registri {Libro mastro} 333, fol. 152; **Registri {Giornale di cassa} 409, fol. 11v**; Geiger 1954, 114)

26 March, L. 9 to Master Giuseppe Arcimboldo for 6 designs of stained-glass windows (AVFDM, Registri {Libro mastro} 333, fol. 152; **Registri {Giornale di cassa} 409, fol. 19**; Geiger 1954, 114)

18 May, L. 9 to Master Giuseppe Arcimboldo for 6 designs of stained-glass windows (AVFDM, Registri {Libro mastro} 333, fol. 152; **Registri {Giornale di cassa} 409, fol. 44v**; Geiger 1954, 114)

22 June, L. 6 to Master Giuseppe Arcimboldo for having painted the Madonna with the façade of the cathedral on a house and garden belonging to the vestry board in Porta Orientale (AVFDM, Registri {Libro mastro} 333, fol. 139; **Registri {Giornale di cassa} 409, fol. 53v;** *Annali* IV, 10)

8 August, L. 12 to Master Giuseppe Arcimboldo for 8 designs of stained-glass windows (AVFDM, Registri {Libro mastro} 333, fol. 152; **Registri {Giornale di cassa} 409, fol. 65**; Geiger 1954, 114)

21 October, L. 3 to Master Giuseppe Arcimboldo for 4 designs of stained-glass windows (AVFDM, Registri {Libro mastro} 333, fol. 152; **Registri {Giornale di cassa} 409, fol. 84;** Geiger 1954, 114 {under the date 21 October})

21 October, L. 1.10 to Master Giuseppe Arcimboldo for having painted three cartoons for the oblation of the measurers and cobblers (Registri {Libro mastro} 333, fol. 114; Registri {Giornale di cassa} 409, fol. 84v)

1553

23 February, L. 3 to Master Giuseppe Arcimboldo for 4 designs of stained-glass windows (AVFDM, Registri {Libro mastro} 333, fol. 154; **Registri {Giornale di cassa} 409, fol. 119v**; indicated without a date and with incorrect page numbers in Geiger 1954, 115)

23 February, L. 4 to Master Giuseppe Arcimboldo for the painting of a cartoon with a tabernacle for last Christmas, and for a drawing of the territory of Volpedo (AVFDM, Registri {Libro mastro} 333, fol. 154; **Registri {Giornale di cassa} 409, fol. 119v**; *Annali* IV, 9, under the date 23 February 1552)

27 September, L. 6 to Master Giuseppe Arcimboldo for 6 designs of stained-glass windows (AVFDM, Registri {Libro mastro} 333, fol. 154; **Registri {Giornale di cassa} 409, fol. 165**; indicated without a date and with incorrect page numbers in Geiger 1954, 115**)**

31 October, L. 5 to Master Giuseppe Arcimboldo for having painted 10 cartoons for the oblation of the porters, carriers, measurers and cobblers (Registri {Libro mastro} 333, fol. 116; Registri {Giornale di cassa} 409, fol. 173)

22 December, L. 5.8 to Master Giuseppe Arcimboldo for 6 designs of stained-glass windows and for the silvering of a staff for the lamps of the high altar (AVFDM, Registri {Libro mastro} 333, fol. 154; Registri {Giornale di cassa} 409, fol. 185v)

1554

8 February, L. 10 to Master Giuseppe Arcimboldo for painting part of the organ doors (AVFDM, Registri {Libro mastro} 334, fol. 185; **Registri {Giornale di cassa} 410, fol. 8**; *Annali* IV, 15)

28 June, L. 6 to Master Giuseppe Arcimboldo for 6 designs of stained-glass windows (AVFDM, Registri {Libro mastro} 334, fol. 202; **Registri {Giornale di cassa} 410, fol. 33v**; indicated without a date in Geiger 1954, 115)

19 July, L. 21 to Master Giuseppe Arcimboldo for having painted the platform, hall and porch of the vestry board (AVFDM, Registri {Libro mastro} 334, fol. 187; **Registri {Giornale di cassa} 410, fol. 40v**; *Annali* IV, 15)

18 August, L. 6 to Master Giuseppe Arcimboldo for 4 designs of stained-glass windows (AVFDM, Registri {Libro mastro} 334, fol. 202; **Registri {Giornale di cassa} 410, fol. 46**; indicated without a date in Geiger 1954, 115)

21 August, L. 5.15 to Master Giuseppe Arcimboldo for having painted the baldachin of the high altar (AVFDM, Registri {Libro mastro} 334, fol. 188; **Registri {Giornale di cassa} 410, fol. 46v**; *Annali* IV, 16)

[14 September, Biagio Arcimboldo q. Pasio, resident in Porta Nuova, Santo Stefano in Nosiggia, and the painter Giovan Angelo Zavattari q. Ambrogio, Porta Vercellina, Santa Maria alla Porta, are present as arbitrators at the drawing up of the agreement following the dispute over the property left by the deceased Bernardino Luini. The agreement has a validity of two months but is renewable (ASM, Notarile 12915; Miller 1989, 14)]

[15 September, payment of L. 319 to Master Andrea Meda (Lomazzo) and associates as recompense for their having gilded and painted the baldachin of the high altar, including the gold (AVFDM, Registri {Libro mastro} 334, fol. 188; **Registri {Giornale di cassa} 410, fol. 50**)]

22 October, Giuseppe Arcimboldo di Biagio, as resident of the parish of Santi Cosma e Damiano (Porta Nuova), summoned by the elder with other neighbours, appoints Luigi Dinali q. Stefano representative of the said parish to swear loyalty to the new duke of Milan, Philip of Habsburg (ASM, Potenze sovrane post 1535, 3, parish of Santi Cosma e Damiano)

[8 November, L. 36 to Master Andrea de Albrisii (Albricci) for having carved a frieze, a crown and a scroll on the altarpiece of the chapel of Santa Corona, including the work of removing the altarpiece and mounting it again (reference to c. 126: L. 36 to Master Andrea de Albrisi for various expenses) (ASM, Santa Corona, Registri 58, c. 88)]

17 November, L. 8.16 to Master Giuseppe Arcimboldo for having painted two insignia of the king of England (Philip of Habsburg) and 2 stools for the altar and for 4 designs for stained-glass windows (AVFDM, Registri {Libro mastro} 334, fol. 189; **Registri {Giornale di cassa} 410, fol. 63**; *Annali* IV, 16)

[19 November, the term of the agreement for the inheritance of the deceased Bernardino Luini of 14 September last is extended for another 22 days. Biagio Arcimboldo now resides in the parish of San Vittore al Teatro, Porta Vercellina (ASM, Notarile 12915; Miller 1989, 15)]

26 November, Arcimboldo is paid for work on Titian's altarpiece of the *Crowning with Thorns* in the chapel of Santa Corona in Santa Maria delle Grazie: "L. 49.10 reckoned to Master Joseph Arcinboldo, taken into account 670 sheets of gold leaf applied to the Altarpiece of the chapel of the Corona alle Gratie, taken into account the gilding L. 36.10, and the rest for the painting, making and ornamentation of said altarpiece, to Messer Jo. Antonio Porro on account, L. XV [sic] viiii ss. X" (with reference to c. 128 (disbursements of the treasurer Antonio Porro): "On said day (26.11.1554) L. 49 ss. 10 paid to Master Joxeph Arcinboldo to set in order the altarpiece of the chapel of Santa Corona alle Gratie, for various expenses, fol. 88" (ASM, Santa Corona, Registri 58, c. 88)

1555

> **[26 August, account that starts on 26 August 1555 (first payment) and ends on 28 May 1556 (balance) in the name of the sculptor Giulio da Oggiono for the construction of a marble tabernacle to be placed above the altar of the sacristy of the church of San Francesco Grande, which serves as chapel of the q. Ottaviano Taverna: paid in all are L. 612.10 (made up of S. 100 + L. 24 for the tabernacle proper, L. 11 for a marble step, L. 5 for various works), with references to various payments to the said Giulio da Oggiono, fols. 175, 181, 189, 192, 202, 203, 204, 205) (ASM, Santa Corona, Registri 58, fol. 170)]**

3 October, L. 9.4 to Master Giuseppe Arcimboldo for painting a *Maestà* for the oblation of the measurers, ducal insignia and other things for the feast of Saint Mary last (**AVFDM, Registri {Libro mastro} 334, fol. 422; Registri {Giornale di cassa} 410, fol. 131;** *Annali* IV, 20)

3 October, L. 33 to Master Giuseppe Arcimboldo for 22 designs of stained-glass windows (AVFDM, Registri {Libro mastro} 334, fol. 203; **Registri {Giornale di cassa} 410, fol. 131;** indicated without a date in Geiger 1954, 115)

> **[22 December, L. 9 to Master Painter Giovan Stefano Arcimboldo for the expenses of the altarpiece of the chapel of the q. Francesco Gallo in the church of Santa Maria alla Porta (reference c. 192, for various expenses), L. VIIII (ASM, Santa Corona, Registri 58, fol. 176)]**

24 December, L. 6 to Master Giuseppe Arcimboldo for 4 designs of stained-glass windows (AVFDM, Registri {Libro mastro} 334, fol. 203; **Registri {Giornale di cassa} 410, fol. 148v;** indicated without a date in Geiger 1954, 115)

1556

31 January, L. 6 to Master Giuseppe Arcimboldo for 6 designs of stained-glass windows (AVFDM, Registri {Libro mastro} 335, fol. 201; **Registri {Giornale di cassa} 411, fol. 2v**; indicated without a date in Geiger 1954, 115)

18 May, L. 6 to Master Giuseppe Arcimboldo for 4 designs of stained-glass windows (AVFDM, Registri {Libro mastro} 335, fol. 201; **Registri {Giornale di cassa} 411, fol. 28v**; indicated without a date in Geiger 1954, 115)

28 May, agreements between the church of San Giovanni Battista in Monza, represented by canon Giovan Angelo Gavanti q. Ambrogio, and the painters Giuseppe Arcimboldo son of Biagio (absent, represented by Master Francesco Crodari da Rosate q. Bartolomeo, Porta Orientale, parish of Santo Stefano in Brolo Intus) and Giuseppe Lomazzo son of Andrea, Porta Nuova, parish of Santo Stefano in Nosiggia (Meda, who agreed with the permission of his father Andrea q. Bernardo); the painters undertook to fresco 8 angels, 4 evangelists on the ceiling and the Tree of Life, the Virgin Mary, Saint John the Baptist and Christ Crucified on the wall, all of the same quality as the figures that adorn the ceiling of Santa Maria presso San Celso located in Porta Ludovica in Milan, the whole for S. 250 including the paint but excluding the scaffolding and accommodation (ASM, Notarile 11801, and copy in ASM, Notarile 8033, no. 9434; Miller 1989, 15)

10 June, ratification of the contract of 28 May last between the church of San Giovanni Battista, i.e. the Cathedral of Monza, and the painters Giuseppe Lomazzo called Meda and Giuseppe Arcimboldo son of Biagio (who was absent at the drawing up of the contract itself, enclosed), resident in Porta Nuova, Santi Cosma e Damiano (ASM, Notarile 8882; Miller 1989, 17)

5 September, L. 3 to Master Giuseppe Arcimboldo for 2 designs of stained-glass windows (AVFDM, Registri {Libro mastro} 335, fol. 201; **Registri {Giornale di cassa} 411, fol. 51**; indicated without a date in Geiger 1954, 115)

5 September, L. 4 to Master Giuseppe Arcimboldo for the painting of 8 cartoons for the oblation of the carriers and cobblers carried out in August (AVFDM, Registri {Libro mastro} 335, fol. 169; Registri {Giornale di cassa} 411, fol. 51)

9 September, payment to Giuseppe Arcimboldo for paintings in the chapel of Ottaviano Taverna in San Francesco: "MDLVI, Inheritance of the quondam Signor Ottaviano Taverna, to give on the day of 9 September L. 60.19 cash to Master Painter Joxeph Arcinboldo for having painted the chapel in the sacristy of Santo Francesco, to Messer Jo. Antonio Porro, on account, L. LX ss. XVIIII" (reference to c. 206: disbursements of the treasurer Antonio Porro: L. 60.19 {and reference to fol. 218} of the inheritance of the q. Ottaviano Taverna) (ASM, Santa Corona, Registri 58, fol. 218)

9 November, L. 6 to Master Giuseppe Arcimboldo for 4 designs of stained-glass windows (AVFDM, Registri {Libro mastro} 335, fol. 201; **Registri {Giornale di cassa} 411, fol. 67v**; indicated without a date in Geiger 1954, 115)

> [The date 1556 appears several times in the stained-glass window with *Scenes from the Life of Saint Catherine of Alexandria* in the cathedral, divided into 48 scenes or episodes]

1557

26 April, L. 12 to Master Giuseppe Arcimboldo for 8 designs of stained-glass windows (AVFDM, Registri {Libro mastro} 335, fol. 202; **Registri {Giornale di cassa} 411, fol. 97v**; indicated without a date in Geiger 1954, 115)

12 June, L. 9 to Master Giuseppe Arcimboldo for 6 designs of stained-glass windows (AVFDM, Registri {Libro mastro} 335, fol. 202; **Registri {Giornale di cassa} 411, fol. 112**; indicated without a date in Geiger 1954, 115)

11 September, L. 39.3 to Master Giuseppe Arcimboldo for painting and gilding 522 poles (AVFDM, Registri {Libro mastro} 335, fol. 171; Registri {Giornale di cassa} 411, fol. 127v)

11 September, L. 4.16 to Master Giuseppe Arcimboldo for painting 8 *Maestà* for the oblations of the carriers and cobblers on 8 August last (AVFDM, Registri {Libro mastro} 355, fol. 171; Registri {Giornale di cassa} 411, fol. 127v)

11 September, L. 5.12 to Master Giuseppe Arcimboldo for painting the Madonna with the façade of the cathedral on the workhouses facing the Ducal Palace, for painting the insignia of the governor Figueroa and for cartoons "mensuratorum broleti" (AVFDM, Registri {Libro mastro} 335, fol. 191; **Registri {Giornale di cassa} 411, fol. 127v**; *Annali* IV, 27)

13 November, L. 9 to Master Giuseppe Arcimboldo for 6 designs of stained-glass windows (AVFDM, Registri {Libro mastro} 335, fol. 202; **Registri {Giornale di cassa} 411, fol. 141v**; indicated without a date in Geiger 1954, 115)

1558

1 March, L. 4 to Master Giuseppe Arcimboldo for having painted the rebuilt wall outside the door of the Cathedral facing the Ducal Palace, and for the insignia of the archbishop (Filippo Archinto) to be placed in the choir of the Cathedral (AVFDM, Registri {Libro mastro} 336, fol. 168; **Registri {Giornale di cassa} 412, fol. 7**; *Annali* IV, 29)

9 December, Giuseppe Arcimboldo receives through his proxy Gabrio da Corte L. 57.10, equal to 10 scudi, as initial payment for the design that he has to execute for the tapestry of the *Death of the Virgin* commissioned from him by Como Cathedral (ASDCo, Fabbrica del duomo, Libri contabili 14 {Mastro Biancho 1557-64}, fol. 114, account of Arcimboldo, and reference to fol. 99, Cassa della Fabbrica, where the same payment is registered)

> [The payment to Arcimboldo, in 1558, also opens, at the Vestry Board of Como Cathedral, the entry concerning the tapestries; in fact the first item relates to the cost of the design commissioned from the painter, a total of 158 lire and 19 soldi, an expense that is registered at the top of the entry; indication given by Ciceri 1811, 99-100, and then more systematically by Monti 1897, 196, and then repeated innumerable times later on **(ASDCo, Fabbrica del duomo, Libri contabili 14 {Mastro Biancho 1557-64}, fol. 114)]**

10 December, deposit with Filippo Candiani of L. 196.10 intended for Arcimboldo and Meda as the balance for the frescoes painted in Monza Cathedral (ASM, Notarile 12825; Miller 1989, 17) (v. 1559, 5 May)

1559
5 May, permission given by the canons of Monza to Filippo Candiani to pay Arcimboldo and Meda the money already deposited with him, L. 196.10, in full payment of the contract and after the painters Gerolamo Figino and Giulio Biglia had approved the work (ASM, Notarile 12825; Miller 1989, 19) (v. 1558, 10 December)

14 December, Giuseppe Arcimboldo receives L. 57.10, equal to 10 scudi, through his proxy Gabrio da Corte as second payment for the design that he has to execute for the tapestry of the *Death of the Virgin* commissioned from him by Como Cathedral (ASDCo, Fabbrica del duomo, Libri contabili 14 {Mastro Biancho 1557-64}, fol. 114 left, account of Arcimboldo, and reference to fol. 144, Cassa della Fabbrica, where the same payment is registered)

1560
18 March, Giuseppe Arcimboldo receives through his proxy Gabrio da Corte L. 43.19 as balance for the design that he has executed for the tapestry of the *Death of the Virgin* commissioned from him by Como Cathedral (ASDCo, Fabbrica del duomo, Registri, Libri contabili 14 {Mastro Biancho 1557-64}, fol. 114, account of Arcimboldo, and reference to fol. 149, Cassa della Fabbrica, where the same payment is registered; ASDCo, Fabbrica del duomo, Registri, Libri di cassa 7 {Libro giornale 1560-70}, unnumbered cc., 18 March 1560)

1561
[23 August, the canvas that Arcimboldo has executed with the design of the *Death of the Virgin* for the tapestry intended for Como Cathedral is taken from Milan to Como (ASDCo, Fabbrica del duomo, Libri contabili 14 {Mastro Biancho 1557-64}, fol. 192, account of the tapestries, and reference to fol. 225, Cassa della Fabbrica, where the same payment is registered; ASDCo, Fabbrica del duomo, Registri, Libri di cassa 7 {Libro giornale 1560-70}, unnumbered cc., 23 August 1561)]

[25 August, the canvas that Arcimboldo has executed with the design of the *Death of the Virgin* for the tapestry intended for Como Cathedral is brought back from Como to Milan (ASDCo, Fabbrica del duomo, Libri contabili 14 {Mastro Biancho 1557-64}, fol. 192, account of the tapestries, and reference to fol. 225, Cassa della Fabbrica, where the same payment is registered; ASDCo, Fabbrica del duomo, Registri, Libri di cassa 7 {Libro giornale 1560-70}, unnumbered cc., 25 August 1561)]

[25 August, Giovanni Karcher, tapestry weaver in the service of the duke of Ferrara but at this moment in Como, receives 40 scudi on account for the weaving of the tapestry representing the *Death of the Virgin* to a design by Giuseppe Arcimboldo, intended for Como Cathedral (ASDCo, Fabbrica del duomo, Libri contabili 14 {Mastro Biancho 1557-64}, fol. 227, account of the tapestry weaver, and reference to fol. 225, Cassa della Fabbrica, where the same payment is registered; ASDCo, Fabbrica del duomo, Registri, Libri di cassa 7 {Libro giornale 1560-70}, unnumbered cc., 25 August 1561)]

[28 August, Gabrio da Corte is reimbursed lire 3.1.6 for the same sum spent by his son on constructing a crate for the transport of the design for the tapestry of the *Death of the Virgin* (ASDCo, Fabbrica del duomo, Libri contabili 14 {Mastro Biancho 1557-64}, fol. 192, account of the tapestries, and reference to fol. 225, Cassa della Fabbrica, where the same payment is registered; ASDCo, Fabbrica del duomo, Registri, Libri di cassa 7 {Libro giornale 1560-70}, unnumbered cc., 28 August 1561)]

[27 November, the canvas on which Arcimboldo has executed the design of the *Death of the Virgin* for the tapestry intended for Como Cathedral is transported from Milan to Pavia and from there to Ferrara (ASDCo, Fabbrica del duomo, Libri contabili 14 {Mastro Biancho 1557-64}, fol. 192, account of the tapestries, and reference to fol. 228, Cassa della Fabbrica, where the same payment is registered; ASDCo, Fabbrica del duomo, Registri, Libri di cassa 7 {Libro giornale 1560-70}, unnumbered cc., 27 November 1561)]

1562
Giuseppe Arcimboldo moves to Vienna at the request of Maximilian of Habsburg (Morigia 1592, 566)

[3 June, the tapestry weaver Giovanni Karcher receives 230 lire and 1 soldo in full payment for weaving the tapestry with the *Death of the Virgin* to a cartoon by Giuseppe Arcimboldo; the same day he is paid for the transport of the hanging from Ferrara to Como (ASDCo, Fabbrica del duomo, Libri contabili 14 {Mastro Biancho 1557-64}, fol. 237, account of the tapestries, and reference to fol. 260, account of the tapestries, with further reference to fol. 266, Cassa della Fabbrica, where the same payment is registered; ASDCo, Fabbrica del duomo, Registri, Libri di cassa 7 {Libro giornale 1560-70}, unnumbered cc., 3 June 1562)]

1563
28 April, in Vienna, Master Giuseppe, painter to His Royal Majesty (Maximilian of Habsburg) has to copy two portraits to a commission from Emperor Ferdinand I; the commission must date from at least the middle of March and the painter is part of the retinue of the king of the Romans, Maximilian. They are two half-length portraits, one of Ferdinand I himself and the other of the widow of Emperor Frederick III, i.e. Eleanor of Portugal (DaCosta Kaufmann 2005, 29)

1566
post-2 June (date of the passport issued at Augsburg): Arcimboldo returns to Milan for a short period

28 August, "Signor Gioseffo [blank] painter of His Majesty the Emperor Maximilian" is present in Sedriano (between Milan and Magenta) as godfather at the baptism of Agostina, daughter of Biagio Mantovani, servant of Signor Ottone Visconti, and Elisabetta Grancina da Poliano; the godmother is Bianca Bariggia (APS, Registro dei battesimi; Cavalieri 2000, 102)

1567
23 May, date of issue of an order for payment of L. 275 in favour of Giuseppe Arcimboldo for the first designs executed for the gonfalon of the city of Milan. Arcimboldo will receive, through his proxy Gerolamo Cisati (or Cesati), L. 223.5.6, 10 October, and L. 51.14.6, 30 December 1567. "L. 275 for a value of S. 50 from ss. 110, paid to Master Painter Josepho Arcimboldo, and for him into the hands of Messer Hieronimo Cisato his proxy, that is on 10 October (1567) L. 223 ss. 5 d. 6, and on 30 December of said year 1567 L. 51 ss. 14 d. 6, as recompense for the work he carried out on the first designs of the aforesaid Gonfalon, by virtue of a commission of 23 May of said year (1567), appear received by said proxy, L. 275" (ASCM, Località Milanesi 309; Colombo Fantini 1987-88, 242)

1576-77
Giuseppe Arcimboldo draws up a will in Milan with the notary Stefano Busti (the notary's documents and account have been partially destroyed and the will is no longer in the file; the information is derived from the subsequent codicils drawn up on 17 March 1581)

1578
13 July, "*Un retratto del Arcimboldo*" is listed in the *post-mortem* inventory of the property of Count Giovanni Anguissola, who died in Como on 26 June 1578. It is likely to have been a portrait painted by Giuseppe Arcimboldo (ASCo, Notarile 1021, Miller 1989, 22)

1581
17 March, Milan, codicils of Giuseppe Arcimboldo q. Biagio, "sequens curiam Serenissimi Imperatoris" but now living in Milan, in Porta Vercellina, parish of San Pietro alla Vigna, of sound mind and body; wishing to make some additions to his last will and testament, drawn up some time in 1576 or 1577 with the notary Stefano Busti, he declares that, should his son Benedetto Arcimboldo die before, at the same time as or even after the testator (but without having reached the age of 18), Giovan Filippo Gherardini will have the entire usufruct for 20 years uninterrupted of all the property of the testator that will be located with the said Gherardini.
Deed attested in the study of the said Gherardini, situated in Porta Vercellina, parish of San Pietro alla Vigna.
Witnesses: Battista del Corno son of Francesco, Porta Nuova, parish of San Pietro in Cornaredo; Giovan Ambrogio Cattaneo q. Andrea, Porta Ticinese, parish of San Michele al Gallo; Antonio Polacini q. Romerio, Porta Vercellina, parish of Santa Maria Podone; Cavalier Giovanni Arcimboldo q. Luigi, Porta Orientale, parish of San Babila Intus; Gian Giacomo Pariani di Antonio, Porta Comasina, parish of San Cipriano.
Co-notaries: Gian Giacomo Borri son of Orfeo, Porta Orientale, parish of Santo Stefano in Brolo; Giulio Cesare Sormani son of Gerolamo, Porta Vercellina, parish of San Pietro sul Dosso (ASM, Notarile 15028, Miller 1989, 22)

1587
post-12 August (date of the payment of

1200 gulden made by the court), Giuseppe Arcimboldo, after two years of requests to this end, obtains permission from Rudolf II to return to Italy for good and settles in Milan, in Porta Vercellina, San Pietro alla Vigna, in the house occupied by Giovan Filippo Gherardini, with his son Benedetto Arcimboldo.

Residents of the house owned by Giovan Filippo Gherardini:
Giovan Filippo Gherardini, clerk of the Health Board, aged 50
Giulia (Litta), his wife, aged 45
Giovan Bernardino, his son, aged 18
Paolo Ambrogio, his son, aged 10
Pompeo, attendant, aged 17
Bianca Bordoni, aged 19
Caterina Carcano, servant, aged 55
Gerolamo Canuti, servant
Benedetto Arcimboldo
Carlo Rizzi, servant
Giuseppe Arcimboldo
Valentino
(ASDM, sez. X, Visitationes, S. Ambrogio XXXV, *Status Animarum*, undated but from some time between 1587 and 1589)

Giuseppe Arcimboldo executes the *Self-portrait on Paper* (dated 1587 and with the number 61 (which probably refers to his age) at the bridge of the nose; Gabinetto di Disegni e Stampe, Palazzo Rosso, Genoa)

1588
28 May, sale and emphyseutic investiture between Giovan Filippo Gherardini and Giuseppe Arcimboldo (ASM, Rubriche notarili 2900, notary Giovan Francesco Maggi q. Giovan Antonio, documents destroyed, Berra 2000, 81, n. 1)

1591
Arcimboldo sends the emperor the *Portrait of Rudolf II as Vertumnus* accompanied by a booklet of poems by various Milanese authors (Giovanni Filippo Gherardini, Gregorio Comanini, Gherardo Borgogni, Bernardino Baldini, Sigismondo Foliano and G.A. from Milan, perhaps Arcimboldo himself), edited by Gherardini, celebrating and explaining both the *Vertumnus* and the *Flora*

In the same year he finishes a picture that associates the four seasons in a single "portrait", which he donates (?) to Gregorio Comanini

1592
1 May, Emperor Rudolf II elevates Giuseppe Arcimboldo to the rank of count palatine

1593
pre-11 July, Giuseppe Arcimboldo acquires from Maurizio Visconti a piece of jasper "of middling size" to make a lid for a vase, paying 100 ducats for it (ASMn, Archivio Gonzaga 1715, fasc. III1, cc. 293-294; Piccinelli 2003, 223-224, no. 460, Maurizio Visconti to Ottaviano Cavriani, from Milan, 26 January 1594)

pre-11 July Giuseppe Arcimboldo designs a writing desk for Rudolf II and entrusts its construction, for the parts in ebony and ivory, to Giuseppe Guzzi; after Arcimboldo's death the desk, which was being constructed in his house, is transferred to the milanese house of the Miseroni family (Morigia 1595 {1619}, 479)

11 July, Giuseppe Arcimboldo dies in Milan at the age of about sixty-six: "*Porte Vercelline, S. Petri ad vineam. Joseph Arcimboldus annorum 66 vel circa ex urine suppressione et calculo in renibus obijt sine pestis signo iudicio Johannes Baptiste Silvatici physici collegiati*" (ASM, Popolazione p.a. 104; Casati 1885, 93)

Cesare Besozzi composes the epitaph for the tomb of Giuseppe Arcimboldo (in San Pietro alla Vigna?):

Iosepho Arcimboldo viro integerrimo, Pictori/Clarissimo, Comitiq. Palatino;/Qui Ferdinando, Maximiliano II, Rodulpho II/Imperatoribus gratissimus semper fuit./Caesar. Besutius tanti viri familiarissimus/L. S.
(Morigia 1595 {1619}, 461). Besozzi had married Giovan Filippo Gherardini's daughter Clara in 1578.

Bernardino Baldini (Baldini 1600, 44) writes a eulogy on the recently deceased Arcimboldo:

Epitaphium Iosephi Arcimboldoi./Integer e vita Ioseph migravit, Olympum/Viseret ut clarum, sidereasq[ue] domos./Caesareus quo pictor, ut hoc effinxit in orbe/Mortaleis, Divum pingat in axe Choros

1587-1593
Arcimboldo sends to the court works by Fede Galizia, which the emperor likes well enough to request others (Borgogni 1598, 39v - 40r)

Arcimboldo advises Giovan Ambrogio Figino to send his works to the court of Rudolf II; the canvas representing *Jupiter Giving Io Turned into a Heifer to Juno as a Mark of Peace* is probably sent but not accepted. Now in the Musei Civici of Pavia, it is signed and dated 1599: "Iussu. Rudol. Caes. Figinus Ping. MDXCIX Mediol." (Ciardi 1968, entry 32, 109-11 and Berra 1998)

Manfred Staudinger

Sources on Arcimboldo at the Habsburg Court

On the court salary of Giuseppe Arcimboldo

The earliest payment of a court salary to the sum of 20 florins per month to Arcimboldo is indicated in the year 1565. On the 31 December he received the last of three payments of that year for a total of 12 months court salary (doc. 5). This is the beginning of a long list of payments made to him documented in court account ledgers

(HZB Volume

20 [1565], fol. 274r [doc. 5];
21 [1566], fol. 277r [doc. 7];
23 [1568], fol. 324r;
24 [1570], fol. 151r, 247v, 556r, 762r;
25 [1571], fol. 80v, 455r, 497v;
27 [1573], fol. 333v;
28 [1574], fol. 350v;
29 [1575], fol. 465v;
31 [1577], fol. 398r [doc. 18];
32 [1581], fol. 309v [doc. 22];
33 [1582], fol. 262v;
34 [1583], fol. 289r;
35 [1584], fol. 304v;
36 [1585], fol. 370r;
37 [1586], fol. 230v;
38 [1587], fol. 190v [doc. 33]),

totalling 70 payments to a sum of at least 6400 florins. Royal household lists, or lists of salary conditions are mostly uncorroborated by documentation and hence of little value.

The abovementioned payments in the year 1565 cover the period from 1st October 1564 up to 30th September 1565. The formulation, that makes no mention of a socalled standing order from the emperor, establishes that it is not the beginning of a salary (see doc. 12). Indeed he received payment of a court salary in 1564, though there is no mention of Arcimboldo in the court accounts ledger of that year. Being the last court accounts ledger under Emperor Ferdinand I. who as is well known died on 25 July 1564 in Vienna, it shows that Arcimboldo did not belong to his court. This is also established through the letters of Adam Swetkowyz to Ferdinand I. (docs. 1 and 3), in which Arcimboldo is described as "His Roman Royal Majesty's Court Painter", i.e. the court painter of Maximilian II.

At the beginning of June 1566 Arcimboldo travelled for more than one and a half years to Italy, probably with some instructions from Maximilian II too. In but a few days he obtained in Augsburg his court salary to the end of May and travelling expenses (docs. 7 and 8) as well as a letter of passage from the imperial chancellery (doc. 9). He received his court salary for the time of his absence from court after his return to Vienna, this requiring a special order from the emperor.

The court account ledgers for the years 1578 to 1580 have been lost, so we don't know exactly when his monthly court salary was raised to 30 florins. The reason for the emperor's granting a rise in Arcimboldo's salary is probably connected with the latter's request from 13 May 1580, to be able to return to Italy (doc. 20). The title of nobility conferred upon him and his son dated 23 May, is to be seen in the same light (doc. 21).

Finally in October 1587 Arcimboldo took leave of the imperial court in Prague. Already in August he received a severance indemnity to the amount of 1500 florins (docs. 30, 31, 32), though with the last payment of his court salary on 2 October there is no indication as to his leaving the royal household (doc. 33). In that his presence at the court was a condition for his receiving a court salary, naturally once in Milan he would receive nothing. Perhaps Arcimboldo was in Prague on Mai 1592 due to the conferment of the title of nobility; at any rate things were considered such, that the emperor decided that Arcimboldo, instead of his court salary should receive a yearly provision of 300 florins. This provision could also be drawn by Arcimboldo in Milan, provided the necessary arrangements for the money transfer in place. We only know of this through the protocol of the court treasury, where the same is recollected by the Emperor's chamber servant Hans Haiden in June 1593 (doc. 37).

Giuseppe Arcimboldo was court painter to Maximilian II and Rudolf II and was until his death 11 July 1593 in Milan a court servant of the emperor.

Documents

Abbreviations:

AVA
: Wien, Österreichisches Staatsarchiv, Allgemeines Verwaltungs-, Finanz- und Hofkammerarchiv

BUB
: Bologna, Biblioteca Universitaria di Bologna, Fondo Ulisse Aldrovandi

FA
: Habsburgisch–Lothringische Hausarchive

HHStA
: Wien, Österreichisches Staatsarchiv, Haus-, Hof- und Staatsarchiv

HKA
: Wien, Österreichisches Staatsarchiv, Allgemeines Verwaltungs-, Finanz- und Hofkammerarchiv, Alte Hofkammer

HZB
: Hofzahlamtsbücher, Vol.

NÖHA
: Niederösterreichische Herrschaftsakten,

ÖNB
: Wien, Österreichische Nationalbibliothek, Handschriften-, Autographen- und Nachlass-Sammlung

RHR-Paßbriefe
: Reichshofrat, Gratialia et Feudalia, Paßbriefe, Faszikel

RHR-Legitimationes
: Reichshofrat, Gratialia et Feudalia, Restitutionis natalium ac legitimationes, Karton

Reichsregister
: Reichskanzlei, Reichsregister

Taxamt
: Reichskanzlei, Reichstaxbücher, vol.

1

Adam Swetkowyz to Emperor Ferdinand I Report on the pictures of Arcimboldo's to be copied

29 March 1563, Vienna

Aller Durchleuchtigister Grossmechtigister Römischer Kayser, zu Vngern vnd Beheim etc. Konig etc. aller genedigister Herr etc.

Eur Rö. Kay. M. genedigisten peuelich des dat[ums] Insprukh den 13. dits, dessen Copj hiebej mit A. hab ich den 22. in vnd[er]thenigisten gehorsam empphang[en], vnd wie Eur Ro. Kay. M. gen[edig]ist peuelhen, aus Eur Kay. M. kunstkamer alhie, Eur M. Conterfehung auff Leinbat ain prust pildt, von angestrihnen harnash gemacht. Desgeleihen in d[er] Purkh zu Neustat, in ainem grossen gebelb bej dem langen Sall, da dj khurn hangen, Kayser Fridrichs gemachl hohloblihister gedachtnus, weilent d[er] Konigin Leonora Augusta von Portugal, Contrafectur zu finden, welihe baidt Conterfecturn d[er] Ro. Ko. M. Hofmaller vnuerzogentlich mit öltrenkhten farben, auff Leinbat tuech abmallen, vnd wan gar getruknett, Eur M. alsopalt woluerwarter auff d[er] post gehorsamist zuvb[er]shikhen etc.

Hab hierauf Eur Rö. Kay. M. gehorsamist ich berichten wöllen, Eur Kay. M. Contrefectur alhie in d[er] kunstkamer zwo all[er]massen gleich formig verhanden sein, alain dj ain im 1548 vnd dj and[er] im 1559 Jar gemacht worden, So nun d[er] Rö. Kö. M. maller sich zuberait vnd teglich ain anfang machen, vnd iner halb 14 tag[en] khaum vertig, nohmals gemelt Contrafectur zu truknen auch etlich tag bedurffen wurde, Ob Eur Kay. M. deren verhanden zween Contrefehungen dj ain zuubershiken gen[edig]ist gefellig sein liesse, möchte mitl[er] weil, dj so d[er] mall[er] alhie vertigen wirt an dj stat d[er] vb[er]shikten gethon werde, Damit würde dj gefar des recht trukhnen, in den vb[er]shiken nit zubesorgen sein. Betrefent aus d[er] purckh zu d[er] Neustat hab ich den 23. dits H[er]n Vlrichen von Scherfenberg geschriben laut copj B. darauff Er mir beiligunt antwort mit C. den 25. dits bej dem Zimerwarter vb[er]shikht, vnd gemelt[er] Zimerwart[er] bericht, bej dem langen Sall, zwen thurn sein darinen gebelb sein mögen, dan dj thuer mit grossen shloss[er]n vershloss[en], darzu Er noch d[er] H[er] von Scherfenberg khain shlüsl hab, vb[er] vil nachfragen hab ich dieselben shlussl lestlich[en] bej d[er] N.O. Camer verpetshierter dabej auch and[er] shlusl mer vnuerpetshierte gefunden, derhalben [fol. 96v] dj Ro. Ko. M. Hern Hansen von Karling gene[dig]ist verornt, nachdem gemelt[er] von Karling in dem 1547 Jar aus gemeltem gebelb dj verhanden an heut sambt dem H[er]n Vlrichen von Sheftenberg daselb gemelt gebelb eroffne vnd samentlich[en] wid[er] verschliessen, vnd ob Er gemelt Conterfectur hieh[er] pringt, sol dieselb zu merer furdrung erstlich[en] abgemalt werden, vnd wurde Eur Kay. M. abconterfectur, von d[er] Conterfectur so hiebeleibt h[er]nach gemacht werden mögen.

Solihes Eur Ro. Kay. M. hab ich vmb merern vnd gene[dig]ist beshait Hiemit anzaigen wöllen, Eur Kay. Mt. mich ganz vnd[er]tenigist vnd gehorsamist peuelhent. Dat[um] Wien den 29 Marcj Im 1563

E. Ro. Kay. Mt. vnd[er]tenigister vnd gehor-samister Diener Adam Swetkowyz

[fol. 98r] Post scriptum

Eur Ro. Kay. M. genedigist[er] peuelih, sambt dem Melaun samen, Hab ich den 22 dits gehorsamist emphang[en], vnd dj drej shcarnezl Eur Kay. M. hof gartner alhie zugestölt, d[er] vermaint dieselb[en] in den Eleffanten garten zu sezen etc.

Den 25 dits hab ich dj an[der]n drej shcarnezl dem gartner zu Eberstorff in peisein des pfleg[er] auch selbst vb[er]antwort, mit anzaigung Eur Kay. M. peuelih nach, neben dem Haus in dj neuen geshut Erden anzusezen etc.

[fol. 98v] [Document description, about:] Adam Swerkhowiz p[er] contrafectur vnd Melaun samen [Records:] O [Date:] Aprilis anno 63.

Der Romischen Kayserlichen auch zu Vngern vnd [Papier zerfallen] Herrn

[Note:] E[xpediert] vnd verantwort den 13. Aprilis 63

[Note:] 5 April. Ao. 63.

HKA, Niederösterreichische Kammer, Rote Nr. 39 [Apr-Jun 1563; 16703], unfol.

2

Official court protocol

April 1563

Adam Swetkhowizn schreiben p[er] contrafectur vnnd Melaun samen, ligt hie verantwurtt. [Bearbeitung:] p[er] w. [Ablage:] O.

HKA, Hoffinanz, Vol. 256-E [1563], fol. 112v.

3

Adam Swetkowyz to Emperor Ferdinand I

Report on the progress of the work of Arcimboldo

28 April 1563, Vienna

Eur Römisch kais. maj. etc. genedigisten pevelih, des datum Insprukh den 13. dits, hab ich den 22. dits in aller undertenigister gehorsam emphangen und denselben nah eur Römisch kais. maj. etc. der zwaer prustpildnus conterfecturen die ain aus der kunstkamer alhie genomen und eingemacht auch verwart und verpetshaft, wie dan eur Römisch kais. maj. etc. dieselb hiebei ich gehorsamist ubershikhe; die ander eur kais. maj. etc. conterfectur haben di kgl. maj. etc. dem maister Josephen, irer maj. etc. maller, abzuconterfehen bevolhen, der nunmals sovil daran vericht, das er inerhalb acht tagen dieselb zu enden hofnung hat und, wie anjezo zu sehen, gar wol damit beshten wierdt. Ob eur kais. maj. etc. diese ubershikhte conterfectur wider an ir ort hierher genedigist verordnen zu shiken, dieweil di jezige conterfectur so pald verfertigt werden mag, pin ich undertenigistes beshaits gewartund. [...] Datum Wien den 28. aprilis 1563.

Undertenigister und gehorsamister diener Adam Swetkowycz.

[Note:] Expedirt und verantwurt den 6. mai 1563.

quoted from: Kreyczi 1887, JKSAK 5, XCIII, Reg. 4344.

quoted as K.u.k. Reichs-Finanz-Archiv, Niederösterreich, Fasc. 16703.

4

Calculation of receipts and disbursements of the court paymaster

Payment to Arcimboldo for pictures

25 September 1565

Josephen Arzimboldo Rom: Kay: Mt: Conterfeter haben die höchsternennt Ro: Kay: Mt: fur etliche Conterfet vnd schöne gmäl, so Er Irer Kay: Mt: gemacht vnd gehorsamist presentiert, 225 Taller [...] jeden per 68 kr [fol. 531v] [...] 255 fl Reinisch bringen [...] raichen zulassen genedigist verordnet. Dieselben hab ich Ime Arzimboldo, auf der Kay: Mt: etc. beuelch, vnd sein Quittung, deren datum am 15.9., vergnuegt vnd bezalt, Idest 255 fl.

HKA, HZB 20 [1565], fol. 531r-531v.

quoted in: Boeheim 1888, JKSAK 7, CXX, Reg. 4994.

quoted in: Geiger 1960, 134.

5

Payment of court salary

31 December 1565

Joseph Arzimboldo, Römischer Kay: Mt: Contterfeter, Hat gleichfals monatlichen 20 fl Hofbesoldung, Die hab ich Ime von 12 Monaten [...] So sich am 1.10.64 angefangen vnnd den 30.9.65 geenndet haben, vnnd in gellt 200 [richtig: 240] fl Reinisch bringen thuen auf 3 seiner verferttigte Quittungen deren dritten dattum den 31.12.65 stet, also vergnuegt. Idest 240 fl.

HKA, HZB 20 [1565], fol. 274r.

6

Calculation of receipts and disbursements of the court paymaster

29 January 1566

Josephen Arzimboldo der Kay: Mt. Conterfeter haben Ir Mt. von besondern genaden wegen, 28 fl 20 kr zuraichen genedigist bewilliget. Dieselben [...] hab ich Ime zuhannden Irer Mt. Camerdiener, vnd oberisten Gwardaroba herrn Hannsen Berchtoldts, vermug beuelchs vnd des Berchtolts Quitung, am 29.1. bezalt, Idest 28 fl 20 kr

HKA, HZB 21 [1566], fol. 611v.

quoted in: Boeheim 1888, JKSAK 7, CXXI, Reg. 5017.

quoted in: Geiger 1960, 135.

7

Payment of court salary

31 May 1566, Augsburg

Joseph Arzimboldo der Römischen Kay: Mt. Conterfeter, hat monatlichen 20 fl Hofbesoldung. Dieselb hab ich Ime von 8 Monaten, Welliche sich den 1.10.1565 angefangen, vnd den 31.5.1566 geendet, bringen in gelt, Benenntlichen 160 fl, laut zwayer verfertigten Quitungen, der lesten datum am 31.5. stet, vergnuegt vnd bezalt, Idest 160 fl

HKA, HZB 21 [1566], fol. 277r.

quoted in: Boeheim 1888, JKSAK 7, CXXII, Reg. 5030.

quoted in: Geiger 1960, 135.

8

Calculation of receipts and disbursements of the court paymaster

Travel allowance for Arcimboldo

2 June 1566, Augsburg

Josephen Arcinnboldo der Röm: Kay: Mt. Conterfeter haben Ir Mt. zu ainer zerung in Italia 100 fl aus genaden zugeben verordnet. Dieselben [...] hab ich Ime Innhallt beuelchs vnd Quitung am 2.6. vergnuegt, Idest 100 fl

HKA, HZB 21 [1566], fol. 658r.

quoted in: Boeheim 1888, JKSAK 7, CXXII, Reg. 5037.

quoted in: Geiger 1960, 135.

9

Letter of passage for Giuseppe Arcimboldo

2 June 1566, Augsburg

Maximilianus etc.

Fideli nobis dilecto, Iosepho Arcimboldo pictori nostro aulico Mediolanum patriam suam profecturo tutum facile et expeditum iter esse clementer cupientes, Equidem a V[estris] Dil[ectioni]b[us] et Deuotionib[us] ceterisq[ue] benigne petimus, ut eund[em] Iosephum quacu[mque] per v[est]ras terras, quarumue demandata uobis etc. e[st] p[re]fectura una cum comitatu suo et suppellectili omni iter facientem et libere dimittatis, et quaecu[mque] ad profectione[m] sua[m] necessaria, iustum pro his diferens precium expeti[]it benigne et beneuolenter suppeditari iubeatis. In eo acturae sunt V[est]rae q[ui]dem Dil[ectiones] et Deuot[iones] [] nobis p[er]grata[m], mutua gra[tia] Caes[are]a n[ost]ra compensandam, vos uero subditi n[ost]ri ex benigniss[im]a voluntate n[ost]ra.

Dat[um] Augustae 2. junij A[nn]o etc. 66.

HHStA, RHR-Passbriefe 1 [A], fol. 177.

quoted in: Voltelini 1894, JKSAK 15, LXVIII, Reg. 11869.

quoted in: Geiger 1960, 137-138.

10

Chamber accounts book

9 March 1569 , Vienna

Denn Neünndten auß Beuelch Irer Kay: Mt. dem Josephen Arcimboldo Hofmaller vermüg aines außzugs vnnd Bekhanndtnuß mit No. 4 gebenn 13 fl 8 kr 2 d.

ÖNB, Cod. 9089, fol. 58v.

quoted in: Boeheim 1888, JKSAK 7, CXXX, Reg. 5163.

quoted in: Geiger 1960, 136.

11

Chamber accounts book

31 May 1570, Prague

Denn Lezten May auß Beuelch Irer Khay: Mt: dem Joseph Arcimbaldo Hoff Maller geben vermüg seiner Bekhanntnuß mit No. 21 100 Tl welliche Ir Mt: Ime auß genaden Raichen laßen, Tuet 113 fl 20 kr.

ÖNB, Cod. 9089, fol. 114r.

quoted in: Boeheim 1888, JKSAK 7, CXLIII, Reg. 5191.

quoted in: Geiger 1960, 136.

12

Payment of court salary

Appointment of Johann de Monte as court painter

14 October 1571

Johannem de Monte, haben die Rom: Khay: Mt: Innhallt beiligunder Ordinanz, von 1.7.71 anzuraiten, mit monatlichen 20 fl Hofbesoldung zw [fol. 641v] derselben Hofmaler gnedigist an vnd aufgenomben. Darauf hab Ich Ime an solicher seiner Hofbesoldung, die gebur von 3 Monaten [bis 30.9.71], Benentlichen 60 fl Reinisch, vermug seiner Quittung am 14.10. zwgestellt.

HKA, HZB 25 [1571], fol. 641r-641v.

13
Calculation of receipts and disbursements of the court paymaster
28 July 1574

Josephen Arcimbaldo, Rom: Khay: Mt. Conterfeter vnd Maller, hab Ich für ettlich gemäll vnd arbaith, so Er auf Ihr Mt. genedigiste verordnung, dem Churfursten zu Sachsen gemacht, Benentlich[en] [fol. 478v] 65 fl Reinisch, Lauth der Khay: Mt. Particular Beuelchs vnd seiner Quittung der datum am 28.7.74 Entricht.

HKA, HZB 28 [1574], fol. 478r-478v.

14
Sealing of parchment-documents
Legitimation for Benedetto Arcimboldo
1575, Vienna

Legimitation für Benedict Arcimbaldo Tax 12 Cronen vnd laut bewilligung mit No 14 Taxfrey.

HHStA, Taxamt 28 [1575], fol. 45r.

15
Calculation of receipts and disbursements of the court paymaster
6 February 1575

Josephen Arcimbaldo Rom: Khay: Mt. Conterfeter vnnd Maller, hab Ich vmb etliche Conterfett, welliche Er hochsternendter Irer Khay: Mt. Lauth ainer verzaichnus hiebey, in Ihr Mt. aigen Camer gemacht, vnd dargeben, 54 Tl, jeden zw 70 kr geraith, thuett Benendtlich[en] [fol. 744r] 63 fl Reinisch, Inhaltt Particular Beuelchs vnnd seiner Quittung der datum am 6.2.75 Enntricht.

HKA, HZB 29 [1575], fol. 743v-744r.

16
Legimitation for Benedetto Arcimboldo
14 July 1575, Prague

Legitimatio pro Benedicto Arcimboldo 14. Jul: 1575.

[Vermerk:] R[egistra]ta et Coll[ationa]ta

Maximilianus etc. Recognoscimus et notum facimus tenore p[re]sentium uniuersis, cum ad sp[l]endorem atq[ue] M[ajes]tatem Caes[are]ae sublimitatis n[ost]rae, ad quam Dei beneficio sumus euecti, magnopere pertinere uideatur, beneficentiae n[ost]rae munera non tenere nimis angustis finibus circumscripta, sed quam latissime in quoscunq[ue] nostros et Sacri Imperij fideles subditos, uasallos et deuotos diffundere, existimamus illud etiam benignitati et clementiae n[ost]rae inprimis consentaneum esse, quod et ijs fauoris et gratiae n[ost]rae plenitudine subueniatur, qui illegitimae geniturae macula aspersi alieno morbo laborantes facile ueniam merentur.

Cum itaq[ue] noster et Sacri Imperij fidelis dilectus Josephus Arcimboldus hum[ili]t[e]r nobis exponendum curauerit, se solutu[m] ex vidua quadam Ottilla olim Thomae Stummeri filia, suscepisse filium nomine Benedictum, cupereq[ue] eundem, cum legitima prole omnino careat, sibi in quibuscunq[ue] facultatibus suis succedere; nobisq[ue] p[ro]inde demisse admodum supplicauerit, ut super huiusmodi natalium defectu clementer dispensare, et quod illegitima procreatio abstulit, de benignitate n[ost]ra Caes[are]a reddendo, ipsum ad o[mn]es honores, officia et successiones habilitare dignaremur.
Nos sane benigne consideratis diuturnis et gratis obsequijs, nobis a p[raefa]to Josepho Arcimboldo multis abhinc annis non sine magna satisfactione n[ost]ra, ac singu- [fol. 155v] lari sua cum laude p[rae]stitis, ac deinceps pari alacritate p[rae]standis, memoratis p[re]cibus deesse non potuimus.

Itaq[ue] ex certa n[ost]ra scientia, a[n]i[m]oq[ue] bene deliberato, ac de Caes[are]ae n[ost]rae potestatis plenitudine p[raefa]tu[m] Josephi Arcimboldi filium naturalem Benedictum, clementer legitimauimus et habilitauimus, ac super memorato naturalium ipsius defectu benigne dispensauimus, et eum iuri naturali primaeuo et ad o[mn]ia iura legitima restituimus, et integre restitutum fore et esse decernimus, omnemq[ue] macula[m] ex eiusmodi genitura contractam tollimus, abstergimus et prorsus abolemus. Dantes et concedentes illi hoc n[ost]ro Caes[are]o indulto plenam potestatem, quod possit, ualeat et debeat pacifice, libereq[ue] et absq[ue] omni impedimento aut illegitimae prolis obiectione, fungi intereße et p[rae]eße o[mn]ibus et singulis actibus publicis et priuatis, officijs, muneribus, Juribus et dignitatibus, et ad illa o[mn]ia nec non quaecunq[ue] beneficia tam Ecclesiastica q[uam] Saecularia, feuda, iudicia, conuentusq[ue] collegia admitti, atq[ue] de domo familia et gente suprano[m]i[n]ati genitoris sui no[m]i[n]ari, haberi, censeri et reputari, tam ab agnatis quam ab alijs quibuscunq[ue] personis, Et quod etiam comp[re]hendatur sub statuto, decreto, constitutione, ordinatione et qualibet voluntate tam Imperiali quam alia quacunq[ue], siue inter uiuos, siue in Vltima voluntate loquente uel [fol. 156r] disponente de legitimis et naturalibus seu de legitimo matrimonio natis et procreatis, quin et nobilitate paterna frui, et potiri, armaq[ue] seu insignia dicti sui parentis habere deferre et gestare, ac scutis, clijpeis, tentorijs, sepulchris, monumentis, parietibus, ostijs, fenestris, lacunaribus, tapetibus, puluinaribus, annulis signatorijs, sigillis, et quibuscunq[ue] rebus insculpere, affigere, appingere et intexere, pro ut ei libuerit, aut neceßitas ipsius postulauerit, ac deniq[ue] caeteris o[mn]ibus et singulis priuilegijs honoribus, p[rae]rogatiuis, p[rae]eminentis, iuribus, indultis, gratijs et concessionibus uti, frui potiri et gaudere, quibus alij ex legitimo matrimonio nati et procreati utuntur, fruuntur, potiuntur et gaudent, consuetudine uel de iure, etiamsi talia forent de quibus hic specialis mentio fieri deberet. Reddentes p[rae]terea ex eadem Caes[are]a n[ost]ra auctoritate et potestatis plenitudine ante no[m]i[n]atum Benedictum Arcimboldum habilem et idoneum ad successionem bonorum iurium et haereditatum, actionumq[ue] paternarum et maternarum, agnatoru[m] et cognatorum atq[ue] etiam extraneorum, ita ut ipse virtute huius dispensationis, legitimationis et habilitationis saepedicto suo parenti Josepho Arcimboldo, ac alijs agnatis et cognatis tam ex Testamento quam ab intestato, ac quibuscunq[ue] donationibus, tam inter uiuos, quam mortis causa, seu alijs institutionibus, substitutionibus, legatis, fidei com[m]issis, dispositionibus et Vltimis Voluntatibus, in q[ui]buslibet bonis paternis, haereditatibus et successionibus per eundem Josephum Ar- [fol. 156v] cimboldum tam emphijtheosis, quam alio quouis titulo ac nomine acquisitis et possessis, non aliter ac si ex legitimo matrimonio prognatus fuisset, succedere possit et debeat, absq[ue] tamen filiorum, haeredum et descendentium legitimorum praeiudicio, sublata etia[m] facultate cuilibet quacunq[ue] dignitate praedito contra p[rae]missa quicq[uam] decernendi, statuendi siue iudicandi: nos enim o[mn]ia et singula contra p[rae]missa facta, gesta et decreta irrita et inania fore decernimus ex nùnc prout ex tùnc, et e conuerso, ipsumq[ue] Benedictum Arcimboldum hac n[ost]ra legitimatione, habilitatione, dispensatione et alijs p[rae]missis plene gaudere uolumus atq[ue] statuimus, non obstantibus in p[rae]missis ulla lege com[m]uni uel speciali aut consuetudine uetustissima, uel priuilegijs Imperialibus aut alijs, sub quacunq[ue] forma uerborum concessis, approbatis uel innouatis, et specialiter in Authent[icis] Quibus mod[is] nat[urales] effi[ciuntur] sui per totum et § naturales si de feudo fuerit controuersia inter do[minum] et ag[natos uasalli] uel qualibet alia constitutione aut lege, scripta siue non scripta, caeterisq[ue] quibuscunq[ue] tam in g[ene]re q[uam] in specie in contrarium facientibus aut alia[m] formam dantibus, etiamsi talia forent de q[ui]bus in p[rae]sentibus specialis mentio fieri deberet, Quibus o[mn]ib[us] et singulis tenores eorum pro expressis habentes, motu proprio, scienter, animoq[ue] bene deliberato, ac de Caes[are]ae n[ost]rae potestatis plenitudine tenore p[raese]ntium in hac duntaxat parte [fol. 157r] derogamus ac sufficienter et totaliter derogatum esse uolumus.

Nulli ergo omnino ho[m]i[n]um, cuiuscunq[ue] status gradus, ordinis, conditionis et dignitatis extiterit liceat hanc n[ost]rae legitimationis, habilitationis, dispensationis restitutionis, concessionis, gr[ati]ae, uoluntatis et decreti paginam infringere, aut ei quouis ausu temerario contraire. Si quis autem hoc attentare p[rae]sumpserit, is n[ost]ram et Sacri Imperij indignationem grauissimam ac poenam ugintj Marcharum auri puri, pro dimidia parte fisco n[ost]ro Imperiali, pro reliqua uero iniuriam passi usibus, o[mn]i spe ueniae sublata, toties, quoties in has parte peccatum fuerit, soluendam sese nouerit incursurum.

Harum testimonio l[ite]rarum, manu p[ro]pria subscriptarum, et Caesarei Sigilli n[ost]ri appensione munitarum Datu[m] Pragae die 14. Julij Anno D[omi]nj 1575.

HHStA, RHR-Legitimationes, Karton 1 [A, B], fol. 155-157.
HHStA, Reichsregister, Maximilian II., Vol. 17 [1571-1576; MF R 63], fol. 394v-396r.
quoted in: Geiger 1960, 138-139.

17
Official court protocol
July 1576

Josephen Arcimboldo aus gnaden 200 fl per caes. noch im verschinen waltag aus gnaden bewilligt.

HKA, Hoffinanz, Vol. 323-E [1576], fol. 269v.

18
Payment of court salary
17 December 1577

Joseph Arcimbaldo Rom: Khay: Mt: Maller vnnd Conterfetter hat monat- [fol. 398v] lichen 20 fl Reinisch hof besoldung. Dieselb hab Ich Ime von ainem ganzen Jahr, oder 12 Monnatten, so sich den 1.11.1575 angefangen, vnnd den 31.10.1576 wider geendet, Benendtlichen 240 fl Reinisch gegen seinner quittungen deren drey sein, der letstern datum am 17.12.1577 vergnüegtt.

HKA, HZB 31 [1577], fol. 398r-398v.

19
Hans Berchtoldt to Wolf Fuert
9 February 1580, Ebersdorf
[fol. 819r]

Verzaichnus mein Hannsen Berchtoldt furnembsten Außgaben bey der Herrschafft Eberstorff Ain ganzes Jar beschehen wieuolgenn

- Erstlichen Mein Hannsen Berchtoldten ganze Jars Besoldung 250 fl

• Item Auf Raumung der wildt pradt wiscn vnd Feexsung derselben Järlich 110 fl
• Item Auf vnd[er]halttung der Laidthundt auf d[as] wenigist Jarlich 100 fl
• Item Auf vnd[er]halttung Fuif Lewen Jarlich Ordinary 520 fl
• Item Auf vnderhaltung des Tiger thier, Lux, Pern, [fol. 819v] Affen, Merdaxl, Indianisch Pappegay, Englische Hundt, Jarlich Beyleyffig 330 fl
HKA, NÖHA, E 8A [Ebersdorf], fol. 819r-820v.
mentioned in: Staudinger 1990, 100 (Pl. 3, note 2).
mentioned in: Staudinger & Irblich 1996, 258 (cat. no. 4711).

20
Official court protocol
13 May 1580, Prague

HofCamer relation auf Josephi Arcimboldi Supp. erlaubnus ins welschlandt, bezalung seiner ausstendig[en] besoldung vnndt bewilligung aines gnadengelts betr. Ligt da aufgehebt vndt ist Ime die Supp. mit geschafftl vmb 100 Taler hinauß gegeb[en]; [Datum:] 13.
HKA, Hoffinanz, Vol. 358-E [1580], fol. 160v.

21
Conferment of nobility on Giuseppe and Benedetto Arcimboldo
23 May 1580, Prague
[mit „[auch: xxx]" werden in Einzelfällen Schreibweisen der zweitgenannten Quelle angegeben]

Nobilitatis Confirmatio cum Armorum melioratione et Saluaguardia pro Josepho Arcimboldo

Rvdolphvs etc.

Fideli nobis dilecto Josepho Arcimboldo gratiam nostram Caesaream ac omne bonum Imperatoriae nostrae benignitatis est non solum de nouo conferendis verum etiam instaurandis et augendis quorumlibet in primis vero eorum ornamentis elementer fauere quos eximia vitae ac morum honestas sijncerumq[ue] de nobis ac Sacro Romano Imperio atq[ue] inclijta n[ost]ra Austriae Domo quouis loco et tempore bene merendi studium prae caeteris commendatos fauoreq[ue] Caesareo dignos reddit.

Consideratis igitur praeter antiquam nobilitatem tuam, egregijs quibus te Josephum Arcimboldum praeditum e[ss]e nouimus cum animi tum ingenij dotibus, diuturnisq[ue] et gratis obsequijs, quae tam Nobis, quam Diuo olim Imperatori Max[imilia]no Secundo domino genitori ac praedecessori n[ost]ro colendissimo aug[ust]ae memoriae a plurimorum iam annorum spatio vtriusq[ue] aulam continue sequendo indefesso studio praestitisti, tuamq[ue] in Nos et sacrum Imperium atq[ue] Inclijtam nostram Austriae Domum fidem inconcussam et praeclarum obseruantiae studium luculenter comprobasti Ita quidem vt non dubitemus, quin et in posterum non solum in eiusmodi bene merendi offitio [auch: officio] constanter perseueraturus. Verum etiam tuis omnibus ad eandem curam aeque capessendam stimulos adhibuturus [auch: adhibiturus] sis praetermittere sane non possumus, quin ad testificandam benignam n[ost]ri in te vicissim animi propensionem conuenienti aliquo virtutibus ac meritis tuis ornamento, quod ad posteros transmissum fidelis seruitutis tuae perpetuum documentum faciat, clementer augendum suscipiamus.

Ac proinde motu proprio, ex certa n[ost]ra scientia animo bene deliberato deq[ue] potestatis nostrae Caesareae plenitudine, tibi praefato Josepho Arcimboldo, acceptam a maioribus tuis nobilitatem, benigne confirmauimus, ratificauimus et innouauimus, prout harum tenore confirmamus, ratificamus, innouamus ac quatenus opus est de nouo concedimus.

Teq[ue] vna cum filio tuo Benedicto per praelibatum Diuum D[omi]n[u]m genitorem n[ost]rum legitimato, ac caeteris, liberis, haeredibus, posteris et descendentibus tuis legitimis in infinitum, masculis ac foeminis ad nomen, ordinem, statum, gradum, caetum et dignitatem nostrorum ac sacri Romani Imperij Nobilium denuo assumimus, attolimus [auch: attollimus] et aggregamus vosq[ue] omnes et singulos iuxta qualitatem sortis humanae Nobiles et tanquam de nobili genere domo et familia procreatos dicimus ac nominamus atq[ue] ab vniuersis cuiuscunq[ue] status, gradus, ordinis, conditionis et dignitatis existant, pro veris Nobilibus dici, nominari, haberi et reputari volumus statuentes praesentiq[ue] edicto nostro Caesareo expresse decernentes, quod tu [fol. 242r] supradicte Josephe Arcimbolde, ac filius tuus Benedictus, omnesq[ue] alij liberi, haeredes et posteri ex te legitime descendentes in infinitum vtriusq[ue] sexus, perpetuis post hac temporibus vbiq[ue] locorum ac terrarum, tam in Judicijs, quam extra in rebus spiritualibus et temporalibus, Ecclesiasticis ac prophanis quibuscunq[ue] etiamsi tales forent de quibus expressa hic mentio fieri deberet, nec non in omnibus et singulis actibus et exercitijs ijsdem honoribus, dignitatibus, officijs, Juribus, libertatibus, Insignibus, priuilegijs, praeeminentijs, gratijs ac praerogatiuis vti, fruj, potiri, et gaudere possitis ac valeatis quibus caeteri nostri et sacri Romani Imperij veri Nobiles, de nobili prosapia a quatuor auis, paternis et maternis geniti, vtuntur fruuntur, potiuntur et gaudent quomodolibet consuetudine vel de Jure.

Quo autem perpetuum huismodi nobilitatis vestrae extet documentum maioreq[ue] beneficio n[ost]ro exornata, clarius in oculos hominum incurrat, eadem potestate nostra Caesarea tibi praenominato Josepho Arcimboldo gentilitia et auita armorum tuorum Insignia non solum laudauimus et approbauimus. Verum etiam ex specialj quadam gratia auximus, amplificauimus atq[ue] locupletauimus, sicuti vigore praesentium laudamus, approbamus, augemus amplificamus, et locupletamus inq[ue] hunc qui sequitur modum deinceps habenda et deferenda clementer concedimus et elargimur.

Scutum quippe crocei siue aurei coloris per medium linea seu trabe rubea ex sinistro angulo inferiori in dexterum superiorem oblique ascendente, ternasq[ue] stellas aureas senis radijs coruscantes, et aequali interuallo positas in se continente dissectum. Cui incumbat galea cancellis heroicis aperta seu (ut vulgo nuncupatur) Tornearia, n[ost]ro beneficio recens adiecta.

Quae diademate aureo super imposito phalerisq[ue] seu lacinijs, ab vtroq[ue] latere croceis siue aureis ac rubeis (quae et ipse septem vtrinq[ue] stellis aureis fulgeant) mixtim circumfusis molliterq[ue] defluentibus redimita sit. E cuius vertice loco eius quo hactenus vsus es, Draconis caerulei, simul exurgent bina Coralliorum quasi cornua ramis hinc inde certo modo dispositis, conspicua. Ita quidem, vt summitatibus suis inuicem auersis vtrinq[ue] reclinare eq[ue] medio ipsorum pubetenus prodire videatur aquila nigra ad dexteram conuersa, rostro flaui coloris aperto linguaq[ue] rubea exerta ac capite corona aurea ornato, insignis.

Quemadmodum haec in medio huius nostri Diplomatis colorib[us] suis rectius depicta ac visui obiecta clarius conspiciuntur. Volentes authoritateq[ue] Caesarea firmiter decernentes quod tu supradicte Josephe Arcimbolde ac filius tuus leg[iti]matus omnesq[ue] alij liberi haeredes ac posteri ex te legitimo matrimonij foedere in infinitum descendentes masculi et foemine iam descripta armorum Insignia perpetuo in omnibus et singulis honestis ac decentibus actibus exercitijs et expeditionibus tam serio quam ioco in hastilibus ludis seu hac tatorum [auch: hastatorum] dimicationibus pedestribus vel aequestribus in bellis, duellis [fol. 242v] singularibus certaminibus et quibuscunq[ue] pugnis, eminus, cominus, in scutis, bannerijs vexillis tentorijs coenotaphijs, sepulchris aedificijs, ostis, parietibus, fenestris, lacunaribus, tapetibus, sigillis monilibus, annulis, totaq[ue] supellectile tam in rebus spiritualibus quam temporalibus et mixtis in locis omnibus, pro rei necessitate et voluntatis vestrae arbitrio aliorum Nobilium armigerorum more libere et absq[ue] vllo impedimento habere gestare, ac deferre ijsdemq[ue] quouis modo vti possitis et valeatis.

Apti quoq[ue] sitis et idonei ad ineundum et recipiendum omnes praerogatiuas gratias, libertates, exemptiones, feuda, Jura, vacationes a muneribus et oneribus quibuscunq[ue] realibus et personalibus siue mixtis ad vtendum deniq[ue] singulis priuilegijs quibus caeteri a nobis et sacro Romano Imperio huiusmodi ornamentis insigniti et feudorum capaces atq[ue] participes vtuntur, fruuntur, potiuntur, et gaudent, quomodolibet consuetudine vel de Jure Porro volentes ie praefatum Josephum Arcimboldum vberiorem beneficentiam nostram experiri Idcirco eadem scientia auctoritateq[ue] et potestate nostra Caesarea, te, vna cum supradicto filio tuo Benedicto omnibusq[ue] rebus ac bonis, quae vel nunc tenes et possides vel in futurum honesto ac legitimo titulo acquires tam mobilibus, quam immobilibus in nostram et Sacri Romani Imperij inclijteq[ue] nostrae Domus Austriae clientelam, protectionem et Salvaguardiam clementer suscepimus et assumpsimus tenoreq[ue] praesentium suscipimus et assumimus.

Volentes ac firmiter decernentes, quod de hinc sis tenearis ac esse debeas vna cum supradicto filio tuo Benedicto Arcimboldo rebusq[ue] ac bonis tuis et ipsius vniuersis sub hac speciali nostra et Imperialis aquilae inclijteq[ue] nostrae Domus Austriacae tuitione protectione et saluaguardia perpetuo saluus protectus et securus ab omni grauamine oppressione atq[ue] onere hospitandorum militum et stipendiariorum, neq[ue] ab vllo Principe, Duce, Marchione, Capitaneo, Magistratu, seu quauis alia persona communitate, vniuersitate siue Collegio contra huiusmodi saluaguardiam nostram vllo modo molestari aut turbari, quinimo omnibus ac singulis priuilegijs immunitatibus, gratijs et praerogatiuis vti, frui, potiri, et gaudere possis ac valeas, quibus alij sub huiusmodi n[ost]ra et Imperij sacri, inclijtaeq[ue] n[ost]rae Domus Austriae saluaguardia, clientela et protectione constituti, vtutur, fruuntur, potiuntur, et gaudent, consuetudine vel de Jure, citra cuiusquam impedimentum aut contradictionum [auch: contradictionem]. Dum modo tamen vnicuiq[ue] actionem aduersus te habenti in locis debitae Jurisdictionis respondeas.

Nulli ergo omnino hominum cuiuscunq[ue] status, gradus, ordinis, conditionis aut praeeminentiae extiterit liceat hanc n[ost]rae confirmationis, ratificationis, locupletationis, tuitionis, protectionis, saluaguardiae, decreti voluntatis et gratiae paginam infringere, aut quouis modo transgredi et violare. Quisquis aut id temerario aliquo ausu attentare praesumpserit is praeter grauissimam n[ost]ram et sacri Romani Imperij indignationem, poenam Quinquaginta Marcharum auri puri, pro dimidia fisco [fol. 243r] seu aerario nostro Imperiali, reliqua vero parte iniuriam passi vsibus aplicandam [auch: applicandam], toties, quoties, contrauentum fuerit, se nouerit ipso facto irremissibiliter incursurum.

Harum testimonio literarum manu nostra subscriptarum sigilliq[ue] nostri Caesarei appensione munitarum. Datum Pragae die vigesima tertia mensis Maij. Anno Domini Millesimo Quingentesimo Octuagesimo.

HHStA, Reichsregister, Rudolf II., Vol. 4 [1576-1584; MF R 67], fol. 241v-243r.
AVA, Adelsarchiv
(R), Arcimboldus 1580, fol. 2-7.
quoted in: Geiger 1960, 139-140.

22
Payment of court salary
8 December 1581

Josephenn Arcimbaldo Rom: Kay: Mat. Conterfetter vnnd Maller hab Ich sein Hofbesoldung der monatlichen 30 fl Reinisch die gebür von 8 monathenn alß vom 1.5.1580 biß 31.12.1580 zuraiten Thüet Benendtlichen 240 fl Reinisch Laüth drey seiner Quitungen derer Letstern Datum den 8.12.1581 Endtricht vnnd bezaldt.

HKA, HZB 32 [1581], fol. 309v.

23
Purchasing journey at the bidding of Emperor Rudolf II
September 1582

Rudolph sendet den Joseph Arcimboldo an den Bürger Raymund zu Kempten, um Antiquitäten und Kunstsachen, die er zum Theile von den Fuggern, auch Thiere und Wundervögel aus der neuen Welt, die Raymund von den Welsern und Hochstettern zu Augsburg erhalten fuer ihn zu bestehen.

quoted from: Archiv für Geschichte 1825, 573.

24
Emperor Rudolf II to Raimund Dorn, Burgher of Kempten
8 September 1582, Augsburg.
[Documet description:] Antiquitates ad 14. vom Jahre 1612. N:Ö: Abth[ei]lung Rudolff

Lieber getrewer. Nachdeme Wir aus ainer verzaichnus, so du dem Edlen vnsern vnd des Reichs Erb Marshalcken vnd lieb[en] get[reuen] Alexandern zu Bappenheim, vnserm Rath vnd bestelten Öbrist[en] zugeshicket, vernom[m]en, das du allerhandt antiquiteten vnd Kunststuck habest, welche du ainem gueten Mann keufflich zustehen zulassen bedacht sein sollest, vnnd wir dann derselben etliche gern sehen vnnd gegen gepurlicher bezalung an vnns bringen wolten, Als haben wir zaigern, vnsern Hof Conterfeter Josephen Arcimboldo, zu dir abgefertigt vnnd Ime beuolhen, dieselben zu sehen, vnnd das Jehnig so Er fur vnns zusein vermainet, vnns zuezubringen. Versehen vnns demnach zu dir hiemit gnedigclich begerendt, Du wollest solche antiquiteten auf vnnser Wagnus und Costen den geringen weeg antweders furderlichst selbst hieher bringen oder doch zum wenigsten yemandts von deinetwegen mit gedachtem vnserm Conterfeter vnd berurten antiquiteten hieher schicken. Wollen wir vnns nit allain [fol. 8v] mit schliessung des Kauffs vnd erstattung alles vncostens der gepur erzaigen, sonder auch solche dein Willfertigkeit geg[en] dir in gnaden anderwerts erkennen, Dat[um] zu Augspurg, den 8. Septemb[ris] Ao etc. 1582

An Reymunden Dorn Burgern zu Kempten.
[Conc. Pap.]
HHStA, FA Hofakten des Ministeriums der Innern, Karton I E 4 II, fol. 8r-8v.
Archiv des k.k. Ministeriums des Innern, I. E. 4. Niederösterreich, ad 14 vom Jahre 1612.
quoted in: Zimerman 1887, JKSAK 5, CLXXII-CLXXIII, Reg. 4565.
quoted in: Geiger 1960, 141.

25
Official court protocol
October 1583, Prague

Anthoni Abundi supplication wegen bezalung ausstendiger 14 monatsoldt, so zu eingang seines diensts ubersehen unnd ime bißher unbezalt blieben, ligt sambt des hoffzallmaisters bericht, herrn vonn Harrachs, des alten Gabrin unnd Josephen Arcimboldo kundtschafften da aufgehebt.

HKA, Hoffinanz, Vol. 379-E [1583], fol. 376r.

26
Ulysses Aldrovandi, Catalogus peregrinarum rerum naturalium
List of pictures of exotic animals, sent by Franziskus Paduanus from Prague
1584, Bologna
[fol. 31r]
Animaliu[m] peregrinoru[m] depictaru[m] catalogus apud Caes: Maest: Imp: que depingi curauit D. Franc[iscus] Paduanus.

Faggiano de India macchiato di bianco
L'Ardilla.
Il Falcon d'India.
+Colombo d'India
Gallo dalla Pietra
Papagallo di Germania
La Regina
+Il Rinocerote
La Tigre.
L'Asino d'Africa.
+Il capriolo d'Africa
+La Capra del Bezar.
+Il Tasso marino.
+Il Ratto d'India e quel di Faraone.
[fol. 31v] Praga
L'Hurone.
Il Gulone.
L'Alce.
Vn toro unicorno.
+La Grue cirrata o cristata

Fuor de l'uso. 237.
+Mus Indicus.
Ichneumon.
Auis ex gruum genere. [eingefügt:] uid[etur] abund[e] obser[uari]
Taurus unicornus.
Forsan Rangifer Cesaris. uel Vnicornus Plini.
BUB, ms 137, tom. 1, fol. 31r-31v.

27
Franciscus Paduanus to Ulysses Aldrovandi, compendium
List of pictures of exotic animals sent by Franziskus Paduanus from Prague
1584, Bologna (Dated: 11.3.1583-8.4.1585)
[fol. 237v]
Animaliu[m] peregrinor[um] depictoru[m] catalogus apud Ces: Maest: Imp: que depingi curauit Ex[cellentissi]mus Ph[ilosoph]us et Med[icu]s D[omi]nus Franc[iscus] Paduanus Foroiulien[sis] [gestrichen: Vienna] Prage

Faggiano dell' Indie macchiato di bianco.
L'Ardilla.
Il Falcon dell' Indie.
Il Colombo dell' Indie.
Il Gallo della pietra.
Il Papagallo di Germania.
La Regina.
Il Rhinocerote.
La Tigre.
L'Asino d'Africa.
Il Capriolo d'Africa
La capra dell Bezoar.
Il Tasso marino.
Il Ratto d'India, et q[ue]l de Faraone.
L'Hurone.
Il Gulone.
L'Alce.
Vn toro unicorno.
La Grue cirrata o cristata.

Fuor del'uso.
[fol. 238r]

Dirigantur haec ad Ex[cellentissimum] Franc[iscum] Paduanu[m] in Maiestatis Ces[areae] Curia per manus Jacobi Scutelarii Medici C[esareae] M[aiesta]tis Vienam uel Pragam.

BUB, ms 136, tom. 10, fol. 237v-238r.

28
Ulysses Aldrovandi. Peregrinarum rerum catalogus.
List of pictures of exotic animals sent by Franziskus Paduanus from Prague
1584, Bologna
10.237
Animalium peregrinorum depictorum apud Imp. catalogus quae depingi curauit Exc[ellentissi]mus Ph[ilosoph]us et Med[icu]s D[ominus] Franciscus Paduanus Foroiuliensis

Faggiano dell'Indie macchiato di bianco.
L'Ardilla.
Il Falcon dell'Indie.
Il Colombo dell'Indie.
Il Gallo della pietra.
Il Papagallo di Germania
La Regina
Il Rhinocerote
La Tigre
L'Asino d'Africa
Il Capriolo d'Africa.
La Capra del Bezuar
Il Tasso marino
Il ratto d'India e q[ue]l di Faraone
L'Hurone
Il Gulone
L'Alce
Vn toro unicorno
La Grue cirrhata o cristata
Fuor dell'uso

BUB, ms 143, tom. 9, fol. 85v-86r.

29
Franciscus Paduanus to Ulysses Aldrovandi, compendium
1585, Bologna (Dated: 1585-1586)
[fol. 1r]

Ex littris D[omini] Franc[isci] d[e] Paduanis, 1585 [...]
[fol. 5r] [...]

Habeo et ego in Delitys auem quam Psittacu[m] Boemicu[m] appellant, curui rostru[m] a Gesnero dicta[m], uiridi, luteo, roseoq[ue] coloribus in cinereo depictam, crates ligneas quascu[n]q[ue] rostro corrodit, id circo ferreis includere necesse est.

Preteritis hisce diebus D[ominus] Meus Baroni d[e] Kinski auem quam uulgo Trapp nominant dono dedit, anseri cinereae plumis et corpore non absimilem at tibijs ulnae altitudinis nitentem a porrigentiu[m] manib[us] panem escellentem uel si in aera proyceretur, rostro retinentem.

Habui et hisce diebus a Josepho Arcimboldo Mediolan[um] Cesaris pictore primario pluriu[m] auiu[m] et quadrupedum peregrinor[um] imagines ad uiuu[m] colorib[us] delineatas ut illas solummodo in tui gratiam effigiare curare[m] sicuti p[er] literas ad Exc[ellentissimu]m Bernardinu[m] Blasettum datas d[e] istor[um] no[min]ibus significaui.
[fol. 5v]

Sed cuiusdam pictoris opera, ut a principio dixi cogor uti, qui me in patientia exe[rce]t et probat. nám fuit adeo negligens quod cum Cesari proximis hisce diebus plantam illam quam Tusai siue Liliu[m] Persicu[m] Car[olus] Clus[ius] lib[ro] rarior[um] stirp[ium] p[er] Pannonia[m] obseruat[arum] 2.o cap. p[rim]o appellat nobilis quidam attullisset nescio quo fabo [richtig: fato] ad huc probe uirens ad manus deuenerit meas, hanc statim illi ad effigiandum obtuli, spopondit, sed postea promissis non stetit nam cum alio nuptiar[?] caussa secessisset p[er] plures abfuit dies, interim flauescentibus floribus, decidentibusq[ue] folijs planta emaciata totaq[ue] corrupta est.

Et quanuis álias te hanc uidisse plantam non ambigam, huius t[ame]n inscitiam certe indignabundus tuli.
BUB, ms 136, tom. 11, fol. 5r, 5v.

30
Calculation of receipts and disbursements of the court paymaster
14 August 1587, Prague

Josephen Arcimbaldo Röm: Kai: Mat. Conterfecter dem haben die höchsternentee Kai: Mat. vmb seiner langwirigen treu vnd Embsigen dienst willen zue ainer wolverdienten gnod vnd hof Abfertigung Benentlichen 1500 fl r. durch hiebeyligunden vom 14.8.87 an mich außgangenen verschloßenen Beuelch raichen zuelassen [fol. 274r] Genedigist bewilligt, Dieselben hab ich im gegen seiner hiebeyligunden Quittung eodem die zuegestelt.
HKA, HZB 38 [1587], fol. 273v-274r.
quoted in: Boeheim 1888, JKSAK 7, CCXXI, Reg. 5475.

31
Emperor Rudolf II to court paymaster Hans Rietman
14 August 1587, Prague
[Concerning:] Der hofzalmaister solle Irer M[ajestät] Cammer Mahler vnd Conterfetter Josephen Arcimbaldo zu ainer hofs abferttigung 1500 fl R gnadengelt bezallen.

Rudolff,

Getrewer Lieber, Wir haben vnnserm Cammer Mohler, Conterfetter vnnd auch getrewen Lieben, Josephen Arcimbaldo vmb seiner Lanngwierig: vnnß erzaigten trew, vnnd embßigen Diennst Willen, zu ainer wol verdienten gnadt, vnnd Hofabferttigung 1500 fl r[einisch], raichen zulassen allerg[nedigi]st Bewilligt, Vnnd Beuelchen Dir hierauf genedigclich du wollest Ime solche ohne ferrern verzug, auß deinen ambts gefellen, Bezallen, Die sollen dir hernach, auf disen vnsern beuelh vnnd seiner quitt[ung] in khünfftig deiner Ambts raittung, für guet Außgab gelegt, vnnd passiert werden, Es beschiecht auch hieran vnnser g[nedigi]ster will vnnd mainung,
Geben den 14. Augusty Ao. 87.
[note:] R[egistrata]
[note:] Collat[ioniert]
HKA, NÖHA, W 61A14a [Wien, Hof, Hofdiener 1521-1716; Rote Nr. 2731], fol. 22r.

32
Official court protocol
14 August 1587, Prague

Der hofzalmaister solle irer mt. camermahler und conterfetter, Josephen Arcimbaldo, zue ainer hofsabferttigung 1.500 fl rh. gnadengelt bezallen.
HKA, Hoffinanz, Vol. 418-R [1587], fol. 255v.

33
Payment of court salary
2 October 1587, Prague

Joseph Arcimbaldo Röm: Kai: Mat. Conterfecter hat monatlich 30 fl Hofbesoldung, vnnd ist derselben von 14 Monaten 5 Tagen, anzwraiten vom 26.7.86 bis 30.9.87 thuet Benentlichen 425 fl gegen hiebey ligunden seinen 6 Quittungen deren letster Datum den 2.10.87 entricht worden.
HKA, HZB 38 [1587], fol. 190v.

34
Palatinate for Giuseppe Arcimboldo
1 May 1592, Prague

Palatinatus pro Josepho Arcimboldo 1. Maij 1592.

Rudolphus Secundus etc.

Nostro et Sacri Imperij Fideli dilecto Josepho Arcimboldo, Sacri Latranensis Palatij, Aulaeq[ue] nostrae Caesareae et Imperialis Consistorij Comiti Palatino, gratiam nostra[m] Caesarea et omne bonum. Peruetusta atq[ue] laudatissima Diuis praedecessoribus nostris Romanorum Imperatoribus consuetudo fuit, ut cum honorum ac dignitatum incrementa ab Imperatoriae Maj[esta]tis splendore tanquam lumen a sole dimanent, singularem adhibuerunt curam, ut in ijs decernendis liberaliores se erga eos praeberent, qui non tantum ab honesto generis origine, sed etiam a praeclaris actionibus et studijs sibi commendarentur, Idq[ue] non solum, ut dignum illi se praemium consecutos sibi gratulari possent, sed ut alij etiam illorum exemplo, quod fieri solet, accensi atq[ue] inflammati ad laudabilia virtutum certamina feruentiore studio nitantur. quam consuetudinem laudatissimam et nos, postquam ad excelsu[m] hoc Imperatoriae sublimitatis fastigium euecti sumus, seruare cupientes, nihil sane libentius facimus, quam ut praesta[n]tium [fol. 2v] virorum, quorum virtus clara habeatur, et merita in suos Principes singularia extent, ornamenta, quantum occasio et ipsorum status fert, augeamus.

Cum itaq[ue] pulchras et elegantes ingenij tui dotes egregiaq[ue] et fidelia multorum annorum obsequia, quibus nos in picturis artificiosis et in alijs rebus plurimis demeruisti atq[ue] etiamnum demereri pergis benigne consideramus, praetermittere noluimus, quin aliquo te singulari benignae uoluntatis nostrae documento sumamus decorandum.
Motu itaq[ue] proprio ex certa nostra scientia animo deliberato Caesareaq[ue] auctoritate et potestate n[ost]ra, te praefatum Josephum Arcimboldum Sacri Lateranensis Palatij, Aulaeque nostrae Caesareae, et Imperialis consistorij Comitem fecimus, creauimus, ereximus, ac Comitatus Palatini titulo clementer insigniuimus, ac aliorum Comitum Palatinorum numero, coetui et consortio adscribimus, adiungimus, et aggregamus.

Decernentes et statuentes quod omnibus et singulis priuilegijs, gratijs, immunitatibus, 7 honoribus, exemptionibus, et libertatibus, vti, frui, potiri, et gaudere possis et debeas, quibus [fol. 3r] coeteri Lateranensis Palatij Comites hactenus vsi, potiti, et gauisi sunt, seu quomodolibet utuntur, fruuntur, potiuntur, et gaudent, consuetudine, uel de Jure.

Dantes, et concedentes tibi antedicto Josepho Arcimboldo, plenam facultatem et potestatem qua possis et ualeas per totum Romanum Imperium, et ubilibet terrarum facere et creare Notarios publicos, seu Tabelliones, ac Judices ordinarios, et omnibus personis quae fide dignae, habiles, et idoneae fuerint (qua in re conscientiam tuam oneramus) Notariatus seu Tabellionatus, et Judicatus ordinarij officium concedere et dare, eosq[ue] et eorum quemlibet, auctoritate Imperiali de praedictis officijs, per pennam et calamarium (prout moris est) inuestire, Recipiendo ab ipsis Notarijs publicis seu Tabellionibus, et Judicibus ordinarijs per te ut praemittitur creandis, et ab eorum quolibet, vice ac nomine Sacri Imperij, et pro ipso Romano Imperio debitum fidelitatis corporale et proprium juramentum, In hunc uidelicet modum: Quod nobis et Sacro Romano Imperio, ac successoribus nostris Romanoru[m] [fol. 3v] Imperatoribus et Regibus legitime intrantibus fideles erunt, nec unquam interfuturi sunt consilio ubi nostrum periculum tractetur, sed bonum et salutem nostram defendent, et fideliter promouebunt, damna nostra sedulo cauebunt et auertent; Praeterea Instrumenta publica, et priuata, ultimas voluntates, testamenta, et quaecunq[ue] Judiciorum acta, ac omnia et singula alia, quae illis, et cuilibet illorum dictorum officiorum ratione facienda uel scribenda occurrent iuste, pure, fideliter, omni simulatione, machinatione, falsitate, dolo, ac fraude remotis, scribent, legent, facient, et dictabunt, non attendendo odium, pecuniam, munera, uel alias passiones, et fauores, scripturas uero in formam publica[m] redigendas, pro locorum consuetudine, et rerum qualitate, in membranis, aut chartis mundis, non abrasis, aut uitiosis fideliter conscribent, et conscribi facient, causasq[ue] hospitalium, et miserabilium personarum, sibi diligenter commendatas habebunt, et promouebunt.

Pontes etiam et vias publicas omnibus modis conseruari, et instaurari curabunt; sententias uero [fol. 4r] et dicta testium, donec publicata fuerint et approbata sub secreto fideliter retinebunt, omniaq[ue] et singula alia recte et iuste facient, atq[ue] exercebunt, quae ad dictum officium quomodolibet pertinebunt. Statuentes Caesareaq[ue] auctoritate nostra firmiter decernentes quod huiusmodi Notarij publici, seu Tabelliones, et Judices ordinarij a te ut supra dictum est, creandi, possint et ualeant per totum Romanum Imperium, et vbilibet locorum, facere, scribere, et publicare, contractus, instrumenta, Judiciorum acta, testamenta, et vltimas voluntates, Matrimoniales, et quascunq[ue] alias literas, simulq[ue] decretum et authoritatem interponere, in omnibus contractibus tale quippiam requirentibus, ac omnia alia facere, et exercere, quae dictum officium Notarij seu Tabellionis, et Judicis ordinarij exigere uidebitur.

Volentes quod omnibus instrumentis et scripturis, per huiusmodi Tabelliones et Notarios publicos, siue Judices ordinarios, per te creandos uel creatos, confectis uel conficiendis, plena ubilubet fides adhibeatur, [fol. 4v] constitutionibus, ordinationibus, et alijs in contrarium facientibus non obstantibus quibuscunq[ue].

Praeterea eadem scientia, authoritate atq[ue] potestate nostra Caesarea, tibi supradicto Josepho Arcimboldo concedimus, et elargimur facultatem, et potestatem, quod possis et ualeas naturales, Bastardos, spurios, Manseres Nothos, incestuosos, copulatiue, uel disiunctiue, ac quoscunq[ue] alios, ex illicito, et damnato concubitu procreatos, et procreandos, masculos et foeminas, quocunq[ue] nomine censeantur, et quemcunq[ue] natalium defectum patiantur, Illustrium tamen Principum, Comitum, et Baronum filijs exceptis viuentibus uel etia[m] mortuis eorum parentibus, ipsisq[ue] absentibus uel praesentibus legitimare, et eos ac eorum quemlibet ad omnia et singula iura legitima restituere et reducere, omnemq[ue] geniturae maculam poenitus tollere, et abolere, restituendo ipsos ad omnia et singula iura successionum et haereditatum bonorum paternorum et maternorum etiam ab intestato, cognatoru[m] et agnatorum, ac ad honores, dignitates, et [fol. 5r] alios quosuis actus legitimos, proinde ac si de vero et legitimo matrimonio procreati essent, obiectione prolis illegitimae prorsus cessante.

Volentes quod ipsorum legitimatio hoc modo facta, habeatur et teneatur pro legitime, et cum omnibus iuris solemnitatibus facta, quarum solennitatum defectus specialiter authoritate nostra supplemus, et suppleri volumus, serioq[ue] firmiter decernimus, quod ipsi legitimandi postquam ut supra legitimati fuerint, sint et esse censeantur, ac nominentur, et nominari possint ac debeant ibiq[ue] locorum uere legitimi, ac legitime nati de familia, agnatione, atq[ue] prosapia parentum suorum, ac arma et insignia eorum ferre et gestare, omnibusq[ue] actibus publicis, et priuatis, officijs, Juribus, honoribus, et dignitatibus quibuscunq[ue] vti, frui, potiri, et gaudere possint, et debeant quibus uere legitimi, et de legitimo coniugio procreati utuntur, fruuntur, potiuntur et gaudent, sine praeiudico tamen filiorum legitimorum, et haeredum ab intestato uenientium.

[fol. 5v] Non obstantibus in praemissis aliquibus legibus, quibus cauetur quod naturales, bastardi, spurij, manseres, nothi, incestuosi, copulatiue uel disiunctiue, uel alij quicunq[ue] ex illicito concubitu procreati, nec possint nec debeant legitimari liberis naturalibus legitimis existentibus, et specialiter in auth[enticis] quibus mod[is] nat[urales] effi[ciuntur] legit[imi] et quib[us] mod[is] nat[urales] effi[ciuntur] sui per totum, et § naturales, si de feu[do] fue[rit] contro[uersia] inter Domi[num] et agna[tos uasalli] et l. inhibebus [etc]. de emancip[atione] lib[erorum] et alijs similibus, neq[ue] etiam obstantibus quibuscunq[ue] locorum statutis, et consuetudinibus, etiamsi tales essent de quibus hoc loci specialis, et expressa mentio fieri deberet, quibus omnibus quatenus obstarent, seu obstare possent, in hoc casu duntaxat, ex certa scientia, et de plenitudine potestatis nostrae derogamus, et sufficienter derogatum esse volumus atq[ue] decernimus.

Similiter ijsdem motu, scientia atq[ue] authoritate tibi sepefato Josepho Arcimboldo concedimus et elargimur plenam facultatem et potestatem, qua possis et ualeas Curatores et [fol. 6r] Tutores constituere, dare, et confirmare, eosdemq[ue] causis legitimis subsistentibus amouere, nec non liberos cuiuscunq[ue] aetatis, et sexus adoptare et arrogare, ac eos adoptiuos, et arrogatos facere et ordinare, rursusq[ue] filios legitimos, et legitimandos, adoptiuosq[ue] et arrogatos, cuiuslibet aetatis, etiam in infantia constitutos emancipare, et á patria potestate liberare, aetatis veniam supplicationibus concedere, seruos manumittere, et adoptionibus, arrogationibus, emancipationibus quibuscunq[ue], omnium et singulorum etiam infantium, et adolescentium, ac manumissionibus quibuslibet. cum, uel sine vindicta, authoritatem et decretum interponere, In omnibus tamen iuris ordine semper seruato.

Mandantes proinde vniuersis et singulis Ecclesiasticis et Secularibus Principibus, Electoribus, Archiepiscopis, Episcopis, Ducibus, Marchionibus, Comitibus, Baronibus, Militibus, Nobilibus, Clientibus, Capitaneis, Vicedominis, Aduocatis, [fol. 6v] Praefectis, Procuratoribus, officinalibus, Questoribus, Ciuium Magistratis, Judicibus, Consulibus, Regum Heroaldis, et Caduceatoribus, ac deniq[ue] omnibus nostris, et Sacri Romani Imperij subditis, ac fidelibus dilectis, cuiuscunq[ue] status, gradus, ordinis, conditionibus, et dignitatis extiterint, ut te sepenominatum Josephum Arcimboldum, omnibus et singulis priuilegijs, gratijs, libertatibus, concessionibus, et iuribus pacifice, quiete, et sine omni prorsus impedimento, vti, frui, potiri et gaudere sinant, atq[ue] id ipsum ab alijs etiam fieri curent.

Si quis autem praesens edictum nostru[m], ausu aliquo temerario tran[s]gredi, et uiolare conatus fuerit, praeter grauissimam nostram et Sacri Imperij indignationem, quinquaginta Marcharum auri puri mulctam Fisco seu Erario nostro Imperiali, et parti laesae ex aequo soluendam se nouerit irremissibiliter incursurum.

Harum testimonio literarum manu nostra subscriptarum, et Caesarei sigilli nostri appensione munitarum. Datum Pragae die 1. Maij Anno D[o]m[ini] 1592

AVA, Adelsarchiv (R), Arcimboldi 1592, fol. 2-6.
HHStA, Reichsregister, Rudolf II., Vol. 23 [1592-1602; MF R 78], fol. 57r-60r.
quoted in: Geiger 1960, 142-143.

35

Rechnungsbuch des Reichstaxamtes
24 July 1592, Prague

Palatinatus pro Josepho Arcimboldo. Tax 40 Cronen, vnnd ist lauth Vrkhundt mit No. 2 Taxfrey [Nachlaß:] 60 fl.

HHStA, Taxamt 71 [1592], fol. 43r.

36

Accounts book of the imperial tax office
October 1592, Prague

Von wegen des Palatinat fürn Joseph Arcimbaldo, so Ir Mtt. haben abgefordert p[er] Schreib-, Schnur- vnnd Siglgelt zalt 13 Tl thun 15 fl 10 kr

HHStA, Taxamt 72 [1592], fol. 63v.

37

Official court protocol
June 1593, Prague

Hanß Haiden erinderung, das ier mt. Josepho Arcimoldo ahnstatt seiner gehabten monatlichen 30 fl besoldung järlich 300 fl provision bewilliget, ligt da aufgehebt und will herr president bey ier mt. selbst deßwegen beschaidt nemben.

HKA, Hoffinanz, Vol. 467-E [1593], fol. 106v.

Bibliography

Albonico 1995
S. Albonico, *Il ruginoso stile. Poeti e poesia in volgare a Milano nella prima metà del Cinquecento*, Milan, 1995

Aldrovandi 1600
U. Aldrovandi, *Ornithologiae tomus alter*, Bononiae, Io. Baptista Bellagamba, 1600

Aldrovandi 1621
U. Aldrovandi, *Quadrupedum omnium bisulcorum Historia*, Ioannes Cornelius Uterverius belga colligere incaepit, Thomas Dempsterus [...] perfecte absolvit, Hieronymus Tamburinus in lucem edidit, Bononiae, Apud Sebastianum Bonhommium, 1621

Aldrovandi 1637
U. Aldrovandi, *De quadrupedibus digitatis viviparis libri tres et de quadrupedibus digitatis oviparis libri duo*, Bartholomaeus Ambrosinus [...] collegit, Sumptibus M. Antonij Berniae, Bononiae, Apud Nicolaum Tebaldinum, 1637

Aldrovandi 1642
U. Aldrovandi, *Paralipomena accuratissima historiae omnium animalium quae in voluminibus Aldrovandi desiderantur*, Bartholomaeus Ambrosinus [...] summo labore collegit, Marcus Antonij Berniae in lucem edidit, Proprijs sumptibus Bononiae, Typis Nicolai Tebaldini, 1642

Alewyn 1985
R. Alewyn, *Das grosse Welttheater. Die Epoche der höfischen Feste*, Munich 1985

Alfons 1957
S. Alfons, *Giuseppe Arcimboldo. En biografisk och ikonografisk studie*, (Symbolister 2/Tidskrift för Konstvetenskap 31), Malmö 1957

Alfons 1987
S. Alfons, *The Museum as Image of the World*, in exhibition catalogue Venice 1987, 67-85

Alpers 1983
S. Alpers, *The Art of Describing. Dutch Art in the Seventeenth Century*, Chicago-London 1983

Ambras 1977
Exhibition catalogue, *Die Kunstkammer*, Kunsthistorisches Museum, Sammlungen Schloß Ambras, Innsbruck 1977

Ambras 1981
Exhibition catalogue, *Die Rüstkammern*, Kunsthistorisches Museum, Sammlungen Schloß Ambras, Vienna 1981

Ambras 2001
Exhibition catalogue, *Alle Wunder dieser Welt. Die kostbarsten Kunstwerke aus der Sammlung Erzherzog Ferdinands II. (1529-1595)*, ed. by W. Seipel, Innsbruck, Vienna 2001

Ambras 2002
Exhibition catalogue, *Werke für die Ewigkeit, Kaiser Maximilian I. und Erzherzog Ferdinand II.*, Kunsthistorisches Museum, Sammlungen Schloß Ambras, Vienna 2002

Ambras 2006
Exhibition catalogue, *Die Entdeckung der Natur. Naturalien in den Kunstkammern des 16. und 17. Jahrhunderts*, ed. by W. Seipel, Vienna 2006

Ames-Lewis 1997
F. Ames-Lewis, "Leonardo's Botanical Drawings", in *Achademia Leonardi Vinci*, 10, 1997, 117-124

Amico 1987
L.N. Amico, "Les céramiques rustiques authentiques de Bernard Palissy", in *Revue de l'art*, 78, 1987, 61-69

Amico 1996a
L.N. Amico, "Bernard Palissy and Saint-Porchaire Ceramics", in *Saint-Porchaire Ceramics*, Washington 1996

Amico 1996b
L.N. Amico, *Bernard Palissy et ses continuateurs: A la recherche du paradis terrestre*, Paris 1996

Annali 1885
Annali della Fabbrica del Duomo di Milano, Milan, Libreria Editrice Brigola, 1877-1885 (voll. 1-5 and Appendix, vol. I), Tipografia Sociale E. Reggiani, 1885 (vol. 6, Appendix, voll. II and Indexes)

Arasse 2006
D. Arasse, "La science divine de la peinture selon Léonard de Vinci", in *L'art de la Renaissance entre science et magie*, ed. by P. Morel, Paris-Rome 2006, 343-356

Arasse, Tönnesman 1997
D. Arasse, A. Tönnesman, *La Renaissance maniériste*, Paris 1997

Argelati 1745
F. Argelati, *Bibliotheca Scriptorum Mediolanensium*, Milan 1745

Arrivabene 1561
A. Arrivabene, *I grandi apparati, le giostre, l'imprese, e i trionfi, fatti nella città di Mantova, nelle nozze dell'Illustrissimo & Eccellentissimo Signor Duca di Mantova, marchese di Monferrato &c. Con tutt'il successo dell'entrata di sua Altezza*, Mantua 1561

Art e Dossier 1987
"Arcimboldi e l'arte delle meraviglie", in *Art e Dossier*, 11, 1987

Auer 2005
A. Auer (ed.), exhibition catalogue Vienna 2005

Augsburg 1980
Exhibition catalogue, *Welt im Umbruch. Augsburg zwischen Renaissance und Barock*, vol. 2, Augsburg 1980, 525f., no. 934

Bairati 1998
E. Bairati, "Note iconografiche su una 'Salome' di Bernardino Luini", in *Itinerari d'arte in Lombardia dal XIII al XX secolo: scritti offerti a Maria Teresa Binaghi Olivari*, ed. by M. Ceriana, Milan 1998, 135-142

Baldini 1600
B. Baldini, *Carminum appendix*, Milan 1600

Ballistreri 1970
G. Ballistreri, "Borgogni (Borgogna), Gherardo", *ad vocem* in *Dizionario Biografico degli Italiani*, Rome, Istituto dell'Enciclopedia Italiana, XII (1970), 766-767

Ballot 1924
M.-J. Ballot, *Musée du Louvre: la céramique française, Bernard Palissy et les fabriques du XVIe siècle*, Paris 1924

Baltrušaitis 1981
J. Baltrušaitis, *Le Moyen âge fantastique. Antiquités et exotismes dans l'art gothique*, Paris 1981 (first ed. 1955)

Bambach 2003
C.C. Bambach, exhibition catalogue *Leonardo da Vinci Master Draftsman*, Metropolitan Museum of Art, New York 2003

Barocchi 1962
P. Barocchi (ed.), *Trattati d'arte del Cinquecento*, Bari 1962, vol. 3

Barocchi 1973
P. Barocchi, *Scritti d'arte del Cinquecento*, vol. II, Milan-Naples 1973

Baroni Vannucci 1997
A. Baroni Vannucci, *Jan van der Straet*, Milan 1997

Barryte 1990
B. Barryte, *The Ill-Matched Couple, Achademia Leonardi Vinci*, III, 1990, 133-139

Barthes 1978
R. Barthes, "Rhétoriqueur et Magicien", in C. Ferrari, *Arcimboldo*, Franco Maria Ricci, Milan 1978, 13-68

Barthes 1980
R. Barthes, *Arcimboldo*, Milan 1980

Barthes 1990
R. Barthes, "Arcimboldo oder Rhéthorique und Magier", in idem, *Der entgegenkommende und der stumpfe Sinn*, Frankfurt a.M. 1990, 136-154

Battisti 1956
E. Battisti, "Alcuni disegni inediti a Madrid", in *Emporium*, CXXIII, 734, 1956, 55-65

Battisti 1989
E. Battisti, *L'antirinascimento. Con un'appendice di manoscritti inediti*, 2 vol., Milan 1989 (first edition 1962)

Battistini 2003
F. Battistini, *L'industria della seta in Italia nell'età moderna*, Bologna 2003

Bauer, Haupt 1976
R. Bauer, H. Haupt (eds.), "Das Kunstkammerinventar Kaiser Rudolfs II., 1607-1611", in *Jahrbuch der Kunsthistorischen Sammlungen in Wien*, vol. 72, 1976, 1-140

Beaufort, Pfaffenbichler 2005
C. Beaufort, M. Pfaffenbichler, *Meisterwerke der Hofjagd- und Rüstkammer, Kurzführer durch das Kunsthistorische Museum*, ed. by W. Seipel, vol. 3, Milan 2005, 30, 162f, cat. no. 56

Becker 1980
J. Becker, *Das Buch im Stilleben-Das Stilleben im Buch*, Stilleben in Europa, Münster-Baden-Baden 1979-80, 448-478

Bedini 1997
S.A. Bedini, *The Pope's Elephant*, Manchester 1997

Beltrami 1911
L. Beltrami, *Luini 1512-1532*, Milan 1911

Benesch 1964
O. Benesch, *Meisterzeichnungen der Albertina: europäische Schulen von der Gotik bis zum Klassizismus*, Salzburg 1964

Berger 1883
A. Berger, "Inventar der Kunstsammlung

des Erzherzogs Leopold Wilhelm von Österreich. Nach der Originalhandschrift im fürstlich Schwarzenberg'schen Centralarchive...", in *Jahrbuch der Kunsthistorischen Sammlungen des Allerhöchsten Kaiserhauses*, vol. I/2, 1883, LXXIX-CLXXVII

Berlin 1995
Exhibition catalogue, *Von allen Seiten schön – Bronzen der Renaissance und des Barock*, Berlin 1995, 226, no. 42, 227, no. 43 (Leithe-Jasper), 320 f., no. 94 (Berger)

Berlin 2006
Exhibition catalogue, *Heiliges Römisches Reich Deutscher Nation 962 bis 1806, Altes Reich und neue Staaten 1495 bis 1806*, Berlin 2006

Berliner 1928
R. Berliner, "Zur älteren Geschichte der allgemeinen Museumslehre in Deutschland", in *Münchner Jahrbuch der bildenden Kunst*, N.F., vol. V, 1928, 237-352

Berns, Rahn 1995
J.J. Berns, Th. Rahn (eds.), *Zeremoniell als höfische Ästhetik in Spätmittelalter und früher Neuzeit*, Tübingen 1995

Berra 1988
G. Berra, "Allegoria e mitologia nella pittura dell'Arcimboldi: la *Flora* e il *Vertumno* nei versi di un libretto sconosciuto di rime", in *Acme*, XLI, II, 1988, 11-39

Berra 1996a
G. Berra, "Un Autoritratto Cartaceo di Giuseppe Arcimboldi", in *Arte Lombarda*, 116, I, 1996, 53-62

Berra 1996b
G. Berra, "Arcimboldi e Caravaggio: 'diligenza' e 'pazienza' nella natura morta arcaica", in *Paragone*, 8-9-10, 55-62

Berra 1998a
G. Berra, "Arcimboldi: le teste 'caricate' leonardesche e le 'grillerie' dell'Accademia della Val di Blenio", in exhibition catalogue Lugano 1998, 57-68

Berra 1998b
G. Berra, "Giuseppe Arcimboldo", in exhibition catalogue Lugano 1998, 200, n. 42

Berra 1998c
G. Berra, "Giovanni Ambrogio Figino, Giove, Giunone ed Io mutata in giovenca", in exhibition catalogue Lugano 1998, 109, 286

Berra 2000
G. Berra, "Arcimboldi, Vincenzo Campi, Figino, Fede Galizia, Caravaggio: congiunture sulla nascita della natura morta in Lombardia", in exhibition catalogue Cremona 2000, 60-85

Berra 2003
G. Berra, in exhibition catalogue *La natura morta italiana da Caravaggio al Settecento*, ed. by M. Gregori, Florence-Milan 2003

Berra 2004
G. Berra, "La 'Medusa tutta serpegiata' del Caravaggio: fonti mitologico-letterarie e figurative", in *Caravaggio la Medusa. Lo splendore degli scudi da parata del Cinquecento*, Milan 2004

Beyer 1983
A. Beyer, "Giuseppe Arcimboldo und die Bühne der Fürsten", in *Giuseppe Arcimboldo, Figurinen, Kostüme und Entwürfe für höfische Feste*, ed. by A. Beyer, Frankfurt a.M. 1983

Beyer 2000
A. Beyer, "Späthumanismus. Zu Aspekten des Fortlebens der Kunst nach dem Ende der Renaissance", in *Späthumanismus. Studien über das Ende einer kulturhistorischen Epoche*, ed. by N. Hammerstein, G. Walther, Göttingen 2000, 287-299

Bianconi 1787
C. Bianconi, *Nuova guida di Milano per gli amanti delle belle arti e delle sacre, e profane antichità milanesi*, Milan 1787

Bibl 1929
V. Bibl, *Maximilian II. Der rätselhafte Kaiser, Ein Zeitbild*, Hellerau 1929

Biffi 1705 (1990)
G. Biffi, *Pitture, scolture et ordini d'architettura*, ed. by M. Bona Castellotti, S. Colombo, Florence 1990 (edition of the manuscript AD XI 35)

Binaghi Olivari 1994
M.T. Binaghi Olivari, "Partita doppia milanese per Tiziano", in *Venezia. Arti*, 8 (1994), 37-46

Birke, Kertèsz 1992
V. Birke, J. Kertész, *Die italienischen Zeichnungen der Albertina. Generalverzeichnis*, vol. 1, Vienna-Cologne-Weimar 1992

Bizzocchi 1995
R. Bizzocchi, *Genealogie incredibili. Scritti di storia nell'Europa moderna*, Bologna 1995

Bőžek 2003
V. Bőžek, "Erzherzog Ferdinand als Statthalter von Böhmen – Residenz, Hof, Alltagsleben und Politik", in exhibition catalogue Vienna 2003, 283-295

Boccardo 1999
P. Boccardo, *I grandi disegni italiani del Gabinetto Disegni e Stampe di Palazzo Rosso a Genova*, Milan 1999

Bock 2005
S. Bock, *Ova struthionis. Die Straußeneiobjekte in den Schatz-, Silber- und Kunstkammern Europas*, Freiburg i. Br.-Heidelberg 2005

Bode 1907
W. von Bode, *Die italienischen Bronzestatuetten der Renaissance*, vol. 1, Berlin 1907, 27

Bode 1922
W. von Bode, *Die italienischen Bronzestatuetten der Renaissance*, vol. 3, Berlin 1922, 45

Boeheim 1888
W. Boeheim (ed.), "Urkunden und Regesten aus der k. k. Hofbibliothek", in *Jahrbuch der Kunsthistorischen Sammlungen des Allerhöchsten Kaiserh*auses, vol. 7, Vienna 1888, XCI- CCCCXIII

Bora 1977a
G. Bora, *Note cremonesi, II: L'eredità di Camillo ed i Campi*, in "Paragone", no. 327, May 1977, 54-88

Bora 1977b
G. Bora, in exhibition catalogue Milan 1977

Bora 1989
G. Bora, "Da Leonardo all'Accademia della Val di Blenio: Giovan Paolo Lomazzo, Aurelio Luini e i disegni degli accademici", in *Raccolta Vinciana*, XXIII, 1989, 73-101

Bora 1998
G. Bora, "Milano nell'età di Lomazzo e di San Carlo: riaffermazione e difficoltà di sopravvivenza di una cultura", in exhibition catalogue Lugano 1998, 37-56

Borgogni 1592
G. Borgogni, *Nuova Scelta di Rime*, Bergamo 1592

Borgogni 1594
G. Borgogni, *Le muse toscane dei diversi nobilissimi ingegni*, Bergamo 1594

Borgogni 1598
G. Borgogni, *La Fonte del Diporto. Dialogo [...] nel quale si raccontano alcuni bellissimi, e morali avenimenti, e si leggono nuove, e diverse poesie, & altre materie curiose*, Per Comin Ventura, Bergamo 1598

Braunschweig 2000
Exhibition catalogue, *Weltenharmonie. Die Kunstkammer und die Ordnung des Wissens*, Braunschweig 2000

Bredekamp 1989
H. Bredekamp, "Grillenfänge von Michelangelo bis Goethe", in *Marburger Jahrbuch für Kunstwissenschaft*, 22, 1989, 169-180

Bredekamp 1993
H. Bredekamp, *Antikensehnsucht und Maschinenglaube. Die Geschichte der Kunstkammer und die Zukunft der Kunstgeschichte*, Berlin 1993

Bredekamp 2003
H. Bredekamp, *Thomas Hobbes. Visuelle Stategien. Der Leviathan: Das Urbild des modernen Staates Werkillustationen und Portraits*, Berlin 2003

Bremond 1995
M.S. de Bremond y Frigola, "Arcimboldo en España", in *Archivo de arte valenciano*, vol. 76, 1995, 75-76

Buck 1981
A. Buck *et al.* (ed.), *Europäische Hofkultur im 16. und 17. Jahrhundert*, 3 vol., Hamburg 1981

Bukovinská 1997
B. Bukovinská, "The Kunstkammer of Rudolf II: Where it Was and What it Looked Like", in exhibition catalogue Prague 1997, 199-208

Bukovinská 2001
B. Bukovinská, "Zum Exotica-Bestand der Kunstkammer Rudolfs II. in Prag", in *Jahrbuch des Kunsthistorischen Museums Wien*, vol. 3, 2001, 205-219

Bukovinská 2005
B. Bukovinská, "The Known and the Unknown Kunstkammer of Rudolf II", in H. Schramm, L. Schwarte, J. Lazardzig, *Collection - Laboratory - Theater. Scenes of Knowledge in the 17th Century*, Berlin-New York 2005, 199-227

Burckhardt 1989
J. Burckhardt, *Die Kultur der Renaissance in Italien (1860)*, Frankfurt a.M. 1989, 397ff.

Calderini 1940
A. Calderini, "Documenti inediti per la storia della Chiesa di S. Francesco Grande in Milano", in *Aevum*, year XIV, fasc. 2-3, April-September 1940, 197-230

Calvesi 1987
M. Calvesi, "Le fonti dell'Arcimboldi e il verde sogno di Polifilo", in "Arcimboldi e l'arte delle meraviglie", in *Art e Dossier*, 11, 1987, 29-34

Camelli 1931
I. Camelli, "La Pinacoteca del Civico Museo. Il catalogo", in *Cremona*, III, (1931), 103-110, 229-234, 305-310, 385-389, 441-445, 523-526

Campbell 1983
A.C. Campbell, *Was lebt im Mittelmeer?*, Stuttgart 1983

Campori 1870
G. Campori, *Raccolta di cataloghi ed inventari inediti*, Modena 1870, 192-202

Canetta 1883
P. Canetta, *Storia del Pio Istituto di S. Corona di Milano*, Milan 1883

Cantaro 1993
M.T. Cantaro, "Aggiornamenti e precisazioni sul catalogo di Lavinia Fontana", *Bollettino d'Arte*, 79 (1993), 85-102

Casati 1885
C. Casati, "Giuseppe Arcimboldi pittore milanese", in *Archivio Storico Lombardo* 1885, 86-94

Cavalieri 2000
F. Cavalieri, "Il patrimonio artistico", in M. Comincino, F. Cavalieri, *Sedriano. Una parrocchia, una comunità*, Sedriano 2000, 93-114

Cavalli-Björkman 2005
G. Cavalli-Björkman, *Målningar på Skokloster*, in *Skoklosters slott under 350 år*, ed. by C. Bergström, Stockholm 2005

Centorio degli Ortensi 1559
A. Centorio degli Ortensi, *I Grandi apparati, e feste fatte in Melano dalli Illust. & Eccell. S. il S. Duca di Sessa Governatore dello Stato di Melano & Capitan generale del Re di Spagna in Italia, & S.*

Marchese di Pescara Generale della Cavalleria leggiera di sua Mae. In Lombardia: in casa dell'Illustr. S. Gio. Battista Castaldo Marchese di Cassano, Appresso di Giovan' Antonio de gli Antonij, Milan 1559
Chabrowe 1970
B. Chabrowe, *Baroque Temporary Structures built for the Austrian Habsburgs*, Ph.D. Dissertation, Columbia University, 1970, 114-22, 180ff.
Christianson 2006
J.R. Christianson, *Tycho Brahe*, in *Danmark og renæssancen 150-1650*, n.p. (Copenhagen) 2006, 174-185
Ciardi 1974
R.P. Ciardi, *Scritti sulle Arti*, Florence 1974, 2 vol., 304
Ciceri 1811
C.F. Ciceri, *Selva di Notizie autentiche risguardanti la fabbrica della Cattedrale di Como con altre memorie patrie, ed analoghe all'argomento*, Como 1811
Clayton 2002
M. Clayton (ed.), *Leonardo da Vinci. The Divine and the Grotesque*, exhibition catalogue London 2002
Clément de Ris 1875
L. Clément de Ris, *Notice des faïences françaises, faïences dites de Henri II, faïences de Bernard Palissy, faïences diverses*, Paris 1875
Coccia 1982
M. Coccia, "Comanini, Gregorio", *ad vocem* in *Dizionario Biografico degli Italiani*, Rome, Istituto dell'Enciclopedia Italiana, XXVIII (1982), 526-528
Cogliati Arano 1980
L. Cogliati Arano, *Disegni di Leonardo e della sua cerchia alle Gallerie dell'Accademia*, Milan 1980
Cogliati Arano 1992
L. Cogliati Arano, in *Leonardo & Venice*, exhibition catalogue ed. by G. Nepi Sciré, P.C. Marani, Venice 1992
Colie 1966
R.L. Colie, *Paradoxia Epidemica. The Renaissance Tradition of Paradox*, Princeton 1966
Cologne-Zurich-Vienna 1996-97
Exhibition catalogue, *Das Capriccio als Kunstprinzip. Zur Vorgeschichte der Moderne von Arcimboldo und Callot bis Tiepolo und Goya. Malerei – Zeichnung – Graphik*, ed. by Ekkehard Mai, Milan 1996
Colombo Fantini 1987-1988
M. Colombo Fantini, "Il gonfalone di Milano", in *Rassegna di Studi e Notizie*, XIV, 1987-1988, 197-248
Comanini 1591 (1962)
G. Comanini, "Il Figino overo del fine della pittura", in P. Barocchi, *Trattati d'arte del Cinquecento fra manierismo e controriforma*, vol. III, Bari 1962 (1591), 237-599
Comanini 1591
G. Comanini, *Il Figino, overo del fine della pittura. Dialogo del Rever[endo] Padre D. Gregorio Comanini ... Ove quistionandosi se'l fine della pittura sia l'utile over oil diletto ... si mostra qual sia imitator più perfetto e che più diletti, il Pittore overo il Poeta*, Mantua 1591
Comanini 1971
G. Comanini, "Il Figino, overo del fine della pittura", in P. Barocchi, *Scritti d'arte del Cinquecento*, I, Milan-Naples 1971
Coppa 1991
S. Coppa, "La diffusione di modelli leonardeschi in alta Lombardia: alcuni esempi", in *I leonardeschi a Milano: fortuna e collezionismo* (conf. proceedings, Milan, 25-26 September 1990, ed. by M.T. Florio, P.C. Marani), Milan 1991, 108-119
Coppa 1992
S. Coppa, "Arcimboldo (Arcimboldi), Biagio", in *Saur – Allgemeines Künstlerlexikon, Vol. 4: Angelin-Ardon*, Munich-Leipzig 1992, 708
Coron 2001
S. Coron, *Livres en bouche. Cinq siècles d'art culinaire francais du quatorzième au dix-huitième siècle*, exhibition catalogue Paris 2001
Crea 1993
E. Crea (ed.), *Hortus pictus dalla raccolta di Ulisse Aldrovandi*, with essays by S. Tugnoli Pattaro, C. Tagliaferri, S. Tommasini, I. Ventura Folli, Rome 1993
Cremades 1998
F. Checa Cremades, "Felipe II: un monarca y su época; un príncipe del Renacimiento", in exhibition catalogue Madrid 1998, 653, no. 268
Cremona 2000
Exhibition catalogue, *Vincenzo Campi: scene del quotidiano*, Cremona 2000
Crescenzi 1640-1647
G.P. de Crescenzi, *Anfiteatro Romano nel quale [...] Si rappresenta la Nobiltà Delle Famiglie Antiche, e Nuove della Regia Città di Milano*, Milan s.d. (1640 or 1647)
Cunnally 1999
J. Cunnally, *Images of the Illustrious: The Numismatic Presence in the Renaissance*, Princeton 1999

D'Ayala 1867
M. D'Ayala, "Vita di Giambattista Castaldo famosissimo guerriero del secolo XVI", in *Archivio Storico Italiano*, series III, vol. V, part I, 1867, 86-124
Danesi Squarzina 1996
S. Danesi Squarzina (ed.), *Natura morta e collezionismo a Roma nella prima metà del Seicento. Italia, Fiandre, Olanda; il territorio di elaborazione dei generi*, Rome 1996, 9-75
De Caro 1978
G. De Caro, "Castaldo, Giovanni Battista", *ad vocem* in *Dizionario Biografico degli Italiani*, Rome, Istituto dell'Enciclopedia Italiana, XXI (1978), 562-566
Delange, Sauzay 1862
C. Delange, A. Sauzay, *Monographie de l'oeuvre de Bernard Palissy, suivie d'un choix de ses continuateurs ou imitateurs*, Paris 1862
della Porta 1586
G.B. della Porta, *De humana physiognomonia*, Vico Equense 1586
Dericks-Tan, Martin 2000
J. Dericks-Tan, G. Martin, *Onans Kinder. Merk-Würdiges zu Sexualität und Fortpflanzung aus Geschichte und Medizin*, Alzenau 2000, 99
di Lorenzo 1989
A. di Lorenzo, "Nuovi documenti per Gaudenzio e i suoi aiuti a Saronno", in *Bollettino della Società Pavese di Storia Patria*, 1989, 215-235
Diemer 1980
P. Diemer, "Materialien zu Entstehung und Ausbau derKammergalerie Maximilians I. von Bayern", in *Quellen und Studien zur Kunstpolitik der Wittelsbacher vom 16. bis zum 18. Jahrhundert*, ed. by Herbert Glaser, Munich-Zurich 1980, 129-158
Diemer 2004
P. Diemer (ed.), *Johann Baptist Fickler, Das Inventar der Münchner herzoglichen Kunstkammer von 1598. Editionsband. Transkription der Inventarhandschrift cgm 2133* (Bayer. Akademie der Wissenschaften, philos.-histor. Klasse, Abhandlungen, N. F., H. 125), Munich 2004
Dijon 2002
Exhibition catalogue, *Praga Magica 1600, L'art à Prague au temps de Rodolphe II*, Dijon 2002
Distelberger 1975
R. Distelberger, "Die Sarachi-Werkstatt und Annibale Fontana", in *Jahrbuch der Kunsthistorischen Sammlungen in Wien*, vol. 71, 1975, 95-164
Distelberger 1978
R. Distelberger, "Beobachtungen zu den Steinschneidewerkstätten der Miseroni in Mailand und Prag", in *Jahrbuch der Kunsthistorischen Sammlungen in Wien*, vol. 74, 1978, 79-152
Distelberger 1985
R. Distelberger, "Gold und Silber, Edelsteine und Elfenbein", in *Renaissance in Böhmen*, ed. by F. Seibt, Munich 1985, 255-287
Distelberger 2000
R. Distelberger, "'Quanta rariora tanta meliora'. Die Faszination des Fremden in Natur und Kunst", in exhibition catalogue Vienna 2000, 19-21
Distelberger 2002
R. Distelberger, "Die Kunst des Steinschnitts. Prunkgefäße, Kameen und Commessi aus der Kunstkammer", in exhibition catalogue Vienna 2002
Dolev 1995
N. Dolev, "Leonardo's Amorphous Imagery and the Arcimboldo Outcome", in *Achademia Leonardi Vinci*, 8, 1995, 129-142
Doni 1549
A.F. Doni, *Disegno*, Venice 1549
Duindam 2004
J. Duindam, "Im Herzen der zusammengesetzten Habsburgermonarchie, Quellen zu einer neuen Geschichte des Hofes, der Regierung und der höfischen Repräsentation", in Pauser, Scheutz, Winkelbauer 2004, 21-32
Duisburg 1994
Exhibition catalogue, *Die Beschwörung des Kosmos. Europäische Bronzen der Renaissance*, Duisburg 1994, 209f., no. 89, 243f., n. 112 (Frosien-Leinz)

Ecouen 1997
Exhibition catalogue, *Une orfèvrerie de terre: Bernard Palissy et la céramique de Saint-Porchaire*, Paris-Ecouen 1997
Edelmayer-Kohler 1992
F. Edelmayer, A. Kohler (eds.), "Kaiser Maximilian II.: Kultur und Politik im 16. Jahrhundert", in *Wiener Beiträge zur Geschichte der Neuzeit*, 19, Vienna 1992
Elias 1981
N. Elias, *Die höfische Gesellschaft*, V ed., Darmstadt 1981
Engert 1864
E. Engert, *Catalog der k.k. Gemälde-Gallerie im Belvedere zu Wien*, Vienna 1864
Engert 1896
E. Engert, *Kurzgefasstes Verzeichnis der kaiserl. Königl. Gemälde-Gallerie*, Vienna 1896
Engerth 1881
E. R. von Engerth, *Kunsthistorische Sammlungen des Allerhöchsten Kaiserhauses. Gemälde. Beschreibendes Verzeichnis*, vol. I, Vienna 1881
Essen-Vienna 1988
Exhibition catalogue, *Prag um 1600. Kunst und Kultur am Hofe Kaiser Rudolfs II.*, 2 vol., Vienna 1988, n. cat. 804
Evans 1973
R.J.W. Evans, *Rudolf II and his World. A Study in Intellectual History*, Oxford 1973
Evans 1979
R.J.W. Evans, *The Making of the Habsburg Monarchy*, Oxford 1979
Evans 1987
R.J.W. Evans, "The Imperial Court in the Time of Arcimboldo", in exhibition catalogue, Venice 1987

Falchetta 1987
P. Falchetta, "Anthology of Sixteenth-Century Texts", in exhibition catalogue Venice 1987, 143-198
Fend, Strolz 1999
D. Fend, M. Strolz, "Arcimboldo's Teste Composte, Report on restoration", in *Jahrbuch des Kunsthistorischen Museums Wien*, 1.1999, 282-290
Ferrari 1978
C. Ferrari, *Arcimboldo*, Milan 1978

Ferrarino, Páez 1974
L. Ferrarino, E. Páez, *Disegni italiani della Biblioteca Nazionale di Madrid*, Madrid 1974
Fichtner 2001
P.S. Fichtner, *Emperor Maximilian II*, New Haven-London 2001
Findlen 1994
P. Findlen, *Possessing Nature. Museums, Collecting, and Scientific Culture in Early Modern Italy*, Berkeley-Los Angeles-London 1994
Findlen 1997
P. Findlen, "Cabinets, Collecting and Natural Philosophy", in exhibition catalogue Prague 1997, 209-219
Findlen 2004
P. Findlen, "The Museum: Its Classical Etymology and Renaissance Genealogy", in *Grasping the World. The Idea of the Museum*, ed. by D. Preziosi, C. Farago, Aldershot 2004, 159-191
Flores, Vassallo, Silva 2004
J. Flores, N. Vassallo e Silva, *Goa and the Great Mughal*, London 2004
Fonteo 1576
G. B. Fonteo (Gio. Battista Fontana de' Conti), *Lettere Spirituali della devota religiosa Angelica Paola Antonia de Negri Milanese, e Vita della medesma*, Rome 1576
Forcione 2003
V. Forcione, "Leonardo's Grotesques: Original and Copies", in exhibition catalogue New York 2003
Forti Grazzini 1982
N. Forti Grazzini, *L'arazzo ferrarese*, Milan 1982
Forti Grazzini 1986
N. Forti Grazzini, *Arazzi del Cinquecento a Como*, Como 1986
Forti Grazzini 1988
N. Forti Grazzini, "Gli arazzi", in *Monza: il Duomo e i suoi tesori*, ed. by R. Conti, Milan 1988, 107-139
Fortunati 1998
V. Fortunati (ed.), exhibition catalogue, *Lavinia Fontana of Bologna, 1552-1614*, Washington D.C. National Museum of Women in the Arts, Milan 1998, 27-28
Frankfurt 1985
Exhibition catalogue, *Natur und Antike in der Renaissance*, Frankfurt a.M. 1985, 204, 534f., no. 258, 204, 543, no. 277 (Gramaccini), 248, 507, no. 219 (Frosien-Leinz), 537, no. 261, 545, no. 282 (Gramaccini)
Frati 1907
L. Frati, *Il Catalogo dei Manoscritti di Ulisse Aldrovandi*, Bologna 1907
Fritz 1983
R. Fritz, *Die Gefäße aus Kokosnuß in Mitteleuropa. 1250-1880*, Mainz 1983
Fučikova 1979
E. Fučikova, *Zur Zeichnung am Prager Hof unter Kaiser Rudolf II*, in exhibition catalogue *Zeichnung in Deutschland*, Stuttgart 1979, vol. 2, 187-192
Fučikova 1985
E. Fučikova, "The Collection of Rudolf II at Prague: Cabinet of Curiosities or Scientific Museum?", in *The Origins of Museums: the Cabinet of Curiosities in sixteenth and seventeenth Century Europe*, ed. by O. Impey, A. MacGregor, Oxford 1985, 49-53
Fučikova 1987
E. Fučikova, "I divertimenti praghesi", in exhibition catalogue Venice 1987, 121-31
Fučikova 1991
E. Fučikova, *Kunst am Hofe Rudolfs II.*, Prague 1991
Fučikova 1997
E. Fučikova (ed.), *Rudolf II and Prague, The Court and the City*, London 1997
Fučikova 2002
E. Fučikova, "Praga magica 1600. L'Art à Prague au temps de Rodolphe II.", in exhibition catalogue Dijon 2002

Gamber 1978
O. Gamber, *Curiositäten und Inventionen aus Kunst- und Rüstkammer, Kunsthistorisches Museum*, Vienna 1978, 22f.
Gamber, Beaufort 1990
O. Gamber, C. Beaufort, *Katalog der Leibrüstkammer, II. Teil, Der Zeitraum von 1530-1560*, Busto Arsizio 1990, 188f.
Garin 1966
E. Garin, *Geschichte und Dokumente der abendländischen Pädagogik*, vol. 2, Hamburg 1966, 205
Geiger 1954
B. Geiger, *I dipinti ghiribizzosi di Giuseppe Arcimboldi. Pittore illusionista del Cinquecento (1527-1593)*, Florence 1954
Geiger 1960
B. Geiger, *Die skurrilen Gemälde des Giuseppe Arcimboldi (1527-1593)*, Wiesbaden 1960, 98f., 17 (ill.)
Genoa 1990
Exhibition catalogue, *Maestri del disegno nelle civiche collezioni genovesi*, ed. by P. Boccardo, Genoa 1990
Genoa 1991
Exhibition catalogue, *Il passato presente. I Musei del Comune di Genova*, ed. by E. Papone, Genoa 1991
Gherardini 1588
G.F. Gherardini, *Alcuni versi [...] nel-l'occasione delle nozze de i molt'Ill.ri S.ri Giulio Dardanone et Zenobia Coria*, Milan 1588
Gherardini 1591
G.F. Gherardini (ed.), *All'invittissimo Cesare Rodolfo secondo. Componimenti sopra li due quadri Flora, et Vertunno, fatti à Sua Sac. Ces. Maestà da Giuseppe Arcimboldo, Milanese*, Milan 1591
Giannini 2000
M.C. Giannini, "Una Chiesa senza arcivescovo. Identità e tensioni politiche nel governo ecclesiastico a Milano (1546-1560)", in *Carlos V y la quiebra del humanismo politico en Europa* (conf. proceedings, Madrid, 3-6 July 2000), Madrid, Societad Estatal para la conmemoraciòn de los centenarios de Felipe II y Carlos V, 2000, 4 vol., IV, 227-279
Giusti 2005
A. Giusti, *Pietra Dura. Bilder aus Stein*, Vienna 2005
Gnann 2004
A. Gnann (ed.), "The era of Michelangelo. Masterpieces from the Albertina", in exhibition catalogue Vienna 2004
Gobiet 1984
R. Gobiet, *Der Briefwechsel zwischen Philipp Hainhofer und Herzog August d. J. von Braunschweig-Lüneburg*, vol. 8, Vienna 1984
Godoy, Leydi 2003
J-A. Godoy, S. Leydi, exhibition catalogue *Parures Triomphales, Le maniérisme dans l'art de l'armure italienne*, Geneve 2003, 424f.
Goffart 2003
W. Goffart, *Historical Atlases. The First Three Hundred Years, 1570-1870*, Chicago-London 2003
Grafton1991
A. Grafton, "Humanism and Science in Rudolphine Prague: Kepler in Context", in idem, *Defenders of the Text: The traditions of Scholarship in an Age of Science, 1450-1800*, Cambridge (Ma)-London 1991, 178-203
Granberg 1911-13
O. Granberg, *Inventaire Général des trésors d'art, peintures & sculptures principalement de maîtres étrangers en Suède*, Stockholm 1911-1913
Graz 1964
Exhibition catalogue, *Graz als Residenz. Innerösterreich 1564-1619*, Graz 1964, 128, no. 323
Greenblatt 1980
S. Greenblatt, *Renaissance Self-Fashioning. From More to Shakespeare*, Chicago-London 1980
Gregori, Bayer 2004
M. Gregori, A. Bayer (eds.) "Pittori della realtà: le ragioni di una rivoluzione da Foppa e Leonardo a Caravaggio e Ceruti", in exhibition catalogue, Cremona-New York 2004
Gries 1994
C. Gries, "Erzherzog Ferdinand II. von Tirol und die Sammlungen auf Schloss Ambras", in *Frühneuzeit-Info*, 1994, no. 5, 7-37
Gripsholm 1988
Masterpieces from Gripsholm Castle, Stockholm 1988
Grote 1994
A. Grote (ed.), *Macrocosmos in Microcosmo. Die Welt in der Stube. Zur Geschichte des Sammelns 1450 bis 1800*, Opladen 1994
Guazzoni 1997
V. Guazzoni (ed.), *La Pinacoteca. Origine e collezioni*, Cremona 1997
Guazzoni 2000
V. Guazzoni, "I figli del Luini", in S. Bandiera, M.T. Florio (eds.), *Bernardino Luini e la pittura del Rinascimento a Milano. Gli affreschi di San Maurizio al Monastero Maggiore*, Milan 2000, 79-91
Gutfleisch, Menzhausen 1989
B. Gutfleisch, J. Menzhausen, "How a Kunstkammer Should Be Formed": Gabriel Kaltemarckt's Advice to Christian I of Saxony on the Formation of an Art Collection, 1587, in *Journal of the History of Collections*, 1, 1987, 3-32

Hajós 2007
G. Hajós, "'Terza Natura' Gartenkunst der Renaissance und des Manierismus", in exhibition catalogue *Gartenlust, Der Garten in der Kunst*, Belvedere Vienna 2007, 41-49
Halsema-Kubes 1977
W. Halsema-Kubes, "Aanwinsten", in *Bulletin van het Rijksmuseum*, 3, 1977, 122
Hammerstein 2000
N. Hammerstein, *Einleitung*, in *Späthumanismus, Studien über das Ende einer kulturhistorischen Epoche*, ed. by N. Hammerstein, G. Walther, Göttingen 2000, 9-18
Hayward 1967
J.F. Hayward, "Wenzel Jamnitzer of Nuremberg. The Mannerist Goldsmiths: 5., Germany", part II, in *The Connoisseur*, vol. 164, no. 661, 1967
Hayward 1976
J. F. Hayward, *Virtuoso Goldsmiths and the Triumph of Mannerism. 1540-1620*, London 1976
Heinz 1963
G. Heinz, "Studien zur Porträtmalerei an den Höfen der österreichischen Erblande", in *Jahrbuch der kunsthistorischen Sammlungen in Wien*, vol. 59, 1963, 99-224
Heinz 1975
G. Heinz, "Das Porträtbuch des Hieronymus Beck von Leopoldsdorf", in *Jahrbuch der kunsthistorischen Sammlungen in Wien*, vol. 71, 1975, 165-310
Helas 1999
Ph. Helas, *Lebende Bilder in der italienischen Festkultur des 15. Jahrhunderts*, Berlin 1999
Hellrigl 2002-03
S. Hellrigl, *Art-Handicap-Art*, Accademia delle Belle Arti di Bologna 2002-03, 32-35
Hendrix, Vignau-Wilberg 1997
L. Hendrix, T. Vignau-Wilberg, *Nature Illuminated. Flora and Fauna from the Court of the Emperor Rudolf II*, London 1997
Hernmarck 1978
C. Hernmarck, *Die Kunst der europäischen Gold- und Silberschmiede 1450-1830*, Munich 1978
Hilger 1969
W. Hilger, *Ikonographie Kaiser Ferdi-*

nands I. (1503-1564), Österreichische Akademie der Wissenschaften, Veröffentlichungen der Kommission für Geschichte Österreichs 3, Vienna 1969

Hofmann 1987
M. Hofmann (ed.), exhibition catalogue, Vienna 1987, 360, no. 45, 370f., no. 74

Honnens de Lichtenberg 1991
H. Honnens de Lichtenberg, *Johann Gregor van der Schardt. Bildhauer bei Kaiser Maximilian II., am dänischen Hof und bei Tycho de Brahe*, Copenhagen 1991, 97, 104ff.

Hookey1969
C. Hookey, *Giovanni Battista Bracelli's Bizzarie di Varie Figure*, M. Phil. Dissertation, Warburg Institute, London 1969

Hope 1987
C. Hope, "Sight Gags – The Arcimboldo Effect: Transformations of the Face from the Sixteenth to the Twentieth Century", in *The New York Review of Books*, vol. 34, no. 14, 24 September 1987, 41-44

Hulten 1987
P. Hulten (ed.), exhibition catalogue, Venice 1987, 52

Hunter-Stiebel 1985
P. Hunter-Stiebel, "A Bronze Bestiary", in exhibition catalogue, New York 1985, 82, n. 65, 86, n. 69

Impey, MacGregor 1984
O. Impey, A. MacGregor (eds.), *The Origins of Museums: the Cabinet of Curiosities in sixteenth and seventeenth Century Europe*, Oxford 1985

Innsbruck 1977
See Ambras 1977

Isella 1993
D. Isella (ed.), *Rabisch / Giovan Paolo Lomazzo e i Facchini della Val di Blenio*, Turin 1993, IX-LXII

Jacquot 1956
J.J. Jacquot (ed.), *Les Fêtes de la Renaissance*, Paris 1956, Vol. 1, 9ff.

Jansen 1988
D.J. Jansen, "Example and Examples: The Potential Influence of Jacopo Strada on the Development of Rudolphine Art", in exhibition catalogue Vienna 1988, 132-146

Jansen 1992
D.J. Jansen, "The Instruments of Patronage: Jacopo Strada at the Court of Maximilian II", in "Kaiser Maximilian II", in *Kultur und Politik im 16. Jahrhundert*, ed. by F. Edelmayer *et al.*, Vienna 1992, 231-245

Janson 1961
H.W. Janson, "'The Image Made by Chance' in Renaissance Thought", in *Essays in Honour of Erwin Panofsky*, ed. by M. Meiss, New York 1961, 254-256

Jones-Davies 1982
M.T. Jones-Davies (ed.), *Le paradoxe au temps de la Renaissance* (conference proceedings), Paris 1982

Jongh 2004
E. de Jongh, "The Symbolism of Fish, Fishermen, Fishing Gear and the Catch", in *Fish. Still Lifes by Dutch and Flemish Masters 1550-1700*, ed. by L.M. Helmus, Utrecht 2004, 76-119

Jordan Gschwend 1991
A. Jordan Gschwend, "A Christal Elephant from the 'Kunstkammer' of Catherine of Austria", in *Jahrbuch der Kunsthistorischen Sammlungen in Wien*, vol. 87/88, 1991, 121-126

Kaufmann 1976a
Th. DaCosta Kaufmann, "Arcimboldo's Imperial Allegories. G.B. Fonteo and the Interpretation of Arcimboldo's Painting", in *Zeitschrift für Kunstgeschichte*, 39/4, 1976, 275-296

Kaufmann 1976b
Th. DaCosta Kaufmann, "Hand-colored Prints and Pseudo-manuscripts: The Curious Case of Codex 7906 of the Österreichische Nationalbibliothek Wien", in *Codices Manuscripti*, 2, 1976, 26-31

Kaufmann 1977
Th. DaCosta Kaufmann, "Arcimboldo au Louvre", in *Revue du Louvre et des Musées de France*, 5/6, 1977, 337-342

Kaufmann 1978a
Th. DaCosta Kaufmann, *Variations on the Imperial Theme in the Age of Maximilian II and Rudolf II*, New York-London 1978

Kaufmann 1978b
Th. DaCosta Kaufmann, "Remarks on the Collections of Rudolf II: the *Kunstkammer* as a Form of *Representatio*", in *Art Journal*, 38, 1978, 22-28

Kaufmann 1982a
Th. DaCosta Kaufmann, "The Eloquent Artist: Towards an Understanding of the Stylistics of Painting at the Court of Rudolf II", in *Leids Kunsthistorisch Jaarboek* I, 1982, 119-148

Kaufmann 1982b
Th. DaCosta Kaufmann, *Drawings from the Holy Roman Empire 1540-1680. A Selection from North American Collections*, exhibition catalogue Princeton 1982

Kaufmann 1983
Th. DaCosta Kaufmann, "'Ancients and Modern' in Prague: Arcimboldo's Drawings for Silk Manufacture", in *Leids Kunsthistorisch Jaarboek* II, 1983, 179-207

Kaufmann 1985a
Th. DaCosta Kaufmann, *L'école de Prague*, Paris 1985

Kaufmann 1985b
Th. DaCosta Kaufmann, "Arcimboldo and Propertius. A Classical Source for Rudolf II as Vertumnus", in *Zeitschrift für Kunstgeschichte*, 48, 1985, 1, 117-123

Kaufmann 1987
Th. DaCosta Kaufmann, "The Allegories and Their Meaning", in exhibition catalogue Venice 1987, 89-109

Kaufmann 1988a
Th. DaCosta Kaufmann, "A tapestry Design by Giuseppe Arcimboldo", in *The Burlington Magazine*, vol. 130, no. 1023, 1988, 428-430

Kaufmann 1988b
Th. DaCosta Kaufmann, "Le opere di Arcimboldo a Monza e la carriera iniziale dell'artista", in *Studi Monzesi*, 3, 1988, 5-17

Kaufmann 1988c
Th. DaCosta Kaufmann, *The School of Prague, Painting at the Court of Rudolf II*, Chicago-London 1988 (revised and expanded from *L'Ecole de Prague, La peinture à la cour de Rodolphe II*, Paris 1985)

Kaufmann 1990a
Th. DaCosta Kaufmann, "Arcimboldo (Arcimboldi), Giuseppe", *ad vocem* in *Allgemeines Künstlerlexikon. Die bildenden Künstler aller Zeit und Völker*, III, Leipzig 1990, 900-902

Kaufmann 1990b
Th. DaCosta Kaufmann, "Arcimboldo's Serious Jokes: 'Mysterious but Long Meaning'", in *The Verbal and the Visual: Essays in honor of William Heckscher*, ed. by K-L. Selig, E. Sears, New York 1990, 57-86

Kaufmann 1993
Th. DaCosta Kaufmann, "Astronomy, Technology, Humanism and Art at the Entry of Rudolf II into Vienna, 1577: The Role of Paulus Fabritius", in *The Mastery of Nature, Aspects of Art, Science, and Humanism in the Renaissance*, Princeton 1993, 136-150

Kaufmann 1995
Th. DaCosta Kaufmann, *Court, Cloister & City. The Art and Culture of Central Europe 1450-1800*, Chicago-London 1995, 184, 191

Kaufmann 1997
Th. DaCosta Kaufmann, in exhibition catalogue Prague 1997

Kaufmann 1998a
Th. DaCosta Kaufmann, "Giuseppe Arcimboldo. The Habsburgs' Leonardo", in *Rudolf II, Prague and the World*, ed. by L. Konečny, B. Bukovinksá, I. Muchka, Papers from the International Conference, Prague 2-4.9.1997, Prague 1998, 169-176, fig. 6

Kaufmann 1998b
Th. DaCosta Kaufmannm, *Caprices of Art and Nature: Arcimboldo and the Monstrous*, in *Kunstform Capriccio. Von der Groteske zur Spieltheorie der Moderne*, ed. by E. Mai, J. Rees, Cologne 1998, 33-51

Kaufmann 1999
Th. DaCosta Kaufmann, "A Gesamtkunstwerk in the Unmaking? The Kunstkammer and the Age of the Bel Composto", in *Actas: Struggle for Synthesis, The Total Work of Art in the 17th and 18th Century*, Simpósio Internacional (1996), vol. II, Lisbon 1999, 389-399

Kaufmann 2002
Th. DaCosta Kaufmann, "'The Stradas' Work on Mills and the Movement of Water in Context", in *L'album fiorentino dei Disegni Artificiali raccolti da Jacopo e Ottavio Strada*, ed. by V. Marchis, L. Dolza, Rome 2002, 1-35, 199-215

Kaufmann 2004a
Th. DaCosta Kaufmann, "Remarks on the Collection of Rudolf II: The Kunstkammer as a Form of Representation", in *Grasping the World. The Idea of the Museum*, ed. by D. Preziosi, C. Farago, Aldershot 2004, 526-537

Kaufmann 2004b
Th. DaCosta Kaufmann, *Toward a Geography of Art*, Chicago-London 2004

Kaufmann 2005
Th. DaCosta Kaufmann, "The Dating of Arcimboldo's First Composite Heads", in *Studia Rudolphina*, 5, 2005, 28-32

Kaufmann 2007
Th. DaCosta Kaufmann, "The Artificial and the Natural: Arcimboldo and the Origins of Still Life", in *The Artificial and the Natural*, ed. by W. Newman, B. Bensaudé, Cambridge 2007

Kaufmann 2007a
Th. DaCosta Kaufmann, "Arcimboldo and the Elector of Saxony", in *Scambio culturale con il nemico religioso. Italia e Sassonia attorno 1600*, ed. by S. Ebert Schifferer, Rome 2007, 27-36

Kaufmann forthcoming
Th. DaCosta Kaufmann, *Arcimboldo's Serious Jokes. Artifice, Naturalism, and the Origins of Still-life Painting*, Chicago forthcoming (2008)

Kemp 1995
M. Kemp, "'Wrought by No Artist's hand': The Natural, the Artificial, the Exotic, and the Scientific in Some Artifacts from the Renaissance", in *Reframing the Renaissance. Visual Culture in Europe and the Latin America 1450-1600*, ed. by C. Farago, New Haven-London 1995, 177-19

Kenner 1893
F. Kenner, "Die Porträtsammlung des Erzherzogs Ferdinand von Tirol", in *Jahrbuch der kunsthistorischen Sammlungen des Allerhöchsten Kaiserhauses*, 14, 1893, 37-186

Kenseth 1991
J. Kenseth (ed.), "The Age of the Marvelous", Hanover, N.H., 1991

Klein 1975
R. Klein, *La forma e l'intelligibile*, Turin 1975

Klein 1999
P. Klein, "Zur Datierung von Gemäldetafeln aus Buchen-, Linde- und Pappelholz", in *Restauratorenblätter*, vol. 19, Vienna 1999, 29-36

Klerck 1999
B. de Klerck, *The Brothers Campi. Images and Devotion. Religious Painting in Six-*

teenth-century Lombardy, trans. Andrew McCormick, Amsterdam 1999
Klier 2004
A. Klier, *Fixierte Natur. Naturabguß und Effigies im 16. Jahrhundert*, Berlin 2004
Kohler 2003
A. Kohler, *Ferdinand I. 1503-1564, Fürst, König und Kaiser*, Munich 2003
Konečny 1995-96
L. Konečny, "Arcimboldo, Christ and Dürer", in the *Bulletin of the National Gallery in Prague*, V-VI, 1995-96, 132-7
Konečny 1997
L. Konečny, "Picturing the Rudolfine Artist", in exhibition catalogue Prague 1997, 107-121
Koreny 1985
F. Koreny, "Albrecht Dürer und die Tier- und Pflanzenstudien der Renaissance", in *Jahrbuch der Kunsthistorischen Sammlungen in Wien*, vol. 82/83, 1986-87, Vienna 1985
Kriegeskorte 1986
W. Kriegeskorte, *Giuseppe Arcimboldo*, Cologne 1986
Kris 1926
E. Kris, "Der Stil "Rustique". Die Verwendung des Naturabgusses bei Wenzel Jamnitzer und Bernard Palissy", in *Jahrbuch der Kunsthistorischen Sammlungen in Wien*, N.F., vol. I, Vienna 1926, 137-208
Kris 1932
E. Kris, "Goldschmiedearbeiten des Mittelalters, der Renaissance und des Barock. Erster Teil. Arbeiten in Gold und Silber", in *Jahrbuch der Kunsthistorischen Sammlungen in Wien* vol. V, Vienna 1932
Kurz 1977
O. Kurz, "Künstlerische Beziehungen zwischen Prag und Persien zur Zeit Kaiser Rudolfs II.", in idem, *The Decorative Arts of Europe and the Islamic East. Selected Studies*, London 1977, 1-22
Kwakkelstein 1994
M. Kwakkelstein, *Leonardo da Vinci as a Physiognomist. Theory and Drawing Practice*, Leiden 1994

Ladner 1932
G. Ladner, *Die Porträtsammlung des Erzherzogs Ferdinand von Tirol, Führer durch die kunsthistorischen Sammlungen in Wien*, ed. by Verein der Museumsfreunde, no. 17, Vienna 1932
Lanzi 1831
L. Lanzi, *Geschichte der Malerei in Italien vom Wiederaufleben der Kunst bis Ende des achtzehnten Jahrhunderts*, vol. II, Lipsia 1831
Latuada 1737-1738 (1995-2000)
S. Latuada, *Descrizione di Milano ornata con molti disegni in rame delle fabbriche più cospicue, che si trovano in questa metropoli*, Milan 1737-1738, 5 voll. (last edition, *La Vita felice*, Milan 1995-2000, 5 voll. + Index)
Laubach 2003
E. Laubach, "Ferdinand I. und das Reich", in exhibition catalogue Vienna 2003, 131-147
Lazius 1558
W. Lazius, *Commentariorum vetustorum numismatum*, Vienna 1558
Lazius 1563
W. Lazius, *Epitome Solenniorum, quae in auspiciarum adventum...*, Vienna 1563
Lazius 1564
W. Lazius, *Commentariorum in genealogiam Austriacam libri duo*, Basel 1564
Lazzari 2000
M.A. Lazzari, "Indagini scientifiche su alcuni dipinti in mostra", in exhibition catalogue Cremona 2000, 141-149
Leeds 2005
Exhibition catalogue, *Bronze – The Power of Life and Death*, Leeds 2005, 66, nn. 12, 13
Legrand, Sluys 1955
F.C. Legrand, F. Sluys, *Arcimboldo et les Arcimboldesques*, Aalter 1955
Lein 2006
E. Lein, "Über den Naturabguss von Schlangen, Kröten, Krebsen und anderen kleinen Tieren", in exhibition catalogue Vienna 2006, 77-78
Leydi 1998
S. Leydi, "Giovan Battista Panzeri, detto Zarabaglia, intagliatore in ferro. E soci", in *Nuovi Studi*, 6 (1998), 31-56
Leydi 1999a
S. Leydi, *Sub Umbra Imperialis Acquiae. Immagini del potere e consenso politico nella Milano di Carlo V*, Florence 1999
Leydi 1999b
S. Leydi, "Il sarto del 'Libro del Sarto': Gian Giacomo del Conte", in exhibition catalogue *Velluti e moda tra XV e XVII secolo*, Milan 1999, 23-30
Lhotsky 1941-45
A. Lhotsky, *Festschrift des Kunsthistorischen Museums zur Feier des fünfzigjährigen Bestandes*, second part, *Die Geschichte der Sammlungen*, Vienna 1941-45
Lhotsky 1971
A. Lhotsky, "Apis Colonna. Fabeln und Theorien über die Abkunft der Habsburger. Ein Exkurs zur Cronica Austrie des Thomas Ebendorfer", in *Aufsätze und Vorträge*, ed. by H. Wagner, H. Koller, Munich 1971, vol. 2
Lietzmann 1987
H. Lietzmann, *Das Neugebäude in Wien, Sultan Süleymans Zelt – Kaiser Maximilians II. Lustschloß*, Munich-Berlin 1987
Lietzmann 1988
H. Lietzmann, "Das Neugebäude und Böhmen", in exhibition catalogue Prague 1988, 176-182
Lindell 1987
R. Lindell, "Marta gentile che'l cor m'ha morto - eine unbekannte Kammermusikerin am Hof Maximilians II.", in *Musicologica Austriaca*, 7, 1987, 59-68
Lindell 1990
R. Lindell, "The wedding of Archduke Charles and Maria of Bavaria in 1571", in *Early Music*, 18/2 (1990), 253-269
Linné 1766
C. von Linné, *Systema naturae per regna tria naturae*, Tomus I, Editio Duodecima, Reformata, Holmiae 1766
Litta 1823
P. Litta, *Famiglie celebri d'Italia*, "Arcimboldi", Milan 1823
Löcher 1962
K. Löcher, *Jakob Seisenegger*, Munich-Berlin 1962
Lomazzo 1584 (1974)
G.P. Lomazzo, *Trattato dell'arte della pittura, scoltura et architectura*, in *Scritti sulle arti*, ed. by R.P. Ciardi, vol. II, Florence, 1974, 7-631, (original edition Milan 1584)
Lomazzo 1587 (2006)
G.P. Lomazzo, *Rime*, ed. by A. Ruffino, Rome 2006 (original edition Milan 1587)
Lomazzo 1589 (1993)
G.P. Lomazzo, *Rabisch*, ed. by D. Isella, Turin 1993 (original edition Milan 1589)
Lomazzo 1590 (1973)
G.P. Lomazzo, *Idea del tempio della pittura*, in *Scritti sulle arti*, ed. by R.P. Ciardi, vol. I, Florence 1973, 241-373 (original edition Milan 1590)
Lomazzo 1973
G.P. Lomazzo, *Scritti sulle arti*, ed. by R.P. Ciardi, vol. 1, Florence 1973, vol. 2, 1974
London 2005
Exhibition catalogue, *From Vulcan's Forge. Bronzes from the Rijksmuseum, Amsterdam 1450-1800*, London 2005
London 2007
Exhibition catalogue, *Xanto. Pottery-Painter, Poet, Man of the Italian Renaissance*, J.V.G. Mallet, Wallace Collection, London 2007
Longo 1979
N. Longo, "Centorio degli Ortensi, Ascanio", *ad vocem* in *Dizionario Biografico degli Italiani*, Rome, Istituto dell'Enciclopedia Italiana, XXIII (1979), 609-611
Lösel 1983
E. Lösel, *Zürcher Goldschmiedekunst vom 13. bis zum 19. Jahrhundert*, Zurich 1983
Louthan 1997
H. Louthan, *The Quest for Compromise. Peacemakers in Counter-Reformation Vienna*, Cambridge 1997
Luchner 1958
L. Luchner, *Denkmal eines Renaissancefürsten. Versuch einer Rekonstruktion des Ambraser Museums von 1583*, Vienna 1958
Lugano 1998
Exhibition catalogue, *Rabisch. Il grottesco nell'arte del Cinquecento. L'Accademia della Val di Blenio, Lomazzo e l'ambiente milanese*, ed. by M. Rossi-Kahn, F. Porzio, C. Apa, Lugano 1998, 141-142, cat. no. 6 (Bert W. Meijer)
Lugli 1983
A. Lugli, *Naturalia et Mirabilia. Il collezionismo enciclopedico nelle Wunderkammern d'Europa*, Milan 1983
Lynch 1964
J.B. Lynch, "Giovanni Paolo Lomazzo's Self-Portrait in the Brera", in *Gazette des Beaux-Arts*, LXIV, 1964, 189-197
Lynch 1968
J.B. Lynch, "Lomazzo's Allegory of Painting", in *Gazette des Beaux-Arts*, LXVIII, 1968, 325-330

Madrid 1998
Exhibition catalogue, *Felipe II. Un monarca y su época, Un príncipe del Renacimiento*, ed. by F. Checa Cremades, Madrid 1998
Madrid 2002
Exhibition catalogue, *Vestidos y armaduras. Roberto Capucci. Moda de ayer y hoy en seda y acero*, ed. by R. Capucci, Madrid 2002, 86f.
Maiorino 1991
G. Maiorino, *The Portrait of Eccentricity. Arcimboldo and the Mannerist Grotesque*, London 1991
Makes 1988
F. Makes, "Enzymatic consolidation of the portrait of Rudolf II as 'Vertumnus' by Giuseppe Arcimboldo with a new multi-enzyme preparation isolated from Antarctic krill (*Euphausia superba*)", in *Göteborg Studies in Conservation*, 1, Göteborg 1988, 49
Malespini 1609
C. Malespini, *Ducento novelle [...] nelle quali si raccontano diversi Avvenimenti così lieti, come mesti & stravaganti*, Venice 1609
Mander 1991
K. van Mander, *Das Leben der niederländischen und deutschen Maler (von 1400 bis ca. 1615). Übersetzung nach der Ausgabe von 1617 und Anmerkungen von Hanns Floerke*, Worms 1991, 339
Mantua 2002
Exhibition catalogue, *Gonzaga. La Celeste Galeria. Le raccolte*, ed. by R. Morselli, Mantua 2002
Marani 1987
P.C. Marani, *Leonardo e i Leonardeschi a Brera*, Florence 1987
Marubbi 2003
M. Marubbi (ed.), *La Pinacoteca Ala Ponzone. Il Cinquecento*, Cinisello Balsamo-Cremona 2003
Marubbi 2004
M. Marubbi (ed.), *La Pinacoteca Ala Ponzone. Dal Duecento al Quattrocento*, Cinisello Balsamo-Cremona 2004
Marzell 1979
H. Marzell, *Wörterbuch der Deutschen*

Pflanzennamen, vol. IV., Stuttgart-Wiesbaden 1979
Maselis, Balis, Marijnjssen 1999
M-C. Maselis, A. Balis, R.H. Marijnissen, *The Albums of Anselmus de Boodt (1550-1632). Natural History Painting at the Court of Rudolph II in Prague*, Tielt 1999
Mazal 1982
O. Mazal, "Tierbilder aus der Ambraser Kunst-und Wunderkammer Erzherzog Ferdinands von Tirol" (Cod. Ser. n. 2669 der Österreichischen Nationalbibliothek), in *Codices Manuscripti*, 8 (1982), 12-38
McGinty 1998
A.B. McGinty, *Stradanus (Jan van der Straet): His Role in the Visual Communication of Renaissance Discoveries, Technologies, and Values*, Ph.D. dissertation, 1974, London 1998
McGrath 1985
E. McGrath, "'Il Senso Nostro': The Medici Allegory Applied to Vasari's Mythological Frescoes in the Palazzo Vecchio", in *Giorgio Vasari: tra decorazione ambientiale e storiografia artistica*, ed. by G.C. Garfagnini, Florence 1985, 130-132
Meganck 2003
T. Meganck, *Erudite Eyes. Artists and Antiquarians in the Circle of Adam Ortelius (1527-1598)*, Ph.D. dissertation, Princeton 2003
Melion 1989
W.S. Melion, "Karel van Mander's, Life of Goltzius'. Defining the Paradigm of Protean Virtuosity in Haarlem around 1600", in *Studies in the History of Art*, 27, 1989, 113ff.
Mette 1990
H.-U. Mette, *Der Nautiluspokal oder Zur objektiven Phantasie einer naturalia.* 2 vol., phil. dissertation, Kiel 1990
Mette 1995
H.-U. Mette, *Der Nautilus-Pokal. Wie Kunst und Natur miteinander spielen*, Munich-Berlin 1995
Migeon 1901
G. Migeon, *Catalogue des faïences françaises et des grès allemands*, Paris 1901
Milan 1977
Exhibition catalogue, *Omaggio a Tiziano: La cultura artistica milanese nell'età di Carlo V*, Milan 1977, 52-54 [notes 58-61], 62-86
Milan 2000
Exhibition catalogue, *Il cinquecento lombardo*, Milan 2000
Milan 2000
Exhibition catalogue, *Il Cinquecento lombardo. Da Leonardo a Caravaggio*, ed. by F. Caroli, Milan 2000
Milan 2005
Exhibition catalogue, *Carlo e Federico. La luce dei Borromeo nella Milano spagnola*, ed. by Paolo Biscottini, Milan 2005
Miller 1989
R.S. Miller, "Note su Giuseppe Arcimboldo, Giuseppe Meda, Giovanni Battista della Rovere ditto il fiammenghino ed altri pittori milanesi", in *Studi Monzesi*, 5, 1989, 3-25
Minges 1998
K. Minges, *Das Sammlungswesen der frühen Neuzeit. Kriterien der Ordnung und der Spezialisierung*, Munster 1998
Mirabile 2005
D. Mirabile, *La committenza della famiglia Rusca nella Lombardia del Rinascimento*, Ph.D. dissertation, Milan 2004-2005
Mogne 2004
P. Mogne, "L'art de la plumasserie", in exhibition catalogue *Le Triptyche aztèque de la Crucifixion*, Paris 2004, 38-79
Mohan, Menu, Mottin 2006
J.P. Mohan, M. Menu, B. Mottin (eds.), *Im Herzen der Mona Lisa - Dekodierung eines Meisterwerkes: eine wissenschaftliche Expedition in die Werkstatt des Leonardo da Vinci*, Munich 2006, 40
Molà 2000
L. Molà, *The Silk Industry of Renaissance Venice*, Baltimore-London 2000
Monbeig-Goguel 1998
C. Monbeig-Goguel, *Francesco Salviati et la bella maniera. Quelques points à revoir*, in conf. proceedings Rome and Paris 1998, Rome 2001, 15-68
Montanari 1994
T. Montanari, "Cristina di Svezia, il cardinale Azzolino e il mercato veronese", in *Ricerche di Storia dell'Arte*, 54, Nov. 1994, 25-52
Monti 1896
S. Monti, *La cattedrale di Como*, Como 1897
Morandotti 2005
A. Morandotti, *Milano profana nell'età dei Borromeo*, Milan 2005
Morel 1998
P. Morel, *Les grotesques. Les figures de l'imaginaire dans la peinture italienne de la fin de la Renaissance*, Paris 1998
Morigia 1592
P. Morigia, *Historia dell'antichità di Milano, divisa in quattro libri*, Venice 1592, 556
Morigia 1593
P. Morigia, *Historia brieve dell'Augustissima casa d'Austria [...]*, Bergamo 1593
Morigia 1595
P. Morigia, *La Nobilità di Milano*, Milan 1595
Morigia 1595 (1619)
P. Morigia, *La Nobiltà di Milano [...]. Aggiuntovi il supplimento in questa nuova impressione del Sig. Girolamo Borsieri*, Milan 1619
Morley 1979
B. Morley, "The Plant Illustrations of Leonardo da Vinci", in *Burlington Magazine*, CXXI, Sept. 1979, 553-560
Moroni 2005
S. Leydi, "Il libro del Sarto", in *Giovan Battista Moroni. Il Cavaliere in nero. L'immagine del gentiluomo nel Cinquecento*, exhibition catalogue Milan 2005, 102-104 no. 6
Moscow 2005
Exhibition catalogue, *Kunstkammer of the Habsburgs. From the collection of the Kunsthistorisches Museum Vienna*, Moscow 2005, 32f., cat. no. 4
Mout 2000
N. Mout, "'Dieser einzige Wiener Hof von Dir hat mehr Gelehrte als ganze Reiche anderer': Späthumanismus am Kaiserhof in der Zeit Maximilians II. und Rudolfs II. (1564-1612)", in *Späthumanismus, Studien über das Ende einer kulturhistorischen Epoche*, Göttingen 2000, 46-64
Mraz 2003
G. Mraz, "Ferdinand I. und sein Wirken im Konflikt der Konfessionen. Reformation und katholische Reform", in exhibition catalogue Vienna 2003, 89-99
Mühlberger 1992
K. Mühlberger, "Bildung und Wissenschaft. Kaiser Maximilian II. und die Universität Wien", in *Kaiser Maximilian II. Kultur und Politik im 16. Jahrhundert*, ed. by F. Edelmayer *et al.*, Vienna-Munich 1992, 203-230
Müller 1983
H. Müller, *Fische Europas*, Radebeul 1983
Müller 1993
J. Müller, *Concordia Pragensis. Karel van Manders Kunsttheorie im Schilder-Boeck. Ein Beitrag zur Rhetorisierung von Kunst und Leben am Beispiel der rudolfinischen Hofkünstler*, Munich 1993, 77ff.
Müller 2004
R. Müller, "Der Fürstenhof in der frühen Neuzeit", in *Enzyklopädie deutscher Geschichte*, vol. 33, Munich 2004
Munich 1994
Exhibition catalogue, *Silber und Gold. Augsburger Goldschmiedekunst für die Höfe Europas*, Munich 1994
Murphy 2003
C.P. Murphy, *Lavinia Fontana: A Painter and her Patrons in Sixteenth-Century Bologna*, New Haven 2003, 164-165

Nepi Scirè 1992
G. Nepi Scirè, "Leonardo and Venice", exhibition catalogue, Venice-Milan 1992, 300, no. 46
Nepi Scirè, Perissa Torrini 2003
G. Nepi Scirè, A. Perissa Torrini (eds.), *I disegni di Leonardo da Vinci e della sua cerchia nel Gabinetto dei Disegni e Stampe delle Gallerie dell'Accademia di Venezia ordinati e presentati da Carlo Pedretti*, Florence 2003
Nerman 1967
G. and A. Nerman, *Catalogo di vendita di disegni antichi*, Florence 1967
Neumann 1966
E. Neumann, *The inventory of the Rudolfin Art Collections from 1607/1611*, in *Analecta Reginensia*, I, Documents and Studies, Stockholm 1966, 262-265
Neumann 1979
J. Neumann, *Die Kunst der Renaissance und der Manierismus in Böhmen*, Prague 1979
New York 1937
Exhibition catalogue, *Fantastic Art, Dada, Surrealism*, ed. By A. H. Barr Jr., New York 1937
Nova *et al.* 2003
A. Nova *et al.* (ed.), *Benvenuto Cellini: Kunst und Kunsttheorie im 16. Jahrhundert*, Cologne 2003
Nowak, Paradiso 1983
R.M. Nowak, J.L. Paradiso, *Walker's Mammals of the World*, 4th ed., Baltimore-London 1983
Nuremberg 1985
Exhibition catalogue, *Wenzel Jamnitzer und die Nuremberger Goldschmiedekunst. 1500-1700*, Nuremberg 1985, 68f., 231ff. nos. 27-30 (Pechstein)

Oestreich 1989
G. Oestreich, *Antiker Geist und moderner Staat bei Justus Lipsius, Der Neostoizismus als politische Bewegung*, Göttingen 1989
Olmi, Tomasi 1993
G. Olmi, L. Tomasi Tongiorgi, *De Piscibus. La bottega artistica di Ulisse Aldrovandi e l'immagine naturalistica*, ed. by E. Crea, in appendix an essay by G. Folena, Rome 1993
Opll 2005
F. Opll, "Neue Erkenntnisse zum ersten Wiener Elefanten", in *Studien zur Wiener Geschichte. Jahrbuch des Vereins für Geschichte der Stadt Wien*, vol. 61, Vienna 2005, 337-343
Oppl 2004
F. Opll, "... ein(e) vorhin in Wien nie gesehene Rarität von jedermann bewundert". Zu Leben, Tod und Nachleben des ersten Wiener Elefanten, in *Studien zur Wiener Geschichte. Jahrbuch des Vereins für Geschichte der Stadt Wien*, vol. 60, Vienna 2004, 229-273
Orsini, Niccoli 2005
R. Orsini, B. Niccoli, *Moda a Firenze 1540-1580. Lo stile di Eleonora di Toledo e la sua influenza*, Florence 2005, 32f.
Orso 1986
S. Orso, *Philip IV and the decoration of the Alcázar in Madrid*, Princeton 1986
Ottino della Chiesa 1956
A. Ottino della Chiesa, *Bernardino Luini*, Novara 1956

Padua 2001
Exhibition catalogue, *Donatello e il suo tempo. Il bronzetto a Padova nel Quattrocento e nel Cinquecento*, 213, no. 56, 216, no. 59 (Leithe-Jasper)

Paliaga 1995
F. Paliaga, "Giovanni Ambrogio Brambilla, 'Le Teste di Carattere' di Leonardo e la commedia dell'arte", in *Raccolta Vinciana*, 26, 1995, 219-254
Paliaga 1997
F. Paliaga, "Le nature morte", in *La Pinacoteca. Origine e collezioni*, ed. by V. Guazzoni, Cremona 1997, 101-103
Paltrinieri 1805
O. Paltrinieri, *Notizie intorno alla vita di Primo del Conte Milanese della Congragazione di Somasca. Teologo al Concilio di Trento a cui si aggiungono quelle di alcuni letterati che furono suoi allievi, le sue lettere e poesie latine e quelle di altri a lui e il dialogo di M. Ant. Majoragio, intitolato Primus Comes seu de Eloquentia*, Rome 1805
Panofsky 1954
E. Panofsky, *Galileo as a Critic of the Arts*, The Hague 1954
Parronchi 1991
A. Parronchi, "Inganni d'ombre", in *Accademia Leonardi Vinci*, vol. IV, 1991, 52-56
Passeri 1937
G.B. Passeri, *Die Künstlerbiographien (um 1678)*, ed. by J. Hess, Leipzig-Vienna 1937, 72
Pauser, Scheutz, Winkelbauer 2004
J. Pauser, M. Scheutz, Th. Winkelbauer (eds.), *Quellenkunde der Habsburgermonarchie (XVI - XVII Jahrhundert), Ein exemplarisches Handbuch, Mitteilungen des Instituts für Österreichische Geschichtsforschung*, Ergänzungsband 44, Vienna-Munich 2004
Pazaurek 1937
G.E. Pazaurek, *Perlmutter*, Berlin 1937
Pedretti 1954
C. Perdetti, "Spigolature aeronautiche vinciane", in *Raccolta Vinciana*, 17, 1954, 117-128
Pedretti 1977
C. Pedretti, "The literary works of Leonardo da Vinci", ed. by J.P. Richter, *Commentary*, vol. 1, Oxford 1977, 174
Pedretti 1980
C. Pedretti, exhibition catalogue *Leonardo da Vinci, Nature Studies from the Royal Library at Windsor Castle*, Florence 1980
Pedretti 2003
C. Pedretti, "Introduzione", in *I disegni di Leonardo da Vinci e della sua cerchia nel Gabinetto dei Disegni e Stampe delle Gallerie dell'Accademia di Venezia ordinati e presentati da Carlo Pedretti*, ed. by G. Nepi Scirè, A. Perissa Torrini, Florence 2003, 13-45
Pedretti, Nepi Scirè 2003
C. Pedretti, G. Nepi Scirè (eds.), *I disegni di Leonardo da Vinci e della sua cerchia nel Gabinetto dei Disegni delle Gallerie dell'Accademia di Venezia*, Florence 2003, 95 (extensive bibliography)
Pedretti, Vecce 1995
C. Pedretti, C. Vecce (eds.), *Leonardo da Vinci, Libro di pittura*, Florence 1995
Peltzer 1926
R.A. Peltzer, "Nicolas Neufchatel und seine Nürnberger Bildnisse", in *Münchner Jahrbuch der bildenden Kunst*, N.F. 3, 1926, 220
Pérez de Tudela, Jordan Gschwend 2001
A. Pérez de Tudela, A. Jordan Gschwend, *Luxury Goods for Royal Collectors: Exotica, Princely Gifts and Rare Animals Exchanged Between the Iberian Courts and Central Europe in the Renaissance (1560-1612)*, in *Jahrbuch des Kunsthistorischen Museums Wien*, 3, Vienna 2001, 1-127
Pérez Sánchez 1964
A.E. Pérez Sánchez, "La 'Primavera' de Arcimboldo, en la Academia de San Fernando", in *Archiv Español de Arte*, 1964, 314-316
Pérez Sánchez 1977
A.E. Pérez Sánchez, *I grandi disegni italiani nelle collezioni di Madrid*, Milan 1977
Pérez Sánchez 1987
A.E. Pérez Sánchez, "L'asse Madrid-Praga", in exhibition catalogue Venice 1987
Perrin 2001
I. Perrin, *Les techniques céramiques de Bernard Palissy*, Paris 2001
Piccinelli 2003
R. Piccinelli, *Le Collezioni Gonzaga. Il carteggio tra Miano e Mantova*, Milan 2003
Pieyre de Mandiargues 1977
A. Pieyre de Mandiargues, *Arcimboldo le Merveilleux*, Paris 1977
Planiscig 1924
L. Planiscig, *Die Bronzeplastiken. Kunsthistorisches Museum in Wien, Publikationen aus der Plastiksammlung*, vol. IV, Vienna 1924, 33, n. 51, 37, nn. 58, 60, 39, nn. 63, 64, 66, 93, n. 163, 194 e sgg., n. 319
Planiscig 1927
L. Planiscig, *Andrea Riccio*, Vienna 1927, 366f.
Planiscig, Kris 1935
L. Planiscig, E. Kris, *Katalog der Sammlungen für Plastik und Kunstgewerbe*, Vienna 1935, 95, no. 6
Pope-Hennessy 1965
J.W. Pope-Hennessy, *Renaissance Bronzes from the Samuel H. Kress Collection*, London 1965, 138, no. 505
Popham, Pouncey 1950
A.E. Popham, P. Pouncey, *Italian drawings in the BM, the fourteenth and fifteenth centuries*, London 1950, I, no. 113, II, pl. CVII
Porzio 1979
F. Porzio, *L'universo illusorio di Arcimboldi*, Milan 1979
Porzio 1990
F. Porzio, "Lombardia 1620 circa. Natura morta delle origini", in *Osservatorio delle arti*, 4, 1990, 118-119
Porzio 1993
F. Porzio, "Fonti carnevalesche del naturalismo nel Cinquecento milanese: alcune ipotesi su Giuseppe Arcimboldi", in *Arte Lonbarda*, 105-107, 1993, 37-42
Prague 1997
Exhibition catalogue, *Rudolf II and Prague. The Court and the City*, ed. by E. Fučikova, Prague 1997
Preiss 1967
P. Preiss, *Giuseppe Arcimboldo*, Prague 1967
Puerari 1951
A. Puerari, *La Pinacoteca di Cremona*, Cremona 1951

Ragotzky, Wenzel 1990
H. Ragotzky, H. Wenzel (eds.), *Höfische Repräsentation. Das Zeremoniell und die Zeichen*, Tübingen 1990
Rampi 2002
E. Rampi, "Artisti e letterati nella Lombardia spagnola", in *Sul Tesin...* 2002, 487-509
Rangström 1992
L. Rangström, *Tournaments and the Dream of Chivalry*, Stockolm 1992, 108
Rauch 2006
M. Rauch, "Steinreich: Gesammeltes aus der Erde", in exhibition catalogue Ambras 2006, 157-158
Rauscher 2004
P. Rauscher, *Zwischen Ständen und Gläubigern. Die kaiserlichen Finanzen unter Ferdinand I. und Maximilian II. (1556-1576), Veröffentlichungen des Instituts für Österreichische Geschichtsforschung*, vol. 41, Vienna-Munich 2004
Reeds 2006
K. Reeds, "Leonardo da Vinci and botanical illustrations: nature prints, drawings, and woodcuts ca. 1500", in *Visualizing medieval medicine and natural history, 1200-1500*, ed. by J.A. Givens *et al.*, Aldershot 2006, 205-237
Reeves 1997
E. Reeves, *Painting the Heavens. Art and Science in the Age of Galileo*, Princeton 1997
Repishti 2002
F. Repishti, "Alcune anticipazioni sul rinnovamento cinquecentesco del duomo. Il contratto per il coro ligneo di San Giovanni Battista a Monza", in *Studi Monzesi*, 11-12, 2002, 51-58
Richter 2006
T. Richter, *Der Berner Silberschatz. Trinkgeschirre und Ehrengaben aus Renaissance und Barock*, Bern 2006
Robinson 1876
J.C. Robinson, *Descriptive catalogue of drawings by the old masters: forming the Collection of John Malcolm of Poltalloch*, II edition, London 1876, no. 320
Rodolf 2001
K. Rudolf, "Exotica bei Karl V., Philipp II. und in der Kunstkammer Rudolfs II.", in *Jahrbuch des Kunsthistorischen Museums Wien*, vol. 3, Vienna 2001, 173-203
Rokitansky 1967
G. Rokitansky, "Ein weiteres Bergrebhuhn aus Österreich", in *Jahrbuch des Naturhistorischen Museums Wien*, 70, 1967, 233-237
Rosenauer 2003
A. Rosenauer (ed.), *Geschichte der bildenden Kunst in Österreich*, vol. 3, Spätmittelalter und Renaissance, Munich 2003
Rossi 1995
M. Rossi, "Ambrogio Arcimboldi. Biografia e schede", in *Pittura in Alto Lario e in Valtellina dall'Alto Medioevo al Settecento*, ed. by M. Gregori, Milan 1995, 256-259
Roth 2000
H. Roth (ed.), *Der Anfang der Museumslehre in Deutschland. Das Traktat "Inscriptiones vel Tituli Theatri Amplissimi" von Samuel Quiccheberg. Lateinisch - Deutsch*, Berlin 2000
Rudolf 1995
K. Rudolf, "Die Kunstbestrebungen Kaiser Maximilians II. im Spannungsfeld zwischen Madrid und Wien. Untersuchungen zu den Sammlungen der Œsterreichischen Habsburger im 16. Jahrhundert", in *Jahrbuch der kunsthistorischen Sammlungen in Wien*, vol. 91, 1995, 165-256

Sacchi 1989
R. Sacchi, "Gaudenzio Ferrari a Milano: i committenti, la bottega, le opere", in *Storia dell'arte*, 67, Sept.-Dec. 1989, 201-218
Sacchi 2005
R. Sacchi, *Il disegno incompiuto. La politica artistica di Francesco II Sforza e di Massimiliano Stampa*, 2 voll., Milan 2005
Sandbichler 2006
V. Sandbichler, "Der Hochzeitskodex Erzherzog Ferdinands II.", in *Jahrbuch des Kunsthistorischen Museums Wien*, vol. 6/7, 2006, 47-89
Santagostino 1671 (1980)
A. Santagostino, *L'immortalità e gloria del pennello*, ed. by M. Bona Castellotti, Milan 1980 (I ed. Milan 1671)
Savio 1905
F. Savio, *Giovanni Battista Fontana o Fonteio scrittore milanese del sec. XVI*, Archivo Storico Lombardo, 4 (32), 1905, 343-375
Saxl 1936
F. Saxl, *Costumes and Festivals of Milanese Society under Spanish Rule*, in Proceedings of Annual Italian Lecture, London 18 November 1936
Schäffer 1911
E. Schäffer, "Un disegno del Luini nell''Albertina' di Vienna", in *Rassegna d'Arte*, XI, 1911, 144
Schallaburg 1976
Exhibition catalogue, *Italienische Klein-*

plastiken, Zeichnungen und Musik der Renaissance. Waffen des 16. und 17. Jahrhunderts, Vienna 1976, 104, nos. 133, 135, 138 (Leithe-Jasper)

Scheicher 1979
E. Scheicher, *Die Kunst- und Wunderkammern der Habsburger*, Vienna-Munich-Zurich 1979

Scheicher 1981
E. Scheicher, "Ein Fest am Hofe Erzherzog Ferdinands II.", in *Jahrbuch der Kunsthistorischen Sammlungen in Wien*, vol. 77 (NF XLI), 1981, 119-154

Scheicher 1995
E. Scheicher, "Zur Ikonologie von Naturalien im Zusammenhang der enzyklopädischen Kunstkammer", in *Anzeiger des Germanischen Nationalmuseums*, 1995, 115-125

Schlegel 1968
U. Schlegel, "Riccios 'Nackter Mann mit Vase' – Zur Bedeutung einer Gruppe italienischer Kleinbronzen", in *FS für Ulrich Middeldorf*, I, Berlin 1968, 350-357

Schlosser 1901
J. von Schlosser, *Die Kunst- und Wunderkammern der Spätrenaissance. Ein Beitrag zur Geschichte des Sammelwesens*, Leipzig 1908, 12, 16f.

Schlosser 1908
J. von Schlosser, *Die Kunst- und Wunderkammern der Spätrenaissance. Ein Beitrag zur Geschichte des Sammelwesens*, Leipzig 1908

Schlosser 1964
J. von Schlosser, *La letteratura artistica. Manuale delle fonti della storia dell'arte moderna*, Florence-Vienna 1964, III edition

Schneider 1994
N. Schneider, *Porträtmalerei. Hauptwerke europäischer Bildniskunst: 1420-1670*, Cologne 1992

Scholten 2001
F. Scholten, "Johan Gregor van der Schardts zelfportret, circa 1573", in *Bulletin van het Rijksmusuem*, 2001, vol. 49, no. 4, 311-324

Schramm, Schwarte, Lazardzig 2005
H. Schramm, L. Schwarte, J. Lazardzig, *Collection - Laboratory – Theater. Scenes of Knowledge in the 17th Century*, Berlin-New York 2005

Schürer 1986
R. Schürer, "Wenzel Jamnitzers Brunnen für Maximilian II. Überlegungen zu Ikonographie und Zweck", in *Anzeiger des Germanischen Nationalmuseums*, 1986, 55-59

Seelig 1986
L. Seelig, "Die Münchner Kunstkammer – Geschichte, Anlage, Ausstattung", in *Jahrbuch der Bayerischen Denkmalpflege*, 40, 1986, 101-138

Seelig 1996
L. Seelig, "Exotics and precious objects mounted by Augsburg goldsmiths", in *The Magazine Antiques*, vol. CL, no. 4, New York 1996, 486-492

Seelig 2001
L. Seelig, "Exotica in der Münchner Kunstkammer der bayerischen Wittelsbacher", in *Jahrbuch des Kunsthistorischen Museums Wien*, vol. 3, 2001, 145-161

Seidel Menchi 1987
S. Seidel Menchi, *Erasmo in Italia*, Turin 1987

Seipel 2002
W. Seipel (ed.), exhibition catalogue Ambras 2002, 108-110

Seipel 2003
W. Seipel (ed.), exhibition catalogue Vienna 2003

Seipel 2005
W. Seipel (ed.), exhibition catalogue Vienna 2005, 164-165

Selvatico 1854
P. Selvatico, *Catalogo delle opere d'arte contenute nella Sala delle Sedute dell'IR Accademia di Venezia*, Venice 1854

Shearman 1967
J. Shearman, *Mannerism*, Harmondsworth 1967

Shell 1995
J. Shell, *Pittori in bottega*, Turin 1995

Siejek, Kirsch 2004
A. Siejek, K. Kirsch, *Die Unterzeichnung auf dem Malgrund, Graphische Mittel und Übertragungsverfahren im 15. – 17. Jhdt*, Siegl Munich 2004, 56-67

Šíp 1969
J. Šíp, "Die Paradieses-Vision in den Gemälden Roelandt Saverys", in *Jahrbuch der Kunsthistorischen Sammlungen in Wien*, 65, 1969, 29-38

Somaini 2003
F. Somaini, "Un prelato lombardo del XV secolo. Il card. Giovanni Arcimboldi vescovo di Novara, arcivescovo di Milano", in *Italia Sacra*, 73, Rome 2003, 3 voll.

Squizzato 2004
A. Squizzato, "Profilo di un collezionista cremonese tra Settecento e Ottocento: il marchese Giuseppe Sigismondo Ala Ponzone", in Marubbi 2004, 17-27

Stainhofer 1566
C. Stainhofer, *Grundliche und Khurtze Beschreibung des alten und jungen Zugs*, Vienna 1566

Staudinger 1990
M. Staudinger, "Études descriptives de zoologie historique", in *Le Bestiaire de Rodolphe II*, ed. by M. Staudinger, H. Haupt, T. Vignau-Wilberg, E. Irblich, Paris 1990

Staudinger 1995
M. Staudinger, "Hans Vermeyen, Kammergoldschmied Kaiser Rudolfs II. in Prag", in *Jahrbuch der Kunsthistorischen Sammlungen in Wien*, vol. 91, 1995, 263-271

Staudinger 1996
M. Staudinger, "Giorgio Liberale. Tierdarstellungen mit besonderer Berücksichtigung der Meeresfauna", in E. Irblich (ed.), exhibition catalogue Vienna 1996, 210-225

Stockhammer 2003
A. Stockhammer, in *Spätmittelalter und Renaissance (Geschichte der bildenden Kunst in Österreich)*, ed. by A. Rosenauer, vol. 3, Munich 2003

Stockholm 1966
Christina, Queen of Sweden, Stockholm Nationalmuseum 1966

Storczer 1992
S.G. Storczer, *Die Handsteinsammlung des Kunsthistorischen Museums in Vienna*, Ph.D. dissertation, Vienna 1992

Strong 1991
R. Strong, *Feste der Renaissance 1450-1650. Kunst als Instrument der Macht*, Freiburg-Würzburg 1991

***Sul Tesin* 2002**
Sul Tesin piantàro i tuoi laureti. Poesia e vita letteraria nella Lombardia spagnola (1535-1706), exhibition catalogue Pavia 2002

Sutter Fichtner 2001
P. Sutter Fichtner, *Emperor Maximilian II*, New Haven-London 2001

Sutton 1987
D. Sutton, "Arcimboldo: Fantasy and Symbolism", in *Apollo* 3, 1987, 231-234

Tainturier 1863
A. Tainturier, *Les Terres émaillées de Bernard Palissy inventeur des rustiques figulines: étude sur les travaux du maitre et de ses continuateurs suivie du catalogue de leur œuvre*, Paris 1863

Thomas 1983
B. and Ch. Thomas, "Dreiprinzengarnitur", in *Jahrbuch der kunsthistorischen Sammlungen in Wien*, vol. 79, 1983

Tokyo, Hiroshima etc. 1994-95
Exhibition catalogue, *Disguised Vision*, ed. by Yamanashi Toshio, Tokyo, Hiroshima etc. 1994-95

Tongiorgi Tomasi, Hischauer 2001
L. Tongiorgi Tomasi, G.A. Hischauer, exhibition catalogue *The flowering of Florence Botanical Art for the Medici*, Washington D.C. 2001, 19-22, no. 22

Toninelli 1997
G. Toninelli, "I conti Ponzoni e la loro collezione d'arte", in Guazzoni 1997, 47-54

Tours, Limoges 2002-03
Exhibition catalogue, *Un bestiaire fantastique, Avisseau et la faïence de Tours (1840-1910)*, Tours, Limoges, Paris 2002

Trevor-Roper 1976
H. Trevor-Roper, *Princes and Artists. Patronage and Ideology at four Habsburg courts, 1517-1633*, London 1976

Trnek 2000
H. Trnek, "'Und ich hab aber all mein lebtag nichts gesehen, das mein hercz also erfreuet hat als diese ding'. Exotica in habsburgischen Kunstkammern, deren Inventare und Bestände", in exhibition catalogue Vienna 2000, 23-47

Trnek 2001
H. Trnek, "Daniel Fröschl – 'kaiserlicher miniathormahler und antiquarius'. Überlegungen zur geistigen Urheberschaft von Konzept und Gliederung des Inventars der Kunstkammer Kaiser Rudolfs II. von 1607-1611", in *Jahrbuch des Kunsthistorischen Museums Wien*, vol. 3, 2001, 221-231

Trunz 1931-1965
E. Trunz, "Der deutsche Späthumanismus um 1600 als Standeskultur", in *Jahrbuch für Geschichte der Erziehung und des Unterrichts*, 20, 1931, 17-53; reproduced in *Deutsche Barockforschung. Dokumentation einer Epoche*, ed. by R. Alewyn, Cologne-Berlin 1966, 147-181

Trunz 1988
E. Trunz, "Späthumanismus und Manierismus im Kreise Kaiser Rudolfs II.", in exhibition catalogue Essen-Vienna 1988

Uhlirz 1895-1896
K. Uhlirz (ed.), *Urkunden und Regesten aus dem Archive der k.k. Reichshauptstadt Residenz-Stadt Wien*, Vienna 1895-1896

Valencia 1999
Exhibition catalogue, *Pintura Europea en colecciones Valencianos*, ed. by F.B. Doménech, Valencia 1999

Vannel, Toderi 2003
F. Vannel, G. Toderi, *Medaglie italiane del Museo Nazionale del Bargello*, vol. I, secoli XV-XVI, Florence 2003

Vasari (ed Milanesi) 1878-1885
G. Vasari, *Le Vite de piú eccelenti pittori scultori ed architettori*, ed. G. Milanesi, 9 voll., Florence 1878-1885

Vasari 1965
G. Vasari, *The Lives of the Painters, Sculptors and Architects*, transl. by A.B. Hinds, London 1965

Venice 1987
Exhibition catalogue, *Effetto Arcimboldo. Trasformazioni del volto nel sedicesimo e nel ventesimo secolo*, ed. by Y. David, (engl. edition: *The Archimboldo Effect*), Venice 1987

Venturelli 1998
P. Venturelli, "'E per tal variar natura è bella'. Arti decorative a Milano tra Leonardo e Lomazzo", in exhibition catalogue Lugano 1998, 77-88

Venturelli 1999
P. Venturelli, *Vestire e apparire. Il sistema vestimentario femminile nella Milano spagnola (1539-1679)*, Rome 1999

Viatte 2003
F. Viatte, "Portraits et grotesques", in *Léonard de Vinci. Dessins et manuscripts*, ed. by F. Viatte, V. Forcione, exhibition catalogue Paris 2003, 169-171

Vienna 1897
Jahrbuch der Kunsthistorischen Sammlungen des Allerhöchsten Kaiserhauses, 18, Vienna 1897
Vienna 1976-1982
Exhibition catalogue, *Porträtgalerie zur Geschichte Österreichs von 1400 bis 1800*, Vienna 1976, second edition 1982
Vienna 1987
Exhibition catalogue, *Der Zauber der Medusa. Europäische Manierismen*, ed. by M. Hofmann, Vienna 1987, 145, no. I/10 (Boeckel, Stengl), 357, no. VIII/36, 367, no. VIII/64, 367, no. VIII/65B (Stengl), 360, no. 45, 370f., no. 74 (Hofmann)
Vienna 1988
Exhibition catalogue, *Antonio Abondio und seine Zeit*, ed. by K. Schulz, Sonderausstellung Kunsthistorisches Museum Münzkabinett, Vienna 1988
Vienna 1989
Exhibition catalogue, *Fürstenhöfe der Renaissance. Giulio Romano und die klassische Tradition*, Vienna 1989, 260ff., no. V/32 (Welzig)
Vienna 1995
Exhibition catalogue, *Natur und Kunst*, ed. by A. Auer, E. Irblich, Vienna 1995
Vienna 1996
Exhibition catalogue, *Thesaurus Austriacus. Europas Glanz im Spiegel der Buchkunst-Handschriften- und Kunstalben von 800 bis 1600*, ed. by E. Irblich, Vienna 1996
Vienna 1999
Exhibition catalogue, *Für Aug' und Ohr: Musik in Kunst- und Wunderkammern*, ed. by W. Seipel, Vienna 1999
Vienna 2000
Exhibition catalogue, *Exotica. Portugals Entdeckungen im Spiegel fürstlicher Kunst- und Wunderkammern der Renaissance*, ed. by W. Seipel, Vienna 2000
Vienna 2003
Exhibition catalogue, *Kaiser Ferdinand I. 1503-1564. Das Werden der Habsburgermonarchie*, ed. by W. Seipel, Vienna 2003
Vienna 2003a
Exhibition catalogue, *Parmigianino und der europäische Manierismus*, ed. by S. Ferino-Pagden, L. Fornari Schianchi, Vienna, Milan 2003
Vienna 2004
Exhibition catalogue, *The era of Michelangelo. Masterpieces from the Albertina*, Vienna, Milan 2004
Vienna 2005
Exhibition catalogue, *Wir sind Helden. Habsburgische Festen in der Renaissance*, Vienna 2005
Vienna 2006
Exhibition catalogue, *Die Entdeckung der Natur. Naturalien aus den Kunstkammern des 16. und 17. Jahrhunderts*, Vienna 2006, 103, 105, nos. 2.46, 2.47, 2.48, 2.49, 2.50 (Kryza-Gersch), 202, no. 17 (Leithe-Jasper)
Vignau-Wilberg 1987
T. Vignau-Wilberg, "Qualche disegni d'importancia. Joris Hoefnagel als Zeichnungssammler", in *Münchner Jahrbuch der Bildenden Kunst*, 38, 1987, 185-214
Vignau-Wilberg 1990
T. Vignau-Wilberg, "Le 'Museum' de l'empereur Rodolphe II et le Cabinet des arts et curiosités", in *Le Bestiaire de Rodolphe II*, ed. by M. Staudinger, H. Haupt, T. Vignau-Wilberg, E. Irblich, Paris 1990, 40-41, 61
Vocelka 1976
K. Vocelka, *Habsburgische Hochzeiten 1550-1600, Kulturgeschichtliche Studien zum Manieristischen Repräsentationsfest*, Vienna-Cologne-Graz 1976

Waddington 1989
R.B. Waddington, "Before Arcimboldo: Composite Portraits on Italian Medals", in *The Medal*, no. 14, 1989, 12-23
Waddington 1993
R.B. Waddington, *Aretino's Satyr. Sexuality, Satire, and Self-Projection in Sixteenth-century Literature and Art*, Toronto-Buffalo-London 1993
Wagner 1985
F. Wagner, "Beschlagene Sraussen-Ayer. Ungewöhnliche Trinkgeschirre des Spätmittelalters und der frühen Neuzeit", in *Kunst und Antiquitäten*, II, 1985, 32-42
Wagner Rieger 1951
R. Wagner Rieger, "Das Wiener Neugebäude", in *Mitteilungen des Instituts für österreichische Geschichtsforschung*, 39, 1951, 136-144
Walz 2000
A. Walz, "Weltenharmonie - Die Kunstkammer und die Ordnung des Wissens", in exhibition catalogue Braunschweig 2000, 9-21
Warnke 1985
M. Warnke, *Hofkünstler. Zur Vorgeschichte des modernern Künstler*, Cologne 1985, 112ff.
Washington 1986
Exhibition catalogue, *Renaissance Master Bronzes from the collection of the Kunsthistorisches Museum Vienna*, Washington DC 1986, 100, no. 16, 214, no. 57 (Leithe-Jasper)
Washington D.C. 2007
Exhibition catalogue *Italian Women Artists from Renaissance to Baroque*, Washington D.C. 2007, no. cat. 26, 152-153
Weihrauch 1967
H. Weihrauch, *Europäische Bronzestatuetten 15.-18. Jh.*, Braunschweig 1976, 321f.
Wescher 1950
P. Wescher, "The 'Idea' in Giuseppe Arcimboldo's Art", in *Magazine of Art*, Jan. 1950, XLII, 3-8
Williamson 1899
G.C. Williamson, *Bernardino Luini*, London 1899
Willingen 1870
A. van Willingen, *Les artistes de Harlem*, Haarlem and The Hague, 1870
Wilson 1983
C.C. Wilson, *Renaissance Small Bronze Sculpture and Associate Decorative Arts at the National Gallery of Art*, Washington D.C. 1983, 75f.
Wilson 2005
T. Wilson, "Un 'intricamento' tra Leonardo ed Arcimboldo", in *Ceramica Antica*, vol. 15, no. 2, 2005, 10-44
Winkelbauer 2003
Th. Winkelbauer, "Ständefreiheit und Fürstenmacht, Länder und Untertanen des Hauses Habsburg im konfessionellen Zeitalter", 2 voll., in *Österreichische Geschichte 1522-1699*, ed. by H. Wolfram, Vienna 2003
Wünsch 1914
J. Wünsch, "Der Einzug Kaisers Maximilians II. zu Wien", in *Berichte und Mitteilungen des Altertum-Verein zu Wien*, 46-48, 1914, 25-31

Zambelli 1963
P. Zambelli, "Baldini, Bernardino", *ad vocem* in *Dizionario Biografico degli Italiani*, Rome, Istituto dell'Enciclopedia Italiana, V, 1963, 481-482
Zapperi 2004
R. Zapperi, *Der wilde Mann von Teneriffa. Die wundersame Geschichte des Pedro Gonzalez und seiner Kinder*, Munich 2004, 61-73, 100-111
Zezza 1999
A. Zezza, "Giovan Battista Castaldo e la chiesa di Santa Maria del Monte Albino: un tondo di Raffaello, un dipinto di Marco Pino e un busto di Leone Leoni a Nocera de' Pagani", in *Prospettiva*, 93-94, January-April 1999, 29-41
Zimmer 1971
J. Zimmer, *Joseph Heintz der Ältere als Maler*, Weißenhorn 1971
Zimmermann 1887
H. Zimmermann, "Urkunden, Acten und Regesten aus dem Archiv des k.k. Ministeriums des Innern", in *Jahrbuch der kunsthistorischen Sammlungen des Allerhöchsten Kaiserhauses*, vol. 5 (1887), CXX-CLXXVI; vol. 7 (1888), XV-LXXXIV
Zimmermann 1889
H. Zimmermann, "Inventare, Acten und Regesten aus der Schatzkammer des Allerhöchsten Kaiserhauses", in *Jahrbuch der Kunsthistorischen Sammlungen des Allerhöchsten Kaiserhauses*, vol. X/2, 1889, CCI-CCCXXVI
Zimmermann 1905
H. Zimmermann, "Das Inventar der Prager Schatz- und Kunstkammer vom 6. Dezember 1621. Nach Akten des K. und K. Reichsfinanzarchivs in Wien", in *Jahrbuch der Kunsthistorischen Sammlungen des allerhöchsten Kaiserhauses*, 25, 1905, XIII-LXXV
Zirfeo 1570
Zirfeo, *Ordentliche Beschreibung: Des gewaltigen, treffentichen und herrlichen Thurnier zu Ross und Fuss. So ... zu Prag in der Alten Stadt den der Enden anwesende Chur und Fürsten zu Ehren gehalten worden ist*, Prag 1570, fol. 16 r
Zittau 2002
Exhibition catalogue, *Welt – Macht – Geist. Das Habsburg und die Oberlausitz*, Zittau 2002
Zwierlein-Diehl 1979
E. Zwierlein-Diehl, *Die antiken Gemmen des Kunsthistorischen Museums in Wien*, vol. 2, Munich 1979

Chloridis carmen etymologicum

VERTVMNVS AD POMONAM:

liberam sane toleramus artem
ut decet Pomona deos, sed audi:
cum tuis pomis mihi tu perenni
sola uoluptas

pinxit Arcimboldus opus stupendum,
iunxit ignotam temere innocenti
sponte Vertumno nitidamque uerno
flore puellam

iam docet nomen, mihi te docenti
crede: VER TEMNO, steriles sed aruis
haec tuos purus timeo furores
ne ferat aestas

POMONA AD VERTVMNVM:

VERTITVR Vertumne globus: nec actum
rite uer temnas timeas nec ortum
tempus aestiuum tibi quo quieta
poma coquentur

ut dedit flores modo uer odoros
sic ferax aestas erit atque fructus
diues autumnus dabit usque uer quos
pectore norat

Flora si nescis Italis uocatur,
atque pictori male qui Viennae
uixit ignoscamus iniqua passo
tempora brumae

An Etymological Poem by Chloris

VERTUMNUS TO POMONA:

Of course we tolerate the liberty of art,
as befits gods, Pomona, but listen:
You, with your fruit, for all my eternity
are my only joy.

Arcimboldo painted an astounding picture:
by himself with innocent Vertumnus
he arbitrarily coupled an unknown maid
resplendent in vernal flowers.

My name says it already, believe me if I say:
spring does not interest me, but I fear that
though I'm true, summer might cover the fields
with your harmful wrath.

POMONA TO VERTUMNUS:

The globe, Vertumnus, is turning:
you should neither scorn the lawfully parted spring
nor fear the summer now begun,
when fruits for you in peace will ripen.

Spring has given you fragrant flowers,
so summer will be fertile,
and rich autumn bear you fruit in plenty,
which spring already had in its heart.

Italians know her as Flora, if you do not know!
And we will pardon the painter,
as he lived miserably in Vienna,
there to suffer winter's wicked weather.

(Translation: David Graham)